Managerial Accounting

Second Edition

Managerial Accounting

Lester E. Heitger, Ph.D., C.P.A.
Graduate School of Business
Indiana University

Serge Matulich, Ph.D., C.P.A.
Roy E. Crummer Graduate School of Business
Rollins College

McGraw-Hill Book Company
New York St. Louis San Francisco Auckland Bogotá Hamburg
Johannesburg London Madrid Mexico Montreal New Delhi Panama
Paris São Paulo Singapore Sydney Tokyo Toronto

MANAGERIAL ACCOUNTING

1234567890 DOCDOC 898765

ISBN 0-07-020211-7

This book was set in Caledonia by Ruttle, Shaw & Wetherill, Inc.
The editors were Jim DeVoe, Scott Amerman, and Jo Satloff;
the designer was Merrill Haber;
the production supervisor was Charles Hess.
New drawings were done by J & R Services, Inc.
Manuscript development was done by Mary Drouin.
R. R. Donnelley & Sons Company was printer and binder.

Library of Congress Cataloging in Publication Data

Heitger, Lester E.
Managerial accounting.

Includes index.
1. Managerial accounting. I. Matulich, Serge.
II. Title.
HF5635.H446 1986 658.1'511 85-11310
ISBN 0-07-020211-7

Contents

Preface

This managerial accounting book is the second edition of a coordinated two-volume financial/managerial set designed for introductory accounting courses. The financial and managerial volumes together offer well-integrated and comprehensive coverage of the fundamentals of financial and managerial accounting. Either volume, however, may be used alone or with other texts. Both books were widely adopted in their first edition, and revised material has been used by the authors and other teachers and is thoroughly class tested.

Our primary objective with the first edition of this book was to write a comprehensive, flexible text that is easy to use by both instructors and students. This second edition continues the same theme while responding to the changing business environment that accounting serves. In writing this second edition, we have listened carefully to adopters, reviewers, editors, and our students, and have also taken into account our own experiences with the book. As a result, we were able to streamline the writing style, rearrange some of the material, and strengthen several key areas of the book such as process costing, production and cost flows, cost behavior and cost analysis, and capital budgeting. In addition we have enhanced an already strong learning support package that is available to students and the corresponding teaching resource support that is available to instructors.

The basic philosophy of the first edition is unchanged. The book is suitable for a second accounting course at either the undergraduate or graduate level with an emphasis on the internal reporting process. The book has been carefully designed to cover a range of material that is sufficiently comprehensive to accommodate various course objectives. The level of coverage in this volume is designed to satisfy the needs of the potential accounting major as well as of those who will not continue with additional accounting courses. A careful balance between conceptual and technical material is maintained because we believe that a combination of basic concepts and practical application of techniques is essential if students are to retain the body of accounting knowledge they will need in other courses and in their future business experiences. The emphasis in the book is on instilling an understanding of how cost data are developed, measured, and used for internal reporting and decision making. Special attention is given to planning, control, and performance reporting.

The book deliberately contains more material than is typically covered in a single semester or quarter. Most instructors like the flexibility afforded by a book that covers the basic managerial accounting concepts and allows them to select additional topics to satisfy their particular course objectives. Although we have made numerous revisions, we have retained the desirable and successful features of the first edition.

ORGANIZATION OF THE TOPICS

The basic organization of the book satisfied most users of the first edition and remains unchanged. The book is divided into five major parts. **Part 1, Developing a Management Accounting Data Base,** introduces students to the managerial accounting environment, the basic concepts of costing, cost behavior, and relevant terminology that students must understand prior to proceeding through the remainder of the book. **Part 2, Cost Behavior and Decision Making,** shows students the importance of cost behavior concepts in developing management accounting reports, making decisions, planning, and evaluating performance. A variety of alternative choice decisions are illustrated.

After obtaining the relevant background in the first five chapters, students are introduced in **Part 3** to the essential concepts of **Planning, Control, and Responsibility Reporting.** Here such topics as budgeting, standard costs, and variance reporting for both manufacturing and nonmanufacturing operations are discussed. Further discussion includes managerial performance reporting, decentralized business operation, pricing of products and services, and capital budgeting. The planning, control, and reporting necessary in not-for-profit organizations are discussed, as is the influence of governmental actions on business.

Part 4, Advanced Managerial Accounting Topics, introduces students to some managerial tools needed in today's complex business environment. These include methods of inventory management, advanced concepts of standard costing, measurement of product costs in a process costing environment, and a variety of quantitative tools used in planning and forecasting future business operations.

Many managerial accounting students have an incomplete financial accounting background. **Part 5** of the book, **Financial Accounting Foundation for Managerial Accounting,** is intended to fill the gap left by financial accounting courses that do not use the financial accounting volume of this series. It consists of financial statement analysis, and the statement of changes in financial position, two topics that are an important part of a manager's accounting background.

Appendix A provides students with an overview of the accounting cycle. This brief review of financial accounting concepts is useful in understanding basic cost flows for students who have not taken financial accounting recently. Appendix B, Time Value of Money, allows students to review compound interest concepts. Following the appendixes are tables of compound interest and present value and a table of areas under the normal curve.

NEW ORGANIZATIONAL FEATURES

There are relatively few changes in the basic organization of the book, but many improvements have been made in the presentation of the material.

a. The entire text has been improved by smoothing out the writing, by devoting a separate chapter to process costing, and by shifting some material among the early chapters.

b. Some numeric examples in the chapters have been revised to make them easier to comprehend and relate to one another.

c. Cost behavior concepts are introduced, discussed, and illustrated in Chapter 2 along with other key cost concepts to facilitate student understanding of product costing and other accounting measurement activities.

d. Process costing has been moved from the appendix to Chapter 3 into a separate chapter to allow instructors more flexibility in teaching product costing material. Process costing can still be taught immediately after the job order costing material in Chapter 3 or it can be taught later in the course or not at all, without loss of continuity.

e. An appendix at the end of the book reviews the fundamental financial accounting concepts and the accounting cycle. This is particularly useful for students who completed the financial accounting course some time prior to taking managerial accounting, or for those whose financial accounting background is weak.

f. Compound interest tables have been expanded to five decimal places and cover more periods and interest rates than in the first edition.

SPECIAL FEATURES OF THE BOOK

Although the initial costing discussions in Chapters 2, 3, and 4 deal primarily with manufacturing operations, other chapters include a reasonable mix of material on service, merchandising, and not-for-profit organizations so that students can obtain a broad general background in managerial accounting and understand the universal applicability of managerial accounting information. Moreover, the material is organized to enable students to integrate their learning into a coherent body of knowledge, rather than to learn what appear to be a number of unrelated topics. For example, cost-volume-profit analysis in Chapter 5 is integrated with a study of alternative choice decisions in Chapter 6, showing students how the analysis is used in decision making. The application of managerial accounting to other than manufacturing operations in Chapter 10 provides the breadth students need to understand the general application of the concepts they study. Difficult topics such as standard costing and process costing are presented clearly at a basic level using easy-to-understand examples. They are then followed by more comprehensive discussions for those who desire more complete coverage.

The chapter dealing with quantitative techniques is especially useful because it focuses on managerial tools that can help to identify cost behavior patterns and to plan and control costs. Although the treatment is elementary, students' basic understanding of these quantitative concepts gives them an edge in other business courses and in their professional work.

The financial accounting material in the last two chapters presents topics that are frequently omitted in financial courses and that are often covered in other accounting textbooks in less than comprehensible terms. Users of this book will find both the teaching and learning of the Statement of Changes in Financial Position greatly enhanced as a result of the approach used to present this material.

LEARNING AIDS

The learning aids that we introduced in the first edition have now become standard features of many other accounting textbooks. These have been retained and improved in the second edition. The learning aids include a brief **chapter overview** and list of **learning objectives** at the beginning of each chapter. **Marginal notes** throughout the book focus the student's attention on important terms, concepts, or ideas. Wide margins allow students to insert their own marginal notes. All figures include an explanatory legend, and the text refers to and explains each figure. A comprehensive **summary** at the end of each chapter reinforces important material, reviews new terminology, and provides an excellent review of the chapter. The summary is followed by a list of **key terms** introduced in the chapter, each referenced to the page number where it was first used. A complete **glossary** is included at the end of the book, with each entry referenced to the chapter where it was first used. The use of **boldface** type and various type styles help students identify and recognize important materials.

END-OF-CHAPTER MATERIAL

The questions, exercises, and problems at the end of each chapter are arranged in the same sequence as the chapter material, and they cover all topics in the chapter. Each chapter also contains one or two cases. To the extent possible, the exercises and problems also are arranged in the order of difficulty, with the shorter and easier problems first.

The exercises are generally short and relatively easy, and they typically cover a single topic or concept. The problems are longer and more challenging, usually integrating several topics or concepts. Far more end-of-chapter material is provided than can be assigned in a single course, making the book very flexible. Assignment material can be suited to any class level, and the book may be used with a different set of assignments in each successive term.

All questions, exercises, problems, and cases are thoroughly coordinated with chapter material, enabling students to obtain guidance from the chapter when attempting a solution. All end-of-chapter material has been designed by the authors and is thoroughly compatible with the text material. It ranges over a wide variety of topics, presents interesting and realistic rather than artificial situations, and offers a variety of learning experiences. Exercises, problems, and cases have been class tested and their solutions thoroughly checked by two independent accounting instructors.

NEW FEATURES IN ASSIGNMENT MATERIAL

At the suggestions of users of the first edition, several improvements have been added to the end-of-chapter material.

a. A greater variety of exercises and problems is included in the second edition than in the first.

b. Materials from CPA and CMA examinations are included in the questions, exercises, and problems where suitable for an introductory course and compatible with the text.

c. Most of the exercises and problems retained from the first edition have been revised and improved, many have been replaced with new materials, and many new items have been added.

d. One or two cases have been added to each chapter. The cases expose students to a relatively complex business situation that incorporates a number of accounting concepts. Cases typically ask students to provide some interpretation and may integrate concepts from earlier chapters. The opportunity for classroom discussion of many accounting topics is afforded by the cases.

INSTRUCTOR'S SUPPLEMENTS

No other accounting textbook offers as much help to the instructor as this one. A comprehensive **Solutions Manual** contains solutions to all questions, exercises, problems, and cases. In addition, this manual provides a wealth of information designed to enhance the planning of courses, selection of assignment material, and presentation of lectures. The manual contains comments on each chapter, suggestions on the teaching approach, and suggested assignment material for a variety of course goals. A brief description of each exercise, problem, and case is provided, together with the time required to complete the solution, the level of difficulty, and the availability of a transparency of the solution.

A **problem-topic grid** in the Solutions Manual offers a complete cross-reference between all exercises, problems, and cases and the topics covered in the chapter, enabling instructors to identify topic coverage of assigned materials. This problem-topic grid is invaluable in planning class assignments and in advising students who request additional practice materials.

A major new innovation in the second edition is the inclusion of a complete set of **lecture notes** for each chapter, covering all chapter topics in outline form and including illustrations and examples of critical issues. The lecture notes are accompanied by **teaching transparencies** for use in class lectures and presentations. They contain examples that emphasize and complement the text without duplicating the examples and figures in the book. With these lecture notes, instructors can prepare polished and professional class presentations in a minimum of time.

Also available is a comprehensive set of **transparencies** of selected exercise, problem, and case solutions, suitable for use with overhead projectors. The very comprehensive book of **examination questions** contains over 1,000 multiple choice, true-false, and matching objective questions and more than 150 test problems including solutions, with time estimates and difficulty levels. The objective test questions are computerized for retrieval and test generation by the Examiner System. All examination material is arranged by chapter and is in a form suitable for duplication directly from the book of examination questions. The quantity of test material far exceeds the requirements of a single course, allowing the instructor to design many different tests on any topic in the book to suit a variety of class levels and goals.

STUDENT SUPPLEMENTS

One of the best study guides in the industry is available to students as a supplement to the textbook. The **Study Guide** is designed to give students a maximum learning experience with a minimum of effort, focusing on the important aspects of each chapter and reinforcing chapter material by means of objective and practical exercises and self-tests. This supplement truly guides students through the most appropriate learning process and enables them to assess their progress and ensure mastery of the materials. Students are given suggestions on how to approach problems and what steps to take to arrive at the correct solutions. Complete answers and explanations are provided in the study guide to all self-test materials and exercises.

Two practice sets are available with this book and may be used to strengthen students' knowledge of procedural materials and provide a framework for integrating managerial accounting concepts from several different chapters. The first practice set, Omni, can be assigned anytime after the first four chapters of the book have been covered. The Omni Corporation practice set, a computerized job order costing practice set, covers one month of operations of a business that manufactures air compressors in a job lot production environment. The set contains all necessary forms, software, and instructions to enable students to obtain a solution by means of a personal computer. The computerized practice set is ideal to help acquaint students with electronic data processing of an accounting system.

The Profit Planning practice set requires the preparation of an annual budget by quarters for a manufacturing firm that uses a standard costing system. Cost-volume-profit analyses are required, and the first quarter performance reports are required for materials, labor, and manufacturing overhead. This practice set is extremely effective in integrating the essential management accounting concepts of standard costs, budgeting, performance reporting, and cost-volume-profit relationships. This practice set can be assigned anytime after the first eight chapters have been covered.

One of the major advantages of the teaching and learning package available with this book is the complete integration and coordination of all elements of the package, made possible because each item was developed, written, and tested by the authors.

FLEXIBILITY

We have tried to make the book as flexible as possible, so that it may be adapted to a variety of course objectives. The material is arranged in a sequence that we found to be logical for a managerial accounting course. It is unlikely, however, that all 20 chapters will be covered in a single semester or quarter. However, the instructor may select any number of topics or entire chapters to omit from a course without loss of continuity, as discussed in the Solutions Manual.

Instructors who arrange their course differently from the chapter sequence in the book will find the book very adaptable and flexible. The quantity of available material permits users to choose those topics that best satisfy specific course objectives and to omit topics that are deemed less important for a particular class. After Chapter 2 instructors have a wide variety of possible topic sequences depending on course objectives and the teaching style and preferences of the instructor. The combination of textbook, instructor's supplements, and student supplements makes the book suitable for many class situations and levels. The material constitutes a complete package that should appeal to the experienced instructor, and it is equally suitable for schools that use student teachers. The book is also suitable for self study, and this leaves room for an instructor to digress, elaborate, and discuss supplementary topics in the classroom.

As used in this book, the pronoun "he" embraces both genders when used without reference to a specific person.

ACKNOWLEDGMENTS

A large number of individuals have contributed to the preparation of this book and supplementary materials. We are grateful to many professors, students, and others for their help, advice, and guidance. Special thanks to Mohammed J. Abdolmohammadi; Jerome Bennet, the E. Clairborne Robins School of Business; Stephen J. Gilmour, Northern Illinois University; Robert E. Holtfreter, Kansas State University; Philip Karpik, University of Illinois at Chicago Circle; Marsha Kertz, San Jose State University; Robert Koehler, Pennsylvania State University; Ronald A. Milne; Vidyapati Singh, Illinois College; and James D. Suver, University of Colorado.

Our special appreciation to N. S. Arunkumar, Lawrence Davis, and Walter Doehring for their help in checking our materials for accuracy. The staff of McGraw-Hill whose help was invaluable in preparing the book and supplements includes Jim DeVoe, Joe Murphy, Mel Haber, Jo Satloff, and Charles Hess.

Members of our families contributed much with their work, suggestions, patience, and sacrifices. We are grateful to the many other people who have helped us to produce the manuscripts and supplements and to make the necessary corrections in the final proofs of the books. Any remaining errors are the sole responsibility of the authors.

Lester E. Heitger
Serge Matulich

Developing a Management Accounting Data Base

part 1

Virtually every major decision made in an organization depends on accounting information. Department heads are responsible for budgets that include costs of materials, labor, building space, and other resources. Production managers need to know how efficiently they are using materials and labor to manufacture products. Marketing managers need to know how effective their marketing programs are in generating sales revenue—is the expense of selling the product too high? Should the product line be dropped? What is the cost of increasing production capacity? Financial managers need information so that they can report profitability and financial position to investors, creditors, taxing authorities, and regulatory agencies. All of these decision makers depend on accounting information, much of which is derived from detailed cost data that accountants develop from daily business activities. The cost data base is particularly useful for preparing managerial reports for internal decision making.

In Chapter 1 we describe the environment of managerial accounting and introduce basic concepts and terms essential to understanding the material in the chapters that follow. In Chapter 2 we present basic cost terminology and discuss how the measurement of costs parallels closely the physical flow of production activities. In addition, Chapter 2 presents cost behavior concepts and discusses the importance of managers' knowing how costs change with respect to changes in the volume of activity. Chapters 3 and 4 describe product costing and the development of the cost accounting data base.

The Managerial Accounting Environment

1

Chapter 1 provides an overview of the managerial accounting environment and the role of managerial accounting in the effective and efficient operation of organizations. When you have completed your study of the chapter, you should understand:

1 The functions of managerial accounting and financial accounting.

2 The nature of decision making and the steps in the decision process.

3 The role of accounting information in the decision process.

4 The function of cost accounting in providing data for financial accounting reports and managerial accounting reports.

5 Characteristics of accounting information and how they are interrelated.

6 The various activities involved in cost accounting.

7 The effect external organizations have on a company's data base.

8 What factors affect the complexity of a firm's cost accounting system.

All organizations require accounting information to manage daily operations, plan future operations, and evaluate past performance. In addition, most organizations must provide external financial information to taxing authorities, shareholders, regulatory agencies, labor unions, and other special interest groups. **Financial accounting** is concerned with providing information to external users. The first volume of this series[1] is about the fundamentals of the external reporting process. The accounting process that provides information primarily for internal use is called **managerial accounting**. This text is primarily about managerial accounting and how accounting information is reported to and used by internal managers.

[1] Serge Matulich and Lester E. Heitger, *Financial Accounting*, 2nd ed. (New York: McGraw-Hill, 1985).

In this chapter we discuss the role of accounting information in making decisions and the way managers use accounting information in the decision process. The nature of managerial accounting is examined along with the environment in which it functions. We also introduce **cost accounting**, which is the process of determining the cost of products or activities, and we discuss the role of costs in external and internal reporting. The chapter concludes with an overview of some of the regulatory groups that have an influence on the development of cost accounting data.

THE DECISION-MAKING PROCESS

We are faced with decisions almost continuously in our personal lives and in business. Many decisions are so routine that we may not even realize they are decisions, such as what clothes to wear each day or what to have for breakfast. Others make us more conscious of the decision process because the decision is made less frequently and is of greater consequence, such as buying a car or choosing a job.

Decisions vary in complexity

Both business and personal decisions vary in complexity and importance. Many decisions require no action at all. For instance, a stockholder may ask a broker for the market price of a stock and as a result of the reply may decide not to sell the stock. Similarly, a production supervisor looks at hourly quality control data and determines that production performance is within acceptable limits, so no action is necessary. Other business decisions, however, are much more complex, such as whether or not to build a new production plant, or whether to make a new line of products or just continue with the products currently being manufactured.

Decision theory affects the way accounting information is prepared

Decision making has been the subject of many research studies, most of which have centered on the structure of the decision process and the role of information in decision making. The body of knowledge on decision making is called **decision theory**. Decision theory directly affects many of the managerial accounting concepts discussed here, and we mention decision theory concepts at various points in the text. Because many business decisions are based on accounting information, it is important to understand the decision-making process and its relationship to accounting information.

Decision making is both an art and a science. It is an art because decisions are made using both subjective and objective data. Decision makers must decide how to combine a variety of inputs to arrive at a logical decision. Decision making is a science because many complex decisions can be reduced to simpler components by means of quantitative methods. For example, many firms examine only a small portion of production output, using statistical techniques to determine whether production processes are operating within acceptable tolerance limits.

The Structure of Decisions

Each individual makes decisions in a slightly different way. However, most people agree that the decision-making process includes the following:

1. Defining the problem
2. Identifying the alternatives
3. Accumulating relevant information
4. Making the decision

Specific problems must be clearly identified before they can be solved

Defining the problem. Perhaps the most important phase of decision making is problem definition, because all of the other activities in the process depend upon this phase. If managers do not have a clear understanding of the **specific** problem at hand, they may spend considerable time and effort identifying alternatives and gathering information that is irrelevant to solving the real problem.

For example, a year-end inventory count reveals a substantial inventory shortage. The plant superintendent immediately suspects employee theft and asks his assistant to determine measures that will eliminate employee theft of inventory. A more careful study of the situation reveals that inventory shortages pertain only to materials used in the production of one of the firm's products. After additional analysis it is discovered that the problem stems from the use of different systems for recording product cost and for transferring inventory items into production.

One type of document, issued by the production engineering department, is used as the basis for transferring inventory items into production. Another document, from the accounting department, is used to record the transfer of inventory costs. A clerk in the inventory storeroom prepares the accounting document based on production requirements no longer in effect. The document used for transferring inventory to production is based on current production engineering requirements. As a result, the two documents do not show the same quantities of inventory for the production of this particular product. Consequently, more inventory goes into production than is recorded, and the shortage is the result of faulty record keeping and not theft.

Incorrectly defined problems waste time and resources, so decision makers should not be too hasty in moving on to the alternatives phase of the decision process. Very complex problems may require much analysis before a clear definition is reached.

The idea stage of decision making

Identifying alternatives. Now that we know the problem, how do we solve it? Usually there is more than one feasible solution. Identifying alternatives is the idea phase of decision making, in which managers can use their ingenuity. Creativity is the watchword in identifying alternatives, and there is no need to be cautious or inhibited in this process because the alternatives are evaluated at a later phase. Unfortunately, previous experience and bias often limit the variety of alternatives that managers identify and evaluate.

Accumulating relevant information. Decision makers may desire a variety of information to assist them in making decisions. Some information may be subjective and some objective; some may be internal to the organization and some may be external. Some information may be based on past costs or events and some may be based on management's expectations about future costs or events.

Only relevant information should be selected

The information used in making decisions must be relevant to the decision at hand. The idea is to select only those items of information that affect the decision and to discard those that do not. In this age of information explosion,[2] decision makers may be inundated with data. Decision theorists refer to this phenomenon as **information overload**. Managers must cautiously select only those items of information that can be assimilated into a logical decision framework.

Information should increase knowledge or decrease uncertainty

Information should increase decision makers' knowledge or reduce their uncertainty. For example, a company manufactures ball bearings which it sells to companies A, B, C, and D. One day a customer calls and says he wants to double his normal monthly order, but the clerk who takes the message cannot remember which company called. Without more information, the sales manager has a 25 percent chance of guessing which company called and a 75 percent chance of guessing the wrong company. When the clerk recalls that he is certain it was not company A, this information increases the chance of guessing correctly to ⅓ and reduces the risk of an incorrect decision to ⅔. Later in the day company C calls to reaffirm its regular monthly order; this additional information reduces the risk of error to 50 percent since only B and D remain as possible choices. The same day a new customer, company E, calls to place an order. This event is not relevant to the question of which company wants to double its order. You can see that relevant information increased knowledge of the situation and reduced the risk of calling the wrong company to verify the doubling of its order.

Making the decision. Once the problem is defined, alternatives are identified, and relevant information is selected, it may appear that making the decision should be simple. Seldom is that the case, particularly for complex decisions. Often no single variable dominates in making the decision. Instead, several important decision criteria interact and affect one another. For example, in choosing a career you may consider economic potential, job satisfaction, lifestyle, advancement potential, geographic location, and other variables. Some careers may rank high for some variables and low for others. The final decision depends on the decision model that you decide to use.

A description of the way that a decision is made is called a **decision model**. Decision models may be quite simple. For example, an investor may decide to buy stock of a company if its earnings per share have increased at least 10 percent a year for the last 3 years. Other variables that may be included in the decision model are earnings ratios or dividend yields. Occasionally even complex problems are decided with simple decision models because managers are unwilling to try more complex tech-

---

[2] The term **information explosion** refers to the expansion of available information of all sorts, primarily due to the tremendous growth in computer technology, in low-cost storage capabilities, and in microcomputers.

niques or because more complex models have not produced better results in the past.

Many routine decisions are made with precise decision models. For example, quality control is performed with sampling procedures that determine when the production process is unsatisfactory and should be investigated. The decision model may be quite simple: Stop production and investigate if more than 3 percent of the products are defective.

Decision models must further the goals of the organization

Whether the decision model is very sophisticated or very simple, it should be designed to further the goals of the organization or individual. Simple as that idea is, it is sometimes lost in the heat of dealing with complex problems. In the final analysis, the quality of a decision is determined by how it affects the achievement of the organization's goals.

THE ROLE OF ACCOUNTING INFORMATION IN DECISION MAKING

Accounting information is objective

The role of accounting information, as well as other types of information, is to increase knowledge or reduce risk. Unlike subjective information, accounting information is quantitative, verifiable information that is very effective in aiding decision makers. For example, a supervisor with 20 years of work experience is of the opinion that assembly line productivity has declined over the last year. Although he may be right, much more useful information is obtained from an accounting report that documents an 8 percent decline in production efficiency, with a resulting increase in product cost of $.30 a unit and a decrease in annual profits of $60,000. As a result, managers frequently assign significant weight to accounting information even when it is supplemented with more subjective data. In short, few organizations can survive, let alone thrive, without reliable accounting information.

The demand for accounting information has grown significantly over the last decade. An important reason has been the declining cost of computer equipment and the increased use of more sophisticated management planning and decision methods. Managers are demanding more detailed accounting data than ever before. The increase in demand for information in general has mushroomed in all organizations; the pressure for more accounting information in particular comes from managers' desire to satisfy both internal information needs and the needs of external information users, especially government. Some of the specific external demands for information are discussed later in this chapter.

Accounting Information Characteristics

Useful accounting information has the following characteristics:

1. Relevance
2. Timeliness
3. Accuracy

Relevance is a very important characteristic of accounting information. It means that accounting information must be useful in considering the specific problem or decision at hand. Relevance is important to external and internal accounting reports, but it particularly affects internal reports. External reports, such as income statements and balance sheets, serve a variety of users for many different types of decisions and are in general relevant for many different purposes.

The benefits of accounting information must exceed the cost of providing it

Relevance has a specific influence on internal accounting reports. Internal reports assist managers in making individual decisions and in evaluating specific problems. Managers may accumulate and report any kind of accounting information they deem useful, and they may use their ingenuity in determining what internal accounting reports are prepared and how frequently—daily, weekly, monthly. The primary limitation on internal reporting is the cost of preparing such reports. **Cost-benefit** refers to the concept that organizations are willing to generate information only if the benefit derived from the information is greater than the cost of providing the information.

Timeliness refers to the need for accounting information to be current. Many types of information lose value rapidly. Financial information is particularly sensitive to the passage of time. Knowing how much a business is currently earning may enable an investor to decide whether or not to invest in the business. If the information is old, the investor's decision may not be made wisely. Similarly, a department store manager may find daily sales information useful in assessing the value of advertising programs as long as the sales information is reported on a timely basis. If the information is a month old when the manager receives it, the information may have little value.

Should we use approximate information now or more precise information later?

Most internal accounting information is sensitive to timing because much of it is used to monitor and control daily operations. Sometimes it is more important to have approximate information immediately than to have precise information later. Precision may have to be sacrificed to achieve timely reporting of relevant information.

Accuracy. Even the most timely information is of little value if it is not accurate. **Accuracy** is therefore an important characteristic of accounting information. For instance, poor estimates of bad debt losses may cause a manager to take inappropriate action in connection with credit-granting policies. Accuracy is a major prerequisite of timely and relevant accounting information. It is important to distinguish between accuracy and precision. A report stating that a company earned $560,000 last year may be accurate, although the precise amount of earnings may be $560,386. On the other hand, earnings reported at $864,932.17 may appear very precise, but the information is of little value if the actual amount is $150,000.

The distinction between accuracy and precision

Many people believe that accounting information is accurate to the last penny. In fact, accounting information involves much estimation and approximation. Accountants estimate the useful life and the salvage value of fixed assets in computing depreciation. They estimate the net amount of receivables that will be collectible, the cost of providing warranty services, and the interest rate for discounting capital lease obligations. Despite the need for estimates, accounting information should be accurate within the constraints imposed on the methods of measurement and the standards applied in producing information.

In addition to being relevant, timely, and accurate, accounting information should be understandable, objective, and unbiased. These characteristics of accounting information are interrelated. Together they provide guidelines for evaluating the usefulness of accounting reports. Such evaluations are particularly appropriate for internal accounting.

Data and Information

The terms *data* and *information* are used frequently in general conversation as well as in many technical disciplines. To ensure a common understanding of the terms, we briefly describe their use in this book.

In decision theory, **information** is data that has been put together into a usable form. This definition of information creates a very individualistic concept of information. For example, a report showing departmental labor costs for one month may be useful to one departmental supervisor, but not to another. With the above definition, the report is information in one case, but not in the other. The term **data** is used to refer to the raw material or building blocks of an information system. **Data base** refers to the foundation of data supporting the information system and drawn on by users to meet information needs.

In this book we use the term *data* in reference to the accumulation and recording of costs. *Information* is used to refer to specific reports or cost analyses.

Characteristics of Managerial Accounting Reports

The distinction between financial accounting and managerial accounting is made primarily on the orientation of the reports. Financial accounting refers to reports that are prepared primarily for external users, such as investors, creditors, regulatory agencies, and taxing authorities. This does not mean that managers of organizations have no use for external reports. For example, net income, earnings per share, and balance sheet ratios are all of interest to many managers. However, external financial statements are prepared **primarily** to satisfy external reporting requirements.

Managerial reports are specific; financial reports are general

Managerial accounting reports, designed to meet the needs of internal users, are situation specific, which means they attempt to fill the information needs of managers with respect to specific problems, decisions, or situations. Sinee relatively few individuals use each managerial accounting report, such reports can be more specific than the general-purpose financial statements that must meet the information needs of many users.

Managerial reports usually are more detailed than external reports. For internal reporting, a firm may develop detailed cost information for each product it produces, but in the external financial statements the firm reports only the total cost of all products produced and sold. Aggregation of information from detailed internal accounting reports is a common characteristic of most external reports.

Another characteristic of managerial reports is their frequency. Many internal reports are prepared monthly, weekly, or even daily. For example, accountants may prepare weekly reports identifying the cost of producing products; they may prepare daily reports on cash receipts and disbursements.

Planning and Control

A major responsibility of managers is to plan and control business operations to ensure that organizational goals are achieved. **Planning** is the process of setting goals, determining what resources are needed, and how best to use them to achieve the goals.

Control is the monitoring of activities to see that organizational goals and objectives are achieved as planned. To control operations, managers compare actual performance with planned performance. Deviations from the plans are investigated to determine their causes and to decide what if any corrective actions should be taken.

Figure 1-1 shows graphically planning and control activities. At the top are the major goals of the organization, established at the highest level of decision making, for example, by the board of directors. An example of such goals is to provide a fair return to investors by manufacturing products in the food products industry. To achieve these goals, management may establish specific operating objectives, such as to produce and sell 2 million boxes of a certain breakfast cereal each month. To achieve the objectives, detailed plans are developed with the help of accounting information. These plans consist of budgets, which describe the amounts of material and labor to be used for making the product; decisions on product pricing; and marketing strategies. Operations are guided by managers in accordance with the detailed plans, and as results are achieved, their costs are measured by accountants. The costs accumulated during operations make up the data needed for preparing accounting reports.

The managerial reports prepared from the cost data form a feedback loop and provide managers with information on how the specific plans of the organization are being met. Managers can compare actual performance with planned operations, and if actual performance deviates from the plans, managers use the information to control performances by making adjustments in operations. The financial reports prepared from the cost data also form a feedback loop. They enable managers to determine whether the specific objectives of the organization are being satisfied. If they are not, the information is used to control operations by changing the plans. Of course, both financial and managerial reports are used at all levels of the organization, but the detailed managerial reports are more relevant for controlling operations at lower levels, whereas the more general financial reports are most suitable for higher-level policy setting.

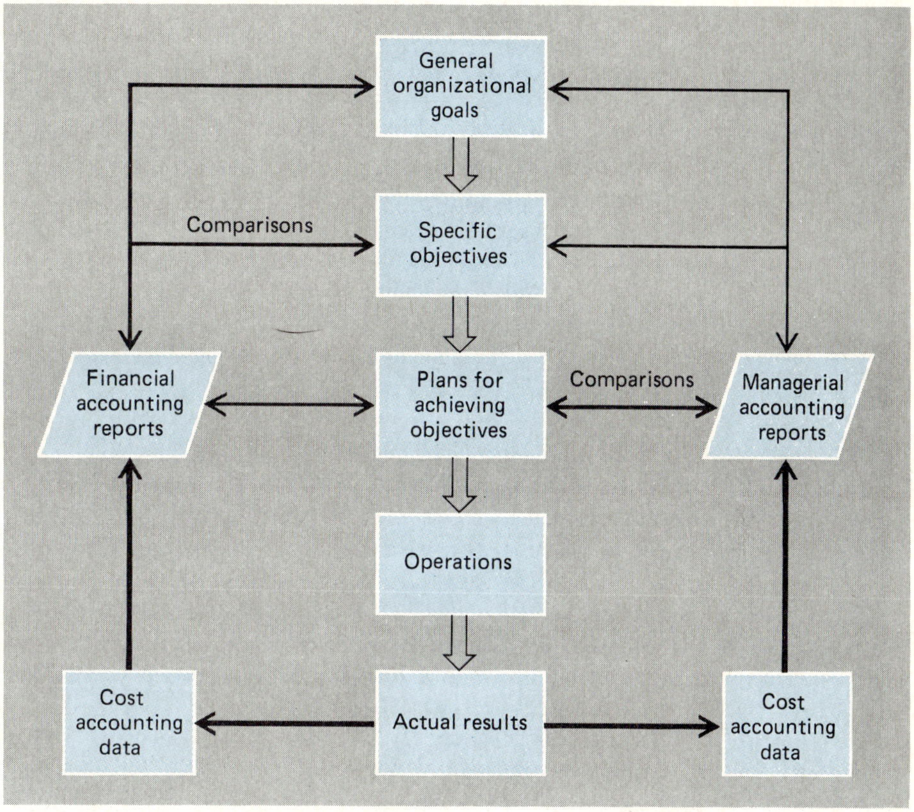

Figure 1-1 **The planning and control process is essential to the successful accomplishment of organizational goals and objectives. Accounting information provides feedback to managers so that they can compare actual results with plans to determine if objectives are being met. Control is achieved by taking action to prevent operations from deviating significantly from plans. The heaviest lines show the most important feedback loops needed for control. All information is used internally, but some is less useful for control purposes, as indicated by the lighter feedback loops which are more relevant for planning.**

Various types of managerial accounting reports are prepared to help managers plan and control operations. Included are reports on the cost of making products, the cost of various marketing and advertising programs, and the cost of employee education and training programs. These managerial accounting reports make it possible for managers to measure the difference between what was planned and what was accomplished. The differences, or **variances**, serve as a basis for coordinating decisions among all managers working toward the same goals, and for taking steps to narrow the differences. Production cost data may demonstrate that it is less expensive for a company to buy boxes from a supplier to package its cereal than to make the boxes in its factory. Inventory cost data indicate whether changes in the insurance and interest costs of carrying inventory require a reduction or increase in inventory.

THE COST ACCOUNTING DATA BASE

In addition to the classifications of financial accounting and managerial accounting, accountants identify cost accounting activities. Unlike financial and managerial accounting, cost accounting does not refer to the reporting process. **Cost accounting** refers to the process of determining the cost of some particular product or activity. Cost accounting data are used for both internal and external reports. Many internal reports present detailed cost information on the production of specific products, such as lamps or knives, or they contain information on the cost of performing some activity, such as preparing a sales invoice. In external reports, cost data are summarized and presented in aggregate. For example, the cost of producing all products sold during the period usually appears as a single number in the income statement.

The cost accounting data base is a key source of accounting information

Because cost data are used in both financial and managerial accounting reports, cost accounting is really part of both classifications of accounting. We present this relationship graphically in Figure 1-2. Notice that cost accounting underlies and supports both financial and managerial reporting. The **cost accounting data base** is the foundation of cost data that supports many accounting activities, particularly in manufacturing firms.

Cost data are vital in preparing and understanding accounting reports, particularly managerial accounting reports. If managers are to use managerial accounting reports effectively in managing a business, they must know how costs are determined and reported. To provide an adequate foundation for understanding and using cost information, Chapters 2 through 4 describe important cost accounting terminology and the fundamentals of determining cost.

Occasionally cost accounting is referred to as **manufacturing accounting**. The need for detailed cost information first became evident in manufacturing firms when product cost data were required to control produc-

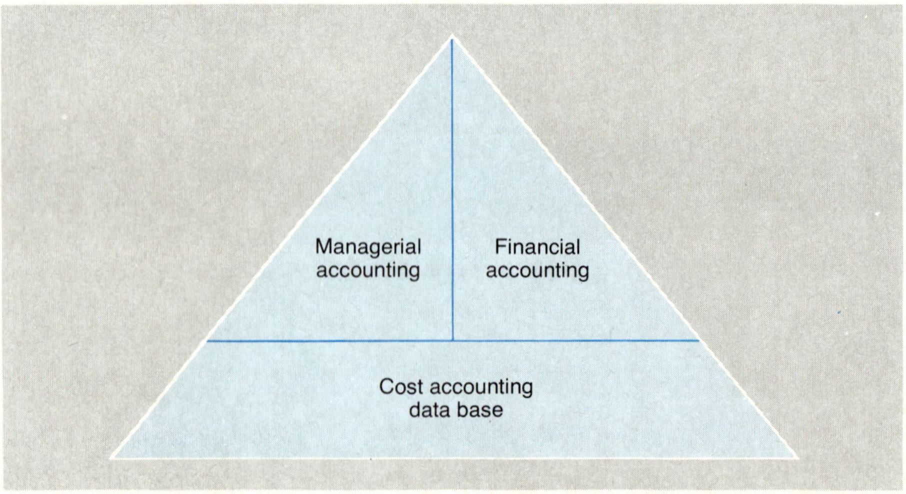

Figure 1-2
The cost accounting data base is the foundation for most internal accounting reports and for much data that is reported in external accounting reports.

tion costs and to establish selling prices. Many cost accounting concepts and techniques were developed in manufacturing industries. However, as product costing methods became more sophisticated, managers turned their attention to determining costs for nonmanufacturing activities. The process of determining costs for things other than tangible products is called **activity costing** or **service costing**.

In this text we highlight only the fundamentals of cost accounting as they relate to the reporting function of managerial accounting. A later course devoted entirely to cost accounting is necessary for those interested in a comprehensive cost background. However, our treatment of cost concepts is sufficient to provide the necessary background for understanding many of the intricacies and problems associated with managerial accounting analysis and reporting. Here we describe basic cost accounting activities and those factors that determine the complexity of a cost system and the volume of cost data generated.

Cost Accounting Activities

Cost accounting is frequently classified into four different activities. They are:

1. Cost determination
2. Cost recording
3. Cost analyzing
4. Cost reporting

Cost determination. The first step in a cost accounting system is **cost determination**, which is just what it sounds like: determining cost for some specific product or activity. Although all activities in a cost system are important, cost determination is critical because the other three activities depend on it. In most cost accounting courses, much time is spent on cost determination procedures and techniques. A substantial part of the next three chapters is devoted to cost determination. The brief introduction given here provides the necessary cost accounting foundation for understanding the nature and use of cost data in the many different types of managerial accounting reports that follow in the rest of the book.

Cost recording. Most cost accounting systems are an integral part of a firm's formal accounting system, with costs recorded in the journal and posted to the ledger. Specific cost recording procedures are not emphasized in this text, although some basic entries are shown in the three chapters dealing with the development of the cost data base.

Cost analyzing. Because accountants develop the cost data, they are usually most capable of analyzing cost information to solve problems, plan operations, or provide advice to managers. Meaningful cost analysis depends heavily upon a clear understanding of the cost-finding methods used in cost accounting. People often attribute totally incorrect characteristics to costs. Throughout this book we describe many common errors caused by incorrect cost assumptions.

Cost reporting. Costs are reported in detail in many internal accounting reports and in aggregate in most external accounting reports. Managers use cost accounting information in varying levels of detail to control costs, to evaluate decisions, and in general to monitor performance. In order to use cost information intelligently and effectively managers must have a good understanding of how costs are measured, what characteristics various costs have, and how costs change with respect to changes in the volume of activity and over time. For these reasons, it is essential for all managers to have a good understanding of cost accounting concepts.

Factors Affecting Cost Accounting Systems

Many different factors determine the complexity of a cost system and the volume of cost data generated. Some of the most important factors are:

1. Size of the firm
2. Number of different products produced
3. Type of production process
4. Management's attitude toward cost information
5. External variables

Size of the firm. The amount of cost data necessary to manage a firm varies with the size of the firm. A firm in which two people manufacture fishing lures in a garage does not require as much cost data as a firm manufacturing fishing lures with 100 employees. In addition, the process of developing cost data is more complex in the larger firm because as an organization gets larger, some costs become more difficult to trace to specific products or activities. In general, the volume of cost data and the complexity of the cost system increases with firm size.

Number of different products produced. If a firm produces only one product, all manufacturing costs can be assigned to it. However, when a firm produces more than one product, the accountant must distribute the manufacturing costs among the various products. Some manufacturing costs, such as the cost of materials, clearly relate to specific products. Other production costs, such as utilities and property taxes, are not so clearly identified with specific products. Usually the number of costs not identifiable with specific products increases with the number of products made.

Type of production process. In cost accounting, costs are assigned to products on the basis of physical production activity. For example, the labor cost of a product is determined by the amount of time employees work on the product and on the wage rate of employees. As long as labor can be identified with specific products, accountants are able to assign labor costs to the products. However, some production processes are so complex that it is difficult to trace production costs to specific products. In such situations accountants cannot assign costs to products easily. As a general rule, the more complex the production process, the more complex is the cost system.

Management's attitude toward cost information. Some cost data are required by virtually all organizations. For instance, even a small manufacturing firm requires some measure of product cost to satisfy taxing authorities when filing tax returns. However, there is a tremendous difference between the bare minimum requirement for cost data and the amount of cost data developed in firms using extensive managerial reporting procedures. The difference between the minimum and the optimum cost system is a function of management's attitude toward cost information. As organizations and the economy become more and more complex, the amount of cost information required to manage a business has continued to increase. As managers at all management levels require more cost information, the size and complexity of cost accounting systems continues to grow.

External variables. Cost data used for internal reporting are fundamentally unaffected by external variables. However, cost data for external reports may be affected by a wide variety of regulatory agencies, such as the Internal Revenue Service, the Federal Trade Commission, and the Securities and Exchange Commission. These organizations are discussed below.

EXTERNAL ORGANIZATIONS AND THE COST DATA BASE

Cost data are used for both internal and external accounting reports; therefore external reporting requirements can have an influence on the kind of data base generated by businesses. For example, businesses with certain types of federal government contracts are required to develop cost data for the contracts in certain prescribed ways. Very large businesses are required to report certain types of information to the Federal Trade Commission. In general, the federal government exercises an important and growing influence over the volume, detail, and form of the cost data base of many firms. In this section we discuss some of the more important organizations that affect cost accounting data bases.

Cost Accounting Standards Board

Each year the federal government spends huge amounts of money purchasing goods and services from private businesses. Some items, such as computer hardware and food for military personnel, are readily available in the market. Potential suppliers of such goods may submit bids when the government advertises the need for them.

Many items, such as nuclear submarines, bridges, and jet fighter airplanes, must be produced by businesses to conform to specifications established by the government. Typically, such goods require developmental work prior to actual production; often it is difficult to estimate accurately what the cost of development and production will be. As a result, government contracts with manufacturers often provide for payment of these costs plus a reasonable profit. In theory, such contracts seem very logical, but in practice much controversy can arise over what costs should be included as the basis for what the government should pay.

To minimize the potential for cost abuses in these kinds of negotiated contracts between manufacturers and the government, Congress created the **Cost Accounting Standards Board (CASB)** in 1970. Basically, the board was created to ensure that the government pays a fair price. Specifically, the CASB was established for the following objectives:

Objectives of CASB

1. Uniformity: Achieve like costs under like circumstances.
2. Consistency: Ensure consistent practices within a firm over time.
3. Comparability: Provide similarity of information and practices among different firms.
4. Neutrality: Achieve fairness with neither bias nor prejudice to either contracting party.

To achieve these objectives the CASB issued cost accounting standards. In 1980 the CASB went out of existence because Congress decided to terminate its funding. By this time it had issued 19 standards on those areas of cost accounting most relevant to negotiated government contracts.[3]

The law that created the Cost Accounting Standards Board required only defense contractors to comply with CASB standards. Subsequently the law was changed so that now virtually all federal government–negotiated contracts of $100,000 or more are governed by the standards. Firms with government contracts that fall under CASB rules are already affected directly. Other firms, however, are affected indirectly because the Internal Revenue Service and the Securities and Exchange Commission have borrowed portions of CASB standards for setting their own reporting requirements. Although the CASB no longer exists, its standards remain in force.

Financial Accounting Standards Board

The **Financial Accounting Standards Board (FASB)** is a professional rule-making body that establishes standards for financial reporting. All publicly held corporations must prepare their external accounting reports in accordance with FASB standards. Because cost accounting information is part of the external financial statements of most organizations, FASB pronouncements have a direct impact on the cost accounting systems of firms.

---

[3] *Cumulative Progress Report to the Congress, 1971–1980,* Cost Accounting Standards Board, November 1980.

Federal Trade Commission

The **Federal Trade Commission (FTC)** may affect a firm's cost accounting system in two ways—through the Robinson-Patman Act and through the lines of business reporting requirements.

Robinson-Patman Act. The Robinson-Patman Act prohibits discriminatory pricing of products of equal grade and quantity when such pricing would reduce competition. The FTC is charged with enforcing this law. The only way a firm can use discriminatory pricing is by showing one of the following conditions is satisfied:

1. The price difference is due to changing market conditions.
2. The price difference was made to match the price difference of competitors.
3. The price difference is directly attributable to the selling firm's cost differences in manufacturing and distributing the product to different customers.

The last reason is commonly used by companies to justify differential pricing and must be supported by detailed cost information.

Lines of business reporting. The FTC has the power to require many large businesses to provide revenue and cost data by business segment instead of just company totals. The business segments are referred to as lines of business and are categorized by a general classification chart provided by the FTC. The purpose of segment or lines of business reporting is to gather business data that may be useful in identifying and eliminating unfair restraint of trade.

The required segment reporting has caused some firms to restructure their cost accounting system to comply with FTC classifications. The cost of gathering and reporting segment data is a point of disagreement between the FTC and some of the reporting firms.

Internal Revenue Service

The **Internal Revenue Service (IRS)** is charged with the responsibility of ensuring that individuals and organizations pay the correct amount of federal income tax. In dealing with businesses, the IRS must sometimes determine accounting procedures for tax purposes. Basically, tax laws allow firms to use generally accepted accounting principles (GAAP) in determining taxable income, but laws also establish certain rules and procedures that affect costs. For instance, the IRS defines product costs as the total cost of production. It encourages consistency in the use of alternative accounting procedures and requires the use of last in, first out (LIFO) inventory valuation for book purposes if it is used for tax purposes. Generally the Internal Revenue Service attempts to avoid tampering with GAAP, but it takes action when it perceives that tax obligations may be misstated.

Securities and Exchange Commission

The **Securities and Exchange Commission (SEC)** is charged primarily with the responsibility of ensuring that the financial statements of publicly held corporations are fair representations of economic position. Like the IRS, the SEC relies heavily on generally accepted accounting principles created by the accounting profession. In addition, the SEC issues accounting pronouncements whenever it feels that some change in accounting practice is necessary to present a correct picture of the economic situation of businesses. Some SEC releases relate to cost accounting activities.

THE CERTIFICATE IN MANAGEMENT ACCOUNTING

Recognition of professional competence is an important aspect of many disciplines. In public accounting a practitioner strives to become a **certified public accountant (CPA)**. To become a CPA, a candidate must pass a rigorous four-part examination that lasts 2½ days. In many states an individual must work some minimum amount of time in public accounting in addition to passing the CPA examination before the certificate is issued.

The CMA—recognition of professional competence

Managerial accounting is somewhat different from public accounting, and in some states only people working in public accounting can be certified as CPAs. To provide a measure of managerial accounting competence, the National Association of Accountants, through its Institute of Management Accounting, offers a **Certificate in Management Accounting (CMA)**. The certificate is earned by passing a five-part 2½-day examination and by meeting work experience requirements. The CMA examination is similar to the CPA examination in format, but the material is more heavily oriented toward internal reporting activities and management information needs. Both CPA and CMA examinations are offered twice a year.

SUMMARY

Organizations require accounting information for internal management and to meet external reporting requirements. **Financial accounting** provides accounting information to external users. **Managerial accounting** refers to the internal reporting process.

Most business decisions depend on accounting information. Decision making should be approached in a logical and systematic manner. The process includes **defining the problem, identifying alternatives, accumulating relevant information**, and **making the decision**. The body of knowledge encompassing decision making is called **decision theory**. A formal description of the way that a decision is made is called a **decision model**.

The role of information is to increase knowledge or decrease risk. Accounting information is useful in fulfilling this role because it is quantitative and verifiable. The demand for accounting information continues to grow.

Accounting information should be relevant, timely, and accurate. **Relevance** means accounting data must satisfy the specific information needs of the user. **Timeliness** refers to the requirement that accounting information be available when it is needed. Financial information is particularly sensitive to loss in value due to the passage of time. **Accuracy** deals with the correctness of accounting reports.

Planning and control are key responsibilities of managers. **Planning** is necessary to achieve the objectives and goals of the organization. **Control** is the monitoring of activities to ensure that planned objectives are met.

Data are the raw materials or source elements of the information system. **Information** is data assembled in usable form. A **data base** is the total data foundation that supports the information system.

Cost accounting is the determination of the cost of specific products or activities. Cost data are used in both internal and external reports. Although detailed cost data are used for internal reports, cost accounting and managerial accounting are not identical. Cost accounting provides data for both the financial and managerial reporting functions.

Cost accounting activities are divided into **cost determination, cost recording, cost analyzing**, and **cost reporting**. An understanding of cost accounting is necessary to use effectively many important managerial accounting reports.

The volume of cost data generated and the complexity of a cost system are affected by the size of the firm, the type of production process, the number of different products produced, management's attitude toward cost accounting information, and external variables. The major external variables are government agencies and regulatory bodies.

The **Cost Accounting Standards Board (CASB)** was created by Congress to establish standards and procedures for negotiated federal government contracts. Although the CASB no longer exists, its standards are still in force, and they make it necessary for many organizations to accumulate and maintain large amounts of cost accounting data.

The **Financial Accounting Standards Board (FASB)** has the responsibility for creating guidelines for financial reporting. Its rules have an impact on the way cost data are accumulated.

The **Federal Trade Commission (FTC)** has the responsibility of ensuring fair trade practices in American business. Two factors that affect the cost accounting system of many companies are the Robinson-Patman Act, which forbids discriminatory pricing practices, and lines of business reporting, which requires some large firms to provide the FTC with revenue and cost data for segments of their businesses. Both types of regulatory action cause firms to generate detailed cost data that might otherwise not be necessary.

The **Internal Revenue Service (IRS)** monitors the operation of the federal tax laws. However, the IRS determines accounting procedures for tax purposes whenever the use of GAAP results in taxable income that is unfair in the eyes of the taxing authorities.

The **Securities and Exchange Commission (SEC)** is devoted to the fair presentation of financial information of publicly held corporations.

Recognition of professional excellence is common in many disciplines. In public accounting, an individual may strive to become a **certified public**

accountant (CPA). In the private sector, managerial accounting excellence is indicated by a **Certificate in Management Accounting (CMA)**. Both certifications require the passing of a comprehensive 2½-day examination.

KEY TERMS

Many new terms commonly used in business and accounting are introduced in this chapter. Most of them are used in subsequent parts of the book. You should become familiar with the terms in the following list. The numbers in parentheses indicate the pages on which the terms first appear.

accuracy *(8)*
activity costing *(13)*
Certificate in Management Accounting (CMA) *(18)*
certified public accountant (CPA) *(18)*
control *(10)*
cost accounting *(12)*
cost accounting data base *(12)*
Cost Accounting Standards Board (CASB) *(15)*
cost analyzing *(13)*
cost-benefit *(8)*
cost determination *(13)*
cost recording *(13)*
cost reporting *(14)*
data *(9)*
data base *(9)*
decision model *(6)*
decision theory *(4)*
Federal Trade Commission (FTC) *(17)*
financial accounting *(3)*
Financial Accounting Standards Board (FASB) *(16)*
information *(9)*
information overload *(6)*
Internal Revenue Service (IRS) *(17)*
managerial accounting *(3)*
planning *(10)*
relevance *(8)*
Securities and Exchange Commission (SEC) *(18)*
service costing *(13)*
timeliness *(8)*

QUESTIONS

1. Distinguish between financial accounting and managerial accounting.
2. Define decision theory. How does it relate to accounting?
3. Identify and briefly describe the basic steps in the decision process.
4. What does the term *information overload* mean?
5. Give an example of a decision model you have used in the last 6 months.
6. How does accounting information fit into the decision process?
7. Describe the characteristics of accounting information.
8. Contrast managerial accounting and cost accounting.
9. Identify four cost accounting activities.
10. What factors affect the complexity of a cost accounting system?
11. Describe the role of planning and control in a business.
12. Describe the role of the Internal Revenue Service in affecting cost accounting systems.
13. Compare the Financial Accounting Standards Board and the Cost Accounting Standards Board.

EXERCISES

Ex. 1-1 **Selecting accounting information.** Mel Jones just started a retail doughnut shop. He makes the doughnuts each night and sells them throughout the next day. He employs two people to help make and sell the doughnuts. Unsold doughnuts from one day are sold at a substantial discount the next day.

Mel thinks the business is doing well so far but he has not maintained very detailed records and has not attempted to compute income for the first month of operations. Mel does not have a business background and now that the business is organized and operating, he comes to you to ask for advice. In particular he would like to know what kind of information he might need to manage his business effectively.

Required: Answer Mel's question, emphasizing the purpose of such information.

Ex. 1-2 **Understanding the role of accounting.** A hospital in a large metropolitan area is owned and operated by a charitable organization. The costs of providing quality health care services have been rising steadily over the past year. With utility costs, medical salaries, medical supplies, and insurance costs rising faster than the cost of living, the hospital posted an operating loss of $1,400,000 for the year. As the hospital administrator, you are concerned about the situation and suggest some immediate steps to reduce the problem. You propose an immediate hiring freeze for nonessential positions, reduced staffing for non–critically ill patient areas of the hospital, a freeze on all new equipment purchases, and across-the-board fee increases of 10 percent.

You present these proposals at the monthly meeting of the hospital's board of directors, which includes key medical personnel. Many doctors and board members are outraged at your suggestions. One board member comments, "We are a charitable hospital. Costs make little difference to us. We want to heal people. If you raise fees, some will be unable to afford our services." The medical chief of staff is even more upset. "I can't treat people with marginal staffing. I think you are forgetting your role in this hospital. We doctors treat people; you are just supposed to push around the accounting numbers and keep all these financial problems out of our hair. If you can't do the job, we can get someone else to do it."

Required: Respond to the board member and doctor and defend your position.

Ex. 1-3 **The role of accounting information.** The Ratherford Stereo Components Company has experienced considerable growth in its first 5 years of operations. Having started with a single retail store, the company now has 17 stores in five states. The owner of the company has a strong marketing background and a keen ability to identify potentially strong market areas. The owner is pleased with the company's growth, but he has watched the changing quarterly financial statements over the years and is concerned about some items. A major concern is the growth in the size of the budget devoted to the accounting function. Recently, while talking to the controller, the owner said, "Why are our accounting system costs growing nearly as fast as company sales? We are working hard to add new stores and generate higher levels of sales, and you're adding new personnel, computers, and management accounting reports nearly as fast. An accounting system is an accounting system; the cost should remain constant from period to period."

Required: Comment in some detail on the owner's thoughts about the firm's accounting system.

Ex. 1-4 Identifying decision-making activities. Below are descriptions of selected activities that occurred recently in a department store. Each activity can be classified as (1) defining the problem, (2) identifying alternatives, (3) accumulating information, or (4) making the decision.

a. The store manager receives the sales report for the month of July and notes that sales are off by 5 percent from last July and 8 percent from expected sales for this July.
b. During a meeting of department heads, the controller reports that July sales in sporting goods are off nearly 50 percent from what was expected. Sporting goods normally has the second-highest departmental sales volume in the store. Excluding sporting goods, July sales in the other departments are only 2 percent short of expected levels.
c. The head of the sporting goods department points out that a new sporting goods discount store opened only a block away on June 28. Heavy advertising and grand-opening specials have drawn away many of the department store's customers.
d. The head of the sporting goods department suggests that the store run a midsummer sale on sporting goods matching or bettering the prices at the new store.
e. The director of marketing thinks a significant reduction in prices in one department would change the flavor of the store and set a dangerous trend. She suggests that a vigorous newspaper and television advertising campaign be launched, emphasizing the reputation and service of the sporting goods department.
f. The head of another department says the store is fighting a losing battle against the tough new competition in sporting goods and recommends that the sporting goods department be eliminated altogether.
g. The controller presents a departmental performance report which indicates that sporting goods still contributed something to the store's profit in July, even though it was not nearly as much as normal.
h. A week after the meeting, the director of marketing reports to the store manager on the cost of the proposed advertising program. A large advertising campaign would reduce the cost of the normal advertising program by 20 percent because of quantity discounts.
i. The assistant controller prepares a cost study showing the reduction in profit margin per dollar of sales if the proposed price reductions are implemented.
j. After careful study of the information, the store manager decides that sporting goods has been an integral part of the store for too long to eliminate the department. Also, it is difficult to measure the effect of customers shopping in other departments when attracted to the sporting goods department for products.
k. The store manager decides that discounts of about half the proposed amount would be acceptable in light of previous sale pricing guidelines. Larger discounts would require the elimination of certain store services.
l. The store manager decides to increase advertising significantly for the next 6 months and periodically to run special discounts on selected items within the store's pricing policy.

Required: List letters *a* through *l* and indicate how each activity should be classified in terms of its role in the decision process.

Ex. 1-5 **Classifying accounting activities.** Following is a list of various accounting activities or events for the Curiali Corporation. Each activity can be classified as either (1) managerial accounting, (2) financial accounting, or (3) cost accounting.

- **a.** Daily time cards are tabulated to determine the amount of time employees spent on each activity.
- **b.** The cost of maintenance supplies is recorded.
- **c.** Weekly labor use reports are sent to production supervisors.
- **d.** A quarterly production output report is sent to the plant manager.
- **e.** The company's quarterly income statement is summarized in the financial news.
- **f.** The company president receives a quarterly profit report for each product line.
- **g.** The company's independent auditors discuss the need for several financial statement footnotes with the controller.
- **h.** A list of materials put into production during the preceding day is sent to the accounting department by the inventory storeroom manager.
- **i.** At the board meeting, the controller presents a special report on the cost of building a new plant in Florida.
- **j.** The controller holds a special meeting of his staff to discuss the proper balance sheet treatment of the company's new lease on computer equipment.

Required: List letters *a* through *j* and indicate how each activity or event should be classified.

Ex. 1-6 **Classifying accounting activities.** Listed below are descriptions of a number of different accounting activities for Howe Manufacturing Company.

- **a.** A special labor efficiency report, to be used in upcoming contract negotiations, is prepared for the company negotiator.
- **b.** The vice president of sales receives a report on the cost of selling each type of product.
- **c.** A quarterly update on the profitability of a new line of business is sent to the bank providing financing for the project.
- **d.** Company sales personnel are provided with reports showing their sales to date for the year compared with their target sales for the same period.
- **e.** Weekly payroll costs are summarized and identified with specific activities.
- **f.** Sales personnel turn in their weekly expense data to the accounting department.
- **g.** The company's independent auditor requests a list of product cost data to be used in the audit that starts next month.
- **h.** The controller and assistant controller discuss how to report the lease for the sales personnel's portable computer terminals on the balance sheet.
- **i.** The company's annual report is issued.
- **j.** The year-end inventory count is taken, and adjustments are made to correct errors.

Required: Identify each activity as managerial accounting (M), financial accounting (F), or cost accounting (C).

PROBLEMS

P. 1-1 Using accounting data to evaluate decisions. Mr. Jones retired from the Navy after 25 years of service. He would like either to find a part-time job or to start a small engine repair shop to supplement his Navy pension. Mr. Jones is offered a part-time job as a security guard at a department store. The job pays $6.50 per hour and requires 30 hours of work per week.

Mr. Jones has done extensive planning for his proposed small engine repair shop and has determined that he could get 15 lawn mowers and other small engine products to repair each week. The average fees for the repairs would be $25 per engine. The average time required to repair each engine would be 2 hours. Mr. Jones expects that the average cost of parts and supplies would be $6 per engine. Other expected costs associated with operating the engine repair business include rent of $100 a month on a large garage, utilities of $60 a month, and insurance of $180 a year.

Required:

a. Analyze the two employment opportunities and determine which one offers Mr. Jones the highest earnings.
b. What other factors might Mr. Jones evaluate in deciding which alternative to choose?

P. 1-2 Identifying relevant accounting information. A man purchased a radio and electronics store from a friend who was retiring. The first thing the new owner did was to prepare a list of inventory items showing the original cost to the business, the current cost to replace the items, the retail price for the items at the time they were purchased, and the current retail price.

		Per Unit			
Item	Quantity	Original Cost	Replacement Cost	Original Price	Current Price
CB radios	10	$90	$35	$150	$80
AM-FM radios	10	48	52	70	80
Tape recorders	8	25	30	50	50
Portable radios	20	18	15	25	22

The new owner is concerned about the data he collected. He lists the following specific observations:

1. CB radio prices have plunged dramatically; CB radios are selling below original cost and obviously should be dropped from the product line.
2. AM-FM radio prices have increased at a rate greater than costs; AM-FM radios should be pushed as the most profitable item.
3. The price of tape recorders has not risen even though their cost has; perhaps the product should be dropped from the store's product line.
4. The price of portable radios has declined, but not by as big a percentage as their cost; therefore, this may be a really good product to sell.

5. Some problems may arise from dropping a product line that is not very profitable.

Required: Respond to each of the owner's observations. Discuss other observations of your own.

P. 1-3 Analysis of business alternatives. Dave Warren works as a welder at an appliance manufacturing plant. He earns $1,700 a month, working an average of 170 hours per month welding appliance frames and panels. In his spare time he makes beautiful wood furniture which he sells at craft shows or through a local furniture dealer. Dave has often thought that he would like to start a small furniture manufacturing business. Recently a business moved out of town, leaving a small manufacturing facility vacant. Dave's neighbor, a loan officer at a local bank, told Dave the bank would be willing to let Dave have the facility for $600 a month rent with no rent charge at all for the first 6 months as an incentive to utilize the facility.

With this incentive, Dave does some detailed planning for other aspects of the business. He decides he would start by making a hardwood table that could be used for a variety of purposes. His estimate of the materials required for **each** table is:

Lumber	$30.00
Adhesives	2.00
Finishing compounds, sealers, and varnish	8.00
Total materials cost	$40.00

Dave estimates that other costs of operating the business would include:

Utilities	$ 220 per month
Taxes and fees	80
Labor (3 employees @ $1,200 a month)	3,600
Maintenance	150
Miscellaneous	350
Total monthly expenses	$4,400

With the above resources, Dave expects to produce 60 tables per month. A regional furniture store chain has offered to buy as many tables as Dave's firm can produce for $150 per table.

Required:

a. Analyze the business alternative and determine whether or not Dave should start the furniture business.

b. What would be Dave's expected hourly earnings in the new business assuming he works 170 hours a month?

c. What other than accounting data might enter into Dave's decision?

P. 1-4 Identifying relevant accounting information. Nolan's department store has used a delivery service to make all local deliveries for many years. The cost of the service averages $.20 per pound this year for the 600,000 pounds of merchandise delivered. The delivery service company plans to raise the rate by 15 percent for next year. The management of the department store is not pleased with the rate increase and thinks of starting the store's own delivery service.

The following data have been gathered:

- An affiliate store in another city currently spends \$.18 a pound for local deliveries.
- Two new delivery trucks would cost \$80,000 each, have a delivery capacity of 500,000 pounds each per year, and would have a salvage value of \$5,000 each at the end of 5 years.
- Other truck costs would average \$.01 per pound for insurance, \$.04 for gas and oil, \$.02 for maintenance, and \$.06 for personnel.
- Costs of loading, storing, and delivering merchandise would amount to \$.05 a pound.
- If the trucks had been purchased last year, they would have cost only \$65,000 each.

Required:

a. Determine the per-pound cost of deliveries if the store starts making its own deliveries. Should the store switch to its own delivery service?

b. Would your answer to part *a* change if deliveries for the next year were 800,000 pounds instead of 600,000 pounds?

c. What data did you choose to ignore in your analysis of parts *a* and *b*? Why?

Cost Flows and Concepts

2

This is an essential chapter in your understanding and use of managerial accounting information. A wealth of terminology and concepts are presented that will prove extremely valuable as you study managerial accounting and the related cost concepts that underlie the managerial reporting process. When you have completed this chapter, you should understand:

1 The concept of cost and the meaning of the term cost objective.

2 The types of costs included in the cost of a manufactured product.

3 The relationship between cost flows and the physical flow of production.

4 The role of product costs in the income statements of various types of businesses.

5 Important managerial accounting terminology and concepts.

6 The way costs change with respect to changes in the volume of activity.

Many types of cost data are used in evaluating performance, making decisions, and helping managers utilize resources effectively. In Chapter 1 we emphasize the importance of cost data in developing accounting reports and the idea that costs of all sorts play an important role in management accounting and in the decision-making process. You also learned that an important function of managerial accounting is to provide cost information in a meaningful way so that managers can make decisions intelligently. The next step in the study of managerial accounting is to become familiar with cost accounting terminology and how costs are determined. The purpose of Chapter 2 is to describe the flow of costs in the production of products, to present basic terminology commonly used in cost accounting and managerial accounting reports, and to describe how costs change with respect to changes in the volume of activity. With this foundation you will be ready for subsequent chapters in which many different kinds of costs are used for preparing managerial accounting reports.

THE CONCEPT OF COST

Cost is the amount of resource given up in exchange for some good or service

In everyday conversation, the term *cost* has many different meanings. From an accounting point of view, **cost** is the amount of resources given up in exchange for some good or service. The resource given up is usually money. An important part of a manager's job is to use company resources as wisely and profitably as possible; therefore, costs are critical components of business decisions and are usually the focus of managerial accounting reports.

The cost of many products and services can be found merely by asking a vendor, or seller, of the product or service. For example, if you want to buy a boat, boat dealers can provide you with the purchase price of various types of boats. The cost of many items, however, is not so readily available. When goods or services are not purchased but instead are produced, determining the cost may be difficult. Instead of a single quoted amount for an item, the cost of a product a firm manufactures itself is a combination of the costs of many resources.

The cost of a manufactured product is more difficult to determine

For example, if you decide to build a boat, you have to determine the cost of all resources used in its production, such as the cost of materials, labor, depreciation on production equipment, and electric power to operate the equipment, all of which are necessary to produce the boat. The costs of some of the production resources, such as fiberglass, resin, and wood, are relatively easy to trace to the boat. Likewise, the cost of employees who work directly on producing the boat is readily identifiable as part of the boat's cost. Some other costs, however, such as heating and electricity for the production plant and maintenance of the production equipment, are not easy to identify with each boat.

Although determining the cost of a product can be difficult, it does not deter organizations from producing goods and providing services. Well-established cost accounting systems and procedures provide the means of measuring costs for a wide variety of uses.

Defining Cost Objectives

To determine the cost of making a particular product or performing a specific activity, it is first necessary to define the cost objective precisely. The **cost objective** is the product or activity whose cost is to be determined. If you want to know the cost of a boat, for instance, you must describe the boat you want. The dealer may have boats priced from $500 to $50,000. The more precise your description of the boat, the better your chance of obtaining the correct price quotation. In business it is just as essential for the accountant to know precisely what the cost objective is. Often it is a product, such as a tire, refrigerator, or backpack. Cost objectives may also

The first step in measuring costs is to define the cost objective

be activities, such as the cost of an advertising campaign or the monthly cost of operating the company's computer. Identifying the cost objectives is often easy, but to ensure that the correct costs are included in measuring the cost of a product, service, or activity, great care must be exercised in describing the cost objective. To illustrate, a person attempting to measure the cost of a year of college education might include:

1. Tuition, room and board
2. Tuition, room and board, and books
3. Tuition, room and board, books, and spending money
4. Tuition, room and board, books, spending money, and transportation
5. All expenditures for college plus the loss of income that would be earned if the student did not attend college

Each of these descriptions of the cost of college education may be appropriate, depending on the way a person plans to use the information. For example, a parent trying to determine the total cash outlay for a year on campus might find item 4 to be the most useful measure of costs. On the other hand, item 1 best describes the contractual amount the college will charge. For any personal example of cost objectives, such as a car, a house, a vacation, or food costs, a variety of different costs can be included. Consequently, it is important to describe the cost objective clearly and completely. This is especially true in businesses that must use cost information for making many decisions.

Cost objectives must state not only the nature of the cost, but also the amount of detail needed or desired. For example, management might be interested in the cost of:

- The total advertising program
- Advertising for a specific product
- Advertising for a specific sales region
- Advertising by region for a specific product
- A variety of other combinations of advertising cost

PRODUCT COSTING

A logical starting point for discussing concepts and procedures used in measuring and reporting costs is with tangible products. For example, how is the cost of making tables, radios, baseballs, or washing machines determined? Although we start by discussing and illustrating costing of tangible products, the same concepts and procedures apply to costing other activities such as marketing, computer services, and personnel services.

Manufacturing Cost Elements

Three basic types of manufacturing costs are identified with the production of goods. They are called **cost elements** and include:

The three types of manufacturing costs

1. Direct materials
2. Direct labor
3. Manufacturing overhead

Material that is directly identifiable with the product

Direct materials are the raw materials that can be directly identified with the production of a specific product. Direct materials become part of the product, such as the handle of a hammer, the wood frame of a sofa, or the steel in an automobile. For many products, direct materials is the largest manufacturing cost element. In some cases it is not possible or economically feasible to identify all materials costs with individual products. For example, the amount of glue used to mount the insignia on an automobile is so insignificant in comparison with the total cost of manufacturing the car that accountants do not identify it as direct material. Such materials are called **indirect materials** and are part of manufacturing overhead costs, discussed below.

Labor cost that can be identified directly with the product

Direct labor is labor that can be specifically identified with the production of a particular product and that contributes directly to completion of the product. Employees putting together the parts of a television set as it moves along the assembly line provide direct labor. Similarly, the cost of an employee painting the outside panels of an air conditioner or drilling bolt holes in an automobile frame is classified as direct labor.

Some labor necessary for the efficient operation of manufacturing activities cannot readily be identified with specific products. For example, employees who move materials from one work location to another and employees who repair and maintain the plant and production equipment are a necessary part of the production process, but their cost cannot be identified as direct labor. This **indirect labor** is part of manufacturing overhead cost.

All necessary costs of manufacturing other than direct materials and direct labor are called manufacturing overhead

Manufacturing overhead (MOH) consists of all **necessary** manufacturing costs other than direct materials and direct labor. Manufacturing overhead contains all of the **indirect costs** in the manufacturing process. Indirect manufacturing costs are necessary production costs, but they cannot be identified with specific products. Many different kinds of manufacturing overhead costs exist, depending on the type of product and the type of production processes used. Although the specific composition of MOH costs varies from firm to firm, many common types of costs are found in most manufacturing operations. In addition to indirect materials and indirect labor, other overhead costs are capacity costs, sometimes called occupancy costs. They include:

- Building rental or depreciation
- Machinery and equipment depreciation or lease cost
- Heat, light, and power costs
- Maintenance costs
- Insurance and taxes on the manufacturing facilities

Other common manufacturing overhead costs are employee fringe benefits, such as health insurance, vacation pay, and pension benefits; supervisory salaries for manufacturing personnel; and inventory handling costs.

Overhead costs are indirect costs of production and by their very nature are not directly identifiable with specific products. Overhead costs are, however, important and necessary manufacturing costs. Accountants must be able to assign these costs to products, and managers must be able to monitor and control overhead costs as they do all other costs of doing business. In Chapters 3 and 4 we discuss the process of assigning overhead costs to products.

Other terms for manufacturing overhead

Other terms for manufacturing overhead are factory burden, factory overhead, manufacturing burden, or simply **burden** or **overhead.** All of these terms are used in business, but we use the term *manufacturing overhead* throughout this text because it is common and best describes the cost.

None of the three basic cost elements is generally more important than the others. The relative importance of each depends on the type of product manufactured and the way it is produced. One product may require more costly material or less skilled labor than another. Many products can be produced in a variety of ways. Some production methods may require much manual labor, whereas others may be highly automated. Frequently managers change production methods, causing a shift in the relative importance of cost elements. For example, a large manufacturer of computer disk drives automates the assembly operations in the production of disk drives. It is common for automation to reduce the relative amount of direct labor cost and increase the relative amount of manufacturing overhead cost. Lower product cost, increased production capacity, more production flexibility, and better production control are but a few reasons why managers alter the mix of production resources.

In discussing direct materials, direct labor, and manufacturing overhead, business managers sometimes combine terms. Direct materials and direct labor together are called **prime cost**. "Prime" refers to the directly traceable nature of the two costs and their significance in cost control, performance evaluation, and decision making. Direct labor and manufacturing overhead together are called **conversion costs** because they are costs of converting raw materials into the finished product.

PRODUCTION FLOWS AND COST FLOWS

The flow of product costs closely parallels the physical flow of production activities

Production supervisors are primarily interested in monitoring and controlling production flows. Accountants are especially interested in determining and reporting the cost flows associated with the production process. Production flow is a physical concept, and cost flow is an accounting concept. The flow of product costs parallels the physical flow of the product through the production process. Accountants assign to products the costs that are incurred as production takes place. The causal relationship between production activity and product cost is most obvious with direct materials and direct labor costs, but the assignment of indirect manufacturing costs is essential as well and is guided by the **matching principle** which requires the matching of expenses with associated revenues. Production costs are assigned to manufactured products, and when the product is sold, the expense of producing the product is matched with the revenue generated by its sale. Throughout this book the matching concept is emphasized as the most important accounting principle in product costing and management reporting.

Visualize the production of a simple product, such as a sledgehammer. A worker picks up a wooden handle and inserts it in the hole of the hammer's head. He then drives a wedge into a slot to keep the handle from falling out of the head. Three materials—the head, the handle, and the wedge—and a certain amount of labor time are required to make the sledgehammer. With the help of labor, the three materials flow together to make up the finished product. Each of the materials has a specific cost, as does the labor time of the worker. When the hammer head is joined to the handle, the sledgehammer's cost is the total of the two separate material costs. When the wedge is added, the cost of the hammer increases by the cost of the wedge. At the same time, the cost of labor also increases the cost of the hammer. The flow of product costs parallels the physical flow of the materials and labor into the product.

The person supervising production is primarily interested in controlling production flows. Are enough handles available? Is the wedge tight enough in each hammer? Is the amount of time spent on assembly excessive? On the other hand, accountants are especially interested in measuring and reporting the cost flows associated with the production process. How much does each handle cost? Is the purchase price of the hammer head higher than management expected? What is the wage of the employee?

The causal relationship between the quantity of production and the amount of direct materials and direct labor costs incurred is clear. But the accountant is also concerned with such questions as: How much manufacturing overhead cost should be assigned to each sledgehammer for indirect costs such as heating, electricity, property tax, and maintenance? As materials, labor, and overhead are converted into a finished product and product costs change during the manufacturing process, the accountant must keep track of these costs in various inventory accounts.

Manufacturing Inventories

In manufacturing firms, inventories typically play a more important role than in other types of business. Service firms have little or no inventory that they hold for resale to customers. Operating supplies and convenience items are carried only to facilitate the main function of providing services. Merchandising firms acquire inventory for resale to customers. A merchandising firm may have many different classifications of inventory and many items within each inventory classification, but all inventory items are ready for sale. They do not require any major modifications, although assembly or other convenience services may be performed in connection with their sale.

A manufacturing firm has three major levels of inventory:

1. Raw materials
2. Work in process
3. Finished goods

The three levels of manufacturing inventories

Raw materials are the basic inputs or ingredients that are converted into final products through the production process. The term *raw materials* does not necessarily mean the most basic of resources, such as lumber and iron ore. Instead raw materials for a manufacturing firm may be partially manufactured products that are processed further. For example, pig iron is the raw material of the forging company that makes sledgehammer heads and sells them to the sledgehammer manufacturer. The final product of the forge is a raw material of the hammer manufacturer. The finished iron hammerhead is the raw material of the sledgehammer manufacturer who buys the heads and wood handles used in the manufacture of the hammers. Most raw materials inventory is used as direct material. A small portion appears as indirect material. A single product may require a large number of different raw materials, and a manufacturer that produces many different products may have thousands of different raw materials items.

Work in process (WIP) is the second level of inventory in a manufacturing firm. It consists of unfinished products that are in the process of being converted into final products, such as the sledgehammer with head and handle joined, but not yet wedged. Many different products can be in work in process simultaneously. For example, a bakery may have a variety of breads, cakes, and doughnuts in process at any given time.

Finished goods. The final level of inventory consists of **finished goods**, which are products ready for sale, such as the completed sledgehammers. Finished goods inventory in a manufacturing firm is similar to merchandise inventory in a merchandising firm. In a multiple-product manufacturing firm, there are many different finished goods inventory items.

PRODUCTION COST CYCLE ILLUSTRATED

As production resources are acquired and used to make products, accountants measure the cost of resources purchased and used and record the transactions and activities in the company's accounting records. The process of accounting for the cost of manufactured products closely parallels the actual physical flow of a product through production. The parallel relationship of accounting and production activities is illustrated in Figure 2-1. The figure shows the physical flow of products through the production process and the corresponding flow of costs through the ledger accounts, from the start of production through the sale of the product. It illustrates a complete cycle for the products cost of a manufacturing firm.

Raw materials purchases are recorded in the Raw Materials Inventory account with a debit, represented in Figure 2-1 by RM_1. The transfer of raw materials costs to production occurs in two ways. Most materials put into production are direct materials and are recorded with a debit to Work in Process, WP_1, and a credit to Raw Materials Inventory, RM_2. When indirect materials are put into production, their costs are recorded with a debit to Manufacturing Overhead, MOH_1, and a credit to Raw Materials Inventory, RM_3. Indirect materials cannot be assigned to the product directly so they become part of manufacturing overhead costs that are assigned to products in a separate step to be discussed shortly.

The cost of manufacturing labor is accounted for in a manufacturing payroll account in a manner similar to the recording of materials costs. Employee wages for the period are charged to Manufacturing Payroll with the entry PY_1. The portion of this account that cannot be assigned directly to products is indirect labor, which is removed from the Manufacturing Payroll account with the credit PY_2 and transferred to Manufacturing Overhead with the debit MOH_2. The labor cost of manufacturing employees who work directly on products is assigned to the Work in Process account with the debit WP_3 and the credit PY_3 to the payroll account.

For most firms, the debits to Manufacturing Overhead for indirect materials and indirect labor are only a small portion of total manufacturing overhead. The greater portion consists of numerous other costs, such as plant depreciation, plant taxes, insurance, heat, electricity, and other indirect manufacturing costs. All of these other overhead items are represented by the debit MOH_3. The charging of MOH to production is accomplished with a debit to Work in Process, WP_2, and a credit to Manufacturing Overhead, MOH_4. With this entry the indirect materials and indirect labor, as well as other manufacturing overhead costs, all become part of the cost of manufactured products.

The Work in Process account contains production costs for all products currently in production. When products are completed, they are transferred to the finished goods inventory, where they are **ready** for sale. When the physical product is completed and transferred to the finished goods inventory storeroom, the cost associated with producing the product is transferred from the Work in Process Inventory account to the Finished Goods

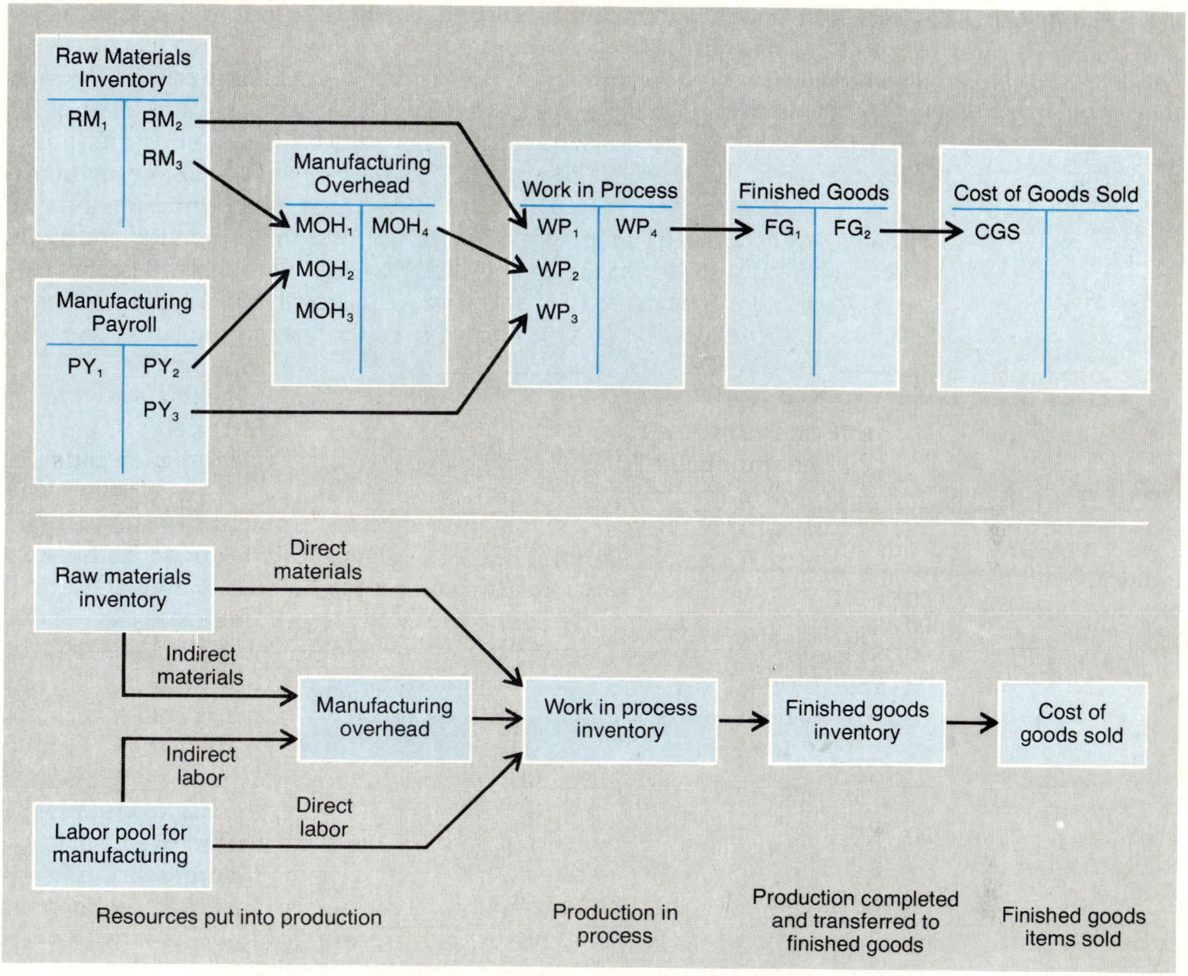

Figure 2-1 The physical flow of products through the production process is paralleled by the flow of costs through the ledger accounts. The matching concept guides accountants in assigning costs to products.

Inventory account. In Figure 2-1, the entry is shown as a debit to Finished Goods, FG_1, and a credit to Work in Process, WP_4.

Costs that are necessary to the production of products are called inventoriable costs and are added to the cost of the product

Keep in mind that both work in process and finished goods inventories contain some costs, such as payroll, utilities, depreciation, and property taxes, that appear as period expenses in nonmanufacturing operations. In nonmanufacturing activities they are expensed because their value is gone. In a manufacturing firm, however, these costs enhance the value of the products on hand. Direct labor and production facilities have converted raw materials into goods that are more valuable than the raw materials from which they were made. This enhancement of value is not realized, however, until the product is sold. Because all of the costs that flow into production increase the value of the product, the costs are said to be inventoriable. **Inventoriable costs** are costs that legitimately can be added to the cost of a manufactured product because they are necessary for the production of the product.

Product costs are expensed when the product is sold

The final step in the product cost flow cycle is the sale of the product. It is the event that causes the product cost to be transferred from the asset account Finished Goods to the expense account Cost of Goods Sold. The cost transfer is dictated by the matching principle, which requires the matching of expenses with associated revenues. The product cost is matched with the revenue generated from the sale of the product. This is accomplished by debiting Cost of Goods Sold, CGS, and crediting Finished Goods Inventory, FG_2, as shown in Figure 2-1. Regardless of how simple or complex the production process is, the basic flow is the same as the one just described.

THE INCOME STATEMENT AND PRODUCT COSTS

Some of the product costs of manufacturing firms are similar to operating costs of other types of businesses. For example, labor and depreciation costs are incurred in both manufacturing and nonmanufacturing activities. But in manufacturing activities these costs become part of the cost of the product and are expensed only when the product is sold, whereas in nonmanufacturing activities they are always expensed in the period in which they occur.

Product Costs and Period Costs

Accountants make a distinction between the cost of manufactured products and the costs incurred in nonmanufacturing activities. **Product costs** are recorded and carried as assets at the time products are made; they become expenses only when the product is sold. **Period costs** are costs of goods and services that are recorded as expenses in the period in which they are consumed.

To make a clear distinction between product and period costs, we look at the way these costs are reported in the income statements of the three basic types of businesses: service firms, merchandising firms, and manufacturing firms.

Service firms. Law firms, certified public accountants, realtors, physicians, hairstyling salons, and dance studios are examples of businesses that sell services rather than products in order to generate revenue. The income statements of service firms are characterized by the fact that they report no product costs. The only deductions from revenue are operating expenses, which are costs that expired during the current accounting period and must be matched with the current period's revenues. The income statement of a service firm may also contain nonoperating revenues and expenses, income taxes, and extraordinary items that we omit to avoid unnecessary details. Figure 2-2 illustrates the income statement of a service business.

Service firms have no product cost

Roosevelt Williams, CPA
Income Statement
For the Year Ended December 31, 1986

Revenue from services		$88,000
Operating expenses:		
Salaries and wages	$38,000	
Office rent	4,800	
Depreciation on furniture and fixtures	2,400	
Professional and educational expenses	2,500	
Supplies	1,600	
Insurance	900	
Utilities	2,200	
Charitable contributions	1,800	
Total operating expenses		54,200
Net income		$33,800

Figure 2-2
The income statement for a service firm has no product expense. Only operating expenses are deducted from revenue to determine net income.

Merchandising firms. Department stores, drug stores, gift shops, and grocery stores are all common examples of merchandising businesses. The Hawthorne Sporting Goods Store, whose income statement is shown in Figure 2-3, is used to illustrate a merchandising income statement. Like all merchandising firms, it must first buy products before it can sell them

Hawthorne Sporting Goods
Income Statement
For the Year Ended December 31, 1986

Sales			$236,500
Less cost of goods sold:			
Beginning inventory 1/1/86		$ 74,000	
Purchases	$142,600		
Less purchase returns	(6,200)		
Add freight-in	2,400		
Net purchases		138,800	
Total goods available for sale		212,800	
Less ending inventory 12/31/86		88,300	
Cost of goods sold			124,500
Gross margin			112,000
Operating expenses:			
Salaries		42,900	
Commissions		4,730	
Building rent		9,600	
Equipment rent		4,800	
Depreciation of furniture and fixtures		3,200	
Advertising		4,400	
Insurance		5,000	
Supplies		2,800	
Utilities		6,000	
Total operating expenses			83,430
Net income			$ 28,570

Figure 2-3
A merchandising firm must buy inventory that it plans to sell for a profit. When the merchandise is sold, it becomes an expense called cost of goods sold. The difference between the cost and the selling price of units sold is called gross margin.

Merchandising firms buy products and resell them for a profit

to its customers. The costs incurred by the merchandising firm in buying products are product costs. When products are sold, the product cost becomes an expense called **cost of goods sold**. At the end of an accounting period, the cost of unsold products is considered an asset because the goods on hand have future economic value. Their cost is called **merchandise inventory** and is reported in the current assets section of the balance sheet. The matching concept dictates when the product cost becomes an expense. If the revenue from the sale of a product is reported in the income statement, then the corresponding cost of that product should be part of cost of goods sold in the same income statement.

In a merchandising firm the main revenue account is called Sales. Associated with sales revenue is the product cost of the sold merchandise. The difference between sales revenue and cost of goods sold is called **gross margin**, and it is calculated before operating expenses are deducted.

Operating expenses, which are deducted from gross margin, include all expenses of the period except product expense. The operating expenses of a merchandising firm are similar to those of a service firm. Differences may occur because of the varying nature of operating activities of businesses. For instance, a merchandising firm has inventory handling expenses and usually more advertising expense than a service firm.

Manufacturing firms make the products they sell

Manufacturing firms. A manufacturing firm also has a product cost that must be subtracted from sales revenue to arrive at gross margin. However, in a manufacturing firm the computation of the product cost is more complex than in a merchandising firm. The next two chapters are devoted to the determination of product costs for manufacturing businesses.

A manufacturing company does not purchase products ready for sale. Instead it purchases a variety of production resources that are combined into a salable product. The flow of costs from Raw Materials through Finished Goods to Cost of Goods Sold is more difficult to identify than the product cost flow of a merchandising firm. In spite of the difficulties, it is important to develop accurate product costs for a variety of management uses. Cost data are the foundation for a multitude of management decisions and accounting reports, as discussed and illustrated throughout this book. Figure 2-4 illustrates a manufacturing business income statement.

To determine the product expense for the period, the cost of products manufactured during the period are added to the cost of beginning finished goods inventory to find total goods available for sale. Next, ending finished goods inventory is subtracted to get cost of goods sold.

The operating expenses of a manufacturing firm may not be significantly different from those of a merchandising or service firm. In a manufacturing firm all operating expenses are nonmanufacturing costs, such as marketing and administrative expenses. These are period costs and are expensed in the period in which they are incurred. All manufacturing costs are product costs and appear as cost of goods sold if the product is sold, or as ending inventory if the product is not sold.

Masston Manufacturing Company
Income Statement
For the Year Ended December 31, 1986

Sales		$792,000
Cost of goods sold:		
Beginning finished goods inventory 1/1/86	$ 82,000	
Add cost of goods manufactured in 1986	442,300	
Total goods available for sale	524,300	
Less ending finished goods inventory 12/31/86	74,200	
Cost of goods sold		450,100
Gross margin		341,900
Operating expenses:		
Salaries, sales and administrative personnel	144,300	
Commissions	34,200	
Depreciation on selling and administrative furniture, fixtures, building, and equipment	68,400	
Advertising	15,000	
Insurance, office	8,600	
Supplies, office	26,500	
Utilities, office	19,900	
Total operating expenses		316,900
Net income		$ 25,000

Figure 2-4
Manufacturing firms convert raw materials into finished products in the production process. The cost of manufacturing the product becomes the product expense in the income statement when the product is sold.

The Schedule of Cost of Goods Manufactured

The cost of products manufactured during the period is called **cost of goods manufactured**. In Figure 2-4 it is shown as $442,300 and it is the cost of the products completed during the period and transferred from work in process to finished goods. The cost of goods manufactured is not an account balance but instead is calculated in a schedule.

The schedule of cost of goods manufactured reports the cost of goods transferred from work in process to finished goods during the period

The **schedule of cost of goods manufactured** describes the cost of the products transferred from work in process to finished goods. It summarizes the product costs that flow through the Work in Process account during a specified time period. Like the income statement, the schedule covers a specific time period. The example in Figure 2-5 covers the calendar year 1986. Sometimes the schedule covers other time periods, such as a month or quarter.

The cost of goods manufactured schedule starts with the beginning work in process inventory. To this amount are added the **production costs for the period**—direct materials, direct labor, and manufacturing overhead. These new manufacturing costs added during the period are called **total manufacturing cost for the period**. The total manufacturing cost for the period plus the beginning work in process inventory together constitute the **total manufacturing costs in production during the period**. At the end of the period, the ending work in process inventory is subtracted from total

Massten Manufacturing Company
Schedule of Cost of Goods Manufactured
For the Year Ended December 31, 1986

Beginning work in process 1/1/86			$ 46,800
Direct materials		$103,450	
Direct labor		152,900	
Manufacturing overhead:			
Depreciation, building	$46,000		
Depreciation, machinery	38,000		
Indirect labor	22,350		
Indirect materials	9,400		
Insurance	12,000		
Salaries	88,100		
Taxes, property	4,200		
Utilities	10,800	230,850	
Total manufacturing cost, 1986			487,200
Total manufacturing costs in production, 1986			534,000
Less ending work in process 12/31/86			91,700
Cost of goods manufactured, 1986			$442,300

Figure 2-5
This schedule summarizes the total cost of manufacturing during the period, the cost of products transferred to finished goods during the period, and the cost of beginning and ending work in process inventories.

manufacturing costs in production to find the cost of goods completed and transferred to finished goods during the accounting period. This number is referred to as the **cost of goods manufactured**. Do not confuse *total manufacturing cost of the period* with *cost of goods manufactured*. The former term identifies the total manufacturing cost of the current period. The latter term describes the cost of the goods actually transferred to finished goods from work in process during the period. The two numbers are identical only when the beginning and ending work in process inventory costs are identical.

Production Resources and Inventory Cost Flows

The production cost flow cycle summarized in the manufacturing income statement and schedule of cost of goods manufactured is illustrated graphically in Figure 2-6. Production resources flow from one inventory level to another until products are completed and sold. The production resources available to a firm are utilized during the period to manufacture products, and the resulting production cost data are used to prepare the income statement and the schedule of cost of goods manufactured.

The Significance of Product Cost

Product cost is an important element in measuring the achievement of merchandising and manufacturing businesses. Variations in product costs can have a significant impact on key measures of performance, such as net income. To illustrate, a condensed income statement is presented below.

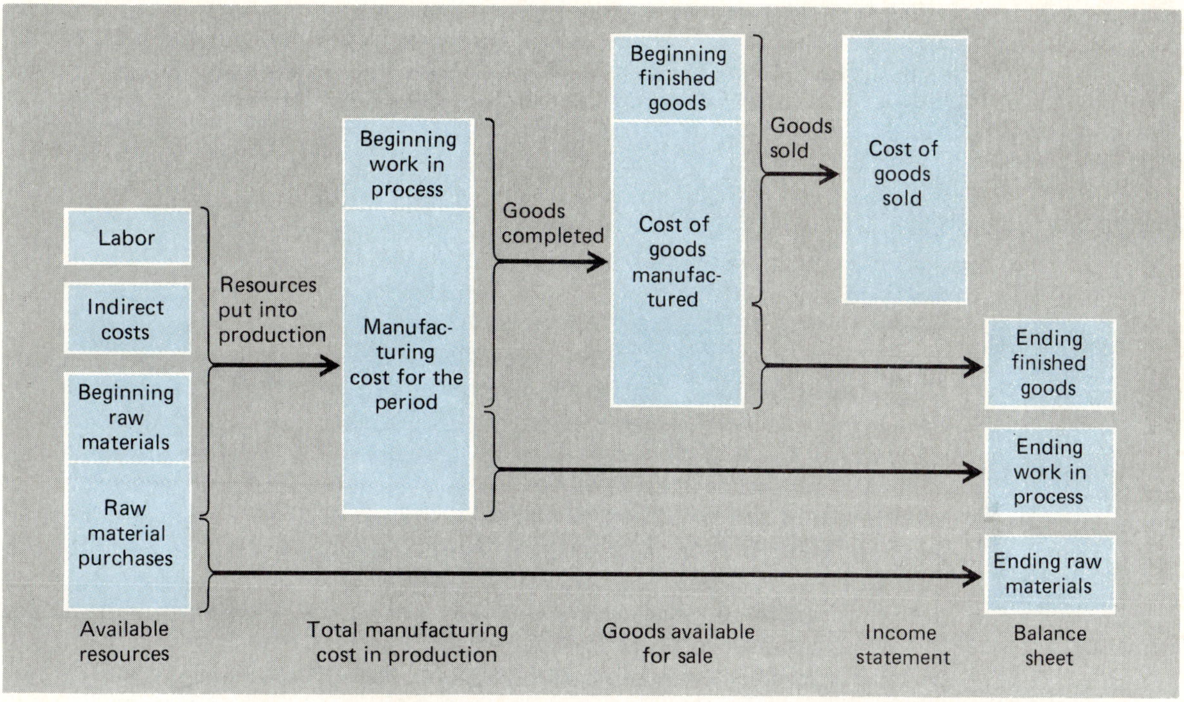

Figure 2-6 The flow of manufacturing costs through inventory accounts to the financial statements. For each level of manufacturing inventory, typically there is some beginning inventory. New resources are added during the accounting period. At the end of the period most of the resources have passed to the next inventory level or to cost of goods sold, but some resources remain in ending inventories.

Sales	$1,000
Cost of goods sold	600
Gross margin	400
Operating expenses	300
Net income	$ 100

Now assume that the product cost increases by 10 percent, or $60 ($600 × .10). All other costs and revenues remain the same. The new income statement is:

Sales	$1,000
Cost of goods sold	660
Gross margin	340
Operating expenses	300
Net income	$ 40

Note that the product cost has increased by 10 percent ($60/$600) and gross margin has declined by 15 percent ($60/$400). However, the really significant change is the 60 percent ($60/$100) decline in net income. You can see that a relatively small change in product cost can cause a very significant change in net income. Period costs can have a similar effect, but typically they are a smaller portion of total costs than product costs and therefore their effect is less pronounced.

COST BEHAVIOR

To provide the variety of cost information needed by management, accountants classify cost information along functional lines and behavioral lines. Costs may be classified according to functions, such as manufacturing, administration, or marketing. Functional cost classifications are useful for many purposes, including external reporting. Classifying costs according to their behavior refers to the way costs change as the volume of activity changes. Many management decisions are affected by **cost behavior**. For example, a manager is evaluating the possibility of eliminating fiberglass canoes from the line of boats the business produces. Very relevant to the decision is information about which costs will be eliminated totally, partially, or not at all. Numerous business decisions require managerial accounting information on the behavior of costs. Consequently, accountants must identify **cost behavior patterns**, and report costs in a way that allows managers to relate the information to specific decision situations.

Managers are very interested in the way costs change with respect to changes in the volume of activity

In this chapter we describe common cost behavior patterns and discuss how they may be useful in business analysis. Chapters 5 and 6 are devoted to the analysis of business situations using cost behavior data.

As the volume of business activity changes, some costs remain constant, some change proportionately, and some change but not proportionally. Although costs behave in many different ways, for most purposes cost behavior can be classified into five common patterns:

Common cost behavior patterns

1. Fixed costs
2. Variable costs
3. Mixed costs
4. Semivariable costs
5. Step function or semifixed costs

Fixed Costs

Costs that don't change with volume are called fixed costs

Fixed costs are costs that do not change with changing levels of activity, that is, they are fixed for all activity levels. For example, the annual rental cost of a manufacturing plant is $24,000, and it remains unchanged regardless of the activity level. Other costs, such as property taxes and depreciation on equipment, typically are unaffected by changing activity levels and are therefore classified as fixed costs.

Figure 2-7 shows graphically the behavior pattern of a fixed cost. With the activity level on the horizontal (X) axis and total cost on the vertical

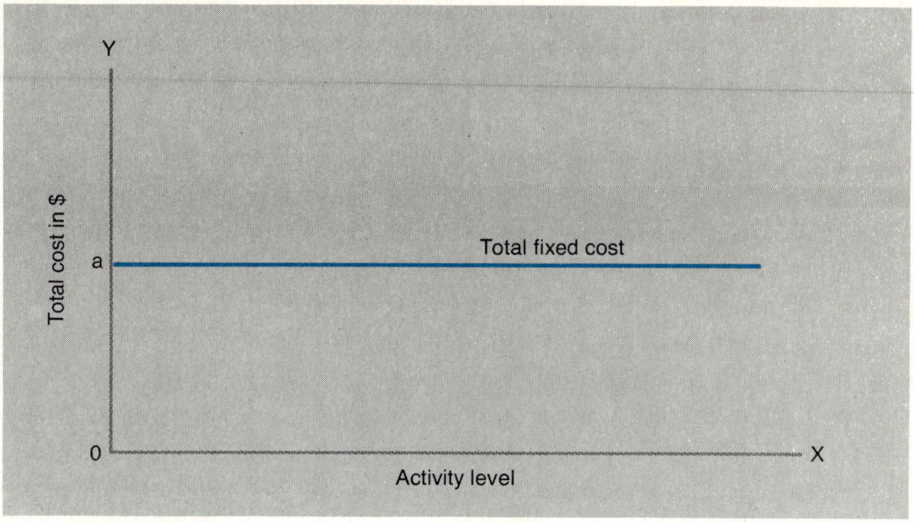

Figure 2-7 **Fixed costs remain constant for all levels of activity and therefore appear as a horizontal straight line. The *Y* intercept *a* represents the amount of fixed cost.**

(Y) axis, a fixed cost is plotted as a horizontal line because the dollar amount of the cost does not change regardless of the level of activity. The amount of fixed cost determines how high the line is on the vertical axis. In this case a, the dollar amount of fixed cost, can be expressed as the equation

$$Y = a$$

This equation says that total cost Y equals a constant fixed cost represented by the letter a. Some costs that usually are fixed include:

- Some manufacturing overhead costs, such as:
  Plant and equipment depreciation
  Property taxes
  Plant and equipment insurance
  Production supervisory salaries
- Some nonmanufacturing costs, such as:
  Depreciation on office facilities and equipment
  Office equipment lease costs
  Supervisory salaries
  Office property taxes
  Advertising
  Office fire insurance
  Rent

Fixed costs typically are assigned to specific cost objectives, such as a product, a department, or an activity. If the fixed cost is assigned to products and production activity is low, each unit of product receives a relatively large amount of the fixed cost; if production activity is high, each unit of product receives a relatively small amount of the fixed cost. To illustrate, $4,000 of monthly rent on the manufacturing plant is assigned to the products produced each month. If 250 bicycles are manufactured in the plant during the month, $16 of the fixed rental cost ($4,000/250 bicycles) is allocated to each bicycle. However, if 400 bicycles are manufactured during the month, each unit is assigned only $10 of plant rental cost ($4,000/400 bicycles). The plant rental cost is fixed at $4,000 for the month, but the amount of cost assigned to each unit of output depends on how many units share the fixed cost.

Sometimes accountants further classify fixed costs as committed fixed costs or discretionary fixed costs. **Committed fixed costs** cannot be easily or quickly eliminated. Typically, they are plant and facility costs such as plant and equipment depreciation, property taxes, long-term leases, and facilities insurance. **Discretionary fixed costs** are costs that can be discontinued at management's discretion in a relatively short time in comparison with committed costs. Typical examples include marketing programs, administrative salaries, research and development costs, systems development costs, and short-term renewable leases.

Variable Costs

Variable costs change proportionately with the volume of activity

Costs that increase directly and proportionately with the volume of activity are called **variable costs**. There is a constant ratio between the change in the cost and the change in the level of activity. For example, if the direct materials cost for a 26-inch men's bicycle is $30, then for each bicycle manufactured, total direct materials cost increases by $30. The total amount of direct materials cost is determined by the number of units produced. Two hundred bicycles have a total direct materials cost of $6,000. Two hundred and one bicycles have a total direct materials cost of $6,030. The $30 increment for materials is the same at all levels of production. The total variable cost increases as the level of activity increases, but the variable cost per unit remains the same. This proportional relationship distinguishes variable cost patterns from other cost behavior patterns and gives rise to the term **directly variable costs** that is used sometimes.

The behavior pattern of variable costs is shown graphically in Figure 2-8. The distance X on the horizontal axis represents the activity level. The distance Y on the vertical axis depicts the total variable cost incurred at each level of activity. For every unit of increase in activity there is a proportionate increase in the cost. The ratio of Y to X is the proportional relationship between the variable cost and the activity level. This ratio is the same for all levels of activity. Therefore, a one-unit change in the volume of activity causes the same total cost change anywhere within the firm's operating capacity.

Variable costs are graphed as a straight line that starts at the origin ($X = 0$ and $Y = 0$) and slopes upward to the right. The general equation for a variable cost line is

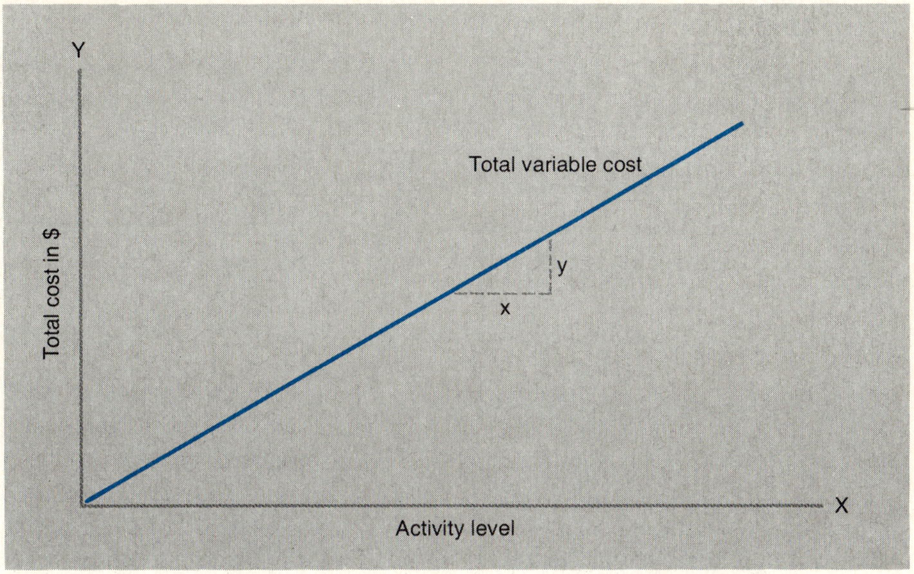

Figure 2-8
Variable costs are shown as a straight line sloping upward to the right. The ratio of *Y* to *X* is the rate of change in the cost caused by a unit change in the volume of activity.

$$Y = bX$$

where Y = total variable cost
b = variable cost per unit of activity
X = activity level measured in units such as direct labor hours or units of output

Using the bicycle example mentioned earlier, with a direct materials cost of \$30 per unit, the variable cost is expressed by the equation

$$Y = \$30X$$

This equation says that the total variable cost of direct materials Y is equal to \$30 times X, the number of bicycles produced. Notice that the ratio of Y to X is equal to b, the slope of the cost line ($Y/X = b$), which is \$30 in this case. If production changes from 400 to 425 bicycles, the change in the activity level is 25 units and the change in total direct materials cost is $(425 \times \$30) - (400 \times \$30) = \$750$. The ratio of the change in direct materials costs to the change in the volume of production is \$750/25 bicycles, or still \$30 per unit. The higher the ratio between variable costs and the volume of activity, the steeper the slope of the cost line.

Expressing cost relationships as equations can be very useful in analyzing costs and making decisions. You should understand the concepts of cost behavior patterns as well as the mathematical representations of the cost patterns.

Variable costs include many different costs:

- Some variable MOH, such as:
  Factory supplies
  Indirect materials
  Payroll taxes on direct labor
  Employee fringe benefits on direct labor
- Direct materials
- Direct labor
- Some nonmanufacturing costs such as:
  Sales commissions
  Office supplies
  Some utility costs

Directly variable costs sometimes are referred to as **manageable costs** because managers often determine whether the costs are incurred. Although many variable costs are controllable by managers, the terms **controllable costs** and **variable costs** are not synonymous. Some variable costs in a manager's sphere of responsibility may not be controllable. For instance, factory supplies used in servicing and maintaining production equipment may vary with the amount of production activity, but the production manager may have no control over the amount of factory supplies used. Conversely, some controllable costs may have cost behavior patterns other than directly variable. For instance, a manager may acquire a 1-year maintenance agreement for hydraulic press equipment. The cost of the maintenance agreement became fixed for the year when the manager made the decision to incur the cost of the service.

Mixed Costs

Mixed costs have both a fixed and a variable component

Costs that cannot be described by a single cost behavior pattern are called **mixed costs**. For purposes of decision analysis managers find it convenient to separate mixed costs into fixed and variable components.

Figure 2-9 illustrates a mixed cost. Fixed costs are shown by a straight line horizontal to the X axis. Variable costs are shown as a sloping line. Total cost is equal to fixed cost plus variable cost. To graph total costs, the line starts on the Y axis at point a, which is the amount of fixed cost. The total cost line slopes upward, indicating that variable costs are added to the fixed costs to equal total costs. In Figure 2-9, the variable cost b is \$30 per unit produced. Because the total amount of variable cost changes with the level of activity, the total cost line slopes upward as the volume of activity increases.

The equations for a fixed cost and a variable cost are combined to find the equation for a mixed cost.

Fixed cost	$Y = a$
Variable cost	$Y = bX$
Mixed cost	$Y = a + bX$

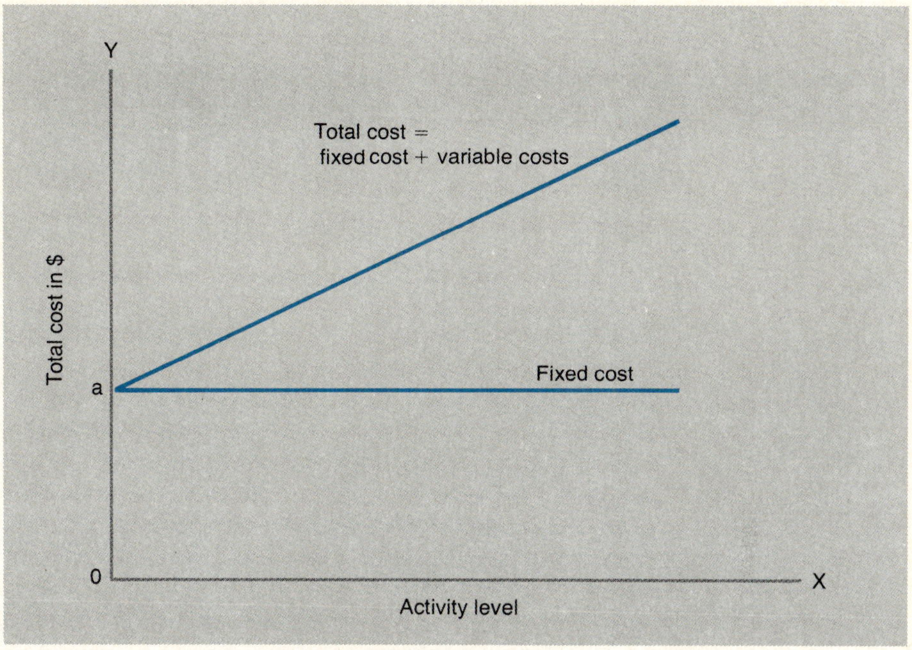

Figure 2-9
Mixed costs contain fixed and variable cost components that may be separated for managerial planning and control purposes.

The mixed cost equation states that the total cost is equal to the fixed cost plus the variable cost. By substituting values for *a* and *b*, we can describe various mixed costs mathematically, which is very useful in planning, analyzing costs, and explaining cost behavior.

The total cost equation for the bicycle example is

$$\text{Total cost} = \text{Fixed cost} + \text{Variable cost}$$
$$Y = a + bX$$
$$= \$4{,}000 + \$30X$$

To find total cost for any level of bicycle production, it is merely necessary to substitute a value for *X*. For instance, the total cost of 600 bicycles is

$$\text{Total cost} = \text{Fixed cost} + (\text{Variable cost per unit} \times \text{Units})$$
$$Y = \$4{,}000 + \$30X$$
$$= \$4{,}000 + \$30(600)$$
$$= \$4{,}000 + \$18{,}000$$
$$= \$22{,}000$$

Many costs exhibit mixed cost characteristics, with some portions of the costs variable and others fixed. The costs of electricity, maintenance, and indirect labor are examples of mixed costs.

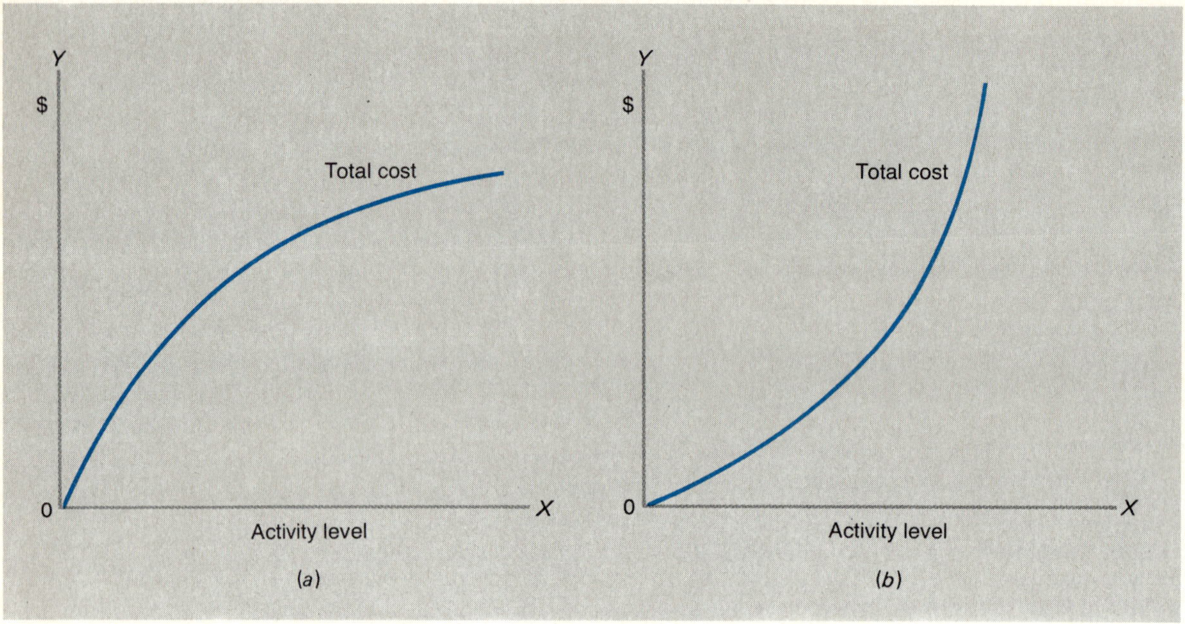

Figure 2-10 Semivariable costs that increase at a decreasing rate are called learning curve costs and are illustrated on the left. Semivariable costs that increase at an increasing rate are shown on the right.

Semivariable Costs

Some costs vary with the volume of activity but not at a constant rate. They are called **semivariable costs**. They can be divided into costs that change at a decreasing rate and costs that change at an increasing rate.

As employees become more familiar with tasks, they become more efficient

In Figure 2-10, part (*a*) shows a semivariable cost that increases at a decreasing rate. This type of cost is referred to as a **learning curve cost**. The term originates from the observed decrease in labor costs that sometimes occurs as employees become familiar with a new task. For example, it may require 3 hours of direct labor to assemble a lawn mower for the first production run of a new type of mower. However, employees may assemble the mowers in 2 hours and 50 minutes on the next run and in 2 hours and 40 minutes on the third run.

Diagram (*b*) in Figure 2-10 shows a semivariable cost that increases at an increasing rate. This type of cost behavior is characterized by larger costs per unit of output as the activity level rises. For example, some forms of energy may be priced to encourage conservation. The price per unit of energy rises as more and more energy is consumed; therefore, the per unit cost of energy used in production rises. Managers should be cautious of this type of cost because it can get out of control quickly. Semivariable costs are discussed further in Chapter 18.

Step Function or Semifixed Costs

Step function costs, sometimes called **semifixed costs**, remain fixed over a range of activity, but beyond some activity level they change usually by

Costs that increase in steps or jumps

intermittent jumps rather than continuously. Many costs exhibit semifixed cost behavior. For example, a firm may increase its production by working overtime or by adding a night shift without increasing the fixed cost of production facilities. But when maximum capacity is reached, increased production can be achieved only by expanding the plant. This causes a jump in the fixed cost of production facilities. Similarly, a firm uses a delivery truck to deliver large appliances sold in the store. Any increase in sales would require the acquisition of a second delivery truck causing the depreciation cost to jump to a higher level. The cost behavior pattern of a semifixed cost is graphed in Figure 2-11.

Figure 2-11 illustrates why the term *step function* is used for semifixed costs. The semifixed cost pattern has characteristics of both variable costs and fixed costs. Like variable costs, step function costs increase with the volume of activity, although not proportionately, and like fixed costs, they remain constant for stretches of activity levels, although not for all levels of activity.

The graph of the cost is the solid horizontal line. The vertical dashed lines, labeled *A*, *B*, and *C*, are the changes in the cost at each step as the level of activity changes. In this illustration the cost changes are not equal. Likewise the intervals of activity between the increases in cost are not equal. The graph of semifixed costs is not continuous; it is broken whenever the cost shifts to another level. Consequently, we cannot describe semifixed costs by a simple mathematical equation. However, this does not prevent managers from identifying and using semifixed costs in decision making.

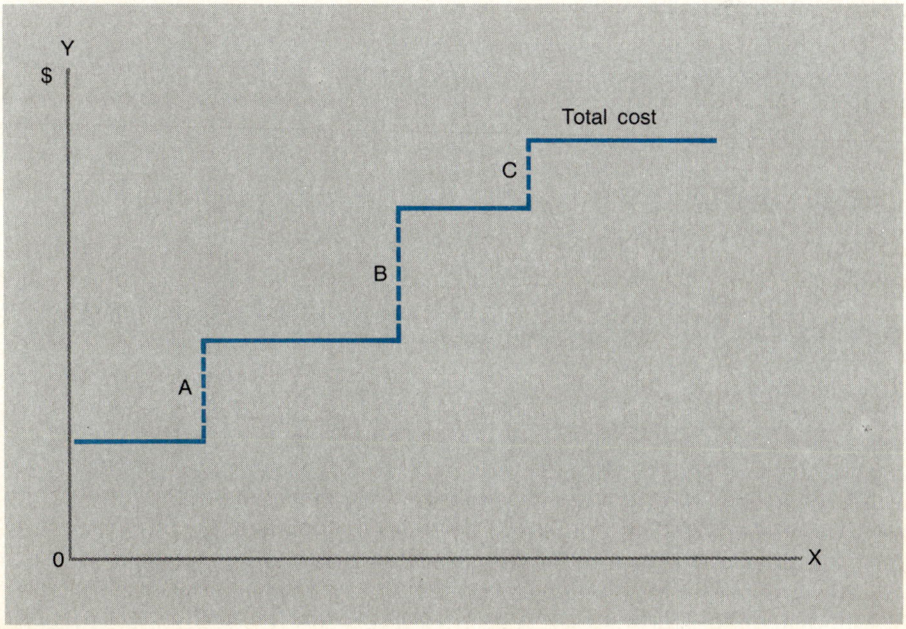

Figure 2-11
Step function costs jump intermittently from one level to another. They remain constant until another change occurs at another level of activity. They are often called semifixed costs.

Cost Behavior Assumptions

The discussion of cost behavior rests on two very important assumptions: the relevant range assumption and the time assumption.

Important assumptions in evaluating cost behavior

The relevant range assumption. No cost actually exhibits the same behavior pattern at all activity levels. The **relevant range assumption** states that the identified cost behavior patterns are correct only for a certain range of activity. Any level of activity above or below the relevant range may have different cost behavior patterns. For example, Figure 2-12 shows cost curves with several different behavior patterns. The diagram on the left depicts a semivariable cost with a learning curve slope from the origin to activity level *A*. From *A* to *B* the cost is directly variable, and above activity level *B* the cost is semivariable, increasing at an increasing rate. The diagram on the right shows a cost that is initially mixed. Between activity levels *C* and *D* the cost is fixed. At *D* the cost jumps to a higher amount, exhibiting a semifixed cost pattern.

In each of these cases, a simple description of the cost curves is not possible. However, very low and very high levels of activity often are not relevant to decision making because there is little chance that those activity levels will occur. The **relevant range** covers the levels of activity that are likely to occur. For example, if the activity level between *A* and *B* is the relevant range in Figure 2-12, then managers can treat the cost as directly variable. The fact that the cost exhibits other behavior patterns outside the

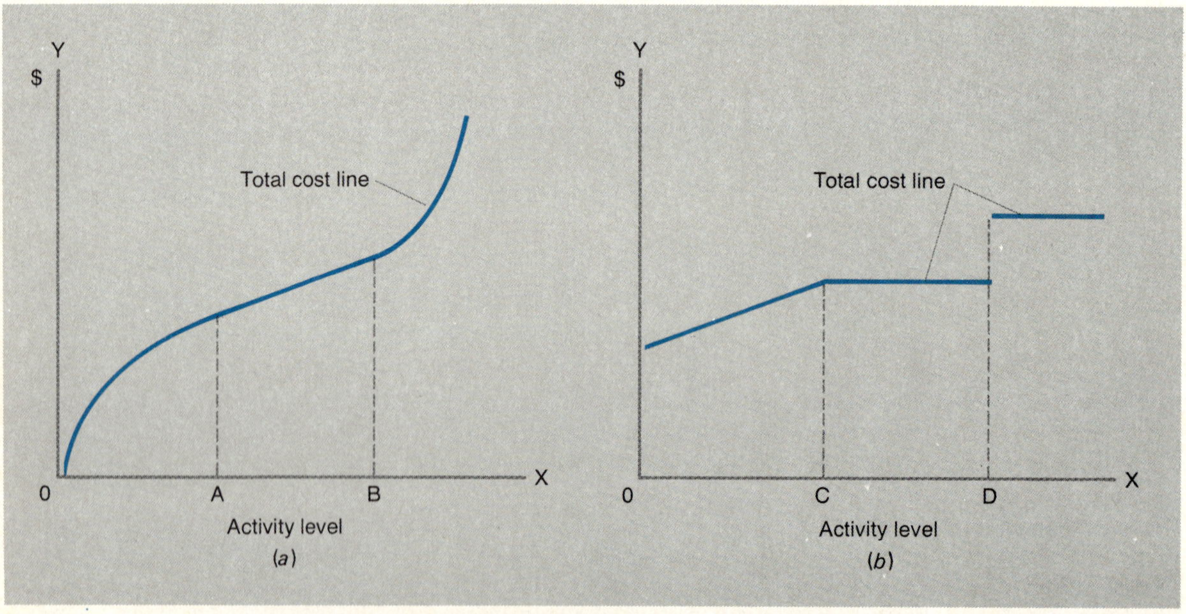

Figure 2-12 Cost behavior patterns are seldom the same for an infinite range of activity. In graph (*a*), the cost is semivariable outside of the relevant range *A* to *B*. In graph (*b*), the fixed cost is semifixed or mixed outside the relevant range *C* to *D*.

relevant range is unimportant as long as the estimate of the relevant range is correct. If the activity level between C and D in Figure 2-12 is the relevant range, then managers can treat that cost as a fixed cost.

The time assumption. A second assumption about cost behavior, called the **time assumption**, states that the identified cost behavior patterns hold true only for a certain period of time. Cost behavior patterns may change over time. Few costs classified as fixed are fixed over the long run. Although they may be fixed for the current year, they may change over a period of years. For example, a 1-year lease on a building is a fixed cost for the year, but it is not as yet fixed for subsequent years. Similarly, a food processor may cause the cost of raw materials to shift from variable to fixed costs by entering into long-term purchase contracts for perishable foods used in production.

Measuring the Volume of Activity

The volume of activity can be measured using a variety of activity measures

The volume of business activity can be measured or expressed in a variety of ways. Number of units produced, dollar volume of sales, number of direct labor hours worked, and number of customers served are all measures of the level of business activity. In analyzing cost behavior, managers must select the measure of business activity that will provide the most accurate estimates of cost behavior patterns. For example, dollar volume of sales may be the best measure of the volume of activity for a department store, whereas number of customers served may be best for a service firm, and perhaps units of production may be most useful for a manufacturing business.

ADDITIONAL COST CONCEPTS

As you probably have learned by now, the term *cost* by itself may be of little use. In many uses, the term *cost* is modified in some way. It is more meaningful to talk about product costs, operating costs, fixed costs, or direct costs than just cost alone. Before moving on to the actual measurement of product costs in Chapter 3 and the use of cost data in managerial accounting reports, we discuss several additional cost concepts and terms that you will find useful.

Cost and Expense

Expense is a timing concept and cost is a valuation concept

The distinction between costs and expenses should be clear to anyone in business. **Cost** is the amount of resource expended for some good or service, and **expense** is the amount of good or service that has expired or has been consumed during a given accounting period. For example, a 1-year fire insurance policy is purchased on August 1 for $2,400. At the end of the year, 5 months of the insurance protection have been used and 7 months of protection remain. The **cost** of the 1-year insurance policy is

\$2,400, but the **expense** of the protection used this year is \$1,000 ($5/12 \times$ \$2,400), leaving an unexpired cost of \$1,400. Similarly, a building is purchased for \$100,000; it has an expected useful life of 10 years with no salvage value, and straight-line depreciation is used. The **cost** of the building is \$100,000, but the **expense** of the building for the first year is \$10,000 of depreciation. Notice that expense is a **timing concept** dictated by the matching principle, whereas cost is a **valuation concept**.

Unit Costs

One of the most widely used pieces of information from a product cost system is the **unit cost**. It is the cost of producing one unit of product or providing one unit of service. Some examples are:

- \$4.50 to give one haircut
- \$9.22 to produce a pair of nylon running shoes
- \$5.81 to process each sales invoice
- \$.48 to produce a 10-inch plastic toy truck

Unit costs are convenient for planning and decision making, but caution is necessary in dealing with them. The fact that accountants have reduced all of the production cost flows to a single unit cost does not mean that it can be used like an external price from vendors. Unit costs, although convenient, have some special characteristics that must be understood.

Most unit costs are averages

The first characteristic of unit costs is that they are almost always average figures. They represent the average cost of producing a product over some time period or during a production run. For example, 5,000 pounds of chocolate candy are produced at a total production cost of \$6,250. The unit cost is \$1.25 per pound, calculated as \$6,250/5,000 pounds, which is the average cost of producing a pound of the chocolate candy. Little can be said about the cost of producing a single pound of candy or about the cost per pound of candy with larger or smaller production runs. A few production processes, such as construction of a bridge, a dam, or a ship, result in a single unit of product, but most unit costs are averages to some degree.

A second characteristic of unit costs is **periodicity**. Unit costs are the result of a production activity for some specific time period. A 5,000-pound batch of candy produced at another time may cost more or less than \$1.25 per pound. Unit costs change as a result of fluctuation in the cost of production resources, differing production efficiencies, changes in management objectives, or other variables. Caution must be exercised to avoid giving long-range predictive characteristics to unit costs.

Cost of Periodic and Perpetual Inventories

Manufacturing firms have a significant amount of resources invested in raw materials, work in process, and finished goods inventories. Because inventories are a significant part of current assets, it is imperative that their costs are reported accurately. The costs of inventories depend on the choice of inventory valuation methods selected and also on the type of inventory system used.

In a **periodic inventory system**, the beginning inventory balance is carried in the Inventory account. All purchases of inventory are recorded in a separate Purchases account. Reductions in inventory are not recorded during the period. At the end of the period, total net purchases are added to beginning inventory to find total inventory available for sale or use. Next, ending inventory is subtracted from total inventory available to arrive at inventory sold or used. To find the ending inventory figure, an inventory count must be taken and the units in inventory must be costed. Usually, first in, first out (FIFO), last in, first out (LIFO), or weighted average methods are used as the cost flow assumptions for costing inventories.

In a **perpetual inventory system**, inventory records are kept for both the inflow and the outflow of inventory items on a continuous basis, and the inventory balance is known at any point in time. Costing the outflow of inventory requires the use of FIFO, LIFO, moving average, or specific identification methods.

Most manufacturing firms use perpetual inventory systems

Most manufacturing firms use a perpetual inventory system for product costing in order to provide timely product cost information. A perpetual inventory system provides better control over inventory shortages caused by inefficiencies or theft. In a periodic system, the amount of inventory used is the residual of an arithmetic operation. In a perpetual system, continuous inventory records are maintained, and inventory counts can be used to verify inventory records. A discussion of periodic and perpetual inventory systems is presented in Chapter 15.

Common Costs

Accountants try to identify costs with specific cost objectives because identifiable costs lend themselves well to analysis and evaluation by management. However, many costs are not readily identifiable with specific cost objectives. Instead they are the **common costs** of two or more cost objectives. For example, a research laboratory supervisor may have responsibility for managing 10 different research projects. The cost of the supervisor's services is shared by all projects and is therefore a common cost of the projects.

Often it is necessary to allocate common costs to cost objectives for reporting purposes

Often it is necessary or desirable to assign part of a common cost to each cost objective benefiting from it. For example, the Internal Revenue Service requires that the product costs used in determining a company's taxable income include all necessary costs of production, both direct and indirect. Therefore costs common to more than one product must be assigned to the various products to determine product cost for reporting net income. In certain situations, managers may find that direct costs are only a small portion of total costs and it may be necessary to assign common costs to cost objectives to aid in the analysis of the cost data in making some decisions. The assignment of common costs to various objectives is called **cost allocation**. Sometimes cost allocation is a simple and logical process. For example, the laboratory supervisor may keep good records of the time spent on each project. Then the total cost of the supervisor can be allocated to the 10 projects in proportion to the time spent on each. When detailed time records are not possible, another cost allocation method may be used for reporting purposes. If cost allocations are based on questionable relationships, the resulting cost data may be of little managerial value. Cost allocations are discussed in Chapter 4.

Controllable Costs

Controllable costs are important for management reporting

An important concept in managerial accounting that strongly influences the development of managerial accounting reports is the concept of controllable cost. Ideally a **controllable cost** is one over which a manager has direct and complete decision authority. Theoretically all costs are controllable by somebody in the organization. The chief executive officer of a firm should be responsible for all company costs. However, identifying responsibility for every cost is difficult at lower levels in the organization's management structure. Therefore, in practice a *controllable cost* is defined as a cost over which a manager has some influence or control. In spite of the difficulty of identifying controllable costs, the concept of controllability strongly influences many managerial accounting activities, such as planning, management reporting, and analysis of performance.

Differential Costs

Costs that differ between decision alternatives are called **differential costs.** For example, if management is evaluating the purchase of either a manual or an automated lathe, both requiring skilled labor costing $12 per hour, the labor rate is not relevant because it is the same for both alternatives. If, however, the manual lathe requires semiskilled labor at $9 per hour and the automated lathe requires skilled labor at $12 per hour, then the labor rate is relevant because it is different for the two alternatives. The difference between the amount of the two labor costs is called **differential cost.** In the above example differential cost is computed as follows:

$$\text{Differential cost} = \text{Cost of one alternative} - \text{Cost of the other alternative}$$
$$= \$12 - \$9 = \$3$$

Opportunity Costs

An **opportunity cost** is the benefit given up by rejecting one alternative and selecting another. For example, if a company decides to use some manufacturing plant space to make wheel bearings, the company must forego the rental income the company could have earned by renting the same space to another company that wanted to use the space for a warehouse. Opportunity costs often are useful in evaluating business decisions.

Sunk Costs

Costs that have been incurred and cannot be changed are called **sunk costs.** Many fixed costs such as depreciation and lease costs are sunk costs and are not relevant in evaluating many types of decisions. For example, the cost of the employee cafeteria in the manufacturing plant is not relevant in evaluating whether to produce or buy steering columns used in the company's manufacturing of tractors. The cost of the cafeteria has already been incurred and will not change regardless of the decision to buy or make the steering columns.

SUMMARY

Cost accounting data provide detailed support for managerial accounting reports. Cost information is univerally applicable to many economic and personal decisions. It is used by all types of business firms and in all types of activities, but is particularly useful in manufacturing operations.

Costs can be determined for a variety of products and activities called **cost objectives**. Typical cost objectives include products, departments, projects, and various services.

Direct materials, direct labor, and **manufacturing overhead (MOH)** are the three basic **cost elements** that make up the cost of a manufactured product. Direct materials and direct labor are identifiable directly with products and together are referred to as **prime costs**. Manufacturing overhead, the **indirect costs** of production, includes all necessary costs of production other than the prime costs, including **indirect materials, indirect labor**, and capacity costs, such as plant and equipment depreciation, insurance and taxes on the production facilities, and utility costs for the manufacturing operations. Manufacturing overhead and direct labor together are called **conversion costs** because they combine to convert raw materials into finished products.

Manufacturing firms have three levels of inventory. **Raw materials** are the basic ingredients of manufactured products. **Work in process (WIP)** consists of products in the process of being produced. **Finished goods** are completed products that are ready for sale, similar to merchandise inventory in a merchandising firm.

The physical flow of production is paralleled by the flow of costs through the ledger accounts. **Product costs** include all necessary costs of production—direct materials, direct labor, and manufacturing overhead. All production costs are recorded first in the Work in Process account. When products are completed, their costs are transferred to the Finished Goods Inventory account. All production costs remain assets as long as the product remains in an inventory account. When a product is sold, its cost is transferred from finished goods to **cost of goods sold**. At the time of sale, the product cost becomes an expense. The expense is matched with the revenue from the sale of the product, satisfying the matching principle. **Period costs** are costs that are expensed in the period in which they are incurred.

The **schedule of cost of goods manufactured** is a summary of manufacturing costs incurred during the accounting period. The schedule starts with the beginning work in process; then current period production costs are added, and ending work in process is subtracted. The resulting amount is called **cost of goods manufactured**, and it represents the total cost of products transferred to finished goods during the accounting period.

Cost behavior patterns are used in making a wide variety of decisions. For accounting purposes several major classifications of cost behavior are useful for planning and control. **Fixed costs** remain constant at all levels of activity. **Variable costs** change directly and proportionately with activity level. **Mixed costs** are composed of fixed and variable costs. **Step function costs**, sometimes called **semifixed costs**, change by intermittent jumps. **Semivariable costs** increase with activity, but at a changing rate. Those that increase at a decreasing rate are called **learning curve costs** and reflect increased efficiency as employees become more familiar with new tasks. Some semivariable costs increase at an increasing rate.

Cost behavior analysis rests on two important assumptions. The **relevant range assumption** states that the identified cost behavior patterns are correct only for a certain range of activity. Outside of that range other cost behavior patterns may prevail. The **time assumption** states that identified cost behavior patterns pertain to a specific period of time. During other time intervals the cost behavior patterns may be different.

Cost is the amount of resource given up for some good or service. **Expense** is the amount of resource used during a given accounting period. For some items cost and expense are the same because the good or service is used in the period purchased. Some items, such as fixed assets, benefit many periods and their annual expense is different from their cost.

A **perpetual inventory system** is used to maintain a continuous record of inventory transactions and is essential in providing timely cost data for managerial accounting reports. With a **periodic inventory system** inventory purchases are recorded in a separate Purchases account. The product expense is not recorded until year-end, when an inventory count is taken to see how much unsold inventory is left. The product expense is determined by subtracting the ending inventory from the total goods available.

The **unit cost** of manufactured products is an **average** cost per unit for some time period or production run. **Controllable costs** refer to costs over which managers have decision authority. They are used to evaluate managers who are responsible for the costs. Costs that differ between decision alternatives are called **differential costs.** An **opportunity cost** is the benefit given up by rejecting one alternative and selecting another. Costs that have been incurred and cannot be changed are **sunk costs.**

KEY TERMS

Much new terminology is introduced in this chapter. The list below consists of terms that you should understand before proceeding to the next chapter. Other new terms are discussed more thoroughly in later chapters. The italic numbers in parentheses indicate the pages on which the terms first appear.

committed fixed cost *(44)*
common cost *(53)*
controllable cost *(54)*
conversion cost *(31)*

cost *(28, 51)*
cost allocation *(54)*
cost behavior *(42)*
cost elements *(30)*
cost objective *(28)*
cost of goods manufactured *(39)*
cost of goods sold *(38)*
differential cost *(54)*
direct labor *(30)*
direct materials *(30)*
discretionary fixed cost *(44)*
expense *(51)*
finished goods *(33)*
fixed cost *(42)*
gross margin *(38)*
indirect costs *(30)*
indirect labor *(30)*
indirect materials *(30)*
inventoriable cost *(35)*
learning curve cost *(48)*
manufacturing overhead (MOH) *(30)*
matching principle *(32)*
merchandise inventory *(38)*
mixed cost *(46)*
opportunity cost *(54)*
overhead *(31)*
period cost *(36)*
periodic inventory system *(53)*
perpetual inventory system *(53)*
prime cost *(31)*
product cost *(36)*
raw materials *(33)*
relevant range assumption *(50)*
schedule of cost of goods manufactured *(39)*
semifixed cost *(48)*
semivariable cost *(48)*
step function cost *(48)*
sunk cost *(55)*
time assumption *(51)*
total manufacturing cost *(39)*
unit cost *(52)*
variable cost *(44)*
work in process (WIP) *(33)*

QUESTIONS

1. What is a cost objective? Give two examples from business and two from your personal life.
2. Describe the three basic cost elements of a manufactured product.
3. What do the terms *prime cost* and *conversion cost* mean?
4. Which is the most important of the cost elements?
5. Describe the different levels of inventory in a manufacturing firm.
6. What is meant by the term *inventoriable cost*?
7. Why is the determination of product cost different in a merchandising firm than in a manufacturing firm?
8. What is the product cost called in the income statement of a service firm?
9. What is the function of the cost of goods manufactured schedule?
10. What is meant by cost behavior patterns and why would managers be concerned with them?
11. The plant manager is having trouble distinguishing between controllable and variable costs. As a cost accountant, how would you explain this issue?
12. Distinguish between fixed and variable costs.
    a. Give a brief definition of each.
    b. Identify the appropriate formula and its components.
    c. Provide two examples of each cost.
13. Describe what is meant by committed and discretionary fixed costs and why it is important for management to be able to identify such costs.
14. "Semifixed and semivariable costs are one and the same; the words are just changed," says the new junior accountant just hired by the firm. As controller for the firm, what would you tell him?

15. What is the rationale behind calling a semivariable cost curve that increases at a decreasing rate a learning curve?
16. Discuss the importance of the relevant range and time assumptions as they relate to cost behavior.
17. Distinguish between a cost and an expense. Give an example of each.
18. Distinguish between a perpetual inventory system and a periodic inventory system. Which is used more often in manufacturing and why?
19. Of what significance is the concept of controllable cost in managerial accounting?

EXERCISES

Ex. 2-1 Determining period and product costs. Below are a number of events and transactions of a manufacturing company that are to be identified as either a product cost or a period cost.

a. Computer lease cost for production scheduling computer
b. Payroll taxes on factory workers
c. Wages of employees working in the raw materials inventory storeroom
d. Factory fire insurance premiums
e. First aid room for factory employees
f. Indirect labor
g. Office equipment lease cost
h. Property taxes, factory
i. Property taxes, office
j. Sales commissions
k. Sales salaries
l. Storage and handling costs for the finished goods inventory
m. The controller's salary
n. The cost of a maintenance contract for hydraulic equipment in the plant
o. Vacation pay for factory workers

Required: Identify each of the items in the list as either a product cost or a period cost.

Ex. 2-2 Measuring and reporting income. Below are financial data for Gurnhart Manufacturing Company for 1984 and 1985.

	1985	1986
Sales	$696,000	$780,000
Marketing and distribution expenses	198,000	217,000
General administrative expenses	103,000	125,000
Beginning finished goods	18,000	72,000
Ending finished goods	72,000	94,000
Current period manufacturing costs	272,000	295,000
Ending work in process inventory	57,000	31,000
Beginning work in process inventory	44,000	57,000

Required: Prepare income statements in good form for each year.

Ex. 2-3 **Use of cost equations.** Below are cost equations for direct labor and direct materials that were developed from last year's gear assembly production data. In the equations X equals units of output.

Direct labor:	$Y = \$12{,}923 + \$3.96X$
Direct materials:	$Y = \$2{,}705 + \$17.03X$

A manager of Limpitt Company asks you to determine the direct labor and material costs of producing 2,500 gear assemblies in the current year.

Required: Calculate the total direct cost of production from the equations provided.

Ex. 2-4 **Describing and using cost behavior data.** Sentery Company, a catalog sales business, has analyzed monthly distribution costs data for the last 3 years. The analysis indicates that variable distribution costs are \$.12 per dollar of sales and fixed costs are \$65,000 per month.

Required:

a. Write a cost equation to describe the company's total monthly distribution cost.
b. Write a cost equation to describe the company's total annual distribution cost.
c. Based on your equation in part *a*, estimate the firm's distribution costs for a month in which budgeted sales are \$3,500,000.
d. Graph the firm's annual distribution cost function.

Ex. 2-5 **Identifying fixed and variable costs.** Below is a list of cost accounts for a manufacturing business.

Advertising
Depreciation, production plant
Depreciation, production equipment
Direct labor
Direct materials
Electricity for the production plant
First aid room
Heating costs for the production plant
Indirect labor
Insurance on office building
Patent royalty on each unit produced
Payroll taxes on production employees
Plant fire insurance
Plant maintenance
Property taxes for the production plant
Sales commission

Required: For each of the costs listed indicate whether it should most likely be classified as a fixed cost or a variable cost.

Ex. 2-6 **Cost of goods manufactured and cost of goods sold.** Following are December 31 ledger account balances from the books of Glendale, Ltd., a manufacturing business. In addition, beginning inventory balances are identified as January 1 account balances.

Ending work in process	$ 43,000
Sales commissions	19,500
Office depreciation	16,000
Manufacturing plant depreciation	40,000
Production supervisors' salaries	85,000
Direct materials	180,000
Indirect labor	25,000
Property taxes (60% factory, 40% office)	30,000
Insurance on finished goods inventory	4,000
Insurance on raw materials	2,000
Utilities (80% factory, 20% office)	20,000
Indirect materials	15,000
Direct labor	200,000
Administrative salaries	120,000
Beginning work in process (January 1)	26,000
Sales	950,000
Sales returns	10,000
Beginning finished goods (January 1)	45,000
Ending finished goods	85,000
Maintenance (90% factory, 10% office)	40,000

Required:

a. Prepare in good form a schedule of cost of goods manufactured for the year.
b. Prepare in good form a schedule of cost of goods sold for the period.

Ex. 2-7 **Missing cost and sales data.** Below are four sets of income statement data, with some items omitted. The four situations are independent.

	A	B	C	D
Sales	$98,000	$80,000	$65,000	$ ____
Beginning finished goods	6,000	9,000	____	12,000
Beginning work in process	4,000	____	____	8,000
Direct materials	20,000	16,000	15,000	____
Direct labor	30,000	20,000	20,000	17,000
Manufacturing overhead	40,000	18,000	25,000	20,000
Ending work in process	12,000	9,000	4,000	7,000
Cost of goods manufactured	____	56,000	65,000	63,000
Ending finished goods	21,000	____	22,000	____
Cost of goods sold	____	____	____	52,000
Gross margin	____	30,000	17,000	33,000
Operating expenses	25,000	____	19,000	____
Net income	$ ____	$12,000	$ ____	$ 9,000

Required: For each situation fill in the missing data.

Ex. 2-8 **Identifying types of costs.** Following is a list of costs to be classified into two categories.

a. Computer lease cost, marketing
b. Controller's salary
c. Depreciation, factory
d. Depreciation, office
e. Direct labor
f. Direct materials
g. Fire insurance, factory
h. Indirect labor
i. Indirect materials
j. Plant superintendent's salary
k. President's salary
l. Property taxes, office
m. Property taxes, factory
n. Utilities, factory

Required: For each cost listed, determine if it should be classified most logically as a fixed or variable cost and also as a product or period cost.

Ex. 2-9 **Distinguishing between costs and expenses.** Below are descriptions of various resource acquisitions by the Doltone Products Company during the year. The company uses straight-line depreciation for all fixed assets.

a. Paid a contractor $350 for snow removal from parking lot.
b. Purchased a 3-year fire insurance policy for $5,400 on October 1.
c. Purchased new word processing equipment for the office on July 1 for $120,000. Cash of $30,000 is paid and a 3-year note payable for $90,000 is issued. The equipment has an expected useful life of 7 years and a salvage value of $15,000.
d. Bought a new front-end loader on April 1 with a list price of $130,000. The company paid $85,000 cash and traded in an old front-end loader that had a market value of $35,000. The new equipment has an expected useful life of 5 years and salvage value of $40,000.
e. Received a bill of $900 on October 15 for September lawn care services.
f. On November 1 purchased a 1-year maintenance agreement on the new word processing equipment for $4,800.
g. Bought a 6-month maintenance agreement on electric typewriters for $1,200 on June 1.
h. Traded land valued at $70,000 for a large parking lot of equal value that is adjacent to the plant.

Required: For each transaction, identify the amount of cost **and** the amount of expense for the year.

Ex. 2-10 **Analyzing changes in product costs.** The condensed income statement of the Tysen Company is presented on the following page.

Tysen Company
Income Statement

Sales (30,000 units)	$450,000
Cost of goods sold	360,000
Gross margin	90,000
Administrative expenses	(30,000)
Marketing expenses	(10,000)
Net income	$ 50,000

The cost of the units sold is broken down as follows:

Direct material—$6.00
Direct labor—$3.75
Manufacturing overhead—$2.25

Required: Determine the percentage change in net income caused by each of the following independent situations *a* through *e*.

a. Selling price increases by 25 percent.
b. Manufacturing overhead cost increases by 25 percent.
c. Direct labor cost rises by 25 percent.
d. Direct materials cost rises by 25 percent.
e. Both selling price and **all** product costs increase by 25 percent.
f. Compute the **per unit change** in profit if both the selling price and all the product costs increased by 25 percent.

Ex. 2-11 Understanding financial statements of a manufacturing firm. The Snyder Furniture Corporation makes a single product, a couch that converts into a bed. It

Snyder Furniture Corporation
Income Statement
For the Year Ended December 31, 1986

Sales		$2,640,000
Less cost of goods sold:		
Beginning finished goods inventory 1/1/86	$ 224,000	
Add cost of goods manufactured in 1986	1,380,000	
Total goods available for sale	1,604,000	
Less ending finished goods inventory 12/31/86	192,000	
Cost of goods sold		1,412,000
Gross margin		1,228,000
Less operating expenses:		
Sales salaries and commissions	268,000	
Administrative salaries	149,000	
Depreciation of office buildings and equipment	161,000	
Insurance	12,500	
Property taxes	17,000	
Office supplies	14,500	
Utilities	29,000	
Total operating expenses		651,000
Net income		$ 577,000

is sold primarily to people living in small apartments. The 1986 income statement for the company is presented on page 62.

During the year Snyder Furniture Corporation made 24,000 units and sold 25,000 units. The beginning work in process inventory had a cost of $236,000 and the ending work in process inventory had a cost of $265,600.

Required:

a. Compute the average unit cost of goods manufactured during the period.
b. Compute the total manufacturing costs incurred during the period.
c. Compute the change in the Finished Goods Inventory account from the beginning to the end of the accounting period.
d. Compute the cost per unit of sales salaries and commissions.
e. Compute the product expenses as a percentage of total expenses for 1986.

Ex. 2-12 Analyzing manufacturing account relationships. Below are partial data from four **independent** income statements. Blanks represent missing data.

	Situation A	Situation B	Situation C	Situation D
Sales	$____	$____	$98,000	$75,000
Beginning finished goods	____	17,000	12,000	____
Beginning work in process	____	9,000	11,000	12,000
Direct materials	26,000	43,000	22,000	31,000
Direct labor	34,000	19,000	33,000	____
Manufacturing overhead	25,000	____	29,000	18,000
Ending work in process	24,000	17,000	____	19,000
Cost of goods manufactured	62,000	73,000	69,000	51,000
Ending finished goods	33,000	____	35,000	14,000
Cost of goods sold	76,000	66,000	____	____
Gross margin	21,000	18,000	____	13,000
Operating expenses	____	14,000	22,000	____
Net income	$ 5,000	$ ____	$30,000	$ 8,000

Required: Fill in the missing data for each situation.

PROBLEMS

P. 2-1 Measuring product costs. Marlene Walker decided to start a fishing lure manufacturing business. During the first year of operations the following transactions and events occurred.

1. Leased a building for $8,400 a year.
2. Bought paint and other materials for $18,500.
3. Incurred electricity and heating bills of $1,900.
4. Leased production machinery for $5,700 a year.
5. Hired an employee for $8 an hour who worked a total of 1,800 hours. The employee worked only on production activities.
6. Bought for $1,200 a typewriter that is expected to last 4 years.
7. Produced 25,000 lures.
8. Sold 22,000 lures for $3.00 each.

9. Had ending raw materials of $1,900.
10. Marketing and distribution costs for the year were $1,240.

Required:
a. Compute the per unit cost of producing the lures during the first year.
b. Compute the cost of goods sold for the year.
c. Compute the net income for the first year of business.
d. If Marlene works 2,200 hours in the business during the year, what are her hourly earnings the first year?
e. Compute the cost of ending finished goods inventory.

P. 2-2 Cost of goods manufactured and the income statement. The general ledger account balances are presented below for the Kluno Corporation as of December 31. Beginning inventory balances are identified by name and are indicated as 1/1 balances.

Administrative salaries	$ 348,250
Advertising	97,500
Beginning finished goods 1/1	192,250
Beginning work in process 1/1	141,750
Depreciation, factory	85,000
Depreciation, office	53,750
Depreciation, factory equipment	140,000
Direct labor	292,750
Direct materials	561,250
Ending finished goods	235,000
Ending work in process	159,500
Fire insurance (70% production plant)	22,250
Indirect labor	48,500
Indirect materials	22,500
Miscellaneous office expense	15,500
Property taxes (60% production plant)	39,000
Raw materials inventory	219,250
Rent, office equipment	28,500
Sales	2,225,000
Sales commissions	89,000
Sales returns and allowances	17,000
Sales salaries	186,250
Utilities (80% production plant)	95,500

All accounts have normal balances.

Required:
a. Prepare a cost of goods manufactured schedule in good form.
b. Prepare an income statement in good form.

P. 2-3 Analyzing manufacturing financial information. You are the auditor for the Kryzchezki Corporation, a manufacturing company. Your analysis of the financial statements and accompanying records of the corporation during the annual audit disclosed some possible errors in the firm's income statement. The income statement and supporting records for the firm are presented below.

Kryzchezki Corporation
Income Statement
For the Year Ended December 31

Sales		$434,000
Less cost of goods sold:		
Beginning work in process inventory Jan. 1	$ 28,100	
Add raw materials purchases for the year	144,650	
Total goods available for sale	172,750	
Less ending raw materials inventory Dec. 31	21,850	150,900
Gross margin		283,100
Less operating expenses:		
Sales salaries	28,450	
Sales commissions	18,350	
Depreciation of office facilities	16,000	
Depreciation of office equipment	7,300	
Insurance (60% on production facilities)	6,000	
Office supplies	3,200	
Utilities (75% for manufacturing operations)	13,800	
Total operating expenses		93,100
Net income		$190,000

The analysis you performed indicated that all of the account balances used in the income statement are correct. In addition, you found that the following accounts did not appear in any of the company's financial reports:

Finished goods inventory Jan. 1	$53,750
Advertising	13,350
Administrative salaries	53,000
Depreciation, production machinery	22,000
Maintenance contract on production equipment	11,000
Maintenance contract on office computer	7,200
Finished goods inventory Dec. 31	49,000

You compute that the cost of goods manufactured during the year was $259,950.

Required: Prepare a corrected income statement for the Kryzchezki Corporation in good form.

P. 2-4 Cost behavior patterns. In an effort to control overhead costs for a large equipment manufacturing firm, you have carefully analyzed three service functions in the manufacturing plant that have not stayed within budget estimates for the last several years. These service functions are maintenance, first aid, and the plant cafeteria. After carefully analyzing 60 months of cost and production data you determine the following costs behavior pattern for each cost:

$$\text{Maintenance cost} = \$60{,}000 + \$2.00X$$
$$\text{First aid cost} = \$45{,}000 + .40X$$
$$\text{Cafeteria cost} = \$30{,}000 + .80X$$

X is the monthly activity expressed in units of production. The total of all other overhead costs can be described by the equation

$$Y = \$165{,}000 + \$4.80X$$

September production is projected at 25,000 units.

Required:

- **a.** Explain the meaning of the maintenance cost equation.
- **b.** Graph the three service department equations on a single graph.
- **c.** What is the expected cost for each service area in September?
- **d.** Write the equation that would describe total manufacturing overhead costs.
- **e.** What are total expected overhead costs for September?

P. 2-5 Measuring and reporting product costs. Fred Staven and Sadie Williams decided to open a homemade fudge shop to produce and sell an outstanding family fudge made by Sadie. Fred invested $2,500 in the business for 30 percent of the profits. Sadie supplied another $500 in cash and provided a place to produce the fudge. Sadie is paid $5.50 per hour for the time she works in the business and is to receive 70 percent of the profits. The business started operating on January 1. During the year the following occurred:

1. Sadie purchased kettles, utensils, a stove, and kitchen equipment needed for large-batch processing. The equipment and installation cost $2,000. The equipment has a 5-year useful life with no salvage value.
2. Sugar, salt, cocoa, vanilla, and other supply purchases for the year cost $16,000.
3. Sadie worked a total of 1,000 hours.
4. 8,000 pounds of fudge were completed.
5. The candy was sold for $3.50 per pound to various candy stores and sweet shops within a 30-mile radius of Sadie's production facility. All candy produced during the period was sold and payment received.
6. Delivery charges amounting to $.05 per pound were paid, and Sadie paid $3,600 for advertising in local newspapers and on radio programs.
7. Sadie determined that her electricity bills were a total of $900 higher this year than last year and there was no utility rate increase.
8. Sadie paid $500 to a secretarial service to handle occasional correspondence, filing of records, and assorted bookkeeping activities.
9. At year-end a physical count showed that $5,200 of supplies inventory was on hand.

Required:

- **a.** Calculate the average unit cost of producing 1 pound of candy during the period.
- **b.** Calculate net income for the business.
- **c.** Determine the amount the partners are entitled to receive as their share of the profits.
- **d.** How much did Sadie actually earn per hour during the year?
- **e.** How much cash is available at year-end for distribution to owners?
- **f.** Why is the cash balance less than the profit, when the beginning cash balance was $3,000?

P. 2-6 Merchandising business income statement and analysis. The Stitchler Department Store is a family-owned merchandising firm that uses a calendar-year accounting period. The company uses a periodic inventory system and the year-end inventory count reveals an ending balance of $203,000. Other year-end account balances are shown in the trial balance. The company is subject to a 40 percent income tax rate. Sixty percent of salary expense is for sales personnel.

Required:

a. Prepare an income statement in good form for Stitchler Department Store.
b. Assuming no dividends are paid, calculate the post-closing balance in retained earnings.
c. Compute the direct cost of selling as a percentage of gross sales, assuming advertising is totally for sales purposes.

Stitchler Department Store
Trial Balance
December 31

	Debit	Credit
Cash	$ 42,000	
Accounts receivable	86,000	
Merchandise inventory 1/1	220,000	
Investments	50,000	
Building	850,000	
Accumulated depreciation, building		$ 210,000
Equipment	92,000	
Accumulated depreciation, equipment		37,000
Accounts payable		45,000
Notes payable		60,000
Mortgage payable		400,000
Capital stock		270,000
Retained earnings		171,000
Sales		940,000
Sales returns and allowances	12,000	
Purchases	479,000	
Purchase returns and allowances		14,000
Freight-in	8,500	
Advertising	63,800	
Commissions	47,000	
Depreciation, building	32,000	
Depreciation, equipment	11,500	
Equipment rent	3,200	
Salaries	96,000	
Utilities	54,000	
Totals	$2,147,000	$2,147,000

P. 2-7 Cost of goods manufactured and the income statement. Below are listed the ledger accounts of the Lendle Company on December 31, with the exception of beginning inventory accounts, which are labeled and identified as being January 1 balances. All accounts have normal balances.

Sales	$2,117,000
Sales salaries	161,000
Sales returns and allowances	136,000
Direct materials	524,000
Ending finished goods inventory	89,000
Beginning work in process inventory (January 1)	67,000
Administrative salaries	279,000
Indirect labor	43,000
Office fire insurance	2,000
Delivery expense for finished products	12,000
Factory property tax	18,000
Direct labor	478,000
Factory fire insurance	7,000
Indirect materials	45,000
Factory supervision	120,000
Office equipment depreciation	4,000
Production equipment depreciation	26,000
Employee fringe benefits (70%, factory employees)	200,000
Advertising	70,000
Beginning finished goods inventory (January 1)	108,000
Ending work in process inventory	93,000

Required:

a. Prepare a schedule of cost of goods manufactured.
b. Prepare an income statement.

P. 2-8 **Interpreting cost of goods manufactured data.** Dellipp Company manufactures bearings. During 1986, the company completed 162,000 bearings and sold 156,000 bearings. Dellipp Company's Raw Materials Inventory account balance on December 31, 1986, was $68,760; $160,560 of raw materials were purchased during the year. Following is the firm's 1986 schedule of cost of goods manufactured.

Dellipp Company
Schedule of Cost of Goods Manufactured
For the Year Ended December 31, 1986

Beginning work in process inventory 1/1/86			$140,640
Direct materials		$175,320	
Direct labor		147,600	
Manufacturing overhead:			
Indirect materials	$13,440		
Indirect labor	16,800		
Depreciation, plant and equipment	49,200		
Salaries, production supervisors	88,080		
Insurance, manufacturing plant	14,040		
Property taxes, manufacturing plant	11,760		
Utilities, manufacturing plant	23,400	216,720	
Total manufacturing cost for 1986			539,640
Total manufacturing cost in production for 1986			680,280
Less ending work in process inventory 12/31/86			113,280
Cost of goods manufactured in 1986			$567,000

Required: Use the data above to answer the following questions and requirements:

a. Compute the average unit cost of bearings manufactured during the year.

b. Compute the balance in the Raw Materials Inventory account on January 1, 1986.

c. Compute the change in the Work in Process Inventory account from the beginning of the accounting period to the end.

d. Determine the total amount of manufacturing cost incurred during the current accounting period.

e. What percentage of manufacturing labor was direct labor?

P. 2-9 Estimating costs from partial data. You have been retained by Braden Company, a small manufacturing firm, to prepare its financial statements for the first 6 months of the year. The financial statements are needed as part of the firm's application for a line of credit. The owner of the company apologized to you about the quality of the company's accounting records. The company's chief accountant left several months ago over a disagreement with the owner. As a result of the accountant's leaving, some information is missing from the accounting records as of June 30. The following data are known.

Finished goods inventory 1/1	$ 40,000
Work in process inventory 1/1	34,000
Raw materials inventory 1/1	31,000
Sales for the first 6 months	950,000
Direct labor cost	350,000

In addition, the following data are estimated.

Factory overhead averages 30 percent of conversion cost.
Material purchases for the 6-month period are $240,000.
Prime costs average 80 percent of cost of goods manufactured.
Gross margin on sales averages 25 percent.
Cost of goods available for sale is estimated at $800,000.
Selling and distribution costs are $112,300.
General administrative expenses are $95,540.

Required: Use the data to estimate the June 30 balance in

a. Raw materials inventory.

b. Work in process inventory.

c. Finished goods inventory.

d. Prepare an income statement in good form for the first 6 months of the year.

P. 2-10 Understanding manufacturing financial statements. Following are the income statement and the schedule of cost of goods manufactured for Riverside Manufacturing, Ltd.

Riverside Manufacturing Ltd.
Income Statement
For the Year Ended December 31, 1986

Sales		$842,300
Less cost of goods sold:		
Beginning finished goods inventory 1/1/86	$ 82,000	
Add cost of goods manufactured in 1986	456,000	
Total goods available for sale	538,000	
Less ending finished goods inventory 12/31/86	105,900	432,100
Gross margin		410,200
Less operating expenses:		
Sales salaries	62,400	
Sales commissions	39,100	
Advertising	22,400	
Administrative salaries	96,500	
Depreciation, office facilities	28,000	
Depreciation, office equipment	37,000	
Insurance	5,000	
Property taxes	12,600	
Office supplies	6,100	
Utilities	15,600	
Total operating expenses		324,700
Net income		$ 85,500

Riverside Manufacturing, Ltd.
Schedule of Cost of Goods Manufactured
For the Year Ended December 31, 1986

Beginning work in process inventory 1/1/86			$ 97,800
Direct materials		$161,300	
Direct labor		142,500	
Manufacturing overhead:			
Indirect materials	$12,600		
Indirect labor	8,400		
Depreciation, manufacturing plant	42,000		
Depreciation, plant equipment	41,000		
Salaries, production supervisors	76,600		
Insurance, manufacturing plant	12,300		
Property taxes, manufacturing plant	14,800		
Utilities, manufacturing plant	22,700	230,400	
Total manufacturing cost for 1986			534,200
Total manufacturing cost in production for 1986			632,000
Less ending work in process inventory, 12/31/86			176,000
Cost of goods manufactured 1986			$456,000

Required: Use the financial data for Riverside Manufacturing, Ltd., to answer the following questions:

a. If the company had been able to sell all of its products, what would have been the cost of goods sold?
b. The raw materials inventory on December 31, 1986, was $84,600. What was the change in total inventory from the beginning to the end of the accounting period?
c. Compute the total manufacturing costs incurred in 1986.
d. In 1986, 105,000 units were sold. Compute the sales commission expense as a percentage of sales dollars and also on a per unit sold basis.
e. Compute the total amount of building depreciation cost for 1986.
f. Raw materials inventory January 1, 1986, was $79,300. What was the total inventory balance on January 1, 1986, for Riverside Manufacturing, Ltd?
g. If 114,000 units of product were transferred from work in process to finished goods during the year, what was the average unit cost to manufacture these products in 1986?
h. What percentage of the company's total costs incurred in 1986 were product costs?

P. 2-11 Merchandising financial reporting. Below is the preclosing trial balance for Kordurva Department Store. The firm uses a periodic inventory system. The year-end inventory count results in an ending inventory balance of $266,000.

Kordurva Department Store
Trial Balance
December 31

	Debit	Credit
Cash	$ 97,000	
Accounts receivable	101,000	
Merchandise inventory 1/1	156,000	
Land	159,000	
Building	950,000	
Accumulated depreciation		$ 404,000
Accounts payable		83,000
Taxes payable		27,000
Notes payable		270,000
Common stock		440,000
Retained earnings		296,000
Sales		985,000
Sales returns and allowances	12,000	
Purchases	548,000	
Purchase returns and allowances		15,000
Freight-in	10,000	
Advertising expense	88,000	
Sales commissions	70,000	
Bad debts expense	16,000	
Equipment rental expense	12,000	
Depreciation expense	45,000	
Administrative salaries	142,000	
Maintenance expense	37,000	
Utilities expense	77,000	
Totals	$2,520,000	$2,520,000

Required:

a. Prepare a cost of goods sold schedule in good form.
b. Prepare an income statement in good form. Use the product expense figure computed in part *a* for cost of goods sold.
c. Calculate the balance in retained earnings after closing all temporary accounts.

P. 2-12 Analyzing the effect of cost allocations. Garcia Construction Company builds bridges, roads, commercial buildings, and other large projects. All projects are administered and accounted for from the firm's central office. The cost of operating Garcia's central office facility is $2,400,000 a year. Administration is a major cost of some projects and this cost must be assigned to all state government contracts in order to charge the correct amount for the construction project.

All contracts with private sector companies are negotiated fixed-price contracts. Construction costs for these projects are accumulated to help management evaluate profitability of projects and the performance of construction supervisors. All state government contracts are based on the total cost of the construction project plus a 15 percent profit margin. Garcia must account for the cost of these projects in order to be paid for the state contracts.

The state government audits Garcia's records for the cost of all state government construction contracts. One point of contention has been the allocation of central office administration costs to state contracts. Garcia has been allocating these costs on the basis of the number of construction labor hours worked on the projects. The state auditor's office believes the office administration costs should be allocated based on the total dollar cost of construction contracts excluding the central office administration costs. Garcia's management argues that this change in the allocation procedure would have no impact on charges to state contracts, but the state auditor's office is not convinced, and cites their belief that because of the extensive use of subcontractors on many private sector contracts, the company does not record as many construction labor hours as would be expected given the total dollar amount of the contract. As a result, the private sector contracts are not assigned their fair share of the office administration costs.

Below are cost and construction labor hour data for each of the construction contracts worked on during the year.

Contract Number	Total Cost Assigned to Contract Excluding Central Office Costs	Construction Labor Hours
State contracts:		
SC-445	$ 2,200,000	140,000
SC-447	3,000,000	200,000
SC-448	800,000	50,000
Other contracts:		
PS-276	1,200,000	20,000
PS-279	500,000	10,000
PS-280	1,500,000	60,000
PS-281	800,000	20,000
Totals	$10,000,000	500,000

Required:

a. Compute the amount of office administration cost charged per construction labor hour using the company's current system.

b. Compute the amount of office administration cost that would be charged per dollar of construction cost using the state auditor's suggested allocation approach.
c. Compute the amount of overhead that would be charged to state contract SC-447 using each of the cost allocation alternatives.
d. Compute the difference in the amount paid to Garcia Construction Company for contract SC-447 using each of the two cost allocation methods.
e. Comment on which of the two alternatives should be used.

CASES

Case 2-1 **Analyzing financial data of a manufacturing firm.** Kaylene Corporation manufactures a single product line of food processors. During 1986, the firm produced 60,000 units and sold 48,000 units. Production costs in 1986 were $950,400 for manufacturing overhead, $458,400 for direct labor, and $614,400 for direct materials. Beginning inventories on January 1, 1986, were $234,000 for raw materials inventory, $285,600 for work in process inventory, and $230,400 for finished goods inventory. Indirect materials used during the year cost $57,000. Below is the year-end trial balance for Kaylene Corporation.

Kaylene Corporation
Trial Balance
December 31, 1986

	Debits	Credits
Cash	$ 164,000	
Accounts receivable	165,000	
Raw materials inventory	115,000	
Work in process inventory	345,600	
Finished goods inventory	369,600	
Investments	226,200	
Building	1,660,000	
Accumulated depreciation, building		$ 510,000
Equipment	640,000	
Accumulated depreciation, equipment		50,000
Accounts payable		165,000
Notes payable		280,000
Mortgage payable		535,000
Capital stock		960,000
Retained earnings		1,032,000
Dividends on common stock	65,000	
Sales		3,456,000
Sales returns and allowances	52,800	
Cost of goods sold	1,824,000	
Advertising	61,200	
Sales commissions	201,600	
Depreciation, building	168,000	
Depreciation, equipment	108,000	
Equipment, rent	30,000	
Administrative salaries	614,400	
Utilities	177,600	
Totals	$6,988,000	$6,988,000

Required:

a. Compute the average sales price of units sold in 1986.
b. Compute the average unit cost of the units sold during 1986.
c. Prepare a cost of goods manufactured schedule in good form for Kaylene Corporation.
d. Prepare an income statement in good form for Kaylene Corporation.
e. Compute the balance in the Retained Earnings account after the books are closed.
f. Compute the average unit cost of the units transferred from work in process to finished goods during 1986.
g. Compute the amount of raw materials purchased during the accounting period.
h. What percentage of Kaylene's total expenses for the period were product expenses?
i. Explain why direct materials, direct labor, and manufacturing overhead do not appear on the company's trial balance. Was this an error on the part of the accountant?

Determining Product Costs

3

The parallel relationship between the physical flow of production activities and the flow of product costs through the ledger accounts is designed to enable the accountant to accumulate product costs and assign them to products as they are produced. In this chapter, we focus on the methods used to measure manufacturing costs and to assign them to specific products. Your understanding of the concepts discussed here is essential to your ability to analyze and use managerial accounting reports. When you have completed the chapter, you should understand:

1 The accounting activities associated with the acquisition and use of production resources.

2 The nature and composition of direct materials, direct labor, and manufacturing overhead.

3 The nature of the two basic types of cost accounting systems: job order costing and process costing.

4 How product costs are determined in a job order costing system.

5 The preparation and use of a job cost sheet.

6 The meaning and use of unit costs in a job order costing system.

7 How manufacturing costs are recorded in a company's accounting system.

In a manufacturing firm's income statement, the calculation of cost of goods sold includes the cost of finished goods manufactured during the period. Because this cost is made up of a large collection of account balances, the income statement must be supported by a schedule of cost of goods manufactured. This schedule reports the cost of all production resources used during the period, as found in various manufacturing control accounts and subsidiary ledger accounts. But how do the data get into the various manufacturing accounts and how are manufacturing costs assigned to specific products? The accountant accumulates these data by carefully monitoring and analyzing the production activities and by gathering information about them from many different source documents as production takes place. The balances of many manufacturing accounts are summarized in the schedule of cost of goods manufactured.

In this chapter we return to the three basic cost elements—**direct materials, direct labor,** and **manufacturing overhead** (MOH)—and look at the way accountants measure and account for each in order to assign them to products. We also discuss job order costing, a product costing system used to determine the cost of specific products. The chapter concludes by illustrating how cost accounting data are recorded in the company's accounting system.

IDENTIFYING AND ACCUMULATING PRODUCTION COSTS

Direct materials, direct labor, and manufacturing overhead are the three components that make up the cost of a manufactured product. But how are these costs measured, identified with a specific product, and recorded in a company's accounting records? Over the years accountants have developed efficient systems for capturing manufacturing costs and assigning them to specific products. They do so by using control accounts and subsidiary ledger accounts in which the costs of materials, labor, and overhead are recorded as these resources are acquired and used in production.

Control Accounts

Control accounts summarize the balances in individual accounts

Control accounts are used to summarize the individual balances in a particular class of accounts. For example, a company's control account for accounts receivable contains the sum of the balances in all the individual accounts receivable owed by customers. Similarly, the firm's control account for accounts payable contains the sum of the balances in all the individual accounts payable owed to suppliers. The control account balances appear on the balance sheet rather than all the individual accounts receivable and accounts payable. Each control account is supported by the detailed subsidiary accounts maintained in a **subsidiary ledger.** For example, a company has the following balances in its individual accounts receivable:

Yellow Company	
900	

Blue Company	
1,200	

Brown Company	
600	

Green Company	
400	

Black Company	
800	

The total of these accounts receivable is $3,900; it can be summarized in a control account for accounts receivable. If this is done, the control account is maintained in the general ledger, and the entire collection of individual accounts is the accounts receivable subsidiary ledger.

Control accounts are used both for convenience and for control. For many reporting purposes it is convenient to list only a single account balance instead of all individual accounts receivable on a firm's balance sheet, although control over individual accounts is important. The subsidiary accounts provide the necessary control, because they are used to determine when specific customers pay their accounts, which customers are in default, and how much to bill each customer at the end of the month.

Control accounts are used widely in managerial accounting

Control accounts are widely used in managerial accounting, especially in manufacturing. Usually they are maintained for raw materials, work in process, finished goods, and manufacturing overhead. Control accounts facilitate the recording and reporting of cost flows, and they contain the data needed for summarizing cost information in management reports.

Materials

The inventory of raw materials is a major asset in manufacturing firms and requires careful management. A discussion of inventory management is found in Chapter 15. Here we discuss the role of raw materials in the production process and trace the flow of costs associated with the physical flow of raw materials in the manufacturing process.

The two basic inventory activities are acquisition and distribution

Two basic activities associated with the flow of raw materials in a manufacturing firm are inventory acquisition and inventory distribution. **Inventory acquisition** includes all of the activities necessary to purchase raw materials and move them into the inventory storage area, called a storeroom or stores area. **Inventory distribution** refers to the process of distributing raw materials from inventory into production.

Inventory acquisition. Figure 3-1 illustrates the activities associated with inventory acquisition and shows the major documents used in the process. These source documents are valuable in identifying costs and providing an audit trail. A good audit trail enables the accountant to trace transactions and activities if problems or errors arise and to verify that the accounting system is functioning properly.

There are several source documents commonly used in inventory acquisition

The inventory acquisition process begins when an item of **raw material** is needed. Perhaps someone in the inventory storeroom observes that an inventory item is at a low level and prepares a **purchase requisition,** which is then sent to the purchasing department. This starts the purchasing process by notifying the purchasing department of the need for the inventory item.

The purchasing department prepares a **purchase order,** which is a document used to place an order with a supplier. The person in charge of the purchasing department is called a **purchasing agent.** In large organizations purchasing may be a highly specialized operation within a large

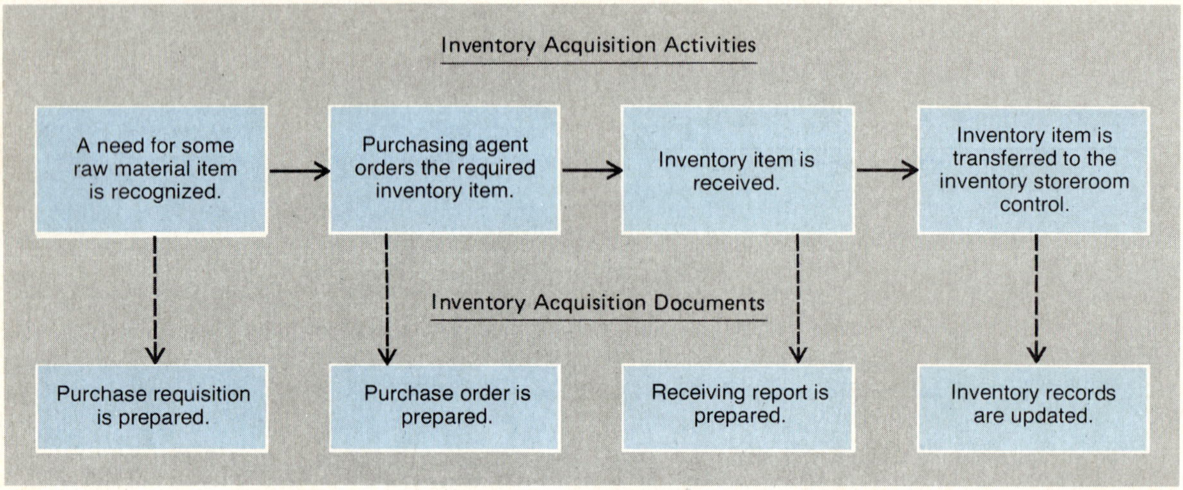

Figure 3-1 Flow of inventory acquisition activities and the source of major inventory acquisition documents. Each activity results in a source document.

purchasing department. In small firms it may be only one of several important functions performed by an individual. In either case, the purchasing agent has prime responsibility for all purchasing activities.

When new materials arrive, a **receiving report** is issued. This document indicates receipt of the item or items and the amount received. A copy of the receiving report is sent to the inventory storeroom for updating inventory records. Updating methods vary widely depending on the record-keeping system. With a manual system, entries are made by hand on inventory cards. In other systems, computerized inventory records might be updated by using a computer terminal in the storeroom.

The purpose of inventory distribution is to get the right materials to the correct production location at the appropriate time

Inventory distribution. The transfer of materials from the inventory storage area to the production areas is called **inventory distribution.** This can be a complex task because it is necessary to have the proper quantity and quality of raw materials in the right place at the right time. Complex production activities complicate the inventory distribution process. A poor inventory distribution system can be very costly in terms of lost production and inefficient use of production facilities. The inventory distribution process is illustrated in Figure 3-2.

A **materials requisition** initiates the flow of raw materials into production. This document indicates the type, quantity, and production location of the required material. This document is useful in determining how much of the material's cost is assigned directly to production as direct materials and how much is assigned to manufacturing overhead as **indirect materials,** which cannot be specifically identified with products. Be careful to differentiate between a purchase requisition and a materials requisition. The former initiates the purchasing process; the latter initiates the internal inventory distribution process.

Labor

Accounting for manufacturing labor is not difficult, but it can be tedious. Detailed individual records must be maintained for each employee, and federal and state governments require a variety of payroll-related reports. Figure 3-3 summarizes graphically the process of accounting for manufacturing labor cost flows.

To measure costs accurately, accountants must be able to identify how production employees spent their time

Identifying manufacturing labor with specific products and assigning labor costs to production is an important cost accounting activity. Accountants must determine what production workers did during their time at work so that labor costs can be identified with products. Documents for identifying employee time, such as **daily time tickets** and **job time tickets,** are accumulated and summarized in reports that show how much work was performed by employees during a particular time period or on a specific project.

Periodically labor data are summarized and reported

Time tickets and other payroll data are summarized periodically in a **labor distribution report,** sometimes called a **labor recapitulation report.** This report identifies the labor cost that should be assigned to each product during the period. Any manufacturing labor not identified with products is **indirect labor.** The data in the labor distribution report are recorded as

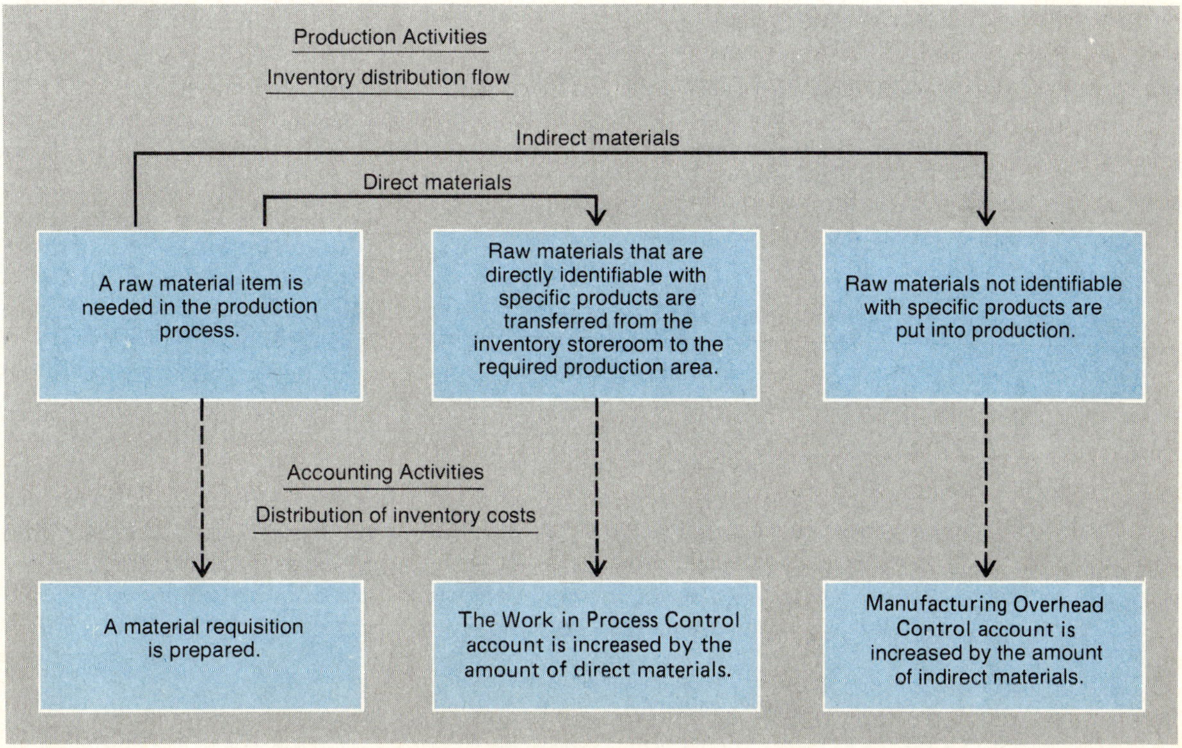

Figure 3-2 **Inventory distribution activities result in source documents used to account for the activities.**

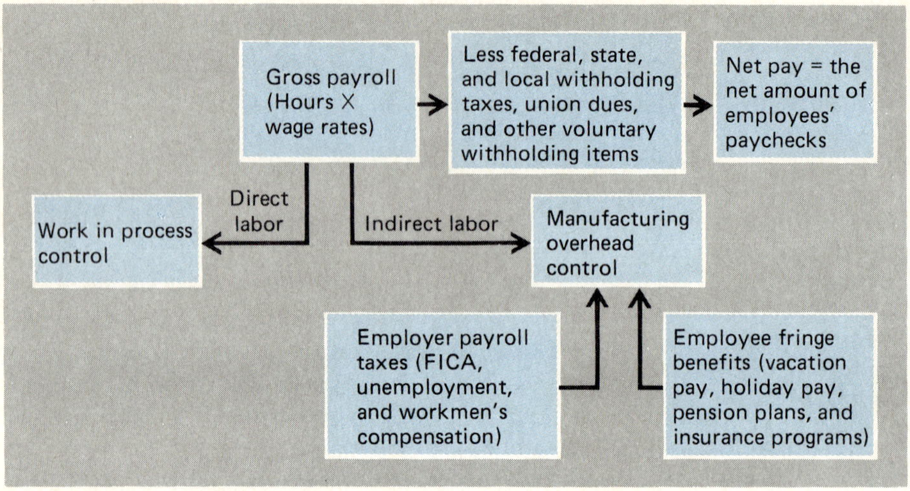

Figure 3-3 Manufacturing labor cost flows.

manufacturing labor costs. Direct labor costs are debited to Work in Process Control, and indirect labor costs are debited to the Manufacturing Overhead Control account.

The total cost of manufacturing labor is more than just gross payroll. Gross payroll is the most visible element of manufacturing labor, but two other elements are also significant. Employer payroll taxes and employee fringe benefits are large parts of total labor cost. These two items have grown in the last 20 years so that now they add 30 to 45 percent of gross payroll to total labor cost in many large businesses. Payroll taxes and employee fringe benefits are usually treated as indirect costs and are charged to Manufacturing Overhead. This approach is simple but it hides a significant portion of payroll cost in the pool of indirect manufacturing costs. In addition, these payroll taxes and employee benefit costs may not get assigned to cost objectives in the correct proportions. To avoid these problems, some firms identify payroll taxes and employee benefit costs with each employee's gross pay and charge the total to direct labor and indirect labor as dictated by each employee's time sheet.

Employee withholdings are not an expense of the employer

Employers are required to withhold from their employees' paychecks amounts for federal income taxes, FICA taxes, and usually state income taxes. In addition, employees may ask their employers to withhold amounts to repay automobile loans, pay unions dues, or pay into savings plans. All of these withholding items are costs to the employees. The labor cost to the employer does not change because of these withholding items, although there is some clerical cost associated with accounting for them. The amounts withheld from employees' checks must be paid to the federal government, state government, unions, insurance companies, and others.

Manufacturing Overhead

By definition indirect costs cannot be identified with specific products. Yet these costs are real and necessary costs of production that often constitute a large part of the cost of manufacturing a product. Managers must monitor and control overhead costs with the same degree of skill they apply to direct manufacturing costs.

Measuring and recording actual overhead. Actual overhead costs are incurred throughout the accounting period. Indirect labor is used to clean and maintain production machinery, electricity is used to light the factory and run the production machinery, and cleaning and lubricating compounds are used as indirect materials in maintaining production operations. As each indirect manufacturing cost is incurred, it is recorded in the account **Manufacturing Overhead Control.** For example, the entry to record the cost of repairing a hydraulic press is as follows:

	Manufacturing overhead control	1,250	
	Cash		1,250
	To record the cost of repairing an		
	A214 hydraulic press serviced by		
	Hydraulics Unlimited.		

The debit to the Manufacturing Overhead Control account is posted to the control account and also to an individual Repairs and Maintenance account in the subsidiary manufacturing overhead ledger. The same procedure is used for all other overhead entries. This allows managers to monitor not just the control account but also the individual overhead accounts. If some account such as Repairs and Maintenance grows unusually large, managers can determine if some action is required.

Assigning overhead costs to products. Recording overhead costs in the Manufacturing Overhead Control account does not accomplish the goal of assigning these costs to specific products. The process of assigning (charging) manufacturing overhead to products is called **applying overhead.**

One way to apply overhead might be to wait until the end of the accounting period and then assign all of the manufacturing overhead costs to the products manufactured during the period. The problem with this approach is that the total cost of the product is not computed until the end of the accounting period, violating the timeliness concept discussed in Chapter 1. Timeliness is especially important in managerial accounting reports that affect daily production and cost control decisions.

A better approach is to assign overhead costs to products as they are produced. However, because overhead costs are not known at the time of production, the amount to be applied must be estimated. From this estimate, the accountant determines a **manufacturing overhead rate,** which is

A manufacturing overhead rate provides a way for assigning overhead costs to products in a timely fashion

a predetermined rate used to assign overhead costs to products. The overhead rate is based on the expected amount of manufacturing overhead costs and the expected quantity of production. For example, the accountant may estimate that total overhead costs for the year will be $400,000 and total direct labor will be 100,000 hours. In this case the predetermined overhead rate is $4 per direct labor hour. For every hour of direct labor used to manufacture the product, $4 of manufacturing overhead cost will be assigned to the product's cost. Other examples of overhead rates are $6 per machine hour used and $10 per unit of production. The process of determining overhead rates is discussed in detail in Chapter 4.

The primary consideration in deciding on an overhead rate is the matching concept, which states that expenses should be matched with revenues generated by business operations. In manufacturing firms, revenues result from the sale of the manufactured products. The largest expense usually is the cost of producing the products, and a major portion of this cost may be overhead. Therefore, the rate used to apply overhead to production should do the best possible job of matching indirect manufacturing costs with products. The selection of a proper overhead application base, such as direct labor hours or machine hours, is an important decision because it directly affects the matching of costs with revenues. Various application bases are discussed in Chapter 4.

The overhead rate is usually decided upon before the accounting period starts. Once the rate is determined, indirect manufacturing costs can be charged to production on a timely basis together with direct materials and direct labor. As production takes place, overhead is applied using the predetermined rate by debiting Work in Process Control and crediting **Manufacturing Overhead Applied.** The overhead applied account accumulates the total amount of overhead **assigned** to products, but this is not the **actual** amount of overhead incurred. Actual overhead costs are debited to the **Manufacturing Overhead Control** account as they are identified.

Notice that there are **two** overhead accounts. Manufacturing Overhead Control contains a debit balance representing actual overhead costs incurred. Manufacturing Overhead Applied contains a credit balance representing overhead applied to products. The cost flow of manufacturing overhead is illustrated in Figure 3-4.

Underapplied and overapplied overhead defined

Underapplied and overapplied overhead. At the end of the accounting period, the debit balance in the Manufacturing Overhead Control account should be about the same dollar amount as the credit balance in the Manufacturing Overhead Applied account. However, the two accounts seldom have **identical** balances. If the balance in the applied account is less than the balance in the control account, overhead is **underapplied,** which is the case in Figure 3-4. That means that the overhead costs assigned to products were somewhat less than the actual amount of overhead costs. Conversely, if the applied account balance is greater than the balance in the control account, overhead is **overapplied;** the amount of overhead costs charged to products was greater than the actual overhead costs.

Credit(s) to Control Accts close them out.

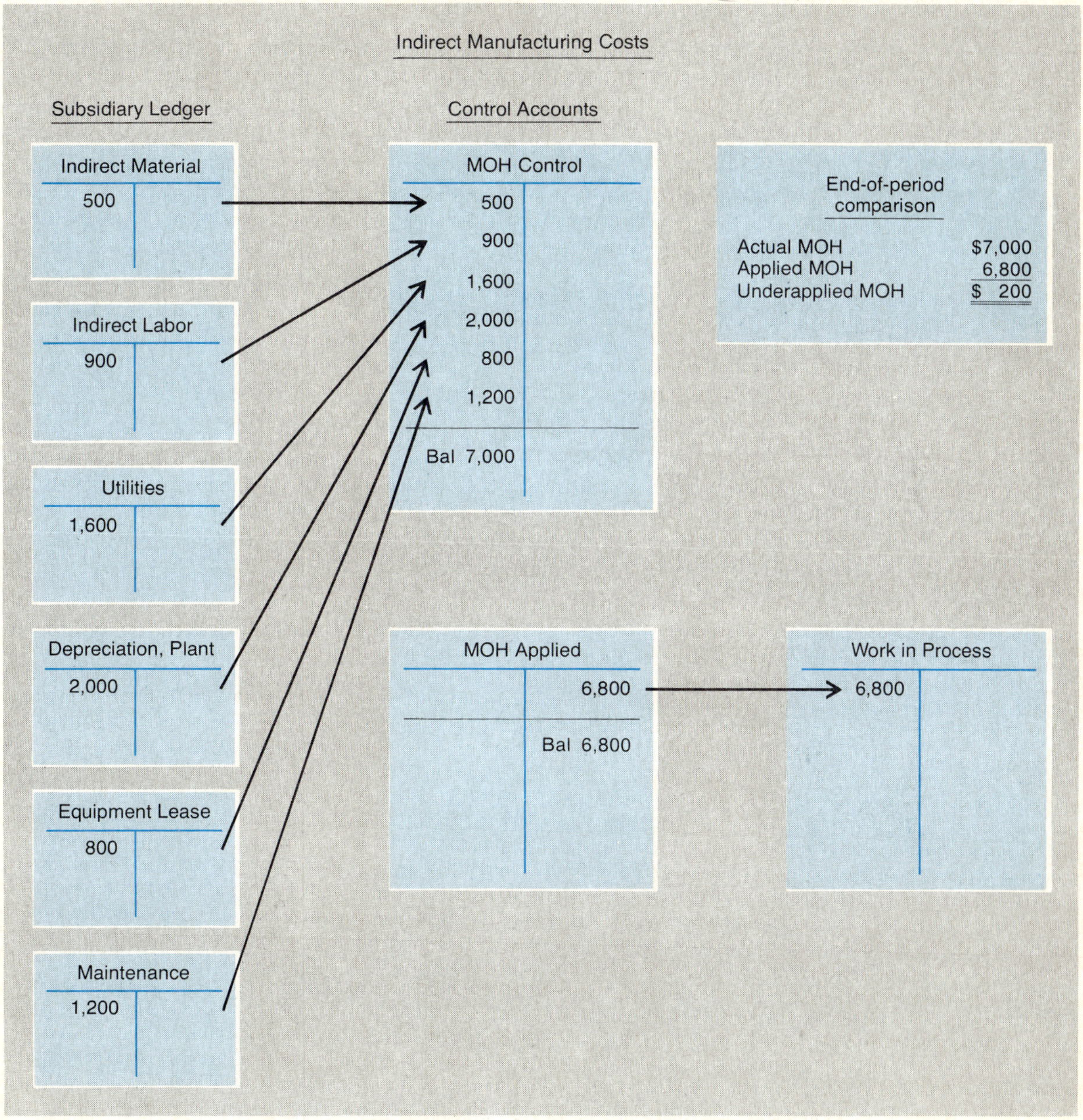

Figure 3-4 Manufacturing overhead cost flows.

Usually the amount of underapplied or overapplied overhead is relatively small. The difference is eliminated by adjusting cost of goods sold in the income statement. If overhead is underapplied, cost of goods sold must be increased; if overhead is overapplied, cost of goods sold must be decreased. The justification for this simple disposition of underapplied or overapplied overhead is twofold:

1. The amounts are immaterial.
2. Typically most of the goods produced during the year are sold by year-end.

Disposing of large amounts of underapplied or overapplied overhead

If underapplied or overapplied overhead is large, financial statements may be distorted when the entire amount is assigned to cost of goods sold. In such cases the product costs should be adjusted to reflect the actual overhead cost. Product costs are found in three accounts—Work in Process Control; Finished Goods Inventory; and Cost of Goods Sold. These three accounts are adjusted to reflect the actual manufacturing overhead cost by spreading the underapplied or overapplied overhead to the accounts in proportion to the relative amount of overhead remaining in each account at year-end. For instance, during the year a company incurs $140,000 in actual manufacturing overhead costs and applies $100,000 of overhead to products. At year-end, overhead is underapplied by $40,000. Of the $100,000 that has been applied to production during the year, $10,000 remains in Work in Process at year-end, $15,000 is in Finished Goods Inventory, and $75,000 has been applied to the products already sold. Therefore, 10 percent, or $4,000, of the underapplied overhead is added to Work in Process; 15 percent, or $6,000, of the underapplied overhead is added to Finished Goods; and 75 percent, or $30,000 is added to Cost of Goods Sold. The determination of whether underapplied or overapplied overhead is large enough to require prorating to inventories and Cost of Goods Sold depends on the judgment of management. Figure 3-5 illustrates graphically the distribution of large underapplied and overapplied overhead.

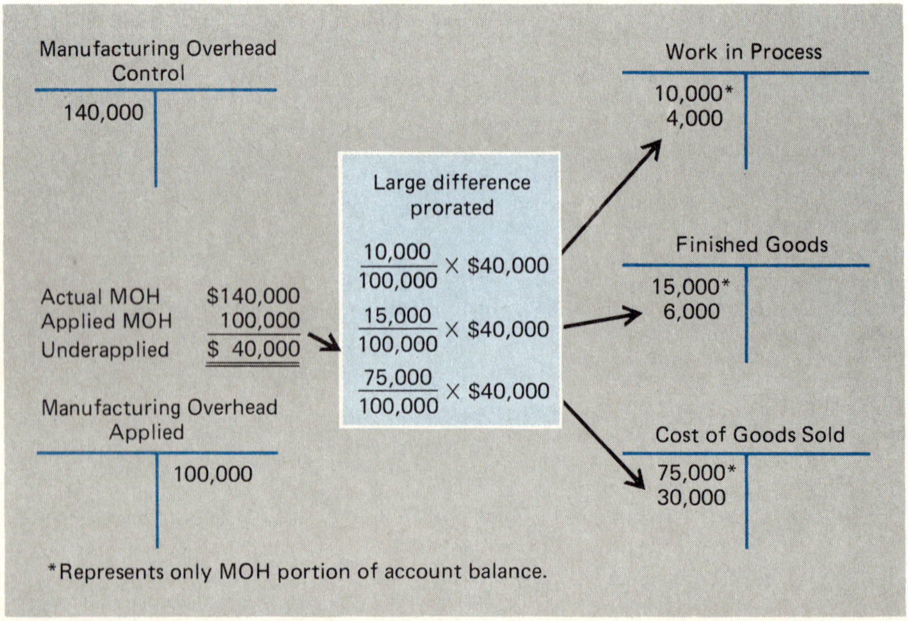

Figure 3-5
Distribution of underapplied and overapplied manufacturing overhead costs.

PRODUCT COSTING SYSTEMS

Two basic product costing systems are used in manufacturing businesses: job order costing and process costing. The system used depends primarily on the way products are manufactured.

Job order costing is used to measure the cost of products manufactured in batches

Job order costing is used to measure the cost of products manufactured in batches or in intermittent production runs. Specialized equipment, personalized products, and some food products such as baked goods are common examples of products that typically are costed using a job order costing system. Companies that do not sell enough of each of their products to require continuous production runs and firms that have seasonal sales patterns use job order costing. For example, a company may make water skis for spring and summer sales and snow skis for fall and winter sales. A company may produce a certain amount of one product, such as 10,000 units, and then produce no more until inventory of the product reaches a level that requires more production. A key characteristic of job order cost systems is that the manufacturing process for each job has a definitely determinable starting and completion time. Accountants start accumulating costs for a job as soon as production is started, and the cost per unit of product is computed when the job is complete.

Process costing is used to measure the cost of products made in continuous production runs

A **process costing** system is used for measuring the cost of products manufactured in continuous-flow production processes. Chemicals, petroleum products, and plastics are common examples of products costed using process costing. Since some units are being started while others are already partially complete and still other units are being completed, there is no distinct starting or completion time for the production activities. To measure unit costs in process costing, it is necessary to measure periodically the amount of resources used in production and the production quantity and unit cost of products manufactured during the period. Although process costing activities are not conceptually difficult, they are a little more complicated to master than job order costing. Either job order costing or process costing is used to measure the cost of manufactured products. In either system, direct materials, direct labor, and manufacturing overhead are identified with the production of specific products. Job order costing is discussed in this chapter and process costing is covered in Chapter 17.

Job Order Costing

In job order costing, a **job cost sheet** is used to accumulate all of the manufacturing costs for a particular product. Figure 3-6 illustrates a job cost sheet for the Blenford Air Moving Systems Company.

Production costs are accumulated in a job cost sheet

Job cost sheets vary significantly in style and form, but all contain the basic cost data shown in Figure 3-6. Job cost sheets contain three distinct sections. The top section of the job cost sheet contains descriptive information about the job and product such as the dates the job was started and completed, the type of product, and the number of units produced. An important item in the job cost sheet is a unique **job number,** which identifies a particular job and distinguishes it from all other jobs the company may manufacture. Job numbers may be simple sequential reference numbers, or they may be more complex code numbers providing much useful processing information. For example, part number, customer number, production priority codes, and production sequencing codes are sometimes included in job numbering systems.

Blenford Air Moving Systems Company
Job Cost Sheet

Date started	8/7/85	Job number	6JL4741
Date completed	8/22/85	Stock number	3L17
Units completed	200	Item	36-inch fan housing

Direct Materials			Direct Labor			Manufacturing Overhead		
Date	Reference	Amount	Date	Reference	Amount	Date	Reference	Amount
8/7/85	MRQ 2112	$3,440	8/10/85	LD 201	$ 482	8/10/85	LD 201	$ 723
8/12/85	MRQ 2189	670	8/17/85	LD 202	1,488	8/17/85	LD 202	2,232
8/19/85	MRQ 2205	230	8/24/85	LD 203	1,250	8/24/85	LD 203	1,875
		$4,340			$3,220			$4,830

Summary of Costs

	Total Cost	Unit Cost
Direct materials	$ 4,340	$21.70
Direct labor	3,220	16.10
Manufacturing overhead	4,830	24.15
Total	$12,390	$61.95

Figure 3-6 An example of a completed job cost sheet.

The middle section of the job cost sheet is used to accumulate the detailed cost data for each of the three cost elements. Direct materials, direct labor, and manufacturing overhead costs are accumulated separately and recorded periodically as shown by the date. The reference column is used to identify the source of the cost data entered in the cost sheet or to provide some other data such as the type of raw materials used or the number of direct labor hours worked.

The bottom section of the job cost sheet is used to summarize the three manufacturing costs of the job and to calulate and report the unit cost of making the product. This part of the cost sheet is prepared when the job is completed and the products are transferred to finished goods inventory. The cost data presented here are used by managers to evaluate production performance, to identify cost trends, to establish product prices, and for a variety of other evaluations or decisions.

Using the Job Cost Sheet

Blenford Air Moving Systems Company, whose job cost sheet is shown in Figure 3-6, manufactures a variety of parts for fans and air-conditioning units for commercial use. The job cost sheet is for the production of two hundred 36-inch fan housings. When the job was started, the accountant entered the starting date on the job cost sheet and assigned a unique job number to the job. In this example, the job number identifies the type of product, the intended use of the product, and a sequential number. The only datum not available on August 7 for the top section of this job cost sheet is the completion date of the job. This must be filled in after the job is finished on August 22.

Production costs of the 200 fan housings are recorded in the cost columns in the middle section of the job cost sheet. The direct materials costs are entered together with the materials requisition numbers (MRQ) to provide a convenient cross reference for auditors and for checking errors. Other firms may have different information in the reference column, such as the type, quantity, or unit cost of the material.

Direct labor costs are assigned to jobs on the basis of Blenford's weekly labor distribution report (LD). The weekly labor cost for each job is entered in the amount column of the direct labor section of the job cost sheet. The date and reference columns indicate the particular labor distribution report (LD) that was the source for the entry. The 200 fan housings required 16 days to complete; this time period included labor costs from three different weekly labor distribution reports. Some businesses indicate in the reference column the hours worked on the job rather than the source document for the entry.

Blenford's overhead rate is 150 percent of direct labor cost. In this example, the application of manufacturing overhead is based on the amount of direct labor cost. Therefore overhead is assigned to the job whenever direct labor cost is charged to the job. In other situations a firm's manufacturing overhead may be applied using some other base, such as the number of machine hours used on the job. In that case a machine utilization report may be the basis for determining the amount of overhead applied to each job, and the overhead may be charged daily, weekly, monthly, or at some other time interval. Regardless of the application base, manufacturing overhead is charged to the job in some systematic and timely manner.

When the job is completed, the direct materials, direct labor, and manufacturing overhead costs are each totaled, and unit costs are computed for each cost element. The unit costs are averages. For example, $21.70 is the average unit cost of materials for the 200 fan housings. Some of the fan housings may have materials costs of $20.50 and others $22.80, but the average materials cost for units produced in this job is $21.70 a unit. Also, the unit costs are for Job number 6JL4741 only. Previous production runs and future production runs of 36-inch fan housings may have higher or lower unit costs. Unit costs are useful and convenient accounting information, but some caution must be exercised to ensure that unit costs are used intelligently in planning and controlling activities and making decisions.

All jobs currently in production have open job cost sheets

Once a job is started, the cost sheet is referred to as an **open job cost sheet.** It remains open until the job is completed. After the summary of costs has been prepared, the cost totals are transferred from Work in Process to Finished Goods. The journal entry to accomplish the transfer for Job number 6JL4741 is

Aug. 22	Finished goods inventory control	12,390	
	Work in process control		12,390
	To record the transfer of costs to finished		
	goods inventory for Job number 6JL4741.		

Costs are summarized when a job is completed and transferred to finished goods inventory

The entry is posted to specific subsidiary accounts as well as to the two control accounts. The subsidiary ledger for work in process consists of **all open job cost sheets.** At any point in time, the balance in the Work in Process Control account should be equal to the total of the costs in the job cost sheets for jobs currently in production. When a job is completed and transferred to finished goods, the summarized job cost sheet is said to be closed. **Closed job cost sheets** are no longer part of work in process, but they may be used for checking product costs, determining cost trends, setting product prices, evaluating employee performance, and establishing bonuses.

Departmental Product Cost Data

The amount of detail provided by accountants in manufacturing cost reports depends on management's information requirements. For example, the managers of one firm may find that the cost information provided in the job cost sheet in Figure 3-6 is all they need to monitor costs, evaluate performance, and make decisions. But what if a manager wants to know how much labor cost was incurred in each department so that changes in labor efficiency can be traced directly to specific departments for appropriate action? If more detail is required, accountants must find a way of providing it. Of course, more information may mean additional accounting expense, but the additional expense is justified in many situations.

Departmental job cost sheets provide more detailed production cost data than a general job cost sheet

Accountants provide more detailed job cost data by preparing a departmental job cost sheet. In addition to identifying costs by element, a **departmental job cost sheet** identifies costs by the department in which they occurred. A departmental job cost sheet is illustrated in Figure 3-7 using Blenford's production of the 36-inch fan housing discussed earlier. The only difference between this and the earlier illustration is that now we identify all costs by the department as well as by cost element.

Blenford Air Moving Systems Company
Job Cost Sheet

Date started 8/7/85
Date completed 8/22/85
Units completed 200

Job number 6JL4741
Stock number 3L17
Item 36-inch fan housing

Department	Direct Materials			Direct Labor			Manufacturing Overhead		
	Date	Reference	Amount	Date	Reference	Amount	Date	Reference	Amount
Cutting and welding	8/7/85 8/12/85	MRQ 2112 MRQ 2189	$3,440 670 $4,110	8/10/85 8/17/85	LD 201 LD 202	$ 482 642 $1,124	8/10/85 8/17/85	LD 201 LD 202	$ 723 963 $1,686
Assembly			0	8/17/85 8/24/85	LD 202 LD 203	$ 846 410 $1,256	8/17/85 8/24/85	LD 202 LD 203	$1,269 615 $1,884
Painting	8/19/85	MRQ 2205	$ 230 $ 230	8/24/85	LD 203	$ 840 $ 840	8/24/85	LD 203	$1,260 $1,260

Summary of Costs

Department	Direct Materials		Direct Labor		Manufacturing Overhead		Total Cost	
	Total	Unit	Total	Unit	Total	Unit	Total	Unit
Cutting and welding	$4,110	$20.55	$1,124	$ 5.62	$1,686	$ 8.43	$ 6,920	$34.60
Assembly	0	0	1,256	6.28	1,884	9.42	3,140	15.70
Painting	230	1.15	840	4.20	1,260	6.30	2,330	11.65
Total	$4,340	$21.70	$3,220	$16.10	$4,830	$24.15	$12,390	$61.95

Figure 3-7 An example of a departmental job cost sheet. Note that the total cost of the product is the same as that in the general job cost sheet in Figure 3-6, but more detailed cost analyses are possible with the departmental job cost sheet.

The product is made in three departments: cutting and welding, assembly, and painting. In other production situations there could be a larger or smaller number of production departments necessary to complete a job. Departmentalization facilitates cost control, aids in achieving the matching concept, and is important in evaluating the performance of departmental production supervisors.

In addition to the total and units costs for materials, labor, and overhead, the total and unit costs for each cost element in each department are calculated at the bottom of the departmental job cost sheet. Changes in production efficiencies or other cost patterns are therefore much easier to identify.

RECORDING COST FLOWS

The cost data accumulated in job cost sheets also must be recorded in the company's ledger accounts

In addition to identifying manufacturing costs with specific products, it is necessary to record the cost data in the company's formal accounting records. Blenford Air Moving Systems Company must record a large number of transactions needed for the production of 36-inch fan housings and the production of many other products. The manufacturing activities listed below are journalized and posted in the general ledger and various subsidiary ledgers. The journal entries are illustrated and a partial general ledger is presented in Figure 3-8 on page 96 with all journal entries posted.

a. Blenford purchased four different materials from a supplier at a total cost of $62,000 on open account.

b. Direct materials totaling $40,000 are transferred from the inventory storeroom into production.

c. Indirect materials costing $4,640 are transferred from the inventory storeroom into production.

d. The weekly payroll for the manufacturing plant is $120,000.

e. A total of $108,000 of the weekly manufacturing payroll can be identified with the production of specific products. The remaining $12,000 is indirect labor cost.

f. Additional weekly payroll costs include $6,900 of FICA taxes, $350 of federal unemployment taxes, and $2,200 of state unemployment taxes.

g. Utility bills of $4,500 for the manufacturing plant are received and paid for 1 month.

h. Monthly rent of $18,000 is paid on leased manufacturing equipment.

i. Property taxes of $9,860 for the manufacturing facility are paid.

j. Manufacturing overhead is applied at the rate of 150 percent of direct labor cost.

k. Products costing $210,000 are completed during the period and transferred to finished goods inventory.

l. Blenford sold products costing $195,000 during the period for a total of $310,000. A perpetual inventory system is used.

m. Monthly depreciation is recorded; $200,000 for the manufacturing plant and $170,000 for manufacturing equipment.

n. At year-end the overhead applied account is closed into the overhead control account.

o. Any underapplied or overapplied overhead is closed into cost of goods sold.

Below, each of these events is analyzed separately, journalized, and posted to ledger accounts.

a. Blenford purchased four different materials from a supplier at a total cost of $62,000 on open account.

a.	Raw materials inventory control	62,000	
	Accounts payable		62,000
	Purchased raw materials on open		
	account.		

Journal entries must be posted to the control accounts and also to the appropriate subsidiary ledger accounts

When the materials are purchased, the total of $62,000 is debited to Raw Materials Inventory Control and credited to Accounts Payable. The total cost is posted to the Raw Materials Inventory Control account in the firm's general ledger. In addition, the inventory is posted to individual accounts in the firm's subsidiary inventory ledger. For example, the $62,000 purchase of raw materials shown in transaction *a* above might consist of the following inventory items, each of which increases a subsidiary account by the amount indicated.

$ 4,800 of JL2—black silicone sealer
$26,400 of KY6—¼-horsepower electric motors
$28,200 of LB9—12-gauge rolled aluminum
$ 2,600 of XX3—cleaning compound

b. Direct materials totaling $40,000 are transferred from the inventory storeroom into production.

b.	Work in process control	40,000	
	Raw materials inventory control		40,000
	Issued direct materials to production.		

c. Indirect materials costing $4,640 are transferred from the inventory storeroom into production.

c.	Manufacturing overhead control	4,640	
	Raw materials inventory control		4,640
	Issued indirect materials to production.		

Indirect production costs are charged to Manufacturing Overhead Control

Transactions *b* and *c* illustrate transfers of raw materials from inventory to production. The materials in transaction *b* can be identified with specific products and their cost is recorded in Work in Process as direct materials. This includes the direct materials used in the 36-inch fan housings posted in the job costs sheet shown earlier. Remember that the job cost sheet is a subsidiary work in process account. The indirect materials in transaction *c* are included in overhead as part of the indirect cost of manufacturing. The $4,640 is posted to the Manufacturing Overhead Control account in the general ledger and also to the Indirect Materials account in the overhead subsidiary ledger. This entry for indirect materials is not posted to a job cost sheet, because overhead costs enter Work in Process when overhead is applied to production, as shown in entry *j*.

d. The weekly payroll for the manufacturing plant is $120,000.

d.	Payroll	120,000	
	Federal withholding tax payable		19,000
	State withholding tax payable		3,900
	FICA tax payable		6,900
	Union dues payable		1,200
	Cash		89,000
	Recorded the weekly payroll and		
	withholding items.		

Entry *d* records the manufacturing payroll for the week. The amounts withheld from the employees' paychecks result from various tax rules and contractual agreements. The key number in the journal entry is the debit of $120,000, which is the gross payroll for the week. This is the amount of payroll cost charged to production either as direct labor in Work in Process Control or as indirect labor in Manufacturing Overhead.

e. A total of $108,000 of the weekly manufacturing payroll can be identified with the production of specific products. The remaining $12,000 is indirect labor cost.

e.	Work in process control	108,000	
	Manufacturing overhead control	12,000	
	Payroll		120,000
	Distributed the payroll costs to		
	production.		

The labor distribution report shows how much of the gross payroll of $120,000 should be assigned to direct labor and indirect labor. Direct labor costs are assigned directly to specific jobs by posting specific job cost sheets

Payroll costs are distributed to production based on the labor summary report

as well as the Work in Process Control account. Indirect labor is charged to the Manufacturing Overhead Control account and to Indirect Labor in the manufacturing overhead subsidiary ledger.

f. Additional weekly payroll costs include $6,900 of FICA taxes, $350 of federal unemployment taxes, and $2,200 of state unemployment taxes.

f.	Manufacturing overhead control	9,450	
	FICA tax payable		6,900
	State unemployment tax payable		2,200
	Federal unemployment tax payable		350
	Recorded payroll taxes imposed on the		
	employer.		

Payroll taxes are an additional cost of employing workers

The various payroll taxes shown in entry *f* are additional costs of labor other than gross payroll. They are posted to individual payroll tax accounts in the manufacturing overhead subsidiary ledger. Some firms may require less detail and use only one payroll cost account for all payroll taxes and other labor-related costs.

g. Utility bills of $4,500 for the manufacturing plant are received and paid for 1 month.

g.	Manufacturing overhead control	4,500	
	Cash		4,500
	Paid utility bills for manufacturing.		

h. Monthly rent of $18,000 is paid on leased manufacturing equipment.

h.	Manufacturing overhead control	18,000	
	Cash		18,000
	Paid rent on leased production		
	equipment.		

i. Property taxes of $9,860 for the manufacturing facility are paid.

i.	Manufacturing overhead control	9,860	
	Cash		9,860
	Paid property tax bills on the production		
	facility.		

Transactions *g*, *h*, and *i* illustrate the process of recording actual manufacturing overhead costs. In each case the cost is charged to the Manufacturing Overhead Control account and to individual overhead subsidiary

Actual overhead costs are accumulated in the Manufacturing Overhead Control account

accounts. The debit balance in the control account continues to accumulate throughout the accounting period. The balance in the account at any point in time is the total amount of actual overhead costs incurred to date.

These three entries illustrate vividly why manufacturing overhead costs are accumulated in a separate overhead account whose balance is not transferred to Work in Process as production takes place. The utility and lease costs are recorded as they are paid this week, but they cover a month of resource use. Property taxes are usually billed twice a year, so the entry is made for a 6-month period. To try to assign these costs to specific products made during a single week could result in inaccurate product costs. In addition, some costs, such as depreciation on production facilities, may be recorded only at year-end. For this reason, actual overhead costs are not allocated to products but instead are assigned using a manufacturing overhead rate and the Manufacturing Overhead Applied account, as illustrated in entry *j*.

j. Manufacturing overhead is applied at the rate of 150 percent of direct labor cost.

j.	Work in process control	162,000	
	Manufacturing overhead applied		162,000
	Applied overhead to products.		

Overhead is assigned to production by debiting Work in Process Control and crediting Manufacturing Overhead Applied

During the week, $108,000 of direct labor cost is incurred and recorded in entry *e*. Therefore, $162,000 of overhead cost is applied to production ($108,000 × 1.5). The debit of $162,000 is posted to the Work in Process Control account and to the individual job cost sheets, such as the one for 36-inch fan housing illustrated earlier. In practice overhead is applied to production on a timely basis during the accounting period, such as daily or weekly. Here we use a weekly entry to coincide with the weekly payroll. Note that the Manufacturing Overhead Applied account accumulates a credit balance throughout the accounting period.

When products are completed and transferred to finished goods inventory, their production costs are transferred from Work in Process Control to Finished Goods Inventory.

k. Products costing $210,000 are completed during the period and transferred to finished goods inventory.

k.	Finished goods inventory	210,000	
	Work in process control		210,000
	Transferred completed products to		
	finished goods.		

l. Blenford sold products costing $195,000 during the period for a total of $310,000. A perpetual inventory system is used.

l.	Cash	310,000	
	Cost of goods sold	195,000	
	Sales		310,000
	Finished goods inventory		195,000
	Recorded sale of finished goods and		
	removed their cost from inventory.		

With a perpetual inventory system, the sale and the product expense are recorded at the same time.

m. Monthly depreciation is recorded; $200,000 for the manufacturing plant and $170,000 for manufacturing equipment.

m.	Manufacturing overhead control	370,000	
	Accumulated depreciation, plant		200,000
	Accumulated depreciation,		
	equipment		170,000
	To record monthly depreciation on		
	manufacturing plant and equipment.		

Closing the overhead accounts

The balances in the Manufacturing Overhead Control account and the Manufacturing Overhead Applied account accumulate throughout the accounting period. By the end of the year, the Manufacturing Overhead Control account has a debit balance of $7,950,000. The Manufacturing Overhead Applied account has a balance of $7,962,000. Actual overhead is $12,000 less than the amount applied. This relatively small difference, .15 percent of actual overhead, is credited to the Cost of Goods Sold account at year-end when the overhead accounts are closed. The necessary entries are as follows:

n. At year-end the overhead applied account is closed into the overhead control account.

n.	Manufacturing overhead applied	7,962,000	
	Manufacturing overhead control		7,962,000
	Closed overhead applied into overhead		
	control.		

o. Any underapplied or overapplied overhead is closed into cost of goods sold.

o.	Manufacturing overhead control	12,000	
	Cost of goods sold		12,000
	Overapplied overhead used to reduce		
	balance in cost of goods sold.		

Figure 3-8 Partial ledger showing the posting of journal entries, closing of the Manufacturing Overhead Applied account to Manufacturing Overhead Control, and adjustment of Cost of Goods Sold for overapplied overhead.

Cash

l.	310,000	d.	89,000
		g.	4,500
		h.	18,000
		i.	9,860

Raw Materials Inventory Control

a.	62,000	b.	40,000
		c.	4,640

Work in Process Control

b.	40,000	k.	210,000
e.	108,000		
j.	162,000		

Finished Goods Inventory

k.	210,000	l.	195,000

Accumulated Depreciation, Plant

		m.	200,000

Accumulated Depreciation, Equipment

		m.	170,000

Union Dues Payable

		d.	1,200

State Unemployment Tax Payable

		f.	2,200

Federal Unemployment Tax Payable

		f.	350

Accounts Payable

		a.	62,000

Federal Withholding Tax Payable

		d.	19,000

State Withholding Tax Payable

		d.	3,900

FICA Tax Payable

		d.	6,900
		f.	6,900

Manufacturing Overhead Control

c.	4,640		
e.	12,000		
f.	9,450		
g.	4,500		
h.	18,000		
i.	9,860		
m.	370,000		
⋮			
Bal.	7,950,000	n.	7,962,000
o.	12,000		

Manufacturing Overhead Applied

		j.	162,000
		⋮	
n.	7,962,000	Bal.	7,962,000

Payroll

d.	120,000	e.	120,000

Sales

		l.	310,000

Cost of Goods Sold

l.	195,000		
⋮			
Bal.	12,427,000	o.	12,000
Bal.	12,415,000		

The cost of goods sold for the period decreases by $12,000. Figure 3-8 shows a partial ledger of Blenford Air Moving Systems Company after all of the above journal entries have been posted.

SUMMARY

Product costs are an integral part of many managerial accounting reports. To understand such reports and use them intelligently in monitoring costs, evaluating performance, and making decisions, it is essential for a manager to have a clear understanding of the nature of product costs and how they are measured and accumulated.

The three costs elements—direct materials, direct labor, and manufacturing overhead—make up the cost of manufactured products. Accountants have developed efficient systems for measuring and accumulating these costs in control accounts and subsidiary accounts. **Control accounts** are used to accumulate total costs whose details are recorded in various **subsidiary ledgers.** Raw Materials Inventory Control, Work in Process Control, and Finished Goods Inventory Control are common inventory control accounts and **Manufacturing Overhead Control** and **Manufacturing Overhead Applied** are common overhead control accounts. Materials purchases are recorded in the account **Raw Materials Inventory Control.** Raw materials acquisition documents consist of **purchase requisitions, purchase orders,** and **receiving reports.** A **materials requisition** is used to start materials from inventory into production. Labor cost entries for recording direct labor and indirect labor are prepared from a **labor distribution report,** which is prepared from payroll records and **daily time tickets** or **job time tickets.** Materials and labor documents are used as a basis for accounting entries and to provide an audit trail.

Manufacturing overhead includes all indirect costs of production. Actual overhead costs are accumulated in the **Manufacturing Overhead Control** account. Typically overhead is applied to production using a predetermined **manufacturing overhead rate** and is recorded in the **Manufacturing Overhead Applied** account. The overhead rate provides timely product cost data and usually is a close approximation of actual overhead costs. Any difference between actual and applied overhead is reconciled at the end of the accounting period. Small differences are used to adjust the Cost of Goods Sold account. Large differences are prorated among Work in Process, Finished Goods, and Cost of Goods Sold.

Job order costing and process costing are two fundamental product costing systems. The choice of the costing system depends on the nature of the production processes. **Process costing** is used to cost continuous-flow production activities. **Job order costing** is used to measure the cost of products manufactured in batches or intermittent production runs with production costs summarized in a **job cost sheet.** Costs are accumulated for each cost element and unit costs are determined for each cost element and in total when a job is complete. Job cost sheets contain a unique **job number,** starting date, completion date, product number, product description, and number of units. Other information may be included on the job cost sheet if managers deem it desirable.

Costs of production are charged to the Work in Process Control account. At the same time, the costs are entered on the appropriate individual job cost sheet. Any job currently in production has an **open job cost sheet.** All open job cost sheets comprise the subsidiary ledger of the Work in Process Control account. When a job is completed, the cost sheet is summarized and the costs of the finished products are transferred from the Work in Process Control account to the Finished Goods Inventory account, resulting in a **closed job cost sheet.** Closed job cost sheets are removed from the work in process control subsidiary ledger.

A **departmental job cost sheet** identifies the department in which each cost was incurred as well as the cost element. It provides management with more detailed cost data and a better basis for control.

The product cost flows identified in job order cost sheets are recorded in the journal and posted to control and subsidiary ledger accounts. Direct costs are charged to Work in Process Control and identified with specific jobs. Indirect costs are charged to Manufacturing Overhead Control. Overhead is assigned to production by debiting Work in Process Control and crediting Manufacturing Overhead Applied. The cost of completed products is transferred to Finished Goods Inventory, by debiting that account and crediting Work in Process Control. Product expense is recorded at the time of sale with a debit to Cost of Goods Sold and a credit to Finished Goods Inventory.

KEY TERMS

applying overhead *(81)*
closed job cost sheet *(88)*
control account *(76)*
daily time ticket *(79)*
departmental job cost sheet *(88)*
direct labor *(76)*
direct materials *(76)*
indirect labor *(76)*
indirect materials *(78)*
inventory acquisition *(77)*
inventory distribution *(77)*
job cost sheet *(85)*
job number *(85)*
job order costing *(85)*
job time ticket *(79)*
labor distribution report *(79)*
labor recapitulation report *(79)*
manufacturing overhead (MOH) *(76)*
Manufacturing Overhead Applied *(82)*
Manufacturing Overhead Control *(81)*
manufacturing overhead rate *(81)*
materials requisition *(78)*
open job cost sheet *(88)*
overapplied overhead *(82)*
process costing *(85)*
purchase order *(77)*
purchase requisition *(77)*
purchasing agent *(77)*
raw material *(77)*
receiving report *(78)*
subsidiary ledger *(76)*
underapplied overhead *(82)*

QUESTIONS

1. What is the function of control accounts? Name the most common control accounts used in manufacturing activities.
2. Distinguish between the inventory acquisition and inventory distribution functions in a manufacturing operation.

3. Identify the primary inventory acquisition documents and describe their purpose.
4. The union negotiator says to the company negotiator, "We just agreed on a $7-an-hour contract. What do you mean it's costing the company $10 an hour for workers?" To what does the $10 figure refer?
5. What is the difference between the Manufacturing Overhead Control account and the Manufacturing Overhead Applied account?
6. What does it mean, in terms of product cost, when manufacturing overhead is underapplied?
7. What is the usual accounting treatment of small amounts of underapplied or overapplied manufacturing overhead?
8. Briefly describe the primary difference between a job order cost system and a process cost system.
9. What is a job cost sheet? What relationship does it have to the Work in Process Control account?
10. Explain the function of a job number.
11. Explain to the president of the company why a departmental job cost sheet should be used when it yields the identical total product cost as a nondepartmental job cost sheet.
12. At the end of the accounting period the Manufacturing Overhead Control account has a debit balance of $145,250, and the Manufacturing Overhead Applied account has a credit balance of $148,155. What is underapplied or overapplied overhead in this case, and what does it mean in terms of product cost?

EXERCISES

Ex. 3-1 **Materials costs flows.** The Petrosky Manufacturing Company uses a perpetual inventory system to account for all inventory transactions. The firm's Raw Materials Inventory account balance on January 1 was $46,760. During the year, the company purchased $178,900 of raw materials. Materials requisitions were filled for $125,300 of direct materials and $21,500 of indirect materials. Of the materials requisitioned, $7,880 were not used and were returned to the inventory storeroom. A year-end inventory count reveals an ending balance in the Raw Materials Inventory account of $77,350.

Required:

a. Compute the December 31 balance in the Raw Materials Inventory account without regard to the physical inventory count.
b. Calculate the cost of materials actually used in production during the year.
c. Calculate the amount of adjustment needed to correct the Raw Materials Inventory Control account so that it conforms to the year-end inventory count.

Ex. 3-2 **Payroll fringe benefits.** The Kulish Construction Company employs one supervisor, two carpenters, four apprentices, and three laborers. They are each paid monthly as follows:

Supervisor	$2,500
Carpenter	2,000
Apprentice	900
Laborer	1,300

All personnel are entitled to a half month of paid vacation time per year which the company accrues each month. Federal income tax withholdings are 20 percent of payroll. All employees except the supervisor belong to a union. The union's monthly dues in the amount of 1.8 percent of salary are withheld by the employer. FICA withholdings are 7 percent of pay. The company contributes $21 per month per employee for a group health and accident insurance plan. The workers work together on construction of one home at a time. Their gross pay is assigned to Construction in Progress and other payroll costs are assigned to Construction Overhead.

Required: Record the payment of the payroll and the employer's other payroll cost.

Ex. 3-3 Identifying labor costs. Jay Williams, an employee of a manufacturing business, prepared the following summary of his job activities for the past week:

	Hours
Assembly on Job 5629	7
Assembly on Job 5626	4
Assembly on Job 5630	8
Assembly on Job 5631	3
Assembly on Job 5633	7
Equipment maintenance	4
Company training program	4
Unassigned	3
Total hours worked	40

Williams's wage rate is $9.50 an hour. The company also pays the following payroll taxes and employee benefits:

Item	Amount
Payroll taxes	12 percent of gross pay
Insurance program	5 percent of gross pay
Retirement program	10 percent of gross pay
Education program	$.50 per hour worked
Vacation and holiday pay	15 percent of gross pay

Required:

a. Compute the amount of direct labor cost that typically would be charged to production for Williams's labor during the week.

b. Compute the amount of indirect labor cost charged to Manufacturing Overhead for Williams.

c. Compute the total labor cost associated with Williams's work for the week.

Ex. 3-4 Product overhead costs. Frainer Company makes home freezers and applies manufacturing overhead to production at the rate of 125 percent of direct labor cost. In January, the company actually produced 1,780 units of product with a labor cost of $102,528. By the end of the year, total labor cost was $1,045,500 and actual overhead cost was $1,268,900.

Required:

a. Determine how much overhead was charged to production in January.
b. Compute the overhead cost per unit for the products produced in January.
c. Compute the underapplied or overapplied overhead for the year.

Ex. 3-5 Payroll costs and bonus. Marsha's Ceramics has two highly skilled employees who design and produce exquisite ceramic pieces. Each earns a salary of $1,495 per month. Each also gets ½ month of paid vacation and a bonus at the end of the year equal to 1 month's pay. The company treats the bonuses and vacation pay as indirect cost. The company deducts 22 percent of salary for federal income tax, 5 percent for state income tax, and 7 percent for FICA tax, and pays 14 percent of gross pay into a pension fund. There is no workmen's compensation or FUTA tax liability.

Required:

a. Record the May payroll.
b. Record the additional payroll costs for May.
c. Record the distribution of the payroll costs.

Ex. 3-6 Using manufacturing overhead costs. Kafer Manufacturing Company applies overhead to products at the rate of $25 per direct labor hour. During 1985, 18,200 actual direct labor hours were worked, and the manufacturing overhead control account had a year-end balance of $512,400.

Required:

a. Compute the amount of applied manufacturing overhead for 1985.
b. Compute the amount of underapplied or overapplied overhead for the year.
c. Compute the actual overhead cost per direct labor hour.

Ex. 3-7 Simple job cost sheet. A materials requisition schedule and a labor distribution report are presented below for the second week of August. Manufacturing overhead is applied to production at the rate of 150 percent of direct labor cost. Job number 8788 was started and completed during the week. Two hundred units were produced.

Materials Requisitions

Date	Job Number	Amount
8/9	8788	$2,400
8/9	8789	2,700
8/10	8787	9,700
8/10	8787	1,300
8/10	8788	1,900
8/11	8790	300
8/12	8786	3,300
8/13	8788	1,400

Labor Distribution 8/13

Job Number	Amount
8786	$3,600
8787	4,000
8788	3,400
8789	1,700
8790	800
8791	1,900

Required: Prepare a job cost sheet in good form for Job 8788.

Ex. 3-8 Working with manufacturing overhead accounts. Arapahoe Basin Manufacturing makes ski bindings in its western slope manufacturing plant. Overhead is applied at the rate of $12 per direct labor hour. The company makes skis in its eastern slope manufacturing plant where manufacturing overhead is applied at the rate of 120 percent of direct labor cost. Below are partial year-end accounting data for each of the manufacturing plants.

	Plant	
	Eastern Slope	Western Slope
Direct labor hours	35,000	18,000
Direct labor cost	$350,000	$ 96,000
Manufacturing overhead control	$390,000	$237,000
Sales	$950,000	$565,000

Required:

a. Compute the amount of applied manufacturing overhead in each plant.
b. Compute the amount of underapplied or overapplied overhead for each plant and for the company as a whole.

Ex. 3-9 Departmental job cost sheet. Kimberly Manufacturing Company makes sandblasting machines. A recent production run of the machines yielded the following data:

Job number: 41457
Number of machines produced: 25
Date started: April 14
Date completed: May 27

	April	May
Department 1:		
Materials	$6,600	$2,600
Direct labor rate	$8.00 per hr	$8.00 per hr
Labor hours	700	800
Department 2:		
Direct labor rate	$7.00 per hr	$7.00 per hr
Labor hours	200	250
Manufacturing overhead rate	150% of DLC	150% of DLC

Required:

a. Prepare in good form a departmental job cost sheet for Job number 41457.
b. If the sandblasting machines are sold for $3,000 each, what is the percentage gross margin on sales for this product?

Ex. 3-10 Identifying errors in accounting for materials. Ristlott Company is a small manufacturing company with a perpetual inventory system. Recently the company hired a new accountant who has not worked for a manufacturing company before. In the first week of work, he made the following entries:

a.	Direct materials	89,300	
	Accounts payable		89,300
	To record the purchase of raw		
	materials on open account.		
b.	Direct materials	1,200	
	Accounts payable		1,200
	Issued $1,200 of compound used to		
	lubricate manufacturing machinery		
	to the maintenance department.		
c.	Raw materials inventory control	2,300	
	Work in process control		2,300
	Issued $2,300 of direct materials		
	to production.		
d.	Raw materials inventory control	750	
	Accounts payable		750
	To record the return of faulty		
	materials to the vendor.		
e.	Accounts receivable	56,000	
	Cost of goods sold		34,000
	Profit on sale		22,000
	To record the sale of goods costing		
	$34,000 for revenue of $56,000.		

The description of each event or activity is correct.

Required: Analyze each of the journal entries to determine if it is correct. For any incorrect entry, identify the error and make the necessary entry to correct the error.

Ex. 3-11 **Preparation of departmental job cost sheet.** Zlonake Company accumulates job costs for its manufacturing operations using departmental job cost sheets. Recently the firm completed Job number 108711, in which 200 stereo tape players were produced. The job was started on February 24 and completed on March 6. Overhead is applied at the rate of 80 percent of direct labor cost. Below are weekly data pertaining to Job number 108711.

Week Ending February 28

Department	Date	Materials Requisition Number	Labor Distribution Report Number	Amount
Fabricating	Feb. 24	RQ3323		$2,220
Fabricating	Feb. 28		LD2/28	1,760
Assembly	Feb. 28	RQ3336		3,250
Assembly	Feb. 28		LD2/28	1,910

Week Ending March 7				
Department	**Date**	**Materials Requisition Number**	**Labor Distribution Report Number**	**Amount**
Assembly	Mar. 7		LD3/7	$1,080
Finishing	Mar. 5	RQ3351		625
Finishing	Mar. 7		LD3/7	1,330

Required: Prepare a departmental job order cost sheet in good form for Job number 108711.

Ex. 3-12 Job cost sheet and gross margin. The Bergoin Company makes windmills used for generating electricity. Because this product is a relatively new alternative power source, it requires a large amount of advertising and other marketing activities. To cover these high marketing costs, the company must generate a 45 percent gross margin on sales. Below are production and cost data for Job number 22765 for 1,000 windmills. Overhead is applied at the rate of $9 per direct labor hour. The labor rate is $7 per hour. Materials requisitions for Job number 22765 include:

Date	Requisition Number	Amount
2/7	1477	$124,000
2/19	1524	96,000
3/2	1590	83,500
3/21	1634	66,500

Labor distribution data pertaining to Job number 22765 are:

Date	Amount
2/15	$ 84,000
2/28	147,000
3/15	164,500
3/31	126,000

Required:

a. Prepare a job cost sheet for Job number 22765.
b. What should the price of the windmill be if the company wants to achieve its target gross margin?

PROBLEMS

P. 3-1 Labor cost of production. Stoney Snord is a stonecutter working for Takonite Quarries, Inc. Stoney earns $9 per hour and normally works 40 hours per week. During the first week of May, Stoney worked 12 hours cutting marble slabs and 20 hours polishing granite. The remaining 8 hours were spent maintaining the cutting and polishing equipment. The company pays $6 per week for health and accident insurance, $12 a week into a guaranteed annual wage fund, 7 percent FICA tax, and 14 percent into a retirement fund for each of its employees.

Required:

a. Compute the direct labor cost to be assigned to processing marble and granite by Stoney.
b. Compute the cost to be assigned to overhead this week for Stoney's work.
c. Compute the total hourly cost of employing Stoney and total hourly cost of Stoney's direct labor if all costs are included in the computations.

P. 3-2 Identifying labor costs. The drill press department of a small manufacturing business has four employees. The company produces a number of different special order products using a job order costing system to account for the manufacturing costs. Employees of the drill press department prepare daily time tickets indicating the time they spent working on jobs, maintaining their machinery, and waiting for new job assignments. Below is the labor summary for the last week of June:

Labor Summary
For the Week of June 23–30

	Job Number					
Employee	**611**	**612**	**613**	**614**	**Machine Maintenance**	**Idle Time**
F. Schultz	26	8	3	-	3	-
M. Singer	11	14	4	-	7	4
P. Granert	-	16	12	8	2	2
L. Martinez	-	-	-	26	7	7
Totals	37	38	19	34	19	13

Drill press department employees are paid $9 an hour and the employer pays the following in payroll taxes and employee benefits:

Employer payroll taxes	12 percent of gross pay
Insurance programs	5 percent of gross pay
Pension program	10 percent of gross pay
Other employee benefits	14 percent of gross pay

Required:

a. Calculate the direct labor cost for the week.
b. Calculate the gross pay for the week.
c. Calculate the cost of indirect labor for the week.
d. Calculate the total amount of labor-related cost that should be charged to Manufacturing Overhead Control for the drill press department.
e. Assuming this is a typical workweek, calculate the total labor cost per hour for each direct labor hour worked.

P. 3-3 Analyzing labor costs. The managers of the Bellnapp Company have just received a labor contract proposal from union leaders. The president wants to make a thorough analysis of the impact of the proposed contract on labor costs. You are the controller for Bellnapp, and you are asked to prepare an itemized listing of labor-related costs for the current contract and the proposed contract. You prepare the following:

Item	Current	Proposed
Wage rate	$6.00/hr	$6.30/hr
Vacation	2 wk	3 wk
Paid holidays	10 days	15 days
Pension fund contribution per employee per week	$24.00	$46.00
Education program contribution per employee per year	0	$144.00

Employees work 40 hours a week at Bellnapp and 20 percent of manufacturing labor is indirect labor. The letter accompanying the union's latest contract proposal states that the union is "interested in the quality of life for its employees rather than monetary issues and consequently is only seeking a 5 percent increase in the wage rate."

Required:

a. Determine the total cost per hour of manufacturing labor for the current contract and the proposed contract.
b. Respond to the union letter that accompanied the most recent union contract proposal.
c. What is the total labor cost for an hour of direct labor with the current contract? With the proposed contract? (Ignore payroll taxes.)

P. 3-4 **Overhead cost computations.** Gilford Manufacturing uses a job order costing system to measure the cost of making its products. Below are cost and activity data for the production of three jobs that were completed during the current week.

	Job Number		
	1193	1198	2001
Direct labor cost, machining	$ 4,000	$ 2,000	$ 5,000
Direct labor cost, assembly	2,000	8,000	1,000
Direct materials cost	24,000	12,000	16,000
Machine hours, machining dept.	800	300	600
Units completed	100	200	300

The firm applies overhead to jobs at the rate of $12 per machine hour in the machining department and at the rate of 150 percent of direct labor cost in the assembly department.

Required:

a. Compute the amount of manufacturing overhead applied to each job.
b. Compute the unit cost of each unit of product.
c. Compute the percentage of total product cost represented by overhead in each job.

P. 3-5 **Using overhead cost data.** Cleveland Catalog Sales Company uses a centralized pool of secretaries to handle typing, filing, and other clerical activities. Many different departments use this central pool. Users of the secretarial pool are charged $15 an hour for a secretary's time. The charge is based on $7 an hour for wages plus $8 an hour for overhead. Overhead includes depreciation on office equipment and furniture and other occupancy costs. During the year the secretarial pool has actual labor cost of $219,000, actual overhead cost of $285,000, and 30,000 hours of labor time.

The director of marketing recently used the pool to have long personalized letters typed to 50 distributors. The charges for the service are as follows:

Materials and postage	$ 32
Typing	300
Total charge	$332

The director of marketing is upset about the amount of the charge. He says, "I can understand the salary charge, but that overhead charge is a lot of accounting funny money. After all we already own the building and typewriters."

Required:

a. Calculate any underapplied or overapplied overhead.

b. What was the total cost of an hour of time in the secretarial pool based on actual costs?

c. How would you justify the charges to the marketing director?

d. If overhead cost is expected to increase 10 percent from this year's actual cost and labor cost is expected to increase 15 percent from the budget figures, what should the new hourly rate be for secretarial services?

P. 3-6 **Labor cost analysis and billing rate computation.** Sam and Janet work for Grimlet Security Company. Sam is a master locksmith and earns $10 per hour. Janet is a journeyman locksmith and earns $8 per hour. They each work 40 hours per week. During the first week of May, Sam worked 20 hours installing locks on a new office building and 16 hours on service calls. The remaining 4 hours he spent on miscellaneous tasks such as store and equipment maintenance. Janet worked 14 hours on the same office building, and handled service calls 18 hours. She spent the remaining 8 hours waiting on customers, setting up display cases, and performing other miscellaneous tasks. The week is considered typical for both employees.

Grimlet Security Company pays $6 per week for accident and life insurance for each of its employees. Also it pays $5 a week into an education and training fund since it must periodically provide its employees with training on new developments in the security industry. The company also pays 7 percent FICA tax, and 13 percent of gross pay into a retirement fund. In order to cover administrative and other operating expenses the company must charge 160 percent of its employees' actual direct labor cost for service calls.

Required:

a. Compute the direct labor cost to be assigned to new lock installations and also to the service calls.

b. Compute the cost to be assigned to overhead this week for Sam and Janet's work.

c. Compute the total hourly cost of employing Sam and Janet and also the total hourly cost of their direct labor if all costs are included in the computations.

d. How much should the company bill its customers for service calls performed by Sam and Janet?

e. Compute a single billing rate for Sam and Janet's service calls, using their individual rates weighted by the time they spend on service calls.

P. 3-7 Accounting for underapplied and overapplied overhead. Jorgenson Company applies manufacturing overhead to production at the rate of 150 percent of direct labor cost. In 1985, it incurred $680,000 in direct labor cost. The year-end balance in the Manufacturing Overhead Control account was $1,211,000. Any differences between applied and actual overhead are assigned to Cost of Goods Sold unless applied overhead is more than 15 percent different than actual overhead. Such significant differences are assigned to Work in Process, Finished Goods, and Cost of Goods Sold in proportion to the total balances in those accounts at year-end. The December 31 balances in those accounts are:

Work in Process		Finished Goods		Cost of Goods Sold	
400,000		500,000		1,600,000	

Required:

a. Compute the amount of applied overhead in 1985.
b. Compute the amount of underapplied or overapplied overhead.
c. Prepare necessary journal entries to close the overhead accounts and dispose of any underapplied or overapplied overhead in accordance with company policy.
d. Repeat part *c* assuming the year-end balance in the Manufacturing Overhead Control account is $1,110,000.

P. 3-8 Journalizing cost flows. Below are transaction data for the Forsythe Tool Company. The company uses a job order costing system to measure the cost of manufacturing its products.

a. Paid the weekly payroll. Gross pay was $26,700; withholding items included $3,240 for federal income tax, $1,565 for FICA tax, $1,725 for state income tax, and $578 for union dues.
b. Other payroll-related items include the employer's share of FICA taxes, and state and federal unemployment taxes of 2.7 percent and .7 percent of gross pay, respectively.
c. Overhead is applied to production at the rate of $5.50 per direct labor hour. During this week's pay period, 2,460 direct labor hours were clocked.
d. A bill for $375 was received from a firm that repaired the hydraulic metal press on Tuesday.
e. Purchased $12,640 of cold rolled steel on open account.
f. Sent $4,800 of steel and $1,750 of lumber from the inventory storeroom to the fabricating department for Job number 14326.
g. Job number 14322 is completed at a cost of $28,442.
h. Direct labor is $24,260 of the gross payroll. The rest is indirect labor.
i. Job number 14322 is delivered to the customer and a bill sent for $39,880.
j. A utility bill is received for $3,600 and paid. Eighty percent of the bill is attributable to the manufacturing activities of the business.
k. Indirect materials in the amount of $945 are issued to production.

Required: Prepare journal entries in good form for each of the transactions described above.

P. 3-9 Identifying transactions from journal entries. Below are journal entries recorded in the journal of the Omitt Company, which manufactures duck decoys in a job order cost system.

a.	Payroll	45,600	
	Federal withholding tax payable		8,500
	FICA tax payable		3,100
	State withholding tax payable		2,200
	Union dues payable		900
	Cash		30,900
b.	Work in process control	37,900	
	Manufacturing overhead control	7,700	
	Payroll		45,600
c.	Raw materials inventory control	13,400	
	Accounts payable		13,400
d.	Accounts receivable	23,500	
	Sales		23,500
	Cost of goods sold	16,200	
	Finished goods inventory control		16,200
e.	Work in process control	4,150	
	Raw materials inventory control		4,150
f.	Work in process control	6,600	
	Manufacturing overhead applied		6,600
g.	Finished goods inventory control	17,960	
	Work in process control		17,960
h.	Manufacturing overhead control	980	
	Raw materials inventory control		980
i.	Property tax expense	1,640	
	Manufacturing overhead control	6,560	
	Cash		8,200
j.	Office supplies expense	435	
	Cash		435

Required: For each of the above journal entries describe the transaction or event that occurred.

P. 3-10 Analyzing product cost data. Alanse Tool and Machine Company makes portable gasoline-powered water pumps. Sales volume for the pumps is not enough to warrant a full-time continuous production process. Instead, the product is manufactured in job lots for inventory. In the last 6 months, the firm has produced six job lots of the water pumps. Currently the pump sells for $160. Because the product requires a lot of advertising to be competitive, management has established a minimum gross margin on sales of 35 percent. Following is a summary of the job cost sheets for the last six production runs of the portable water pump.

Job No.	Date Completed	Units Produced	Direct Materials	Direct Labor	Overhead Applied	Total Cost
54211	1/12	1,000	$ 32,000	$ 24,000	$ 36,000	$ 92,000
54243	2/25	600	22,800	15,600	23,400	61,800
54256	3/12	1,800	72,000	50,400	75,600	198,000
54269	3/31	2,500	105,000	80,000	120,000	305,000
54289	4/14	2,200	94,600	74,800	112,200	281,600
54301	5/24	1,900	85,500	68,400	102,600	256,500
Total		10,000	$411,900	$313,200	$469,800	$1,194,900

Required:

a. Has the cost of the water pumps fluctuated enough to cause concern about the price of the product? Analyze the cost data presented and support your answer with a cost analysis.

b. What should the price of the pumps be to meet the minimum gross margin requirement?

P. 3-11 (CMA) Understanding manufacturing overhead concepts. is a manufacturing company with a fiscal year that runs from July 1 to June 30. The company uses a job order accounting system for its production costs.

A predetermined overhead rate based upon direct labor hours is used to apply overhead to individual jobs. A flexible budget of overhead costs was prepared for the 1985–1986 fiscal year as shown below.

Direct labor hours	100,000	120,000	140,000
Variable overhead costs	$325,000	$390,000	$455,000
Fixed overhead costs	216,000	216,000	216,000
Total overhead	$541,000	$606,000	$671,000

Although the annual ideal capacity is 150,000 direct labor hours, company officials have determined 120,000 direct labor hours as normal capacity for the year.

The information presented below is for November 1985. Jobs 77-50 and 77-51 were completed during November.

Inventories November 1, 1985	
Raw materials and factory supplies	$ 10,500
Work in process (Job 77-50)	54,000
Finished goods	112,500

Purchases of raw materials and factory supplies	
Raw materials	$135,000
Factory supplies	15,000
Materials and supplies requisitioned for production	
Job 77-50	45,000
Job 77-51	37,500
Job 77-52	25,500
Supplies	12,000
Total requisitioned materials and factory supplies	$120,000

Factory direct labor hours	
Job 77-50	3,500 DLH
Job 77-51	3,000 DLH
Job 77-52	2,000 DLH
Labor costs	
Direct labor wages	$ 51,000
Indirect labor wages (4,000 hours)	15,000
Supervisory salaries	6,000
Building occupancy costs (heat, light, depreciation, etc.)	
Factory facilities	6,500
Sales offices	1,500
Administrative offices	1,000
Total building occupancy costs	$ 9,000

Factory equipment costs	
Power	$ 4,000
Repairs and maintenance	1,500
Depreciation	1,500
Other	1,000
Total factory equipment costs	$ 8,000

1. The predetermined overhead rate to be used to apply overhead to individual jobs during the 1985–86 fiscal year is

   a. $3.25 per DLH.
   b. $4.69 per DLH.
   c. $5.05 per DLH.
   d. $5.41 per DLH.
   e. Some rate other than those shown above.

Note: Without prejudice to your answer to question 1 assume the predetermined overhead rate is $4.50 per direct labor hour. Use this amount in answering questions 2 through 6.

2. The total cost of Job 77-50 is

   a. $81,750.
   b. $135,750.
   c. $142,750.
   d. $146,750.
   e. Some amount other than those shown above.

3. The factory overhead costs applied to Job 77-52 during November were

   a. $9,000.
   b. $47,500.
   c. $46,500.
   d. $8,000.
   e. Some amount other than those shown above.

4. The total amount of overhead applied to jobs during November was
   a. $29,250.
   b. $38,250.
   c. $47,250.
   d. $56,250.
   e. Some amount other than those shown above.
5. Actual factory overhead incurred during November 1985 was
   a. $38,000.
   b. $41,500.
   c. $47,500.
   d. $50,500.
   e. Some amount other than those shown above.
6. At the end of the last fiscal year (June 30, 1985), Baehr Company had the following account balances:

Overapplied overhead	$ 1,000
Cost of goods sold	980,000
Work in process inventory	38,000
Finished goods inventory	82,000

   The most common treatment of the overapplied overhead would be to
   a. Prorate it between Work in Process Inventory and Finished Goods Inventory.
   b. Prorate it between Work in Process Inventory, Finished Goods Inventory, and Cost of Goods Sold.
   c. Carry it as a deferred credit on the balance sheet.
   d. Carry it as miscellaneous operating revenue on the income statement.
   e. Credit it to Cost of Goods Sold.

P. 3-12 Using product cost data. Kenndlton Company has a policy of evaluating product prices once a year. The company manufactures accessories for pleasure boats. It prices its products as low as possible to maintain a competitive sales position and still earn a reasonable profit. The desired target price for products provides a 35 percent gross margin on sales although competition sometimes forces less profitable pricing. However, the minimum acceptable gross margin on sales is 25 percent.

The company's leading volume product is its teak swim platform which is installed on the stern of the boats. The current selling price is $110 per unit. Below are cost data for the five production runs of the product during the last year.

Job No.	Date Completed	Units Produced	Materials	Labor	Overhead	Total Cost
7765	3/14	2,500	$ 72,500	$ 62,500	$ 50,000	$185,000
7783	3/29	1,000	31,000	30,000	24,000	85,000
7798	4/17	3,500	105,000	84,000	66,500	255,500
7812	5/10	2,000	62,000	54,000	44,000	160,000
7845	6/11	1,000	32,000	32,000	26,000	90,000
Total		10,000	$302,500	$262,500	$210,500	$775,500

Required:

a. Use the data to determine what the price should be, based on:

1. The cost of the first production run (Job number 7765).
2. Average unit cost for the year.
3. Unit cost of the most recent production run.

b. Do the cost data suggest to you any trends in costs or significant variables that may affect the cost of the product? Explain.

c. Of the prices computed in part *a*, which one would you select? Explain.

P. 3-13 Understanding cost flows. On January 1, 1986, the Candlelever Company opened a new division that makes projector bulbs for slide projectors. The firm started operation with no beginning inventories and during the year the division started 110,000 units. By year-end, 94,000 units were completed and 84,000 bulbs were sold for $21.20 each. In 1986, $344,800 of raw materials was put into production of which $17,600 was indirect materials. Production payroll cost for the year was $210,000, with 90 percent of this being direct labor. Overhead is applied at the rate of 140 percent of direct labor cost. At the end of 1986, the Work in Process Control account had a balance of $71,840 made up of $26,400 of direct materials, $19,800 of direct labor, and $25,640 of applied manufacturing overhead. Actual overhead for 1986 was $230,400.

Required:

a. Calculate the cost of goods manufactured in 1986.

b. Calculate the total amount of production costs charged to Work in Process Control during 1986.

c. Calculate the average unit cost for each cost element and the average unit cost in total for units completed in 1986.

d. Calculate the total applied overhead for 1986.

e. Using the average unit cost of completed units in 1986, calculate the year-end balance in the Finished Goods Inventory Control account.

f. Calculate underapplied or overapplied manufacturing overhead for 1986.

P. 3-14 Departmental job cost sheets information. Scott's Bay Toy Company uses departmental job cost sheets to monitor and control production costs for its job shop manufacturing operations. Summaries are prepared weekly for labor and materials. The labor distribution summary and the materials requisition summary are presented on page 114 for the week of April 14–18. Both reports identify the job number and the department for the resources used. In Job number 165, the company made 100 toy robots for its general stock.

Overhead is applied to jobs using the following rates:

Fabricating	75% of direct labor cost
Welding	$6 per direct labor hour
Machining	$6 per direct labor hour
Assembly	$6 per direct labor hour

The four jobs listed were all started during the week and were the only jobs in process during the week. Only Job number 165 was completed by the end of the week.

The company's normal gross margin is 40 percent but on high-technology

Scott's Bay Toy Company
Labor Distribution Report
For the Week Ended April 18

Employee	Department	Hours Charged to Job Number 163	164	165	166	Hours Assigned to MOH	Total Hours
S. Johnson	Fabricating	–	–	10	28	2	40
C. Brooks	Fabricating	–	–	20	16	4	40
A. Brula	Fabricating	–	–	23	13	4	40
B. Evans	Welding	11	10	15	–	3	39
T. Terry	Welding	–	9	9	17	5	40
K. Kelley	Machining	–	6	5	19	6	36
E. Kafer	Machining	21	–	15	4	–	40
C. Germer	Assembly	–	13	19	–	8	40
L. Hagg	Assembly	12	–	17	4	3	36
P. Palmer	Assembly	15	–	–	14	3	32
Total hours		59	38	133	115	38	383

Wage Rates

Fabricating	$8.00 per hour
Welding	9.00
Machining	9.00
Assembly	7.00

Scott's Bay Toy Company
Summary of Materials Requisitions
For the Week of April 14–18

Date	Materials Requisition Number	Job Number	Department	Amount
4/14	972	165	Fabricating	$ 700
4/14	973	166	Fabricating	3,900
4/15	974	163	Welding	350
4/16	975	164	Assembly	1,130
4/16	976	163	Welding	175
4/17	977	166	Fabricating	2,160
4/17	978	165	Fabricating	950
4/17	979	165	Welding	600
4/18	980	164	Assembly	2,060
4/18	981	165	Assembly	675
4/18	982	MOH	General	210

products the company requires a 60 percent gross margin because of the higher marketing costs and costs of defective units returned by customers.

Required:

a. Prepare a departmental job cost sheet in good form for Job number 165.

b. Compute the required selling price for the toy robots.
c. Compute the cost of work in process at the end of the week.

P. 3-15 Analyzing cost flows with T accounts. Below is a partial list of ledger accounts for the Barthome Manufacturing Company on December 31, 1986. Some data are missing from the accounts as shown by the ? signs that appear in some of the accounts. Manufacturing overhead is applied to production at the rate of 80 percent of direct labor cost.

Raw Materials Inventory Control

Bal. 1/1	23,000	1986 Credits	55,000
1986 Debits	48,000		
Bal. 12/31	?		

Finished Goods Control

Bal. 1/1	?	1986 Credits	105,000
1986 Debits	?		
Bal. 12/31	19,000		

Work in Process Control

Bal. 1/1	15,000	1986 Credits	86,000
Direct mtl.	51,000		
Direct labor	?		
Applied MOH	?		
Bal. 12/31	43,000		

Cost of Goods Sold

1986 Debits	?		

Manufacturing Overhead Control

1986 Debits	32,000		

Manufacturing Overhead Applied

		1986 Credits	28,000

Manufacturing Payroll

1986 Debits	38,000	1986 Credits	?

Sales

		1986 Credits	165,000

Required: From the partial list of general ledger accounts presented above determine:

a. The amount of applied manufacturing overhead in 1986.
b. The amount of direct labor cost assigned to production during 1986.
c. The amount of indirect material costs incurred during 1986.
d. The amount of indirect labor cost incurred during the period.
e. The cost of goods sold for 1986.
f. The ending balance in Raw Materials Inventory Control on December 31, 1986.
g. The beginning balance in Finished Goods Control on January 1, 1986.
h. The amount of underapplied or overapplied overhead for 1986.
i. The cost of goods manufactured for 1986.
j. The 1986 gross margin on sales percentage.

P. 3-16 Comprehensive cost flows using T accounts. Below is the 1986 beginning trial balance of the B & C Manufacturing Company.

B & C Manufacturing Company
Trial Balance
January 1, 1986

	Debit	Credit
Cash	$ 67,000	
Accounts receivable	145,000	
Raw materials inventory	84,000	
Work in process inventory	105,000	
Finished goods inventory	91,000	
Prepaid expenses	12,000	
Land	25,000	
Building and equipment	600,000	
Accumulated depreciation		$ 245,000
Accounts payable		110,000
Mortgage payable		230,000
Capital stock		200,000
Retained earnings		344,000
Total	$1,129,000	$1,129,000

B & C Manufacturing Company uses a job order costing system to accumulate production costs for the products the company manufactures. Withholding from employees' paychecks include 7 percent for FICA taxes, 20 percent for federal income tax, and 5 percent for state income tax. Employer payroll taxes are 7 percent of gross payroll for FICA taxes and 3 percent for unemployment taxes. All payroll withholding items and employer payroll taxes are paid during the year. Below are summarized transactions for the year.

a. Raw materials costing $263,000 were purchased on open account.
b. Direct materials costing $167,000 and indirect materials costing $34,000 were put into production during 1986.
c. Heat, light, and power costs for the year were $60,000. Production facilities used 80 percent of the utility resources. All utility bills were paid during the year.
d. Depreciation for the year was $90,000, 85 percent of which pertained to production equipment and building space.
e. Marketing and administrative salaries were $150,000. (Be sure to record the employer's payroll taxes as well as the payroll.)
f. The company paid 1986 property taxes of $25,000, of which 70 percent were for production facilities.
g. Production wages were $325,000. (Be sure to record the employer's payroll taxes as well as the payroll.)
h. Ninety percent of the production payroll was direct labor.
i. Manufacturing overhead was applied to production at the rate of 90 percent of direct labor cost.
j. Advertising and other marketing expenses for the year of $22,000 were paid.

k. A $24,000 bill for plant insurance was received and paid. Ninety percent of the insurance cost was for production facilities.
l. Products costing $654,000 were sold for $988,000 on open account.
m. The company received and paid a bill totaling $18,000 for a factory maintenance agreement with an outside contractor.
n. Ending work in process on December 31, 1986, was $91,000.
o. Customers payments on accounts receivable during 1986 were $996,000.
p. B & C Manufacturing Company paid $281,000 on its accounts payable.
q. All payroll taxes and withholding items were paid by year-end.
r. Prepaid expenses of $8,000 weree used up during 1986. They all were marketing expenses.
s. Paid $20,000 of interest and $30,000 of principal on the mortgage payable.

Required:

a. Prepare a set of T accounts and enter the beginning trial balance amounts. (Be certain to leave space for additional T accounts that will be necessary to record transactions that occurred during 1986.)
b. Enter the 1986 transactions directly into the firm's ledger accounts. (You will need to create some new accounts not found in the firm's beginning trial balance.)
c. Prepare a pre-closing trial balance for December 31, 1986.
d. Prepare the 1986 income statement.
e. Prepare the balance sheet for December 31, 1986.
f. Prepare a journal entry to close the two overhead accounts.

CASES

Case 3-1 **Job order costing accounting cycle.** Harbor Springs Furniture Company is known for its high-quality products. Many of the products are manufactured as special orders. Some are manufactured for general stock. All production is in job lots and a job order costing system is used to measure product costs. At the end of April, the company had three jobs in production. The production costs to date on these jobs are shown on the open job costs sheets (pages 118 and 119). Manufacturing overhead is applied to products at the rate of 80 percent of direct labor cost. Overhead is applied at the time direct labor is charged to jobs.

Expected sales for the year are $840,000 and expected annual operating expenses are $156,000. The company has a net investment in assets of $945,000. The April 30 inventory balances are $34,600 in Finished Goods and $27,900 in Raw Materials. During the first week of May the following transactions and events took place:

May 2 Purchased lumber costing $2,600, vinyl covering costing $900, and foam padding costing $700, all from the same supplier.
May 2 Started Job number 8745 to make office lounge chairs for Slater Company. Issued $1,550 of direct materials to the job on requisition number MRQ12774.
May 3 Issued $900 of materials to Job number 8743 as reported in MRQ12775.
May 3 Issued $360 of cleaning compound and $175 of lubricating material to the factory maintenance department on MRQ12776.
May 4 Started the production of folding chairs for open stock with Job number 8746. Issued $1,880 of materials to production with MRQ12777.

May 5 Completed Job number 8741, the production of 100 bar stools.
May 5 Received property tax bill for $8,500. Eighty percent is for the production facility.
May 6 Completed Job number 8743, which yielded 50 desk chairs.
May 7 The weekly gross manufacturing payroll was $9,200. Federal withholding is 15 percent, state withholding is 4 percent, FICA tax is 7 percent, and other withholding is 3 percent. Employer payroll taxes total 11 percent of gross payroll.
May 7 The weekly labor distribution report showed the following direct labor costs. All other labor costs are indirect labor.

Job	Amount
8741	$ 600
8743	1,200
8744	1,800
8745	1,600
8746	2,700

May 7 Sold Job number 8743 on open account for $190 per unit.

Open Job Cost Sheets on April 30:

Harbor Springs Furniture Company
Job Cost Sheet

Date started 4/25 — Job number 8741
Date completed — Quantity 100
Product Bar stools — Customer Stock

Direct Materials			Direct Labor			Manufacturing Overhead		
Date	**Reference**	**Amount**	**Date**	**Reference**	**Amount**	**Date**	**Reference**	**Amount**
4/25 4/28	MRQ12765 MRQ12772	$2,100 800	4/30	LD 4/30	$1,400	4/30	LD 4/30	$1,120

Harbor Springs Furniture Company
Job Cost Sheet

Date started 4/28 — Job number 8743
Date completed — Quantity 50
Product Desk chairs — Customer Cranston Corp.

Direct Materials			Direct Labor			Manufacturing Overhead		
Date	**Reference**	**Amount**	**Date**	**Reference**	**Amount**	**Date**	**Reference**	**Amount**
4/28	MRQ12770	$2,700	4/30	LD 4/30	$ 800	4/30	LD 4/30	$ 640

Harbor Springs Furniture Company
Job Cost Sheet

Date started 4/29
Date completed
Product Folding chairs

Job number 8744
Quantity
Customer Kramer College

Direct Materials			Direct Labor			Manufacturing Overhead		
Date	**Reference**	**Amount**	**Date**	**Reference**	**Amount**	**Date**	**Reference**	**Amount**
4/29	MRQ12773	$2,100	4/30	LD 4/30	$ 600	4/30	LD 4/30	$ 480

Required:

a. Compute the April 30 balance in Work in Process Control.
b. Journalize the transactions for the first week of May.
c. Post all necessary data to the appropriate job cost sheets.
d. Complete any job cost sheets for finished jobs.
e. Compute the balance in the Work in Process account at the end of the first week in May.
f. Compute the total balance in inventory accounts at the end of the first week in May.
g. Compute the gross margin on sales percentage for Job number 8743.
h. Assuming the gross margin on sales percentage on Job number 8743 is standard for the company, compute the expected profit for the year.
i. Based on the data available, discuss the performance of the company.

Manufacturing Overhead and Cost Allocation

4

Many business costs are not easy to identify with specific cost objectives such as products or service contracts. You now understand some of the challenges of assigning indirect manufacturing costs to products; many other cost measurements require all the skills and ingenuity of accountants in order to report accurately the cost of making products and providing services. When you have completed the chapter, you should understand·

1 The nature of costs that are common to several cost objectives, and why they occur.

2 Why it is necessary to assign common costs to cost objectives.

3 How common costs are allocated to cost objectives.

4 The development and use of manufacturing overhead rates.

5 The use of departmental manufacturing overhead rates.

6 The nature of joint products and how their production costs are measured.

7 Various methods of allocating joint costs.

The assignment of common costs to cost objectives is called cost allocation

Common costs are costs that cannot be identified readily with specific cost objectives. Such costs provide a challenge for accountants who must determine how the common costs should be included in managerial accounting reports and how they should be assigned to products and activities. The assignment of common costs to cost objectives is called **cost allocation.**

Decision makers need a variety of cost figures to assist them in making various management decisions. For example, external users of accounting information require cost information that is condensed and summarized, whereas corporate managers need very detailed cost data for daily operating decisions. No single cost figure will suffice for making every type of managerial decision. Production, pricing, purchasing, performance evaluation, and budgeting decisions each require accounting information containing somewhat different cost data.

In this chapter we discuss the nature of common costs and common cost allocation procedures in manufacturing businesses. A manufacturing example is used to illustrate the development of overhead rates and overhead cost allocations. Also, we examine the allocation of common costs to joint products.

THE NATURE OF COMMON COSTS

Causes of common costs

Common costs often are a large portion of total manufacturing costs and they occur for a variety of reasons. Some are caused by the organizational structure of the company, others by manufacturing processes that make it impossible to identify some manufacturing costs directly with specific products. If the management of a company decides that it can achieve better control over costs or that the firm can earn a larger profit by separating operations into several departments or divisions, it may find that some costs that are identifiable with the whole company are not easily identifiable with individual operating units. Property taxes and insurance on the entire production facilities are examples of common costs that are shared by several cost objectives because managers decided to change the structure of the organization and need reports on the performance of each unit. For product costing and some types of management reports the cost of the property taxes and insurance together with other common costs are logically allocated to the various operating units.

Indirect manufacturing costs are common costs because they cannot be identified directly with individual products. Some products, such as gasoline and fuel oil, are not distinguishable as separate products early in the production process. Instead they appear as one product until some point in the manufacturing process where the products separate. Such products are called **joint products** or **by-products.** All manufacturing costs incurred before the products separate are identifiable with the group of products, but not with specific products in the group. Therefore, all production costs before the point of separation are common to the group of products being produced. Joint products are discussed in detail later in this chapter.

COST ALLOCATIONS IN MANAGEMENT REPORTING

Common costs should not be allocated arbitrarily

Cost allocation consists of deciding what part of indirect costs belong to each cost objective. Allocation of common costs to cost objectives should not be arbitrary but should be based on the matching principle. In order to satisfy the matching principle, the accountant must find a meaningful causal relationship between the cost objective and the cost to be allocated to the objective. For example, heating costs may be allocated to departments based on the square feet of floor space occupied by each department because, in general, heating cost is directly related to the amount of space that is heated.

Not all accountants believe that common costs should be allocated to cost objectives. Some argue that most cost allocations are arbitrary and as such cloud the issues of evaluating performance, making decisions, and providing general information. Of course, for some reporting purposes there is no choice. Income statements must include full product costs with both direct and indirect costs of production. The Internal Revenue Service accepts only full cost income statements for reporting taxable income. Cost-plus contracts require numerous cost allocations. In short, cost allocations are often needed to satisfy reporting requirements. When allocations are made, they should reflect the matching principle, causal relationships, and common sense.

Common costs should not be allocated for some business reporting situations

Some situations require allocation of all common costs; others require allocation of only part of the common costs. In some cases the management decision is most easily made when no cost allocation is made. For example, in the evaluation of production line supervisors, it may make little sense to allocate computer service charges for production scheduling to each supervisor if supervisors have no control over those costs. Similarly the allocation of personnel service costs, accounting service costs, or other corporate expenses to line managers or to cost objectives may have little value in evaluating performance, in establishing product prices, or in deciding whether to make or buy production parts. These and many other decisions affected by cost allocations are discussed in later chapters. In this chapter, we look at situations that require cost allocations.

MANUFACTURING OVERHEAD COSTS

Manufacturing overhead costs, such as depreciation on plant and equipment, utilities, maintenance, indirect materials, and indirect labor, are necessary but indirect costs of production; they are incurred to provide and maintain the necessary production facilities and in general to facilitate the manufacture of products made by the firm. Even though these costs cannot be identified directly with specific products, they are an essential part of the cost of manufacturing products. Like other manufacturing costs, overhead costs must be included in the cost of products for pricing, performance evaluation, and other product-related decisions. Accountants therefore have developed methods of assigning overhead costs to products in some logical fashion. The assignment of overhead starts with the development of appropriate overhead rates.

Manufacturing Overhead Rates

The application of manufacturing overhead to products is simple if managers can wait until the end of an accounting period to assign overhead

Predetermined overhead rates provide timely assignment of overhead costs to production

costs. However, two problems arise from such a policy. If the accounting period is long, such as a year, product costs are not timely enough to be of much use in decision making. If the period is short, such as a month, timely measures are obtained, but they are often distorted by seasonal factors. For example, in northern regions heating and lighting costs are higher in January than in July. Consequently, accountants need a timely method of assigning overhead costs to products, but one that minimizes the problem of short-run or seasonal overhead cost fluctuations. Therefore managers estimate the overhead costs and the amount of production for the accounting period and establish an overhead application rate based on these estimates. The application rate is used to assign overhead costs to products during the accounting period. Typically the amount of overhead applied to products is not identical to the amount of actual overhead cost incurred, but it is close enough for making management decisions. Any discrepancies between actual and applied overhead are adjusted at the end of the accounting period.

Steps in Accounting for Manufacturing Overhead

The development and use of a manufacturing overhead system includes the following steps:

1. Prior to the beginning of the accounting period, estimates are made of the expected production level and the expected total overhead cost for the next period, usually a year.
2. From these estimates, a **manufacturing overhead rate** is established. Sometimes this rate is called the **predetermined overhead rate** to emphasize the fact that it is based on estimates of the future year's activities. For example, the budgeted overhead rate for the next accounting year might be $6 per machine hour or 150 percent of direct labor cost.
3. Manufacturing overhead is applied to products using the predetermined overhead rate and actual measures of production, and the total amount of overhead applied is accumulated in the MOH Applied account.
4. Actual overhead costs are accumulated during the accounting period in the MOH Control account.
5. At the end of the accounting period, the applied overhead is compared with the actual overhead to determine the amount of overhead that has been overapplied or underapplied.

Developing the Manufacturing Overhead Rate

A predetermined manufacturing overhead rate is calculated from estimated figures. First the total manufacturing overhead cost, or **budgeted overhead cost,** for the accounting period is estimated. Then the production volume for the period (or **budgeted volume of activity**) is estimated.

The overhead rate is calculated by dividing the budgeted overhead cost for the period by the budgeted volume of activity

Estimates of future costs and volumes of activity involve uncertainty and may be difficult to make accurately. Nevertheless, experienced managers are able to develop predetermined overhead rates that provide a close match between the actual overhead costs incurred and the amount of overhead applied to production. Once the estimates of costs and volume of activity have been made, the calculation of the overhead rate is simple:

$$\text{Manufacturing overhead rate} = \frac{\text{Estimated manufacturing overhead cost}}{\text{Estimated volume of activity}}$$

The activity measure is called the overhead application base

The estimated volume of activity may be expressed in terms of various measures of activity. Units of output, direct labor hours, and machine hours are frequently used activity measures. The activity measure is referred to as the **overhead application base.**

We illustrate the computation of a manufacturing overhead rate by assuming that a manufacturing firm expects to produce 20,000 wooden porch swings next year. Based on past production experience, 5 hours of direct labor will be required for each swing. Estimated manufacturing overhead costs for the period are $300,000. Using these estimates, the manufacturing overhead rate can be computed using either units of production or direct labor hours as the application base.

Units of production:

$$\frac{\text{Total estimated MOH}}{\text{Total estimated units of production}} = \frac{\$300{,}000}{20{,}000 \text{ units}} = \$15 \text{ per unit}$$

Direct labor hours:

$$\begin{aligned}\text{Total estimated labor hours} &= \text{Units of production} \times \text{Labor hours per unit}\\ &= 20{,}000 \text{ porch swings} \times 5 \text{ hours per swing}\\ &= 100{,}000 \text{ labor hours}\end{aligned}$$

$$\frac{\text{Total estimated MOH}}{\text{Total estimated labor hours}} = \frac{\$300{,}000}{100{,}000 \text{ hours}} = \$3 \text{ per direct labor hour}$$

Selecting an Overhead Application Base

Logically, overhead should be assigned to products in proportion to the amount of overhead resources used in production. But how is this matching of costs accomplished when accounting for overhead? The selection of an appropriate application base is critical in developing good product costs. If only one type of product is manufactured, overhead could be assigned to products merely by dividing the total overhead cost by the number of units manufactured. Many companies, however, manufacture a variety of products, and the overhead costs incurred benefit all of them. If a company produces refrigerators and electric carving knives, a simple units of output measure would assign too little overhead to refrigerators and too much to electric carving knives. Logic tells us that overhead should be assigned to these products using some application base other than units produced. A common measure should be used that assigns the proper proportion of overhead costs to each product. For example, if 1 direct labor hour is required to make one electric carving knife and 10 hours are needed to make one refrigerator, using direct labor hours, overhead costs may be assigned to products in proportion to the amount of overhead resources used in production. Overhead costs may also be assigned on the basis of direct labor cost, machine hours, or other measures, discussed below.

Matching is the key to selecting the overhead application base

The most important principle in selecting the application base is the **matching principle.** The direct costs of production are relatively easy to match with products. It is just as desirable to match indirect costs with products to ensure the proper measurement of income and proper balance sheet valuations. The very fact that manufacturing overhead is an indirect cost causes some people to believe that the matching principle does not apply, but overhead costs are significant costs of production and should be matched with the revenue from the completed product just as direct costs are. The application of overhead is an attempt to match the indirect costs of manufacturing with the benefits derived from those costs. The benefits are, of course, the revenue from the sale of manufactured products whose completion is made possible, in part, by the indirect costs of production.

In addition to satisfying the matching principle, the application base should be easy to use and to understand and should provide timely product cost information. Following are some of the more common overhead application bases.

Direct labor hours is easy to understand and use

Direct labor hours (DLH). Direct labor hours is a popular application base that is easy to understand and apply. Often it does a good job of matching overhead costs with products and it is used as an application base by a large number of manufacturing firms. Direct labor hours and direct labor cost application bases are popular in production situations in which there is a close tie between the amount of manufacturing overhead costs incurred and the amount of labor used. Many overhead costs, such as labor fringe benefits, are related directly to the quantity of labor used in production. Others, such as machinery operating costs and machine maintenance costs for equipment operated by direct labor, are related to some degree to the quantity of labor time. To illustrate the computation of a direct labor hours application base, we assume that the estimated manufacturing overhead costs for the year are \$260,000 and the estimated number of direct labor hours for the year are 40,000. The calculation of the overhead rate is

$$\frac{\text{Total budgeted MOH}}{\text{Total budgeted direct labor hours}} = \frac{\$260{,}000}{40{,}000\ \text{DLH}}$$

$$= \$6.50 \text{ per direct labor hour}$$

Using this overhead rate, $6.50 of overhead cost is added to the cost of production for every direct labor hour charged to production. Notice the use of budgeted MOH instead of estimated MOH in the above equation. Both terms mean the same thing and are used to refer to expected cost and expected volume of activity.

Direct labor cost (DLC). **Direct labor cost** is an application base similar to direct labor hours. Often this application base satisfies the criteria of matching, ease of understanding, and ease of application. Typically, the choice between a labor hours base and a labor cost base is made on convenience considerations rather than on theoretical grounds. Using the same example of $260,000 for budgeted MOH and a budget of $200,000 for direct labor cost, the calculation of the overhead rate is

$$\frac{\text{Total budgeted MOH}}{\text{Budgeted direct labor cost}} = \frac{\$260{,}000}{\$200{,}000}$$

$$= 1.3, \text{ or } 130\% \text{ of direct labor cost}$$

With the above overhead application base, $1.30 of manufacturing overhead cost is added to production for every dollar of direct labor cost assigned to production.

Units of production. In some production situations an overhead rate based on the **units of production method** may do a good job of matching overhead costs with products. With this method each unit of product is assigned the same amount of manufacturing overhead cost. This base should be used only if production consists of a single product or a relatively homogeneous set of products. For example, if a manufacturer builds 40-foot fiberglass boat hulls, all of which are similar, and this is the company's only product, an overhead rate based on units of production may provide very accurate product costs. On the other hand, if the company produces boats ranging in size from 12-foot prams to 50-foot cruisers, a rate based on units of production would assign a disproportionate amount of overhead to the small boats. The large boats use significantly more manufacturing overhead resources; therefore more costs should be assigned to them. To illustrate a units of production base, we assume estimated production of 10,000 units of homogeneous product. The overhead rate is calculated as follows:

$$\frac{\text{Estimated MOH}}{\text{Estimated units of production}} = \frac{\$260{,}000}{10{,}000 \text{ units}} = \$26 \text{ per unit}$$

Machine hours (MH). An overhead rate based on machine hours can be used when production is performed primarily on machines or when machine-related costs make up a large portion of overhead costs. This application base requires gathering machine use data. In some cases the collection of such data may be automated. The additional cost of data collection is warranted if the result is an overhead rate that does a good job of matching. With an estimated 25,000 machine hours budgeted for the period, the calculation of the overhead rate is

$$\frac{\text{Estimated MOH}}{\text{Estimated machine hours}} = \frac{\$260{,}000}{25{,}000 \text{ MH}} = \$10.40 \text{ per machine hour}$$

This overhead rate requires that for every hour of machine time used on a product, $10.40 is added to its cost for overhead.

Materials cost. Sometimes manufacturing overhead costs are related closely to direct materials costs. In that case, a rate calculated on the basis of direct materials may be warranted. The rate is usually expressed as a percentage of direct materials cost. Relatively few situations lend themselves to a direct materials application base compared to the other bases discussed. An example is a drug manufacturing process requiring many specialized materials that result in high materials handling and storage costs. In some situations a direct materials base can yield a manufacturing overhead rate that accurately matches overhead costs with products. If the direct materials cost is estimated at $160,000, the manufacturing overhead rate is

$$\frac{\text{Estimated MOH}}{\text{Estimated direct materials cost}} = \frac{\$260{,}000}{\$160{,}000}$$

$$= 1.625, \text{ or } 162.5\% \text{ of direct materials cost}$$

For every dollar of direct materials assigned to production, $1.625 of overhead is added to the cost of production.

Applying Overhead

Overhead is applied to production using the predetermined overhead rate and the actual volume of activity

The manufacturing overhead rate is determined before the accounting period begins using estimated overhead costs and an estimated volume of activity. Once the accounting period begins, manufacturing overhead is applied to products by multiplying the **overhead rate** times the **actual volume of production.** For example, a firm with an overhead rate of 150 percent of direct labor cost charged $60 of direct labor cost to a product. The amount of overhead assigned to the product is $90, computed as $60 × 1.50. The predetermined overhead rate is 150 percent of direct labor cost, and the measure of actual production is $60 of direct labor cost. The entry to apply overhead is

	Work in process control	90	
	Manufacturing overhead applied		90
	Applied overhead to production.		

Departmental Overhead Rates

Departmental overhead rates may provide more accurate product costs

In some production situations one overhead rate for an entire manufacturing plant may do a satisfactory job of matching overhead costs with all products that are manufactured. In some cases, however, a single rate may apply too much overhead to some products and not enough to others. For instance, machining and metal fabricating departments require expensive production machinery with large utility, maintenance, and insurance costs, whereas assembly and finishing departments, which may be labor-intensive, require relatively inexpensive production facilities. If a single overhead rate is used, products made primarily in the machining and metal fabricating departments will not be charged enough for manufacturing overhead costs and those products made primarily in the assembly and finishing departments will be charged too much for manufacturing overhead costs. To avoid this problem, managers may create more than one overhead rate for a manufacturing plant, with each rate designed to assign overhead costs to products accurately.

Separate overhead rates may be developed for each department or production activity, or for groups of departments that have similar overhead cost characteristics. For example, all machining production activities might have one overhead rate, all assembly activities another rate, and finishing yet another rate. The number of separate manufacturing overhead rates is limited only by management's information needs and the cost of creating and using separate rates.

Products are manufactured in producing departments

Service departments support production

Producing departments and service departments. Most departments in a manufacturing plant are directly involved in the production of the firm's products and are classified as **producing departments.** Typical production activities include metal fabrication, machining, drilling, assembly, and painting. Some departments do not make products but provide services that are essential for the production activities. These **service departments** include maintenance, toolroom, inventory storeroom, and first aid. Service departments make production possible or more efficient; therefore their costs are part of the total cost of the product.

Using departmental overhead rates. The development and use of departmental overhead rates is similar to that of a single comprehensive overhead rate. The following steps are required:

1. The overhead rate is determined for each department before the accounting period starts.
2. Overhead is applied to production during the accounting period using departmental overhead rates.
3. Actual overhead costs are accumulated for each department during the accounting period.
4. At the end of the period, underapplied and overapplied overhead are computed for each department as well as in total.

To create **departmental overhead rates,** the budgeted overhead cost for each department is divided by the budgeted volume of activity in that department. Some overhead costs, such as depreciation or lease cost on machinery in a particular department, are easily identifiable as overhead costs of that department. Other overhead costs are not so readily identifiable with individual departments. For example, the salary of the production plant manager is common to all of the departments in the manufacturing plant. Similarly utilities, insurance, property taxes, and plant depreciation costs are common to the various departments. These common overhead costs must be allocated to the various departments to compute a manufacturing overhead rate for each department.

Budgeted data are used to calculate the overhead rates

Before the accounting period starts, **estimates** are made for factory utilities, plant depreciation, property taxes, and all other manufacturing overhead costs. Overhead costs that are clearly identifiable with specific manufacturing departments are assigned directly to those departments. All other estimated overhead costs are allocated to departments in a systematic manner so that total departmental overhead cost can be used to compute overhead. When the accounting period is over, **actual** manufacturing overhead costs are assigned to departments in the same manner used to assign estimated overhead costs.

Cost allocations to departments should reflect a causal relationship between the department and the cost. For example, factory heating costs often are closely related to the volume of space heated. Therefore, factory heating costs may be allocated based on the square footage of floor space in each department. The cost of the plant's first aid department may be allocated to departments in proportion to the number of employees in each department. Fire insurance premiums may be allocated to departments in proportion to the value of the insured assets in each department. Square feet, number of employees, investment value, and other variables used to allocate costs to departments are called **allocation bases.** Allocation bases are used both to allocate budgeted costs and to assign actual costs to departments. Be careful to distinguish between allocation bases and application bases. The former are used to allocate actual or budgeted costs to departments or other cost objectives, whereas the latter are used to apply overhead costs to products.

DEPARTMENTAL OVERHEAD RATES ILLUSTRATED

To help you understand how departmental overhead rates are determined and used, we present an example using the Winthrop Manufacturing Company. The company has two service departments—maintenance and inventory storeroom—and three producing departments—metal fabricating, assembly, and finishing. In this example:

1. Budgeted manufacturing overhead is allocated to the departments, and departmental overhead rates are computed.

2. Predetermined overhead rates and actual measures of production activity are used to determine the amount of applied overhead.
3. Underapplied or overapplied overhead is calculated for each department at the end of the accounting period.

In this example there are nine overhead costs, each of which must be assigned to the five departments. The total budgeted manufacturing overhead costs for the period and the allocation bases to be used are presented in Figure 4-1.

Figure 4-1 Manufacturing overhead costs must be allocated to the individual factory departments to determine budgeted departmental overhead. The allocations should be made using allocation bases that best satisfy the matching principle.

Winthrop Manufacturing Company
Budgeted Manufacturing Overhead Costs
For the Year Ending December 31, 1986

Cost Item	Amount	Allocation Base
Indirect materials	$ 20,000	Past utilization ratios
Indirect labor	40,000	Past utilization ratios
Fuel oil (heating)	10,000	Square footage of floor area
Electricity	20,000	Square footage of floor area
Payroll fringe benefits	100,000	Number of employees
Fire insurance	4,000	Value of the investment
Property taxes	12,000	Value of the investment
Plant depreciation	40,000	Square footage of floor area
Machine depreciation	54,000	Specific identification
Total	$300,000	

Setting Departmental Overhead Rates

The first step in creating the departmental manufacturing overhead rates is to assign all of the estimated overhead costs to departments. One cost category, machine depreciation, can be identified directly with each department. All other overhead costs in this example are allocated to the departments using the allocation bases in Figure 4-1. The estimated amounts for each allocation base, shown in Figure 4-2, are used as the base for allocating budgeted overhead costs to departments. To obtain these allocation bases, managers estimate the number of employees in each department for the coming year, the number of square feet of floor space in each department, and so on. The budgeted data in Figure 4-1 and the budgeted amounts for each allocation base in Figure 4-2 are used to determine the budgeted overhead cost in each department.

Allocating budgeted overhead. The budgeted overhead costs in Figure 4-1 and the estimated allocation bases in Figure 4-2 are used to prepare the departmental cost allocations in Figure 4-3.

Each cost in Figure 4-1 is allocated first to the five departments in the manufacturing plant (two service departments and the three producing

Winthrop Manufacturing Company
Budgeted Activity Levels and Allocation Bases
For the Year Ending December 31, 1986

	Service Departments		Producing Departments			
Allocation Base	**Mainten-ance**	**Inventory Storeroom**	**Metal Fabricating**	**Assembly**	**Finishing**	**Total**
Past indirect materials use	30%	5%	20%	30%	15%	100%
Past indirect labor use	5%	7.5%	37.5%	37.5%	12.5%	100%
Square footage of floor area	1,000	2,000	8,000	5,000	4,000	20,000
Number of employees	6	4	15	15	10	50
Value of the investment	$100,000	$150,000	$500,000	$100,000	$150,000	$1,000,000
Maintenance hours	—	—	6,000	2,000	2,000	10,000
Materials requisitions	—	—	400	400	200	1,000
Machine hours			20,000			
Direct labor hours				25,000		
Direct labor cost					$100,000	

Figure 4-2 Once allocation bases have been selected, the activity level must be estimated for each allocation base. Each item of data in this schedule is an estimate of a future level of activity or a future value.

Budgeted overhead costs are allocated to both service and producing departments

departments). The first two costs, indirect materials and indirect labor, are allocated on the basis of past use of the resource as obtained from historical data. For example, the quantity of indirect materials used last year might be the basis for the allocation, or the average quantity used in the past several years might be computed. Historical data are useful in forecasting only if the current situation is similar to those in which the data originated. If necessary, past data should be modified to reflect any expected changes in the production environment.

In this example the proportion of indirect materials and indirect labor used by each department is expressed as a percentage. The allocation of the $20,000 of budgeted indirect materials cost is shown below.

Department	Budgeted Indirect Materials Cost (See Figure 4-1)	×	Department Allocation (See Figure 4-2)	=	Allocated Departmental Cost for Indirect Materials (See Figure 4-3)
Maintenance	$20,000		30%		$ 6,000
Inventory storeroom	20,000		5		1,000
Metal fabricating	20,000		20		4,000
Assembly	20,000		30		6,000
Finishing	20,000		15		3,000
Total			100%		$20,000

Winthrop Manufacturing Company
Schedule of Budgeted Overhead Costs
For the Year Ending December 31, 1986

Cost Item	Amount from Figure 4-1	Service Departments: Maintenance	Service Departments: Inventory Storeroom	Producing Departments: Metal Fabricating	Producing Departments: Assembly	Producing Departments: Finishing
Indirect materials	$ 20,000	$ 6,000	$ 1,000	$ 4,000	$ 6,000	$ 3,000
Indirect labor	40,000	2,000	3,000	15,000	15,000	5,000
Fuel oil	10,000	500	1,000	4,000	2,500	2,000
Electricity	20,000	1,000	2,000	8,000	5,000	4,000
Payroll fringe benefits	100,000	12,000	8,000	30,000	30,000	20,000
Fire insurance	4,000	400	600	2,000	400	600
Property taxes	12,000	1,200	1,800	6,000	1,200	1,800
Plant depreciation	40,000	2,000	4,000	16,000	10,000	8,000
Machine depreciation	54,000	4,900	3,600	27,000	13,900	4,600
Total	$300,000			112,000	84,000	49,000
Maintenance department cost allocation to producing departments based on estimated maintenance hours		$30,000		18,000	6,000	6,000
Inventory storeroom cost allocations to producing departments based on estimated materials requisitions			$25,000	10,000	10,000	5,000
Total estimated departmental overhead				$140,000	$100,000	$ 60,000
divided by estimated activity level				20,000 MH	25,000 DLH	$100,000
Budgeted overhead rate				$7/machine hour	$4/direct labor hour	60% of direct labor cost

Figure 4-3 Using the budgeted overhead costs in Figure 4-1 and the budgeted allocation bases in Figure 4-2, budgeted overhead costs are computed for each service department and each producing department. Next, service department costs are allocated to the producing departments to arrive at the budgeted departmental overhead costs. Finally, the budgeted overhead costs are divided by the budgeted activity levels to find the overhead rates.

The indirect materials cost allocated to each department is shown in the right column at the bottom of page 131 and is entered on the first line of Winthrop's schedule of budgeted overhead costs in Figure 4-3. Indirect labor is allocated in a similar manner using the percentage of past indirect labor used by each department.

The cost of fuel oil used for heating is allocated on the basis of budgeted square feet of floor space for each department. In this case no convenient ratio is available as with indirect materials and indirect labor. However, the budgeted data for departmental square footage are readily available, and the allocation ratios are easily computed. Figure 4-2 shows that the plant has a total of 20,000 square feet for all departments. The allocation ratio is found by dividing each department's estimated area by the total number of square feet.

Department	Ratio	Department Allocation
Maintenance	1,000/20,000	5%
Inventory storeroom	2,000/20,000	10
Metal fabricating	8,000/20,000	40
Assembly	5,000/20,000	25
Finishing	4,000/20,000	20
Total		100%

Note that all allocation percentages sum to 100 percent. Once we have these percentages, we proceed as we did with indirect materials and indirect labor. The fuel oil allocations are shown on the schedule of budgeted overhead costs in Figure 4-3.

Square footage is also the allocation base for electricity and plant depreciation. The square footage ratios just calculated are therefore used to allocate budgeted costs for electricity and plant depreciation by multiplying each cost by the square footage percentage.

Payroll fringe benefits constitute a large overhead item for Winthrop. An allocation based on the number of employees in each department is logical. The allocation percentages are again computed from the data in Figure 4-2. When the total of 50 employees is divided into each department's budgeted number of employees, the departmental allocation percentages are 12, 8, 30, 30, and 20 percent, respectively, for the five departments. Using these percentages, you should calculate the allocation of budgeted payroll fringe benefit costs and compare them with the results in Figure 4-3.

Fire insurance and property taxes are closely related to the investment value of the insured and taxed tangible assets. Consequently, the estimated value of the investment in each department is used to allocate these two costs. You should compute the allocation ratios for value of the investment and calculate the allocation for fire insurance and property taxes so that you can compare your answers with the amounts in Figure 4-3.

The last cost is machine depreciation. Most machinery is identifiable with specific departments, so depreciation can be assigned to the department where each asset resides. Depreciation data are found in fixed asset records. In our example they are given, so there is no way for you to verify the amounts.

The sum of each department's column in Figure 4-3 is the amount of overhead allocated to each department. At this point, however, we are not yet ready to compute the overhead rates. The service departments perform no direct production functions, but we need a way to charge their overhead costs to products. Therefore, all service department costs must now be allocated to the three producing departments.

Service department costs are allocated to the producing departments

Allocating service department costs. Service department costs are allocated to producing departments in much the same way that manufacturing overhead costs are allocated to all five departments. As always the allocations should be strongly influenced by the matching principle. Winthrop Manufacturing Company uses maintenance hours as its measure of the amount of maintenance service performed for each department. Similarly, the number of materials requisitions filled for each department is used to measure inventory storeroom services. These two allocation bases are used to distribute maintenance department costs and inventory storeroom costs to producing departments.

The allocation process used in this example is called **direct allocation,** meaning that service department costs are allocated directly to producing departments. No service department costs are allocated to other service departments, even though the maintenance department may perform some work for the inventory storeroom, and the inventory storeroom may fill materials requisitions for the maintenance department. When interservice department activities are significant, some cost distortions can occur with direct allocation. Accountants try to minimize such distortions by using **reciprocal allocation,** which is a more complicated approach requiring the use of linear algebra and yielding more accurate results. Although we use only direct allocation in this text, you should be aware that other techniques may be used in practice.

Computing the Overhead Rate

Figure 4-3 shows how service department costs are allocated to the producing departments and added to arrive at total budgeted overhead costs for each production department. Each department's total budgeted overhead cost is divided by its budgeted activity level to determine the departmental overhead rates. For example, in the metal fabricating department the total budgeted overhead cost of $140,000 is divided by the budgeted application base of 20,000 machine hours, yielding an overhead rate of $7 per machine hour. Similarly, for the assembly department, budgeted direct labor hours are divided into budgeted overhead costs to find the overhead rate of $4 per direct labor hour. Finally, the finishing department's manufacturing overhead rate is found by dividing budgeted overhead costs for the department by budgeted direct labor cost for the department, yielding a rate of 60 percent of direct labor cost.

You may have noticed that in this example each of the departments uses a different type of application base for assigning overhead cost to production. This is done to illustrate the use of three different application bases. A firm can use a single type of application base, such as direct labor hours, and still have separate departmental overhead rates.

Using Departmental Overhead Rates

Overhead is applied to production in each department using departmental overhead rates

Departmental overhead rates are determined before the accounting period begins. Once the accounting year starts, these rates are used to apply overhead to production. For every machine hour logged in the metal fabricating department, $7 of manufacturing overhead cost is assigned to production, and for every direct labor hour worked in the assembly department, $4 of manufacturing overhead cost is assigned to production. For every dollar of direct labor cost charged to production in the finishing department, $.60 of manufacturing overhead cost is charged to production.

Each time overhead is applied to production, the Work in Process Control account is debited and the Manufacturing Overhead Applied account is credited for the amount of manufacturing overhead charged to production. With departmental rates, there is a Manufacturing Overhead Applied account for each department. For example, during 1 day of production at Winthrop Manufacturing Company, 100 machine hours are worked in the metal fabricating department, 120 hours of direct labor are worked in the assembly department, and $500 of direct labor cost are incurred in finishing. The journal entries to record overhead applied for the day in each department are

	Work in process control, metal	700	
	fabricating		
	MOH applied, metal fabricating		700
	Applied overhead in metal fabricating,		
	100 × $7 = $700.		
	Work in process control, assembly	480	
	MOH applied, assembly		480
	Applied overhead in assembly,		
	120 × $4 = $480.		
	Work in process control, finishing	300	
	MOH applied, finishing		300
	Applied overhead in finishing,		
	$500 × .60 = $300.		

Measuring Actual Departmental Overhead Costs

Accounting for manufacturing overhead requires two distinct functions; one is the assignment of manufacturing overhead costs to products and the other is the accumulation of actual overhead costs as they are incurred. You just saw how departmental overhead rates are computed and applied. Now we turn to the measurement of actual manufacturing overhead costs for each department. These actual overhead costs can be compared with the applied overhead to determine the amount of underapplied or overapplied overhead in each department.

Actual departmental overhead costs are determined similarly to budgeted overhead except that actual data are used

The process of assigning actual overhead costs to departments is much like that of assigning budgeted overhead costs. The primary difference is that now we use actual data rather than estimated data. Costs such as machine depreciation or repair of machinery may be identified with and assigned to specific departments. All common overhead costs, on the other hand, cannot be identified with specific departments and must be allocated to the departments. The manufacturing overhead costs that are either assigned or allocated to departments are the **actual** costs that have been incurred. Also, the amounts used as allocation bases to assign costs to departments are actual measures. For example, management can actually measure the amount of square feet that each department has and count the number of employees in each department.

To illustrate the process of determining actual overhead costs for departments, we present actual overhead costs in Figure 4-4 and actual allocation base amounts in Figure 4-5. The data presented in Figures 4-1 and 4-2 and the data presented in Figures 4-4 and 4-5 are similar except that the former are budgeted data and the latter are actual data.

The schedule showing the allocation of actual overhead costs to departments is presented in Figure 4-6. You may want to compute the cost allocations for several of the cost items to verify your understanding of cost allocation procedures. The actual service department costs are allocated to the three producing departments in the same manner as budgeted data so that all actual overhead costs are assigned to the producing departments.

Winthrop Manufacturing Company
Actual Manufacturing Overhead Costs
For the Year Ending December 31, 1986

Cost Item	Amount	Allocation Base
Indirect materials	$ 25,000	Actual materials requisitions
Indirect labor	40,000	Actual payroll reports
Fuel oil	16,000	Square footage of floor area
Electricity	24,000	Square footage of floor area
Payroll fringe benefits	120,000	Number of employees
Fire insurance	4,000	Value of the investment
Property taxes	16,000	Value of the investment
Plant depreciation	40,000	Square footage of floor area
Machine depreciation	55,000	Specific identification
Total	$340,000	

Figure 4-4
This figure is identical to Figure 4-1 except that actual rather than budgeted overhead costs are presented here.

Winthrop Manufacturing Company
Actual Activity Levels and Allocation Bases
For the Year Ending December 31, 1986

Allocation Base	Service Departments: Maintenance	Service Departments: Inventory Storeroom	Producing Departments: Metal Fabricating	Producing Departments: Assembly	Producing Departments: Finishing
Indirect materials use	28.40%	3.60%	20.00%	32.00%	16.00%
Indirect labor use	5.00%	3.75%	35.00%	40.25%	16.00%
Square footage of floor area	1,000	2,000	8,000	5,000	4,000
Number of employees	6	6	20	18	10
Value of the investment	$100,000	$150,000	$500,000	$100,000	$150,000
Maintenance hours			7,000	2,000	1,000
Materials requisitions			600	400	200
Machine hours			24,500		
Direct labor hours				26,000	
Direct labor cost					$102,000

Figure 4-5 **This schedule contains actual measures of activity levels for the allocation bases.**

Winthrop Manufacturing Company
Schedule of Actual Overhead Costs
For the Year Ending December 31, 1986

Cost Item	Amount from Figure 4-4	Service Departments: Maintenance	Service Departments: Inventory Storeroom	Producing Departments: Metal Fabricating	Producing Departments: Assembly	Producing Departments: Finishing
Indirect materials	$ 25,000	$ 7,100	$ 900	$ 5,000	$ 8,000	$ 4,000
Indirect labor	40,000	2,000	1,500	14,000	16,100	6,400
Fuel oil	16,000	800	1,600	6,400	4,000	3,200
Electricity	24,000	1,200	2,400	9,600	6,000	4,800
Payroll fringe benefits	120,000	12,000	12,000	40,000	36,000	20,000
Fire insurance	4,000	400	600	2,000	400	600
Property taxes	16,000	1,600	2,400	8,000	1,600	2,400
Plant depreciation	40,000	2,000	4,000	16,000	10,000	8,000
Machine depreciation	55,000	4,900	4,600	27,000	13,900	4,600
Total	$340,000			128,000	96,000	54,000
Maintenance department cost allocations to producing departments based on **actual** maintenance hours		$32,000		22,400	6,400	3,200
Inventory storeroom cost allocations to producing departments based on **actual** material requisitions			$30,000	15,000	10,000	5,000
Total **actual** departmental overhead				$165,400	$112,400	$62,200

Figure 4-6 **Actual departmental overhead costs are determined following the same procedures used to find budgeted departmental overhead. The only difference is that this figure contains actual data, whereas Figure 4-3 shows budgeted data.**

Total Applied Overhead

Earlier we illustrated journal entries for applying overhead to production in each of Winthrop's three producing departments. Such journal entries are made on a timely basis throughout the accounting period. The credits to the manufacturing overhead applied accounts for each department accumulate throughout the year, and at year-end the amount of overhead applied in each department can be read from the ledger account balances for each department.

In the Winthrop example, the total applied manufacturing overhead in each department is summarized for the entire year in Figure 4-7. In each department, the amount of applied overhead is equal to the departmental overhead rate times the actual activity level for the period, as measured by the application base in the department. For example, the metal fabricating department used 24,500 actual machine hours (Figure 4-5), and the overhead rate is $7 per machine hour, as calculated in Figure 4-3. Multiplying the actual machine hours used by the $7 rate results in $171,500 of overhead applied to production in the metal fabricating department during the accounting period. Applied overhead costs in assembly and finishing are computed in a similar way, as shown in Figure 4-7.

Underapplied and Overapplied Overhead

At the end of the accounting period, the actual overhead in **each** department is compared with the applied overhead in **each** department to determine underapplied overhead or overapplied overhead.

Comparing actual and applied overhead. It is a simple process to compare **actual** overhead in Figure 4-6 with **applied** overhead computed in Figure 4-7 to find underapplied or overapplied overhead for each department. In

Winthrop Manufacturing Company
Schedule of Underapplied and Overapplied Overhead
December 31, 1986

Department	Overhead Rate	×	Actual Activity Level	=	Applied Manufacturing Overhead	−	Actual Manufacturing Overhead from Figure 4-6	=	Underapplied (Overapplied) Overhead
Metal fabricating	$7/MH		24,500 MH		$171,500		$165,400		$(6,100)
Assembly	$4/DLH		26,000 DLH		104,000		112,400		8,400
Finishing	60% of DLC		$102,000 DLC		61,200		62,200		1,000
Total					$336,700		$340,000		$3,300

Figure 4-7 **In each department, applied overhead is equal to the overhead rate times the actual level of activity for the overhead application base. Underapplied or overapplied overhead is the difference between the actual overhead and the applied overhead in each department.**

the metal fabricating department the actual amount of overhead cost incurred is $165,400, and the amount applied is $171,500. The difference of $6,100 is the amount of **overapplied** overhead in the department, which in this case means that the amount of overhead applied to products in the metal fabricating department was larger than the amount of manufacturing overhead cost actually incurred in the department. Applied overhead was 3.7 percent ($6,100/$165,400) more than the actual overhead cost in metal fabricating. In effect the actual cost of the products made in the department is somewhat lower than the cost recorded in the accounts. The final column of Figure 4-7 indicates the underapplied or overapplied overhead in each department and in total. Notice that the manufacturing overhead is **underapplied** in the other two departments, which means that the amount of overhead applied to products was less than the amount of manufacturing overhead cost actually incurred in the department. Underapplied overhead is unfavorable because a department actually incurred more overhead cost than was applied to products. Overapplied overhead is favorable because a department incurred less actual overhead than was applied.

The difference between applied overhead and actual overhead is underapplied or overapplied overhead

Adding the departmental underapplied and overapplied overhead, we find net underapplied overhead of $3,300. With actual overhead of $340,000, the amount is underapplied by only about 1 percent of actual overhead cost. Typically, a 1 percent variance is considered small, but in our example the individual departmental fluctuations are much greater. Metal fabricating is 3.7 percent overapplied, and assembly is 7.5 percent underapplied. Large underapplied and overapplied overhead may be netted out when only one total overhead figure is calculated. But when departmental overhead variances are available, managers can investigate the reasons for any discrepancy between applied and actual overhead and can deal with any problems disclosed. One reason for the difference may be the use of inappropriate budgeted overhead rates.

JOINT PRODUCTS AND BY-PRODUCTS

Common examples of joint products and by-products

In some cases it is not possible to produce a single product without obtaining other products. For example, in the wood products industry it is not possible to produce plywood without producing sawdust. At one time sawdust was burned as a waste product, but now it is pressed into particle board and sold. Similarly, in the food industry a beef carcass provides hide and internal organs in addition to the main cuts of meat. Crude oil is processed into gasoline, kerosene, fuel oil, and other oil products. When more than one product results from the production process, the products are either joint products or by-products.

The distinction between joint products and by-products is not always clear, but it is usually made on the basis of relative economic value. Joint products have relatively large economic value and are the main products in the production process. By-products have relatively small economic value and are less significant in comparison with the value of the main products. In some cases the distinction is difficult. A general rule, but one that cannot be applied in every situation, is

> If the value of the product is so small that it has no effect on the decision to produce or not to produce the entire product group, it is a **by-product;** if it does affect the decision to produce, it is a **joint product.**

For example, the sawdust produced in the sawing of logs would probably be considered a by-product and the lumber a main product. Gasoline, kerosene, and fuel oil are normally viewed as joint products. Because joint products are significantly more important than by-products, and affect many more decisions, we limit our discussion in this chapter to joint products.

The point in the production process where individual products are identifiable is called the split-off point

Common costs occur with joint products because some of the manufacturing costs occur prior to the time that the products can be identified individually. The **split-off point** is the point in the production process where products separate. Individual products become identifiable at the split-off point, and their production costs can be measured separately. Prior to the split-off point, all production costs are common to all of the joint products. These common costs are called **joint costs.**

Figure 4-8 illustrates the production flows for a company producing three joint products and a by-product. In the first two processes, blending and settling, the products are indistinguishable. Therefore, all production costs in the two process centers are joint costs because they are common to all three joint products. At the end of production in the second process center, the three joint products split off, or separate. All costs incurred after the split-off point are identifiable with each individual product. Product A goes right from split-off to finished goods inventory. Product B goes to a curing process after split-off and then to finished goods. Product C requires two additional processes before reaching finished goods, and the manufacturing process results in a by-product.

The total cost of joint products includes both joint costs and **costs after split-off,** which are the usual product costs discussed in Chapters 2 and 3. The manufacturing costs incurred after split-off can be identified with the individual products. Joint costs, however, cannot be identified with each product and therefore must be allocated to joint products to determine the manufacturing cost of each joint product. In our example, the cost of the by-product may be minor and is therefore not separated from the cost of product C. If the by-product cost is significant, it might be treated as another joint product with its separate cost.

Joint costs are allocated to products

The inability to identify joint costs with specific joint products does not reduce the importance of the costs. However, accounting for joint production entails the additional step of allocating joint costs in order to measure product costs. The resulting product costs require careful interpretation. Because the full cost of products is required for many accounting purposes, such as external reporting, some method of allocating joint costs is necessary.

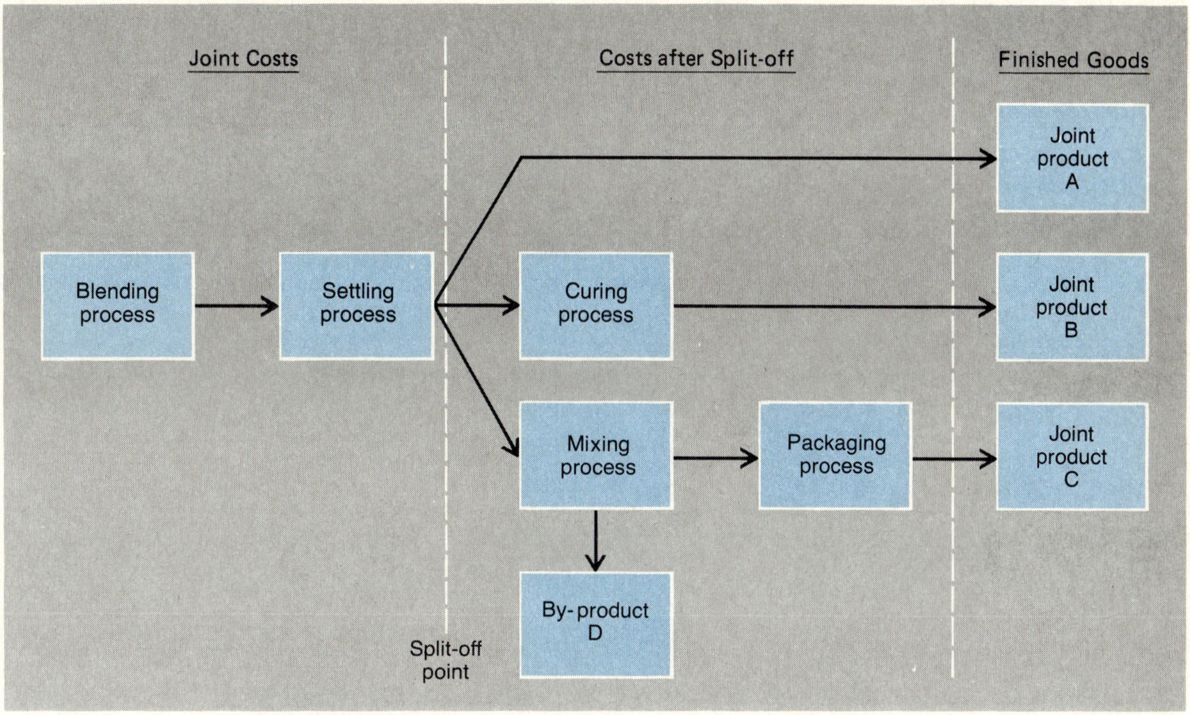

Figure 4-8 **The split-off point is critical in joint product costing because all production costs incurred before the split-off point are indistinguishable between products.**

Joint Product Cost Allocation

Although the allocation of joint costs to individual products should satisfy the matching principle, the association between joint product costs and specific product revenues is not clear. A good match between product revenue and product cost is not always possible, and joint cost allocation procedures vary widely. In this chapter we present four joint cost allocation methods and examine their effects on product costs.

JOINT PRODUCT ILLUSTRATION

Greengrow Company manufactures three types of fertilizers in a joint production process. The production and sales data for August, tabulated in Figure 4-9, are used to determine product costs. Product costing for joint products is divided into two steps:

1. Identify the costs of each product after split-off.
2. Allocate the joint costs of production to the products.

We are primarily concerned with step 2 in this example.

Greengrow Company
Schedule of Production and Sales Data
For the Month of August

Item	Grow	Grow-U	Grow-U-Plus	Total
Produced	60,000 bags	30,000 bags	10,000 bags	100,000 bags
Sold	60,000 bags	30,000 bags	10,000 bags	100,000 bags
Sales price	$4 per bag	$8 per bag	$12 per bag	
Cost after split-off	$60,000	$120,000	$30,000	$210,000

Joint cost = $240,000

Figure 4-9 **Three products are manufactured in this joint production process. Over half of the total manufacturing cost is joint cost that must be allocated to the three products to get a full cost for the products.**

Physical Units Allocation Method

The physical units joint cost allocation method is easy to understand and use

A common and easy-to-use joint allocation approach is the **physical units allocation method,** sometimes called the **units of output method.** In this example a bag of fertilizer is the output unit. The $240,000 of joint cost is allocated to the three products in proportion to the number of bags of each type of fertilizer produced. With total production of 100,000 bags, the joint cost is allocated according to the following computations.

Grow: $\frac{60{,}000 \text{ bags}}{100{,}000 \text{ bags}} \times \$240{,}000 = \$144{,}000$

Grow-U: $\frac{30{,}000 \text{ bags}}{100{,}000 \text{ bags}} \times \$240{,}000 = \$\ 72{,}000$

Grow-U-Plus: $\frac{10{,}000 \text{ bags}}{100{,}000 \text{ bags}} \times \$240{,}000 = \$\ 24{,}000$

An alternative way of computing the joint cost allocations with the physical units method is to divide the $240,000 joint cost by the 100,000 total units of output to find the joint cost of $2.40 per unit. This unit cost is multiplied by the number of units of each product to obtain the total joint cost allocation for each product.

The costs after split-off also are assigned to the products, and the total product cost is found as illustrated in Figure 4-10. The distinction between joint cost and cost after split-off is important because joint cost is an allocated cost and is treated differently from cost after split-off in many management decisions. Such decisions are discussed in Chapter 6. Here we focus only on the allocation method. As shown in the figure, the **total** joint cost allocated to each product is different, but the joint cost **per unit** is $2.40 for each product. The total product costs are used for many external reporting purposes. However, one must interpret such costs cautiously.

Greengrow Company
Product Cost Schedule Using Physical Units Allocation Method
For the Month of August

	Joint Cost		Cost after Split-Off		Total Product Cost	
Product	**Total**	**Per Unit**	**Total**	**Per Unit**	**Total**	**Per Unit**
Grow	$144,000	$2.40	$ 60,000	$1.00	$204,000	$3.40
Grow-U	72,000	2.40	120,000	4.00	192,000	6.40
Grow-U-Plus	24,000	2.40	30,000	3.00	54,000	5.40
Total	$240,000		$210,000		$450,000	

Figure 4-10 The physical units allocation method is easy to understand and use. Each unit of product receives an identical amount of joint cost.

The physical units method of joint cost allocation is easy to use and understand, but it can yield questionable product costs if the sales values of the joint products or their costs after split-off are significantly different.

Sales Value Allocation Method

The sales value method incorporates the products' final market value in the allocation of joint costs

The **sales value method** allocates joint costs to products in proportion to the amount of sales revenue generated by each joint product. The sales revenue contributed by each of the joint products is found by multiplying the number of units of each joint product manufactured times its sales price. Using the data in Figure 4-9, the total sales value is computed as follows:

Product	Quantity Produced	Unit Price	Sales Value
Grow	60,000 bags	$ 4/bag	$240,000
Grow-U	30,000	8	240,000
Grow-U-Plus	10,000	12	120,000
Total sales value			$600,000

Joint costs are assigned to each product in proportion to its share of the total sales value. For example, $96,000 of joint cost is allocated to the product Grow. The amount is computed as ($240,000/$600,000 of total sales value) × $240,000 of joint cost. The $96,000 of allocated joint cost is divided by the 60,000 bags of output to find the joint cost of $1.60 per unit. The joint costs of the other two products are computed in the same manner and are reported in the product cost schedule in Figure 4-11.

Comparing the product cost schedule for the sales value method with the product cost schedule for the physical units method provides some

Greengrow Company
Product Cost Schedule Using Sales Value Allocation Method
For the Month of August

	Joint Cost		Cost after Split-Off		Total Product Cost	
Product	Total	Per Unit	Total	Per Unit	Total	Per Unit
Grow	$ 96,000	$1.60	$ 60,000	$1.00	$156,000	$2.60
Grow-U	96,000	3.20	120,000	4.00	216,000	7.20
Grow-U-Plus	48,000	4.80	30,000	3.00	78,000	7.80
Total	$240,000		$210,000		$450,000	

Figure 4-11 With the sales value method of joint cost allocation, the joint cost allocated to each product is different than with the physical units method but the costs after split-off are the same.

interesting information. The joint cost allocations are different, but the costs after split-off are the same. It is easy to forget that the costs after split-off do not change just because the method of allocating joint costs is different.

Combining the allocated joint costs with the costs after split-off yields the total product cost for each of the joint products. Each joint product has a different unit cost, depending on which method of joint cost allocation is used.

A logical question is, "Which of the two joint cost allocation methods is correct?" or better, "Which of the two methods is preferred for allocating joint costs?" Neither is clearly correct or incorrect. Which method is preferred depends on the given production situation, and on the reporting needs of management.

Net Realizable Value at Split-Off

Net realizable value at split-off is used to allocate joint costs

Another popular method of joint cost allocation is **net realizable value at the point of split-off,** sometimes shortened to the **net realizable value method.** With this method, each product is assigned joint costs in proportion to its net realizable value at the split-off point. **Net realizable value** is the sales value at split-off minus any selling and distribution costs. Many joint products have a ready market value at the split-off point, although the market value at split-off is less than the value if processed to completion. Note that net realizable value is merely used to allocate joint costs to products. There is no intent to sell the products at split-off; they still may be processed beyond the split-off point to completion.

If there is a readily determinable market value at split-off, the costs to market and distribute the product are estimated and subtracted from the market value to compute the net realizable value at split-off. The three products in our example are assumed to have net realizable values at split-off as follows:

Product	Net Realizable Value at Split-Off
Grow	$120,000
Grow-U	100,000
Grow-U-Plus	80,000
Total net realizable value at split-off point	$300,000

The net realizable value data are used to allocate joint costs to the joint products in proportion to their net realizable value at split-off as follows:

Product	Percentage of NRV at Split-Off	×	Total Joint Cost	=	Allocated Joint Cost
Grow	$120,000/$300,000		$240,000		$ 96,000
Grow-U	100,000/ 300,000		240,000		80,000
Grow-U-Plus	80,000/ 300,000		240,000		64,000
Total allocated joint cost					$240,000

The allocated joint costs are presented in the product cost schedule in Figure 4-12 for the net realizable value joint cost allocation method.

Greengrow Company
Product Cost Schedule Using Net Realizable Value at Split-Off
For the Month of August

	Joint Cost		Cost after Split-Off		Total Product Cost	
Product	**Total**	**Per Unit**	**Total**	**Per Unit**	**Total**	**Per Unit**
Grow	$ 96,000	$1.60	$ 60,000	$1.00	$156,000	$2.60
Grow-U	80,000	2.67	120,000	4.00	200,000	6.67
Grow-U-Plus	64,000	6.40	30,000	3.00	94,000	9.40
Total	$240,000		$210,000		$450,000	

Figure 4-12 **Net realizable value at split-off allocates joint costs based on the market value of the products before any value is added to the products by processing after the point of split-off.**

Gross Profit Allocation Method

The **gross profit allocation method,** sometimes called the **constant percentage method,** is used to allocate joint costs so that all products in the group of joint products have the same percentage of gross profit. For

Each product has the same percentage gross margin

example, if the entire group of joint products generates a 30 percent gross profit on sales, then each product is assigned a **total product cost** of 70 percent of its selling price. A product selling for $10 would have a total unit cost of $7 per unit, and a product with a price of $6 would have a total unit cost of $4.20. Each product has a gross profit of 30 percent; ($10 − $7)/$10 = 30 percent and ($6 − $4.20)/$6 = 30 percent.

The objective of the gross profit method is to assign joint costs to products so that each has the same percentage of gross profit. This is accomplished by determining the overall gross profit for the group of joint products and allocating joint costs so that the joint cost and the costs after split-off for each product yield an equal percentage of gross profit for all products in the joint product group. The gross profit approach rests on the assumption that the decision to produce the products was made for the entire product group and therefore all products in the group should have the same gross margin.

The first step in the process is to determine the gross profit of the group of joint products by estimating the sales revenue of the entire product group and deducting the total cost of the products. To illustrate, the total cost of Greengrow Company's August production is $450,000 ($240,000 joint cost and $210,000 cost after split-off). Total sales value is $600,000 as computed earlier with the sales value method.

The proportion of total product costs to total sales value is 75 percent ($450,000/$600,000), which means that gross margin from the entire group of products is 25 percent of sales. To assign the appropriate joint cost to each product, it is first necessary to decide what the product's total product cost should be to yield a gross margin of 25 percent. The cost after split-off is then deducted from the total cost to arrive at the amount of joint cost to be allocated to each product. The total cost of each product, based on the gross margin percentage, is calculated as follows:

Product	Sales Value		Ratio		Total Product Cost
Grow	$240,000	×	.75	=	$180,000
Grow-U	240,000	×	.75	=	180,000
Grow-U-Plus	120,000	×	.75	=	90,000
Total	$600,000	×	.75	=	$450,000

The total product cost includes both joint costs and costs after split-off. Since the cost after split-off is identified with each product, it is a simple process to allocate joint costs to each product. Either of the following basic relationships may be used:

$$\text{Allocated joint cost} + \text{Cost after split-off} = \text{Total cost}$$

or

$$\text{Allocated joint cost} = \text{Total cost} - \text{Cost after split-off}$$

Greengrow Company
Product Cost Schedule Using Gross Profit Allocation Method
For the Month of August

	Joint Cost		Cost after Split-Off		Total Product Cost	
Product	**Total**	**Per Unit**	**Total**	**Per Unit**	**Total**	**Per Unit**
Grow	$120,000	$2.00	$ 60,000	$1.00	$180,000	$3.00
Grow-U	60,000	2.00	120,000	4.00	180,000	6.00
Grow-U-Plus	60,000	6.00	30,000	3.00	90,000	9.00
Total	$240,000		$210,000		$450,000	

Figure 4-13 With the gross profit allocation method, joint costs are allocated in a way that yields identical percentage gross margins for each product. Here the gross margin is 25 percent of sales.

Total cost is shown above, and cost after split-off is given in Figure 4-9 on page 142. The amount of joint cost to be allocated to each product is

Product	Total Product Cost	−	Cost after Split-Off	=	Allocated Joint Cost
Grow	$180,000		$ 60,000		$120,000
Grow-U	180,000		120,000		60,000
Grow-U-Plus	90,000		30,000		60,000

The results of the above computations are summarized in a product cost schedule in Figure 4-13.

Compare the difference in product costs between the four joint cost allocation methods. Which of the product costs is correct? Depending on management's use of the product cost information, any of the costs can be correct. If some other method of joint cost allocation were used, it might yield still different product costs.[1] The allocation of joint costs to products makes total unit product costs difficult to evaluate and use in some types of management decisions. The greater the proportion of allocated joint costs to total production cost, the more caution managers must exercise when using total product cost figures. We elaborate on this issue in Chapter 6, where we discuss other aspects of joint product costs.

Joint Product Inventory Mix

In addition to the problem of allocating joint product costs, managers are also faced with the problem of managing joint product inventories. In many joint product manufacturing situations, the product mix cannot be changed

[1] Methods other than the four illustrated in this chapter are also used in practice.

significantly. The result is that some of the joint products may be selling well, while others are experiencing weak markets. For example, a petroleum company may experience a high demand for fuel oil and lower demand for gasoline during the winter months. In the summer the reverse may be true. To the extent possible, managers may try to change the production mix in order to obtain more of the product that is in demand.

If joint products sell in proportions different from the production proportion, inventory management can be a problem

Changing the production mix for joint products is not always possible, however, and when it is possible, it often is not economically feasible. For example, in spite of the strong market for chicken breasts and legs, it is impossible to increase the production of these two products without increasing the production of wings, backs, necks, hearts, and gizzards proportionately.

SUMMARY

Common costs are costs shared by more than one cost objective. Sometimes common costs are a large portion of total product cost and must be assigned to cost objectives in a logical manner. The assignment of common costs is called **cost allocation.** Allocations should reflect a meaningful causal relationship between the cost objective and the cost.

Manufacturing overhead is a major common cost. Typically overhead is applied using a **budgeted overhead rate,** also called a **predetermined overhead rate.** The overhead rate is obtained by dividing the **budgeted overhead cost** by the **budgeted volume of activity.** Many different activity levels can be used, including direct labor hours, direct labor cost, units of production, machine hours, and materials cost. The choice of an **application base** is influenced strongly by the matching principle.

Sometimes a single overhead rate for an entire plant does a poor job of assigning overhead cost to products. Therefore, **departmental overhead rates** may be used.

Departmental overhead rates are used to allocate overhead costs to departments. Any **service department** costs must be allocated to **producing departments. Direct allocation** of service department costs is not as accurate as **reciprocal allocation,** but it is simpler to perform. The departmental cost allocations must be done twice: once, before the accounting period starts, with **budgeted** data to set the departmental overhead rates, and again at the end of the accounting period with **actual** data to find actual departmental overhead costs. **Actual overhead** is compared with **applied overhead** to find **underapplied** and **overapplied overhead** for each department.

Joint products are indistinguishable in the production process until a point in the production process called the **split-off point.** Costs incurred prior to the split-off point are called **joint costs.** Beyond the split-off point they are called **costs after split-off.** Joint costs are common costs that must be allocated to the joint products. Costs after split-off can be identified with specific products. The method of joint product cost allocation can have a major influence on the final product costs. Joint cost allocation is accomplished using the **physical units allocation method,** also called the

units of output method; the **sales value method**; the **net present value method**; or the **gross profit method**, sometimes called the **constant percentage method.**

Total product costs resulting from different allocation methods should not be viewed as correct or incorrect because alternative joint cost allocation methods can yield strikingly different product costs.

Managers are concerned with joint product mix as well as product cost allocation. Changing the product mix is not always feasible or possible, even if some of the products are hard to sell.

KEY TERMS

actual overhead *(136)*
allocation base *(129)*
application base *(124)*
applied overhead *(138)*
budgeted activity level *(123)*
budgeted overhead cost *(123)*
budgeted overhead rate *(123)*
by-product *(121)*
common costs *(120)*
constant percentage method *(145)*
cost allocation *(120)*
costs after split-off *(140)*
departmental overhead rates *(129)*
direct allocation *(134)*
gross profit allocation method *(145)*
joint costs *(140)*
joint products *(121)*
net realizable value method *(144)*
net realizable value at the point of split-off *(144)*
overapplied overhead *(139)*
overhead rate *(123)*
physical units allocation method *(142)*
predetermined overhead rate *(123)*
producing departments *(128)*
reciprocal allocation *(134)*
sales value method *(143)*
service departments *(128)*
split-off point *(148)*
underapplied overhead *(139)*
units of output method *(142)*
units of production method *(126)*

QUESTIONS

1. What are common costs and why do they occur?
2. Give some examples of common costs.
3. Discuss the relationship between common costs, cost objectives, and cost allocation.
4. What is a predetermined manufacturing overhead rate and why is it used?
5. Name three overhead application bases and give an example of where each might be appropriate.
6. What factors should managers consider in selecting an overhead application base?
7. Why should managers consider using departmental overhead rates?
8. Distinguish between producing and service departments.
9. To what does the term *direct allocation* refer?
10. A manager in a company comments, "I understand these product cost figures, but I don't know what this $5,500 underapplied overhead figure means." As the controller, explain in understandable terms.

11. Distinguish between budgeted overhead, actual overhead, and applied overhead.
12. Describe joint products and joint costs.
13. Is there any reason to separate joint costs from costs after split-off in developing product costs? Explain.
14. What kind of inventory problem may arise from the production of joint products?
15. Is the gross profit method or the physical units method the correct way of allocating joint costs?

EXERCISES

Ex. 4-1 Computing manufacturing overhead rates. Hanover High-Tec, Inc., manufactures test tubes, beakers, and other glass products for chemical laboratories. Below are budgeted production costs for the coming year. A number of budgeted activity measures are listed also.

Budgeted costs:			
Direct labor			$125,000
Direct materials			93,000
Manufacturing overhead:			
Indirect labor		$16,000	
Indirect materials		17,000	
Factory utilities		22,000	
Factory property taxes		7,000	
Factory insurance		6,000	
Factory depreciation		38,000	
Production equipment depreciation		31,000	
Production supervisor's salaries		52,000	
Production employee's benefits		11,000	
Total budgeted overhead			200,000
Total budgeted production costs			$418,000
Other budgeted data:			
Machine hours	10,000		
Direct labor hours	16,000		
Units of output	500,000		

Required: Compute a manufacturing overhead rate based on

a. Direct labor cost.
b. Direct labor hours.
c. Units of production.
d. Machine hours.
e. Direct materials cost.
f. Prime cost.

Ex. 4-2 **A variety of application bases.** The Custom Rubber Stamp Company prepared the following budget for next year's operations:

Budgeted costs:		
Direct labor		$ 32,560
Direct materials		34,200
Manufacturing overhead:		
Variable	$30,200	
Fixed	10,500	40,700
Total		$107,460
Other budgeted data:		
Machine hours	5,700	
Direct labor hours	4,400	
Units of output	13,300	

Required: Compute a manufacturing overhead rate based on

a. Direct labor hours.
b. Machine hours.
c. Units of production.
d. Direct labor cost.
e. Direct materials cost.
f. Prime cost.

Ex. 4-3 **Overhead journal entries.** Lodoun Manufacturing Company produces lamp bases using a job order costing system. During 1986 the company completed 32,000 units of product, using 6,400 direct labor hours and incurring the following manufacturing costs:

a. Direct labor, $66,000
b. Indirect labor, $25,000
c. Direct materials, $28,000
d. Indirect materials, $13,000
e. Utilities paid in cash with a debit to utility expense, $9,000
f. Property taxes, $3,800
g. Depreciation on manufacturing equipment, $7,000

Overhead is applied using direct labor hours as the application base. The budget for 1986 called for 6,000 direct labor hours and total overhead of $48,000. Overapplied or underapplied overhead is assigned to cost of goods sold at the end of each year.

Required: Prepare journal entries to record work in process and actual and applied overhead and to close the overhead accounts at the end of the year.

Ex. 4-4 **Computing budgeted departmental overhead costs.** Louderford Paper Company identifies three departments in its manufacturing operations. The sole service department is maintenance. The two producing departments are fabricating and assembly. Below are budgeted overhead costs and activity data for the coming year.

	Maintenance	Fabricating	Assembly
Number of employees	9	36	15
Asset valuation	$40,000	$560,000	$120,000
Direct labor hours	—	80,000	30,000
Units of product	—	212,000	188,000
Square feet of space	2,000	18,000	5,000

	Overhead Cost	Allocation Base
Supervision	$ 30,000	Number of employees
Administration	240,000	Number of employees
Depreciation	90,000	Asset value
Utilities	45,000	Square feet of space

Maintenance department costs are allocated to the two producing departments on the basis of units of product.

Required: Prepare a schedule of cost allocations to departments showing the total budgeted overhead costs in each of the producing departments for the budget year.

Ex. 4-5 Departmental overhead allocation. Lelanii Manufacturing Company operates with three departments: stores, production, and finishing. Following are budgeted data for the coming year:

	Stores	Production	Finishing
Number of employees	10	34	16
Asset valuation	$80,000	$560,000	$160,000
Direct labor hours	—	74,900	36,000
Shipping cost			163,300
Units of product	—	225,000	275,000
Square feet of space	3,200	20,800	8,000

	Overhead Cost	Allocation Base
Supervision	$ 60,000	Number of employees
Administration	264,000	Number of employees
Depreciation	100,000	Asset value
Rent	48,000	Square feet of space
Utilities	50,000	Square feet of space

Stores department costs are allocated to the other two departments on the basis of units of product. The overhead rate for the production department is based on direct labor hours, and for the finishing department on shipping cost.

Required: Prepare a schedule to determine the overhead rate for the production and finishing departments after stores department costs have been allocated to the two departments.

Ex. 4-6 **Underapplied and overapplied departmental overhead.** Avalon Business Machines Company uses departmental overhead rates to apply manufacturing overhead to products. The firm has four production departments. The year-end balances in the departmental overhead accounts are as follows.

MOH Control, Machining	
586,000	

MOH Applied, Machining	
	544,000

MOH Control, Assembly	
271,000	

MOH Applied, Assembly	
	225,000

MOH Control, Finishing	
319,000	

MOH Applied, Finishing	
	377,000

MOH Control, Painting	
188,000	

MOH Applied, Painting	
	172,000

Required: Prepare a schedule identifying the amount of underapplied and overapplied overhead for each department and in total. For each department and in total, express underapplied and overapplied overhead as a percentage of actual overhead.

Ex. 4-7 **Physical units and sales value joint cost allocation.** The Lendle Division of the Catawahl Chemical Company makes products used in preserving grains and other food products. Many of the firm's products are made in joint production processes. One such product group is called the phenol group and is designated by a PH product code. PH-111 sells for $10 per gallon, PH-222 sells for $16 per gallon, and PH-444 sells for $32 per gallon. The firm just completed a production run of the phenol group, which resulted in joint costs of $100,000 and the following production quantities and costs after split-off:

Product	Output in gal	Sales Price per gal	Costs after Split-Off	Net Realizable Value at Split-Off
PH-111	6,000	$10.00	$18,000	$ 6.00
PH-222	13,000	16.00	52,000	10.00
PH-444	1,000	32.00	10,000	14.00

Total joint cost = $100,000

Required: Prepare a schedule of product costs using

a. The physical units joint cost allocation method.

b. The sales value joint cost allocation method.

Ex. 4-8 Net realizable value and gross profit joint cost allocation. Refer to the data in Exercise 4-7.

Required: Prepare a schedule of product costs using

a. The net realizable value at split-off joint cost allocation method.

b. The gross profit joint cost allocation method.

Ex. 4-9 Joint cost allocation using net realizable value at split-off. A company makes paints which it sells to industrial users. The paints are manufactured in joint production processes. The Salvo line of paints is used for metals. The joint production of this line results in three different paints, each of which has different characteristics and special uses. Each paint in the line requires some processing beyond the split-off point to add corrosion inhibitors, hardeners, and other required paint characteristics. Although the products are processed beyond the split-off point, each has a ready market at the split-off point if management chooses to sell at that point in the production process. Following are April data on production quantity, sales value at split-off, and the final market selling prices for each product.

	Product		
	SA-1	**SA-2**	**SA-3**
Gallons produced	3,000	6,000	1,000
Price per gallon	$5.00	$8.00	$14.00
Costs after split-off	$3,000	$9,000	$5,000
Net realizable value at split-off	$3.00	$5.00	$11.00

Total joint cost = $20,000

Required: Compute the total and per unit joint costs, costs after split-off, and total product costs using net realizable value at split-off to allocate joint costs.

Ex. 4-10 Joint product costing. A company makes bulk modeling clay which it sells to schools and craft shops in 5-pound packages. The clay is manufactured in a joint production process that yields various grades of clay. The cheaper grades of clay are used for modeling but cannot be baked. The more expensive grades of clay are used for pottery and other fired products. The special features of each grade of clay result from the processing that occurs after the point of split-off. Below are production data for a production run of clay just completed.

Product	Pounds Produced	Selling Price	Costs after Split-Off
CLAY-A	52,500	$2.40	$16,800
CLAY-AA	45,000	3.00	7,200
CLAY-AAA	27,500	4.50	13,200

Total joint cost = $140,000

Required: Prepare a schedule of product costs for the three products using:

a. The physical units method of joint cost allocation.

b. The sales value method of joint cost allocation.

Ex. 4-11 Physical units joint cost allocation. The Buzbee Honey Company produces artificial sweeteners to be used as sugar supplements. A continuous-flow production process is used that yields four joint products. The products split off at the end of production in department 5, and three products go on for more processing before being transferred to finished goods. Cost data and other details for the month of February are presented below.

Total joint cost = $180,000

Product	Quantity (Pints)	Sales Price per Pint	Cost after Split-Off
Buzie I	200,000	$ .40	$40,000
Buzie II	100,000	.60	0
Buzie III	80,000	2.00	12,000
Buzie-Whamo	20,000	5.00	28,000

Required: Using the physical units method of joint cost allocation, compute the joint cost per unit, cost after split-off per unit, and total cost per unit.

Ex. 4-12 Gross profit joint cost allocation. The Far West Milling Company processes soybeans into meal, oil, and animal feed. A 60-pound bushel yields an average of 45 pounds of meal, 10 pounds of oil, and 5 pounds of animal feed. Before split-off, average processing costs are $.50 per bushel, and the average cost of soybeans is $7 per bushel. After split-off additional processing costs are $35 per ton for meal, $50 per ton for oil, and $25 per ton for animal feed. The selling prices of the products are $230 per ton for meal, $.45 per pound for oil, and $130 per ton for animal feed. The company processed 1,200 tons of soybeans in August. There are 2,000 pounds in a ton.

Required: Prepare a schedule of product costs for soybean processing in August using the gross profit method of joint cost allocation.

Ex. 4-13 Understanding overhead account balances. Below are partial data for overhead costs and activity levels for three **independent** companies.

	Collins	Pipkin	Patton
Budgeted overhead cost	$600,000	$ ______	$952,000
Actual overhead cost	682,300	______	982,000
Applied overhead	657,600	660,000	______
Budgeted activity level	240,000 DLH	100,000 DLH	______
Actual activity level	______	120,000 DLH	276,000 DLH
Underapplied or (overapplied) overhead	______	$(12,000)	$ 43,600

Required: Find the missing values for each of the companies.

PROBLEMS

P. 4-1 Overhead costs. Omega Enterprises applies overhead to production using an overhead rate based on direct labor hours. The following cost and production estimates were made before the year started:

Units produced	500,000
Machine hours	20,000
Direct labor hours	40,000
Direct labor cost	$160,000
Manufacturing overhead	$280,000

At the end of the year, the accounts showed the following information:

Units produced	400,000
Machine hours	17,000
Direct labor hours	35,000
Direct materials	$500,000
Direct labor cost	$140,000
Manufacturing overhead	$231,000

Required:

a. Calculate the overhead rate.
b. Calculate the total amount of cost assigned to production during the year.
c. Determine the amount of overapplied or underapplied overhead.
d. How small would the actual activity level have to be in order to have underapplied factory overhead when actual overhead is $231,000?

P. 4-2 Underapplied or overapplied overhead. The following cost and production estimates were made by Limoon Company prior to the start of the accounting year:

Manufacturing overhead	$560,000
Direct labor hours	80,000
Machine hours	40,000
Production in units	500,000
Direct labor cost	$320,000

By the end of the year the following actual data were recorded:

Units produced	400,000
Machine hours used	32,000
Direct labor hours used	70,000
Direct labor cost	$280,000
Direct materials cost	$800,000
Manufacturing overhead cost	$462,000

Required:

a. Compute the overhead rate assuming the application base is direct labor hours.
b. Compute the overhead rate assuming the application base is machine hours.

c. Compute the total amount of cost assigned to production during the year with each application base.
d. Determine the amount of underapplied or overapplied overhead for each application base.
e. Determine the actual activity level the company would require in order to have no underapplied or overapplied overhead for each application base.

P. 4-3 **Computing and using manufacturing overhead rates.** Below are annual budgeted production and cost data for the two manufacturing divisions of the Mazzarini Products Company.

	Assembly Division	Finishing Division
Production quantity	10,000 units	12,500 units
Direct labor hours	160,000	125,000
Machine hours	100,000	50,000
Direct labor cost	$1,280,000	$1,250,000
Budgeted overhead cost	$800,000	$500,000

Following are actual production data:

	Assembly Division	Finishing Division
Production quantity	11,000 units	14,000 units
Direct labor hours	178,000	132,000
Machine hours	113,000	53,000
Direct labor cost	$1,495,000	$1,340,000
Actual overhead cost	$894,300	$543,400

Required:
a. Calculate overhead rates for each division using units of output, direct labor hours, direct labor cost, and machine hours.
b. Calculate the amount of overhead applied in each division using each of the overhead application rates from part *a*.
c. Calculate the underapplied or overapplied overhead for each division using **each** of the application rates from part *a*.

P. 4-4 **Overhead application and year-end disposition.** Skorinski Company is a manufacturer with two production divisions. The overhead application base in the assembly division is direct labor cost and the overhead application base in the finishing division is machine hours. Below are budgeted and actual overhead costs and activity levels. Underapplied or overapplied overhead larger than 10 percent of actual overhead cost is considered large and is allocated to the affected accounts.

Budgeted Data

	Division	
	Assembly	**Finishing**
Production quantity	10,000 units	50,000 units
Direct labor hours	80,000 hours	120,000 hours
Direct labor cost	$720,000	$900,000
Direct materials	$450,000	$650,000
Machine hours	60,000 hours	40,000 hours
Overhead cost	$900,000	$680,000

Actual Data

	Division	
	Assembly	**Finishing**
Production quantity	9,400 units	56,000 units
Direct labor hours	79,000 hours	122,000 hours
Direct labor cost	$715,000	$940,000
Direct materials	$432,000	$654,000
Machine hours	57,000 hours	43,000 hours
Overhead cost	$911,000	$687,000

Required:

a. Calculate the amount of applied overhead in each division for the period.

b. Calculate the underapplied or overapplied overhead for each division and in total.

c. Prepare a journal entry to dispose of any underapplied or overapplied overhead.

P. 4-5 Comprehensive departmental overhead. Following are budgeted data for three production departments—machining, forging, and milling.

Cost Item	Budgeted Amount	Allocation Base
Fire insurance	$ 6,000	Value of investment
Plant depreciation	15,000	Square footage
Telephone	5,000	Number of extensions
Payroll taxes	10,000	Number of employees
Indirect labor	36,000	Past utilization rate
Utilities	18,000	Square footage

Budgeted Overhead Allocation Bases

	Service Departments		Production Departments		
	Repair Shop	Supply Department	Machining	Forging	Milling
Past indirect labor use	10%	10%	25%	35%	20%
Square footage	1,000	1,000	4,000	2,000	2,000
Number of phone extensions	3	7	5	5	5
Value of investment	$30,000	$20,000	$60,000	$ 40,000	$50,000
Number of employees	8	5	17	10	10
Repair shop service hours			10,000	6,000	4,000
Number of supply requisitions			460	160	370
Machine hours			19,000		
Direct labor cost				$100,000	
Direct labor hours					16,000

Repair shop service hours are used to allocate repair shop costs to producing departments, and number of supply requisitions is used for supply department allocations.

The following information is available at year-end:

	Machining	Forging	Milling
Actual activity level	17,000 machine hr	$97,000 DLC	15,000 DLH
Actual MOH cost	$35,000	$32,000	$19,400

Required:

a. Prepare a schedule of cost allocations to departments.

b. Calculate overhead rates for each of the three production departments using machine hours, direct labor cost, and direct labor hours, respectively, as the application bases.

c. Calculate the amount of underapplied or overapplied overhead for the three producing departments and in total.

P. 4-6 Computing departmental manufacturing overhead rates. Following are budgeted overhead cost and activity data for Plasticast Corporation. The company operates with two service departments and three production departments. The schedule of budgeted costs indicates the allocation base used by the company to assign costs to departments. The company uses direct allocation of service department costs. Maintenance hours are used to allocate maintenance department costs, and materials requisitions are used to allocate inventory department costs to production departments.

Plasticast Corporation
Budgeted Manufacturing Overhead Costs
For the Quarter Ending June 30

Indirect materials	$ 50,000	Direct labor hours
Employee services	112,500	Number of employees
Electric power	37,500	Square feet of floor space
Casualty insurance	25,000	Value of investment
Fuel oil	50,000	Square feet of floor space
Plant depreciation	25,000	Square feet of floor space
Total	$300,000	

Plasticast Corporation
Budgeted Activity Measures
For the Quarter Ending June 30

	Maintenance	Inventory	Mixing	Casting	Finishing	Total
Number of employees	5	5	15	10	15	50
Square feet of space	2,000	8,000	15,000	15,000	10,000	50,000
Value of investment	$140,000	$260,000	$580,000	$820,000	$200,000	$2,000,000
Machine hours			10,000	5,000	8,000	23,000
Maintenance hours			4,000	3,200	800	8,000
Materials requisitions			200	200	600	1,000
Direct labor hours			6,000	4,000	10,000	20,000

The allocation bases for computing budgeted overhead rates are machine hours for the mixing department and direct labor hours for the casting and finishing departments. By the end of the quarter the following were the actual results of operations for the three production departments.

	Mixing	Casting	Finishing
Direct labor hours	5,100	4,800	10,200
Machine hours	11,000	5,200	7,900

Required:

a. Prepare a schedule of budgeted departmental overhead costs and compute the departmental manufacturing overhead rates.

b. Compute the amount of manufacturing overhead cost applied in the first quarter in each of the three production departments.

P. 4-7 Creation and use of departmental overhead rates. Takiti Manufacturing Company operates with two service departments—supplies and maintenance—and two production departments—production and packaging. Following are budgeted activity and cost data for the coming year:

	Supplies	Maintenance	Production	Packaging
Number of employees	10	12	34	16
Asset valuation	$80,000	60,000	$500,000	$160,000
Direct labor hours	—	—	35,300	27,700
Shipping cost	—	—	—	$228,800
Units of product	—	—	240,000	260,000
Square feet of space	2,040	1,360	22,100	8,500

	Budgeted Overhead	Allocation Base
Administration	$316,800	Number of employees
Supervision	72,000	Number of employees
Depreciation	100,000	Asset value
Rent	50,000	Square feet of space
Utilities	60,000	Square feet of space

Service department costs are allocated to the other two departments on the basis of units of product. The overhead rate for the production department is based on direct labor hours, and for the packaging department on shipping cost. Actual results of operations for the year are summarized below.

	Supplies	Maintenance	Production	Packaging
Number of employees	10	11	35	14
Asset valuation	$80,000	60,000	$500,000	$160,000
Direct labor hours	—	—	35,000	27,700
Shipping cost	—	—	—	$226,500
Units of product	—	—	249,600	270,400
Square feet of space	2,040	1,360	22,100	8,500

	Actual Overhead	Allocation Base
Administration	$300,000	Number of employees
Supervision	75,000	Number of employees
Depreciation	100,000	Asset value
Rent	50,000	Square feet of space
Utilities	64,000	Square feet of space

Required:

a. Prepare a schedule to determine the overhead rate for the production and packaging departments after service department costs have been allocated using direct allocation.

b. Prepare a schedule showing the actual amount of overhead in production departments.

c. Compute the amount of underapplied or overapplied overhead for the year.

P. 4-8 Accounting for joint products. You have just been hired as the chief cost accountant for the J&M Company. Its major product group is four food processing solutions, which are produced in a joint production process. The four products, K1, K2, K3, and K4, sell for $5, $7, $10, and $15 per gallon respectively.

September production yielded 25,000 gallons of K1, 20,000 gallons of K2, 10,000 gallons of K3, and 5,000 gallons of K4. Joint costs were direct materials of $140,000, direct labor of $50,000, and manufacturing overhead of $80,000. Products K1 and K2 are sold at split-off, but K3 and K4 required additional processing costs of $20,000 and $40,000 respectively.

The company uses the physical units method to allocate joint cost to products, but some managers have asked why K1 and K2 have the same product cost when they sell for different prices. One accountant suggested that the gross profit method may be a better way of allocating joint product costs. At the beginning of September, the company had the following inventory quantities and costs for K products:

Product	Quantity	Unit Cost	Total Cost
K1	6,000	$ 4.30	$ 25,800
K2	8,000	4.30	34,400
K3	5,000	6.20	31,000
K4	4,000	11.50	46,000
Total			$137,200

During September, the company sold 22,000 gallons of K1, 16,000 gallons of K2, 13,000 gallons of K3, and 6,000 gallons of K4.

Required:

a. Compute the cost of ending inventory using the physical units method of joint cost allocation.

b. Compute the cost of ending inventory using the gross profit method of joint cost allocation.

c. Compute the total gross margin for the K products sold during September using the company's current policy for costing joint products.

P. 4-9 Joint product costing. Kevelar Plastics Company makes three resins used in the manufacture of very tough plastics. During the first week of January the firm manufactured 1,000 gallons of Resflex, 3,000 gallons of Reslin, and 6,000 gallons of Reslon. The joint costs for the production were $18,000 for direct materials, $9,000 of direct labor, and $13,000 of manufacturing overhead. The costs after split-off were $5,600 for Resflex, $5,400 for Reslin, and $12,000 for Reslon. The selling prices of the products are $18, $10, and $7 per gallon respectively. If the products were sold at the point of split-off their net realizable values would be $12 per gallon for Resflex, $8 for Reslin, and $4 for Reslon.

Required: Prepare a schedule of product costs using the following joint cost allocation methods:

a. Physical units.

b. Sales value.

c. Gross profit.

d. Net realizable value at split-off.

P. 4-10 Analyzing the impact of different joint costing methods. Petro-Edge Corporation manufactures specialized oils and lubricants for the aviation industry. One product group, manufactured in a joint production process, is the Lub-eez group used for a variety of harsh-climate lubrication conditions. During April the company manufactured 100,000 gallons of Lub-eez-1, 60,000 gallons of Lub-eez-2, and 40,000 gallons of Lub-eez-3. Costs after split-off were $80,000, $90,000, and $160,000 respectively for the three products. Joint costs for the month were $360,000. The selling prices of the three products are $3.00, $5.00, and $9.00 per gallon respectively. On April 1 the company had the following inventory of Lub-eez products:

Product	Quantity	Cost
Lub-eez-1	40,000 gallons	$2.60 per gal
Lub-eez-2	23,000	3.50
Lub-eez-3	8,000	5.50

During April the company sold 110,000 gallons of Lub-eez-1, 64,000 gallons of Lub-eez-2, and 36,000 gallons of Lub-eez-3. The company uses a FIFO perpetual inventory system.

Required:

a. Prepare a schedule of product costs using the physical units joint cost allocation method.

b. Compute the cost of ending inventory for each product and for the Lub-eez product group.

c. Compute the percentage gross margin on sales for the April sales of the Lub-eez products for each product and for the product group in total.

d. Prepare a schedule of product costs using the sales value method of joint product cost allocation.

e. Answer parts *b* and *c* again using the product cost data from the sales value method of cost allocation.

f. Analyze the data from parts *c*, *d*, and *e* and determine which cost allocation method is more valuable in analyzing the performance of the products.

P. 4-11 Using various joint product costing methods. Laughlin Ag-Products, Ltd., offers an extensive line of soil and crop products. This month the company started production of a new line of grass herbicides intended to control a variety of field grasses. The new line of herbicides is manufactured in a joint production process which yields three herbicides, each designed to control certain types of grasses. During the first month of production the firm made 300,000 gallons of GFC-1, 180,000 gallons of GFC-2, and 120,000 gallons of GFC-3. The selling prices of the three herbicides were $2.80 per gallon for GFC-1, $6 a gallon for GFC-2, and $24 per gallon for GFC-3. At the end of the month ending inventories were 50,000 gallons, 80,000 gallons, and 30,000 gallons respectively. Joint production costs were $1,920,000 and the following additional production costs were incurred after the point of split-off:

GFC-1	0
GFC-2	$360,000
GFC-3	$600,000

Required: Prepare a detailed schedule of product costs for the products using:

a. The physical units method of joint cost allocation.
b. The gross profit method of joint cost allocation.
c. The sales value method of joint cost allocation.

Using your product cost data from parts *a, b,* and *c*:

d. Compute the cost of ending inventory using each of the joint costing methods used above.
e. Using **each** of the joint cost allocation methods computed in parts *a, b,* and *c*, compute the total gross margin for GFC-2 for the first month of production.

P. 4-12 (AICPA) Joint product costing. In its three departments Amaco Chemical Company manufactures several products:

- In department 1 the raw materials amanic acid and bonyl hydroxide are used to produce Amanyl, Bonanyl, and Am-Salt. Amanyl is sold to others who use it as a raw material in the manufacture of stimulants. Bonanyl is not salable without further processing. Although Am-Salt is a commercial product for which there is a ready market, Amaco does not sell this product, preferring to submit it to further processing.
- In department 2 Bonanyl is processed into the marketable product, Bonanyl-X. The relationship between Bonanyl used and Bonanyl-X produced has remained constant for several months.
- In department 3 Am-Salt and the raw material colb are used to produce Colbanyl, a liquid propellant that is in great demand. As an inevitable part of this process Demanyl is also produced. Demanyl was discarded as scrap until discovery of its usefulness as a catalyst in the manufacture of glue; for 2 years Amaco has been able to sell all of its production of Demanyl.

In its financial statements Amaco states inventory at the lower of cost (on the first in, first out basis) or market. Unit costs of the items most recently produced must therefore be computed. Costs allocated to Demanyl are computed so that after allowing for packaging and selling costs of $.04 per pound no profit or loss will be recognized on sales of this product.

Certain data for October follow:

Raw Materials	Pounds Used	Total Cost
Amanic acid	6,300	$5,670
Bonyl hydroxide	9,100	6,370
Colb	5,600	2,240

Conversion Costs (Labor and Overhead)	
Department 1	$33,600
Department 2	3,306
Department 3	22,400

		Inventories, Pounds		
Products	Pounds Produced	September 30	October 31	Sales Price per Pound
Amanyl	3,600			$ 6.65
Bonanyl	2,800	210	110	
Am-Salt	7,600	400	600	6.30
Bonanyl-X	2,755			4.20
Colbanyl	1,400			43.00
Demanyl	9,800			.54

Required: Prepare for October the schedules listed below. Supporting computations should be prepared in good form. Round answers to the nearest cent.

a. Cost per pound of Amanyl, Bonanyl, and Am-Salt produced—relative sales value method.

b. Cost per pound of Amanyl, Bonanyl, and Am-Salt produced—physical units cost method.

c. Cost per pound of Colbanyl produced. Assume that the cost per pound of Am-Salt produced was $3.40 in September and $3.50 in October.

CASE

Case 4-1 Joint product analysis. Rico Plastics Company makes plastics and resins used widely in the toy manufacturing industry. During March the company manufactured 4,000, 6,000, and 15,000 gallons respectively of Goo, Goo-gum, and Goo-frum in a joint production process. The selling prices of the products are $10 per gallon for Goo, $5 for Goo-gum, and $2 for Goo-frum. Production costs were $50,000 of joint cost and costs after split-off of $4,000, $12,000, and $12,000 respectively.

The company's policy is to produce only products that generate a 20 percent or greater gross margin on sales. The new sales manager is concerned about the profitability of Goo-frum. The company uses the physical units method of joint product costing, and recent production reports have shown that Goo-frum may be violating company gross margin policy.

Any costs after split-off can be eliminated entirely if a single product is dropped, and all joint costs can be eliminated entirely if an entire product group is dropped.

Required:

- **a.** Prepare a product cost schedule for March production of this group of joint products using the company's product costing methods.
- **b.** Analyze each product to determine if it is achieving company gross margin requirements.
- **c.** Prepare any additional product costing schedules you think may be useful in analyzing these products.
- **d.** Prepare a written analysis of what the company should do about these products. Support your decision with relevant cost data.

Cost Behavior and Decision Making

part 2

Cost data are essential elements in the development of managerial accounting reports, but the mere existence of a cost accounting data base does not ensure useful management reports. Different decisions and performance evaluations require a variety of types of accounting information. A key criterion in selecting accounting data for managerial reports is relevance. Knowing how costs change with respect to changes in the volume of activity is an important factor in determining the relevance of the data in decision making.

Chapter 5 discusses methods of estimating the common cost behavior patterns presented in Chapter 2. Cost behavior data and characteristics are used to show the relationship between the volume of business activity and the amount of profit or loss earned. In Chapter 6 common types of business decisions involving the use of cost behavior information are discussed, showing how managers choose between alternative choices of action. Making correct choices often means the difference between profits and losses.

Cost-Volume-Profit Analysis

5

Chapter 5 builds on the cost behavior concepts you learned earlier; these concepts are used to evaluate the way costs and profits change with changes in the volume of activity. The concepts presented in this chapter are essential to your understanding of many management reports discussed later in the book. When you have completed the chapter, you should understand:

1. Several methods that managers use to evaluate costs and determine their cost behavior patterns.
2. The nature of cost-volume-profit analysis and how it is used by managers.
3. Break-even analysis in units and sales dollars.
4. How changes in cost-volume-profit variables affect the analysis of cost-volume-profit relationships.
5. Graphic cost-volume-profit analyses.
6. How cost-volume-profit analyses are performed for multiple products or services.

Classifying costs by functions, such as manufacturing or nonmanufacturing, prime or conversion, sales salaries or administrative salaries, is useful for evaluating cost trends, measuring the cost of a product or service, and evaluating performance. But many managerial decisions cannot be made easily by using costs classified by functions. Many decisions are improved significantly if costs are classified according to behavior.

The five cost behavior patterns discussed in Chapter 2—fixed costs, variable costs, mixed costs, semivariable costs, and step function costs—are all useful in helping managers evaluate performance and make informed business decisions. The primary impediment to the use of cost behavior data in business is the lack of accurate cost behavior data. The general ledgers of most businesses are arranged along functional business lines such as manufacturing, administration, marketing, or computer services. Therefore it is usually necessary for managers to analyze cost data from the ledger in order to determine how specific costs behave. Systematic analysis of cost behavior patterns provides managers with many useful statistical measures and other information.

COST ESTIMATION METHODS

Managers use a variety of methods to determine cost behavior patterns

A number of cost estimation methods are available to managers. Some are relatively simple to use and may provide adequate estimates of cost behavior patterns and cost predictions needed for planning and control purposes. Sophisticated analysis methods are more complex but may provide better cost estimates that can be interpreted statistically. Here we discuss some of the more common cost analysis methods; Chapter 18 provides an in-depth presentation of some powerful cost analysis methods.

Intuition and Professional Experience

Quantitative cost analysis methods are useful managerial tools, but sometimes there is no substitute for experience. Personnel with extensive service and a proven record of successful cost prediction are often invaluable in identifying cost patterns and predicting cost levels. They often are able to integrate a complex array of causal variables into a useful prediction system. Some individuals making decisions have track records that are too good to deny.

High-Low Method

The high-low method is easy to use

A simple and widely used cost estimation technique is the **high-low method,** which uses the highest and lowest costs and their associated activity levels to isolate the fixed and variable components of a mixed cost. To illustrate, below are monthly cost and activity data for a 6-month period:

Month	Cost	Labor Hours
January	$54,000	2,100
February	56,000	2,300
March	62,000	2,400
April	58,000	1,900
May	44,000	1,500
June	50,000	1,700

The variable cost is estimated first

The data indicate that costs vary somewhat with changes in the volume of activity. The costs at low levels of activity are less than the costs at high levels of activity. However, what the precise relationship is between the cost and the volume of activity is not evident. The high-low method is used to isolate the fixed and variable components of the cost. For the 6-month period, we select the highest cost and the lowest cost. These occur in March and May, respectively. We divide the change in the cost, which is \$62,000 − \$44,000, by the corresponding change in the activity level, computed as 2,400 hours − 1,500 hours. The calculation yields the per unit variable cost b in the total cost formula $Y = a + bX$, where Y is the total cost, a is the fixed cost, and b is the variable cost per unit of activity.

$$b = \frac{\$62{,}000 - \$44{,}000}{2{,}400 \text{ hours} - 1{,}500 \text{ hours}}$$

$$= \frac{\$18{,}000}{900 \text{ hours}}$$

$$= \$20 \text{ per labor hour}$$

The value of b indicates that for every labor hour worked, the cost increases by \$20. Knowing the variable cost, we can calculate the fixed cost a by substituting the variable cost of \$20 per hour into the total cost formula for either the highest or lowest level of activity. In March, when the volume of activity was 2,400 labor hours, the total cost was \$62,000. We find the fixed cost as follows:

$$\text{Total cost} = \text{Fixed cost} + \text{Variable cost}$$

$$Y = a + bX$$

$$\$62{,}000 = a + \$20(2{,}400 \text{ hours})$$

$$\$62{,}000 = a + \$48{,}000$$

$$a = \$14{,}000$$

If we use May cost data instead of March, we find the same amount of fixed cost. The variable cost is 1,500 labor hours times \$20 per hour, or \$30,000. Total cost of \$44,000 minus variable cost of \$30,000 yields the fixed cost, \$14,000.

It is possible that the highest cost does not occur at the highest activity level or the lowest cost does not occur at the lowest activity level. In such cases, the manager using the high-low method must determine whether to use the highest and lowest cost or the highest and lowest volume of activity in the cost analysis. Managers should select the data that they believe will provide the best estimates of cost behavior.

Sometimes the high-low method yields poor estimates

The high-low method is a simple cost analysis tool that yields the fixed and variable components of a mixed cost, but the estimates it yields are not always sufficiently precise. If the linear relationship between the cost and the measure of activity is not strong, the resulting fixed and variable cost estimates may not be accurate. Managers using the high-low method have no way of knowing if the estimated costs are accurate or inaccurate. This problem can be avoided by using more sophisticated methods discussed later in this chapter and in Chapter 18.

Scatter Diagram

A scatter diagram allows managers to see cost patterns

Often it is useful to present cost data graphically for various levels of activity. A graph may enable managers to see relationships between costs and activity that are not readily apparent by looking at numbers. A graph of cost and activity data, called a **scatter diagram,** typically shows the total cost on the vertical axis and the volume of activity on the horizontal axis. Each datum is plotted on the graph as illustrated in Figure 5-1. The term *scatter diagram* comes from the way that the data are scattered across the graph. The purpose of a scatter diagram is to aid in identifying the cost behavior pattern of a set of cost data.

The data in Figure 5-1 are those used in the high-low method discussed earlier. A strong linear relationship among the six data points is evident. The variable cost rate b can be approximated by drawing a line through the points so that it intersects the vertical axis. In Figure 5-1, the intersection is shown as point a, which is the graphic estimate of the fixed cost. As you can see, it is very close to the $14,000 fixed cost estimate obtained with the high-low method.

In this example it is easy to draw a line through the set of data points because there is a strong linear relationship between the costs and the level of activity. Sometimes the relationship between costs and the volume of activity is not strong, as illustrated in Figure 5-2. In that case there is no point in trying to analyze the data graphically.

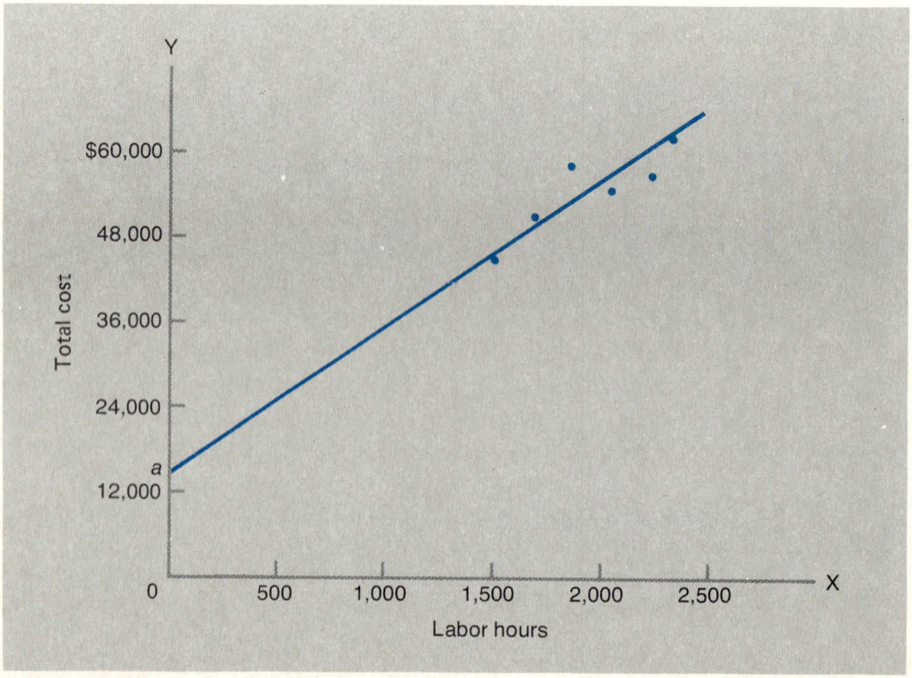

Figure 5-1
Scatter diagrams help managers spot cost behavior patterns by visual observation of the data. This example shows a mixed cost situation with a strong linear relationship.

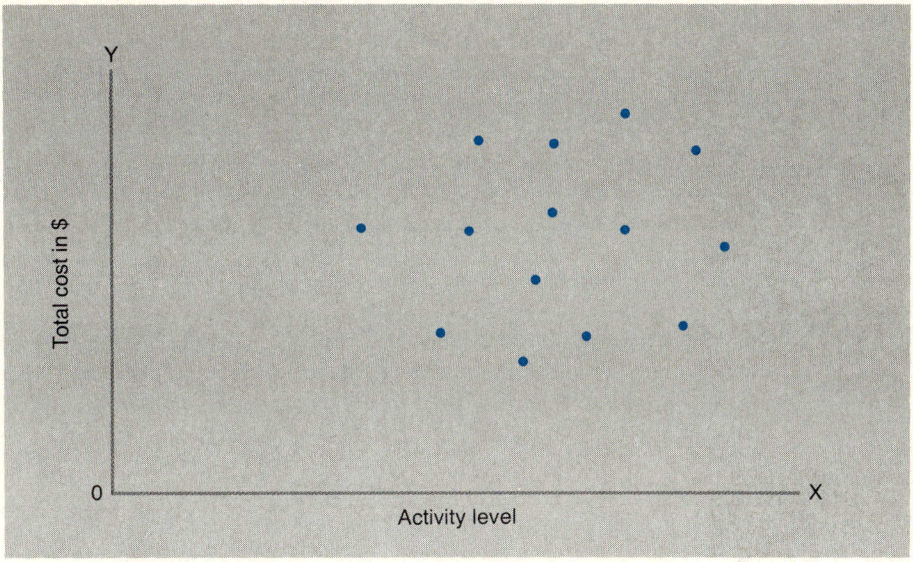

Figure 5-2
This scatter diagram shows no obvious cost pattern. Other analyses are required to determine the cost behavior.

Regression-Correlation Analysis

Regression-correlation analysis is a powerful cost analysis tool

One of the most powerful and useful methods for cost analysis and prediction is regression-correlation analysis, **Regression-correlation analysis** is a statistical method used to determine the nature and strength of the relationship between costs and the volume of activity. No other quantitative tool has as wide an applicability to accounting data analysis. Its appeal stems from its ability to use one or more activity variables to analyze and predict the value of another variable, such as cost. Regression-correlation analysis is a two-step process involving:

1. Determination of the nature of the association between two or more variables
2. Determination of the strength of the relationship between the variables

Regression-correlation embodies a broad spectrum of statistical analysis tools, including simple linear regression, multiple regression, and curvilinear regression. All have potential application to cost planning and control. In this chapter, however, we discuss only simple linear regression; we cover other regression concepts in Chapter 18.

In **simple linear regression** two variables are analyzed. The **independent variable** is usually some measure of activity such as units produced, volume of sales, or labor hours worked. The value of the **dependent variable** depends on the value of the independent variable and on the relationship between the two variables as described by a mathematical equation. In cost analysis, the dependent variable typically is some cost.

Typically, regression-correlation analysis is used to analyze historical cost data. The results of the analysis may be useful in making estimates or predictions of future costs and activity levels. For example, employee fringe benefits may be related to the number of hours worked. A company may use regression-correlation analysis to measure the relationship between the independent variable and the dependent variable. The cost is the dependent variable because its value depends on the number of labor hours worked and the relationship between labor hours and fringe benefit costs.

Computing the regression line. The **regression line** is the line whose equation best describes the linear relationship between the independent variable and the dependent variable. The linear regression line has the form of the traditional equation for a straight line:

The regression line describes the linear relationship between two variables

$$Y_c = a + bX$$

where:

Y_c = the value of the dependent variable computed from a specific value for the independent variable.
a = the constant, which is the point where the regression line crosses the Y axis. It is the value of Y_c when $X = 0$.
b = the slope of the regression line. It describes the change in the value of Y_c for each unit change in the value of X. If Y_c increases when X increases then the slope of the regression line is positive. If Y_c decreases when X increases, the slope of the regression line is negative.
X = the value of the independent variable.

Figure 5-3 illustrates a regression line described by the equation $Y_c = 5 + 2X$. In this case, $a = 5$ and $b = 2$. For any value of X, Y is equal to 5 + 2 times the value of X. The regression line was computed from the 10 data points shown on the graph. The straight line is drawn so that the absolute vertical distance between the line and each data point is the smallest possible. In other words, no other straight line can be drawn through the set of data that would reduce the total vertical distance between the data points and the regression line, so the line is referred to as the **line of best fit.**

How strong is the relationship between variables?

The actual calculation of the regression line is discussed in Chapter 18. The regression line describes the **relationship** that exists between the dependent and the independent variable, but it does not say how good the relationship is, that is, how strong is the linear relationship between the independent variable and the dependent variable? Although the regression line is the best-fitting straight line that can be drawn through a set of data, it is possible that no regression line can do a very good job of

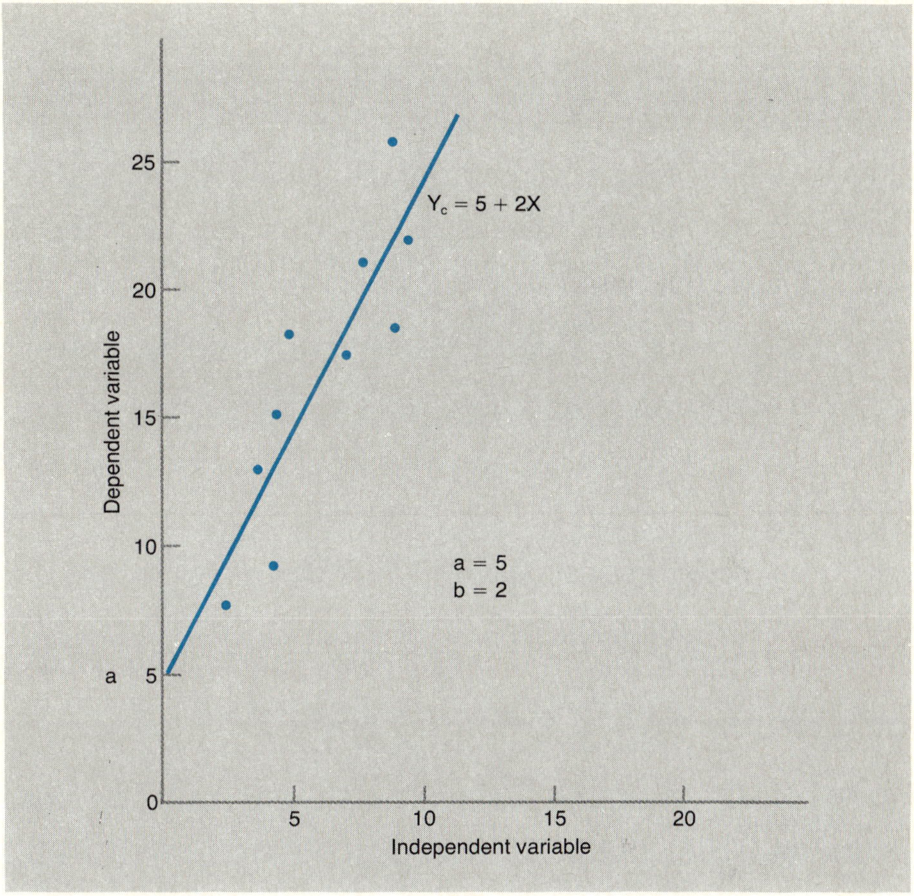

Figure 5-3 **Graph of a regression line showing the constant, *a*, where the regression line crosses the *Y* axis, and the slope of the regression line, *b*, which is the change in the value of *Y* for each unit change in the value of *X*.**

fitting the data. The scatter diagram in Figure 5-2 illustrates a poor linear relationship, whereas the one in Figure 5-1 shows a strong linear relationship.

The **coefficient of correlation,** denoted as *r*, measures the degree of association between the dependent and the independent variables. It ranges in value from +1, representing perfect positive correlation, to −1, representing perfect negative correlation. Positive correlation means that as the independent variable increases or decreases so does the dependent variable. Negative correlation means that as the independent variable increases, the dependent variable decreases, and vice versa. Figure 5-4 illustrates the general relationship between *r*, the regression line, and the data.

The closer *r* is to +1 or −1, the stronger the relationship is between the dependent and the independent variables. As *r* gets closer to zero it indicates a weaker relationship. The sign of *r* indicates only the direction of the relationship, not the strength.

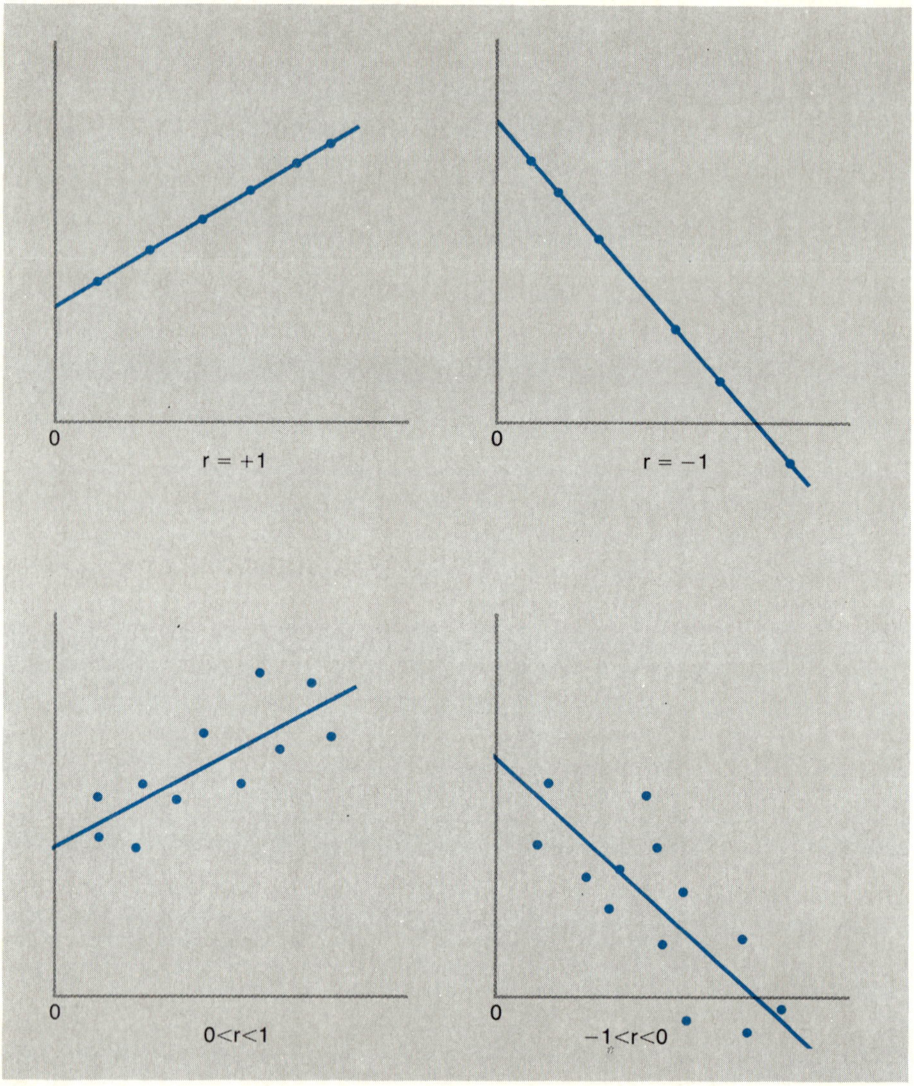

Figure 5-4
Graphs showing the general slopes and data distributions for correlations ranging from perfect positive correlation, +1, to perfect negative correlation, −1.

Measuring the strength of the linear relationship between variables

Values of r must be interpreted carefully. An r of .8 does not indicate twice as good a linear relationship as an r of .4; the larger value actually indicates a relationship that is four times as strong as the smaller value. Similarly, an r of .75 is nine times as strong as an r of .25. As r doubles, the relationship increases by 2^2, and as r triples the relationship increases by 3^2. To make the interpretation of r more meaningful, therefore, the coefficient of correlation is often converted to the **coefficient of determination,** which is calculated as r^2, thereby eliminating the sign of r and enabling a more easily understood comparison to be made between the resulting values.

The coefficient of determination is another measure of how well the regression line fits the data. A coefficient of .9 shows a fit that is twice as strong as an r^2 of .45 and three times as strong as an r^2 of .3.

Association versus causation. When analyzing two variables, such as the distribution cost of a product and the volume of sales for the product, there may be a strong temptation to state that the **cause** of any change in distribution cost is the change in the volume of sales. We must remember, however, that regression-correlation analysis measures the nature of association between two variables, usually based on historical data. But association—even strong association—does not prove cause-and-effect relationship. Many strong statistical associations exist that certainly suggest causal relationships but do not prove them. Regression-correlation analysis can provide much useful evidence, but the manager must determine the ultimate use of the information.

Using Regression-Correlation Analysis

The computation of regression lines and coefficients of correlation and determination take time if done manually, but computers can analyze large amounts of cost data in a short time. Such analyses can disclose which cost and activity relationships are the strongest and, therefore, most useful in planning and controlling costs. For example, in an effort to control manufacturing overhead costs, a manager runs three different linear regressions, each using monthly manufacturing overhead costs as the dependent variable. The independent variables are direct labor hours for the first regression analysis, machine hours for the second, and units produced for the third. Each of the three analyses yields a regression equation with a fixed and a variable cost component. The coefficients of correlation for the three analyses are

Direct labor hours	.82
Machine hours	.70
Units produced	.64

The strongest linear relationship is between manufacturing overhead costs and direct labor hours. With this information, the manager may decide to use direct labor hours rather than machine hours or units produced for estimating overhead costs. But the strength of the relationship is not the only factor the manager evaluates. For example, if machine hours had a stronger r than direct labor hours, management may still decide to use direct labor hours as the basis for estimating overhead costs if direct labor hour data are easier to accumulate than machine hour data.

Estimating costs with regression data. For the example with direct labor hours as the independent variable, we assume that the regression line equation is

$$Y_c = \$73{,}500 + \$1.20X$$

The company uses the regression data to estimate manufacturing overhead costs for the budget and for the computation of a manufacturing overhead rate. If the company expects to use 52,500 direct labor hours during the budget year, the estimated manufacturing overhead cost is

$$\begin{aligned} Y_c &= \$73{,}500 + \$1.20(52{,}500 \text{ hr}) \\ &= \$73{,}500 + \$63{,}000 \\ &= \$136{,}500 \end{aligned}$$

The manufacturing overhead rate based on direct labor hours is

$$\begin{aligned} \text{MOH rate} &= \frac{\$136{,}500}{52{,}500 \text{ DLH}} \\ &= \$2.60 \text{ per DLH} \end{aligned}$$

COST-VOLUME-PROFIT RELATIONSHIPS

CVP looks at how costs and profits change with changing volumes of activity

Cost behavior information is used by managers to evaluate performance, to prepare budgets, to evaluate decisions, and to monitor and control business activities. Among the important uses of cost behavior information is **cost-volume-profit (CVP)analysis,** which deals with the way costs and profits change as the volume of activity changes. Cost-volume-profit analysis ranges from simple break-even analysis to complex analyses with multiple products and many changes in variables. We start with basic CVP analyses and continue in this and the next chapter with a comprehensive coverage of the topic.

Break-Even Analysis

At the break-even point, revenues equal expenses

The **break-even point** is the level of activity at which **total costs** equal **total revenues,** leaving no profit or loss. A break-even point may be computed for a product, a group of products, a division, an entire company, or any other carefully defined objective. At the break-even point revenues from the product equal the total costs of producing, selling, and distributing the product. Both the fixed and the variable costs of manufacturing and nonmanufacturing operations must be included in the calculation of the break-even point. The unifying characteristic of all costs used in the analysis is that all are identifiable with the cost objective in the analysis.

To illustrate, Samson Company is evaluating the introduction of a new lawn sprinkler with an expected selling price of $5 per unit, variable cost of $3 per unit, and fixed cost of $10,000. Total revenue is the number of units sold times $5 per unit, and total variable cost is $3 per unit times the number of units sold. The break-even point occurs where total revenue equals total cost and profit is zero, as computed below.

$$\begin{aligned} \text{Revenue} &= \text{Total cost} \\ &= \text{Fixed cost} + \text{Variable cost} \end{aligned}$$

or

$$R = FC + VC$$

Substituting, we solve for the break-even point in units, X:

$$\$5X = \$10{,}000 + \$3X$$

Solving for X

$$\begin{aligned} \$5X - \$3X &= \$10{,}000 \\ \$2X &= \$10{,}000 \\ X &= \frac{\$10{,}000}{\$2 \text{ per unit}} \\ &= 5{,}000 \text{ units} \end{aligned}$$

The break-even point is expressed in units because the variable X represents units. It is easy to convert the break-even point into sales dollars by multiplying units by the selling price, yielding

$$5{,}000 \text{ units} \times \$5 \text{ per unit} = \$25{,}000$$

The **contribution margin** (**CM**) of a product is the difference between its selling price and its variable cost. It is the amount of revenue that the sale of each unit contributes toward covering fixed costs and generating profits. Initially, the contribution margin covers fixed costs, but once the break-even point is reached the contribution margin provides income. The break-even point can be computed using the contribution margin, as follows:

$$\begin{aligned} \text{Contribution margin} &= \text{Selling price} - \text{Variable cost} \\ &= \$5 - \$3 \\ &= \$2 \end{aligned}$$

$$\text{Break-even point} = \frac{\text{Fixed cost}}{\text{Contribution margin}}$$

Substituting:

$$\begin{aligned} \text{Break-even point} &= \frac{\$10{,}000}{\$2 \text{ per unit}} \\ &= 5{,}000 \text{ units} \end{aligned}$$

In some CVP analyses, specific unit selling price and unit variable cost data are not available. For example, an analyst may have only data on total sales and total variable costs without any information on number of units sold. In the illustration above, fixed costs are $10,000 and variable costs are 60 percent of selling price. The break-even point can be computed in sales dollars, Y, as follows:

$$\begin{aligned}
\text{Revenue} &= \text{Total cost} \\
&= \text{Fixed cost} + \text{Variable cost} \\
Y &= \$10{,}000 + .6Y \\
Y - .6Y &= \$10{,}000 \\
.4Y &= \$10{,}000 \\
Y &= \frac{\$10{,}000}{.4} \\
&= \$25{,}000
\end{aligned}$$

The relationship between total costs and total revenue can be shown graphically in a **cost-volume-profit graph,** also called a **cost-volume-profit chart** or **CVP chart,** such as the one illustrated in Figure 5-5. The chart has a total cost line and a total revenue line. The cost line is composed of the fixed cost of $10,000 plus the $3 per unit variable cost. The total revenue line is $5 a unit. The break-even point occurs where the two lines intersect.

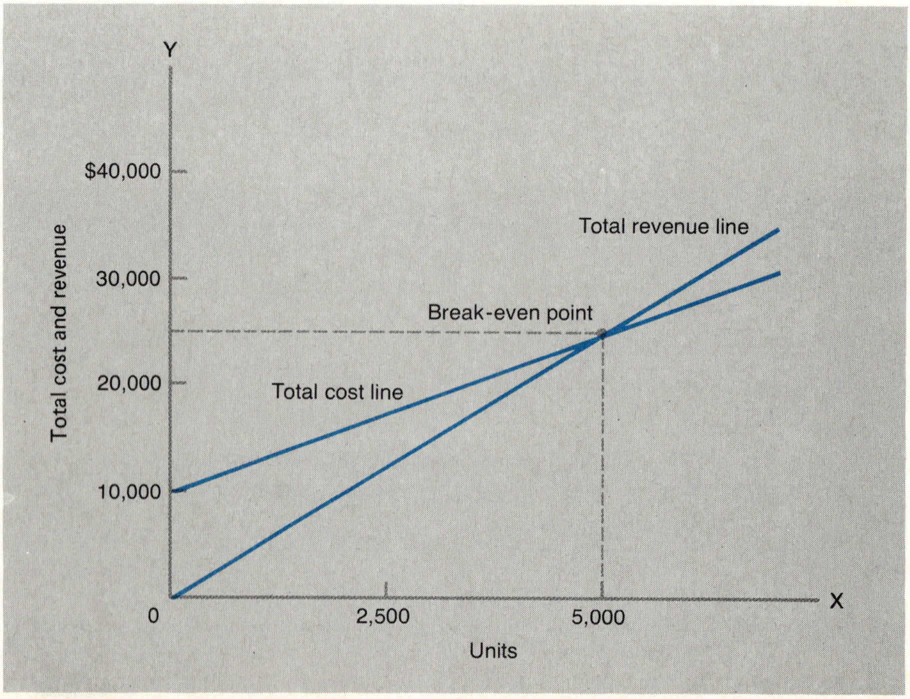

Figure 5-5
A graph is useful in showing the break-even point. The fixed cost is eventually covered because the revenue line has a steeper slope than the variable cost line. The difference between the slope of the revenue line and the variable cost line is the contribution margin, which in this example is $5 − $3 = $2.

Extensions of Break-Even Analysis

For a new firm or a new product line, breaking even may be an important short-term goal. But there are many other objectives in business that can be evaluated effectively using CVP analyses, including:

1. Achieving a target net income
2. Changing fixed costs
3. Changing variable costs
4. Changing selling price
5. Changing management strategies

There are many more analyses in CVP than break-even

Achieving a target net income. Although breaking even is a desirable initial hurdle, it is not the ultimate goal of a profit-seeking enterprise. Investors do not commit resources to businesses that promise zero return. Instead managers strive to earn a profit that yields an acceptable level of return on owners' investments.

Cost-volume-profit analysis can be used to determine the level of activity necessary to cover fixed costs and achieve a target level of income. If the target income is expressed in a dollar amount, it is merely added to the fixed cost and the required activity level is computed. To illustrate, Samson Company decides that $8,000 of net income is required. The number of lawn sprinklers needed to earn $8,000 of income is

$$\begin{aligned} \text{Sales} &= \text{Variable costs} + \text{Fixed costs} + \text{Profit} \\ \$5X &= \$3X + \$10{,}000 + \$8{,}000 \\ \$5X - \$3X &= \$18{,}000 \\ \$2X &= \$18{,}000 \\ X &= 9{,}000 \text{ units} \end{aligned}$$

or $$9{,}000 \times \$5 = \$45{,}000 \text{ of sales}$$

Target income can be expressed as a dollar amount or a percentage of sales

Target income may be expressed as a percentage of sales revenue rather than a dollar amount of income. In the above example, suppose that the desired target income is 20 percent of sales revenue. Variable cost is 60 percent of the selling price, so the required level of activity to achieve the target income is

$$\begin{aligned} Y &= .6Y + \$10{,}000 + .2Y \\ Y &= .8Y + \$10{,}000 \\ Y - .8Y &= \$10{,}000 \\ .2Y &= \$10{,}000 \\ Y &= \frac{\$10{,}000}{.2} \\ &= \$50{,}000 \text{ of sales} \end{aligned}$$

or $$\frac{\$50{,}000}{\$5 \text{ per unit}} = 10{,}000 \text{ units}$$

The problem can also be solved in units directly by noting that the target net income is 20 percent of selling price; 20 percent of \$5 = \$1. That means \$1 of each unit's sales revenue is designated as required net income. Then

$$\$5X = \$3X + \$10{,}000 + \$1X$$
$$X = 10{,}000 \text{ units}$$

Changing fixed costs. The term **fixed cost** implies costs that do not change. However, many fixed costs are discretionary and can be changed in the near future if management desires. In addition, managers often know about some fixed costs, such as property taxes, that are expected to increase in the near future. Managers often use cost-volume-profit analysis when evaluating discretionary cost decisions or planning for a new committed fixed cost, such as a property tax increase.

The analysis of changing fixed costs incorporates any anticipated fixed cost changes into the CVP equation. Continuing our example, we assume that fixed costs for the next year are expected to increase by \$5,000. The new fixed cost used in the analysis is \$15,000, and the new break-even point is

$$\$5X = \$15{,}000 + \$3X$$
$$\$2X = \$15{,}000$$
$$X = 7{,}500 \text{ units}$$

The CVP effect of the increase in fixed cost can be evaluated by dividing the expected fixed cost increase of \$5,000 by the contribution margin of \$2 per unit. The result is 2,500 units, the amount that the break-even point must increase from the original level of 5,000 units to accommodate the higher fixed cost. Using this approach, the new break-even point is

$$\text{New break-even point} = \text{Old break-even point} + \text{Volume required to cover additional fixed cost}$$
$$= 5{,}000 \text{ units} + 2{,}500 \text{ units}$$
$$= 7{,}500 \text{ units}$$

Changing variable costs. The costs of raw materials, labor, and other variable costs of production resources often change as resource prices increase or production efficiencies change. Changes in variable costs are incorporated into the CVP analysis with a simple modification in the variable cost component of the break-even equation. For example, if variable costs increase by \$.75 per unit, the new unit variable cost is \$3.75. The calculation of the break-even point is

$$\$5X = \$10{,}000 + \$3.75X$$
$$\$1.25X = \$10{,}000$$
$$X = \frac{\$10{,}000}{\$1.25}$$
$$= 8{,}000 \text{ units}$$

The $.75 increase in variable cost is 15 percent of the selling price; but it is also 37.5 percent of the original $2 contribution margin. The new, lower contribution margin results in a higher break-even volume. It takes more units of sales to cover the $10,000 of fixed costs.

Changing selling price. A change in the selling price has an effect on the break-even point similar to that caused by a change in variable cost. They both affect the contribution margin needed to cover fixed cost. If market conditions require a $.40 drop in the price of the product, to $4.60, the new break-even point is

$$\$4.60X = \$3X + \$10{,}000$$
$$\$1.60X = \$10{,}000$$
$$X = 6{,}250 \text{ units}$$

or

$$6{,}250 \text{ units} \times \$4.60 \text{ per unit} = \$28{,}750 \text{ of sales}$$

Changing management strategies. By evaluating the changes in cost-volume-profit variables individually, it is easy to see the effect of each on the break-even point. In practice, however, several variables may change simultaneously. Multiple changes are not difficult to analyze, but sometimes it is difficult to visualize the impact of several changes at once.

Often more than one CVP variable will change in the analysis

To illustrate multiple changes, we combine several variable changes into a single CVP analysis. Management is facing an increase in labor costs, which would increase variable costs of production. The company has two alternatives that will allow it to maintain its target level of profit of $9,000. It can increase the price to compensate for the increased cost, but an increase in price may cause a decrease in the volume of sales. The other alternative is to acquire new equipment that will automate some of the production and thus reduce variable labor costs. The new equipment would add $20,000 per year to the current annual fixed costs of $10,000, but variable costs would decrease from $3.00 to $2.60 per unit. The level of sales required to achieve the target profit of $9,000 with this alternative is computed as follows:

- Increase fixed costs from $10,000 to $30,000.
- Decrease variable costs from $3.00 to $2.60 per unit.
- Achieve target profit of $9,000, with no change in selling price.

$$\$5X = \$2.60X + \$30{,}000 + \$9{,}000$$
$$\$5X - \$2.60X = \$39{,}000$$
$$\$2.40X = \$39{,}000$$
$$X = \frac{\$39{,}000}{\$2.40}$$
$$= 16{,}250 \text{ units}$$

An alternative strategy is to increase the selling price to $5.50 per unit. To counteract any decline in sales volume that may result, a new advertising and marketing campaign would be required that would raise fixed costs by $8,000 per year and variable costs to $4.25 per unit.

- Increase fixed costs from $10,000 to $18,000.
- Increase variable costs from $3.00 to $4.25 per unit.
- Achieve target profit of $9,000, with an increase in selling price from $5.00 to $5.50.

$$\$5.50X = \$4.25X + \$18{,}000 + \$9{,}000$$
$$\$1.25X = \$27{,}000$$
$$X = 21{,}600 \text{ units}$$

The sales required to meet the target net income in the first alternative is $81,250, the target volume of 16,250 units times the $5 selling price. Target revenue for alternative 2 is $118,800 (21,600 units × $5.50). Which of the two alternatives should management choose? The computation of the target sales levels for the two alternatives does not provide an obvious decision. Other analyses and information may be necessary. For example, if the target profit can be reached in either case, the second alternative may be better because it has a greater margin of safety. The concept of margin of safety is discussed later in this chapter. Managerial accounting information provides managers with much relevant information for decision making, but it seldom provides the decision itself. Instead, managers must use the data from accounting reports and combine them with other information to make intelligent decisions.

Graphic CVP Analysis

CVP charts allow visual analyses of CVP relationships

Many managers find that graphic analyses and presentations of accounting information are more informative and more quickly understood than some conventional accounting reports. Commonly cited advantages of graphic presentations are

1. Managers with a low tolerance for financial data often are able to understand financial information presented graphically.
2. A range of activity rather than a static situation can be presented.
3. More information can be presented and understood without information overload.
4. The solutions to some complex analyses are made simpler and more understandable.

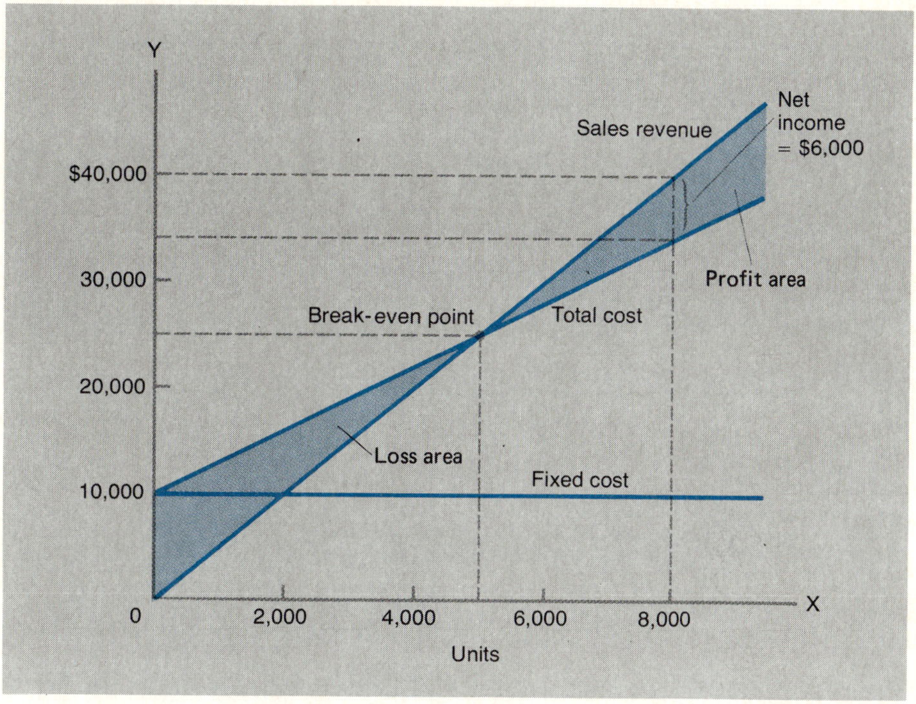

Figure 5-6
This cost-volume-profit chart illustrates the relationships of the cost data used in our break-even computations. Notice how easy it is to evaluate a wide range of activity levels with a visual presentation of the data.

The CVP chart shown in Figure 5-6 presents the CVP relationships illustrated in our initial break-even example on page 179: Fixed cost is \$10,000, variable cost is \$3 per unit, and selling price is \$5 per unit. The break-even point is read on the horizontal axis in units or on the vertical axis in sales dollars. The 5,000 units and \$25,000 coincide with the answers computed earlier. In addition to the break-even point, the graph shows profit and loss possibilities at various volumes of activity. For instance, at 8,000 units profit is \$6,000, shown by the vertical distance between the total revenue line and the total cost line.

Charts illustrating CVP changes. Any of the CVP analyses discussed in the chapter can be illustrated graphically. The four CVP charts in Figure 5-7 illustrate the graphic analysis of each of the variable changes in the cost-volume-profit analyses presented earlier. Each chart shows the original example of breaking even with fixed cost of \$10,000, variable cost of \$3 per unit, and a selling price of \$5 per unit. In addition, each chart illustrates a change in one of the variables and the effect of the change on the break-even point or on target profit. Chart (*a*) illustrates the addition of \$8,000 of target profit to the analysis; chart (*b*) shows a \$5,000 increase in fixed cost; chart (*c*) illustrates an increase of \$.75 per unit in variable cost; and chart (*d*) shows the decrease in selling price from \$5.00 to \$4.60. These graphic solutions can be verified by comparing them with computational analyses.

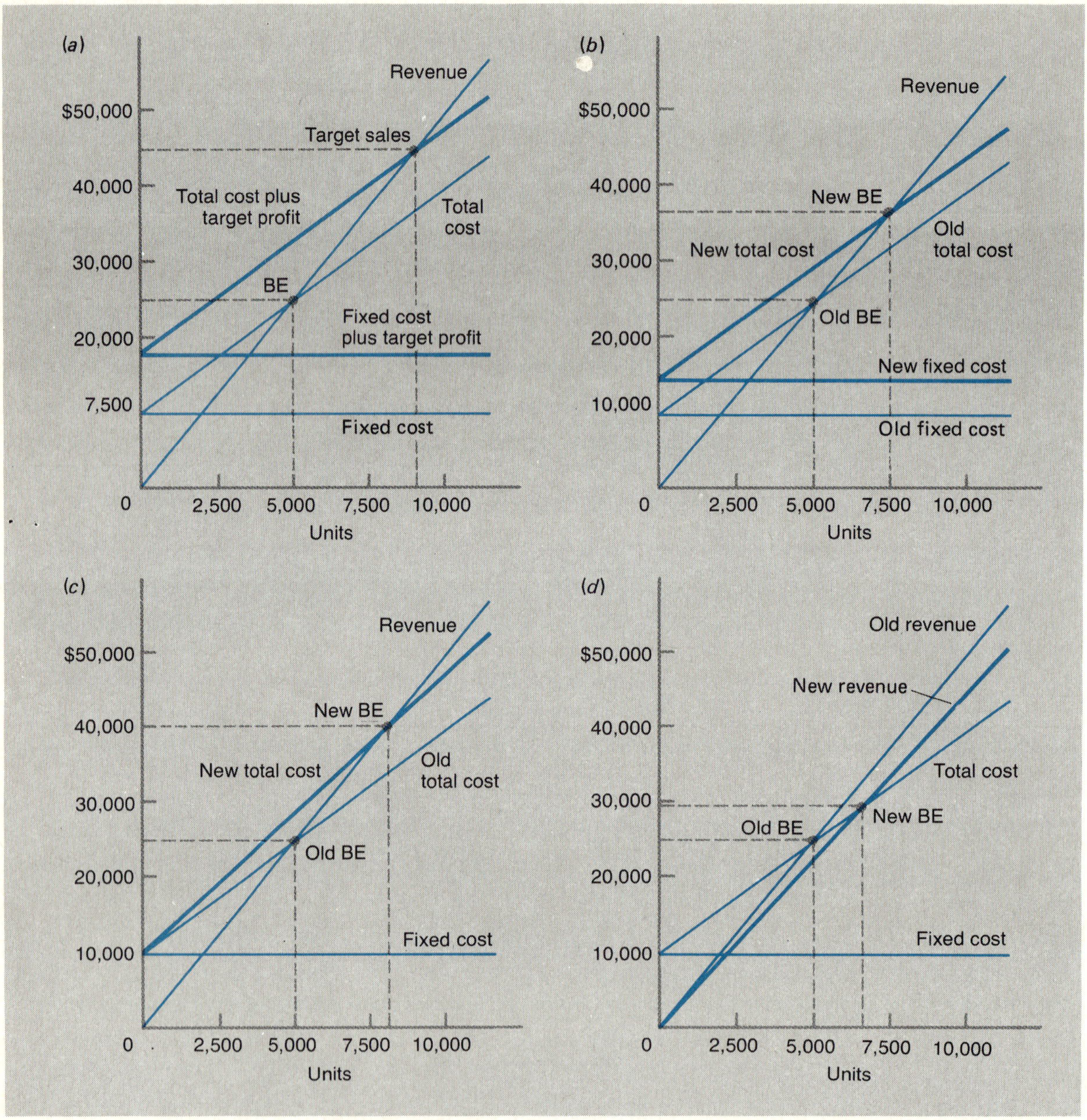

Figure 5-7 **CVP charts depicting the effect on the break-even point (BE) of changes in the data used to analyze cost-volume-profit relationships. The four charts illustrate: (*a*) adding a target profit, (*b*) increasing the amount of fixed cost, (*c*) increasing the per unit variable cost, and (*d*) decreasing the selling price.**

One limitation of graphs is that it is often difficult to determine a precise answer to break-even or other CVP analyses. Poorly drawn graphs may be of little use to managers. However, for some managerial purposes, visualizing CVP relationships is more important than computing precise answers.

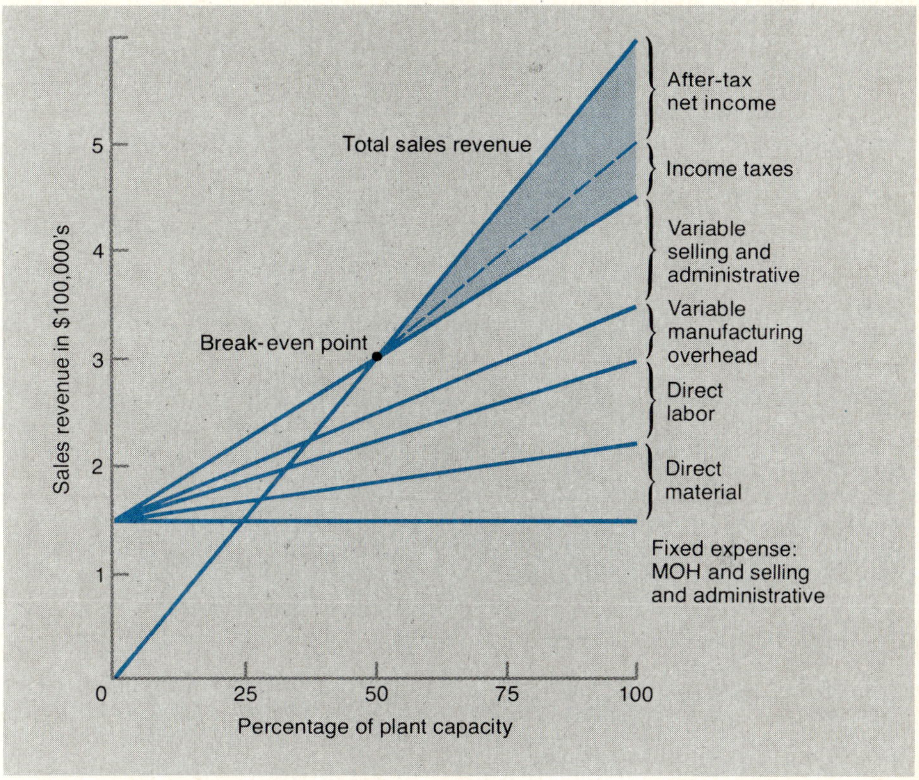

Figure 5-8
Detailed CVP charts provide managers with more analytic capabilities. Charts may be color coded or enhanced in other ways to provide better comprehension of the data.

Cost-volume-profit charts can include more details and information to provide more specific fixed and variable cost data. In Figure 5-8, fixed costs are $150,000, and variable costs are 50 percent of selling price. The break-even point is at $300,000 of sales, or 50 percent of plant capacity. This CVP chart reports several categories of variable costs, providing much information about the significance of each. The income tax line starts at the break-even point because income taxes are levied on net income. Like other internal management reports, CVP charts are limited only by the ingenuity of management and the cost-benefit relationship between the information in the report and the cost of preparing it.

A profit-volume chart highlights the break-even point and profit and loss

Profit-volume chart. A variation of cost-volume-profit charts is the **profit-volume chart,** which highlights the break-even point and profitability. A profit-volume chart is presented in Figure 5-9 using the same data found in Figure 5-6. The horizontal axis represents activity levels, and the vertical axis is the profit in dollars. Because any activity level below the break-even point yields a loss, the vertical axis has negative as well as positive values. Instead of revenue and total cost, the diagonal line is contribution margin, which is $5 − $3 in this example. The slope of the line is therefore $2 per unit. At the zero level of activity, there is a $10,000 loss because revenue is zero, variable cost is zero, but fixed cost is $10,000. By comparing the vertical distance between the contribution margin line and the

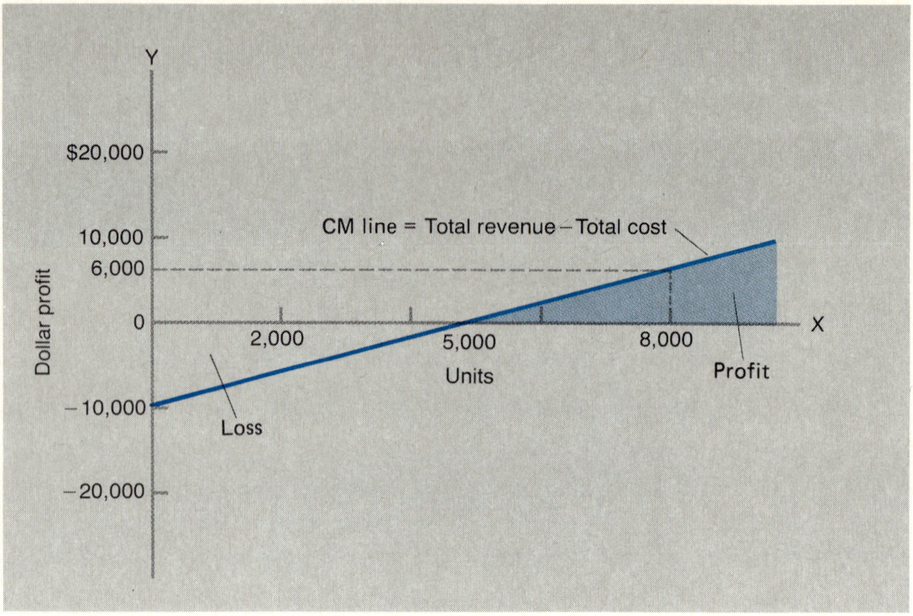

Figure 5-9
Profit-volume charts provide quick visual responses to break-even and profitability questions, although they lose some of the detailed cost and revenue information found on CVP charts.

horizontal axis, the profit or loss can be seen for various activity levels. The advantage of the profit-volume chart is that the profit and loss information is readily apparent.

The **contribution margin line** is the difference between total revenue and total variable cost. It touches the vertical axis at the point where the activity level is zero and all fixed costs are covered. The value of the vertical axis intercept in our example is

$$\begin{aligned}\text{Profit} &= \text{Total revenue} - \text{Total cost}\\ &= (\text{Units} \times \text{Sales price})\\ &\qquad - (\text{Fixed cost} + \text{Units} \times \text{Variable cost per unit})\\ &= (0 \times \$5) - [\$10{,}000 + (0 \times \$3)]\\ &= 0 - (\$10{,}000 + 0)\\ &= -\$10{,}000\end{aligned}$$

As you see, the contribution margin line intercepts the vertical axis at an amount equal to the negative value of the fixed cost. In fact this relationship is always true because both revenue and variable cost equal zero at the zero activity level. Therefore, at that point the loss (negative profit) is equal to the fixed cost that is incurred whether or not any activity takes place.

From its origin the contribution margin line slopes upward and to the right. The angle of the slope is determined by the contribution margin, so the higher the contribution margin, the steeper the slope. The profit or loss for any activity level can be read from the chart. At the 8,000-unit activity level, the profit-volume chart shows a profit of $6,000, just as in Figure 5-6.

Break-Even Analysis and the Relevant Range Assumption

CVP analyses outside the relevant range may be of little value

Cost-volume-profit relationships cannot be expected to be valid in all ranges of activity. They hold only for a relevant range of activity in which a business operates. All costs in CVP analysis are assumed to fall into fixed or variable categories and all costs and revenues are represented with straight lines. Some accountants believe a more realistic representation of costs and revenues is provided by a graph such as the one in Figure 5-10. This graph shows a curvilinear total cost line and a total revenue line with changing behavior patterns. The two curves cross twice and yield two different break-even points, *A* and *B*. The shaded area represents the profitable operating range.

Although the curves in Figure 5-10 represent realistic cost behavior, the graph includes activity levels that are outside of the relevant range, which means they have little or no chance of occurring. The relevant range is between X_1 and X_2 on the activity scale. In that range the two curves approximate straight lines and the total cost curve can be extended to the vertical axis to graph a mixed cost function. As long as CVP analyses are restricted to the relevant range, the straight-line assumption works well to provide managers with valid information.

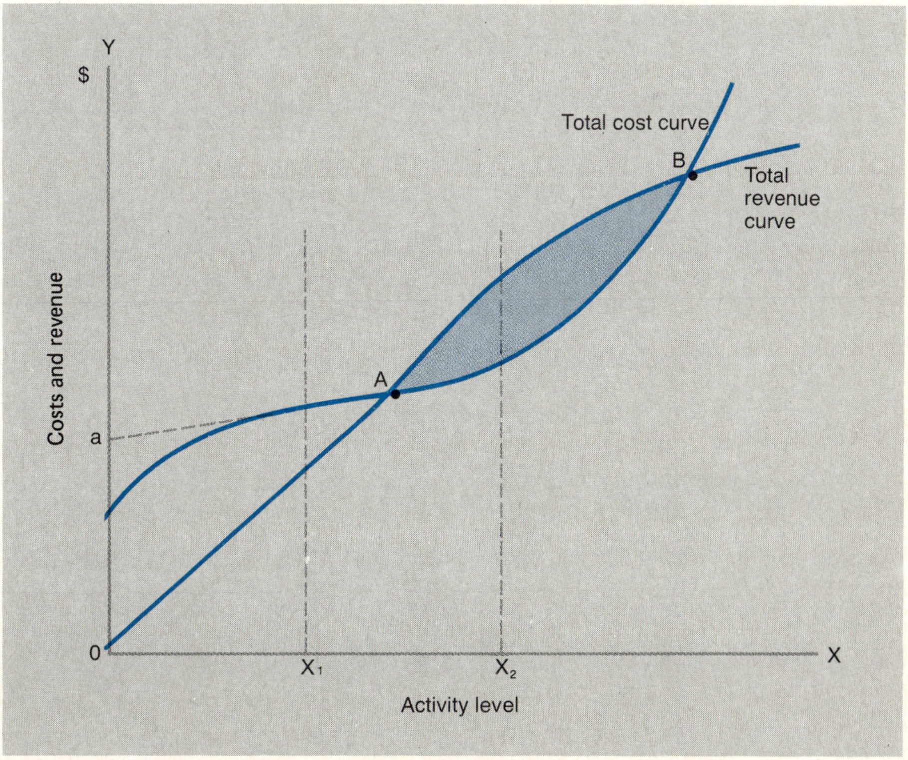

Figure 5-10
The accountant's view of the total cost and revenue curves may be somewhat limited, but it has proved useful in a wide variety of management planning, control, and decision activities. Note the relevant range within which linear relationships can be assumed.

Margin of Safety Ratio

The **margin of safety ratio** is a measure of the difference between the actual level of activity and the break-even point expressed as a percentage of sales. The ratio is computed as follows:

$$\text{Margin of safety (MS)} = \frac{\text{Actual sales} - \text{Break-even sales}}{\text{Actual sales}}$$

The range of possible values for the ratio is from $-\infty$ to $+1$. A positive value means the firm is operating above the break-even level of activity. To illustrate, a firm has actual sales of 24,000 units and a break-even point of 15,000 units.

$$\text{Margin of safety} = \frac{24{,}000 - 15{,}000}{24{,}000} = .375, \text{ or } 37.5\%$$

The margin of safety ratio may also be computed using projected data rather than actual data. For example, a company projects sales of $400,000 and a break-even sales level of $260,000; the expected margin of safety ratio is

$$\text{Margin of safety} = \frac{\text{Budgeted sales} - \text{Break-even sales}}{\text{Budgeted sales}}$$

$$= \frac{\$400{,}000 - \$260{,}000}{\$400{,}000}$$

$$= \frac{\$140{,}000}{\$400{,}000} = .35, \text{ or } 35\%$$

To illustrate the use of the margin of safety ratio, we refer to the two alternatives described on page 184. For the first alternative, the acquisition of new equipment, fixed cost is $30,000, variable cost is $2.60 per unit, and the selling price is $5 per unit. For the second alternative, the implementation of a new marketing program, fixed cost is $18,000, variable cost is $4.25 per unit, and the price is $5.50 per unit. The required sales level to achieve a target profit of $9,000 is 16,250 units with the first alternative and 21,600 units with the second alternative. If the target sales levels for both alternatives seem attainable, what is a reasonable basis for choosing between the two alternatives? First we compute the break-even point for each alternative.

Alternative 1

$$
\begin{aligned}
\text{Break-even sales} &= \text{Fixed costs} + \text{Variable costs} \\
\$5X &= \$30{,}000 + \$2.60X \\
\$2.40X &= \$30{,}000 \\
X &= 12{,}500 \text{ units}
\end{aligned}
$$

Alternative 2

$$
\begin{aligned}
\text{Break-even sales} &= \text{Fixed costs} + \text{Variable costs} \\
\$5.50X &= \$18{,}000 + \$4.25X \\
\$1.25X &= \$18{,}000 \\
X &= 14{,}400 \text{ units}
\end{aligned}
$$

The break-even analysis does not show which alternative is preferable. But we can obtain additional information by solving for the margin of safety ratios:

Alternative 1

$$
\text{MS} = \frac{\text{Expected sales} - \text{Break-even sales}}{\text{Expected sales}}
$$

$$
= \frac{16{,}250 - 12{,}500}{16{,}250} = .23, \text{ or } 23\%
$$

Alternative 2

$$
\text{MS} = \frac{\text{Expected sales} - \text{Break-even sales}}{\text{Expected sales}}
$$

$$
= \frac{21{,}600 - 14{,}400}{21{,}600} = .33, \text{ or } 33\%
$$

How do we use this additional information? Figure 5-11 illustrates the margin of safety ratio concept. Diagram (*a*) presents alternative 1. Both the break-even point and the target profit level are identified. To calculate the margin of safety ratio, the difference between expected and break-even activity, represented by the distance ***m***, is divided by the expected activity, represented by the distance ***n***. Alternative 2 is presented in diagram (*b*) of Figure 5-11. The margin of safety for alternative 2 is $\boldsymbol{m'/n'}$.

The margin of safety ratio is a measure of risk

If managers feel equally confident about achieving the target profit sales level, they may adopt the second alternative. Its level of expected sales is further above its break-even level of activity. Managers may con-

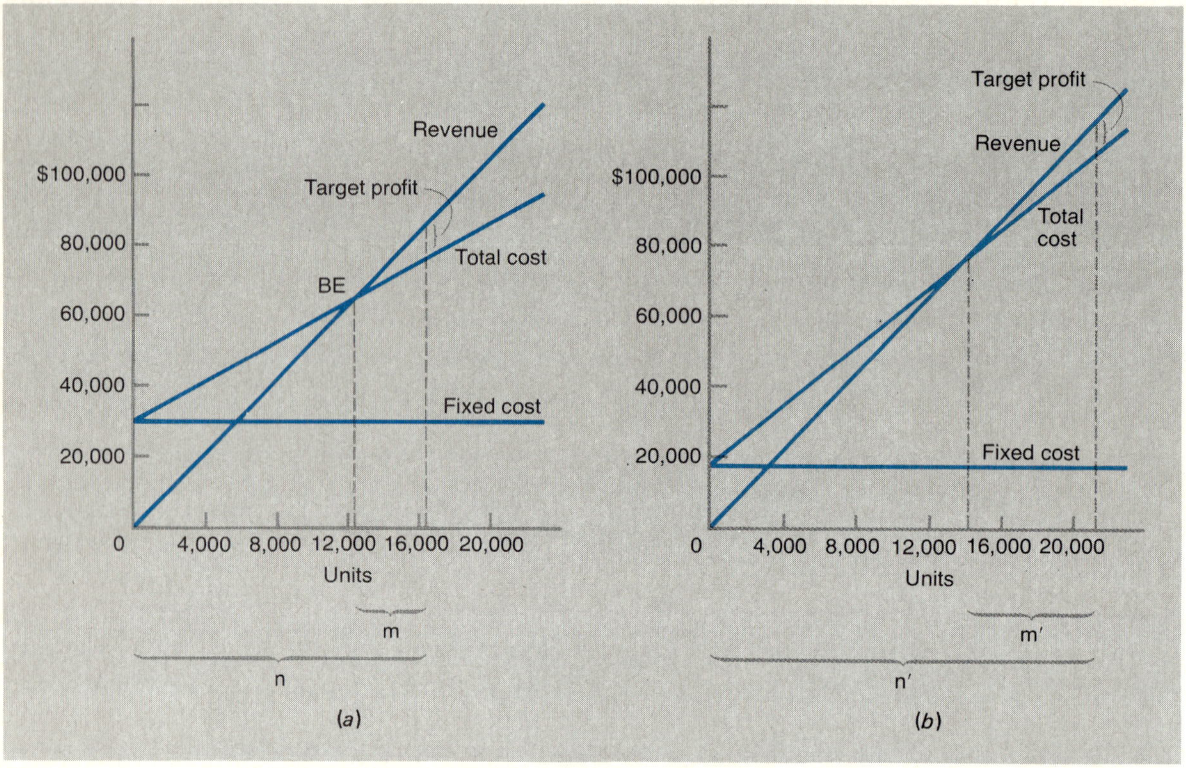

Figure 5-11 A graphic description of the margin of safety ratio. The two graphs show the break-even point (BE) and expected activity levels for two decision alternatives. The activity levels used to compute the margin of safety for each situation are on the horizontal axis.

sider alternative 2 less risky than alternative 1. Often the margin of safety ratio is used as a measure of risk because it measures the relative amount of actual activity level above or below the break-even activity level. The larger the margin of safety ratio, the safer the situation, as there is less risk of staying above the break-even point.

The interpretation of the margin of safety ratio depends on the individual using it and the type of decision being made. As in all ratio analysis, no absolute parameters can be established. The significance of any particular value for a margin of safety ratio varies among industries, managers, and decision situations. Nonetheless, as the ratio approaches 1, the situation becomes safer in terms of breaking even. As the ratio approaches 0, the risk of not breaking even increases. Negative ratios mean that the break-even point has not yet been reached. For example, if actual sales are 7,500 units and break-even sales are 9,000 units, the ratio is

$$\frac{7{,}500 - 9{,}000}{7{,}500} = \frac{-1{,}500}{7{,}500} = -.20, \text{ or } -20\%$$

MULTIPLE-PRODUCT BREAK-EVEN ANALYSIS

When a firm produces more than one product, break-even and other CVP analyses may require some additional computations and involve some limiting assumptions. If fixed cost cannot be identified with specific products, then the break-even analysis is performed for the group of products. To illustrate multiple-product break-even analysis, we use the following data:

	Product		
	A	B	C
Selling price	$10	$21	$25
Variable cost	8	14	18
Contribution margin	2	7	7
Contribution margin as a percent of selling price	20%	33.3%	28%
Percentage of total sales in terms of units	20%	50%	30%

Total fixed cost = $42,000

Break-Even Computations

Computing the average contribution margin of the group of products

Each product has a different selling price and variable cost. One problem in computing the break-even point is the lack of a single contribution margin that can be divided into the $42,000 fixed cost to find the break-even point. The problem is solved by computing an average contribution margin based on the expected percentage of total sales for each product. The unit contribution margin of each product is multiplied by its expected percentage of sales as follows:

A	$2 × .20 =	$ .40
B	7 × .50 =	3.50
C	7 × .30 =	2.10
Average contribution margin		$6.00

The $6 average contribution margin is the average of the individual product contribution margins weighted by their expected portion of total unit sales. No single sale results in a $6 contribution margin, but the average contribution margin based on the expected sales mix is $6 per unit.

An alternative method of finding the average contribution margin is to compute the weighted average selling price and weighted average variable cost and subtract one from the other to find the average contribution margin. Figure 5-12 shows the computations.

If the computations are based on historical sales and cost data, the results are **weighted averages.** If expected sales and cost data are used in the computations, the results are called **expected values.**

The expected sales price of $20 and the expected contribution margin of $6 do not equal any product price or contribution margin. The expected

Product	Sales Frequency	Sales Price	Expected Value	
	Average Sales Price			
A	.20	$10	$ 2.00	
B	.50	21	10.50	
C	.30	25	7.50	
Average sales price				$20.00
	Average Variable Cost			
A	.20	$ 8	$ 1.60	
B	.50	14	7.00	
C	.30	18	5.40	
Average variable cost				14.00
Average contribution margin				$ 6.00

Figure 5-12 Computation of expected contribution margin using the expected selling price and expected variable cost.

price of $20 is an **average.** We compute the break-even point for total sales in units as fixed costs divided by expected contribution margin.

$$\text{Break-even point} = \frac{\$42{,}000}{\$6} = 7{,}000 \text{ total units}$$

The break-even point can be computed in sales dollars by dividing the contribution margin ratio into the fixed costs. With expected sales price of $20 and expected contribution margin of $6, the contribution margin ratio is $6/$20, or 30 percent. Break-even in sales dollars is

$$\text{Break-even point} = \frac{\$42{,}000}{.30} = \$140{,}000 \text{ of total sales}$$

Multiple-product break-even analysis requires sales mix information

A multiple-product break-even point rests upon the critical assumption that the relative sales frequencies will occur. If the sales mix is different from the 20 percent, 50 percent, and 30 percent used in the computations, the calculated break-even point will be wrong.

The 7,000 units represent sales of all three products. To find the break-even point for each product, we multiply the break-even point in total units by the sales mix of the products.

The break-even level of sales for individual products

A	7,000 units × .20	= 1,400
B	7,000 units × .50	= 3,500
C	7,000 units × .30	= 2,100
Total break-even sales		7,000

The computation in sales dollars is as follows:

1,400 units × $10	=	$ 14,000
3,500 units × $21	=	73,500
2,100 units × $25	=	52,500
Total sales revenue		$140,000

Multiproduct break-even analysis assumes that fixed costs cannot be identified specifically with individual products. In our example the $42,000 fixed cost is assumed to be common to all three products. Where fixed costs can be identified with products, each product is assigned its appropriate fixed cost, and multiproduct break-even analysis is reduced to a set of single-product break-even computations.

SUMMARY

Cost behavior concepts are essential in understanding management accounting reports and in making many types of decisions and performance evaluations. **Cost-volume-profit (CVP) analysis** is a powerful management tool used to relate activity levels to changing costs and profits. The first step in CVP analysis is to determine a firm's cost behavior patterns. In addition to using the knowledge of experienced employees, the high-low method, the scatter diagram method, and regression-correlation techniques are used. The **high-low method** compares the change in cost and corresponding change in the volume of activity between the highest and lowest costs to obtain the variable cost rate and the fixed cost. **Scatter diagrams** are plots of cost data used to identify cost patterns. **Regression-correlation analysis** is a statistical method for relating two or more variables. **Simple linear regression** relates a single dependent variable to a single independent variable. The **independent variable** is given or derived from historical data. The **dependent variable** is so called because its value depends on the value of the independent variable and the relationship between the two variables as described by an equation. In cost analysis the dependent variable is usually cost and the independent variable is some measure of activity.

Regression-correlation analysis is a two-step process. The first step is to compute the **regression line,** which is a line whose equation best describes the linear relationship between the dependent and the independent variable. It is also called the **line of best fit.** Once computed, the regression line can be used to predict any value of the dependent variable, given some value of the independent variable.

Correlation analysis measures the strength of the relationship between the two variables. The **coefficient of correlation** is denoted as r, whose value ranges between -1 and $+1$. Positive correlation means that the dependent and independent variables move in the same direction. Negative correlation means that they move in opposite directions. The relationship between the variables is strong if r is close to -1 or to $+1$, and it is weaker as r approaches zero. To make interpretation of r easier, we usually convert it to r^2, which is called the **coefficient of determination.**

Break-even analysis is used to find the activity level at which total cost equals total revenue. The selling price minus variable cost is called the **contribution margin,** which can be divided into fixed cost to find the break-even point. Changes in fixed cost, target net income, variable cost, and selling price can be incorporated in CVP analysis. **Cost-volume-profit charts** assist managers in understanding and using CVP information. **Profit-volume charts** highlight the break-even point and profitability.

The **margin of safety ratio** measures the difference between the actual activity level and the break-even activity level expressed as a percentage of actual activity. The ratio is an indication of risk showing that the risk of reaching the break-even point decreases as the ratio approaches 1.

When a break-even analysis is made for multiple products, a single contribution margin is computed. With historical data it is a **weighted average contribution margin;** when using projected data, it is an **expected contribution margin.** The average contribution margin is used to compute the break-even point in total units or sales dollars, which can then be used to find individual product break-even points. Multiple-product break-even analysis rests heavily upon the accuracy of the sales mix information.

KEY TERMS

break-even point *(178)*
coefficient of correlation *(175)*
coefficient of determination *(176)*
contribution margin *(179)*
correlation analysis *(173)*
cost-volume-profit analysis *(178)*
cost-volume-profit (CVP) chart *(180)*
dependent variable *(173)*
expected contribution margin *(193)*
high-low method *(170)*
independent variable *(173)*
line of best fit *(174)*
margin of safety ratio *(190)*
profit-volume chart *(187)*
regression-correlation analysis *(173)*
regression line *(174)*
scatter diagram *(172)*
simple linear regression *(173)*
weighted average contribution margin *(193)*

QUESTIONS

1. What is meant by cost behavior patterns and why would managers be concerned with such things?
2. What is a scatter diagram and of what use is it to business managers?
3. While walking through the cost accounting department, the vice president of finance hears you mention the high-low method to a coworker. He asks you if that is a horse-race betting system. What is your response?
4. What is the purpose of using regression-correlation analysis?
5. Explain the two steps in regression-correlation analysis.
6. "Cost-volume-profit analysis and break-even analysis are two names for the same thing." React to this statement.

7. What is the purpose of using graphic presentations of accounting information? What specific advantages are there to using CVP charts?
8. How does a profit-volume chart differ from a CVP chart?
9. Why does the graph in Figure 5-10 show two break-even points? Is the accountant's view of break-even incorrect?
10. What is the margin of safety ratio and what information does it provide?
11. What effect does the relative sales frequency of products have on multiple-product break-even analysis?

EXERCISES

Ex. 5-1 Scatter diagram. Below are production cost data for Howe Corporation, which makes metal folding tables.

Units Produced	Direct Labor Cost	Facility Cost
80	$1,100	$520
150	1,600	800
120	1,500	570
60	700	500
210	1,750	910
190	1,700	850
140	1,600	600

Required: Plot the cost data on a scatter diagram and use the graph to estimate the direct labor cost and facility cost of producing orders of 100 units and 200 units.

Ex. 5-2 High-low cost estimates. The following are data on the cost of producing india ink linens by the Fineline Drafting Service:

Month	Linens Completed	Total Cost
March	51	$ 6,955
April	78	9,408
May	116	13,000
June	65	8,320
July	99	11,512
August	83	9,864

Required:

a. Use the high-low method to estimate the total cost formula for preparing linens.

b. Estimate the cost of preparing linens for a month of average activity.

Ex. 5-3 Understanding regression-correlation information. The manager of Flatone Brass Instruments Company believes that the company's utility costs are strongly correlated with production. He wants to develop a method of predicting utility costs with some reliability. Following are data collected over a 7-month period:

Utility Costs (× $100)	Hundreds of Units Produced
$11	8
9	8
16	6
23	10
13	8
8	4
12	9

Using the utility cost and production data, the manager computes the following regression line:

$$Y = \$539 + \$1.07X$$

where utility cost is the dependent variable and units produced is the independent variable. The coefficient of determination for the data is .232425.

Required:

a. Explain the meaning of the regression line presented above.
b. Estimate the total utility cost for the production of 600 units.
c. Evaluate and discuss the quality of the estimate you made in part *b*.

Ex. 5-4 Regression-correlation concepts. Wayfarer Hospital's controller is concerned about significant cost increases that have occurred over the last several years. Many doctors, nurses, administrators, and other hospital personnel have offered possible explanations for the cost increases. The suggested causes center around increases in patients served and inflation in general. The controller decided to use regression-correlation analysis to provide additional data for her analysis of costs. She analyzed total monthly medical-surgical costs and activity variables over the last several years and found the following relationships:

Activity Variable	Fixed Cost	Variable Cost per Unit	Coefficient of Determination
Patients served	$236,000	$456	.72
Patient days	144,000	132	.79
Physician hours	356,000	49	.43
Nursing hours	379,000	20	.51

Estimated activity levels for the coming year are 2,500 patients served, 8,800 patient days, 12,000 physician hours, and 32,000 nursing hours.

Required:

a. Write the regression line equation for each of the regression analyses summarized above.

b. Estimate the total medical-surgical costs for the coming year using **each** of the activity variables presented above.
c. In your opinion, which of your cost estimates in part *b* is most reliable? Explain.

Ex. 5-5 Computing the break-even point. The Heat Treating Division of the Georgian Company is evaluating a proposed steel treatment process designed to reduce corrosion. The treatment would require leasing several machines at a total annual cost of $85,000. A maintenance agreement and other fixed costs associated with the proposed new treatment would total $35,000. Expected variable costs for the treatment are $.02 per pound of steel. The firm plans to charge $60.00 per ton for the service.

Required: Compute the break-even point in units and dollars for the proposed steel treatment process.

Ex. 5-6 Break-even point and target profit. Bludon Company manufactures a product that it sells for $125. The variable cost to manufacture the product is $70 per unit and the variable cost to market and distribute the product is $15 per unit. The company has fixed manufacturing costs of $1,200,000 and fixed selling and administrative costs of $400,000. Management's current profit objective is to earn $120,000 of income. The new financial vice president proposed a target income of 15 percent on sales.

Required:

a. Calculate the break-even volume of activity both in units and in dollars.
b. Calculate the required volume of sales in units and in dollars to earn the firm's current target income.
c. Calculate the required volume of sales in units and in dollars to earn the vice president's proposed target profit.

Ex. 5-7 CVP pricing analysis. The Paradise Tavern is open from 11 A.M. to 12 midnight Monday through Thursday and from 11 A.M. to 2 A.M. Friday and Saturday. The tavern does a good business from 8 to 12 midnight Monday through Thursday and after 5 P.M. on Friday and Saturday. In an effort to increase sales, the owner of the tavern is evaluating a proposal to have a happy hour from 5 to 8 P.M., when all drinks would be two-for-the-price-of-one. The owner calculated the following data:

1. Monday through Thursday sales average $120 per day.
2. Variable cost of drinks averages 30 percent of price.
3. Fixed costs equal $3,500 a month.
4. Average sales from 5 to 8 P.M. on Friday and Saturday are $400 per day.

Required:

a. Calculate the Paradise Tavern's break-even point in annual sales with the current pricing system.
b. How much would sales have to increase with the happy hour proposal to warrant the new pricing policy?
c. What other variables might the owner evaluate?

Ex. 5-8 **Simple break-even analysis.** Moonbeam Company is the exclusive Montana distributor for a small manufacturer of alcohol-powered compact automobiles. The only model currently available is the Moonshine 85P, which sells for $6,000 and for which Moonbeam pays $4,500. Moonbeam's other variable costs are sales commissions, dealer preparation, and advertising, which together amount to $600 per car. Fixed costs are $10,800 per month. In June the company sold 10 cars and in July it sold 18.

Required:

a. Calculate the monthly break-even sales volume.
b. Calculate monthly net income for June and July.
c. Find the rate of return on sales for July.

Ex. 5-9 **Break-even point and the margin of safety ratio.** A manufacturing firm sold 95,000 bearing assemblies for $5 each. The assemblies require $2.80 of variable manufacturing costs and $.50 of variable marketing and distribution costs. Fixed manufacturing costs were $88,000 and fixed operating expenses were $48,000. The company is evaluating a proposal to raise the price of the bearing assemblies by $.50.

Required:

a. Calculate the current break-even point for the firm.
b. Calculate the current margin of safety ratio for the firm.
c. Calculate the break-even point with the proposed price increase.
d. Assuming the number of units sold does not decline with the increased price, calculate the new margin of safety ratio.

Ex. 5-10 **(CMA) Profit-volume graphic analysis.** The SAB Company uses a profit-volume graph similar to the one shown below to represent the cost-volume-profit relationships of its operations. The vertical (Y) axis is the profit in dollars and the horizontal (X) axis is the volume in units. The diagonal line is the contribution margin line.

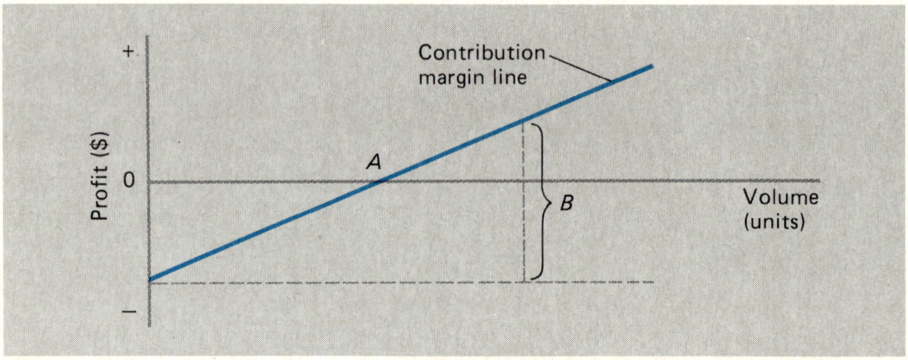

Required:

1. Point *A* on the profit-volume graph represents

   a. The point where fixed costs equal sales.
   b. The point where fixed costs equal variable costs.
   c. A volume level of zero units.
   d. The point where total costs equals total sales.
   e. The point where the rate of contribution margin increases.

2. The vertical distance from the dashed line to the contribution margin line denoted as *B* on the profit-volume graph represents

   a. The total contribution margin.
   b. The contribution margin per unit.
   c. The contribution margin rate.
   d. Total sales.
   e. The sum of the variable and fixed costs.

3. If SAB Company's fixed cost were to increase,

   a. The contribution margin line would shift upward parallel to the present line.
   b. The contribution margin line would shift downward parallel to the present line.
   c. The slope of the contribution margin line would be more pronounced (steeper).
   d. The slope of the contribution margin line would be less pronounced (flatter).
   e. The contribution margin line would coincide with the present contribution margin line.

4. If SAB Company's variable costs per unit were to increase but unit selling price stays constant,

   a. The contribution margin line would shift upward parallel to the present line.
   b. The contribution margin line would shift downward parallel to the present line.
   c. The slope of the contribution margin line would be more pronounced (steeper).
   d. The slope of the contribution margin line would be less pronounced (flatter).
   e. The slope of the contribution margin line probably would change but how it would change is not determinable.

5. If SAB Company decided to increase its unit selling price to offset exactly the increase in the variable cost per unit,

   a. The contribution margin line would shift upward parallel to the present line.
   b. The contribution margin line would shift downward parallel to the present line.
   c. The slope of the contribution margin line would be more pronounced (steeper).
   d. The slope of the contribution margin line would be less pronounced (flatter).
   e. The contribution margin line would coincide with the present contribution margin line.

Ex. 5-11 **Using CVP relationships.** While Ms. Martin was out her secretary received a call from Mr. John, who said, "Ms. Martin wanted some figures from me before I leave for Washington. Please give her this information: We break even at 1,200 units and our fixed costs are $20,160. These are quarterly figures. Last quarter the return on sales was 7 percent. Our contribution margin is steady at 35 percent."

When Ms. Martin returned she looked at the figures and said, "I wanted a lot more. Why didn't he give me sales and profit for the quarter? Call Mr. John back and get that information, and also find out variable cost per unit." When the secretary called back, Mr. John was already gone, so she asks you to look at the figures and help her get the rest of the information.

Required: Use the available data to find variable cost per unit, number of units sold, sales revenue, and net income for the quarter.

Ex. 5-12 **Break-even point and margin of safety.** Drifling Company's income statement as of year-end is as follows:

Sales (20,000 units)	$180,000
Variable expenses	110,000
Contribution margin	70,000
Fixed expenses	52,500
Net income	$ 17,500

Management is dissatisfied with the results and plans the following changes for the coming year:

1. Implement a new marketing program that would increase fixed costs by $9,600 and variable cost by $.50 per unit. The new program is expected to increase unit sales by 15 percent.
2. Increase sales price by 5 percent to help meet the additional marketing expense.

You have been hired as a consultant to determine the feasibility of such changes.

Required:

a. Calculate the old and new break-even points and margin of safety ratios.
b. Calculate the net income with the proposed changes.

Ex. 5-13 **Multiple-product break-even analysis.** Video Concepts, Inc., manufactures videotapes for use in video recorders. The company makes three grades of tapes—TH750, TH900, and TH1200. Below are production and sales data for the year.

Product	Sales Price	Variable Costs	Contribution Margin	Expected % of Units Sold
TH750	$5.00	$3.00	$2.00	60
TH900	7.00	4.50	2.50	30
TH1200	9.00	6.00	3.00	10
				100

Fixed costs were:

Manufacturing	$1,230,000
Administration	385,000
Marketing and distribution	500,000
Total fixed costs	$2,115,000

Required:

a. Calculate the break-even point in units and dollars for each product.

b. Calculate the volume and sales in total units and total sales dollars necessary to achieve a 30 percent return on sales.

PROBLEMS

P. 5-1 Scatter diagram and the high-low method. Rollins Company is preparing its overhead rate for the coming year. Below are overhead costs and machine hours for the first 8 months of the current year.

Month	Machine Hours	MOH Cost
January	50,000	$525,000
February	52,000	530,000
March	67,000	555,000
April	77,000	590,000
May	54,000	540,000
June	60,000	560,000
July	75,000	600,000
August	80,000	648,000

Rollins Company uses machine hours to apply overhead costs to production. The estimated number of machine hours for the coming year is 800,000.

Required:

a. Carefully plot the overhead cost data on a scatter diagram and draw a cost estimation line.

b. Use the high-low method to calculate the fixed and variable cost components for manufacturing overhead.

c. Calculate the manufacturing overhead rate for the next year.

P. 5-2 High-low method and cost estimation. Doorite Department Store uses both television and newspaper advertising to promote its products and good service image. The marketing director has accumulated 8 weeks of sales revenue and advertising cost data.

Week	Television Ads	Sales Dollars	Newspaper Ads
1	$2,640	$ 78,000	$1,620
2	2,000	60,000	900
3	3,360	67,000	1,520
4	6,000	110,000	1,900
5	4,040	97,000	1,820
6	4,400	83,000	1,780
7	5,020	85,000	1,680
8	4,600	100,000	1,840

The marketing director has contracted for $4,400 of television advertising and $1,600 of newspaper advertising for the next week.

Required:

a. Use the high-low method to calculate the fixed amount of sales and the variable sales per dollar of television advertising.
b. Use the high-low method to calculate the fixed amount of sales and the variable sales per dollar of newspaper advertising.
c. Calculate the expected level of sales for next week using expected television advertising costs and your fixed and variable cost data from part *a*.
d. Calculate the expected level of sales for next week using the expected level of newspaper advertising and the fixed and variable cost data you calculated in part *b*.
e. Which of the two sales estimates do you believe is most accurate? Why?

P. 5-3 CVP analysis with income statement data. Beloitte Manufacturing, Ltd., has the following income statement for the year just completed:

Beloitte Manufacturing, Ltd.
Income Statement
For the Year Just Ended

Sales (60,000 units)		$540,000
Cost of sales:		
Direct labor	$120,000	
Direct materials	90,000	
Variable MOH	30,000	
Fixed MOH	80,000	320,000
Gross margin		220,000
Variable selling expenses	50,000	
Fixed selling expenses	37,000	
Variable general and administrative expenses	70,000	
Fixed general and administrative expenses	33,000	190,000
Net income		$ 30,000

A proposed marketing campaign, which should double unit sales next year, is expected to add $50,000 of fixed cost and $.50 per unit of variable cost. A 20 percent increase in direct materials costs is expected next year and a new labor agreement will increase direct labor costs by 10 percent.

Required:

a. Compute the current unit contribution margin.
b. Compute the current break-even point in units and sales dollar.
c. Compute the current margin of safety ratio.
d. Excluding the marketing campaign, what effect will the expected cost changes have on the break-even point?
e. Should Beloitte Manufacturing, Ltd., use the marketing campaign? Support your answer with computations.

P. 5-4 Regression-correlation analysis for a county government. The board of supervisors of Hyumid County has collected some statistics on interest rates and number of building permits issued in the county in the past 9 years. The supervisors are concerned about the figures because interest rates this year are averaging 15 percent.

Year	Building Permits	Interest Rates
1977	2,210	9.6
1978	2,040	10.0
1979	2,560	9.1
1980	1,950	11.3
1981	1,740	11.6
1982	1,820	10.9
1983	1,530	12.5
1984	1,440	12.3
1985	1,200	13.8

The county controller ran a regression-correlation analysis on the building permit and interest rate data and found a coefficient of determination of .868082 and the following regression line:

$$Y = 4{,}804.80 - 264.62X$$

In the above equation the number of building permits is the dependent variable and the percentage interest rate is the independent variable.

Required:

a. Compute the expected number of building permits in the county for interest rates of 13, 14, 15, and 16 percent.
b. Comment on the reliability of your estimates in part *a*.
c. What does the negative sign of b mean?
d. Because b is negative, shouldn't the value of r^2 also be negative? Explain.

P. 5-5 CVP chart and changing variables. Cordova Company manufactures basketballs that are sold to retailers at $10 each. Unit variable costs are

Direct materials	$2.50
Direct labor	1.50
Variable MOH	1.00
Variable selling	1.50
Variable administrative	.50
Total	$7.00

Fixed costs are

Manufacturing overhead	$400,000
Selling	300,000
Administrative	200,000
Total	$900,000

This year's sales were 350,000 units. The company's desired net income is $6000 before taxes. The firm is evaluating a marketing program designed to help achieve the firm's target net income. The program would increase fixed costs by $145,000 and variable costs by $.25 a unit.

Required:

a. Calculate the break-even point in units and sales dollars.
b. Prepare a detailed cost-volume-profit chart, carefully labeled, based on the current situation.
c. Compute the margin of safety ratio for the current year.
d. Ignoring the marketing program, compute the sales level that will satisfy Cordova's net income requirement.
e. Compute the break-even point with the marketing program.
f. If the marketing program is implemented and sales are precisely enough to achieve the firm's minimum net income requirement, what is the margin of safety ratio?

P. 5-6 Analyzing CVP relationships. Below are cost and price data for five **independent** situations.

	A	B	C	D	E
Fixed costs	$315,000	$256,000	$239,000	$557,000	$____
Sales price	40	____	27	37	12
Variable costs/unit	25	17	____	29	8
Target profit	____	24,000	111,000	83,000	5,000
Required activity level in units	25,000	20,000	70,000	____	9,000

Required: Provide the missing values.

P. 5-7 Business decisions using CVP analysis. Julia Johnson, chief investment analyst for Crafton Company, has a file on a local doughnut shop that is for sale. The revenue and expense data for the most recent year are as follows:

Sales (30,000 dozen doughnuts)	$60,000
Less expenses:	
Variable	24,000
Fixed	39,000
Net loss	$(3,000)

The selling price of the shop is $50,000. It is estimated that sales could be increased by 15 percent if the shop remained open 3 more hours each night. This would have no effect on unit variable cost, but fixed costs would increase by $6,000 per year. The baking process has been a bottleneck in the production of doughnuts. An automatic doughnut machine would greatly increase productive capacity and reduce variable cost to $.40 a dozen. The machine would add $20,000 to annual fixed costs.

Required: Julia gives you the file and asks you to:

a. Calculate the current break-even point.
b. Calculate the current margin of safety ratio.
c. Calculate the minimum acceptable sales level for Crafton to purchase the doughnut shop assuming current operating conditions and assuming that Crafton requires a 30 percent before-tax profit on sales.
d. Determine whether the doughnut shop should stay open 3 hours later each night.
e. Calculate the new break-even point assuming the new machine is purchased.

P. 5-8 Break-even point and profit with regression analysis. Pied Piper Company owns a unique process for exterminating rats from cities. Its fees are based on a city's population. The company charges a fee of $15,000 per city plus $1 per person. Below are revenue and operating data for the last six contracts.

City	Operating Cost	Rat Population	Total Revenue
Hummel	$ 70,000	400,000	$ 55,000
Hamilot	125,000	1,500,000	165,000
Himmel	80,000	500,000	85,000
Homily	90,000	1,000,000	130,000
Hamlet	110,000	1,350,000	140,000
Humer	115,000	1,200,000	120,000

The company is negotiating a contract with the city of Hamelin, which has a population of 110,000. The rat population is estimated at 1,100,000. Using regression-correlation analysis on the data above, Pied Piper Company has computed a regression cost line where Y equals operating cost and X equals the number of rats in the city. This cost line is

$$Y = \$52,816 + \$.05X$$

Required:

a. Develop a total revenue line from the data provided.
b. Calculate the break-even point in units and dollars for the company's operations based on your estimates in part *a*.
c. Use the city population and estimate of rat population for Hamelin to determine the expected profit or loss on the contract.

P. 5-9 (CMA) CVP with cost and price changes and target profit. Laraby Company produces a single product. It sold 25,000 units last year with the following results:

Sales		$625,000
Variable costs	$375,000	
Fixed costs	150,000	525,000
Income before taxes		100,000
Income taxes (45%)		45,000
Net income		$ 55,000

In an attempt to improve its product, Laraby is considering replacing a component part that has a cost of $2.50 with a new and better part costing $4.50 per unit in the coming year. A new machine would also be needed to increase plant capacity. The machine would cost $18,000 with a useful life of 6 years and no salvage value. The company uses straight-line depreciation on all plant assets.

Required:

1. What was Laraby Company's break-even point in units last year?
   a. 6,000.
   b. 15,000.
   c. 21,000.
   d. 18,000.
   e. None of the above responses is correct.

2. How many units of product would Laraby Company have had to sell in the last year to earn $77,000 in net income after taxes?
   a. 29,000.
   b. 23,000.
   c. 22,700.
   d. 29,300.
   e. None of the above responses is correct.

3. If Laraby Company holds the sales price constant and makes the suggested changes, how many units of product must be sold in the coming year to break even?
   a. 15,300.
   b. 18,750.
   c. 19,125.
   d. 21,000.
   e. None of the above responses is correct.

4. If Laraby Company holds the sales price constant and makes the suggested changes, how many units of product will the company have to sell to earn the same net income after taxes as last year?
   a. 31,625.
   b. 31,250.
   c. 33,500.
   d. 25,300.
   e. None of the above responses is correct.

5. If Laraby Company wishes to maintain the same contribution margin ratio, what selling price per unit of product must it charge next year to cover the increased materials costs?
   a. $27.00.
   b. $25.00
   c. $32.50.
   d. $28.33.
   e. None of the above responses is correct.

P. 5-10 (AICPA) CVP analysis. The president of Beth Corporation, which manufactures tape decks and sells them to producers of sound reproduction systems, anticipates a 10 percent wage increase on January 1 of next year to the manufacturing employees (variable labor). He expects no other changes in costs. Overhead will not change as a result of the wage increase. The president has asked you to assist him in developing the information he needs to formulate a reasonable product strategy for next year.

You are satisfied by regression analysis that volume is the primary factor affecting costs and have separated the mixed costs into their fixed and variable segments. You also observe that the beginning and ending inventories are never materially different. Current operating capacity is 5,300 units.

Below are the current year data assembled for your analysis:

Current selling price per unit	$ 80.00
Variable cost per unit:	
Material	$ 30.00
Labor	12.00
Overhead	6.00
Total	$ 48.00
Annual volume of sales	5,000 units
Fixed costs	$51,000

Required: Provide the following information for the president using cost-volume-profit analysis:

a. What increase in the selling price is necessary to cover the 10 percent wage increase and still maintain the current profit-volume-cost ratio?

b. How many tape decks must be sold to maintain the current net income if the sales price remains at $80.00 and the 10 percent wage increase goes into effect?

c. The president believes that an additional $190,000 of machinery (to be depreciated at 10 percent annually) will increase present capacity by 30 percent. If all tape decks produced can be sold at the present price and the wage increase goes into effect, how would the estimated net income before capacity is increased compare with the estimated net income after capacity is increased? Prepare computations of estimated net income **before** and **after** the expansion.

P. 5-11 CVP analysis. The managers of Dormin Corporation are meeting to discuss the latest monthly report, which showed that sales of 6,250 kilograms of Zlotym, the company's brand of polyester, yielded only a 7 percent return on sales. The material sold for $30 per kilogram and had a variable cost of $19.50. The company's management wants to determine if it is possible to improve profit, and the president is asking for suggestions. Following are some responses:

1. "If we spend $2,500 a month advertising a 3 percent price reduction we should be able to increase unit sales volume 6 percent," suggests the marketing manager.
2. "We could get rid of that automatic blender that we rent for $6,500 per month. Going back to manual blending would increased direct labor cost $.50 per kilogram, but it should increase profits," says the production manager.
3. One of the production-line workers, who had just come in to change a burned-out light bulb in the meeting room, overheard the production manager's remark and said, "Get rid of that blender and get one of them new control units with the mixture selector. That'll save you $.50 a kilo." The production manager agreed that the control unit would produce a saving but noted that it rents for $4,000 per month.
4. The vice president suggested leaving production facilities alone. "I think a $2 decrease in price will give us a 16 percent increase in sales volume, and that's probably all we need."
5. The treasurer said, "We need a target profit of 10 percent of sales. Let's leave operations as they are and offer the salespeople an additional $1.50 commission on each kilo they sell. That will give them some incentive to increase the volume of sales."

Required:

a. Calculate fixed costs and break-even volume with the current situation.

b. Evaluate each of the five suggestions separately as independent situations by computing profit, return on sales, and break-even volume if the suggested changes are adopted.

P. 5-12 (CMA) Multiple-product CVP analysis. Hewtex Electronics manufactures two products—tape recorders and electronic calculators—and sells them nationally to wholesalers and retailers. The Hewtex management is very pleased with the company's performance for the current fiscal year. Projected sales through December 31, 1985, indicate that 70,000 tape recorders and 140,000 electronic calculators will be sold this year. The projected earnings statement, which appears on page 211, shows that Hewtex will exceed its earnings goal of 9 percent on sales after taxes.

The tape recorder business has been fairly stable the last few years, and the company does not intend to change the tape recorder price. However, the competition among manufacturers of electronic calculators has been increasing. Hewtex's calculators have been very popular with consumers. In order to sustain this interest in its calculators and to meet the price reductions expected from competitors, management has decided to reduce the wholesale price of its calculator from \$22.50 to \$20.00 per unit effective January 1, 1986. At the same time the company plans to spend an additional \$57,000 on advertising during fiscal year 1986. As a consequence of these actions, management estimates that 80 percent of its total revenue will be derived from calculator sales as compared to 75 percent in 1985. As in prior years, the sales mix is assumed to be the same at all volume levels.

The total fixed overhead costs will not change in 1986, nor will the variable overhead cost rates (applied on a direct labor hour base). However, the cost of materials and direct labor is expected to change. The cost of solid state electronic components will be cheaper in 1986. Hewtex estimates that materials costs will drop 10 percent for the tape recorders and 20 percent for the calculators in 1986. However, direct labor costs for both products will increase 10 percent in the coming year.

Hewtex Electronics
Projected Earnings Statement
For the Year Ended December 31, 1985

	Tape Recorders		Electronic Calculators		
	Total Amount (000 omitted)	Per Unit	Total Amount (000 omitted)	Per Unit	Total (000 omitted)
Sales	\$1,050	\$15.00	\$3,150	\$22.50	\$4,200.0
Production costs:					
Materials	280	4.00	630	4.50	910.0
Direct labor	140	2.00	420	3.00	560.0
Variable overhead	140	2.00	280	2.00	420.0
Fixed overhead	70	1.00	210	1.50	280.0
Total production costs	630	9.00	1,540	11.00	2,170.0
Gross margin	\$ 420	\$ 6.00	\$1,610	\$11.50	2,030.0
Fixed selling and administrative					1,040.0
Income before income taxes					990.0
Income taxes (55%)					544.5
Net income					\$ 445.5

Required:

a. How many tape recorder and electronic calculator units did Hewtex Electronics have to sell in 1985 to break even?
b. What volume of sales is required if Hewtex Electronics is to earn a profit in 1986 equal to 9 percent on sales after taxes?
c. How many tape recorder and electronic calculator units will Hewtex have to sell in 1986 to break even?

CASES

Case 5-1 **Multiproduct CVP analysis.** The Bluewater Fishing and Supply Company produces a variety of fishing equipment. The fishing rod division has three products. Unit price and cost data are presented below.

	Product		
	Graphite	Lightweight Fiberglass	Regular Fiberglass
Selling price	$40.00	$25.00	$15.00
Variable production costs	15.00	11.00	7.50
Variable selling costs	3.00	2.00	1.50
Variable administrative costs	2.00	2.00	2.00

The fishing rod division has the following fixed costs:

Fixed manufacturing overhead	$ 65,000
Fixed selling	25,000
Fixed administrative	45,000
Total fixed cost	$135,000

The new president of Bluewater is very interested in seeing that each division of the company contributes its fair share to the profit of the firm. Recent quarterly

Fishing Rod Division
Quarterly Income Statement
First Quarter, 1985

	Product			
	Graphite	Lightweight Fiberglass	Regular Fiberglass	Total
Sales in units	1,000	1,200	900	3,100
Sales revenue	$40,000	$30,000	$13,500	$83,500
Less variable costs:				
Variable manufacturing	(15,000)	(13,200)	(6,750)	(34,950)
Variable selling	(3,000)	(2,400)	(1,350)	(6,750)
Variable administrative	(2,000)	(2,400)	(1,800)	(6,200)
Product contribution margin	$20,000	$12,000	$ 3,600	35,600
Less fixed costs:*				
Fixed manufacturing				(16,250)
Fixed selling				(6,250)
Fixed administrative				(11,250)
Division net income				$ 1,850

One-fourth of the annual fixed costs for the division is assigned to each quarter.

Fishing Rod Division
Quarterly Income Statement
Second Quarter, 1985

	Product			
	Graphite	Lightweight Fiberglass	Regular Fiberglass	Total
Sales in units	500	1,000	3,000	4,500
Sales revenue	$20,000	$25,000	$45,000	$90,000
Less variable costs:				
Variable manufacturing	(7,500)	(11,000)	(22,500)	(41,000)
Variable selling	(1,500)	(2,000)	(4,500)	(8,000)
Variable administrative	(1,000)	(2,000)	(6,000)	(9,000)
Product contribution margin	$10,000	$10,000	$12,000	32,000
Less fixed costs:				
Fixed manufacturing				(16,250)
Fixed selling				(6,250)
Fixed administrative				(11,250)
Division net income (loss)				$ (1,750)

profit reports have raised serious doubts in the president's mind about the operations of the fishing rod division. The quarterly reports are as shown here.

The fishing rod divisional manager estimates that the sales mix in units for the third quarter will be 20 percent for graphite rods, 30 percent for lightweight fiberglass rods, and 50 percent for regular fiberglass rods. The marketing manager estimates that a new advertising campaign emphasizing the more expensive products would provide a sales mix of 30 percent graphite rods, 40 percent lightweight rods, and 30 percent regular rods. The advertising program would increase annual fixed costs by $16,200. The variable selling costs are composed entirely of sales commissions.

The president of Bluewater was not pleased with the first-quarter profit in the fishing rod division, which was only 2.2 percent of sales. However, in the second quarter a net loss was incurred in spite of the fact that unit sales increased 45 percent and dollar sales increased 7.8 percent. The president suspects gross mismanagement of the production operations, but before he takes action he calls you in, as an expert, to evaluate the situation.

Required:

a. Explain the lower profit yet higher sales of the second quarter.
b. Compute the break-even point for the third quarter in total sales dollars and unit sales assuming the division manager's estimated sales mix.
c. Compute the annual break-even point for each product assuming the advertising program is implemented.
d. Compute estimated margin of safety ratios for 1985 for parts *b* and *c*. Expected sales in 1985 are 16,000 units.
e. Evaluate the division's sales commission structure.

Case 5-2 Analysis of a multiple-service company. The Birchbark Guide Service offers packaged 3-day, 6-day, and 12-day canoe and hiking trips into wilderness areas of Canada. A good deal of preparation, such as equipment packing, trip planning, customer equipment orientation, and administrative correspondence and scheduling, precedes each of these trips regardless of length. The result is that the per-day cost of the trips is lower for the longer trips. All of the cost difference cannot be reflected in the pricing system, or prices would appear unfair to many potential customers. In addition, many 12-day-trip customers are former customers from the shorter trips. Management therefore looks on the 3-day trip as something of a service to generate customer loyalty and repeat trips that are longer. Below are the current price and cost data for the trips.

	3-Day Trip	6-Day Trip	12-Day Trip
Price	$75	$140	$250
Variable costs:			
Food	15	30	60
Supplies	9	18	36
Packing, cleaning, orientation, correspondence, etc.	36	42	49
Total variable cost	$60	$ 90	$145

Fixed costs include:

Depreciation on canoes, tents, sleeping bags, and other equipment	$13,000
Depreciation on store facilities and equipment	9,000
Property taxes, power costs, and other facility fixed costs	7,000
Administrative, marketing, and supervisory fixed costs	31,000
Total fixed costs	$60,000

The owners of Birchbark Guide Service have accumulated some trip data for the past 5 years. During that period 45 percent of the trips sold were 3-day trips, 30 percent were 6-day trips, and 25 percent were 12-day trips. Last year Birchbark sold 1,500 trips, which generated $207,375 in revenue but yielded only a $12,000 net income before tax. The owners are not satisfied with the performance, and they hire you to help analyze the situation. The owners believe that the trip mix would change to 20, 40, and 40 percent, respectively, for the 3-, 6-, and 12-day trips if the prices were dropped to $120 for the 6-day trip and $225 for the 12-day trip.

The owners also believe that many customers are afraid to chance a long trip into the wilderness without experience. A better advertising brochure could assist in convincing potential customers that longer trips are more economical and interesting. The owners think the 20 percent, 40 percent, 40 percent sales mix also can be achieved with the new brochures without a price reduction. The cost of the advertising program would be $15,000 a year.

Required:

a. Compute the unit contribution margin of each product.

b. Compute the price per day of each length trip. Compute the average variable cost per day of each length trip.

c. Using the average sales mix described above, compute the break-even point in total trips, in trips of each length, and in sales dollars.

d. If the owners' expected trip mix is correct with lower prices, and a new advertising brochure is not used, should the pricing changes be made?

e. Should Birchbark use the brochure rather than a price reduction?

Relevant Costs and Alternative Choice Decisions

6

Cost data are useful in evaluating most business decisions. But what kinds of costs are most useful in decision making? This chapter uses the cost behavior concepts introduced in Chapter 2 and the cost-volume-profit concepts in Chapter 5 to look specifically at the decision-making process. Concepts from this chapter are useful in many management reporting situations. When you have completed this chapter, you should understand:

1 The concept of alternative choice decisions.

2 The nature and use of relevant costs.

3 How two-alternative decisions are analyzed.

4 How cost indifference points are computed and used in analyzing alternatives.

5 How to analyze various alternative choice decisions such as make-buy, special order, and pricing decisions.

6 What a price indifference point is and how it is used in evaluating pricing decisions.

7 The nature of multiple-alternative decisions and how they are evaluated.

Relevance is one of the three basic characteristics of accounting information. **Relevance** refers primarily to the usefulness of accounting information in making decisions. Different individuals make decisions in different ways and there is no universal measure of relevance for all types of accounting information. However, some types of accounting information generally are more useful than others in making various kinds of business decisions. The purpose of this chapter is to present the concept of relevant costs and to relate it to decision making. Some of the more common business decisions are used to illustrate how relevant cost data are identified and used in decision making. We define relevant costs and then discuss how they are used to choose among alternative choices of action. Decisions involving two alternatives are discussed and illustrated first, followed by decisions involving three alternatives.

RELEVANT COSTS

Many types of accounting information are useful to managers. Unit costs of production may be useful in determining product prices, sales volume may indicate the success of a recent advertising program, balance sheet ratios may influence dividend payment decisions, and earnings per share figures may influence capital-raising decisions. Although many kinds of information are used by managers to make decisions, almost all business decisions are influenced by cost information.

Relevant costs provide information essential for decision making

Some costs are classified according to function, such as manufacturing or nonmanufacturing. Some are classified according to their behavior, such as fixed or variable. Sometimes functional and behavioral cost classifications are combined in describing costs such as fixed marketing costs or variable manufacturing costs. Not all costs are of equal importance in making decisions, and managers must identify those that are useful in specific situations. Such costs are called **relevant costs.** Costs that are relevant to a decision vary with the type of decision and the person making the decision. However, most people attribute two basic characteristics to relevant costs:

1. They are expected future costs.
2. They differ between decision alternatives.

Expected future costs are costs that are expected to occur during the time period covered by the decision. For example, a manager evaluating the cost of producing a new product during the next year uses the labor, materials, and overhead costs expected during the next year. Past or historical costs are relevant to the decision only if they are expected to continue in the future, or are used as the basis for predicting the future costs.

Relevant costs are expected future costs that are different between decision alternatives

Costs that **differ between decision alternatives** often are useful in analyzing decisions, but costs that are identical for each alternative have no impact on the decision. For example, if management is evaluating the purchase of either a manual or an automated drill press, both of which require skilled labor costing $10 per hour, the labor rate is not relevant because it is the same for both alternatives. If, however, the manual drill press requires semiskilled labor at $8 per hour and the automated drill press requires skilled labor at $10 per hour, then the labor rate may be relevant because it is different for the two alternatives. The difference between the amount of the two costs is called **differential cost.** In the above example differential cost is computed as follows:

$$\text{Differential cost} = \text{Cost of one alternative} - \text{Cost of the other alternative}$$
$$= \$10 - \$8 = \$2$$

ALTERNATIVE CHOICE DECISIONS

Many of the decisions discussed in this chapter are frequently referred to as alternative choice decisions. **Alternative choice decisions** are situations with two or more courses of action from which the decision maker must select the best alternative. In the broadest sense, virtually all decisions are alternative choice decisions. For instance, should you continue watching television or start doing your homework? This decision involves choosing between two alternatives. Similarly, during spring vacation should you go to Florida to sunbathe, Colorado to ski, or home to relax? A decision involving more than two alternatives is called a **multiple-alternative decision.**

There are many types of alternative choice decisions

Some decisions are based primarily on judgment, with little or no analytical data. Others involve systematic decision models. Some accounting data are useful in reaching most business decisions, and cost data are particularly useful in analyzing many alternative choice decisions.

The variety of alternative choice decisions is limitless. Some business examples are:

1. Should we manufacture or buy automobile windshields?
2. Should we sell a joint product at the split-off point or process it further?
3. Should we raise the price of a product or maintain the current price?
4. Should we keep our copying machine or acquire a faster one?
5. Should we produce the new fan wheels with semiautomated welding equipment or should we use fully automated welding equipment?
6. Should we accept a special order for a product below our normal selling price?

The analyses of these and other types of alternative choice decisions are often aided by relevant cost data. The discussions that follow illustrate a variety of alternative choice decisions and the types of costs relevant to each decision.

TWO-ALTERNATIVE DECISIONS

Decisions that involve choosing between two alternative courses of action are common. For instance, a sales manager is evaluating the choice of purchasing either a portable microcomputer or a portable computer terminal for all sales personnel. Sometimes one of the alternatives being evaluated is the current situation. For example, a plant manager is evaluating a sophisticated new telephone and intercom system. The new system offers several advantages, but the current telephone system is far less expensive.

To illustrate some important concepts in analyzing two-alternative decisions, we use Endline Corporation, which produces a variety of toy products. The firm is planning to produce a plastic dump truck to sell for $5. The management of Endline must decide between two methods of producing the dump trucks.

Method A requires leasing a plastic molding machine for $6,000 per year and purchasing a $2,000 annual maintenance contract on the equipment. Method B requires a more expensive automatic machine that has a higher maintenance contract but requires less labor to operate. The expected costs of the two production methods are listed in Figure 6-1.

All of the costs for the two plans are expected future costs, and they therefore satisfy one of the criteria for relevant costs. However, not all of the costs differ between the alternative production methods. Costs that are the same for each method are not relevant. Occupancy costs and materials costs are expected to be identical for the two methods. Three costs are expected to be different, and the differential amounts for these three costs are shown in the far right column of Figure 6-1. The three differential costs in our example meet both relevant cost characteristics.

Because the occupancy and materials costs are the same whether

Endline Corporation
Expected Production Costs for Plastic Dump Trucks
For Two Possible Production Methods

	Method A	Method B	Differential Fixed Cost
Fixed costs:			
Occupancy costs	$ 4,000	$ 4,000	$ 0
Maintenance contract	2,000	3,000	1,000
Machine lease costs	6,000	29,000	23,000
Total	$12,000	$36,000	$24,000

	Method A	Method B	Differential Variable Cost
Variable costs:			
Materials	$1.00	$1.00	$ 0
Labor	2.50	1.00	1.50
Total	$3.50	$2.00	$1.50

Figure 6-1
The relevant costs for comparing alternative courses of action are the costs that differ between alternatives. Here the differential costs are shown in a separate column.

Only relevant costs should be used in evaluating alternatives

management adopts method A or B, these costs will not affect the decision. However, the other three costs should be useful in making the decision. The maintenance contract and machine lease cost for production method B is $24,000 a year higher than with method A, but the variable cost of labor is $1.50 per unit less. The management of Endline Corporation has a choice between lower fixed cost and higher variable cost for A or higher fixed cost and lower variable cost for B.

If the decision is based solely on profits, the company will choose the plan that yields the higher net income. Because the selling price is the same for both production methods, production costs determine any difference in profit between the two alternatives. For example, if Endline expects sales of 13,000 trucks in the first year of production, the following analysis can be made:

		Method A		Method B
Sales	13,000 @ $5.00	$65,000		$65,000
Less fixed costs		(12,000)		(36,000)
Variable costs	13,000 @ $3.50	(45,500)	13,000 @ $2.00	(26,000)
Profit		$ 7,500		$ 3,000

At 18,000 units of sales, however, the results are as follows:

		Method A		Method B
Sales	18,000 @ $5.00	$90,000		$90,000
Less fixed costs		(12,000)		(36,000)
Variable costs	18,000 @ $3.50	(63,000)	18,000 @ $2.00	(36,000)
Profit		$15,000		$18,000

At 13,000 units, method A yields a higher profit, and at 18,000 units, method B is more profitable. In each case the profit is determined by applying the activity level to the cost data found in Figure 6-1. Although this approach provides an answer for both activity levels, it does **not** yield a general solution to the problem of selecting the appropriate production method.

The Cost Indifference Point

A general solution is found by using the relevant costs in Figure 6-1. At low levels of activity, Endline should use method A because the lower fixed costs more than compensate for higher variable costs. Eventually, however, the lower fixed costs are more than offset by the higher variable

The total cost of two alternatives is identical at the cost indifference point

costs, and then B becomes more profitable. The question is, at what level of activity does the choice shift from one production method to the other? The answer is the point where the lower fixed costs of A are offset **exactly** by its higher variable costs. This point is called the **cost indifference point;** it is the activity level at which the cost is identical for both of the two alternatives. The cost indifference point is computed by setting the cost formulas for each production method equal to each other as follows:

$$\text{Total cost of method A} = \text{Total cost of method B}$$

$$\begin{matrix}\text{Total fixed} \\ \text{cost A}\end{matrix} + \begin{matrix}\text{Total variable} \\ \text{cost A}\end{matrix} = \begin{matrix}\text{Total fixed} \\ \text{cost B}\end{matrix} + \begin{matrix}\text{Total variable} \\ \text{cost B}\end{matrix}$$

$$\$12{,}000 + \$3.50X = \$36{,}000 + \$2.00X$$

$$\$1.50X = \$24{,}000$$

$$X = 16{,}000 \text{ units}$$

At 16,000 units, both methods provide identical production costs and therefore yield the same profit. The lower fixed costs make A the more profitable production method below 16,000 units. Above 16,000 units, production method B is more profitable. At precisely 16,000 units, management is indifferent between the two plans. We can verify these conclusions by calculating the profit for each plan at 16,000 units and also just above and below this level of production. The calculations are presented in Figure 6-2.

Figure 6-2
The cost indifference point can be verified by substituting into each cost function values just above and just below the cost indifference point. With method A total cost is higher above the indifference point, whereas with method B total cost is higher below the indifference point.

	Method A		
Activity level	15,990	16,000	16,010
Sales	$79,950	$80,000	$80,050
Less:			
Fixed costs	(12,000)	(12,000)	(12,000)
Variable costs	(55,965)	(56,000)	(56,035)
Profit	$11,985	$12,000	$12,015
	Method B		
Activity level	15,990	16,000	16,010
Sales	$79,950	$80,000	$80,050
Less:			
Fixed costs	(36,000)	(36,000)	(36,000)
Variable costs	(31,980)	(32,000)	(32,020)
Profit	$11,970	$12,000	$12,030

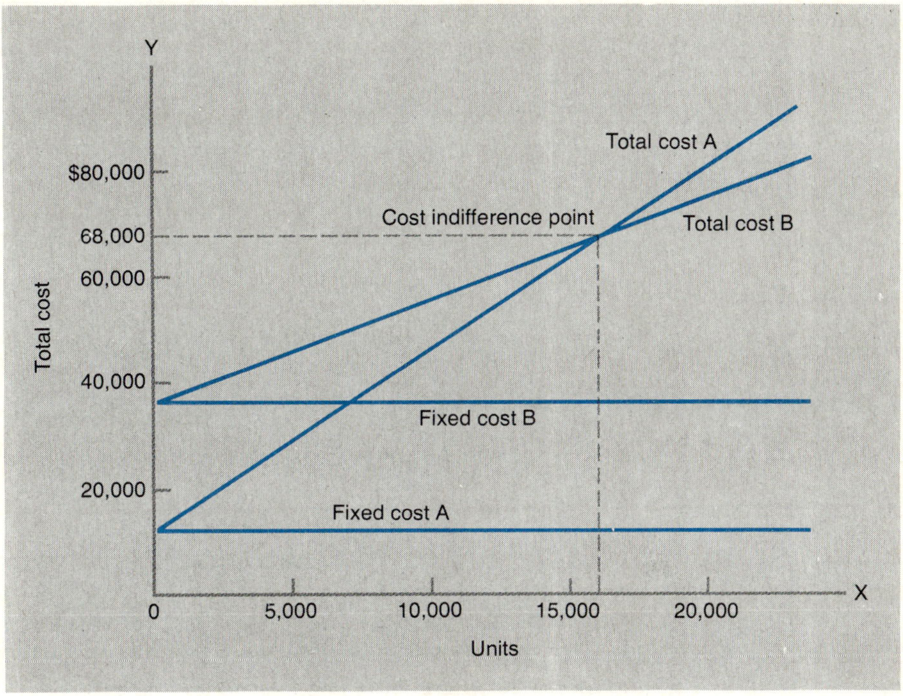

Figure 6-3
The total cost lines cross at the cost indifference point. The higher fixed cost of B is eventually offset by its lower variable cost.

The cost indifference point is presented graphically in Figure 6-3. Because of the lower fixed cost of method A, initially its total cost line is lower than the total cost line of method B. However, the higher variable cost of A causes the total cost line of A to have a steeper slope. Eventually, at the cost indifference point, the lower fixed cost of method A is entirely offset by its higher unit variable cost.

An alternative method of calculating the cost indifference point is to use only differential costs, identified in the far right column of Figure 6-1. The calculations are as follows:

$$\begin{aligned}\text{Cost indifference point} &= \frac{\text{Differential fixed cost}}{\text{Differential variable cost}}\\ &= \frac{\$36{,}000 - \$12{,}000}{\$3.50 - \$2.00 \text{ per unit}}\\ &= \frac{\$24{,}000}{\$1.50 \text{ per unit}}\\ &= 16{,}000 \text{ units}\end{aligned}$$

The graphic solution of the cost indifference point using differential costs is presented in Figure 6-4. The differential fixed cost is $24,000 ($36,000 − $12,000). The slope of the differential variable cost line is $1.50 per unit ($3.50 − $2.00). The differential variable cost exactly offsets the differential fixed cost at 16,000 units.

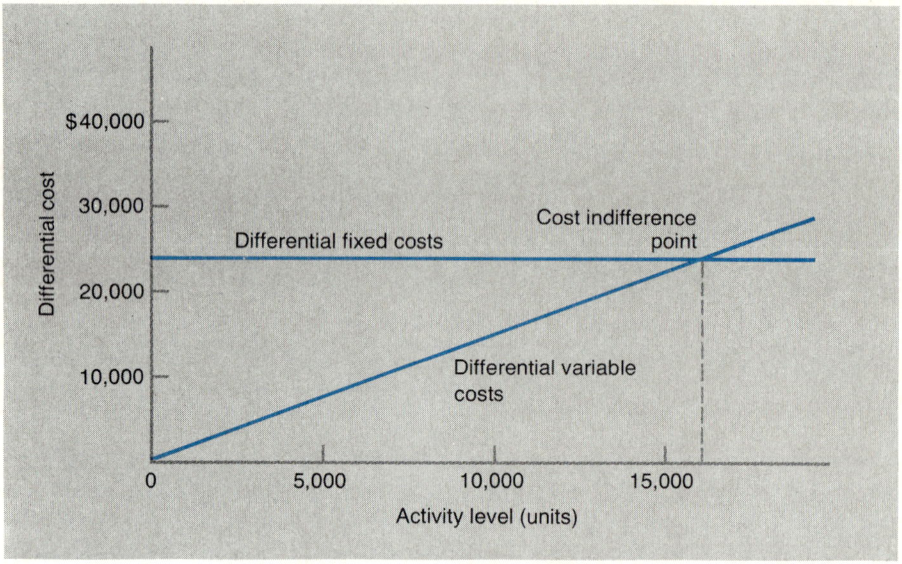

Figure 6-4
The advantage of lower fixed costs for production method A is eventually offset by its higher variable costs. At 16,000 units the two production methods have identical costs. Above 16,000 units method B has the lower total cost.

Notice that when the total cost equation is used to solve for the cost indifference point, the algebraic computations reduce the variables to the differential variable cost of $1.50 and the differential fixed cost of $24,000.

$$\$1.50X = \$24{,}000$$

Cost indifference points may be used to analyze alternative production methods, marketing plans, or quality control programs. Likewise, whether to make or buy a product, whether to process a product further or sell it at split-off, and whether to accept or reject an order at a selling price below normal are all examples of decision alternatives that may require the use of relevant costs and cost indifference points. Before illustrating several types of alternative choice decisions, we briefly discuss the distinction between break-even points and cost indifference points.

Break-Even Point Compared with Cost Indifference Point

The break-even point is the activity level at which total revenue equals total cost. The fixed and variable cost of the product and its selling price are used to compute the break-even point using the formula

$$\text{Selling price} \times \text{Units} = \text{Fixed cost} + \text{Variable cost} \times \text{Units}$$

On the other hand, the cost difference formula is

$$\text{Total cost of one alternative} = \text{Total cost of the other alternative}$$

Using the Endline Corporation data, two break-even points must be computed, one for each production method.

Production method A break-even point:

$$\$5X = \$12{,}000 + \$3.5X$$
$$\$1.5X = \$12{,}000$$
$$X = 8{,}000 \text{ units}$$

Production method B break-even point:

$$\$5X = \$36{,}000 + \$2X$$
$$\$3X = \$36{,}000$$
$$X = 12{,}000 \text{ units}$$

Cost indifference point analysis compares the costs of two alternatives

The cost indifference point is computed by equating the total costs of the two plans or by dividing the differential variable costs into the differential fixed costs. Using either approach we find that the cost indifference point of 16,000 units for the toy dump trucks is well above either break-even point in this example. The two break-even points and the cost indifference point are diagramed in Figure 6-5.

Break-even analysis compares the total cost and total revenue of a single alternative

Several important characteristics of cost indifference points are evident in Figure 6-5. Indifference point C occurs where the two **cost lines** intersect, that is, where the total cost is identical for the two alternatives. Break-even points A and B occur where the **total revenue line** intersects each of the total cost lines. The two analyses provide complementary, but different, information. Both may be useful in reaching a decision. For example, if expected sales are 17,000 units, the cost indifference analysis indicates that method B should be selected because it yields a higher net income than method A. However, if the risk of operating below the break-even point is high, managers may choose alternative A because it has a greater margin of safety. The margin of safety ratios for the two plans are

Method A

$$\text{Margin of safety ratio} = \frac{17{,}000 \text{ units} - 8{,}000 \text{ units}}{17{,}000 \text{ units}} = .53, \text{ or } 53\%$$

Method B

$$\text{Margin of safety ratio} = \frac{17{,}000 \text{ units} - 12{,}000 \text{ units}}{17{,}000 \text{ units}} = .29, \text{ or } 29\%$$

Management may be willing to forgo the expected extra income from B for the added safety of A.

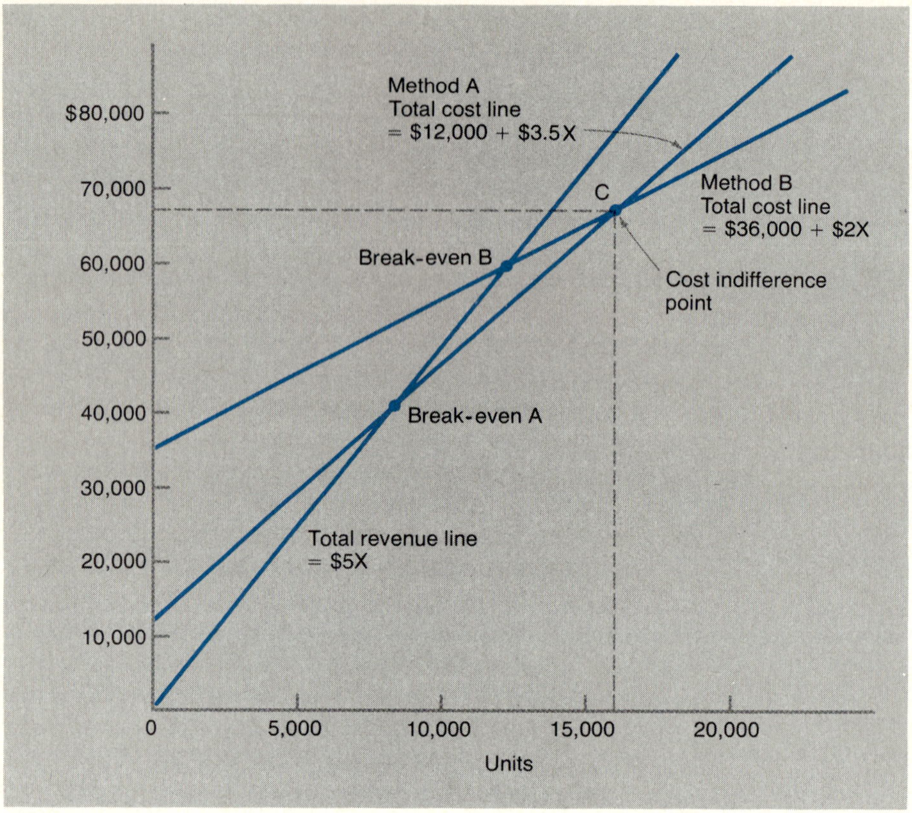

Figure 6-5
The break-even points occur where the revenue line crosses the total cost line of each alternative. The cost indifference point occurs where the two total cost lines intersect.

USING RELEVANT COSTS

You can see that cost indifference points may be used to select between two decision alternatives and how break-even points enter into the decision-making process. Now we turn to several specific types of business decisions and illustrate the use of relevant costs.

Make-Buy Decisions

A common alternative choice situation is a **make-buy decision,** in which the decision maker chooses between buying and manufacturing a product. For example, should an automobile manufacturer buy windshields or manufacture them, or should a brewer grow its own grains or purchase them? Make-buy decisions often involve tangible products, but some deal with administrative or service activities. For example, a firm may send its employees to executive development seminars or it may develop its own inhouse education program.

The analytical process for evaluating make-buy decisions requires isolating the costs relevant to the decision at hand. In make-buy decisions many cost data are in the form of unit costs, such as expected unit cost if an item is manufactured and expected unit price if it is purchased. Since manufacturing costs contain both fixed and variable components, it may be difficult to determine the costs that differ between alternatives, and unit costs must be used with caution to ensure valid comparisons.

We illustrate make-buy decisions with Mighty-Mite Tractors, a manufacturer of garden tillers. Currently the company purchases transmission subassemblies used in production. The current purchase price of $80 a unit is expected to increase to $90 next year. The company is operating at 70 percent of capacity and could manufacture the transmission subassemblies in its excess space. Additional fixed costs of $25,000 a year would be required to lease machinery and equipment. Management estimates a need of 5,000 units next year. Estimated cost data for the manufacture of the transmissions are presented in Figure 6-6.

Sunk costs are not relevant in making decisions

The unit cost data indicate that manufacturing the transmissions would cost $2 per unit more than buying them. However, the unit cost figure contains some costs that are not relevant to the decision, namely the allocated fixed cost. Capacity costs of $60,000 will be incurred whether the transmissions are manufactured or purchased. Such costs are called **sunk costs** because they have already been incurred and cannot be changed. Most committed fixed costs are sunk costs and are not relevant to the decision process. In the Mighty-Mite Tractors example, allocated fixed overhead costs are neither differential costs nor expected future costs and therefore fail both tests of relevant costs. The relevant unit cost is $80, which is the total unit cost of $92 less the allocated fixed manufacturing overhead cost of $12. The company can save $10 per unit by producing the subassemblies rather than buying them. Notice that the expected purchase price is used in the analysis. Historical costs are used for many types of internal and external reports, but for decision analysis, historical costs are useful only as indicators of future costs. In the example the cost of the transmissions is expected to increase to $90 a unit from the current $80.

Another type of relevant cost is **opportunity cost,** which is the benefit given up by rejecting one alternative and selecting another. For example,

Mighty-Mite Tractors
Estimated Production Costs
Transmission Subassemblies

Cost Item	Units	Unit Cost	Total Cost
Direct material	5,000	$25	$125,000
Direct labor	5,000	30	150,000
Variable MOH	5,000	20	100,000
Additional fixed MOH	5,000	5	25,000
Allocated fixed MOH	5,000	12	60,000
Total		$92	$460,000

Purchase alternative: 5,000 units @ $90 = $450,000

Figure 6-6
Estimated production cost data for 5,000 transmission subassemblies.

Opportunity cost is the benefit forgone by rejecting one alternative to accept another

if the management of Mighty-Mite Tractors decides to manufacture transmission subassemblies, it must forgo the use of the space for some other production alternative. The $10 per unit saving created by producing rather than buying transmissions results in a $50,000 annual saving ($10 × 5,000 units). However, an alternative use of the facilities may be to produce engine blocks at a saving of $15 per unit over the expected purchase price. If management expects to produce 5,000 units, the cost savings is $75,000 for the year ($15 × 5,000 units). Here the opportunity cost of producing the transmissions is $75,000 because the company must forgo the production of engine blocks, which would save $75,000.

Joint Product Decisions

In the discussion of joint product costs in Chapter 4, we distinguished between allocated joint costs and costs after split-off. Now we discuss how these costs are used in decision making. Joint product decision making is illustrated using Placerton Products Company, which produces two cleaning products, K-X and K-O, in a joint production process. The products are sold in gallon jugs. Both products require processing beyond the split-off point before they are ready for sale. Figure 6-7 presents a product cost schedule using both the physical units and sales value methods of joint cost allocation.

Figure 6-7 This figure illustrates the difference between unit costs of joint products as a consequence of using different methods of allocating joint costs. As with other decisions, the relevant costs for joint product decisions are future-oriented differential costs.

Placerton Products Company
Schedule of Joint Product Costs
For the Month of February

Physical Units Method

Product	Sales Price	Gallons Produced	Joint Cost		Cost after Split-Off		Total Product Cost	
			Total	Per Unit	Total	Per Unit	Total	Per Unit
K-O	$2	50,000	$62,500	$1.25	$18,000	$ .36	$ 80,500	$1.61
K-X	5	10,000	12,500	1.25	12,000	1.20	24,500	2.45
Totals			$75,000		$30,000		$105,000	

Sales Value Method

Product	Sales Price	Gallons Produced	Joint Cost		Cost after Split-Off		Total Product Cost	
			Total	Per Unit	Total	Per Unit	Total	Per Unit
K-O	$2	50,000	$50,000	$1.00	$18,000	$ .36	$ 68,000	$1.36
K-X	5	10,000	25,000	2.50	12,000	1.20	37,000	3.70
Totals			$75,000		$30,000		$105,000	

As with other alternative choice decisions, relevant costs play an important role in making joint product decisions. In general, joint product decisions can be categorized as those affecting a single joint product and those affecting the entire group of joint products. Typically, allocated joint costs are **not** relevant in making single product decisions, but they **are** relevant in analyzing decisions affecting the group of joint products. For example, another company markets a new product that competes directly with K-X. To remain competitive, the price of K-X must be reduced to $3.25. Should Placerton continue to produce K-X? The total product cost data in the last column of Figure 6-7 indicate two different conclusions.

Total Product Cost for K-X

Joint Cost Allocation Method	Unit Cost	New Price	Decision
Physical units method	$2.45	$3.25	Keep producing
Sales value method	3.70	3.25	Stop producing

The two decisions conflict because irrelevant cost data are used in the analysis. If the company continues to manufacture K-O, the allocated joint cost is not relevant because the total joint cost will still be incurred and will be assigned to the single product. Therefore, joint costs should not be used in this type of decision analysis. In this case the relevant cost for the production of K-X is the cost after split-off of $1.20 per unit. It is the only cost that differs between producing and not producing the product. The decision to stop or continue production should be made by comparing the new selling price of $3.25 with the cost after split-off of $1.20. The decision is to continue producing K-X because it contributes $2.05 ($3.25 − $1.20) per unit toward covering joint costs. If K-X were discontinued, the $12,000 cost after split-off would be eliminated, but all joint costs would remain. The resulting gross margin calculations are:

	Both Products	Single Product
Revenue	$132,500	$100,000
Less joint cost	(75,000)	(75,000)
Cost after split-off	(30,000)	(18,000)
Gross margin	$ 27,500	$ 7,000

Allocated joint costs are not relevant to single product decisions

The difference of $20,500 in gross margin is the 10,000 units of K-X produced times the $2.05 per gallon difference between the product selling price and the per unit cost after split-off. Not only is the allocated joint cost not relevant to the decision, but if it is used it leads to an incorrect decision and the subsequent loss of $20,500 of income. The above analysis assumes that K-X has no value at the split-off point.

Should the product be sold at the split-off point or processed further?

Some joint products have a market value at the split-off point as well as after further processing. Let us assume that K-O can be sold for $1 a gallon without processing beyond the split-off point. The company must decide if K-O should be sold at the split-off point or processed further. What costs are relevant for this analysis? For an individual product decision, only differential costs are relevant. If Placerton sells K-O at the split-off point, the revenue declines from $2 a gallon to $1, and cost declines by $.36 a gallon because there is no processing after split-off. Since the decline in revenue is greater than the decrease in cost, the product should be processed to completion. This decision is verified by analysis comparing the original situation and selling K-O at the split-off point:

Product K-O

	Process after Split-Off	Sell at Split-Off	Difference
Revenue	$150,000	$100,000	$50,000
Less joint cost	(75,000)	(75,000)	—
Cost after split-off	(30,000)	(12,000)	(18,000)
Gross margin	$ 45,000	$ 13,000	$32,000

The decline in revenue is $.64 a gallon more than the decline in cost ($1.00 − $.36). There are 50,000 gallons produced, so total gross margin would decline by $32,000, computed as $.64 × 50,000 gallons.

Assuming a different situation, K-X can be sold at the split-off point for $2.75 per gallon, or processed further and sold for $3.25 per gallon. If it is sold at split-off, the cost after split-off can be eliminated. In this situation revenue would decline by $.50 per gallon, but cost after split-off would decline by $1.20 per gallon. The net effect is a $.70 per gallon increase in gross margin, or a $7,000 total increase in profit ($.70 × 10,000 gallons). Therefore, the product should be sold at the split-off point. This can be verified by preparing a gross margin schedule for both products.

Product K-X

	Process after Split-Off	Sell at Split-Off	Difference
Revenue	$132,500	$127,500	$ 5,000
Less joint cost	(75,000)	(75,000)	—
Cost after split-off	(30,000)	(18,000)	(12,000)
Gross margin	$ 27,500	$ 34,500	$ (7,000)

Joint costs become relevant when one of the alternatives is to discontinue production of all the joint products in the group. To illustrate, Pla-

When should a firm discontinue producing an entire group of joint products?

certon Products Company has a policy of producing only products whose gross margin is at least 22 percent of selling price because a smaller gross margin does not cover marketing and administrative expenses. If the price of K-X declines to $3.25, the total revenue from all products is

Product	Units	Price	Revenue
K-O	50,000 gal	$2.00	$100,000
K-X	10,000 gal	$3.25	32,500
Total revenue			$132,500

The required gross margin on this group of joint products is $29,150, which is $132,500 × .22. To satisfy company policy, the revenue must cover all product costs plus $29,150 of required gross margin. The analysis is as follows:

Revenue	$132,500
Less joint costs	(75,000)
Cost after split-off	(30,000)
Target gross margin	(29,150)
Revenue deficit below minimum gross margin	$ (1,650)

In this situation the joint cost becomes a relevant cost because it is differential between producing both products and producing neither product. Given the company's policy on gross margin, the two products should not be produced.

Pricing Decisions

Pricing decisions are essential to the successful operation of all profit-seeking firms. Such firms must establish and revise the prices they charge to their customers for products and services. Even not-for-profit organizations may have to make pricing decisions, such as setting university tuition, establishing park user fees, and charging for a fishing license. Pricing is such an important topic that we devote all of Chapter 12 to pricing concepts and decisions. Here, however, we introduce the concept of relevant accounting information as it relates to pricing decisions.

A decision to change a price typically affects the number of units sold, the total sales revenue for the product, and product profitability. Managers may change a price to respond to competition, to increase product profitability, or to affect the volume of sales. Whatever the reason for the price change, the important question is, how will the price change affect sales volume and product profitability?

What effect does a price change have on sales volume?

Often it is very difficult to anticipate the precise effect of a price change. However, some general comments about pricing may be useful. A price increase makes the product less desirable to consumers, usually causing a decrease in the number of units sold. If the increase in price and the decrease in demand result in an increase in total revenue, the demand for the product is said to be **inelastic.** If an increase in the price and the corresponding decrease in the number of units sold results in a decrease in total revenue, the demand for the product is said to be **elastic.** For example, the demand for liquor in the United States is very inelastic because the quantity sold does not change significantly with increases in the price. The demands for tobacco products, basic food staples, and electric energy are relatively inelastic.

Products with ready substitutes have elastic demand. For instance, if one oil company raised the price of gasoline significantly above prices for the same grade of gasoline of other companies, most customers would switch to the lower-priced brands.

In many situations it is difficult to predict the precise impact of a change in the selling price of a product. For example, a manufacturer of basketballs sells them for $16 each. A price increase of $2 each is being evaluated. Management expects some decrease in the number of units sold, but there is controversy over the amount of the decline in sales because the **demand elasticity** of the product is not known. In such cases managers need data that can help them to decide whether to maintain the current price or raise it. One type of information is the price indifference point.

At the price indifference point the new price yields the same profit as the old price

The **price indifference point** is the level of sales with the new selling price that provides the identical **profit** achieved with the old selling price and old unit sales volume. For example, if the basketball manufacturer earned a $60,000 profit by selling 25,000 basketballs at $16 each, the price indifference point for the $18 selling price is the sales volume that will provide the same $60,000 profit.

To illustrate price indifference, we use the income statement presented in Figure 6-8. Steadler Manufacturing Company sells basketballs to dealers for $16 each. If the selling price is increased to $18, the volume of sales is expected to decline. The company is willing to increase the price if the resulting net income is greater than the $60,000 the company currently earns on the basketballs. The question is, how far can the volume of sales decline before the price indifference point is reached?

The solution is found using cost-volume-profit concepts. The target net income is $60,000. The solution is found by setting the total new revenue equal to the total costs plus target income.

Figure 6-8

Price indifference is based on the net income figure, which is $30,000 in this example.

Steadler Manufacturing Company
Income Statement
For the Year Ended December 31, 1985

Sales:	25,000 units @ $16	$400,000
Less: Variable cost	25,000 units @ $10	(250,000)
Fixed cost		(90,000)
Net income		$ 60,000

$$\text{Total revenue} = \text{Total costs} + \text{Target net income}$$

$$\begin{aligned}(\text{New selling price})(\text{Units sold}) = {} & (\text{Variable cost})(\text{Units sold}) \\ & + \text{Fixed cost} + \text{Target net income}\end{aligned}$$

Substituting and solving for X, the number of units sold, we get

$$\begin{aligned}\$18X &= \$10X + \$90{,}000 + \$60{,}000 \\ \$8X &= \$150{,}000 \\ X &= 18{,}750 \text{ basketballs}\end{aligned}$$

To check the answer, we compute net income at 18,750 units with the new selling price:

Revenue	18,750 × $18 =	$337,500
Less variable cost	18,750 × $10 =	(187,500)
Fixed cost		(90,000)
Net income		$ 60,000

The price indifference point of 18,750 units is the volume of sales at which the new price generates a profit equal to the profit at the old sales volume and old price. If management expects the sales volume with the new price to be below the price indifference point, the price increase should be rejected because profit will decline. Conversely the price change should be implemented if the expected sales volume with the price increase is greater than the price indifference point because profit will increase. For example, if 21,000 units of sales are expected at the new $18 selling price, profits for Steadler Manufacturing Company would be $78,000, or $18,000 higher than at the old price. The price indifference point provides a major benefit for management: Demand elasticity is hard to estimate, but it is relatively easy for many managers to decide whether or not the volume of sales will reach the price indifference point if the price is changed. As with cost indifference points, other factors affect the decision, such as the firm's public image, employee job security, and competitor actions.

The price indifference point is shown graphically in Figure 6-9. It occurs where net income with the new $18 price is identical to the $60,000 net income with the old $16 price. Both the new and the old price lines are graphed. The $60,000 profit is realized with the old price at 25,000 units. The profit is denoted as the distance n on the graph. Profit of $60,000 with the new price is achieved at a sales volume of 18,750 units. The profit with the new price is denoted by m on the graph. Of course, m and n are identical.

The higher price provides a higher contribution margin which results in a lower break-even point and a lower margin of safety ratio. For example, the break-even point was 15,000 basketballs, computed as $90,000/$6 per unit contribution margin. With the new price the break-even point is 11,250 basketballs, computed as $90,000/$8 per unit contribution margin.

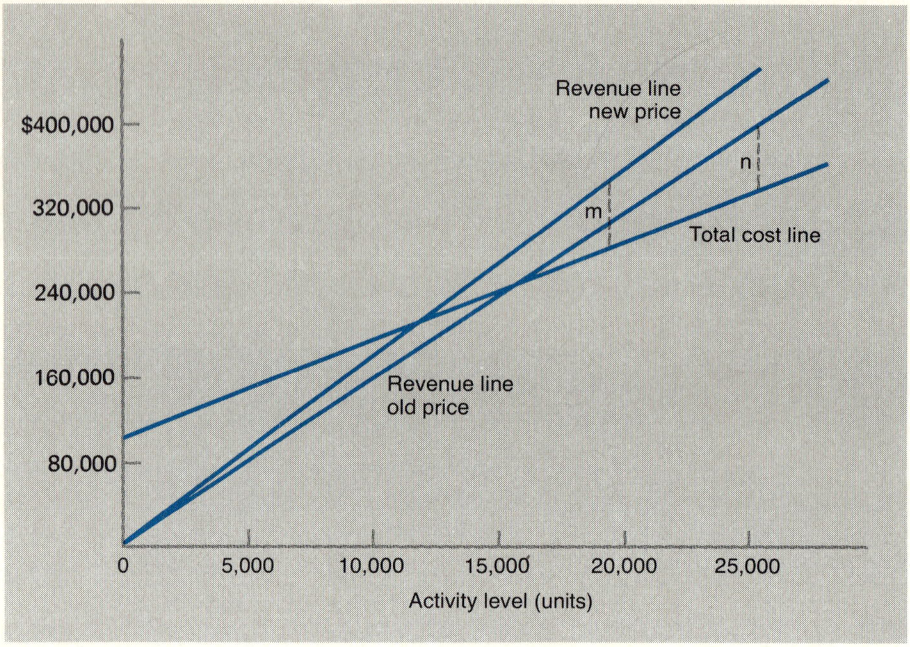

Figure 6-9
At the current price of $16, the net income of $60,000 is reached at a volume of 25,000 units. The same profit is achieved at a volume of 18,750 units with the new $18 price. Thus, 18,750 units is the price indifference point for the price increase.

Figure 6-10 presents another way of graphing this analysis. The fixed cost plus current or target net income is shown as a horizontal line representing the amount that must be covered by the contribution margin. The new price of $18 provides a contribution margin of $8. The old price of $16 provides only a $6 contribution margin. Both contribution margin lines start at the origin on the graph. However, the new contribution margin line increases faster than the old one and intersects the fixed cost plus net income line at 18,750 units. The old CM line intersects at 25,000 units. Figure 6-10 yields the same results as Figure 6-9; however, the contribution margin graph often is easier to read.

A variety of factors may be included in the analysis. For example, Steadler plans to raise the price of the basketballs to $20 but will improve the quality of the basketballs by using a tougher cover. The company estimates the proposed changes will increase marketing and production fixed costs by $10,000 and variable costs by $2 a unit. The analysis is performed as before.

$$\begin{aligned}\text{(New price)(Number of units)} = {} & \text{(New variable cost)(Number of units)} \\ & + \text{Old fixed cost} + \text{Additional fixed cost} \\ & + \text{Target profit}\end{aligned}$$

Substituting values and solving:

$$\begin{aligned}\$20X &= \$12X + \$90{,}000 + \$10{,}000 + \$60{,}000 \\ \$8X &= \$160{,}000 \\ X &= 20{,}000 \text{ units}\end{aligned}$$

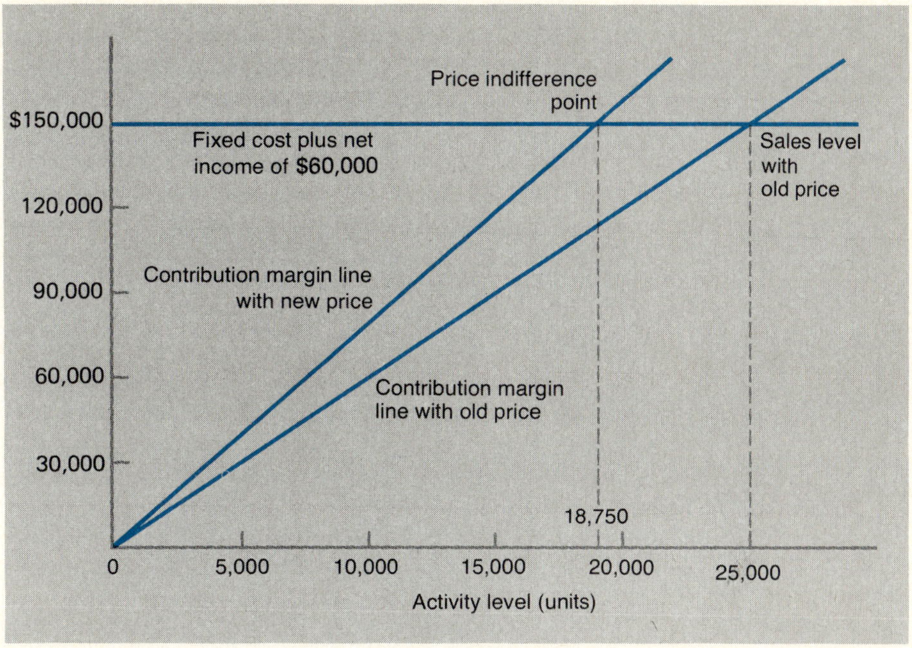

Figure 6-10
An alternative graphic approach to Figure 6-9 is to add the target net income to the fixed cost and then to graph the new and old contribution margin lines. The new CM line reaches the target net income line at 18,750 units, whereas the old CM line crosses the target net income line at 25,000 units.

The price indifference point in this illustration tells us that if expected sales at the new price and cost are greater than 20,000 units, then the new price and associated costs should be implemented. Often it is difficult to estimate accurately the sales level with a new selling price, but with a price indifference point, a pricing decision can be made without a precise estimate of sales level. In evaluating the $20 selling price and additional production and marketing costs for the basketballs, Steadler management may be uncertain of a specific sales estimate but believes that a range of 21,500 units to 23,000 units is reasonable. In spite of the inability to settle on a specific sales estimate, the management of Steadler can accept the new pricing and production plan because the lowest point in the range of sales estimates is still above the price indifference point.

The price indifference point is a two-alternative analysis

Notice that the comparison is between two pricing alternatives, the old and the new price. Although we add some cost changes, there are still only two distinct alternatives being evaluated. The price indifference point does not establish a price, but it assists managers in evaluating the alternatives.

Special Orders

All business opportunities should not be evaluated in the same way. For example, special orders or one-time orders often have different characteristics than recurring orders. As a result, each order should be evaluated based on costs relevant to the situation and the goals of the company.

For example, the Divine Fudge Company is operating at only 60 percent of capacity due to slow holiday season sales. A national organiza-

It may be logical to evaluate some orders differently than others

tion of high school bands approaches Divine Fudge with an offer to buy 1 million quarter-pound fudge bars at $.55 each, to be sold by high school band members to raise money. The fudge bars can be produced using the firm's current excess capacity. The company's chief accountant prepares the following cost estimates for the production and sale of the bars:

	Total Cost	Unit Cost
Direct materials	$250,000	$.25
Direct labor	100,000	.10
MOH (60% is allocated fixed MOH)	250,000	.25
Variable selling and administrative cost	50,000	.05
Total	$650,000	$.65

A glance at the unit cost data indicates that Divine Fudge Company would lose $.10 a bar, or $100,000, by accepting this special order. But allocated fixed overhead costs are not relevant to this decision because fixed overhead costs will be incurred whether the order is accepted or rejected. A more relevant cost analysis is as follows:

Direct materials	$.25
Direct labor	.10
Variable MOH (40% of total)	.10
Variable selling and administrative cost	.05
Total	$.50

Using only relevant costs in the analysis shows that accepting the order adds $.05 per bar, or $50,000, to the firm's profit. If no other factors affect the decision, the order should be accepted.

A major influence on special order pricing decisions is the effect on regular customers who are paying more than the special order customers for products or services. They may demand price reductions or stop buying from the firm. Another problem is that some special order customers may decide to become regular customers, but still expect the lower price. The Robinson-Patman Act serves as another obstacle to special order pricing. Basically, this law states that price differentiation between customers is illegal unless the price differences can be justified by cost differences.

MULTIPLE-ALTERNATIVE DECISIONS

Decisions involving more than two alternatives are called multiple-alternative decisions

Multiple-alternative decisions require the analysis of three or more alternatives in the decision. The decision process is more complicated for two reasons. First, more information must be gathered and analyzed with a large number of alternatives, sometimes resulting in **information overload,** which means that the decision maker has more information than can be reasonably absorbed. The second problem is that the computations and interpretation of the cost analyses are more complicated.

Although multiple alternatives introduce some complications, a logical analysis can be performed. Break-even points and cost indifference points can be computed, but with multiple alternatives, several cost indifference points may exist. Remember that a cost indifference point is the volume of activity at which total cost is identical for two alternatives. With multiple alternatives **each** alternative is compared with **every other** alternative to determine the cost indifference point for each pair of alternatives.

To illustrate the analysis of multiple alternatives, we use the example of the Lost County Court System. For each person brought before the court, a search of criminal records is made and a case report is prepared. Currently the entire process is done manually. Two other methods of doing the work have been suggested. One method requires the use of semiautomatic equipment and reduces labor time. A second method is almost fully automated and reduces labor even more. Both of the proposed methods require the leasing of equipment. In addition, the equipment requires periodic maintenance and repair, which are covered by a maintenance agreement. The court administrator must choose between keeping the current system or switching to one of the two new systems. Data for the three alternatives are presented in Figure 6-11.

Lost County Court System
Cost Analysis of Three Case Processing Methods

	Alternatives		
	A Manual	B Semi-automatic	C Fully Automatic
Monthly fixed costs:			
Occupancy	$1,500	$1,500	$ 1,500
Maintenance contract	0	500	1,000
Equipment lease	0	2,500	10,000
Total	$1,500	$4,500	$12,500
Unit variable costs:			
Supplies	$ 4	$ 8	$2
Labor	20	6	2
Total	$24	$14	$4

Alternative A: Current manual system
Supply cost is $4 per report.
Each report requires 5 hours of labor.
Labor rate is $4 per hour.

Alternative B: Semiautomated system
Supply cost is $8 per report.
Machine must be leased for $2,500 a month.
Each report requires 1 hour of labor.
Labor rate is $6 per hour.

Alternative C: Automated system
Supply cost is $2 per report.
Machine lease cost is $10,000 a month.
Each report requires 15 minutes of labor.
Labor rate is $8 per hour.

Figure 6-11
These are cost data for three alternative ways of processing the clerical work for cases brought before the Lost County Court System. With three choices the alternatives must be compared two at a time. Therefore, A must be compared with B, B with C, and A with C.

The first step is to compute the cost indifference point for each possible combination of alternatives using relevant cost data. Comparing the current manual system (alternative A) with the semiautomatic system (alternative B) yields cost indifference point AB.

$$\text{Cost indifference point AB} = \frac{\text{Differential fixed cost}}{\text{Differential variable cost}}$$

$$= \frac{\$4{,}500 - \$1{,}500}{\$24/\text{case} - \$14/\text{case}}$$

$$= \frac{\$3{,}000}{\$10/\text{case}}$$

$$= 300 \text{ cases}$$

This indifference point provides precisely the same type of information as in the two-alternative situations discussed earlier. With three alternatives, however, two other possible cost indifference points must be calculated. Therefore, we compute the cost indifference points for the manual system compared with the fully automated system, denoted AC, and for the semiautomated system compared with the fully automated system, denoted BC.

The comparison of the current manual system with the fully automated system yields indifference point AC.

$$\text{Cost indifference point AC} = \frac{\$12{,}500 - \$1{,}500}{\$24/\text{case} - \$4/\text{case}}$$

$$= \frac{\$11{,}000}{\$20/\text{case}}$$

$$= 550 \text{ cases}$$

The comparison between the semiautomated system and the fully automated system yields indifference point BC.

$$\text{Cost indifference point BC} = \frac{\$12{,}500 - \$4{,}500}{\$14/\text{case} - \$4/\text{case}}$$

$$= \frac{\$8{,}000}{\$10/\text{case}}$$

$$= 800 \text{ cases}$$

With two alternatives it is fairly easy to see that at activity levels below the indifference point the alternative with lower fixed costs and higher variable costs should be used. Above the indifference point there is a shift to the alternative with higher fixed costs because these costs are more than offset by lower variable costs. With multiple alternatives the concept is the same, but the comparison must be made for all the alternatives, not just two.

Select the alternative that yields the lowest total cost at the expected level of operations

Benefits are identical for the three alternatives but costs differ, so the objective is to select the alternative with the lowest total cost. Each alternative has the lowest total cost over **some** range of activity, which is determined by computing all cost indifference points. The best alternative is selected by determining the range of activity for which each alternative has the lowest cost and then determining in which range of activity the expected volume of activity occurs. If the choice is based solely on cost, management should select the alternative that provides the lowest total cost at the expected activity level.

The graph in Figure 6-12 shows the total cost line for each of the three alternatives. The intersections of the total cost lines are the cost indifference points. Alternative A, the current manual system, has the lowest cost from 0 to 300 cases. The other two cost lines are above it in this range of activity. Alternative B, the semiautomated system, offers the lowest cost from 300 to 800 cases. Above 800 cases the lower variable cost of the fully automated system makes it the most economical. The lowest cost for all levels of activity is shown by the heavy colored line in the diagram. Notice that indifference point AC is irrelevant because at that level of activity, the lower cost of alternative B renders the AC comparison meaningless.

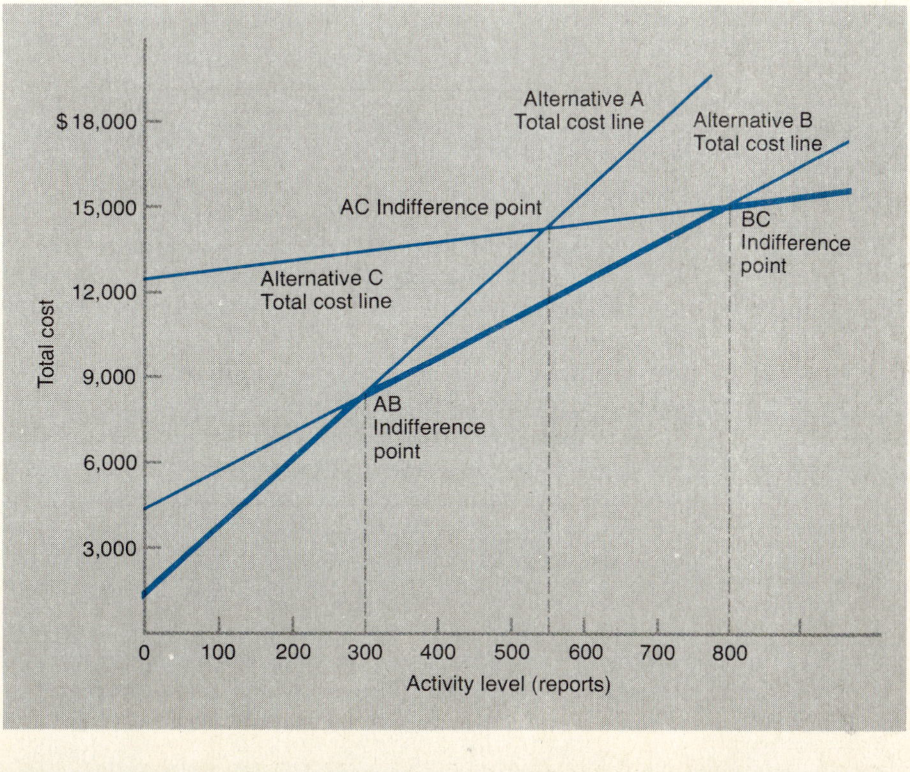

Figure 6-12
Three cost functions are graphed here. The minimum cost is the lowest cost line at all times. Here we start with alternative A, switch to alternative B at the AB cost indifference point, and switch to alternative C at the BC indifference point. A switch always occurs at a cost indifference point. The lowest cost path is highlighted with a heavy colored line.

At this point in the analysis there is not yet sufficient information to arrive at a decision. The cost information says:

With 0 to 300 cases use alternative A.

With 300 to 800 cases use alternative B.

Above 800 cases use alternative C.

To make the decision, the administrator must determine the most likely activity level that will occur in the future. The past history of the court's report-processing activity may be a good indicator of what can be expected. If the number of reports processed in the past remained fairly stable or showed a steadily increasing trend, good projections of future activity may be possible. Analysis of the past, however, may indicate that the number of reports processed fluctuates in a wide range, spanning more than one of the alternatives analyzed above. In that case, projections may be only marginally useful. In addition, the decision maker may have to modify the above findings. For example, alternative C may be the most desirable, but it may be politically unfeasible to eliminate the jobs of current employees. If the present caseload is 600 cases, alternative B appears most desirable, but C may be the better choice due to expected growth in the caseload. At 600 cases, alternative C would save money over the current manual system and at 800 cases it would become the most cost-effective system. Whatever the other factors, cost analysis for multiple alternatives is usually very beneficial.

Additional alternatives add complexity to cost analysis at a geometric rate. For instance, four alternatives may have 6 cost indifference points and five alternatives may have 10 cost indifference points. The possible number of separate cost indifference points for multiple alternatives is $n(n - 1)/2$, where n equals the number of alternatives. In this text we do not exceed three decision alternatives.

SUMMARY

Alternative choice decisions involve situations with two or more courses of action from which the decision maker must select the best alternative. Important components in the decision process are **relevant costs,** which are expected future costs that differ between decision alternatives. Costs that differ between decision alternatives are referred to as **differential costs.**

A **cost indifference point** is the volume of activity at which the costs of two decision alternatives are identical. The cost indifference point is used to compare two alternative methods of producing the same product or two alternative methods of providing the same service. Management's estimates of the activity level and the cost indifference point are used to select the best alternative based on cost.

The break-even point and the cost indifference point are two different measures. The former uses costs and revenue to measure the activity level necessary for the contribution margin to cover fixed costs. The latter uses costs only to determine the activity level at which the costs of two alternatives are identical.

Make-buy decisions involve choosing between producing an item and purchasing it. Such decisions require care when using unit production costs because unit costs may include many nondifferential costs. The correct decisions should be based only on relevant costs.

Joint product decisions should be separated into single product decisions and group product decisions. Costs after split-off are relevant for single product decisions. Joint costs become relevant only when one alternative is to terminate the production of the set of joint products.

Pricing decisions are difficult to make because a change in the price affects the volume of sales and total revenue, but the effect cannot be determined without knowing the **demand elasticity** of the product. A product has **elastic demand** if total revenue falls with a price increase. A product has **inelastic demand** if total revenue increases with a price increase. A **price indifference point** is the sales level at which the company's net income with the new price is identical to net income with the old price and sales volume. Pricing decisions may be made by estimating the expected sales volume and comparing it with the price indifference point.

Multiple-alternative decisions involve more than two alternatives. There are three possible cost indifference points for three alternatives and as many as six for four alternatives. The number of cost indifference points increases geometrically with the number of alternatives. The manager selects the alternative that yields the lowest cost at the expected volume of activity. However, the interpretation of multiple indifference points is complicated, and the additional data may lead to **information overload,** making it hard to integrate the data into a logical decision model.

KEY TERMS

alternative choice decisions *(217)*
cost indifference point *(220)*
demand elasticity *(230)*
differential cost *(216)*
elastic demand *(230)*
inelastic demand *(230)*
information overload *(234)*
make-buy decision *(224)*
multiple-alternative decision *(217)*
opportunity cost *(225)*
price indifference point *(230)*
relevant cost *(216)*
sunk cost *(225)*
two-alternative decisions *(217)*

QUESTIONS

1. What does the term *relevance* mean in reference to accounting information?
2. What are relevant costs? How are they distinguishable from other costs?
3. What is meant by alternative choice decisions? Give some business and personal examples.
4. What is meant by the term *multiple alternatives*? If a manager is deciding between five alternatives, how many separate cost indifference points are possible?

5. Describe cost indifference points and explain their usefulness in decision making.
6. As the company controller, you provide the company president with relevant cost data on the purchase of 10 new lathes. He says, "What do you mean, the $9 an hour we pay lathe operators is not relevant? I don't care what kind of lathes we buy, I am going to be interested in the amount we pay our lathe operators." Respond to the president.
7. Distinguish between a cost indifference point and a break-even point.
8. Why must managers use product costs cautiously when evaluating make-buy decisions?
9. When deciding between selling a joint product at the split-off point and processing further, what costs are relevant?
10. How is a price indifference point different from a cost indifference point?
11. "A price indifference point tells us what price should be used for a product." Comment.

EXERCISES

Ex. 6-1 Cost indifference point. Below are the projected cost data for the production and sale of lighted marine compasses. Two production methods are being evaluated. Each results in an identical quality product, but they have different costs.

	Process A	Process B
Prime costs	$10/unit	$14/unit
Variable MOH	3	2
Variable selling and administrative	2	2
Selling price	25	25
Total fixed manufacturing	$44,000	$20,000

Required:

a. Calculate the cost indifference point.
b. At what levels of activity should each production method be used?

Ex. 6-2 Calculation of cost indifference point. Corbin Products, Ltd. operates a water purification plant for the city of Torbin. The company is paid a fee based on the number of gallons processed. The company's management is evaluating the acquisition of some new treatment equipment for one phase of its operations. Below are estimated cost data for the current and proposed water treatment equipment.

	Current	Proposed
Fixed costs:		
Annual depreciation	$32,000	$71,000
Maintenance contract	12,500	22,500
Insurance and other fixed costs	5,500	9,000
Variable costs per 1,000 gallons treated:		
Labor	$.38	$.13
Fuel	.08	.05
Supplies and other variable costs	.04	.02

Required:

a. Compute the cost indifference point.

b. If Corbin Products, Ltd. expects to process 190,000,000 gallons of water during the next year, should the current or the proposed equipment be used?

Ex. 6-3 **Cost indifference point analysis.** Spencer Manufacturing Company is planning the construction of a new manufacturing plant to make wheel assemblies for its boat trailer division. Management is evaluating two types of plants. One is highly automated, requiring a relatively small amount of labor and providing highly efficient operations. The other plant requires more labor per wheel assembly but the plant investment is much lower than the highly automated plant. Below are estimated data for the two production plants.

	Plant A	Plant B
Variable costs per unit:		
Prime costs	$ 8	$ 5
Variable MOH	3	2
Fixed costs:		
Plant depreciation	45,000	65,000
Equipment depreciation	25,000	140,000
Utilities	15,000	40,000
Maintenance	10,000	25,000

Required:

a. Compute the cost indifference point.

b. Describe the logical course of action for all levels of activity based solely on cost.

c. Present a graphic analysis of the cost indifference point.

d. What other factors might enter into management's decision?

Ex. 6-4 **Break-even point and cost indifference point.** Nutty World, Inc., is evaluating two alternative methods of processing roasted cashew nuts. One method is a fully automatic shelling, roasting, and packaging machine, and the other method is partially automated with some manual operations. Both methods will produce the identical product, a 2-pound tin of cashews that sells for $6. Below are cost data for the two processing methods.

	Automated	Semiautomated
Variable cost per 2-lb tin	$2.80	$3.60
Fixed expenses	$42,000	$27,000

Required:

a. Compute the break-even point in units for both alternatives.

b. Calculate the cost indifference point for the two production methods.

c. Prepare a complete graphic analysis of the alternatives.

Ex. 6-5 Cost indifference point and break-even point. Following are cost data pertaining to different methods of mining road salt:

	Continuous Mining Equipment	Brine Solution Method
Variable costs per ton:		
Labor	$10.00	$ 4.00
Materials	.50	.80
Overhead	4.50	5.20
Total	$15.00	$10.00
Fixed costs:		
Equipment depreciation	$400,000	$ 600,000
Maintenance	200,000	300,000
Other overhead	200,000	300,000
Total	$800,000	$1,200,000

Salt is sold for $35 per ton. Last year the salt mine operated 225 days, with average production of 400 tons a day. The company expects the same volume of activity this year.

Required:

a. Compute the break-even point for each method.
b. Compute the cost indifference point.
c. Based on last year's production, which method should be used?

Ex. 6-6 Decision making with cost indifference point. The management of Robinstein's Department Store is evaluating methods of automating the customer billing system with the intention of improving the collection time on receivables. The selection has been narrowed to two billing systems. Bill-Fast would require leasing equipment for $6,000 a month. A maintenance contract and other fixed costs would amount to another $2,000 a month. Monthly variable costs including forms and other supplies would cost $.35 per customer. Other variable costs such as labor cost to run the equipment would be $.15 per customer. Speed-O-Bill is a more sophisticated and faster system. However, it is more costly to lease and maintain. The monthly lease cost for Speed-O-Bill is $15,000. Maintenance and other fixed costs are $5,000 a month. Monthly variable costs per customer would be $.30.

Required:

a. Compute the cost indifference point for the two alternatives.
b. Describe the decision you would make based solely on the cost indifference point.
c. Compute the total monthly cost of *each* system if there are 50,000 customer bills per month.

Ex. 6-7 Make-buy decision. Brumley Company makes the Bumble-Bee depth finder used by bass fishermen and others. Currently Brumley Company buys the display units used in the manufacture of the depth finders. The display units are now purchased for $14.00 each from a supplier, but Brumley was informed of a 10 percent price increase effective next year. The engineering department of the company has developed a proposal to manufacture the display units rather than buy them. Estimated cost data for the production of the units are as follows:

Direct materials	$ 8.00
Direct labor	4.50
Applied variable overhead	2.00
Applied fixed overhead	4.50
Total cost	$19.00

Of the estimated fixed overhead cost, $1.50 is for lease costs on new equipment that would have to be acquired if the display units are manufactured. The rest of the applied fixed overhead cost is for depreciation on the production plant and facilities. The firm is currently operating at 65 percent of capacity and the production of the display units would increase that to 75 percent of capacity. Brumley Company expects to produce 30,000 depth finders next year. No other alternatives are currently available for the excess space.

Required:

a. Determine if Brumley Company should make or buy the display units.

b. If the management of Brumley Company does not take your advice in part *a*, what would be the cost of the incorrect decision?

Ex. 6-8 Joint product decision analysis. Del-Mar Company manufactures chemical products in joint production processes. Kolon-G, used in food processing, is one of three products produced in a joint production process. Kolon-G currently sells for $18 per gallon. The cost of Kolon-G using the physical units joint cost allocation method is $15, of which $6 is cost after split-off. The product's unit cost is $13 using the sales value joint cost allocation method. The chemical could be sold at the split-off point for $12 and 80 percent of the product's cost after split-off could be eliminated.

Required:

a. Should the product be sold at the split-off point?

b. The marketing manager is concerned about a competitor's new product that may require a price reduction for Kolon-G. If the firm has to lower the selling price of Kolon-G to $11 per gallon, should the firm continue to produce and market the product?

Ex. 6-9 Pricing analysis. Stricklen Company sells a variety of boating and recreational accessories. A new product introduced last year is wooden canoe paddles which the company sells for $9 each. Production costs for the paddles are $5 of prime cost and $2 of applied overhead. About 25 percent of the overhead cost is variable. Variable selling and administrative costs associated with the paddles are $.50 per unit. During the first year, 10,000 paddles were produced and sold.

Company managers would like to increase the company's share of the canoe paddle market. They are convinced that a price reduction is necessary to accomplish that goal. Currently the company is operating at about half of its production capacity for canoe paddles. Production facilities and equipment to produce an additional 10,000 canoe paddles a year can be leased for $12,000. Management is evaluating a price reduction of $1 per unit.

Required:

a. At what sales volume would management be indifferent between the current selling price and the proposed selling price?
b. If sales would increase to 19,000 with the proposed price reduction and to 27,000 if the price is reduced to $7.50, what price should the company charge for canoe paddles this year?

Ex. 6-10 Price indifference point. Canadian Woods Treasures Company manufactures wool blankets which it sells for $80 each. At that price the company was able to earn a profit of $90,000 last year on sales of 8,000 units. Variable costs during the year were $50 a blanket, and fixed costs were $150,000. The demand for these quality blankets is high, and the company is evaluating a price increase to $90.

Required:

a. What is the price indifference point?
b. Should the price be raised if sales with the new price are expected to be 7,000 units?
c. If the price is increased and the expected sales level occurs, what is the net income for the year?

Ex. 6-11 Special order decision. MKS Marine Products, Inc., manufactures marine engines used primarily in recreational boats. Recently a company with several marine parks around the country offered to buy one hundred 50-horsepower outboard motors for $850 each. The motors are sold to dealers for $1,300 each. MKS is currently operating at 65 percent of capacity on its 50-horsepower line and could handle this order without exceeding capacity.

	Costs for 1,000 Units	Unit Cost
Direct materials	$ 400,000	$ 400
Direct labor	160,000	160
Manufacturing overhead (30% variable)	300,000	300
Marketing (50% variable)	150,000	150
Administrative (10% variable)	140,000	140
	$1,150,000	$1,150

Required:

a. Should the company accept the offer? Support your answer.
b. Compute the difference in net income that will result based on your decision in part *a*.

Ex. 6-12 **Multiple-alternative analysis.** McCaulley Company manufactures electric motors. Management is evaluating three methods of coil winding and assembly for the production of its 50-horsepower electric motors. Estimated cost data for the three alternatives are as follows:

	Method		
	A-10	A-25	A-50
Variable costs per motor:			
Direct materials	$ 40	$25	$18
Dirct labor	35	29	25
Variable MOH	33	24	20
Total	$108	$78	$63
Fixed costs per year:			
Equipment depreciation cost	$136,000	$250,000	$340,000
Maintenance contract on equipment	44,000	50,000	110,000
Total	$180,000	$300,000	$450,000

Required:

a. Compute the cost indifference points for the three alternatives.

b. Graph the costs for each of the alternatives. Draw a dark line along the lowest cost path of the three alternatives.

c. Describe the range of activity at which each alternative should be used.

Ex. 6-13 **(AICPA) Analyzing several alternatives.** You have been engaged to assist the management of the Arcadia Corporation in arriving at certain decisions. Arcadia has its home office in Ohio and leases factory buildings in Texas, Montana, and Maine, all of which produce the same product. The management of Arcadia has provided you with a projection of operations for 1986, the forthcoming year, as follows:

	Total	Texas	Montana	Maine
Sales	$4,400,000	$2,200,000	$1,400,000	$800,000
Fixed costs:				
Factory	1,100,000	560,000	280,000	260,000
Administrative	350,000	210,000	110,000	30,000
Variable costs	1,450,000	665,000	425,000	360,000
Allocated home office costs	500,000	225,000	175,000	100,000
Total	3,400,000	1,660,000	990,000	750,000
Net profit from operations	$1,000,000	$ 540,000	$ 410,000	$ 50,000

The sales price per unit is $25.

Due to the marginal results of operations of the factory in Maine, Arcadia has decided to cease operations and sell that factory's machinery and equipment by the end of 1985. Arcadia expects that the proceeds from the sale of these assets would be greater than their book value and would cover all termination costs.

Arcadia, however, would like to continue serving its customers in that area if it is economically feasible and is considering one of the following three alternatives:

1. Expand the operations of the Montana factory by using space presently idle. This move would result in the following changes in that factory's operations:

	Increase over Factory's Current Operations
Sales	50%
Fixed costs:	
Factory	20%
Administrative	10%

Under this proposal, variable costs would be $8 per unit sold.

2. Enter into a long-term contract with a competitor who will serve that area's customers. This competitor would pay Arcadia a royalty of $4 per unit based upon an estimte of 30,000 units being sold.
3. Close the Main factory and not expand the operations of the Montana factory.

Total home office costs of $500,000 will remain the same under all conditions.

Required:
In order to assist the management of Arcadia Corporation to determine which alternative is most economically feasible, prepare a schedule computing Arcadia's estimated net profit from total operations that would result from each of the following methods:

a. Expansion of the Montana factory.
b. Negotiation of long-term contract on a royalty basis.
c. Shutdown of Maine operations with no expansion at other locations.

PROBLEMS

P. 6-1 Two-alternative graphic analysis. Megawand Products, Ltd. manufactures home freezers. A new line of freezers requires a type of compressor not currently manufactured by the company. Two alternatives are to buy the compressors from a supplier or build a new facility for making the compressors.

One company has offered to build the specialized compressor for an annual fixed fee of $800,000 plus $70 per compressor. If Megawand builds its own production facility for the compressors, the estimated production costs are as follows:

Annual fixed cost:	
Depreciation, equipment	$900,000
Supervision	240,000
Occupancy costs	200,000

Variable cost per unit:	
Materials	$28.00
Labor	6.00
Variable overhead	6.00

Estimated annual need for the compressors is 15,000 units.

Required:

a. Carefully graph the total cost lines of the two alternatives.
b. Compute the cost indifference point.
c. Describe the appropriate course of action suggested by the cost indifference point for all activity levels.
d. Compute the total cost for the compressors at the expected level of activity using the most cost-effective course of action.
e. Compute the cost of selecting the incorrect alternative assuming the expected activity level occurs.

P. 6-2 Two-alternative analysis. The management of Verona Company is evaluating two methods for assembling the sensing devices for a metal detector that the company manufactures. One method of assembly requires many manual operations and a relatively small amount of investment in plant and equipment. An alternative assembly method uses less labor but requires a higher grade of material and a larger investment in plant and equipment.

Sales estimates for the coming year indicate the firm will need 13,000 metal detector sensing devices. Below are estimated cost data for the two proposed production methods.

	Automatic	Manual
Variable costs per unit:		
Materials	$5.00	$4.00
Labor and variable overhead	2.00	9.00
Fixed manufacturing costs:		
Plant depreciation	$30,000	$26,000
Machine depreciation and lease	56,000	4,000
Other	15,000	5,000

Required:

a. Compute the cost indifference point.
b. Graph the cost data and identify the cost indifference point.
c. What is the cost saving or loss of using the manual system if the company achieves its expected level of activity?
d. Answer part *c* again assuming 10,000 units are produced.

P. 6-3 Cost indifference points. The controller of Melburn Products seeks your advice on whether to replace its current manual assembly operation with an automated assembly line. The automated system would be much faster, use fewer employees, and reduce waste caused by errors. However, more skilled personnel would be needed to operate the system, and it involves a sizable annual lease cost. The data for the manual and automated systems are given on the following page.

	Manual	Automated
Variable costs:		
Materials	$ 8.00/unit	$6.00/unit
Labor	16.00/unit	9.00/unit
Variable MOH	6.00/unit	5.00/unit
Fixed costs:		
Occupancy	$150,000/yr	$160,000/yr
Machinery lease	—	290,000/yr

There is some concern that it is too late in the model year to change the assembly operation. If the company waits until the beginning of next year, it expects the varible costs to rise by 10 percent and the fixed costs by 6 percent. Next year's sales estimate is 33,000 units.

Required:

a. At what level of production should Melburn Products switch to the automated system based on current costs?

b. Graph the current year's cost data for the two alternatives.

c. Given the expected cost increases and sales for next year, decide if the assembly operation should be automated next year.

P. 6-4 Analyzing two computer alternatives. Medington Department Store uses a computer to process all of its credit sales transactions and to update customer accounts on a timely basis. The store averages 27,000 customer accounts. Daily credit sales transactions are input on terminals and weekly summaries are run. Updated customer records are printed weekly and given to customer information employees, who respond to all customer questions and complaints about accounts. Currently the store averages three requests per year per customer for account information.

A major problem with the current system is its lack of timeliness. Customer credit sales transactions early in one week are not available to customer information employees until the next week. This information lag creates many problems in dealing with customers. Management is evaluating two alternatives to eliminate this timeliness problem. Both alternatives are new computer systems. Each system has slightly different characteristics and costs but both will provide the information needed for timely customer data. Below are cost data for the two systems, including the lease of a separate computer for each system.

	Data-Sort	Data-Trex
Annual fixed costs:		
Lease cost	$34,000	$22,000
Maintenance cost	7,000	4,000
Insurance cost	4,000	2,000
Occupancy costs	8,000	7,000
Variable cost per inquiry:		
Labor cost	$1.60	$1.20
Supply cost	.30	.60
Other variable costs	.10	.40

Required:

a. Determine which information system is most cost-effective for Medington Department Store.

b. If the number of requests for customer account information rises to four per year per customer, which system should be used?

c. If the store selects the computer system you suggested in part *a*, and actual account requests per customer average four per year, what is the cost of the decision?

P. 6-5 Break-even, cost, and price indifference points. Two different methods of producing a new product are being evaluated by the Schwartz Company. A new plant facility will be needed for either production method. However, one method requires a significantly higher plant and equipment investment while providing a lower variable cost of production. Sales estimates for the first year of production are 30,000 units at a price of $80 each. Below are estimated cost data for the two production plans:

	Method A	Method B
Variable costs:		
Direct materials	$20	$22
Direct labor	17	8
Variable overhead	8	5
Variable marketing, distribution, and administration	5	5
Annual fixed costs:		
Depreciation, equipment	$70,000	$200,000
Depreciation, production facilities	90,000	120,000
Other fixed overhead	20,000	30,000
Marketing, distribution, and administration	90,000	90,000

Required:

a. Compute the cost indifference point.

b. Compute the break-even point for the two alternatives.

c. Compute the net income for the first year given the expected sales level and the more cost-effective production method.

d. Compute the price indifference point for a $10 increase in the price of the product.

P. 6-6 Two-alternative analysis. The McClellen Fence Company has been in business 40 years selling and installing chain link fences. The company employs four full-time installers as well as three part-time employees who supplement their other income by working for McClellen during busy periods. Last year McClellen sold and installed 34,000 feet of chain link fence at an average price of $4 per foot. The company expects sales to increase by 10 percent this year, with prices and costs remaining the same. Recently the company hired a consulting firm to suggest methods of improving the company's shrinking profit margin. The consultants returned with a plan that involved leasing new, more efficient installation equipment that would greatly reduce the amount of manual labor involved in setting posts and stretching fence. The owner of the company is concerned about any actions that would require terminating part-time or full-time employees. Following are data on the current and proposed systems:

	Current	Proposed
Variable cost per 100 ft of fence:		
Labor	$120	$ 40
Materials	180	210
Total	$300	$250
Fixed costs:		
Equipment	$3,000	$15,000
Other	2,000	3,000
Total	$5,000	$18,000

Required:

a. Compute the break-even point for both the current and the proposed installation methods.

b. Compute the cost indifference point for the two alternatives.

c. Given the sales expectations, what is the cost effect of keeping the employees and continuing use of the old system instead of the proposed system?

d. A reevaluation of the labor estimates indicates that the estimated labor cost should be 25 percent higher than originally estimated for both alternatives. What is the effect on the cost indifference point?

P. 6-7 Joint product decisions. The Pearly Waters Perfume Company manufactures various qualities of perfumes and colognes. One popular line of colognes includes three products that result from a joint production process. Below are data from the most recent month of production.

Product	Price	Quantity	Joint Cost	Cost after Split-Off	Total Cost
Evergreen	$ 4	10,000	$2.80	$2	$4.80
Morning Flower	10	6,000	2.80	4	6.80
Evening Flower	15	4,000	2.80	5	7.80

As the new controller, you are called into the president's office with the director of marketing. The president says, "I don't understand your product cost report. Either we are selling our largest-volume product at a loss, or the product cost data are all wrong. Now which is it?"

Required:

a. Respond to the president's question.

b. Another company has just introduced a product that competes directly with Morning Flower. To compete successfully with the other company's product, the price of Morning Flower cologne must be reduced to $6. Should the company do so and sell below cost?

c. If Pearly Waters has a policy of maintaining a gross margin of 20 percent on sales, what would your answer be in response to the price reduction in part *b*.

d. What is the minimum price for which Morning Flower can sell and still meet the 20 percent product gross margin for the group of products?

P. 6-8 Two-alternative comprehensive problem. Jolly Jaws Amusement Park charges $.40 each for all rides in the park. Variable costs amount to $.08 per ride, and fixed costs are $320,000. Last season's net income was $64,000 on sales of $480,000. Rising costs have cut sharply into net income for Jolly Jaws for the last 2 years. This season management again expects cost increases of 25 percent for variable costs, and 10 percent for fixed costs. To help offset these increases, management is considering raising the price of a ride to $.50.

Required:

a. How many rides did Jolly Jaws sell last year?
b. If the price increase is not implemented, what is the expected net income for this season assuming the same volume of activity?
c. Compute the price indifference point for the new ride price.
d. Compute the break-even point for this season using (1) the old price, (2) the new price.
e. Should management raise the price of a ride if the price increase will reduce ride volume 10 percent from last season's level?
f. What is the expected net income for Jolly Jaws for this year based upon your decision in part *e*?

P. 6-9 Special order decision analysis. Karoom Manufacturing recently built a large addition to its manufacturing facilities. Company management expects to utilize all of the new production space within 2 years with new business. However, in the short run the company has a significant amount of excess production capacity. To help utilize this space, the director of marketing suggests seeking new customers in other countries and selling them products at bargain prices. As a test case the director of marketing has proposed selling 10,000 of the KL40 fire extinguisher to a French company for $35 each. These same units are sold to domestic customers for $50 each. The president of the company has asked the controller to assemble data on the product, and the accountant presents the following product performance report.

KL40 Fire Extinguisher
Product Profitability Statement
Fourth Quarter 1985

Sales (5,000 units @ $50)		$250,000
Direct materials	$60,000	
Direct labor	50,000	
Manufacturing overhead	70,000	
Product cost		180,000
Gross margin		70,000
Marketing and distribution	40,000	
Administrative	20,000	60,000
Profit		$ 10,000

At the meeting to discuss the feasibility of the special order, the accountant noted that 40 percent of the overhead cost was variable. Also, 60 percent of the marketing costs and 15 percent of the administrative costs are variable. Half of the variable marketing and distribution cost is for commissions and the rest is the variable cost of processing the order and shipping it. The marketing director does not think the company will have to pay commissions on the special order.

Required:

a. What is the fire extinguisher's profit per unit as indicated by the product profitability report?
b. Determine if the special order should be accepted. Show supporting analysis data.
c. If the order is accepted, what is the effect on the company's income?

P. 6-10 (CMA) Special order decision. Anchor Company manufactures several different styles of jewelry cases. Management estimates that during the third quarter of 1987 the company will be operating at 80 percent of normal capacity. Because the company desires a higher utilization of plant capacity, the company will consider a special order.

Anchor has received special order inquiries from two companies. The first order is from JCP Inc., which would like to market a jewelry case similar to one of Anchor's cases. The JCP jewelry case would be marketed under JCP's own label. JCP Inc. has offered Anchor $5.75 per jewelry case for 20,000 cases to be shipped by October 1, 1987. The cost data for the Anchor jewelry case that would be similar to the specifications of the JCP special order are as follows:

Regular selling price per unit	$9.00
Costs per unit	
Raw materials	$2.50
Direct labor: .5 hr @ $6.00	3.00
Overhead: .25 machine hr @ $4.00	1.00
Total costs	$6.50

According to the specifications provided by JCP Inc., the special order case requires less expensive raw materials. Consequently, the raw materials will only cost $2.25 per case. Management has estimated that the remaining costs, labor time and machine time, will be the same as for the Anchor jewelry case.

The second special order was submitted by the Krage Co. for 7,500 jewelry cases at $7.50 per case. These jewelry cases, like the JCP cases, would be marketed under the Krage label and have to be shipped by October 1, 1987. However, the Krage jewelry case is different from any jewelry case in the Anchor line. The estimated per unit costs of this case are as follows.

Raw materials	$3.25
Direct labor: .5 hr @ $6.00	3.00
Overhead: .5 machine hr. @ $4.00	2.00
Total costs	$8.25

In addition, Anchor will incur $1,500 in additional setup costs and will have to purchase a $2,500 special device to manufacture these cases; this device will be discarded once the special order is completed.

The Anchor manufacturing capabilities are limited to the total machine hours available. The plant capacity under normal operations is 90,000 machine hours per year or 7,500 machine hours per month. The budgeted fixed overhead for 1987 amounts to $216,000. All manufacturing overhead costs are applied to production on the basis of machine hours at $4.00 per hour.

Anchor will have the entire third quarter to work on the special orders. Management does not expect any repeat sales to be generated from either special order. Company practice precludes Anchor from subcontracting any portion of an order when special orders are not expected to generate repeat sales.

Required: Should Anchor Company accept either special order? Justify your answer and show your calculations.

P. 6-11 Evaluating several alternatives. The Whiskey-Island Salt Company mines road salt year-round and stores it in huge piles on an 80-acre storage site. During 8 months of the year demand for road salt can be handled at the main warehouse storage facility. However, during 4 winter months the company must use the salt stored in the field to meet most of the demand.

Last winter the Whiskey-Island Salt Company used front-end loaders to load the salt into highway department salt trucks. The company rented the loaders since they are used heavily only for 4 months of the year. In past years the company rented whatever was available. Last year the company used three GW-6 and two GW-9 loaders. This year it is making a systematic analysis of the alternatives. Management has narrowed the choice to three loaders, whose data are presented below.

	Front-End Loaders		
	GW-6	GW-9	GW-12
Capacity in tons per hour	80	160	240
Operator wages per hour	$8	$10	$12
Other hourly operating costs	$4	$6	$8
Monthly lease cost per machine	$1,350	$3,700	$6,600
Monthly diesel/hydraulic maintenance agreement per machine	$150	$300	$400

During the peak 4-month period the truck-loading operation runs two 8-hour shifts, 25 days a month. The company expects to load an average of 192,000 tons a month during the 4 winter months. A systems engineer suggests that the firm look into an automated loading system to handle the loading activities for the 80-acre storage site. The automated system would require several gigantic hoppers and a sophisticated conveyor belt system. A system large enough to handle current demand would require an annual fixed cost of $95,000 and would have a variable loading cost of $.02 per ton.

Required:

a. Analyze the three alternatives for front-end loaders and suggest the best alternative.

b. What is the total and per-ton cost of loading salt for the 4-month period using the alternative you recommended in part *a*?

c. Assuming last year's costs were the same as this year's, how much more did the company pay for winter loading activities than was necessary if all machines were run full-time?

d. Analyze the automatic loading system and decide if it should be implemented.

P. 6-12 Multiple-alternative decision. The McWilliams Company's Central Services department is evaluating new copying machines to replace the firm's current copier, which is worn out. The analysis of alternative machines has been narrowed to three, and the estimated costs of operating them are shown below.

	Cost per 100 Copies		
	Copy-A	Copy-B	Copy-C
Materials cost	$6	$4	$2
Labor cost	$8	$3	$2
Annual lease cost	$3,000	$5,800	$10,000

Required:

a. Compute the cost indifference points for the three alternatives.

b. What do the cost indifference points suggest as a course of action in this case?

c. If management expects to need 87,000 copies next year, which copier would be most economical?

d. If management estimates a need for 87,000 copies in making its selection and only 35,000 copies are actually made, what is the cost of estimating the demand incorrectly?

e. Graph the costs for the three copiers, identifying the cost indifference points.

P. 6-13 (CMA) Three-alternative analysis. Valbec Company manufactures and distributes dollhouses. The toy industry is a seasonal business. Therefore, a large portion of Valbec's sales occur in the late summer and fall.

The projected sales in units for 1987 are shown in the schedule on page 255. With a sales price of $10 per unit, the total sales revenue for 1987 is projected at $1.2 million. Valbec scheduled its production in the past so that finished goods inventory at the end of each month, exclusive of a safety stock of 4,000 dollhouses, would equal the next month's sales. One-half hour of direct labor time is required to produce each dollhouse under normal operating conditions. Using the production schedule followed in the past, the total direct labor hours per month that would be required to meet the 1987 sales estimate are also shown in the schedule opposite.

The production schedule followed in the past requires the scheduling of overtime hours for any production over 8,000 units (4,000 direct labor hours) in 1 month. While the use of overtime is feasible, the Valbec management has decided that it should consider two other possible alternatives: (1) Hire temporary help from an agency during the peak months, or (2) expand its labor force and adopt a level production schedule. The use of a second shift was not considered because management believed the community would not support this alternative.

Factory employees are paid $6 per hour for regular time; the fringe benefits average 20 percent of regular pay. For hours worked in excess of 4,000 hours per month, employees receive time and one-half; however, fringe benefits only average 10 percent on these additional wages. Past experience has shown that when overtime is required, labor inefficiencies do occur during overtime, at the rate of 5 percent of overtime hours; this 5 percent inefficiency was not included in the direct labor hour estimates presented in the schedule.

Rather than pay overtime to its regular labor force, Valbec could hire temporary employees when production exceeds 8,000 units per month. The temporary workers can be hired through an agency at the same labor rate of $6 per hour, but there would be no fringe benefit costs. Management estimates that the temporary workers would require 25 percent more time than the regular employees to produce the dollhouses.

If Valbec goes to a level production schedule, the labor force would be expanded. However, no overtime would be required The same labor rate of $6 per hour and fringe benefit rate of 20 percent would apply.

The manufacturing facilities have the capacity to produce 18,000 dollhouses per month. On-site storage facilities for completed units are adequate. The estimated annual cost of carrying inventory is $1 per unit. Valbec is subject to a 40 percent income tax rate.

Valbec Company
Projected Sales and Planned Production
For the Year Ended December 31, 1987

	Projected Sales (in units)	Direct Labor Hours Required[1]
January	8,000	4,000
February	8,000	4,000
March	8,000	4,000
April	8,000	4,000
May	8,000	5,000
June	10,000	6,000
July	12,000	6,000
August	12,000	6,500
September	13,000	6,500
October	13,000	6,000
November	12,000	4,000
December	8,000	4,000[2]
Total	120,000 units	60,000 hours

[1] This schedule does not incorporate any additional direct labor hours resulting from inefficiencies.
[2] Sales for January 1988 are projected at 8,000 units.

Required:

a. Prepare an analysis that compares the costs associated with each of Valbec Company's three alternatives:

   1. Schedule overtime hours.
   2. Hire temporary workers.
   3. Expand labor force and schedule level production.

b. Identify and discuss briefly the noncost factors and the factors which are difficult to cost that Valbec Company should consider in conjunction with the cost analysis prepared in requirement *a* before a final decision is made relative to the three alternatives.

CASE

Case 6-1 Comprehensive two-alternative decision. A private university with a current enrollment of 12,000 students is reviewing cost and revenue data for the past academic year. Student tuition is $3,600 a year. Tuition normally covers 75 percent of university expenditures. The remaining 25 percent comes from endowments and contributions. During the last academic year fixed costs amounted to $30,000,000. The rest of the costs varied with student enrollment. Costs have been rising more rapidly than tuition or contributions, and the university just broke even last year. A tuition increase is being contemplated. The budget committee thinks endowment revenues and contributions will remain constant at last year's level for the next several years.

The fixed costs are expected to increase $3,000,000, and variable costs are expected to increase 10 percent. The president of the university tells the budget committee that he expects a new $5,000,000 grant in addition to the normal contributions for each of the next 5 years from a large corporation owned by an alumnus of the university. The university has been postponing a number of major capital improvement and building projects.

Required:

a. How much could student enrollment drop for the university still to break even if tuition is raised to $4,200 a year and the grant is not received? Ignore the expected cost increases.
b. How would receipt of the grant affect your answer to part *a*?
c. If the grant is received and tuition is raised to $4,200, how much money would the university have available the first year for capital improvements and building with student enrollment of 11,200 and the expected cost increases?
d. If the grant is received and costs increase as predicted for the coming academic year, what tuition should the university charge to break even with its current enrollment of 12,000 students?
e. Compute the required tuition rate as in part *d*, but provide $4,040,000 for capital improvements.

Planning, Control, and Responsibility Reporting

part 3

Managing a business in today's economic environment is a complex and difficult task. Professional managers plan every phase of business operations in advance and must ensure, by means of carefully developed control procedures, that plans are carried out. Managers accomplish the planning and control function by assigning to different persons the responsibility for specific segments of business operations. Information must be provided about the accomplishment of goals and about progress toward achieving predetermined managerial plans. Such information is included in specialized managerial reports, many of which are accounting reports discussed in this part of the book.

Much managerial planning and control involves short-range business goals, such as the number of units of a product to be produced next year. Chapter 7 discusses the way such business goals are developed by means of combining many separate budgets into a master budget. Once the budget is prepared, control over operations is accomplished by comparing the budgeted plans with actual operating results and by taking corrective action when necessary. Chapter 8 discusses the use of standards in measuring the costs of materials and labor used to produce goods and services. Chapter 9 deals with the more difficult problems of measuring and controlling the indirect costs of goods and services and the preparation of budgets at several levels of activity.

Measuring and reporting performance often must be done for many separate segments of business. Chapter 10 discusses the measurement of a specific business segment's contribution to overall business profits. Chapter 11 discusses the various approaches to dividing a business into specific centers of responsibility.

In addition to the short-range plans that deal with immediate problems of day-to-day business operations, long-range plans are also prepared by managers. Pricing of products, or planning a new production facility, may require looking many years into the future. Chapter 12 discusses the many factors that enter into the determination of the price of a product or service. Chapter 13 is devoted to capital budgeting, which is the planning of new products and investment in production facilities. Chapter 14 discusses planning, control, and responsibility reporting of not-for-profit organizations such as governments and hospitals. It also illustrates how the actions of government influence business operations ranging from current production to price setting and capital budgeting.

Budgeting: The Planning and Control Process

7

This chapter introduces basic budgeting concepts and presents the framework of the budgeting process. When you have completed this chapter, you should understand:

1 The purpose and characteristics of budgeting.

2 That planning and control are the two functions of budgeting.

3 The nature of the master budget and how it is developed.

4 The process used to review budgets.

5 How budgets affect the performance of employees and managers.

6 Why budget performance reports are a key component of control.

Like many accounting terms, **budgeting** is used commonly in our everyday language. The news media discuss budgets of federal, state, and local governments, and many people describe a variety of resource allocation decisions, ranging from vacation planning to the purchase of food and clothing, as budgeting. The purpose of this chapter is to introduce the framework of the budgeting process, define budgeting terms, and provide a clear understanding of the concepts of budgeting. Although the primary emphasis in this chapter is on business budgeting, most of the concepts are applicable to nonbusiness activities.

THE FUNDAMENTALS OF BUDGETING

A **budget** is a comprehensive, formal plan, expressed in quantitative terms, describing the expected operations of an organization over some future time period. A budget deals with a specific entity, covers a specific future time period, and is expressed in quantitative terms.

Quantitative Plan

Often budgets contain material describing the various programs and activities planned by the company. In this chapter, however, we are interested primarily in the way that cost and revenue estimates of the activities are expressed by the budget. All planned projects and activities for the organization are reduced to the common denominator of money and other quantitative measures, such as units of input or output.

Budget Entity

Budgets may be prepared for any organization or part of an organization

The entity concept, so important in financial accounting, is essential to budgeting also. A specific budget must apply to a clearly defined accounting entity. For budgeting purposes the entity may consist of a small part of a business, a single activity, or a specific project. Budgets may be prepared for a section, division, or department of a business, or for activities such as a new product design or advertising campaign. The concept of a budget entity applies to individuals as well. For example, a student interested in budgeting the cost of a first year's college education should not include in the budget the cost of a 3-week vacation or the purchase of an $800 guitar. Although these two expenditures may be costs of the period, they are not college education expenses.

Mary Drummer plans a trip to Florida over Christmas vacation. She estimates the amounts she expects to spend for the trip, as shown in Figure 7-1. Her plan (budget) has four cost categories. This budget is **only** for Mary's trip to Florida in December 1986. It does not include the costs of others who might travel with her or other trips or activities that she may plan for December 1986.

A budgeting entity can be as specific as a single project, such as Mary's Florida trip, or it can be a broader activity, such as the cost of a year at college. Of course, a budget might cover a broader situation than either of the above examples, such as the budget for an entire manufacturing firm or for the United States government. The important concept is that one

Figure 7-1
A very simple budget. Most people find it necessary to do some personal budgeting although the budgeting process may be very informal.

Mary Drummer
Budget for a Christmas Vacation to Florida
December 10–21, 1986

My share of the fuel	$ 60.00
My share of the lodging	105.00
Food costs	100.00
Souvenirs and miscellaneous	50.00
Total vacation budget	$315.00

Murphy Manufacturing Company
Departmental Labor Budget
1986

Department	Shearing	Machining	Finishing	Assembly	Total
Direct labor	$126,000	$220,000	$142,000	$108,000	$596,000
Indirect labor	44,000	80,000	30,000	18,000	172,000
Allocated service department labor	21,000	34,000	28,000	15,000	98,000
Total	$191,000	$334,000	$200,000	$141,000	$866,000

Figure 7-2 **Budgets for businesses require systematic procedures for developing and reviewing the budget. Departmental budgets require managers to delineate carefully the functions and activities of each department.**

must first define **precisely** the budget entity and only then can one start preparing the budget.

Organizations must clearly define each entity for which they prepare budgets. For example, if a firm prepares departmental budgets, the functions and activities of each department must be carefully delineated. Figure 7-2 is a departmental labor budget for Murphy Manufacturing Company; it shows the amount to be paid for labor in each department and the total for the entire company. Here the budget is just for departmental labor. A budget for all departmental activities would include labor, materials, maintenance, and many other costs.

Future Time Period

Many financial figures are meaningless unless they are couched in some time reference. Income statements are annual, quarterly, or monthly. A job offer of $30,000 is of little value without knowing if the figure represents pay for a month, a year, a lifetime, or some other time period. We might assume the $30,000 is an annual salary. In accounting, however, time references should be clearly stated.

Budgets are estimates of future economic events

Budgets should express the expected financial consequences of programs and activities planned for a specified period of time. Annual budgets are widespread. Since most organizations prepare annual reports to satisfy reporting requirements of the Internal Revenue Service, Securities and Exchange Commission, lending institutions, and others, annual budgets provide a convenient framework for comparing planned results with actual results.

In addition to annual budgets, budgets for many other time periods are prepared. Long-term plans may be prepared for 2, 3, 5, or more years in the future. Long-term budgets are usually less detailed than annual budgets. It is more difficult to prepare detailed plans for periods far from the present.

Frequently budgets are prepared for shorter time periods, such as quarters or months. Management of some resources such as cash may require weekly or daily budgets. Short-range budgets allow quick responses to problems as they rise.

REASONS FOR BUDGETING

Budgets offer a variety of benefits to organizations. Some common benefits of budgeting include the following:

1. Requires periodic planning.
2. Fosters coordination, cooperation, and communication.
3. Forces quantification of proposals.
4. Provides a framework for performance evaluation.
5. Creates an awareness of business costs.
6. Satisfies legal and contractual requirements.
7. Orients a firm's activities toward organizational goals.

Periodic Planning

Budgets provide a systematic uniform process for planning

Virtually all activities require some planning to ensure efficient and effective use of scarce resources. Some people are compulsive planners who continuously update plans that have already been made and plan for new activities and functions. At the other extreme are people who do not like to plan and therefore find little or no time to get involved in the planning process. The budgeting process closes the gap between these two extremes by creating a formal planning framework that provides specific, uniform periodic deadlines for each phase of the planning process. People who are not attuned to the planning process must still meet budget deadlines. Of course, planning does not guarantee success. People must execute the plans, but careful planning is an important prerequisite to the accomplishment of many activities.

Coordination, Cooperation, and Communication

Planning by individual managers does not ensure an optimum plan for the entire organization. The budgeting process, however, provides a vehicle for the exchange of ideas and objectives among people in the various organizational segments. The budget review process and other budget communication networks should minimize redundant and counterproductive programs by the time the final budget is approved.

Quantification

Because we live in a world of limited resources, virtually all individuals and organizations must ration their resources. The rationing process is easier for some than for others. Each person and each organization must compare the costs and benefits of each potential project or activity and choose those that result in the most appropriate resource allocation decisions.

Measuring costs and benefits requires some degree of quantification. Profit-oriented firms make dollar measurements for both costs and benefits. This is not always an easy task. For example, the benefits of an advertising campaign are increased sales and a better company image, but it is difficult to estimate precisely the additional sales revenue caused by a particular advertising campaign, and it is even more difficult to quantify the improvements in the company image. In not-for-profit organizations, such as government agencies, quantification of benefits can be even more difficult. For example, how does one quantify the benefits of better police protection, more music programs at the city park, or better fire protection, and how should the benefits be evaluated in allocating resources to each activity? Despite the difficulties, resource allocation decisions necessitate some reasonable quantification of the costs and benefits of the various projects under consideration.

Performance Evaluation

Managers need to know what is expected of them

Budgets are estimates of future events, and as such they serve as estimates of acceptable performance. Managerial performance in each budgeting entity is appraised by comparing actual performance with budgeted projections. Most managers want to know what is expected of them so that they may monitor their own performance. Budgets help to provide that type of information. Of course, managers can also be evaluated on other criteria, but it is valuable to have some quantifiable measure of performance.

Cost Awareness

Accountants and financial managers are concerned daily about the cost implications of decisions and activities, but many other managers are not. Production supervisors focus on output, marketing managers on sales, and so forth. It is easy for people to overlook costs and cost-benefit relationships. At budgeting time, however, all managers with budget responsibility must convert their plans for projects and activities to costs and benefits. This cost awareness provides a common ground for communication among the various functional areas of the organization.

Legal and Contractual Requirements

Some organizations are required to budget. Local police departments, for example, cannot ignore budgeting even if it seems too much trouble, and the National Park Service would soon be out of funds if its management decided not to submit a budget this year. Some firms commit themselves to budgeting requirements when signing loan agreements or other operating agreements. For example, a bank may require a firm to submit an annual operating budget and monthly cash budgets throughout the life of a bank loan.

Goal Orientation

Budgets should reflect plans to achieve organization goals

Resources should be allocated to projects and activities in accordance with organization goals and objectives. Logical as this may sound, it sometimes is difficult to relate general organization goals to specific projects or activities. Many general goals are not operational—meaning that it is difficult to determine the impact of specific projects on the achievement of the general goals of the organization. For example, organization goals may be stated as follows:

1. Generate a satisfactory profit.
2. Maintain sufficient liquidity.

Organization goals and objectives should be created and stated formally

The terms "satisfactory" and "sufficient" mean different things to different people. A major prerequisite to goal-oriented budgeting is the development of a formal set of operational goals. Some organizations do not have formally defined goals, and even those that do often have only general goals for the entire organization. Major operating units may function without written or clearly defined goals or objectives. Sometimes the unwritten objectives of a supervisor or group of managers represent unstated or undefined objectives that may or may not dovetail with the general objectives of the organization. The undefined objectives might be used in preparing the budget, even if only subconsciously. Such informal structures may jeopardize the firm's ability to utilize its scarce resources optimally.

A logical first step toward effective budgeting is to formalize the goals of the organization. Starting at the top, general organization goals should be as specific as possible, carefully established, and written. Next, each major unit of the organization should develop more specific operational goals. The process should continue down the organization structure to the lowest level of budget responsibility. This goal-development process requires management at all levels to resolve difficult issues, but it results in a budgeting framework that is much more likely to be effective.

It is not necessary for all goals to be defined with precision, and at high levels of management numerous goals may be stated in very general terms. For example, the loosely defined goals listed above may be stated more precisely to make them operational, and they may be combined with additional goals as follows:

1. Generate a return on investment of 15 percent or more.
2. Maintain a current ratio of 1.8 or more.
3. Provide valuable products to society.
4. Provide jobs for the community.

The last two items on this list can be satisfied whether or not the organization achieves the first two goals, which are now stated in operational terms. The two operational goals can be used to establish organization goals at lower levels that are compatible with the main objectives. For example, budget proposals for the acquisition of computer equipment can be evaluated more easily if detailed operating objectives are available. The goals of the data processing department should be consistent with the objective of earning a 15 percent return and maintaining a 1.8 current ratio. It is, of course, entirely possible that some goals are not relevant to all departments. Some examples of goals for the computer department are

1. Provide corporate users with data processing services of quality equal to or greater than services that could be purchased from external sources.
2. Provide corporate users with data processing services at a cost equal to or less than the cost of comparable services from external sources.
3. Provide data processing services to any internal corporate user who can justify the cost of the service.
4. Charge all corporate users (through the budget process) the total cost of the services used.

Defining goals for not-for-profit organizations may be more difficult than for profit-seeking firms due to the inability to quantify some objectives. For example, the goals of a government agency may be

1. Maximize community benefits, given the amount of available resources.
2. Minimize the cost of providing a given level of service.

When budgets are prepared, however, the decision must still be made on the actual amount to be spent on a particular service or the amount of resources to be used for a specific project.

FUNCTIONS OF BUDGETING

Planning is the entire process of creating the budget

The two basic functions of budgeting are planning and control. **Planning** encompasses the entire process of preparing the budget, from the initial ideas through the development of the budget. Planning is the process that most people think of when the term "budgeting" is mentioned. The majority of the time and effort devoted to budgeting is expended in the planning stage. Careful planning provides the framework for the second function of budgeting.

Control is the comparison of actual results with budgeted data, evaluation of the differences, and taking corrective actions to adjust for differences when necessary. The comparison of budgeted and actual data can occur only after actual accounting data have been accumulated. For ex-

Control is the process of ensuring that plans are achieved

ample, January production and cost data are necessary to compare with the January production budget to measure the difference between plans and accomplishments. The comparison of actual results with budget expectations is often referred to as **performance reporting.** The term *control* does not merely refer to cost minimization; instead it refers to the ability to monitor activities and take corrective action when actual results differ from expectations. The budget acts as a gauge against which managers compare actual costs and revenues.

The planning function of budgeting is a future-based activity using estimates to enhance the management of scarce resources. Control, on the other hand, requires use of the current budget to monitor activities and take corrective actions. Typically it is more pleasant to plan for the future than to explain what went wrong when comparisons show unfavorable performance. However, the control phase is where managers can learn from the mistakes indicated by the performance reports and can improve future planning and performance.

THE MASTER BUDGET

The total budget package of an organization is called the master budget

The **master budget** is the total budget package for an organization; it is the end product of the budget preparation process. The master budget consists of all the individual budgets for each part of the organization aggregated into one overall budget for the entire organization. The exact composition of the master budget depends somewhat on the type and size of the business. However, all master budgets represent the organization's overall plan for the budget period in question. Figure 7-3 identifies the basic components of a master budget for a manufacturing firm.

Manufacturing Firm
Master Budget

- Operating budget
  - Sales budget
  - Budget of ending inventories
  - Production budget
    - Materials budget
    - Direct labor budget
    - Manufacturing overhead budget
  - Budgeted cost of goods sold
  - Administrative expense budget
  - Marketing expense budget
  - Budgeted net income from operations
  - Budgeted nonoperating items
  - Budgeted income statement
- Financial budget
  - Capital expenditure budget
  - Cash budget
  - Budgeted balance sheet
  - Budgeted statement of changes in financial position

Figure 7-3
A typical master budget for a manufacturing firm. Master budgets for other types of organizations also include an operating budget and a financial budget, although the components of each may vary. For example, a merchandising firm does not prepare a production budget.

The components of the master budget form the firm's detailed operating plan for the coming year. We first examine each of the components individually, then show a comprehensive illustration of a master budget.

The master budget is divided into two major categories: the operating budget and the financial budget. The **operating budget** includes revenues, product costs, operating expenses, and other components of the income statement. The **financial budget** includes the budgeted balance sheet, cash budget, capital expenditure budget, and other budgets used in financial management. A large part of the financial budget is determined by the operating budget and the beginning balance sheet.

Operating Budget

The operating budget is composed of the income statement elements. A manufacturing business budgets both manufacturing and nonmanufacturing activities. Below we discuss the various elements of the operating budget of a manufacturing firm.

The sales budget is prepared first and influences most other operating budget components

Sales budget. The **sales budget** is the first budget to be prepared. It is usually the most important budget because so many other budgets are directly related to sales and are therefore largely derived from the sales budget. Inventory budgets, production budgets, personnel budgets, marketing budgets, administrative budgets, and other budget areas are all affected significantly by the amount of revenue that is expected from sales.

Sales budgets are influenced by a wide variety of factors, including general economic conditions, pricing decisions, competitor actions, industry conditions, and marketing programs. In an effort to develop an accurate sales budget, firms employ many experts to assist in sales forecasting.

Often the sales budget starts with individual sales representatives or sales managers predicting sales in their particular area. The basic sales data are aggregated to arrive at a raw sales forecast that is then modified to reflect many of the variables mentioned previously. The resulting sales budget is expressed in dollars and must include sufficient detail on product mix and sales patterns to provide the information necessary for making decisions about changes in inventory levels and production quantities.

Budget of ending inventories. Inventories comprise a major portion of the current assets of many manufacturing firms. Separate decisions about inventory levels must be made for raw materials, work in process, and finished goods. Raw material scarcities, management's attitude about inventory levels, inventory carrying costs, inventory ordering costs, and other variables may all affect inventory level decisions. Managers may use the inventory management techniques discussed in Chapter 15, or they may make simple seat-of-the pants decisions about inventory. In either case decisions on inventory levels must be made before production budgets can be finalized.

Production budget. The production quantity budget initiates the development of the production budget. The materials budget, direct labor budget, and manufacturing overhead budget are all derived from the production quantity budget. Together these budgets are called the **production budget.** Managers incorporate current and expected inventory levels and sales estimates into the materials budget. Monthly **materials budgets** reflect sales patterns and the time required between ordering and receiving materials.

The **direct labor budget** is instrumental in production planning and personnel management. Managers evaluate any changes in the type of labor talent needed as a result of changes in the mix of products manufactured and sold. Likewise, firms must plan for changing labor requirements caused by cyclical production patterns. Significant swings in production demand during the year cause much greater problems in planning for labor than for materials and manufacturing overhead.

The **manufacturing overhead budget** includes all indirect costs of manufacturing discussed in Chapters 3 and 4. Included are indirect materials, indirect labor, capacity costs for the production facility, and indirect production support costs. It is important to separate the fixed and variable components of manufacturing overhead costs so that the cost estimates are reliable at the expected production level.

Budgeted cost of goods sold. For a manufacturing firm cost of goods sold is the production cost of products that are sold. Consequently, the **cost of goods sold budget** follows directly from the production budget. The cost of goods sold figure is different from the production budget figure because it is affected by beginning and ending inventories.

Administrative expense budget. The expected administrative costs for an organization are presented in the **administrative expense budget.** The administrative expense budget may contain many fixed costs, some of which may be avoidable if subsequent operations indicate some cost cuts are necessary. These avoidable costs, sometimes called **discretionary fixed costs,** include such items as research and development, employee education and training programs, and portions of the personnel budget. Fixed costs that cannot be avoided during the period are called **committed fixed costs.** Mortgage payments, bond interest payments, and property taxes are classified as committed costs. Variable administrative costs may include some personnel costs, a portion of the utility costs, computer service bureau costs, and supplies costs.

Marketing expense budget. Sales volume is determined, to some degree, by the marketing effort. Consequently, the **marketing expense budget** is prepared, at least in part, early in the budgeting process when the sales budget is being prepared. Some marketing costs, such as marketing management salaries and machinery and building depreciation for marketing, do not vary directly with sales volume. Other marketing costs, such as sales commissions and product distribution costs, may vary with the level of sales volume. Marketing costs for some consumer products, such as toothpaste, are very high and in some cases even may exceed the cost of producing the product. In such cases the marketing budget is obviously a very important budget.

The budgeted income statement shows the planned profit for the period

Budgeted income statement. The **budgeted income statement** is the combination of all of the preceding budgets. This budget shows the expected revenues and expenses from operations during the budget period. Budgeted income is a key figure in the firm's profit plan and reflects a majority of the firm's commitment of talent, time, and resources for the period.

A firm may have **budgeted nonoperating items** such as interest on investments or gains or losses on the sale of fixed assets. Usually they are relatively small, although in large firms the dollar amounts can be sizable. If nonoperating items are expected, they should be included in the firm's budgeted income statement. Income taxes are levied on actual, not budgeted, net income, but the budget plan should include expected taxes; therefore, the last figure in the budgeted income statement is budgeted after-tax net income.

The operating budget outlined in Figure 7-3 is for a manufacturing firm, but other types of organizations have similar operating budgets. A merchandising firm, such as a department store, has no production budget. The cost of goods sold budget comes directly from merchandise inventory and the merchandise purchases budget. The type and proportion of marketing costs may be different for a merchandising firm than for a manufacturing firm.

Operating budgets of service firms, such as dry-cleaning establishments, lawyers, and computer service firms, are somewhat different because service firms have no product cost. The major components are revenue from services and operating expenses.

The operating budgets for public-sector organizations such as governments, and for not-for-profit institutions such as universities, are also similar in form to the one described. Of course, the nature of the revenues and costs is different. Public-sector budgeting is discussed in Chapter 14.

Financial Budget

The **financial budget** consists of the budgeted capital expenditures, the cash budget, the balance sheet, and the statement of changes in financial position. Although there are some differences in operating budgets of manufacturing, merchandising, and service firms, very little difference exists among financial budgets of these entities.

Capital budgeting is long-range planning

Capital expenditure budget. Capital budgeting is the planning of investments in major resources like plant and equipment, and other types of long-term projects, such as employee education programs. The **capital expenditure budget** or **capital budget** describes the capital investment plans for an organization for the budget period. It contains some of the most critical budgeting decisions of the organization. Typically capital expenditures are relatively large in comparison with operating expenditures and have a long-term impact on the organization and the achievement of its goals.

Capital expenditure projects have useful lives in excess of one accounting period, and like other budget proposals, they are evaluated in light of the organization's goals and objectives. However, the length of the time period of capital projects and the relative size of the expenditures warrant detailed and careful analysis. A number of specialized analytical tools have been developed for making capital budgeting decisions. These are discussed in some detail in Chapter 13.

Cash budget. A major goal of all organizations is liquidity, which is the ability to pay debts when they come due. Even government organizations must pay their bills and other obligations on time. Meeting cash obligations is not as simple as it may appear. Profitability and liquidity do not necessarily go hand in hand. Some firms experience their most critical liquidity problems when they go from a break-even position to profitability. At that time growing receivables, inventories, and capacity cost requirements may create cash shortages.

Planning cash flows is an essential management function in all organizations

The **cash budget** is a very useful tool in cash management. Managers estimate all expected cash flows for the budget period. The typical starting point is cash from operations, which is net income adjusted for noncash items, such as depreciation. All nonoperating cash items are also included. Purchases of land and equipment, sales of bonds and common stock, and acquisition of treasury stock are a few examples of nonoperating items affecting the cash budget. The net income figure for an accounting period usually is very different from the cash flow for the period because of nonoperating cash flow items or changes in working capital.

For many firms, annual cash budgets do not provide short enough time intervals to satisfy management's cash planning needs. Monthly, weekly, and even daily cash budgets may be necessary for meeting management information requirements. The frequency of cash budgets depends on management's planning needs and the potential for cash management problems.

Cash management is intended to optimize cash balances; this means having enough cash to meet liquidity needs and not having so much cash that profitability is sacrificed. Excess cash should be invested in earning assets and should not be allowed to lie idly in the Cash account. Cash budgeting is useful in dealing with both types of cash problems.

Budgeted balance sheet. The **budgeted balance sheet**, sometimes called the **budgeted statement of financial position**, is derived from the budgeted balance sheet at the beginning of the budget period and the expected changes in the account balances reflected in the operating budget, capital expenditure budget, and cash budget. It is necessary to use a budgeted balance sheet for the beginning of the period because the new budget is

The budgeted balance sheet reflects important relationships among account balances

prepared before the previous accounting period has ended. When the budgeted balance sheet for the coming accounting period is prepared, there may be several months left in the current accounting period.

The budgeted balance sheet is more than a collection of residual balances resulting from other budget estimates. Undesirable projected balances and account relationships may cause management to change the operating plan. For instance, if a lending institution requires a firm to maintain a certain minimum current ratio and debt/equity ratio, the budget must reflect these requirements. If it does not, the operating plan must be changed until the agreed requirements are met.

Budgeted statement of changes in financial position. The final element of the master budget package is the statement of changes in financial position. It has emerged as a useful tool for managers in the financial planning process. This statement is usually prepared from data in the budgeted income statement and changes between the estimated balance sheet at the beginning of the budget period and the budgeted balance sheet at the end of the budget period.

Graphic Depiction of the Budgeting Process

Figure 7-4, on page 272, shows graphically the flow process in the development of the master budget for a manufacturing firm. The master budget example that follows should clarify the steps required to prepare the budget package. After studying the entire example, return to Figure 7-4 and follow the example through the flow diagram.

MASTER BUDGET ILLUSTRATED

A single example that illustrates all the budgets

The master budget can be a large document even for a small organization. The simple example that follows gives some indication of the potential size and complexity of the master budget of a business. The example illustrates a **fixed** or **static budget** prepared for a single expected level of activity. Flexible budgeting, which involves various activity levels, is discussed in Chapter 9.

The example is the master budget for Fable Manufacturing Company for the year 1986. The company produces and sells two products, a birch captain's chair and an oak rocking chair. Each product requires one raw material and some direct labor for production. Production requirements are given below.

		Quantity per Unit of Product	
Resource	**Price**	**Captain's Chair**	**Rocking Chair**
Birch lumber	$1.60/bd ft	10 bd ft	—
Oak lumber	$2.00/bd ft	—	12 bd ft
Direct labor	$6.00/hr	2 hr	3 hr

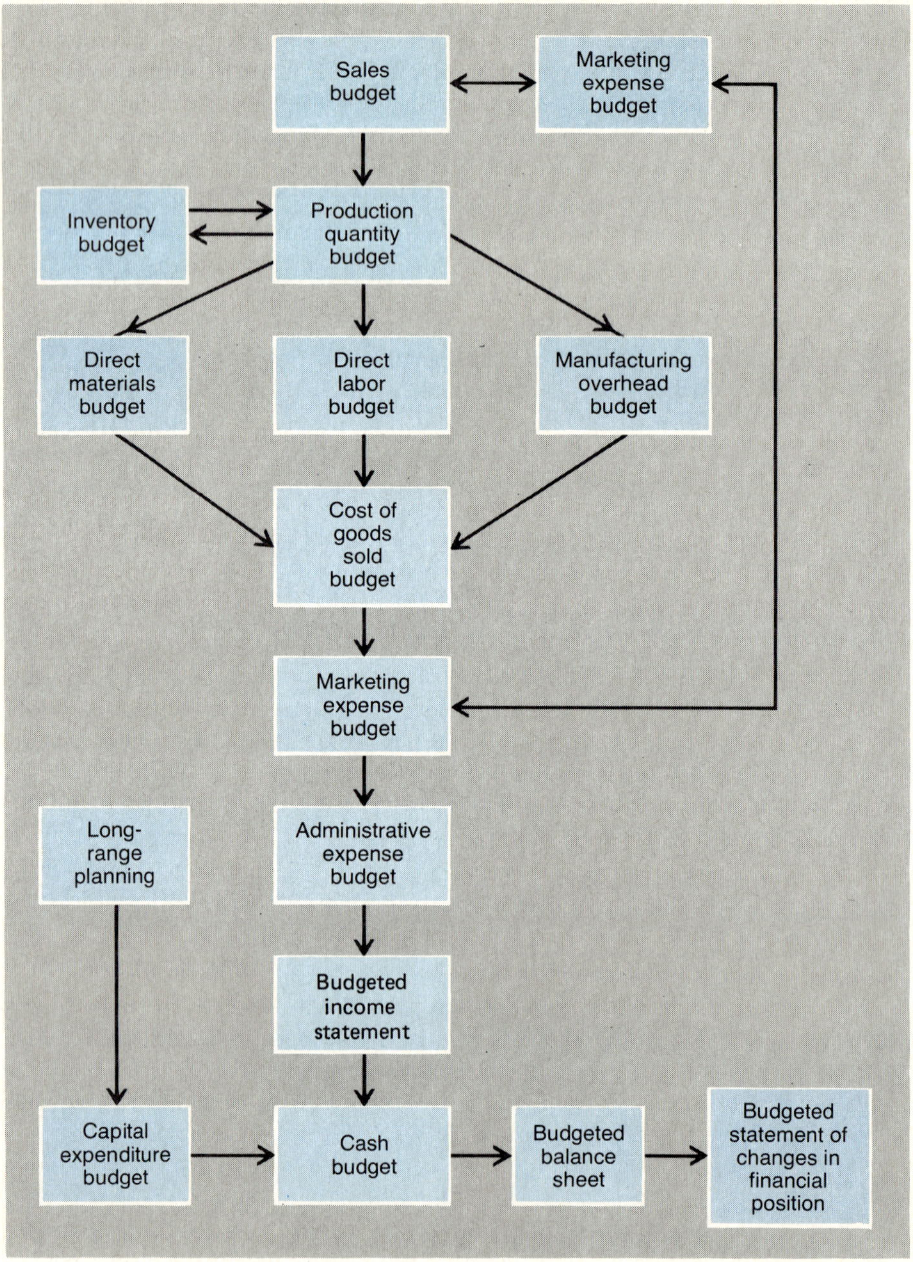

Figure 7-4
The development of the master budget is a somewhat sequential process in which information from one budget is input for another budget. However, some elements of the budgeting package, such as the capital expenditure budget, are somewhat independent.

The first step is to prepare the sales budget in terms of both quantities and dollars, as shown in Figure 7-5. The sales dollars appear in the budgeted income statement, and the quantities are essential to the production budget. We have divided the budget into quarters. Fable Manufacturing Company's two products have cyclical sales patterns as is evident from the quarterly figures but not from the yearly total. A single annual budget would not be very useful for planning Fable's production.

Fable Manufacturing Company
Sales Budget
For the Year Ending December 31, 1986

	Captain's Chairs		Rocking Chairs		Company Total	
	Units	Amount	Units	Amount	Units	Amount
Quarter 1	2,000	$ 120,000	5,000	$ 450,000	7,000	$ 570,000
Quarter 2	6,000	360,000	2,000	180,000	8,000	540,000
Quarter 3	5,000	300,000	1,000	90,000	6,000	390,000
Quarter 4	4,000	240,000	7,000	630,000	11,000	870,000
Yearly total	17,000	$1,020,000	15,000	$1,350,000	32,000	$2,370,000

Figure 7-5 Sales budget prepared by quarters in units and in dollars. The fluctuations in the quarterly amounts would be hidden if only annual figures were presented.

The ending inventory budget in Figure 7-6 is based on expected sales and management's policy on inventory levels. Fable's policy is to have enough ending inventory to meet 25 percent of next quarter's budgeted sales. For instance, the budgeted finished goods inventory of captain's chairs for the end of the first quarter is 25 percent of budgeted second-quarter sales, or .25 × 6,000 = 1,500 chairs. The budgeted inventory for the end of the second quarter is 25 percent of budgeted third-quarter sales, or .25 × 5,000 = 1,250 chairs. The budgeted ending inventories for rocking chairs are computed in the same way.

Fable Manufacturing Company
Ending inventory Budget—Finished Goods
For the Year Ending December 31, 1986

	Quarter			
Finished Goods*	**1**	**2**	**3**	**4†**
Captain's chairs	1,500	1,250	1,000	500
Rocking chairs	500	250	1,750	1,250

* 25% of budgeted sales for the next quarter.
† Sales for first quarter 1987 are expected to be the same as for first quarter 1986.

Figure 7-6 Budgeted ending finished goods inventories for each quarter are determined by expected sales levels and desired supplies of each inventory item. Inventory levels may be determined using inventory management techniques discussed in Chapter 15.

Fable Manufacturing Company
Production Quantity Budget
For the Year Ending December 31, 1986

	Quarter 1	2	3	4	Year Total*
Captain's Chairs					
Budgeted sales in units	2,000	6,000	5,000	4,000	17,000
Desired ending inventory	1,500	1,250	1,000	500	500
Total requirements	3,500	7,250	6,000	4,500	17,500
Beginning inventory	800†	1,500	1,250	1,000	800†
Budgeted production	2,700	5,750	4,750	3,500	16,700
Rocking Chairs					
Budgeted sales in units	5,000	2,000	1,000	7,000	15,000
Desired ending inventory	500	250	1,750	1,250	1,250
Total requirements	5,500	2,250	2,750	8,250	16,250
Beginning inventory	1,200†	500	250	1,750	1,200†
Budgeted production	4,300	1,750	2,500	6,500	15,050

* Figures in the rows for budgeted sales and budgeted production add across to the "year total" column, but those in the inventory rows and the total requirements row do not. Ending inventory is the same as the fourth-quarter figure, and beginning inventory is the same as the first-quarter figure.
† Estimated beginning inventory.

Figure 7-7 The production quantity budget is determined from beginning and ending inventory requirements and quarterly sales estimates. This budget is the primary determinant of the amounts in all the other production budgets.

The production quantities in Figure 7-7 are determined from budgeted sales plus ending inventory requirements minus beginning inventory. Production quantities must be computed for both products. To illustrate, the production quantity budget for rocking chairs for the first quarter is prepared as follows:

Budgeted first-quarter sales of rocking chairs	5,000 units
Add budgeted finished goods ending inventory	500
Total requirements	5,500
Less beginning finished goods inventory	(1,200)
Budgeted production quantity for the first quarter	4,300 units

The first-quarter beginning finished goods inventory is estimated in the budget of the preceding period. In the other three quarters the beginning finished goods inventory for each quarter is the ending finished goods inventory of the preceding quarter. In the second quarter the production quantity is calculated as follows:

Budgeted second-quarter sales of rocking chairs	2,000 units
Add budgeted finished goods ending inventory	250
Total requirements	2,250 units
Less beginning inventory (ending inventory of previous quarter	(500)
Budgeted production quantity for second quarter	1,750 units

The production quantity for captain's chairs is prepared in the same manner. Note the fluctuation in production from quarter to quarter caused by the fluctuation in sales. Clearly an annual production budget would be inadequate for the company's planning and control needs.

Sometimes the ending inventory budget for raw materials can be prepared when the finished goods ending inventory budget has been prepared. But Fable's policy for ending raw materials inventory is based on the production quantity budget. Consequently, the production quantity budget is prepared first and then the budgeted ending inventory levels for raw materials are determined, as shown in Figure 7-8. Company policy is to maintain ending raw materials inventories equal to 50 percent of the amount required for the next quarter's production. To illustrate, the budgeted ending inventory for birch lumber for the first quarter is as follows:

Second-quarter budgeted production of captain's chairs	5,750 units
Required amount of birch lumber per chair	10 bd ft
Required amount of birch lumber for second-quarter production	57,500 bd ft
Fifty percent inventory requirement	.50
Required first-quarter ending inventory of birch lumber	28,750 bd ft

Ending inventories for oak lumber are computed the same way. The first-quarter ending inventory of oak lumber is

Second-quarter budgeted production of rocking chairs	1,750
Required amount of oak lumber per rocking chair	12 bd ft
Required amount of oak lumber for second-quarter production	21,000 bd ft
Fifty percent inventory requirement	.50
Required first-quarter ending inventory of oak lumber	10,500 bd ft

Figure 7-8
Raw materials inventory levels. Each item must be estimated from expected production and must comply with company policy on minimum levels of inventories.

Fable Manufacturing Company
Ending Inventory Budget—Raw Materials
For the Year Ending December 31, 1986

	Quarter			
Raw Material*	**1**	**2**	**3**	**4†**
Birch lumber (bd ft)	28,750	23,750	17,500	13,500
Oak lumber (bd ft)	10,500	15,000	39,000	25,800

* Ending raw materials each quarter must equal 50% of the raw material needed for the next quarter's budgeted production. Quantities are in board feet.
† Assume first-quarter production in 1987 will equal first-quarter production in 1986.

The materials budget in Figure 7-9 indicates the expected materials purchases for the period, using the budgeted production quantity and the required quantity of raw materials in ending inventory. Of course, some of the materials requirement will be met with beginning inventory. The computation is

	Required material for budgeted current-quarter production
+	Required ending inventory
−	Beginning inventory
=	Budgeted purchases

The amount of material required for budgeted production during the quarter is the number of units of budgeted production for the quarter multiplied

Fable Manufacturing Company
Materials Budget
For the Year Ending December 31, 1986

	Quarter 1	Quarter 2	Quarter 3	Quarter 4	Year Total
Birch Lumber					
Material requirements in bd ft for current quarter's production*	27,000	57,500	47,500	35,000	167,000
Ending inventory requirements	28,750	23,750	17,500	13,500	13,500
Total requirements	55,750	81,250	65,000	48,500	180,500
Less beginning inventory	10,500†	28,750	23,750	17,500	10,500
Current-period purchases	45,250	52,500	41,250	31,000	170,000
Unit purchase price	× $1.60	× $1.60	× $1.60	× $1.60	× $1.60
Total cost of purchases, birch lumber	$ 72,400	$ 84,000	$ 66,000	$ 49,600	$272,000
Oak Lumber					
Material requirements in bd ft for current quarter's production‡	51,600	21,000	30,000	78,000	180,600
Ending inventory requirements	10,500	15,000	39,000	25,800	25,800
Total requirements	62,100	36,000	69,000	103,800	206,400
Less beginning inventory	24,600†	10,500	15,000	39,000	24,600
Current-period purchases	37,500	25,500	54,000	64,800	181,800
Unit purchase price	× $2.00	× $2.00	× $2.00	× $2.00	× $2.00
Total cost of purchases, oak lumber	75,000	51,000	108,000	129,600	363,600
Total cost of material purchases	$147,400	$135,000	$174,000	$179,200	$635,600

* Budgeted production for the quarter times 10 bd ft of birch lumber for each captain's chair.
† Estimated beginning inventory.
‡ Budgeted production for the quarter times 12 bd ft of oak lumber for each rocking chair.

Figure 7-9 The materials purchases budget is based on required beginning and ending inventory levels and planned production for each quarter. Material quantity is converted to dollars by multiplying by the purchase price for each raw material.

Fable Manufacturing Company
Direct Labor Budget
For the Year Ending December 31, 1986

	Quarter 1	2	3	4	Year Total
Captain's Chairs					
Budgeted production	2,700	5,750	4,750	3,500	16,700
Direct labor hours per unit	×2	×2	×2	×2	×2
Required direct labor hours	5,400	11,500	9,500	7,000	33,400
Hourly rate	×$6	×$6	×$6	×$6	×$6
Direct labor cost	$ 32,400	$ 69,000	$ 57,000	$ 42,000	$200,400
Rocking Chairs					
Budgeted production	4,300	1,750	2,500	6,500	15,050
Direct labor hours per unit	×3	×3	×3	×3	×3
Required direct labor hours	12,900	5,250	7,500	19,500	45,150
Hourly rate	×$6	×$6	×$6	×$6	×$6
Direct labor cost	77,400	31,500	45,000	117,000	270,900
Total direct labor cost	$109,800	$100,500	$102,000	$159,000	$471,300
Total direct labor hours	18,300	16,750	17,000	26,500	78,550

Figure 7-10 The direct labor budget is merely an extension of the production quantity budget in Figure 7-7. Production quantities are multiplied by the labor requirement for each product produced.

by the amount of raw material needed for each unit. Since there are two raw materials, the company must make the computation for each raw material for all four quarters.

The direct labor budget, illustrated in Figure 7-10, is prepared from the production quantity budget and labor rate data. The budgeted quantity of production for each quarter is multiplied by the required amount of labor needed to produce each unit. Two hours of direct labor are required to produce one captain's chair and 3 hours of direct labor are needed to produce one rocking chair. These required labor hours are multiplied by the quarterly production quantity of each product to compute the direct labor budget for each product. Then the direct labor hours and direct labor costs for each product are added to find the totals for the period.

We have ignored numerous factors that could complicate the direct labor budget, such as differing labor costs and the inability to increase or decrease the labor pool significantly. These are very real budgeting variables, but we omit them to simplify this illustration in order to concentrate on the basic budgeting concepts.

Manufacturing overhead is divided into fixed and variable components, as shown in the manufacturing overhead budget in Figure 7-11. The total variable cost fluctuates with the production level. Fable uses direct labor hours as its measure of production activity. The budgeted amounts

Fable Manufacturing Company
Manufacturing Overhead Budget
For the Year Ending December 31, 1986

	Quarter				
Manufacturing Overhead	**1**	**2**	**3**	**4**	**Year Total**
Variable costs:					
Indirect materials	$ 9,150	$ 8,375	$ 8,500	$ 13,250	$ 39,275
Indirect labor	18,300	16,750	17,000	26,500	78,550
Employee fringe benefits	36,600	33,500	34,000	53,000	157,100
Payroll taxes	9,150	8,375	8,500	13,250	39,275
Utilities	10,980	10,050	10,200	15,900	47,130
Maintenance	7,320	6,700	6,800	10,600	31,420
Total variable costs	91,500	83,750	85,000	132,500	392,750
Fixed costs:					
Supervision	18,000	18,000	18,000	18,000	72,000
Depreciation	24,000	24,000	24,000	24,000	96,000
Maintenance	9,000	9,000	9,000	9,000	36,000
Property taxes*	4,912	4,913	4,912	4,913	19,650
Insurance	3,000	3,000	3,000	3,000	12,000
Total fixed costs	58,912	58,913	58,912	58,913	235,650
Total manufacturing overhead costs	$150,412	$142,663	$143,912	$191,413	$628,400

$$\text{Manufacturing overhead rate} = \frac{\$628{,}400}{78{,}550 \text{ DLH}} = \$8.00/\text{hr}$$

For cash flow purposes it is assumed that expenses are paid evenly over the 4 quarters as follows:

$$\frac{\$628{,}400 - \text{Depreciation of } \$96{,}000}{4 \text{ quarters}} = \frac{\$532{,}400}{4} = \$133{,}100/\text{quarter}$$

* The budgeted property tax of $19,650 amounts to $4,912.50 per quarter. Budgets are made up of estimated figures, and managers often round them to whole dollars; therefore, the quarterly amounts of $4,912 and $4,913 are alternated for the four quarters.

Figure 7-11 Variable manufacturing overhead budget based on the number of units produced each quarter. The overhead rate contains fixed and variable components.

of variable overhead costs are based on the following estimated relationships:

	Estimated Variable Overhead Cost per Direct Labor Hour
Indirect materials	$ .50
Indirect labor	1.00
Employee fringe benefits	2.00
Payroll taxes	.50
Utilities	.60
Maintenance	.40
Total	$5.00

Budgeted variable overhead is computed for each overhead cost by multiplying the budgeted activity level for the quarter times the estimated amount of cost per direct labor hour for the overhead cost. For example the budgeted indirect materials cost of $9,150 for the first quarter, as shown in Figure 7-11, is computed by multiplying 18,300 budgeted direct labor hours (Figure 7-10) times $.50 per direct labor hour. The other variable overhead costs are computed the same way. For example, the costs of three overhead items for the second quarter are computed as follows:

	Indirect Materials	Indirect Labor	Employee Fringe Benefits
Budgeted DLH for the second quarter	16,750	16,750	16,750
Estimated cost per direct labor hour	×$.50	×$1.00	×$2.00
Budgeted overhead amount	$8,375	$16,750	$33,500

Fixed overhead is determined by using past experience and knowledge of any expected changes. In this example, five fixed overhead costs are given which total $58,912 a quarter. Notice that depreciation of $24,000 is not a cash expense. To estimate cash outflow caused by overhead costs, depreciation is subtracted from total overhead. The remaining overhead cost is divided by 4 to spread the cash outflow evenly over the four quarters. The overhead cash outflow of $133,100 per quarter appears in the cash flow budget presented in Figure 7-17. In this example we spread the cash outflow from overhead evenly over the four quarters merely for the sake of convenience. In practice the budget should reflect the expected cash flow, and some quarters may have greater cash outflows than others. For example, winter heating costs may cause higher overhead costs during the winter quarter.

To arrive at the cost of goods sold budget (Figure 7-12), the budgets for total production, direct materials, direct labor, and manufacturing overhead plus beginning and ending finished goods inventory are used. Beginning inventory must be estimated because the end of the current year has not yet been reached when the budget is prepared. However, since year-end is near, the estimates may be quite accurate. The basic format for computing cost of goods sold is

	Estimated finished goods inventory at beginning of budget year
+	Expected production during budget year
=	Total cost of units available
−	Cost of expected ending finished goods inventory
=	Cost of goods sold

The administrative expense budget in Figure 7-13 is not divided into quarters. Many of the administrative expenses are fixed or semivariable, so quarterly budgets may not improve cost control for this cost area. For convenience we assume that the administrative expenses are paid evenly over the four quarters.

Fable Manufacturing Company
Cost of Goods Sold Budget
For the Year Ending December 31, 1986

	Captain's Chairs		Rocking Chairs		Total
Beginning inventory in units*	800		1,200		
Unit cost†	×$42		×$65		
Cost of beginning inventory		$ 33,600		$ 78,000	$ 111,600
1986 production*	16,700		15,050		
Unit cost‡	×$44		×$66		
Total production cost		734,800		993,300	1,728,100
Total available		768,400		1,071,300	1,839,700
Less ending inventory in units§	500		1,250		
Unit cost	×$44		×$66		
Cost of ending inventory		22,000		82,500	104,500
Cost of goods sold		$746,400		$ 988,800	$1,735,200

* Production quantity budget (Figure 7-7).
† Estimated unit cost for beginning inventory.
‡ Budgeted product costs are computed as follows:

	Captain's Chairs		Rocking Chairs	
Direct material	10 bd ft @ $1.60	$16	12 bd ft @ $2	$24
Direct labor	2 hr @ $6	12	3 hr @ $6	18
Manufacturing overhead	2 hr @ $8	16	3 hr @ $8	24
Total		$44		$66

§ Ending finished goods inventory budget (Figure 7-6).

Figure 7-12 **The cost of goods sold budget is derived from the cost of beginning inventory and the budgeted costs of production for the period. A FIFO inventory flow is assumed.**

Fable Manufacturing Company
Administrative Expense Budget
For the Year Ending December 31, 1986

Administrative salaries	$120,000
Clerical salaries	55,000
Insurance	8,000
Maintenance	17,000
Office supplies	9,000
Property taxes	7,000
Depreciation on office and equipment	24,000
Total administrative expenses	$240,000

It is assumed that administrative expenses are paid evenly over the four quarters as follows:

$$\frac{\$240{,}000 - \$24{,}000 \text{ depreciation}}{4 \text{ quarters}} = \$54{,}000 \text{ per quarter cash outflow}$$

Figure 7-13 **In this budget, administrative expenses are assumed to be spread equally over all four quarters, but in some cases they may vary throughout the year. A budget should reflect the expected cost behavior.**

Fable Manufacturing Company
Marketing Expense Budget
For the Year Ending December 31, 1986

Marketing sales and commissions	$110,000
Clerical salaries	46,000
Advertising	30,000
Entertainment	11,000
Insurance	4,000
Maintenance	12,000
Office supplies	9,000
Property taxes	4,000
Travel	16,000
Depreciation on office equipment	18,000
Total marketing expense	$260,000

It is assumed that marketing expenses are paid evenly over the four quarters as follows:

$$\frac{\$260{,}000 - \$18{,}000 \text{ depreciation}}{4 \text{ quarters}} = \$60{,}500 \text{ per quarter cash outflow}$$

Figure 7-14
The marketing expense budget includes some costs, such as commissions, that vary with sales. However, here we assume a constant marketing cost for each quarter to simplify the illustration.

The budgeting of marketing expense is similar to the budgeting of administrative expense. Some marketing expenses, such as sales commissions, vary directly with sales; others are fixed. In this example marketing expenses are spread evenly over the four quarters, as shown in Figure 7-14.

One of the most eagerly awaited budgets is the budgeted income statement, shown in Figure 7-15. It is the end product of the profit plan

Fable Manufacturing Company
Budgeted Income Statement
For the Year Ending December 31, 1986

	From Figure		
Sales	7-5		$2,370,000
Cost of goods sold	7-12		1,735,200
Gross margin on sales			634,800
Administrative expense	7-13	$240,000	
Marketing expense	7-14	260,000	
			500,000
Income before tax			134,800
Income tax*			60,660
Net income†			$ 74,140

* A 45% effective tax rate is assumed.
† There are no nonoperating items.

Figure 7-15
The budgeted income statement is a key document in the profit plan. If the net income is unsatisfactory, management may revise the budget.

Fable Manufacturing Company
Capital Expenditure Budget
For the Year Ending December 31, 1986

	Quarter				
Project	**1**	**2**	**3**	**4**	**Year Total**
Delivery equipment*	$43,000			$86,000	$129,000
Office equipment†	6,000	$ 6,000	$6,000	6,000	24,000
Manufacturing equipment‡	22,000	22,000			44,000
Total expenditures§	$71,000	$28,000	$6,000	$92,000	$197,000

* Purchase one delivery truck in the first quarter and two more in the fourth quarter to help with peak sales.
† Replace all desk calculators with new printout calculators and acquire new electric typewriters during the year.
‡ Purchase four new high-speed welders as soon as they can be delivered.
§ We assume cash outlays for capital expenditure items. Financing portions of major projects is common. That topic is covered in Chapter 13.

Figure 7-16 Capital expenditure budgets reflect the company's long-range planning strategy.

and provides useful numbers in evaluating target net income or other measures of expected performance. If the budgeted net income figure is disappointing to management, it may be necessary to revise all of the budgets in an effort to generate a profit plan that satisfies management's expectations.

The elements of the budgeted income statement come from other budgets already prepared. Detailed information about sales, product cost, and administrative and selling expense can be found in the supporting budgets. The budgeted income tax is estimated and in this example is based on a rate of 45 percent.

Fable's capital expenditure budget, shown in Figure 7-16, is small, but it illustrates the process of determining the impact of capital expenditures on cash flow. A more extensive treatment of this topic is found in Chapter 13.

The cash budget, shown in Figure 7-17, is critically important because it helps managers to avoid cash shortages or cash surpluses. The data for the cash budget are taken from many of the budgets previously prepared. Assumptions have to be made about the timing of receivable collections and expense payments based on past experience and expected changes in the future. For examples such as this one, the assumptions must be stated.

The budgeted income statement ties together the December 31, 1985, and the December 31, 1986, balance sheets. At the time the budget is prepared, the current operating year has not yet ended. Therefore, the balance sheet for the end of the current year must be estimated. Fable Manufacturing Company's beginning and ending budgeted balance sheets

Fable Manufacturing Company
Cash Budget
For the Year Ending December 31, 1986

	Quarter				
	1	2	3	4	Year Total
Beginning balance	$ 31,000[a]	$ 82,200	$120,100	$ 25,500	$ 31,000[a]
Collections from sales[b]:					
Prior quarter × .3	228,000	171,000	162,000	117,000	678,000
Current quarter × .7	399,000	378,000	273,000	609,000	1,659,000
Total cash available without financing	658,000	631,200	555,100	751,500	2,368,000
Less disbursements:					
Direct materials[c]	147,400	135,000	174,000	179,200	635,600
Direct labor[d]	109,800	100,500	102,000	159,000	471,300
Manufacturing overhead[e]	133,100	133,100	133,100	133,100	532,400
Administrative expense[f]	54,000	54,000	54,000	54,000	216,000
Marketing expense[g]	60,500	60,500	60,500	60,500	242,000
Total disbursements	504,800	483,100	523,600	585,800	2,097,300
Net cash available	153,200	148,100	31,500	165,700	270,700
Capital expenditures[h]	71,000	28,000	6,000	92,000	197,000
Ending cash balance	$ 82,200	$120,100	$ 25,500	$ 73,700	$ 73,700

[a] Estimated beginning balance.
[b] From Figure 7-5; it is assumed that 70% of cash is collected during the quarter of the sale and the remaining 30% the following quarter. Estimated fourth quarter sales, 1985 = $760,000.
[c] From Figure 7-9; it is assumed that materials are paid for in the quarter in which they are purchased.
[d] From Figure 7-10; it is assumed that labor is paid for in the quarter in which it is utilized.
[e] From Figure 7-11; $157,100 − $24,000 depreciation = $133,100.
[f] From Figure 7-13.
[g] From Figure 7-14.
[h] From Figure 7-16.

Figure 7-17 **Cash budgets are critically important. Here we present quarterly cash budgets, but many firms prepare monthly or weekly cash budgets.**

are presented in Figure 7-18. The account balances in the 1986 statement are different from those in the 1985 statement, reflecting the plans detailed in the operating budget and other financial budgets. Finally the budgeted statement of changes in financial position, shown in Figure 7-19, is prepared from the beginning and ending balance sheets, from the income statement, and from data in other budgets, such as the capital expenditure budget, that show expected cash flows.

The Fable Manufacturing Company master budget example is not large or complicated. Still, there are many individual budgets and they require many computations. It should be clear that preparation of a complete master budget for an actual organization is a major task.

Fable Manufacturing Company
Budgeted Balance Sheet
December 31,1985

Assets			
Current assets:			
Cash		$ 31,000	
Accounts receivable		228,000	
Raw materials inventory		66,000	
Finished goods inventory		111,600	
Total current assets			$ 436,600
Fixed assets:			
Land		60,000	
Buildings	$780,000		
Less accumulated depreciation, building	200,000	580,000	
Equipment	383,000		
Less accumulated depreciation, equipment	96,000	287,000	927,000
Total assets			$1,363,600
Liabilities and Stockholders' Equity			
Stockholders' equity:			
Common stock		$600,000	
Retained earnings		763,600	$1,363,600
Total liabilities and stockholders' equity			$1,363,600

Figure 7-18 **The budgeted balance sheets for December 31, 1985, and December 31, 1986, show the expected account balances at the beginning and end of the budget period.**

Fable Manufacturing Company
Budgeted Statement of Changes in Financial Position
For the Year Ending December 31, 1986

Sources of cash from operations:		
Net income		$ 74,140
Add items not requiring the use of cash		
Depreciation	$138,000	
Decrease in finished goods inventory	7,100	
Increase in taxes payable	60,660	205,760
Total		279,900
Less items not providing cash		
Increase in accounts receivable	33,000	
Increase in raw materials inventory	7,200	40,200
Total cash provided by operations		239,700
Uses of cash:		
Purchase of new equipment		197,000
Increase in cash balance		$ 42,700

Figure 7-19 **A budgeted statement of changes in financial position.**

Fable Manufacturing Company
Budgeted Balance Sheet
December 31, 1986

Assets

	From Figure			
Current assets:				
Cash	7-17		$ 73,700	
Accounts receivable	7-5		261,000*	
Raw materials inventory	7-8		73,200†	
Finished goods inventory	7-6		104,500‡	
Total current assets				$ 512,400
Fixed assets:				
Land			60,000	
Buildings		$780,000		
Less accumulated depreciation, building		290,000	490,000	
Equipment		580,000		
Less accumulated depreciation, equipment		144,000	436,000	986,000
Total assets				$1,498,400

Liabilities and Stockholders' Equity

Current liabilities:		
Taxes payable		$ 60,660
Stockholders' equity:		
Common stock	$600,000	
Retained earnings	837,740	1,437,740
Total liabilities and stockholders' equity		$1,498,400

* 30% of fourth-quarter budgeted sales.
† 13,500 bd ft of birch lumber @ $1.60/bd ft = $21,600 + 25,800 bd ft oak lumber @ $2.00/bd ft = $51,600, for a total of $73,200.
‡ 500 captain's chairs at a cost of $44 each + 1,250 rocking chairs at a cost of $66 each (500 × $44) + (1,250 × $66) = $104,500.

Figure 7-18 (***Continued***)

The Profit Plan

The profit plan best describes the operating part of the master budget

The term **profit plan** is sometimes used to refer to a master budget. *Profit plan* probably best describes the operating part of the master budget of a profit-oriented firm. However, it can be argued that the entire master budget of profit-oriented firms is the total profit plan for the firm. The operating budget shows details of budgeted net income, but the financial budgets, such as cash and capital expenditure budgets, are also an integral part of the overall profit planning of the firm.

Naturally the term *profit plan* is not suitable for public-sector firms. Organizations such as a fire department do not generate a net income. For public-sector organizations, **master budget** is the more logical term for the total budget package. Because we are concerned with both public- and private-sector organizations, we use *master budget* predominantly. However, be aware of *profit plan* because it is used occasionally in practice.

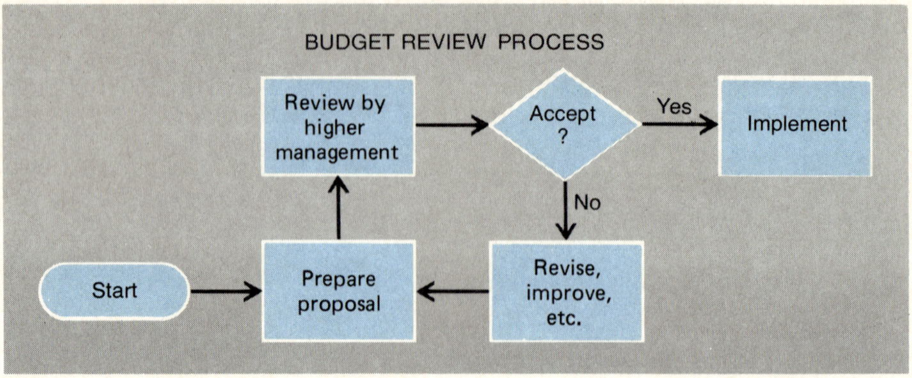

Figure 7-20
There are many types of budget review systems. This example is typical of the budget review process.

The Budget Review Process

The budget plan determines the allocation of resources within the organization. Typically the resources available are less than the demand for the resources. Consequently, there should be some systematic process for evaluating all proposals relating to the budget. The process of systematically evaluating budget proposals is referred to as the **budget review process.**

In the early planning stages budget review may not be a formal process. Sometimes a few people or even a single individual makes the budgeting decisions. For example, production line supervisors may determine resource allocations within their department. Next a plant budget committee may evaluate budget proposals for all production supervisors. The budget proposals for the entire plant go to a division budget committee, and the final budget review is made by a budget committee of the controller and corporate vice presidents.

The budget review process varies among organizations. Even within a single firm, different budget review processes may be used in various segments of the firm and at various levels of responsibility. However, the basic review process is fairly standard. Figure 7-20 shows the general flow in the budget review process.

CONTROL THROUGH BUDGETING

Performance reports are used to compare the actual results with the expected results presented in the budget

An important part of the control function of budgeting is the comparison of budgeted data with actual operating results. The comparisons are presented in periodic **budget performance reports.** The reports may be prepared as frequently as management desires but, as with other types of information, they are costly. Consequently, reports should be prepared only when the information can be cost-benefit justified. In the Fable Manufacturing Company example quarterly budgets are prepared. To illustrate performance reporting, we present hypothetical cost data for the first quarter of 1986 for manufacturing overhead. The report appears in Figure 7-21.

During the quarter Fable produced 3,200 captain's chairs and 5,200 rocking chairs. The budget figures and the actual cost figures for the quarter are presented in Figure 7-21. The actual cost figures are a product of the accounting system and can be obtained only after the budget period has elapsed. The right-hand column shows the differences between the budget and actual data. These differences are called **variances** because they show the variation between expected and actual results. Variances are favorable if actual costs are less than budgeted costs; they are unfavorable if actual costs are greater than budgeted costs. Variances are used extensively in management accounting in performance reporting.

Fable Manufacturing Company
Manufacturing Overhead Performance Report
First Quarter 1986

Manufacturing Overhead	Budget	Actual	Variance (Favorable) Unfavorable
Variable costs:			
Indirect materials	$ 9,150	$ 10,800	$ 1,650 U
Indirect labor	18,300	19,000	700 U
Employee fringe benefits	36,600	45,200	8,600 U
Payroll taxes	9,150	11,400	2,250 U
Utilities	10,980	13,500	2,520 U
Maintenance	7,320	7,100	(220)F
Total variable costs	91,500	107,000	15,500 U
Fixed costs:			
Supervision	18,000	18,000	0
Depreciation	24,000	24,000	0
Maintenance	9,000	9,500	500 U
Property taxes	4,912	5,200	288 U
Insurance	3,000	3,300	300 U
Total fixed costs	58,912	60,000	1,088 U
Total manufacturing overhead costs	$150,412	$167,000	$16,588 U

Figure 7-21
A manufacturing overhead quarterly performance report. Detailed timely performance reports provide managers with a framework for identifying potential problem areas.

We use a U to designate unfavorable variances and an F and parentheses ( ) to denote favorable variances. In practice the U and F are usually omitted because the parentheses are well understood. The total overhead variance is $16,588 unfavorable, which is approximately 11 percent of actual overhead cost. Part of the explanation of this variance may be that actual production was different than expected during the quarter. Variances caused by changes in the level of activity are discussed in Chapter 9.

The total net variance may have little value for cost control purposes without the more detailed information in the report. Individual favorable and unfavorable variances may net out large variances of real importance. Therefore, the item-by-item variance information must be evaluated in detail to determine managerial performance and to make specific cost control decisions.

The mere existence of a performance reporting system does not assure the existence of a true control process. Control suggests a means for encouraging successful budget performance and discouraging unfavorable performance. Performance reporting alone does not assure that employees will strive toward budget objectives. Instead budget performance must be tied to the organization's reward structure. That means promotions, pay raises, bonuses, fringe benefits, and other rewards must be determined, at least in part, by employee budget performance.

Participative Budgeting

Budgets should not be imposed on managers

Most budgeting experts agree that budgets should not be imposed by top-level management but instead should be prepared with the active participation of middle- and lower-level managers who are responsible for their individual budgets. **Participative budgeting** does not mean that each manager can choose exactly what goes into the budget; it means that managers with budget responsibility have an opportunity to explain and defend their respective budget proposals.

Human Behavior and Budgets

It is difficult to discuss the control aspect of the budgeting process without mentioning behavioral implications. Budget control is based on the concept that managers are held responsible for activities they manage. Performance reports reflect the degree of achievement of plans as embodied in the budget. A variety of human reactions occur, however, to even the most carefully prepared performance reports. To minimize adverse behavioral problems, care should be taken to develop and administer budgets appropriately. Budgets should not be used as a hammer to demand unattainable performance from employees. The best safeguard against unrealistic budgets is participative budgeting.

SELLING THE BUDGET

Budget proposals must be sold to the budget review committee

Accountants are concerned primarily with preparation of the entire master budget, but marketing managers, production supervisors, purchasing officers, and other nonfinancial managers are interested mainly in the preparation of their budgets and in their ability to sell their budgets to higher-level management. **Selling the budget** means convincing the budget review committee that a particular budget proposal should be accepted. For some managers selling the budget is the single most important activity in their entire job because if they fail at this task, even a tremendous management effort cannot obtain desired results.

With such an awesome description of the importance of selling the budget, one might conclude that it is an exceedingly difficult process. Not so! Actually the process requires a mixture of logic and diligence. There is no precise formula for success, but the following are some common suggestions:

1. Know your audience.
2. Make a professional presentation.
3. Quantify the material.
4. Avoid surprise.
5. Set priorities.

Know Your Audience

A large part of the budget-selling strategy may be determined by the nature of the budget review audience, whether it is one person or a group of people. Information that may prove essential to the successful budget approval effort includes:

1. Strategies that have succeeded or failed in the past
2. Pet peeves or special likes of review members
3. A variety of other committee characteristics

Make a Professional Presentation

Not all managers approach the budgeting process with the same level of enthusiasm. By the time budget review arrives, some managers just want to get it over with. Such an attitude can easily show during the budget review process. Review committees may interpret such attitudes as disdain for their job and their management function in general. Often the result is unfavorable action on the budget proposals under review.

A professional presentation includes:

An enthusiastic and polished presentation

A neat, concise, and understandable budget proposal

Ample supporting documentation

A willingness and ability to answer relevant questions

Quantify the Material

Because most resource allocation decisions are in some way affected by their cost-benefit relationships, it is necessary to quantify both the costs and benefits of virtually all budget proposals. Cost estimation is seldom easy, but it is usually far easier than the measurement of benefits. Even in the private sector, benefits are not always easy to measure in terms of the corporate goals of profitability and liquidity. In the not-for-profit sector, benefit measurement is even more difficult. For example, how does one measure the benefits of 20 new park rangers, 10 new police cars, or a decorative fountain in the city park? Obviously the quantification process would be different for each of these, and direct comparisons could be inconclusive. Yet, such comparisons may be necessary in arriving at final budget allocations.

It is easy to dismiss the value of quantification when the resulting numbers are hard to compare with other budget proposals, or the numbers are hard to verify. Nevertheless, some quantitative support typically is better than just general statements about the desirability of the budget proposal. Budget salesmanship should be approached with the same ingenuity that is found in the external marketing effort. If certain budget proposals have benefits that are difficult to quantify directly, various types of statistics might support the projects in an indirect way. For example, if a police department wants to justify 10 new police officers, it might offer supporting statistics on rising population in the community, rising crime rates, or relatively low per-capita police cost ratios. None of the suggested statistics measure direct benefits, but they may be more useful in swaying a budget review committee than some vague statement about the value of more officers. Statistics that are not direct measures of benefits can be used widely in both the public and private sector when supporting budget proposals.

Avoid Surprises

Avoiding surprises means avoiding surprises to the review committee as well as to the ones presenting the budget. Brand new proposals and information are hard to sell to a budget review committee. Anything startlingly new should be introduced and developed long before the final review process.

Surprises to managers presenting the budgets most often occur during the questioning process or when a budget proposal is more detailed than prior budgets. To minimize this problem, budget presentations should be carefully rehearsed in great detail. The rehearsal might include a realistic or even pessimistic mock review committee. The mock review should ask pointed and difficult questions. Sometimes knowing the answer to a relatively immaterial question is enough to secure a favorable opinion.

Set Priorities

Few managers receive a totally favorable response to all budget requests. In a world of limited resources, wants exceed available resources, and managers should be prepared for a budget allocation that is somewhat different from the initial request. Typically all proposed budget items are not equally desirable. Some projects and activities are essential; others are highly desirable. Some would be nice but are really not essential.

Priority systems established by the managers of each budgeting entity before the review process starts aid in structuring the budget proposal so that important items are funded first. Setting priorities avoids embarrassing questions and last-minute decision crises that affect the quality of a professional presentation.

SUMMARY

A **budget** is a comprehensive quantitative plan for the utilization of an entity's resources for some specific time period. The activity or function represented by the budget must be carefully defined. Budgets force periodic planning, improve coordination and communication, and require quantification of plans. In addition, a budget provides a performance measurement framework, creates cost awareness, and provides goal orientation.

Planning and control are the two basic functions of budgeting. **Planning** involves the entire budget development process. **Control** is exercised by comparing actual results with budgeted data. The reporting process alone does not ensure control; it merely provides performance measures. Control is exercised by tying budget performance to the organization's reward structure.

The total budget package for an organization is called the **master budget.** It includes the operating budget and the financial budget. The **operating budget** describes the expected results of future operations of the organization. For a manufacturing firm it includes budgeted sales, inventories, materials, direct labor, manufacturing overhead, cost of goods sold, administrative expenses, marketing expenses, and net income. The **financial budget** includes the budgeted capital expenditures, cash flows, balance sheet, and changes in financial position.

Participative budgeting refers to the active involvement of lower- and intermediate-level managers in the budgeting process. Budgets should not be imposed but rather should be developed with the input of all managers with budget responsibility.

Selling the budget refers to the process of securing approval for budget proposals. Some suggestions for selling the budget include knowing the audience, making professional presentations, quantifying the materials, avoiding surprises, and setting priorities.

KEY TERMS

administrative expense budget *(268)*
budget *(259)*
budget entity *(260)*
budget performance reports *(286)*
budget review process *(286)*
budgeted balance sheet *(270)*
budgeted income statement *(269)*
budgeted nonoperating items *(269)*
budgeted statement of changes in financial position *(271)*
budgeted statement of financial position *(270)*
capital expenditure budget *(269)*
cash budget *(270)*
control *(265)*
cost of goods sold budget *(268)*
direct labor budget *(268)*
financial budget *(269)*
fixed budget *(271)*
manufacturing overhead budget *(268)*

marketing expense budget *(268)*
master budget *(266)*
materials budget *(268)*
operating budget *(267)*
participative budgeting *(288)*
performance reporting *(266)*
planning *(265)*
production budget *(268)*
profit plan *(285)*
sales budget *(267)*
selling the budget *(288)*
static budget *(271)*
variances *(287)*

QUESTIONS

1. What are the basic characteristics of budgeting?
2. Define and describe the budget review process.
3. Explain the functions of budgeting.
4. How do long-term budgets differ from annual budgets?
5. What is meant by the term "goal-oriented budgets"? What practical implications does the term have in the budgeting process?
6. Define, compare, and contrast the terms *master budget* and *profit plan.* What significance does the term *profit plan* have for public-sector organizations?
7. Which budget is prepared first and why?
8. "Budgets are important in profit planning for private-sector firms, but budgets are costly and time-consuming frills in not-for-profit organizations." Respond.
9. Describe and illustrate the concept of a budgeting entity.
10. What is participative budgeting?
11. "Since the capital expenditure budget is not part of the budgeted income statement, it would not be considered part of the profit plan." Respond.
12. What factors would affect the frequency of production budget preparation?
13. Of what value is budget performance reporting? What behavioral implications are there with performance reports?
14. What is meant by selling the budget? Describe the budget selling process.

EXERCISES

Ex. 7-1 Sales and cash receipts budgets. Management expects *Antique World* magazine sales to be 80,000 copies in the first quarter of 1986, and sales are expected to increase by 10 percent each successive quarter of 1986. The magazine sells for $3 per copy, but the company plans to increase the price to $3.50 per copy starting with the July issue. All sales are on open account. The company expects to collect 80 percent of all accounts in the quarter of sale and the balance in the following quarter. The accounts receivable balance on December 31, 1985, is $51,000.

Required:

a. Prepare an annual sales budget by quarters.
b. Prepare a schedule of quarterly cash collections.

Ex. 7-2 Inventory purchase budget. Conveyor Systems manufactures conveyor belt systems for manufacturing and merchandising operations. Two types of electric motors, a 25-horsepower and a 40-horsepower, are used in the production of the systems. Expected quarterly demand for the two motors is as follows:

	Quarter	25-Horsepower	40-Horsepower
Year 1	1	250	100
	2	350	150
	3	200	140
	4	150	80
Year 2	1	200	120

Fluctuations in production schedules and in lead time between placing orders and receiving products have resulted in a management policy of having ending inventory each quarter equal to 30 percent of next quarter's estimated use.

Required: Prepare a purchase quantities budget for the model year.

Ex. 7-3 **Direct labor budget.** The Yellowwood Ceramic Arts Company produces hand-molded and painted ceramic pieces for lawn and garden decorations. Below are budgeted quarterly production quantity data for 1986 and labor requirements for each of the three products produced.

Budgeted production in units is

	Quarter				
Product	**1**	**2**	**3**	**4**	**Total**
Fawn	2,000	4,000	8,000	6,000	20,000
Deer	1,000	4,000	6,000	4,000	15,000
Raccoon	500	1,000	2,000	1,500	5,000

Labor requirements at the rate of $6 per hour are

Product	Labor Hours
Fawn	2
Deer	3
Raccoon	4

Required: Prepare a direct labor budget for the company for 1986 assuming no beginning and ending inventories.

Ex. 7-4 **Manufacturing overhead budget.** Geo-Scan Industries is developing its manufacturing overhead budget for the coming year. Relevant data from past experience and current budget expectations are given below.

	Type I Scanner	Type II Scanner
Sales budget	2,000	5,000
Labor requirement per unit	15 hr	10 hr

Manufacturing overhead expected cost relationships are:

Fixed costs:	
Depreciation, manufacturing facilities	$35,000
Supervision, manufacturing	30,000
Fixed portion of other manufacturing costs	15,000
Variable costs:	
Indirect materials	$.10 per direct labor hr
Indirect labor	.15 per direct labor hr
Utilities	.30 per direct labor hr
Maintenance	.05 per direct labor hr

Required:

a. Prepare a manufacturing overhead budget at the expected level of activity.
b. Prepare a manufacturing overhead rate using direct labor hours as the application base.

Ex. 7-5 **Purchase quantity budget.** The Markland Tire Store is a retail tire distributor selling three basic tires—nylon cord, steel-belted radials, and fiberglass-belted radials. Expected sales for the first 4 months of 1986 are

	Quantity			
Tire	**January**	**February**	**March**	**April**
Nylon cord	100	200	300	400
Steel-belted	500	600	800	900
Fiberglass-belted	200	200	300	400

The December 31, 1985, inventory of tires is 60 nylon cords, 100 steel-belted radials, and 180 fiberglass-belted radials. The company policy for 1986 is to have inventory at month-end equal to 40 percent of next month's expected demand.

Required: Prepare a purchase quantity budget for each of the first 3 months of 1986.

Ex. 7-6 **Labor budget.** Presented below are labor requirements for the manufacture of two different models of videotape recorder-players.

Type of Labor	Model 660	Model 880	Labor Rate
Setup and machining	4 hr	6 hr	$7
Assembly	6 hr	10 hr	9
Testing and packaging	2 hr	3 hr	6

The production quantity budget for the four quarter is

Product	March	April	May
Model 660	600	500	350
Model 880	400	350	300

Required: Prepare a monthly labor budget identifying each type of labor.

Ex. 7-7 Cash receipts schedule. Below are 6 months of budgeted sales data for the Rico Department Store.

Month	Budgeted Sales
January	$100,000
February	90,000
March	120,000
April	150,000
May	160,000
June	160,000

The store has experienced the following sales and collection patterns. The store sells 60 percent of the merchandise on credit. Credit collections are as follows: 40 percent in the month of the sale; 30 percent in the month after the sale; 26 percent 2 months after the sale plus a 2 percent late charge. Four percent of credit sales are never collected. A $12,000 note payable must be paid April 14. A note receivable of $32,000 will be collected on June 29 with 10 percent annual interest for a 6-month period.

Required: Prepare a cash receipts schedule for April, May, and June.

Ex. 7-8 Materials purchase budget. Harrison Products Company manufactures and sells liquid fertilizer in 2.5-gallon bottles. Two raw materials, powdered nitrate and a mineral solution, are used in the production of the fertilizer. The nitrate is purchased for $.60 a pound, and the mineral solution for $.80 a gallon. The production of a 2.5-gallon bottle of fertilizer requires 4 pounds of nitrate and 2 gallons of mineral solution. January 1, 1986, inventories include 4,800 pounds of nitrate and 2,400 gallons of mineral solution. The company policy is to maintain inventory at the end of each quarter equal to 20 percent of the required quantity for next quarter's production. Budgeted production for the first quarter of 1987 is 5,000 units (bottles of fertilizer). Budgeted quarterly production for 1986 is listed below.

Quarter	Budgeted Production
1	3,000 units
2	8,000 units
3	5,000 units
4	4,000 units

Required: Prepare Harrison Products Company's 1986 materials purchase budget by quarters for each raw material.

Ex. 7-9 Manufacturing overhead budget and rate. William Ravenwood owns and manages a small manufacturing business that makes standard and energy-efficient control units for hot water heaters. Mr. Ravenwood is working on the manufacturing overhead budget for the firm for the coming year. The following estimates were made:

	Budgeted Sales per Unit	Labor Requirement per Unit
Standard controls	12,000	.3 hour
Energy-efficient controls	36,000	.2 hour

Overhead

Fixed:	
Depreciation of building	$400 per year
Utilities	$120 per year
Property tax	$ 70 per year
Variable:	
Indirect materials	$.10 per direct labor hour
Utilities	$.15 per direct labor hour

Required:

a. Prepare a manufacturing overhead budget.
b. Calculate the manufacturing overhead rate using direct labor hours as the application base.

Ex. 7-10 Budget performance report. Hebron City Parks Department prepares an annual budget and a year-end performance report. Below are the department's 1986 budget and corresponding actual revenue and cost data.

	Budget	Actual
Resources:		
Appropriations	$45,000	$43,000
Fees from admissions	6,000	6,300
Fees from programs	2,500	2,600
Total resources	$53,500	$51,900
Expenditures:		
Salaries	$14,500	$14,500
Seasonal wages	18,000	17,400
Equipment	8,500	8,400
Supplies	6,000	7,700
Utilities	2,500	3,100
Miscellaneous	4,000	3,550
Total expenditures	$53,500	$54,650

Required: Prepare a budget performance report for 1986.

Ex. 7-11 Production and overhead budgets. Sales of Geodata Company's 28-inch fiberglass relief globes are budgeted as follows:

April	800
May	600
June	700
July	500

April 1 beginning inventory is 150 globes. The desired ending inventory each month is 30 percent of expected sales for the next month. Each globe requires 6 hours of direct labor. Estimated variable overhead cost per direct labor hour is as follows:

Indirect materials	$ .40
Indirect labor	1.20
Fringe benefits	1.80
Payroll taxes	.60
Other	1.00

Fixed overhead of $178,500 per year is allocated equally to each month.

Required:

a. Prepare a production quantity budget for April, May, and June.
b. Prepare a direct labor budget for the 3 months.
c. Prepare a manufacturing overhead budget for the 3 months.

Ex. 7-12 Overhead budget and performance report. Zebek Company has budgeted 3,840 machine hours of production for March. Variable overhead is allocated to production using machine hours as the allocation base as follows:

Indirect materials	$ .60
Indirect labor	1.20
Fringe benefits	1.80
Payroll taxes	.40
Utilities	.55
Maintenance	.45

Fixed overhead for March was budgeted at $15,000. By the end of March the following actual cost data were accumulated:

Indirect materials	$ 2,450
Indirect labor	4,510
Fringe benefits	6,840
Payroll taxes	1,500
Utilities	2,305
Maintenance	1,790
Fixed overhead	14,680

Required:

a. Prepare an overhead budget for March.
b. Prepare an overhead budget performance report for March.

PROBLEMS

P. 7-1 **Sales and production budget.** Wilderness Way Manufacturing produces hiking boots and mountaineering boots. The hiking boots sell for $50 a pair, and the mountaineering boots sell for $95 a pair. Management expects to sell 20,000 pairs of hiking boots and 5,000 pairs of mountaineering boots during 1986. Annual boot sales are distributed over the year as follows:

Quarter	Percentage of Annual Sales
1	10
2	30
3	40
4	20

Since all boots are handmade, the company finds it difficult to adjust to periodic jumps in demand. To avoid shipping delays and customer dissatisfaction, management's policy is to carry a finished goods inventory that at the end of each quarter is equal to 40 percent of the next quarter's expected demand. Expected beginning inventory for the year is 800 pairs of hiking boots and 200 pairs of mountaineering boots. In 1987 boot sales are expected to be the same as in 1986.

Required:

a. Prepare a sales budget by quarters for each product and in total.
b. Prepare an ending inventory quantity budget for each product.
c. Prepare a quarterly production quantity budget for each product.

P. 7-2 **Ending raw materials inventory budget.** The Support Division of the Wayfarer Boat Company manufactures a variety of items used in the Assembly Division of the company. The SD-10 boat seat is used in the manufacture of several of the company's boats. Below is the quarterly production quantity budget for the coming year for the SD-10 boat seats.

Production Quantity Budget for SD-10 Boat Seats
For Four Quarters Ending December 31

	Quarter			
	1	2	3	4
Budgeted sales	6,000	8,000	9,000	7,000
Desired ending inventory	1,000	1,500	2,000	1,800
Total requirement	7,000	9,500	11,000	8,800
Less beginning inventory	800	1,000	1,500	2,000
Budgeted production	6,200	8,500	9,500	6,800

The SD-10 seat requires the following materials and ending inventories:

Material	Quantity	Required Ending Inventory at End of Previous Quarter
Metal tubing	10 ft	20%
Plywood	2.5 sq ft	10%
Vinyl	12 sq ft	20%
Foam padding	2 lb	50%

The percentages in the above schedule indicate how much of each quarter's material requirement should be in the ending inventory of the previous quarter. Beginning inventories are expected to be as follows:

Metal tubing	11,000 ft
Plywood	1,800 sq ft
Vinyl	15,000 sq ft
Foam padding	5,000 lb

Required: Prepare a budget of raw materials ending inventory for the first three quarters of the budget year.

P. 7-3 Sales and production budgets. Henderson Corporation makes a driveway sealing compound that it sells in 5-gallon cans for $50 per can. Company sales personnel have estimated annual sales of 3,600 units divided among the quarters as follows:

First quarter	1,000 units
Second quarter	1,100
Third quarter	800
Fourth quarter	700

Operating capacity of the manufacturing facilities is 900 units per quarter. Production of more than 900 units requires additional costs. Production cost is $30 per unit and there would be a 20 percent increase in cost for units in excess of 900 per quarter. The production manager is evaluated on the cost of production, whereas the sales manager is evaluated on the basis of sales revenue. The sales manager claims that if he had only 900 units to sell in each of the first two quarters, the unsatisfied customers would switch to new products and sales in each of the last two quarters would be 50 units less than estimated.

Required: Prepare sales and production budgets to determine how production should be scheduled and to resolve the conflict between the sales and production managers.

P. 7-4 Sales region quarterly sales budget. Kay Products, Inc., uses sales region quarterly sales budgets to plan inventory requirements and marketing strategies. The company sells two products and sales are divided into five sales regions. Each regional sales manager prepares a sales forecast in units. When necessary, the sales forecasts are modified at company headquarters. The products, Kay-1 and Kay-2, sell for $20 and $30, respectively. The regional sales managers' forecasts for 1986 are presented below:

Region	Kay-1	Kay-2
Northeast	4,000	8,000
Southeast	9,000	5,000
Midwest	10,000	15,000
Southwest	5,000	2,000
Northwest	6,000	10,000

Corporate management thinks poor weather in the Midwest and Northeast will reduce regional sales levels by 10 percent in the Northeast and 20 percent in the Midwest. Annual sales for both products are spread over the four quarters in the following percentages:

	Percentage of Annual Sales				
	Quarter				
	1	2	3	4	Total Percentage
Northeast	10	40	30	20	100
Southeast	20	20	20	40	100
Midwest	15	30	30	25	100
Southwest	25	20	20	35	100
Northwest	10	50	30	10	100

Required: Prepare a quarterly sales budget for each product by sales region and for the company in total.

P. 7-5 Materials and labor budgets. Leatherford Table Company makes oak office tables. Below are materials and labor cost and quantity data.

Resources	Quantity	Unit Cost
Oak lumber	40 bd ft	$ 3.20 per bd ft
Stain	.5 gal	12.00 per gal
Finishing compound	1 gal	19.00 per gal
Cutting labor	1.5 hr	7.00 per hr
Assembly labor	6 hr	8.00 per hr
Finishing labor	5 hr	9.00 per hr

Expected monthly sales for the first 4 months of 1986 are

Month	Sales
January	200
February	250
March	300
April	400
May	400

The company's policy is to have finished goods ending inventories each month equal to 20 percent of expected sales for next month and raw materials ending inventory equal to 30 percent of expected production needs for next month. Expected inventories for January 1, 1986, are

Item	Quantity	Unit Cost
Oak tables	40 tables	$300 per table
Oak lumber	8,400 bd ft	3 per bd ft
Stain	45 gal	12 per gal
Finishing compound	120 gal	19 per gal

Required:

a. Prepare a production quantity budget for January, February, and March.
b. Prepare a materials use budget for January, February, and March.
c. Prepare a materials purchases budget for January, February, and March.
d. Prepare a direct labor budget for January, February, and March.

P. 7-6 Cash budget. The Haley Dry Goods Company runs a chain of general-merchandise department stores in the upper Midwest. The average markup on merchandise inventory is 50 percent. Haley prepares quarterly sales budgets and company policy is to have an ending merchandise inventory equal to 1¼ times the next quarter's budget sales. Haley's budget committee has developed the following data:

1. Budgeted quarterly sales for 1986:

Quarter	Sales
1	$ 600,000
2	900,000
3	750,000
4	1,200,000

2. January 1, 1986, expected beginning merchandise inventory, at cost, $500,000.
3. Sales:

40% for cash (2% cash discount)
60% on credit of which:

60% collected in quarter of sale
30% collected in following quarter after sale
6% collected in second quarter after sale
4% never collected

4. Merchandise inventory purchases:

30% paid in quarter of purchase
70% paid in following quarter

5. Other budgeted expenses for 1986:

Quarter	Expense
1	$180,000
2	220,000
3	200,000
4	260,000

Of the other budget expenses, 90 percent are paid in the quarter in which they are incurred, and the remaining 10 percent are paid in the following quarter. The 1985 quarterly data are as follows:

Quarter	Sales	Other Expenses
1	$ 540,000	$170,000
2	820,000	205,000
3	700,000	190,000
4	1,000,000	240,000

6. Bank loan payments of $25,000 must be made at the end of the second and fourth quarters.
7. Estimated first-quarter sales, 1987 = $660,000.
8. Expected cash balance on January 1, 1986 = $160,000.
9. Fourth-quarter merchandise purchases in 1985 are $500,000.

Required: Prepare a quarterly cash budget for Haley Dry Goods Company.

P. 7-7 **(CMA) Cash and inventory budget.** The Russon Corporation is a retailer whose sales are all made on credit. Sales are billed twice monthly, on the tenth of the month for the last half of the prior month's sales and on the twentieth of the month for the first half of the current month's sales. The terms of all sales are 2/10, net 30. Based on past experience, the collection of accounts receivable is as follows:

Within the discount period	80%
On the 30th day	18%
Uncollectible	2%

Russon's average markup on its products is 20 percent of the sales price. The sales value of shipments for May and the forecast for the next 4 months are:

May (actual)	$500,000
June	600,000
July	700,000
August	700,000
September	400,000

Russon purchases merchandise for resale to meet the current month's sales demand and to maintain a desired monthly ending inventory of 25 percent of the next month's sales. All purchases are on credit with terms of net 30. Russon pays for one-half of a month's purchases in the month of purchase and the other half in the month following the purchase. All sales and purchases occur uniformly throughout the month.

1. How much cash can Russon Corporation plan to collect from accounts receivable collections during July?
   a. $574,000. **b.** $662,600. **c.** $619,000. **d.** $608,600.
   e. None of the above.
2. How much cash can Russon plan to collect in September from sales made in August?
   a. $337,400. **b.** $343,000. **c.** $400,400. **d.** $280,000.
   e. None of the above.

3. The budgeted dollar value of inventory on August 31 will be:
   a. $110,000. b. $80,000. c. $120,000. d. $100,000.
   e. Some amount other than those given above.
4. How much merchandise should Russon plan to purchase during June?
   a. $520,000. b. $460,000. c. $500,000. d. $580,000.
   e. None of the above.
5. The amount Russon should budget in August for the payment for merchandise is:
   a. $560,000. b. $500,000. c. $667,000. d. $600,000.
   e. None of the above.

P. 7-8 Comprehensive budget. Jane Hubbard retired from her job several years ago. As a hobby she makes stuffed animals that she sells to friends and neighbors. The demand for her products is especially heavy before the holidays, so she usually plans full-scale production for October and November, during which time she hires a helper. She plans to spend $100 each month in October and November for advertising "Mother Hubbard's Stuffed Animals." She plans to limit production to two products with the following sales and production data:

	Sales Forecast		Quantity and Cost of	
Product	**No. of Units**	**Sales Price**	**Beginning Inventory**	**Ending Inventory**
Panda	50	$110	8 @ $90	10 units
Pig	20	95	5 @ $77	6 units

Resources Required

		Required Use	
Materials	**Cost**	**Panda**	**Pig**
Black cloth	$8 per yd	1.5 yd	—
White cloth	6 per yd	1 yd	2 yd
Pink cloth	7 per yd	—	1 yd
Stuffing	1 per lb	4 lb	5 lb
Owner's labor	8 per hr	4 hr	3 hr
Hired labor	5 per hr	2 hr	2 hr

Expected Inventories of Raw Materials

Material	Beginning Inventory	Ending Inventory
Black cloth	10 yd	12 yd
White cloth	8 yd	10 yd
Pink cloth	5 yd	8 yd
Stuffing	20 lb	30 lb

Manufacturing overhead is $5 per labor hour.

Required: Prepare the following budgets for Mother Hubbard's Stuffed Animals:

- **a.** Sales budget.
- **b.** Production quantity budget.
- **c.** Materials use budget.
- **d.** Materials purchases budget.
- **e.** Direct labor budget.
- **f.** Schedule of product costs per unit using FIFO.
- **g.** Cost of goods sold budget.
- **h.** Budgeted income statement.

P. 7-9 **Budget performance reporting.** Biothon Company manufactures keyboards for computer terminals. Estimated sales for the first 4 months of 1986 are presented below.

January	6,000 units
February	7,000
March	8,000
April	7,500

The ending inventory of keyboards on December 31, 1985, is expected to be 2,000 units. The desired ending inventory of finished goods each month is 40 percent of next month's expected sales. Each unit requires 5 hours of direct labor costing $9 per hour. Fixed overhead of $1,879,200 per year is allocated equally to each month. Estimated variable overhead per direct labor hour is

Indirect materials	.50
Indirect labor	1.20
Fringe benefits	1.70
Payroll taxes	.60
Other expenses	1.10

By the end of January the company had produced 7,000 units using 35,350 hours of labor. Actual overhead was as follows:

Indirect materials	$ 17,200
Indirect labor	40,000
Fringe benefits	60,000
Payroll taxes	21,300
Other expenses	36,100
Fixed overhead	160,000

Required:

- **a.** Prepare a production quantity budget for the first quarter of 1986.
- **b.** Prepare a direct labor budget for the first quarter.
- **c.** Prepare a manufacturing overhead budget for the first quarter.
- **d.** Prepare a budget performance report for labor and overhead for January.

P. 7-10 Comprehensive manufacturing budget. Kafer Corporation makes two products, Y and Z. The following production and sales data are for the 1986 budget year.

Sales Forecast for 1986

Product	Units	Price	Expected Beginning Inventory	Desired Ending Inventory
Y	5,000	$ 80	800 units	1,000 units
Z	2,000	100	500	300

Manufacturing Resources	Unit	Cost	Production Requirements for Each Product	
			Y	Z
RS1	lb	$2 per lb	2 lb	—
RS2	lb	3 per lb	3 lb	2 lb
RS3	gal	5 per gal	1 gal	2 gal
RS4	gal	3 per gal	—	2 gal
General labor	hr	5 per hr	4 hr	2 hr
Skilled labor	hr	8 per hr	—	3 hr

Raw Materials	Expected Desired Beginning Inventory	Ending Inventory
RS1	600 lb	800 lb
RS2	1,000 lb	1,500 lb
RS3	2,000 gal	1,000 gal
RS4	200 gal	200 gal

The manufacturing overhead rate is $4 per direct labor hour. The company uses FIFO inventory.

Required:

a. Prepare a sales budget.
b. Prepare a production quantity budget.
c. Prepare a direct materials use budget.
d. Prepare a direct materials purchases budget.
e. Prepare a direct labor budget.
f. Prepare a cost of goods sold budget assuming a beginning inventory unit cost of $38 for Y and $70 for Z.

P. 7-11 Comprehensive budget. Rec-Furniture produces redwood picnic tables and benches. Forecasted data on sales, production requirements, and inventory levels are given on page 306. First in, first out (FIFO) inventory is used.

1986 Sales Forecast

Product	Units	Price
Picnic tables	1,200	$180
Benches	3,000	45

Manufacturing Requirements

Resource	Cost or Rate	Quantity: Table	Quantity: Bench
Redwood	$2.50 per bd ft	36 bd ft	10 bd ft
Sealer	9.00 per gal	1 gal	1 qt
Bolts	.20 each	15 bolts	6 bolts
Assembly labor	7.00 per hr	3 hr	1 hr
Finishing labor	5.00 per hr	1 hr	¼ hr

Inventory Item	Expected Beginning Inventory	Expected Cost
Picnic tables	70 tables	$125.00 per table
Benches	100 benches	35.00 per bench
Redwood	18,000 bd ft	2.50 per bd ft
Sealer	600 gal	9.00 per gal
Bolts	8,800 bolts	.20 each

The manufacturing overhead rate is $2 per direct labor hour. Desired ending inventory levels in 1986 are 10 percent of 1986 budgeted demand for finished goods and 20 percent of 1986 budgeted use for raw materials.

Required:

a. Prepare a sales budget.
b. Prepare a production quantity budget.
c. Prepare a direct materials budget.
d. Prepare a direct labor budget.
e. Prepare a cost of goods sold budget.

P. 7-12 (AICPA) Comprehensive cash budget. Modern Products Corporation, a manufacturer of molded plastic containers, determined in October 1986 that it needed cash to continue operations. The corporation began negotiating for a 1-month bank loan of $100,000 which would be discounted at 14 percent per annum on November 1. In considering the loan the bank requested a projected income statement and a cash budget for the month of November.

The following information is available:

1. Sales were budgeted at 120,000 units per month in October 1986, December 1986, and January 1987 and at 90,000 units in November 1986. The selling price is $2 per unit. Sales are billed on the fifteenth and on the last day of each month on terms of 2/10, net 30. Past experience indicates sales are even throughout the month and 50 percent of the customers pay the billed amount within the discount period. The remainder pay at the end of 30 days, except for bad debts, which average ½ percent of gross sales. On its income statement the corporation deducts from sales the estimated amounts for cash discounts on sales and losses on bad debts.
2. The inventory of finished goods on October 1 was 24,000 units. The finished goods inventory at the end of each month is to be maintained at 20 percent of sales anticipated for the following month. There is no work in process.
3. The inventory of raw materials on October 1 was 22,800 pounds. At the end of each month the raw materials inventory is to be maintained at not less than 40 percent of production requirements for the following month. Materials are purchased as needed in minimum quantities of 25,000 pounds per shipment. Raw materials purchases of each month are paid in the next succeeding month on terms of net 30 days.
4. All salaries and wages are paid on the fifteenth and on the last day of each month for the period ending on the date of payment.
5. All manufacturing overhead and selling and administrative expenses are paid on the tenth of the month following the month in which incurred. Selling expenses are 10 percent of gross sales. Administrative expenses, which include depreciation of $500 per month on office furniture and fixtures, total $33,000 per month.
6. The standard cost of a molded plastic container, based on "normal" production of 100,000 units per month, is as follows:

Materials—½ pound	$ .50
Labor	.40
Variable overhead	.20
Fixed overhead	.10
Total	$1.20

Fixed overhead includes depreciation on factory equipment of $4,000 per month. Overapplied or underapplied overhead is included in cost of sales.

7. The cash balance on November 1 is expected to be $10,000.

Required: Prepare the following for Modern Products Corporation assuming the bank loan is granted. (Do not consider income taxes.)

a. Schedules computing inventory budgets by months for
   1. Finished goods production in units for October, November, and December.
   2. Raw materials purchases in pounds for October and November.

b. A projected income statement for the month of November.

c. A cash forecast for the month of November showing the opening balance, receipts (itemized by dates of collection), disbursements, and balance at end of month.

P. 7-13 (AICPA) Production budget with a variance analysis report. The Wyoming Division of Reid Corporation produces an intricate component part used in Reid's major product line. The division manager has been concerned recently by a lack of coordination between purchasing and production personnel and believes that a monthly budgeting system would be better than the present system.

Wyoming's division manager has decided to develop budget information for the third quarter of the current year as a trial before the budget system is implemented for an entire fiscal year. In response to the division manager's request for data that could be used to develop budget information, the division controller accumulated the following data:

Sales. Sales through June 30, 1986, the first 6 months of the current year, are 24,000 units. Actual sales in units for May and June and estimated unit sales for the next 4 months are as follows:

May (actual)	4,000
June (actual)	4,000
July (estimated)	5,000
August (estimated)	6,000
September (estimated)	7,000
October (estimated)	7,000

Wyoming Division expects to sell 60,000 units during the year ending December 31, 1986.

Direct materials. Data on the materials used in the component are shown in the schedule below. The desired monthly ending inventory for all direct materials is to have sufficient materials on hand to produce the next month's estimated sales.

Direct Material	Units of Direct Materials per Finished Component	Cost per Unit	Inventory Level 6/30/86
#101	6	$2.40	35,000 units
#211	4	3.60	30,000 units
#242	2	1.20	14,000 units

Direct labor. Each component must pass through three different processes to be completed. Data on direct labor are presented below.

Process	Direct Labor Hours per Finished Component	Cost per Direct Labor Hour
Forming	.80	$8.00
Assembly	2.00	5.50
Finishing	.25	6.00

Factory overhead. The division produced 27,000 components during this 6-month period through June 30, 1986. The actual variable overhead costs incurred during this 6-month period are shown below. The division controller believes the variable overhead costs will be incurred at the same rate during the last 6 months of 1986.

Supplies	$ 59,400
Electricity	27,000
Indirect labor	54,000
Other	8,100
Total variable overhead	$148,500

The fixed overhead costs incurred during the first 6 months of 1986 amounted to $93,500. Fixed overhead costs are budgeted for the full year as follows:

Supervision	$ 60,000
Taxes	7,200
Depreciation	86,400
Other	32,400
Total fixed overhead	$186,000

Finished goods inventory. The desired monthly ending inventory in units of completed components is 80 percent of the next month's estimated sales. There are 5,000 finished units in the inventory on June 30, 1986.

Required:

a. Prepare a production budget in units for the Wyoming Division for the third quarter ending September 30, 1986.

b. Without prejudice to your answer in requirement *a*, assume the Wyoming Division plans to produce 18,000 units during the third quarter ending September 30, 1986, and 60,000 units for the year ending December 31, 1986.

1. Prepare a direct materials purchase budget in units and dollars for the third quarter ending September 30, 1986.
2. Prepare a direct labor budget in hours and dollars for the third quarter ending September 30, 1986.
3. Prepare a factory overhead budget for the 6-month period ending December 31, 1986.

c. Assume Wyoming Division actually produced 38,000 components during the 6-month period of July 1–December 31, 1986, and incurred variable overhead of $203,300 and fixed overhead of $95,000. Evaluate Wyoming Division's performance for the last 6 months of 1986 with respect to its control of factory overhead costs. Show and explain briefly any supporting calculations used in your evaluation.

CASE

Case 7-1 Comprehensive manufacturing budget

Carbo Chemical Company manufactures four types of cleaning compound with special grease-cutting abilities. All four products, which are sold in cans, are manufactured from basic inputs of petroleum distillates and ketones, but each product is cooked and distilled various lengths of time to bring out certain cleaning properties. For inventory identification purposes, petroleum distillates are called M1 and ketones are called M2. Budgeted sales and production data for 1986 are presented on page 310. The company uses a FIFO inventory system.

Product	Sales Forecast in Cans	Unit Price	Expected Inventory, 1/1/86	Expected Cost per Can
Nefle	30,000	$11	2,000	$ 4
Nefle-Plus	11,000	14	1,000	7
Nefle-Pro	8,000	16	500	8
Nefle-Whamo	7,000	19	500	11

	Direct Materials Quantity		
Product	M1	M2	Direct Labor
Nefle	2 gal	—	.4 hr
Nefle-Plus	2 gal	1 gal	.7 hr
Nefle-Pro	3 gal	—	.9 hr
Nefle-Whamo	3 gal	1 gal	1.2 hr

Direct labor cost: $6 per hr
Materials costs:
M1: $1.00 per gal
M2: $1.50 per gal
Manufacturing overhead: $3 per labor hr
Expected beginning inventories of raw materials on 1/1/86
M1: 20,000 units @ $1.00 per gal
M2: 2,000 units @ $1.50 per gal
Desired ending inventories:
Finished goods—15% of 1986 budgeted sales
Raw materials—20% of 1986 budgeted use for production
Marketing and administrative expense budget data:
Fixed costs:

Marketing	$40,000
Administrative	60,000

Variable costs:

Marketing	10% of sales
Administrative	5% of sales + 10% of direct labor cost

Required:

a. Prepare a sales budget.
b. Prepare a finished goods ending inventory budget.
c. Prepare a production quantity budget.
d. Prepare a materials use budget.
e. Prepare a materials purchases budget.
f. Prepare a direct labor budget.
g. Prepare a cost of goods sold budget.
h. Prepare a marketing and administrative expense budget.
i. Prepare a budgeted income statement.

Standard Costs

8

Standard cost accounting systems are used by many companies for planning and controlling operations. Standards are useful in detailed planning, cost control, performance measurement, and pricing decisions. When you have completed this chapter, you should understand:

1 The nature and use of standard costs.

2 The types and purposes of standard costs.

3 The development of standards.

4 The operation of a standard cost system.

5 The computation of direct materials and direct labor variances.

6 The concept and procedures of reporting standard cost variances.

Standards are carefully predetermined measures of excellence used in measuring performance or achievement. We use many types of standards in all walks of life. For example, in sports a .300 batting average is used to measure a baseball player's batting ability, or par on a golf course is used to measure golfing skill. Similarly, colleges use a specific grade-point average as an indication of academic achievement. In each of these examples an individual's performance is measured against some predetermined standard. The standard provides a quick and convenient means of performance appraisal.

In business, standards provide a framework for detailed and timely performance reporting, which is essential in monitoring and controlling daily business activities. The emphasis in this chapter is on the use of standards in business. We discuss the purpose of standards, the development of standards, and the operation of a standard cost system.

STANDARD COSTS DEFINED

Standard costs are benchmarks of efficient performance

Standard costs are carefully predetermined costs created by management and used as a basis for comparison with actual costs. Like all standards, standard costs are measures of achievement. Consequently, managers must use care to ensure that the standards are appropriate measures of performance that encourage attainment of organizational goals.

Standard costs are composed of two parts, a quantity and a cost. To illustrate, the Kindell Machine Tool Company produces plywood packing crates to package its products. Production of the crates requires the following resources:

Resource	Quantity	Cost
¾-in plywood	20 sq ft per crate	$ .40 per sq ft
Labor	30 min per crate	$6.00 per hr

Management has set some **standards** on the cost of producing the crates by estimating the quantity and cost of materials and labor. The estimates are management's idea of what should be required to produce a crate. As the crates are constructed, these standards can be compared with the actual quantity and cost of material and labor, and management can determine whether production performance is different from the standards. Standards are more detailed measures of performance than budgets and provide a useful framework for timely management reporting.

Measuring the standard cost of one unit of output

The standard cost of one crate is computed easily by multiplying the standard quantity of inputs times their standard costs and adding them up.

Resource	Quantity	Unit Cost	Total Cost
Plywood	20 sq ft	$ .40/sq ft	$ 8.00
Labor	.5 labor hr	$6.00/hr	3.00
Standard cost/unit			$11.00

During 1 month 500 crates were manufactured. The actual resources used to produce the 500 crates were:

Resource	Quantity	Cost
Plywood	10,400 sq ft	$ .38 per sq ft
Labor	240 hr	$6.20 per hr

Variance is the difference between standard cost and actual cost

The data show the firm paid less than the standard cost for the plywood but more than the standard cost for labor. The difference between the standard and actual cost of materials is called a **material price variance** and the difference between the standard and actual cost of labor is called a **labor rate variance.** Both variances highlight the same type of cost difference, which results from a difference between the standard and actual **cost** of resources. Because the purchase price of plywood was less than the standard price, the material price variance is **favorable.** The labor rate variance is **unfavorable** in the illustration because the amount paid to employees was $.20 per hour more than standard.

A second type of variance deals with the **quantity** of resources used rather than their cost. Quantity variances are not quite as obvious as price variances because the quantity standards are expressed in terms of one unit of output, but during the month many units are produced. It is therefore not obvious whether the 10,400 square feet of plywood used is more or less than the standard quantity. To determine the variance, we must first multiply the number of units produced by the standard quantity per unit.

	Units Produced	×	Unit Standard Quantity	=	Total Standard Quantity	Actual Quantity	Difference
Plywood	500		20		10,000	10,400	400
Labor	500		.5		250	240	10

Variances are unfavorable when actual costs are more than standard costs

The 500 crates require 20 square feet of plywood each, or a total standard quantity of 10,000 square feet. The company actually used 10,400 square feet of plywood, or 400 square feet more than standard. The cost of using 400 square feet too much plywood is 400 times the standard cost of $.40 per square foot, or $160. Because too much plywood is used the **material quantity variance** is **unfavorable.** Unfavorable variances mean actual costs are greater than standard costs.

Favorable variances occur when actual costs are less than standard costs

The standard quantity of labor is 250 hours for the 500 crates manufactured. Actual hours worked are only 240. The company used 10 less labor hours than standard. The cost savings to the company is 10 hours times $6 per hour, or $60. The **labor efficiency variance** is **favorable** because less than the standard quantity of labor was used to make the crates. Favorable variances mean actual costs were lower than standard costs.

Recording Costs in a Standard Cost System

Many manufacturing firms incorporate standard costs into their formal accounting system of journals and ledgers. Whenever possible, costs are recorded at the standard amount, and variances are recorded when they can be identified. For example, when Kindell Machine Tool Company purchased 10,400 square feet of plywood at $.38 per square foot on open account, the journal entry to record the purchase was:

	Materials inventory (plywood)	4,160	
	Material price variance		208
	Accounts payable		3,952
	Bought 10,400 square feet of plywood at		
	$.38 per square foot for a total cost		
	of $3,952. Recorded at standard cost		
	of $.40 per sq ft.		

Unfavorable variances are recorded with a debit

The purchase is recorded at the **standard** cost of $.40 per square foot of plywood rather than the actual cost of $.38 a square foot. Accounts Payable is credited for the amount owed because the vendor is not concerned with Kindell's standard cost for plywood but only with the amount agreed upon as a purchase price. The difference between the standard cost and actual cost is the variance that is recorded in a variance account. In this case Kindell paid less than the standard price for plywood, so the variance is favorable and is recorded with a credit. Unfavorable variances are recorded with debits. If a variance account contains some favorable variances (credits) and some unfavorable variances (debits) during an accounting period, the debits and credits are netted to find an ending balance. A debit balance means a **net unfavorable variance** and a credit balance indicates a **net favorable variance.**

Favorable variances are recorded with a credit

The debit and credit relationship of variance accounts can be logically derived from your study of financial accounting. An unfavorable variance means that actual costs are greater than standard. The debit balance in the variance account is in effect an extra expense. Expense accounts normally have debit balances. Just the reverse is true for favorable variances.

THE PURPOSE OF STANDARDS

Many business functions are facilitated by the use of standards. Specifically, standard costs provide the following benefits for businesses:

1. Cost control
2. Pricing decisions
3. Performance appraisal
4. Cost awareness
5. Management by objective

Cost Control

Monitoring and controlling the costs of production, marketing, and administrative activities are among the primary functions of managers. Cost control is not merely the minimization of costs; it is identifying costs with their benefits and ensuring that the costs are justified, given the benefits derived. Standard costs provide a useful framework for cost control.

Standard costs allow the timely comparison of actual costs with standard costs

Typically, standards are expressed in terms of one unit of output. In the plywood crate example, standards are defined as the quantity and cost of direct material and direct labor per crate. When standards are expressed in terms of a single unit of output, they can be used to measure cost performance for any number of units. Managers can compare actual costs with standard costs as frequently as desired—monthly, weekly, daily, or for each work shift. As long as production output can be measured and actual cost accumulated, cost performance can be measured.

The great value of standards in cost control is that they enable managers to compare actual costs with desired costs on a timely basis. Timely reporting of differences between actual and standard costs allows managers to take appropriate action to correct problems and maintain desired performance. Without standards many cost control problems are undetected until considerable damage occurs.

Pricing Decisions

Costs usually influence a company's product pricing decisions. Products such as agricultural commodities sell at prices determined by the market in which they are traded. A seller of wheat, oats, soybeans, or hogs decides whether or not to sell at the market price, but he does not determine the price. Most products, however, do not sell in the same type of market as agricultural products. Instead companies attempt to differentiate their products from those of other companies in order to be able to establish a price that will cover all costs of making and distributing the product and earn an acceptable rate of return on capital invested. Claims that a product is bigger, better, prettier, more efficient, or in some other way more desirable than other products are designed to convince customers that the asking price is justified. When the cost of a product is used to determine its selling price, standard costs often are used instead of actual costs to make the pricing decision because standard costs reflect the desired or expected cost of a product, whereas actual costs may include efficiencies or inefficiencies of production that are not expected to prevail and that cannot be anticipated when the pricing decision is made.

Standard costs are also used for the **internal pricing** of goods and services, often called **transfer pricing.** A **transfer price** is the amount charged by one segment of a business to another segment for a product or service. For example, one division of a company manufactures wheels that are transferred to another division of the company to be used in the manufacture of lawn carts. The wheels are an output of the first division and an input to the second division.

The transfer price is the amount used to record the transfer of wheels from one division to the other, as if the first division sold the wheels and the second one purchased them. The pricing of such transfers within the company allows managers to evaluate the operations and performance of divisions. Transfer prices may be based on actual costs, standard costs, market prices, or other bases. When cost is used as the transfer price, the best basis is standard cost because it eliminates the transfer of inefficiencies from one division to another. In Chapter 11 we discuss transfer pricing in more detail.

Performance Appraisal

Employee performance evaluation is a difficult task involving many different variables, some of which are subjective and therefore difficult to use in comparing employees. When standards are established for performance evaluation, they provide tangible measures that can be applied uniformly to all personnel. For example, the standard labor time for performing various production activities may be used to evaluate the efficiency of employees. Similarly, production department supervisors may be evaluated on how close their departments came to achieving standards. Standards can be effective in performance evaluation if employees have a clear understanding of the standards and the way they are used. In addition, employees must be given timely reports evaluating their performance. The timely reports are possible because the standards are readily available for quick comparison and reporting.

Cost Awareness

Accountants and financial managers are aware of the costs associated with the activities of the business, because they deal with them daily. Many other employees, however, have little or no awareness of costs. They may be concerned with increasing daily production, improving employee morale, and improving production efficiency, all of which have an impact on costs, but many employees do not understand the cost consequences of these activities. Standard costs and standard cost performance reports inform employees about the cost implications of their actions. Such cost awareness may result in better employee efforts at cost control.

Management by Objective (MBO)

Management by objective (MBO), also called **management by exception,** is a simple yet powerful concept that requires managers to establish specific objectives for all business activities. When activities fall within the desired performance levels, little management action is necessary. When performance varies significantly from desired levels, managers take appropriate action.

Many organizations find that MBO works best when a detailed standard cost system is used. Standards provide the quick, ready reference for identifying and reporting variances from acceptable performance levels.

TYPES OF STANDARDS

Several different types of standards used in business include:

1. Ideal standards
2. Basic standards
3. Currently attainable standards

Ideal standards reflect the most optimistic expectations of management. Ideal standards can be achieved only with perfect operating conditions, such as no idle time, no breakdowns, no inventory shortages, and no employee errors—in other words, no production problems of any sort. Such production utopias are very rare, if they exist at all. Managers use ideal standards as measures of optimum performance. Personnel are not expected to achieve the standards, but rather to come as close as possible. Sometimes ideal standards are used as a basis for setting more realistic performance measures.

Basic standards provide a framework for comparing performance over a period of years. They are sometimes called **long-range standards** because once created, they are used for several years or longer. Performance trends are easier to spot when standards remain the same. However, rapidly rising resource costs and changing production technology often make basic standards difficult to use. As a result, not many firms use basic standards.

The most commonly used type of standard is currently attainable standards

Currently attainable standards are the most commonly used standards. They represent benchmarks for **efficient** production **in the current environment.** Currently attainable standards are not as stringent as ideal standards because they allow for normal production problems, such as equipment maintenance, downtime, random employee errors, and occasional inventory shortages. Still, currently attainable standards represent desirable performance.

THE STANDARD COST SYSTEM

Three fundamental activities in a standard cost system are:

1. Standard setting
2. Accumulation of actual costs
3. Variance analysis

Standard setting. The first step in a standard cost system is the creation of the standards to be used as a basis for measuring performance. **Standard setting** is an important activity because poorly conceived standards result in inappropriate measures of performance. Standard setting is not a one-time activity. As resource costs and production methods change, revision of the standards is necessary. In many firms standards are evaluated on a regular basis, such as annually or every 6 months.

Accumulation of actual costs. A standard cost system does not eliminate the need for accumulating actual production costs. Actual costs are compared with standard costs to determine variances. In manufacturing, actual costs are accumulated in a job order or a process costing system. With nonmanufacturing activities, actual costs also are accumulated and compared with standards established for nonmanufacturing activities.

Variance analysis. A **variance** occurs when actual costs differ from standard costs. Variances are expressed in total dollar amounts and separated into specific classifications to facilitate cost analysis and control. **Variance analysis** is a systematic process of identifying variances and reporting them to management. Variance reports provide managers with detailed data useful in making daily decisions. For example, when the material and labor variances for plywood packing crates are reported, managers can use the reports to determine whether the company may be better off purchasing finished crates instead of building them.

SETTING STANDARDS

To set standards, managers must have engineering data and historical cost and quantity data. These inputs must be combined logically with individual value judgments to arrive at the most useful standards.

The Process of Setting Standards

Companies establish standards in many different ways. The possibilities range from a single person setting all standards by intuition to firms with committees that use a variety of management science and engineering tools to set standards. A combination of methods and techniques is used in most large organizations. We discuss some of these to give you the flavor of the standard-setting process.

The standards committee. It is unlikely that any one individual can understand all of the issues relevant to setting standards in all parts of a business. Therefore, it is common to form a **standards committee** which establishes and monitors standards for the firm. Ideally the committee represents a cross section of all segments of the firm that are affected by the standards. Often a key member of the committee is the controller or some other member of the accounting department.

Technical input. At the mention of standards, some people immediately visualize an industrial engineer with a stopwatch, carefully observing every move of a production employee in a manufacturing plant. Although such **time and motion studies** are used as aids in setting some standards, they are but one type of input. Other technical inputs are **simulation studies,** which involve models of the activity or operations being studied by the standards committee. **Pilot production projects** are frequently used with new products to manufacture a small amount of output and generate some actual production data that are used in setting standards. **Learning curves,** discussed in Chapter 18, are mathematical models that describe the decreasing labor time, and corresponding cost, required for the production of a product or service. Learning curve effects are experienced most often in the production of new products or the providing of new services.

Past experience. Often the immediate past is the best predictor of the near future. Past experience is very useful in establishing new standards. Past results are tangible and verifiable. Although many sophisticated prediction tools are available, managers may give heavy weight to past experience in setting standards for future production.

Other inputs. Management decisions often affect employees, consumers, and the general public. Standard setting is no exception. In particular, employees and labor unions are keenly interested in the relation of standards and labor efficiency. Many labor-management confrontations arise over standard-setting decisions, such as the amount of labor time allowed to assemble a product. Unresolved disputes about standards may result in strikes or other job actions by employees. Standard-related disputes must be settled before workable standards are created. The resulting standards represent management's belief of what costs **should be,** tempered by the environment within which the firm operates.

STANDARD COST VARIANCE ANALYSIS

Variance analysis addresses two issues

Variances occur whenever actual costs differ from standard costs. **Variance analysis** is the systematic evaluation of variances to provide managers with useful information for measuring efficiency and improving performance. Variance analysis is performed in order to answer two general questions:

1. What is the amount of difference between actual and standard costs?
2. Why did the difference occur?

The first questions deals with the measurement of the variance, which is basically a computation process. Accountants accumulate actual cost data and compare them with the standards to find the variances.

The second question addresses the cause of the variances. For instance, in the packing crate example, why was the labor cost $6.20 per hour rather than the standard rate of $6.00 per hour? Did the personnel manager hire a new, more expensive worker, or was a more expensive worker taken from another task and assigned to producing crates? Perhaps something else caused the labor rate variance. Often the question of why the variance occurred is the more difficult of the two questions to answer. Sometimes variances result from a complex interaction of human and physical variables. For instance, the unfavorable material quantity variance of 400 square feet resulted from the following sequence of events:

Many factors may interact to cause variances

1. Inventory control personnel overlooked the reorder point for ¾-inch plywood, and the company ran out of plywood.
2. The production supervisor decided to substitute ¾-inch particle board for the plywood. Employees in the cutting department are not used to working with particle board and made more than the normal number of cutting mistakes.
3. The supervisor in the cutting department was angry because he was not consulted about the material substitution. He told his employees not to worry about material waste because they should not have to work with particle board.

The many variables affecting the use of materials do not complicate the computation of the material quantity variance, but they do complicate the process of explaining the variances and of taking the necessary action to correct the problem. Although accounting reports provide valuable information, additional information is required. The analyst needs a clear understanding of the operations and personnel affecting each variance. To achieve this understanding, a firm may assign an accountant to a specific location in the plant who is then responsible for identifying, measuring, and reporting variances for the particular location. Such decentralization of the accounting activity is designed to provide more meaningful accounting information by making the accountant familiar with specific production activities.

In this text we discuss primarily the computation and reporting of variances. The more complex issue of explaining their cause is beyond the scope of this text.

The Computation of Variances

Variances can be computed for all three of the basic cost elements—direct materials, direct labor, and manufacturing overhead. The computation of variances for materials and labor is quite similar. Manufacturing overhead variances require different and somewhat more complex computations. In this chapter we discuss variance analysis for direct materials and direct labor. Manufacturing overhead variances are discussed in Chapter 9.

Variances are expressed in dollar amounts and are denoted as favorable or unfavorable. For example, \$350 favorable and \$500 unfavorable are two variances. The size or amount of the variances are \$350 and \$500, and the favorable and unfavorable express the direction of the variance. A variance is not complete without both types of information. Sometimes the symbols F and U are used to designate favorable and unfavorable variances in variance analysis reports.

Failure to identify whether a variance is favorable or unfavorable is a serious oversight in a managerial report. Often managers attach significantly different weights to variances depending on whether the variance is favorable or unfavorable. For example, a company policy may be to investigate any unfavorable variances greater than \$100 and any favorable variances greater than \$400.

To illustrate variance analysis, we use the Natural-Wood Products Company. Two of its products are oak coffee tables and redwood table lamps. The April production of these two products is used to illustrate the computation and reporting of variances. The discussion is illustrated with production data for oak coffee tables. The reporting of variances is illustrated with both products. The standard costs for the two products are presented in Figure 8-1.

Variances are computed for April by comparing actual April cost data with the standard costs for the products. Actual cost data are presented in Figure 8-2.

Natural-Wood Products Company

Resource	Standard Input Quantity	Standard Input Price	Standard Output Cost
Standard Cost for One Oak Coffee Table			
Direct materials:			
Oak lumber	8 bd ft	$ 2.50/bd ft	$20.00
Finishing varnish	.5 gal	18.00/gal	9.00
Standard cost of direct materials			29.00
Direct labor:			
Cutting and Assembly Department	3 hr	$ 8.00/hr	24.00
Finishing Department	2 hr	6.00/hr	12.00
Standard cost of direct labor			36.00
Manufacturing overhead	5 DLH	$ 6.00/DLH	30.00
Total standard cost of an oak coffee table			$95.00
Standard Cost for One Redwood Table Lamp			
Direct materials:			
Redwood lumber	4 bd ft	$3.00/bd ft	$12.00
Electrical fixture	1 unit	9.00/unit	9.00
Standard cost of direct materials			21.00
Direct labor:			
Forming and Finishing Department	2 hr	$8.00/hr	16.00
Manufacturing overhead	2 machine hr	$5.00/machine hr	10.00
Total standard cost of a redwood table lamp			$47.00

Figure 8-1
These are standard costs and quantities for the production of oak coffee tables and redwood table lamps. The standard quantities are for the production of one unit of product.

During April, 2,000 oak coffee tables and 1,500 redwood lamps are produced by the Natural-Wood Products Company. Using the standard costs from Figure 8-1 and the actual cost data from Figure 8-2, it is easy to calculate the **total** variance.

(Units produced × Unit standard cost) − Actual cost = Total variance

Oak tables: (2,000 × $95) − $189,720 = Total variance

$190,000 − $189,720 = $280 F

Redwood lamps: (1,500 × $47) − $72,460 = Total variance

$70,500 − $72,460 = $1,960 U

Natural-Wood Products Company
Schedule of Actual Costs for April

2,000 Oak Coffee Tables

Resource	Actual Input Quantity	Total Cost
Oak lumber	16,800 bd ft	$ 45,360
Finishing varnish	1,040 gal	17,160
Cutting and assembly labor	5,400 hr	40,500
Finishing labor	3,900 hr	29,100
Manufacturing overhead	9,300 hr	57,600
Total actual costs for oak coffee tables		$189,720

1,500 Redwood Table Lamps

Resource	Actual Input Quantity	Total Cost
Redwood lumber	5,600 bd ft	$14,950
Electrical fixtures	1,550 units	13,950
Forming and finishing labor	3,300 hr	27,060
Manufacturing overhead	3,300 hr	16,500
Total actual costs for redwood table lamps		$72,460

Figure 8-2 Actual costs for oak tables and redwood lamps are accumulated so that they can be compared with standards. Actual product costs are developed as described in Chapter 3.

The total **standard** cost for the 2,000 oak coffee tables manufactured in April is $190,000. **Actual** production cost in April was $189,720, which is less than standard, yielding a $280 favorable total variance for the product. The actual cost of redwood table lamps is greater than the standard cost during April, resulting in a $1,960 unfavorable variance for redwood lamps. These total variances provide some information about production efficiency. However, more detailed variance information is needed to manage daily operations, evaluate performance, and address specific production problems. The total variance can be separated into more specific variances for each element of cost.

Materials and Labor Variances

Typically, two variances are identified for direct materials and two for direct labor. The variances are called **price** and **quantity variances** for direct materials and **rate** and **efficiency variances** for direct labor. Although the names of the materials and labor variances are different, the computation of the variances is similar. Figure 8-3 shows the cost relationships used in computing direct materials and direct labor variances.

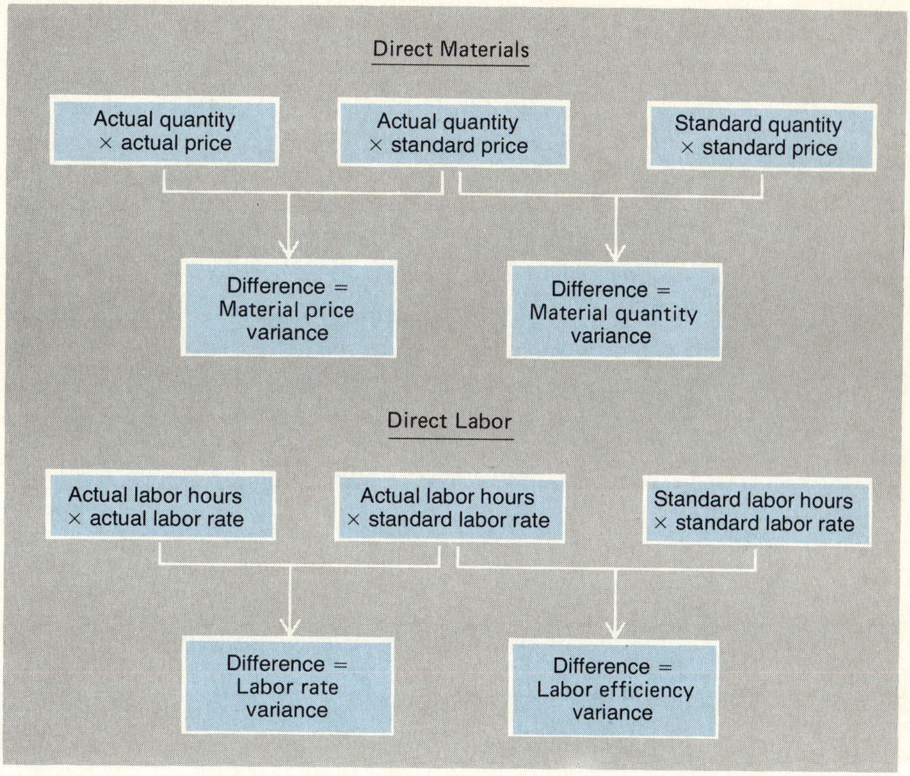

Figure 8-3
The same types of computations are used to calculate direct materials variances and direct labor variances, although different names are used for the variances.

DIRECT MATERIAL VARIANCES

The discussion below covers material price and quantity variances, followed by a graphic presentation. In addition to computing the variances, we show how standard costs and variances are recorded in the books of account.

Material Price Variance

Did we pay more or less for material than we should have?

The **material price variance** measures the amount of variance from standard that occurs because the price paid for raw materials is different from the standard cost. If the actual materials cost is greater than standard, the price variance is unfavorable. A favorable price variance occurs if the cost of materials is less than standard. The computation of the material price variance is shown in Figure 8-3.

(Actual quantity × Standard price) − (Actual quantity × Actual price)

= Material price variance

Because the standard price and the actual price are both multiplied by the actual quantity, the formula can be simplified to

Actual quantity × (Standard price − Actual price) = Material price variance

or

Actual quantity × Difference in price = Material price variance

In Figure 8-1 we find the standard quantities and standard prices for the resources used in the production of oak coffee tables. Actual materials used in April (shown in Figure 8-2) are 16,800 board feet of oak lumber at $2.70 per board foot and 1,040 gallons of varnish at $16.50 a gallon.

Actual quantity × (Standard price − Actual price)

= Material price variance

Oak lumber: 16,800 bd ft × ($2.50 − $2.70) = $3,360 U

Varnish: 1,040 gal × ($18.00 − $16.50) = $1,560 F

The journal entries to record the purchase of the two raw materials on open account are as follows:

	Inventory control, oak lumber	42,000	
	Material price variance	3,360	
	Accounts payable		45,360
	Purchased 16,800 board feet of oak		
	lumber at $2.70 per board foot; standard		
	cost, $2.50 per board foot.		
	Inventory control, varnish	18,720	
	Material price variance		1,560
	Accounts payable		17,160
	Purchased 1,040 gallons of varnish at		
	$16.50 per gallon; standard cost, $18.00		
	per gallon.		

The material is recorded in the inventory control account at the actual quantity times its standard cost. Any variance from the standard cost is recorded in the material price variance account. The debit to the material price variance account for the purchase of oak lumber indicates that the material cost is $3,360 more than standard, and the credit of $1,560 indicates that the varnish price was less than standard.

In this example only one material price variance account is used, which now has a debit balance of $1,800, indicating a net unfavorable material price variance in April for materials used in the production of oak coffee tables. Sometimes a separate variance account is used for each type of material. The amount of detail used in classifying and recording variances depends on the information needs of management and on the cost of gathering the additional cost data.

Sometimes it is not convenient to compare the actual and standard price of materials because the material is purchased for varying prices during the period. To illustrate, Figure 8-1 identifies the standard quantities and costs for redwood lamps. During April, 5,600 board feet of redwood lumber are purchased and used. The total cost is $14,950, so the average cost per board foot of the redwood is $2.6696428. Instead of using a long decimal fraction, it is easier to use the general price variance formula stated earlier.

$$(\text{Actual quantity} \times \text{Standard price}) - (\text{Actual quantity} \times \text{Actual price}) = \text{Material price variance}$$

Redwood lumber:

$$(5{,}600 \times \$3.00) - \$14{,}950 = \text{Material price variance}$$
$$\$16{,}800 - \$14{,}950 = \$1{,}850 \text{ F}$$

There are two general types of material price variances. One occurs because the purchase price of a raw material is different from its standard cost. This type of price variance typically is identified and recorded at the time of purchase. The second type of price variance occurs when one raw material is substituted for another raw material that has a different standard cost. For example, the standard for the production of packing crates calls for C-D grade plywood with a cost of $.40 per square foot, but a temporary inventory shortage of this item necessitates the use of B-C grade plywood at a standard cost of $.45 per square foot. The $.05 per square foot difference causes an unfavorable material price variance in the production of the packing crates. Typically this type of variance is identified and recorded when the material is put into production, whereas the former type is recorded at the time of purchase, because the material substitution is not known at the time the material is purchased.

Material Quantity Variance

The **material quantity variance** measures the amount of variance caused by using more or less materials than standard. More material than standard is an unfavorable variance and less than standard is a favorable variance.

The computation of the material quantity variance is quite simple and is taken directly from the general cost relationships in Figure 8-3.

The formula for computing the material quantity variance

(Standard quantity × Standard price) − (Actual quantity × Standard price)
= Material quantity variance

This can be shortened to

(Standard quantity − Actual quantity) × Standard price
= Material quantity variance

or

Difference in quantity × Standard price = Material quantity variance

The standard material quantity is the amount of material that **should have** been used to produce the number of units manufactured during the period. For example, the standard quantities of the two raw materials used in making 2,000 coffee tables in April are

Oak lumber:

2,000 × 8 bd ft = 16,000 bd ft

Varnish:

2,000 × .5 gal = 1,000 gal

Actual material quantities used in April were 16,800 board feet of oak lumber and 1,040 gallons of varnish. The material quantity variances are computed as follows:

(Standard quantity − Actual quantity) × Standard price
= Material quantity variance

Oak lumber:

(16,000 bd ft − 16,800 bd ft) × $2.50/bd ft = $2,000 U

Varnish:

(1,000 gal − 1,040 gal) × $18.00/gal = $ 720 U

Like other variances, the material quantity variance should be isolated and recorded as soon as possible. If quantity variances can be identified at the time that materials are put into production, the entries for April production of oak coffee tables are as follows:

	Work in process, materials	40,000	
	Material quantity variance	2,000	
	Inventory control, oak lumber		42,000
	Put oak lumber into production and		
	recorded material quantity variance.		
	16,000 bd ft × $2.50 per bd ft = $40,000.		
	16,800 bd ft × $2.50 per bd ft = $42,000.		
	Work in process, materials	18,000	
	Material quantity variance	720	
	Inventory control, varnish		18,720
	Put varnish into production and		
	recorded material quantity variance.		
	1,000 gal × $18 = $18,000.		
	1,040 gal × $18 = $18,720.		

Sometimes it is not possible to identify material quantity variances at the time materials are put into production. A quantity variance can be calculated only when the amount of production for the period can be measured. That may be impossible before the end of the period or at least until well after the materials have been added. If that is the case in the production of coffee tables, the input of raw materials is recorded at actual quantities as follows:

	Work in process, materials	42,000	
	Inventory control, oak lumber		42,000
	Put oak lumber into production.		
	16,800 bd ft × $2.50 per bd ft = $42,000.		
	Work in process, materials	18,720	
	Inventory control, varnish		18,720
	Put varnish into production.		
	1,040 gal × $18 = $18,720.		

When production is completed and transferred to finished goods, the entries for the **materials portion** of the product are:

	Finished goods inventory	40,000	
	Material quantity variance	2,000	
	Work in process, materials		42,000
	Transferred work in process to finished		
	goods and recorded material quantity		
	variance. 16,000 bd ft × $2.50 per bd ft		
	= $40,000.		

	Finished goods inventory	18,000	
	Material quantity variance	720	
	Work in process, materials		18,720
	Transferred work in process to finished goods and recorded material quantity variance. $1,000 gal × $18 per gal = $18,000.		

In practice the amount transferred to Finished Goods also includes direct labor and manufacturing overhead. However, here we identify only the materials to highlight the material quantity variance. Notice that the amount charged to the product and the amount of the variances are the same in the end regardless of when the variance is identified. The timing of variance recognition affects management's ability to use the variances, but not the size of the variances. Timely variance information may, however, increase efficiency, which could affect total variances favorably.

Graphic Solution

The variances discussed in the previous examples are illustrated graphically in Figure 8-4, which shows in the left graph the standard and actual costs for oak lumber used in April for the production of coffee tables. Standard and actual prices are plotted on the vertical axis, and standard and actual quantities on the horizontal axis. The standard cost is the colored area formed by the standard price of $2.50 and the standard quantity of 16,000 board feet of lumber.

The actual price is greater than the standard price, and the actual quantity of material used is greater than the standard quantity. Therefore, actual cost is greater than standard as shown by the rectangle formed by the actual price of $2.70 and the actual quantity of 16,800 board feet of oak lumber. The difference in area between the standard cost rectangle and the actual cost rectangle is the total materials variance for oak lumber. It is composed of the price variance and the quantity variance. The price variance is the difference between standard and actual prices multiplied by the actual quantity ($.20 × 16,800 board feet = $3,360) and is the cross-hatched area at the top of the rectangle. The material quantity variance is the difference between standard and actual quantities times the standard price (800 board feet × $2.50 = $2,000) and is represented by the double cross-hatched area on the right side of the rectangle.

The variances for varnish are presented in diagram *b* in Figure 8-4. The form is similar to diagram *a* except that the price variance is favorable. The price variance is the difference between standard and actual prices multiplied by the actual quantity ($1.50 × 1,040 gallons = $1,560). Note that this variance extends beyond the total standard cost area shown in

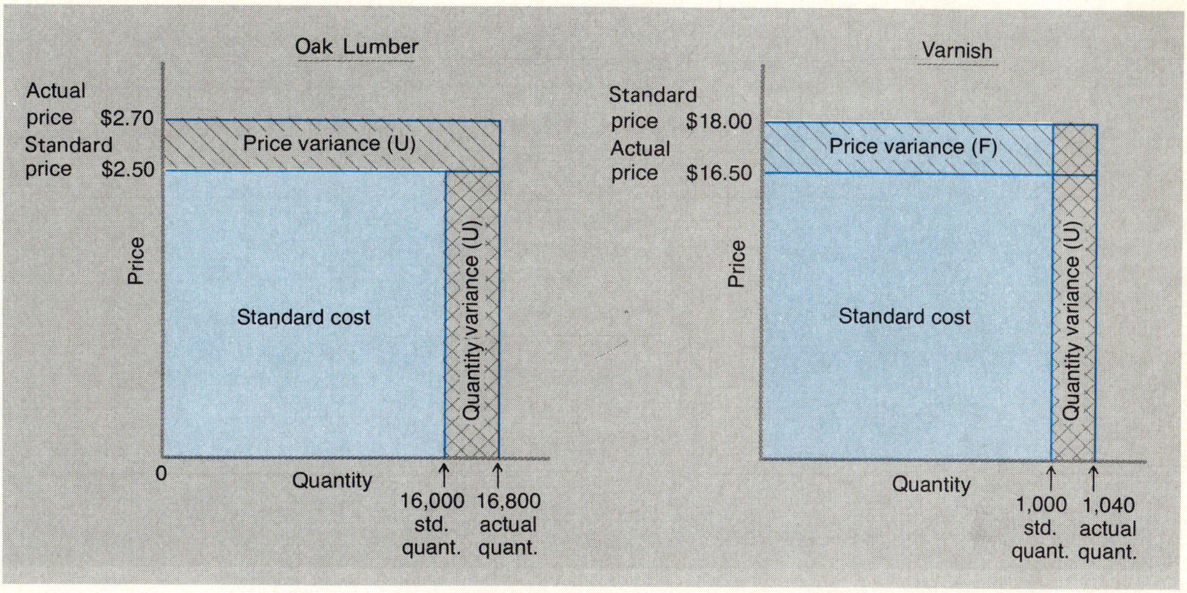

Figure 8-4 **The total standard cost for any quantity of production is merely the unit standard cost multiplied by the production quantity. The total standard cost is represented by the colored rectangle. All unfavorable variances lie outside the colored standard cost area. All favorable variances lie within the colored standard cost area.**

color. This occurs because more than the standard quantity of material was used, but the purchase price was favorable on the entire quantity used, not just the standard quantity. Because the material quantity used was more than standard, the quantity variance is unfavorable. The quantity variance is the difference between the standard and actual quantities times the standard price (40 gallons × \$18.00 = \$720). Some of the favorable price variance is offset by part of the unfavorable quantity variance. As a result, the total variance for varnish is \$1,560 F − \$720 U = \$840 F.

DIRECT LABOR VARIANCES

The computation of direct labor variances is very similar to that of direct materials variances. However, there are some differences between labor and materials in setting standards, in the controllability of the variances, and in the timing of the variance reports. Consequently, we treat labor and materials separately and give different names to their variances in order to reflect better the specific information they convey.

Labor Rate Variance

The **labor rate variance** isolates the portion of the total labor variance that is caused by the actual labor rate's being different from the expected (standard) labor rate. It is computed the same way as the material price variance. The formula is

The labor rate variance is similar to the material price variance

(Actual hours × Standard rate) − (Actual hours × Actual rate)
= Labor rate variance

The formula can be shortened to

Difference in rate × Actual hours = Labor rate variance

We continue with the example of the April production of oak coffee tables. The amount of labor used in cutting and assembly was 5,400 hours at $7.50 per hour; the finishing department used 3,900 hours at a total cost of $29,100. Computing the rate variances we have

(Standard rate − Actual rate) × Actual hours = Labor rate variance

Cutting and assembly department:

($8.00 − $7.50) × 5,400 hr = $2,700 F

Dividing the 3,900 hours of finishing department labor into the total cost of $29,100 yields an actual hourly rate of $7.4615384. Rather than use this long decimal fraction, we use the general form of the rate variance formula.

(Actual hours × Standard rate) − (Actual hours × Actual rate)
= Labor rate variance

Finishing department:

($6.00 × 3,900 hr) − $29,100 = Labor rate variance
$23,400 − $29,100 = $5,700 U

The variance is unfavorable because the rate actually paid for labor was higher than the standard rate.

Labor Efficiency Variance

Labor efficiency: Did we use more or fewer labor hours than standard?

The **labor efficiency variance** identifies the amount of the total labor variance caused by using more or less labor than the standard quantity. The term **efficiency** expresses the idea that labor is used favorably if fewer hours than standard are used to make a product. Conversely, labor is used inefficiently if more labor hours than standard are used.

As with the standard quantity of materials, the standard number of direct hours cannot be determined without knowing the quantity of production for the period. In our example, 2,000 coffee tables are produced in April, so the standard number of direct labor hours is

Units produced × Standard hours per unit

= Standard quantity of direct labor hours

Cutting and assembly department:

2,000 × 3 hr = 6,000 labor hr

Finishing department:

2,000 × 2 hr = 4,000 labor hr

The computation of the efficiency variance is very similar to the computation of the material quantity variance. The formula is

(Standard hours × Standard rate) − (Actual hours × Standard rate)

= Labor efficiency variance

The formula can be shortened to

Difference in hours × Standard rate = Labor efficiency variance

The labor efficiency variances for coffee tables are calculated as follows:

(Standard labor hours − Actual labor hours) × Standard rate

= Labor efficiency variance

Cutting and assembly department:

(6,000 hr − 5,400 hr) × $8.00 = $4,800 F

Finishing department:

(4,000 hr − 3,900 hr) × $6.00 = $ 600 F

If the efficiency variances can be determined at the time the payroll is distributed to production (recorded in Work in Process), the journal entries to record the direct labor and the rate and efficiency variances are:

Cutting and assembling labor:

	Work in process, labor	48,000	
	Labor efficiency variance		4,800
	Labor rate variance		2,700
	Payroll		40,500
	Recorded direct labor and the labor		
	variances.		

Finishing labor:

	Work in process, labor	24,000	
	Labor rate variance	5,700	
	Labor efficiency variance		600
	Payroll		29,100
	Recorded direct labor and the labor		
	variances		

The Work in Process account is debited for the standard cost of labor; the Payroll account is credited for the actual cost because that is the amount paid regardless of the standards.

If the labor efficiency variance cannot be determined at the time that labor cost is charged to production, the entries would be as follows:

Cutting and assembling labor:

	Work in process, labor	43,200	
	Labor rate variance		2,700
	Payroll		40,500
	Recorded direct labor and the labor rate		
	variance.		

Finishing labor:

	Work in process, labor	23,400	
	Labor rate variance	5,700	
	Payroll		29,100
	Recorded direct labor and the labor rate		
	variance.		

Later, when the efficiency variances have been determined, the entries to transfer the **labor portion** of WIP to Finished Goods are

Cutting and assembling labor:

	Finished goods inventory	48,000	
	Labor efficiency variance		4,800
	Work in process, labor		43,200
	Transferred work in process to finished		
	goods and recorded the labor efficiency		
	variance.		

Finishing labor:

Finished goods inventory	24,000	
Labor efficiency variance		600
Work in process, labor		23,400
Transferred work in process to finished goods and recorded the labor efficiency variance.		

The attempt is always to record product costs at standard. If that is not possible when the product costs are recorded in Work in Process, then they are converted to standard costs when they are transferred from Work in Process to Finished Goods.

Graphic Solution

The labor rate and efficiency variances just computed are presented graphically in Figure 8-5. Both the rate and efficiency variances are favorable in the cutting and assembly department; therefore they appear within the colored area of the total standard cost. The finishing department has a favorable efficiency variance and an unfavorable rate variance, so the efficiency variance is colored, but the rate variance lies outside the colored standard cost area.

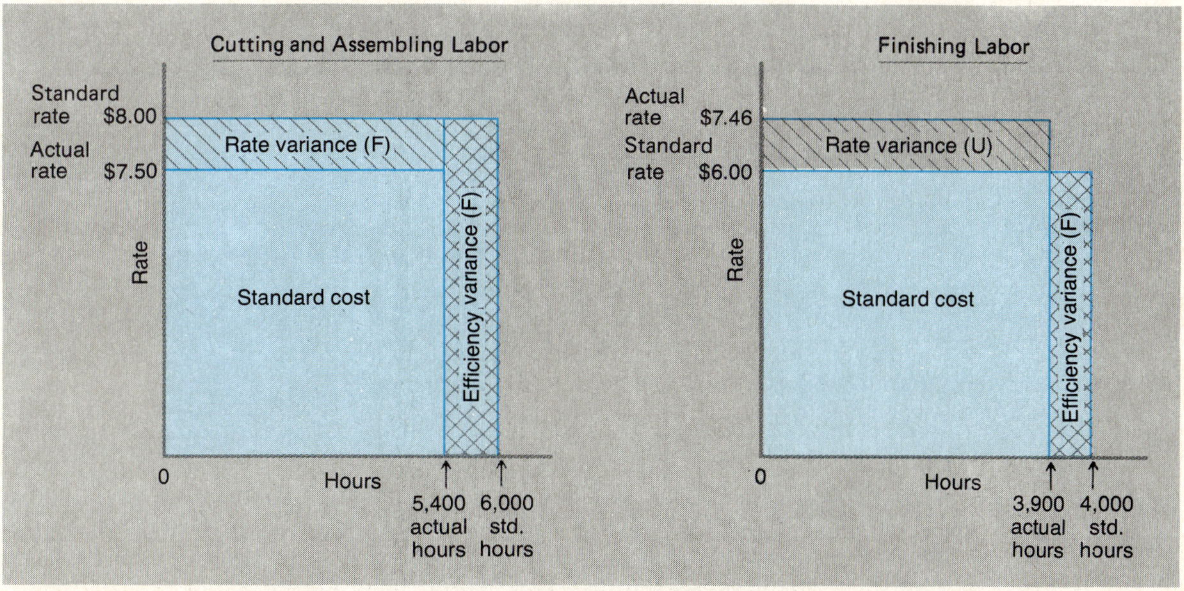

Figure 8-5 **Labor variances are similar to materials variances except for slightly different terminology for the variances. Both the rate and the efficiency variance are within the colored standard cost area for the cutting and assembly department because both variances are favorable. In the finishing department only the efficiency variance is favorable.**

VARIANCE ANALYSIS AND REPORTING

Variance analysis reports are internal accounting reports

As with other internal reports, the preparation of variance analysis reports is not guided by a rigid set of reporting requirements. Instead variance reports are developed to meet the specific information needs of managers. The content, format, and timing of variance reports differ among firms. The only limitation is that reports must be cost-benefit–justified.

To illustrate variance reporting, we continue the Natural-Wood Products example. Oak coffee table variances, together with April variances for redwood table lamps, are used to illustrate production variance reports for manufacturing operations. April variances for redwood lamps are derived from standard and actual cost data presented in Figures 8-1 and 8-2 and are summarized in Figure 8-6, but the calculations are not shown.

Variances for Redwood Table Lamps

Material	Price Variance	Quantity Variance
Redwood lumber	$1,850 F	$1,200 F
Electrical fixtures	0	450 U
Labor	**Rate Variance**	**Efficiency Variance**
Forming and finishing department	$660 U	$2,400 U

Figure 8-6 The materials and labor variances for redwood table lamps are summarized in this figure. The variances are computed in the same way as the variances for oak tables. Using the standards from Figure 8-1 and the actual cost data from Figure 8-2, you should compute several of the lamp variances to be certain you understand the procedure.

Direct Materials Variance Reporting

A direct materials variance report is illustrated in Figure 8-7. This report presents the material price variance first, grouping each material with the product for which it is used. Subtotals for material price variances are given for each product, and a total materials variance is computed. Next, the material quantity variances are presented using a similar grouping to highlight the variances for each product. Finally, the price and quantity variances are summed to show a total direct materials variance. The exact format of this report is not critical. The report shows one of many possible logical organizations of direct materials variance data.

Natural-Wood Products Company
Performance Report—Direct Materials
April

Material	Actual Quantity @ Actual Price	Actual Quantity @ Standard Price	Material Price Variance		
	Material Price Variance				
Oak Coffee Tables					
Oak lumber	$45,360	$42,000	$3,360 U		
Varnish	17,160	18,720	1,560 F		
Material price variance for oak coffee tables				$1,800 U	
Redwood Table Lamps					
Redwood lumber	14,950	16,800	1,850 F		
Electrical fixtures	13,950	13,950	0		
Material price variance for redwood tables lamps				1,850 F	
Total material price variance during April					$ 50 F

Material	Actual Quantity @ Standard Price	Standard Quantity @ Standard Price	Material Quantity Variance		
	Material Quantity Variance				
Oak Coffee Tables					
Oak lumber	$42,000	$40,000	$2,000 U		
Varnish	18,720	18,000	720 U		
Material quantity variance for oak coffee tables				$2,720 U	
Redwood Table Lamps					
Redwood lumber	16,800	18,000	1,200 F		
Electrical fixtures	13,950	13,500	450 U		
Material quantity variance for redwood table lamps				750 F	
Total material quantity in April					1,970 U
Total direct material variance in April					$1,920 U

Figure 8-7 **This is a typical direct materials performance report. The exact form of the report is not critical as long as the report is logical, understandable, and meets the information needs of managers.**

Direct Labor Variance Reporting

A direct labor variance report is illustrated in Figure 8-8. This report is organized similarly to the direct materials report. The labor rate and efficiency variances are grouped according to product. Product subtotals are shown, as are totals for the monthly labor rate variance and monthly labor efficiency variance. The final figure is the total direct labor variance for April.

Natural-Wood Products Company
Performance Report—Direct Labor
April

	Labor Rate Variance				
Department	**Actual Hours @ Actual Rate**	**Actual Hours @ Standard Rate**	**Labor Rate Variance**		
Oak Coffee Tables					
Cutting and assembly	$40,500	$43,200	$2,700 F		
Finishing	29,100	23,400	5,700 U		
Labor rate variance for oak coffee tables				$3,000 U	
Redwood Table Lamps					
Forming and finishing	27,060	26,400	660 U		
Labor rate variance for redwood table lamps				660 U	
Total labor rate variance during April					$3,660 U

	Labor Efficiency Variance				
Department	**Actual Hours @ Standard Rate**	**Standard Hours @ Standard Rate**	**Labor Efficiency Variance**		
Oak Coffee Tables					
Cutting and assembly	$43,200	$48,000	$4,800 F		
Finishing	23,400	24,000	600 F		
Labor efficiency variance for oak coffee tables				$5,400 F	
Redwood Table Lamps					
Forming and finishing	26,400	24,000	2,400 U		
Labor efficiency variable for redwood table lamps				2,400 U	
Total labor efficiency variance during April					3,000 F
Total direct labor variance in April					$ 660 U

Figure 8-8 The labor performance report is similar to the direct materials report. Variances should be reported on a timely basis so that problems can be investigated and solved before they cause significant losses.

Manufacturing Overhead Variance Reporting

A manufacturing example is not complete without manufacturing overhead as a cost element. Consequently, we include overhead cost data in this example. The total overhead variance for each product is presented without a detailed analysis of the variance at this time. The analysis of overhead variances is postponed until the next chapter.

Figure 8-9 shows the computation of standard overhead for each product and a comparison of standard overhead with the actual manufacturing overhead given in Figure 8-2. The standard amount of overhead cost is merely the overhead rate multiplied by the standard number of hours for the number of units produced. Direct labor hours is used to apply overhead

Natural-Wood Products Company
Schedule of Manufacturing Overhead Variance
April

Product	Standard Hours	MOH Rate	Standard Amount of MOH	Actual Amount of MOH	MOH Variance
Oak coffee tables	10,000 DLH	$6/DLH	$60,000	$57,600	$2,400 F
Redwood table lamps	3,000 machine hr	$5/machine hr	15,000	16,500	1,500 U
Total manufacturing overhead variance for April					$ 900 F

Figure 8-9 **Manufacturing overhead is often a significant product cost. Overhead variances should be reported on a timely basis so that costs can be monitored and controlled. A schedule of total overhead variance is presented here. Detailed variance analyses for manufacturing overhead are presented in Chapter 9.**

to the oak coffee tables. Adding up the standard hours of cutting and assembling labor and finishing labor required to produce 2,000 units yields a total of 10,000 standard hours. Multiplying by the overhead rate of $6/DLH for coffee tables gives a standard overhead cost of $60,000. Since actual MOH is $2,400 less, there is a $2,400 favorable variance. The same procedure is used to find the manufacturing overhead standard cost and variance for redwood lamps. The presentation in Figure 8-9 merely identifies the total manufacturing overhead variance.

Comprehensive Variance Reporting

The variance information in Figures 8-7 through 8-9 may be summarized in a single comprehensive report, as shown in Figure 8-10, which presents a monthly product variance analysis report.

Natural-Wood Products Company
Product Variance Analysis Report
April

Variance	Oak Tables	Redwood Lamps	Total
Material price variance	$1,800 U	$1,850 F	$ 50 F
Material quantity variance	2,720 U	750 F	1,970 U
Total material variance	4,520 U	2,600 F	1,920 U
Labor rate variance	3,000 U	660 U	3,660 U
Labor efficiency variance	5,400 F	2,400 U	3,000 F
Total labor variance	2,400 F	3,060 U	660 U
Manufacturing overhead variance	2,400 F	1,500 U	900 F
Total April variance	$ 280 F	$1,960 U	$1,680 U

Figure 8-10 **This report summarizes all of the production variances for the two products. The report provides managers with a quick overview of production performance in a single report.**

The product variance analysis report summarizes all of the production variances associated with each product. Although some detail is lost in comparison with the other variance reports, much variance information is concentrated in one report and is identified with specific products. Product variance reports may be very useful for some management decisions, such as product pricing, make-buy decisions, and evaluating managers with specific product responsibility. In later chapters we discuss the use of variance data and other managerial information in making these types of decisions.

Standard Costs and the Financial Statements

Actual costs must be reported on external financial statements

Generally accepted accounting principles require using actual costs in external accounting reports such as the income statement and the balance sheet. Therefore, even though standards are used to determine product costs internally, standard costs cannot be used for costing inventories in the balance sheet or for cost of goods sold in the income statement. Often actual costs and standard costs are very close, yielding relatively small variances. In such situations standard costs may be used in the financial statements because the standard costs **closely approximate** the actual costs, and the difference is not material. Any small variances usually are netted out against cost of goods sold in the income statement.

Occasionally variances are very large. Perhaps some raw material becomes scarce and the price rises sharply, fuel costs rise rapidly, or some other major cost change occurs. Whatever the reason, standard costs may not be reported in financial statements when they vary significantly from actual costs. Instead, the accounts must be adjusted to reflect **actual costs.** Variance accounts must be closed into the accounts that are affected by the variances. Materials variances typically affect raw materials inventory, work in process inventory, finished goods inventory, and cost of goods sold. Labor and overhead variances affect only the latter three accounts.

Large variances must be prorated over the accounts affected

Disposition of large variances. When variance accounts are closed into Inventory and Cost of Goods Sold, the amount assigned to each account is determined by the relative amount of the resource remaining in each account at year-end. For example, $1,000,000 of direct labor was charged at standard to production during the year. At year-end the following amounts of direct labor costs remain in the accounts:

Work in process	$ 100,000	10%
Finished goods	200,000	20%
Cost of goods sold	700,000	70%
Totals	$1,000,000	100%

The labor rate variance for the year is $160,000 unfavorable; the labor efficiency variance is $180,000 unfavorable. In this situation the accounts are closed as follows:

	Work in process inventory	34,000	
	Finished goods inventory	68,000	
	Cost of goods sold	238,000	
	Labor rate variance		160,000
	Labor efficiency variance		180,000
	Allocated unfavorable variances to the		
	affected accounts: 10% of $340,000;		
	20% of $340,000; 70% of $340,000.		

Each of the accounts affected by the labor variance receives a pro rata cost adjustment. When all variance accounts are closed with entries such as this one, the inventory and cost of goods sold accounts reflect actual costs.

SUMMARY

Standard costs are carefully predetermined costs. They are convenient measures of performance. A standard is composed of two parts, a quantity and a cost. Standards are used for cost control, pricing decisions, performance appraisal, cost awareness, and **management by objective. Ideal standards** are very tight, reflecting a production utopia. **Basic standards** are created for use over periods of several years. **Currently attainable standards** reflect desirable performance, given normal production problems. Currently attainable standards are the most widely used type of standard.

There are three basic activities in a standard cost system. They are **standard setting, accumulating actual costs,** and **variance analysis. Standard setting** is an important task involving many variables. Typically, standards are set by a standards committee with representation from all parts of the organization affected by the standards. Inputs from engineering and technological studies assist the committee in setting standards. Management's objectives in setting standards are tempered by environmental factors such as employee attitudes, union negotiations, and economic conditions. Standards must be revised frequently to remain current if they are to be used for performance evaluation.

Most firms incorporate their standard cost system into their formal accounting system. Product costs are **recorded at standard,** and any difference is recorded in a variance account. **Unfavorable variances** have debit balances, and **favorable variances** have credit balances.

Variance analysis is the systematic evaluation of variances to provide managers with useful information. Variance analysis is performed for all three types of manufacturing cost elements. Variance analysis answers two questions: What is the amount of the variance? Why did the variance occur?

The first question is answered by performing computations on data gathered in the standard cost system. The answer to the second question requires subjective evaluations of the operations and cost data, and the answer often is more art than science.

A variance is expressed as a dollar amount and is identified as favorable or unfavorable. **Favorable variances** mean that actual costs or quantities are less than standard. **Unfavorable variances** mean that actual costs or quantities are greater than standard. A **material price variance** measures the amount of variance from standard caused when the actual price of material is different from the standard price. A **material quantity variance** results from using more or less material than the standard amount. The **labor rate variance** is similar to the material price variance and the **labor efficiency variance** is like the material quantity variance.

Once computed, variances should be reported in a manner that provides management with a maximum amount of useful information. Variance reports are tailored to the information requirements of management, and many formats are possible.

Technically only actual costs may be reported in external financial statements. However, if variances are small, standard costs may be used for the financial statements because they closely approximate actual costs. Any minor variance is netted against cost of goods sold. If variances are large, the affected accounts must be adjusted to reflect actual costs.

KEY TERMS

basic standards *(317)*
currently attainable standards *(317)*
efficiency *(330)*
favorable variance *(313)*
ideal standards *(316)*
internal pricing *(315)*
labor efficiency variance *(313)*
labor rate variance *(312)*
learning curves *(318)*
long-range standards *(317)*
management by exception *(316)*
management by objective (MBO) *(316)*
material price variance *(312)*
material quantity variance *(313)*
standard cost *(312)*
standard setting *(317)*
standards *(312)*
standards committee *(318)*
transfer pricing *(315)*
unfavorable variance *(313)*
variance *(317)*
variance analysis *(317)*

QUESTIONS

1. Define what is meant by the term *standard cost* and explain its relevance to internal and external reporting.
2. Identify and discuss the major reasons for using a standard cost system.
3. Differentiate between ideal, basic, and currently attainable standards.
4. What are the functions of a standards committee?
5. When and how are standards revised?
6. What two main questions are addressed by variance analysis?
7. What variances are computed for direct materials and direct labor? What do they mean?
8. As a new corporate controller, respond to a manager's remarks made at your first Monday morning meeting: "These weekly variance reports must be cost-

ing us a lot of money. Let's just prepare them once a quarter. As long as the information on the reports is correct, who cares when we get them?"

9. What is the normal balance in a material price variance account?
10. Comment on the following statement made by an assembly worker to his supervisor: "Standards are just pressure devices used by management to criticize employees. Nobody ever achieves the standards."
11. Briefly describe the three basic activities of a standard cost system.
12. Discuss the disposition of the balances in variance accounts in the closing of the books at year-end.
13. Identify which of the four variances—material price, material quantity, labor rate, labor efficiency—would be most useful in evaluating the following and explain why:

    a. Purchasing manager
    b. Production supervisor
    c. Personnel manager

14. Compare and contrast the application of manufacturing overhead to products in a standard cost system and in an actual cost system.
15. Comment on the following statements:

    a. All variances are bad.
    b. All variances should be investigated.
    c. Only unfavorable variances should be investigated.

16. How are standard costs treated for purposes of external financial reporting?

EXERCISES

Ex. 8-1 **Direct material variances.** The Demorist Manufacturing Company has created standard costs for the production of its birch dining room table. Material standards are 50 board feet of birch at $1.75 a board foot. During November the company purchased 4,800 board feet of birch at a total cost of $9,140. The company made 80 birch tables using 3,880 board feet of birch.

Required: Compute material price and quantity variances.

Ex. 8-2 **Direct labor variances.** Cornella Company makes high-pressure gas valves. The direct labor standards for the grinding department operation are presented below.

Standard labor rate	$12 per hour
Standard labor time	1.5 hours per valve

December production of valves in the grinding department was 5,400 units. Direct labor cost in the department was $95,250 for 7,700 direct labor hours.

Required: Compute the direct labor variances for the grinding department of Cornella Company.

Ex. 8-3 Computing and graphing direct labor variances. Ormsbee Company incurred the following standard and actual labor costs for the month:

Standard labor rate: $7/hour
Actual labor rate: $8/hour
Standard amount of labor for the output produced: 6,000 labor hours
Actual labor hours: 6,200

Required:

a. Compute the direct labor variances for Ormsbee Company.
b. Prepare a graphic analysis of the direct labor variances.

Ex. 8-4 Computing and graphing direct material variances. Worthland Incorporated has determined the following material standards for the production of swim platforms:

Standard material quantity	14 board feet of teakwood
Standard material price	$5.00 per board foot

During the first week of January, 240 swim platforms were manufactured using 3,150 board feet of teakwood at a total cost of $16,400.

Required:

a. Compute the material variances for the first week of January.
b. Prepare a graphic analysis of the material variances.

Ex. 8-5 Materials variances and journal entries. Mendoza, Ltd., established the following materials standards for the production of valve switches:

Material	Units	Unit Cost
Rubber tubing	3 in	$.04/in
Aluminum contacts	2 in	$.15/in

Purchases of raw materials in April are as follows:

Rubber tubing	1,000 ft	$ 504.00
Aluminum contact stock	1,000 ft	$1,680.00

May production required 405 feet of rubber tubing and 235 feet of aluminum contact materials in order to produce 1,500 valve switches.

Required:

a. Compute the materials variances for Mendoza, Ltd.
b. Journalize the purchase of materials and the transfer of materials into production.

Ex. 8-6 Interpreting standard costing journal entries. The following journal entries were made to assign direct materials and direct labor cost to production for the week:

	Work in process, materials	51,400	
	Material quantity variance	700	
	Inventory control		52,100
	Work in process, labor	74,000	
	Labor rate variance	1,900	
	Labor efficiency variance		4,800
	Payroll		71,100

Required: Examine the above entries and answer the following questions:

a. What was the standard cost of the direct materials put into production?
b. Was the material quantity variance favorable or unfavorable?
c. What was the actual cost of direct labor?
d. What was the standard cost of direct labor?
e. What was the total direct labor variance?
f. Is the labor efficiency variance favorable or unfavorable?

Ex. 8-7 Labor variances. Merlin Company uses three types of labor in the production of its long-span welded trusses. Critical welds are performed by master welders, and less critical welds by journeymen. Cutting, temporary fastening, and other tasks are done by apprentices. The standards for one size of truss are as follows:

Master welder	2 hours @ $15/hour
Journeyman	3 hours @ $12/hour
Apprentice	6 hours @ $7/hour

During May, two journeymen welders were sick for several days and their work had to be performed by master welders and apprentices. Actual production in May provides the following data:

Trusses completed: 150

Labor used:	Time	Cost
Master welder	340 hours	$5,338
Journeyman	390 hours	4,661
Apprentice	920 hours	5,750

Required: Compute the labor variances for each type of labor for May production of trusses.

Ex. 8-8 Using standard costs. Following are basic and supplementary data on the mowing operations of Green-Yard Lawn Care Company:

1. The company has set a labor standard of 1.25 hours per 5,000 square feet of lawn for mowing and trimming. The standard wage rate is $4.50 per hour. During the first 2 months of the mowing season Green-Yard mowed 4,800,000 square feet of lawn; 1,420 hours of labor were used at a cost of $7,100.
2. Green-Yard computes labor hours for mowing by having employees record starting and finishing times for each lawn. Employees spend some time driving the equipment trucks between jobs. On the average, employees mow lawns only 62½ percent of their workday. In addition to wages, employees receive vacations and fringe benefits amounting to 20 percent of their salary.

Required:

a. Compute the labor rate and efficiency variances based only on the data in paragraph 1.
b. With the additional information in paragraph 2, calculate the total standard labor cost for mowing a 5,000-square-foot lawn.

Ex. 8-9 Product costs and the revision of standards. Americ Corporation, which produces 20-horsepower electric motors, is currently negotiating a new labor agreement with its employees. The new wage rate is agreeable to both labor and management and calls for increases of $.50 an hour in each of the next 2 years. However, a major disagreement in the negotiations is the speed of the assembly line. Union negotiators are demanding a decrease in the assembly line speed from 15 feet a minute to 12 feet a minute. All direct labor activities are performed on the assembly line.

Current standard costs for one electric motor are:

Direct material		$ 44
Direct labor	4 hr @ $6/hr	24
MOH	4 DLH @ $8/DLH	32
Total		$100

Union negotiators point out that in the second year of the contract the labor rate will be only $7 an hour, a 16.7 percent increase over the current rate. Since labor accounts for only 24 percent ($24/$100) of the current product cost, the cost increase of the product caused by labor is really 4 percent (.24 × .167). Furthermore, the union argues that management should not be so concerned with the assembly line speed, which is a nonfinancial item that has no effect on product cost. Material costs and the MOH rate are expected to remain constant even with increased production hours.

Required:

a. Prepare management's case on the impact of the union's proposal on the standard cost of the product.
b. The current selling price of each motor is $160. What price would the company have to charge to achieve the same percentage gross margin that it is earning on the current price, if the union's proposed standards are accepted?

Ex. 8-10 **Computing and recording variances.** The Avco Company manufactures dining room tables with the following standard prime costs per unit:

Direct material	10 bd ft @ $3/ft	$30
Direct labor	5 hr @ 5/hr	25
Total		$55

The following events took place in May:

1. Purchased 60,000 board feet of lumber on open account at $2.80 a board foot.
2. Put 116,000 board feet of lumber into production for 11,000 tables.
3. Direct labor used in producing the tables cost $249,100 for 53,000 actual hours worked.
4. The 11,000 tables are completed and transferred to finished goods. (Record the transfer of prime costs only.)

Required: Prepare journal entries for the above transactions, identifying variances when possible.

Ex. 8-11 **Interpreting recorded variances.** The following journal entries were recorded by Sigmet Company in August:

	Work in process control	128,094	
	Material quantity variance	1,731	
	Material price variance		1,350
	Raw materials inventory		128,475
	Put 11,250 units of Brandex into		
	production.		
	Work in process control	18,688	
	Labor rate variance	143	
	Labor efficiency variance		384
	Payroll		18,447
	Used 2,860 hours of labor in production.		

Required:

a. Compute the actual and standard unit cost of material.
b. Compute the standard quantity of material.
c. Compute the actual and standard labor rate.
d. Compute the standard quantity of labor.

Ex. 8-12 **Standard costs with an incentive plan.** Flapart Company's three production employees work under an incentive wage plan. The company manufactures rotor blade assemblies that are sold to another company for use in their production operations. The standard wage rate is $12.50 per hour. The standard production output is 20 rotor blade assemblies per employee per 40-hour week. Any worker completing more than 20 units per week is given a bonus of $10 for each additional unit. The production record for the week of July 19 is provided below.

Worker	Units Assembled	Wages Paid
A	23	$565
B	14	480
C	29	640

The company charges direct labor at standard and any difference between actual and standard labor as a labor rate or efficiency variance.

Required:

a. Prepare a direct labor performance report for the week showing the amount of variances for each worker and the production department.

b. Prepare the journal entry to record the week's direct labor costs and variances.

Ex. 8-13 **(AICPA) Analyzing standard cost variances.** Milner Manufacturing Company uses a job order costing system and standard costs. It manufactures one product whose standard cost is as follows:

Materials	20 yards at $.90 per yard	$18
Direct labor	4 hours at $6 per hour	24
Total factory overhead	Applied at the rate of 5⁄6 of direct labor cost	20
Variable selling and administrative expense		12
Fixed selling and administrative expense		7
Total cost per unit		$81

The standard costs are based on normal activity of 2,400 direct labor hours. Actual activity for the month of October was as follows:

Units produced		500
Materials purchased	18,000 yards at $.92 per yard	$16,560
Materials used	9,500 yards	
Direct labor	2,100 hours at $6.10 per hour	12,810
Total factory overhead		11,100

Required: Compute the following variances for the month of October:

a. Direct material price variance.

b. Direct material quantity variance.

c. Direct labor rate variance.

d. Direct labor efficiency variance.

e. Total manufacturing overhead variance.

PROBLEMS

P. 8-1 Material and labor variances. Renseleer, Incorporated, manufactures heavy construction equipment. A heavy foam insulation is applied under the engine cover of the company's K-18 grader to abate noise and protect engine parts. Below are labor and material standards for installing the foam insulation.

Labor	3 hours	@ $12.00 per hour
Material	40 pounds	@ $ .50 per pound

During April the company manufactured 350 K-18 graders using 13,400 pounds of insulation and 980 labor hours. Renseleer, Incorporated, purchased 16,000 pounds of insulation at a total cost of $8,490 and the actual cost of direct labor for installing insulation was $11,140.

Required:

a. Compute the material variances.
b. Compute the labor variances.
c. Prepare journal entries to record the variances.

P. 8-2 Computing material and labor variances. Rollins Company makes RUF-COAT, a tar-based roof covering used primarily on commercial buildings. Standard prime costs per can of RUF-COAT are presented below.

Materials:		
Base	4 gal @ $ 2.50/gal	$10.00
Drying agents	1 qt @ 12.00/gal	3.00
Coloring agents	1 lb @ 2.00/lb	2.00
Total material costs		15.00
Direct labor	1 hr @ $ 7.00/hr	7.00
Standard prime cost		$22.00

August production of RUF-COAT yielded 6,000 cans of output and the firm incurred the following production costs:

Materials:		
Base	25,000 gal @ $ 2.80/gal	$ 70,000
Drying agents	1,600 gal @ 11.00/gal	17,600
Coloring agents	5,500 lb @ 2.20/lb	12,100
Total material costs		99,700
Direct labor	5,500 hr @ 6.80/hr	37,400
Total prime costs		$137,100

Required:

a. Calculate material price and quantity variances.
b. Calculate the labor rate and efficiency variances.
c. Calculate the actual per-unit direct cost of RUF-COAT in August.

P. 8-3 Understanding standard cost variances. Below is the trial balance of the Kelley Company.

Kelley Company
Trial Balance
December 31, 1986

	Debit	Credit
Cash	$ 60,000	
Accounts receivable	80,000	
Inventory	120,000	
Plant and equipment	800,000	
Accumulated depreciation		$ 300,000
Accounts payable		30,000
Notes payable		70,000
Common stock		100,000
Retained earnings		546,000
Sales		500,000
Cost of goods sold	275,000	
Administrative expenses	85,000	
Marketing expenses	60,000	
Material price variance	36,000	
Material quantity variance	16,000	
Labor rate variance		28,000
Labor efficiency variance	42,000	
Totals	$1,574,000	$1,574,000

Required: Use the data provided to calculate:

a. The standard cost of products sold.
b. The actual cost of products sold.
c. Net income based on standard cost.
d. Net income based on actual cost.
e. Total variance expressed as a percentage of total standard cost.
f. The percentage decrease in income caused by the variances.

P. 8-4 Direct labor variances. Fine Furniture Company manufactures a white oak china cabinet that has the following direct labor standard costs:

Fabricating and assembly	8 hr @ $ 8/hr	$ 64
Finishing	6 hr @ 10/hr	60
Total direct labor cost		$124

Actual results for the month:

1. The number of china cabinets produced is 200.
2. Fabricating and assembly labor is 1,700 hours at a total cost of $14,450.
3. Finishing labor is 1,150 hours at a total cost of $11,270.

Required:

a. Calculate the total labor variance.
b. Compute the direct labor rate and efficiency variances for both departments.
c. Graph the fabricating and assembly department variances.

P. 8-5 Setting and evaluating standards. Dunnlevy Manufacturing Company is in its first year of production of a new line of outdoor gas grills. Unfamiliar with this type of product, Dunnlevy management is worried about the appropriateness of labor standards. Four production process centers are used to manufacture the gas grills. Labor standards are presented below together with actual hours used for the first 6 months of production.

Process	Hours per Unit	Total Actual Hours Used
Machining	1.5	4,500
Drilling	.5	1,900
Painting	.5	1,200
Assembling	2.0	4,000
Total	4.5	11,600

The number of gas grills produced during the 6-month period is 2,500.

Required:

a. Compute the total number of standard direct labor hours.
b. Compute the direct labor variances in terms of labor hours for each process and express the variances as a percentage of standard hours.
c. Evaluate the labor standards management established for the production of gas grills.

P. 8-6 Identifying and using variances. Green Mountain Falls Nursery provides lawn care services, including lawn fertilizing. The company has developed standards for its services to help control costs and provide information for pricing decisions. The following standards are used for fertilizing lawns.

Per 5,000 square feet of lawn:

Labor time	1 hr
Labor rate	$4.40 per hr
Material quantity	50 lb
Material cost	$18 per 100 lb

During the first quarter of the year actual lawn fertilizing data for Green Mountain Falls Nursery were:

Total area fertilized: 2,100,000 sq ft
Labor: 540 hr at a cost of $1,974
Material: 25,200 lb at a cost of $4,284

Required:

a. Compute the material price and quantity variances.
b. Compute the labor rate and efficiency variances.
c. If the average lawn size is 7,500 square feet, what should Green Mountain Falls Nursery charge for fertilizing in order to set the price at double the standard cost for labor and material?
d. What would your answer be for part *c* if actual costs were used instead of standard costs?
e. Do the variances indicate that any activities should be evaluated?

P. 8-7 Direct materials variances. Universal Company manufactures cast housings for a variety of uses. The castings are made by mixing several ingredients which are then solidified in molds. The mix of ingredients depends on the properties each casting requires. There is some freedom to substitute a higher-cost material for one that costs less without impairing the quality of the casting. However, substituting low-cost materials for high-cost is generally not possible.

Two of the company's castings have the following material quantity standards:

Casting	Material A	Material B	Material C
Type AB	8 units	4 units	—
Type BC	—	5 units	2 units

Standard prices of materials are: A, \$3 per unit; B, \$2.80 per unit; and C, \$1.00 per unit. Following are data on March purchases of materials and production of 1,000 units of Type AB castings and 2,000 units of Type BC castings:

Materials purchases:

	Units	Cost
A	25,000	\$74,000
B	10,000	30,000
C	40,000	38,800

Materials use:

Product	A	B	C
Type AB	7,000	4,500	—
Type BC	3,000	8,000	4,100

Material A was used for production of Type BC castings because it was brought to the mixing site for Type BC castings by mistake.

Required:

a. Compute the material purchase price variance.
b. Compute the material price variances for the use of materials and the material quantity variances for Type AB castings.
c. Compute the material price variances for the use of materials and the material quantity variances for Type BC castings.

P. 8-8 Unit standard and actual costs and variance analysis. Rudyards Bakery is famous for its all-natural-ingredients sour cream coffee cake. Standard data for a 100-cake batch are presented below for materials and labor.

Direct Materials	Quantity	Cost	Total
Sugar	25 lb	$ .20/lb	$ 5.00
Eggs	12 dozen	.80/dozen	9.60
Flour	50 lb	.22/lb	11.00
Sour cream	8 gal	6.00/gal	48.00
Baking soda	½ lb	.40/lb	.20
Salt	1 lb	.20/lb	.20
Standard cost for direct materials			74.00
Direct labor	4 hr	$6.50/hr	26.00
Total standard direct materials and direct labor cost			$100.00

During June Rudyards Bakery produced 2,500 sour cream coffee cakes with the following production costs:

Direct Materials	Quantity	Cost	Total
Sugar	650 lb	$ .22/lb	$ 143
Eggs	300 dozen	.75/dozen	225
Flour	1,300 lb	.25/lb	325
Sour cream	220 gal	6.25/gal	1,375
Baking soda	12.5 lb	.40/lb	5
Salt	10 lb	.20/lb	2
Actual cost for direct materials			2,075
Direct labor	96 hr	$6.25/hr	600
Total actual direct materials and direct labor cost			$2,675

Required:

a. What is the standard direct materials and direct labor cost for one sour cream coffee cake?

b. What is the actual prime cost for one coffee cake?

c. What is the total materials variance for June?

d. What is the total labor variance for June?

e. Calculate material price and quantity variances for sugar, eggs, flour, and sour cream.

f. Calculate the labor rate and efficiency variances.

P. 8-9 Variance analysis with unit standard and actual ccsts. Roth Manufacturing produces men's clothing in a job-shop production environment. Roth attaches the appropriate store label to the clothes during production and sells directly to several retail stores. A major product of Roth's is wool sport coats that have the following standards:

Wool material	3 yd @ $8.00/yd	$24.00
Lining material	2 yd @ 1.50/yd	3.00
Direct labor	3 hr @ 6.00/hr	18.00
MOH applied at the rate of $5 per direct labor hour		15.00

A recent job run of 1,000 sport coats was completed with the following costs:

Wool material	2,900 yd @ $7.80/yd	$22,620
Lining material	2,200 yd @ 1.40/yd	3,080
Direct labor	3,300 hr @ 6.20/hr	20,460
MOH actual		16,500
Total cost of job		$62,660

Required:

a. What is the standard cost of one sport coat?
b. What is the actual cost of one sport coat for the job just completed?
c. Compute the material price and quantity variances.
d. Compute the labor rate and efficiency variances.

P. 8-10 Comprehensive standard cost variance reporting. Herbert Company makes leather coats and shoes and uses standard costs to monitor and control production costs. Presented below are standards for both products.

Standard Cost	Input Quantity	Input Cost	Standard Cost of Output	
Coats				
Direct materials:				
Leather	3 yd	$12.00/sq yd	$36.00	
Buckles	1 unit	$ 1.50/each	1.50	
Standard cost of direct materials				$37.50
Direct labor:				
Cutting	2 hr	$ 5.50/hr	11.00	
Sewing	1 hr	$ 7.00/hr	7.00	
Standard cost of direct labor				18.00
Manufacturing overhead		$ 3.00/DLH		9.00
Total standard cost of a leather coat				$64.50
Leather shoes (per pair)				
Direct materials:				
Leather	2 sq ft	$ 5.00/sq ft	$10.00	
Soles	2 units	$ 1.00/unit	2.00	
Standard cost of direct materials				$12.00
Direct labor:				
Cutting	1 hr	$ 4.00/hr	4.00	
Sewing	1 hr	$ 5.00/hr	5.00	
Standard cost of direct labor				9.00
Manufacturing overhead		$ 1.00/DLH		2.00
Total standard cost of a pair of leather shoes				$23.00

Because a different quality of leather is used for the two products, the standard price for the two types of leather is different. Similarly, the types of labor skills required for each product vary, resulting in different standard hourly rates for the two products even though they are produced in the same processing departments.

During June, 11,000 units of leather coats and 11,000 pairs of leather shoes were produced. The actual costs incurred are presented below.

	Actual Input Quantity	Total Input Cost
Leather coats:		
Leather	36,000 yd	$417,600
Buckles	11,200 units	18,480
Cutting labor	21,000 hr	130,200
Sewing labor	11,500 hr	77,050
Manufacturing overhead	32,500 hr	91,000
Total actual cost of leather coats		$734,330
Leather shoes:		
Leather	24,000 sq ft	$115,200
Soles	22,500 units	24,750
Cutting labor	10,500 hr	43,575
Sewing labor	12,000 hr	63,600
Manufacturing overhead	22,500 hr	20,250
Total actual cost of leather shoes		$267,375

Required: From the data on actual and standard costs, prepare the following reports in good form:

a. Performance report—direct materials.
b. Performance report—direct labor.
c. Schedule of manufacturing overhead variance.
d. Comprehensive product variance analysis report.

P. 8-11 **Disposition of variances.** Following is **part** of the pre-closing trial balance of Verilee Company:

Verilee Company
Trial Balance
December 31

	Debit	Credit
Raw materials inventory	$ 400,000	
Work in process inventory	1,000,000	
Finished goods inventory	1,250,000	
Sales		$7,540,240
Cost of goods sold	4,000,000	
Material purchase price variance		18,900
Material quantity variance	82,600	
Direct labor rate variance	97,800	
Direct labor efficiency variance		1,900
Total manufacturing overhead variance		0
Administrative salaries	189,750	

An analysis of various accounts indicates the following proportion of products costs in each:

	Work in Process	Finished Goods	CGS
Direct materials	15%	20%	15%
Direct labor	50	8	35
Manufacturing overhead	35	72	50

Company policy is to distribute individual variances to Cost of Goods Sold if they are less than 2 percent of CGS, and to all product cost accounts if they are 2 percent or more of CGS.

Required: Distribute the balances in the variance accounts to Raw Materials Inventory, Work in Process, Finished Goods, and Cost of Goods Sold in accordance with company policy.

P. 8-12 **(CMA) Problem analysis using standard cost variances.** The Lenco Co. employs a standard cost system as part of its cost control program. The standard cost per unit is established at the beginning of each year. Standards are not revised during the year for any changes in material or labor inputs or in the manufacturing processes. Any revisions in standards are deferred until the beginning of the next fiscal year. However, in order to recognize such changes in the current year, the company includes planned variances in the monthly budgets prepared after such changes have been introduced.

The following labor standard was set for one of Lenco's products effective July 1, 1986, the beginning of the fiscal year.

Class I labor	4 hr	@ $ 6.00	$24.00
Class II labor	3 hr	@ 7.50	22.50
Class V labor	1 hr	@ 11.50	11.50
Standard labor cost per 100 units			$58.00

The standard was based upon the quality of material that had been used in prior years and what was expected to be available for the 1986–87 fiscal year. The labor activity is performed by a team consisting of four persons with class I skills, three persons with class II skills, and one person with class V skills. This is the most economical combination for the company's processing system.

The manufacturing operations occurred as expected during the first 5 months of the year. The standard costs contributed to effective cost control during this period. However, there were indications that changes in the operations would be required in the last half of the year. The company had received a significant increase in orders for delivery in the spring. There was an inadequate number of skilled workers available to meet the increased production. As a result, the production teams, beginning in January, would be made up of more class I labor and less class II labor than the standard required. The teams would consist of six class I persons, two class II persons, and one class V person. This labor team would be less efficient than the normal team. The reorganized teams work more slowly so that only 90 units are produced in the same time period that 100 units would normally be produced. No raw materials will be lost as a result of the change in the labor mix. Completed units have never been rejected in the final inspection process. This is expected to continue.

In addition, Lenco was notified by its material supplier that a lower-quality material would be supplied after January 1. One unit of raw material normally is required for each good unit produced. Lenco and its supplier estimated that 5 percent of the units manufactured would be rejected upon final inspection due to defective material. Normally, no units are lost due to defective material.

Required:

a. How much of the lower-quality material must be entered into production in order to produce 42,750 units of good production in January with the new labor teams? Show your calculations.
b. How many hours of each class of labor will be needed to produce 42,750 good units from the material input? Show your calculations.
c. What amount should be included in the January budget for the planned labor variance due to the labor team and material changes? What amount of this planned labor variance can be associated with the (1) material change; and (2) the team change? Show your calculations.

P. 8-13 **(AICPA) Comprehensive standard costing.** Conti Pharmaceutical Company processes a single compound-product known as NULAX and uses a standard cost accounting system. The process requires preparation and blending of three materials in large batches with a variation from the standard mixture sometimes necessary to maintain quality. Conti's cost accountant became ill at the end of October 1986 and you were engaged to determine standard costs of October production and explain any differences between actual and standard costs for the month. The following information is available on the blending department:

1. The standard cost card for a 500-pound batch shows the following standard costs:

	Quantity	Price	Total Cost	
Materials:				
Mucilloid	250 pounds	$.14	$35	
Dextrose	200 pounds	.09	18	
Ingredients	50 pounds	.08	4	
Total per batch	500 pounds			$ 57
Labor:				
Preparation and blending	10 hours	$3.00		30
Overhead:				
Variable	10 hours	$1.00	10	
Fixed	10 hours	.30	3	13
Total standard cost per 500-pound batch				$100

2. During October 410 batches of 500 pounds each of the finished compound were completed and transferred to the packaging department.
3. Blending Department inventories totaled 6,000 pounds at the beginning of the month and 9,000 pounds at the end of the month (assume both inventories were completely processed but not transferred and consisted of materials in their standard proportions). Inventories are carried in the accounts at standard cost prices.

4. During the month of October the following materials were purchased and put into production:

	Pounds	Price	Total Cost
Mucilloid	114,400	$.17	$19,448
Dextrose	85,800	.11	9,438
Ingredients	19,800	.07	1,386
Totals	220,000		$30,272

5. Wages paid for 4,212 hours of direct labor at $3.25 per hour amounted to $13,689.
6. Actual overhead costs for the month totaled $5,519.
7. The standards were established for a normal production volume of 200,000 pounds (400 batches) of NULAX per month. At this level of production variable factory overhead was budgeted at $4,000 and fixed factory overhead was budgeted at $1,200.

Required:

a. Prepare a schedule presenting the computation for the blending department of:

   1. October production in both pounds and batches.
   2. The standard cost of October production itemized by components of materials, labor, and overhead.

b. Prepare schedules computing the differences between actual and standard costs and analyzing the difference as:

   1. Materials variances (for each material) caused by
      (*a*) Price differences.
      (*b*) Quantity differences.
   2. Labor variances caused by
      (*a*) Rate difference.
      (*b*) Efficiency difference.
   3. Total overhead variance.

CASE

Case 8-1 Production evaluation with standard costs

Jefferson Commercial Products manufactures air-conditioning and air-moving units for commercial users. The company has recently introduced a new rooftop air-conditioning unit, the AC550, which in its first year of sales accounted for 40 percent of sales volume. However, this large sales volume has not improved the firm's quarterly earnings report. Management is very concerned about the firm's overall performance and in particular the performance of the AC550, which it hopes will provide a much needed improvement in company profits. You have been called in to investigate the problem and provide your expert opinion on the

Standards for an AC550 Air Conditioner

Direct materials:					
Galvanized steel	2 tons	@	$ 500/ton	=	$1,000
Copper	.6 ton	@	2,200/ton	=	1,320
Paint	3 gal	@	15/gal	=	45
Controls	1 unit	@	260/unit	=	260
Motors	1 unit	@	550/unit	=	550
Standard cost of direct materials					3,175
Direct labor:					
Cutting and forming department	45 hr	@	$ 8/hr	=	360
Coil department	15 hr	@	9/hr	=	135
Painting department	3 hr	@	7/hr	=	21
Assembly department	50 hr	@	8/hr	=	400
Standard cost of direct labor					916
Manufacturing overhead applied at the rate of $10/direct labor hour					1,130
Total standard cost of AC550 unit					$5,221

Production Cost AC550—January through June

	Quantity	Cost
Direct materials:		
Galvanized steel	720 tons	$ 388,800
Copper	270 tons	648,000
Paint	720 gal	9,360
Controls	305 units	76,250
Motors	300 units	186,000
Actual cost of direct materials		1,308,410
Direct labor:		
Cutting and forming department	15,200 hr	110,700
Coil department	5,000 hr	45,000
Painting department	840 hr	5,712
Assembly department	17,000 hr	121,500
Actual cost of direct labor		282,912
Actual manufacturing overhead		390,000
Total actual cost of production for AC550		$1,981,322

situation. AC550 standard cost data are presented above together with actual production cost data for the last 6 months.

January through June operating data are as follows:

1. 300 AC550 units are produced and sold at a price of $9,400 each.

2. Commissions to salespeople on AC550 units are 5 percent of selling price rather than the normal company rate of 3 percent.
3. Advertising cost for the 6-month period is $120,000.
4. The AC550 unit is a very sophisticated air-conditioning system that requires a heavy commitment of time by the engineering department and key administrative people. For most of the company's products, engineering and administrative costs amount to about 15 percent of the selling price. For AC550 units, management feels the percentage is about 20 percent.

Required:

a. Prepare a direct materials performance report.
b. Prepare a direct labor performance report.
c. Prepare a manufacturing overhead schedule of variance.
d. Prepare a product variance analysis report.
e. What is the actual unit product cost of the AC550 unit?
f. Prepare a product income statement for January through June for the AC550 product.
g. If the company requires a 15 percent profit on sales including all costs, what should be the selling price using the above actual cost data?
h. In evaluating the performance of this new product and its profit potential, what factors other than the standard cost variance analysis would you consider?

Flexible Budgeting and Manufacturing Overhead Variance Analysis

9

The cost behavior concepts presented in Chapter 2 and the basic budgeting concepts from Chapter 7 are combined in this chapter to provide a dynamic management planning and control system called flexible budgeting. A natural extension of flexible budgeting is overhead variance analysis, which was introduced in Chapter 8. The topic is discussed in depth in this chapter. When you have completed this chapter, you should understand:

1 The distinction between fixed and flexible budgets.

2 The purpose of flexible budgets and how they are used.

3 The use of flexible budgets in performance evaluation.

4 The effect of fixed cost on manufacturing overhead rates.

5 The detailed analysis of manufacturing overhead variances.

The planning and control framework provided by a budgeting system is an essential element of effective management. In many organizations **fixed budgets** are tools that offer managers the ability to plan and control operations and to evaluate performance. If, however, the actual volume of activity achieved by a firm is significantly different from the volume of activity planned in the fixed budget, the fixed budget may be less useful to managers than desired.

Actual activity may differ significantly from budgeted activity because of an unexpected strike, cancellation of an order, an unexpected large new production contract, or other factors. When actual results differ considerably from plans, a fixed budget may not be particularly effective in supporting managers. In a business that frequently experiences wide variations in its volume of activity, a **flexible budget,** which is a collection of several budgets prepared for a variety of activity levels, may be more useful. When activity levels fluctuate, flexible budgets provide managers with more useful information for planning and a better basis for comparing performance than a fixed budget.

In this chapter we discuss and illustrate the preparation and use of flexible budgets in planning, in monitoring performance, and in analyzing manufacturing overhead variances.

FIXED BUDGETING

Fixed budgets are prepared for a single level of activity

A **fixed budget,** sometimes called a **static budget,** contains data for a single volume of activity. The master budget for the Fable Manufacturing Company illustrated in Chapter 7 was based on expected production volume of 2,700 captain's chairs and 4,300 rocking chairs. The fixed budget performance report for manufacturing overhead was based on this level of production. The report, presented in Figure 7-21, is re-created in Figure 9-1. It indicates an 11 percent unfavorable overhead variance for the first quarter of the year. Does this report do a good job of measuring performance in this case?

As indicated in Chapter 7, the actual production quantity of captain's chairs was 19 percent higher than budgeted, and production of rockers was 21 percent higher than budgeted. Because fixed costs remain constant at all levels of activity, and variable costs change with changing volumes of activity, we expect higher costs with higher volumes of activity. In this example, the fixed budget says little about what first-quarter manufacturing overhead costs should have been for the volume of activity that occurred. Such information, however, is available in a flexible budget. Below we look at this illustration again, using a flexible budget to evaluate performance.

FLEXIBLE BUDGETING

Flexible budgets cover a range of activity

A **flexible budget,** also called a **dynamic budget,** is prepared for more than one level of activity. For example, a firm may prepare budgets for 10,000, 11,000, and 12,000 units of production. The purpose of preparing budgets for multiple activity levels is to provide managers with information about a range of activity in case the actual volume of activity differs from the expected level. Managers continue to rely heavily on the budget based on the expected level of activity for planning materials acquisitions, labor needs, and other resource requirements, but the flexible budget provides additional information useful in modifying plans if operating data indicate that some other level of activity will occur. When performance reports are prepared, actual results are compared with a budget based specifically on the level of activity actually achieved.

Characteristics of Flexible Budgets

Flexible budgets have several desirable characteristics. They

1. Cover a range of activity
2. Are dynamic
3. Facilitate performance measurement

Flexible budgets cover a range of activity. Forecasts of future events always involve some uncertainty. Managers want to minimize the effect of uncertainty in planning and decision making. A flexible budget does not reduce the probability that fluctuations in activity level will occur, but it does offer managers information about the effect of changes in activity levels. Accurate predictions of activity levels are sometimes hard to make, and many managers find they make more effective decisions with the aid of flexible budgets.

Some organizations experience stable activity levels or activity levels that are predictable. For example, a firm may have sales growth rates of 9 to 10 percent for 10 years in a row. In such a case the expected activity level and associated revenues and costs may be relatively easy to estimate, and a fixed budget may be all that is needed. Other firms may experience widely fluctuating business activity, with some years of dramatic growth and other years of declining sales. Among the most important factors influencing business stability is type of business. For example, tourist businesses are strongly affected by weather conditions and by general economic conditions. Staples industries, such as food, are influenced less by economic conditions. Of course, an individual food business, such as a single grocery store, may experience significant fluctuations due to growing or declining neighborhood population, managerial actions, or other variables. For businesses with widely fluctuating activity, flexible budgets provide essential managerial information.

An important step in developing a flexible budget is the selection of the range of activity covered by the flexible budget. Managers want information about activity levels that are **likely** to occur. Often one activity level at each extreme of the relevant activity range is selected, with one or more in between. The most likely activity level is the primary source of data for planning business operations.

Flexible budgets help managers adjust plans when the expected level of activity does not occur

Flexible budgets are dynamic. Flexible budgets allow managers to adjust plans easily when activity differs from the expected level. With flexible budget data, it is easy to adjust budget estimates on a timely basis to reflect activity fluctuations. Such budgets address "what is" rather than "what was" or "what was expected." This dynamic nature of flexible budgets makes them a very useful decision-making tool for management.

Flexible budgets facilitate performance measurement. Measuring efficiency is an important role of performance reporting. Fixed budgets are useful for measuring effectiveness such as the achievement of a $1,000,000 sales goal. In some cases, however, fixed budgets do not identify efficiency. For example, was the per-unit cost of marketing the product less than or more than the $.60 per unit expected cost? A flexible budget highlights efficiency measures because it answers the question, "What should the results be, given the actual level of activity?" For an illustration, refer to Figure 9-1. The report shows an unfavorable overhead variance of $16,588 for the first quarter of the year. The fixed budget is based on estimated production of 2,700 captain's chairs and 4,300 rocking chairs. The actual cost of $167,000 resulted from making 3,200 captain's chairs and 5,200 rocking chairs. Naturally, with more production than planned, overhead is more than planned, but how much more than the original fixed budget should the overhead cost be? The answer to this question is determined by preparing a new budget for the actual level of activity using the cost relationships used in developing the original budget. This new budget is compared with actual costs in the budget performance report.

Performance reports are based on a budget at the volume of activity that occurred

To illustrate a flexible budget performance report we continue the Fable Manufacturing Company overhead example in Figure 9-1. On the basis of the expected production of 2,700 captain's chairs and 4,300 rocking chairs, the company calculated the following number of direct labor hours, which were used to apply overhead and develop the overhead budget.

Captain's chairs	2,700 × 2 hr =	5,400
Rocking chairs	4,300 × 3 hr =	12,900
Total budgeted direct labor hr	=	18,300

Using the same standard hours per unit, expected labor hours for the actual production activity were 22,000 hours, as shown below.

Captain's chairs	3,200 × 2 hr =	6,400
Rocking chairs	5,200 × 3 hr =	15,600
Total budgeted direct labor hr	=	22,000

The fixed budget in Figure 9-1 was prepared using 18,300 direct labor hours, and the flexible budget is prepared using 22,000 direct labor hours. Both the fixed and flexible overhead budgets are prepared using fixed overhead cost data from Chapter 7 as well as the variable overhead data presented below.

	Cost per Direct Labor Hour
Indirect materials	$ .50
Indirect labor	1.00
Employee fringe benefits	2.00
Payroll taxes	.50
Utilities	.60
Maintenance	.40
Total variable overhead cost	$5.00

In preparing the fixed budget, each variable overhead cost was multiplied by 18,300 direct labor hours, which is the number of direct labor

Fable Manufacturing Company
Manufacturing Overhead Performance Report
First Quarter

Manufacturing Overhead	Fixed Budget for 18,300 DLH	Actual Cost	Variance (Favorable) Unfavorable
Variable costs:			
Indirect materials	$ 9,150	$ 10,800	$ 1,650
Indirect labor	18,300	19,000	700
Employee fringe benefits	36,600	45,200	8,600
Payroll taxes	9,150	11,400	2,250
Utilities	10,980	13,500	2,520
Maintenance	7,320	7,100	(220)
Total variable costs	91,500	107,000	15,500
Fixed costs:			
Supervision	18,000	18,000	—
Depreciation	24,000	24,000	—
Maintenance	9,000	9,500	500
Property taxes	4,912	5,200	288
Insurance	3,000	3,300	300
Total fixes costs	58,912	60,000	1,088
Total manufacturing overhead	$150,412	$167,000	$16,588

Figure 9-1
Fixed budget performance report for manufacturing overhead activities.

hours budgeted for the quarter. For instance, indirect materials were budgeted at $9,150 ($.50 × 18,300 DLH). On the other hand, a flexible budget performance report can be prepared using an overhead budget based on the 22,000 direct labor hours actually worked. In this budget each variable overhead cost is multiplied by 22,000 direct labor hours to arrive at the cost expected to be incurred at that level of production. For example, indirect materials are budgeted at $11,000 ($.50 × 22,000 DLH). The flexible budget for the actual level of activity is shown in Figure 9-2 and is computed by multiplying each of the variable cost items by 22,000 direct labor hours and adding the fixed costs of $58,912 shown in Figure 9-1. The fixed part of overhead cost is expected to remain the same at all activity levels. The performance report is completed by listing the actual costs and comparing them with the flexible budget data.

Flexible budgets provide a better measure of efficiency than fixed budgets

Compare the variances in Figure 9-1 with those in Figure 9-2. The two performance reports show very different results. The fixed budget report identifies an unfavorable total variance of $16,588, which is 11 percent of total budgeted overhead costs. The flexible budget variance report shows a favorable variance of $1,912, which is 1.3 percent of total budgeted overhead cost in the flexible budget. In this case the flexible budget variance report provides a better measure of efficiency, because the budgeted costs are based on the actual activity level of 22,000 direct

Fable Manufacturing Company
Manufacturing Overhead Performance Report
First Quarter

Manufacturing Overhead	Flexible Budget for 22,000 DLH	Actual Cost	Variance (Favorable) Unfavorable
Variable costs:			
Indirect materials	$ 11,000	$ 10,800	$ (200)
Indirect labor	22,000	19,000	(3,000)
Employee fringe benefits	44,000	45,200	1,200
Payroll taxes	11,000	11,400	400
Utilities	13,200	13,500	300
Maintenance	8,800	7,100	(1,700)
Total variable costs	110,000	107,000	(3,000)
Fixed costs:			
Supervision	18,000	18,000	—
Depreciation	24,000	24,000	—
Maintenance	9,000	9,500	500
Property taxes	4,912	5,200	288
Insurance	3,000	3,300	300
Total fixed costs	58,912	60,000	1,088
Total manufacturing overhead	$168,912	$167,000	$(1,912)

Figure 9-2
Flexible budget performance report for manufacturing overhead activities for the same period covered by the fixed budget report in Figure 9-1.

labor hours. Efficiency measures must answer the question, "How good was performance, given the actual level of activity?" Whenever actual and budgeted activity are significantly different, a flexible budget variance analysis report provides a better measure of efficiency than a report based on a fixed budget.

FLEXIBLE BUDGETING ILLUSTRATED

The preceding discussion illustrates the need for flexible budget performance reports and how the reports are prepared using actual costs and the actual activity level. Now we illustrate the development of a flexible budget before the accounting period begins. We use the Willimett State College Student Health Center to illustrate flexible budgeting, from the development of a flexible budget to the preparation of performance reports.

The health center serves students enrolled in the college. Most patients require outpatient services, but facilities are available for students requiring hospitalization. The center has a small permanent professional staff that is supplemented by local doctors and nurses who work part-time as needed. As a result, a portion of the salaries is fixed and some of the medical salaries cost varies with the number of students served.

Steps in the Flexible Budgeting Process

The following steps are needed to develop a flexible budget:

1. Determine the range of activity the budget should cover.
2. Determine the cost behavior patterns for each cost included in the budget.
3. Select the activity levels for which budgets will be prepared.
4. Prepare the flexible budget using the cost behavior data and the selected activity levels.

What levels of activity should the flexible budget cover?

Step 1. Selecting the range of activity the flexible budget will cover is important because cost behavior patterns may be different in different ranges of activity. For example, the building lease cost may be fixed from 0 to 25,000 student visits a year, but beyond 25,000 visits additional space must be leased, causing a jump in the lease cost from $18,000 to $30,000 annually. This **relevant range** concept is discussed in Chapter 2. It makes little sense to analyze costs and revenues for activity levels that have little chance of occurring because they are beyond the relevant range.

Step 2. Cost behavior patterns must be determined for each cost included in the budget. Typically firms analyze historical cost data using techniques discussed in Chapters 5 and 18, such as the high-low method, scatter diagrams, linear regression analysis, or other methods. Behavior patterns suggested by historical cost data are modified to reflect known or expected changes, such as expected payroll tax increases, new pension fund contributions, and increased property tax rates. Usually the behavior pattern for each cost is described in terms of fixed and variable components.

In this example the activity measure is the number of student visits to the health center. Other measures of activity, such as the number of medical staff hours, could be used, but in this case management feels that student visits is the most appropriate measure. The health center manager selects an activity range of 12,000 to 20,000 student visits for the budget year. This relatively wide activity range is selected because student enrollment figures for the coming year are not yet available. Also, the national health service is predicting a major flu epidemic during the year. If the flu epidemic strikes the campus, health service visits next year will be noticeably higher than this year's level of 15,000.

The health center identifies 10 different costs and determines the behavior pattern of each. Figure 9-3 shows a scatter diagram analysis of health center maintenance costs for the last 10 years. Regression analysis indicates that $20,000 of maintenance cost is fixed and $1.50 per student visit is variable. Similar analyses are made for each of the health center costs. Figure 9-4 summarizes the results of the cost behavior analysis for each cost.

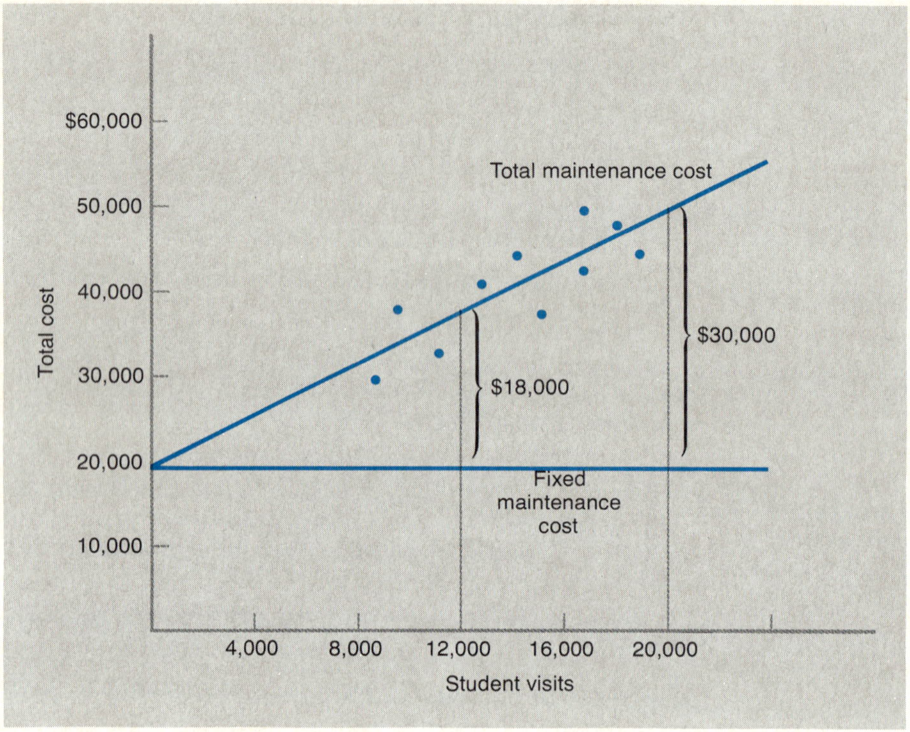

Figure 9-3
Scatter diagram of maintenance costs for the health center of Willimett State College.

Step 3. Using data in Figure 9-4, budgets are prepared for the activity levels that management selects within the relevant range. In this example budgets are prepared for three activity levels—12,000, 16,000, and 20,000 student visits. The number of budgets prepared for different activity levels

Willimett State College
Student Health Service
Estimated Cost Behavior Patterns
For the Fiscal Year 1986–1987

Cost	Fixed Cost	Variable Cost per Student Visit
Administrative salaries	$35,000	—
Medical and nursing salaries	80,000	$8.00
Other salaries	28,000	2.50
Medical supplies	6,000	5.00
External laboratory fees and other medical fees	—	1.00
Building lease	18,000	—
Utilities	6,500	.50
Maintenance	20,000	1.50
Computer services	12,000	.75
Employee fringe benefits	34,500	1.75

Figure 9-4
Cost behavior for the 10 cost pools used by the health center for budgeting and costing purposes. Most are mixed costs.

is a matter of managerial preference, which is influenced by the cost-benefit relationship of preparing more budgets. However, the cost of preparing budgets for different activity levels is not high once cost behavior data have been developed. The health center could prepare a budget with increments of 1,000 visits throughout the relevant range of activity, but for our purposes three activity levels are sufficient.

Step 4. The preparation of a flexible budget is easy once the cost behavior patterns are determined and the budgeted activity levels are selected. Figure 9-5 shows the fixed and variable costs for each of the selected levels of activity.

Administrative salaries are entirely fixed and are therefore constant at $35,000 for all three activity levels. Medical and nursing salaries have a fixed component of $80,000 and a variable component of $8 per student visit. Therefore, the variable part of this cost is $8 × 12,000, or $96,000, at the 12,000-visit level; $8 × 16,000, or $128,000, at the 16,000-visit level; and $8 × 20,000, or $160,000, for 20,000 visits. Similarly the cost category "Other salaries" has a fixed component of $28,000 plus a variable amount that increases at the rate of $2.50 per student visit to the health center.

Other costs have fixed and variable components just as medical and nursing salaries do. The total cost is found in each case by combining the fixed and variable costs as described above. Like administrative salaries, building lease cost is completely fixed, whereas external laboratory and other medical fees are entirely variable.

Willimett State College
Student Health Service
Flexible Budget
For the Fiscal Year 1986–1987

	Activity Level (Number of Student Visits)					
	12,000		16,000		20,000	
Cost	**Fixed**	**Variable**	**Fixed**	**Variable**	**Fixed**	**Variable**
Administrative salaries	$ 35,000	—	$ 35,000	—	$ 35,000	—
Medical and nursing salaries	80,000	$ 96,000	80,000	$128,000	80,000	$160,000
Other salaries	28,000	30,000	28,000	40,000	28,000	50,000
Medical supplies	6,000	60,000	6,000	80,000	6,000	100,000
External laboratory fees and other medical fees	—	12,000	—	16,000	—	20,000
Building lease	18,000	—	18,000	—	18,000	—
Utilities	6,500	6,000	6,500	8,000	6,500	10,000
Maintenance	20,000	18,000	20,000	24,000	20,000	30,000
Computer services	12,000	9,000	12,000	12,000	12,000	15,000
Employee fringe benefits	34,500	21,000	34,500	28,000	34,500	35,000
Total	$240,000	$252,000	$240,000	$336,000	$240,000	$420,000

Figure 9-5 **A flexible budget for the health center, identifying fixed and variable cost components.**

Willimett State College
Student Health Service
Flexible Budget
For the Fiscal Year 1986–1987

	Activity Level (Number of Student Visits)		
Cost	**12,000**	**16,000**	**20,000**
Administrative salaries	$ 35,000	$ 35,000	$ 35,000
Medical and nursing salaries	176,000	208,000	240,000
Other salaries	58,000	68,000	78,000
Medical supplies	66,000	86,000	106,000
External laboratory fees and other medical fees	12,000	16,000	20,000
Building lease	18,000	18,000	18,000
Utilities	12,500	14,500	16,500
Maintenance	38,000	44,000	50,000
Computer services	21,000	24,000	27,000
Employee fringe benefits	55,500	62,500	69,500
Total	$492,000	$576,000	$660,000

Figure 9-6
The fixed and variable cost data in Figure 9-5 are combined into a single amount for each cost at each activity level.

Fixed and variable costs are totaled for each activity level when all of the costs have been budgeted. The fixed costs remain constant for all levels of activity, and the variable costs increase as the level of activity increases. Usually fixed and variable costs are combined in the final version of a flexible budget, as illustrated in Figure 9-6, which combines the fixed and variable cost data in Figure 9-5.

The form of the flexible budget presented in Figure 9-6 is very common, but with this format it is not obvious what the fixed and variable cost components are. However, it is simple to determine the cost behavior from the flexible budget using the high-low method. For each cost, the difference in cost is divided by the difference in activity level to find the variable cost. Then the variable cost for one activity level is substituted into the mixed cost formula to find the fixed cost. To illustrate, we use the medical and nursing salaries from the flexible budget in Figure 9-6.

$$\text{Variable cost} = \frac{\text{Cost at one activity level} - \text{Cost at another activity level}}{\text{Difference in activity level}}$$

$$= \frac{\$208{,}000 - \$176{,}000}{16{,}000 \text{ students} - 12{,}000 \text{ students}}$$

$$= \$8 \text{ per student visit}$$

Using the mixed cost formula for 12,000 student visits and substituting the variable cost figure, we have

$$
\begin{aligned}
\text{Total mixed cost} &= \text{Fixed cost} + \text{Variable cost} \\
\$176{,}000 &= \text{Fixed cost} + (12{,}000 \text{ students} \times \$8) \\
\$176{,}000 &= \text{Fixed cost} + \$96{,}000 \\
\\
\text{Fixed cost} &= \$80{,}000
\end{aligned}
$$

The same $80,000 fixed cost results if the variable cost per student is substituted into the formula for 16,000 or 20,000 student visits. The fixed and variable cost component for other costs can be computed in the same way. For example, the computation for medical supplies is

$$
\begin{aligned}
\text{Variable cost} &= \frac{\$86{,}000 - \$66{,}000}{16{,}000 \text{ students} - 12{,}000 \text{ students}} \\
&= \frac{\$20{,}000}{4{,}000 \text{ students}} = \$5 \text{ per student}
\end{aligned}
$$

$$
\begin{aligned}
\text{Fixed cost} &= \$66{,}000 - (12{,}000 \text{ students} \times \$5) \\
&= \$66{,}000 - \$60{,}000 \\
&= \$6{,}000
\end{aligned}
$$

Budget performance reports are prepared periodically by comparing the actual results of the period with the budgeted data for the period. But which of the several flexible budgets should be used in preparing the performance report? With flexible budgeting, actual results are compared with a budget prepared for the volume of activity that actually occurred. To illustrate, during the year the student health center had 18,500 student visits. If a budget for this level of activity already exists, then a performance report is prepared from the budget data already available. If the actual activity level was not budgeted previously, a new budget is prepared. It may appear strange that a budget is prepared after the reporting period is ended, but this budget is used expressly for performance reporting and is not a plan for future operations. The flexible budget performance report for the health center is prepared by using the data from Figure 9-4 and the activity level of 18,500 student visits. Actual cost data are found in the ledger accounts of the health center. The report is presented in Figure 9-7.

The right column of Figure 9-7 shows variances computed for each cost and in total. Several costs show relatively large variances, although the total variance of $2,500 favorable is quite small.

The value of the flexible budget performance report becomes evident when the data are analyzed. If the actual cost of $626,000 is compared with the budget based on 16,000 visits (see Figure 9-6), the variance is $50,000 unfavorable. A comparison of actual data with the budget based on 20,000 visits yields a favorable variance of $34,000. The two comparisons provide widely differing results. The logical approach is to compare actual results with a budget based on the actual level of activity.

Willimett State College
Student Health Service
Flexible Budget Performance Report
For the Fiscal Year 1986–1987

Cost	Budget for 18,500 Students*	Actual Cost	Variance (Favorable) Unfavorable
Administrative salaries	$ 35,000	$ 37,000	$ 2,000
Medical and nursing salaries	228,000	236,900	8,900
Other salaries	74,250	67,000	(7,250)
Medical supplies	98,500	96,000	(2,500)
External laboratory fees and other medical fees	18,500	21,250	2,750
Building lease	18,000	18,000	—
Utilities	15,750	19,250	3,500
Maintenance	47,750	39,250	(8,500)
Computer services	25,875	21,375	(4,500)
Employee fringe benefits	66,875	69,975	3,100
Total	$628,500	$626,000	$(2,500)

* Actual activity level = 18,500 student visits.

Figure 9-7
A flexible budget performance report is developed by preparing a budget for the actual activity level of 18,500 student visits and comparing budgeted with actual cost data for the year.

MANUFACTURING OVERHEAD FLEXIBLE BUDGETING

Flexible budgets are particularly useful in helping managers understand overhead costs

Flexible budgets provide managers with a valuable planning and control framework for many types of organizations and activities, but they are particularly useful in helping managers to establish manufacturing overhead rates and to analyze overhead variances. Flexible budgets are especially pertinent for overhead costs because a significant portion of overhead is fixed and the rest varies with the volume of activity.

We use the Hornebrook Structural Steel Company to illustrate the development of a manufacturing overhead rate and later to discuss overhead variance analysis. The range of activity selected by Hornebrook Structural Steel Company for its flexible budget is 15,000 to 30,000 direct labor hours. The company experiences large sales fluctuations because its products are used primarily in the construction industry. Sales tend to be depressed during periods of little construction activity and high when construction activity picks up. The range of 15,000 to 30,000 direct labor hours is management's estimate of what the company might experience, with 25,000 hours being the expected activity level. Using this range of activity, manufacturing overhead cost behavior patterns are analyzed for each cost shown in Figure 9-8.

The cost data in Figure 9-8 are used to develop a flexible budget for each level of activity that management chooses. In this example, four activity levels are illustrated—15,000, 20,000, 25,000, and 30,000 direct labor hours. Fixed and variable costs are budgeted for each level of activity for each overhead cost. The flexible budget is presented in Figure 9-9.

Hornebrook Structural Steel Company
Estimated Cost Behavior Patterns
For Manufacturing Overhead
For the Year 1987

Cost	Fixed Cost	Variable Cost per Direct Labor Hour
Indirect materials	—	$.50
Indirect labor	—	.70
Factory supplies	$12,000	.30
Maintenance	25,000	.60
Utilities	4,000	.80
Computer services	6,000	.10
Property taxes	5,000	—
Insurance	3,000	.10
Supervision	25,000	.90
Depreciation, production plant	30,000	—
Depreciation, production equipment	40,000	—

Figure 9-8
Cost behavior data for Hornebrook's manufacturing overhead costs. Three costs are fixed, two are directly variable, and six are mixed costs.

As expected, the total fixed cost remains constant for all levels of activity, and the total variable cost increases with activity level. The rate of increase is $4 per direct labor hour, which is determined easily by applying the high-low method to the cost data of any two activity levels.

The manufacturing overhead rate is calculated by dividing the budgeted volume of activity into the budgeted overhead cost, as discussed in Chapter 4. For example, at the 15,000-hour level, the budgeted overhead cost ($150,000 + $60,000) divided by 15,000 hours yields an overhead rate of $14 per direct labor hour. In Chapter 4 a fixed budget was used to arrive at overhead cost, and only one set of budgeted data was available, yielding a single overhead rate. Now we have budgeted data for four activity levels, each of which yields a different overhead rate. Which should be used to apply overhead to production?

Normally only one overhead rate is calculated. In Figure 9-9, we show a rate for each activity level in order to explain some characteristics of overhead cost and to help you understand overhead variance analysis later in the chapter. Typically the overhead rate is based on the firm's **normal capacity,** which is the expected activity level for the period, assuming normal operating conditions. In the Hornebrook example, normal capacity is 25,000 direct labor hours. Therefore, the overhead rate is

$$\text{MOH rate} = \frac{\text{Budgeted manufacturing overhead}}{\text{Budgeted activity level}}$$

$$= \frac{\$250{,}000}{25{,}000 \text{ DLH}} = \$10/\text{DLH}$$

The overhead rate has a fixed and a variable component

This overhead rate contains the fixed and variable components of the total overhead cost. Figure 9-9 shows that at 25,000 direct labor hours, the $250,000 of budgeted overhead cost is composed of $150,000 of fixed cost and $100,000 variable cost. Therefore, the $10 overhead rate at this level of activity consists of $6 per hour of fixed overhead ($150,000/25,000 DLH) and $4 per hour of variable overhead ($100,000/25,000 DLH).

Total fixed cost remains constant; fixed cost per unit declines with higher volumes of activity

Note that although the total variable cost changes proportionately with the volume of activity, variable cost of $4 per hour remains the same throughout the relevant range. On the other hand, total fixed cost is $150,000 at all activity levels, but the fixed cost per unit declines as it is spread over a larger number of direct labor hours. At 15,000 direct labor hours, the fixed part of the overhead rate is $10 per direct labor hour ($150,000/15,000 DLH). At 20,000 direct labor hours, the fixed overhead rate is $7.50 per DLH ($150,000/20,000 DLH). The total overhead rate is calculated for each level of activity in the flexible budget by adding the fixed overhead rate to the $4 per DLH variable rate. Hornebrook's overhead rate would be $14/DLH if normal capacity were 15,000 hours, $11.50/DLH at 20,000 hours, and $9/DLH at 30,000 hours, as shown in Figure 9-9. The difference in the overhead rate is caused **entirely** by the amount of

Hornebrook Structural Steel Company
Manufacturing Overhead Flexible Budget
For the Year 1987

	Activity Level (Direct Labor Hours)							
	15,000		20,000		25,000		30,000	
Cost	**Fixed**	**Variable**	**Fixed**	**Variable**	**Fixed**	**Variable**	**Fixed**	**Variable**
Indirect materials	—	$ 7,500	—	$10,000	—	$ 12,500	—	$ 15,000
Indirect labor	—	10,500	—	14,000	—	17,500	—	21,000
Factory supplies	$ 12,000	4,500	$ 12,000	6,000	$ 12,000	7,500	$ 12,000	9,000
Maintenance	25,000	9,000	25,000	12,000	25,000	15,000	25,000	18,000
Utilities	4,000	12,000	4,000	16,000	4,000	20,000	4,000	24,000
Computer service charges	6,000	1,500	6,000	2,000	6,000	2,500	6,000	3,000
Property taxes	5,000	—	5,000	—	5,000	—	5,000	—
Insurance	3,000	1,500	3,000	2,000	3,000	2,500	3,000	3,000
Supervision	25,000	13,500	25,000	18,000	25,000	22,500	25,000	27,000
Depreciation, production plant	30,000	—	30,000	—	30,000	—	30,000	—
Depreciation, production equipment	40,000	—	40,000	—	40,000	—	40,000	—
Total	$150,000	$60,000	$150,000	$80,000	$150,000	$100,000	$150,000	$120,000
Manufacturing overhead per direct labor hour	$10/DLH	$4/DLH	$7.50/DLH	$4/DLH	$6/DLH	$4/DLH	$5/DLH	$4/DLH
Manufacturing overhead rate	$14/DLH		$11.50/DLH		$10/DLH		$9/DLH	

Figure 9-9 **A manufacturing overhead flexible budget with fixed and variable cost components separated. The overhead rate used for applying overhead costs to production during the period depends on the level of activity that management considers most relevant.**

fixed overhead prorated over each direct labor hour. This concept is important in overhead variance analysis.

The manufacturing overhead flexible budgeting data provide some interesting information. For instance, at the estimated normal capacity of 25,000 direct labor hours, the overhead rate is $10 per DLH. Once this overhead rate is selected, it is used to apply overhead to products as they are manufactured. But if the firm's normal capacity actually turns out to be 20,000 direct labor hours, the correct overhead rate is $11.50 per DLH. A product requiring 12 direct labor hours would be charged $120 of manufacturing overhead cost at the 25,000-hour level of activity, when $138 is the correct amount. In this situation, using the $10 per hour overhead rate results in recording a product cost that is $18 less than the actual cost of making the product.

Flexible budgets allow managers to understand why inaccurate costs are recorded for products and to analyze the effects of such errors, which are caused by estimation errors. With a fixed budget we know that the overhead rate is wrong if normal capacity is estimated incorrectly, but the effect on product costs is not clear. In addition to providing valuable information for establishing overhead rates and for analyzing the effect of different activity levels on product costs, flexible budgets are useful in analyzing manufacturing overhead variances. Their usefulness is particularly enhanced when combined with a standard cost system.

MANUFACTURING OVERHEAD VARIANCE ANALYSIS

The process of analyzing the difference between standard and actual costs, called **variance analysis,** can be applied to overhead costs just as we applied it to direct materials and direct labor in Chapter 8. Direct materials and direct labor are variable costs only; they contain no fixed component. On the other hand, overhead includes relatively large amounts of fixed costs as well as some variable costs, making the analysis of overhead variances somewhat more complicated. Without flexible budgets it is difficult to assess the impact on overhead costs of activity levels that differ from the budgeted level.

The purpose of overhead variance analysis is the same as that of other types of variance analysis: to determine how much actual results differ from expected outcomes and why the variance occurred. To illustrate **manufacturing overhead variance analysis,** we continue to use the example of Hornebrook Structural Steel Company. The following additional information is necessary:

1. The normal capacity of 25,000 direct labor hours is based on production of 12,500 tons of steel at a standard of 2 direct labor hours per ton.
2. Actual production in 1987 is 12,000 tons.
3. Actual direct labor hours worked is 24,400.
4. Actual manufacturing overhead cost in 1987 is $242,000.

Applying Overhead in a Standard Cost System

When an **actual** cost system is used, manufacturing overhead is applied to production by multiplying the overhead rate times the **actual** level of activity, with activity measured in terms of the overhead application base. If the overhead rate is based on direct labor hours, overhead is applied based on the number of direct labor hours actually worked.

Overhead is applied based on standard hours in a standard cost system

In a **standard** cost system the same basic concepts apply. But instead of applying overhead based on actual direct labor hours or machining hours, the overhead rate is multiplied by the **standard** direct labor hours given the actual amount of production achieved. For example, the overhead rate is $5 per direct labor hour and 2 direct labor hours is the standard for each unit produced. Ten units are produced using 23 **actual** direct labor hours. Standard hours for 10 units is 20 direct labor hours, so the amount of applied overhead in a standard cost system is $100 for the 10 units (10 units × 2 DLH × $5 per DLH). In an actual cost system the amount of applied overhead for the 10 units is $115, which is 23 actual direct labor hours × $5 per DLH.

In the Hornebrook example, production of 12,000 tons of steel used 24,400 actual direct labor hours, but the overhead applied to production for the output was based on 24,000 standard direct labor hours (12,000 tons × 2 standard hours per ton). Overhead variance analysis will help us understand the effects of using more actual direct labor hours than standard, producing less steel than budgeted, and applying the overhead costs using a different number of direct labor hours than expected.

Measuring Total Overhead Variance

In a standard cost system the total overhead variance is the difference between actual overhead and applied overhead. Actual overhead of $242,000 is found in the Manufacturing Overhead Control account. Applied manufacturing overhead is found in the Manufacturing Overhead Applied account.

In this example the applied overhead and total overhead variance are computed as follows:

$$\text{Applied overhead} = \text{Actual output} \times \frac{\text{Standard hours}}{\text{per unit of output}} \times \text{Overhead rate}$$

Applied overhead	= 12,000 tons × 2 hr/ton × $10/hr
	= $240,000
Actual overhead	= 242,000
Manufacturing overhead variance	= $ 2,000 unfavorable

The overhead variance can be diagramed as follows:

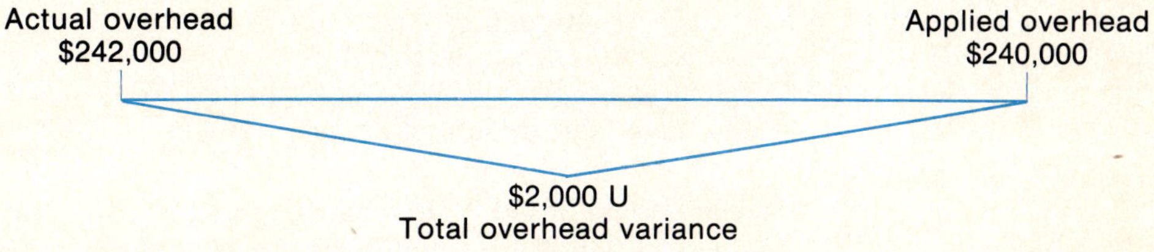

The variance is unfavorable for Hornebrook because actual overhead is greater than the standard amount of overhead. In practice the total variance can be determined by comparing actual overhead, which is the ending balance in the Manufacturing Overhead Control account, with the balance in the Manufacturing Overhead Applied account. For this example the account balances are

MOH Control		MOH Applied	
242,000			240,000

Total overhead variance can be divided in several ways

Knowing only the total overhead variance is not especially useful for controlling overhead costs and evaluating performance. Just as the direct materials variance was divided into price and quantity variances and the direct labor variance was divided into rate and efficiency variances, so too overhead variances can be divided into more specific measures. There are several approaches to overhead variance analysis. We describe two common approaches that use flexible budgets in the analysis process. They are called the two-variance method and the three-variance method.

Two-Variance Method

The **two-variance method** isolates the variance that is controllable by management and the variance caused by operating at an activity level other than the budgeted volume of activity. The computations can be diagramed as follows:

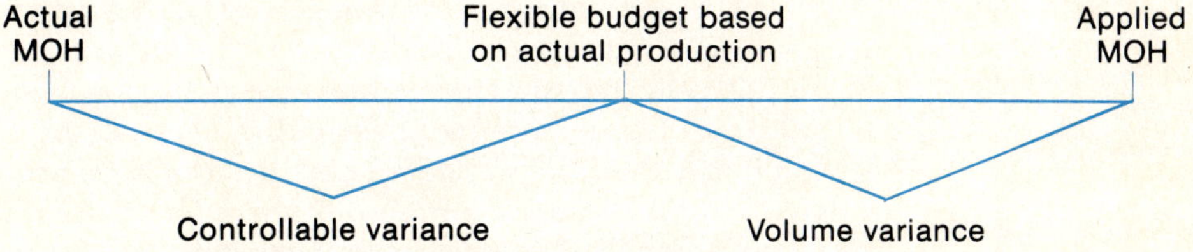

Actual manufacturing overhead of $242,000 is found in the Manufacturing Overhead Control account. A flexible budget based on actual output is a new budget that is prepared for performance evaluation after actual production is known. For variance analysis purposes, we need the fixed and variable portion of this budget. The budget is determined as follows:

Actual production	12,000 tons
Standard direct labor hr/ton	2 hr/ton
Total standard direct labor hours, given the amount of actual production	24,000 hr

$$\text{Flexible budget based on actual output} = \left(\text{Standard hours} \times \text{Variable overhead cost per hour}\right) + \text{Fixed overhead cost}$$

Variable cost: 24,000 hr × $4/hr =	$ 96,000
Fixed cost	+ 150,000
Flexible budget based on actual output	$246,000

The flexible budget based on actual output shows what overhead costs **should have been** at the **actual** production volume.

With direct labor hours as the overhead application base, and using a standard cost system, applied overhead is standard hours times the overhead rate. In this example applied overhead is 24,000 hr × $10/hr = $240,000. Substituting actual overhead, applied overhead, and the new flexible budget into the overhead variance diagram, we get:

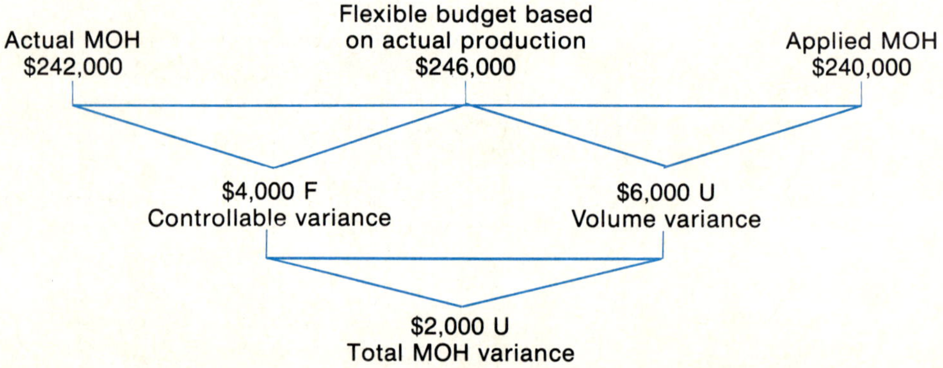

The **controllable variance** is the difference between actual overhead and a flexible budget based on actual output. The variance is called controllable because it is a deviation of actual costs from budgeted costs over which managers can exercise some control. Therefore this variance is a benchmark of managerial performance, because a flexible budget based on output reflects expected achievement for managers. In this case the $4,000 controllable variance is favorable because the actual overhead cost is $4,000 less than the budgeted cost for the 24,000-standard-hour level of activity. In other words, Hornebrook spent less for overhead than expected, given the amount of product manufactured.

The **volume variance** occurs because actual production differs from the budgeted amount of production. The volume variance deals with the fixed part of the overhead rate and it occurs whenever the actual output is different than expected output. Remember that the $10 per hour overhead rate of Hornebrook was based on a budgeted activity level of 25,000 direct labor hours. The rate was composed of two parts, a $4 per hour variable component and a $6 per hour fixed component, as shown in Figure 9-9.

The volume variance results from producing more or less than the expected volume of production

The variable component is $4 per hour throughout the relevant range, but the fixed component of $6 per hour is the $150,000 fixed cost spread over 25,000 hours of expected activity. But if more or less than 25,000 standard direct labor hours were used, then more or less than $150,000 of fixed overhead was applied to production. With only 24,000 standard hours used to apply overhead, as in the Hornebrook example, less than $150,000 of fixed overhead has been assigned to products. The amount assigned to production in this case is $144,000 of fixed overhead ($6 per hour × 24,000 standard hours). Activity was 1,000 hours short of the budgeted activity level, and the variance of $6,000 is 1,000 hours times the $6 per hour fixed overhead component. The variance is unfavorable because the standard amount of fixed overhead is $144,000 and the actual fixed overhead is $150,000, or $6,000 more than applied using the standard overhead rate.

Three-Variance Method

The **three-variance method** is used to isolate a spending variance, an efficiency variance, and a volume variance. The spending and efficiency variances are the controllable variance from the two-variance method separated into two components. The spending variance results from spending more or less than budgeted for overhead, given the amount of production input—in this case direct labor hours actually worked. The efficiency variance is caused by using a different number of labor hours than standard—that is, by working more or less efficiently than expected. The volume variance in the three-variance approach is the same as for the two-variance method. The following diagram shows the computations:

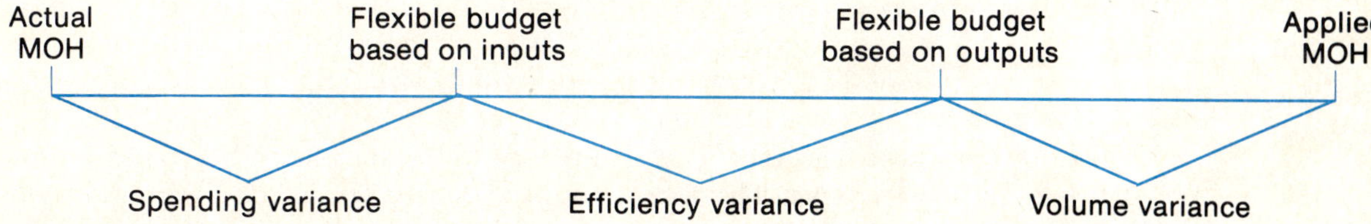

Typically, activity level is measured in terms of direct labor hours, machine hours, or some other activity variable. In our example direct labor hours is the activity measure used for the budget. Therefore production outputs are measured in terms of standard direct labor hours and production inputs are in terms of actual direct labor hours. A budget based on inputs means a budget based on actual direct labor hours, and a budget based on outputs means a budget based on standard direct labor hours. A flexible budget based on actual hours is computed as follows:

$$\text{Flexible budget based on inputs} = \left(\text{Actual hours} \times \text{Variable overhead cost per hour}\right) + \text{Fixed overhead cost}$$

Variable cost: 24,400 hr × $4/hr	$ 97,600
Fixed cost	+ 150,000
Flexible budget based on actual hours	$247,600

The flexible budget based on standard hours is $246,000, as computed for the two-variance method. Applied overhead is $240,000, and actual overhead is $242,000, the same as before. Substituting these numbers into the analysis we get:

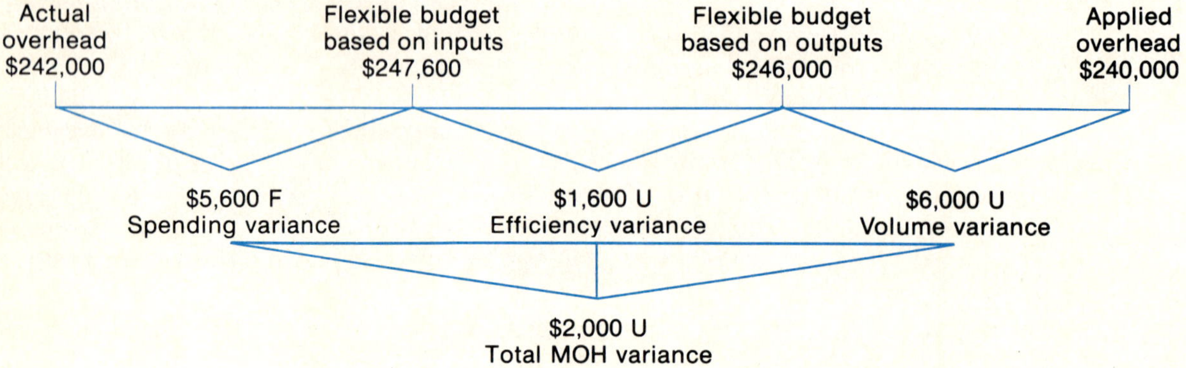

The **spending variance** addresses the question, "How much should have been spent on overhead, given the actual input?" It is a comparison of actual overhead with a flexible budget based on actual hours. In this example the actual overhead is $5,600 less than the budget amount and therefore is favorable.

The overhead efficiency variance measures the impact on overhead cost of using more or fewer hours than standard

The **efficiency variance** measures the amount of overhead variance attributable to using more or less inputs than allowed by the standards, given the amount of production. If actual hours worked are fewer than standard hours, the efficiency variance is favorable. An unfavorable variance occurs when actual hours exceed standard hours; this is the case in the Hornebrook example. Actual hours are 24,400, whereas standard hours are 24,000. When the difference of 400 hours is multiplied by the **variable** overhead rate of $4 per hour, the unfavorable efficiency variance of $1,600 is obtained.

The **volume variance** is the same as computed and discussed in the two-variance analysis. The terms **capacity variance** and **denominator variance** sometimes are used to describe the volume variance. Summing the three variances results in a $2,000 unfavorable total overhead variance, as with the two-variance method. Of course, the two-variance and three-variance methods always yield the same total variance for any particular set of data. The different variance analysis methods merely divide the total variance in different ways.

The controllable variance measures the amount that actual overhead cost differs from the budget based on the output produced. The spending variance measures the amount that actual overhead differs from a budget based on the inputs. The difference between the spending and controllable variances is the efficiency variance that results when inputs differ from outputs. The two-variance method addresses performance using a budget based on standard hours as a basis for measurement. The three-variance method uses budgets based on actual and standard hours as a basis of performance measurement. Neither method is necessarily better than the other. Both are widely used in business, and the choice rests with man-

Type of Analysis	Calculation	Variance Amount	Explanation
Two-Variance Method			
Controllable variance	Actual MOH − Flexible budget, standard hours		Spent less on overhead than planned, given the number of units actually produced.
	$242,000 − $246,000	$4,000 F	
Volume variance	Flexible budget, standard hours − Applied MOH		The volume in terms of standard hours was 1,000 hours below normal capacity
	$246,000 − $240,000	6,000 U	
Total variance		$2,000 U	
Three-Variance Method			
Spending variance	Actual MOH − Flexible budget, actual hours		Spent less on overhead than planned for the amount of input (hours worked).
	$242,000 − $247,600	$5,600 F	
Efficiency variance	Flexible budget, actual hours − Flexible budget, standard hours		Used more hours than allowed by the standards for the quantity of goods produced.
	$247,600 − $246,000	1,600 U	
Volume variance	Flexible budget, standard hours − Applied MOH		The volume in terms of standard hours was 1,000 hours below normal capacity.
	$246,000 − $240,000	6,000 U	
Total variance		$2,000 U	

Figure 9-10 A comparison of the computation and meaning of the different overhead variances.

agers' preferences and information needs. Other ways of measuring and interpreting the fixed overhead variance are advocated by some accountants. The two different overhead variance analysis methods discussed here are sufficient for our purposes.

The two-variance and three-variance methods, their calculation, and their interpretation are summarized and illustrated in Figure 9-10.

Analysis of Individual Overhead Accounts

Individual overhead accounts can be analyzed in the same way as overhead in total

Thus far we have analyzed overhead variances for the total manufacturing overhead accounts. However, the same analysis can be prepared for each individual cost included in overhead. In the Hornebrook example the overhead control account consists of 11 different costs that are maintained in a subsidiary ledger. The balance in the 11 accounts at year-end total to the control account balance of $242,000. An analysis identical to that of the total overhead account can also be prepared for each of the overhead accounts. To illustrate, $41,500 is the actual balance in the overhead subsidiary ledger for maintenance.

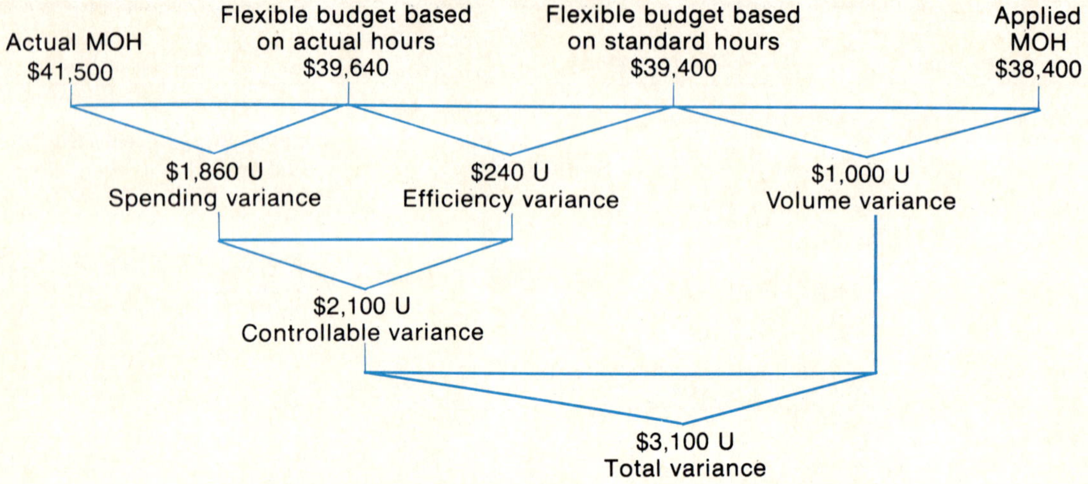

The budget based on actual hours is 24,400 hours times the variable rate for maintenance, which is $.60 per hour, plus the fixed maintenance cost of $25,000 as shown in Figure 9-8. The same procedure is used to compute the budget based on 24,000 standard hours. The fixed and variable components for each cost in the Hornebrook example are found in Figure 9-8. When a single cost item is being analyzed, the overhead rate used is the rate for that single item. Here maintenance has a fixed cost of $25,000 plus a variable rate of $.60 per hour. Dividing the fixed cost by the normal capacity of 25,000 hours yields a fixed rate of $1 per hour; adding the variable component, we have a rate of $1.60 per DLH for maintenance. Using this rate, we compute $38,400 of applied overhead (24,000 hours × $1.60 per hour). Note that here applied overhead refers to the amount of maintenance overhead applied. Applied overhead may be calculated in the same way for the other 10 overhead costs.

The other overhead costs can be analyzed in the same way. For instance, Figure 9-8 shows the cost behavior for utilities cost, and the actual cost is $22,800. The variance analysis using the three-variance method is

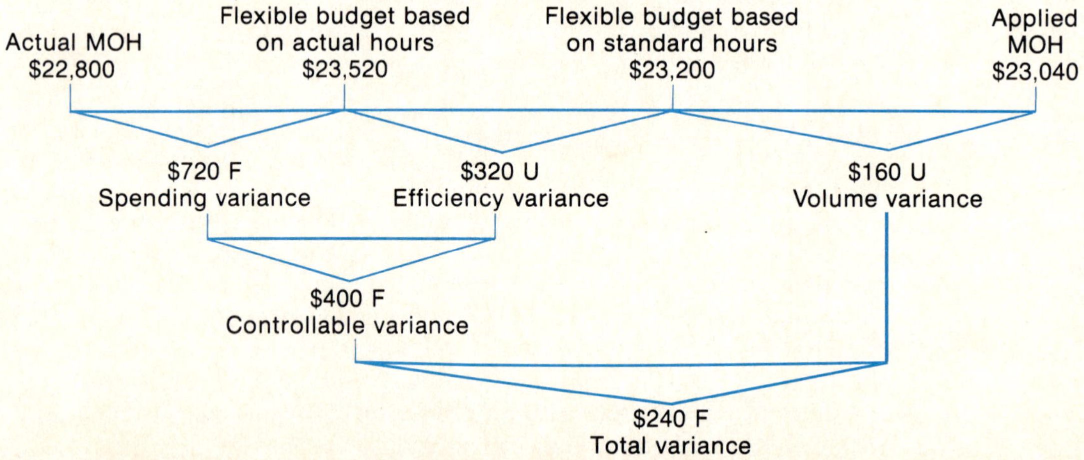

Hornebrook Structural Steel Company
Detailed Analysis of Overhead Variances
For the Year 1987

Cost	Variance: Spending	Efficiency	Volume	Total
Indirect materials	$2,500 F	$ 200 U	$ 0	$2,300 F
Indirect labor	1,080 F	280 U	0	800 F
Factory supplies	720 F	120 U	480 U	120 F
Maintenance	1,860 U	240 U	1,000 U	3,100 U
Utilities	720 F	320 U	160 U	240 F
Computer service charges	840 F	40 U	240 U	560 F
Property taxes	100 U	0	200 U	300 U
Insurance	740 F	40 U	120 U	580 F
Supervision	960 F	360 U	1,000 U	400 U
Depreciation, production plant	0	0	1,200 U	1,200 U
Depreciation, production equipment	0	0	1,600 U	1,600 U
Total	$5,600 F	$1,600 U	$6,000 U	$2,000 U

Figure 9-11
A detailed variance analysis report for manufacturing overhead costs.

If each cost is analyzed in the same way as maintenance and utilities and the variances are totaled, the net variances are identical to the amounts computed when the total overhead variance is analyzed. To illustrate, each of the actual overhead costs is listed below:

Indirect materials	$ 9,700
Indirect labor	16,000
Factory supplies	18,600
Maintenance	41,500
Utilities	22,800
Computer service charges	7,600
Property taxes	5,100
Insurance	4,700
Supervision	46,000
Depreciation, production plant	30,000
Depreciation, production equipment	40,000
Total	$242,000

The variance analysis for each overhead cost is summarized in Figure 9-11. If you wish, you may use the data above to compute the variances for one or more of the overhead costs to be certain that you understand the process.

USING MANUFACTURING OVERHEAD VARIANCES

As with other variance analysis, the primary purpose of manufacturing overhead variance analysis is to provide relevant information to managers

Overhead variance analysis helps managers monitor and control overhead costs as they do other costs

for planning, control, and performance measurement. Because overhead costs are by their nature indirect costs, they are more difficult to manage than direct production costs. Managers are interested in any overhead variance information that can help them efficiently manage overhead costs. The separation of variances into those dealing with fixed costs and those dealing with variable costs is important. Fixed cost variances, such as the volume variance, deal with issues of production capacity. If managers find that volume variances are consistently unfavorable, it may mean that the firm has too much production capacity and should attempt to reduce this capacity either by selling facilities or temporarily leasing some production space.

The controllable variance and the spending and efficiency variances address variable overhead costs, some of which are controllable by managers. By monitoring these variances carefully, managers may be able to modify the use of indirect labor, utilities, and other variable overhead resources to adjust for changes in the volume of activity.

SUMMARY

A major benefit of budgeting is the control over operations that is exercised through the comparison of actual results with the budget by means of budget performance reporting. Performance reports are most useful when budget data are based on an activity level that closely approximates the level of activity actually achieved. A useful method of developing relevant budget data is **flexible budgeting,** which means that budgets are prepared for more than one level of activity. Performance reports can then be prepared from a budget based on the actual level of activity. Flexible budgets are dynamic because they cover a range of activity, and they facilitate efficiency measurement.

The first step in flexible budgeting is to determine the range of activity to be covered by the budget. Next, cost behavior patterns are identified for all costs for the activity range of the budget. Management selects a number of activity levels within the range of the budget, and budgets are prepared for each selected activity level. Actual operating data are accumulated for the period and compared with budget data for the activity level achieved.

Flexible budgets are useful in developing manufacturing overhead rates and analyzing overhead variances. A flexible budget allows managers to distinguish between the variable and fixed components of overhead cost. Total variable overhead costs change proportionately with activity levels and therefore are a constant component of the overhead rate throughout the relevant range of the flexible budget. The total fixed overhead cost is constant throughout the relevant range and results in a declining overhead rate as the activity base is increased and the constant fixed cost is spread over more activity.

As with other variance analyses, manufacturing overhead variance analysis addresses the issues of the magnitude and cause of the variance. Total overhead variance may be divided into several components. The **two-variance method** isolates a controllable and a volume variance. The **controllable variance** measures the amount that actual overhead differs from the standard amount, given the number of units produced. It is the difference between actual overhead and a flexible budget based on actual output. The **volume variance** is the difference between a flexible budget based on standard hours and applied overhead. It shows the result of operating at a volume above or below normal capacity.

The **three-variance method** identifies spending, efficiency, and volume variances. The **spending variance** is a comparison between actual overhead and a flexible budget based on actual input. It measures the amount that actual overhead differs from planned overhead for the number of hours actually worked. The **efficiency variance** is the difference between standard and actual hours times the variable overhead rate. It describes the amount of overhead variance attributable to using more or fewer labor hours than standard. The **volume variance** is the same as the one computed in the two-variance method.

KEY TERMS

capacity variance *(378)*
controllable variance *(376)*
denominator variance *(378)*
dynamic budget *(360)*
efficiency variance *(378)*
fixed budget *(359)*
flexible budget *(360)*
manufacturing overhead variance analysis *(373)*
normal capacity *(371)*
relevant range *(365)*
spending variance *(378)*
static budget *(360)*
three-variance method *(377)*
two-variance method *(375)*
volume variance *(376)*

QUESTIONS

1. Define and contrast fixed budgeting and flexible budgeting.
2. Briefly describe the characteristics of a flexible budget.
3. What are the steps involved in the flexible budgeting process?
4. What is meant by the relevant range and how does it affect the development of a flexible budget?
5. What does the volume variance measure? How do you determine whether the volume variance is favorable or unfavorable?
6. "Why are you having Jones waste time and money preparing a budget for last quarter's operations? We already know what happened last quarter, and 3 months earlier you convinced me that we should waste our time preparing four budgets for the quarter instead of one. I gave in then, but this is too much." Explain to the new vice president why another budget is needed in addition to the flexible budget already prepared earlier.
7. What variance is identified by comparing a flexible budget based on inputs with a flexible budget based on outputs?
8. Distinguish between the spending variance and the controllable variance.
9. What is the efficiency variance? Why does it occur?
10. Are the overhead efficiency variance and the labor efficiency variance the same thing? Explain.
11. "Tell the new accountant I just hired that he made a mistake. This variance report shows an efficiency variance for direct labor and another one for manufacturing overhead. Doesn't he know where the efficiency variance belongs?" Respond to this statement.

EXERCISES

Ex. 9-1 Preparing a flexible budget. Bayview Department Store uses a flexible budgeting system to plan and monitor operations. Using historical accounting data, the firm's accountant has accumulated the following costs.

Item	Fixed Cost	Variable Cost per Sales Dollar
Advertising	$ 8,500	—
Building lease cost	15,000	$.02
Commissions	—	.08
Cost of goods sold	—	.40
Employee fringe benefits	6,000	.04
Equipment rent	4,500	—
Insurance	2,400	.01
Maintenance	6,400	—
Miscellaneous	2,000	.02
Property taxes	3,800	—
Salaries and wages	68,000	—
Utilities	5,400	.03

Required: Prepare a flexible budget for the Bayview Department Store using sales levels of $300,000, $350,000, and $400,000.

Ex. 9-2 Flexible budget performance report. Refer to the flexible budget and cost data presented in Exercise 9-1 for the Bayview Department Store. The following actual sales and expenses occurred during the budget year.

	Actual
Sales	$362,000
Advertising	9,700
Building lease cost	24,300
Commissions	27,600
Cost of goods sold	137,700
Employee fringe benefits	22,200
Equipment rent	6,900
Insurance	5,500
Maintenance	8,800
Miscellaneous	6,200
Property taxes	3,500
Salaries and wages	66,000
Utilities	17,900
Total expenses	336,300
Net income	$ 25,700

Required: Prepare a flexible budget performance report for the year.

Ex. 9-3 Manufacturing overhead flexible budget and overhead rate. Below are summarized cost behavior data for the manufacturing overhead activities of a small firm. The company uses units of output as its measure of activity and as the base for applying manufacturing overhead to products.

	Fixed Costs	Variable Costs per Unit
Indirect materials	$ 3,500	$.40
Indirect labor	4,000	.30
Factory utilities	8,000	.15
Factory insurance	3,600	—
Factory property taxes	12,900	—
Maintenance	5,000	.15
Depreciation, manufacturing equipment	10,000	—
Depreciation, manufacturing plant	14,000	—
Employee benefits	—	.60
First aid room	4,000	.05
Cafeteria for the manufacturing plant	8,000	.35
Manufacturing supervisory salaries	26,000	.20

Required:

a. Prepare a flexible budget for manufacturing overhead costs for 30,000, 40,000, and 50,000 units of activity.

b. If 40,000 units is the normal capacity, determine the manufacturing overhead rate for the period.

Ex. 9-4 Developing a flexible budget. Hillsdale Hospital operates a cafeteria for visitors, outpatients, and staff. The manager of the cafeteria wants to prepare a flexible budget because the cafeteria experiences significant differences in the number of meals it serves from one month to the next. Cost behavior data for the cafeteria are presented below.

	Costs	
	Fixed	Variable per Meal
Wages	$160,000	$ .30
Rental expense	20,000	—
Food costs	—	2.20
Utilities	4,000	.20
Maintenance	18,000	.20
Insurance	10,000	—
Supplies	10,000	.30

Average revenue per meal served is $4.50.

Required:

a. Prepare a flexible budget for the cafeteria using 150,000, 175,000, and 200,000 meals served as activity levels.

b. At what level of activity does the cafeteria break even?

Ex. 9-5 Fixed and flexible budget performance reports. Seidler University Student Bookstore made the following cost estimates for budgeting purposes:

Cost Item	Fixed	Variable per Dollar of Sales
Product cost	—	$.60
Employee wages	$16,000	.14
Supervisory salaries	25,000	.02
Supplies	1,000	.01
Utilities	3,000	.02
Rent	6,000	.01
Insurance	4,000	—

In 1986 the bookstore experienced the following results:

Sales	$350,000
Product cost	(217,000)
Employee wages	(66,000)
Supervisory salaries	(33,000)
Supplies	(4,000)
Utilities	(8,500)
Rent	(9,500)
Insurance	(4,000)
Profit	$ 8,000

Required:

a. Prepare a fixed budget performance report based on an estimated sales level of $300,000.

b. Prepare a flexible budget performance report.

Ex. 9-6 Two-variance manufacturing overhead analysis. The Columbus Musical Instruments Company uses direct labor hours to apply manufacturing overhead costs to production. The company's 1986 budgeted manufacturing overhead cost is $800,000, of which $320,000 is fixed cost. The company's normal capacity is 100,000 direct labor hours.

At the end of 1986, the firm had a balance of $832,400 in its Manufacturing Overhead Control account. Direct labor hours actually worked were 106,400 and standard hours for the production output achieved were 104,200.

Required: Prepare a two-variance analysis of overhead for the Columbus Musical Instruments Company.

Ex. 9-7 Three-variance manufacturing overhead analysis. Refer to the Columbus Musical Instruments Company data in Exercise 9-6.

Required: Use the data to prepare a three-variance analysis of manufacturing overhead for the Columbus Musical Instruments Company.

Ex. 9-8 Identifying favorable and unfavorable MOH variances. Jonas Manufacturing Company uses direct labor hours as the basis for applying manufacturing overhead to production. Below are budgeted, actual, and standard direct labor hours for three separate manufacturing divisions of the firm. The company uses a standard costing system in all divisions and uses the three-variance method of analyzing manufacturing overhead variances.

	Division		
	A	B	C
Budgeted hours	22,000	30,000	15,000
Actual hours	24,000	31,000	15,400
Standard hours	24,800	30,500	14,900

Required: For **each** firm determine the direction (favorable or unfavorable) of the manufacturing overhead efficiency variance, volume variance, and labor efficiency variance.

Ex. 9-9 Understanding overhead cost relationships. Piney Island Manufacturing, Inc., uses the three-variance method to analyze manufacturing overhead variances. Manufacturing overhead variances for the fiscal year just ended were computed as follows:

Spending	$8,600 U
Efficiency	3,600 F
Volume	8,000 F

The manufacturing overhead application rate for the year was $16 per machine hour, of which $6 per machine hour was the variable component. The year-end balance in the firm's Manufacturing Overhead Control account was $165,000, and standard machine hours for the year were 11,300.

Required: From the above data compute:

a. The fixed part of the overhead rate.
b. Budgeted machine hours.
c. Actual machine hours.
d. Applied manufacturing overhead.
e. The total amount of fixed overhead cost.

Ex. 9-10 The impact of overhead costs. A manufacturing company applies overhead to production using an overhead rate of $10 per direct labor hour. The rate is based on total budgeted overhead of $600,000, of which $450,000 is fixed cost. The company has been using 60,000 direct labor hours as its normal capacity for establishing its overhead rate.

Actual manufacturing overhead during the current year was $562,500, and the actual volume of activity was 45,000 direct labor hours. For the past several years the firm's activity level has been around 45,000 direct labor hours rather than the

60,000 used as the measure of normal capacity. Several key managers feel that competition and the economy in general have had a permanent effect on the company's normal capacity, and they consequently feel that 45,000 direct labor hours should be used as the firm's normal capacity in establishing the overhead rate.

The company has a government contract for the production of a tank stabilizer bar. The contract calls for a price equal to actual manufacturing cost plus 40 percent. The completed job included prime costs of $90,000 and required 4,000 direct labor hours.

Required:

a. Determine the fixed and variable components of the company's current manufacturing overhead rate.
b. Compute the manufacturing overhead rate if the correct normal capacity is 45,000 direct labor hours.
c. Compute the price of the government contract using the new normal capacity of 45,000 direct labor hours.

Ex. 9-11 (CMA) Overhead variances. King Company estimates that it will operate its manufacturing facilities at 800,000 direct labor hours for the year. The estimate for total budgeted overhead is $2,000,000. The standard variable overhead rate is estimated to be $2 per direct labor hour or $6 per unit. The actual data for the year are presented below:

Actual finished units	250,000
Actual direct labor hours	764,000
Actual variable overhead	$1,610,000
Actual fixed overhead	$392,000

Required: Respond to the following questions by selecting the best answer.

1. The variable overhead spending variance for the year is

   a. $2,000 F. b. $10,000 U. c. $82,000 U. d. $110,000 U.
   e. some amount other than those shown above.

2. The variable overhead efficiency variance for the year is

   a. $28,000 U. b. $100,000 U. c. $110,000 U.
   d. determined from information other than given above.
   e. some amount other than those shown above.

3. The fixed overhead spending variance for the year is

   a. $8,000 F. b. $10,000 U. c. $17,000 U. d. $74,000 U.
   e. some amount other than those shown above.

4. The fixed overhead volume variance for the year is

   a. $7,000 U. b. $25,000 U. c. $41,667 U. d. $18,000 F.
   e. some amount other than those shown above.

Ex. 9-12 **(AICPA) Analyzing overhead variances.** Milner Manufacturing Company uses a job order costing system and standard costs. It manufactures one product whose standard cost is as follows:

Materials: 20 yards at \$.90 per yard	\$18
Direct labor: 4 hours at \$6 per hour	24
Total factory overhead: Applied at the rate of 5/6 of direct labor cost (the ratio of variable MOH costs to fixed MOH costs is 3 to 1)	20
Variable selling and administrative expense	12
Fixed selling and administrative expense	7
Total cost per unit	\$81

The standard costs are based on normal activity of 2,400 direct labor hours. Actual activity for the month of October was as follows:

Units produced		500
Materials purchased	18,000 yards at \$.92 per yard	\$16,560
Material used	9,500 yards	
Direct labor	2,100 hours at \$6.10 per hour	12,810
Total factory overhead		11,100

Required: Compute the following:

a. The variable factory overhead rate per direct labor hour and the total fixed factory overhead based on normal activity.
b. The controllable overhead variance.
c. The volume overhead variance.

Ex. 9-13 **(CMA) Three-variance overhead analysis.** Standard Company has developed standard overhead costs based on a capacity of 180,000 direct labor hours as follows:

Standard overhead costs per unit:

Variable portion	2 hours @ \$3 =	\$ 6
Fixed portion	2 hours @ \$5 =	10
Total overhead cost		\$16

During April, 85,000 units were scheduled for production; however, only 80,000 units were actually produced. Following are April data:

Actual direct labor cost incurred was \$644,000 for 165,000 actual hours of work.

Actual overhead incurred totaled \$1,378,000: \$518,000 variable and \$860,000 fixed.

All inventories are carried at standard cost.

Required: Respond to the following questions by selecting the best answer.

1. The overhead spending variance for April was

a. \$15,000 U. **b.** \$23,000 U. **c.** \$38,000 F. **d.** \$38,000 U.
e. some amount other than those given above.

2. The overhead efficiency variance for April was

   a. $15,000 U. b. $23,000 U. c. $38,000 F. d. $38,000 U.
   e. some amount other than those given above.

3. The fixed overhead budget spending variance for April was

   a. $40,000 U. b. $40,000 F. c. $60,000 F. d. $60,000 U.
   e. some amount other than those given above.

4. The fixed overhead volume variance for April was

   a. $60,000 U. b. $60,000 F. c. $100,000 F. d. $100,000 U.
   e. some amount other than those given above.

PROBLEMS

P. 9-1 **Flexible budget performance report.** The Snyder Shoe Shop uses a flexible budget to plan operations and measure performance. Below are budgeted and actual data for the shop for 1986. The company uses sales dollars as its measure of activity.

	Flexible Budget		Actual Results
Sales	$800,000	$1,000,000	$850,000
Cost of goods sold	480,000	600,000	493,000
Depreciation	15,000	15,000	15,000
Supervisory salaries	45,000	45,000	42,000
Commissions	120,000	150,000	119,000
Advertising	36,000	40,000	42,000
Maintenance	20,000	23,000	21,000
Utilities	18,000	20,000	24,000
Insurance	14,000	15,000	14,000
Total expenses	748,000	908,000	770,000
Profit	$ 52,000	$ 92,000	$ 80,000

Required: Prepare a flexible budget variance analysis report.

P. 9-2 **Flexible budget analysis for a manufacturing firm.** M-V Company is planning to use a flexible budgeting system to plan and control its operations. The firm's data analysis expert has accumulated the preceding 2 years' cost data for use in the cost analysis. The data are presented at the top of page 391.

Required:

a. Prepare a schedule showing the cost behavior formula for each of the costs presented based on direct labor hours.
b. Prepare a flexible budget for 45,000, 48,000, and 51,000 direct labor hours for 1987.

	1985	1986
Direct labor hours	40,000	50,000
Sales	$1,800,000	$2,250,000
Direct labor cost	320,000	400,000
Direct materials	480,000	600,000
Depreciation	80,000	80,000
Property taxes	30,000	30,000
Maintenance	140,000	160,000
Utilities	55,000	65,000
Supervision	120,000	125,000
Administration	208,000	210,000
Marketing	270,000	315,000

c. Actual activity for the year was 49,500 direct labor hours, which provided a profit of $260,000. Using flexible budgeting analysis, what is the total variance from expected profit?

P. 9-3 Flexible budget performance report. Evergreen Art Studio sells a wide variety of art supplies in a small resort community. The studio also offers art lessons in a variety of media for beginners and advanced students. About 60 percent of the studio's income is derived from the sale of art supplies and the remaining income is from art lessons. The volume of business depends a lot on the number of visitors to the resort community, which in turn is affected significantly by the weather. Cindy Evans, the manager of the art studio, thinks that total sales of products and services will be $300,000 in 1986. Cindy asked her accountant to prepare some cost data to help her plan and evaluate the performance of the art studio. The accountant prepared the following schedule of costs, with variable costs expressed in amount per sales dollar.

	Fixed Costs	Variable Costs
Supervisory salaries	$35,000	
Wages and commissions	45,000	$.10
Product expense	—	.25
Studio lease	24,000	.03
Insurance	4,000	—
Depreciation, furniture and equipment	5,000	—
Maintenance	6,000	.02
Teaching supplies	1,000	.09
Office supplies	500	.01
Employee benefits	9,500	.03
Utilities	1,800	.01
Miscellaneous	2,000	.01

During 1986, the Evergreen Art Studio had sales of $350,000 that resulted in the following income statement:

Evergreen Art Studio
Income Statement
For the Year Ended December 31, 1986

Sales		$350,000
Supervisory salaries	$36,500	
Wages and commissions	77,000	
Product expense	85,800	
Studio lease	34,500	
Insurance	4,000	
Depreciation, furniture and equipment	5,500	
Maintenance	12,200	
Teaching supplies	30,500	
Office supplies	3,800	
Employee benefits	22,200	
Utilities	5,000	
Miscellaneous	5,900	322,900
Net income		$ 27,100

Required:

a. Prepare a flexible budget performance report for the Evergreen Art Studio for 1986.

b. At what level of sales does the studio break even?

P. 9-4 Flexible budget performance report. The city of Hershfield owns and operates its own electric power company, which supplies electricity for the area. The company is not expected to earn a normal profit, but rates are set so as to meet all costs, with a small surplus remaining to cover unexpected costs or other contingencies. Budget and actual data for 1986 are shown below.

Hershfield Municipal Power Company
Flexible Budget
For the Year 1986

	Budgeted Kilowatt Hours		Actual Results Kilowatt Hours
	60 million	**80 million**	**75 million**
Revenue	$2,700,000	$3,600,000	$3,375,000
Labor	580,000	740,000	665,000
Maintenance	240,000	260,000	240,000
Coal	1,200,000	1,600,000	1,615,000
Depreciation	250,000	250,000	250,000
Supplies	110,000	140,000	128,500
Supervision	150,000	160,000	146,500
Insurance	20,000	20,000	21,000
Miscellaneous	90,000	110,000	126,000
Profit	$ 60,000	$ 320,000	$ 183,000

Required: Prepare a flexible budget variance analysis report.

P. 9-5 Flexible budget and budget analysis. Malstrom Industries plans to start using flexible budgeting for its 3-year-old farm grain wagon manufacturing division. Costs that are completely fixed are depreciation, $160,000; property taxes, $40,000; and insurance, $18,000. Completely variable costs include direct material of $700 per wagon and direct labor of $400 per wagon. Each wagon requires 40 direct labor hours. Wagons sell for $1,800 each. Other costs are mixed, with fixed and variable components. Below are 1984 and 1985 data for the mixed cost items.

	1984	1985
Direct labor hours	100,000	120,000
Indirect materials	$ 60,000	$ 70,000
Indirect labor	105,000	121,000
Utilities	85,000	99,000
Maintenance	100,000	108,000
Supervision	200,000	204,000
Miscellaneous overhead	60,000	64,000
Administrative	430,000	436,000
Marketing	370,000	424,000

Required:

a. Prepare a schedule showing the cost behavior pattern of each mixed cost.

b. Prepare a flexible budget for the division for 1986 using production levels of 3,000, 3,200, and 3,400 wagons. Assume these activity levels are within the relevant range of the cost behavior patterns experienced in 1984 and 1985.

c. Actual sales for 1986 were 3,350 wagons, yielding a profit of $682,000. Using flexible budget data, determine the total variance from expected profit.

P. 9-6 Using overhead cost relationships. Below are standard cost data for the production of wheelbarrows for Ramshee Corporation:

Labor time	1½ hr per wheelbarrow
Labor rate	$8 per hr
Overhead rate	$10 per labor hr
Fixed manufacturing overhead	$90,000
Normal capacity	15,000 direct labor hr

During the year actual production was 10,500 wheelbarrows, actual overhead cost was $152,000, and actual hours worked was 15,200.

Required:

a. Calculate the variable part of the overhead rate.

b. Calculate the standard conversion cost of each wheelbarrow.

c. Compute the manufacturing overhead variances using the three-variance method.

d. Compute the direct labor efficiency variance.

e. Explain why the labor efficiency variance and the overhead efficiency variance are different.

P. 9-7 Two- and three-variance overhead analysis. Rico Concrete Products manufactures concrete garden ornaments and figures. The company uses a standard cost system and applies overhead using a direct labor hours application base. Normal capacity is 10,000 direct labor hours. The overhead rate of $6 per hour is split on a ⅓ to ⅔ basis between variable and fixed overhead costs, respectively. During the accounting year just completed, the following occurred:

Actual overhead cost	$60,000
Actual direct labor hours	9,800
Standard direct labor hours	10,300

Required:

a. Prepare a two-variance analysis of overhead variances.
b. Prepare a three-variance analysis of overhead variances.

P. 9-8 Two methods of computing manufacturing overhead variances. Hilo Drilling Equipment Company makes drill bits for oil-drilling activities. The Deloid Division makes the firm's DB-220 bit, which has budgeted production of 4,000 units for 1987. The company uses machine hours to apply manufacturing overhead to production and each drill bit requires 6 hours of machine time. The variable overhead rate is $5 per machine hour and budgeted fixed manufacturing overhead is $108,000 for 1987.

During 1987, 4,150 DB-220 bits were manufactured using 25,460 actual machine hours. The balance in the Manufacturing Overhead Control account at year-end was $226,780.

Required:

a. Compute manufacturing overhead variances using the two-variance method.
b. Compute manufacturing overhead variances using the three-variance method.

P. 9-9 Interpreting overhead variances. Following are overhead data for the Blackwell Company:

Manufacturing overhead rate:	
Variable	$2 per direct labor hr
Fixed	$3 per direct labor hr
Budgeted direct labor hours	30,000

The three-variance method of analyzing overhead yields the following:

Spending variance	$6,000 U
Efficiency variance	3,000 U
Volume variance	1,500 U

Required: From the data above determine:

a. Standard hours.
b. Actual hours worked.
c. Applied overhead.
d. Actual overhead.
e. Controllable variance.

P. 9-10 (AICPA) Flexible budgeting and performance reports. Department A is one of 15 departments in the plant and is involved in the production of all the six products manufactured. The department is highly mechanized, and as a result its output is measured in direct machine hours. Variable (flexible) budgets are utilized throughout the factory in planning and controlling costs, but here the focus is upon the application of variable budgets only in department A. The following data covering a time span of approximately 6 months were taken from the various budgets, accounting records, and performance reports (only representative items and amounts are utilized here):

- On March 15, 1986, the following variable budget was approved for the department; it will be used throughout the 1987 fiscal year, which begins July 1, 1986. This variable budget was developed through the cooperative efforts of the department manager, his supervisor, and certain staff members from the budget department.

1987 Variable Budget—Department A

Controllable Costs	Fixed Amount per Month	Variable Cost per Direct Machine Hour
Employee salaries	$ 9,000	
Indirect wages	18,000	$.07
Indirect materials		.09
Other costs	6,000	.03
Totals	$33,000	$.19

- On May 5, 1986, the annual sales plan and the production budget were completed. In order to continue preparation of the annual profit plan (which was detailed by month) the production budget was translated to planned activity for each of the factory departments. The planned activity for department A was:

	For the 12 Months Ending June 30, 1987				
	Year	July	Aug.	Sept.	Etc.
Planned output in direct machine hours	325,000	22,000	25,000	29,000	249,000

- On August 31, 1986, the manager of department A was informed that his planned output for September had been revised to 34,000 direct machine hours. He expressed some doubt as to whether this volume could be attained.

- At the end of September 1986 the accounting records provided the following actual data for the month for the department:

Actual output in direct machine hours	33,000
Actual controllable costs incurred:	
Employee salaries	$ 9,300
Indirect wages	20,500
Indirect materials	2,850
Other costs	7,510
Total	$40,160

Required: The requirements relate primarily to the potential uses of the variable budget for the period March through September 1986.

a. What activity base is utilized as a measure of volume in the budget for this department? How should one determine the range of the activity base to which the variable tasks per direct machine hours are relevant? Explain.

b. The high-low method was utilized in developing this variable budget. Using indirect wage costs as an example, illustrate and explain how this method would be applied in determining the fixed and variable components of indirect wage costs for this department. Assume that the high-low budget values for indirect wages are $19,400 at 20,000 direct machine hours and $20,100 at 30,000 direct machine hours.

c. Explain and illustrate how the variable budget should be utilized:

1. In budgeting costs when the annual sales plan and production budget are completed (about May 5, 1986, or shortly thereafter).
2. In budgeting a cost revision based upon a revised production budget (about August 31, 1986, or shortly thereafter).
3. In preparing a cost performance report for September 1986.

P. 9-11 Overhead variance relationships. B and B Enterprises manufactures electronic sensing devices used in quality control programs. The standard direct labor time for each sensing device is 8 hours. Manufacturing overhead is applied to production at the rate of $5 per direct labor hour.

Budgeted production for 1986 was 2,500 units. Budgeted fixed cost was $60,000. During 1986, 2,375 sensing devices were actually produced. The following overhead variances were computed using the three-variance method of overhead variance analysis.

Spending variance	$7,800 U
Efficiency variance	4,000 U
Volume variance	3,000 U

Required: Using the above data compute:

a. Budgeted direct labor hours.

b. Standard direct labor hours.

c. The amount of applied overhead.

d. The balance in the Manufacturing Overhead Control account at the end of 1986.

e. The actual direct labor hours worked.

f. The amount of overhead cost that should have been incurred given the number of units produced.

P. 9-12 (AICPA) Comprehensive standard costing problem with two-variance overhead analysis. Conti Pharmaceutical Company processes a single compound product known as NULAX and uses a standard cost accounting system. The process requires preparation and blending of three materials in large batches with a variation from the standard mixture sometimes necessary to maintain quality. Conti's cost accountant became ill at the end of October 1986 and you were engaged to determine standard costs of October production and to explain any differences between actual and standard costs for the month. The following information is available on the blending department:

1. The standard cost card for a 500-pound batch shows the following standard costs:

	Quantity	Price	Total Cost	
Materials:				
Mucilloid	250 pounds	$.14	$35	
Dextrose	200 pounds	.09	18	
Ingredients	50 pounds	.08	4	
Total per batch	500 pounds			$ 57
Labor:				
Preparation and blending	10 hours	$3.00		30
Overhead:				
Variable	10 hours	$1.00	10	
Fixed	10 hours	.30	3	13
Total standard cost per 500-pound batch				$100

2. During October, 410 batches of 500 pounds each of the finished compound were completed and transferred to the packaging department.
3. Blending department inventories totaled 6,000 pounds at the beginning of the month and 9,000 pounds at the end of the month (assume both inventories were completely processed but not transferred and consisted of materials in their standard proportions). Inventories are carried in the accounts at standard cost.
4. During October the following materials were purchased and put into production:

	Pounds	Price	Total Cost
Mucilloid	114,400	$.17	$19,448
Dextrose	85,800	.11	9,438
Ingredients	19,800	.07	1,386
Totals	220,000		$30,272

5. Wages paid for 4,212 hours of direct labor at $3.25 per hour amounted to $13,689.
6. Actual overhead costs for the month totaled $5,519.
7. The standards were established for a normal production volume of 200,000 pounds (400 batches) of NULAX per month. At this level of production variable factory overhead was budgeted at $4,000 and fixed factory overhead was budgeted at $1,200.

Required:

a. Prepare a schedule presenting the computation for the blending department of:

1. October production in both pounds and batches.
2. The standard cost of October production itemized by components of materials, labor, and overhead.

b. Prepare schedules computing the differences between actual and standard costs and analyzing the differences as:

1. Materials variances for each material caused by
   (*a*) Price differences.
   (*b*) Quantity differences.
2. Labor variances caused by
   (*a*) Rate difference.
   (*b*) Efficiency difference.
3. Overhead variances caused by
   (*a*) Controllable factors.
   (*b*) Volume factors.

P. 9-13 Comprehensive standard cost variance analysis. Heather Candy Factory makes valentine candy. Below are production standards for candy production.

Standards		
Materials	**Quantity**	**Price**
Sugar	6 lb/10-lb carton of output	$ .06/lb
Syrup	1 gal/10-lb carton of output	2.60/gal
Flavoring	1 qt/10-lb carton of output	4.00/gal
Coloring	1 pt/10-lb carton of output	6.00/gal
Labor	**Quantity**	**Rate**
Blending	4 hr per 100-lb case	$5.50/hr
Cooking	2 hr per 100-lb case	5.00/hr
Manufacturing Overhead		
Fixed cost	$21,000	
Variable cost	$4.00/DLH	
Expected level of activity	3,500 hr	

During the year the following production volume and costs occurred.

Actual Results for the Period		
Produced	60,000 lb of Valentine candy	
Material	**Quantity**	**Cost**
Sugar	37,000 lb	$ 2,960
Syrup	5,800 gal	20,300
Flavoring	1,400 gal	5,460
Coloring	700 gal	3,920
Labor	**Hours**	**Cost**
Blending	2,500	$13,250
Cooking	1,050	5,460
Total manufacturing overhead		$35,000

Note: There are 2 pints in a quart, 4 quarts in a gallon.

Required:

a. Compute the material price and quantity variances.
b. Determine the labor rate and efficiency variances.
c. Compute overhead variances using the two-variance method.
d. Find the standard cost of 1 pound of Valentine candy.
e. Compute the actual cost of 1 pound of Valentine candy.

P. 9-14 (CMA) Performance evaluation with flexible budgeting. The Jason Plant of Cast Corporation has been in operation for 15 months. Jason employs a standard cost system for its manufacturing operations. The first 6 months' performance was affected by the usual problems associated with a new operation. Since that time the operations have been running smoothly. Unfortunately, however, the plant has not been able to produce profits on a consistent basis. As the production requirements to meet sales demand have increased, the profit performance has deteriorated.

The plant production manager commented at a staff meeting in which the plant general manager, the corporate controller, and the corporate budget director were in attendance that the changing production requirements make it more difficult to control manufacturing expenses. He further noted that the budget for the plant, included in the company's annual profit plan, was not useful for judging the plant's performance because of the changes in the operating levels. The meeting resulted in a decision to prepare a report which would compare the plant's actual manufacturing expense performance with a budget of manufacturing expense based on actual direct labor hours in the plant.

The plant production manager and the plant accountant studied the cost patterns for recent months, and volume and cost data from other Cast plants. Then they prepared the following flexible budget schedule for a month with 200,000 planned production hours, which at standard would result in 50,000 units of output. The corporate controller reviewed and approved the flexible budget.

	Amount	Per Direct Labor Hour
Manufacturing expenses		
Variable		
Indirect labor	$160,000	$ .80
Supplies	26,000	.13
Power	14,000	.07
Variable cost per unit		$1.00
Fixed		
Supervisory labor	64,000	
Heat and light	15,000	
Property taxes	5,000	
Total fixed costs	$284,000	

The manufacturing expense reports prepared for the first 3 months after the flexible budget program was approved were pleasing to the plant production manager. They showed that manufacturing expenses were in line with the flexible budget allowance. This was also reflected by the report prepared for November, which is presented below, when 50,500 units were manufactured. However, the plant was still not producing an adequate profit because the variances from standard costs were quite large.

Jason Plant
Manufacturing Expenses
November 1986
220,000 Actual Direct Labor Production Hours

	Actual Costs	Allowed Costs	(Over) Under Budget
Variable			
Indirect labor	$177,000	$176,000	$(1,000)
Supplies	27,400	28,600	1,200
Power	16,000	15,400	(600)
Fixed			
Supervisory labor	65,000	64,000	(1,000)
Heat and light	15,500	15,000	(500)
Property taxes	5,000	5,000	0
Totals	$305,900	$304,000	$(1,900)

Required:

a. Explain the advantages of flexible budgeting over fixed budgeting for cost control purposes.

b. Calculate the excess amount over standard spent on manufacturing expense items during November 1986. Analyze this excess amount into those variances due to:
   1. efficiency.
   2. spending.

c. Explain what the management of Jason Plant should do to reduce:
   1. the efficiency variance.
   2. the spending variance.

P. 9-15 **Standard cost variances.** The Efflin Division of the Maudlin Company makes folding chairs. The standard costs for the production of the chairs are presented below.

Direct materials: 10 feet of tubular steel @ $.40 per foot	$ 4.00
5 square feet of steel @ $.30 per square foot	1.50
Direct labor: 1.5 hours @ $9.00 per hour	13.50
Manufacturing overhead: 1.5 hours @ $6.00 per hour	9.00
Total standard cost of one folding chair	$28.00

The manufacturing overhead rate is based on expected production of 4,000 chairs. The variable part of the overhead rate is $2.00 per hour. During the period 4,200 chairs were manufactured. The division incurred the following production costs.

Direct materials: 47,300 feet of tubular steel, cost	$ 17,974
20,200 square feet of steel, cost	6,666
Direct labor: 5,900 hours, cost	55,460
Manufacturing overhead: actual cost	35,480
Total manufacturing costs	$115,580

Required:

a. Compute the direct material price and quantity variances.
b. Compute the direct labor rate and efficiency variances.
c. Compute the manufacturing overhead spending, efficiency, and volume variances.
d. Compute the total amount of variance and compute the total variance as a percentage of standard cost.
e. Prepare a report showing the savings caused by the efficiency of production labor for the period.

CASE

Case 9-1 Flexible budget analysis for a manufacturing business

Home-spun Industries manufactures modular homes in its Indiana manufacturing plant. The modular homes sell for $38,000 each. Analysis of production and marketing data shows that direct materials costs are $13,200 per unit and direct labor costs are $7,000 per unit. Each modular home requires 700 direct labor hours at standard.

Fixed costs for the year are $130,000 for property taxes, $180,000 for insurance, $250,000 of building depreciation, and $220,000 of equipment depreciation. A flexible budget is presented on page 402 for accounts that include both fixed and variable components.

Direct labor hours	120,000	150,000
Indirect materials	$180,000	$210,000
Indirect labor	270,000	330,000
Maintenance	360,000	375,000
Utilities	300,000	345,000
Production supervision	405,000	412,500
Miscellaneous	165,000	187,500
Administration	660,000	675,000
Marketing and distribution	540,000	600,000

An engineering consulting firm recently completed a study of Home-spun Industries' production operations and has made recommendations that if implemented should cut $400,000 from the firm's fixed production costs and 10 percent from the firm's total variable costs.

Required:

a. Prepare a schedule showing the cost behavior for the mixed costs.
b. Prepare a flexible budget for Home-spun Industries using activity levels of 175, 225, and 275 modular homes.
c. During the year, 250 modular homes were produced and sold yielding a profit of $197,400. Using the flexible budget data, determine the total variance from expected profit at that production level.
d. Compute the variance as a percentage of total expected costs.
e. At the current level of expected costs, how many units must the company sell to break even?
f. Assuming the consulting firm's cost-cutting plan can be achieved, what will be the new expected break-even level?
g. Assuming the expected cost savings are achieved from the consulting firm's recommendations, what would be the expected profit at production and sales of 240 units?

Costing Nonmanufacturing Activities and the Contribution Approach to Costing

10

Nonmanufacturing activities comprise a significant portion of the economic activity in this country, and it is essential that managers efficiently manage these activities. Of course costs play a major role in nonmanufacturing activities just as they do with manufactured products. When you have completed the chapter, you should understand:

1 The similarities and differences between costing manufacturing and nonmanufacturing activities.

2 The nature of segment reporting and how performance is measured for different parts of a business.

3 The form and content of the different types of segment performance reports.

4 The concept of variable costing, sometimes called direct costing.

5 The similarities and differences between variable costing and absorption costing.

6 The determination of product costs using both variable and absorption costing.

7 The different types of information provided by variable and absorption costing income statements.

8 The cause of any difference in net income between variable and absorption costing for a particular year.

Most of our discussions of cost measurement and reporting concepts are illustrated with manufacturing situations. This is done because cost accounting systems were first used in manufacturing operations and because costing tangible products is easy to understand. In this chapter, we turn our attention to costing of nonmanufacturing activities, which currently constitute a significant portion of all economic activity. Service firms, merchandising firms, and even the nonmanufacturing activities of manufacturing firms are included in this segment of the economy. Marketing, general administration, engineering, and accounting are examples of nonmanufacturing activities. In the first part of this chapter we discuss the costing of nonmanufacturing activities, noting the similarities and differences between costing for manufacturing and nonmanufacturing activities. The two types of activities are combined when we turn to segment reporting. The concept of contribution margin, introduced in Chapter 5, is extended to segment reporting and product costing.

COSTING NONMANUFACTURING ACTIVITIES

Costing manufacturing activities typically involves measuring the total cost of making some product or part of a product and dividing the total cost by the amount of output to find the unit cost of production. Unfortunately, not all nonmanufacturing activities lend themselves equally well to cost measurement. Most manufacturing activities are systematic and repetitive. The output is a single product or a set of homogeneous products. Many **nonmanufacturing activities** are not repetitive. For example, administrators, marketing managers, engineers, and other office personnel spend considerable time monitoring activities, analyzing problems, and making decisions. Although the types of problems and decisions may recur, these activities are not nearly as systematic and repetitive as most manufacturing activities. Because of these differences in the nature of activities, costing nonmanufacturing activities can be divided into two separate categories: costing repetitive activities that lend themselves to unit cost calculations, and segment reporting whereby costs are reported for parts of the organization.

Costing Repetitive Activities

Some nonmanufacturing activities are repetitive and generate a relatively homogeneous service or activity. Examples are the preparation of purchase orders, sales invoices, and checks, or making phone calls in a telephone marketing survey. Repetitive activities, whether they are manufacturing or

Repetitive activities can be costed like manufactured products

nonmanufacturing, lend themselves to detailed cost measurement and the determination of unit costs. The process is simple. First, the cost objective must be carefully defined; next, all direct costs are assigned to the cost objective; and finally, any indirect costs necessary for the activity are allocated to the cost objective.

We illustrate the costing of repetitive nonmanufacturing activities with the Home Market Sales Company, a catalog mail-order sales business. Each day orders received in the mail are sent to the order processing department, where product descriptions and numbers are verified with catalog information and a sales invoice is prepared. Management wants to measure the cost of processing orders. Data have been accumulated for the order processing department for the year. Using these data, we compute the average unit cost of processing orders. The direct costs include direct labor and the cost of the sales invoice. In addition, there are a number of indirect costs that cannot be identified with individual orders. Indirect costs for nonmanufacturing activities are treated similarly to indirect manufacturing costs. The cost of processing 30,000 orders is summarized in Figure 10-1.

Orders processed	30,000
Hours worked	18,000
Hourly rate	$ 5
Invoice forms cost (31,200 invoices)	7,800
Indirect supplies and materials	4,000
Utilities cost	6,000
Depreciation, building	4,000
Depreciation, equipment	2,000
Payroll fringe benefits	18,000
Other departmental indirect costs	8,000

Home Market Sales Company
Order Processing Costs
For the Year Ended December 31, 1986

	Total Cost	**Unit Cost***
Direct costs:		
Direct materials, invoice form	$ 7,800	$ .26
Direct labor	90,000	3.00
Total direct costs	97,800	3.26
Indirect costs:		
Indirect supplies and materials	4,000	
Utilities	6,000	
Depreciation, building	4,000	
Depreciation, equipment	2,000	
Payroll fringe benefits	18,000	
Other departmental indirect costs	8,000	
Total indirect costs	42,000	1.40
Total cost of processing orders	$139,800	$4.66

* Based on a total of 30,000 orders processed.

Figure 10-1
Order processing is a repetitive activity at Home Market Sales Company, and therefore unit costs can be determined in the same way as for a manufactured product. The unit costs are average unit costs for the year.

The computation of unit costs for processing a sales order is similar to the computation of units costs for a manufactured product. The direct costs are similar to prime costs and the indirect costs are similar to manufacturing overhead. The resulting unit cost is an average unit cost of processing orders during the year.

Standards for Nonmanufacturing Activities

Standard costs can be used for nonmanufacturing activities

The cost report in Figure 10-1 shows the average unit cost of processing one order but it does not indicate how the cost compares with management's expectations for the activity. Repetitive homogeneous activities, such as order processing, may be monitored and evaluated using standard costs in much the same manner as manufacturing activities. For example, the Home Market Sales Company has established the following standards for the order processing activity.

Standard costs per invoice processed:

Direct materials: 1 invoice form per order @ $.20 each

Direct labor: 35 minutes per order @ $5.25 per hour

Indirect cost: Allocated at the rate of $2.30 per direct labor hour

Actual results for the period were as follows:

Direct materials: Used 31,200 invoices at a cost of $.25 each

Direct labor: Used 18,000 hours at $5.00 per hour

Indirect costs: Incurred $42,000 of indirect costs

Using the standard and actual cost data, it is easy to construct a standard cost variance analysis report as shown in Figure 10-2. The material price variance for invoices is computed by subtracting the actual price of $.25 from the standard price of $.20 and multiplying by the 31,200 actual invoices used. The $1,560 variance is unfavorable because the company paid $.05 more than standard. The material quantity variance for invoices is also unfavorable because the company used 1,200 more invoices than standard in processing. The amount of the variance is $240, which is the 1,200 extra invoices used times their standard cost of $.20 each.

The labor rate variance is the difference between the standard and actual rates times the number of hours worked. The actual rate is $.25 an hour lower than standard, yielding a $4,500 favorable rate variance. The standard quantity of labor is 35 minutes per order. However, 18,000 actual hours were used to process the 30,000 orders. That is .6 hour per order, or .6 × 60 minutes = 36 minutes per order. The efficiency variance is 1 minute unfavorable times the 30,000 orders processed, which is 30,000 minutes, or 500 hours. Multiplying by the standard rate of $5.25 an hour yields a $2,625 unfavorable labor efficiency variance.

Home Market Sales Company
Variance Analysis Report for Order Processing
For the Year Ended December 31, 1986

Direct materials:		
Material price variance	($.20 − $.25) × 31,200	= $1,560 U
Material quantity variance	(30,000 forms − 31,200 forms) × $.20	= 240 U
Total materials variance		1,800 U
Direct labor:		
Labor rate variance	($5.25 − $5.00) × 18,000 hr	= 4,500 F
Labor efficiency variance	[(35 min − 36 min) × 30,000]/ 60 min/hr × $5.25	= 2,625 U
Total labor variance		1,875 F
Indirect costs:		
Standard indirect cost	17,500 hr × $2.30 = $40,250	
Actual indirect cost	42,000	
Indirect cost variance		1,750 U
Total variance for the year for order processing activities		$1,675 U

Figure 10-2 **Standard costs can be used to measure the performance of repetitive nonmanufacturing activities such as the order processing activity reported here.**

Indirect costs are assigned to order processing activities at the rate of $2.30 per standard labor hour. The 30,000 orders require 35/60 hours × 30,000 orders, or 17,500 standard hours. Multiplying 17,500 hours by the rate of $2.30 per hour yields $40,250, the standard amount of indirect cost for the year. The actual indirect cost is $42,000, which results in a $1,750 unfavorable variance. Total variance for the year for order processing is $1,675 unfavorable.

Although variance analysis reports are not common in nonmanufacturing activities, such reports are useful to managers. The detailed data can be used to identify cost trends, to highlight problem areas, and in general to monitor and control costs. The variance report presented in Figure 10-2 covers an entire year, but more timely reports, such as weekly or monthly, can be prepared. If the variance for any cost component indicates that management's attention is needed, action can be taken before serious problems develop. For example, the purchasing agent may decide that the high price of order forms warrants buying the forms from a new, less expensive supplier. The unfavorable labor efficiency variance may be the result of hiring less skilled employees than expected when the standards were established. However, the new employees were paid below-standard wages, yielding a net favorable labor rate variance. Managers can perform these and other analyses by evaluating performance reports and using other information about the personnel and activities covered by the performance report.

SEGMENT REPORTING

For the many nonmanufacturing activities that are not repetitive or that do not result in a homogeneous set of services, detailed standards and unit cost determinations are not feasible. Nonetheless, nonrepetitive activities require monitoring and controlling just as repetitive activities do. In many cases cost control is achieved by accumulating costs for each of the various segments of the firm, such as a department, a division, a marketing region, or any other part of an organization that management chooses to identify as a cost objective.

Segment reporting measures the performance of the various parts of an organization

Segment reporting is the process of reporting the performance of various parts or activities of an organization. How the organization is divided into segments for which reports are prepared depends on the information needs of management. Some examples of segment reports are as follows:

Income statements for each division of a company
Product profitability reports
Product profitability reports for sales regions
Departmental cost reports

Segment reports often combine the costs of manufacturing and nonmanufacturing activities. For example, division income statements and product profitability reports include product costs and costs of marketing and administrative activities.

The Business Segment Reporting Process

The variety and frequency of accounting reports for business segments is limited only by management's information requirements and its ability and desire to pay the cost of preparing the reports. The steps in preparing segment reports include the following:

Steps in measuring segment costs

1. Identify the cost objective.
2. Assign direct costs to the cost objective.
3. Allocate indirect costs to the cost objective.

Identify the cost objective. It is not difficult to define the cost objective for a single manufactured product or a repetitive homogeneous activity. With a business segment as the cost objective, the process can be more challenging. For example, if management is interested in determining the cost of marketing a particular product in one sales region of the country, the costing process may be complicated because some marketing efforts promote several products and other marketing programs benefit several sales regions. Identifying each dollar spent on marketing with specific marketing cost objectives can be complex. Therefore, accountants should utilize the knowledge of managers from all parts of the organization in an effort to identify as clearly as possible each cost objective to ensure that only appropriate costs are assigned to the objective.

Assign direct costs. Costs that are specifically identifiable with the cost objectives, such as direct materials and direct labor, are assigned directly to each cost objective. Typically these are variable costs that change proportionately with the volume of activity. Not all direct costs are variable, however; some direct costs for nonmanufacturing activities are fixed. For example, a $2 million annual contract for television advertising is a fixed cost directly identifiable with the marketing cost objective. Many cost objectives have fixed costs that are directly traceable to a specific activity.

Allocate indirect costs. Indirect costs are those that are necessary but not directly traceable to the cost objective. Some nonmanufacturing activities have significant indirect costs. A data processing department, for example, has a large amount of occupancy cost, equipment cost, and management cost, all of which are indirect. As with manufactured products, indirect costs of nonmanufacturing activities should be assigned to cost objectives using the matching principle as a guide.

Once the cost objective has been identified, assigning direct costs and allocating indirect costs must be accomplished in some systematic manner. There are two approaches commonly used to assign and allocate costs to segments, the full costing approach and the contribution approach. Both are used for segment reporting; the choice depends on the needs of management.

THE FULL COSTING APPROACH TO SEGMENT REPORTING

Full costing assigns all cost of production to products

Full costing, also called **absorption costing,** assigns all costs of production—direct and indirect, fixed and variable—to the product or other cost objective. Alternatively, the **contribution approach** to costing is the process of assigning only the variable costs to the cost objective. We explain full costing below and cover the contribution approach later in the chapter. The emphasis in full costing is on the functional classification of costs into categories, such as direct labor, indirect labor, utilities, and depreciation, or manufacturing and nonmanufacturing. Full costing often is used in segment reporting.

The Full Costing Approach Illustrated

We use Longmount Diversified Products to illustrate full cost segment reporting. Longmount is a manufacturing firm whose products are manufactured in two divisions. The Business Machines Division produces a business calculator and a programmable scientific calculator. The Home Products Division manufactures toaster ovens and blenders. The company's management uses segment reports to evaluate performance. Reports include a division income statement and a product profitability statement.

Longmount Diversified Products
Division Sales and Cost Data
For the Fiscal Year Ended August 31, 1986

	Division	
	Business Machines	**Home Products**
Units sold	10,000	31,000
Weighted average unit sales price	$86.00	$40.00
Weighted average unit manufacturing costs:		
Direct materials	$12.00	$8.00
Direct labor	10.00	5.00
Manufacturing overhead	23.00	7.81
Operating expenses:		
Marketing	$126,000	$174,000
Distribution	60,000	102,000
Administrative	82,000	152,000
Corporate expenses not directly identifiable with divisions		$180,000

Figure 10-3 **The unit sales price and unit cost data are the weighted average for the products manufactured in each division. For example, the $86 price in the Business Machines Division is the weighted average selling price of the business calculators and programmable calculators sold by that division. Also, note that some expenses are classified as corporate expenses.**

A **division income statement** identifies the income provided by each division. Revenue and expenses are identified separately for each division, and then added to arrive at totals for the corporation. Division data for the fiscal year are presented in Figure 10-3 and the division income statement is shown in Figure 10-4. All revenues and expenses are identified with a division when possible. Expenses not identifiable with specific divisions are deducted from the corporate total to arrive at corporate net income.

How much profit does each product provide?

A **product profitability statement** isolates profits for individual products or product lines. In Figure 10-5, cost and quantity data of the Business Machines Division are shown for each product: various direct and indirect costs are allocated to the two types of calculators. As an organization is divided into smaller and smaller parts, more costs become common costs that are not identifiable with specific segments of the business. For example, the Business Machines Division has $80,000 of costs that are identifiable with the division, but not with specific products within the division. The income statement in Figure 10-4 indicates that $126,000 of marketing costs were incurred by the Business Machines Division. Of this amount, $108,000 can be identified with the two calculators and assigned to them, as shown in Figure 10-5. The remaining $18,000 of marketing costs cannot be identified with either calculator and is therefore shown separately as part of division expenses of $80,000.

Longmount Diversified Products
Division Income Statement
For the Fiscal Year Ended August 31, 1986

	Division		
	Business Machines	**Home Products**	**Company Total**
Sales	$860,000	$1,240,000	$2,100,000
Less cost of goods sold	450,000	645,000*	1,095,000
Gross margin	410,000	595,000	1,005,000
Less operating expenses:			
Marketing	126,000	174,000	300,000
Distribution	60,000	102,000	162,000
Administrative	82,000	152,000	234,000
Total operating expenses	268,000	428,000	696,000
Division income	$142,000	$ 167,000	309,000
Corporate expenses			180,000
Net income			$ 129,000

* Rounded.

Figure 10-4 A division income statement highlights the profit contributed to the company's total profit by each division. Income of the divisions does not equal total company profit because some expenses that cannot be identified with divisions must be deducted from the company total to find corporate net income.

Longmount Diversified Products
Business Machines Division
Product Sales and Cost Data
For the Fiscal Year Ended August 31, 1986

	Product		
	Business Calculator	**Programmable Calculator**	**Division Expenses***
Units sold	8,000	2,000	
Sales price/unit	$70.00	$150.00	
Average unit manufacturing costs:			
Direct material	$15.00	$25.00	
Direct labor	8.00	20.00	
Manufacturing overhead	14.50	30.00	
Operating expenses:			
Marketing	$68,000	$40,000	$18,000
Distribution	29,000	9,000	22,000
Administrative	23,000	19,000	40,000
Total division expenses			$80,000

* Expenses identifiable with the division, but not with specific products.

Figure 10-5 Product cost and sales data for each product are necessary to prepare product profitability reports. Longmount's Business Machines Division has only two products, business calculators and programmable calculators.

Longmount Diversified Products
Business Machines Division
Product Profitability Statement
For the Fiscal Year Ended August 31, 1986

	Product		
	Business Calculator	Programmable Calculator	Division Total
Sales	$560,000	$300,000	$860,000
Less cost of goods sold	300,000	150,000	450,000
Gross margin	260,000	150,000	410,000
Less operating expenses:			
Marketing	68,000	40,000	108,000
Distribution	29,000	9,000	38,000
Administrative	23,000	19,000	42,000
Total operating expenses	120,000	68,000	188,000
Product profitability	$140,000	$ 82,000	222,000
Less division expenses*			80,000
Division net income			$142,000

* Division expenses not identifiable with products consist of $18,000 marketing, $22,000 distribution, and $40,000 administration.

Figure 10-6 **Here product profitability is measured using the full cost of products, which means both fixed and variable manufacturing costs are included in the product cost.**

Figure 10-6 illustrates the product profitability statement for the Business Machines Division. Division expenses are subtracted from total product profit to arrive at division profit. Naturally this figure must be the same as the division's profit shown in the division income statement in Figure 10-4.

THE CONTRIBUTION APPROACH TO SEGMENT REPORTING

Although the full costing approach is widely used, many people believe that much valuable managerial information is missing from full cost reports. Some accountants suggest that costs should be reported according to behavior patterns, such as fixed and variable, because behavioral cost classifications are far more useful to managers for internal decision making.

The contribution approach reports costs by behavior pattern

As discussed in Chapter 2, costs may be classified into behavior patterns, such as variable, fixed, semivariable, and semifixed. These classifications are used in Chapters 2, 5, and 6 to analyze cost-volume-profit relationships and to make various types of business decisions. Segment reporting based on cost behavior is referred to as the **contribution approach.** Contribution approach reporting can provide managers with a wealth of decision-support information not available in full cost reports. For example, identifying variable costs separately allows managers to evaluate the effect of declining sales volume on segment profitability. Similarly, reporting all fixed costs separately gives managers some information about the cost of closing or discontinuing segments of the organization.

The Contribution Approach Illustrated

We continue the Longmount Diversified Products example to illustrate the contribution approach to segment reporting. Additional data are provided so that three different contribution approach reports can be prepared. These are

Common types of contribution reports

1. A division contribution statement
2. Product contribution statement
3. Sales region contribution statement

A **division contribution statement** describes the amount of contribution margin provided by each division of a firm. This concept of **contribution margin** is the same concept used in cost-volume-profit analysis. The only difference is that here we apply contribution margin to a division, whereas with CVP analysis contribution margin is computed for a single product. Sales and cost data are presented for Longmount's two divisions in Figure 10-7.

Longmount Diversified Products
Division Sales and Cost Data
For the Fiscal Year Ended August 31, 1986

	Division	
	Business Machines	**Home Products**
Units sold	10,000	31,000
Weighted average unit sales price	$86.00	$40.00
Weighted average unit variable costs:		
Manufacturing	$30.00	$15.00
Marketing	8.60	4.00
Distribution	3.00	2.00
Administrative	1.20	2.00
Fixed costs directly identifiable with the division:		
Manufacturing	$150,000	$180,000
Marketing	40,000	50,000
Distribution	30,000	40,000
Administrative	70,000	90,000

Figure 10-7 **It is necessary for all costs to be divided into fixed and variable components in order to prepare contribution approach reports. Here are the fixed and variable costs by division for Longmount. The unit variable costs are the weighted average unit variable costs for the products manufactured in each division.**

Longmount Diversified Products
Division Contribution Statement
For the Fiscal Year Ended August 31, 1986

	Division		
	Business Machines	**Home Products**	**Company Total**
Sales	$860,000	$1,240,000	$2,100,000
Less variable manufacturing expenses	300,000	465,000	765,000
Manufacturing contribution margin	560,000	775,000	1,335,000
Less other variable expenses:			
Variable marketing	86,000	124,000	210,000
Variable distribution	30,000	62,000	92,000
Variable administrative	12,000	62,000	74,000
Total	128,000	248,000	376,000
Contribution margin	432,000	527,000	959,000
Less division fixed expenses:			
Fixed manufacturing	150,000	180,000	330,000
Fixed marketing	40,000	50,000	90,000
Fixed distribution	30,000	40,000	70,000
Fixed administrative	70,000	90,000	160,000
Total	290,000	360,000	650,000
Division contribution	$142,000	$ 167,000	309,000
Corporate expenses			180,000
Net income			$ 129,000

Figure 10-8 A division contribution statement highlights the contribution margin provided by each division. Cost behavior information by division is useful for many managerial decisions, such as determining whether to close a marginally profitable division.

Measuring division performance with the contribution approach

Division contribution statements. Data from Figure 10-7 are used to prepare the division contribution statement shown in Figure 10-8. First, variable manufacturing costs for each division are deducted from the division's sales revenue to yield the manufacturing contribution margin. Next, the variable expenses of nonmanufacturing activities are deducted, yielding the contribution margin. Finally, fixed expenses directly identifiable with each division are subtracted to arrive at the division's contribution toward covering corporate expenses and generating corporate profit. Corporate expenses include the general administrative expenses of operating the corporate offices. These expenses are necessary in the operations of the company, but they are not identifiable with specific divisions.

Product contribution statement. A **product contribution statement** presents an analysis of the contribution margin for each product of a division. Such a report is useful in making many management decisions on product pricing, sales strategy, and production scheduling, or on discontinuing a product line. The form of the product contribution statement is similar to that of the division contribution statement. The primary difference is the cost objective, which is the product instead of a division of the business.

The preparation of a product contribution statement requires sales and cost data for each product included in the report. The example presented here is the Business Machines Division of Longmount Diversified Products. Product data for the year are presented in Figure 10-9.

The product contribution report is presented in Figure 10-10. Because the division produces only two products, and both are included in the report, the sales and variable cost figures total to the amount shown in the Business Machines column of the division contribution report. If only part of the division's products were analyzed in the product contribution report, the amounts would not have the same total.

The computations of the manufacturing contribution margin and the contribution margin are similar to the computations in the division contribution statement except that in the product contribution statement both

Longmount Diversified Products
Business Machines Division
Product Sales and Cost Data
For the Fiscal Year Ended August 31, 1986

	Product		
	Business Calculator	**Programmable Calculator**	**Division Expenses***
Units sold:			
Eastern region	4,500	1,000	
Western region	3,500	1,000	
Sales price	$70	$150	
Unit variable costs:			
Manufacturing	$25	$50	
Marketing	7	15	
Distribution	3	3	
Administrative	1	2	
Fixed costs directly identifiable with the product:			
Manufacturing	$70,000	$60,000	$ 20,000
Marketing	12,000	10,000	18,000
Distribution	5,000	3,000	22,000
Administrative	15,000	15,000	40,000
Total division expenses			$100,000

* Fixed expenses identifiable with the division, but not with specific products.

Figure 10-9 Product contribution reports require cost behavior data for individual products. Here we present cost and sales data for the Business Machines Division.

Longmount Diversified Products
Business Machines Division
Product Contribution Statement
For the Fiscal Year Ended August 31, 1986

	Product		
	Business Calculator	**Programmable Calculator**	**Division Totals**
Sales	$560,000	$300,000	$860,000
Less variable manufacturing expenses	200,000	100,000	300,000
Manufacturing contribution margin	360,000	200,000	560,000
Less other variable expenses:			
Variable marketing	56,000	30,000	86,000
Variable distribution	24,000	6,000	30,000
Variable administrative	8,000	4,000	12,000
Contribution margin	272,000	160,000	432,000
Less fixed direct expenses:			
Fixed manufacturing	70,000	60,000	130,000
Fixed marketing	12,000	10,000	22,000
Fixed distribution	5,000	3,000	8,000
Fixed administrative	15,000	15,000	30,000
Product contribution	$170,000	$ 72,000	242,000
Less division fixed expenses*			100,000
Division contribution			$142,000

* Division fixed expenses not identifiable with products consist of $20,000 manufacturing, $18,000 marketing, $22,000 distribution, and $40,000 administrative.

Figure 10-10 Product contribution reports help managers to evaluate cost-volume relationships and to make decisions about marketing, production priorities, and dropping product lines. Compare this report with the product profitability report in Figure 10-6.

margins are computed for each product. Conversely, the computation of the product contribution is somewhat different from the computation of the division contribution, because some of the fixed expenses that can be directly identified with the division cannot be specifically identified with the individual products. For instance, administrative cost pertains to the general administration of the division rather than to specific products. Similarly, some advertising may promote the division's calculators in general rather than a specific product. The result is that only a part of the division fixed expenses is assigned to products, leaving some division expenses that are common to all the division's products. These division expenses are similar to the corporate expenses in the division contribution statement. After division expenses are deducted, the division contribution remains. This amount is equal to the amount shown in the division contribution statement for the Business Machines Division in Figure 10-8.

A sales region statement reports the amount of contribution provided by each sales region

Sales region contribution statement. **A sales region contribution statement** reports the amount of contribution margin provided by each sales region. Sometimes the costs of marketing and distribution vary significantly between sales regions. For example, a sales office servicing the Plains states and Rocky Mountain states may experience significantly higher marketing and distribution costs than the New York State sales office because of the travel and shipping costs caused by low population densities in the West. Cost data by sales regions are useful in planning sales strategies and supervising marketing activities in general.

Longmount divides its sales activity into an Eastern and a Western region. Unit sales data by region in Figure 10-9 are used in Figure 10-11 to present an analysis of contribution margin by sales region.

Longmount Diversified Products
Business Machines Division
Sales Region Contribution Statement

	Region		
	Eastern	**Western**	**Division Total**
Sales	$465,000	$395,000	$860,000
Less variable manufacturing expenses	162,500	137,500	300,000
Manufacturing contribution margin	302,500	257,500	560,000
Less other variable expenses:			
Variable marketing	33,500	52,500	86,000
Variable distribution	7,500	22,500	30,000
Variable administrative	6,500	5,500	12,000
Total variable expenses	47,500	80,500	128,000
Contribution margin	255,000	177,000	432,000
Less fixed expenses:			
Fixed marketing	6,000	6,000	12,000
Fixed distribution	6,000	12,000	18,000
Total fixed expenses	12,000	18,000	30,000
Sales region contribution	$243,000	$159,000	402,000
Less division fixed expenses not assignable to sales regions*			260,000
Division contribution			$142,000

*Division fixed expenses not assignable to sales regions consist of $150,000 manufacturing, $28,000 marketing, $12,000 distribution, and $70,000 administrative.

Figure 10-11 **Differential marketing, distribution, and administrative costs for different sales regions can cause a significant difference in the contribution margin of products sold in those regions. Sales region contribution reports often present important contribution data that are buried in division contribution reports.**

Selling price and variable manufacturing costs are identical for each region. However, variable marketing and distribution costs are significantly higher in the Western region than in the Eastern region. The variable costs shown in Figure 10-9 for marketing and distribution activities are weighted averages of the following unit variable costs in each region:

	Eastern Region	Western Region
Business calculator:		
Marketing	$ 4.67/unit	$10.00/unit
Distribution	1.44/unit	5.00/unit
Programmable calculator:		
Marketing	12.50/unit	17.50/unit
Distribution	1.00/unit	5.00/unit

The regional unit costs result in a lower per unit contribution margin for products sold in the Western region. Given a choice, management would prefer to sell units in the Eastern region, and during periods of peak demand, priorities may be set in filling orders.

An important point is illustrated by the fixed expenses section of the sales region report. A comparison of the fixed cost data in Figure 10-9 and the fixed costs in Figure 10-11 discloses that few division fixed expenses are assignable to the sales regions. In this example none of the fixed manufacturing expenses or administrative expenses are identifiable with the sales regions, and only a portion of the marketing and distribution fixed expenses are assigned to the regions. Typically, fewer fixed costs of a division are identifiable with sales regions than are identifiable with products because costs are incurred to manufacture or sell a product in general rather than to manufacture and sell it in a specific region. In some cases a larger portion of the marketing and distribution costs may be identified with the regions than in our example, and occasionally some fixed manufacturing costs may be assigned to a sales region when a plant serves a specific region. However, the general statement holds that division fixed costs are less identifiable with sales regions than with product lines.

THE CONTRIBUTION APPROACH TO PRODUCT COSTING: VARIABLE COSTING

In the above discussion of the full costing approach and the contribution approach to segment performance reporting we do not examine in detail the effect of these two costing methods on product costs. Now we look specifically at product costs and the effect of each reporting method on the measurement of product costs, the reporting of net income, and the types of information provided.

Absorption Costing

Absorption costing, also called **full costing,** includes in the product cost all necessary costs of production—both direct and indirect, fixed and variable. Direct materials, direct labor, and **all** manufacturing overhead are product cost elements. Fixed overhead costs are absorbed by the product and become part of ending inventory and cost of goods sold. Absorption costing is the generally accepted method of product costing for purposes of external reporting. Although the terms *full costing* and *absorption costing* are used interchangeably, *absorption costing* is the more common of the two, and we use it in the discussion that follows.

Variable Costing

Variable costing includes only variable costs of production in product cost

Variable costing, often called **direct costing,** assigns only the variable costs of manufacturing to products. Direct materials, direct labor, and the **variable** portion of manufacturing overhead are included in inventory, and fixed manufacturing overhead costs are expensed in the period in which they are incurred, together with all nonmanufacturing expenses. Although the term *direct costing* is frequently used, *variable costing* describes the process more accurately, because indirect variable overhead costs are part of the product cost.

The key issue is, What costs should be assigned to products?

The main controversy between the two methods centers on what costs should be **inventoried** (assigned to products). Absorption costing advocates believe that all necessary costs of production should be included in product cost—both direct and indirect, fixed and variable. Variable costing advocates, on the other hand, maintain that a cost should be inventoried **only** if incurring the cost now eliminates the necessity of incurring it in the future. For example, adding direct materials to a unit of product now eliminates the need of adding the same materials to the same unit later. On the other hand, fixed capacity costs, such as depreciation on plant and equipment, are not avoidable in future periods because of current-period production.

The characteristics of variable costing income statements

A variable costing income statement highlights cost behavior characteristics. It provides managers with information about the effect on costs and profits of changes in the volume of activity. Comparing variable costs with revenue provides contribution margin information. Variable costing is one of several reporting methods generally classified as **contribution approach reporting.**

Variable and Absorption Costing Illustrated

Perhaps it is easiest to understand the similarities and differences between absorption and variable costing by studying a parallel example. We use Higgens Industries, Ltd., to illustrate variable and absorption costing. Figure 10-12 presents 4 years of production, cost, and sales data. In this example selling price, fixed costs, and variable costs per unit remain con-

Higgens Industries, Ltd.
Sales and Cost Data
Years 1 Through 4

	Year 1	Year 2	Year 3	Year 4
Sales in units	45,000	50,000	55,000	50,000
Production in units	55,000	55,000	45,000	45,000
Direct materials per unit	$4	$4	$4	$4
Direct labor per unit	$5	$5	$5	$5
Variable MOH per unit	$3	$3	$3	$3
Fixed MOH	$400,000	$400,000	$400,000	$400,000
Variable selling and administrative per unit	$2	$2	$2	$2
Fixed selling and administrative	$220,000	$220,000	$220,000	$220,000
Sales price per unit	$32	$32	$32	$32
Beginning inventory in units	0	10,000	15,000	5,000

Figure 10-12 **Sales and cost data for a 4-year period are shown. All costs are identified as fixed or variable. In this example variable costs per unit and total fixed costs remain constant.**

stant during the 4-year period, although the number of units produced and sold varies. Such cost and price stability is somewhat unrealistic but makes it easier to understand the differences and similarities between variable and absorption costing. A later example has varying costs and selling prices.

The first step in preparing variable and absorption costing income

Higgens Industries, Ltd.
Unit Product Cost Data
Years 1 Through 4

	Year 1	Year 2	Year 3	Year 4
Variable manufacturing costs:				
Direct materials	$ 4	$ 4	$ 4	$ 4
Direct labor	5	5	5	5
Variable MOH	3	3	3	3
Product cost using variable costing	12	12	12	12
Add prorated fixed overhead cost	8	8	8	8
Production cost using absorption costing	$20	$20	$20	$20

Figure 10-13 **Unit variable manufacturing costs constitute the total product cost in variable costing income statements. Product cost with absorption costing includes a prorated portion of fixed manufacturing overhead costs.**

statements is to compute the unit cost of the product for both costing methods. The computations are shown in Figure 10-13 with cost data obtained from Figure 10-12. The variable manufacturing costs consist of direct materials, direct labor, and variable manufacturing overhead. In this example variable manufacturing costs are $12 a unit in each of the 4 years. With the variable costing method, the $12 is the entire unit cost of the product. With the absorption costing method, a portion of the fixed manufacturing overhead cost must be allocated to the product in addition to the $12 variable cost.

The amount of fixed overhead allocated to each unit of product is determined by the amount of fixed cost and the number of units used in estimating the level of activity. Higgens uses 50,000 units as its estimate of normal annual production during the 4-year period. The fixed overhead cost per unit is $400,000/50,000 units, or $8 per unit. Adding the fixed overhead component to the variable unit cost of $12 yields a total unit cost of $20.

The unit cost is identical for all 4 years because the fixed and variable costs remained constant. If the costs changed, the unit costs would be different each year, but the computational procedures would be the same. The income statements in Figure 10-14 are prepared from the product cost data in Figure 10-13 and the sales and cost data in Figure 10-12.

Absorption costing income statement. The data for the income statements are taken from Figure 10-12. The sales revenue in each year is the number of units sold times the selling price of $32 per unit. In the absorption costing income statement, cost of goods sold is the number of units sold times the full cost of $20 per unit. Underapplied and overapplied overhead occur because actual production levels are somewhat different from the normal level of 50,000 units used for setting the overhead rate. In the first 2 years, 55,000 units are produced and $440,000 of fixed overhead (55,000 units × $8/unit) is applied to production. Actual fixed MOH is $400,000, or $40,000 less. Therefore, $40,000 must be deducted from total cost of goods sold. In years 3 and 4, production is only 45,000 units. As a result, less overhead was applied than was actually incurred. Actual fixed overhead is $400,000, but only $360,000 (45,000 units × $8/unit) was applied, causing underapplied overhead of $40,000. As discussed in Chapter 4, these overhead variances typically are charged or credited to the Cost of Goods Sold account if the amounts are small. Otherwise the underapplied or overapplied overhead is prorated between Cost of Goods Sold, Finished Goods, and Work in Process. Here we assume that the amounts are small. The variable selling expense is units sold times $2 per unit, and the fixed selling expense is a constant $220,000 per year regardless of the sales volume.

Variable costing income statement. The variable costing income statement shows the same annual revenue amounts as the absorption costing income statement, because revenue is not affected by the choice of costing

Higgens Industries, Ltd.
Absorption Costing Income Statement
For Years 1 Through 4
(All figures in thousands)

	Year 1	Year 2	Year 3	Year 4
Sales	$1,440	$1,600	$1,760	$1,600
Cost of goods sold	900	1,000	1,100	1,000
Underapplied (overapplied) MOH	(40)	(40)	40	40
Gross margin	580	640	620	560
Variable selling and administrative	90	100	110	100
Fixed selling and administrative	220	220	220	220
Total operating expenses	310	320	330	320
Net income	$ 270	$ 320	$ 290	$ 240

Higgens Industries, Ltd.
Variable Costing Income Statement
For Years 1 Through 4
(All figures in thousands)

	Year 1	Year 2	Year 3	Year 4
Sales	$1,440	$1,600	$1,760	$1,600
Variable product cost	540	600	660	600
Manufacturing contribution margin	900	1,000	1,100	1,000
Variable selling and administrative	90	100	110	100
Contribution margin	810	900	990	900
Fixed MOH	400	400	400	400
Fixed selling and administrative	220	220	220	220
Total fixed expenses	620	620	620	620
Net income	$ 190	$ 280	$ 370	$ 280

Figure 10-14 **The difference in net income in any particular year between absorption costing and variable costing is caused by the fixed manufacturing overhead costs that are carried from one period to the next through inventory. Fixed overhead costs included in ending inventory using absorption costing are transferred out of the period, thus reducing period expenses and increasing net income. Fixed manufacturing overhead costs in beginning inventory increase period expenses and reduce net income.**

methods. However, the rest of the income statement looks quite different. The variable product cost of $12 per unit is subtracted from sales revenue to obtain the **manufacturing contribution margin.** Variable selling and administrative costs are deducted to arrive at the **contribution margin (CM).** This is the same contribution margin discussed in connection with cost-volume-profit analysis, only here it appears in total. The average unit contribution margin could be computed by dividing the total CM by the units **sold.** For instance, in year 1 the average contribution margin is $810,000/45,000 units = $18 per unit.

All fixed expenses are subtracted from the contribution margin to determine net income. Absorption costing and variable costing result in different net incomes for each of the 4 years. With absorption costing net income is higher in years 1 and 2 and lower in years 3 and 4 than with variable costing net income.

Comparing absorption costing and variable costing. The difference in net income in any given year between the two costing methods is caused entirely by the fixed manufacturing overhead of $8 per unit that is absorbed by the products and included in beginning and ending inventories when absorption costing is used. With this method fixed MOH is assigned to products and is expensed only when the products are sold. The ending inventory therefore contains current fixed overhead costs that are not expensed until a future period.

For example, Figure 10-15 shows the quantity and cost of beginning and ending inventory for both absorption and variable costing. The physical quantity of ending finished goods inventory is identical for both costing methods. However, the unit cost is $8 higher using absorption costing. At the end of year 1, when 10,000 units remain in inventory, $80,000 (10,000 units × $8/unit) of fixed overhead is transferred from year 1 to year 2. With variable costing all of the fixed overhead cost is expensed in the year in which it is incurred, resulting in an $80,000 lower net income in year 1.

The difference in net income is caused by fixed overhead that is part of product cost with absorption costing but not with variable costing

Each year the difference in net income between absorption and variable costing can be explained by the amount of fixed overhead in inventory that is transferred from one accounting period to another using the absorption costing method. The fixed overhead costs that are in beginning and ending inventory are summarized in Figure 10-16.

Because there is no beginning inventory in year 1, no fixed overhead cost is transferred in from prior periods. Ending inventory of 10,000 units with $8 per unit fixed overhead has the effect of transferring $80,000 of fixed overhead out of year 1. Since all fixed overhead was expensed with variable costing, absorption costing net income is $80,000 higher. The $80,000 in fixed overhead transferred out of year 1 is transferred into year 2 in beginning inventory. This alone would make absorption costing net income $80,000 lower than variable costing net income in year 2, but $120,000 of year 2 fixed overhead is transferred out of year 2 via ending inventory. The result is a $40,000 higher net income in year 2 using

Higgens Industries, Ltd.
Schedule of Beginning and Ending inventory
Under Absorption Costing and Variable Costing

	Year 1	Year 2	Year 3	Year 4
Absorption Costing				
Beginning inventory:				
Number of units	0	10,000	15,000	5,000
Unit cost	—	$20	$20	$20
Total cost	—	$200,000	$300,000	$100,000
Ending inventory:				
Number of units	10,000	15,000	5,000	0
Unit cost	$20	$20	$20	—
Total cost	$200,000	$300,000	$100,000	—
Variable Costing				
Beginning inventory:				
Number of units	0	10,000	15,000	5,000
Unit cost	—	$12	$12	$12
Total cost	—	$120,000	$180,000	$60,000
Ending inventory:				
Number of units	10,000	15,000	5,000	0
Unit cost	$12	$12	$12	—
Total cost	$120,000	$180,000	$ 60,000	—

Figure 10-15 **The difference in the value of the ending inventory beween absorption costing and variable costing is due entirely to the fixed manufacturing overhead cost that is assigned to products under absorption costing. In this example the fixed overhead cost is $8 per unit.**

Higgens Industries, Ltd.
Schedule of Fixed Overhead Costs Included in
Beginning and Ending Inventory Under Absorption Costing

	Year 1	Year 2	Year 3	Year 4
Fixed MOH transferred into the period in beginning inventory	0	$ 80,000	$120,000	$40,000
Fixed MOH transferred out of the period in ending inventory	$80,000	120,000	40,000	0
Causes absorption costing net income to be	$80,000 higher	$ 40,000 higher	$ 80,000 lower	$40,000 lower

Figure 10-16 **The difference in net income in any particular year between absorption costing and variable costing is caused by the fixed manufacturing overhead costs that are carried from one period to the next through inventory. Fixed overhead costs included in ending inventory are transferred out of the period, thus reducing period expenses and increasing net income. Fixed manufacturing overhead costs in beginning inventory increase period expenses and reduce net income.**

absorption costing. Similarly, the $120,000 of fixed overhead transferred into year 3 is partially offset by the $40,000 of fixed overhead included in year 3 ending inventory using absorption costing. The result is an $80,000 lower net income in year 3 with absorption costing. Finally, in the fourth year $40,000 of fixed overhead costs is transferred into the period, but none can be transferred out because there is no ending inventory. The result is a $40,000 lower net income in year 4 using absorption costing. Total net income for the 4-year period is identical with both methods because there is no beginning inventory in year 1 and no ending inventory in year 4.

Net Income

Year	Absorption	Variable
1	$ 270,000	$ 190,000
2	320,000	280,000
3	290,000	370,000
4	240,000	280,000
Total	$1,120,000	$1,120,000

There is no fixed overhead to be transferred into year 1 or out of year 4. For any reporting period, whether a single year or a series of reporting periods, if there is no beginning and no ending inventory, the net income is the same for absorption and variable costing.

To reinforce your understanding of absorption and variable costing and to emphasize the point that inventoried fixed MOH costs are the only cause of differences between absorption and variable costing net income,

Higgens II Industries, Ltd.
Sales and Cost Data
Years 1 Through 4

	Year 1	Year 2	Year 3	Year 4
Sales in units	45,000	50,000	55,000	50,000
Production in units	55,000	55,000	45,000	45,000
Direct materials per unit	$3	$3	$4	$5
Direct labor per unit	$4	$5	$5	$6
Variable MOH per unit	$3	$4	$5	$5
Fixed MOH	$400,000	$400,000	$450,000	$450,000
Variable selling and administrative per unit	$2	$2	$3	$3
Fixed selling and administrative	$200,000	$220,000	$240,000	$250,000
Sales price per unit	$30	$32	$34	$35
Beginning inventory in units	0	10,000	15,000	5,000

Figure 10-17 **Higgens II parallels the Higgens example, but in this second illustration the fixed and variable costs and sales price fluctuate. This figure presents data similar to those found in Figure 10-12.**

Figure 10-18
In the Higgens II example, product costs change from year to year. The computation procedures for measuring product costs and net income, however, are the same as in the first illustration.

Higgens II Industries, Ltd.
Unit Product Cost Data
Years 1 Through 4

	Year 1	2	3	4
Variable manufacturing costs:				
Direct materials	$ 3	$ 3	$ 4	$ 5
Direct labor	4	5	5	6
Variable MOH	3	4	5	5
Product cost using variable costing	10	12	14	16
Add prorated fixed MOH cost	8	8	9	9
Production cost using absorption costing	$18	$20	$23	$25

Higgens II Industries, Ltd.
Absorption Costing Income Statement
For Years 1 Through 4
(All figures in thousands)

	Year 1	2	3	4
Sales	$1,350	$1,600	$1,870	$1,750
Cost of goods sold	810	980	1,220	1,240
Underapplied (overapplied) MOH	(40)	(40)	45	45
Gross margin	580	660	605	465
Variable selling and administrative	90	100	165	150
Fixed selling and administrative	200	220	240	250
Total operating expenses	290	320	405	400
Net income	$ 290	$ 340	$ 200	$ 65

Figure 10-19
This figure parallels Figure 10-14. The primary difference is that a number of cost and revenue elements are changing from year to year, whereas only production and sales quantities changed in the earlier example.

Higgens II Industries, Ltd.
Variable Costing Income Statement
For Years 1 Through 4
(All figures in thousands)

	Year 1	2	3	4
Sales	$1,350	$1,600	$1,870	$1,750
Variable product cost	450	580	740	790
Manufacturing contribution margin	900	1,020	1,130	960
Variable selling and administrative	90	100	165	150
Contribution margin	810	920	965	810
Fixed MOH	400	400	450	450
Fixed selling and administrative	200	220	240	250
Total fixed costs	600	620	690	700
Net income	$ 210	$ 300	$ 275	$ 110

we use the example of Higgens II Industries, Ltd. The production and sales quantities are identical to those in the Higgens Industries, Ltd., example, but costs and selling prices fluctuate. Figures 10-17 through 10-21 exactly parallel Figures 10-12 through 10-16. Even with varying costs and revenues the entire difference in net income in any particular year is caused by fixed overhead being transferred from one accounting period to another by absorption-costed inventories.

Figure 10-20 Again the sole difference in ending inventory values between variable and absorption costing are the fixed production costs assigned to absorption costing inventories. Here the amounts are $8 a unit in years 1 and 2 and $9 a unit in years 3 and 4.

Higgens II Industries, Ltd.
Schedule of Beginning and Ending Inventories
Under Absorption Costing and Variable Costing

	Year 1	Year 2	Year 3	Year 4
Absorption Costing				
Beginning inventory:				
Number of units	0	10,000	15,000	5,000
Unit cost	—	$18	$20	$23
Total cost	—	$180,000	$300,000	$115,000
Ending inventory:				
Number of units	10,000	15,000	5,000	0
Unit cost	$18	$20	$23	—
Total cost	$180,000	$300,000	$115,000	—
Variable Costing				
Beginning inventory:				
Number of units	0	10,000	15,000	5,000
Unit cost	—	$10	$12	$14
Total cost	—	$100,000	$180,000	$70,000
Ending inventory:				
Number of units	10,000	15,000	5,000	0
Unit Cost	$10	$12	$14	—
Total cost	$100,000	$180,000	$70,000	—

Figure 10-21 As with the earlier example, the total difference in net income in any given year is caused by the amount of fixed manufacturing costs transferred into the period through beginning inventory and transferred out of the period through ending inventory.

Higgens II Industries, Ltd.
Schedule of Fixed Overhead Costs Included in
Beginning and Ending Inventory Under Absorption Costing

	Year 1	Year 2	Year 3	Year 4
Fixed MOH transferred into the period in beginning inventory	0	$ 80,000	$120,000	$45,000
Fixed MOH transferred out of the period in ending inventory	$80,000	120,000	45,000	0
Causes absorption costing net income to be	$80,000 higher	$ 40,000 higher	$ 75,000 lower	$45,000 lower

SUMMARY

Nonmanufacturing activities are an important part of the economy and require the same type of monitoring and control as manufacturing activities. Order processing, invoice preparation, and data entry are repetitive activities and can be costed in much the same way as manufactured products. Standards can be established for repetitive nonmanufacturing activities and timely variance reports can be prepared.

Nonrepetitive activities require cost control as well. Often costs are accumulated for specific segments of a firm. **Segment reports** assist managers in evaluating performance in the various parts of the firm. As with other cost objectives, the basic approach in segment cost reporting is to identify the cost objective, assign direct costs, and allocate the indirect costs. **Full cost** segment reports use the basic full costing approach to cost determination.

An alternative method of segment reporting uses the **contribution approach.** With this method the emphasis is on cost behavior rather than functional cost classifications. Variable costs are subtracted from revenue to find the **contribution margin.** Fixed costs are deducted from the contribution margin to arrive at the **division contribution** or **product contribution.** Advocates of the contribution approach believe that this method provides managers with cost data that are more useful for decision making.

The contribution approach may be used for product costing as well as for segment reporting. Products may be costed using **absorption costing,** sometimes called **full costing,** in which all production costs, including fixed overhead costs, are assigned to products. Costs that are assigned to products are called **inventoriable costs.** With the contribution approach, only variable costs are assigned to products. Direct materials, direct labor, and variable manufacturing overhead constitute the product cost. All fixed overhead costs are expensed in the period in which they are incurred. This method of product costing is called **variable costing** or **direct costing.**

Differences in reported net income between variable and absorption costing occur because fixed overhead costs are carried from one accounting period to the next through ending inventory. If there are no beginning or ending inventories, the two costing methods yield identical net income, although the income statement format and information content are different.

KEY TERMS

absorption costing *(409)*
contribution approach *(409)*
contribution margin *(413)*
direct costing *(419)*
division contribution statement *(413)*
division income statement *(410)*
full costing *(409)*
inventoriable costs *(419)*
manufacturing contribution margin *(423)*
nonmanufacturing activities *(404)*
product contribution statement *(414)*
product profitability statement *(410)*
sales region contribution statement *(417)*
segment reports *(408)*
variable costing *(419)*

QUESTIONS

1. "Costs for nonmanufacturing activities are of no concern to manufacturing firms." Comment.
2. Name some common nonmanufacturing activities.
3. What characteristics should an activity have in order for accountants to compute unit costs for the activity?
4. The president of a firm said to the controller, "Today I received a report from the standards-setting committee indicating it was creating standards for our order processing department. Why? Aren't standards for manufacturing departments?" Respond to the president.
5. What is segment reporting? Give some examples.
6. What are the basic functions in the segment reporting process?
7. What is meant by the "contribution approach" to reporting?
8. How does a product contribution statement differ from a product profitability statement? Which is more useful?
9. A manager said to the chief cost accountant, "If contribution margin is so important, why do you bother to include fixed expenses in the contribution reports at all?" Answer for the chief cost accountant.
10. Describe absorption costing and variable costing.
11. "Contribution margin and manufacturing contribution margin are the same thing." Comment.
12. What is the cause of a difference in net income between variable and absorption costing in any particular year?
13. What effect do fluctuating fixed and variable production costs have on the difference in the net income between variable and absorption costing?

EXERCISES

Ex. 10-1 **Costing service activities.** The Portage Amusement Company operates a series of amusement parks in the South. In an effort to control rising costs, management has undertaken a program of costing all activities. One activity, selling tickets for rides, is of particular interest because many managers thought of the activity as almost costless. Below are cost data for the last 3-month period, when 5 million tickets were sold.

Wages of ticket sellers	$25,000
Printing cost per 1,000 tickets	$1
Depreciation and maintenance on ticket booths	$2,500

Required:

a. What is the cost of selling 10,000 tickets?
b. If tickets sell for $.50 each, what is the cost of ticket selling expressed as a percentage of ticket revenue?

Ex. 10-2 **Service activity costing.** Megabend Department Stores recently switched to an automated order input system for all catalog sales. Data entry is performed in a separate department with 12 terminal operators and one supervisor. Data are input and edited on cathode ray tube (CRT) terminals and various daily order status reports are generated at the end of each workday. Below are cost data for the department for May, the first month of operations, when 42,000 orders were processed.

Terminal operators' wages	$16,380
Supplies	2,100
Supervisor's salary	3,300
Utilities	1,780
Depreciation, building	700
Computer terminal lease cost	1,220
Other equipment lease cost	560
Allocated corporate costs	5,040
Total department cost	$31,080

Data Service, Ltd. has offered to provide the order entry services for catalog sales for the department store at a rate of $.70 per order.

Required:

a. Prepare a cost report for the data entry activity of Megabend Department Store for May.

b. Should the department store continue to provide its own order entry services or should it acquire the services from the outside vendor? What factors other than costs might enter into your evaluation?

Ex. 10-3 Business region labor variance reports. Septic-Service, Inc. provides a variety of septic system installation and care services. The firm has developed standard costs for some of its more standard services. Labor standards for septic field installations are 12 hours per field at $10 per hour. During June the firm experienced the following costs and activities in the two regions in which it operates, the Northern and Southern.

	Northern Region	Southern Region
Fields installed	600	800
Hours worked	6,950	10,700
Wages expense	$76,880	$99,450

Required: Prepare a labor variance report for each region.

Ex. 10-4 Product contribution report. The Whittier Fan Company makes fans for home ventilation. Cost and sales data for the two fans manufactured in the Home Products Division of the company are shown at the top of page 431.

	Product: 18-inch	Product: 30-inch	Total
Sales in units	500	300	
Sales price	$400	$260	
Unit variable costs:			
Manufacturing	$180	$110	
Other variable costs	40	25	
Fixed costs directly identifiable with products:			
Manufacturing	$42,000	$20,000	$62,000
Other fixed costs	26,000	8,000	34,000
Division expenses not identifiable with products			$26,000

Required: Prepare a product contribution statement for the Home Products Division of the Whittier Fan Company.

Ex. 10-5 Sales region contribution statement. Refer to the data in Exercise 10-4 for the Home Products Division of the Whittier Fan Company. The following data are pertinent to the development of a sales region contribution statement.

	Northern Region	Southern Region
Sales in units:		
18-inch fan	400	100
30-inch fan	120	180
Other variable costs:		
18-inch fan	$35.00	$60.00
30-inch fan	17.50	30.00
Fixed costs:		
Other fixed costs	$18,000	$16,000

Fixed costs not identifiable with sales regions:	
Manufacturing	$62,000
Others	6,000
Divisional expenses	20,000

Required: Prepare a sales region contribution statement in good form for the Home Products Division of the Whittier Fan Company.

Ex. 10-6 Product contribution report. The 1986 product cost and sales data for the Garden Division of the Home Products Company are shown on page 432. The division manufactures two electric hedge-trimming tools. The model 250 is for normal gardening use, and the model 300 is a heavy-duty unit.

	Product		
	Model 250	Model 300	
Sales in units	1,000	2,000	
Sales price	$ 70	$ 40	
Unit variable costs:			
Manufacturing	25	10	
Marketing	6	5	
Distribution	3	3	
Administrative	2	1	
Fixed costs directly identifiable with products:			
Manufacturing	12,000	8,000	
Marketing	6,000	4,000	
Distribution	3,000	3,000	
Administrative	5,000	6,000	
Division expenses not identifiable with products			$22,000

Required: Prepare a product contribution statement in good form for the Garden Division of the Home Products Company.

Ex. 10-7 **Variable costing income statement.** The Grand Traverse Manufacturing Company manufactures coffee makers that it sells through an affiliation of department stores. Following are production cost and quantity data and sales data for 1986. There was no beginning inventory.

Quantities:	
Units sold	60,000
Units manufactured	80,000
Costs and revenues:	
Selling price/unit	$12
Direct materials/unit	3
Direct labor/unit	2
Variable MOH/unit	2
Variable selling and administrative/unit	1
Budgeted and actual fixed manufacturing overhead	$140,000
Fixed selling and administrative	$80,000
Normal capacity in units	80,000

Required: Prepare the 1986 variable costing income statement in good form for the Grand Traverse Manufacturing Company.

Ex. 10-8 **Absorption costing income statement.** Refer to the Grand Traverse Manufacturing Company data presented in Exercise 10-7. Assume that all underapplied or overapplied overhead is assigned to Cost of Goods Sold.

Required: Prepare the 1986 absorption costing income statement in good form for the Grand Traverse Manufacturing Company.

Ex. 10-9 **Interpreting absorption and variable costing data.** Dublin Company uses absorption costing for all of its external reporting requirements. The firm's president, however, is interested in some of the information that is provided by variable costing income statements. Below are absorption costing and variable costing product cost data for beginning inventory and current-year production.

	Units	Variable Unit Cost	Absorption Unit Cost
Beginning inventory	9,000	$12	$17
Ending inventory	13,000	$13	$20
Normal capacity	40,000		
Actual production	40,000		

There is no underapplied or overapplied manufacturing overhead.

Required: Use the data to determine

a. The cost of ending inventory using variable costing.
b. The cost of ending inventory using absorption costing.
c. The number of units sold.
d. The difference in net income between the two product costing methods.

Ex. 10-10 **Variable and absorption costing income statement.** Largen Company manufactured 60,000 metal bookcases during 1986. Prime cost was $22 per unit, variable overhead $6 per unit, and variable selling and administrative cost $3 per unit. Fixed manufacturing overhead cost was $300,000 and fixed selling and administrative cost was $220,000. During the year, 55,000 units were sold for $50 each. Beginning inventory was 6,000 units with variable manufacturing costs of $25 and applied fixed overhead of $4 per unit. Normal capacity is 60,000 bookcases a year. The FIFO inventory method is used.

Required:

a. Prepare a variable costing income statement in good form for the Largen Company.
b. Prepare an absorption costing income statement in good form for the Largen Company.

Ex. 10-11 **Two-year variable and absorption costing.** Production quantity and cost data and sales quantity and revenue data for the Irvine Company are shown on page 434. Normal capacity for the company is 80,000 units a year and the firm uses the FIFO inventory method. Underapplied or overapplied manufacturing overhead is assigned to Cost of Goods Sold.

	Year 1	Year 2
Production in units	80,000	60,000
Sales in units	50,000	80,000
Prime cost per unit	$13	$13
Variable MOH per unit	5	5
Variable selling and administrative	3	3
Fixed MOH (budgeted and actual)	$400,000	$400,000
Fixed selling and administrative	300,000	300,000
Selling price per unit	$40	$40
Beginning inventory in units	30,000*	?

* The cost of beginning inventory is the same as the cost of production in year 1 for both the variable costing and absorption costing methods.

Required:

a. Prepare a schedule of variable costing net income for both years.
b. Prepare a schedule of absorption costing net income for the 2 years.
c. Prepare a schedule to reconcile the difference between absorption costing and variable costing net income for each of the years.

Ex. 10-12 **(CMA) Absorption costing income from a variable costing statement.** The vice president for sales of Huber Corporation has received the income statement for November 1986. The statement has been prepared on the direct cost basis and is reproduced below. The firm has just adopted a direct costing system for internal reporting purposes.

Huber Corporation
Income Statement
For the Month of November 1986
(000 omitted)

Sales		$2,400
Less variable standard cost of goods sold		1,200
Manufacturing margin		1,200
Less: Fixed manufacturing cost at budget	$600	
Fixed manufacturing cost spending variance	0	600
Gross margin		600
Less fixed selling and administrative costs		400
Income before taxes		$ 200

The controller attached the following notes to the statements.

- The unit sales price for November averaged $24.
- The standard unit manufacturing costs for the month were

Variable cost	$12
Fixed cost	4
Total cost	$16

The unit rate for fixed manufacturing costs is a predetermined rate based on a normal monthly production of 150,000 units.
- Production for November was 45,000 units in excess of sales.
- The inventory on November 30 consisted of 80,000 units.

The vice president for sales is not comfortable with the direct cost basis and wonders what the net income would have been under the prior, absorption cost basis.

Required:

a. Present the November income statement on an absorption cost basis.

b. Reconcile and explain the difference between the direct costing and the absorption costing net income figures.

c. Explain the features associated with direct cost income measurement that should be attractive to the vice president for sales.

Ex. 10-13 **(AICPA) Absorption and direct costing income statements.** Flear Company has a maximum productive capacity of 210,000 units per year. Normal capacity is 180,000 units per year. Standard variable manufacturing costs are $11 per unit. Fixed factory overhead is $360,000 per year. Variable selling expenses are $3 per unit and fixed selling expenses are $252,000 per year. The unit sales price is $20.

The operating results of 1986 are: sales, 150,000 units; production, 160,000 units; beginning inventory, 10,000 units; and net unfavorable variance for standard variable manufacturing costs, $40,000. All variances are written off as additions to or deductions from standard cost of goods sold.

Required:

a. Prepare formal income statements for 1986 using

1. Absorption costing.
2. Variable costing.

b. Briefly describe the reasons for the difference in net income between the two income statements.

PROBLEMS

P. 10-1 **Costing service activities.** Van-Tastic, Inc., has a professional cleaning and waxing service for custom vans. The company charges $80 for washing, cleaning, and waxing a van. The cleaning compound and the paste wax are accounted for as direct materials. All other materials, such as water and buffing pads, are treated as indirect charges. All labor is direct labor except for the shift supervisor's salary. Below are cost data for the month of July, when 300 vans were serviced.

Supervisor's salary	$ 1,500
Employee wages	11,520
Cleaning compound	1,140
Paste wax	1,725

Depreciation on equipment	$ 1,050
Utilities (including water)	1,800
Building lease cost	900
Buffing pads	750
Miscellaneous	450

In addition to the operating costs listed above, the company must pay a franchise fee of 10 percent of gross revenue to the national chain that advertises and provides other support.

Required:

a. Prepare a detailed report for the cost of waxing vans during July.
b. Compute the company's profit for July.

P. 10-2 **Service activity cost analysis.** Goshen Garden Care Company provides lawn care services. Lawn cutting is the major revenue service for the firm. During May, the firm cut 5,000 lawns with an average size of 7,000 square feet. Below are revenue and cost data for lawn-cutting services provided in May.

Revenue	$80,000
Advertising	4,000
Building rent	7,200
Depreciation, mowing equipment	6,000
Depreciation, service trucks	8,000
Gasoline	1,200
Insurance	1,400
Labor cost	28,000
Miscellaneous	1,500
Supervisory salaries	2,400
Supplies	800
Utilities	1,600
Total expenses	$62,100

The company accountant treats labor cost as a direct cost and all other costs as indirect costs of the lawn-cutting service.

The average lawn size cut by the firm has been increasing each year. The manager of the lawn-cutting service believes that next year the average lawn size cut will be 8,000 square feet.

Required:

a. Prepare a May cost report for the lawn-cutting service of the Goshen Garden Care Company.
b. Compute the lawn care service's income for the month.
c. Compute the cost per square foot of cutting lawns in May.
d. If the firm wants to maintain its current revenue-to-cost ratio for lawn cutting, compute the required average revenue per lawn next year assuming no change in the cost per square foot of cutting lawns.

P. 10-3 Division income statement. The Halstead Boat Company produces and sells boats in two separate divisions, the Canoe Division and the Fishing Boat Division. Below are division sales and cost data for the year.

	Division	
	Canoe	**Fishing Boat**
Sales in units	1,500	2,000
Average unit selling price	$ 400	$ 700
Average unit manufacturing costs:		
Direct materials	120	240
Direct labor	50	80
Manufacturing overhead	50	120
Operating expenses:		
Marketing	80,000	140,000
Distribution	25,000	60,000
Administrative	60,000	110,000

Corporate expenses not directly identifiable with divisions are $140,000.

Required: Prepare a full cost division income statement in good form.

P. 10-4 Product profitability r[illegible] Product sales and cost data are presented below for the Canoe Division of the Halstead Boat Company mentioned in Problem 10-3. The company produces three different canoes.

	Canoes		
	13-Foot Lightweight	**17-Foot Standard**	**20-Foot Camp**
Sales in units	200	1,000	300
Selling price	$ 380	$ 395	$ 430
Average unit manufacturing costs:			
Direct materials	90	117	150
Direct labor	59	47	54
Manufacturing overhead	59	47	54
Operating expenses:			
Marketing	3,800	19,750	6,450
Distribution	2,500	12,000	3,800
Administrative	8,000	16,000	8,000

Division expenses not identifiable with individual products are $84,700.

Required: Prepare a product profitability report in good form.

P. 10-5 Division contribution statement. The Melotone Musical Instruments Company manufactures stringed musical instruments in two divisions, the Guitar Division and the Violin Division. Sales and cost data are presented below for the fiscal year ended September 30.

Corporate expenses not identifiable with divisions are $14,000.

	Guitar Division	Violin Division
Units sold	1,000	250
Average unit sales price	$ 300	$ 600
Average unit variable costs:		
Manufacturing	120	220
Marketing	27	55
Distribution	13	30
Administrative	5	5
Fixed expenses identifiable with divisions:		
Manufacturing	54,000	26,000
Marketing	16,000	9,500
Distribution	8,000	3,000
Administrative	19,000	16,000

Required: Prepare a division contribution statement for the Melotone Musical Instruments Company.

P. 10-6 Product contribution statement. Melotone Musical Instruments Company prepares product contribution analysis reports on a monthly basis. Below are product sales and cost data for September for the Guitar Division.

	Type of Guitar	
	Standard	Classic
Units sold	800	200
Selling price	$ 225	$ 600
Unit variable costs:		
Manufacturing	90	240
Marketing	18	63
Distribution	10	25
Administrative	5	5
Fixed expenses identifiable with products:		
Manufacturing	30,000	16,000
Marketing	6,000	8,000
Distribution	2,500	2,000
Administrative	3,000	2,000

Division expenses not identifiable with individual products are $27,500.

Required: Prepare a product contribution statement for the Guitar Division of Melotone.

P. 10-7 Sales region contribution statement. Melotone Musical Instruments Company divides its marketing effort into three sales regions. The sales regions have varying marketing, distribution, and administrative expenses. Below are relevant data for the Melotone Standard guitar in the three regions. Refer to Problem 10-6 for manufacturing costs and selling price.

	Sales Region		
	Northern	**Southern**	**Western**
Units sold	100	300	400
Variable expenses:			
Marketing	$ 24	$ 20	$ 15
Distribution	20	8	9
Administrative	9	5	4
Fixed expenses:			
Marketing	4,000	8,000	10,000
Distribution	2,000	2,500	3,000
Administrative	1,000	1,000	2,000

Fixed expenses identifiable with the Melotone Standard guitar, but not identifiable with sales regions, are $8,000.

Required: Prepare a sales region contribution analysis for the Melotone Standard guitar.

P. 10-8 Using absorption and variable costing data. Below are summarized product cost data for the Mesa Company. The firm uses the FIFO inventory method to cost all inventory flows. Budgeted and actual fixed overhead costs are the same for the year.

	Units	Prime Cost	Applied Overhead
Beginning inventory	8,000	$12/unit	$10/unit ($3 variable)
Ending inventory	5,000	$14/unit	$11/unit ($3 variable)
Normal capacity	30,000		

Underapplied overhead = $12,000 (all fixed overhead)

Required: Use these data to determine:

a. The total amount of fixed overhead during the current year.

b. The difference in net income between absorption and variable costing for the year.

c. The number of units produced during the period.

d. The number of units sold during the period.

e. The cost of ending inventory using variable costing.

P. 10-9 Understanding absorption and variable costing information. Below are sales, production, and cost data for the Denton Company.

Sales (9,000 units)	$945,000
Manufacturing costs for the units produced:	
Prime cost	378,000
Variable MOH	126,000
Fixed MOH	150,000
Operating expenses:	
Variable selling expense	81,000
Fixed selling expense	67,500
Fixed administrative	135,000

During the year, 10,500 units were produced, which is 500 more than normal capacity. There were 2,000 units in beginning inventory, with a variable manufacturing cost of $45 per unit. Fixed MOH included in the beginning inventory was $13.50 per unit.

Required: From the above data determine:

a. The number of units in ending inventory.
b. The cost of ending inventory using absorption costing.
c. The cost of ending inventory using variable costing.
d. The company's gross margin percentage.
e. The company's total manufacturing contribution margin.
f. The company's contribution margin as a percentage of sales.
g. The difference in net income between the two costing methods.

P. 10-10 Variable and absorption costing over 4 years. Carmel Manufacturing Company manufactures wheel covers. The company's normal capacity is 50,000 units per year. Following are 4 years of sales, cost, and production data.

	Year 1	Year 2	Year 3	Year 4
Sales in units	50,000	50,000	50,000	50,000
Production in units	60,000	80,000	20,000	50,000
Fixed MOH	$400,000	$400,000	$400,000	$400,000
Fixed selling and administrative	$100,000	$100,000	$100,000	$100,000
Direct materials	$2/unit	$2/unit	$2/unit	$2/unit
Direct labor	$4/unit	$4/unit	$4/unit	$4/unit
Variable MOH	$4/unit	$4/unit	$4/unit	$4/unit
Variable selling and administrative	$3/unit	$3/unit	$3/unit	$3/unit
Unit price	$25	$25	$25	$25
Beginning inventory in units	0			

Required:

a. Prepare a schedule of unit product costs for the 4 years using variable and absorption costing.

b. Prepare a schedule of beginning and ending inventories for both methods for each of the 4 years.
c. Prepare a schedule of net income for the 4-year period using both variable and absorption costing.
d. Prepare a schedule reconciling the difference in net income between the two methods.

P. 10-11 **(AICPA) Product contribution analysis.** The president of Eastern Company wants guidance on the advisability of eliminating product C, one of the company's three similar products, or investing in new machinery to reduce the cost of product C in the hope of reversing product C's operating loss sustained in 1986. The three similar products are manufactured in a single plant in about the same amount of floor space and the markets in which they are sold are very competitive.

Below is the condensed statement of operating income for the company and for product C for the year ended October 31, 1986.

Eastern Company
Statement of Operating Income
For the Year Ended October 31, 1986

	All Three Products	Product C
Sales	$2,800,150	$350,000
Cost of sales:		
Raw materials	565,000	80,000
Labor		
Direct	1,250,000	150,000
Indirect	55,000	18,000
Fringe benefits (15% of labor)	195,750	25,200
Royalties (1% of product C sales)	3,500	3,500
Maintenance and repairs	6,000	2,000
Factory supplies	15,000	2,100
Depreciation (straight-line)	25,200	7,100
Electrical power	25,000	3,000
Scrap and spoilage	4,300	600
Total cost of sales	2,144,750	291,500
Gross profit	655,400	58,500
Selling general and administrative expenses:		
Sales commissions	120,000	15,000
Officers' salaries	32,000	10,500
Other wages and salaries	14,000	5,300
Fringe benefits (15% of wages, salaries, and commissions)	24,900	4,620
Delivery expense	79,500	10,000
Advertising expense	195,100	26,000
Miscellaneous fixed expenses	31,900	10,630
Total selling, general, and administrative expenses	497,400	82,050
Operating income (loss)	$ 158,000	$ (23,550)

Required:

a. Disregarding income taxes, prepare a schedule showing the contribution of product C to the recovery of fixed costs and expenses (marginal income) for the year ended October 31, 1986. Assume that each element of cost and expense is entirely fixed or variable within the relevant range and that the change in inventory levels has been negligible.

b. Assume that in fiscal 1986 the variable costs and expenses of product C totaled $297,500 and that its fixed costs and expenses amounted to $75,100. Prepare a schedule computing the break-even point of product C in terms of annual dollar sales volume. Sales for 1986 amounted to $350,000.

c. The direct labor costs of product C could have been reduced by $75,000 and the indirect labor costs by $4,000 by investing an additional $340,000 (financed with 5 percent bonds) in machinery with a 10-year life and an estimated salvage value of $30,000 at the end of the period. However, the company would have been liable for total severance pay costs of $18,000 (to be amortized over a 5-year period), and electrical power costs would have increased $500 annually.

Assuming the information given above in part *b*, prepare a schedule computing the break-even point of product C in terms of annual dollar sales volume if the additional machinery had been purchased and installed at the beginning of the year.

P. 10-12 Comprehensive variable and absorption costing problem. Grogen Industries manufactures depth finders used primarily by fishermen. The product is sold to retail establishments. Normal production and sales levels are 20,000 units a year. Early in 1986 the company's union contract expired. A long strike ensued that lasted into the spring of 1987. Anticipating the strike, Grogen used overtime in 1985 to accumulate a large inventory by the time the strike occurred. The management of Grogen has always used absorption costing for financial reporting. There is some interest, however, in knowing what effect direct costing would have on reported income, particularly during unusual times, such as the long strike. Presented below are sales and cost data for the years 1984–1988.

	1984	1985	1986	1987	1988
Production in units	20,000	35,000	1,000	15,000	20,000
Sales in units	20,000	20,000	20,000	20,000	20,000
Selling price/unit	$ 45	$ 48	$ 50	$ 52	$ 56
Prime cost/unit	10	13	11	12	13
Variable MOH/unit	6	6	7	7	8
Variable selling and administrative costs/unit	4	4	5	5	6
Fixed MOH	210,000	210,000	180,000	240,000	280,000
Fixed selling and administrative costs	200,000	200,000	200,000	210,000	240,000

Beginning inventory in 1984 was 10,000 units with an absorption cost of $245,000. With variable costing the inventory cost was $150,000.

Required:

a. Prepare a schedule of unit product costs for the 5-year period using both variable and absorption costing.
b. Prepare a schedule of beginning and ending inventories using both variable and absorption costing.
c. Prepare income statements in schedule form for the years 1984–1988 using both variable and absorption costing.
d. Prepare a schedule to reconcile the difference between variable and absorption costing net income.

CASES

Case 10-1 (AICPA) Contribution analysis for products

The Marcia Company, your client, has asked your assistance in determining an economical sales and production mix of its products for 1986. The company manufactures a line of dolls and a doll dress sewing kit.

The company's sales department provides the following data:

Product	Estimated Demand for 1986 (Units)	Established Net Price (Units)
Laurie	50,000	$5.20
Debbie	42,000	2.40
Sarah	35,000	8.50
Kathy	40,000	4.00
Sewing kit	325,000	3.00

To promote sales of the sewing kit there is a 15 percent reduction in the established net price for a kit purchased at the same time that a Marcia Company doll is purchased.

From accounting records you develop the following data:

1. The production standards per unit:

Product	Material	Labor
Laurie	$1.40	$ .80
Debbie	.70	.50
Sarah	2.69	1.40
Kathy	1.00	1.00
Sewing kit	.60	.40

2. The labor rate of $2.00 per hour is expected to continue without change in 1986. The plant has an effective capacity of 130,000 labor hours per year on a single-shift basis. Present equipment can produce all of the products.
3. The total fixed costs for 1986 will be $100,000. Variable costs will be equivalent to 50 percent of direct labor cost.
4. The company has a small inventory of its products that can be ignored.

Required:

a. Prepare a schedule computing the contribution to profit of a unit of each product.

b. Prepare a schedule computing the contribution to profit of a unit of each product per labor dollar expended on the product.

c. Prepare a schedule computing the total labor hours required to produce the estimated sales units for 1986. Indicate the item and number of units that you would recommend be increased (or decreased) in production to attain the company's effective productive capacity.

d. Without regard to your answer in part *c*, assume that the estimated sales units for 1986 would require 12,000 labor hours in excess of the company's effective productive capacity. Discuss the possible methods of providing the missing capacity. Include in your discussion all factors that must be taken into consideration in evaluating the methods of providing the missing capacity.

Case 10-2 (CMA) Product line decision analysis

The Scio Division of Georgetown Inc. manufactures and sells four related product lines. Each product is produced at one or more of the three manufacturing plants of the division. Presented on page 445 is a product line profitability statement for the year ended December 31, 1985, which shows a loss for the baseball equipment line. A similar loss is projected for 1986.

The baseball equipment is manufactured in the Evanston plant. Some football equipment and all miscellaneous sports items also are processed through this plant. A few of the miscellaneous items are manufactured, and the remainder are purchased for resale. The items purchased for resale are recorded as materials in the records. A separate production line is used to produce each product line.

A schedule (opposite) presents the costs incurred at the Evanston plant in 1985. Inventories at the end of the year were substantially identical to those at the beginning of the year.

The management of Georgetown Inc. has requested a profitability study of the baseball equipment line to determine if the line should be discontinued. The marketing department of the Scio Division and the accounting department at the plant have developed the following additional data to be used in the study:

1. If the baseball equipment line is discontinued, the company will lose approximately 10 percent of its sales in each of the other lines.
2. The equipment now used in the manufacture of baseball equipment is quite specialized. It has a current salvage value of $105,000 and a remaining useful life of 5 years. This equipment cannot be used elsewhere in the company.
3. The plant space now occupied by the baseball equipment line could be closed off from the rest of the plant and rented for $175,000 per year.
4. If the line is discontinued, the supervisor of the baseball equipment line will be released. In keeping with company policy he would receive severance pay of $5,000.
5. The company has been able to invest excess funds at 10 percent per annum.

Required:

a. Should Georgetown Inc. discontinue the baseball equipment line? Support your answer with appropriate calculations and qualitative arguments.

b. A member of the board of directors of Georgetown Inc. has inquired whether the information regarding the discontinuance of product lines should be included in the financial statements on a regular monthly basis for all product lines. Draft a memorandum in response to the board mem-

Product Line Profitability—1985
(000 omitted)

	Football Equipment	Baseball Equipment	Hockey Equipment	Miscellaneous Sports Items	Total
Sales	$2,200	$1,000	$1,500	$500	$5,200
Cost of goods sold:					
Material	400	175	300	90	965
Labor and variable overhead	800	400	600	60	1,860
Fixed overhead	350	275	100	50	775
Total	1,550	850	1,000	200	3,600
Gross profit	650	150	500	300	1,600
Selling expense:					
Variable	440	200	300	100	1,040
Fixed	100	50	100	50	300
Corporate administrative expenses	48	24	36	12	120
Total	588	274	436	162	1,460
Contribution to corporation	$ 62	$ (124)	$ 64	$138	$ 140

Evanston Plant Costs—1985
(000 omitted)

	Football Equipment	Baseball Equipment	Miscellaneous Sports Items	Total
Material	$100	$175	$ 90	$ 365
Labor	100	200	30	330
Variable overhead:				
Supplies	85	60	12	157
Power	50	110	7	167
Other	15	30	11	56
Total	150	200	30	380
Fixed overhead:				
Supervision*	25	30	21	76
Depreciation†	40	115	14	169
Plant rentals‡	35	105	10	150
Other§	20	25	5	50
Total	120	275	50	445
Total costs	$470	$850	$200	$1,520

* The supervision costs represent salary and benefit costs of the supervisors in charge of each product line.
† Depreciation cost for machinery and equipment is charged to the product line on which the machinery is used.
‡ The plant is leased. The lease rentals are charged to the product lines on the basis of square feet occupied.
§ Other fixed overhead costs are the cost of plant administration and are allocated arbitrarily by management decision.

ber's inquiry. Your memorandum should (1) state why or why not this information should be included in the regular monthly financial statements distributed to the board and (2) detail the reasons for your response.

Decentralized Operations and Responsibility Accounting

11

Most organizations find that separating the organization into smaller segments enhances the efficiency and effectiveness of managing the business. An important role of managerial accounting is to report on the performance of business segments. This chapter deals specifically with the performance measurement of business segments and incorporates many cost and performance reporting concepts of previous chapters. When you have completed this chapter, you should understand:

1. The concepts of decentralization and the reasons for decentralizing.
2. The nature and purpose of responsibility accounting.
3. The types of responsibility centers and when each is used.
4. How to prepare various responsibility reports.
5. The role of transfer pricing in performance reports.
6. The computation and use of the different types of transfer prices.

In many small organizations decision making is characterized by one individual making virtually all the important decisions. As an organization grows, it becomes difficult, even impossible, for a single person to make all decisions. Instead some decisions should be delegated to other managers, providing them with decision authority for specific areas of operations. For example, the owner of a small variety store employing four salesclerks may make all purchasing, pricing, advertising, personnel, and other decisions. As the store grows into a department store, some of the inventory purchasing decisions are assigned to department heads because the owner cannot be knowledgeable about all product lines sold in the store and must devote more time to the growing amount of accounting data and to financial planning. When a new store is opened in a neighboring town, the new store manager may be assigned authority to make even more decisions. With authority comes responsibility, which means that managers are held accountable for their decisions. Ideally managers are granted decision authority commensurate with their responsibility,

Decentralization is the process of separating an organization into smaller, more manageable units

The need to delegate decision authority and responsibility to subordinates occurs because as organizations grow, centralized decision making can become unwieldy. Often it becomes necessary to separate the organization into more manageable units. This separation is known as **decentralization.** Managers of decentralized operations are given decision authority and are held responsible for the results of their decisions. An important function of managerial accounting in decentralized organizations is reporting the performance of managers. The term **responsibility accounting** refers to the accounting process that reports how well managers meet their responsibilities.

The purpose of this chapter is to introduce the concepts of decentralization and responsibility accounting. Many costing concepts from previous chapters and income measurement concepts from financial accounting affect the discussion of responsibility reporting. Some of the more common responsibility accounting reports are illustrated and practical problems are discussed. We also cover transfer pricing, an issue that can create major challenges in measuring division performance.

RESPONSIBILITY ACCOUNTING

Responsibility accounting reports on the performance of business segment managers

Responsibility accounting rests on the premise that individuals should be held accountable for their performance and the performance of their subordinates. This concept guides accountants in the accumulation and reporting of operating results by areas of responsibility. Responsibility accounting embodies a number of important assumptions:

1. Managers should be held responsible for the activities occurring in the area of the organization over which they exercise control.
2. Managers should strive to meet the goals and objectives established for them and for their segment of the organization.
3. Managers should participate in establishing the goals against which their performance is measured.
4. Goals should be attainable with efficient and effective performance.
5. Performance reports and feedback to managers should be timely.
6. The role responsibility accounting plays in the company's reward structure should be clearly stated.

Benefits of decentralized organizations and responsibility accounting systems

Responsibility reporting may have little importance for small organizations, but as firms grow larger control and evaluation become more difficult. In such situations decentralization and responsibility accounting are beneficial because:

1. Organizations are separated into units of manageable size.
2. Decisions are made at the level at which managers are uniquely aware of the problems and information relevant to the decision.
3. Decisions can be made on a more timely basis.
4. Managers' morale and level of job satisfaction are higher because of their active participation in decision making.
5. Responsibility center managers have an opportunity to gain valuable managerial skills that in turn provide the firm with a pool of potential top management personnel.
6. Managers are motivated to act in a manner most beneficial to the firm.

TYPES OF RESPONSIBILITY CENTERS

Responsibility centers can be classified in a variety of ways. Three classifications commonly used are cost centers, profit centers, and investment centers.

The type of responsibility center used for measuring segment performance depends on the type of business situation. The report should measure appropriately the performance of responsibility center managers. For example, if a manager is responsible for the costs of a department but has no control over revenues, the responsibility report should be limited to costs and should not include profits. Below we discuss the nature of the different types of responsibility centers.

Cost Centers

Managers are held responsible for costs incurred in their segment of the organization

A **cost center** is a segment of an organization in which a manager is held responsible for the costs incurred in the segment. Cost center managers have control over some or all of the costs in their segment of the business, but not over revenues. The cost center is the most widely used form of responsibility center because many different types of business segments can be identified as cost centers. An entire marketing department, a sales region, or a single sales representative can be defined as a cost center.

For example, the customer service department of a retail store provides services that help generate and maintain profits. Although the customer service department is an important element in the successful operation of the store, it is difficult, if not impossible, to measure the precise effect of the department on profits. Consequently, the customer service department is viewed as a cost center. The most important characteristic of a cost center is that costs **controllable** by the management of the cost center can be identified, because the managers of cost centers are held responsible for the costs over which they have control.

It seems reasonable to expect cost center managers to accept responsibility for the costs that they or their subordinates control. However, it is not always easy to identify costs with individual cost centers. The issue of what costs should be charged to cost centers is critical in evaluating cost center managers, and it certainly influences the control of corporate costs in general.

Guidelines in charging costs. The importance of determining what costs to assign to cost centers is underlined by the attention it has been given by accounting organizations. The Committee on Cost Concepts and Standards of the American Accounting Association considered this problem and formulated the following guidelines for deciding what costs should appropriately be charged to responsibility center managers:

Guidelines for assigning costs to responsibility centers

1. The person having authority over both the acquisition and the use of a service should be charged with the cost of the service.
2. The persons who can significantly influence the amount of costs through their own action may be charged with such costs.
3. Persons who cannot significantly influence the amount of cost through their own direct action may be charged with those elements with which management desires them to be concerned, so that they will help to influence those who are responsible.[1]

A desired benefit from decentralization and a responsibility accounting system is the motivation of managers to act in a way most beneficial to the firm as a whole. Thus costs should be identified and assigned in a way that has the most desired impact on employee motivation. The American Accounting Association Committee on Cost Concepts and Standards commented on this problem:

> The basis of measurement used in providing cost data for control is often a matter of management discretion and an important consideration in motivation. Different bases may significantly affect the way in which different individuals are motivated. For this reason, the basis of measurement selected should be consistent with the type of motivation desired. For example, different types of motivation may result when maintenance costs are charged to a responsibility center on the basis of: (1) a rate per maintenance labor hour, (2) a rate per job, or (3) a single amount per month.[2]

Cost responsibility is common in organizations and forms the nucleus for many managerial accounting reports. For example, product cost reports often are used both for product costing and for evaluation of department managers. Standard cost variance analysis reports are based on cost responsibility. The number and variety of cost responsibility reports is large. An example of a cost responsibility performance report is presented in Figure 11-1. The top portion of the report summarizes production variances

---

[1] "Committee on Cost Concepts and Standards," *Accounting Review*, April 1956, p. 189.
[2] Ibid.

Marine Products Production Division
Division Performance Report
For the Fiscal Year Ended October 31

Department	Standard Costs	Actual Costs	Variance
Machining	$ 540,000	$ 620,000	$ 80,000
Welding	380,000	440,000	60,000
Assembly	450,000	480,000	30,000
Finishing	190,000	160,000	(30,000)
Painting	220,000	200,000	(20,000)
Total	$1,780,000	$1,900,000	$120,000

Marine Products Assembly Department
Department Performance Report
For the Fiscal Year Ended October 31

Cost	Standard Costs	Actual Costs	Variance
Direct materials	$200,000	$245,000	$45,000
Direct labor	160,000	150,000	(10,000)
Manufacturing overhead	90,000	85,000	(5,000)
Total	$450,000	$480,000	$30,000

Figure 11-1 Segment reports are prepared with the level of detail required by the managers using the reports. The total variances used in the division performance report are separated into variances by cost component in the department reports. Even more detail might be used in reporting the activities of a particular production operation within a department.

for five production departments. The bottom portion of the report shows the production variances for each cost element for the assembly department of the Production Division. In practice a complete set of department production reports is prepared. In addition, detailed variance reports are prepared for each product. Each report is at least part of the basis for managerial cost performance measurement.

Profit Centers

Managers are responsible for both revenues and costs in a profit center

A **profit center** is a segment of a business in which a manager is held responsible for both costs and revenues. A profit center may be viewed as a business within a business. The chief aim of the business as a whole—earning a profit—is also the main concern of each profit center manager. Ideally, if each of the profit centers maximizes its profits, then the profits of the firm as a whole will be maximized. However, this idea is not necessarily true. Sometimes the maximization of profits by one division causes harm to another division. If interdivision activities are impaired by profit-maximizing actions of divisions, the entire company may suffer. For example, if one division of a company maximizes its profits by selling more product than the production division of the company can manufacture, the firm may experience significant production cost increases for overtime pay and other production inefficiencies.

Evaluation as a profit center can be quite useful if a business segment has the characteristics of a profit center. For example, the home appliance department of a department store may be treated as a profit center because both costs and revenues are identifiable with the department and to a large degree are controllable by department personnel and management. The key is to determine the type and amount of authority and responsibility that are assigned to a responsibility center manager and to develop the type of responsibility reports that best measure the performance of the manager.

Criteria for profit center responsibility. Some business segments do not have the necessary characteristics to be evaluated as profit centers. For example, the accounting department provides essential services to the firm, but its effect on revenues and profits is impossible to measure. Three criteria should be present for a company to have decentralized profit responsibility:

Profit centers should only be used when the business segment lends itself to profit measurement

1. It must have two or more units for which separable measures of revenue and expense are obtained.
2. The management of these units must have considerable control over the units' expense and revenue. (Presumably authority to influence profit must accompany any true responsibility for the size of the profit.)
3. Each unit's profit must be calculated and reported regularly to top management, and the results of this calculation must be considered by top management as part of its evaluation of the unit's performance.[3]

Dealing with common costs. The calculation of a profit center's profit is very similar to the calculation of profit for an individual firm. The primary difference is that often there are some costs that are difficult to identify with specific profit centers because the costs are common to several profit centers. For example, some benefits of corporate administration, research and development, and centralized computer services are shared by all segments of a firm. These common costs are sometimes allocated to each of the profit centers, but if the allocations are made arbitrarily, the resulting

[3] John Mauriel and Robert Anthony, "Misevaluation of Investment Center Performance," *Harvard Business Review*, March–April 1966, p. 99.

Ramjet Fuel Corporation
Division Income Statement
For the Fiscal Year Ended October 31

	Division			Company Total
	X	Y	Z	
Sales	$450,000	$250,000	$300,000	$1,000,000
Less cost of goods sold	225,000	88,000	105,000	418,000
Gross margin	225,000	162,000	195,000	582,000
Less operating expenses:				
Advertising	26,000	15,000	23,000	64,000
Commissions	18,000	11,000	9,000	38,000
Rent	20,000	18,000	8,000	46,000
Salaries	90,000	70,000	60,000	220,000
Utilities	12,000	8,000	4,000	24,000
Division income	59,000	40,000	91,000	190,000
Less allocated corporate expenses:				
Administrative	36,000	20,000	24,000	80,000
Research and development	18,000	10,000	12,000	40,000
Income before taxes	5,000	10,000	55,000	70,000
Income tax (40%)	2,000	4,000	22,000	28,000
Net income	$ 3,000	$ 6,000	$ 33,000	$ 42,000

Figure 11-2 **A profit center manager directs a business within a business. The key ingredient in establishing successful profit centers is that authority is commensurate with responsibility. Typically, comparison of profit center performance is most meaningful if allocated corporate expenses are excluded from the analysis.**

profit figures may be useless. Consequently, division profit reports often present profit before allocation of corporate common costs followed by profit after allocations have been made.

Figure 11-2 illustrates a company's division income statement for its three profit centers. All expenses specifically identifiable with a division are deducted from the division's sales revenue to find division net income before deducting allocated corporate expenses. Next, corporate expenses common to the three divisions are allocated to each division using an allocation base that management believes does a good job of matching the costs with the benefits derived by each division. In this example, corporate expenses are allocated to divisions in proportion to the amount of sales each division achieved. For instance, Division X had 45 percent of total company sales. Therefore, $36,000 of administrative expense and $18,000 of research and development expense, representing 45 percent of the total amount of each cost, are allocated to Division X. Notice that Division X has the highest dollar sales volume and the second-highest division net income before allocation of corporate common costs, but after the allocation Division X has the lowest profit. Shifts in relative profit performance caused by common cost allocations should be evaluated carefully. For example, Division X covers $54,000 ($36,000 + $18,000) in allocated corporate expenses. If these common expenses are fixed expenses, eliminating Division X would leave the remaining two divisions with an additional $54,000 of expenses to cover before any profit could be earned.

Investment Centers

Managers are evaluated on the rate of return on the investment

An **investment center** is a business segment whose managers are held responsible for the return on the resources invested in the segment. Total profit alone may not be a good measure of a division's performance because typically profit is related to the amount of resources available to earn the profit. Business segments with a lot of assets should earn more profit than business segments with less assets. To illustrate the issue, Division A reports an annual profit of $100,000 and Division B reports a profit of $50,000 for the same year. However, Division A has $1,000,000 in assets and Division B has $200,000 in assets. Division A has a return on assets of 10 percent, whereas Division B's return is 25 percent. Because of this type of situation, some managers suggest the use of investment centers for evaluating business segments.

In an investment center the evaluation emphasis shifts from the profit figure to a measure of rate of return. The computation of an investment center's rate of return on assets is simple.

$$\text{Return on investment} = \frac{\text{Investment center income}}{\text{Investment center assets}}$$

There are many possible measures of investment base

For example, if earnings are $60,000 and assets are $400,000, the rate of return on investment is $60,000/$400,000 = 15 percent. Clearly the division's profit figure is a basic element in calculating the investment center's rate of return, and the problems of isolating revenues and expenses are still of great importance. The other basic element in calculating an investment center's rate of return is the investment base. Many different investment bases may be used, including the following:

1. Total gross assets, which includes all assets of the division without regard to contra-asset accounts, such as Accumulated Depreciation.
2. Total net assets, which includes all assets of the division less any contra-asset accounts.
3. Total net assets employed, which includes all of the division's net assets that are employed in the production of division profit. Investments and other nonoperating assets are excluded from this base.
4. Stockholders' equity, which highlights the return to investors and includes contributed capital as well as earnings retained in the business. This asset base is applicable only to wholly owned sub-

sidiaries or branches if they are operated as a division of the parent company.

5. Others. Almost any other measure of investment base can be used if it is deemed appropriate by management. Working capital and fixed assets are two examples of other possible bases for measuring return on investment.

Clearly, the percentage return on investment depends on the investment base selected. To illustrate the computation of return on investment using each of the investment bases listed above, we use the Downtown Department Store, a wholly owned subsidiary corporation of Consolidated Department Stores. Downtown Department Store is operated as a division of Consolidated, which uses return on investment (ROI) as a measure of division performance. The trial balance for the division is presented in Figure 11-3.

Downtown Department Store
Trial Balance
October 31, 1986

	Debit	Credit
Cash	$ 25,000	
Accounts receivable	75,000	
Merchandise inventory	250,000	
Land held for investment	100,000	
Building	500,000	
Accumulated depreciation, building		$ 250,000
Equipment	200,000	
Accumulated depreciation, equipment		150,000
Patents	50,000	
Accounts payable		40,000
Taxes payable		10,000
Mortgage payable		50,000
Capital stock		250,000
Retained earnings		250,000
Sales		1,000,000
Cost of goods sold	450,000	
Advertising expenses	50,000	
Commission expenses	80,000	
Machine rental expenses	40,000	
Insurance expenses	20,000	
Salaries expenses	120,000	
Utilities expenses	40,000	
Total	$2,000,000	$2,000,000

Figure 11-3 **This is the year-end trial balance of a department store that is a wholly owned subsidiary of Consolidated Department Stores. The subsidiary is operated as a division of the parent company.**

First we compute the division's net income, which in this example is sales revenue of \$1,000,000 less total expenses of \$800,000, yielding a net income of \$200,000. Income is divided by the investment bases selected to find return on investment.

Total gross assets. An investment base that is easy to use and understand is gross assets. It includes all asset accounts without deducting contra-asset accounts, such as Accumulated Depreciation. The investment base is found by adding up the balances in the asset accounts of the division, which for Downtown Department Store amount to \$1,200,000. The return on investment using gross assets is

$$\text{Return on investment (ROI)} = \frac{\text{Net income}}{\text{Investment base}}$$

$$= \frac{\$200{,}000}{\$1{,}200{,}000} = .1667, \text{ or } 16.67\%$$

Total net assets. Sometimes a more useful measure of investment base is total net assets, particularly when facilities are old and almost fully depreciated. This asset base is computed by totaling the balances in the asset accounts and subtracting the balances in the contra-asset accounts. For Downtown Department Store this figure is \$800,000 (total assets of \$1,200,000 less accumulated depreciation of \$250,000 and \$150,000). The rate of return on investment for total net assets is as follows:

$$\text{ROI} = \frac{\$200{,}000}{\$800{,}000} = .25, \text{ or } 25\%$$

Total net assets employed. A division may own assets that are not used in its normal productive activities. For example, a company may invest excess cash in land that it intends to sell in several years. If such assets constitute a relatively large amount of total assets, they may distort the division's rate of return on the amount invested in operations of the division. To eliminate the problem, the asset base may be limited to assets employed in normal operating activities. For example, Downtown's ROI is based on net assets employed. Net assets are \$800,000, but that amount includes \$100,000 of land held for investment that is not used in the division's normal activities as a department store. Therefore, the investment base using net assets employed is \$800,000 minus \$100,000 of land, or \$700,000, and the rate of return on net assets employed is

$$\text{ROI} = \frac{\$200{,}000}{\$700{,}000} = .286, \text{ or } 28.6\%$$

Stockholders' equity. A popular measure of investment base is stockholders' equity. It is composed of contributed capital and earnings retained in the business. This investment base can be used only by segments that are independent entities, such as branches or subsidiaries with separate owners' equity accounts. Downtown Department Store is a wholly owned subsidiary of Consolidated Department Stores and is operated as a division investment center. Return on investment based on owners' equity is computed as

$$\text{Return on investment} = \frac{\text{Net income}}{\text{Capital stock} + \text{Retained earnings}}$$

ROI on owners' equity can be computed on the beginning balance, the ending balance, or an average

But what value do we use for these capital accounts? Do we use their beginning balance, their ending balance, or an average? The answer is that any of these can be used depending on what management believes is the best measure of division performance. We assume in this example that there were no transactions in the capital stock account during the year. Using the beginning balances in the capital accounts, ROI is

$$\text{ROI} = \frac{\$200{,}000}{\$250{,}000 + \$250{,}000} = .40, \text{ or } 40\%$$

If we use the ending balance in the owners' equity accounts, ROI is

$$\text{ROI} = \frac{\$200{,}000}{\$250{,}000 + \$250{,}000 + \$200{,}000} = .286, \text{ or } 28.6\%$$

An alternative to using either the beginning or the ending balance is to use an average. The beginning and ending balances can be averaged, or a monthly average can be computed if there were a lot of capital transactions during the year. Here we average the beginning and ending balances.

$$\text{ROI} = \frac{\$200{,}000}{\$250{,}000 + (\$250{,}000 + \$450{,}000)/2} = .333, \text{ or } 33.3\%$$

Other bases. Other investment bases may be used and managers should select the base deemed most appropriate for measuring performance and making decisions. For example, inflation has increased significantly the cost of constructing new production facilities, making historical asset costs of little value in measuring ROI performance. To illustrate, Downtown Department Store estimates a current market value of $2,500,000 for its assets. The return on investment using current market values is

$$\text{ROI} = \frac{\$200{,}000}{\$2{,}500{,}000} = .08, \text{ or } 8\%$$

The rate of return based on current market values is less than a third of the rate computed using total net assets, which is a historical cost measure.

This type of measurement problem is common among firms with heavy fixed cost investments. In recent years the cost of building a facility has doubled every 4 to 6 years in some areas of the country, and the current values of many facilities are many times higher than book value, or even original cost, for some plant assets.

Residual Income

Residual income is a combination of investment centers and profit centers

Residual income combines profit center and investment center concepts. With residual income, management establishes a target profit or target rate of return for the business segment. Any income in excess of the target level is the **residual income.** To illustrate, the target rate of return for Downtown Department Store is 20 percent on total net assets. Total net assets are \$800,000, so the target net income is \$800,000 × .20 = \$160,000. The residual income for the store is

$$\begin{aligned} \text{Residual income} &= \text{Actual net income} - \text{Target net income} \\ &= \$200{,}000 - \$160{,}000 \\ &= \$40{,}000 \end{aligned}$$

The residual income approach does not necessarily eliminate the problem of comparing the performance of large and small divisions. For example, a company has three divisions, each of which earns a 25 percent return on its total net assets. However, the residual incomes of the divisions are significantly different. Below are the data for the three divisions.

	Division		
	X	Y	Z
Total net assets	\$100,000	\$500,000	\$1,000,000
Net income	25,000	125,000	250,000
ROI on net assets	25%	25%	25%
Target net income (15% of net assets)	\$ 15,000	\$ 75,000	\$ 150,000
Residual income (net income − target net income)	10,000	50,000	100,000

Each division earned the same rate of return on net assets, and each has the same percentage target net income requirement. Still the residual income measures are dramatically different among the divisions. This approach has a tendency to highlight the divisions that generate the largest dollar profits for the firm.

TRANSFER PRICING

A transfer price is the amount charged for some good or service sold between business segments

One of the primary obstacles to meaningful division performance measurement is caused by the transfer of goods and services between divisions. If each division dealt only with organizations external to the firm, prices for the goods and services would be determined by the market. However, in many decentralized businesses, divisions deal with other divisions of the firm. Often the output of one division is the raw material of another division, and so on until the final product of the company is sold to outside customers. The issue raised by interdivisional transfers of products and services is, What should be the amount used to record the transfer of the product or service between divisions? This amount is called a **transfer price,** or sometimes a **charge-back** or **internal price.** The transfer pricing dilemma has been described very well as follows:

> If a divisionalized company could arrange its affairs so that its divisions had no dealings of any kind with each other it would have removed one of the principal complexities of divisional profit measurement. It would also, however, have lost a valuable feature of decentralization, namely, the capacity to enjoy the fruits of division of labor and of specialization while simultaneously benefiting from integration to a greater or lesser degree. The fact that a divisionalized company is more than the sum of its parts is evidenced through the intricate pattern of interdivisional relationships which can establish itself within a large decentralized company.[4]

A transfer price is the amount at which goods and services are transferred between segments of a business. It is an internal price—the amount one responsibility center charges another responsibility center within the firm for a product or service. The importance of transfer prices for a given firm depends primarily on the importance of the transactions between the segments of the firm. If interdivisional transfers are minimal, the transfer price has little effect on the measurement of segment performance. Substantial amounts of interdivisional transfers mean that the type of transfer price can have a dramatic effect on reported performance.

Transfer Pricing Methods

There are many different transfer pricing methods

Many different transfer pricing methods are used in practice. The selection of a transfer pricing method is determined by the reporting needs of the business. For instance, one company may treat its automobile pool for executives and employees as a profit center and use a market price for car rentals. Another company may treat its automobile pool as a cost center and charge cost for the use of vehicles. No one method is better than the others, although market price seems to be the method cited most often as being closest to the ideal transfer price. Commonly used transfer pricing methods include

---

[4] David Solomons, "Divisional Performance: Measurement and Control," Financial Executives Research Foundation, New York, 1965, p. 160.

1. Market price
2. Modified market price
3. Actual cost
4. Standard cost
5. Modified cost
6. Negotiated price
7. Target profit
8. Others

Market price is the most widely accepted transfer price

Market price. **Market price** is the ideal transfer price because it is determined by parties that are external to the firm and dealing at arm's length with one another. When market price is used for internal transfers, the most objective measure of value is employed in charging for the goods or services exchanged. The market price is the one that would prevail if profit centers were in fact separate firms. It is the price that the selling division would receive if it sold to external customers, and it is the price that the buying division would have to pay if it bought from external suppliers.

A problem with the market price method is that some goods and services transferred between divisions do not have a ready market price. A product or service may be specially made or may have special characteristics that make any outside market price only a rough estimate of its market value. For example, a patented circuit board for a calculator produced by one division of a firm and sold to another division is not manufactured anywhere else in the world. Similarly, the supplying division may provide a more personalized service than the buying division could expect from an external supplier. Sometimes centralized corporate data processing centers provide other segments of a firm with far more personalized information processing services than can be obtained from an external time-sharing firm. Faster turnaround from data input to reports and more relevant report information are two commonly mentioned features attributed to corporate data processing centers. Such specialized service differentiates internal data processing centers from external services.

Sometimes even when there is a market price for a product or service sold between divisions, the market price is not used as the transfer price. Instead the market price is modified to reflect the specific situation involved in the intracompany transfers of products and services.

Modified market price. When there is an appropriate outside market, the market price is sometimes reduced to make allowance for the reduced selling effort and transportation expense that often characterize interdivisional transfers. This reduced price is called a **modified market price.** The justification is that if the selling division incurs less cost in making a sale to another division, some of the saving should be passed on to the buying division. In addition, other variables, such as special production requirements or inventory carrying costs, may be factors considered in charging a modified market price.

When there is no outside market for a product, a market price for a close substitute product is sometimes used. The market price of the substitute product may be modified to reflect a realistic estimate of a market price for the firm's product. For example, if a firm uses high-quality material to manufacture specialized cold-weather-resistant bearings, the transfer price for the bearings may be set above the market price of a similar but lower-quality bearing to reflect the difference in production costs.

Actual cost. **Actual cost,** sometimes called **historical cost,** is a popular transfer pricing method when market price is not feasible. Two frequently cited advantages of a historical cost transfer price are that it is definitely determinable and readily available. Given the discussion of costs in previous chapters, an obvious question is, Which costs are used for actual cost transfer prices? Typically, "actual cost" refers to an absorption cost transfer price, meaning that all direct and indirect costs—both fixed and variable—are included in product cost. Exceptions are discussed later in the chapter.

Historical cost transfer prices are limited by the fact that a profit center cannot be evaluated on a profit basis if its revenue is merely a recovery of cost. It is even difficult to evaluate a cost center using historical cost transfer prices because all efficiencies and inefficiencies are passed on to the buying segments of the firm.

Standard cost. A **standard cost transfer price** has the advantage of isolating efficiency measures in the producing division. The price to the buying division is based on expected efficient performance. Standard costs reveal inefficient operations early so that they are not carried through to the final product. Compared to actual costs, standard costs are particularly effective with interdivisional transfers because an actual cost transfer price allows the seller to recover all costs, including inefficiencies, and there may be little incentive to operate efficiently. Standard cost transfer prices provide the incentive because responsibility center managers are evaluated on standard cost variance reports.

Modified cost. Many variations of cost are used as a basis for establishing transfer prices. A cost-based transfer price that is adjusted in some way is called a **modified cost** transfer price. A common transfer pricing model is **cost-plus**, whereby some amount is added to the cost of the product or service in arriving at the transfer price. The amount added may be fixed, such as $5 a unit, or it may be a percentage, such as 15 percent of cost.

When actual costs are used as the basis for a cost-plus transfer price, there is little incentive for efficiency on the part of the selling division. In fact, if the model is expressed in terms of cost plus a percentage, the selling division can generate greater profits by incurring more costs. If standard costs are used as the base for cost-plus transfer prices, the selling division cannot profit from its own inefficiencies. The transfer price is determined by the standard cost plus the additional amount.

Partial cost transfer prices may lead to uneconomical use of some resource

Another form of modified cost transfer price is **partial cost,** which charges buying divisions only part of the total cost of providing the product or service. Many partial cost transfer prices are used, such as **marginal cost, prime cost,** and **variable cost.** In theory, partial cost includes all values between zero and full cost. Often partial cost transfer prices are used to encourage the use of some service or facility. For example, some firms with large centralized computer installations have excess capacity when a new computer is acquired. The computer requires a large commitment of fixed costs with relatively small amounts of variable operating costs. To increase the utilization of the computer, users are charged a low rate for services. The amount charged usually is only a portion of the total cost of operating the computer.

Most partial cost transfer prices are intended to encourage use, but only to a point. For example, if a low transfer price for computer services increases computer use too much, another, larger computer may have to be acquired, thus causing another large cash outlay. Therefore, partial cost transfer prices must be monitored closely to ensure that organizational goals are not violated. Beyond a desired level of use, a new form of transfer pricing system may be adopted. Many firms change their transfer price from partial cost to full cost, or even to cost-plus, as excess capacity dwindles. Typically the switch to full cost slows the growth in demand for services but does not eliminate the growth altogether..

Segment managers must have the ability to bargain and use outside markets

Negotiated price. A **negotiated transfer price** is one that is determined by bargaining between buyer and seller. A negotiated price suggests an arm's-length bargaining process such as one would encounter when dealing with entities external to the firm. For the process to work appropriately, the entities must have freedom to bargain. If agreement is not reached on the transfer price, the entities should have the ability to enter external markets. In the absence of such power, the negotiation approach may break down. If the buying and selling divisions must deal solely with each other, a bilateral monopoly exists. Economic analysis indicates that such a situation is indeterminant, which means no logical solution can be derived. In such cases management may impose a transfer price on the parties in question.

Target profit can be based on standard or actual costs

Target profit. Sometimes a transfer price is based on a target profit, such as 15 percent of standard costs or 10 percent of actual costs. **Target profit transfer prices** attempt to provide reasonable or desired profit levels for divisions when a market price is not available or when other transfer pricing methods would yield unsatisfactory results. To illustrate, refer to the following data for a manufacturing division of a corporation:

	Cost	
	Standard	**Actual**
Units produced	—	10,000
Manufacturing expenses	$80,000	$98,800
Operating expenses	20,000	30,000

If company policy is to provide a division profit of 20 percent on sales with standard cost as the base, the transfer price is found by computing the total revenue (TR) required to yield the target profit and then dividing total revenue by units produced. In this example the computation is

$$\text{Total revenue} = .2\ (\text{Total revenue}) + \text{Total standard cost}$$

$$\begin{aligned} TR &= .2\ TR + \$80{,}000 + \$20{,}000 \\ .8\ TR &= \$100{,}000 \\ TR &= \$125{,}000 \end{aligned}$$

Total revenue of $125,000 is required to generate a 20 percent profit on sales using standard cost as the basis for measuring profit. The transfer price is the total required revenue divided by the number of units produced.

$$\begin{aligned} \text{Transfer price} &= \$125{,}000/10{,}000 \text{ units} \\ &= \$12.50 \text{ per unit} \end{aligned}$$

If actual cost is used to measure profit, the transfer price is computed in the same way except that actual cost is substituted for standard cost. To illustrate, company policy is to base the transfer price on a target profit of 8 percent of sales using actual cost as the base. The total required revenue is

$$\text{Total revenue} = .08\ (\text{Total revenue}) + \text{Total actual cost}$$

$$\begin{aligned} TR &= .08\ TR + \$98{,}800 + \$30{,}000 \\ .92\ TR &= \$128{,}800 \\ TR &= \$140{,}000 \end{aligned}$$

The transfer price is

$$\begin{aligned} \text{Transfer price} &= \$140{,}000/10{,}000 \text{ units} \\ &= \$14.00 \text{ per unit} \end{aligned}$$

The process of computing target profit transfer prices is more difficult if the division sells part of its output in an outside market. To illustrate, 20 percent of the division's output is sold in an outside market at $16.50 per unit and the remaining 80 percent is sold internally. What transfer price yields a 20 percent profit on sales using standard costs to measure profit? Since standard costs and the target profit percentage have not changed from the original example, the total required revenue is still $125,000.

$$\begin{aligned} TR &= .20\ TR + \$80{,}000 + \$20{,}000 \\ TR &= \$125{,}000 \end{aligned}$$

However, now some of the revenue is generated from sales in the outside market. The amount of revenue is

$$10{,}000 \text{ units} \times 20 \text{ percent} \times \$16.50 \text{ per unit} = \$33{,}000$$

The amount of revenue that must be generated by the transfer price from sales to other divisions is the total revenue required less the revenue from the outside market.

$$\begin{aligned}\text{Required internal sales revenue} &= \$125{,}000 - \$33{,}000 \\ &= \$92{,}000\end{aligned}$$

The transfer price is computed by dividing the required revenue from internal sales by the number of units sold internally.

$$\begin{aligned}\text{Transfer price} &= \$92{,}000/8{,}000 \text{ units} \\ &= \$11.50 \text{ per unit}\end{aligned}$$

Others. We have discussed the most common methods of transfer pricing, but managers may use any type of transfer price deemed useful in motivating employees toward achieving organization goals. Some firms have developed sophisticated mathematical models for transfer pricing. Such methods as linear programming produce transfer prices whose apparent precision promotes favorable motivation among employees.

Transfer Pricing Illustrated

We illustrate some of the more common transfer pricing methods with Peachgrove Appliance Manufacturing, which produces refrigerators and stoves in a decentralized organization. The Motor Division supplies motors to the Refrigerator Division. In the open market similar motors can be purchased for $70 each. Below are some recent cost data for the Motor Division.

Cost Item	Standard Cost	Actual Cost
Direct materials	$10	$14
Direct labor	15	18
Variable MOH	5	8
Fixed MOH	20	20

The market transfer price is $70 per unit. If management reduces market price 20 percent to reflect the absence of marketing costs, the transfer price is

$$\$70 - (\$70 \times .2) = \$70 - \$14 = \$56$$

With actual cost as a transfer price, we merely sum the costs of production and get a transfer price of $60. Based on standard cost, the transfer price is $50. The difference results from the unfavorable variances of $10 per motor.

Using actual product cost plus 20 percent, the transfer price is

$$\$60 + (\$60 \times .2) = \$72$$

and using standard product cost plus 20 percent the transfer price is

$$\$50 + (\$50 \times .2) = \$60$$

Other examples of transfer prices include actual variable cost or standard prime cost.

Direct materials	+	Direct labor	+	Variable overhead		
$14	+	$18	+	$8	=	$40
Direct materials	+	Direct labor				
$10	+	$15			=	$25

SUMMARY

As an organization grows, centralized decision making can become unwieldy. Often it is necessary to separate the decision process into more manageable units. This separation is known as **decentralization.** Managers of decentralized operations are given decision authority and are held responsible for the results of their decisions. **Responsibility accounting** is used to report on segment activity. It rests on the premise that managers should be responsible for the activities over which they have decision authority.

Cost centers, profit centers, and investment centers are the three basic forms of **responsibility centers. Cost centers** are decentralized units whose managers are responsible for the cost of operating the unit. Cost centers are very common because they can be used for any kind of segment in large or small organizations. The major problem is identifying the **controllable costs** in each center.

In **profit centers** managers are held responsible for expenses **and** revenues. Each profit center is a business within a business. Ideally the maximization of segment profits results in maximization of corporate profit.

Investment centers carry the profit center approach one step further by measuring the rate of return on the resources invested in the business segment. Often it is difficult to decide what investment base to use. Some common bases are **total gross assets, total net assets, total net assets employed,** and **stockholders' equity.**

Residual income is a variation of the profit center and investment center methods. Each division is assigned a target profit or percentage. Any profit above the target level is the residual income.

An issue in segment performance measurement is the transfer of goods and services between business segments. If such transfers are significant, the question of how much to charge for the transferred goods and services is crucial in evaluating management performance. Many different **transfer prices** are used, and none is accepted as universally correct.

Market price is determined by pricing mechanisms external to the firm. **Modified market price** is the market price of an identical or similar product changed to reflect a more realistic estimate of the situation. **Actual cost** is the historical cost of producing the product or service transferred. It allows inefficiencies to be transferred out of the producing segment of the firm. **Standard cost** eliminates the problem of transferring the cost of inefficiency from one department to the next. **Modified cost** uses either historical or standard cost as a base from which to adjust for target profits or other factors. **Negotiated transfer prices** allow the trading parties to participate directly in price setting. However, a bilateral monopoly may occur, in which case top management must intercede to set the transfer price. **Target profit** transfer prices are based on a desired level of net income or return on investment. The transfer price is set at a level that is intended to yield the target profit.

KEY TERMS

actual cost *(460)*
charge-back *(458)*
controllable cost *(448)*
cost center *(448)*
cost plus *(460)*
decentralization *(447)*
historical cost *(460)*
internal price *(458)*
investment center *(453)*
market price *(459)*
modified cost *(460)*
modified market price *(459)*
negotiated price *(461)*
partial cost *(461)*
profit center *(450)*
residual income *(457)*
responsibility accounting *(447)*
responsibility centers *(448)*
return on investment (ROI) *(453)*
standard cost *(460)*
stockholders' equity *(456)*
target profit *(461)*
total gross assets *(455)*
total net assets *(455)*
total net assets employed *(455)*
transfer price *(458)*

QUESTIONS

1. Why do firms decentralize?
2. What is meant by the term *responsibility accounting*? What assumptions are embodied in responsibility accounting?
3. Briefly describe the basic types of responsibility centers. Which type is most widely used? Why?
4. What is a controllable cost and how does this concept affect the assignment of costs to responsibility centers?

5. "Profit centers are great, a business within a business. Each minibusiness maximizes its profits, so the entire business maximizes profit." Do you agree?
6. Why might division performance evaluation be better using investment centers rather than profit centers?
7. Identify five investment bases that are used in investment center analysis.
8. What is residual income?
9. Define transfer pricing and explain why it is necessary in responsibility reporting.
10. Name five methods of transfer pricing. Which method is correct?
11. "My performance report might mean something if my division did not have to buy all our raw material from other divisions and then get charged those ridiculous prices that someone in corporate headquarters sets. It is just a funny money game we play." Comment.

EXERCISES

Ex. 11-1 Return on investment. Laughtenburg Corporation's Commercial Products Division reported the following data and asset balances for the year 1986:

Sales	$1,500,000
Prime costs	660,000
Overhead	240,000
Operating expenses	200,000
Total gross assets	3,000,000
Contra-asset accounts	1,400,000 -
Land held for investment	400,000

There are no beginning or ending inventories.

Required: Compute the return on investment for the Commercial Products Division using as the investment base:

a. Total gross assets.
b. Net assets. - 1,400,000
c. Net assets employed.

Ex. 11-2 Computing residual income. Refer to the data on the Commercial Products Division of Laughtenburg Corporation presented in Exercise 11-1.

Required: Compute the residual income for the division using target income of:

a. $220,000. 180 K
b. 18 percent of sales. 130k 400K - 18%(1,5 mill)
c. 12 percent of gross assets employed. 88 K 400k - 12%(3 mill 400 k)

Ex. 11-3 ROI using owners' equity. Droast Department Store uses return on owners' equity to measure performance. During the past year the company had sales of $1,880,000, product expenses of $870,000, and operating expenses of $660,000. The January 1 owners' equity balances were $800,000 in Capital Stock and $600,000 in Retained Earnings. The December 31 balance in Capital Stock was $980,000. The company operates on a calendar year and no dividends were paid during the year.

Required: Compute the return on owners' equity using:

a. The beginning balance of owners' equity.
b. The ending balance of owners' equity.
c. The average balance of owners' equity.

Ex. 11-4 **ROI performance measurement methods.** The end-of-period trial balance of Fort Company is presented below.

Fort Company
Trial Balance
December 31, 1986

	Debit	Credit
Cash	$ 20,000	
Accounts receivable	18,000	
Inventory	70,000	
Building	92,000	
Accumulated depreciation, building		$ 40,000
Accounts payable		12,000
Mortgage payable		28,000
Capital stock		30,000
Retained earnings		70,000
Sales		150,000
Cost of goods sold	58,000	
Advertising	12,000	
Sales salaries and commissions	16,000	
Administrative salaries	34,000	
Office operation expense	7,000	
Miscellaneous expense	3,000	
Totals	$330,000	$330,000

Required: Compute the return on investment for the Fort Company using as the investment base:

a. Total gross assets.
b. Total net assets.
c. Beginning owners' equity.
d. Ending owners' equity.

Ex. 11-5 **Evaluating division performance.** Rayburn Corporation is a decentralized specialized sales company. Each division competes with the other divisions for resources and for management rewards. Below are some summarized data.

	Division		
	X	Y	Z
Sales	$1,000,000	$800,000	$500,000
Net income	100,000	120,000	80,000
Assets	600,000	600,000	320,000

Required:

a. For each division compute sales as a percentage of assets.
b. For each division compute the rate of return on assets.
c. Which division had the best performance? Why?

Ex. 11-6 Alternative ROI measures. Following is the year-end trial balance of the Hofstra Company. The company closes its books on December 31. There were no stock transactions during the year.

	Debit	Credit
Current assets	$ 200,000	
Fixed assets	900,000	
Accumulated depreciation		$ 350,000
Land held for investment	300,000	
Current liabilities		50,000
Long-term liabilities		210,000
Capital stock		240,000
Retained earnings		400,000
Dividends	50,000	
Sales		750,000
Cost of goods sold	340,000	
Operating expenses	210,000	
Totals	$2,000,000	$2,000,000

Required: Compute return on investment using:

a. Gross assets.
b. Net assets.
c. Gross assets employed.
d. Net assets employed.
e. Beginning owners' equity
f. Ending owners' equity.

Ex. 11-7 Asset base and performance measurement. Hoppleworth Products started operations 8 years ago on the East Coast. Business grew rapidly, and soon product demand outstripped production facilities. The company opened a new plant of identical size and capacity on the West Coast 2 years ago. Each plant serves its geographic area and is operated as a separate division. Below are operating data for the most recent year.

	Eastern Division	Western Division
Sales	$1,000,000	$1,000,000
Manufacturing expenses	500,000	600,000
Marketing expenses	100,000	100,000
Administrative expenses	200,000	200,000
Current assets	200,000	200,000
Fixed assets (gross)	1,000,000	2,000,000
Accumulated depreciation	800,000	400,000

Since the East Coast plant was built, construction costs have doubled. The entire difference in manufacturing expenses is due to higher depreciation costs at the West Coast plant.

Required:

a. Compute return on investment for each division based on total net assets.
b. Compute return on investment for each division based on total gross assets.
c. What is your evaluation of the two divisions?

Ex. 11-8 **Working backward from ROI data.** The Small Appliance Division of Heatherow Company had income of $90,000 for the year just completed. The division's annual performance report showed a return on net assets of 12 percent. The division has accumulated depreciation of $400,000 and no other contra-asset accounts.

Required:

a. Compute the amount of gross assets for the Small Appliance Division.
b. Compute the division's return on gross assets.

Ex. 11-9 **Cost-based transfer prices.** The McClurey Company operates a decentralized manufacturing business. The company's main product is electric winches used primarily by farmers and outdoor enthusiasts on the front of trucks and other vehicles. Several different divisions manufacture components of the winch and transfer them to the Assembly Division, where the units are assembled and transferred to finished goods inventory. The Housing Division manufactures cast-iron housings for the winches. There is no market price for the specific housing manufactured in the division, and the company has used a variety of cost-based transfer prices through the years. Standards have been developed for the production of housings, and below are standard and actual cost data for the Housing Division for the fiscal year ending March 31.

	Standard	Actual
Production quantity	—	10,000
Direct materials	$150,000	$190,000
Direct labor	120,000	150,000
Manufacturing overhead	180,000	190,000
Administration	—	130,000
Marketing and distribution	—	80,000

Required: Compute the unit transfer price for the winch housings using each of the following:

a. Standard product cost.
b. Actual product cost.
c. Standard product cost plus 30 percent.
d. Total actual cost.

Ex. 11-10 **Computing transfer prices.** The Ribbon Division of the 5Q Products Company sells all of its output to the Sales Division of the company. The only product of the Ribbon Division is computer ribbons that are sold in boxes of 12. The retail price of the ribbons is $55 per box. Production quantity and cost data are presented on page 470 for the fiscal year just completed.

Computer ribbons manufactured (in dozens)	90,000
Direct material	$1,260,000
Direct labor	720,000
Manufacturing overhead (of which 20 percent is variable)	600,000
Operating expenses (of which 30 percent is variable)	900,000

Required: Compute the transfer price for a box of computer ribbons using:

a. Variable product cost.
b. Full product cost.
c. Total cost.
d. Total variable cost.
e. Full product cost plus 30 percent.
f. Total cost plus 20 percent.

Ex. 11-11 **Target profit and modified market transfer prices.** Refer to the data in Exercise 11-10 on the Ribbon Division of the 5Q Products Company.

Required:

a. Compute the transfer price for a box of a dozen ribbons based on a final market sales price less 30 percent for marketing and distribution costs incurred in the Sales Division.
b. Compute the transfer price for a box of a dozen ribbons using a target profit of 15 percent of total costs.
c. Compute the net income for the Ribbon Division using each of the transfer prices computed above.

Ex. 11-12 **(CMA) ROI and goal congruence.** The Notewon Corporation is a highly diversified company which grants its division executives a significant amount of authority in operating the divisions. Each division is responsible for its own sales, pricing, production, costs of operations, and the management of accounts receivable, inventories, accounts payable, and use of existing facilities. Cash is managed by corporate headquarters; all cash in excess of normal operating needs of the divisions is transferred periodically to corporate headquarters for redistribution or investment.

The division executives are responsible for presenting requests to corporate management for investment projects. The proposals are analyzed and documented at corporate headquarters. The final decision to commit funds to acquire equipment, to expand existing facilities, or for other investment purposes rests with corporate management. This procedure for investments projects is necessitated by Notewon's capital allocation policy.

The corporation evaluates the performance of division executives by the return-on-investment (ROI) measures. The asset base is composed of fixed assets employed plus working capital exclusive of cash.

The ROI performance of a division executive is the most important appraisal factor for salary changes. In addition, the annual performance bonus is based on the ROI results, with increases in ROI having a significant impact on the amount of the bonus.

The Notewon Corporation adopted the ROI performance measure and related compensation procedures about 10 years ago. The corporation did so to increase the awareness of division management of the importance of the profit-asset relationship and to provide additional incentive to the division executives to seek investment opportunities.

The corporation seems to have benefited from the program. The ROI for the corporation as a whole increased during the first years of the program. Although the ROI has continued to grow in each division, the corporate ROI has declined in recent years. The corporation has accumulated a sizable amount of cash and short-term marketable securities in the past 3 years.

The corporation management is concerned about the increase in the short-term marketable securities. A recent article in a financial publication suggested that the use of ROI was overemphasized by some companies, with results similar to those experienced by Notewon.

Required:

a. Describe the specific actions division managers might have taken to cause the ROI to grow in each division but decline for the corporation. Illustrate your explanation with appropriate examples.

b. Explain, using the concepts of goal congruence and motivation of division executives, how Notewon Corporation's overemphasis on the use of the ROI measure might result in the recent decline in the corporation's return on investment and the increase in cash and short-term marketable securities.

c. What changes could be made in Notewon Corporation's compensation policy to avoid this problem? Explain your answer.

Ex. 11-13 **Transfer prices for government services.** Central Data Systems, a government agency of Big City, provides data processing services for all branches of the city government. The city uses a full cost transfer price to charge for the use of intracity services. However, a continuing debate centers on the base to be used in the full cost charge for data processing services. During the year just ended, Central Data Systems incurred total costs of $2,000,000. The following measures of service activity were accumulated for the year:

Activity Measure	Total Annual Use for the Activity Measure
Core hours of time	4,000
Pages of printed output	10,000,000
Punch cards processed	20,000,000
Tape drive hours	10,000
Disc drive hours	20,000
Terminal connect hours	250,000

Below are total computer-utilization data for the year for two departments of city government.

	Department	
	Police	City Planning
Core hours of time	500	100
Pages of printed output	200,000	1,000,000
Punch cards processed	100,000	1,500,000
Tape drive hours	1,000	5,000
Disc drive hours	4,000	500
Terminal connect hours	100,000	10,000

Required:

a. Compute the transfer price for services rendered by Central Data Systems using each of the activity measures as a charging base.
b. Calculate the computer charge to the police department and city planning department based on each of the transfer prices computed in part *a*.
c. What observations and suggestions do you have concerning the transfer price?

PROBLEMS

P. 11-1 **Measuring division performance.** Below is the year-end trial balance of the Fainer Division of the Morrosen Manufacturing Company. Fainer is a wholly owned subsidiary that is operated as a division and is evaluated with all of the other divisions of the decentralized firm.

	Debit	Credit
Cash	$ 40,000	
Marketable securities	35,000	
Accounts receivable	75,000	
Inventory	100,000	
Plant	1,325,000	
Accumulated depreciation, plant		$ 375,000
Land held for investment	400,000	
Patents	100,000	
Current liabilities		175,000
Long-term liabilities		400,000
Common stock		225,000
Retained earnings		800,000
Dividends	150,000	
Sales		700,000
Cost of goods sold	350,000	
Operating expenses	100,000	
Totals	$2,675,000	$2,675,000

Required: For parts *a* through *d*, compute the rate of return on investment using:

a. Total net assets employed.
b. Total gross assets.
c. Beginning owners' equity.
d. Ending owners' equity.
e. Calculate the residual income, assuming a target return of 20 percent on gross assets employed.

P. 11-2 **Division performance trends.** The Grand Island Auto Equipment Company is organized into three divisions operated as investment centers. Data for 3 years for the Shock Absorber Division are as follows:

	1986	1985	1984
Sales	$1,210,000	$1,100,000	$1,000,000
Cost of goods sold	700,000	600,000	500,000
Operating expenses	300,000	250,000	200,000
Current assets	150,000	120,000	100,000
Fixed assets	2,000,000	2,000,000	2,000,000
Accumulated depreciation	1,400,000	1,100,000	800,000

Required:

a. Compute net income for each year.
b. Compute return on investment for each year using total gross assets.
c. Compute return on investment for each year using total net assets.
d. What is the trend in the division's performance?

P. 11-3 Ranking segment performance. Orlando Corporation is a decentralized manufacturing company with three production divisions. Following is a schedule of sales and cost data for the accounting year just completed.

	Division		
	A	B	C
Sales	$225,000	$ 90,000	$600,000
Cost of goods sold	105,000	37,500	360,000
Operating expenses	90,000	30,000	150,000
Current assets	75,000	30,000	120,000
Land held for investment	—	120,000	—
Fixed assets (gross)	180,000	150,000	750,000
Accumulated depreciation	90,000	15,000	525,000
Current liabilities	15,000	22,500	60,000
Long-term liabilities	22,500	—	37,500

Required: Compute the following:

a. Net income for each division.
b. ROI using gross assets.
c. ROI using net assets.
d. ROI using gross assets employed.
e. Residual income using a target income of 15 percent of net assets.
f. Income as a percentage of sales.
g. Prepare a chart ranking the divisions for each of the performance measures.

P. 11-4 Interpreting ROI. Pueblo Company's Plastics Division had a return on investment on gross assets of 15 percent for the year. The division's return on investment on net assets was 20 percent, and on net assets employed ROI was 24 percent. The division's net income for the year was $450,000 and residual income was $85,000. The only contra-asset accounts the division has are accumulated depreciation accounts.

Required: Compute:

a. The target income used in computing residual income.
b. The company's gross assets.
c. The company's total amount of accumulated depreciation.
d. The amount of assets not employed in the business.

P. 11-5 ROI on owners' equity with stock transactions. The Day Company had 1986 earnings of $600,000 and paid dividends of $250,000 during the year. The company's stock records on January 1, 1986, showed 10,000 shares of its $20 par value stock issued and outstanding. Additional paid-in capital on the stock was $600,000. The beginning balance in the Retained Earnings account was $550,000. Day Company has no preferred stock. During 1986 the firm had the following common stock transactions.

March 1	Issued 1,000 shares for $120 each.
May 1	Issued 3,000 shares for $140 each.
October 1	Issued 1,000 shares for $150 each.

On January 1, 1986, the company's stock was trading for $106 per share and on December 31, 1986, the market price of the stock was $157 per share.

Required: Compute the ROI on owners' equity using:

a. The beginning balance in Owners' Equity.
b. The ending balance in Owners' Equity.
c. The average balance in Owners' Equity with a monthly average for the calculations.

P. 11-6 Computing and using transfer prices. The Power-Lite Division of Outside Products manufactures batteries that it sells primarily to the Lantern Division for inclusion with that division's main product. Last year 20 percent of the batteries were sold to other companies at a price of $1 each. The remaining batteries went to the Lantern Division. Cost data for the year are presented for Power-Lite.

Units produced	500,000
Manufacturing costs	$300,000
Marketing costs	10,000
Administrative costs	50,000

Required:

a. What should be the transfer price for the batteries if the company uses:
   1. Market price?
   2. Market price less marketing costs?
   3. A transfer price that will yield a net income of 10 percent on sales for Power-Lite?
   4. Product cost plus 40 percent?
b. Prepare a schedule showing the Power-Lite Division's net income for each of the transfer pricing alternatives computed.

P. 11-7 Transfer pricing with various objectives. The Pop-Up Popcorn Company is separated into three divisions: Popcorn Production, Popcorn Preparation, and Caramel Corn. The Production Division sells 60 percent of its products to the other two divisions and the rest to outside customers. The price to outside customers is

$.80 per pound. Relevant data for last year's popcorn production are presented below.

Production	500,000 lb
Direct materials	$ 80,000
Direct labor	100,000
Indirect production costs	60,000
Marketing expenses	25,000
Administrative expenses	75,000

Required:

a. Compute the transfer price for the sale of popcorn to the Preparation Division and Caramel Corn Division assuming:

1. The objective of the Production Division is just to cover all costs.
2. The objective of the Production Division is to generate a profit of 15 percent on sales.
3. The transfer price is market price less the marketing expense, all of which is for external sales.

b. What is the Production Division's profit using the transfer price computed in part *a*, number 3?

P. 11-8 Transfer pricing analysis. The Starrock Boat Company makes a variety of boats in a decentralized environment with three operating divisions. The Engine Division manufactures a four-cylinder, 160-horsepower engine used to power the inboard-outboard units assembled in the Boat Division of the company. Each division is operated as an investment center. The transfer price used by the company is standard product cost plus 28 percent. Following are standard and actual cost data for the production of the 5,000 engines manufactured during the period.

	Standard	Actual
Direct materials	$1,450,000	$1,690,000
Direct labor	1,375,000	1,555,000
Manufacturing overhead	1,100,000	1,005,000
Operating expenses	—	650,000

Required:

a. Compute the transfer price for the engines using the company's usual transfer pricing model.

b. Compute the net income for the Engine Division using the transfer price computed in part *a*.

c. What would the net income have been if the Engine Division had experienced no variances during the period?

d. Compute the net income for the division using a transfer price of actual product cost plus 18 percent.

P. 11-9 (CMA) Decentralized organizations. Edwin Hall, chairman of the board and president of Arrow Works Products Company, founded the company in the mid-1970s. He is a talented and creative engineer. Arrow Works was started with one of his inventions, an intricate diecast item which required a minimum of finish work. The item was manufactured for Arrow Works by a Gary, Indiana, foundry. The product sold well in a wide market.

The company issued common stock in 1982 to finance the purchase of the Gary foundry. Additional shares were issued in 1985 when Arrow purchased a fabricating plant in Cleveland to meet the capacity requirement of a defense contract.

The company now consists of five divisions. Each division is headed by a manager who reports to Hall. The Chicago Division contains the product development and engineering department and the finishing (assembly) operation for the basic products. The Gary plant and Cleveland plant are the other two divisions engaged in manufacturing operations. All products manufactured are sold through two selling divisions. The Eastern Sales Division is located in Pittsburgh and covers the country from Chicago to the East Coast. The Western Sales Division, which covers the rest of the country, is located in Denver. The Western Sales Division is the newest operation and was established just 8 months ago.

Hall, who still owns 53 percent of the outstanding stock, actively participates in the management of the company. He travels frequently and regularly to all of the company's plants and offices. He says, "Having a business with locations in five different cities spread over half the country requires all my time." Despite his regular and frequent visits he believes the company is decentralized, with the managers having complete autonomy. "They make all the decisions and run their own shops. Of course they don't understand the total business as I do, so I have to straighten them out once in a while. My managers are all good men, but they can't be expected to handle everything alone. I try to help all I can."

The last 2 months have been a period of considerable stress for Mr. Hall. During this period, John Staple, manager of the fabricating plant, was advised by his physician to request a 6-month sick leave to relieve the work pressures that had made him nervous and tense. This request had followed by 3 days a phone call in which Hall had directly and bluntly blamed Staple for the lagging production output and increased rework and scrap of the fabricating plant. Hall made no allowances for the pressures created by the operation of the plant at volumes in excess of normal and close to its maximum rated capacity for the previous 9 months.

Hall thought he and Staple had had a long and good relationship prior to this event. Hall attributed his loss of temper in this case to his frustration with several other management problems that had arisen in the past 2 months. The sales manager of the Denver office had resigned shortly after a visit from Hall. The letter of resignation stated that he was seeking a position with greater responsibility. The sales manager in Pittsburgh asked to be reassigned to a sales position in the field; he did not feel he could cope with the pressure of management.

Required:

- **a.** Explain the difference between centralized and decentralized management.
- **b.** Is Arrow Works Products Company decentralized, as Edwin Hall believes? Explain your answer.
- **c.** On the basis of the facts presented in the problem, could the events which have occurred over the past 2 months in Arrow Works Products Company have been expected? Explain your answer.

P. 11-10 Transfer prices for services. Paradise State Park has been plagued by vandalism recently. There are no funds available to hire permanent security officers to patrol the park. However, there is a general contingency fund with enough resources to hire temporary security people to patrol the park for a while until the vandalism is controlled. Private security firms have bid for the job, with a low bid of $25 per patrol hour, including patrol vehicles. The state police have heard of the situation and offered to patrol the park. In return the park must pay the state police out of the special contingency fund. State police cost and activity data for the year are as follows.

	Police Hours	Cost
State police in total	1,000,000	$15,000,000
State police patrol division	400,000	7,200,000

Of the patrol division's cost, 60 percent is variable.

Required:

a. Compute the transfer price for the state police patrol service if:
   1. Park officials can convince the state police that full cost for state police activities in general is the appropriate transfer price.
   2. State police can convince park officials that full cost for the patrol division is the appropriate transfer price.
   3. State police can convince park officials that outside market price less a normal profit of 20 percent is the appropriate transfer price.
   4. Park officials can convince the state police that the appropriate transfer price is the variable part of the patrol division cost plus an incentive of 20 percent of the variable cost.

b. If the contingency fund can provide $27,000 for this project, how many patrol hours can the park purchase using each of the transfer prices computed above?

P. 11-11 Using trial balance data to measure division performance. The Fernald Company manufactures toys which it sells to stores and wholesalers. The Dollhouse Division is a wholly owned subsidiary of the company. Corporate management evaluates division managers on the basis of division performance. Recently, there has been a lot of discussion about what measure of division performance is most useful. To illustrate the differences in various performance measures, you have been asked to compute the return on investment using a number of the more popular ROI measures. The Dollhouse Division trial balance is given on page 478.

Required: Compute the return on investment for the Dollhouse Division using each of the following investment bases:

a. Net assets.
b. Gross assets.
c. Working capital.
d. Sales.
e. Beginning owners' equity.
f. Ending owners' equity
g. Average owners' equity.
h. Residual income based on a target income of 10 percent of net assets.

Dollhouse Division
Trial Balance
December 31, 1986

	Debit	Credit
Cash	$ 4,000	
Accounts receivable	12,000	
Inventory	18,000	
Prepaid assets	2,000	
Building	82,000	
Accumulated depreciation, building		$ 17,000
Equipment	32,000	
Accumulated depreciation, equipment		13,000
Accounts payable		8,000
Taxes payable		8,000
Notes payable		11,000
Mortgage payable		23,000
Capital stock		25,000
Paid-in capital in excess of par		5,000
Retained earnings		20,000
Sales		136,000
Cost of goods sold	56,000	
Advertising	12,000	
Sales salaries and commissions	9,100	
Administrative salaries	28,000	
Office insurance	1,100	
Office property taxes	2,500	
Office utilities	3,300	
Office maintenance	4,000	
Totals	$266,000	$266,000

P. 11-12 **Determining and using transfer prices.** The Hot Iron Steel Company has a Mining Division and a Steel Production Division. Currently the Mining Division sells 60 percent of its output to the Steel Production Division and 40 percent in the outside market. The market price for iron ore is $100 a ton. Production and cost data for the Mining Division are presented below.

Output	500,000 tons
Direct labor	$12,000,000
Depreciation and depletion	10,000,000
Other production costs	10,000,000
Marketing	1,000,000
Administration	8,000,000

Required:

a. Compute the transfer price for iron ore, assuming:
   1. A total cost transfer price is used for all iron ore sold to the Steel Production Division.
   2. The objective of the Mining Division is to recover all division costs.
   3. A market price less marketing cost.

4. The objective of the Mining Division is to earn 10 percent on sales.

b. What is the Mining Division's net income using each of the transfer prices computed above?

P. 11-13 **Alternative transfer prices.** The Glass Division of Winthrop Motors manufactures windshields that it sells primarily to the Assembly Division of the firm, but some units are sold in the open market. During 1986 the Glass Division manufactured 50,000 windshields of which 10,000 were sold to other companies at a price of $65. Cost data for 1986 operations were as follows.

Direct materials	$ 550,000
Direct labor	900,000
Manufacturing overhead	1,200,000
Administrative	180,000
Marketing and distribution	80,000

Required: For parts *a* through *e*, compute the transfer price for windshields assuming management's objective is to:

a. Transfer units at full product cost.

b. Transfer units at the market price less 15 percent to reflect the lower marketing and distribution costs of internal sales.

c. Cover all costs of making, marketing, and administering the windshields.

d. Generate a target profit of 10 percent on total costs for the division.

e. Transfer units at market price.

f. Compute the Glass Division's net income for 1986 using each of the transfer prices computed above.

P. 11-14 **(CMA) Analysis of transfer pricing alternatives.** The Lorax Electric Company manufactures a large variety of systems and individual components for the electronics industry. The firm is organized into several divisions, with division managers given the authority to make virtually all operating decisions. Management control over division operations is maintained by a system of division profit and return on investment measures which are reviewed regularly by top management. The top managers of Lorax have been quite pleased with the effectiveness of the system they have been using and believe that it is responsible for the company's improved profitability over the last few years.

The Devices Division manufactures solid-state devices and is operating at capacity. The Systems Division has asked the Devices Division to supply a large quantity of integrated circuit IC378. The Devices Division currently is selling this component to its regular customers at $40 per hundred.

The Systems Division, which is operating at about 60 percent capacity, wants this particular component for a digital clock system. It has an opportunity to supply large quantities of these digital clock systems to Centonic Electric, a major producer of clock radios and other popular electronic home entertainment equipment. This is the first opportunity any of the Lorax divisions have had to do business with Centonic Electric. Centonic Electric has offered to pay $7.50 per clock system.

The Systems Division prepared an analysis of the probable costs to produce the clock systems. The amount that could be paid to the Devices Division for the integrated circuits was determined by working backward from the selling price. The cost estimates employed by the division reflected the highest per-unit cost the Systems Division could incur for each cost component and still leave a sufficient margin so that the division's income statement could show reasonable improvement. The cost estimates are summarized below.

Proposed selling price		$7.50
Costs excluding required integrated circuits (IC378)		
Components purchased from outside suppliers	$2.75	
Circuit board etching—labor and variable overhead	.40	
Assembly, testing, packaging—labor and variable overhead	1.35	
Fixed overhead allocations	1.50	
Profit margin	.50	6.50
Amount that can be paid for integrated circuits IC378 (5 @ $20 per hundred)		$1.00

As a result of this analysis, the Systems Division offered the Devices Division a price of $20 per hundred for the integrated circuit. This bid was refused by the manager of the Devices Division because he felt the Systems Division should at least meet the price of $40 per hundred that regular customers pay. When the Systems Division found that it could not obtain a comparable integrated circuit from outside vendors, the situation was brought to an arbitration committee that had been set up to review such problems.

The arbitration committee prepared an analysis that showed that $.15 would cover variable costs of producing the integrated circuit, $.28 would cover the full cost including fixed overhead, and $.35 would provide a gross margin equal to the average gross margin on all the products sold by the Devices Division. The manager of the Systems Division reacted by stating, "They could sell us that integrated circuit for $.20 and still earn a positive contribution toward profit. In fact, they should be required to sell at their variable cost—$.15—and not be allowed to take advantage of us."

Lou Belcher, manager of Devices, countered by arguing, "It doesn't make sense to sell to the Systems Division at $20 per hundred when we can get $40 per hundred outside on all we can produce. In fact, Systems could pay us up to almost $60 per hundred and they would still have a positive contribution to profit."

The recommendation of the committee, to set the price at $.35 per unit ($35 per hundred), so that Devices could earn a "fair" gross margin, was rejected by both division managers. Consequently, the problem was brought to the attention of the vice president of operations and his staff.

Required:

a. What is the immediate economic effect on the Lorax Company as a whole if the Devices Division were required to supply IC378 to the Systems Division at $.35 per unit—the price recommended by the arbitration committee? Explain your answer.

b. Discuss the advisability of intervention by top management as a solution to transfer pricing disputes between division managers such as the one experienced by Lorax Electric Company.

c. Suppose that Lorax adopted a policy of requiring that the price to be paid in all internal transfers by the buying division would be equal to the variable costs per unit of the selling division for that product and that the supplying division would be required to sell if the buying division decided to buy the item. Discuss the consequences of adopting such a policy as a way of avoiding the need for the arbitration committee or for intervention by the vice president.

CASE

Case 11-1 Comprehensive transfer pricing analysis

Hummer Sewing Machine Company is a decentralized manufacturing company in which all major component parts are made by separate divisions that are operated as profit centers. The motors for the sewing machines are made by the MTO Division of the Company. The MTO Division has more capacity than required to satisfy production needs for the company's sewing machines. During 1986, the division sold 30 percent of its motors to other companies at a price of $20 each and the rest were sold to the Assembly Division of the Hummer Sewing Machine Company. The industry average for marketing and distribution costs of this type of motor is 20 percent of selling price.

The MTO Division made 25,000 motors during 1986 and incurred the following total standard manufacturing costs and actual operating expenses.

Direct materials	$150,000	
Direct labor	100,000	
Manufacturing overhead	80,000	
Total production cost variances	40,000	Unfavorable
Operating expenses:		
Selling and distribution	20,000	
Administrative	80,000	

Evaluation of the production standards has led to the decision to increase production standard costs by 10 percent for the coming year. Market analysis indicates a 6 percent price increase is logical for the motors. With the new standard costs, management of the MTO Division expects variances from standard will average 5 percent unfavorable. No changes are expected in selling and distribution expenses or administrative expenses. Production and sales quantities are expected to be the same as in 1986.

Required: Compute the required transfer price for the sewing machine motors for each of the following **independent** assumptions: The transfer price should

a. Be based on 1986 standard product cost.
b. Be based on 1986 actual product cost.
c. Be based on 1987 standard product cost.
d. Be based on 1987 expected actual product cost.
e. Be based on 1987 market price.
f. Be based on 1987 market price modified for lower marketing and distribution costs.
g. Provide a 6 percent profit on 1987 expected total costs.

h. Prepare a schedule showing the MTO Division's net income for each of the 1987-base transfer pricing alternatives.
i. Comment on the logic of management's establishing new standards that are expected to yield an unfavorable variance of 5 percent.

Accounting Data and Pricing Decisions

12

The pricing of products and services involves complex decisions that many organizations must undertake. This chapter discusses the economic framework and the accounting concepts used in establishing selling prices of an organization's products and services. When you have completed the study of this chapter you should understand:

1. The fundamental economic framework in price determination.
2. Four basic economic market models.
3. Variables that affect pricing decisions.
4. Several pricing models commonly used in business.
5. The calculation of prices with commonly used pricing models.

All profit-oriented firms and many not-for-profit organizations must establish prices for their goods and services. Setting prices for goods and services requires an understanding of relevant concepts as well as an ability to apply those concepts in the complex economic environment in which organizations operate. In this chapter we discuss the economic framework and accounting concepts used in establishing prices for the products and services sold by an organization.

Selling price is the amount charged customers for some product or service

The pricing decision is one of the more interesting decisions that managers must make. **Pricing** refers to the assignment of a selling price to a product or service provided by a firm. Sometimes the term **price** refers to the **purchase price** of some resource acquired by a firm, but this is more precisely a **cost** to the purchasing firm. In this chapter we discuss **selling price,** which is the amount charged customers for some product or service.

Pricing activities are more extensive than many people realize. It is easy to visualize the need to price each product in a store, but all organizations that provide a service for a fee or sell products must decide on the amount to charge for **each** service or product. A construction firm must decide how much to bid on a building contract. A physician must establish a price for examinations, X-rays, and other services. When people decide whether to accept jobs that pay specific salaries, they are pricing their services. The Postal Service, a not-for-profit organization, sets prices on mail services, and local governments establish prices for marriage licenses.

Once a price is established for a product or service, the pricing decision is not over. Prices must be continuously reevaluated to ensure that they reflect management's pricing objectives in light of current costs, market conditions, and competitor actions. Some prices may remain in effect for a year or more; others may change rapidly. Stamp and coin dealers change some prices daily. Automobile manufacturers may change prices several times a year. Pricing decisions are dynamic, and they are a necessary, continuing activity of virtually all organizations.

In the first part of the chapter, we discuss the nature of pricing decisions and of the entities that set prices. We introduce the economic framework in which pricing decisions take place so that you understand the reasons behind pricing decisions. The basic economic concepts play a role in production and pricing decisions discussed in the second part of the chapter, in which we illustrate specific pricing models commonly used by businesses.

THE ECONOMICS OF PRICING

Pricing decisions may be influenced by internal factors, such as costs and profit objectives, and by external factors, such as competitors' pricing actions or regulatory pricing guidelines. Some factors that may influence pricing decisions include

Factors influencing pricing decisions

- Cost data
- Revenue and profit objectives
- Type of product or service
- Type of industry
- Management style
- Pubic image
- Government influence
- Competitor actions
- Type of market
- Economic trends

How do the above factors interact and result in a pricing decision? The answer depends on the individual making the decision. Each decision maker incorporates pricing variables into the decision process in a different way. One person may weigh economic trends and industry averages heavily and may ignore government pressure for price restraint. Another may use government pricing guidelines as the primary variable in establishing new prices. Whatever the decision style of the individual, many pricing decisions are couched, at least in part, in the general framework of economic pricing theory. The discussion that follows is an overview of pricing, but it is only a brief presentation of the economic theory underlying pricing decisions.

The way prices are established depends on the market in which goods are traded. Economists describe several types of markets, including:

1. Perfectly competitive markets
2. Monopolistic competition
3. Oligopoly
4. Monopoly

Perfectly Competitive Markets

A market is **perfectly competitive** if it has the following characteristics:

Assumptions underlying perfectly competitive markets

1. The goods traded are homogeneous, which means that the product of one seller is identical, in the opinion of the buyers, to the products of other sellers.
2. Market participants, whether buyers or sellers, cannot individually influence the market price of the products by their actions.
3. There is freedom of entry and exit, which means that anyone may enter or leave the market at any time by offering or withholding resources.
4. Market participants have complete and perfect knowledge of prices and resource costs.

Very few products have perfectly competitive markets if all four characteristics are strictly interpreted. However, if the last two conditions are slightly relaxed, a number of products may be classified as trading in perfectly competitive markets. Such a classification is useful for analyzing prices and pricing decisions. The stock market is viewed by some economists as being nearly perfectly competitive. Probably the most notable products selling in almost perfectly competitive markets are farm commodities such as corn, wheat, cattle, and hogs.

Supply is the amount that suppliers in aggregate are willing to sell at each market price

The prices in perfectly competitive markets are determined by supply and demand. **Supply** is the total amount of product all suppliers are willing to sell at each possible selling price. **Demand** is the total amount all buyers are willing to purchase at each possible price. Figure 12-1 shows the supply and demand schedules for corn. These schedules are the amount of product that sellers are willing to supply and that buyers are willing to buy at specific prices. At a price of $200 a metric ton, suppliers are willing to produce 180,000 metric tons of corn; at $190 a ton, they will produce only 170,000 metric tons. At lower prices even less corn will be produced.

Supply and Demand Schedules for Corn

Price per Metric Ton	Quantity Supplied in Thousands of Tons	Quantity Demanded in Thousands of Tons
$200	180	60
190	170	70
180	156	84
170	135	100
160	120	120
150	88	140
140	65	165
130	43	190

Figure 12-1 **Supply and demand schedules for a commodity that trades in a perfectly competitive market. At higher prices demand is small but supply is large. At lower prices demand is large but supply is small because fewer suppliers find it economically feasible to produce the commodity.**

Demand is the amount that buyers in aggregate are willing to buy at each market price

The demand for a product is inversely affected by price, which means that as the price increases, demand for the product decreases. For example, the demand schedule in Figure 12-1 shows that at $200 per metric ton, purchasers are willing to buy only 60,000 tons of corn. At $190 per ton, they are willing to buy 70,000 tons. As the price declines, demand increases because buyers are willing to acquire more corn at lower prices.

The supply and demand schedules may be graphed as shown in Figure 12-2. The supply schedule slopes up and to the right, showing a willing-

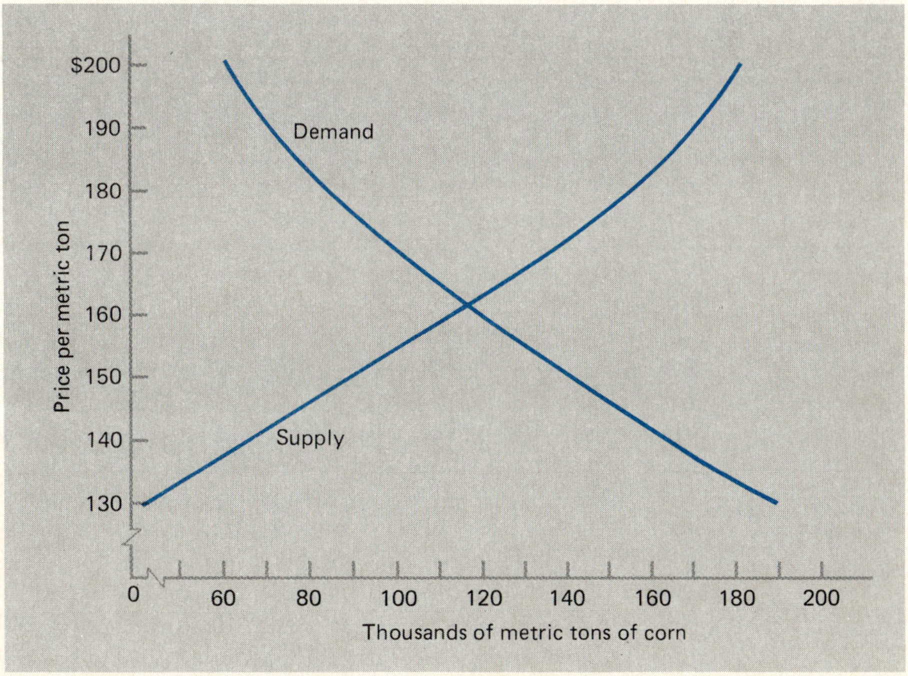

Figure 12-2 **Supply and demand curves plotted from the data in Figure 12-1. Market equilibrium occurs where the curves intersect. At that price, supply is sufficient to satisfy all demand because suppliers and buyers agree on both price and quantity.**

Schedule of Production Costs for a Single Producer of Corn

Metric Tons Produced	Total Cost	Marginal Cost
0	$ 100	—
1	190	$ 90
2	260	70
3	320	60
4	370	50
5	418	48
6	470	52
7	535	65
8	615	80
9	715	100
10	840	125
11	995	155
12	1,195	200
13	1,455	260
14	1,785	330

Figure 12-3
An individual producer decides on the best course of action by evaluating the market price and production costs. This production schedule shows that marginal cost declines from zero to 5 metric tons and then increases as production increases.

ness on the part of producers to supply greater quantities at higher prices. The graph of the supply schedule is called a **supply curve.** The demand schedule may be graphed in the form of a **demand curve,** which slopes down and to the right as shown in Figure 12-2, indicating an increase in demand as the price of a product declines.

Market equilibrium occurs when the quantity supplied and the quantity demanded are equal at a particular price

The only point where the buyers and sellers are in total agreement is where the two curves intersect. The point of intersection, called the **market equilibrium,** yields the price *P*—$160 a metric ton in this example—and the quantity purchased *Q*—120,000 metric tons of corn.

The $160 price and 120,000-ton quantity are determined by all participants in the market. By definition, no single buyer or seller can influence the market. If a seller attempts to charge more than $160 for a ton of corn, the purchaser will buy from someone else. A lower price than $160 makes no sense because individual suppliers can sell their entire supply at the market price in a perfectly competitive market. Therefore, the demand curve for an **individual** supplier in a perfectly competitive market is a horizontal straight line at the selling price. This demand curve is illustrated in Figure 12-5, discussed later. Note the difference between the demand curve for an **individual** producer and the demand curve in Figure 12-2 for **all** sellers in the market.

Since individual suppliers cannot influence the price of a product, their only decision is to decide how much to produce. Using the selling price and production data, each supplier must determine the optimum amount to produce and sell, which is the production level where profit is greatest. To illustrate, Figure 12-3 presents cost data for a supplier with 200 acres available for corn production.

Figure 12-4
This schedule shows that profit increases up to 11 metric tons of production, then declines above that level. At this level of production, marginal cost equals marginal revenue and profit is maximized.

Schedule of Revenue, Costs, and Net Income for a Single Producer of Corn

Metric Tons Produced	Total Revenue	Total Cost	Net Income
0	$ 0	$ 100	$(100)
1	160	190	(30)
2	320	260	60
3	480	320	160
4	640	370	270
5	800	418	382
6	960	470	490
7	1,120	535	585
8	1,280	615	665
9	1,440	715	725
10	1,600	845	755
11	1,760	995	765
12	1,920	1,195	725
13	2,080	1,455	625
14	2,240	1,785	455

The supplier has certain fixed costs, such as property taxes, and some variable production costs, such as seed and fertilizer. The corn yield can be varied by planting different amounts of the acreage, thereby using more or less fertilizer, labor, and seed, and by using varying amounts of labor, fertilizer, and herbicides per acre cultivated. The cost data for various levels of production appear in Figure 12-3. The **marginal cost** is the amount of cost increase caused by a unit increase in output. For example, if production increases from 7 metric tons to 8 metric tons, total cost increases from $535 to $615 per ton, an increase of $80. The $80 marginal cost applies only to the 8-ton production level. At other production levels the marginal cost is different. The optimum strategy is to produce at the level where marginal cost equals marginal revenue. **Marginal revenue** is the additional revenue obtained by selling one additional unit of product. In a perfectly competitive market, marginal revenue is equal to price, so the optimal strategy is to produce at the level where marginal cost equals price. Beyond this point the next metric ton of corn produced will cost more to produce than the price it will bring in the market. This strategy is illustrated graphically in Figure 12-5 and is verified by the schedule in Figure 12-4, which shows revenue, cost, and net income.

Marginal cost is the additional cost of producing one more unit

Marginal revenue is the additional revenue from selling one more unit

In Figure 12-5 the marginal cost line crosses the $160 price line at just above 11 metric tons of corn. At this quantity, net income is greatest, as shown in Figure 12-4. Production of less than 11 tons or more than 11 tons yields less net income. Note that this illustration is an example of economic theory that works in aggregate terms. For the individual producer, it is often very difficult to know the marginal revenue and marginal cost. The price of many commodities changes frequently as a result of

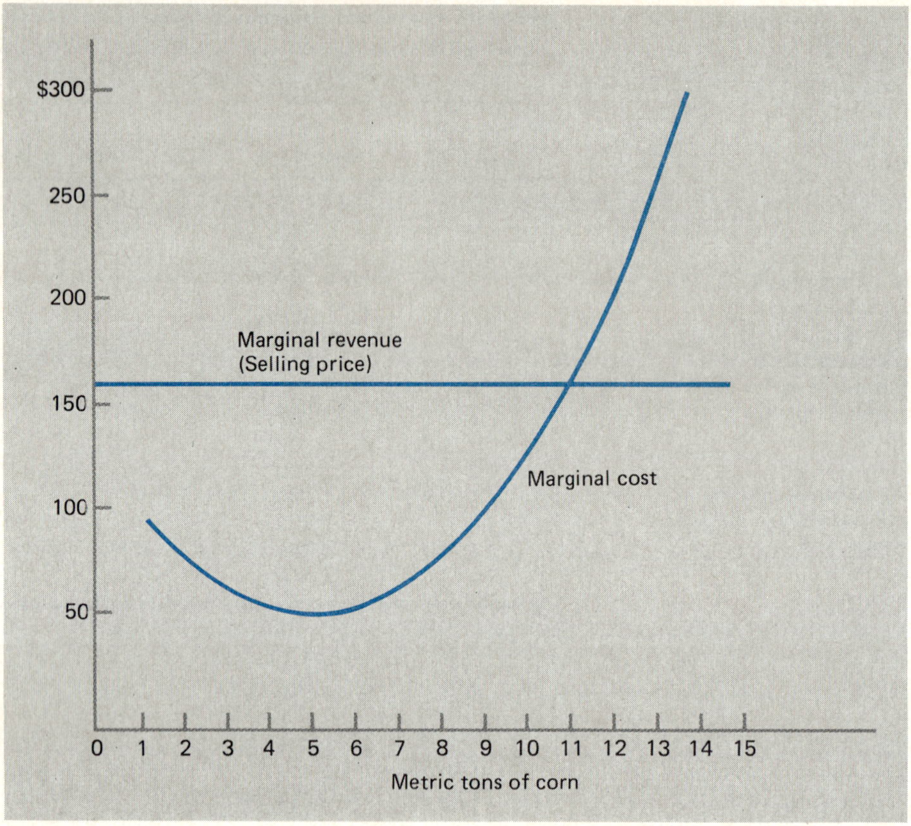

Figure 12-5
In a perfectly competitive market, an individual producer's marginal revenue is the selling price, which plots as a horizontal line. To maximize profit, the producer should continue to supply the product until marginal revenue equals marginal cost.

weather conditions, political atmosphere, changes in supply and demand, and other factors. Once a producer has made a commitment to a specific amount of production, the quantity produced cannot be increased, and it can be decreased only by withholding part of the production from the market. In practice, individual producers apply the aggregate economic theory by modifying it with specific individual pricing models discussed later in this chapter.

Monopolistic Competition, Monopoly, and Oligopoly

Producers try to get some monopolistic characteristics into their competing products

Most products are not sold in perfectly competitive markets because they do not satisfy the homogeneity characteristic of perfect competition. Businesses make an effort to differentiate their products from the products of other companies. They do so by patenting unique features of their products or by making their products function or perform differently than competing products. In addition, companies advertise their products, claiming they are bigger, better, faster, prettier, more practical, easier to use, more colorful, easier to pay for, and so forth. Such differentiation creates a somewhat different type of market and pricing framework, including monopolistic competition, monopoly, and oligopoly.

Monopolistic competition occurs when there are many sellers of similar, but not identical, products in the market. No single seller is able to exercise a perceptible influence over the market price of the similar products. Breakfast cereals, appliances, and furniture are examples of monopolistic competition. **Monopoly** occurs when a firm is the sole supplier of some product. There are no competing products in the market. Electric utilities and gas utilities are common examples. An **oligopoly** exists when several large sellers dominate a market and compete against one another. The automobile industry and the steel industry are examples of oligopolies.

Monopolistic competition. The economic solution to the product pricing decision in other than perfectly competitive markets rests on the same principle of maximizing net income that is achieved when marginal revenue equals marginal cost. The difference between a perfectly competitive market and other types of markets is the shape of the revenue curves. In a perfectly competitive market, a single seller faces a horizontal demand curve. That means the firm can sell as many units of product as it chooses at the market price. The horizontal demand curve is also the marginal revenue curve. Each additional unit of sales adds the same amount to total revenue as the last unit sold. In other types of markets, **each** supplier faces a downward-sloping demand curve similar to the **aggregate** demand curve in a perfectly competitive market.

Individual demand curves in other than perfectly competitive markets slope downward

The downward-sloping demand curve occurs because the firm attempts to differentiate its product from competing brands. Differentiation may take place if the firm provides different features for the product, such as a different appearance, more functions, or less complicated controls, or advertises in order to build brand loyalty and make the product's existence known to a large number of consumers. For example, one automatic dishwasher costs more than another, but it is quieter. A buyer may be willing to pay the higher price in order to obtain less noise, but if the price is much higher, the customer may forgo quiet operation in order to save money. There is a range of price variation within which customers will not switch from one product to another. As the price increases, some, but not all, customers may switch to other products, reducing the amount demanded. If the price is decreased, some competitors' customers will be attracted.

The following examples illustrate the general pricing model for monopolistic competition. The quantity and revenue data in Figure 12-6 are used to derive the demand curve facing the individual producer. The quantity demanded by purchasers varies inversely with the product price. High prices mean few units are purchased, and low prices result in more units being purchased. The total revenue column in Figure 12-6 is merely the selling price times the number of units demanded at each price. Marginal revenue is the amount added to total revenue by the sale of one additional unit.

The data in Figure 12-6 are graphed in Figure 12-7. Total revenue

Figure 12-6
The demand for a product in monopolistic competition increases as the price declines. To increase unit sales, the supplier must reduce prices. In this example, as total revenue increases, marginal revenue declines.

Schedule of Demand, Total Revenue, and Marginal Revenue

Price	Quantity Demanded	Total Revenue	Marginal Revenue
$1,200	0	$ 0	$ 0
1,100	1	1,100	1,100
1,000	2	2,000	900
900	3	2,700	700
800	4	3,200	500
700	5	3,500	300
600	6	3,600	100
500	7	3,500	(100)
400	8	3,200	(300)
300	9	2,700	(500)
200	10	2,000	(700)
100	11	1,100	(900)

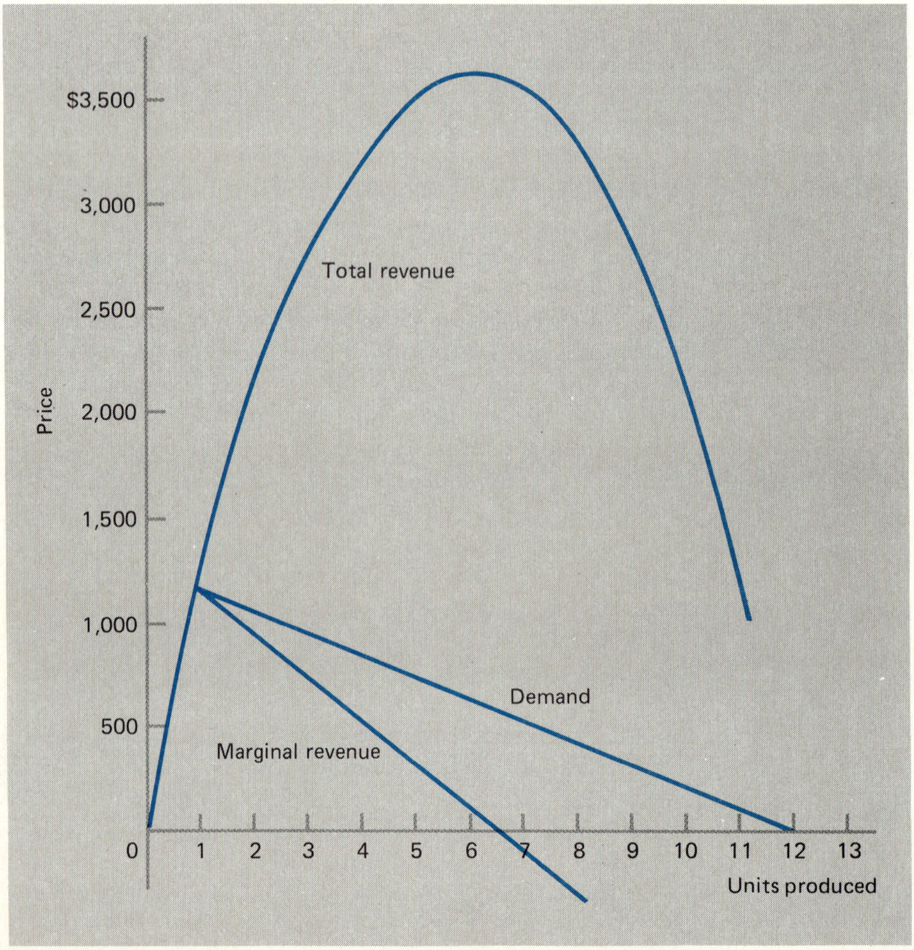

Figure 12-7
The data in Figure 12-6 are plotted here showing the downward-sloping demand curve, marginal revenue curve, and the total revenue curve. The total revenue curve starts to decline when marginal revenue reaches zero.

Schedule of Production, Total Cost, and Marginal Cost

Quantity Produced	Total Cost	Marginal Cost
0	$1,000	—
1	1,300	$ 300
2	1,600	300
3	2,000	400
4	2,500	500
5	3,100	600
6	3,800	700
7	4,600	800
8	5,500	900
9	6,500	1,000
10	7,600	1,100
11	8,800	1,200

Figure 12-8
Schedule of production costs and marginal cost for a product that sells in monopolistic competition. Marginal cost is the difference in total cost between any two levels of production.

starts at zero and rises to a peak of $3,600 at six units. Marginal revenue is $1,100 at one unit and declines throughout because selling price must be lowered to generate more demand for the product. The demand curve shows how many units will be purchased at each price.

As with perfectly competitive markets, the supplier sells the product as long as the marginal revenue is greater than the marginal cost. Figure 12-8 shows the production cost data for the firm at each level of activity. The total cost and marginal cost data are graphed in Figure 12-9.

The marginal revenue and marginal cost curves are combined in Figure 12-10, where the vertical scale is changed to accentuate the slope of the curves. At $500 per unit, four units of product will be sold, and at this price and volume, net income is maximized. If the producer raises or lowers the price, net income decreases. Using the cost and revenue data in Figures 12-6 and 12-8, the producer can set the optimal selling price.

Monopoly. If a business is the only producer of a product for which there is a demand, it controls the price for the product. This does not mean that it can set any price, for at some high price level there will be no demand for its product. If the product satisfies a basic need for which demand is high, a very high price may be commanded. If the product is something that people can easily do without, a high price will drive customers away.

A monopoly must submit to regulation

When prices are high relative to production costs, profits are also high, and this attracts other producers into the market, destroying the monopoly. In the case of some products, such as utility services, it is more economical and efficient to have one large producer provide the service than to have many small, inefficient producers. Consequently, monopoly power may be granted to a single producer in exchange for some guarantee that prices will be reasonable. Reasonable prices are usually ensured by setting a

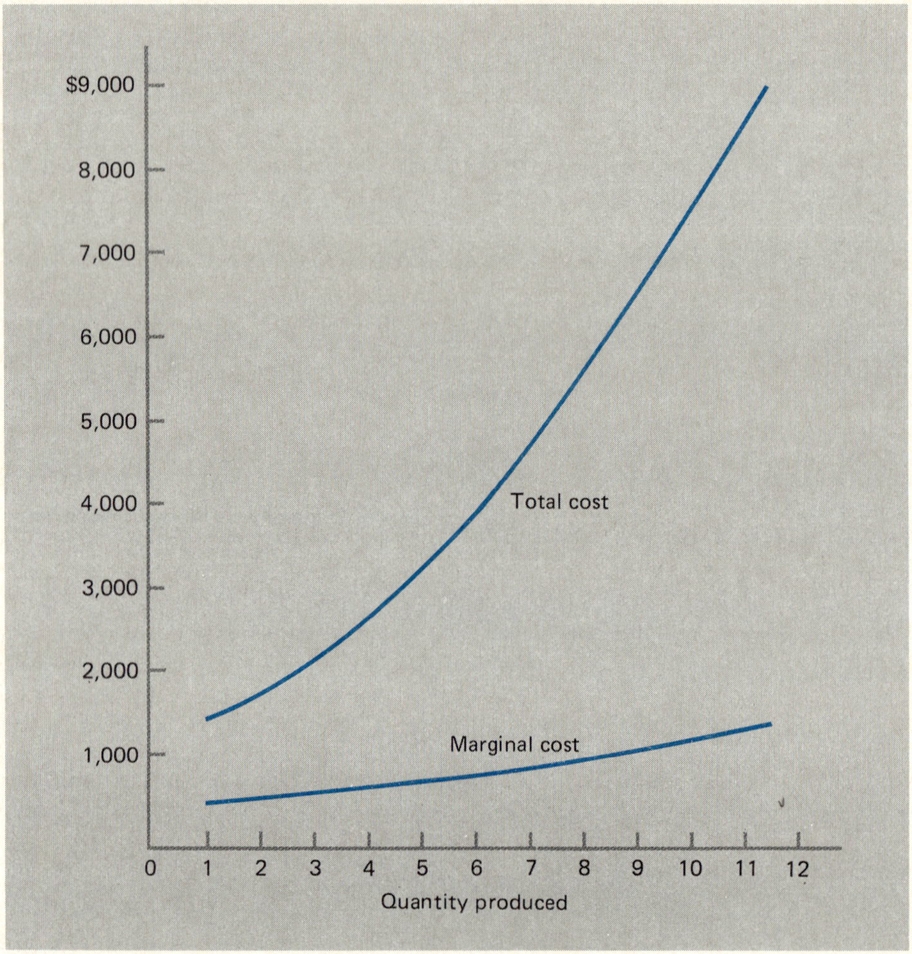

Figure 12-9
Graph of production costs shown in Figure 12-8. The marginal cost curve is increasing because the total cost curve is increasing at an increasing rate.

legal ceiling beyond which prices may not be raised or by having a regulatory body establish prices.

Once the price has been set for a monopoly, the firm's production decision is the same as under monopolistic competition. The demand curve is downward-sloping because there is some substitution possible among products offered by monopolies. Customers may choose to heat their homes using electric power, natural gas, a wood-burning fireplace, or a combination of all three. A monopoly is usually able to maintain its prices at the highest possible level allowed by law, and in such cases it only needs to decide how much to produce, just as in a perfectly competitive market. But monopoly status usually carries with it the obligation for the business to satisfy demand completely given the established price. In exchange for price control and requirements to satisfy demand, monopolies are guaranteed prices that produce a reasonable profit.

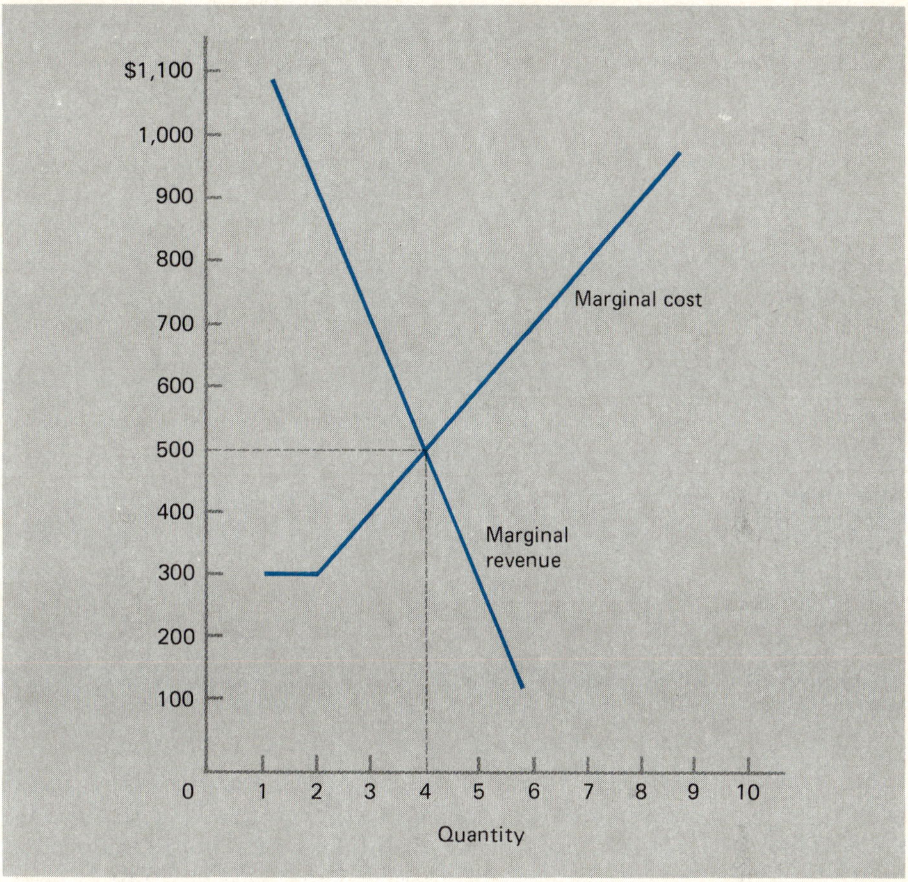

Figure 12-10 **Marginal cost plotted in Figure 12-7 and marginal revenue plotted in Figure 12-9 are combined here to show the production level that maximizes profit. The vertical scale is changed to accentuate the slopes of the curves.**

Given the constraints under which they operate, monopolies must monitor and control their costs carefully. As production and operating costs increase and profit margins decline, monopolies request price increases from their regulatory agencies, and must justify such price increases by providing adequate cost data as supporting evidence. In theory, the pricing of products or services provided by monopolies ensures a fair price and efficient operation. In practice, however, much waste may occur if costs are allowed to proliferate, and if rate-setting agencies automatically approve price increases without careful scrutiny of costs and their appropriateness.

Oligopoly. An oligopoly market consists of several large suppliers, any one of which is large enough to affect the market price. As a result, the demand curve of one firm may be directly affected by the pricing actions of other sellers in the market. For example, if one producer of aluminum

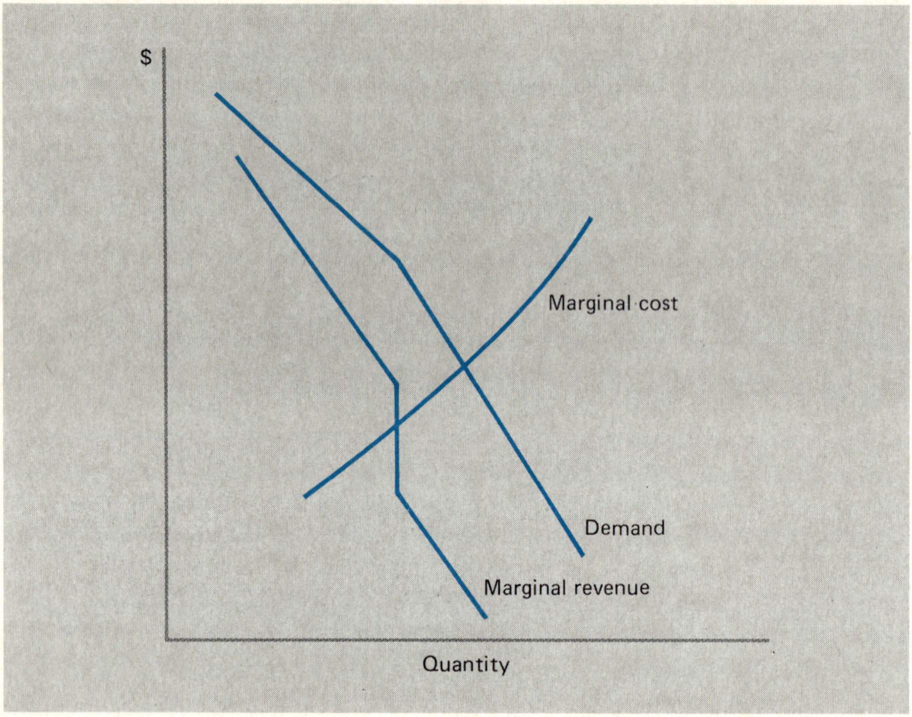

Figure 12-11
A kinked demand curve for a company that competes in an oligopolistic market. A price change by one firm may have a dramatic impact on the demand of competing firms.

An oligopoly is a group of relatively large firms that together dominate a market

lowers its price, the demand for other producers' aluminum declines when buyers shift to the lower-priced producer. This buyers' shift may cause the demand curve for an oligopolistic firm to undergo sharp changes when going from one price to another, as is shown in the **kinked demand curve** illustrated in Figure 12-11. There are various solutions to determining price in oligopolistic markets, depending upon the nature of the firms in the market, their relationship to one another, and the attitude of each firm's management about pricing. A **price leader** in effect establishes the price, and the **price follower** merely adopts the price set by the leader. With this approach, a price follower is confronted with a horizontal demand curve, as in perfectly competitive markets. The problem for the price leader is to set prices at the level that will maximize its profits considering that the price followers will be trying to sell all they can at the same price.

Elasticity of Demand

When an individual firm faces a downward-sloping demand curve, the shape of the curve often determines the pricing policy to be adopted. A downward-sloping demand curve means that a higher price makes the goods less desirable to customers and a lower price makes them more desirable. At any point on the demand curve for an individual supplier, the quantity and the price together will produce a specific amount of revenue. If the price is increased, the quantity demanded will decrease, but the total revenue with the new price and quantity may be more or less than with the old price and quantity.

Demand elasticity determines the change in revenue from a change in price

If a price increase and a corresponding decrease in quantity produce an increase in total revenue, the demand for the product is said to be **inelastic.** If the price increase results in a decrease in total revenue, demand is said to be **elastic.** Demand elasticity is measured by the ratio of the percentage change in quantity to the percentage change in price. For example, a product sells for \$100 and at this price the quantity demanded is 100 units. Total revenue in this case is \$10,000. At a price of \$101 per unit, only 99 units are demanded, and at a price of \$99 per unit, 101 units are demanded. In this price and quantity range, demand elasticity is 1, computed as follows:

$$\text{Demand elasticity} = \frac{\text{Percentage change in quantity}}{\text{Percentage change in price}}$$

$$= \frac{1/100}{\$1/\$100} = 1$$

If demand is elastic, revenue is increased by lowering the price

When demand elasticity is 1, a small change in price will produce a change in quantity just large enough to leave total revenue unchanged. When demand elasticity is greater than 1, demand is **elastic** and a **decrease** in price increases total revenue. When demand elasticity is less than 1, demand is **inelastic** and an **increase** in price increases total revenue. For example, a product has the demand curve shown in Figure 12-12. At \$10 per unit the quantity demanded is 10 units and total revenue is \$100, shown by the shaded area in the figure. If the price is increased to \$11.40, only 9 units will be demanded, but total revenue will increase to \$102.60. At this point on the demand curve, demand elasticity is less than 1, computed as follows:

$$\text{Demand elasticity} = \frac{1/10}{\$1.4/\$10} = .71$$

Because demand is inelastic, the price can be increased in order to increase total revenue. The area in Figure 12-12 enclosed with the dashed lines is the total revenue with the new price. The revenue lost, shown by the small vertical rectangle on the right, is less than the revenue gained, shown by the small horizontal rectangle at the top.

An increase in total revenue does not always mean an increase in profit. Profits may decline if the marginal cost of production is greater than the marginal revenue earned by selling additional units. For example, demand for a \$10 product is 20 units and demand elasticity is greater than 1, which means that a decrease in price should increase total revenue. When price is reduced by \$1.20, demand increases by 4 units. Variable

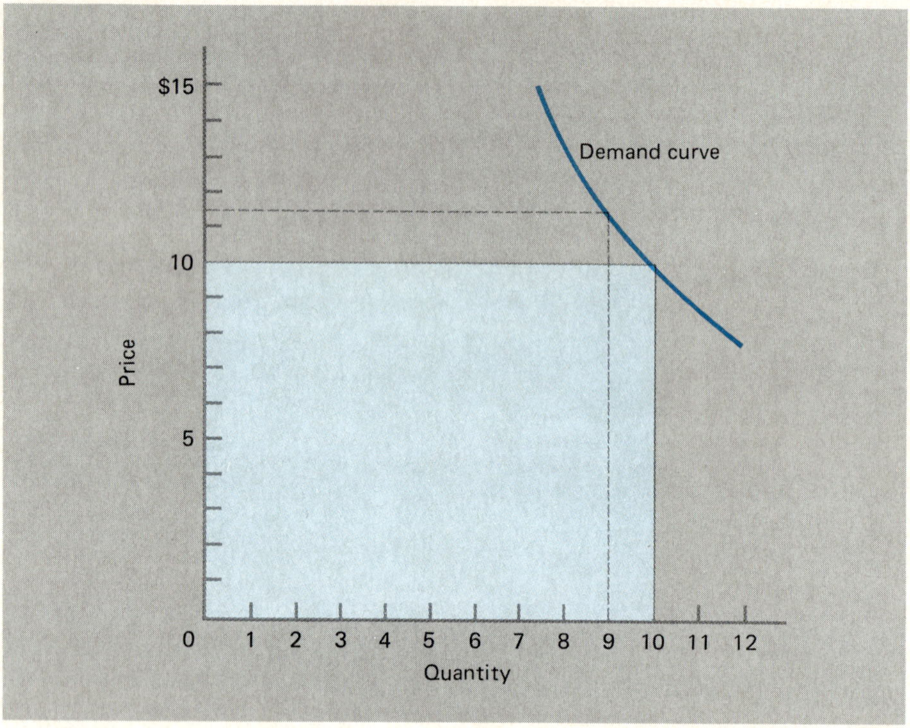

Figure 12-12 The effect of demand elasticity can be seen by comparing the total revenue at two different prices. When demand is inelastic, an increase in price causes an increase in total revenue. The additional revenue represented by the rectangle added at the top is more than the lost revenue represented by the smaller rectangle on the right.

cost of production is $5 per unit and fixed cost is $50. In this case, a decrease in price increases revenue but does not increase profit:

	Old Price		New Price	
Revenue	$10 × 20 units	$200	$8.80 × 24 units	$211.20
Variable cost	$5 × 20 units	(100)	$5.00 × 24 units	(120.00)
Fixed cost		(50)		(50.00)
Profit		$ 50		$ 41.20

When producers attempt to differentiate their products, they are really trying to make the demand for the product less elastic. Some products, such as tobacco and electric power, have very inelastic demand. Tobacco products trade in competitive markets and an individual producer cannot easily increase the price, because consumers would switch to other brands. But if prices are increased on all tobacco products, demand decreases very slightly. For this reason, taxes placed on products such as tobacco and liquor have no appreciable effect on demand. For this reason also, producers in monopoly markets have controlled prices. An electric utility could establish exorbitant prices for electric power before the demand for power would become elastic.

Demand elasticity is an essential element in pricing decisions. When a new product is developed, the producer may use the strategy of price skimming or the strategy of market penetration, depending on the elasticity of demand.

Pricing strategies on new products

Price skimming is the strategy of setting very high prices while the product is new and production quantity is small. This strategy takes advantage of those customers who will pay a high price to be the first with a new product. At this stage in the product's life, demand is very inelastic. Products such as ballpoint pens and electronic watches have gone through a period of price skimming. When the ballpoint pen was invented the unit price was about $15, and some early electronic watches sold for more than $1,000 each. Price skimming sometimes is used to recover initial research and development costs before increased competition forces prices lower.

Market penetration is a strategy of setting prices quite low in order to develop a strong customer base before other producers come in with competing products, or because other producers are already well established. Introductory offers on new food products and free samples are attempts at market penetration. Another example is the bargain price for charter membership at a new racquet club. Members joining the club after the charter offer expires pay a higher price.

Some Modifying Variables

The economic models just discussed are useful to managers in making pricing decisions, but the models are only basic frameworks. They are based on theories that apply to aggregate market situations and assume that businesses attempt to maximize profits. Many variables affect the pricing of any particular product. Some key variables that have a modifying effect on economic models are profit satisfaction, government influence, model limitations, and inferior goods.

Satisfactory profits may be less than maximum profits

Profit satisfaction. One of the primary assumptions in economic theory is that managers attempt to maximize profits. Without such an assumption, many types of economic analysis are impossible, but in the modern environment of business, profit maximization may not be possible. Even the word "profit" elicits unfavorable comments from some people, and the term "profit maximization" sometimes has the connotation of unwarranted or excessive profits. Economists argue that excessive profits cannot last long because new resources would flow into the market to take advantage of the high profits, thus increasing supply and forcing down prices and profits. In our economy, the free flow of resources from one market to another does not exist in all markets. For example, utilities have exclusive franchises to serve certain geographic areas, and some industries, such as steel, require such huge capital investments that resources do not flow freely into such industries. Therefore, many people argue that excessive or unfair profits sometimes do occur.

Unfavorable public sentiment toward excessive profits and direct intervention by governmental agencies have led firms from a goal of profit maximization to a more tempered description of profit objectives. The terms **satisfactory profit** and **target profit** describe a level of profits that provides a reasonable return on invested capital, but not an excessive return. Some people maintain that the goal of management historically has been to earn a satisfactory profit in light of the business and social environment within which a firm operates. Target profit levels may reflect the maximum profit the firm strives to achieve given the constraints of the business environment, and such profit objectives may result in product prices somewhat different from the prices suggested by economic models.

Government influence. Some firms sell products whose prices are directly or indirectly affected by federal, state, or local governments. During the late 1970s, most energy products, such as gas and oil sold by national firms, had prices established by federal government agencies, or the firms had to seek approval for any product price increase. Electric utilities typically must secure approval for rate increases from some state agency or rate-setting organization. Sometimes local government agencies also must approve changes in utility rates. In some states hospital price increases must be sanctioned by an agency of the state. On occasion, government representatives have indirectly affected prices by criticizing industries for price increases. This action, called **jawboning,** has sometimes been used effectively by presidents to reduce proposed price increases in the steel industry and other industries.

Governments may affect pricing decisions in many different ways

The list of products and services whose prices are affected by one or more agencies of government is lengthy. Often it is the business firm that wants to maintain government price controls. For example, in the early 1980s, the trucking industry vigorously opposed deregulation for fear of competition moving into the industry. When airline industry regulation was substantially reduced in the late 1970s, a large number of small independent airlines established routes at reduced prices, taking considerable business from the previously regulated major airlines, and causing some of the airlines to sustain substantial losses. The key issue here is that businesses are part of a total economic environment in which government plays an important role. The intelligent manager stays abreast of government actions affecting the operation of the business, including those actions affecting pricing decisions.

Model limitations. A **model** is an abstract representation of something in the real world. Models are useful because they allow us to cut away irrelevant details and get at the fundamental issues of the subject being modeled. But modeling has some serious limitations. A model must be a good representation of the item or activity being modeled. The most sophisticated model can be totally useless if care is not taken to ensure a proper fit with the subject. This limitation holds for pricing models as well as for other types of models.

A model should be a good representation of the item or activity modeled

An additional modeling limitation is that of gathering relevant and accurate data for use in the model. Pricing models require cost and revenue data that are projections of the future. Revenue data require estimation of consumer behavior with changing prices. Any estimate is difficult and risky, but estimates based on the expected actions of others are even more difficult than internal projections. The economic models described earlier in this chapter such as perfectly competitive, oligopoly, and monopoly require a knowledge of supply and demand functions in order to set optimal prices. Because the exact form of these functions is usually not known, managers often set prices that are more or less than optimal. A wide variety of prices may therefore exist for similar goods in markets that are characterized by monopolistic competition, and even in markets that approach perfect competition.

Giffen's paradox

Inferior goods. Not all supply and demand situations can be described satisfactorily by the general economic models already discussed. Various special cases occur. One is referred to as **inferior goods,** or **Giffen's paradox.** An inferior good is a product for which the quantity demanded varies directly with changes in price for the product. A price increase causes an increase in the quantity demanded, and a price decrease causes a decline in the quantity demanded. No class of products can be generally classified as inferior goods, but some products occasionally seem to possess such demand characteristics.

One plausible explanation for the inferior goods effect is the adage "You get what you pay for." Many consumers equate quality and price; high-priced items are assumed to be high-quality items. Although such a relationship is often true, it is by no means universally true. There are numerous cases of firms that raised the price of a product significantly without changing the product, and they experienced a sharp increase in the number of units sold. One case involved a service firm that was having trouble selling its services. As a desperation measure the firm tripled its service rates, and sales volume increased 400 percent.

These exceptions to traditional economic explanations of supply and demand, although interesting, should not be used in the general analysis of pricing decisions. The exceptions should be used only where they are known to apply, or where their existence is strongly suspected.

PRICING MODELS IN BUSINESS

Armed with the knowledge of general economic relationships described by the economic models, managers must make pricing decisions for specific products. Typically, managers select specific product pricing models that they feel will convert a general economic model into a model usable for pricing individual products. Some of the more common pricing models are discussed below.

Cost-Based Pricing Models

Many pricing models are based on cost relationships. For example, a merchant may set prices by adding 50 percent to the cost paid for the merchandise. A university may estimate its total operating cost for the coming academic year and set tuition rates by dividing estimated student enrollments into the total estimated cost.

Cost is an important variable in making pricing decisions

Prices based on costs are popular because they are easy to use and easy to understand. Prices can be explained easily to management and government agencies if necessary. Cost data are readily available from the accounting system, and little if any additional data need be gathered and assimilated to utilize cost-based pricing models. In addition, cost-based models are intuitively logical to many people. It seems reasonable that there should be a direct relationship between the cost of a product or service and the price charged. Although the cost-price relationship does not always exist, economic theory tells us it should exist over the long run.

Price may be set at cost plus some amount or percentage

Cost-plus models. A very simple and widely used cost-based pricing model is referred to as cost-plus. With **cost-plus,** a certain amount or percentage is added to the product cost to determine its selling price. The obvious question is, Which cost should be used? The term *cost* can refer to a variety of possible costs, such as full cost, variable cost, standard cost, and others. Any cost-plus model must clearly identify the cost to be used.

Product cost is a common cost-plus pricing model. For example, Hawkeye Hardware prices all products at cost plus 60 percent. The following products just received are priced below.

Product	Invoice Cost	Markup (60%)	Selling Price
Hammers	$ 5.00	$3.00	$ 8.00
Saws	7.50	4.50	12.00
Drills	16.25	9.75	26.00
Pipe wrenches	6.25	3.75	10.00

The same type of calculations can be used to price a manufactured product, except that the manager cannot merely refer to an invoice for the cost of the product. Instead, the manager must use the firm's accounting records to determine the manufacturing cost of the product. To illustrate, below are the summarized data from a job cost sheet for the production of 150 power mowers. The manufacturer sells these mowers to dealers for product cost plus 40 percent.

Resource	Total Cost	Units Produced	Unit Cost
Direct materials	$18,900	150	$126
Direct labor	10,500	150	70
Applied overhead	12,600	150	84
Total manufacturing cost	$42,000		$280

Selling price per unit = $280 + .4($280) = $392

When product cost is used as the basis for pricing, the addition to cost, or markup, must cover all operating expenses and generate a satisfactory profit. Often, managers must experiment with the values used in the pricing model until a satisfactory level of profit is achieved.

Total cost. A total cost pricing model includes both product costs and operating costs. This is a common approach to pricing government contracts. For example, a contract may establish a price of total cost plus 15 percent. The cost part of the price allows the firm to recover all costs associated with the contract, and the 15 percent is the profit on the contract.

Total cost pricing models are popular for government contracts because the government frequently purchases goods or services for which there is no other ready market. For example, nuclear submarines and antiaircraft guns cannot be sold to the general public. Frequently, it is impossible to predict accurately the cost of such specialized products. If a price were to be established when the contract was signed, it could be much too high, in order to allow for unknown production problems, or it could be much too low, causing the manufacturer to suffer a loss. The purpose of total cost–based contracts is to provide a fair price and a fair profit that are advantageous to both parties.

A difficulty with total cost pricing is the measurement of total cost. If the producing firm manufactures only a single product for the purchaser, the costing problem is simple, but most firms produce a variety of products for different customers. For example, Boeing Corporation produces aircraft for the federal government and it sells a variety of products to private-sector customers. Although multiple customers and multiple products complicate the process of determining costs, the total cost of the contract can be computed. As discussed in Chapter 10, cost can be determined for repetitive nonmanufacturing activities and assigned to the contract for services using cost allocation procedures discussed in Chapters 2 and 4. As always, the guiding principle for the cost allocation is the matching principle. Even relying on the matching principle, managers sometimes encounter cost determination problems. The Cost Accounting Standards Board (discussed in Chapter 1) was created to standardize the cost determination process and to minimize costing problems for federal government cost-plus contracts.

We illustrate cost-plus pricing with the example of General Tektonics Corporation, which has a government contract to produce an earthquake-forecasting device. The contract price is total cost plus 12 percent. Total cost is defined as manufacturing cost plus 30 percent of the firm's administrative costs. Production data for contract and administrative costs are:

Manufacturing costs:	
Direct materials	$ 660,000
Direct labor	980,000
Applied overhead	1,460,000
Total administrative costs	2,400,000

The contract price for the device is computed as follows:

Manufacturing cost	$3,100,000
Allocated administrative costs ($2,400,000 × .3)	720,000
Total contract cost	3,820,000
Add .12 contract profit	458,400
Contract price	$4,278,400

Standard cost pricing models isolate efficiencies and inefficiencies of a manufacturing firm

Standard cost. Actual cost pricing provides a difficult managerial dilemma—the higher the cost, the greater the profit. In many cases this means that more profit can be earned with inefficient than with efficient operations. For example, if a contract price is set at total cost plus 20 percent, $3 million of total cost yields a profit of $600,000. However, if more inefficient operations yield a total cost of $4 million, the contract profit rises to $800,000. There is a double incentive to assign unnecessary or unwarranted costs to contracts. First, the costs are covered by the contract rather than by other activities of the firm, making the other activities more profitable. Second, these extra costs raise the profit on the cost-plus contract. Even contracts using fixed fees, such as total cost plus $100,000 or product cost plus $250,000, provide little incentive for cost control when cost coverage is a basic part of the contract.

Standard costs provide a framework for eliminating the problem of rewarding inefficiency. Standard cost pricing models place the burden of production efficiency on the manufacturer. The price to the buyer reflects only costs from efficient operations plus the agreed-upon profit. Even standards are not always successful, however, because it is difficult to establish standards for new and complicated products and activities. An example of a standard cost-plus pricing system is presented below. The pricing model is standard manufacturing cost plus 75 percent.

	Unit Cost		
Resource	**Standard Cost**	**Actual Cost**	**Variance**
Direct materials	$13	$12	$(1)F
Direct labor	18	24	6 U
Applied overhead	12	16	4 U
Total	$43	$52	$ 9 U

Price = $43 + .75($43) = $75.25

If the model were actual manufacturing cost plus 75 percent, the price would be $91 ($52 + .75 × $52). The difference of $15.75 is 21 percent higher than the price based on standard costs. When standard cost pricing models are used, variances must be monitored carefully to ensure that prices reflect realistic production costs. If large variances persist, the pricing model may have to be modified.

The contribution approach to pricing depends on variable costs

Contribution approach pricing models. Another approach to cost-plus pricing is **contribution approach pricing,** but this approach is significantly different from full cost pricing. As with other applications of the contribution approach in managerial accounting, we are concerned with identifying all costs that vary with the product or service being priced. Fixed costs are **not** allocated to the product, service, or contract.

The contribution approach is appealing for a variety of reasons. One is the ease of seeing the relationship between prices and costs that vary directly with sales. Cost allocations that may be complicated or that may be based on questionable causal relationships are not necessary with the contribution approach. The contribution pricing method appeals to some customers who are suspicious of allocated fixed costs. Often a customer would rather pay some multiple of variable costs than a much smaller percentage of a cost figure that includes fixed cost allocations. Whatever the reasons, many products are priced using the contribution approach.

A simple example follows. Rydless Machinery Company manufactures a small riding lawn mower as one of its many products. It sets selling prices at variable costs plus 125 percent of variable cost. Variable cost data for the mower are presented below:

Resource	Unit Variable Cost
Direct materials	$ 80
Direct labor	50
Variable MOH	70
Variable selling expense	35
Variable administrative expense	5
Total variable cost	$240

Selling price = $240 + 1.25($240) = $540

The contribution approach to pricing ignores fixed costs in the pricing model. Consequently, there is some danger of overlooking fixed costs altogether. Although fixed costs are not assigned to cost objectives under the contribution approach, they must be taken into account in determining the amount to be added to variable costs to arrive at the price. The amount added must provide enough revenue to cover all of the fixed costs plus provide a satisfactory profit. Fixed costs are important in the contribution approach to pricing, but they are treated in a different manner than with full cost pricing models.

Target Profits

Target profits are satisfactory profits

Earlier we discussed the concept of satisfactory profits. Satisfactory profit levels are target profits that managers use as a general guide for establishing prices or as the prime pricing variable, as in utility rate setting. Targets may be established as specific dollar amounts, such as $2,300,000, or in relation to other variables, such as 10 percent of sales or a 15 percent return on net assets, as discussed in Chapter 11. Once the target profit is determined, prices are computed by dividing the expected activity level into the target profit.

To illustrate target profit pricing, assume three attorneys who have just formed a partnership are trying to determine an appropriate hourly fee for their services. They estimate they will incur the following expenses during the coming year:

Secretarial salaries	$30,000
Building and equipment lease	14,000
Utility expenses	7,000
Other expenses	24,000
Total	$75,000

In addition to the above expenses, each of the attorneys wants to earn $35,000 the first year. The three attorneys together expect a total of 3,000 hours of billable time during the year. The rate required to cover all expenses and reach the target profit is calculated as follows:

Total expenses	$ 75,000
Target profit (3 × $35,000)	105,000
Total	$180,000/3,000 hours = $60 per hour

The partners must now examine the $60 per hour price to determine whether it is feasible. If competing firms charge much less, the attorneys may have to lower their profit expectations; on the other hand, they may find $60 to be so low that potential clients stay away, thinking that such low-priced services cannot be very good. The latter situation is an example of Giffen's paradox, discussed earlier in the chapter.

Special Orders

Each special order should be evaluated individually

All business opportunities cannot be evaluated in the same way. The specific characteristics of each opportunity must be examined. For example, a one-time **special order** may provide a company with an opportunity to utilize some excess capacity. The selling price of the units in the special order may be different from the normal selling price, but that does not necessarily mean the order should be rejected. Instead, it should be evaluated carefully to see how it impacts on total company profit and other company goals.

To illustrate, we again use Rydless Machinery Company, which produces a variety of parts for the automobile industry. The normal selling price for its automobile generator is $72 each. Recently, an outboard motor manufacturer offered to buy 2,000 generators for $55 per unit.

Rydless currently has excess capacity, and the generators could be produced without incurring any additional fixed costs. This would be a one-time order. The outboard motor manufacturer normally produces its own generators, but new production equipment is being installed in the production facility, causing a temporary interruption in production. The following cost estimates were prepared for the production of the 2,000 units.

Cost Item	Total Cost	Unit Cost
Direct materials	$ 60,000	$30
Direct labor	20,000	10
Manufacturing overhead (60% fixed)	30,000	15
Selling and administrative (80% fixed)	20,000	10
Total	$130,000	$65

A quick evaluation of the unit cost data indicates that the company would lose $20,000 (2,000 units × $10 per unit) if the special order is accepted at $55 per unit. But fixed overhead cost and fixed selling and

Some data are not relevant in evaluating special orders

administrative costs are irrelevant to this decision because they will be incurred whether the order is accepted or rejected. A more relevant analysis is to identify those costs that would occur only if the project is accepted:

Cost Item	Unit Cost
Direct materials	$30
Direct labor	10
Variable overhead (40% of $15)	6
Variable selling and administrative (20% of $10)	2
Total unit cost	$48

Accepting the order would provide a $7 per unit contribution margin ($55 selling price − $48 variable cost). Therefore, the special order would increase company profit by $14,000 (2,000 units × $7 per unit).

Managers may need to evaluate other factors in making special order pricing decisions. A major concern is the effect on regular customers. If regular customers are paying more for the same products and services, they may demand price reductions or stop buying from the firm. Another problem is that some special order customers may decide to become regular customers, and changes in the price may become necessary. The Robinson-Patman Act, discussed in Chapter 1, serves as another obstacle to special order pricing. This law states that price differentiation between customers is illegal unless the price difference can be justified by cost differences.

Loss Leader Pricing

Loss leaders attract customers who buy normally priced products

An old merchandising joke states, "We lose a little on every unit we sell, but we make it up in volume." It does not require any business experience to realize that such a merchandising policy quickly leads to disaster. However, the policy of selling a product at a small loss may be an effective approach in some circumstances. For example, most grocery stores offer weekly specials on certain items that are temporarily priced well below normal prices, perhaps even below cost. Products priced below cost are called **loss leaders,** and their function is to attract customers to the store. Hopefully, customers will purchase enough regularly priced merchandise along with the loss leaders to warrant the low prices on special products. Of course, some people purchase only the specially priced items, but in aggregate, customers usually buy a satisfactory mix of products.

Not all businesses are capable of using loss leader pricing. Ideally, the business should sell a large variety of products that customers purchase on a regular basis. Firms selling expensive products, such as appliances and automobiles, typically are not able to use loss leaders. Most people do not buy one car below dealer cost and several more at the regular price. A form of loss leader pricing is attempted when dealers or manufacturers offer popular options such as power steering, power brakes, or air-conditioning well below regular prices. The intent is to attract customers by the low prices on desirable options and induce them to buy the automobile.

SUMMARY

Pricing refers to the assignment of selling prices to products or services. Pricing decisions are necessary in all profit-oriented organizations and in many not-for-profit organizations. Many factors affect prices, but pricing decisions are made within the framework of general economic models. The type of pricing model used depends on the type of market in which products are traded.

A **perfectly competitive market** is characterized by homogeneous products, free mobility of resources, and perfect information among participants, none of whom can influence market prices. Prices are determined by supply and demand. **Supply** is the total aggregate quantity of goods or services that suppliers are willing to provide at each possible price. The graph of a supply function is called a **supply curve. Demand** is the total aggregate quantity of goods or services that purchasers are willing to buy at each possible price. The graph of a demand function is called a **demand curve.** The **market equilibrium** is the quantity at which supply equals demand; it is the intersection of the supply and demand curves.

In a perfectly competitive market, individual suppliers face a horizontal demand curve at the market price and can sell as many units of product as they choose at that price. The quantity a supplier will provide is determined by the firm's cost schedule. Each firm maximizes its net income if it sells its products until the marginal cost of supplying the last unit equals the marginal revenue. **Marginal cost** is the amount of cost increase caused by a unit increase in output. **Marginal revenue** is the amount of increase in revenue caused by the sale of one additional unit. In a perfectly competitive market, marginal revenue is the selling price.

Monopolistic competition, monopoly, and oligopoly are three other market types. **Monopolistic competition** occurs where there are many sellers of similar, but not identical, products, and no single seller can influence market prices. **Monopoly** exists when a firm is the sole supplier of a product. **Oligopoly** results when several large sellers dominate a market and compete with one another. The pricing decision in each of these three markets is to maximize profits at the level of sales where marginal cost equals marginal revenue. The individual seller faces a downward-sloping demand curve rather than a horizontal one. Therefore, to increase the volume of sales, a seller must lower the price. Oligopolies may face a **kinked demand curve.** A price decrease by one firm causes a sharp drop in the quantity demanded from other firms. Prices are often set by the **price leader,** and the same price is charged by the remaining firms, which are **price followers.**

At any point on the demand curve, demand for a product may be elastic or inelastic. **Demand elasticity** is measured as the ratio of percentage change in quantity to the percentage change in price along the demand curve. If an increase in price creates more revenue at the new quantity, demand is **inelastic** and demand elasticity is less than 1. If an increase in price creates less revenue, demand is **elastic** and demand elasticity is greater than 1. **Price skimming** is the strategy of setting high prices on a new product when demand for it is inelastic. New products with elastic demand may benefit from a strategy of **market penetration** pricing, which means setting below normal prices to establish a broad customer base.

Most firms do not maximize profits in the strict sense. Instead, firms strive to earn a satisfactory profit that yields a desirable return on capital. Government influence or control affects some pricing decisions. Economic models have limitations because they are abstract representations of the real world. If the model is a poor representation or the data used are inaccurate or inappropriate, the model is of little value. Additionally, the demand for some products does not take the form of a typical demand curve in economics. With **inferior goods,** for example, the quantity demanded decreases as price decreases.

We select specific models for making pricing decisions. **Cost-plus** models use the cost of the product plus an amount or percentage to arrive at the selling price. The cost base may be the product cost, total cost, or standard cost. Total costs are often used in government cost-plus contracts. Standard costs are popular pricing models because the buyer is not charged for seller inefficiencies.

Contribution approach pricing uses only variable costs in establishing prices. Fixed costs do not enter directly into the price, but they must be covered by the price before profits can be realized. **Target profits** can be expressed in dollar amounts or as return on investment, but the target profit measure must be converted to expected sales quantities and mix to establish prices.

In setting prices for **special orders,** managers may choose to sell below full cost as long as variable costs are covered. Caution must be exercised to guard against antagonizing regular customers or violating the law. Some businesses may entice customers into their stores by offering **loss leaders** at very low prices, perhaps even below cost. Customers usually purchase enough regularly priced merchandise to make the loss leaders worthwhile.

KEY TERMS

contribution approach pricing *(502)*
cost-plus pricing *(500)*
demand *(484)*
demand curve *(486)*
demand elasticity *(495)*
elastic demand *(495)*
inelastic demand *(495)*
inferior goods *(499)*
kinked demand curve *(494)*
loss leaders *(505)*
marginal cost *(487)*
marginal revenue *(487)*
market equilibrium *(486)*
market penetration *(497)*
monopolistic competition *(489)*
monopoly *(489)*
oligopoly *(489)*
perfectly competitive market *(484)*
price follower *(494)*
price leader *(494)*
price skimming *(497)*
pricing *(482)*
purchase price *(482)*
selling price *(482)*
special order *(504)*
supply *(484)*
supply curve *(486)*
target profit pricing *(497)*

QUESTIONS

1. Distinguish between purchase price and selling price.
2. Give several examples of pricing decisions in not-for-profit organizations.
3. Identify six factors that often influence pricing decisions.
4. Identify the basic types of product markets.
5. What characteristics must a market have to be classified as perfectly competitive?
6. Describe a supply schedule and a supply curve.
7. "Don't give me any of the economics stuff; we set our own prices around this company." Comment.
8. What is a market equilibrium point and what information does it provide?
9. In a perfectly competitive market, how do individual suppliers determine the quantity of product they will supply?
10. What are the characteristics of a monopolistic competition market?
11. What is a monopoly market? Give an example.
12. Define marginal revenue and marginal cost.
13. What is a kinked demand curve and to what kind of market does it apply?
14. Briefly describe several variables that modify the general economic pricing models.
15. Identify and briefly describe the basic cost-oriented pricing models.
16. What is meant by the contribution approach to pricing?
17. "I do not like to bother with fixed costs, so I really like the contribution approach pricing models." Comment.
18. The president said to the sales manager, "Special orders should be priced like all other orders; we cannot show any favoritism in this company." Do you agree? Explain.
19. "Loss leader pricing! Are you crazy? We cannot make any money selling below cost. We may need a new pricing specialist." As the pricing specialist, defend yourself.

EXERCISES

Ex. 12-1 **Graphic analysis in a perfectly competitive market.** A farmer produces wheat on a small farm. Below is the cost schedule for his wheat production.

Bushels Produced	Total Cost	Marginal Cost
0	$1,000	—
100	1,300	$300
200	1,600	300
300	1,700	100
400	1,850	150
500	2,050	200
600	2,300	250
700	2,600	300
800	2,950	350
900	3,350	400
1,000	3,800	450
1,100	4,300	500

Required:

a. If the market price for wheat is $4.30 a bushel, how much wheat should the farmer supply?
b. What is the farmer's net income at the optimum production level?
c. Graph the solution to this problem.

Ex. 12-2 **Interpreting supply and demand functions.** A polymer extrusion can be manufactured by using either chemical X or chemical Y as one of its components. There is a limited demand for the extrusion and limited other uses for the two chemicals. The demand schedule for the two chemicals is therefore the same, but their supply schedules differ, as shown below:

Chemicals X and Y		Chemical X		Chemical Y	
Price	**Demand**	**Price**	**Supply**	**Price**	**Supply**
$25	20	$24	90	$15	108
20	26	16	70	13	90
15	36	13	60	12	70
10	50	5	30	9	28
5	71	4	20	8	10
2	90				

Required:

a. Diagram the supply and demand functions of the two chemicals.
b. Use your diagram to determine which chemical is easier to manufacture.

Ex. 12-3 **Graphing supply and demand curves.** Below are price, supply, and demand data for a mineral ore.

Price per Ton	Quantity Supplied (In thousands of tons)	Quantity Demanded (In thousands of tons)
$20	400	20
18	380	50
16	360	75
14	330	100
12	300	130
10	260	160
8	220	220
6	160	270
4	100	340
2	20	450

Required:

a. Use the data to graph supply and demand curves.
b. Determine the market equilibrium point.

Ex. 12-4 **Optimum production strategy.** Digmore Mines extracts a mineral ore whose output sells in a perfectly competitive market at $18 per ton. Production cost data, as collected by management, appear below:

Production (In tons)	Total Production Cost	Marginal Cost
300	$ 3,950	—
500	4,800	$ 850
700	5,700	900
800	6,700	1,000
900	7,800	1,100
1,000	9,100	1,300
1,100	10,600	1,500
1,200	12,400	1,800
1,300	14,800	2,400
1,400	17,800	3,000
1,500	21,000	3,200

Required:

a. Determine the optimum production strategy for the company.
b. Compute net income at the optimum strategy.
c. Compute net income at a production level of 1,400 tons.

Ex. 12-5 **Using economic data.** Below are production cost data for an individual firm producing ore in a perfectly competitive market. The market price for the ore is $12 per ton.

Quantity Produced (In tons)	Total Production Costs	Marginal Cost
0	$ 2,000	—
100	2,400	$ 400
200	2,900	500
300	3,500	600
400	4,200	700
500	5,000	800
600	5,900	900
700	6,900	1,000
800	8,000	1,100
900	9,200	1,200
1,000	10,600	1,400
1,100	12,200	1,600
1,200	14,000	1,800

Required:

a. What is the optimum strategy for this producer?
b. What is the supplier's net income with the optimum strategy?
c. What is the supplier's net income if 1,000 tons are produced and sold?

Ex. 12-6 **Elasticity of demand.** Marthaller Company has determined that its new electronic pocket checkers game has the following demand schedule:

Demand	Price
22	$91
23	88
24	85
25	80
26	76
27	73
28	70
29	68

Required:

a. Determine the elasticity of demand at each price.

b. Decide at what price the product should be sold in order to maximize total revenue.

Ex. 12-7 **Cost-plus product pricing.** Filly, Buster & Co. produces bicycle frames which are sold to bicycle manufacturers. The company uses a standard cost system and has collected the following data on two types of frames:

	Deluxe		Extralite	
	Actual Cost	Standard Cost	Actual Cost	Standard Cost
Direct materials	$25	$24	$45	$48
Direct labor	16	15	22	21
Variable MOH	9	7	12	11
Allocated fixed MOH	10	10	16	14
Units produced		1,000		900
Marketing and administrative		$30,000		$40,000

The manager wants to know the difference in product price between two alternative pricing methods.

Required: Use the above data to compute the price of the products if the pricing strategy is to charge

a. Full product cost plus 50 percent.

b. Standard product cost plus 50 percent.

Ex. 12-8 **Cost-plus pricing.** The Shiny Coat Cat Food Company prices its products at full product cost plus 80 percent. Below are production and cost data for the three products manufactured by the company.

	Dry Food in a Bag	Canned Seafood Dinner	Moist Pouch Dinner
Units produced	10,000	6,000	4,000
Direct materials	$6,500	$900	$ 800
Direct labor	1,000	300	400
Manufacturing overhead	1,500	600	1,000
Marketing	4,000	500	500
Administrative	2,000	500	500

Required: Use the data above to determine selling prices for each product.

Ex. 12-9 **Special order pricing.** The Deep Beep Company manufactures depth finders for fishermen. The most inexpensive model sells for $80, has variable production costs of $40 per unit, commission cost of $6 per unit, and variable distribution cost of $4 per unit. Fixed manufacturing costs associated with this model of depth finder are $100,000. Sales of the depth finders are 4,000 units a year. A bass-boat manufacturer has offered to buy 1,200 units at $60 each. This order would require a one-time cost of $18,000 to lease extra space and equipment until the order is completed. However, the normal commission of $6 per unit and the variable distribution cost would be eliminated.

Required:

a. Decide whether the special order should be accepted and support your decision with calculations.
b. If the regional distribution representative for the bass-boat manufacturer's area demands his commission, should the order be accepted?

Ex. 12-10 **Target profit product pricing.** David took a woodworking course as a senior in high school and decided to spend the summer after graduation making wooden hobbyhorses in order to earn some money for college expenses. He expected to be able to make 50 horses per month and to earn at least $600 per month. By the end of the first month of summer he had built 40 horses and decided that it was not possible to do more in 1 month. But all 40 horses sold easily at $30 each, and David had a waiting list of customers. However, he felt that for a month's work he had not earned very much money, so he went through his receipts of materials, accumulated some data, and made some time estimates to come up with the following figures:

Cost of lumber	$ 615
Paint	480
Glue, screws, and miscellaneous	240
Cost of tools and equipment	1,800
Expected useful life	5 years

David estimates that of the materials purchased he used ⅔ for the horses sold and still has ⅓ left for future production.

Required: Determine the selling price that David should charge in order to achieve his target profit.

Ex. 12-11 **Pricing analysis.** Greta has a $700-a-month summer job offer as a cost analyst for a construction company. An alternative is to offer swimming lessons to children, in her neighbor's pool. The neighbor will let Greta use the pool for lessons during the day for $180 a month. Greta likes the outdoors and would rather give swimming lessons than work in an office, but she needs all the money she can earn to return to college in the fall. Greta can schedule four 1-hour lessons per weekday in groups of five children each and can give lessons 22 days per month.

Required:

a. How much does Greta have to charge each student per lesson to equal her summer job offer?

b. If the maximum rate for group swimming lessons is $1.25 an hour and four group lessons are all that can be scheduled during a day, how large must the group be for Greta to match her salary offer?

Ex. 12-12 **Cost-plus pricing strategies.** Fletcher Company produces a small home copier that it sells by mail order. The company uses a standard cost system and has collected the following data on its model SLO-1 copier:

	Actual Cost	Standard Cost
Direct materials	$96	$92
Direct labor	38	34
Variable MOH	26	24
Allocated fixed MOH	30	35
Units produced	3,500	

The manager wants to explore several product pricing strategies.

Required: Use the above data to compute the price of the products if the pricing strategy is to charge:

a. Variable product cost plus 90 percent.
b. Standard variable cost plus 90 percent.
c. Prime cost plus 115 percent.

Ex. 12-13 **Special order pricing.** Morgan Manufacturing Company's Electric Motor Division manufactures compressor motors for the Compressor Division. The motors are transferred to the Compressor Division at $155 per unit, which includes direct cost of $90 per unit, indirect manufacturing cost of $35, and a markup to cover administrative costs of $320,000, of which 10 percent is variable. Normal production is 8,000 units per year.

The company has been approached by a manufacturer of electric-powered lawn mowers who offers to pay $143 per unit for a special order of 1,000 motors. The order would require a one-time investment of $8,000 for leasing extra space and equipment to complete the order.

Required:

a. Decide if the order should be accepted and support your decision with calculations.
b. If the special order also requires $7.50 per unit for shipping the motors, should the order be accepted?

Ex. 12-14 **Cost-based pricing.** The Old Salt Seafood Palace uses a standard cost system. It has accumulated the following data for its specialty, Lobster Thermidor à la Heitger, which is currently priced at $12.50:

	Actual Cost	Standard Cost
Lobster	$ 5.75	$ 5.40
Other ingredients	2.25	2.00
Direct labor	.90	.80
Allocated indirect costs	2.30	1.80
Total cost	$11.20	$10.00

After examining these data, the manager became concerned about the price of the dinner, which is very popular with patrons. He decides to investigate several pricing options.

Required: Determine the price of the dinner using:

a. Actual food cost plus 90 percent.
b. Standard food cost plus 100 percent.
c. Total cost plus 25 percent.
d. Total standard cost plus 40 percent.
e. Standard direct cost plus 60 percent.
f. Actual direct cost plus 60 percent.

PROBLEMS

P. 12-1 Graphing supply and demand. Below are price, supply, and demand data for two ores, both of which are used to refine a rare earth element. Buyers can use either ore to refine the desired element, but the concentration of the element in one type of ore is different from that in the other.

Price	Supply for Ore A	Supply for Ore B	Demand for Ores A and B
$ 5			940
7	100		780
8	220		760
10	400	120	620
15	700	400	400
20	920	560	260
25	1,100	700	160
30		800	100

Required:

a. Develop a graph of the supply and demand curves for the two ores.
b. Use your diagram to determine market equilibrium for the two ores and discuss which ore is more concentrated and which one is easier for suppliers to provide.

P. 12-2 Equilibrium supply and demand. A chemical used in small quantities in the production of certain medicines has the following supply and demand function:

Price	Demand	Price	Supply
$26	18 kg	$24	120 kg
22	30	19	100
18	42	14	76
14	60	10	51
10	80	6	30
5	110	5	10

Required:

a. Graph the supply and demand functions for the chemical.
b. Use your graph to determine the market equilibrium price and quantity.

P. 12-3 Determining market equilibrium and elasticity. The supply and demand functions for soybeans are provided below.

Price per Bushel	Millions of Bushels Supply	Millions of Bushels Demand
$6.60	20	70
7.00	31	60
7.30	40	49
7.90	55	37
8.20	60	30
8.70	70	18

Required:

a. Compute the market equilibrium.

b. Find the elasticity of demand at the equilibrium point if the quantity demanded is 100,000 bushels less than the equilibrium quantity.

P. 12-4 Cost-plus pricing. A retired man builds beautiful wooden dollhouses as a hobby and to supplement his income. He charges enough to cover lumber costs and give himself a little for his efforts. His wife tells him he is not charging enough to cover his costs, so he accumulates the following data:

	Expected Costs per House		Actual Costs per House
Lumber	$20		$35
Paint	2		1
Glue, fittings, and miscellaneous supplies and expenses	—		6
Total materials cost	$22		$42
Labor time	20 hr		30 hr
Equipment cost		$2,500	
Expected useful life of equipment		10 yr	
Dollhouses produced per year		25	

The man had been charging $45 each for the dollhouses and had a long waiting list of customers. Several people have suggested the price could be more than doubled without a noticeable decline in the demand for the dollhouses.

Required:

a. If the man merely wants to recover all his actual costs, what should be the price?

b. If the man wants $1.50 an hour for his time plus actual costs, what should be the price for his product?

c. If an alternative use of the man's basement workshop is to rent the space as a small apartment for $1,200 a year, what is the full cost price for each dollhouse including the required labor rate?

P. 12-5 **Cost-price analysis.** Kool-Komfort Air-Conditioning Company manufactures a full line of home air-conditioners. Management is contemplating entering the recreational vehicle air-conditioning market with a new model designed for use in travel trailers and motor homes. The model would have a maximum selling price of $500, given the size and quality of the unit. At that price, marketing estimates indicate a sales level of 5,000 units. Product engineers estimate new fixed manufacturing costs of $300,000 annually if the product is produced. Any new product must generate a minimum pretax profit of 15 percent of sales to be accepted. Management estimates variable marketing and administrative expenses of 10 percent of sales and fixed marketing and administrative costs of $225,000.

Required:

a. What is the maximum per unit variable manufacturing cost that would still justify production of the new product?

b. If variable manufacturing costs are 10 percent less than the maximum computed in part *a* and the variable MOH costs amount to ⅙ of the total variable manufacturing costs, how much is prime cost per unit?

c. Assuming the variable manufacturing cost data in part *b*, what is the net income?

P. 12-6 **Price analysis.** The Brown County White Lightning Factory manufactures a brew of amazing flavor. No other firm has a product of similar character. The firm seems to be able to sell all it can produce at the current price of $12 a gallon. Variable costs are $4 a gallon, and fixed costs are $25,000 a year. At current capacity the firm is able to produce 5,000 gallons a year. An increase of $15,000 a year in fixed costs would double capacity. However, the price would have to be lowered to $10.50 a gallon to sell all of the output.

A national distributor approaches Brown County White Lightning with an offer to buy 50,000 gallons at $9 a gallon. If the offer is accepted, an investment in plant and equipment of $1,000,000 would be required, adding $135,000 in annual fixed costs to the original amount of $25,000. The company requires an 8 percent return on newly invested capital.

Required:

a. Should the firm expand the operations to 10,000 gallons? Support your answer.

b. If the company doubles its present capacity, what is the minimum the company can charge for White Lightning and be at least as well off as before the expansion?

c. Should the company accept the offer to sell 50,000 gallons at $9? Support your answer.

P. 12-7 **Special order.** Fridgstrom, Inc., manufactures quality redwood picnic tables that it sells to garden stores for $120 each. Last year the company produced and sold 8,000 picnic tables. Sales and cost data for the year are given at the top of the next page.

Fridgstrom, Inc., received an offer from a department store chain to purchase 2,000 picnic tables for $95 each. This special order would require the temporary lease of some production space and equipment. The building and equipment lease cost and setup costs for the special order would amount to $8,000.

Sales: 8,000 units @ $120		$960,000
Manufacturing costs:		
Direct material	$480,000	
Direct labor	200,000	
Manufacturing overhead (20% variable)	120,000	800,000
Gross margin		160,000
Operating expenses:		
Marketing (80% variable)	70,000	
Administrative (all fixed)	64,000	134,000
Net income		$ 26,000

Required

a. Should the special order be accepted if there are no marketing and administrative costs associated with the order?

b. What is the effect on net income of accepting the special order?

c. Should the special order be accepted if only half of the variable marketing cost can be eliminated?

d. Assuming the situation described in part *c*, what is the effect on net income of accepting the order?

P. 12-8 Analysis of selling price for a new product. Innovation, Inc. has recently developed a new camera that produces instant holographic pictures. The camera is expected to have a limited appeal in the consumer hobby market. The product pricing committee is meeting to determine the potential of the new camera and to determine its selling price.

The sales manager wants the camera priced at $60 each to be appealing to as wide a market as possible. Market penetration is expected to be slow at first but should increase as users start appreciating the camera's features. The sales manager believes that sales should be 1,000 units in the first year, 2,000 in the second year, and 2,400 per year in subsequent years.

The production manager says that variable cost of the camera is $50 each and the company cannot afford to sell its products for a 17 percent contribution margin. He thinks the price of the camera should be at least $90 each, but admits that at this price sales would probably be 10 percent less than estimated by the sales manager.

The sales manager points out that the camera is not a primary revenue item. For each camera sold, the company can expect to sell 20 rolls of film per year. This film sells for $10 per roll and has a variable cost of $3. Fixed cost is $300,000 per year.

Required: Prepare a schedule of expected sales and income for the first 3 years under each of the pricing options and decide which price should be charged for the camera.

P. 12-9 Sales volume, pricing, and target profits. For many years Ye Ole Corner Drug Store has used a pricing formula of product cost plus 120 percent. In the last several years the store has lost sales volume and experienced sharply declining profits. Following is the income statement for the most recent year:

Ye Ole Corner Drug Store
Income Statement
For the Year Ended October 31

Sales		$88,000
Less cost of goods sold		40,000
Gross margin		48,000
Operating expenses:		
Advertising	$ 4,000	
Depreciation, store	3,600	
Equipment rental	2,100	
Insurance	1,800	
Miscellaneous	1,500	
Salary and wages	30,000	
Utilities	4,000	47,000
Net income		$ 1,000

The owner of the store thinks profits may be increased by reducing the product prices and increasing sales volume.

Required: For parts *a*, *b*, and *c* assume operating expenses remain at $47,000.

a. If a new pricing formula of product cost plus 80 percent increases sales quantity by 30 percent, should this new pricing formula be used?

b. What would your answer be to part *a* if the new pricing formula resulted in a 60 percent increase in sales?

c. What is the required sales volume to generate a target net income of $15,000 if the pricing formula is product cost plus 80 percent?

d. Someone suggests that the store could become a small discount drugstore for the area by pricing all products at product cost plus 40 percent. This pricing strategy would require additional operating expenses of $23,000 a year, and the owner wants an annual profit of $30,000 to make such major changes. What sales volume is required for the proposed change to be acceptable?

P. 12-10 **Determining selling price and supply.** The Whizzer Toy Company has developed a new toy rocket that is expected to sell as a fad item for one season only. The rocket is operated by a fuel capsule that produces a lot of smoke, makes a loud noise, and sends the rocket shooting 50 feet into the air. The company expects that the sale of each kit would produce additional sales of 25 boxes of fuel capsules at $3 per box. Each box contains 10 capsules. The variable cost of each fuel capsule is $.10 and the variable cost of each rocket kit is $50. Market research discloses that the demand schedule for the kits is as follows:

Price	Demand	Price	Demand
$90	5,000	$70	8,000
89	5,500	64	8,500
87	6,000	57	9,000
84	6,500	50	9,500
80	7,000	42	10,000
75	7,500		

Required: Determine the optimum price the company should charge and the supply it should produce for the market.

P. 12-11 (CMA) Analyzing the expected results of pricing alternatives. Aplet Inc. purchased Avcont Company in 1975 during Aplet's expansion period. The subsidiary has been quite profitable until recently. Beginning in 1983 the market share dropped, costs increased primarily due to increased prices of inputs, and the profits turned into losses. The income statements for 1983 and 1984 are presented along with an estimate of the 1985 income made in October 1985.

Avcont Company
Income Statement for Years Ending December 31
(000 omitted)

	1983	1984	1985 (est.)
Industry unit sales	1,300	1,200	1,200
Avcont unit sales	120	110	110
Sales	$1,200	$1,100	$1,100
Less variable expenses:			
Raw materials	175	170	175
Labor	210	215	225
Manufacturing overhead	100	99	100
Selling	125	115	120
Administrative	50	50	60
	660	649	680
Variable contribution margin	540	451	420
Less fixed expenses:			
Manufacturing*	200	210	230
Selling*	125	140	145
Administrative*	135	145	145
	460	495	520
Net income (loss)	$ 80	$ (44)	$ (100)

*Depreciation and amortization included in fixed expenses:

	1983	1984	1985
Manufacturing	$60	$70	$70
Selling	5	6	6
Administrative	8	8	9
Total depreciation	$73	$84	$85

The subsidiary management is optimistic about the volume of sales for 1986. Recent sales promotion efforts seem to be beneficial, and Avcont expects to increase unit sales 10 percent during 1986 even though industry volume is expected to decline to 1,100,000 units. However, Avcont management also knows its variable cost rates will increase 10 percent in 1986 over 1985 levels.

Avcont management wants to take action to reverse the unsatisfactory results the company has been experiencing. One proposal under consideration is to increase the price of Avcont's product. Some members of management believe that the market might accept an 8 percent increase in prices at this time without affecting the expected 10 percent increase in unit sales volume, because no price increases have taken place in this market since 1982. Several other companies are also considering price increases for 1986.

Other members of Aplet management question the feasibility of a price increase because Avcont is operating in an industry that is experiencing declining sales. In addition, the marketing department believes a price increase will have an impact on the expected increase in unit sales volume during 1986. Its estimate of the possible outcomes on unit sales and the related probabilities for the 8 percent price increase are as follows:

Increase (Decrease) in 1986 Unit Sales Volume	Probability
10%	.4
5	.3
0	.2
(5)	.1
	1.0

Required:

a. Calculate Avcont Company's profits for 1986 if the 8 percent price increase takes place and unit sales volume increases 10 percent.

b. Will the 8 percent price increase and 10 percent volume increase reduce Avcont Company's need for funds from the corporate treasury during 1986? Explain your answer.

c. What are Avcont Company's expected profits for 1986 if the probabilistic sales data assembled by the marketing department are used?

d. A member of the analysis team made the following observation to support his recommendation for a price increase: "Inflationary pressures make it reasonable for a company to forecast increased costs, increased product prices, and increased or at least constant volume because consumers can be expected to accept the product price increases." Comment on the validity of this statement for planning purposes.

CASES

Case 12-1 Cost analysis and target profit pricing

White Rim Outfitters runs pack and float trips into the canyon country of southeast Utah and northeast Arizona. The company offers 3-, 7-, and 14-day trips. Cost per day varies with the length of the trip due to large front-end costs for organizing and outfitting each trip, whether it lasts 3, 7, or 14 days. Cost data for last year are given at the top of page 521.

White Rim has the philosophy of keeping the 3-day-trip price as low as possible in the hope of generating repeat business for the longer trips.

Required:

a. Compute the price for each trip using 200 percent of direct costs as a model.

b. Use the average daily direct cost of all trips as a basis for pricing each trip and apply the 200 percent model used in part *a*.

	Trip Length			
	3 Days	**7 Days**	**14 Days**	**Total**
Number of customers	200	100	50	350
Direct cost of trips:				
Outfitting costs	$10,000	$ 6,000	$ 4,000	$ 20,000
Guide costs	8,400	10,500	11,600	30,500
Supplies costs	3,600	4,200	4,200	12,000
Miscellaneous costs	2,000	1,000	500	3,500
Total direct costs	$24,000	$21,700	$20,300	66,000
Other expenses:				
Marketing				16,000
Trip research				8,000
Licenses, taxes, etc.				2,000
General administrative				28,000
Total other expenses				54,000
Total expenses				$120,000

c. Using last year's volume and mix of trips, compute the required daily price for trips and the price or each type of trip, assuming a $30,000 target profit is required and all costs remain the same.

d. If the company sets the price of the 3-day trip at direct costs plus 50 percent, what must be the prices for the other trips to generate the $30,000 target profit?

Case 12-2 Analyzing cost and pricing data.

Beachfront State Park requested funds from the state legislature to build a badly needed breakwater to prevent further beach erosion. The estimated cost of the proposed project is $298,800. The legislature made a special appropriation of $200,000 to start the project, but park officials believe the project must be completed this year to prevent irreversible damage. Currently the park charges $.50 per person admission to the park. Park management has the power to raise fees up to $1.25 without special permission. Below are cost and revenue data for the park for the last year, when 150,000 people visited the park.

Revenue:	
Admission fees	$ 75,000
Legislative appropriations	300,000
Expenses:	
Normal maintenance	90,000
Park personnel salaries	202,000
Supplies	40,000
Utilities	25,000
Miscellaneous	18,000

This year appropriations and all costs are expected to rise 8 percent. The number of visitors has risen by 20 percent in each of the last 3 years, and a similar increase is expected this year. However, it is anticipated that for every $.05 increase in price, the increase in visitors will be 1 percent less than expected (for example, a $.05 increase in price means the increase in visitors would be 19 percent, and a $.10 price increase would mean an increase in park visitors of 18 percent).

The additional funds required to build the breakwater must come from higher fees from park users and cost savings in other areas. To minimize the impact on park users, $35,000 of normal maintenance programs will be postponed, and $8,000 of utilities and miscellaneous expenses will be eliminated. The funds saved will be used in the breakwater project.

Required:

a. What admission price must each park visitor be charged to pay for the breakwater if all of the above assumptions hold?

b. What would your answer to part *a* be if actual cost savings from operations totaled only $35,725 instead of $43,000?

Capital Budgeting 13

This chapter covers capital budgeting, which is the process of determining what capital expenditures a company should make. Capital expenditures often are long-term commitments of significant amounts of resources and involve long-range policy decisions. When you have completed this chapter, you should understand:

1. The nature and characteristics of the capital budgeting process.
2. The activities involved in capital budgeting.
3. The types of capital budgeting evaluation models and their characteristics.
4. How to use each of the capital budgeting evaluation models.
5. Factors other than the capital budgeting evaluation models that may enter into capital budgeting decisions.
6. What effect taxes have on project evaluation.

A capital budget reflects the long-range goals of an organization

Capital budgeting is the process of identifying, evaluating, planning, and financing major investment projects of an organization. Decisions to expand production facilities, acquire new production machinery, buy a new computer, or remodel the office building are all examples of capital expenditure decisions. Capital budgeting decisions made now determine to a large degree how successful an organization will be in achieving its goals and objectives in the years ahead. Capital budgeting plays an important role in the long-range success of many organizations because of several characteristics that differentiate it from most other elements of the master budget.

First, most capital budgeting projects require relatively **large commitments of resources.** Major projects, such as plant expansion or equipment replacement, may involve resource outlays in excess of annual net income. Relatively insignificant purchases are not treated as capital budgeting projects even if the items purchased have long lives. For example, the purchase of 40 electronic calculators at $35 each for use in the office would probably be treated as a period expense by most firms, and the purchase decision would be made by a manager with responsibility for office operating expenses.

Usually capital investments require large amounts of resources for a long period of time

Second, most capital expenditure decisions are **long-term commitments;** projects last more than 1 year, and many extend over 5, 10, or even 20 years. The longer the life of the project, the more difficult it is to predict the project's revenues, expenses, and cost savings.

A third characteristic is that capital budgeting decisions are **long-term policy decisions** and should rest firmly on organization policies on growth, marketing, industry share, social responsibility, and other matters.

In this chapter we discuss in general the capital budgeting process and then concentrate on the most common methods of evaluating proposed capital budgeting projects. We also examine capital rationing, which deals with the issue of making capital budgeting decisions with a limited amount of available resources.

THE CAPITAL BUDGETING PROCESS

The long-range effect that many capital expenditures have on an organization and the required size of the investment of many capital expenditures dictate a careful, systematic analysis of investment alternatives. A business often has far more investment alternatives than it can fund. A capital expenditure evaluation system is necessary to ensure that all capital investment proposals are evaluated in light of organization goals so that the most desirable investments are undertaken. Capital budgeting procedures vary among firms, but the process generally involves the following activities:

Activities of the capital budgeting process

1. Identification of potential capital budgeting projects
2. Estimation of project benefits and costs
3. Evaluation of proposed projects
4. Development of the capital expenditure budget based on project acceptance criteria
5. Reevaluation of projects after acceptance

Identification of Projects

The first phase of capital budgeting is the identification of capital budgeting projects. In large organizations investment proposals are prepared by each segment of the firm. Managers attempt to satisfy the most pressing capital investment needs of their departments. For example, a production division requests new drill presses because the machines now in use are old and require frequent repairs. The marketing division proposes acquiring portable computer terminals for sales representatives to speed up the order entry process. Top management proposes a new companywide computer-based information processing system to improve decision making throughout the company. Together all capital investment proposals comprise the set of potential investments from which management attempts to select the optimum investments, given the organization's goals and available investment funds.

Estimation of Project Benefits and Costs

Sometimes it is difficult to estimate costs and benefits for long-term projects

Capital budgets include such projects as plant expansions, employee education programs, replacement of major items of equipment, and acquisition of a new computer. Each acceptable project must meet acceptance criteria established by management. For example, a plant supervisor wants to replace a punch press with a new model. The supervisor must show not only that the new equipment is faster, but also that it provides sufficient savings over its useful life to justify its cost. The analysis of the new equipment is based on estimates of cost and future benefits. Such estimates may be difficult, particularly for long-term projects. For example, a house that cost $90,000 five years ago may cost $150,000 today, and the cost of constructing a 20,000-square-foot production plant may increase from $1,000,000 to $1,800,000 in 5 years. What is your estimate of the change in housing prices over the next 20 years? Many plant facilities projects involve 20-year forecasts, yet the estimates must be made now so that the project may be evaluated together with other investment proposals.

Evaluation of Projects

Organizations must have a logical, systematic process for evaluating all capital budgeting proposals

Capital investment projects may cover a short period of time or range beyond 20 years; they may involve a few thousand dollars or millions of dollars. Some projects are expected to improve profits directly through higher sales or lower costs, whereas others promise indirect benefits, such as improvement in employee morale from a new employee cafeteria. Capital expenditure projects impact on organizations in many different ways; consequently all projects must be evaluated systematically and each project's costs and benefits measured so that the most desirable projects are accepted. The evaluation process should include as much relevant project data as possible. To provide managers with relevant information there are a variety of project evaluation methods, whose strengths and weaknesses are discussed later in the chapter.

Development of the Capital Expenditure Budget

The capital expenditure budget includes all investment proposals that have been approved for the budget period. The budget may simply be a listing of the projects and the amounts of the investments, or it may provide descriptive data about the projects. Regardless of the format of the budget, it is the end result of management's decisions on capital investments.

The decisions that result in the budget are strongly influenced by information obtained during the evaluation phase of the capital budgeting process, but the evaluation process seldom provides the actual selection decision for investment proposals. Managers must decide on the amount of resources to be used for capital expenditures and must set priorities to meet company objectives.

An analysis of each proposal's costs and benefits may be supplemented by an analysis of other variables, such as the behavioral impact of accepting or rejecting a project. For example, rejecting all investment proposals of a particular division may have undesirable consequences even if the proposals do not meet the firm's criteria of acceptability. Approving several proposals of a particular division may appear to some managers as favoritism, although all proposals offered by the division meet the criteria of the firm. In addition, to evaluate a particular project, other criteria may have to be examined to prevent an undesirable consequence from what might appear to be a desirable project. For example, a proposal to automate the assembly process may be economically feasible, but if it is implemented employee productivity in other production functions may decline because of support for assembly employees who have lost their jobs.

Reevaluation of Projects

All estimates of future events are risky, and capital expenditure predictions are particularly so, because of the long-term nature of the projects. Consequently, once projects are accepted, they should be reviewed periodically to determine if they are achieving original expectations.

Many firms are so busy evaluating new investment proposals and managing daily activities that they find little time to reevaluate projects accepted in prior periods. Reevaluation has two benefits. First, evaluation of previous project estimates may improve the quality of new project estimates. For example, one supervisor may always underestimate project costs or overestimate labor productivity. A second possible advantage is that reevaluation of previously accepted projects may indicate that some current projects should be liquidated to finance new projects under evaluation. A formal system for evaluating the feasibility of terminating an operating project is called **capital abandonment analysis.**

PROJECT EVALUATION METHODS

Project evaluation provides managers with information relevant for making capital budgeting decisions but, as we discussed in Chapter 1, relevance depends upon the person making the decision. Different decision makers require different types of information. In capital budgeting, decision makers may use one or more project evaluation methods in order to secure various types of project information. In this chapter we discuss the following evaluation methods:

1. Discounted cash flow methods
   a. Internal rate of return
   b. Net present value
   c. Profitability index
2. Payback
3. Payback reciprocal
4. Accounting rate of return

DISCOUNTED CASH FLOW METHODS

Discounted cash flow (DCF) methods of project evaluation depend on the time value of money for evaluating capital budgeting projects. *Discounted cash flow* refers to the fact that all projected cash inflows and outflows for a capital budgeting project are discounted to their present value using an appropriate interest rate. Two discounted cash flow methods are generally used in capital budgeting. One is called the internal rate of return (IRR) method, and the other is called the net present value (NPV) method. Both methods focus on the timing of the cash flows over the entire life of the project. The spotlight is on the *cash flows* as opposed to accounting measures of revenue and expense.

Discounted cash flow project evaluation methods are based on the time value of money

All discounted cash flow methods are based on the *time value of money,* which means that an amount of money received now is worth more than an equal amount of money received in the future. Money in hand can be invested to earn a return. For example, $100 invested now at 12 percent will accumulate to $112 by the end of 1 year [$100 + ($100 × .12)]. It accumulates to $125.44 at the end of the second year [$112 + ($112 × .12)]. Clearly then, $100 today is worth more than $100 two years from today. To be precise, $79.72 invested now at 12 percent interest will accumulate to $100 at the end of 2 years. Therefore, $79.72 is the **present value (pv)** of $100 received 2 years from now if money can be invested at 12 percent. The time value of money is a very important concept involving compound interest. If you are not familiar with time value of money concepts, study the appendix at the end of the book before proceeding further.

We assume all cash flows occur at the end of the period

To simplify the process of evaluating proposals using discounted cash flows, the assumption is often made that cash flows or cost savings from a project occur at the end of an accounting period. Although the assumption is somewhat unrealistic, it is commonly made because it produces good results that are not materially different from more precise calculations.

Internal Rate of Return (IRR)

The IRR is the interest rate that equates the present values of the cash inflows and outflows

The **internal rate of return (IRR)** is the interest rate that discounts an investment's future cash flows to the present so that the present value of cash inflows exactly equals the present value of the cash outflows. For example, if a project costs $10,000 and is expected to yield cash inflows of $2,000 per year for the next 8 years, the internal rate of return is that interest rate which discounts the eight future annual cash inflows of $2,000 to a present value of $10,000. The IRR is not given; it must be computed. Once the IRR is found for a specific project, management can decide whether the rate is sufficiently high to make the project acceptable. Usually the minimum acceptable rate of return is the firm's **cost of capital,** which is the rate a business must pay for the use of funds. The process of measuring the cost of capital is discussed later in this chapter.

To illustrate, Joplin Products Company is evaluating the purchase of an automatic package-labeling machine. The machine would eliminate the manual labeling process now used by the company. The estimated net cash saving is $10,000 a year for 5 years. At the end of 5 years, the machine will be obsolete and will have no salvage value.

The purchase price of the machine is $32,000. If the machine is acquired, it will cost $242 to rewire part of the plant's electrical system. The purchase is subject to a 4 percent sales tax. The initial cash outflows are the cost of the machine, which amounts to $33,522 calculated as follows:

Machine price	$32,000
Sales tax @ 4%	1,280
Electrical wiring	242
Total cost	$33,522

The objective is to determine the interest rate that will discount the present value of the expected cash savings for the machine to the present value of the machine's cost. The cash outflows totaling $33,522 all occur at the time of purchase. Therefore, the present value of the outlay is the cash paid. The inflows, or in this case cash savings, occur over a period of 5 years. Since the cash inflows are the same for all 5 years of the investment, they are an annuity. Graphically the situation is as follows:

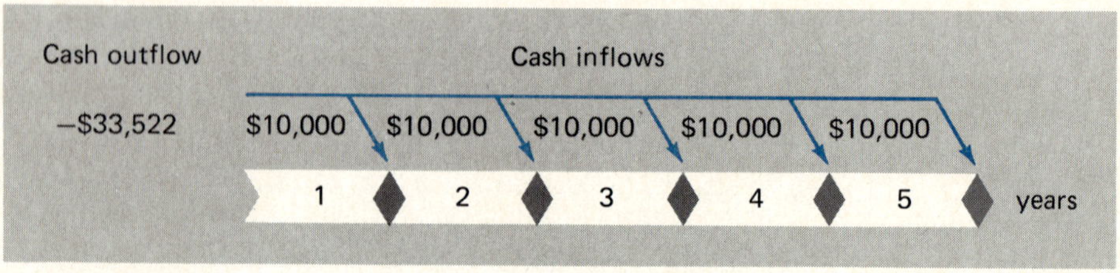

We want to find the interest rate i at which the present value of an annuity of five rents of $10,000 is equal to $33,522.

$$\text{Present value (PV)} = \text{Rent} \times f(i = ?, n = 5)$$

$$\$33{,}522 = \$10{,}000 \times f(i = ?, n = 5)$$

$$f = \frac{\$33{,}522}{\$10{,}000} = 3.35220$$

Using the value of f, the annuity factor, and the table for the present value of an annuity, we find for $n = 5$ the value 3.35216 in the 15 percent column. This value is very close to the computed value of 3.35220. Therefore, 15 percent is the IRR.

What does the 15 percent rate mean in evaluating the project? It tells management that the labeling machine project yields an investment return of 15 percent. If Joplin Products is evaluating other investment proposals, the IRR may be used as a ranking system. For instance, other projects may yield estimated returns of 9 percent, 11 percent, 12 percent, and 17 percent. The labeling project yields the second highest estimated return. If Joplin accepts projects based on their rate of return, the labeling machine would be the second project accepted.

Cost of capital is the rate a firm must pay for the use of its funds

However, the mere ranking of projects by rate of return does not determine which projects to accept or reject. Management should accept only those projects that yield an **acceptable** rate of return. They are projects that **yield a higher rate of return than the company pays for its capital.** A business must pay for the use of money in the form of interest and dividend payments to investors. The cost of obtaining funds is called the **cost of capital.** Any investment that yields a rate of return greater than the cost of capital should be accepted because the project will increase the value of the firm. In the above example, the labeling machine would be an acceptable investment if Joplin's cost of capital is less than 15 percent.

Many investment projects do not conveniently coincide with an annuity factor in the table. Instead the computed annuity factory falls somewhere between interest rates in the table. To illustrate, we assume the annual cash savings on the labeling machine are \$9,000 a year instead of \$10,000. The computed annuity factor is

$$\frac{\$33{,}522}{\$9{,}000} = 3.72467$$

The table for the present value of an annuity of five rents shows that the factor lies between 10 and 11 percent. Management may use the nearest whole percent as the IRR, in this case 11 percent. If this is not sufficiently precise, a more exact return can be calculated by interpolation as follows:

	Annuity Factors	
At 10%	3.79079	3.79079
Computed		3.72467
At 11%	3.69590	
Difference	.09489	.06612

The total difference between the factors for 10 and 11 percent is .09489. The annuity computed for the investment proposal is .06612 different from the 10 percent annuity. The portion of interest that is above the 10 percent value is .06612/.09489 = .7 percent. Adding .7 percent to 10 percent, we get 10.7 percent as the IRR for this project. This, of course, is an approximation. A precise computation of the internal rate of return is easy with the aid of a computer or even a fairly simple electronic calculator.

Nonuniform cash flows make manual computation of the IRR tedious

Nonuniform cash flows. Some projects yield unequal cash flows over the project's life. For example, a project may cost $40,000 and provide cash savings of $10,000, $20,000, and $24,000, respectively, in each of the next 3 years. When cash flows are not uniform, an interest rate cannot be found using annuity tables. Instead trial-and-error methods or a computer can be used to find the IRR. If the IRR is computed manually, the first step is to select an interest rate that seems reasonable and then compute the present value of the individual cash flows using that rate. If the present value of the cash inflows is greater than the present value of the cash outflows, then the interest rate used is too low—that is, the IRR is higher than the interest rate selected. A higher interest rate is then chosen, and the present value of the cash flows is computed again. If the new interest rate yields a negative value, then a lower interest rate is selected. The process is repeated until the present value of the cash inflows is equal to the present value of the cash outflows. Finding the rate of return using trial-and-error methods can be tedious, but a computer can accomplish the task quite easily.

To illustrate finding the internal rate of return with unequal cash flows, we assume that the labeling machine in the previous example will yield the following annual savings:

Year	Cash Savings
1	$18,000
2	12,000
3	10,000
4	5,000
5	5,000

First an interest rate is selected. There is no formula for making a good first estimate of the interest rate, but experience in solving this type of problem enhances the quality of initial estimates. For this example we choose 16 percent. Each cash flow is evaluated separately, using the present value of $1 table. We find the present value of $18,000 discounted for 1 year at 16 percent, the present value of $12,000 discounted for 2 years at 16 percent, and so on.

If the net present value is positive, the interest rate selected is lower than the IRR

	Discount Factor (16%)	× Cash Savings =	Present Value of Cash Savings
Year 1	.86207	$18,000	$15,517.26
Year 2	.74316	12,000	8,917.92
Year 3	.64066	10,000	6,406.60
Year 4	.55229	5,000	2,761.45
Year 5	.47611	5,000	2,380.55
Present value of cash savings			35,983.78
Present value of cash outflow			33,522.00
Difference			$ 2,461.78

The present value of the cash inflow is $2,461.78 higher than the present value of the cash outflow. Therefore, the rate of return on the project must be higher than 16 percent.

The next interest rate chosen is 22 percent. Once again this is just a guess at the IRR. We proceed as before.

	Discount Factor (22%)	× Cash Savings =	Present Value of Cash Savings
Year 1	.81967	$18,000	$14,754.06
Year 2	.67186	12,000	8,062.32
Year 3	.55071	10,000	5,507.10
Year 4	.45140	5,000	2,257.00
Year 5	.37000	5,000	1,850.00
Present value of cash savings			32,430.48
Present value of cash outflow			33,522.00
Difference			$ (1,091.52)

The present value of the cash savings is $1,091.52 lower than the present value of the cash outflow. Consequently, the IRR must be somewhere between 16 and 22 percent. Because the 22 percent rate provides a smaller absolute difference between the present values of the cash flows, the rate is closer to 22 percent than to 16 percent. Next we try 20 percent.

	Discount Factor (20%)	× Cash Savings =	Present Value of Cash Savings
Year 1	.83333	$18,000	$14,999.94
Year 2	.69444	12,000	8,333.28
Year 3	.57870	10,000	5,787.00
Year 4	.48225	5,000	2,411.25
Year 5	.40188	5,000	2,009.40
Present value of cash savings			33,540.87
Present value of cash outflow			33,522.00
Difference			$ 18.87

The 20 percent interest rate discounts the cash savings to within $18.87 of the initial cash outflow, which means that 20 percent is a close approximation of the IRR for the project.

The IRR method assumes that cash inflows are reinvested at the IRR of the project

Internal rate of return characteristics. The IRR method specifically addresses the time value of money and the timing of cash flows. The important variable is cash flows; accounting concepts of income measurement, such as depreciation, play no role in evaluating projects except as they affect cash flows. Furthermore, the method assumes that cash receipts are reinvested at the internal rate of return of the project. For example, cash received from a project with a rate of return of 35 percent is assumed to be reinvested to yield a 35 percent rate of return. This reinvestment assumption may be optimistic for high-yielding investments because cash received from one project may have to be reinvested in less profitable new projects.

Net Present Value (NPV)

The NPV method discounts all cash flows at the firm's cost of capital

The **net present value** (**NPV**) method is another discounted cash flow project evaluation method. With this method, all cash inflows and outflows are discounted at a minimum acceptable rate of return, usually the firm's cost of capital. If the present value of the cash inflows is greater than the present value of the cash outflows, the project is acceptable.

To illustrate, we use the Joplin Products Company labeling machine example with a cost of \$33,522 and annual cash savings of \$10,000 for each of 5 years. Joplin's cost of capital is 12 percent. The present value of the cash outflow is \$33,522. The present value of the cash inflows is \$10,000 each year discounted at the rate of 12 percent.

With uniform cash flows, the present value (PV) is computed using the present value of an annuity of five payments of \$10,000 each at 12 percent; the NPV is calculated as follows:

$$PV = \$10{,}000 \times f(n = 5,\ i = 12\%)$$

$= \$10{,}000 \times 3.60478 =$ Present value of cash inflows	\$36,048
Less present value of cash outflows	33,522
Net present value of the project	\$ 2,526

A positive NPV means the project earns a rate of return higher than the firm's cost of capital

The net present value of the project is \$2,526, which means the labeling machine is an acceptable project given Joplin's 12 percent cost of capital. A positive net present value means that the company will earn a higher rate of return on its investment than it has to pay for the use of its capital. The net effect is that the present value of the earnings exceed by \$2,526 the amount paid for the use of the funds to finance the investment. If Joplin's cost of capital was higher than 12 percent, the decision might be to reject the project. For instance, if the cost of capital is 16 percent, the net present value of the labeling machine project is as follows:

Present value of cash inflows: \$10,000 × 3.27429	\$32,743
Less present value of cash outflows	33,522
Net present value of the project	\$ (779)

In this case, the net present value of the proposed project is negative, indicating the project should be rejected. Here the return from the investment is $779 less than the cost of the funds used for the project. The reason the net present value is negative in this case is because the cost of capital is 16 percent instead of 12 percent. The cash inflows from the investment remain constant, but the company has to pay more for capital to finance the project. The project is discounted using a higher interest rate. This result should be expected if you recall the earlier computation of the internal rate of return for the project. The IRR is 15 percent, but the cost of capital is 16 percent, so the project does not meet this minimum return. Both evaluation methods provide a reject decision, given the 16 percent cost of capital and the cash flow data for the machine.

If an investment has a salvage value, the money received from the sale of the investment is a cash inflow in addition to any revenues or cost savings generated by the project during the final year of use. For example, if the labeling machine is expected to have a salvage value of $3,000 at the end of 5 years, the cash inflow would be $10,000 in cost savings for year 5 plus $3,000 of salvage value. The entire $13,000 is discounted at the cost of capital of 12 percent. A salvage value increases the value of an investment, but since the cash from the sale of the investment is received at the time the investment is sold, the present value of the salvage may be small. In the case of the labeling machine, the $3,000 salvage value has a present value of $1,702.29 ($3,000 × .56743). High discount rates and long-lived projects may cause even a large salvage value to have an insignificant present value.

With nonuniform cash flows it is easier to compute NPV than IRR

Unlike the internal rate of return method, no additional complexities are encountered with the net present value method when cash flows are irregular. All cash flows are discounted at the firm's cost of capital whether the cash flows are identical each year or different. To illustrate, assume a cost of capital of 12 percent and annual cash savings of $18,000, $12,000, $10,000, $5,000, and $5,000, respectively, for the 5 years. The computation of the net present value is as follows:

	Discount Factor	Cash Savings	Present Value of Cash Savings
Year 1	.89286	$18,000	$16,071.48
Year 2	.79719	12,000	9,566.28
Year 3	.71178	10,000	7,117.80
Year 4	.63552	5,000	3,177.60
Year 5	.56743	5,000	2,837.15
Present value of cash inflows			38,770.31
Present value of cash outflow			33,522.00
Net present value of the project			$ 5,248.31

With irregular cash flows the computations using the NPV method are easier than the IRR method because there is no need to use trial and error to find the solution.

NPV assumes all cash inflows are invested at cost of capital

Net present value characteristics. Like the internal rate of return method, the net present value method relies on the time value of money and the timing of cash flows in evaluating projects. All cash flows are discounted at the cost of capital, and NPV assumes that all cash inflows from projects are reinvested at the cost of capital. Net present value is simple to use and is especially convenient with nonuniform cash flows.

Profitability Index (PI)

The net present value of a project is a function of the discount rate, the timing of the cash flows, and the size of the cash flows. Other things being equal, large investment proposals yield larger net present values. For example, two projects have the following cash flows:

Year	Small Machine	Large Machine
0	−$25,000	−$100,000
1	+ 10,000	+ 40,000
2	+ 10,000	+ 40,000
3	+ 10,000	+ 40,000
4	+ 10,000	+ 40,000

The PI converts investment alternatives to NPV per dollar of investment

Using a cost of capital of 14 percent, the net present values of the two machines are $4,137 and $16,548, respectively, so the large machine appears to be the more attractive project. Logic tells us, however, that the projects should be equally attractive investments because the cash flows of the larger machine are merely a multiple of 4 of the smaller machine's cash flows. To adjust the analysis for the size of the cash flows, we can calculate a **profitability index (PI)**, which is the ratio of the present value of the cash inflows to the present value of the cash outflows. In this example the profitability indexes are

$$\text{Profitability index} = \frac{\text{Present value of cash inflows}}{\text{Present value of cash outflows}}$$

$$\text{Profitability index of small machine} = \frac{\$29{,}137}{\$25{,}000} = 1.17$$

$$\text{Profitability index of large machine} = \frac{\$116{,}548}{\$100{,}000} = 1.17$$

The purpose of the profitability index is to provide a basis for comparison between projects of differing sizes. The higher the profitability index, the more desirable the project in terms of return per dollar of investment. A profitability index of 1.0 is the cutoff point for accepting projects. A profitability index less than 1.0 indicates a negative net present value for the project.

OTHER METHODS OF EVALUATING CAPITAL EXPENDITURE PROJECTS

Discounted cash flow methods are popular for evaluating capital expenditure projects, because they are based on the time value of money and the cost of capital has been high in recent years. But other methods of project evaluation are also used by some managers. Three other methods that are commonly used are payback, payback reciprocal, and accounting rate of return. None of these three methods uses discounted cash flows in the analysis.

Payback

Payback measures how long it takes to recover the cost of the investment

The **payback method,** sometimes called the **payout method,** is a computationally simple project evaluation approach that has been used for many years. The procedure is to determine how long it takes a project to return the cost of the original investment. For example, a retail store currently uses a delivery service. The store can purchase two delivery trucks at a cost of \$35,000 each. After deduction of operating and maintenance expenses, the two trucks will save a total of \$20,000 a year in delivery expenses for the next 6 years. After 6 years the trucks will be worn out and will be scrapped without any salvage value. The payback computation is

$$\text{Payback} = \frac{\text{Initial cost}}{\text{Annual cash savings}}$$

$$= \frac{\$70{,}000}{\$20{,}000 \text{ per year}} = 3.5 \text{ years}$$

The cost of the trucks will be recovered in 3½ years. The payback period itself does not provide an accept-reject decision. Managers must assess the significance of the payback period in selecting investment alternatives. If several projects are being evaluated, projects may be accepted in the order of quickest payback. Alternatively the firm may decide to invest only in projects with a certain maximum payback period, such as 3 years or less. During periods of economic instability or when it is hard to raise money by borrowing or selling stock, some businesses choose capital investment projects that are expected to return the invested funds in a year or two.

Some managers feel that payback provides a measure of risk. Often cash flows expected in the near future are more certain than more distant cash flows; therefore, a quick payback period indicates a less risky project. An additional argument for payback is that earlier payback is desirable because cash is more valuable now than later.

Payback computations are slightly different if cash inflows are not uniform from one year to the next. For instance, we assume the truck example mentioned earlier has higher cash savings in earlier years because of lower maintenance costs on new trucks.

Year	Yearly Cash Savings	Cumulative Cash Savings
1	$30,000	$ 30,000
2	30,000	60,000
3	20,000	80,000
4	20,000	100,000
5	10,000	110,000
6	10,000	120,000

Payback period = \$30,000 for year 1 + \$30,000 for year 2 + \$10,000 for ½ of year 3
= 2½ years

The process is merely to add up the cash savings starting with year 1 until the investment is recovered. Only half of the cash saving available in year 3 is needed to complete paying back the original investment.

Bailout measures how quickly the investment can be recovered from the combination of cash inflows and the salvage value

Bailout. The payback method of project evaluation is particularly sensitive to the recovery of investment outlays. A logical extension of payback is the bailout concept. **Bailout** measures how quickly the investment outlay can be recovered from the combination of cash savings and the salvage value of the investment at any point in time. To illustrate, refer to the original truck example with a cost of \$70,000 and annual cash savings of \$20,000 a year. At the end of 6 years, the salvage value of the trucks is zero; but clearly, when the trucks are newer, they have a market value, which continues to decline throughout their useful life. The chart below summarizes the estimated annual cash savings and salvage values for the trucks each year.

Year	Yearly Cash Savings	Cumulative Cash Savings	Year-End Salvage Value	Total of Salvage Value + Cash Savings
1	$20,000	$ 20,000	$45,000	$ 65,000
2	20,000	40,000	30,000	70,000
3	20,000	60,000	20,000	80,000
4	20,000	80,000	10,000	90,000
5	20,000	100,000	5,000	105,000
6	20,000	120,000	0	120,000

At the end of 2 years, the cash savings of \$40,000 and the salvage value of \$30,000 allow the firm to recover its original investment. The cost recovery of 2 years can be achieved only by terminating the project, hence the term *bailout*. Payback assumes the continuation of the project until the payback period has been reached.

Payback characteristics. A primary advantage of the payback method is its simplicity. No interest rates need to be estimated, and present value computations are not required. The only question is, How soon will the investment be recovered? An additional strength cited by supporters of payback is that it is a reasonable surrogate for risk. The longer one must wait for cash, the less certain one is that the cash will be received. Therefore, quick investment recovery is one measure of a low-risk project.

Payback ignores the timing of cash flows and all cash flows after the payback period

One criticism of payback is that no provision is made for the time value of money. All cash received during the payback period is of equal value in analyzing the project. A more serious issue is that cash flows occurring after the payback period are totally ignored. For example, two projects have the following cash flows:

Project X	$(80,000)	$10,000	$30,000	$40,000	$15,000	0	0	
Project Y	$(80,000)	$25,000	$25,000	$25,000	$25,000	$25,000	$25,000	
	0	1	2	3	4	5	6	yr

A manager using the payback method would prefer project X with a payback of 3 years over project Y with a payback of more than 3 years. But in the payback computation, the timing of the cash flows during the payback period is ignored. The larger early cash receipts for project Y can be reinvested. Also, project Y has $70,000 of cash receipts after the payback period, and project X has only $15,000. Yet these cash flows never enter into the project evaluation using payback.

The Payback Reciprocal

Payback reciprocal is a rough estimate of the IRR

A simple method of estimating the internal rate of return from a project is the **payback reciprocal,** which is 1 divided by the payback period. For example, a project has an initial cash outlay of $20,000 followed by 10 years of annual cash savings of $5,000. The payback period is $20,000/$5,000 per year, or 4 years. The payback reciprocal is

$$\text{Payback reciprocal} = \frac{1}{\text{Payback period}} = \frac{1}{4} = .25, \text{ or } 25\%$$

An initial cash outlay of $20,000 followed by 10 years of $5,000 cash inflows yields an internal rate of return of 21.4 percent, computed by using the table for the present value of an annuity of $1. The internal rate of return of 21.4 percent is 3.6 percent lower than the estimated internal rate of return computed by using the payback reciprocal. The payback reciprocal is always higher than the internal rate of return. However, if the life of the cash flows is at least twice the payback period, the payback reciprocal is a reasonable estimate of the rate of return. If the life of the cash flows is less than twice the payback period, the IRR estimate is very poor. To illustrate, the payback on the original labeling machine example is $33,522/$10,000 per year = 3.35 years. The payback reciprocal is 1/3.35 = 29.9 percent compared with the IRR of 15 percent, computed earlier. The life of the cash flows of 5 years is only 1.65 years beyond the payback period, which is significantly less than the required minimum of twice the payback period for a reasonable estimate of IRR.

Payback reciprocal characteristics. The payback reciprocal is easy to calculate and provides a reasonable estimate of the internal rate of return under some conditions. If the payback period is short and the investment period is long, the method can save computation time. However, a limitation of the method is that it should be used only with uniform cash flows. With nonuniform cash flows, the payback reciprocal can be a poor estimate of the internal rate of return regardless of the life of the investment project.

Accounting Rate of Return (ARR)

The accounting rate of return method is based on traditional accounting measures of income and investment

The **accounting rate of return (ARR)** method of evaluating capital budgeting projects is so named because it parallels traditional accounting concepts of income and investment. A project is evaluated by computing a rate of return on the investment using accounting measures of net income. The formula for the accounting rate of return is

$$\text{ARR} = \frac{\text{Annual revenue from project} - \text{Annual expenses of project}}{\text{Project investment}}$$

For example, Wort Doughnut Company is evaluating the acquisition of an automatic doughnut-making machine. The machine costs $20,000 and has a 5-year useful life with no salvage value. It is expected to add $10,000 of incremental revenue and $2,600 of additional operating expenses annually. Straight-line depreciation is used. Incremental net income is as follows:

Revenue		$10,000
Less operating expenses	$2,600	
Less depreciation expense	4,000	6,600
Incremental income		$ 3,400

All the capital budgeting evaluation methods discussed in this chapter are based on cash flows rather than accounting measures of income. Consequently, noncash items, such as depreciation, did not enter into the analysis. With the accounting rate of return method, however, accounting income is the prime element in the evaluation process and depreciation is used in determining income.

$$\text{ARR} = \frac{\text{Annual revenue from project} - \text{Annual expenses of project}}{\text{Project investment}}$$

$$= \frac{\$10{,}000 - \$2{,}600 - \$4{,}000}{\$20{,}000} = \frac{\$3{,}400}{\$20{,}000} = .17\text{, or }17\%$$

Some advocates of the accounting rate of return method argue that the investment should not be measured at its initial cost of $20,000, but rather at the **average investment** for the life of the project. The average investment is the average book value of the asset over its useful life. It is easily calculated by adding the beginning and ending book values and dividing by 2. The beginning value is the cost of $20,000, and the ending value is the salvage value of $0. Therefore, the average investment is ($20,000 + $0)/2, or $10,000. Using this investment base the accounting rate of return is

$$\text{ARR} = \frac{\$10{,}000 - \$2{,}600 - \$4{,}000}{\$10{,}000} = .34, \text{ or } 34\%$$

Clearly there is a significant difference between the computed rate depending on the choice of investment base. The controversy over the appropriate investment base is much the same as discussed in Chapter 11 in connection with determining the investment base for investment center evaluation. A firm must select the most appropriate base, given its reasons for measuring the investment rate of return.

The accounting rate of return method provides managers with a basis for comparing investment alternatives. Projects may be ranked according to their accounting rates of return. Capital budgeting funds may be allocated to projects starting with the highest rate of return and going down the ranking until all investment funds are allocated. An alternative is to establish a minimum accounting rate of return for all projects. Each division or department is assigned a certain amount of investment funds as long as each project satisfies a minimum accounting rate of return.

Accounting rate of return characteristics. The accounting rate of return method is supported on the grounds that it closely parallels accounting concepts of income measurement and investment return. However, strong criticism is leveled against this method because it totally ignores the timing of cash flows, the duration of cash flows, and the time value of money.

OTHER FACTORS INFLUENCING CAPITAL BUDGETING DECISIONS

Managers consider information other than the project evaluation models

Capital project acceptance criteria may be established for each project evaluation method. The IRR method requires deciding on some minimum rate of return for acceptable projects; with the NPV method, projects are acceptable if they have a positive net present value. Payback requires deciding on a maximum time period to repay the investment, and ARR requires a minimum accounting rate of return for a project. Acceptance criteria, however, are only a starting point in the decision to accept or reject a project. Most managers use information provided by the various evaluation methods as general guidelines in making capital expenditure decisions. The final decision involves more than just ranking the alternatives or selecting those that qualify. Many other factors are examined and considered by management. Some of the considerations that may modify capital budgeting decisions are discussed below.

Economic Conditions

Changes in economic conditions affect business operations and the way managers make business decisions. If managers believe that the economy is slowing down, they may be reluctant to make capital investments because the demand for the project's product or service may not materialize. A decline in economic activity may mean a reduction of sales and an increase in idle capacity, with a corresponding decrease in earnings. On the other hand, during good economic conditions, managers may perceive the need to expand capital investments in order to take advantage of the increase in demand for products and the resulting increase in sales. Managers may also build substantial excess productive capacity now to avoid increased construction costs in the future.

The way economic changes affect a business often depends on the nature of the business. For example, luxury items and recreational products typically experience a decline in demand during economic downturns, whereas staples, such as food and fuel, tend to be relatively unaffected and experience stable demand. On the other hand, the demand for staples does not increase significantly during economic upturns when luxury goods experience strong demand. The demand for some products is affected by particular economic conditions even when the economy is booming. For example, during gasoline shortages sales of recreational vehicles are strongly curtailed.

Each firm must evaluate the effect of economic conditions on its own capital budgeting decisions. For example, a grocery store pressed by competition from a new nearby store may experience falling sales and profits. Consequently, management may postpone a decision to install new electronic cash registers until it is clear the store can survive the competition. Similar actions are common among individuals. If you have just started a new job and really want and need a new car, you may postpone the purchase until you are confident you will succeed in the job.

When cash shortages loom on the horizon, management often looks to the capital expenditure budget for spending cuts. During severe economic downturns the news media carry many reports of companies that have sharply curtailed capital expenditures from originally planned levels.

Growth Policies

Many progressive companies have a significantly larger number of profitable investment opportunities than can be managed successfully. Rather than accept all profitable projects, a firm accepts as many as it can manage effectively, starting with the most profitable projects. Some managers find it hard to reject investment projects that look profitable, especially if they evaluate each proposal independently. However, unmanaged growth can turn potentially profitable investments into unprofitable mistakes. Managers must ascertain the volume of growth that can be effectively managed by the firm and must develop a capital budgeting policy accordingly.

Risk Evaluation

Risk is a key factor in evaluating projects

Risk is an integral part of all business and professional activities. Business risk refers to the possibility that desired outcomes may not be achieved. In capital expenditure analysis, expected cash flows are discounted at a target rate of return to find the net present value, the internal rate of return may be calculated, or perhaps the payback period is computed. In any case, the estimated cash flows are the basis for the evaluation. Cash flows are easier to predict for some projects than for others. For example the management of a fast-food chain with 40 restaurants in operation can probably predict cash flow better for a proposed new restaurant than the management of another restaurant chain just beginning business.

In capital budgeting, **risk** is usually defined in terms of the potential amount of fluctuations in a project's cash inflows. The more potential variability of the cash flows, the riskier the project. A problem is that none of the capital budgeting models have an explicit adjustment for risk. About the only feature is that most of the models discussed place a premium on earlier rather than later cash receipts. However, there is no measure of the possible variability of the cash flows in the models. Two projects may have identical expected cash flows; one project's cash flows may be virtually certain, and the other project's cash flows may be very volatile. The projects would be ranked equal using each of the evaluation methods, although one is clearly more desirable from a risk point of view. Profitable projects that managers view as too risky may be dropped from the capital expenditure budget. Managers prefer less risk over more risk if the rates of return on projects are equal. Risky projects must offer potentially greater returns in order to be viewed as attractive investment alternatives. Sometimes firms consider high-risk, high-return projects as a separate investment category. For instance, a company may perform a separate investment analysis to evaluate investments in new potentially profitable companies that are seeking capital. Money invested in new high-risk firms is called **venture capital.** People providing venture capital accept the high risk of losing their investment but also expect the opportunity for large returns.

Intuitive Factors

Capital budgeting project evaluation methods do not necessarily provide optimum capital budgeting decisions. Years of experience in a business plus good business intuition are valuable elements in capital budgeting. Consequently, the capital expenditure budget may reflect decisions based on inputs other than the capital budgeting models. Less structured methods of project evaluation often are referred to as seat-of-the-pants techniques, intuitive techniques, or "by-gut-and-by-golly" techniques. Whatever the name, many managers with good performance records rely on such techniques and do not use formal capital budgeting evaluation models.

Capital Rationing

Sometimes managers must select the most attractive investments from among many acceptable projects

The process of selecting the more desirable projects among many profitable investments is called **capital rationing.** Like any rationing it is designed to maximize the benefits available from using scarce resources. In this case the scarce resources are funds available for capital investments, and the benefits are returns on the investments. The process sounds simple enough. Rank the investments in order of profitability and accept the most profitable projects until the investment funds are exhausted. The problem is how to rank the projects. To illustrate, refer to Figure 13-1, which shows expected cash flows of five different projects being evaluated.

The Connelly Company has approximately $140,000 to invest in the five potential projects. Cash flow data are presented for projects A through

	Project				
Year	A	B	C	D	E
0	$(52,189)	$(50,197)	$(40,000)	$(20,000)	$(89,882)
1	10,000	5,000	30,000	15,000	20,000
2	10,000	5,000	20,000	10,000	20,000
3	10,000	10,000	10,000	5,000	20,000
4	40,000	10,000	—	—	20,000
5	—	20,000	—	—	20,000
6	—	20,000	—	—	20,000
7	—	20,000	—	—	20,000
8	—	50,000	—	—	20,000
9	—	—	—	—	20,000
10	—	—	—	—	20,000

	Project Evaluation Method			
Project	Internal Rate of Return	Net Present Value	Profitability Index	Payback
A	10.0%	$ (6,485)	.88	3.55 yr
B	20.0%	12,678	1.25	5.01 yr
C	28.9%	7,785	1.19	1.50 yr
D	28.9%	3,893	1.19	1.50 yr
E	18.0%	10,494	1.12	4.49 yr

Figure 13-1 Estimated cash flows for five investment projects. Only project E has uniform cash flows. Evaluation data for the five projects using four different evaluation methods show the relative desirability of each project.

Project Rank	Project Evaluation Method: Internal Rate of Return	Net Present Value	Profitability Index	Payback
1	C and D	B	B	C and D
2	—	E	C and D	—
3	B	C	—	A
4	E	D	E	E
5	A	A	A	B

Figure 13-2 A ranking of the five projects using four evaluation methods. Each method suggests a different ranking of the investment alternatives.

E. The projects have lives that range from 3 to 10 years. Connelly estimates its cost of capital at 15 percent.

Managers want as much data as possible to assist in making the investment decisions. Therefore, four different evaluation methods are used. Summarized at the bottom of Figure 13-1 are the internal rate of return, net present value, profitability index, and payback period evaluations for all five projects. Neither the payback reciprocal nor the accounting rate of return method is used because four of the five projects have nonuniform cash flows, and this severely limits the usefulness of the rate of return computed with these methods.

Analysis of the data in Figure 13-1 indicates that there is no consensus as to the most desirable and the least desirable projects. On the whole, the five projects vary significantly in ranking with each evaluation method. The data in Figure 13-1 are used to develop the ranking chart presented in Figure 13-2.

The projects with the highest internal rate of return rank third and fourth using net present value. The most desirable project using NPV ranks last using payback. Other interesting relationships can be found by scrutinizing Figures 13-1 and 13-2.

The obvious question is, Which ranking is correct? Unfortunately there is no obvious answer. Each evaluation method has some advocates who believe the information provided by that method is the most useful for making capital budgeting decisions. Most financial analysts support the use of discounted cash flow evaluation methods because these methods incorporate the time value of money into the analysis. But internal rate of return, net present value, and profitability index are all discounted cash flow methods. A major differentiating variable is the assumption about the reinvestment rate for cash inflows generated by projects. The IRR model assumes cash inflows are reinvested at the IRR for that project, whereas the NPV model assumes cash inflows are reinvested at the cost of capital. Each reinvestment rate assumption has some advocates. In summary, there is no correct answer to the ranking question, only opinions of managers. Each must select the evaluation system and ranking method considered most useful.

TAXES AND CAPITAL BUDGETING

Taxes affect cash flows and must be included in capital budgeting analyses

Taxes are expenses of doing business. Consequently, managers must take tax effects into account when analyzing capital expenditure alternatives. That is, projects should be evaluated using estimated after-tax cash flows. To illustrate, Baytown Plumbing Company is evaluating the installation of a radio communications system in its fleet of five trucks with a base unit in the company's office. In addition, the company would install a minicomputer with a terminal. Employees would use the radio to call in the arrival and completion time for each job. The dispatcher would use the computer terminal to develop quickly the correct charges for the job using standard times and rates for the job. The accounts receivable file would be searched by the computer to determine whether the customer in question had any outstanding balance with the plumbing company. The dispatcher would then radio the correct bill to the plumbers, and the customer would receive the bill for the job before the plumber left. With the radio equipment and minicomputer, the entire billing process would take less than 2 minutes. In addition, the dispatcher would be able to assign new jobs without the plumbers' returning to the office. This would save many hours of travel time. The cost of the new equipment is \$24,000, and installation cost is \$1,000. A full-time radio dispatcher would have to be hired at a cost of \$13,000 a year. The new dispatching system would minimize trips back to the office for new assignments and allow the firm to make an estimated 80 additional service calls a month. The average revenue per service call is \$30, and average parts and supply cost is \$5 per call. The company's income tax rate is 40 percent. All the new equipment has a 5-year useful life and no salvage value.

The cash outflows of \$25,000 for the equipment and installation are made when the equipment is purchased. The cash flows associated with the project for **each** of the 5 years of useful life are as follows:

Revenue:	80 calls × \$30/call × 12 months =	\$28,800
Expenses:		
Parts and supplies:	80 calls × \$5/call × 12 months =	(4,800)
Dispatcher's salary		(13,000)
Net cash flows from project before taxes		\$11,000

This part of the analysis is not different from earlier discussions except that revenue and expenses are identified separately. Note that the \$11,000 is the net cash inflow from the project, ignoring taxes, and is not accounting net income. To calculate accounting net income, depreciation expense is included. The tax expense is calculated using the 40 percent tax rate. For tax purposes the company is required to use a 5-year life under the accelerated cost recovery system (ACRS), passed by Congress in 1981 with the Economic Recovery Tax Act. Mandatory ACRS rates are presented in Figure 13-3. With ACRS depreciation, any expected salvage value at the end of the asset's useful life is ignored. The ACRS percentage from the

Asset Amortization Schedules in Percent Under the Accelerated Cost Recovery System

	Equipment				18-Year Real Property											
	Class life in years				Month (in first recovery year) property is placed in service											
Year	**3**	**5**	**10**	**15**	**1**	**2**	**3**	**4**	**5**	**6**	**7**	**8**	**9**	**10**	**11**	**12**
					The applicable percentage is:											
1	25	15	8	5	9	9	8	7	6	5	4	4	3	2	1	0.4
2	38	22	14	10	9	9	9	9	9	9	9	9	9	10	10	10.0
3	37	21	12	9	8	8	8	8	8	8	8	8	9	9	9	9.0
4		21	10	8	7	7	7	7	7	8	8	8	8	8	8	8.0
5		21	10	7	7	7	7	7	7	7	7	7	7	7	7	7.0
6			10	7	6	6	6	6	6	6	6	6	6	6	6	6.0
7			9	6	5	5	5	5	6	6	6	6	6	6	6	6.0
8			9	6	5	5	5	5	5	5	5	5	5	5	5	5.0
9			9	6	5	5	5	5	5	5	5	5	5	5	5	5.0
10			9	6	5	5	5	5	5	5	5	5	5	5	5	5.0
11				6	5	5	5	5	5	5	5	5	5	5	5	5.0
12				6	5	5	5	5	5	5	5	5	5	5	5	5.0
13				6	4	4	4	5	4	4	5	4	4	4	5	5.0
14				6	4	4	4	4	4	4	4	4	4	4	4	4.0
15				6	4	4	4	4	4	4	4	4	4	4	4	4.0
16					4	4	4	4	4	4	4	4	4	4	4	4.0
17					4	4	4	4	4	4	4	4	4	4	4	4.0
18					4	3	4	4	4	4	4	4	4	4	4	4.0
19						1	1	1	2	2	2	3	3	3	3	3.6

* ACRS cost recovery table for 18-year real property (18-year, 175% declining balance, assuming mid-month conversion.)

Figure 13-3 **Cost recovery rates enacted by the Economic Recovery Tax Act of 1981 and modified in 1984. The depreciation rate is a specified percentage each year. Each column adds up to 100 percent. Salvage value is not used with ACRS. The 10-year and 15-year classes of equipment are for utility property only. Real estate is amortized over 18 years, with the annual percentage depending on the month it was placed in service.**

schedule is multiplied times the asset's cost. The calculation of taxable income and income taxes for each of the 5 years of the project is as follows:

	Year 1	Year 2	Year 3	Year 4	Year 5
Net pretax cash savings	$11,000	$11,000	$11,000	$11,000	$11,000
Less depreciation	3,750	5,500	5,250	5,250	5,250
Taxable income	7,250	5,500	5,750	5,750	5,750
Tax rate	× .40	× .40	× .40	× .40	× .40
Income tax	$ 2,900	$ 2,200	$ 2,300	$ 2,300	$ 2,300

Subtracting the taxes from the net cash savings yields the following:

	Year 1	Year 2	Year 3	Year 4	Year 5
Before-tax cash savings	$11,000	$11,000	$11,000	$11,000	$11,000
Less income taxes	2,900	2,200	2,300	2,300	2,300
After-tax cash savings	$ 8,100	$ 8,800	$ 8,700	$ 8,700	$ 8,700

Depreciation affects taxable income and therefore cash flows

The above illustrates an important point. Depreciation does not require a cash outlay, but it does affect cash flows because of its effect on taxes. Once the net-of-tax cash flows are determined, the evaluation is made as before. If Baytown Plumbing's cost of capital is 14 percent, the net present value of the project is as follows:

	14 Percent Discount Factor	Cash Savings	Present Value of Cash Savings
Year 1	.87719	$8,100	$ 7,105.24
Year 2	.76947	8,800	6,771.34
Year 3	.67497	8,700	5,872.24
Year 4	.59208	8,700	5,151.10
Year 5	.51937	8,700	4,518.52
Present value of cash inflows			29,418.44
Present value of cash outflow			25,000.00
Net present value of the project			$ 4,418.44

The profitability index is

$$\frac{\text{Present value of cash inflows}}{\text{Present value of cash outflows}} = \frac{\$29{,}418.51}{\$25{,}000.00} = 1.18$$

ESTIMATING THE COST OF CAPITAL

A business pays for the use of money in the form of interest or dividends. Businesses obtain funds from many sources, each with a different cost. Interest and dividend rates vary for bonds, mortgages, notes payable, preferred stock, and common stock. Theoretically, the cost of capital can be computed as the weighted average of the rates paid to various investors. For many firms, however, the cost of capital is difficult to compute because it may change with changes in the economy, government actions, and changes in the risk of various types of investments. Consequently, the cost of capital can only be estimated. Estimation methods vary and can be very complex. We present only the basic concepts of computing the weighted average cost of capital for a firm.

In return for the capital provided by investors, companies pay dividends to shareholders and interest to creditors. Given the amount of the dividends and interest, and many other variables, such as the amount of earnings, state of the economy, and tax rates, investors place a value on the equity and debt instruments of a company. To estimate the cost of capital, it is necessary to relate the **market value** of the debt and equity instruments to their **market return.** The following example illustrates the process.

Cost of Common Stock

Petosky Corporation has outstanding 50,000 shares of no-par common stock which trades in the stock market at \$40 per share. The company currently pays a cash dividend of \$6 per share annually. The cost of common stock to the company is expressed as a percentage rate computed as follows:

$$\text{Cost of common stock} = \frac{\text{Dividend per share}}{\text{Market price per share}}$$
$$= \frac{\$6}{\$40}$$
$$= .15\text{, or 15 percent}$$

The computation is nothing more than the company's dividend yield expressed as a percentage. This percentage is the current rate investors demand for providing the company with equity capital. Because the amount of earnings and the company's dividend policy may change, the figure above is also subject to change. In addition, the cost of funds depends on investor expectations about company performance and dividend policy, their knowledge about the company's earnings and the amount retained for expansion and potential future dividends, and their evaluation of investment risk. As investor expectations and evaluations change, the dividend yield changes also.

Cost of Preferred Stock

The cost of preferred stock is also the stock's dividend yield. Typically, a company pays the required preferred dividend, which usually does not change over the life of the preferred stock. Therefore the preferred dividend yield is usually more stable than the common dividend yield. The preferred dividend yield does change, however, when changes in interest rates cause the price of preferred stock to move up or down.

Petosky Corporation has outstanding 10,000 shares of \$9 preferred stock which currently trades in the market at \$90 per share. The cost of the preferred stock is

$$\text{Cost of preferred stock} = \frac{\text{Preferred dividend per share}}{\text{Market price of preferred share}}$$
$$= \frac{\$9}{\$90}$$
$$= .10\text{, or 10 percent}$$

Cost of Long-Term Debt

Companies typically have many types of long-term debt with different costs. Except for differences in interest rates, the cost of each is computed the same way. Interest is a tax-deductible expense; its actual cost is less than the interest rate paid. Therefore the company's tax rate must be included in the computation of the cost of long-term debt.

Petosky Corporation has outstanding $1,000,000 of 12 percent bonds which trade in the market at their face value. The company is subject to a 35 percent tax rate. Its true interest cost is therefore

$$\begin{aligned}\text{True interest cost} &= \text{Interest rate} \times (1 - \text{Tax rate})\\ &= .12\,(1 - .35)\\ &= .078, \text{ or } 7.8 \text{ percent}\end{aligned}$$

In all cases, the market value of the debt rather than the book value should be used, so that the interest rate computed is the company's actual cost of borrowing rather than the coupon rate of the bonds. Similar calculations may be made for other types of debt such as mortgages, notes, and leases.

Weighted Average Cost of Capital

We are now ready to compute the weighted average cost of capital for Petosky Corporation. We need to know what proportion of its capitalization is debt, preferred, and common equity. To compute the cost of capital we multiply the cost of each individual type of capital by the percentage weight of each type of capitalization, based on market values.

Type of Capitalization	Market Value	Proportion ×	Cost =	Weighted Cost
Long-term debt	$1,000,000	10/39	.078	.0200
Preferred stock	900,000	9/39	.100	.0231
Common stock	2,000,000	20/39	.150	.0769
Total capitalization	$3,900,000	Cost of capital		.1200

Problems immediately become apparent. For many types of securities, there is no market price from which the cost of capital can be computed. The relative proportion of long-term debt and equity capitalization may not remain the same over time. Changes in company policy, government action, state of the economy, and risk perception of investors all tend to change the relationships that affect the cost of capital. Still, managers can obtain some approximation of the cost of capital in order to use the estimate for capital budgeting purposes.

SUMMARY

Capital budgeting decisions typically are long-term commitments of large amounts of resources and thus involve long-term policy decisions. Consequently, they are a major factor in determining the long-range success of an organization. Capital investments require a systematic decision procedure that includes the identification of investment alternatives, estimation of project benefits and costs, evaluation of capital budgeting projects in a systematic way, development of the capital expenditure budget, and reevaluation of projects after acceptance. Projects should be selected using decision criteria that are compatible with organization goals.

With **discounted cash flow (DCF)** methods, the **time value of money** is used to evaluate investments. The **internal rate of return (IRR)** is the rate earned by a project. It is the interest rate which discounts the cash inflows to a **present value (PV)** that is equal to the present value of cash outflows. If the IRR is higher than the company's cost of capital, the project is acceptable. The **cost of capital** is the amount a company must pay for the use of money. Another discounted cash flow method is the **net present value (NPV)** method, in which all cash flows are discounted at the firm's cost of capital. If the net present value is positive, the project is acceptable. Projects with nonuniform cash flows may be evaluated using either the net present value method or the internal rate of return method. The **profitability index (PI)** is used to convert all net present value computations to a measure of NPV per dollar of investment and thus provides a basis for comparing projects of differing sizes.

The **payback** method, sometimes called the **payout** method, measures how quickly the original investment is recovered. It is a quick and easy method of project evaluation, but it ignores the time value of money and all cash flows after the payback period. **Payback reciprocal** is a rough approximation of the IRR and is computed as 1/payback period. For the payback reciprocal to be a reasonable estimate of IRR, the life of the project must be at least twice the payback period and only uniform cash flow can exist. **Bailout** is similar to the payback method but includes the project's salvage value at the end of each period.

The **accounting rate of return (ARR)** method is based on accounting concepts of income measurement and investment base to compute a rate of return. The timing of cash flows and the time value of money are totally ignored.

The process of selecting the most desirable projects is called **capital rationing.** Some factors affecting capital budgeting decisions are economic conditions, growth policies, risk evaluation, intuitive factors, and capital structure.

It is difficult to select the correct projects for the capital budget. Different evaluation methods may yield different rankings of the projects. Capital expenditure decisions should include calculations of tax effects, which in turn must involve depreciation calculations, although depreciation itself has no cash flow consequences.

To use the project evaluation methods effectively, it is necessary to have some idea of the cost of capital, but measuring the cost of capital can be complex. Typically, market values and yields of common stock, preferred stock, and long-term debt are used in the computation. In the case of debt, the after-tax interest cost should be used. When the cost of each individual source of funds is established, a weighted average cost for the entire organization is computed.

KEY TERMS

accounting rate of return (ARR) *(538)*
average investment *(539)*
bailout *(536)*
capital abandonment analysis *(526)*
capital budgeting *(523)*
capital rationing *(542)*
cost of capital *(528)*
discounted cash flow (DCF) *(527)*
internal rate of return (IRR) *(528)*
net present value (NPV) *(532)*
nonuniform cash flows *(530)*
payback *(535)*
payback reciprocal *(537)*
payout *(535)*
present value (PV) *(527)*
profitability index (PI) *(534)*
risk *(541)*
time value of money *(527)*
venture capital *(541)*

QUESTIONS

1. What characteristics do capital budgets have that cause management to spend much time and effort preparing them?
2. Briefly describe the five activities involved in the capital budgeting process.
3. What is meant by *discounted cash flow* methods? Name two capital budgeting methods that are based on discounting of cash flows.
4. Define the internal rate of return.
5. What effects do nonuniform cash flows have on the manual computation of IRR?
6. Compare and contrast the net present value method with the internal rate of return method of evaluating capital projects.
7. Describe cost of capital and explain how it pertains to net present value and the internal rate of return.
8. What is the profitability index and why is it used?
9. Defend the use of payback as a capital budgeting evaluation method.
10. Is the timing of cash flows relevant to payback analysis? Discuss.
11. What is the payback reciprocal? What requirements must be met for the payback reciprocal to be of any use?
12. How does the accounting rate of return method differ from the other capital budgeting methods?
13. What does *capital rationing* mean?
14. Identify variables other than capital budgeting evaluation models that influence capital budgeting decisions.
15. Explain how it is possible to have a set of capital budgeting projects ranked differently by the different capital budgeting evaluation methods.
16. "Depreciation is a noncash item and consequently does not affect the analysis of investment proposals using discounted cash flow methods." Comment.
17. What is the cost of capital? How can it be estimated?

EXERCISES

Ex. 13-1 **Internal rate of return.** Pipkin Company is evaluating a proposal to acquire robot assembly units for the West Coast Manufacturing Division. Each unit costs $31,500, and the sales tax is 5 percent. The cost of installing units is $975 each.

The assembly units have a useful life of 6 years, and the division managers want to acquire four units. Annual labor and other cost savings of all four units are expected to be $36,000 for the life of the units. The company evaluates capital projects using the internal rate of return and rejects projects with an IRR less than 16 percent.

Required: Compute the internal rate of return for the robot units and determine if they should be acquired.

Ex. 13-2 **Interpolation of internal rate of return.** Cofferine Company is thinking about acquiring a new conveyor belt line for production parts. The line would cost $162,000 and would provide an estimated annual cash savings of $36,800 for the next 8 years, at which time the belt line would be worn out and would have no salvage value.

Required: Compute the internal rate of return rounded to one decimal place.

Ex. 13-3 **Present value and profitability index.** Below are cash flow data for two investment projects that are being evaluated.

	Investment Project	
Year	Machine X	Machine Y
0	−$250,000	−$100,000
1	+ 90,000	+ 45,000
2	+ 90,000	+ 45,000
3	+ 90,000	+ 45,000
4	+ 90,000	+ 45,000
5	+ 90,000	+ 45,000

The company uses a target rate of return of 20 percent for evaluating investment proposals.

Required:

a. Compute the net present value for each machine.
b. Compute the profitability index for each machine.

Ex. 13-4 **Net present value analysis.** J & J Radiator Repair has operated in an old garage for over 10 years. A reputation for quality service at a fair price has pushed business past current capacity. A. J. Jones, owner of the business, would like to build a new facility that would double business capacity. The total cost of the new facility, including equipment, would be $200,000, not including land costing $25,000. The estimated useful life of the facility is 10 years; at the end of the period, the facility and land are expected to have a value of $50,000. The current garage can be sold for $60,000. Jones can obtain funds at 15 percent interest. Jones estimates that net cash receipts will increase by $32,000 a year as a result of increased capacity.

Required:

a. Compute the net present value of the project.
b. Should the project be accepted? Explain.

Ex. 13-5 **Payback and payback reciprocal.** A manager is evaluating an investment proposal that costs $100,000 and has expected annual cash inflows of $25,000 for 8 years.

Required:

a. Compute the payback period.
b. Compute the payback reciprocal.

Ex. 13-6 **Accounting rate of return.** Sauna City Sales Company is evaluating a plan to expand its showroom space by 30 percent and its warehouse space by 10 percent. The expansion would cost $200,000 and would have a useful life of 20 years, with no salvage value. The firm uses straight-line depreciation. The expected increase in revenue is $55,000 a year, and cash expenses are $20,000 a year.

Required:

a. Compute the accounting rate of return.
b. If Sauna City requires a 15 percent accounting rate of return, should the project be accepted?

Ex. 13-7 **Maximum investment to achieve a desired rate of return.** The Webberville Toy Company is contemplating marketing a new toy. The company expects the product to be marketable for 5 years. Expected net cash inflows from the product are as follows:

Year	Net Cash Flow
1	$ 40,000
2	60,000
3	50,000
4	30,000
5	10,000
Total	$190,000

The company uses 25 percent as the minimum required return on new products.

Required: What is the maximum the toy company should invest in the production of the new toy, assuming no salvage value on any of the investment?

Ex. 13-8 **ARR, payback, NPV, and PI for a single project.** Donlevey Hardware Store currently has four cash registers in the store, all of which are fully depreciated. The owner is evaluating the possibility of purchasing two new electronic cash registers at a cost of $10,000 each. The new machines are much faster than the old cash registers and would free some employees to help customers. The owner estimates that new cash registers will save $6,000 a year over their useful life in personnel costs. Maintenance and other operating costs will total $1,000 a year on the new machines. The machines have a useful life of 10 years, with no salvage value. The current cash registers will be scrapped. The firm uses straight-line depreciation. Donlevey's cost of capital is 12 percent.

Required:

a. Compute the accounting rate of return based on total investment.
b. Compute the payback period.
c. Compute the net present value.
d. Compute the profitability index.

Ex. 13-9 Understanding capital project analysis. Following are data on a capital project being evaluated by the management of Luke Coldenhot Company.

	Project M
Annual cost saving	$10,000
Useful life	16 years
IRR	22 percent
Profitability index	1.12
NPV	?
Cost of capital	?
Cost of project	?
Payback	?
Salvage value	0

Required: Find the missing values.

Ex. 13-10 Using capital budgeting concepts. Following are data on a capital project with equal annual cash savings being evaluated by the management of Schloope Company.

	Project KRAK
Cost	$101,400
Payback	5.07 years
Annual cost saving	?
Useful life	?
Cost of capital	?
NPV	?
IRR	19 percent
PI	1.14
Salvage value	0

Required: Find the missing values.

Ex. 13-11 IRR and payback reciprocal with taxes. Haverforth Company is evaluating a proposal to acquire an inventory handling system. The system would save the company $70,000 a year in inventory handling costs. The system has an expected useful life of 5 years with no salvage value. It costs $90,510 and requires a maintenance contract that costs $20,000 a year. The company has an effective income tax rate of 46 percent.

Required:

a. Compute the internal rate of return for the project.
b. Compute the estimated rate of return using the payback reciprocal.

Ex. 13-12 Two accounting rates of return. Ketterling Company is planning to buy a store building for $355,000. The building has an estimated life of 20 years and a salvage value of $20,000. Of the purchase price, $15,000 is allocated to the land and the remainder to the building. The company plans to use straight-line depreciation. Annual revenue from the building is expected to be $200,000 and operating expenses are estimated at $125,000, not including depreciation.

Required:

a. Compute the accounting rate of return using actual cost as a base.
b. Compute the accounting rate of return using average cost as a base.

Ex. 13-13 Cost of capital. Baffer Company has outstanding $800,000 face value of 14 percent, 20-year bonds which trade in the bond market at par. The remainder of its long-term debt consists of $400,000 of 12 percent mortgages whose face value is considered to be fair value. It has outstanding 10,000 shares of $100 par $7 preferred stock which trades in the market at $70 per share. Also outstanding are 10,000 shares of common stock with a market price of $40 per share. The company pays a cash dividend of $3.20 on the common shares. The Retained Earnings balance is $900,000. The company is subject to a 40 percent income tax rate.

Required: Compute the weighted average cost of capital.

PROBLEMS

P. 13-1 Five project evaluation methods. Following are cash flow data for an investment that is being evaluated by Carlisle Company.

Year	Cash Flow
0	−$114,200
1	+ 40,000
2	+ 40,000
3	+ 40,000
4	+ 40,000

The company's cost of capital is 12 percent.

Required: Compute the:

a. Payback period.
b. Payback reciprocal.
c. Internal rate of return.
d. Net present value.
e. Profitability index.

P. 13-2 Net present value project evaluation. Sullivan Custom Welding is considering the purchase of an automatic spot-welding machine. It costs $10,000 and has an 8-year useful life. Annual net cash inflow of $2,500 is expected from new business, and it is expected the machine will have a salvage value of $1,000. Sullivan's cost of capital is 15 percent, and the company uses the net present value method of evaluating investments.

Required:

a. Should Sullivan Custom Welding acquire the welding machine?
b. The owner of the welding business is not confident of the estimated net cash flow from new business. If actual net cash flow turns out to be $2,000 a year, should the welding machine be purchased?
c. What is the minimum annual net cash flow from the investment that the company must have to accept the project?

P. 13-3 Project evaluation using NPV, PI, and payback period. Yard Beautiful Nursery has four employees who plant trees and shrubs on a full-time basis. Currently the company uses a large flatbed truck and a pickup truck for all planting deliveries.

A new truck with a small hydraulic crane can be purchased for $54,000. It would have a useful life of 8 years and a salvage value of $6,000. If the new truck is purchased, the company can maintain its current level of operations with only two employees engaged in full-time planting. The savings in personnel costs would be $9,000 per year for each employee. Operating and maintenance costs on the new truck are expected to be $4,000 per year higher than on the old trucks. The old trucks, which have a book value of zero, would be sold for a total of $2,000. The company has a tax rate of 40 percent and uses straight-line depreciation for all depreciable assets and for estimating after-tax cash flows. Yard Beautiful requires a 15 percent return on investments.

Required:

a. Compute the net present value for the new truck.
b. Compute the profitability index.
c. Compute the payback period.

P. 13-4 **Capital investment analysis.** Bovine Company is evaluating a proposal to acquire an automated welding machine for its small parts assembly department. The equipment costs $68,000, plus the company would have to pay a 5 percent sales tax on the purchase and spend $2,000 for freight and installation. The equipment has a useful life of 10 years and is expected to produce cost savings of $15,750 per year. There is no salvage value. Company policy is not to fund any capital project whose internal rate of return is below the company's 16 percent cost of capital.

Required:

a. Compute the net present value of the project.
b. Compute the profitability index.
c. Find the internal rate of return to the nearest percent.
d. Compute the payback on the project.
e. Compute the payback reciprocal.

P. 13-5 **Project evaluation and ranking.** A firm is evaluating three alternative investment proposals each requiring a $60,000 initial cash outlay. Each project has an expected useful life of 6 years. Below are expected net cash inflows over the life of the projects. Observing the data, one manager comments, "Clearly project C is the best choice; it yields far more cash than the others." The firm's cost of capital is 20 percent.

	Investment Proposal		
Year	A	B	C
1	$ 50,000	$ 20,000	$ 10,000
2	10,000	20,000	10,000
3	10,000	20,000	10,000
4	10,000	20,000	10,000
5	10,000	20,000	10,000
6	10,000	20,000	90,000
Total	$100,000	$120,000	$140,000

Required:

a. Evaluate and rank the projects using payback and net present value. Do you agree with the manager's evaluation? Discuss your answer.

b. Would your ranking of the projects change if the firm's cost of capital was 10 percent?

P. 13-6 Maximum investment for a project. The High Peaks Sporting Goods Store has been plagued by numerous burglaries over the last 3 years. To keep insurance premiums at a reasonable level and protect a $1,000,000 inventory, the store hired a night watchman. The watchman has solved the burglary problem, but he costs the firm $12,000 a year. He is occasionally absent from work due to sickness or bad weather. A security systems company has offered to sell the store a system that would eliminate the need for the night watchman. The system has an expected useful life of 15 years. The security system's salesperson is computing the cost of the system and will present a bid this week. The management estimates cost of capital at 16 percent.

Required:

a. What is the maximum bid the store should accept?

b. If the bid is $64,000, should the store accept it?

c. If the actual life of the security system is 12 years instead of 15, does it have any effect on your answer in part *b*?

P. 13-7 Net present value of two capital projects. Blossen Company produces molded plastic appliance housings. Its molds are wearing out and need replacing. The company is evaluating two suppliers' proposals for replacement molds. Supplier A is offering to replace the company's molds with new molds costing $310,000. The supplier will allow $15,000 on the company's old molds as a trade-in. The new molds have a useful life of 5 years and a salvage value of $10,000. Using the new molds, the company estimates net cash inflows of $95,000 per year.

Supplier B is offering replacement molds costing $330,000 and is willing to allow $10,000 as a trade-in on the old molds. The new molds have a useful life of 7 years and a salvage value of $10,000. Since these molds require more maintenance than those of supplier A, the company estimates that its net cash inflows from using the molds would be only $90,000 per year. The company evaluates its capital projects using the net present value method with an estimated cost of capital of 20 percent.

Required:

a. Compute the net present value of each project.

b. Compute the profitability index for each.

c. Decide which supplier's molds should be acquired.

P. 13-8 Project ranking with four project analysis methods. Dune and Ryan, Incorporated, is evaluating four investment opportunities. The company estimates its cost of capital at 14 percent. Below are cash flow data for the investments.

	Estimated Annual Cash Flows			
Year	A	B	C	D
0	–$82,228	–$90,000	–$78,242	–$50,000
1	20,000	15,000	15,000	10,000
2	20,000	15,000	15,000	10,000
3	20,000	15,000	15,000	10,000
4	20,000	15,000	15,000	10,000
5	20,000	15,000	15,000	10,000
6	20,000	15,000	15,000	38,117
7	—	15,000	15,000	—
8	—	53,337	15,000	—
9	—	—	15,000	—
10	—	—	15,000	—

Required:

a. For each project calculate:

1. The payback period.
2. The internal rate of return.
3. The net present value.
4. The profitability index.

b. Prepare a schedule ranking the investments in order of preference using each of the evaluation methods in part *a*.

P. 13-9 Evaluation and ranking of several proposals. Gridly is evaluating three investment proposals for equipment used in the production of Plexiglas containers. He obtains the following cash outflow and inflow data from companies that are willing to provide appropriate equipment. His required rate of return is 15 percent.

Year	Vendor A	Vendor B	Vendor C
0	$(6,435)	$(7,000)	$(10,140)
1	1,500	1,500	1,950
2	1,500	1,500	1,950
3	1,500	1,500	1,950
4	1,500	1,500	1,950
5	1,500	1,500	1,950
6	1,500	1,500	1,950
7	1,500	1,500	1,950
8	0	1,500	1,950
9	0	1,500	1,950
10	0	1,500	1,950
11	0	0	1,950
12	0	0	1,950

Required:

a. Compute the payback on each project.
b. Compute the net present value on each project.
c. Compute the profitability index on each project.
d. Compute the internal rate of return on each project to the nearest whole percentage.
e. Rank the projects in order of preference using each of the evaluation methods.

P. 13-10 **Project evaluation with increasing costs.** Starburg Manufacturing Company is concerned about the rising cost of labor. The assembly phase of its small appliance manufacturing business is almost totally manual. The engineering department has developed a plan to automate 80 percent of the assembly operation. The cost of the proposed project is $2.2 million. The expected life of the automated system is 10 years, after which time the system will be scrapped without any salvage value. If the system is implemented, labor costs should decline by 60 percent and direct materials costs should fall by 5 percent due to greater production efficiencies. Current-year labor and materials costs are $500,000 and $200,000 respectively. Over the life of the project, management expects labor costs to rise 10 percent a year and materials costs 8 percent a year. Starburg's cost of capital is 15 percent. Ignore taxes.

Required:

a. Compute the expected cost savings for the life of the project.
b. Compute the net present value of the project.
c. Should the project be accepted?
d. If there were no cost increases at all, should the project be accepted?

P. 13-11 **Capital rationing.** The following projects are being evaluated by Grummett Company, which has $100,000 available for capital investment. The company's cost of capital is 16 percent. The available projects have the following costs and internal rates of return:

Project	Cost	IRR
A	$10,000	20.0%
B	20,000	18.5
C	20,000	18.0
D	30,000	17.0
E	60,000	17.5

The company evaluates projects using the IRR method. The president says she wants the greatest possible IRR on capital projects. The vice president argues that he would prefer the greatest dollar return even if the IRR is less than optimal.

Required:

a. Determine the best combination of investments.
b. Discuss the merits of your combination and the merits of the president's and vice president's arguments.

P. 13-12 **New product project evaluation.** Graph-O-Tron, Inc., has acquired the patent rights to a new, very fast vector cathode-ray tube computer terminal. The terminal is very attractive to organizations, such as utilities, highway departments, and land-use planning organizations, that use geography and geographic locations in their management information systems. Graph-O-Tron is operating near capacity and would require a new production facility to produce the new terminal. The cost of the plant and other facilities would be $6,200,000. The expected useful life is 8 years, with an estimated salvage value of $1,400,000. Expected unit manufacturing costs are as follows:

Direct material	$280
Direct labor	270
Variable overhead	30
Variable selling and administrative	120

The product is expected to have an 8-year life cycle, after which it will be technologically obsolete. At a selling price of $1,400 per unit, expected sales for the 8-year period are as follows:

Year	Expected Sales (Units)
1	2,000
2	4,000
3	5,000
4	5,000
5	4,000
6	3,000
7	2,000
8	2,000

Heavy advertising and promotional costs are required to penetrate the market quickly before competition reacts to the new product. During the first 2 years of the product's life, such costs would be $300,000 a year, and they would decrease to $100,000 per year for the last 6 years.

Other fixed costs, including straight-line depreciation, would amount to $800,000 a year. The firm's average income tax rate is 40 percent.

Graph-O-Tron requires a 25 percent return on investment for a product that is as risky as the new terminal.

Required:

a. Using the net present value method, evaluate the investment project.

b. If Graph-O-Tron, Inc., uses its normal required rate of return of 16 percent instead of the 25 percent rate for risky projects, would the project be acceptable?

P. 13-13 **(CMA) Equipment replacement analysis.** Wisconsin Products Company manufactures several different products. One of the firm's principal products sells for $20 per unit. The sales manager of Wisconsin Products has stated repeatedly that he could sell more units of this product if they were available. In an attempt to substantiate his claim, the sales manager conducted a market research study last year at a cost of $44,000 to determine potential demand for this product. The study indicated that Wisconsin Products could sell 18,000 units of the product annually for the next 5 years.

The equipment currently in use has the capacity to produce 11,000 units annually. The variable production costs are $9 per unit. The equipment has a book value of $60,000 and a remaining useful life of 5 years. The salvage value of the equipment is negligible now and will be zero in 5 years.

A maximum of 20,000 units could be produced annually on the new machinery which can be purchased. The new equipment costs $300,000 and has an estimated useful life of 5 years with no salvage value at the end of 5 years. Wisconsin Product's production manager has estimated that the new equipment would provide increased production efficiencies that would reduce the variable production costs to \$7 per unit.

Wisconsin Products Company uses ACRS 5-year depreciation on all of its equipment for tax purposes. The firm is subject to a 40 percent tax rate, and its after-tax cost of capital is 15 percent.

The sales manager felt so strongly about the need for additional capacity that he attempted to prepare an economic justification for the equipment although this was not one of his responsibilities. His analysis, presented below, disappointed him because it did not justify acquiring the equipment.

Required Investment

Purchase price of new equipment		\$300,000
Disposal of existing equipment:		
Loss on disposal	\$60,000	
Less tax benefit (40%)	24,000	36,000
Cost of market research study		44,000
Total investment		\$380,000

Annual Returns

Contribution margin from product:	
Using the new equipment [18,000 × (\$20 − \$7)]	\$234,000
Using the existing equipment [11,000 × (\$20 − \$9)]	121,000
Increase in contribution margin	113,000
Less average depreciation	60,000
Increase in before-tax income	53,000
Income tax (40%)	21,200
Increase in income	31,800
Less 15% cost of capital on the additional investment required (.15 × \$380,000)	57,000
Net annual return of proposed investment in new equipment	\$ (25,200)

Required:

a. The controller of Wisconsin Products Company plans to prepare a discounted cash flow analysis for this investment proposal. The controller has asked you to prepare corrected calcuations of

1. The required investment in the new equipment
2. The recurring annual cash flows

Explain the treatment of each item of your corrected calculations that is treated differently from the original analysis prepared by the sales manager.

b. Calculate the net present value of the proposed investment in the new equipment.

P. 13-14 (CMA) Evaluation of acquiring or constructing new equipment. Edwards Corporation is a manufacturing concern that produces and sells a wide range of products. The company not only mass produces a number of products and equipment components but also is capable of producing special-purpose manufacturing equipment to customer specifications.

The firm is considering adding a new stapler to one of its product lines. More equipment will be required to produce the new stapler. There are three alternative ways to acquire the needed equipment: (1) purchase general-purpose equipment, (2) lease general-purpose equipment, (3) build special-purpose equipment. A fourth alternative, purchase of the special-purpose equipment, has been ruled out because it would be prohibitively expensive.

The general-purpose equipment can be purchased for $125,000. The equipment has an estimated salvage of $15,000 at the end of its useful life of 10 years. At the end of 5 years the equipment can be used elsewhere in the plant or be sold for $40,000.

Alternatively, the general-purpose equipment can be acquired by a 5-year lease for $40,000 annual rent. The lessor will assume all responsibility for taxes, insurance, and maintenance.

Special-purpose equipment can be constructed by the Contract Equipment Department of the Edwards Corporation. While the department is operating at a level that is normal for the time of year, it is below full capacity. The department could produce the equipment without interfering with its regular revenue-producing activities.

The estimated departmental costs for the construction of the special-purpose equipment are

Materials and parts	$ 75,000
Direct labor	60,000
Variable overhead (50% of DLC)	30,000
Fixed overhead (25% of DLC)	15,000
Total	$180,000

Corporation general and administrative costs average 20 percent of direct labor cost.

Engineering and management studies provide the following revenue and cost estimates (excluding lease payments and depreciation) for producing the new stapler depending upon the equipment used:

	General-Purpose Equipment		Self-Constructed Equipment
	Leased	Purchased	
Unit selling price	$5.00	$5.00	$5.00
Unit production costs:			
Materials	1.80	1.80	1.70
Conversion costs	1.65	1.65	1.40
Total unit production costs	3.45	3.45	3.10
Unit contribution margin	1.55	1.55	1.90
Estimated unit volume	40,000	40,000	40,000
Estimated total contribution margin	$62,000	$62,000	$76,000
Other costs:			
Supervision	$16,000	$16,000	$18,000
Taxes and insurance	—	3,000	5,000
Maintenance	—	3,000	2,000
Total	$16,000	$22,000	$25,000

This type of equipment is subject to ACRS 5-year depreciation. At the end of 5 years the special purpose machine can be sold for $30,000.

The company uses an after-tax cost of capital of 10 percent. Its marginal tax rate is 40 percent.

Required:

a. Calculate the net present value for each of the three alternatives that Edwards Corporation has at its disposal.

b. Should Edwards Corporation select any of the three options, and if so, which one? Explain your answer.

CASE

Case 13-1 New-product capital investment decision

Headly Power Products is planning to create a new Heat Pump Division to manufacture and market a quality, energy-efficient heat pump. Headly is a respected name in the production of power tools and equipment, but heat pump production would be an entirely new line. Management believes a major promotional effort would be required to get good market penetration. Estimated promotional costs for the first 15 years of the product are as follows:

Year	Promotional Expense
1–3	$800,000
4–5	400,000
6–15	200,000

The product would have unit variable manufacturing costs of $1,200 and variable selling and administrative costs of $300 per unit. The selling price would be $2,500 each. Additional plant and office facilities would be required at a cost of $12,000,000. Other divisional fixed expenses, **not** including depreciation, would be $700,000 a year. The firm's income tax rate averages 40 percent, and 25 percent is the minimum acceptable rate of return on new product investments because of their risk. Accelerated cost recovery system depreciation for 18-year real estate must be used for tax purposes. At the end of 15 years the plant and office facilities can be sold for book value.

Management expects to sell the product for 15 years. Expected annual sales are as follows:

Year	Sales per Year (Units)
1	3,000
2	5,000
3–5	6,000
6–15	4,000

Required:

a. Prepare a report for the management of Headly Power Products describing and documenting the course of action you suggest.

b. What would your recommendation be if the company's cost of capital is 15 percent? Show supporting computations.

c. Explain the reason for any change in your recommendation between parts *a* and *b*.

The Public Sector and Not-for-Profit Budgeting

14

The not-for-profit sector is a large and growing component of our economy. This sector affects businesses and individuals directly through taxes and spending decisions and also through government policies and regulations. Because of the significant impact on all of us, it is important that you understand the nature of the not-for-profit sector and how it affects business. When you have completed this chapter you should understand:

1 The size and importance of the public sector.

2 Similarities and differences between budgeting for profit-seeking firms and not-for-profit organizations.

3 The need for a public sector.

4 The objectives of public finance.

5 Fiscal policy and monetary policy and the relationship between the two.

6 The impact of government activities on the private sector.

7 The framework and terminology of the federal government's PPBS budgeting system.

The not-for-profit sector is sometimes called the public sector

Entities such as federal, state, and local governments, universities, foundations, hospitals, churches, and museums make up the **not-for-profit sector** of our economy. Not-for-profit organizations provide services for the general public or some designated group of society, with the primary intent of serving the public rather than generating a profit. The not-for-profit area is sometimes referred to as the **public sector,** but that term is not sufficiently broad because it includes only public institutions, such as governments, whereas not-for-profit entities include many private organizations as well.

Although our discussion focuses primarily on the public sector, much of it also applies to other not-for-profit entities.

The relative importance of not-for-profit organizations in the economy has changed dramatically in the last decade. From the formation of our country until 1940, this segment of the economy accounted for one-sixth or less of the nation's total economy. Since that time, however, the growth of not-for-profit economic activity has been staggering, both in its absolute dollar amount and in its relative share of the economy. By far the most dramatic increase has been in governmental activities, with the federal government leading the way. Today government and other not-for-profit activities account for nearly half of all economic activity in this country. With not-for-profit spending in excess of one trillion dollars ($1,000,000,000,000) a year, it is logical that we devote a portion of the book to this part of the economy.

Many of the concepts discussed in this book are applicable to not-for-profit entities. Virtually all of the cost measurement, relevant cost, budgeting, cost analysis, and other concepts presented in earlier chapters are relevant to all types of organizations in the management of their operations and the measurement of their performance, whether or not they are profit-seeking.

The significance of the public sector

The purpose of this chapter is to discuss some accounting and managerial issues that relate specifically to not-for-profit organizations. Special attention is given to the federal government budgeting process, because it accounts for such a large portion of the economy and because it affects the budgeting process of many states, cities, and other not-for-profit organizations.

Since virtually all not-for-profit organizations must prepare budgets, we start this chapter by presenting the characteristics and procedures of budgeting that are unique to the not-for-profit area. We illustrate important basic budgeting concepts, introduced in Chapter 7, as they relate specifically to not-for-profit activities. In addition, an overview is presented of the government financing and expenditure process, referred to as *public finance*.

There are two reasons for devoting a large portion of the chapter to public finance and governmental budgeting: First, the federal government is responsible for well over half of all not-for-profit expenditures; second, federal government financing and spending decisions have a significant impact on business decisions and activities in the **private sector.** Therefore, this chapter should help you to understand how budgeting in the not-for-profit sector affects planning and decision making in the private sector.

The first part of the chapter deals with budgeting for not-for-profit organizations. Similarities and differences between not-for-profit and private sector budgeting are examined, and program budgeting is illustrated. Next, we present an overview of the way public finance affects public and private entities. Finally, after discussing the influence of government policies on business, we examine the budgeting system used by the federal government and some state and local governments.

THE BUDGETING PROCESS

The fundamentals of budgeting are identical for profit and not-for-profit organizations. In both cases budgeting plays a vital role in planning, monitoring, and controlling the effective and efficient use of scarce resources.

Revenue Budgets

A key element of all budgets is budgeted revenue. It is the primary determinant of all the expenditures in the rest of the budget. In profit-oriented firms, revenue is a key determinant of profit, which is the primary goal of the firm. In most not-for-profit organizations, however, revenue is not the primary benefit. Instead, revenue is used to finance various activities that generate desired benefits. For example, a city police department's revenue is determined primarily by the amount of money appropriated for the police department by the city council. In addition, some federal and state money may be provided for special programs and activities. The revenue provided for the police department determines, to a large degree, the size of the police force and the quality of its services. The benefits are derived by the citizens in the form of police protection and through community education and service programs offered by the police department.

In addition to revenue appropriated by the city council in a budget, some entities obtain revenue from a variety of other sources. For example, Figure 14-1 shows the revenue budget for the current year and the coming fiscal year for Fairview City. For the 1986–87 fiscal year, the city expects revenue from a number of different sources including taxes, fees for services, government programs, and investments.

Revenue sources

The detail in the revenue budget allows the city to evaluate each revenue source separately. Some revenue sources are more susceptible to fluctuations or prediction errors than others. For example, water sales, sewage service fees, and property taxes are less likely to fluctuate significantly with economic conditions than city sales tax revenue. Similarly, the likelihood of receiving federal government grants may depend on political attitudes in the nation's capital and on other variables outside the control of city officials.

Like a business, the city must determine the probabilities that projected revenues may be different from actual revenues. Variances could have a serious effect on the operation of city services. City officials may, therefore, attempt to identify a range of possible revenue levels for each revenue classification and establish alternative spending plans for the various levels of revenue. The alternative budgets should identify which programs would be curtailed or eliminated in the event of revenue shortages and which programs would be expanded or added with revenue surpluses.

Fairview City
Budgeted Revenue
For the Fiscal Year 1986–87

	Current Budget 1985–86	Approved Budget 1986–87
Taxes:		
Property tax	$3,600,000	$4,300,000
City sales tax	740,000	790,000
Total taxes	4,340,000	5,090,000
Fees and assessments:		
License fees	26,000	29,000
Recreational fees	43,000	46,000
Water sales	1,267,000	1,592,000
Sewage service	1,811,000	2,165,000
Refuse collection	548,000	599,000
Miscellaneous	45,000	49,000
Total fees and assessments	3,740,000	4,480,000
Other revenues:		
Federal government grants and appropriations	450,000	220,000
Investment income	36,000	30,000
Sale of city property	144,000	—
Total other revenue	630,000	250,000
Total revenue	$8,710,000	$9,820,000

Figure 14-1 **This is the revenue budget for a relatively small city with a variety of income sources. By preparing a detailed revenue budget, city managers can monitor actual revenue receipts and compare them with budgeted amounts. If differences occur between budgeted and actual revenue, city management may be able to adjust spending or change revenue collections.**

Expenditure Budgets

Expenditure budgets state how the organization plans to spend its resources during the budget period. As with private industry, the format of the budget and nature of the expenditures are dictated somewhat by the type of organization. The Fairview City budget is separated into 12 functional activities. The summary budget for these activities is presented in Figure 14-2, which shows the current budget year as well as the budget for the next fiscal year.

Detailed expenditure budgets are needed for monitoring and managing operations

The summary expenditure budget provides an overview of the resources allocated to each major activity of the city. However, this budget is of little use in planning and controlling daily operations of any one of the activities, such as the city transit system or the city school system. Instead, detailed operating budgets are required for each activity. Figure 14-3 illustrates the operating budget for the fire department. The total for the current year of $874,000 is the same amount that appears in the summary expenditure budget for the department.

Fairview City
Summary Expenditure Budget
For the Fiscal Year 1986–87

	Current Budget 1985–86	Approved Budget 1986–87
City council	$ 120,000	$ 125,000
City office facilities	460,000	490,000
City transit system	433,000	400,000
Court system	360,000	430,000
Fire department	874,000	982,000
Parks and recreation department	327,000	394,000
Police department	1,288,000	1,392,000
Refuse collection department	736,000	887,000
School system	2,745,000	2,990,000
Sewage and treatment plant	563,000	795,000
Streets department	480,000	510,000
Water department	324,000	425,000
Total expenditures	$8,710,000	$9,820,000

Figure 14-2 **The expenditure budget states how the organization plans to spend its resources. It can be prepared at whatever level of detail management deems necessary and cost-effective.**

Fairview City
Fire Department Budget
For the Fiscal Year 1986–87

	Current Budget 1985–86	Approved Budget 1986–87
Clerical wages	$ 35,000	$ 38,000
Education and training	56,000	52,000
Equipment operating expenses	28,000	32,000
Equipment purchases	120,000	175,000
Firemen's salaries	320,000	355,000
Gasoline	12,000	14,000
Insurance	15,000	15,000
Maintenance, buildings	13,000	18,000
Maintenance, equipment	86,000	67,000
Miscellaneous	22,000	25,000
Payroll taxes and fringe benefits	64,000	77,000
Supervisory salaries	62,000	66,000
Supplies	14,000	15,000
Uniform allowances	6,000	7,000
Uniform cleaning	3,000	4,000
Utilities	18,000	22,000
Total expenditures	$874,000	$982,000

Figure 14-3 **To manage the financial matters of the fire department, it is necessary to have more detail than the single number in the summary expenditure budget in Figure 14-2.**

Budgets provide an excellent framework for monitoring and controlling costs of government operations. All too often, however, they are viewed merely as devices for securing resources. Once the budget is approved, there may be a tendency to ignore it and simply use the resources provided by it without any effort to measure the cost-benefit relationships of the activities. In such cases, the benefits of control from the budgeting process are lost. The control aspects are important, however, because resources are scarce and only a limited amount may be available for specific purposes.

Budget Performance Reports

Once approved, the budget becomes an operating plan that must be followed by the governmental unit. For example, if a city council approves $4,200,000 for the parks and recreation department, city management cannot simply decide to use part of the funds for road maintenance. If planning is a worthwhile activity, then comparing actual results with the budget to see whether the plans were carried out is also worthwhile. Such comparisons are made in performance reports prepared by accountants to show how the planned activity was accomplished and how the accomplishment compared with the original plan. Figure 14-4 presents a performance report for the fire department for the 1985–86 fiscal year.

Fairview City
Fire Department Performance Report
For the Fiscal Year 1985–86

	Budget 1985–86	Actual 1985–86	Unfavorable (Favorable) Variance
Clerical wages	$ 35,000	$ 32,500	$ (2,500)
Education and training	56,000	47,000	(9,000)
Equipment operating expenses	28,000	29,700	1,700
Equipment purchases	120,000	144,000	24,000
Firemen's salaries	320,000	316,000	(4,000)
Gasoline	12,000	11,000	(1,000)
Insurance	15,000	14,500	(500)
Maintenance, buildings	13,000	19,200	6,200
Maintenance, equipment	86,000	94,800	8,800
Miscellaneous	22,000	27,300	5,300
Payroll taxes and fringe benefits	64,000	62,700	(1,300)
Supervisory salaries	62,000	67,000	5,000
Supplies	14,000	16,000	2,000
Uniform allowances	6,000	5,400	(600)
Uniform cleaning	3,000	3,200	200
Utilities	18,000	22,600	4,600
Totals	$874,000	$912,900	$ 38,900

Figure 14-4
A budget performance report can be as useful in the not-for-profit sector as it is for the profit-seeking firm. This example is a fixed budget performance report.

PROGRAM BUDGETING

Line budget defined

The master budget of a business, illustrated in Chapter 7, is developed along functional lines. Business functions such as marketing, manufacturing, and administration are major entities in the master budget. This form of budget is called a **line budget** or **functional budget.** Line budgeting is popular because it closely parallels the lines of responsibility in the organization chart, and it facilitates the performance measurement of managers. The budget for each part of the organization provides a convenient framework for developing performance reports.

The Nature of Program Budgets

For not-for-profit organizations, line budgeting is not always a useful framework for monitoring costs and measuring cost-benefit relationships. A form of budgeting that often provides better information is **program budgeting,** with budgets prepared for programs or outputs of the organization.

Program budgeting identifies costs with outputs or objectives of the organization

The distinguishing characteristic of program budgeting is that the focal point in budget preparation and cost control is the program or goal rather than a functional or organizational unit. For example, a school system may prepare budgets for individual school programs, such as primary education, secondary education, student enrichment programs, adult education, and athletic programs. The amount of detail in the program budget depends on management's needs. For instance, the budget for adult education programs may be divided into vocational training programs, cultural enrichment programs, and community safety programs. Later you will see that program budgeting may be instrumental in identifying changes in an organization's structure that would facilitate the achievement of goals. To contrast line and program budgeting, refer to Figure 14-5.

Figure 14-5 shows the current and proposed budgets for the Fairview City police department. The budget at the top is a line budget for the department, and the budget at the bottom is a program budget for the same department. The line budget identifies 17 functional activities of the police department. The program budget is divided into six programs. Costs are identified with programs rather than with functions. As with line budgeting, some costs may not be clearly identifiable with a single program in the budget. Such common costs are allocated to the appropriate programs in a logical manner using cost allocation concepts discussed in Chapters 4, 10, and 11.

In business organizations, most activities are intended to contribute to the firm's profit objective, and the benefits from these activities are measured in the income statement. In not-for-profit organizations, there is typically no common measure of program success. For example, a city government uses a variety of programs to achieve many diverse goals, such as education, fire and police protection, city sanitation, and recreation. Success of the various programs cannot be measured in dollars. Instead, the number of high school diplomas, reduced crime rates, enrollments in

Fairview City Police Department
Line Budget
For the Fiscal Year Ending June 30

	Current Budget 1985–86	Proposed Budget 1986–87
Administrative salaries	$ 123,000	$ 132,000
Building maintenance salaries	26,000	28,000
Building maintenance supplies	15,000	16,000
Clerical salaries	36,000	38,000
Crime lab supplies	18,000	22,000
Employee education programs	32,000	28,000
Insurance	25,000	30,000
Miscellaneous expenses	16,000	24,000
Office supplies	21,000	23,000
Payroll taxes and employee benefits	92,000	104,000
Police car and equipment maintenance	82,000	98,000
Police car operation	126,000	183,000
Police car purchases	94,000	66,000
Police officers' salaries	520,000	534,000
Transportation	25,000	22,000
Uniform allowances and cleaning	11,000	13,000
Utilities	26,000	31,000
Total expenditures	$1,288,000	$1,392,000

Fairview City Police Department
Program Budget
For the Fiscal Year Ending June 30

	Current Budget 1985–86	Proposed Budget 1986–87
Community crime prevention programs	$ 89,000	$ 102,000
Drug abuse education program	95,000	115,000
School safety program	48,000	55,000
Criminal investigation	382,000	410,000
Criminal proceedings	110,000	120,000
Community patrol program	564,000	590,000
Totals	$1,288,000	$1,392,000

Figure 14-5 **A line budget is most commonly used. The cost categories follow the lines of responsibility in the organization chart. A program budget identifies costs by outputs or goals and is very useful in comparing costs and benefits during project evaluations.**

recreational programs, or attendance at symphony concerts are measures of success. If resources are to be allocated among various programs in ways that maximize total benefits to the citizens of the city, there must be a method of comparing program benefits with program costs. Since benefits are measured for programs rather than for organizational lines, it stands to reason that costs should be identified with programs also, so that direct analyses can be made.

Advantages of Program Budgeting

Why use program budgeting?

The primary advantage of using program budgeting is that it facilitates cost-benefit analysis for programs in which benefits are measured in something other than dollars. If benefits are measured for projects, then the costs should be identified for each project as well, so that logical resource allocations can be made. For example, the benefit of a late-night police patrol through residential areas is a 20 percent reduction in burglaries, and the cost of the patrols is \$200,000 annually. Other benefits and costs are identified specifically for this program. If a program budgeting system were not used, the cost of the late-night patrols would be buried in a line budget among personnel costs, gasoline costs, patrol car operating costs, and others.

When costs are expressed in dollars and the benefits are described in other terms, such as decreased crime, the measures are not directly comparable. However, additional analysis might yield statistics that make comparisons possible. For example, 20 percent fewer burglaries means 90 fewer burglaries for the city. City crime statistics show that the average loss from a burglary is \$2,600. Therefore, the estimated reduction in burglary losses from the program is \$234,000 (90 × \$2,600). Of course, there are other benefits as well, such as a feeling of security among citizens, a better image for the city, and pride in the police department.

Sometimes managers of not-for-profit organizations think that quantification of program benefits is of little use. General arguments praising the value of quality education, safer streets, or better recreational facilities have merit, but perhaps are not enough to secure project funding when compared with specific quantified benefits of competing projects. In a world of scarce resources, not-for-profit entities must evaluate program costs and benefits just as businesses do, so that intelligent resource allocation decisions can be made.

Line-Program Budget

A combination line-program budget provides cost information by function and also by program. An example of this type of budget presentation is shown in Figure 14-6 using the data from the Fairview City police department budget in Figure 14-5.

Combining line and program budgeting gives the best of both worlds

The program budget is presented in the columns and the line budget appears in the rows. The data presented in the combined line-program budget offer greater detail than either the line budget or the program budget separately. Notice that only the 1985–86 fiscal year is presented in Figure 14-6. Another report is required to present the proposed budget for the 1986–87 fiscal year in a similar format. The combined budget provides

Fairview Police Department
Line-Program Budget
For the Fiscal Year 1985–86

	Crime Prevention	Drug Education	School Safety	Criminal Investigation	Criminal Proceedings	Community Patrol	Totals
Administrative salaries	$ 8,000	$ 9,000	$ 3,000	$ 47,000	$ 8,000	$ 48,000	$ 123,000
Building maintenance salaries	2,000	1,500	1,500	11,000	3,000	7,000	26,000
Building maintenance supplies	2,500	1,000	1,000	5,500	2,000	3,000	15,000
Clerical salaries	4,000	1,000	2,000	16,000	7,000	6,000	36,000
Crime lab supplies	500	500	—	12,000	1,000	4,000	18,000
Employee education programs	2,000	3,000	1,500	15,500	3,000	7,000	32,000
Insurance	1,000	1,000	1,000	6,000	2,000	14,000	25,000
Miscellaneous expenses	500	500	500	4,000	3,000	7,500	16,000
Office supplies	500	500	500	6,000	5,000	8,500	21,000
Payroll taxes and employee benefits	7,500	8,500	3,500	27,000	9,500	36,000	92,000
Police car and equipment maintenance	3,000	2,000	2,000	17,000	5,000	53,000	82,000
Police car operation	4,500	3,500	3,000	16,000	6,500	92,500	126,000
Police car purchases	7,000	7,000	7,000	14,000	7,000	52,000	94,000
Police officers' salaries	42,000	52,000	17,000	161,000	38,000	210,000	520,000
Transportation	1,000	2,000	2,500	9,000	6,000	4,500	25,000
Uniform allowances and cleaning	1,000	1,000	1,000	2,500	1,500	4,000	11,000
Utilities	2,000	1,000	1,000	12,500	2,500	7,000	26,000
Totals	$89,000	$95,000	$48,000	$382,000	$110,000	$564,000	$1,288,000

Figure 14-6 **A combined line-program budget provides budget information using both approaches. This type of budget provides managers with detailed cost information that may be useful in planning and controlling costs.**

cost information on programs and on functions and shows the amount of cost planned for each function of each program.

PUBLIC FINANCE

Public finance defined

Public finance is the entire area of government economic activity, including resource allocations, income distribution, and the financing of government operations. In total, public finance activities affect both the public and private sectors. In this section we present the fundamentals of governmental budgeting, and discuss the nature of public finance activities and their impact on private sector business.

A budget is a comprehensive quantitative plan for utilizing the resources of an entity for some period of time. Budgeting is used to allocate scarce resources in a way that optimizes the achievement of organizational goals. To a large degree, federal, state, and local government taxing and expenditure decisions determine resource allocations and income distribution. For example, an increase in Social Security taxes takes money out of the hands of taxpayers, and an increase in Social Security benefits puts money into the hands of recipients. Similarly, increases in tax deductions caused by liberalized depreciation guidelines for new business assets are designed to encourage business investment and increase job opportunities for workers. Most people and businesses are affected by taxing and spending decisions, and members of Congress are aware of the impact their decisions have on individuals, businesses, and the entire economy.

Taxation by Governments

Taxation is a carefully guarded power of governments

The ability to tax is an important power of government. To a large degree, taxing powers determine the influence government has over the economy. The founding fathers of the United States were very cautious in granting taxing powers to the federal government, and the Constitution specifically describes the types of taxes that can and cannot be levied. It was not until 1913 that the Sixteenth Amendment was passed, allowing direct taxation of income without apportionment of the tax among the states according to population. In 1917 the first personal income tax law was passed. Even then, the federal income tax only affected relatively few citizens. It was not until World War II that the income tax became broadly based among the population. From the start of the war to the end, the number of income taxpayers increased from 8 million to 60 million.

The federal income tax and the FICA (Social Security) tax are the two largest sources of federal revenue. For many years, the income tax was by far the biggest tax source, but FICA taxes have grown dramatically in recent years. Now FICA taxes rival the personal income tax as a source of government revenue, and many employees and employers find the FICA tax their biggest tax burden. Other federal taxes include excise taxes, inheritance taxes, and import taxes. State and local governments also levy taxes such as income taxes, sales taxes, property taxes, payroll taxes, inheritance taxes, and gasoline taxes. In total, the public sector raises over $1 trillion per year through taxation and other assessments.

The Need for a Public Sector

The public sector performs services that cannot be done privately

A logical question might be, Why does the public sector exist and what does it do with the vast wealth of resources it collects? The public sector exists to fill the voids not serviced by the private sector and to ensure that the private sector operates in a way that is acceptable to society. Many government services, such as parks, highways, police protection, national defense, and national archives, are not available from the private sector. The market mechanism does not provide for regulatory agencies, such as the Securities and Exchange Commission, the Federal Energy Regulatory Commission, or the Federal Trade Commission.

Federal government rules and regulations affect virtually every facet of business life, including external accounting requirements, health and safety standards, transportation costs, energy costs, employee taxes, and countless other items. Government activities, rules, and regulations often have an impact on business decisions about investments, number and types of employees to hire, types of products to produce, plant locations, and transportation systems used. Currently the public sector commands a tremendous amount of resources, and directly and indirectly influences private sector business in many ways. The government's significant role in the economy will continue in the future; therefore, it is important to understand the processes of government budgeting and resource allocation.

Public Finance Objectives

The basic policy objectives of public finance are:

Basic objectives of public finance

1. Allocation
2. Distribution
3. Stabilization

Allocation. The first policy objective deals with providing socially desirable goods and services not made available through the private sector. **Allocation** policy determines what goods and services should be provided and in what quantity. In the public sector, resource allocations are made primarily through the process of voting. Citizens vote for people to represent them in government, and the representatives in turn vote on projects and proposals in Congress, in state legislatures, and in city councils. Allocation decisions in the aggregate have a tremendous impact on our economy and on society. In the private sector the "voting" is done with dollars. Consumers tell suppliers how to allocate resources by spending on the various products and services supplied by the private sector. Typically, consumers are able to adjust their voting patterns more quickly in the private sector than in the public sector, but the process is quite similar.

What goods and services are provided by the public sector?

Distribution. The second policy objective addresses the issue of who should receive the economic benefits of society. **Distribution** is the process of collecting taxes and using the money to provide government benefits to citizens. The private sector strongly influences income distribution by providing jobs and by distributing profits to owners. However, the impact of government distribution policies is significant. Graduated income taxes take a larger portion of a wage earner's income as wages increase. FICA taxes are paid to the government by wage earners and distributed to recipients who are not employed or who earn a small amount. Many tax programs are designed to tax people earning higher incomes on the assumption that such people are better able to bear the tax burden. Many

Who receives the benefits of government?

expenditures are designed primarily to help lower-income people because they are most in need of the services. Frequently, distribution policy decisions are based on establishing a lower limit on poverty or an upper limit on wealth.

Government tries to maintain a stable economy

Stabilization. The objective of stabilization policy is to see that the economy runs smoothly. **Stabilization** is the use of economic theory to smooth out excessive fluctuations in economic activities. Economic theory implies that a stable economy characterized by an acceptable level of growth without widely fluctuating economic conditions is most conducive to high employment, stable prices, and reasonable income levels. To minimize fluctuations and wide swings known as depression, inflation, recession, and booms, the government has two basic instruments that may be used to stabilize the economy. They are fiscal policy and monetary policy.

Fiscal Policy

Congress controls fiscal policy—taxing and spending

Fiscal policy pertains to the taxing and spending actions of government. Although taxing and spending together constitute fiscal policy, Congress seldom specifically ties the two functions together. However, both taxing and spending affect the economy. For instance, during periods of high inflation, Congress may raise taxes to reduce the quantity of money available for the purchase of goods and services. Another possibility is to reduce government spending, thereby keeping money out of the economy.

Fiscal actions may have a dramatic impact on businesses. For instance, a manager may postpone an investment because a special tax break on investments is expected shortly, or a company may buy more automated production equipment to avoid higher payroll taxes and a higher minimum wage. Fiscal decisions can create significant changes in economic conditions, particularly for certain segments of the economy. For example, government energy policies and tax breaks brought boom times to insulating firms during the energy shortages in the late 1970s.

Fiscal policy of the federal government is a powerful economic tool with a strong impact on the economy. It is also difficult to implement quickly because it takes time for Congress to enact new tax legislation or new spending programs. When fast action is needed to stabilize the economy, or to counteract the poor timing of fiscal policy, the government has monetary policy at its disposal.

Monetary Policy

The Federal Reserve Board controls monetary policy

Monetary policy deals with the quantity and the cost of money in the economy. Monetary policy is therefore in the hands of a government central bank called the **Federal Reserve System.** The Federal Reserve System is governed by the **Federal Reserve Board,** a body of appointed officials who are largely independent of government control or influence.

The Federal Reserve Board, often referred to as the **Fed,** may change the money supply in the economy by buying and selling government securities in the market, by raising or lowering the interest rates it charges banks for loans, or by raising or lowering bank reserve requirements. Reserve requirements dictate the amount of funds each member bank must keep on reserve with the Fed. When the requirements are high, the amount of money available to banks is not as great as when reserve requirements are low. The Fed can act very quickly to change the quantity of money and interest rates and thus can use monetary policy to fine-tune the economy as necessary to keep it relatively stable.

When the Federal Reserve Board raises the bank interest rate, its actions almost always mean higher interest rates to businesses and consumers. The result is that the cost of borrowing becomes too high for some people and businesses, and purchases are postponed or eliminated. When interest rates and reserve requirements are high, money becomes hard to borrow, resulting in what is sometimes called a "credit crunch." At such times businesses in the housing, automobile, and major appliance industries may experience sharp declines in sales because their products are usually sold on credit.

THE EFFECT OF GOVERNMENT INFLUENCE

Government taxing and expenditure activities affect our lives in many ways. We may not be fully aware of the effect of some taxes because most taxes are not paid the way a utility bill or store charge account is paid. Instead, many taxes are somewhat hidden. Gasoline taxes are included in the price of the fuel; sales tax is part of the total cost of the purchase; income taxes and FICA taxes are withheld from paychecks; excise taxes are buried in the purchase price of certain products; and property taxes may be part of house payments. Taxpayers should not lose sight of the taxes they pay to government units. Taxes pay for government services and, as with other outlays for purchases, there should be justification for the resources spent. Such justification is provided in the form of budgets, which elected officials must approve before tax money can be spent.

The federal government affects our lives in many ways

Some tax laws have a direct measurable effect on citizens. For instance, a $50 per person tax credit has a direct effect on the tax burden of each taxpayer, whereas a tax credit on a new home has no effect on a taxpayer who is not in the market for a new home.

Expenditure legislation, such as Social Security payments and welfare payments, are direct benefits to individuals; but many other expenditures have a more indirect effect on the population. It is easy to see that a monthly Social Security check of $480 provides an annual income of $5,760 to the recipient. It is harder to determine the specific value to individuals of a new missile, the space shuttle, highway construction, or the creation of a new national park in Alaska. But government officials must evaluate the benefits of such programs and compare them with the costs of the programs to make intelligent spending decisions.

Effects on Businesses

Government policies affect businesses as well as individuals. Businesses are subject to many types of taxes in addition to income taxes. In order to continue earning profits, businesses must view taxes and other government assessments as part of the cost of doing business and must pass on these costs to customers in the form of prices. Pricing decisions are therefore influenced by government actions.

Businesses react quickly to changes in government policy

Fiscal and monetary policies can be used effectively by governments through their influence on businesses. As interest rates are increased by the Fed, businesses curtail borrowing or expansion. When the government wants to stimulate the economy, it may induce expansion by providing tax benefits to businesses, such as the investment credit and rapid depreciation of fixed assets. Businesses react to such policies by shifting resources in directions that will minimize their tax burden or place them in a better competitive position.

In addition to influencing business by means of tax legislation, governments also affect business by demanding many types of reports, the cost of which must also be reflected in the price of products.

Government Demand for Information from Business

In the past 10 years there has been a significant increase in the amount and types of information that businesses must provide to government. Some of this information is summarized and used to report general business conditions. Other information is used to monitor adherence to government rules and regulations. Some is used for research by government staffs or private individuals.

Government information needs require businesses to collect many types of data

The impact on businesses of government requirements for business data is both indirect and direct. The indirect impact occurs when the analysis of business data results in new government rules and regulations that affect the operations of businesses. The direct impact occurs from specific reporting requirements that cause a business to modify the way it gathers and reports information.

In most cases government information requirements are for financial data. Sometimes firms must modify their financial information system to satisfy government reporting requirements. Some common effects on a company's information system are a more detailed data base, different data base structure, or different reporting characteristics than the business would have for its own use.

More detailed data base. Numerous government reporting requirements have caused some businesses to develop a more detailed cost data base than they previously had. For example, during the period of the Economic

Stabilization Policy of the mid-1970s, some companies were unable to get price increase approval from the Price Commission solely because the cost data provided by the companies were not detailed enough to prove that the price increase was cost justified. As a result, many companies started to accumulate more detailed cost data primarily to satisfy future information requirements the government might make.

The Cost Accounting Standards Board developed very specific requirements for reporting costs of government contracts. Some firms found that they had to modify their cost accounting data base and develop a detailed cost data base for nonmanufacturing activities to comply with the CASB reporting requirements. Similar examples can be cited for other government organizations which require detailed reporting, such as the Federal Trade Commission and the Internal Revenue Service.

Different data base structure. The accounting data base consists of the basic data from which internal and external reports are developed. The structure of the data base—that is, the way data are organized and stored—is determined by such factors as efficiency of updating the data base, efficiency of retrieving needed data, and reporting requirements. Whenever government requires information that is significantly different from the information normally generated by the business, there is a possibility that the company will have to modify its data base structure to satisfy the new reporting requirement. For example, the Federal Trade Commission requires some large businesses to report revenues and expenses for various categories of business, such as domestic and foreign, or by type of product. These lines of business reports may be different from those used by some businesses for their own reporting purposes.

Another example of government reporting requirements that necessitates changes in the data base structure of some companies is the need to be able to locate products or customers geographically. Including information about geographic location adds a complex dimension to the structure of the data base. For example, some hospitals and other health care institutions are required to report health care costs and patient treatment data for illness categories by geographic location of the patient. Product warranty requirements may necessitate keeping location data for products or customers. There is a possibility that the government will greatly expand its demand for geographic data. Congress has considered comprehensive legislation that requires an extensive land-use planning data base for each state. The logical extension of such legislation is to add business data on customers, sales, employment, pollution, and so on, to the data base.

Different reporting characteristics. The frequency, detail, and format of internal reports are dictated by the information needs of managers, which may change with new government requirements. For example, if very detailed product cost information is needed to justify price increases, a firm may change its cost accounting system and internal cost reporting system to provide managers with necessary cost details on a timely basis. Another example is a need to report salary data by race and sex to ensure compliance with affirmative action programs, although such data are not necessary for costing purposes.

FEDERAL GOVERNMENT BUDGETING

All federal resource allocation (spending) decisions are made by the Congress of the United States. It is often said that Congress controls the purse strings of the nation, but much of the information for congressional decisions is provided by the federal government budgeting process. The federal government budgeting system also strongly influences the budgeting processes and procedures of many state and local governments.

Although government expenditures are financed basically by taxes, taxing and expenditure decisions typically are not specifically tied together. Usually the taxing and expenditure decisions only merge when total revenues (taxes) and total expenditures are compared to determine whether the budget balances or provides an acceptable deficit. Frequently the federal government operates at a deficit, which means spending programs exceed tax revenues. Deficits are covered by borrowing money, usually in the form of bonds or other government securities, most of which are sold to citizens and companies within the United States. Seldom does Congress specifically address the financing of projects, except in the very broadest sense of how the project will affect the budget deficit. One exception is the FICA program, which is specifically financed by FICA taxes. In general, however, Congress passes tax legislation and spending legislation separately without tying specific expenditures and tax laws together.

In 1965, President Johnson announced the introduction of a new budgeting system in the federal government called the **planning, programming, budgeting system (PPBS).** It is also identified as PPB. The purpose was to provide a systematic process for developing and analyzing budget proposals and for completing the final budget package. As the title implies, PPBS is based on program budgeting, but it encompasses more than just the concept of program budgeting. The PPBS includes systematic procedures for the accounting, programming, and evaluation processes. It has been suggested that PPBS has five distinguishing features:

Components of PPBS

1. Program accounting
2. Multiyear costing
3. Detailed description of activities
4. Zero-base budgeting
5. Benefit-cost analysis[1]

---

[1] Leonard Merewitz and Stephen H. Sosnick, *The Budget's New Clothes* (Chicago: Markam Publishing Company, 1973), pp. 2–108.

Program Accounting

A basic requisite of program budgeting is an ability to attach accounting data to specific programs to show the resources used or budgeted for each objective. The process of accumulating costs by programs is referred to as **program accounting.** A program accounting system must be capable of accumulating historical costs by program and of developing projected program costs. Under PPBS, four types of costs are required to be accumulated for programs: past costs, current year costs, budget year costs, and future costs. **Past costs** are program costs for the last fiscal year. **Current year costs** are program costs for the current fiscal year. **Budget year costs** are proposed program costs for the coming fiscal year, and **future costs** are anticipated expenditures for the program covering 4 or more years in the future.

Multiyear Costing

Multiyear costing is the process of identifying costs with a project for the life of the project rather than just for the next budget year. This is not a new budgeting concept. It has been used for many years by businesses to evaluate capital expenditure projects. The logic for multiyear costing in capital expenditure decisions is that most projects require large outlays benefiting many future periods. However, in conventional budgets, few items in the operating budget are evaluated in light of expected outlays beyond the current budget period. Without multiyear costing, some budget proposals may be accepted with only a small portion of the relevant cost data available for analysis.

Often, government programs have life spans covering many accounting periods. Consequently, it is logical to evaluate projects based on costs and benefits over their entire expected life rather than just for 1 year. Like all long-range estimates, multiyear costing of programs becomes more subjective the longer the estimate. Nevertheless, multiyear costing is often cited as one of the major contributions of PPBS because it gives a better picture of program alternatives. Occasionally a proposed program requires very small expenditures initially, followed by very substantial outlays in later years. For example, the growth in Social Security payments since the start of the program has been tremendous.

Detailed Description of Activities

The planning, programming, budgeting system is intended to provide uniform systematic data for evaluating ongoing programs and new programs alike by providing a detailed description of each activity. An important attribute of PPBS is the uniform application of systematic procedures throughout the federal government budgeting system. Each program requires six specific steps, resulting in information that helps to implement the program in accordance with the planning, programming, budgeting system.

First, objectives must be established for each program. **Objectives** are the basic goals or desired outcomes of the program. Next, each program must have **targets,** which are specific short-term expectations for the program. Then the program director must identify the **selections made,** which are the specific operating plans of the program. The selections made must be supported by a description of the **alternatives reviewed,** with a discussion of why the alternatives were rejected in favor of the selected plans. **Outputs** are the current benefits or results achieved by the program and should relate directly to the targets. Finally, the detailed description of activities must include a discussion of **effectiveness,** which is the measure of how well targets and objects were achieved. Figure 14-7 illustrates a hypothetical detailed description of activities for the Maritime Administration of the Department of Commerce.

Notice that all components of PPBS are included in the description of activities. Outputs are the measurable results of the programs. In this case 700 new skilled laborers were trained. In other programs outputs may be measured in higher reading levels of elementary students, improved grain

Maritime Administration
Maritime Readiness
Detailed Description of Activities

Objective:	Maintain a well-rounded maritime capability to provide military support during times of crisis and to provide a strong commerce base for international trade.
Target:	Provide 1,000 new shipbuilding jobs annually for American citizens.
Selection made:	Let $200,000,000 of new contracts to United States shipbuilders for Navy ships.
Alternatives:	Offer a 20 percent wage subsidy to firms training new employees. Develop a government training program to teach shipbuilding skills by repairing older Navy ships.
Output:	A total of 700 new employees received skilled labor classifications in the shipbuilding industry.
Effectiveness:	A total of 1,300 people started a company job training program in shipbuilding during the year. Of these, 600 dropped out, were terminated, or required more training before being classified as skilled labor.

Figure 14-7
This is a hypothetical detailed description of activities for the Maritime Administration.

prices, or many other variables. Effectiveness measures compare the output with input. In this example the inputs and outputs are people in a training program. In other cases they may be measured in dollars; for instance, a job training program may cost $2,458 per graduate.

Zero-Base Budgeting

All budget programs, even existing ones, are reviewed each year under zero-base budgeting

Implemented with PPBS in 1965, **zero-base budgeting** means that each project or program must start the budget evaluation process with no commitment of resources. Instead of the old budget as a base, a zero base is assumed, and every item in the budget must be justified on its own merit, not simply because it existed previously. Each project must be proved worthy of funding, or it is rejected regardless of whether it is a new proposal or a program of long standing.

Governments operate on budgets that must be approved prior to the beginning of each fiscal year. Before PPBS, the previous budget was a convenient starting point for a new budget because it consisted of revenues and expenditures that had already been approved once before. The new budget usually was a revision of the old budget, with most of the items increased to allow for a growing economy, rising population, or inflation. Such a budgeting process is generally known as **incremental budgeting** because the new budget consists of the old one with an increment. Budget increments based on the inflation rate, increases in appropriations, a fixed percentage, or any other across-the-board increment to the budget beg the question of a true budget evaluation process. As a result of incremental budgeting, there is a tendency for budgets to become ever larger, and it is difficult to eliminate unsuccessful or inefficient programs once they are included in a budget. Many government budgets are routinely prepared by using the previous budget as a base and modifying the figures to suit expectations.

With zero-base budgeting, it is conceivable, although unlikely, that major program classifications, such as national defense or the space program, could be terminated if they proved to be undesirable. Typically, such major programs are sufficiently important to continue receiving congressional support and funding without substantial modifications. Still, there is a natural appeal to the idea that programs of all sorts and durations should be evaluated annually. Obsolete or ineffective programs should be terminated and resources should be shifted to new, justifiable programs. Zero-base budgeting is an alternative to incremental budgeting.

Although it is conceptually attractive, zero-base budgeting is not always easy to apply in practice. Programs currently in operation are hard to eliminate or curtail. They may involve long-term commitments or fixed investments that cannot easily be shifted to other areas. For example, military weapons systems, once developed, have little market value if a new system is developed. Program participants with vested interests in the program can cite prestige, hardship, tradition, or countless other reasons for maintaining the program.

Benefit-Cost Analysis

Benefit-cost analysis integrates the four features of PPBS—program accounting, multiyear costing, detailed description of activities, and zero-base budgeting—into a decision framework. Here the term "decision framework" is used somewhat loosely because often no formal decision model is developed. However, all program proposals are evaluated in terms of benefits and costs. Proposals with the highest benefit-cost ratios are accepted first, and other programs are delayed or canceled. The difficult question is, How are benefit-cost ratios determined?

Although program costs are sometimes difficult to measure, program benefits are even harder to determine for many government projects. How does one compare the value of a program that helps a few people a great deal with a program that helps many people a little? How do the benefits of increased defense spending compare with a 10 million acre national park in Alaska? What is the benefit-cost ratio of a program that reduces unemployment by 50,000 people and costs the taxpayers $1,900,000,000?

Questions like these are not simple, but they must be answered if government is to achieve policy goals effectively. The entire budgeting system collapses if we arrive at the last step and cannot make sound resource allocation decisions based on solid benefit-cost analyses supported by relevant factual data.

The planning, programming, budgeting system emphasizes quantitative benefit-cost analysis. Quantitative measures of some sort are frequently available if intuition and persistence are applied. Quantitative analysis does not necessarily mean dollar-for-dollar benefit-cost comparisons. For example, many types of unemployment statistics may be evaluated in considering a full-employment program; and park visitation statistics, population densities, and changing recreational patterns may be cited in developing a case for new park facilities.

The Status of PPBS

Probably no other budgeting phenomenon swept the country, even the world, as PPBS did in the late 1960s and early 1970s. Government officials and others raved about it as the new system that would ensure effective and efficient government. In 1966, California adopted the system and renamed it programming and budgeting (PAB). Many state and local governments rushed to pattern their budgeting system after PPBS, or at least to use some of its features. The rush to PPBS has been referred to as the "PPB epidemic."[2]

Is PPBS accomplishing its goals?

Unfortunately, the planning, programming, budgeting system has not fulfilled all of the great expectations held for it. There have been some successes from time to time in various government agencies with parts of

---

[2] Ibid., p. 2.

PPBS, but in aggregate the system has not produced as much improvement in government budgeting as was expected. The most common reasons cited for the difficulties with PPBS are costs, government size, government organization, and difficult measurement problems.[3]

PPBS costs. Any accounting and budgeting system must be benefit-cost justifiable. The planning, programming, budgeting system, with its intricate detail, devotion to full disclosure of all alternatives, need for justification of currently operating programs, and requirement for quantitative measures in benefit-cost analysis, is very expensive and time-consuming. Some people feel that the idea is superior but the economic realities of operating the system are prohibitive.

Government size. The federal government is huge and growing larger every year. All private sector businesses, including General Motors and American Telephone and Telegraph, are dwarfed by the size of the federal government. The coordination of large businesses is very difficult; the coordination of all federal government activity is truly mind-boggling. The major purpose of PPBS was to help coordinate resource allocation decisions, but the sheer size of the federal government may preclude any chance of complete success. A comprehensive plan like PPBS for a small firm would require a lot of work; for the federal government PPBS is a massive undertaking.

Government organization. Some programs cut across several organizational units, and some government segments house many different programs, causing critics to argue that government is just not organized in a way that is conducive to program budgeting. Some believe a required feature of PPBS is reorganization along lines that facilitate the process of program accounting and budgeting, but major reorganization of the federal government is a very complex political issue.

Difficult measurement problems. Many of the measurements required in PPBS are very difficult to make. Particularly difficult are long-range cost and benefit estimates. So many different benefit measures are used for the myriad of government programs that it is perplexing to attempt to integrate the benefit-cost analysis of each program into a logical structure for comparing all alternative programs.

The Future of PPBS

Any criticism of PPBS must be tempered by the realization that planning, coordinating, and controlling any organization the size of the federal gov-

[3] Aaron Wildavsky, *The Politics of the Budgetary Process* (Boston: Little, Brown and Company, 1974), pp. 181–208.

ernment is tremendously difficult. Any general criticism can be countered with the question, What system would operate more effectively and efficiently than PPBS? For the near future, it appears that the current system will continue to be used, with only minor modifications from time to time to improve the system or to remedy perceived problems.

SUMMARY

Not-for-profit organizations are an important segment of the economy, with total expenditures exceeding $1 trillion. By far the largest element in the not-for-profit sector is government, particularly the federal government. Budgeting is vital to the effective and efficient utilization of resources in the **public sector.** Most budgeting concepts and procedures are the same regardless of the type of organization.

The **revenue budget** influences the number, size, and quality of programs in not-for-profit organizations, but revenue is not a goal in itself. It is merely the means for operating various programs that in turn provide the desired benefits. The **expenditures budget** is the organization's plan for using the resources at its disposal. Budgets should be prepared in sufficient detail to provide adequate control over the resources of not-for-profit organizations. Typically, control includes timely performance reporting.

Line budgets are prepared using functional lines or the organization structure as the budget framework. Typical categories in a line budget include accounting, maintenance, divisions, and departments. **Program budgets** identify costs and benefits for goals or programs, such as education, crime prevention, or recreation. The primary advantage of program budgeting is the ability to compare the cost of a program with its benefits. Some organizations use both line and program budgeting to take advantage of each system.

Public finance refers to the financing of government activities, resource allocations, and income distribution. Three basic policy objectives in public finance are allocation, distribution, and stabilization. **Allocation** is concerned with the quantity and types of goods and services to be provided. **Distribution** addresses the issue of who should receive the economic benefits of society and in what amount. Stabilization actions attempt to keep the economy running smoothly. Stabilization is accomplished by means of fiscal and monetary policies. **Fiscal policy** is implemented by taxing and spending decisions. **Monetary policy** is implemented by the Federal Reserve System, which controls interest rates and bank reserve requirements.

An important element of governmental decision making is its budgeting activity. The **planning, programming, budgeting system (PPBS)** is a program budgeting system with five distinguishing features: program accounting, multiyear costing, detailed description of activities, zero-base budgeting, and benefit-cost analysis. **Program accounting** is a system capable of accumulating costs by program or goal. **Multiyear costing** means identifying costs for the life of the project, not merely for the current budget period. **Detailed description of activities** is the careful delineation of the proposed program's goals, targets, selections, alternatives, output, and effectiveness measures. **Zero-base budgeting** requires all activities to be evaluated each year whether the activity is a newly proposed or an old program. **Benefit-cost analysis** requires all proposals to be evaluated in a quantitative systematic manner.

The planning, programming, budgeting system has had a dramatic impact but its initial expectations have not been fully realized. Some reasons for the lack of complete success are high cost; the size of the government, which is too large to utilize comprehensive budgeting effectively; the fact that the government is not organized along program lines; and the large number of projects whose benefits are difficult to measure and compare.

KEY TERMS

allocation *(574)*
benefit-cost analysis *(583)*
distribution *(574)*
Federal Reserve Board (Fed) *(575)*
Federal Reserve System *(575)*
fiscal policy *(575)*
functional budget *(569)*
incremental budgeting *(582)*
line budget *(569)*
line-program budget *(571)*
monetary policy *(575)*
multiyear costing *(580)*
not-for-profit sector *(563)*
planning, programming, budgeting system (PPBS) *(579)*
private sector *(564)*
program accounting *(580)*
program budget *(569)*
public finance *(572)*
public sector *(563)*
stabilization *(575)*
zero-base budgeting *(582)*

QUESTIONS

1. Distinguish between public sector organizations and private sector organizations. Give several examples of each.
2. "Look, Sam, we are a city government. We are not in business to make a profit. We do not want a lot of detailed data on revenue estimates; just give us your guess about how much total revenue we can expect next year." Comment on this statement.
3. Describe program budgeting and compare it with line budgeting.
4. "Performance reports are for profit-oriented firms; such reports are a waste of effort in public sector organizations." Do you agree? Explain.
5. Define the term *public finance*.
6. Give a brief description of the development of the federal income tax in this country.
7. What is the purpose of a public sector in a capitalistic society?
8. Briefly describe the three basic objectives of public finance.
9. Discuss the role of fiscal policy in stabilization. What characteristics does fiscal policy have?
10. What is monetary policy? How does it relate to fiscal policy and the stabilization objective?
11. What is PPBS? Briefly describe the steps in PPBS.

12. What is program accounting and what does it involve?
13. What is the purpose of a detailed description of activities and what information is included?
14. What is zero-base budgeting? What is its origin? What are its strengths and weaknesses?
15. Discuss the status of the PPB system.

EXERCISES

Ex. 14-1 Identifying line and program budget items. Plainfield school system uses both line and program budgeting in planning and managing its activities. Below is a list of cost categories used by the school system. Some of the items are from the program budget and some are from the line budget.

a. Depreciation, equipment
b. Administrative salaries
c. Textbooks
d. Utilities
e. School supplies
f. Athletic programs
g. Teacher salaries
h. Primary education
i. Secondary education
j. School bus costs
k. Student enrichment
l. Adult education
m. Heating
n. Driver training

Required: For each item listed, determine if it most likely came from the line budget or the program budget.

Ex. 14-2 Impact of government action on business. Polybord Corporation is a small manufacturing firm which produces printed circuit boards that it sells to about a dozen clients who make home computers, electronic games, and other electronic products. Competition is keen, with many small firms operating in the field, because entry into the business is relatively easy and requires little capital. The firm depends heavily on bank financing for its operations. It employs 150 production people.

Required: Describe what effect the following government actions might have on the operations of the firm:

a. The Federal Reserve Board increases bank reserve requirements.
b. New legislation requires all firms with more than 100 employees to report the amount of tax-free contributions that employees make into company-operated retirement systems. Up to now, only the employer's contribution to such systems had to be reported to the government.
c. New taxes are imposed on the importation of electronic components from foreign countries.

Ex. 14-3 Identifying program benefits. The fire chief and his employees are very eager to acquire a new, fast, efficient fire truck. The truck costs $260,000, and the city council has been reluctant to approve the request. In the past, arguments in favor of the truck have always been general statements about the need, and the council has requested more quantitative measures of benefit. The fire chief hires you as a consultant to help prepare the department's case.

Required: Discuss some possible measures of benefits. Be specific. Develop hypothetical data to illustrate your case.

Ex. 14-4 **Tax structure.** On the way home from work Frank heard an interview on the radio in which a researcher said the average citizen earning $25,000 a year pays nearly 40 percent of the earnings in taxes. Frank, who earns $24,000 a year, was shocked at that number and immediately went to his den to find copies of last year's tax return. After adding up his state and federal income tax payments, he found that these two amounted to 24 percent of his salary. Frank wondered how his tax burden could be so different from what the researcher stated.

Required: Discuss what might account for the difference Frank found. Use numbers to illustrate your point.

Ex. 14-5 **Incremental budgeting.** The intramural department of Nonsuch College has proposed the following changes in the current year's budget as the budget for the next academic year:

Item	Change	Current Budget
Administrative salaries	8% increase	$ 70,000
Student wages	4% increase	10,000
Supplies	15% increase	30,000
Equipment	10% decrease	20,000
Utilities	20% increase	12,000
Miscellaneous	10% increase	8,000
Total		$150,000

Required:

a. Prepare the intramural department's budget for the next academic year based on the proposal above.
b. Compute the total percentage difference between the current year's budget and next year's budget.

Ex. 14-6 **Relating government actions to public finance objectives.** Below are a number of actions and decisions from various branches of the federal government. Each of them is intended to satisfy one of three policy objectives—allocation, distribution, or stabilization.

a. Congress passes a bill to increase the amount of the investment credit on new machinery.
b. The Fed increases the interest rate it charges member banks for loans.
c. The National Parks Service announces the creation of a nationwide campfire program for all parks in the system.
d. Congress increases the FICA tax rate.
e. Congress passes a bill to create jobs for the hard-core unemployed.
f. A new sailing ship is purchased for the Naval Academy.
g. Congress increases medical benefits to the elderly.
h. The President signs a bill to build 50 new strategic bombers.
i. Congress passes a 5 percent income tax surtax to help curtail inflationary spending.
j. Reserve requirements for Federal Reserve member banks are lowered.
k. Congress raises Social Security benefits.
l. The Federal Reserve raises reserve requirements to tighten the money supply.

Required: Indicate whether the objective of each action is best classified as allocation, distribution, or stabilization.

Ex. 14-7 **Determining program benefits.** The head of the parks and recreation department of a city has proposed a free swimming lesson program for children between the ages of 3 and 14. The estimated cost of the program is $36,000, primarily composed of instructor salaries. The city council, already operating with a tight budget, is not very interested in adding a new service without any source of revenue.

Required: Develop a presentation to the city council to support the addition of the free swimming classes. Provide specific arguments where possible and develop hypothetical data to support your position.

Ex. 14-8 **Understanding budgeting data.** The director of personnel services for a large university has been preparing a budget for the next fiscal year. The university administration has provided department heads with a budget policy statement indicating that the maximum budget increase for any department will be 4 percent, and all increases will be carefully evaluated because of a shortage of funds. The director of personnel services, with the help of staff, has developed the following budget that, in the department head's opinion, satisfies the university's guidelines. The director is very pleased with the budget proposal, because it continues the policy of switching from typewriters to word processing equipment and allows for the hiring of qualified personnel to operate the new equipment. All of this can be accomplished with the new budget without violating the university's tight budget guidelines.

Personnel Services
Operating Budget

	Current Budget	Proposed Budget	Percentage Change
Supplies	$ 20,000	$ 20,400	2% increase
Maintenance	15,000	13,800	6% decrease
Utilities	18,000	18,720	4% increase
Equipment purchases	100,000	115,000	15% increase
Employee wages	180,000	201,600	12% increase
Miscellaneous	10,000	9,700	3% decrease
Average change in the budget*			4% increase

* Percentage change computed as follows:

$$\text{Average change} = \frac{2 - 6 + 4 + 15 + 12 - 3}{6 \text{ items}} = +4 \text{ percent}$$

Required: As the coordinator of departmental budgets, you are required to evaluate each budget to see that it satisfies university guidelines. Evaluate the personnel department budget and comment on its acceptability.

Ex. 14-9 **Program budgeting.** A line budget has always been used at Tidal Pool State Park. A recent directive from state headquarters informed all park managers to prepare a program budget for the next year. Below is the proposed line budget for the coming year along with information about the percentage of line item costs assignable to each program.

Tidal Pool State Park
Proposed Line Budget

Personnel salaries	$200,000
Housing costs	50,000
Utilities	25,000
Supplies	30,000
Vehicle costs	40,000
Clothing and other allowances	5,000
Total	$350,000

Percentage of Costs Assignable to Each Program

	Educational Programs	Park Protection	Repairs and Maintenance	Park Administration
Personnel salaries	30%	30%	20%	20%
Housing costs	20	30	20	30
Utilities	20	10	30	40
Supplies	40	10	30	20
Vehicle costs	15	50	30	5
Clothing and other allowances	20	30	20	30

Required: Prepare a program budget for the next budget year.

Ex. 14-10 Incremental budget. The Middleview Community Action Center is a not-for-profit community service program that provides a variety of services to the elderly and needy in the community. Included are free transportation to medical services, inexpensive meals, education programs, and other supportive programs. Below is the budget for the current year.

Middleview Community Action Center
Expenditure Budget
1986

Administrative salaries	$ 75,000
Building maintenance	6,000
Employee wages	82,000
Equipment purchases	5,000
Food costs	20,000
Supplies	6,000
Utilities	17,000
Vehicle maintenance	9,000
Vehicle operating costs	12,000
Total expenditures	$232,000

The management of the center expects vehicle operating costs to rise 15 percent in 1987. The average age of the vehicle will be 5 years in 1987, and some major repairs will be necessary. Management expects vehicle maintenance to increase 40 percent. The maintenance employee agreement calls for an 8.5 percent wage increase in 1987, and administrative employees will receive a 9 percent raise. Food costs are expected to increase 12 percent, utility costs 15 percent, and all other costs 8 percent.

Required:

a. Prepare the 1987 expenditure budget for the Middleview Community Action Center.

b. Compute the total percentage change in the budget from the 1986 budget.

Ex. 14-11 **Combined line and program budget.** The Good City Police Department traditionally has prepared a line budget. Now there is discussion about using a program budget as well in an effort to control activities better and do a better job of securing resources from the city council. Below are the proposed line budget for the coming year and estimated data concerning the percentage of line item costs assignable to each of the four major programs of the police department.

Good City Police Department
Proposed Budget

Salaries	$525,000
Patrol car costs	250,000
Supplies	125,000
Utilities	50,000
Miscellaneous	44,000
Total	$994,000

Percentage of Costs Assignable to Each Program

	Crime Prevention	Criminal Investigation	Criminal Proceedings	Community Education
Salaries	60%	20%	10%	10%
Patrol car costs	70	20	2	8
Supplies	20	30	20	30
Utilities	10	60	20	10
Miscellaneous	30	25	20	25

Required: Prepare a combined line-program budget proposal for the coming year.

PROBLEMS

P. 14-1 **Budget performance report.** Budgeted and actual 1985–86 data for the Fairview City fire department are as follows:

	Approved Budget 1985–86	Actual Costs 1985–86
Clerical wages	$ 38,000	$ 39,400
Education and training	52,000	49,700
Equipment operating expenses	32,000	36,300
Equipment purchases	175,000	164,000
Firemen's salaries	355,000	358,100
Gasoline	14,000	12,200
Insurance	15,000	15,900
Maintenance	85,000	94,800
Miscellaneous	25,000	29,900
Payroll taxes and fringe benefits	77,000	79,600
Supervisory salaries	66,000	66,000
Supplies	15,000	12,700
Uniform allowances and cleaning	11,000	10,900
Utilities	22,000	24,800
Totals	$982,000	$994,300

Required: Prepare a performance report in good form for the fire department.

P. 14-2 **Revenue budget.** Harte-Knox University had the following revenue for the 1985–86 academic year:

Tuition: 2,000 students @ $2,500 per student	$ 5,000,000
State appropriations	3,000,000
Contributions	1,000,000
Investment revenues	400,000
Fees and assessments	600,000
Total revenue	$10,000,000

For the 1986–87 academic year, student enrollments are expected to increase 5 percent, and student tuition will be raised 8 percent. State appropriations are based on the estimated number of students enrolled, and it is estimated that state appropriations will rise 4 percent per student. Contributions are expected to rise 5 percent in 1986–87. A large portion of the investments was sold this year to finance the construction of a multipurpose center; therefore, investment revenue will decline by 60 percent. Student fees and assessments will increase 25 percent per student to help pay for the cost of constructing and operating the new multipurpose center.

Required: Prepare a revenue budget for Harte-Knox University for the 1986–87 academic year.

P. 14-3 **Expenditure budget.** Harte-Knox University had the following expenditure budget during the 1985–86 academic year:

Faculty salaries	$ 3,500,000
Other employee salaries	1,640,000
Educational supplies	260,000
Buildings maintenance	2,600,000
Utilities	800,000
Miscellaneous	1,200,000
Total expenditures	$10,000,000

There were 2,000 students in 1985–86. Student enrollment is expected to grow 5 percent in 1986–87. Faculty staffing will increase in the same ratio as student enrollments, and faculty raises are expected to average 6 percent for the academic year. Other employee salaries are covered by a labor agreement calling for an 8 percent raise during the 1986–87 academic year; however, new laborsaving equipment will allow a 10 percent decrease in the number of other employees. Rapidly rising paper costs and other supply items are expected to increase supply costs by 15 percent per student. Building maintenance costs should continue their trend of a 9 percent per year increase, and a major overhaul of the air-conditioning system will increase costs an additional $450,000 in 1986–87. A 12 percent rise in utility rates will be in effect during the 1986–87 academic year. Miscellaneous items are expected to increase 8 percent.

Required: Prepare an expenditure budget for Harte-Knox University.

P. 14-4 **Revenue budget for a university.** Bergstown College is a state-supported college with a current enrollment of 4,000 students. During the current year, the state provided $1,200 per student. Student tuition is $40 per credit hour, and a normal load is 30 credit hours per year. Contributions for the year were $3,200,000. Student fees were $25 per student and room and board charges were $1,400.

In planning for the next academic year, the financial management committee is evaluating the college's revenue sources. The committee expects student enrollments to increase 12 percent because a small private college in the area just closed. In addition, state appropriations are expected to increase 2 percent per student. To offset rising costs, the tuition will be increased by 12.5 percent, and room and board rates will increase 8 percent. Student fees will increase to $40, primarily to cover significant increases in insurance charges for the student health center. Current year contributions are the result of a significant fund drive effort aimed at raising money to make badly needed repairs and improvements. The campaign will not be continued next year and contributions are expected to fall 30 percent from the current year.

Required: Prepare a revenue budget in good form for Bergstown College for the next year.

P. 14-5 **Revenue budget.** Batesfield Community Hospital provides medical services for a three-county region. During the last accounting year the hospital's revenue consisted of the following:

Medical-surgical (70,000 patient days)	$ 7,000,000
Cardiac care (4,200 patient days)	1,050,000
Laboratory fees (100,000 lab orders)	1,300,000
Emergency room (20,000 emergency room visits)	1,500,000
Outpatient (22,500 outpatient visits)	1,125,000
Total revenue	$11,975,000

The activity measure for each revenue item is indicated in parentheses. Patient days are used to measure activity for medical-surgical services and cardiac care services. Number of lab orders is the activity measure for laboratory revenues. Emergency room and outpatient revenues are related to the number of patient visits to each. The financial manager of the hospital has arrived at each of these activity measures after careful study of the relationships between various activity measures and each type of revenue. Analysis indicates that there is a strong direct relationship between the amount of revenue and the level of activity for each of the revenue classifications.

The financial manager is ready to prepare the revenue budget for the next accounting year and has determined the following: A rate increase recently approved by the board of directors will increase the revenue per patient day by $8.50 in medical-surgical and by $9.00 in cardiac care. In addition, laboratory revenue will increase by an average of $1.75 per order, emergency room revenue by an average of $2.00 per patient, and outpatient revenue by an average of $3.00 per patient.

Medical-surgical patient days are expected to increase by 12 percent during the next year. A new cardiac care unit in a neighboring hospital will decrease patient days for that unit by about 20 percent. New home construction in the area is expected to increase both emergency room and outpatient visits by 10 percent. Management expects laboratory orders to increase 8 percent.

Required: Prepare a revenue budget in good form for the Batesfield Community Hospital.

P. 14-6 Expenditure budget. The golf course division of the city parks and recreation department is responsible for the management and maintenance of four golf courses throughout the city, and the division operates with its own budget. The person who usually prepared the golf course division's budget retired recently. You have been hired during the summer months to prepare a budget for the new fiscal year that starts on September 1. Discussions with parks and recreation personnel, study of the past budgets, and a careful review of accounting documents disclose a number of items important in the preparation of the budget for the next fiscal year.

Each golf course has a crew of groundkeepers who mow and water the greens and fairways and keep the courses in good conditions. Three of the courses have ground crews of 8 people and one course has a crew of 12. Crew members' average wage is $6 per hour, and they average 1,600 hours of work a year in this South Florida community. Payroll taxes and employee benefits cost 18 percent of gross pay. Each course has a groundkeeper supervisor who receives a salary of $19,000 a year. The salary is $4,000 higher for the supervisor at the larger golf course. The payroll taxes and employee benefits cost 23 percent of gross wages for the supervisors. Grass-cutting equipment and other groundkeeping equipment is leased at a cost of $41,000 per year. Maintenance is included in the lease agreement.

The golf pros at each of the four courses are paid $22,000 each. There are 14 clerks who work an average of 1,200 hours per year selling products and collecting green fees in the pro shops of the courses, and each receives $5 per hour. Both the golf pros and the pro shop clerks receive employee benefits that average 20 percent of gross wages. Utilities are expected to be $27,000 next year, and insurance will be $14,000.

Rental golf carts are leased at a total cost of $108,000. Supplies and products sold in the pro shop next year should cost $54,000. No change is expected in the level of inventories in the pro shops. Business supplies, which cost $1,600 this year, are expected to increase by 15 percent next year. Miscellaneous costs are expected to increase about 20 percent from last year's budget of $7,500.

Required: Prepare a detailed expenditure budget for the golf course division for the next budget year.

P. 14-7 **Program budget.** The Barklay City Police Department has a highly respected residential patrol program that has resulted in an extremely low crime rate in residential areas. As a general rule, police need one patrol route for every 300 residences. A patrol route requires two patrol shifts, each with one officer. One police car is required for each patrol route. Total actual patrol time on a route is 14 hours a day. The data available for patrol costs for the program in 1985 are:

Patrol routes	32
Average salary of officers	$11,000
Gasoline cost per patrol car	$1.20 per hour
Annual maintenance cost per patrol car	$350

Six of the current patrol cars will have to be replaced in 1986. New patrol cars have a net cost of $8,200. The price the city pays for gasoline will increase 5 percent in 1986, and maintenance costs are expected to rise 8 percent. The wage agreement calls for a 7 percent increase in officers' salaries in 1986. New housing developments have added 900 new residences to the city's patrol area.

Required: Prepare the 1986 budget for this patrol program, identifying salary costs, gasoline costs, maintenance costs, and the cost of new patrol cars.

P. 14-8 **Budget performance report.** Below is the expenditure budget for the 1985–86 school year for the Fontana County School System.

Item	1985–86 Budget
Administrative salaries	$ 180,000
Teachers' salaries	980,000
Other salaries	110,000
Maintenance costs	70,000
School supplies	80,000
Utilities	42,000
Transportation	210,000
Medical and legal	40,000
Furniture	80,000
Equipment	25,000
Miscellaneous	23,000
Bond retirement	60,000
Total	$1,900,000

At the end of the school year, an office clerk prepared the following listing of account balances:

Item	1985–86 Actual
Administrative salaries	$ 172,000
Teachers' salaries	1,004,000
Other salaries	104,000
Maintenance costs	126,000
School supplies	92,000
Utilities	38,000
Transportation	226,000
Medical and legal	34,000
Furniture	25,000
Equipment	27,000
Miscellaneous	29,000
Bond retirement	60,000
Total	$1,937,000

Required:

a. Prepare a detailed budget performance report for the year for the Fontana County School System.

b. What budget items appear to need investigation?

P. 14-9 **Expenditure budget.** Following are data relevant to the preparation of the 1986 budget for the refuse collection department. The department can provide weekly refuse collection for 1,600 houses with one collection unit, which consists of one truck, one driver, and two collection people dumping refuse into the truck. Drivers receive $12,000 a year and collection people $11,000 a year. Each truck uses $3,600 a year in fuel and oil and requires average annual maintenance costs of $600. Each year 50 percent of the trucks require new tires at a cost of $800 a truck. Total insurance costs are $26,000 a year. Administrative costs for 1986 are expected to rise 9 percent from their 1985 level of $210,000. In 1985, refuse is collected from 40,000 houses. That number is expected to increase 4 percent in 1986. Other items include:

Cost	1985 Budget
Electricity	$ 30,000
Building maintenance	65,000
Payroll taxes	140,000
Miscellaneous	25,000

Management expects electricity to increase 10 percent because of a program to light up truck lots all night to discourage vandalism. In addition, the electricity rate is scheduled to rise 14 percent on January 1, 1986. A new building maintenance agreement has been signed with an outside contractor for 1986. It calls for more thorough cleaning and more preventive maintenance. The new agreement costs $87,000 for the year. Payroll taxes will go up 16 percent in 1986. It is expected that the miscellaneous category will continue its annual growth of 8 percent. A new truck costs $95,000.

Required: Prepare a detailed expenditure budget for the refuse collection department for 1986.

P. 14-10 **Program budget.** The athletic department of Monrovia State College wants to start an intercollegiate basketball team for women. The department is trying to determine the first-year cost of such a program. Some relevant data follow.

The team will have 14 players, each on a scholarship costing $4,000. The new coach will be one of the current physical education teachers. She will become the full-time basketball coach in addition to her current duties and will receive 40 percent more than her current salary of $18,000 a year. Other costs include:

	Cost per Player
Uniforms	$260
Shoes	90
Supplies	150
Medical	60

In addition, an old locker room will be remodeled at a cost of $12,000. New equipment will cost $7,200. A trainer will work part-time for $4,500 a year. Travel costs should run about $1,200 per year per traveler. On average, 17 people will be traveling to games off campus.

Required: Prepare a detailed budget for the first year of the new basketball program.

P. 14-11 Program budget. Monrovia State College is a liberal arts college that has never offered business courses. In recent years students have expressed a considerable amount of interest in taking some business courses. In response to this interest, the faculty has developed a proposed business minor. The faculty believes that the business minor will attract students to campus who might otherwise have attended other colleges. Thus any loss of student enrollments in other disciplines of the college because of students taking the business minor will be more than offset by new students attending the college. The minor would require the establishment of the following courses:

Course	Estimated Annual Student Enrollment
Accounting 101—Financial	180
Accounting 102—Managerial	150
Accounting 201—Intermediate	60
Accounting 204—Income tax	60
Marketing 101—Introduction	120
Marketing 103—Retailing	60
Management 101—Policy	120
Management 201—Production	60
Business Law 102—Contracts	270

The college averages one faculty member for every 120 student enrollments. The average cost of hiring faculty to staff the new business minor would be $18,000 each. In addition, health care, retirement program, and other fringe benefits amount to 25 percent of faculty salaries. Two secretaries would have to be hired for the business faculty at a cost of $6,500 each per year plus 12 percent in fringe benefits. Supply costs average $5.50 per student enrollment. Currently, excess classroom space is available to handle the new business enrollments, but office space is at a premium. A large house on the edge of campus was willed to the college. It will be remodeled at a cost of $60,000 for faculty office space. Utility costs for the new offices will average $360 per month.

Required:

a. How many business faculty members are required to staff the new program?

b. Prepare a detailed budget for the cost of the new program for the first year.

c. If student tuition for courses is $250 a class, does the program appear to be economically feasible?

P. 14-12 (AICPA) Public school budget. The board of education of the Victoria School District is developing a budget for the school year ending June 30, 1986. The budgeted expenditures follow:

Victoria School District
Budgeted Expenditures
For the Year Ended June 30, 1986

Current operating expenditures:			
Instruction:			
General	$1,401,600		
Vocational training	112,000	$1,513,600	
Pupil service:			
Bus transportation	36,300		
School lunches	51,700	88,000	
Attendance and health service		14,000	
Administration		46,000	
Operation and maintenance of plant		208,000	
Pensions, insurance, etc.		154,000	
Total current operating expenditures			$2,023,600
Other expenditures:			
Capital outlays from revenues		75,000	
Debt service (annual installment and interest on long-term debt)		150,000	
Total other expenditures			225,000
Total budgeted expenditures			$2,248,600

The following data are available:

1. The estimated average daily school enrollment of the school district is 5,000 pupils, including 200 pupils enrolled in a vocational training program.
2. Estimated revenues include equalizing grants-in-aid from the state of $150 per pupil. The grants were established by state law under a plan intended to encourage raising the level of education.
3. The federal government matches 60 percent of state grants-in-aid for pupils enrolled in a vocational training program. In addition the federal government contributes toward the cost of bus transportation and school lunches a maximum of $12 per pupil based on total enrollment within the school district but not to exceed 6⅔ percent of the state per-pupil equalization grants-in-aid.
4. Interest on temporary investment of school tax receipts and rents of school facilities is expected to be $75,000 and is earmarked for special equipment acquisitions listed as "Capital outlays from revenues" in the budgeted expenditures. Cost of the special equipment acquisitions will be limited to the amount derived from these miscellaneous receipts.
5. The remaining funds needed to finance the budgeted expenditures of the school district are to be raised from local taxation. An allowance of 9 percent of the local tax levy is necessary for possible tax abatements and losses. The assessed valuation of the property located within the school district is $80,000,000.

Required:

a. Prepare a schedule computing the estimated total funds to be obtained from local taxation for the ensuing school year ending June 30, 1986, for the Victoria School District.

b. Prepare a schedule computing the estimated current operating cost per regular pupil and per vocational pupil to be met by local tax funds. Assume that costs other than instructional costs are assignable on a per capita basis to regular and vocational students.

c. Without prejudice to your solution to part *a*, assume that the estimated total tax levy for the ensuing school year ending June 30, 1986, is $1,092,000. Prepare a schedule computing the estimated tax rate per $100 of assessed valuation of the property within the Victoria School District.

CASE

Case 14-1 Analysis of a budget performance report

Recently the police department has had some difficulty acquiring all of the resources believed essential for quality services to the community. A young police officer who had an accounting course several years ago suggested that the department might have more success if it took a professional approach in the budgeting process. The officer suggested that the department might start by preparing a performance report for the year just completed. He believed this extra effort, which was not required by the city council, would display the professional competence of the department. Below is the budget performance report that the officer prepared, followed by the letter that accompanied the report.

Police Department
Expenditure Budget
Performance Report
1985–86

	Budget	Actual	Variance
Accounts payable	$ —	$ 45,000	$ 45,000 F
Accounts receivable	—	7,200	7,200 U
Administrative salaries	125,000	129,000	4,000 U
Building maintenance	46,000	54,000	8,000 U
Cash	—	65,000	65,000 F
Clerical salaries	68,000	66,500	1,500 U
Depreciation, equipment	—	13,000	13,000 F
Employee benefits	85,000	96,000	11,000 U
Equipment lease cost	22,000	24,000	2,000 U
Equipment purchases	140,000	60,000	80,000 F
Miscellaneous	42,000	26,000	16,000 F
Police officers' salaries	690,000	733,000	43,000 F
Patrol car maintenance	78,000	57,000	21,000 F
Patrol car purchases	240,000	560,000	320,000 F
Payroll taxes	94,000	104,000	8,000 U
Professional training programs	45,000	42,000	3,000 F
Utilities	36,000	49,000	13,000 U
Totals	$1,711,000	$2,130,700	$551,300 F

We are pleased to present a budget performance report for the city police department. This report is evidence of our faith in the budgeting process, and we are especially pleased by the outstanding performance of the department as reflected in the performance report. Although the report speaks for itself, there are several items we want to mention.

Accounts receivable and accounts payable did not appear in the expenditure budget sent to us by the city controller, apparently an oversight on her part. We have included these important items in our report. Note that we have been able to postpone payment on a number of our open accounts, accumulating a balance of $45,000 by year-end. In these days of high interest, that is quite an accomplishment, and we have indicated this with a favorable variance. Unfortunately, we have $7,200 in outstanding receivables from officers, mostly for travel advances to education programs. This, of course, is unfavorable. We also listed our cash balance of $65,000 on the performance report. This is clearly favorable, but cash did not appear on our original budget.

We were surprised to see no depreciation on the budget and, therefore, decided to add it to the performance report. We had considerable discussion about whether depreciation should be favorable or unfavorable. Finally we concluded that since this was an improvement to the reporting system, it should be a favorable variance. We are particularly pleased with the efforts of our chief of police in securing new police officer lines. This additional amount spent for the security of the community is certainly a favorable variance. A major success of the budget year was a large fleet purchase of patrol cars. The department was planning to buy cars over a 3-year period, but a fleet purchase at a significant saving was made this year. Although the total cost of the purchase was much more than the budget, it will save a great deal of money over the next several years. Therefore, this is clearly a favorable variance.

As you can see, through shrewd management and careful cost control, the department was able to generate over a half million dollars in favorable budget variances. The city council can count on the police department to be just as diligent in the use of its resources in future years.

Required:

a. As the city controller, write a detailed analysis of the police department's expenditure budget performance report.
b. Prepare a correct performance report in good form.

Advanced Managerial Accounting Topics

part 4

The successful management of a business depends heavily on the managerial accounting fundamentals presented in earlier parts of this book. Managers rely on accounting information, measurements, and reports, but they also utilize experience and a good knowledge of business and economic conditions to guide the operations of a business. Research done on management and decision making has resulted in new, more sophisticated managerial tools and techniques that many managers are able to use in their work. Some of these new tools are quantitative methods and other managerial techniques that supplement intuition and experience and provide objective support for decisions. This section of the book presents some important concepts and tools used for cost evaluation and decision analysis.

Chapter 15 presents some quantitative models used in inventory management and illustrates methods for determining when and how much inventory to order. Standard cost-variance analysis, discussed earlier, is extended in Chapter 16 to include analysis of multiple material and labor inputs in manufacturing operations and also some advanced variance concepts used in nonmanufacturing operations. Chapter 17 discusses process costing, which is used to measure product costs for continuous-flow production processes. A number of important quantitative tools used in identifying cost behavior patterns and forecasting future operations are presented in Chapter 18. This chapter presents concepts that allow managers to maximize information from a set of cost data.

Inventory Planning, Control, and Valuation

15

Inventory planning and control is an essential function of management for merchandising and manufacturing firms and for not-for-profit organizations such as universities and hospitals. Inventory valuation plays a key role in the measurement of income and balance sheet values. When you have completed this chapter, you should understand:

1. The nature of inventory planning and control and the reasons it is important.
2. The procedures and methods used in inventory management.
3. Typical costs associated with inventory.
4. The methods used to determine the amount and timing of inventory orders.
5. The use of quantitative techniques in planning and controlling inventory.
6. The reasons for and the assumptions underlying inventory valuation.
7. The methods used in valuing periodic and perpetual inventory.

In many merchandising and manufacturing firms inventories are one of the largest dollar investments. Consequently inventories of goods must be carefully managed to ensure that they are being used as efficiently as possible and in accordance with management's policies. Determining the types of inventory to buy, the optimum inventory order size, and the best time to reorder inventory are common types of inventory decisions. Also, managers must plan the most efficient ways of storing, handling, and using inventories. Inventory management is an important activity involving production engineers, systems engineers, industrial engineers, financial managers, and accountants. The primary role of accountants is to supply relevant inventory cost data to managers for use in managing operations.

In this chapter we discuss inventory planning and control. We present the general model for choosing the best inventory order size and discuss the issues involved in selecting the optimum time to reorder inventory. Finally, we discuss inventory valuation, which is essential to inventory costing procedures.

INVENTORY PLANNING AND CONTROL

Like all assets, inventory must be managed to ensure it is being used efficiently in accomplishing company goals

All assets have economic value and require some planning and control to ensure that they are used in accordance with organization goals. Engineers, for example, carefully schedule manufacturing activities to make the best use of production facilities, and information systems managers develop operating procedures and controls to maximize the company benefits from computer resources and to ensure that unauthorized use of the system does not occur. Some assets require more management attention than others because of their nature or importance. For example, cash is essential to the operations and liquidity of the firm and is useful to everyone. Managers spend much time and effort planning cash receipts and disbursements to ensure a desirable level of cash on hand, and to prevent cash from being lost, stolen, or misused.

Inventory is an asset that commands much attention of managers in merchandising and manufacturing firms. Two characteristics make inventory planning and control necessary. First, inventory usually represents a large investment of resources, and inventory constantly circulates. Unlike fixed assets, inventory is used and replenished frequently. In manufacturing operations raw materials flow to work in process and are converted to finished goods that are then sold. In a merchandising firm the various inventory items are sold and new items are purchased to replenish the inventory.

The Nature of Inventory Planning and Control

Inventory must be sold in order to generate revenue. In a manufacturing firm, raw materials must first be converted into finished goods before products can be sold. Money invested in inventory is money that cannot be invested in other earning assets such as production or sales facilities. Therefore, it is necessary to ensure that excessive amounts of resources are not invested in inventories.

The purpose of inventory management is to minimize the cost of inventory without impairing the efficient flow of production and sales activities. Managers attempt to maintain an optimal investment in inventory that balances the costs of ordering and carrying inventory with the costs of not having enough inventory. This balance is achieved by determining the optimum size of an inventory order and the optimum time for placing each order. The quantity of inventory on hand and the frequency and size of inventory orders are directly related to inventory costs.

Inventory costs. Inventory decisions are affected by the cost of ordering inventory and the cost of carrying inventory, as well as by the costs of not having enough inventory on hand. Below are common types of inventory cost that are incurred in addition to the actual cost of the inventory itself.

There are many costs associated with inventory

Inventory ordering costs:

- Costs of acquiring recent price quotations
- Costs of preparing and approving a purchase order
- Costs of receiving shipments and checking against purchase orders
- Costs of recording the purchase and moving the new inventory into storage

Inventory carrying costs:

- Cost of money invested in inventory
- Heat, light, power, and depreciation costs for inventory storage facilities
- Inventory handling costs
- Inventory insurance costs
- Cost of taxes on inventory
- Costs of spoilage, obsolescence, and deterioration

Inventory shortage costs:

- Cost of lost sales
- Cost of inefficient production runs
- Cost of substituting more expensive raw materials
- Penalty costs for late completion of contracts

Inventory **ordering costs** and inventory **carrying costs** are used to compute the optimum size inventory order, discussed in the next section. Inventory **shortage costs** are included in determining the optimum reorder point for inventory items. In addition to these two important inventory topics, several practical considerations are discussed, such as how sensitive the optimum inventory order quantity is to changes in the values of different variables.

ECONOMIC ORDER QUANTITY (EOQ)

The EOQ is the optimum order size to minimize the total cost of inventory

The **economic order quantity (EOQ)** is the order size for some particular inventory item that results in the lowest total inventory cost for the period. **Total inventory cost** consists of inventory ordering costs and inventory carrying costs. An EOQ may be computed for each inventory item.

The optimum order quantity for an inventory item is achieved when the total cost of inventory is minimized. The minimum cost occurs when the cost of ordering inventory is equal to the cost of carrying inventory. These inventory cost relationships are shown in Figure 15-1.

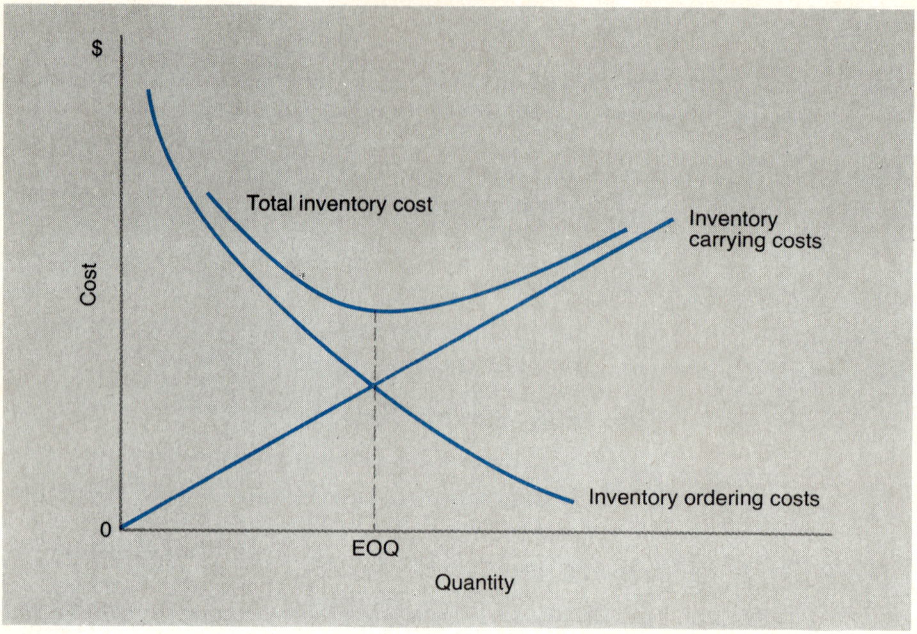

Figure 15-1 **Diagram of inventory ordering and carrying costs. As the order size is increased, the total inventory ordering cost decreases and the total inventory carrying cost increases. Minimum total cost is reached at the order size for which ordering cost equals carrying cost. This order size is called the economic order quantity (EOQ).**

The EOQ occurs where the cost of ordering inventory equals the cost of carrying inventory

When the order size is small, total ordering costs are high because orders must be placed frequently, but total carrying costs are low because relatively small amounts of inventory are on hand at any particular point in time. When orders are large, total ordering costs are low but carrying costs are high because the average amount of inventory on hand is relatively large. The total inventory cost curve, which is merely a combination of ordering and carrying cost curves, is lowest at the intersection of the ordering and carrying cost curves. Any point other than the EOQ yields a higher total inventory cost for the period.

Several methods for finding the EOQ are available. One is trial and error, which requires computing the total inventory costs at various order sizes. Eventually the EOQ can be found or closely approximated by repeating the computation enough times. Another approach is to graph the costs. Although both methods can be used, the first is time-consuming and the second lacks precision.

A third approach is to calculate the optimum order size mathematically using a method called the economic order quantity (**EOQ**) **model,** which yields the **optimum order quantity** with a single set of calculations. The model is

The economic order quantity model

$$EOQ = \sqrt{\frac{2AP}{UI}}$$

where:

A = quantity of inventory required for the period
P = cost of placing one order
U = unit cost of item
I = inventory carrying costs expressed as a percentage of unit cost

The economic order quantity model is a mathematical equation that describes the relationships between ordering costs and carrying costs for inventory in reference to order size. The model rests on several important assumptions:

EOQ model assumptions

1. There is a known constant demand.
2. Ordering costs are known and remain constant.
3. Carrying costs are known and remain constant.
4. Production and inventory capacity is unlimited.

In spite of the somewhat restrictive assumptions, the model can provide managers with some useful information in planning inventory and making ordering decisions.

EOQ Illustrated

To illustrate the computation of the economic order quantity, we use the Samplewood Wholesale Tire Company, which is open Monday through Friday except for a 2-week vacation period and 10 holidays. The firm operates a total of 240 business days a year. Below are demand and cost data for its most expensive steel-belted radial tire.

Average daily demand	50
Selling price	\$95/tire
Cost	\$60/tire
Ordering cost	\$500/order
Carrying cost	20 percent of unit cost

It is easy to solve for the EOQ using the above data. The quantity required for the year (A) is 50 tires a day times 240 business days, or 12,000 tires. The cost of ordering (P) is \$500 per order. The carrying cost (I) is 20 percent of the \$60 unit cost (U), or \$12. Substituting these values into the EOQ model, we have

$$\text{EOQ} = \sqrt{\frac{(2)(12{,}000)(\$500)}{(\$60)(.2)}}$$

$$= \sqrt{\frac{\$12{,}000{,}000}{\$12}}$$

$$= \sqrt{1{,}000{,}000}$$

$$= 1{,}000 \text{ tires}$$

Total inventory cost is the sum of ordering cost and carrying cost

Determining inventory costs. The economic order quantity—that is, the order size that minimizes the total inventory cost for this particular tire—is 1,000 units. Total inventory cost for the year for this inventory item is merely the carrying cost plus the ordering cost. In this example ordering cost is $500 times the number of orders placed, and carrying cost is 20 percent times the cost of the average amount of inventory for the period. The number of orders placed during the year can be determined by dividing the EOQ into the number of units required for the period:

$$\text{Number of orders} = \frac{A}{\text{EOQ}}$$

$$= \frac{12{,}000 \text{ units}}{1{,}000 \text{ units per order}}$$

$$= 12 \text{ orders}$$

$$\text{Ordering cost} = \frac{A}{\text{EOQ}} \times P$$

$$= \frac{AP}{\text{EOQ}}$$

$$= \frac{(12{,}000 \text{ units})(\$500 \text{ per order})}{1{,}000 \text{ units per order}}$$

$$= \$6{,}000$$

Carrying cost is a function of the average amount of inventory on hand multiplied by the carrying cost rate. The average inventory on hand is the order size divided by 2.

$$\text{Average inventory} = \frac{\text{EOQ}}{2}$$

$$= \frac{1{,}000 \text{ units}}{2}$$

$$= 500 \text{ units}$$

$$\text{Carrying cost} = \frac{\text{EOQ}}{2} \times UI$$

$$= \frac{1{,}000 \text{ units}}{2} \times (\$60)(.2)$$

$$= \$6{,}000$$

At the EOQ, the cost of ordering for the period ($6,000) equals the carrying cost for the period ($6,000). By combining carrying cost and ordering cost, we can determine the total inventory cost for the period:

$$\text{Total inventory cost} = \frac{AP}{\text{EOQ}} + \frac{\text{EOQ}}{2} \times UI$$

The general equation for the total cost of inventory is

$$\text{Total inventory cost} = \frac{AP}{Q} + \frac{Q}{2} \times UI$$

where Q refers to any size order quantity, not just the EOQ.

Substituting the values from the tire company example, we find the total inventory cost for the steel-belted radial tires at the EOQ of 1,000 units:

$$\begin{aligned}\text{Total inventory cost} &= \frac{(12{,}000)(\$500)}{1{,}000} + \frac{1{,}000}{2} \times (\$60)(.2) \\ &= \$6{,}000 + \$6{,}000 \\ &= \$12{,}000\end{aligned}$$

This total inventory cost of $12,000 is the lowest possible inventory cost the company can achieve for this particular inventory item. Any other order size yields a higher total inventory cost. To illustrate, Figure 15-2 shows inventory costs for several other order sizes above and below the EOQ of 1,000 units. Order sizes near the EOQ yield inventory costs near the optimum amount, illustrating the relatively flat nature of the inventory total cost curve near the EOQ point.

Samplewood Wholesale Tire Company
Schedule of Inventory Costs at Various Order Sizes

Order size	400	600	800	1,000	1,200	1,400	1,600
Average inventory size	200	300	400	500	600	700	800
Number of inventory orders	30	20	15	12	10	8.6	7.5
Ordering cost	$15,000	$10,000	$ 7,500	$ 6,000	$ 5,000	$ 4,300	$ 3,750
Carrying cost	2,400	3,600	4,800	6,000	7,200	8,400	9,600
Total inventory cost	$17,400	$13,600	$12,300	$12,000	$12,200	$12,700	$13,350

Figure 15-2 **Any inventory order size other than the EOQ yields a higher total inventory cost. However, order sizes close to the EOQ provide relatively low inventory costs, illustrating the relatively flat nature of the inventory total cost curve near the EOQ point.**

Cost Estimation and Model Sensitivity

What is the cost of incorrectly estimating one or more inventory variables?

Often it is difficult to make precise estimates of the variables used in computing the economic order quantity. For instance, total demand for the year may fluctuate significantly from one year to the next, or carrying costs may be hard to measure because of fluctuating interest rates. To determine the effect of incorrect estimates of variables used in the model, managers often compute the EOQ several times, each time substituting a new value for one of the important variables. By comparing the results of the several computations of EOQ, managers may be able to determine how sensitive the model is to changes in the value of the model variables. For example, Samplewood is not confident about its demand estimate of 50 tires a day, but management is confident that demand will be at least 40 and less than 60 tires a day. The two extremes of 40 and 60 can be substituted in the EOQ model, one at a time, to see what effect the difference in demand estimates has on the EOQ. We proceed as before:

40 tires a day

$$A = 40 \text{ tires per day} \times 240 \text{ days} = 9{,}600 \text{ tires}$$

$$\begin{aligned}\text{EOQ} &= \sqrt{\frac{(2)(9{,}600)(\$500)}{(\$60)(.2)}}\\ &= \sqrt{\frac{\$9{,}600{,}000}{\$12}}\\ &= \sqrt{800{,}000}\\ &= 894.4 \text{ tires}\end{aligned}$$

60 tires a day

$$A = 60 \text{ tires per day} \times 240 \text{ days} = 14{,}400 \text{ tires}$$

$$\begin{aligned}\text{EOQ} &= \sqrt{\frac{(2)(14{,}400)(\$500)}{(\$60)(.2)}}\\ &= \sqrt{\frac{\$14{,}400{,}000}{\$12}}\\ &= \sqrt{1{,}200{,}000}\\ &= 1{,}095.4 \text{ tires}\end{aligned}$$

These computations give management some information about what effect its demand estimate has on the optimum order size. But what impact do differing demand estimates have on inventory cost? Since the optimum order quantity is computed using estimates of demand, unit cost, ordering cost, and carrying cost, if any of the estimates are wrong the EOQ will be incorrect. If the incorrect EOQ is used for inventory decisions, the total inventory cost will be greater than if the correct EOQ had been calculated and used in managing inventory. To illustrate, suppose the actual demand for tires is 40 a day rather than 50. The optimum order size with demand of 40 tires a day is 894, which yields a total inventory cost of $10,733:

$$\begin{aligned}\text{Total inventory cost} &= \frac{AP}{Q} + \frac{Q}{2} \times UI \\ &= \frac{(9{,}600)(\$500)}{894} + \frac{894}{2} \times (\$60)(.2) \\ &= \$5{,}369.1 + \$5{,}364 \\ &= \$10{,}733\end{aligned}$$

If managers use the EOQ of 1,000 based on a demand estimate of 50 tires per day, when actual demand is 40 tires per day, the total inventory cost is $10,800:

$$\begin{aligned}\text{Total inventory cost} &= \frac{(9{,}600)(\$500)}{1{,}000} + \frac{1{,}000}{2} \times (\$60)(.2) \\ &= \$4{,}800 + \$6{,}000 \\ &= \$10{,}800\end{aligned}$$

The difference between the total inventory cost using the correct EOQ—$10,733—and the total inventory cost using the incorrect order quantity—$10,800—is $67, which is the cost of incorrectly estimating the demand. The difference in inventory cost of $67 is the result of not placing the optimum size orders, which occurred because demand was incorrectly estimated.

The sensitivity of other variables can be tested as well. The carrying cost of 20 percent in our example has a possible range of 16 to 24 percent. What effect would these different carrying costs have on the EOQ? Again we substitute each of these two values in the EOQ model, leaving the other values unchanged.

16 percent carrying cost

$$\begin{aligned}\text{EOQ} &= \sqrt{\frac{(2)(12{,}000)(\$500)}{(\$60)(.16)}} \\ &= \sqrt{\frac{\$12{,}000{,}000}{\$9.6}} \\ &= \sqrt{1{,}250{,}000} \\ &= 1{,}118 \text{ units}\end{aligned}$$

24 percent carrying cost

$$\text{EOQ} = \sqrt{\frac{(2)(12{,}000)(\$500)}{(\$60)(.24)}}$$

$$= \sqrt{\frac{\$12{,}000{,}000}{\$14.4}}$$

$$= \sqrt{833{,}333}$$

$$= 912.9$$

As before, we can determine the cost of incorrectly estimating the value of one of the variables in the economic order quantity equation. For instance, suppose the actual inventory carrying cost is 24 percent rather than the original estimate of 20 percent. Let us determine the effect on inventory cost of using the original estimate of a 20 percent inventory carrying cost if the actual carrying cost is 24 percent. The EOQ is 912.9 if carrying cost is 24 percent. The total inventory cost using this optimum order size is

$$\text{Total inventory cost} = \frac{AP}{Q} + \frac{Q}{2} \times UI$$

$$= \frac{(12{,}000)(\$500)}{912.9} + \frac{912.9}{2} \times (\$60)(.24)$$

$$= \$6{,}572.5 + \$6{,}572.9$$

$$= \$13{,}145$$

The EOQ of 1,000 was calculated with the incorrect carrying cost estimate of 20 percent. The total inventory cost using the EOQ of 1,000 and the actual carrying cost of 24 percent is computed as follows:

$$\text{Total inventory cost} = \frac{(12{,}000)(\$500)}{1{,}000} + \frac{1{,}000}{2} \times (\$60)(.24)$$

$$= \$6{,}000 + \$7{,}200$$

$$= \$13{,}200$$

The difference in total inventory cost ($13,200 − $13,145) is $55, representing the additional cost caused by using a nonoptimum inventory order quantity, which resulted from not estimating inventory carrying costs correctly. If management had known carrying cost was 24 percent, the quantity ordered would have been 913 units each time an order was placed.

In both situations just illustrated the model is not very sensitive to estimation errors. In the first case estimated daily tire sales are 25 percent higher than actual sales—(50 tires − 40 tires)/40 tires. However, the total inventory cost using an EOQ based on the incorrect demand estimate is only .6 percent higher—($10,800 − $10,733)/$10,733—than the optimum total inventory cost. Similarly, the estimated carrying cost is 16.7 percent lower than actual carrying cost—(24 percent − 20 percent)/24 percent. The resulting total inventory cost using an EOQ based on the incorrect carrying cost is only .4 percent more than the optimum total inventory cost—($13,200 − $13,145)/$13,145.

If the cost of estimation error is large, managers will devote time and resources to improving estimates

When model sensitivity is very low, as in these two illustrations, managers cannot justify spending significant amounts of time and money refining estimates of demand and carrying cost. If the EOQ model is sensitive to estimation errors, however, such errors can cause significant unanticipated costs. In such cases, managers generally try to avoid excessive inventory costs by making more accurate estimates of the variables used in the EOQ model.

EOQ and Not-for-Profit Organizations

EOQ analysis rests solely on costs and quantities and therefore is applicable to not-for-profit organizations

In the Samplewood example the selling price of the tire is given, but it was not used in the computation of EOQ. It is an irrelevant datum for EOQ analysis. The primary reason for its inclusion is to distinguish between purchase price (cost) and selling price. Economic order quantity computations require **cost** and **quantity** data only. Consequently, EOQ analysis is applicable to all types of organizations. For example, a municipal government uses a centralized purchasing and inventory system that handles supplies for all city facilities. One supply item is paper towels for use in city buildings and public rest rooms. The following data pertain to this inventory item:

Annual use	1,800 cases
Purchase price	$20/case
Ordering cost	$90/order
Carrying cost	18% of purchase price

Solving for the optimum order size yields 300 cases as follows:

$$\text{EOQ} = \sqrt{\frac{(2)(1{,}800)(\$90)}{(\$20)(.18)}}$$

$$= \sqrt{90{,}000}$$

$$= 300 \text{ cases}$$

The municipal government can minimize its inventory cost for paper towels by placing six orders a year (1,800/300 = 6), each for 300 cases.

Determining Optimum Production Lots

The EOQ model can be used in job order costing situations to determine the optimum size production run. The model is the same except that we substitute setup costs for ordering costs and unit cost of production for unit purchase price. To illustrate, we assume a firm manufactures products in job lots and this year expects to sell 10,000 units of its 27-gallon cooler. The unit manufacturing cost of the cooler is $10. Setup costs of $625 include labor for making machine settings, installing the new dies, and other costs of setting up the production run of the coolers. The cost of storing and handling units is estimated at 20 percent of production cost. In this case the variables needed to compute the optimum production run are:

A = 10,000 units demanded during the year
U = production cost is $10 per unit
P = cost of setting up the production run
I = inventory carrying cost

$$\text{Optimum size production run} = \sqrt{\frac{2\,AP}{UI}}$$

$$= \sqrt{\frac{2\text{ (10,000 units) (\$625)}}{\text{(\$10 per unit) (.20)}}}$$

$$= \text{2,500 units}$$

The number of job runs during the year will be:

$$\text{Number of job runs} = \frac{\text{Total demand}}{\text{Optimum size production run}}$$

$$= \frac{\text{10,000 units}}{\text{2,500 units per run}}$$

$$= \text{4 production runs}$$

THE REORDER POINT

The inventory level at which a new order is placed is called the reorder point

The economic order quantity provides a manager with information about the optimum order size for a particular item of inventory, but it does not provide information about when the order should be placed. The **reorder point** is the inventory level at which a new order is placed. If a firm has the ability to buy and receive inventory items instantly, a new order is placed when there are no more units on hand. In such a case, inventory purchases and use would appear as shown in Figure 15-3 for the tire dealer. As soon as the company runs out of inventory, it orders and receives the

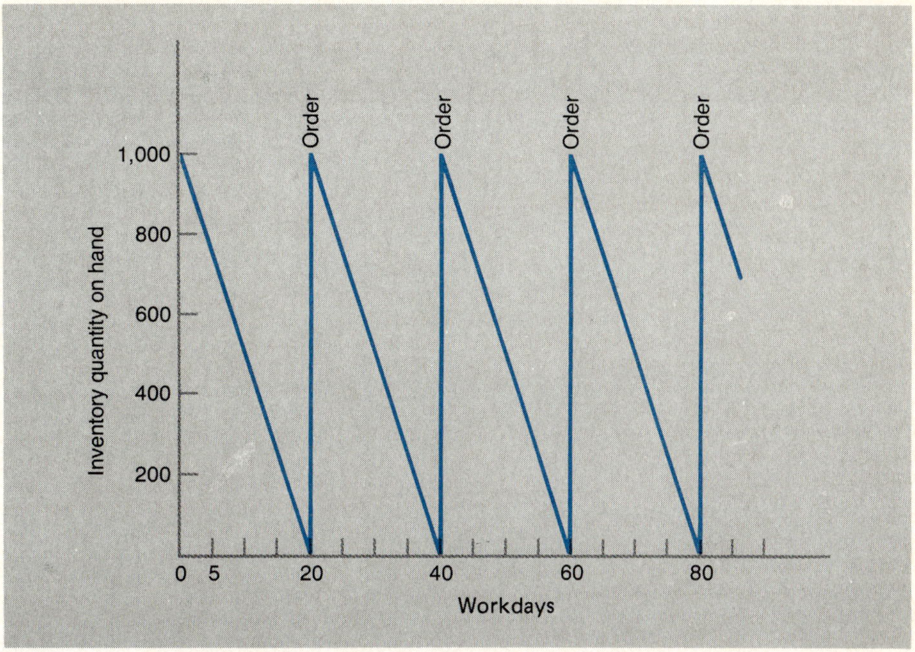

Figure 15-3 **An order is placed when the inventory quantity reaches zero. The quantity on hand then increases to 1,000, the EOQ. Then the quantity declines at the rate of 50 units a day until 20 days later when the inventory quantity has again reached zero. A new order is placed and the cycle begins again.**

EOQ of 1,000 units. The quantity of inventory on hand increases to 1,000 units and declines at the rate of 50 tires per day until zero is again reached. Then the cycle begins anew.

Lead time demand is the amount of inventory required between the time the order is placed and the time it is received

Unfortunately, few firms are able to get instant deliveries. Some time is required between placing an order and receipt of the goods. This time period is called **lead time,** sometimes abbreviated **LT.** If the lead time is known and daily demand is known, the reorder point is easy to find. The Samplewood Wholesale Tire Company example has a lead time of 8 days for tire orders. The daily demand is 50 tires. The **lead time demand,** or **demand during lead time,** is 8 × 50 = 400 tires. If Samplewood plans to receive a new tire shipment just as the inventory reaches zero, it should place an order when the inventory level reaches 400 tires. The inventory flow and timing of inventory orders are shown graphically in Figure 15-4. A new order is placed at an inventory level of 400 tires, 8 days before inventory reaches zero.

Inventory Under Uncertainty

The use of lead time and lead time demand in the analysis of reorder point assumes a known constant demand and lead time. Often one or both of these fluctuate and are not known. Demand in particular is difficult to

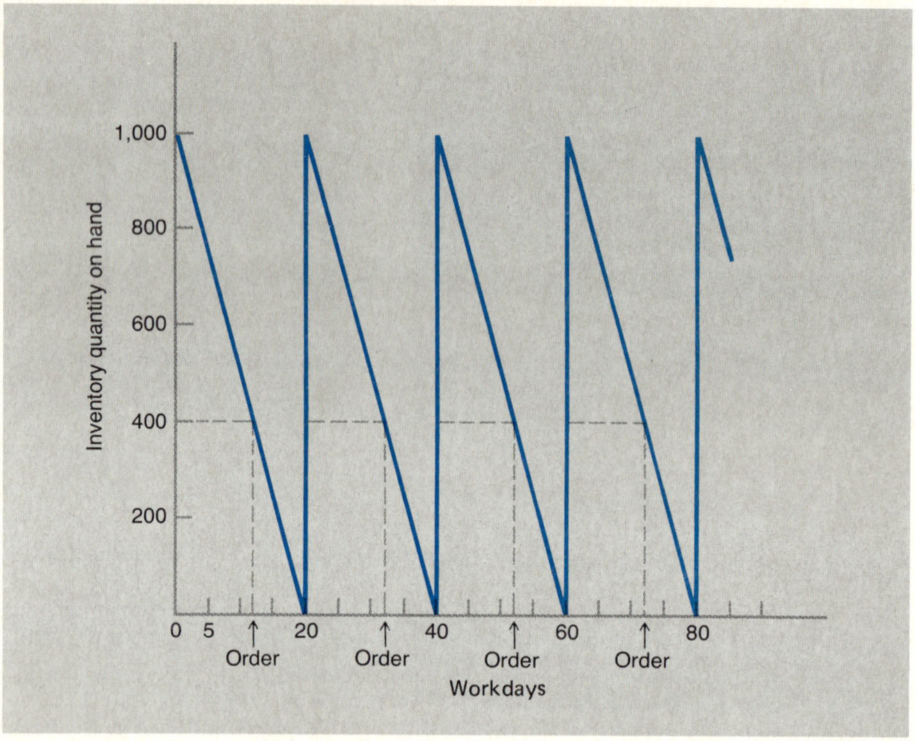

Figure 15-4
With daily demand of 50 tires and lead time of 8 days, a new order must be placed when the inventory level reaches 400 tires, 8 days before stockout.

predict, because it can change from day to day. Delivery on inventory is affected by the supplier's inventory levels and operating efficiency, as well as by variations in delivery schedules of shippers and common carriers.

A stockout occurs when we run out of inventory

When lead time or demand are uncertain, the analysis of the inventory reorder point is complicated. A firm must consider the possibility of running out of inventory, a situation known as a **stockout.** Typically stockouts have a cost. The cost a firm incurs because it runs out of some inventory item is called **stockout cost.** With merchandise inventory or finished goods inventory, stockout costs are likely to be lost profit on potential sales, customer ill will, or the loss of customers altogether. Raw materials inventory stockouts may cause expensive start-up costs, production inefficiencies, a switch to more expensive raw materials, or penalty costs for late delivery of contracted goods. Often it is difficult to estimate stockout costs. For instance, how does a firm know exactly how many sales were lost rather than postponed because of a stockout? Stockout costs are very real costs even if they are hard to measure.

Safety stock is extra inventory to avoid stockouts

In an effort to avoid stockout costs, firms sometimes carry a **safety stock,** which is additional inventory above what is needed for average demand. Safety stock is a cushion that management uses to avoid an interruption of normal activities due to stockouts. Sometimes managers establish the amount of safety stock arbitrarily. For instance, Samplewood may establish a safety stock of 100 tires to guard against heavy demand or late deliveries of orders. The firm places its order when the inventory level reaches 500 tires, which is the average demand of 50 tires times 8 days' lead time plus the safety stock of 100 tires.

Establishing arbitrary safety stocks can be costly. If a safety stock of 100 tires is established, the annual inventory carrying cost is increased by

$$100 \times \$60 \times .2 = \$1,200$$

Since the total annual inventory cost of this particular item is $12,000 without the safety stock, the total cost with the 100-unit safety stock is $13,200, or 10 percent higher. Perhaps $1,200 does not sound like a large amount of money, but if the same safety stock policy is used for all inventory items, the cost may be very large indeed.

The optimum inventory strategy is to increase safety stock as long as the cost of carrying the additional inventory is less than the expected cost of stockouts. The **expected stockout cost** is the cost of the stockout multiplied by its probability of occurring. For example, the cost of a 1-day stockout for the steel-belted radial tire is the gross margin lost on 1 day's sales. With a selling price of $95 and a cost of $60, gross margin is $35 per unit. Expected demand of 50 units per day means that a 1-day stockout results in a stockout cost of $35 × 50 units, or $1,750. Management estimates that with no safety stock, there is a 30 percent chance of a stockout. The expected cost of a stockout is

$$\begin{aligned}\text{Expected stockout cost} &= \text{Stockout cost} \times \text{Probability of stockout}\\ &= \$1,750 \times .30\\ &= \$525\end{aligned}$$

How much should a firm pay to carry safety stock?

The optimum strategy is to carry just enough safety stock so that the cost of carrying the safety stock equals the expected cost of a stockout. With a carrying cost of $12 per unit ($60 × .20), the optimum safety stock is 43.75, or 44 tires ($525/$12 per tire). With a 30 percent chance of a stockout, the arbitrary 100-unit safety stock is excessive. A 44-unit safety stock has a carrying cost of $525, which is the expected cost of the stockout. Incurring more cost by having a larger safety stock is not warranted. Sophisticated statistical models may be developed to address the issue of optimum safety stocks and reorder points. Such models are beyond the scope of this chapter.

INVENTORY VALUATION

As discussed in Chapters 2 and 3, the physical flow of inventory is paralleled by the flow of inventory costs through the accounting system. Managers must decide how those costs are to be measured. Inventory valuation methods are covered in financial accounting texts, but we review them here because inventory valuation has a direct effect on many costing activities.

Physical Flow of Inventory

The physical flow of business inventories may occur in a variety of ways. Some businesses find it necessary to rotate their stock of inventory so that fresh goods are always available. For example, in a paint store, the oldest cans of paint are placed at the front of the shelves so that they will sell first, preventing inventory from spoiling or deteriorating with age. The usual rule for moving inventory is first in, first out (FIFO). Some inventories, however, follow a last-in, first-out (LIFO) pattern. For example, if coal is stored in a pile, the inventory removed from the pile is the latest inventory purchased, because coal obtained earlier is at the bottom of the pile.

Cost-Flow Assumptions

Accountants are interested primarily in inventory cost flows rather than in the physical flow of inventory

The physical movement of inventory is not of importance to the accountant; the flow of inventory costs, however, is. Inventory cost flows affect the value of ending inventories and the amount charged to Cost of Goods Sold. Consequently, both the balance sheet and the income statement are affected directly by inventory cost flows.

Inventory cost-flow assumptions

Accounting for inventory cost flows is relatively simple if the costs of raw materials and merchandise inventories do not fluctuate and the cost of producing finished goods inventory does not vary. However, it is common for inventory costs to vary, sometimes significantly. The accountant must decide which costs should be assigned to ending inventory and which should be charged to production or Cost of Goods Sold. A number of costing alternatives are used. **First in, first out (FIFO)** assigns the most recent cost to Inventory and the oldest costs to Cost of Goods Sold. **Last in, first out (LIFO)** assigns the most recent costs to Cost of Goods Sold and the oldest costs to Inventory. A third alternative is to assign an **average cost** to Inventory and Cost of Goods Sold. The inventory cost flow does not have to follow the physical movement of inventory. Inventory valuation using FIFO, LIFO, or average cost should satisfy the matching concept.

VALUATION OF PERIODIC INVENTORIES

In periodic inventory systems, used primarily by merchandising firms, purchases of inventory are recorded in a Purchases account rather than directly in the Inventory account. When merchandise is sold, the sales revenue is recorded but no product cost is recorded in Cost of Goods Sold. Cost of goods sold is calculated at the end of the accounting period, when financial statements are prepared.

In a mechandising firm the beginning inventory balance and the Purchases account balance together represent the cost of goods available for sale. In order to calculate the cost of goods sold, a physical count is made of merchandise remaining on hand. Next the ending inventory is valued by assigning to each unit a cost based on some cost-flow assumption such as FIFO, LIFO, or weighted average. The value of ending inventory is deducted from the cost of goods available for sale to yield cost of goods sold.

To illustrate the various inventory methods, we use Boltek Corporation's inventory for the month of July. The beginning balance consists of 18 units costing $10 each. During July the company purchased 32 additional units as follows:

July 1 beginning balance	18 units @ $10.00	$180.00
July 11 purchased	10 units @ 10.50	105.00
July 25 purchased	12 units @ 11.00	132.00
July 30 purchased	10 units @ 12.00	120.00
Total goods available	50 units	$537.00

During July the company sold 30 of the 50 units available for sale, leaving an ending inventory of 20 units. Sales were as follows:

July 3 sale	8 units
July 17 sale	5 units
July 28 sale	17 units
Total sales	30 units

In order to prepare financial statements, Boltek Corporation must assign values to the 20 units in ending inventory and the 30 units sold. The value depends on the inventory method used by the company and on the cost-flow assumption adopted. We first consider valuation of periodic inventories. Perpetual inventory systems are covered later in this chapter.

First In, First Out (FIFO)

The FIFO method is logically appealing because it follows the actual physical movement of many kinds of goods. With a beginning inventory of $180 and total purchases of $357 during July, total cost of goods available for sale is $537. The physical count of inventory reveals 20 units remaining on hand. With FIFO valuation we assume that these 20 units consist of the **latest** units acquired. The ending inventory is as follows:

10 units from the July 30 purchase @ $12.00	$120.00
10 units from the July 25 purchase @ 11.00	110.00
20 units	$230.00

Cost of goods sold is $307, calculated as follows:

Goods available for sale	$537
Less ending inventory	230
Cost of goods sold	$307

Last In, First Out (LIFO)

With LIFO inventory valuation in a periodic system, the 20 units remaining on hand are assumed to be the **earliest** units acquired. They consist of the beginning balance and part of the first units purchased during the month.

18 units from the beginning balance	@ $10.00	$180.00
2 units from the July 11 purchase	@ 10.50	21.00
20 units		$201.00

Cost of goods sold is $336 in this case.

Goods available for sale	$537
Less ending inventory	201
Cost of goods sold	$336

Weighted Average

The weighted average cost of the inventory available in July is obtained by dividing the total cost of inventory, including the beginning balance and July purchases, by the total units available for sale.

$$\frac{\text{Cost of goods available for sale}}{\text{Number of units available for sale}} = \frac{\$537}{50 \text{ units}} = \$10.74/\text{unit}$$

Cost of ending inventory is $214.80 calculated as

$$20 \text{ units} \times \$10.74 = \$214.80$$

Cost of goods sold is $322.20 calculated as

$$30 \text{ units} \times \$10.74 = \$322.20$$

VALUATION OF PERPETUAL INVENTORIES

In a perpetual inventory system, the Inventory account contains a current record of all inventory transactions. Such a system is particularly useful in a manufacturing firm, where current production cost data are vital. A per-

A perpetual inventory system is essential to timely cost accounting information in manufacturing businesses

petual inventory system allows the firm to charge inventory costs to production as soon as the inventory is used. Each acquisition of raw materials and each transfer to work in process is recorded in the Inventory account as the transactions occur. The Inventory account is current, hence the name "perpetual."

As in a periodic system, purchases in a perpetual system are recorded at their cost. When raw materials inventory is put into production, its cost is transferred from the Raw Materials Inventory account to the Work in Process account. If the cost of raw materials is changing over time, some cost-flow assumption must be made. Perpetual systems may be maintained using specific identification, FIFO, LIFO, or moving average. The examples that follow deal with merchandise inventory, but the discussion applies equally well to transfers of raw materials to WIP, transfers of WIP to finished goods, and the sale of finished goods.

Specific Identification

Specific identification requires an ability to follow the physical flow of each inventory item and its cost from acquisition through use or sale. The method is appropriate when each item of inventory can be separately identified and therefore has a cost that applies only to that item. Specific identification is used with unique and costly items, such as jewelry, automobiles, or custom-made products.

First In, First Out (FIFO)

Inventory cost flow with perpetual FIFO is illustrated in Figure 15-5. The units remaining in inventory are always assumed to be those purchased

Boltek Corporation
FIFO Perpetual Inventory Record

		Purchases			Sales			Balance	
Date	Explanation	No. of Units	Unit Cost	Total Cost	No. of Units	Unit Cost	Total Cost	No. of Units	Total Cost
July 1	Balance	18	$10.00	$180.00				18	$180.00
3	Sold 8 units				8	$10.00	$ 80.00	10	100.00
11	Bought 10 units	10	10.50	105.00				20	205.00
17	Sold 5 units				5	10.00	50.00	15	155.00
25	Bought 12 units	12	11.00	132.00				27	287.00
28	Sold 17 units				5	10.00	50.00		
					10	10.50	105.00		
					2	11.00	22.00	10	110.00
30	Bought 10 units	10	12.00	120.00				20	230.00

Figure 15-5 **The FIFO cost flow closely approximates the physical flow of many inventory items. In a perpetual system each inflow and outflow of inventory is recorded at the time of the transfer.**

Boltek Corporation
LIFO Perpetual Inventory Record

		Purchases			Sales			Balance	
Date	Explanation	No. of Units	Unit Cost	Total Cost	No. of Units	Unit Cost	Total Cost	No. of Units	Total Cost
July 1	Balance	18	$10.00	$180.00				18	$180.00
3	Sold 8 units				8	$10.00	$ 80.00	10	100.00
11	Bought 10 units	10	10.50	105.00				20	205.00
17	Sold 5 units				5	10.50	52.50	15	152.50
25	Bought 12 units	12	11.00	132.00				27	284.50
28	Sold 17 units				12	11.00	132.00		
					5	10.50	52.50	10	100.00
30	Bought 10 units	10	12.00	120.00				20	220.00

Figure 15-6 **The primary advantage of LIFO is that current costs are matched with current revenues. Consequently LIFO has definite tax advantages during periods of rising prices.**

most recently. After the July 17 sale of five units, the 15 units remaining on hand consist of the most recent 10 units acquired on July 11, and five units from the beginning balance. Similarly the sale of 17 units on July 28 first exhausts five units from the beginning balance, then 10 units acquired next on July 11, and finally two units purchased most recently on July 25.

If you compare the perpetual FIFO ending inventory balance with the periodic FIFO ending inventory balance, you can see that the two are identical. With FIFO valuation, periodic and perpetual systems both produce the same ending inventory cost.

Last In, First Out (LIFO)

With perpetual LIFO, when a sale takes place the cost of the latest acquisition is transferred from Inventory to Cost of Goods Sold. Figure 15-6 illustrates a perpetual LIFO system. The first sale of eight units reduces the initial balance to 10 units, but subsequent sales all consist of the units purchased more recently. Therefore the sale of 17 units on July 28 consists of the 12 units obtained on July 25 plus five units obtained on July 11. Of the original 18 units, 10 units at a cost of $10 each still remain in inventory at the end of the period.

Notice the difference in ending inventory under the perpetual and periodic systems when LIFO valuation is used. The cost of ending inventory with the periodic system is $201. With the perpetual system the cost is $220 because some of the units on hand are valued at the most recent purchase costs. Perpetual LIFO and periodic LIFO often produce different inventory valuations.

Boltek Corporation
Moving Average Perpetual Inventory Record

		Purchases			Sales			Balance		
Date	Explanation	No. of Units	Unit Cost	Total Cost	No. of Units	Unit Cost	Total Cost	No. of Units	Unit Cost	Total Cost
July 1	Balance	18	$10.00	$180.00				18	$10.00	$180.00
3	Sold 8 units				8	$10.00	$ 80.00	10	10.00	100.00
11	Bought 10 units	10	10.50	105.00				20	10.25	205.00
17	Sold 5 units				5	10.25	51.25	15	10.25	153.75
25	Bought 12 units	12	11.00	132.00				27	10.5833	285.75
28	Sold 17 units				17	10.5833	179.92	10	10.5833	105.83
30	Bought 10 units	10	12.00	120.00				20	11.2915	225.83

Calculation of average costs:
July 11, $205.00/20 units = $10.25 per unit
July 25, $285.75/27 units = $10.5833 per unit
July 30, $225.83/20 units = $11.2915 per unit

Figure 15-7 The moving average inventory costs are between FIFO and LIFO costs. In a perpetual system a new average cost is computed every time more units are added to the inventory. Units transferred out of inventory are costed at the most recently computed average cost.

Moving Average

An average cost perpetual inventory system requires computing a new average cost each time additional inventory is purchased. This **moving average** is a weighted average of the units on hand after each acquisition. The procedure is illustrated in Figure 15-7. For example, the average cost of the units on hand after the July 11 purchase included 10 units at $10 each and 10 units at $10.50 each. The average cost is $10.25, calculated by dividing the total cost of $205 by 20 units.

The units removed from inventory are valued at the average cost at the time of sale or use. With costs increasing over time, the moving average cost also increases, but it always lags somewhat behind the current cost of inventory. As usual, the average cost valuation falls somewhere between FIFO and LIFO valuation.

SUMMARY AND COMPARISON OF INVENTORY VALUATION METHODS

The six inventory values obtained in the previous examples are summarized in Figure 15-8. Assuming total sales of $500, gross margin varies from $164 to $193, depending on the inventory system and the cost-flow assumption applied in valuing the ending inventory.

Clearly the selection of an inventory valuation method has a significant effect on inventory values, product costs, and the determination of net income. If managers could select an inventory valuation method at will

Boltek Corporation
Gross Margin Calculations

Perpetual Inventory Systems

	FIFO	Moving Average	LIFO
Sales	$500.00	$500.00	$500.00
Beginning inventory	180.00	180.00	180.00
Purchases	357.00	357.00	357.00
Goods available for sale	537.00	537.00	537.00
Less ending inventory	230.00	225.83	220.00
Cost of goods sold	307.00	311.17	317.00
Gross margin	$193.00	$188.83	$183.00

Periodic Inventory Systems

	FIFO	Weighted Average	LIFO
Sales	$500.00	$500.00	$500.00
Beginning inventory	180.00	180.00	180.00
Purchases	357.00	357.00	357.00
Goods available for sale	537.00	537.00	537.00
Less ending inventory	230.00	214.80	201.00
Cost of goods sold	307.00	322.20	336.00
Gross margin	$193.00	$177.80	$164.00

Figure 15-8 Of the three inventory valuation systems, only FIFO always yields the same inventory cost using either a perpetual or periodic inventory system. Can you explain the differences in inventory costs between perpetual and periodic inventory for LIFO and average inventory?

The selection of an inventory valuation method may have a significant effect on the determination of net income

and change methods whenever they wished, they could easily manipulate reported income, but the **consistency** principle, which requires the consistent application of accounting principles and methods over time, prevents such manipulation. You should be aware of the strengths and weaknesses of each of the inventory valuation methods.

Specific identification. The advantage of specific identification is that it provides good matching of product costs and revenues. The disadvantage is the possibility of income manipulation. Managers may, in some situations, have the ability to adjust gross profit by selecting which units of an inventory item to deliver to a customer. Moreover, the method cannot be used with many types of inventory.

First in, first out. By far the most popular method, FIFO has the advantage of being easy to understand and apply. It tends to conform to the physical movement of inventory and results in reporting inventories on the balance sheet at a cost that is close to the current purchase price. During periods of rising prices the net income reported is higher than with other valuation methods.

The FIFO method of valuation has several disadvantages. When prices are rising, the higher net income results in a higher income tax expense. Current revenues tend to be matched with old costs, implying that the company is able to earn a higher profit than is actually possible with current costs. To replace the inventory used or sold, the business must pay the latest prices. The higher profits reported by matching current revenues with older costs are known as **inventory profits.** During periods of rising prices, inventory profits make a company appear more profitable than is actually the case.

Last in, first out. The most important advantage of LIFO is the lower tax expense incurred during periods of rising prices. Net income tends to be stated more nearly in current terms, because revenues are matched with current rather than old product costs. The lower tax expense results in improved cash flows.

The LIFO method has some serious disadvantages. If it is used for a number of years, balance sheet inventory values tend to become grossly understated, because inventories are reported at costs that existed several years ago. If the company has to reduce its inventory below the amount normally on hand, product costs calculated with old values appear abnormally low. In that case, high profits result from the artificially low product costs.

During periods of rising prices, net income tends to be lower with LIFO. Although this results in a tax advantage, reduced earnings per share tend to be viewed unfavorably by shareholders. The Internal Revenue Service requires that companies choosing LIFO for tax purposes must also use it for reporting purposes. A company has no choice but to report the lower income if it wants the tax savings offered by LIFO.

Average cost methods. Inventory valuations at average cost are among the least popular methods. They seem to have all the disadvantages of LIFO and FIFO, and few advantages. Neither net income nor ending inventories are shown at current values.

SUMMARY

Inventory is a major asset in many merchandising and manufacturing firms and must be carefully monitored and controlled. Inventory analysis requires the use of inventory ordering costs, carrying costs, and shortage costs. In addition, the costs of inventory must be determined by one of several cost-flow assumption methods: FIFO, LIFO, or average cost.

The **economic order quantity (EOQ)** is the inventory order size that minimizes total inventory cost for the period. It is achieved when inventory ordering costs equal inventory carrying costs. Trial-and-error computations and graphic techniques may be used to find the EOQ, but the most precise and efficient method is to use the EOQ model. The model is an inventory cost minimization technique that is equally applicable to businesses and not-for-profit organizations.

Estimation of model variables may be difficult. If a range of values is more realistic for some variable, the extreme values may be substituted into the model to find their impact on the EOQ. The cost of incorrect estimates can be computed and various sensitivity measures can be made by managers.

The **reorder point** is the inventory level at which management places a new order. The time between placing an order and its delivery is called **lead time.** The amount of units demanded (used) during lead time is called **lead time demand.** If demand and lead time are known, the order is placed when the inventory level equals lead time demand.

With uncertainty there is the possibility of a **stockout**, or running out of inventory, which typically results in a **stockout cost.** To avoid stockout costs, firms maintain additional quantities of inventory called **safety stock.** Safety stocks add carrying costs to the total inventory cost. The optimum reorder point equates the cost of carrying safety stock with the **expected stockout cost.** A sophisticated analysis of the inventory reorder point problem requires the use of probabilities and statistical inference.

The valuation of inventories and calculation of the cost of goods sold depends on the cost-flow assumption used in measuring inventory costs. **First in, first out (FIFO)** valuation assumes that the ending inventory consists of the goods acquired most recently. **Last in, first out (LIFO)** valuation assumes that the goods acquired most recently are the first goods used or sold, and the ending inventory is therefore valued at the earliest cost. It is also possible to adopt an **average** cost-flow assumption, or to value inventories on a **specific identification** basis.

The FIFO valuation method produces the same results whether perpetual or periodic inventory systems are used. With LIFO valuation, there can be a difference in value with different inventory systems. During periods of rising prices LIFO results in a close match between costs and revenues and produces a lower gross margin than FIFO. On the other hand, balance sheet valuation of inventory is usually out of date. The FIFO method produces balance sheet valuations that are close to current costs, but the method may not produce a good match between current costs and current revenues on the income statement, and results in the reporting of **inventory profits.**

KEY TERMS

average cost *(618)*
carrying costs *(605)*
consistency *(624)*
economic order quantity (EOQ) *(605)*
EOQ model *(606)*

expected stockout cost *(617)*
first in, first out (FIFO) *(618)*
inventory profits *(625)*
last in, first out (LIFO) *(618)*
lead time (LT) *(615)*
lead time demand (LTD) *(615)*
moving average *(623)*
optimum order quantity *(606)*
ordering costs *(605)*
reorder point *(614)*
safety stock *(616)*
shortage costs *(605)*
specific identification *(621)*
stockout *(616)*
stockout costs *(616)*
weighted average *(620)*

QUESTIONS

1. Why is inventory planning and control important?
2. Describe briefly three types of inventory costs associated with economic order quantity and reorder point computations.
3. What is the economic order quantity and how is it computed?
4. Define inventory carrying cost, inventory ordering cost, total inventory cost, and average inventory size.
5. Discuss the limitations and assumptions of the EOQ model.
6. "Hey, we're running a city government here, not a business. We're not trying to make a profit, so forget this inventory management stuff." Reply.
7. What is meant by a reorder point? What factors affect the inventory reorder point?
8. How does uncertainty affect inventory management?
9. Discuss the relationship between inventory physical flow and cost flow, and relate them to the accounting function.
10. Describe perpetual inventory and periodic inventory systems.
11. Do FIFO perpetual and FIFO periodic always yield the same inventory valuation? Do LIFO perpetual and LIFO periodic always yield the same inventory valuation?
12. Distinguish between the weighted average and moving average methods of inventory valuation.
13. Compare the effect of LIFO and FIFO inventory valuation on the income statement and balance sheet in periods of rising and falling prices.

EXERCISES

Ex. 15-1 **Economic order quantity.** J & L Sloan Company estimates the demand for its CQ10 bearings at 50,000 units a year. The bearings cost $6 each. Ordering cost is $90 per order and carrying cost is 24 percent of product cost.

Required:

a. Compute the economic order quantity.
b. How many orders a year will the company place if it orders the economic order quantity?

Ex. 15-2 **EOQ and inventory cost.** Horthen Appliance Store sells about 375 console model 25-inch television sets per year. The price of the sets is $800 and the units cost the store $600 each. Costs of ordering are $125 per order and carrying costs are 25 percent of unit cost, comprised mostly of insurance and financing costs for inventory.

Required:

a. Compute the economic order quantity.
b. Compute the total cost of the inventory.

Ex. 15-3 Economic order quantity and inventory cost. Below are cost and demand data for a china hutch sold by a large eastern furniture wholesaler:

Demand in units	800
Unit cost	$500
Carrying cost as a percentage of unit cost	25%
Cost of placing an order	$125

Required:

a. Compute the economic order quantity.
b. Determine how many orders will be placed during the year.
c. Find the minimum total cost of ordering and carrying inventory.

Ex. 15-4 EOQ and ordering costs. Folsom River Products is contemplating the use of economic order quantity analysis to optimize inventory ordering activities and minimize inventory cost. Below are data for three products the company sells:

	Product		
	RS2	PM3	SNZ
Annual demand in units	24,500	16,000	5,000
Cost per unit	$50	$20	$10
Cost to place an order	$100	$60	$40
Carrying cost as a percent of product cost	20%	15%	16%

Required:

a. Compute the EOQ for each product.
b. Determine the number of orders placed annually for each of the products.
c. Compute the total annual inventory ordering costs for the three products combined.

Ex. 15-5 Optimal safety stock. Josine's Pipe Shoppe sells Blue Velvet pipe tobacco. Average daily demand for the product is 60 pouches. Selling price is $4.00 per pouch and cost is $2.50 per pouch. Inventory carrying cost is 15 percent. Inventory shortages cause lost sales because customers can go to other tobacco shops in the area. Without a safety stock there is a 20 percent chance the store will experience a stockout of Blue Velvet tobacco. There is a 10 percent chance the stockout will last a second day.

Required: Compute the optimal safety stock for Blue Velvet pipe tobacco.

Ex. 15-6 EOQ and sensitivity analysis. The Lake County School System purchases school supplies for the entire school system and distributes them from a central supply facility. Each year, 10,000 packs of construction paper are used. The paper costs $2 a pack. Ordering costs are $22.50 and carrying costs are estimated at 10 percent of purchase price.

Required:

a. Compute the economic order quantity for construction paper.

b. If actual use for the year increased to 12,000 packs, find the cost of incorrectly estimating demand.

c. If paper use is actually 10,000 packs but the price of construction paper averages $2.50 a pack, determine the cost of incorrectly estimating the purchase price.

Ex. 15-7 Cost of estimation error. The Blusky Swimming Pool Company manufactures above-ground swimming pools of various sizes. Several large-model pools require XM42Z filter pumps, which the company buys from a supplier for $100 each. Estimated annual use of the pumps is 4,000 units and carrying cost is estimated at 16 percent of unit cost. Ordering cost is $80 per order. Using the above estimates, the EOQ for the pumps is computed as 200 units. During the year extremely strong demand for large swimming pools pushed the need for the pumps to 6,250 units.

Required: Compute the cost of incorrectly estimating demand.

Ex. 15-8 Inventory valuation with a periodic system. Bismarck Company uses a periodic inventory system. It maintained the following record of purchases and sales of the 16.5V dual-phase transformer:

Date				
Jan. 1	Beginning inventory	120 @	$18.00	$2,160.00
Mar. 3	Purchases	30	18.50	555.00
May 22	Sold 80 units			
Jun. 1	Purchases	60	19.20	1,152.00
Aug. 8	Sold 80 units			
Oct. 18	Purchases	40	21.00	840.00

Required: Compute the cost of ending inventory and cost of goods sold using:

a. First in, first out.

b. Last in, first out.

c. Weighted average.

Ex. 15-9 Periodic and perpetual inventory valuation. The following inventory record is maintained by Gretel Company:

Mar. 1	Beginning balance	20 units @ $125	$2,500
7	Sold 8 units		
16	Purchases	10 units @ 130	1,300
28	Sold 6 units		

Required:

a. Assuming that the company maintains a periodic inventory system, calculate the cost of ending inventory and cost of goods sold using FIFO and LIFO.

b. Assuming that the company maintains a perpetual inventory system, calculate the cost of ending inventory and cost of goods sold using FIFO and LIFO.

Ex. 15-10 **Inventory valuation with a perpetual system.** Mandan Corporation uses a perpetual inventory system. It maintained the following record of purchases and uses for 7-pound alnico magnets:

Feb. 2	Beginning inventory	80 @	$24.40	$1,952.00
Mar. 22	Used 50 units			
May 17	Purchases	60	25.60	1,536.00
June 8	Used 40 units			
Aug. 30	Purchases	30	26.80	804.00

Required: Compute the cost of ending inventory and the amount of inventory added to work in process using:

a. First in, first out.
b. Last in, first out.
c. Moving average.

Ex. 15-11 **Inventory valuation.** Rollington Manufacturing Company maintains a periodic inventory system for its finished goods. Following is the record for one of its rolamite assemblies:

June 1	Beginning balance	300 @	$108	$32,400.00
4	Added from WIP	200	112	22,400.00
11	Sold 240 units			
17	Added from WIP	100	111	11,100.00
23	Sold 190 units			
29	Added from WIP	400	115	46,000.00
30	Sold 120			

Required: Calculate the cost of ending inventory and cost of goods sold using

a. FIFO inventory valuation.
b. LIFO inventory valuation.
c. Weighted average inventory valuation.

Ex. 15-12 **Inventory valuation with a perpetual system.** Lorrain Manufacturing Company uses a perpetual inventory system for its raw materials. It maintained the following record of alnico magnets purchased and used in the manufacture of a large machine tool component.

Date				
Jan. 1	Beginning inventory	120 @	$180	$21,600
3	Purchases	30	185	5,550
12	Issued 80 units			
15	Purchases	60	192	11,520
18	Issued 90 units			
28	Purchases	40	210	8,400

Required: Compute the amount of direct material added to work in process assuming use of the following inventory valuations:

a. FIFO
b. LIFO
c. Moving average, rounded to three decimal places.

PROBLEMS

P. 15-1 Inventory analysis. Melvin Product Company uses 4,000 cans of roof tar per month in its roofing operations. The tar costs $10 per can, and inventory carrying cost is 20 percent of product cost. Ordering cost is $80 per order and lead time is 15 days. The company operates 273 days per year. It maintains a 3-day supply of safety stock.

Required:

a. Compute the EOQ for roof tar.
b. Determine the total inventory cost at the EOQ.
c. Determine the expected lead time demand.
d. Determine the reorder point for roof tar.
e. Compute the cost of providing the safety stock.
f. Compute total inventory cost with the safety stock.

P. 15-2 EOQ and cost of inventory. Corbin Company's deluxe cordless telephone sells for $79.95 and costs $40 each. Last year the company sold 85,000 units. The supplier recently announced a price increase of $5 per unit, and management of Dayle estimates that as a result of a selling price increase to $89.95 the demand for the telephone this year will decline 10 percent. It costs $400 to place an order and the carrying cost of the deluxe telephones is 12 percent of cost. The supplier has indicated that due to increased processing costs, it will accept orders only in round lots of 1,000 units at the quoted $45 price. An additional charge of $50 per order is made on any fractional orders.

Required:

a. Compute the economic order quantity.
b. Compute the total cost of inventory if the EOQ is ordered.
c. Compute the total cost of inventory if each order is rounded to the nearest round lot of 1,000 units.
d. What order size should the company place?

P. 15-3 Inventory analysis. The Ski-King Shop sells a variety of water sports equipment. An important sales item is a molded life jacket. It costs $30 and sells for $50. The shop sells about 1,000 life jackets in the 250 days the shop is open each year. Ordering costs are $37.50 an order, and carrying costs are 25 percent of purchase price. Lead time on ordering the jackets is 5 business days. The manager of the shop is very conscious of the problem of losing customers because of stockouts. Therefore, he carries a 15-day safety stock of this type of life jacket.

Required:

a. Compute the economic order quantity for the life jackets.
b. Find lead time demand.
c. Find the reorder point.
d. Determine the cost of carrying the safety stock.
e. If actual demand for the year were 1,500 jackets, compute the cost of estimating the wrong amount of demand.

P. 15-4 Planning inventory activities. The Florida Outdoor Marina sells 10,000 cases of outboard motor oil a year. Oil costs $12 a case, inventory carrying costs are 10 percent of oil cost, and inventory ordering costs are $60 per order. Average lead time for orders is 10 days and average daily demand is 27 cases.

Required:

a. Compute the EOQ for outboard motor oil.
b. Determine the total inventory cost at the EOQ.
c. Determine the expected lead time demand.
d. If the marina wants a safety stock of 5 days' demand, determine the reorder point for outboard motor oil.
e. Compute the cost of providing the safety stock.
f. Compute total inventory cost with the safety stock.

P. 15-5 Inventory analysis in the public sector. The Inverness County Highway Department uses a centralized fueling operation for all department vehicles. Each year the department uses 200,000 gallons of gasoline purchased for $1.00 a gallon. Gasoline orders are made through the county purchasing department and the highway department is charged $60 per order for the purchasing service. Carrying costs are estimated at $.06 a gallon per year. There are 250 workdays in the year. Lead time on gasoline orders is 5 workdays. Gasoline use is fairly constant, but some fluctuations occur because of crisis situations such as severe weather. To guard against gasoline stockouts during emergencies, the department keeps a 15-working-day safety stock of gasoline.

Required:

a. Compute the optimum order quantity for gasoline for the highway department.
b. Determine expected lead time demand.
c. Determine the reorder point.
d. Compute the annual inventory cost for the department.
e. A severe winter caused actual gasoline use to be 250,000 gallons. Find the cost of the incorrect estimation of gasoline use.

P. 15-6 Inventory analysis under uncertainty. The Home-Grown Fence Company installs chain-link fences in southern California. In a year it uses 25,000 rolls of chain-link fence. Each roll costs $120. Orders for fence rolls are placed directly with the manufacturer and require 20 business days to fill. Ordering cost is $60 and carrying cost is estimated to be 10 percent of purchase price. The company operates 250 business days a year—5 days a week except for 2 weeks a year when the company closes for vacation. The company experiences a reasonably stable demand for fencing. A 2-week safety stock is desired by management.

Required:

a. Find the EOQ for the fence inventory.
b. Find the expected lead time demand for chain-link fence.
c. Determine the reorder point.
d. Compute the minimum expected stockout cost.
e. If the actual carrying cost is 18 percent, find the cost of using the 10 percent annual carrying cost in computing EOQ.

P. 15-7 EOQ and reorder point. The Bloominggulch Paint Company sells 60,000 gallons of latex house paint each year. Cost of the paint is $10 a gallon. Management estimates that inventory carrying costs are 15 percent and the cost of ordering is $72. Order lead time averages 5 days and average daily demand is 200 gallons per business day. Management wants a safety stock of 10 days.

Required:

a. Compute the EOQ for latex paint.
b. Determine how many latex paint orders the store should place per year.
c. Find the reorder point.
d. Compute the total inventory cost using the reorder point computed in part *c*.

P. 15-8 Periodic inventory system. Maryanne Garden Farm uses a periodic inventory system to account for its inventory of liquid fertilizer. At the beginning of planting season the farm had 16,000 gallons of fertilizer on hand which cost $13,760. Purchases and use of the fertilizer during the next 5 months were as follows:

March	Used 10,000 gallons	Purchased 23,000 @ $.84/gal
April	Used 17,000 gallons	Purchased 11,000 @ .88/gal
May	Used 14,000 gallons	Purchased 13,000 @ .90/gal
June	Used 12,000 gallons	Purchased 10,000 @ .93/gal
July	Used 13,000 gallons	Purchased 12,000 @ .92/gal

Required: Calculate the cost of inventory used and the cost of ending inventory using

a. FIFO.
b. LIFO.
c. Weighted average.

P. 15-9 Perpetual inventory system. Following is Frummer Company's record on the purchases and sales of one type of electronic home organ. The company maintains a perpetual inventory system.

Date	Transaction	Quantity	Unit Cost	Total Cost
Jan. 1	Beginning balance	12	@ $3,200	$38,400
7	Sold 5 organs			
12	Purchases	3	3,450	10,350
19	Sold 3 organs			
22	Purchases	6	3,500	21,000
23	Sold 4 organs			
25	Sold 5 organs			
28	Purchases	4	3,540	14,160

Required: Compute the cost of ending inventory and cost of goods sold for January to the nearest cent, using

a. FIFO.
b. LIFO.
c. Moving average.

P. 15-10 Valuation of manufactured inventories. Moldifome Corporation recently established a new department to produce molded foam packaging materials for packing sensitive electronic instruments and components. Production started in July. During the next two quarters the company experienced the following costs, production, and sales:

	Transferred from WIP	Cost per Unit	Units of Sales	Selling Price
July	40,000	$3.00	20,000	$5.00
August	60,000	3.20	55,000	5.25
September	50,000	3.40	60,000	5.50
October	70,000	3.50	57,000	5.70
November	72,000	3.60	65,000	5.85
December	78,000	3.75	83,000	6.00

The company uses a periodic inventory system for finished goods. It incurred the following operating expenses in the new department:

Third quarter	$250,000
Fourth quarter	$340,000

Required:

a. Prepare income statements for the department for each of the two quarters assuming that the company uses FIFO inventory valuation for its finished goods. Also calculate net income for the 6-month period.

b. Prepare income statements for the department for each of the two quarters assuming that the company uses LIFO inventory valuation for its finished goods. Also calculate net income for the 6-month period.

c. Prepare a single income statement for the 6-month period assuming the company uses LIFO inventory valuation for finished goods.

d. Explain any difference in net income between the income statement in part *c* and the total net income in part *b*.

P. 15-11 Perpetual inventory valuation. Consolidated Spacecraft Company uses a special radioactive alloy in one of its new manufacturing processes. After 1 month of operation the controller asked the company president which inventory valuation method should be used for this raw material. The president noted that the price of the material has been rising rapidly, and asked the controller to prepare a schedule using several valuation methods for comparison, prior to settling on a single method.

The company uses a perpetual inventory system for all its raw materials. Following is a record of the number of grams of alloy purchased and put into production during March.

Date	Transaction	Grams		Unit Cost
Mar. 1	Purchased	450	@	$ 90
6	Issued	220		
13	Purchased	200		94
16	Purchased	300		95
19	Issued	400		
25	Purchased	350		98
30	Issued	380		
31	Purchased	200		100

Required: Prepare a schedule showing the valuation of inventory and calculate ending inventory and cost of goods transferred to work in process, using

a. First in, first out.
b. Last in, first out.
c. Moving average, rounded to three decimal places.

P. 15-12 **Inventory valuation with perpetual and periodic systems.** Aurora Company makes sensitive electronic components, many of which require the use of precious metals. Following is a record of the company's purchases and use of gold during a 3-month period:

Date		Transaction	Troy Ounces		Cost per Ounce
June	1	Balance	40	@	$590
	6	Issued	(22)		
	23	Purchased	30		575
July	16	Purchased	20		595
	29	Issued	(30)		
Aug.	5	Purchased	35		610
	19	Issued	(35)		
	21	Purchased	20		580
	30	Issued	(18)		

Required: Compute the ending inventory and amount of raw materials issued to work in process assuming the company uses

a. First in, first out with a perpetual inventory system.
b. Last in, first out with a perpetual inventory system.
c. First in, first out with a periodic inventory system.
d. Last in, first out with a periodic inventory system.

P. 15-13 **(AICPA) FIFO, LIFO, and average inventory valuation.** The controller of the Investor Corporation, a retail company, made three different schedules of gross margin for the first quarter ended September 30, 1986. These schedules appear below.

	Sales ($10 per Unit)	Cost of Goods Sold	Gross Margin
Schedule A	$280,000	$118,550	$161,450
Schedule B	280,000	116,900	163,100
Schedule C	280,000	115,750	164,250

The computation of cost of goods sold in each schedule is based on the following data:

	Units	Cost per Unit	Total Cost
Beginning inventory, July 1	10,000	$4.00	$40,000
Purchase, July 25	8,000	4.20	33,600
Purchase, August 15	5,000	4.13	20,650
Purchase, September 5	7,000	4.30	30,100
Purchase, September 25	12,000	4.25	51,000

The president of the corporation cannot understand how three different gross margins can be computed from the same set of data. As controller, you have explained to him that the three schedules are based on three different assumptions concerning the flow of inventory costs; i.e., first-in, first-out; last-in, first-out; and weighted average. Schedules A, B, and C were not necessarily prepared in this sequence of cost-flow assumptions.

Required: Prepare three separate schedules computing cost of goods sold and supporting schedules showing the composition of the ending inventory under each of the three cost-flow assumptions.

P. 15-14 **(CMA) Analysis of changing from FIFO to LIFO inventory valuation.** The management of Stark Products Company has asked its accounting department to describe the effect upon the company's financial position and its financial statements of accounting for inventories on the LIFO rather than FIFO basis during 1985 and 1986. The accounting department is to assume that the change to LIFO would have been effective on January 1, 1985, and that the initial LIFO base would have been the inventory value on December 31, 1984. Presented below are the company's financial statements and other data for the years 1985 and 1986 when the FIFO method was in fact employed.

	Financial Condition as of		
	12/31/84	**12/31/85**	**12/31/86**
Cash	$ 67,700	$121,300	$176,050
Accounts receivable	40,000	54,000	61,750
Inventory	69,000	75,000	84,000
Other assets	114,000	114,000	114,000
Total assets	$290,700	$364,300	$435,800
Accounts payable	$ 23,000	$ 30,000	$ 36,400
Other liabilities	40,000	40,000	40,000
Common stock	140,000	140,000	140,000
Retained earnings	87,700	154,300	219,400
Total equities	$290,700	$364,300	$435,800

	Income for Years Ended	
	12/31/85	**12/31/86**
Sales	$540,000	$617,500
Less Cost of goods sold	294,000	355,000
Other expenses	135,000	154,000
Total expenses	429,000	509,000
Income before income taxes	111,000	108,500
Less income taxes (40%)	44,400	43,400
Net income	$ 66,600	$ 65,100

Other data:

1. Inventory on hand at 12/31/84 consisted of 30,000 units valued at $2.30 each.

2. Sales (all units sold at the same price in a given year):

   1985—120,000 units @ $4.50 each
   1986—130,000 units @ $4.75 each

3. Purchases (all units purchased at the same price in a given year):

   1985—120,000 units @ $2.50 each
   1986—130,000 units @ $2.80 each

4. Income taxes at the effective rate of 40 percent are paid on December 31 each year.

Required: Name the account(s) presented in the financial statements which would have different amounts for 1986 if LIFO rather than FIFO had been used and state the new amount for each account that is named.

CASES

Case 15-1 **(CMA) Estimation of inventory model parameters.** Evans Inc., is a large wholesale distributor which deals exclusively in baby shoes. Due to the substantial costs related to ordering and storing the shoes, the company has decided to employ the economic order quantity method (EOQ) to help determine the optimum quantities of shoes to order from the different manufacturers. The EOQ formula is

$$\text{EOQ} = \sqrt{\frac{2AP}{UI}}$$

where:

EOQ = optimum number of units per purchase order
A = annual demand
U = purchase price per unit
P = cost of placing an order
I = annual carrying cost per dollar of investment in inventory

Before Evans Inc., can employ the EOQ model, they need to develop values for two of the cost parameters—ordering costs (P) and carrying costs (I). As a starting point, management has decided to develop the values for the two cost parameters by using cost data from the most recent fiscal year, 1986.

The company placed 4,000 purchase orders during 1986. The largest number of orders placed during any one month was 400 orders in June and the smallest number of orders placed was 250 in December. Selected cost data for these two months and the year for the purchasing, accounts payable, and warehousing operations follow.

	Costs for High Activity Month (June; 400 orders)	Costs for Low Activity Month (December; 250 orders)	Annual Costs
Purchasing department:			
Purchasing manager	$ 1,750	$ 1,750	$ 21,000
Buyers	2,500	1,900	28,500
Clerks	2,000	1,100	20,600
Supplies	275	150	2,500
Accounts payable dept.:			
Clerks	2,000	1,500	21,500
Supplies	125	75	1,100
Data processing	2,600	2,300	30,000
Warehouse:			
Supervisor	1,250	1,250	15,000
Receiving clerks	2,300	1,800	23,300
Receiving supplies	50	25	500
Shipping clerks	3,800	3,500	44,000
Shipping supplies	1,350	1,200	15,200
Freight out	1,600	1,300	16,800
Totals	$21,600	$17,850	$240,000

The purchasing department is responsible for placing all orders. The costs listed for the accounts payable department relate only to the processing of purchase orders for payment. The warehouse costs reflect two operations—receiving and shipping. The receiving clerks inspect all incoming shipments and place the orders in storage. The shipping clerks are responsible for processing all sales orders to retailers.

The company leases space in a public warehouse. The rental fee is priced according to the square feet occupied during a month. The annual charges during 1986 totaled $34,500. Annual insurance and property taxes on the shoes stored in the warehouse amounted to $5,700 and $7,300 respectively. The company pays 8 percent a year for a small amount of short-term, seasonal bank debt. Long-term capital investments are expected to produce a rate of return of 12 percent after taxes. The effective tax rate is 40 percent.

The inventory balances tend to fluctuate during the year depending upon the demand for baby shoes. Selected data on inventory balances are shown below.

Inventory, January 1, 1986	$160,000
Inventory, December 31, 1986	120,000
Highest inventory balance (June)	220,000
Lowest inventory balance (December)	120,000
Average monthly inventory	190,000

The boxes in which the baby shoes are stored are all approximately the same size. Consequently, the shoes all occupy about the same amount of storage space in the warehouse.

Required:

a. Using the 1986 data, determine estimated values appropriate for

1. *P*—cost of placing an order.
2. *I*—annual carrying cost per dollar of investment in inventory.

b. Should Evans Inc., use the cost parameters developed solely from the historical data in the employment of the EOQ model? Explain your answer.

Case 15-2 **(CMA) Analyzing the impact of inventory valuation methods.** The Elof Co. is considering changing its inventory valuation method from the first in, first out method (FIFO) to the last in, first out method (LIFO) because of the potential tax savings. However, management wishes to consider all of the effects on the company, including its reported performance, before making the final decision.

The Inventory account, currently valued on the FIFO basis, consists of 1,000,000 units at $7.00 per unit on January 1, 1985. There are 1,000,000 shares of common stock outstanding as of January 1, 1985. The cash balance on January 1, 1985 is $400,000.

The company has made the following forecasts for the period 1985 through 1987.

	1985	1986	1987
1. Unit sales (in millions of units)	1.1	1.0	1.3
2. Sales price per unit	$10	$10	$12
3. Unit purchases (in millions of units)	1.0	1.1	1.2
4. Purchase price per unit	$7	$8	$9
5. Annual depreciation (in thousands of dollars)	$300	$300	$300
6. Cash dividends per share	$0.15	$0.15	$0.15
7. Cash payments for additions to and replacement of plant and equipment (in thousands of dollars)	$350	$350	$350
8. Income tax rate	40%	40%	40%
9. Operating expense (exclusive of depreciation) as a percent of sales	15%	15%	15%
10. Common shares outstanding (in millions)	1	1	1

Required:

a. Prepare a schedule which illustrates and compares the following data for Elof Co. under the FIFO inventory method and under the LIFO inventory method for 1985, 1986, 1987, assuming the company would begin LIFO at the beginning of 1985.

1. Year-end inventory balances.
2. Annual net income after taxes.
3. Earnings per share.
4. Cash balance.

Assume all sales are collected in the year of sale and all purchases, operating expenses, and taxes are paid during the year incurred.

b. Using the data in the question, your answer to requirement *a*, and any additional issues you believe need to be considered, prepare a report to recommend whether or not Elof Co. should change to the LIFO inventory method. Be sure to support your conclusions with appropriate arguments.

Standard Costs Extended: Mix and Yield Variances

16

Standard cost variance analysis, discussed in Chapter 8, is useful in providing timely cost control and management performance information. The basic standard costing concepts in Chapter 8 are extended in this chapter to include the analysis of varying the proportion of production resource inputs and the analysis of standard cost variances for nonmanufacturing activities. When you have completed this chapter, you should understand:

1. The various types of variance analysis measurements used with manufacturing activities.
2. How to compute the various types of production variances.
3. The separation of material quantity and labor efficiency variances into mix and yield variances.
4. How standard cost variances are measured for marketing activities.
5. The computation of marketing variances.

The standard cost discussion in Chapter 8 shows how a standard cost system produces information for strategic planning, cost control, and performance measurement. In this chapter we extend standard cost concepts to include production situations not covered earlier. We use standards to measure the cost effects of varying combinations of materials and labor production inputs. We also apply standard cost performance reporting to some nonmanufacturing activities.

PERFORMANCE REPORTING FOR MANUFACTURING ACTIVITIES

Many complex manufacturing activities that require numerous types of materials and several kinds of labor require sophisticated cost measurement and performance reporting processes. Before we discuss more complex standard costing concepts, we review briefly the basic standard costing concepts with an example designed to highlight the relationship between resource inputs and production outputs. We then use this same example to present the new standard costing concepts.

Standard Costing Illustrated

To illustrate comprehensive variance analysis, we use the Dixie Chocolate Company, a manufacturer of high-quality candy. One of Dixie Chocolate Company's specialty products is a dark chocolate cream, produced in 4,000-pound batches. The company uses standard costs to set selling prices and to monitor production costs and activities. First we illustrate direct material price and quantity variances and direct labor rate and efficiency variances. Then we separate the direct material quantity variance and the direct labor efficiency variance into more detailed variances to provide managers with additional information to help monitor and control prime production costs.

Standard cost data. The Dixie Chocolate Company's dark chocolate cream candy is packaged in 10-pound cartons and shipped to stores in 100-pound cases. The product is priced at 250 percent of standard prime cost (direct materials + direct labor). A schedule of standard costs for the product is presented in Figure 16-1.

Dixie Chocolate Company
Schedule of Standard Costs
For Dark Chocolate Creams

Standards

Material	Quantity per 10-lb Carton	Price
Cocoa syrup	3.0 quarts	$9.00 per gallon
Milk	.9 gallon	1.50 per gallon
Liquid sugar	1.0 quart	3.00 per gallon
Flavoring	.1 gallon	6.50 per gallon
Labor	**Quantity per 100-lb Case**	**Rate**
Skilled labor	4 hours	$9.00 per hour
General labor	2 hours	4.50 per hour

Figure 16-1
This schedule presents the standard costs and quantities for direct materials and direct labor.

Standard cost data may be expressed in any unit management finds convenient and useful. In Figure 16-1 materials standards are presented in terms of 10-pound cartons and labor standards are presented in terms of 100-pound cases. To perform variance analysis, however, it is convenient to convert standards to common units of measure.

Unit standard costs. Either pounds, cartons, or cases could be used as the unit for measuring costs. In this example we use the pound as the unit measure and convert the standards in Figure 16-1 to costs per pound of product. Material quantity standards are expressed in terms of input per 10-pound carton, and material input prices are expressed in terms of price per gallon of input. To find the **cost** of materials **per pound of candy,** we need to multiply the **quantity** of input **per pound** of output times the **price** per gallon of input for each of the four inputs.

Material	Quantity		Input Price		Cost per Pound
Cocoa syrup	.75 gal/10 = .075 gal	×	$9.00 per gal	=	$.675
Milk	.90 gal/10 = .090 gal	×	1.50 per gal	=	.135
Liquid sugar	.25 gal/10 = .025 gal	×	3.00 per gal	=	.075
Flavoring	.10 gal/10 = .010 gal	×	6.50 per gal	=	.065
Total materials cost per pound					$.95

Labor standards are expressed in terms of 100-pound cases and must be divided by 100 and multiplied by the hourly rate to find the **labor cost per pound of candy.**

Labor	Quantity		Hourly Rate		Cost per Pound
Skilled labor	4 hr/100 = .04	×	$9.00 per hr	=	$.36
General labor	2 hr/100 = .02	×	4.50 per hr	=	.09
Total labor cost per pound					$.45

The total prime cost of the product is $1.40 per pound, the sum of the materials and labor costs calculated above. Now that we have a standard prime cost per pound of candy, we can calculate the standard price of the product, which is the prime cost times 250 percent, or $3.50 per pound ($1.40 × 2.50).

Standard cost data should be converted to common units to facilitate variance analysis

Conversion of standard cost data to a common unit of measure facilitates variance analysis. The data should be expressed in the most appropriate physical units. When the costs are converted to common units, as above, it is easy to see the relative proportion of the various costs. For example, you can see that liquid sugar is a much cheaper input per pound of candy than cocoa syrup, and that general labor is much less costly than skilled labor. These relationships become important when we analyze mix and yield variances.

Variance Reports

Variance analysis reports the difference between standard and actual costs

Variance analysis measures the fluctuation of actual costs from standards, and managers attempt to explain the cause of variances, particularly if they are large. Generally, a manager's ability to interpret variances is affected by the content, timeliness, and detail of the variance reports. Variance reports require actual production data in addition to standards. The **actual** costs of producing 60,000 pounds of candy in the first quarter of 1986 are shown in Figure 16-2. These data are compared with the standards in Figure 16-1. Variances are computed and reported to management on a timely basis so that managers can use the data to correct inefficiencies and measure performance.

The difference between standard and actual cost is the material price variance

Material variances. Material variances are typically divided into a price variance and a quantity variance. When there are multiple inputs, such as the four raw materials in this example, the variances are calculated for each material. The **price variance** for each input is the difference between the standard and actual cost of the material times the actual quantity used or purchased. The **quantity variance** for each material is the difference between the standard and actual quantity of material multiplied by the standard cost. Figure 16-3 presents the material variances for the period.

The standard and actual unit costs for each material are obtained directly from the standard cost schedule in Figure 16-1 and the actual cost schedule in Figure 16-2. To obtain the standard quantities, however, it is

Dixie Chocolate Company
Schedule of Actual Costs for Dark Chocolate Creams
First Quarter, 1986

Production = 60,000 pounds of candy

Material	Quantity	Cost
Cocoa syrup	4,100 gallons	$9.40 per gallon
Milk	6,000 gallons	1.75 per gallon
Liquid sugar	1,400 gallons	2.60 per gallon
Flavoring	800 gallons	6.30 per gallon
Total materials	12,300 gallons	

Labor	Quantity	Cost
Skilled labor	2,500 hours	$23,500
General labor	1,050 hours	5,040
Total labor	3,550 hours	$28,540

Figure 16-2
This schedule presents the actual direct materials and direct labor costs for the first quarter of 1986.

Dixie Chocolate Company
Materials Variances for Dark Chocolate Creams
First Quarter 1986

Material Price Variance

Price variance = (Standard cost − Actual cost) × Actual quantity

Cocoa syrup	= ($9.00 − $9.40) × 4,100 gal =	$1,640 U	
Milk	= (1.50 − 1.75) × 6,000 gal =	1,500 U	
Liquid sugar	= (3.00 − 2.60) × 1,400 gal =	560 F	
Flavoring	= (6.50 − 6.30) × 800 gal =	160 F	
Total material price variance			$2,420 U

Material Quantity Variance

Quantity variance = (Standard quantity − Actual quantity) × Standard price

Cocoa syrup	= (4,500 gal − 4,100 gal) × $9.00 =	$3,600 F	
Milk	= (5,400 gal − 6,000 gal) × 1.50 =	900 U	
Liquid sugar	= (1,500 gal − 1,400 gal) × 3.00 =	300 F	
Flavoring	= (600 gal − 800 gal) × 6.50 =	1,300 U	
Total material quantity variance			1,700 F
Total materials variance			$ 720 U

Figure 16-3
A material price and quantity variance report. Price and quantity variances are computed for each material.

The difference between standard and actual quantity is the material quantity variance

necessary to refer to the unit cost data calculated earlier. The actual quantity of each input is given in Figure 16-2. The standard quantity is obtained by multiplying the standard quantity per pound of output by the production of 60,000 pounds for the period. For example, the standard quantity for cocoa syrup is .075 gallon per pound of finished product. The standard quantity for the period's production level is .075 gallon/pound × 60,000 pounds, or 4,500 gallons of syrup. The standard quantities for each of the other resources are calculated in the same manner.

The labor rate and efficiency variances are similar to the material price and quantity variances

Labor variances. When multiple labor classifications are used, a separate labor rate and labor efficiency variance is computed for each labor classification. The **rate variance** is the difference between standard and actual labor rates, multiplied by the actual number of hours worked. The **efficiency variance** is the difference between the standard and actual hours for the output achieved times the standard rate. Figure 16-4 presents the labor variance report.

The schedule of actual results in Figure 16-2 provides the total labor hours for each labor classification. Labor costs for each type of labor are expressed in total dollars. This is common because most firms have employees working for various rates in any particular labor classification. Labor costs for each labor classification are accumulated each pay period and the total is reported at the end of the period. Although some skilled

Dixie Chocolate Company
Direct Labor Variances for Dark Chocolate Creams
First Quarter 1986

Labor Rate Variance

Rate variance	= (Standard rate − Actual rate) × Actual hours		
Skilled labor	= ($9.00 − $9.40) × 2,500 hours =	$1,000 U	
General labor	= (4.50 − 4.80) × 1,050 hours =	315 U	
Total labor rate variance			$1,315 U

Labor Efficiency Variance

Efficiency variance	= (Standard hours − Actual hours) × Standard rate		
Skilled labor	= (2,400 − 2,500) × $9.00 =	$900 U	
General labor	= (1,200 − 1,050) × 4.50 =	675 F	
Total labor efficiency variance			225 U
Total labor variance			$1,540 U

Figure 16-4
A direct labor rate and efficiency variance report.

employees earn more than others, for variance analysis we are concerned with the average cost of skilled employees and not with their individual earnings. Similarly, we need the average cost of an hour of general labor. We can calculate these costs from the actual data given, and then use them to calculate variances. For the first quarter of 1986 the average rates paid for skilled and general labor were:

Skilled labor rate: $23,500/2,500 hours = $9.40 per hour
General labor rate: $ 5,040/1,050 hours = $4.80 per hour

We compare the actual and standard labor rates to find the labor rate variance, as shown in the labor variance report in Figure 16-4.

The efficiency variance requires the computation of standard hours. Earlier we calculated the standard amount of labor per pound of chocolate cream candy. We multiply the standard quantity of labor per pound times the actual production quantity to determine the standard labor hours for each classification of labor. The calculations are as follows:

Skilled labor = .04 hr/lb × 60,000 lb = 2,400 hours

General labor = .02 hr/lb × 60,000 lb = 1,200 hours

The standard hours computed above are compared with actual hours in Figure 16-4 to compute the labor efficiency variance.

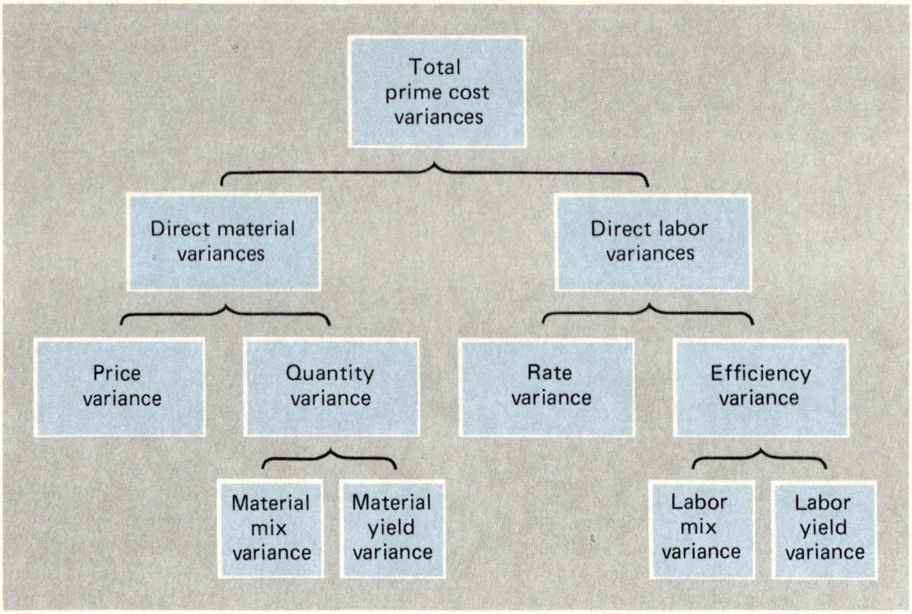

Figure 16-5 **This diagram shows the component parts of direct materials and direct labor variances. The material quantity variance and the labor efficiency variance can each be separated into mix and yield variance components that provide more specific information about the use of materials and labor quantities.**

Extending Variance Analysis

With multiple inputs, quantity and efficiency variances can be separated into mix and yield variances

The material and labor variances illustrated in Figures 16-3 and 16-4 provide useful information for managers. However, in situations with multiple resources used in the production of a product or service, additional information can be obtained by separating the material quantity variance and labor efficiency variance into two components. The purpose of this additional variance analysis is to provide information about the economic consequences of varying the relative amounts of inputs used in production. Figure 16-5 illustrates the relationship of mix and yield variances to the material quantity and labor efficiency variances. The diagram also shows the breakdown of the total prime cost variance into its various component parts.

The Dixie Chocolate Company example has four raw materials and two labor classifications whose standard quantities per pound of candy were calculated earlier. It is possible, however, to produce a pound of candy of approximately the same quality with a somewhat different mix of materials or labor. When the mix of resources changes, mix and yield variances can be calculated to determine the cost effect of these changes.

MIX VARIANCES AND YIELD VARIANCES

Sometimes it is possible to vary the proportion or mix of inputs in the production of a product or service without impairing the nature or quality of the product or service. For example, a roofing contractor may install a roof using two experienced roofers and three apprentice roofers, or the contractor may install the roof using three experienced roofers and one apprentice. When there is a change in the mix of labor from the standard or expected mix, managers often want to know what the cost of that change is.

Similarly, it is common for the mix or proportion of material inputs to change from the standard mix. For example, a bakery may be able to reduce the amount of sour cream and increase the amount of milk in the production of a batch of Danish pastry. The relative proportion of inputs may vary from standards for a variety of reasons, including:

Causes of difference in the mix of inputs

1. Shortages of a particular labor or material resource
2. Attempts by managers to reduce production costs
3. Human error
4. Random error

When variances from the standard mix occur, accountants can measure a mix variance and a yield variance by dividing the material quantity variance and the labor efficiency variance each into two parts. The **mix variance** measures the amount of cost variance caused by using a different **proportion** of inputs than defined by the standards. The **yield variance** measures the amount of cost variance caused by using more or fewer **total** inputs than standard.

Mix and Yield Variances for Materials

We repeat below the calculation of the per-pound standards for materials given earlier for the Dixie Chocolate Company:

	Standard Quantity per Pound of Output	Cost per Gallon	Cost per Pound of Candy
Cocoa syrup	.075 gal	$9.00	$.675
Milk	.090 gal	1.50	.135
Liquid sugar	.025 gal	3.00	.075
Flavoring	.010 gal	6.50	.065
Total	.200 gal		$.95

The $.95 a pound standard material cost for candy occurs with the standard mix of materials described above. On the **average**, .2 or ⅕ gallon of material input is required for 1 pound of product output. The average cost of a gallon of input given the standard mix of materials is $4.75 per gallon. (At the standard mix per 10 pounds of candy there are 2 gallons of input at a total cost of $9.50; therefore, the average cost of 1 gallon of input is $9.50/2 gallons, or $4.75.) The average cost of inputs at the standard mix and price is called the **average standard cost** of material inputs. Using the standard and actual costs and quantities it is possible to compute the material mix variance and the material yield variance.

Material mix variance. The **material mix variance** measures the amount of variance caused by using a different mix of material inputs than the standard proportion of inputs. The objective of measuring the mix variance is to determine the economic consequences of changes in the mix of materials.

High-cost inputs have a standard cost higher than the average standard cost of all inputs

We define the **average standard cost** of material inputs as the average cost of materials given the mix of inputs at the standard quantities. Any material whose standard cost is higher than the average standard cost of inputs is referred to as a **high-cost input.** Any material whose standard cost is lower than the average standard cost of material inputs is referred to as a **low-cost input.** The mix variance is favorable for a high-cost material if less than the standard quantity of that material is used in making the product; it is unfavorable if more than the standard quantity of the material is used. The reverse is true for a low-cost material: For a low-cost material, the material mix variance is favorable when more than the standard quantity is used in making the product and unfavorable if less than the standard quantity of the material is used. The material mix variance formula is

$$\text{Mix variance} = (\text{Standard quantity} - \text{Actual quantity}) \times (\text{Standard cost of the individual input} - \text{Average standard cost of all inputs})$$

Calculating the material mix variance. The material mix variance for the candy example is presented in the top half of Figure 16-6. The average standard cost of materials is $4.75 per gallon as shown earlier. Each raw material that has a standard cost higher than $4.75 per gallon is a high-cost input, and each raw material that has a standard cost less than $4.75 is a low-cost input. In the candy example cocoa syrup and flavoring are high-cost inputs, and liquid sugar and milk are low-cost inputs.

The comparison of standard and actual quantity for each material in the mix variance is identical to that of a material quantity variance analysis. The standard quantity of each raw material is merely the amount of material that **should have been used** given the quantity of output. It is computed by multiplying actual output by the standard quantity per unit of output for each raw material. For example, the standard quantity of cocoa syrup is 4,500 gallons (60,000 pounds of output × .075 gallon of cocoa syrup per pound of candy), and the standard quantity of milk is 5,400 gallons (60,000 pounds × .09 gallon per pound of output). These per-unit standards were computed earlier; actual quantities used for each material are given in Figure 16-2 on page 643.

Dixie Chocolate Company
Material Mix and Yield Variances
First Quarter 1986

Material Mix Variance

Mix variance = (Standard quantity − Actual quantity) × (Standard cost − Average standard cost)

Cocoa syrup	(4,500 gal − 4,100 gal)($9.00 − $4.75) =	$1,700 F	
Milk	(5,400 gal − 6,000 gal)($1.50 − $4.75) =	1,950 F	
Liquid sugar	(1,500 gal − 1,400 gal)($3.00 − $4.75) =	175 U	
Flavoring	(600 gal − 800 gal)($6.50 − $4.75) =	350 U	
Mix variance			$3,125 F

Material Yield Variance

Yield variance = (Actual input × Average standard cost of inputs) − (Actual output × Standard cost of output)

12,300 gallons × $4.75 per gallon	= $58,425	
Less 60,000 pounds × $.95 per pound	= 57,000	
Yield variance		1,425 U
Material quantity variance		$1,700 F

Figure 16-6 **The direct material quantity variance is separated into mix and yield variances. The total of the mix and yield variances equals the quantity variance.**

In a mix variance, using less high-cost inputs or more low-cost inputs than standard is favorable

To find the mix variance, the difference between standard and actual quantities is multiplied by the difference between the **standard cost of each material** and the **average standard cost,** which in this example is $4.75 per gallon. For instance, during the first quarter of 1986, Dixie used 400 gallons less cocoa syrup than standard. Cocoa syrup is a high-cost input because it has a standard cost of $9 per gallon, which is $4.25 per gallon higher than the average standard cost of $4.75. The computation gives a $1,700 favorable variance (400 gallons × $4.25 per gallon difference). This **mix variance** is favorable because the company used less than the standard quantity of a high-cost input. In other words, if the company is able to substitute a low-cost input for cocoa syrup, which is a high-cost input, a net cost savings should result.

The second raw material, milk, has a standard quantity of 5,400 gallons, but 6,000 gallons were used. Milk is a low-cost item, costing $1.50 per gallon, or $3.25 a gallon less than the average standard cost of inputs. If more than the standard quantity of a low-cost input is used, a favorable variance occurs. You may wonder how one can obtain a favorable variance by using more than the standard quantity of an input. Logic tells us that we would be better off if less milk had been used. However, a certain quantity of raw material is required to produce 1 pound of chocolate candy.

The mix variance measures the effect of changing the relative amounts of materials, not the effect of changing the quantity of an individual material. If changing the proportion of material means reducing the quantity of a high-cost material and increasing the quantity of a low-cost material, the variance from this change in mix is favorable, because the cost per pound of output will be lower if other inputs remain constant. Therefore, the mix variance for milk is $1,950 favorable (600 gallons × $3.25 per gallon less than the average standard cost of inputs).

The remaining two inputs are analyzed in the same fashion as cocoa syrup and milk. Dixie used less liquid sugar than standard, but sugar is a low-cost material relative to the average cost of inputs. Using less than average of a low-cost input yields an unfavorable mix variance. Finally, the company used more than the standard quantity of flavoring, which is a high-cost resource. The result is an unfavorable mix variance for flavoring. If each variance computation is made in strict algebraic fashion, all positive outcomes are favorable mix variances (F) and all negative outcomes are unfavorable mix variances (U). For example:

All positive outcomes are favorable mix variances and all negative outcomes are unfavorable mix variances

Mix variance = (Standard quantity − Actual quantity) × (Standard cost − Average standard cost)

Cocoa syrup	= (4,500 − 4,100)($9.00 − $4.75)			
	= (400) × ($4.25)	= $1,700	=	$1,700 F
Milk	= (5,400 − 6,000)($1.50 − $4.75)			
	= (−600) × (−$3.25)	= $1,950	=	1,950 F
Liquid sugar	= (1,500 − 1,400)($3.00 − $4.75)			
	= (100) × (−$1.75)	= −$175	=	175 U
Flavoring	= (600 − 800)($6.50 − $4.75)			
	= (−200) × ($1.75)	= −$350	=	350 U

This approach works every time if the analysis is structured as above. If the **order** of any set of variables is reversed, however, the sign will be incorrect.

Material yield variance. **Yield** can be described as the amount of output derived from a certain amount of input. The **material yield variance** is the difference between the actual and the expected yield from some actual amount of input. For example, the Dixie Chocolate Company expects a yield of 5 pounds of dark chocolate from each gallon of input, as calculated on page 647 (.2 gallon of input per pound of candy means 5 pounds of candy for 1 gallon of input.) Actual production output can be compared with actual inputs to measure the yield variance. The yield variance for the Dixie Chocolate Company is presented in Figure 16-6 on page 649. It is computed as follows:

Yield variance = (Actual quantity of inputs during the period
× Average standard cost of inputs)
− (Actual quantity of outputs for the period
× Standard cost of outputs)

The actual input of 12,300 gallons is merely the sum of the quantities of the four materials used during the period as shown in Figure 16-2 on page 643. The expected output from this quantity of input is 61,500 pounds of candy (12,300 gallons of input/.2 gallon of input per pound of candy). The company's yield of candy was 1,500 pounds short of standard (61,500 pounds of output at standard − 60,000 pounds of actual output). The standard materials cost is $.95 per pound of candy; therefore the yield variance is $1,425 unfavorable (1,500 pounds × $.95 per pound). The yield variance is unfavorable because the company did not get as much output as it should have based on the standards. An easy method of computing the material yield variance is to multiply the **actual inputs** times their **average standard cost** and compare that amount with the **actual outputs** times their **standard material cost.** If the outputs at standard cost are more than the inputs at average standard cost, the material yield variance is favorable. If the reverse is true, the material yield variance is unfavorable.

The yield variance is the difference between actual and expected yield for a specified amount of input

When the favorable mix variance of $3,125 and the unfavorable yield variance of $1,425 are combined, the result is the material quantity variance of $1,700 F shown in Figure 16-3. Often a favorable mix variance caused by substituting a lower-cost material for a higher-cost one is partially or entirely offset by an unfavorable yield variance. The lower-cost material may create more waste, shrinkage, or some other production problem.

Interpreting the variances. Material price, mix, and yield variances help managers isolate the cost effects of modifying the mix of inputs. However, the mere calculation of variances does not complete the variance analysis process. Typically management wants to determine the cause of changes in the input mix and the effect of those changes on costs and product quality. The input mix may have been altered from standard because of temporary or permanent resource scarcity, changing resource prices, human errors, random errors, or attempts at improving production methods or costs. Input mix changes may also affect product quality. The manager must determine the nature or cause of the variances before appropriate actions can be taken.

Investigation by managers may determine that product quality is adversely affected by a particular change in input mix. The savings in input cost may be more than offset by the decline in gross margin from lost sales. Another investigation might indicate that a new materials distribution system has been ineffective in supplying production operations with the correct type and quantity of materials. Machinery malfunctions, production employee errors, computer programming errors for the production activity, or faulty materials are other possible causes of input mix changes. Analysis of the causes of mix changes and the appropriate management action are determined by the nature of the situation being analyzed. In many cases mix and yield variances are an important part of the total variance analysis.

Mix and Yield Variances for Labor

Mix and yield variances can be computed when there are multiple labor classifications

Sometimes managers are able to modify the mix of labor used to produce a product or service. A construction company may use apprentice carpenters instead of journeymen carpenters to frame houses, or a manufacturer may use less-skilled labor for assembly activities when standards call for skilled labor. Changes from the expected mix of labor resources may occur because of labor shortages, changes in production schedules, attempts to reduce costs, strikes, and for other reasons. Whatever the cause of using a mix of labor other than standard, it is usually desirable to know the economic effect. A labor efficiency variance may not provide managers with the kind of information needed to manage labor resources effectively. The labor efficiency variance may be divided into a labor mix variance and a labor yield variance to provide more detailed labor variance information. Figure 16-7 presents the labor mix and yield variances for the Dixie Chocolate Company.

Labor mix variance. The standard hours for each classification of labor are

Standard hours = Standard quantity per unit × Output

Skilled labor = .04 hour per pound × 60,000 pounds = 2,400 hours

General labor = .02 hour per pound × 60,000 pounds = 1,200 hours

The average standard rate for labor is the weighted average cost of labor using the standard mix of labor resources. It can be determined in two ways. One is to weight the cost of each labor classification by the relative amount of hours used in production. In this example, for each hour of general labor 2 hours of skilled labor are used. Therefore, the weighted average cost of labor is:

2 hours	× $9.00	=	$18.00
1 hour	× 4.50	=	4.50
3 hours		=	$22.50

Weighted average ($22.50/3 hr) = $7.50/hr

Another method is to use the standard cost of labor for 1 pound of candy and convert the cost to a labor cost per hour.

Dixie Chocolate Company
Labor Mix and Yield Variances
First Quarter 1986

Labor Mix Variance

Mix variance = (Standard hours − Actual hours) × (Standard rate − Average standard rate)

Skilled labor	(2,400 hr − 2,500 hr)($9.00 − $7.50) =	$150 U	
General labor	(1,200 hr − 1,050 hr)($4.50 − $7.50) =	450 U	
Mix variance			$600 U

Labor Yield Variance

Yield variance = (Actual hours × Average standard rate) − (Output × Standard cost of output)

	3,550 hours × $7.50 per hour =	$26,625	
	60,000 pounds × $.45 per pound =	27,000	
Yield variance			375 F
Labor efficiency variance			$225 U

Figure 16-7 **In some situations it may be appropriate to separate the labor efficiency variance into a mix and a yield variance. The Dixie Chocolate Company had a favorable labor yield variance, but it was more than offset by an unfavorable labor mix variance caused by using a higher proportion of expensive labor.**

	Quantity per pound	× Labor Rate	= Cost per Pound
Skilled labor	= .04 hr per pound ×	$9.00	= $.36 per pound
General labor	= .02 hr per pound ×	$4.50	= .09 per pound
Total labor	= .06 hr per pound		$.45 per pound

Labor cost using the standard labor mix is $.45 per pound for .06 hour of labor; therefore, 1 hour of labor at the average standard rate is $.45/.06 hour, or $7.50 per hour. By comparing the average standard labor cost of $7.50 per hour with the two standard labor rates, you can see that skilled labor is a high-cost resource whose rate is greater than average, and general labor is a low-cost resource.

During the first quarter of 1986, Dixie used more skilled labor and less general labor than required by the standards. With a greater proportion of a high-cost resource used, the skilled labor mix variance is unfavorable. Similarly, less general labor was used than standard, but general labor is a low-cost labor resource. Therefore, it also has an unfavorable mix variance. The total labor mix variance is $600 unfavorable.

Labor yield variance. The labor yield variance is similar to the material yield variance. The inputs, in this case total actual hours worked, are multiplied by the average standard wage rate. Subtracted from this amount is the output multiplied by its standard cost for labor. A special note of caution is needed here: The output is expressed in the same units as used in the material variance—a pound of candy in our example—**but** the **standard cost of the output** refers to the standard cost of the labor used to produce the candy. Therefore, we multiply the 60,000 pounds of output by the standard labor cost of $.45 per pound, whereas we used the $.95 per pound standard material cost when computing the material yield variance. The 3,550 actual labor hours are taken from the schedule of actual costs in Figure 16-2. The computation of the yield variance is shown in Figure 16-7. The $375 favorable yield variance indicates that the output achieved was greater than expected based on the hours of labor used.

Interpreting the variances. In this example the favorable **labor yield variance** of $375 is more than offset by the unfavorable **labor mix variance** of $600. The net result, of course, is the $225 unfavorable **labor efficiency variance** shown in Figure 16-4. Typically a higher proportion of skilled labor results in a favorable labor yield variance. The objective is to generate a large enough labor yield variance to more than offset an unfavorable labor mix variance. Just the reverse is true if management attempts to reduce production costs by substituting lower-cost labor for higher-cost labor. Under these conditions management hopes to create a large enough mix variance to more than offset an unfavorable yield variance that might occur.

PERFORMANCE REPORTING FOR NONMANUFACTURING ACTIVITIES

Standards may be used for many nonmanufacturing activities

Most of the standard cost discussion in this and previous chapters is illustrated with manufacturing examples. Although standards are widely used in planning and controlling manufacturing activities, standards are also applicable in many other types of business activities. Some marketing and administrative activities may be monitored using standard costs. The ingenuity of managers and the nature of the cost-benefit relationships are the primary limitations on the type and amount of standard cost information a firm can develop. Our purpose here is to illustrate the use of standard cost variance analysis reports for nonmanufacturing activities. The example presented is for marketing activities.

Business firms can establish standards for marketing activities such as sales volume, unit prices, product sales mix, and contribution margin. To illustrate, consider the example of the Country Road Bike Shoppe, which sells three types of bicycles: a twelve-speed, a five-speed, and a single-speed model. The company establishes standards for sales mix, sales volume, variable costs, and contribution margins. Standards for sales and contribution margins for 1986 are presented in Figure 16-8.

The **standard unit variable cost** includes product cost, marketing cost, and any variable administrative costs per unit of product. The **standard unit contribution margin** is the sales price less the variable cost per unit, and the **total standard contribution margin** is the unit contribution margin times the expected sales volume in units. The average unit selling price is merely the weighted average price of all the budgeted units of sales at the expected sales volume and sales mix. No single product sells for $165, but on the **average** a sale results in $165 of revenue. Similarly, the **average standard contribution margin** of $66 per unit is the weighted average contribution margin on expected sales.

With a variety of products available for sale, we can define high-profit items and low-profit items. A **high-profit item** is a product whose contribution margin is greater than the average standard contribution margin; a **low-profit item** is a product whose contribution margin is less than the average standard contribution margin. In our example, twelve-speed bicycles are high-profit products and five-speed and single-speed bicycles are low-profit items.

Figure 16-9 presents the actual results for the bicycle shop for the year. As is often the case, actual results are somewhat different from expectations. Sales volumes and contribution margins for each product differ from those expected, resulting in a lower average unit selling price and a

Country Road Bike Shoppe
Budgeted Sales and Contribution Margins
For the Year 1986

Bicycle Model	Unit Sales Price	Sales Volume in Units	Sales	Unit Variable Cost	Unit Contribution Margin	Total Contribution Margin
Twelve-speed	$260	200	$ 52,000	$143	$117	$23,400
Five-speed	150	700	105,000	93	57	39,900
Single-speed	80	100	8,000	53	27	2,700
Totals		1,000	$165,000			$66,000

Average unit selling price = Sales/Sales volume in units
= $165,000/1,000 units
= $165 per unit

Average contribution margin = Total contribution margin/Sales volume in units
= $66,000/1,000 units
= $66 per unit

Figure 16-8 The Country Road Bike Shoppe creates standards for sales volume, sales mix, and contribution margin. The standards are presented here.

Country Road Bike Shoppe
Actual Sales and Contribution Margin Data
For the Year 1986

Bicycle Model	Unit Sales Price	Sales Volume in Units	Sales	Unit Variable Cost	Unit Contribution Margin	Total Contribution Margin
Twelve-speed	$260	300	$ 78,000	$150	$110	$33,000
Five-speed	145	600	87,000	92	53	31,800
Single-speed	90	300	27,000	56	34	10,200
Totals		1,200	$192,000			$75,000

Average unit selling price = Sales/Sales volume in units
= $192,000/1,200 units
= $160 per unit

Average unit contribution margin = Total contribution margin/Sales volume in units
= $75,000/1,200 units
= $62.50 per unit

Figure 16-9 **Actual sales results are presented above in the same format used to present the standards.**

lower average unit contribution margin than standard. However, the total contribution margin is $75,000, or $9,000 higher than expected. Although a manager can often obtain some information from the standard and actual data in reports such as Figures 16-8 and 16-9, systematic analysis of variances typically provides far more information for decision making. In this example we discuss three variances: a contribution margin variance, a sales quantity variance, and a mix variance.

Contribution Margin Variance

The contribution margin variance is the difference between the expected and the actual contribution margin

A **contribution margin variance** measures the amount of variance caused by the actual contribution margin being different from the expected contribution margin. The contribution margin variance is computed as follows:

Contribution margin variance = (Standard contribution margin per unit
− Actual contribution margin per unit)
× Actual units sold

The contribution margin variance analysis for Country Road Bike Shoppe is presented in Figure 16-10 together with the sales quantity and sales mix variances.

The expected and actual contribution margins for each product are presented in Figures 16-8 and 16-9. The difference between expected and actual contribution margin is multiplied by the actual quantity sold. The

Country Road Bike Shoppe
Sales Variance Analysis Report
For the Year 1986

Contribution Margin Variance

(Standard contribution margin − Actual contribution margin) × Actual units

Twelve-speed ($117 − $110)(300 units) = $2,100 U		
Five-speed ($ 57 − $ 53)(600 units) = 2,400 U		
Single-speed ($ 27 − $ 34)(300 units) = 2,100 F		
Total contribution margin variance		$ 2,400 U

Sales Quantity Variance

(Total expected sales − Total actual sales)
× Average standard contribution margin

(1,000 units − 1,200 units)($66)	13,200 F

Sales Mix Variance

(Expected sales in units − Actual sales in units)
× (Expected contribution margin per unit of product
− Average standard contribution margin)

Twelve-speed (200 units − 300 units)($117 − $66) =	$5,100 F	
Five-speed (700 units − 600 units)($ 57 − $66) =	900 F	
Single-speed (100 units − 300 units)($ 27 − $66) =	7,800 U	
Total mix variance		1,800 U
Total variance		$ 9,000 F

Figure 16-10 **This performance report isolates the contribution margin variance, the quantity variance, and the mix variance.**

contribution margin variance addresses the question, Given the actual sales, how much different would profit have been if the expected contribution margin had occurred rather than the actual contribution margin? For instance, if the contribution margin for twelve-speed bicycles had been the standard of $117 a unit instead of the actual contribution margin of $110, the company's profit would have been $2,100 higher ($7 × 300 twelve-speed bicycles). Likewise profit could have been $4 a unit higher if five-speed bicycles had attained their expected unit contribution margin. Since 600 five-speed bicycles were sold, the company's profit was $2,400 lower because of the lower-than-expected contribution margin. A higher-than-standard contribution margin is achieved for single-speed bicyles, which in total provide $2,100 more profit than would be the case with the standard contribution margin. The total of $2,400 U is the net result of all the contribution margin variances. It tells us that fluctuations from the standard contribution margins have decreased profit by $2,400 in 1986.

Sales Quantity Variance

The sales quantity variance looks at the total units sold and the average profit per unit

The **sales quantity variance,** like the yield variance, deals with total quantities rather than with specific products of the sales mix. The sales quantity variance addresses the question, Did we sell more or less total units than expected? This variance is an **effectiveness** measurement. More units than standard means a favorable variance, and less units than standard means an unfavorable variance. The sales quantity variance should not be confused with the material quantity variance, which is primarily an **efficiency** measure that asks, Did we use more or less material than we should have, given the amount of production? The sales quantity variance is determined by the difference between expected and actual sales and the average contribution margin:

$$\text{Sales quantity variance} = \left(\begin{matrix}\text{Total expected}\\ \text{units of sales}\end{matrix} - \begin{matrix}\text{Total actual}\\ \text{units of sales}\end{matrix}\right) \times \left(\begin{matrix}\text{Average standard contribution}\\ \text{margin per unit}\end{matrix}\right)$$

The sales quantity variance in Figure 16-10 is a large favorable variance, because the bicycle store sold 20 percent more bicycles than expected. Notice that the sales quantity variance does not consider the mix of the units sold. High-profit and low-profit items are equally important in computing the quantity variance. Variances caused by selling a different product mix than expected are discussed next.

Sales Mix Variance

With sales mix, the objective is to sell more of the high-profit items instead of the low-profit items

The **sales mix variance** measures the profit consequences of selling products in amounts different from the expected sales mix. In terms of sales mix only, managers generally want to increase the sales of high-profit items relative to the sales of low-profit items. For any particular volume of sales, managers prefer to sell a greater proportion of high-profit items and a smaller proportion of low-profit items. Therefore, a favorable mix variance occurs whenever sales of a high-profit item exceed expected sales or whenever sales of a low-profit item fall short of expected sales. Unfavorable sales mix variances occur when sales of low-profit items exceed the standard quantity or sales of high-profit items are less than expected. Note that the sales mix variance has characteristics similar to a production mix variance, where the object is to use more low-cost inputs and less high-cost inputs. The computation of the sales mix variance is as follows:

$$\text{Sales mix variance} = \left(\begin{matrix}\text{Expected sales}\\ \text{in units}\end{matrix} - \begin{matrix}\text{Actual sales}\\ \text{in units}\end{matrix}\right) \times \left(\begin{matrix}\text{Expected}\\ \text{contribution margin}\\ \text{per unit of product}\end{matrix} - \begin{matrix}\text{Average standard}\\ \text{contribution margin}\\ \text{per unit of all products}\end{matrix}\right)$$

Figure 16-10 includes the sales mix variance at the bottom of the report. The expected sales quantities and contribution margins and the average standard contribution margin are found in Figure 16-8. Actual sales quantities and contribution margins are presented in Figure 16-9.

One hundred more twelve-speed bicycles were sold than expected, and because the twelve-speed bicycle is a high-profit item this results in a favorable mix variance of $5,100. Five-speed bicycles, a low-profit item, fall 100 units short of standard sales, yielding a favorable mix variance of $900. More single-speed bicycles were sold than expected, but single-speeds are low-profit products. More than standard sales of a low-profit product means an unfavorable sales mix variance, in this case $7,800 U. The total sales mix variance is $1,800 unfavorable, indicating that the net effect of selling a product mix different from the expected one is $1,800 unfavorable.

Some people have difficulty understanding why selling more of a low-profit item yields an unfavorable variance. The point to remember is that the mix variance measures only the effect of selling a different sales mix from what was expected. The effect of sales volume changes is dealt with in the quantity variance. Consequently, if a low-profit item sells more than the standard quantity, it appears as a favorable quantity variance and an unfavorable mix variance. To illustrate, the bicycle shop sold 200 more single-speed bicycles than expected. This resulted in an unfavorable mix variance of $7,800—200 bicycles × ($27 − $66) a bicycle. However, it also contributed $13,200 of favorable sales quantity variance (200 bicycles × $66 a bicycle). The net effect is that selling the 200 additional single-speed bicycles contributed an additional $5,400 of profit to the shop. Whenever variance analysis is performed, the analyst must constantly be aware of precisely what is being measured by the analysis.

With the sales mix variance, negative outcomes are favorable and positive outcomes are unfavorable

Earlier we mentioned that if production mix variances are solved using algebraic rules, all positive answers mean favorable variances and all negative answers mean unfavorable variances. Just the **reverse** is true for sales mix variances. Positive outcomes are unfavorable variances and negative outcomes are favorable variances. The reason for the difference is that production mix attempts to minimize cost, while sales mix attempts to maximize profits.

SUMMARY

Standard cost variance analysis reports provide managers with much detailed and useful information for planning and controlling many types of business activities. Material and labor variances are widely used and often provide managers with adequate variance information to make intelligent decisions about material use and about the management of production activities. However, when multiple inputs are used to produce a product and the mix of inputs can be varied, variance analysis reports may need to be expanded. The material quantity variance and labor efficiency variance can be divided into mix and yield variances.

A **material mix variance** measures the effect of using a proportion of material inputs that differs from the standard mix of materials. The **material yield variance** measures the cost effect of using more or less total inputs than required by standards.

In terms of the mix of resources, managers prefer to use more low-cost inputs and fewer high-cost inputs, which results in a favorable mix variance. A **high-cost input** is one whose standard cost is greater than the **average standard cost** of inputs. The size of the mix variance is determined by the difference between the standard and the actual quantity and the difference between the standard cost of the input and the average standard cost of all inputs.

The yield variance is used to compare the inputs at standard cost with the outputs at standard cost. Actual inputs are multiplied by the average standard cost of inputs, and outputs are multiplied by the standard cost per unit of output.

Usually managers are interested in determining the cause of changes in the input mix and the cost effect of such changes. Factors influencing input mix are human error, random error, resource shortages, and attempts to reduce costs. Part of the information used by managers to determine the cause and cost effect of input mix changes consists of mix and yield variances.

Labor mix and **labor yield variances** can be computed for the labor efficiency variance if multiple labor classifications are used to produce the product. The computational process is the same as for material mix and yield variances except that labor data are substituted for material data.

Many nonmanufacturing activities can benefit from a good standard cost system. If standards are created for sales volume, sales price, sales mix, and variable costs, then several detailed variance analyses can be performed. Included are contribution margin variances, sales quantity variances, and sales mix variances.

The **contribution margin variance** measures the difference in profit or contribution margin when actual contribution margins are different from expected contribution margins. The **sales quantity variance** measures the effect of selling more or less **total** units than expected. The variance is based solely on the total number of units sold regardless of the mix of units, and the computation is based on the weighted average profit of all products. The **sales mix variance** measures the impact on profits of selling a different mix of products from the standard sales mix. A favorable variance occurs when more than the standard amount of a high-profit product is sold or when less than the standard amount of a low-profit product is sold. High or low profit is determined by the profit margin of individual products compared with the weighted average profit margin for the standard product mix.

KEY TERMS

average standard contribution margin *(655)*
average standard cost *(648)*
contribution margin variance *(656)*
high-cost input *(648)*
high-profit item *(655)*
labor efficiency variance *(644)*
labor mix variance *(652)*
labor rate variance *(644)*
labor yield variance *(654)*
low-cost input *(648)*
low-profit item *(655)*
material mix variance *(648)*
material price variance *(643)*
material quantity variance *(643)*
material yield variance *(650)*
mix variance *(647)*
sales mix variance *(658)*
sales quantity variance *(658)*
total contribution margin *(655)*
unit contribution margin *(655)*
unit variable cost *(655)*
variance analysis *(643)*
yield variance *(647)*

QUESTIONS

1. Helen Morgan was hired recently as the controller in a manufacturing firm. One of her first actions was to develop a standard cost system for the company. Her first weekly standard cost variance analysis report, presented below, summarized the cost of variances for one of the company's products. The company president, not familiar with standard costs and variances, commented, "I cannot tell what it cost to produce this product." Explain briefly the meaning of the variances and compute the product cost for the president.

Units produced	1,000
Standard cost	$80 per unit
Material price variance	$1,500 U
Material quantity variance	$2,500 U
Labor rate variance	$2,000 U
Labor efficiency variance	$1,800 F

2. How do mix and yield variances relate to material quantity or labor efficiency variances?
3. What kind of situations lend themselves to mix and yield variance analysis? How does a mix and yield variance analysis assist managers in such situations?
4. How can using more than the standard amount of some resource produce a favorable variance?
5. Cite several reasons why the actual mix of production resources used may differ from the standard mix of production resources.
6. The monthly variance analysis reports have just been released. The assembly line report shows:

Labor mix variance	$26,000 U
Labor yield variance	$37,400 F

The assembly line supervisor states, "I knew we should not have hired all those skilled workers. Look at the horrible labor mix variance we generated." Do you agree with the supervisor's assessment? Explain.

7. "Standard costs are for manufacturing activities, not for marketing and administration. Standards for nonmanufacturing activities serve no useful purpose and waste a lot of time." Respond to the preceding remarks.
8. Describe the nature and use of a contribution margin variance analysis.
9. A regional sales manager just received a monthly sales performance report and is concerned about having an unfavorable sales mix variance on a product for which sales were double the expected amount. How can there by an unfavorable variance on a product whose sales were significantly higher than standard?
10. "A sales mix variance and a production mix variance are the same variance for two different types of activities." Respond.

EXERCISES

Ex. 16-1 Material price and quantity variances. Able Company uses four raw materials in its production of weight benches. Standard costs are given below.

	Material Standards per Unit	
Resource	**Quantity**	**Cost**
Tubular steel	25 ft	$.90/ft
Plywood	6 sq ft	.80/sq ft
Foam padding	8 sq ft	.40/sq ft
Vinyl	10 sq ft	.25/sq ft

	Actual Results	
Resource	**Quantity**	**Cost**
Tubular steel	21,100 ft	$.85/ft
Plywood	5,200 sq ft	.94/sq ft
Foam padding	6,150 sq ft	.36/sq ft
Vinyl	7,600 sq ft	.28/sq ft

Weight benches produced = 800 units.

Required:

a. Compute the material price variance.
b. Compute the material quantity variance.

Ex. 16-2 Labor rate and efficiency variances. Hawthorne, Ltd., identifies three labor classifications for employees who manufacture oak rolltop desks. Labor standards for the desk are:

Labor Classification	Standard Hours	Labor Rate
Cutting	8 hours per desk	$8.00 per hour
Assembly	10	7.00
Finishing and crating	6	7.50

April production was 900 desks. The actual labor costs incurred were:

Labor Classification	Hours Worked	Total Labor Cost
Cutting	7,760 hours	$60,528
Assembly	8,700	62,640
Finishing and crating	5,600	42,560

Required:

a. Compute the labor rate variance for April.

b. Compute the labor efficiency variance for April.

Ex. 16-3 Direct material and direct labor variances. Following are standard and actual cost data for the production of a driveway sealer compound that is sold in 5-gallon cans.

Standards

Material:	
Silicate compounds	3 pounds per can @ $.80 per pound
Petroleum solvents	2 gallons per can @ $.50 per gallon
Labor:	
Skilled	¼ hour per can @ $9.00 per hour
General	⅒ hour per can @ $4.50 per hour

Actual Results

Production	25,000 cans
Material:	
Silicate compounds	72,000 pounds, cost $61,200
Petroleum solvents	51,000 gallons, cost $24,480
Labor:	
Skilled	6,000 hours, cost $55,500
General	2,400 hours, cost $11,040

Required:

a. Compute the material price and quantity variances.

b. Compute the labor rate and efficiency variances.

Ex. 16-4 Basic material mix and yield variances. A chemical products company has the following raw materials standards for the production of one batch of its product, Zoleene-X. A typical production batch yields 7,500 cans of output.

Material	Quantity	Price	Total Cost
Zelvon-1	3,750 gal	$6.00/gal	$22,500
Zoline-4	2,250 gal	3.00/gal	6,750
Zuklar-3	1,500 gal	9.00/gal	13,500
Totals	7,500 gal		$42,750

During November, 42,000 cans of Zoleene-X were produced and the following materials quantities and costs were incurred.

Material	Quantity	Price	Total Cost
Zelvon-1	24,750 gal	$ 5.70/gal	$141,075
Zoline-4	13,200 gal	3.45/gal	45,540
Zuklar-3	6,750 gal	10.50/gal	70,875
Totals	44,700 gal		$257,490

Required: Compute the material mix and yield variances for the production of Zoleene-X.

Ex. 16-5 **Material mix and yield variances.** A company produces a high-fiber axle grease for high-speed bearings. The grease is produced in 5,000-gallon vats. Below are standard cost data for materials for 5,000 gallons of output:

Material	Quantity	Input Cost	Total Cost
MQ	1,000 gal	$3.00/gal	$ 3,000
MR	3,500 gal	1.50/gal	5,250
MZ	1,500 gal	2.50/gal	3,750
Totals	6,000 gal		$12,000

During the month of April, 24,000 gallons of axle grease were produced and the following materials costs were incurred:

Material	Quantity	Input Cost	Total Cost
MQ	5,000 gal	$3.20/gal	$16,000
MR	18,000 gal	1.40/gal	25,200
MZ	6,000 gal	3.00/gal	18,000
Totals	29,000 gal		$59,200

Required: Compute the mix and yield variances for the April production of axle grease.

Ex. 16-6 **Material quantity, mix, and yield variances with shrinkage.** A company produces an adhesive compound by mixing two substances together. Materials standards for the product are

8 gallons of petroleum distillates ZG7	@ $ .60	=	$4.80
2 gallons of ketone compound YG7	@ 1.20	=	2.40
10 gallons of standard mix			$7.20

Each 10 gallons of standard mix yields 9 gallons of adhesive.

During October, 18,000 gallons of adhesive were manufactured using 14,500 gallons of petroleum distillates and 4,600 gallons of ketone compounds.

Required:

a. Calculate the material quantity variance.

b. Calculate the material mix and yield variances.

Ex. 16-7 **Understanding material variances.** The Swortage Company makes Moblies. Below are the standard material quantities and prices for the production of one Mobly.

Standard materials for the production of one Mobly:

Material T: 3 units @ $4 per unit
Material W: 5 units @ $3 per unit

The following summary of data are taken from the materials variance report for May, when 1,100 Moblies were manufactured:

Material price variance for T	$ 875.00 U
Quantity variance for T	800.00 U
Material price variance for W	1,160.00 F
Material quantity variance for W	900.00 U
Material yield variance	1,687.50 U
Material mix variance for W	112.50 F

Required: Calculate

a. The total material price variance.
b. The total material mix variance.
c. The material mix variance for T.
d. The standard quantity of material W for May.
e. The actual quantity of W used in May.
f. The actual cost per unit of W.
g. The total material variance for May.

Ex. 16-8 Labor efficiency, mix, and yield variances. Crosstown Roofing Company has created standard costs for residential roofing projects. The standard labor costs are given below for roofing an average house of 1,500 square feet.

Labor Classification	Hours	Rate
Skilled roofer	30	$12 per hour
Apprentice roofer	20	8
Laborers	10	5

During the past month the company installed 22 residential roofs using the following labor.

Labor Classification	Hours
Skilled roofer	630
Apprentice roofer	410
Laborers	350

Required:

a. Compute the labor efficiency variance for the month.
b. Compute the labor mix and yield variances.

Ex. 16-9 Sales variances. Fern decided to open a lemonade stand in her front yard during summer vacation. Her mother built her a stand from scrap lumber she found in the garage. Fern planned to sell two drinks. Her estimates of sales for the summer are presented below:

Product	Price per Glass	Sales in Units	Unit Variable Cost
Lemonade	$.30	600	$.21
Fruit punch	.20	400	.06

Based on the above, Fern expected to earn a profit of $110 during the summer. However, her actual profit was $124 despite the fact that she sold much less of the high-price drink and sold fewer total drinks than she expected. Being a fifth-grader, Fern has not had any accounting, and she asks you to explain why she made more money with fewer sales. Actual sales data are presented below.

Product	Price per Glass	Sales in Units	Unit Variable Cost
Lemonade	$.30	300	$.19
Fruit punch	.20	650	.06

Required:

a. Prepare a variance report including contribution margin, sales quantity, and sales mix variances.

b. Explain to Fern what your variance report means to her in terms of the performance of her business.

Ex. 16-10 **Analyzing marketing variances.** A manufacturing company makes three different sizes of bass boats. The 14-foot boat sells for $2,600, the 16-foot boat for $3,800, and the 18-foot boat for $6,100. The budget for the first quarter calls for production and sales of one hundred 14-foot boats, two hundred fifty 16-foot boats, and one hundred fifty 18-foot boats, for a total of 500 units. Manufacturing costs are $1,600 for the 14-foot, $2,400 for the 16-foot, and $3,800 for the 18-foot boat. Variable marketing and distribution costs are 10 percent of selling price.

During the first quarter of the year, actual production and sales were one hundred twenty 14-foot boats, two hundred twenty 16-foot boats, and two hundred 18-foot boats. Unit manufacturing costs were $1,650, $2,300, and $3,950, respectively, for the three types of boats. All boats were sold at their expected prices.

Required:

a. Compute the expected gross margin for the bass boat line for the first quarter of the year.

b. Prepare a marketing variance analysis, based on variances from gross margins.

Ex. 16-11 **Computing marketing variances.** H & M Corporation has budgeted the following sales for its doll product line:

Product	Quantity	Price	Cost	Margin	Total Margin
Pam Dream Doll	40,000	$3.50	$2.00	$1.50	$ 60,000
Pam Beach Doll	30,000	6.00	3.50	2.50	75,000
Pam Cowgirl Doll	20,000	4.00	2.00	2.00	40,000
Pam Party Doll	10,000	9.00	5.00	4.00	40,000
Totals	100,000				$215,000

Actual sales during the summer were as follows:

Product	Quantity	Price	Cost	Margin	Total Margin
Pam Dream Doll	42,000	$3.50	$1.80	$1.70	$ 71,400
Pam Beach Doll	35,000	6.50	3.80	2.70	94,500
Pam Cowgirl Doll	9,000	4.00	2.10	1.90	17,100
Pam Party Doll	12,000	9.50	5.20	4.30	51,600
Totals	98,000				$234,600

Required: Prepare a detailed analysis of the marketing variances, isolating the contribution margin variance, the sales quantity variance, and the sales mix variance.

Ex. 16-12 **(CMA) Computing standard quantities.** Danson Company is a chemical manufacturer which supplies industrial users. The company plans to introduce a new chemical solution and needs to develop a standard product cost for this new solution.

The new chemical solution is made by combining a chemical compound (nyclyn) and a solution (salex), boiling the mixture, adding a second compound (protet), and bottling the resulting solution in 10-liter containers. The initial mix, which is 10 liters in volume, consists of 12 kilograms of nyclyn and 9.6 liters of salex. A 20 percent reduction in volume occurs during the boiling process. The solution is then cooled slightly before 5 kilograms of protet are added; the addition of protet does not affect the total liquid volume.

The purchase prices of the raw materials used in the manufacture of this new chemical solution are as follows:

Nyclyn	$1.30 per kilogram
Salex	1.80 per liter
Protet	2.40 per kilogram

Required: Determine the standard quantity for each of the raw materials needed to produce a 10-liter container of Danson Company's new chemical solution and the standard materials cost of a 10-liter container of the new product.

PROBLEMS

P. 16-1 **Material price and quantity variances.** Arlington Company makes merchandising display cases that have the following materials standards:

Lumber	30 bd ft	@	$ .60 per bd ft
Glass	20 sq ft	@	2.00 per sq ft
Casement material	30 ft	@	1.10 per ft
Glue	.5 gal	@	8.00 per gal

Arlington Company made 60 display cases during January, incurring the following materials costs:

Item Purchased	Quantity Purchased	Total Cost	Quantity Used
Lumber	2,200 bd ft	$1,430	1,890 bd ft
Glass	800 sq ft	1,680	1,140 sq ft
Casement material	2,600 ft	2,652	1,740 ft
Glue	60 gal	525	42 gal

Required:

a. Compute the January material price variance for each of the materials used in the production of the display cases.

b. Compute the January material quantity variance for each of the materials used in the production of display cases.

P. 16-2 Direct labor rate and efficiency variances. Standard labor costs and times are presented below for the production of microcomputers.

Labor Classification	Direct Labor per Computer	Hourly Wage Rate
Molding	2.0	$ 9.00
Assembly	8.0	14.00
Testing	1.5	11.00
Finishing & packaging	2.5	12.00

The company manufactured 8,000 microcomputers during the first month of the quarter and 7,200 units were shipped to customers. The following labor costs were incurred in manufacturing the computers:

Labor Classification	Total Labor Hours	Total Labor Cost
Molding	16,900	$ 148,720
Assembly	61,300	876,590
Testing	11,200	127,680
Finishing & packaging	22,700	265,590
Totals	112,100	$1,418,580

Required:

a. Compute the labor rate variance for the month for each classification of labor and in total.

b. Compute the labor efficiency variance for the month for each labor classification and in total.

P. 16-3 Material price, mix, and yield variances. Smedley Smalsh had been producing high-quality garden fertilizer for many years. Until recently he never worried about production variances. But tough economic conditions are causing him some concern. He therefore called in a consultant to help him set production standards. But just looking at the standards for a typical 4-ton production run does not help. He calls you in to analyze April production data. Below are the standards as well as the production data for April 1986.

Standards

Raw Material	Price/Gallon	Gallons	Total Cost
B	$ 2.00	800	$1,600
Y	12.00	300	3,600
Z	8.00	100	800
Totals		1,200	$6,000

Expected yield from inputs = 4 tons

Actual Production

Raw Material	Price/Gallon	Gallons	Total Cost
B	$ 2.20	4,600	$10,120
Y	11.00	1,200	13,200
Z	9.00	700	6,300
Totals		6,500	$29,620

Actual yield = 20 tons

Required: Analyze the material price, mix, and yield variances using the production data.

P. 16-4 Price, mix, and yield variances for direct materials. Petry Manufacturing Company makes a wood glue for commercial use. The product is manufactured in batches of 5,000 gallons. It requires three raw materials. The standard quantities and costs for a batch are presented below.

Material	Quantity	Material Cost	Total Cost
KTN-2	5,000 lb	$3.00/lb	$15,000
KTR-4	17,500 lb	1.50/lb	26,250
KZX-5	7,500 lb	2.50/lb	18,750
Totals	30,000 lb		$60,000

During October the company produced 14,000 gallons of glue and incurred the following materials costs:

Material	Quantity	Material Cost	Total Cost
KTN-2	16,500 lb	$3.20/lb	$ 52,800
KTR-4	53,000 lb	1.40/lb	74,200
KZX-5	15,000 lb	3.00/lb	45,000
Totals	84,500 lb		$172,000

Required:

a. Compute the material price variances.
b. Compute the material quantity variances.
c. Compute the material mix variance.
d. Compute the material yield variance.
e. Compute the actual materials cost per unit of output.

P. 16-5 Labor mix and yield variances. Healthfield Manufacturing Company developed a plan to provide day care for children of its employees. The plan was based on an estimated 1,200 children in the day-care program. It included the following personnel requirements for children's care:

40 professional instructors @ $700 per month
20 teachers' aides @ $400 per month

The first month of operating the day-care center, 1,440 students enrolled in the program and the following labor resources were used:

37 professional instructors @ $730 per month
39 teachers' aides @ $420 per month

Required:

a. Compute the labor rate variance for each class of instructor and in total.
b. Compute the labor mix and yield variances.
c. Compute the expected and the actual instructor cost per student.

P. 16-6 Analysis of labor variances for professional services. Elec-Tec-Instruments, Ltd., planned to review and evaluate all product engineering specifications and standard costs for all its products. The purpose of the review was to detect errors or omissions, update requirements to reflect the current production environment of the firm, and provide more uniform decisions on standards and engineering specifications that had been developed over a number of years. This rather large project could not be undertaken solely by the company's current personnel without disrupting normal business activities. Therefore, college juniors studying engineering and accounting were hired for the summer to help with the job. In addition, some of the company's clerical staff were used. Professional staff from the engineering department and accounting department supervised student and clerical employees and made all evaluations and modifications of standards and specifications. Students and clerical employees cross-referenced standards with engineering specifications checked for numerical errors, classified data by product type and production activity, and generally served the professional staff in whatever capacity possible for completing the project.

Elec-Tec-Instruments established the following labor standards for the project:

Type of Labor	Expected Labor Time	Expected Labor Cost
Professional staff	3,000 hours	$45,000
Clerical	1,200 hours	6,000
Students	7,800 hours	31,200

Number of products to be reviewed = 300

During the project, management decided to train students to perform some of the easier evaluation functions in an effort to relieve professional staff members for their regular job activities. In early September the project was completed. The company accumulated the following data related to the project:

Type of Labor	Actual Labor Time	Actual Labor Cost
Professional staff	2,800 hours	$39,200
Clerical	1,400 hours	7,350
Students	10,000 hours	42,000

Number of products reviewed = 320

Required:

a. Compute unit standards for input and output.
b. Compute the labor rate and efficiency variances for the project.
c. Compute labor mix and yield variances from the data.
d. Compute the economic consequence of shifting students to activities originally planned for professional staff.

P. 16-7 **Labor variance analysis for a service activity.** The Longly County School Board has decided to establish an extensive achievement testing program for all students in the third, sixth, and ninth grades. The purpose of the program is to measure the performance of students in the school system against statewide averages. Teachers will do some of the testing, but outside help must be hired to handle much of the individual testing. Substitute teachers or teachers' aides can be hired to assist in testing but they are less efficient because they are not as familiar with each student or with the testing procedures as regular teachers. Expected time and personnel costs for testing the estimated 1,500 students are:

	Hours	Rate
Teachers	600	$7 per hour
Substitutes	2,100	6 per hour
Aides	3,300	4 per hour

During the current school year, 1,700 students were tested. A shortage of qualified substitute teachers required the use of more teacher's aides in the testing program than expected. Actual costs for the year are as follows:

	Hours	Cost
Teachers	600	$ 4,680
Substitutes	1,400	9,100
Aides	5,100	21,675
Total	7,100	$35,455

The school board is interested in data on the cost of the program compared with the original cost estimates. Also, the board would like to know the effect of the necessary modification in the staffing of the program.

Required:

a. Calculate the average standard labor cost, standard hours per student, and expected labor cost per student based on original estimates of cost.
b. Calculate the total variance of the labor cost for the program.
c. Compute labor rate and efficiency variances.
d. Prepare a labor mix and yield variance report and explain the meanings of these variances to the school board.

P. 16-8 **Prime cost variance analysis.** Jordan Corporation makes a variety of food products. Included is a beef stew, which is packaged in 2-pound cans. Production standards for beef stew are presented below for a normal cooking vat of 2,000 pounds of stew:

Material	Quantity (Pounds)	Cost per Pound	Total Cost
Beef	500	$1.71	$ 855
Beef broth	800	.20	160
Potatoes	500	.12	60
Tomato paste	300	.40	120
Sugar	100	.15	15
Total	2,200		$1,210

Labor	Hours	Rate	Total Cost
Mixing	24	$5.00	$120
Cooking	16	8.00	128
Total	40		$248

In the past month, 7,000 cans of beef stew were produced. The following production costs were incurred:

Material	Quantity (Pounds)	Cost per Pound	Total Cost
Beef	3,200	$1.80	$5,760
Beef broth	6,000	.18	1,080
Potatoes	3,600	.09	324
Tomato paste	2,200	.44	968
Sugar	600	.15	90
Total	15,600		$8,222

Labor	Hours	Rate	Total Cost
Mixing	150	$5.20	$ 780
Cooking	125	8.40	1,050
Total	275		$1,830

Required:

- **a.** Calculate the standard prime cost for one can of beef stew.
- **b.** Compute the material price and quantity variances.
- **c.** Determine the labor rate and efficiency variances.
- **d.** Find the material mix and yield variances.
- **e.** Compute the labor mix and yield variances.

P. 16-9 Multiple-input variance analysis. The By-Cracky-Snacky Company manufactures a variety of snack foods, including pretzel sticks, whose production standards are listed below for an 800-pound batch:

Material	Quantity (Pounds)	Unit Cost per Pound	Total Cost
Flour	600	$ .14	$ 84
Shortening	250	.48	120
Butter	100	1.20	120
Yeast	10	1.40	14
Salt	40	.15	6
Total	1,000		$344

Labor	Hours	Rate	Total Cost
Skilled	4	$8 per hour	$32
General	2	$4 per hour	8
Total	6		$40

The company packages pretzel sticks in 1-pound bags and sells them to wholesalers for 175 percent of standard prime cost. In November the company produced 9,000 pounds of pretzel sticks. Actual production costs were:

Material	Quantity (Pounds)	Total Cost
Flour	7,000	$ 840
Shortening	3,000	1,500
Butter	1,000	1,350
Yeast	110	132
Salt	420	63
Total	11,530	$3,885

Labor	Hours	Total Cost
Skilled	40	$336
General	30	126
Total	70	$462

Required:

a. Compute the material quantity and price variances.
b. Find the labor rate and efficiency variances.
c. Determine the material mix and yield variances.
d. Compute the price to wholesalers per bag of pretzels.

P. 16-10 Marketing variances analysis. The manager of the sporting goods department of the Big Bay Department Store recently decided to carry a line of downriggers used for deep-water trolling for lake trout and salmon. The downrigger line includes an electric-powered model that sells for $300, a manual model with a clutch and digital depth reader for $150, and a basic model for $80. The three units cost $160, $100, and $50 respectively. Each unit has commission and other variable costs associated with its sales and service, which amount to 10 percent of selling price. The department manager estimated he would sell 50 units a month during the 6-month fishing season. The expected sales mix of the downriggers was 20 percent, 50 percent, and 30 percent respectively.

The Big Bay Department Store started selling downriggers in April and during the first month 55 units were sold. The sales mix was 6 of the $300 model, 20 of the $150 model, and 29 of the $80 model. The manager of the sporting goods department was very pleased with the number of units sold, but the chief accountant for the store reported that the new product line failed to provide the expected amount of contribution margin. This was surprising to the department manager given the number of units sold and the fact that the units were all sold for their expected price. The store accountant noted that the cost of the units was actually $170, $85, and $52 respectively, instead of the expected amounts.

Required:

a. Compute the expected total product contribution for the new line of downriggers.
b. Prepare a detailed variance analysis for the downriggers for April.
c. Compute the actual product contribution for the month of April.
d. Explain to the sporting goods department manager why the expected product contribution was not achieved.

P. 16-11 Marketing variances. Vergouven Home Appliance Store sells three types of refrigerator-freezer units. The standard model has 15 cubic feet with a freezer at the top. The deluxe model is 18 cubic feet and frost-free and has an ice maker. The side-by-side model is 25 cubic feet and frost-free, and has an ice maker and 10 cubic feet of freezer space. In an effort to plan and control operations better, the store has prepared the following schedule of expected sales of refrigerators:

Refrigerator	Sales in Units	Price	Sales	Unit Variable Cost	Unit Contribution Margin	Total Contribution Margin
Standard	100	$400	$ 40,000	$300	$100	$10,000
Deluxe	300	600	180,000	420	180	54,000
Side-by-side	100	900	90,000	600	300	30,000
Total	500		$310,000			$94,000

During the year the store had the following refrigerator sales:

Refrigerator	Sales in Units	Price	Sales	Unit Variable Cost	Unit Contribution Margin	Total Contribution Margin
Standard	120	$410	$ 49,200	$290	$120	$14,400
Deluxe	360	560	201,600	420	140	50,400
Side-by-side	70	880	61,600	620	260	18,200
Total	550		$312,400			$83,000

Required: Prepare a variance analysis report for the store isolating the contribution margin variance, quantity variance, and sales mix variance.

P. 16-12 Sales variance analysis. Folsom Products Company sells four different types of microwave oven cookware. Presented below are expected and actual sales data for the four products.

Expected Data

Product	Units	Unit Price	Sales	Unit Variable Cost	Total Variable Cost	Contribution Margin
4-piece set	2,000	$20	$ 40,000	$8	$ 16,000	$12
Bacon-tray	6,000	10	60,000	6	36,000	4
Vegetable-dish	8,000	8	64,000	6	48,000	2
3-piece set	4,000	15	60,000	5	20,000	10
Total	20,000		$224,000		$120,000	

Fixed cost = \$35,000

Expected net income = Sales − Variable cost − Fixed cost

= \$224,000 − \$120,000 − \$35,000 = \$69,000

Actual Data

Product	Units	Unit Price	Sales	Unit Variable Cost	Total Variable Cost	Contribution Margin
4-piece set	3,000	\$20	\$ 60,000	\$9	\$ 27,000	\$11
Bacon-tray	5,000	9	45,000	6	30,000	3
Vegetable-dish	9,000	8	72,000	5	45,000	3
3-piece set	4,000	15	60,000	6	24,000	9
Total	21,000		\$237,000		\$126,000	

Fixed cost = \$35,000

Actual net income = \$237,000 − \$126,000 − \$35,000 = \$76,000

Required: Compute the contribution margin variance, sales quantity variance, and sales mix variance.

P. 16-13 (CMA) Computing and interpreting materials variances. The LAR Chemical Co. manufactures a wide variety of chemical compounds and liquids for industrial uses. The standard mix for producing a single batch of 500 gallons of one liquid is as follows:

Liquid Chemical	Quantity (in Gallons)	Cost (per Gallon)	Total Cost
Maxan	100	\$2.00	\$200
Salex	300	.75	225
Cralyn	225	1.00	225
Totals	625		\$650

There is a 20 percent loss in liquid volume during processing due to evaporation. The finished liquid is put into 10-gallon bottles for sale. Thus, the standard materials cost for a 10-gallon bottle is \$13.00.

The actual quantities of raw materials and the respective cost of the materials placed in production during November were as follows:

Liquid Chemical	Quantity (in Gallons)	Total Cost
Maxan	8,480	\$17,384
Salex	25,200	17,640
Cralyn	18,540	16,686
Totals	52,220	\$51,710

A total of 4,000 bottles (40,000 gallons) were produced during November.

Required:

a. Calculate the total raw material variance for the liquid product for November and then further analyze the total variance into a:

1. Material price variance.
2. Material mix variance.
3. Material yield variance.

b. Explain how LAR Chemical Co. could use each of the three material variances—price, mix, yield—to help control the cost to manufacture this liquid compound.

P. 16-14 Comprehensive standard cost variance analysis. The Hardrock Candy Company manufactures a number of different products in its Bloomingulch production facility. Below is the production information for the fourth quarter for its Christmas candy:

Standards

Material	Quantity	Price
Sugar	6 lb/10-lb carton of output	$ .06/lb
Syrup	1 gal/10-lb carton of output	2.60/gallon
Flavoring	1 qt/10-lb carton of output	4.00/gallon
Coloring	1 pt/10-lb carton of output	6.00/gallon
Labor	**Quantity**	**Rate**
Blending	4 hr per 100-lb case	$5.50/hr
Cooking	2 hr per 100-lb case	5.00/hr

MOH

Fixed cost	$21,000
Variable cost	$4.00/DLH
Expected level of activity	3,500 hr

Actual Results for the Period

Produced	60,000 lb of Christmas candy	
Material	**Quantity**	**Cost**
Sugar	37,000 lb	$ 2,960
Syrup	5,800 gal	20,300
Flavoring	1,400 gal	5,460
Coloring	700 gal	3,920
Labor	**Hours**	**Cost**
Blending	2,500	$13,250
Cooking	1,050	5,460
MOH		
$35,000		

Note: There are 2 pints in a quart, 4 quarts in a gallon.

Required:

a. Compute the material price and quantity variances.
b. Determine the labor rate and efficiency variances.
c. Compute overhead variances using the two-variance method.
d. Compute the standard cost of 1 pound of Christmas candy.
e. Compute the actual cost of 1 pound of Christmas candy.

CASE

Case 16-1 **(CMA) Comprehensive variance analysis.** The Markley Division of Rosette Industries manufactures and sells patio chairs. The chairs are manufactured in two versions—a metal model and a plastic model of a lesser quality. The company uses its own sales force to sell the chairs to retail stores and to catalog outlets. Generally, customers purchase both the metal and plastic versions.

Markley Division
Operating Results for the First Quarter

	Actual	Budget	Variance Favorable (Unfavorable)
Sales in units:			
Plastic model	60,000	50,000	10,000
Metal model	20,000	25,000	(5,000)
Sales revenue:			
Plastic model	$630,000	$500,000	$130,000
Metal model	300,000	375,000	(75,000)
Total sales	930,000	875,000	55,000
Less variable costs:			
Manufacturing (at standard):			
Plastic model	480,000	400,000	(80,000)
Metal model	200,000	250,000	50,000
Selling:			
Commissions	46,500	43,750	(2,750)
Bad debt allowance	9,300	8,750	(550)
Total variable costs (except variable manufacturing variances)	735,800	702,500	(33,300)
Contribution margin (except variable manufacturing variances)	194,200	172,500	21,700
Less other costs:			
Variable manufacturing costs variances from standards	49,600	—	(49,600)
Fixed manufacturing costs	49,200	48,000	(1,200)
Fixed selling and administrative costs	38,500	36,000	(2,500)
Corporation offices allocation	18,500	17,500	(1,000)
Total other costs	155,800	101,500	(54,300)
Division operating income	$ 38,400	$ 71,000	$ (32,600)

The chairs are manufactured on two different assembly lines located in adjoining buildings. The division management and sales department occupy the third building on the property. The division management includes a division controller responsible for the division's financial activities and the preparation of reports explaining the differences between actual and budgeted performance. The controller structures these reports so that the sales activities are distinguished from cost factors and each can be analyzed separately.

The operating results for the first 3 months of the fiscal year as compared to the budget are presented on the previous page. The budget for the current year was based upon the assumption that Markley Division would maintain its present market share of the estimated total patio chair market (plastic and metal combined). A status report had been sent to corporate management toward the end of the second month indicating that division operating income for the first quarter would probably be about 45 percent below budget; this estimate was just about on target. The division's operating income was below budget even though industry volume for patio chairs increased by 10 percent more than was expected at the time the budget was developed.

The manufacturing activities for the quarter resulted in the production of 55,000 plastic chairs and 22,500 metal chairs. The costs incurred by each manufacturing unit are presented below.

Raw Materials (stated in equivalent finished chairs)

	Quantity	Price	Plastic Model	Metal Model
Purchases:				
Plastic	60,000	$5.65	$339,000	
Metal	30,000	$6.00		$180,000
Use:				
Plastic	56,000	$5.00	280,000	
Metal	23,000	$6.00		138,000
Direct labor:				
9,300 hours @ $6.00 per hour			55,800	
5,600 hours @ $8.00 per hour				44,800
Manufacturing overhead:				
Variable:				
Supplies			43,000	18,000
Power			50,000	15,000
Employee benefits			19,000	12,000
Fixed:				
Supervision			14,000	11,000
Depreciation			12,000	9,000
Property taxes and other items			1,900	1,300

The standard variable manufacturing costs per unit and the budgeted monthly fixed manufacturing costs established for the current year are as follows:

	Plastic Model	Metal Model
Raw materials	$5.00	$ 6.00
Direct labor:		
1/6 hour @ $6.00 per DLH	1.00	
1/4 hour @ $8.00 per DLH		2.00
Variable overhead:		
1/6 hour @ $12.00 per DLH	2.00	
1/4 hour @ $8.00 per DLH		2.00
Standard variable manufacturing cost per unit	$8.00	$10.00
Budgeted fixed costs per month:		
Supervision	$4,500	$3,500
Depreciation	4,000	3,000
Property taxes and other items	600	400
Total budgeted fixed costs for month	$9,100	$6,900

Required:

a. Explain the variance in Markley Division's contribution margin attributable to sales activities by calculating the:

1. Sales price variance.
2. Sales mix variance.
3. Sales volume variance.

b. What portion of sales volume variance, if any, can be attributed to a change in Markley Division's market share?

c. Analyze the variance in Markley Division's variable manufacturing costs ($49,600) in as much detail as the data permit.

d. Based upon your analyses prepared for parts *a*, *b*, and *c*,

1. Identify the major cause of Markley Division's unfavorable profit performance.
2. Did Markley's management attempt to correct this problem? Explain your answer.
3. What other steps, if any, could Markley's management have taken to improve the division's operating income? Explain your answer.

Process Costing

17

Some products are manufactured in batches, in which case their costs are accumulated using a job order costing system, discussed in Chapter 3. Other products are manufactured in continuous-flow production processes and their costs are accumulated using a process costing system. In this chapter we present process costing. When you have finished this chapter you should understand:

1. The nature of process costing and its similarities and differences with job order costing.
2. The purpose of cost of production reports and how they are prepared.
3. The measurement of production output in continuous-flow production activities.
4. The use of FIFO and weighted average for costing production flows.
5. The preparation and use of summary product cost reports.

Process costing is a system for measuring and reporting the cost of manufactured products that are produced in continuous-flow production processes. Chemicals, plastics, petroleum fuels, and many other products are produced in continuous-flow production processes and are accounted for using process costing. In contrast, job order costing is used to measure the cost of products that are produced in batches or intermittent production runs. With job order costing, costs are totaled and unit costs are computed when the job is completed. In process costing there is no specific time when all units are completed. Instead, as some units are completed others are being started and still others are in various stages of production. Regardless of the costing system, managers require timely product cost information. Consequently, accountants must provide periodic reports of product costs in process costing situations.

PROCESS COSTING ACTIVITIES

A number of specific steps are needed to create and operate a process costing system.

Steps in developing and operating a process costing system

1. Establish specific process costing centers.
2. Determine the time period to be covered by the product cost reports.
3. Accumulate actual manufacturing costs for each process center for the reporting period.
4. For each process center measure the quantity of product produced during the reporting period.
5. Compute unit costs for each process center using the manufacturing cost and output data gathered in steps 3 and 4.
6. Prepare the product cost reports.

Establishing Process Costing Centers

In a process costing system, accountants divide the production activity into specific identifiable processes, each of which is called a **process center.** Process centers must be clearly identified before any process costing activity can take place. For example, the manufacturer of 21-inch floor model fans divides the production process into metal fabricating, drilling, welding, painting, assembly, and testing. The output of the first process center is the input for the next process center, and so forth. The output of the last process center is the final product, the 21-inch fan, that is sold to customers. Each of these production activities is a separate production function for which accountants accumulate costs and measure unit costs of production. A process center is distinguished by three characteristics:

Characteristics of process centers

1. Some specific identifiable production activity is performed.
2. The same type and amount of work is performed on all units passing through the process center.
3. Only one type of product passes through each process center.

In process costing, process centers are the focal point for accumulating manufacturing costs and measuring the amount of output. To determine the cost of a product it is necessary to measure the cost of production in each process center. The number of separate process centers necessary to complete a product depends on many factors, such as the type of product, the complexity of the production process, and the management of the manufacturing activities. One type of product may require only two or three process centers to complete; others may require 15 or more process centers. The number of process centers needed to manufacture a product determines the amount of cost accounting work that must be done and the volume of cost data supplied to managers, but the cost accounting concepts and activities are similar for simple and complex process costing situations.

There is a distinction between process centers and production departments in job order costing. Production departments are used to manufacture a variety of products from many different jobs, and each product may have different kinds of work performed. In a process center, on the other hand, only one type of product is produced, and identical work is performed on each unit passing through the process center. A production department may have many process centers each performing specific work on a particular product. For example, a company makes five different types of computer terminals whose costs are accounted for using a process costing system. All of the terminals require assembly, but each type of terminal requires somewhat different assembly operations. Although all of the terminals are assembled in the assembly department, the company establishes a separate assembly process center for **each** type of computer terminal. The assembly department then consists of five process centers. It prepares five cost of production reports. Each report is identified according to the department as well as by product. Therefore several cost of production reports may be labeled as assembly department reports, and each would identify a different product to show precisely which process center is reported. In addition each product has process centers in other departments for additional necessary manufacturing activities.

Determining Reporting Intervals

In job order costing, unit costs are computed when the job is completed; with continuous-flow production there is a constant flow of products through the manufacturing process. The convenient starting and completion points found in job order costing do not exist in continuous-flow production. But managers need frequent, detailed cost accounting reports to manage daily operations, and therefore such reports must be prepared periodically while production is still occurring in continuous production flows.

Product cost information must be timely to be useful to managers

How frequently cost accounting reports should be provided depends on the cost of preparing the reports and the benefits derived from them. Some companies prepare product cost reports once a month, others once a week, and in some cases reports may be prepared daily. Whatever the reporting interval, the timing of the reports must be determined before the process accounting system can function because accountants must plan the necessary cost accounting activities.

Accumulating Manufacturing Costs

The costs of direct materials, direct labor, and manufacturing overhead are accumulated separately for **each** process center for the period. If process centers are clearly defined, these manufacturing costs can be assigned easily to the appropriate process center. Similarly, if the report timing interval is clearly defined and understood, manufacturing costs of one period will not be erroneously included in another reporting period.

Measuring Production Output

Unit costs are computed by dividing production output into the manufacturing costs, but in a continuous production process with some units just started, others almost completed, and still others already finished, how does one measure production output? Accountants have developed methods of converting all production for the period into a single measure of production output.

In a process costing system output is measured in equivalent units

To measure the amount of production, clearly we include the units started and completed during the reporting period. But what do we do with the units started last period and the units that are only partially completed at the end of this period? Partially completed units cannot logically be treated as whole units or we would overstate the amount of manufacturing work accomplished during the period. On the other hand these units cannot be ignored because some work was done on them, and some of the manufacturing costs of the period were incurred in working on these units. Ignoring these partially completed units would clearly understate the period's production. The logical solution is to measure the amount of work done on the partially completed units and express that work effort in terms of whole units of output, which accountants call **equivalent units of production** or **equivalent whole units** or just **equivalent units.** The concept of equivalent units is shown graphically in Figure 17-1.

Figure 17-1 illustrates the measurement of production output for June for a company that manufactures camping trailers. At the beginning of June there were four camping trailers in beginning work in process inventory, already ¾ complete. During June the trailers in beginning inventory were completed and eight more units were started and completed. In addition, five trailers were started during the month but only partially finished by June 30. The units in ending work in process inventory are 40 percent complete at the end of the month. During June the company did the ¼ remaining work on the four units in beginning inventory, which is 1 equivalent unit of work (.25 × 4 units). The eight units started and completed during the month are already expressed as whole units, and the amount of work done on ending inventory is 2 equivalent units (5 trailers × 40 percent completion). Summing the amount of work during the month, we get 11 equivalent units (1 + 8 + 2).

Computing Unit Costs

Unit costs of production are measured by dividing the total manufacturing costs of the period by the number of units produced during the period. In a job order costing system, it is easy to measure the unit costs because the calculations are not made until the job is completed. The completion of the job rather than a specific time interval is the key to the measurement of unit costs.

In process costing, unit costs are determined for a **particular reporting period** by dividing the total manufacturing costs for the reporting period by the number of equivalent units for the period.

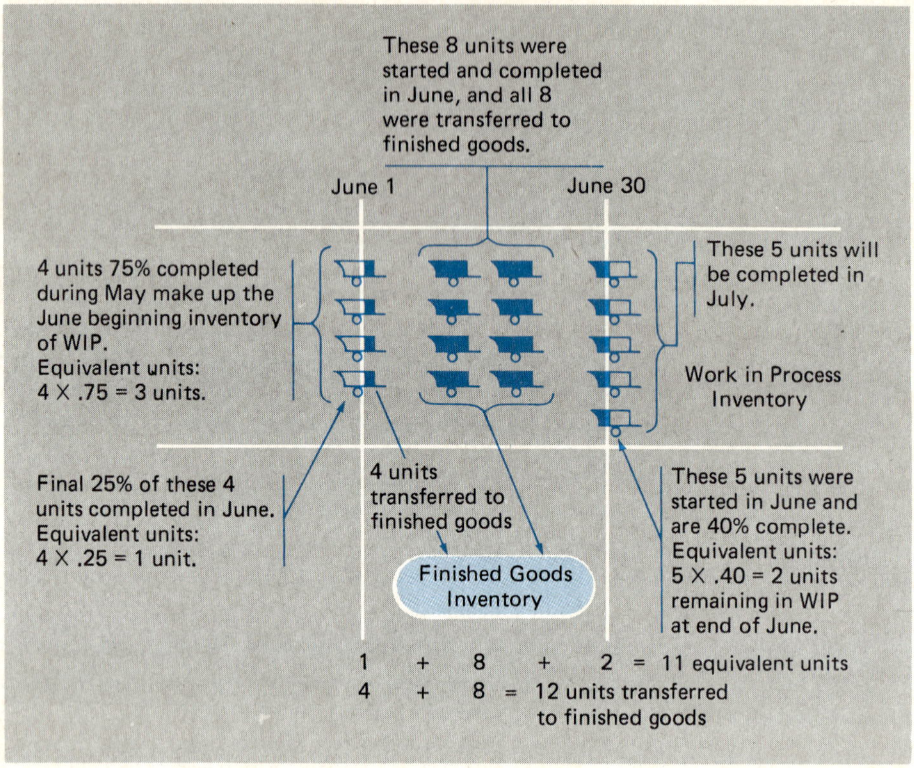

Figure 17-1
In process costing the accountant must measure the amount of production for the period in order to compute unit costs. The production quantity for the period includes the completion of beginning work in process inventory, the units started and completed during the period, and the work done on ending work in process inventory.

Typically unit costs are computed separately for each cost element. The number of equivalent units used to calculate unit costs for direct materials may be different from the number of equivalent units used to compute unit costs for direct labor or manufacturing overhead. For example, all materials may be added to a product as soon as it is started into production, but the work necessary to assemble, weld, buff, and otherwise complete the product may not be done right away. Therefore units in ending work in process may be complete in terms of materials but only partially complete in terms of the conversion process.

Preparing Product Cost Reports

Cost of production reports are prepared for a particular process center for a specific period of time

Product costs are reported periodically such as weekly or monthly in a **cost of production report.** This report summarizes cost and production quantity data for a specific process center for a particular reporting period. The report includes total manufacturing costs, the production quantity, and unit costs. A cost of production report is somewhat similar to a job order cost sheet, but instead of reporting costs for the job, it reports costs for a specific time period.

An important distinction between a cost of production report and a job order cost sheet is that a cost of production reports summarizes the production activity for a single process center. If six process centers are needed to complete the production of a particular product, six cost of production reports provide the detailed product cost data. On the other hand, a job cost sheet contains a summary of all the cost data for the manufacture of a product in a particular job. The characteristics of job cost sheets and cost of production reports are compared below:

Item	Job Order Costing	Process Costing
Timing of the report	Prepared when the job is completed	Prepared periodically to satisfy management's information needs
Manufacturing costs to be reported	All production costs for the product	Production costs only for a particular process center
Measurement of the output	Number of units produced with the job	Number of units started and completed during the period plus the equivalent number of whole units represented by partially completed units

Notice the difference in the timing of product costs between job order costing and process costing. The job cost sheet is summarized and unit costs of the product are reported only when the job is completed. In process costing unit product costs are reported periodically as desired by management. Figure 17-2 on page 686 illustrates the product costing activities for job order costing and process costing.

PROCESS COSTING ILLUSTRATED

To understand well the nature and concepts of process costing it is necessary to study carefully a process costing example. We use Fergus Valve Company to illustrate product costing in a process costing system. We examine the June 1986 production activity for the firm's R2 gas valve. This valve is manufactured in three process centers—machining, assembly, and finishing. The company purchases rough iron castings that are ground, drilled, and polished in the machining process center. Then, in the assembly process center, the necessary fittings are added to the valves. Finally, in the finishing process center, the valves are treated with rust inhibitors, buffed, and packaged.

First Process Center: No Beginning Work in Process

There was no beginning work in process inventory in the machining process center on June 1. June production activities were as follows.

Job Order Costing System		
Beginning of Production		End of Production
Job Is Started	**Job Is in Production**	**Job Is Completed**
A job cost sheet is created.	Costs are incurred and accumulated on the job sheet and recorded in the company's books.	The job cost sheet is summarized and unit costs are computed for the product. Product costs are transferred from the Work in Process Control account to the Finished Goods Control account.

Process Costing System		
Beginning of the Reporting Period	**During the Reporting Period**	**End of the Reporting Period**
Units already in production are not complete. Manufacturing costs already incurred were recorded in last period.	Units already in production are completed. Additional units are started. Manufacturing costs are accumulated as incurred. Completed units are transferred to finished goods. Units started but not completed remain in work in process inventory.	Production quantity is measured for each process center. Costs of production for the period are divided by production quantity to obtain unit costs. A cost of production report is prepared.

Figure 17-2 In job order costing, production costs are accumulated for the life of the job and unit costs are computed and reported when the job is completed. In process costing, product costs are measured and reported periodically.

Conversion is direct labor and manufacturing overhead together

Machining process center production data. During June, 10,000 valves were put into production, of which 9,000 were completed and transferred to the next process center. On June 30, 1,000 valves were in ending work in process inventory in machining with all material added and 40 percent of the direct labor and manufacturing overhead completed. The term **conversion** is often used to refer to direct labor and manufacturing overhead together when the percentage of completion is identical for the two. We can state that in machining, conversion of the 1,000 units in ending work in process inventory is 40 percent complete, meaning that 40 percent of the total required labor is done and 40 percent of the total overhead has been applied to the product. Production costs in the machining process center for June were $12,000 of direct materials, $7,520 of direct labor, and $9,400 of manufacturing overhead.

Developing the cost of production report. Using these cost and production data, the June cost of production report for the machining process center

Fergus Valve Company
Cost of Production Report
R2 Gas Valve
June
Machining Department

Units to account for:		**Units accounted for:**	
Units started in June	10,000	Transferred out	9,000
		Ending work in process inventory	1,000
Total units to account for	10,000	Total units accounted for	10,000

	Cost	Equivalent Units	Unit Cost
Costs to account for:			
Materials	$12,000	10,000	$1.20
Labor	7,520	9,400	.80
Manufacturing overhead	9,400	9,400	1.00
Total costs to account for	$28,920		$3.00

Costs accounted for:			
Transferred to next department	9,000 @ $3.00 =		$27,000
Ending work in process inventory:			
Materials	1,000 @ 1.20 =	$1,200	
Labor	400 @ .80 =	320	
Manufacturing overhead	400 @ 1.00 =	400	1,920
Total costs accounted for			$28,920

Schedule of Equivalent Units

	Materials	Conversion
Units started and completed during the period	9,000	9,000
Materials in ending work in process:		
1,000 units with 100% of the material added	1,000	
Conversion of ending work in process:		
1,000 units with 40% conversion		400
Equivalent units of output for the period	10,000	9,400

Figure 17-3 The June cost of production report for the machining process center of the Fergus Valve Company. Carefully observe the general format of the report.

is prepared and presented in Figure 17-3. The title of the report identifies the type of report, the process center, and the time period covered by the report. The top portion of the cost of production report describes the physical flow of units; the middle section reports the production costs incurred and shows the computation of unit costs. This section of the report also shows the disposition of the manufacturing costs. The calculation of equivalent units is shown in the schedule at the bottom of the cost of production report.

The physical flow of units through the process center is reported at the top of the cost of production report. **Units to account for** reports the total number of units in production in the process center during the period, in this example the month of June. Because there were no units in beginning work in process on June 1, the only source of units is the 10,000 units started during the month. The **units accounted for** section describes the disposition of the units in production. Most are transferred out of the process center to the next production process or to finished goods if this is the last process center. The remaining units are those not yet completed that are the process center's ending work in process inventory at the end of the reporting period. In the machining process center the 10,000 total units are divided between the 9,000 units transferred to assembly and the 1,000 in ending work in process inventory on June 30.

The **costs to account for** section reports the manufacturing costs incurred in the process center during the period and also the unit cost of production for the period in the process center. As with job order costing, the quantity of production is divided into production costs to find the unit cost of production. Typically, unit costs are reported for each of the cost elements and in total.

Equivalent units are divided into production costs to find unit costs of production for the period

To compute unit costs it is necessary to determine the amount of costs and the number of units produced in the process center during the period. The cost amounts are derived from various sources, such as materials requisitions and labor distribution reports, just as in job order costing; however, measuring the quantity of production is somewhat different. In job order costing the number of units produced is measured when the job is completed. In process costing measuring the quantity of production is not so simple because the production is continuous, with some units started and completed during the period and other units only partially completed during the period. Accountants must measure the number of **equivalent units** of production as described earlier.

In the machining process center, measuring June production quantity is relatively simple because there was no beginning work in process inventory. The 9,000 units transferred out had to be started and completed during June. In addition to the 9,000 whole units of production, some work has been done on the 1,000 units in ending work in process inventory. Forty percent conversion means that ⅖ of the required labor and overhead costs already have been expended on the partially completed units. Another way of viewing the situation is that 60 percent of conversion is still required to complete the 1,000 units. Total equivalent units for conversion (direct labor and manufacturing overhead together) amount to 9,400 units, which is the sum of the 9,000 units started and completed during June and the 400 equivalent units (1,000 units × 40 percent) of conversion already done on ending work in process by the end of June. The computation of equivalent units for both materials and conversion is shown in the **schedule of equivalent units** at the end of the cost of production report. The equivalent units for materials in the machining process center are 1,000 for ending work in process because the only raw material is the rough iron casting and it is added at the beginning of production in the process center. Therefore all 10,000 units started during the period are complete in terms of material for the machining process center.

Computing unit costs. Unit costs are computed by dividing the equivalent units of production into the costs for the period. This means that the total cost of materials is divided by 10,000 units but the total costs of labor and overhead are divided by 9,400 equivalent units. The unit costs obtained in this way are added to arrive at the total unit cost. In machining the total is $3.00 per unit. The unit costs are averages for the month of June. Unit costs for prior or future periods may be different. Typically, managers compare cost of production reports from month to month to identify cost fluctuations and cost trends.

Costs are assigned to units transferred out and to units in ending work in process inventory

Reporting cost flows. The **costs accounted for** section of the report describes what happened to the costs identified in the costs to account for section. Costs are accounted for in two ways. First, the cost of completed goods is transferred to the next production department or to finished goods. Second, the cost of goods not completed remains in the process center as ending work in process inventory.

In the machining department 9,000 units are completed and transferred out at a cost of $3.00 per unit. That accounts for $27,000 of the $28,920 total cost. Ending inventory of 1,000 units consists of 1,000 equivalent units of material and 400 equivalent units of labor and overhead. Multiplying the equivalent units in ending inventory by their appropriate unit costs, the cost of ending inventory is $1,920. The cost transferred out plus the cost of ending inventory is $28,920, the total cost to account for. The cost accounted for must always equal the cost to account for. Occasionally small rounding errors may arise if unit costs are not even numbers, and a small rounding adjustment may be necessary so that the two totals balance.

The costs of production resources used are recorded in a Work in Process Control account for each process center. For example, a total of $28,920 of costs was charged to the machining process center during June. Process center managers responsible for these costs are held accountable for production efficiency in each process center. As products are completed and sent to the next process center, the production costs associated with the products are transferred with the units. The costs accounted for section of the report describes the disposition of production costs. For example, in the machining process center there was $28,920 of costs to account for. What happened to those costs? The report tells us that $27,000 of the costs was transferred to the next process center with the 9,000 completed units and the remaining $1,920 stayed with the 1,000 units of ending work in process inventory.

Second Process Center: Beginning WIP and Units Transferred In

In the second process center, assembly, fittings are added to the R2 gas valve castings that were transferred in from the machining process center. The materials are added early in the assembly process. Completed units are transferred to the finishing process center. The assembly process center has two characteristics not found in the first process center. First, the assembly process center has beginning work in process on June 1. The existence of beginning work in process creates some accounting issues which are discussed in connection with the second process center.

Second, some costs are transferred into assembly from the first process center. These **transferred in costs** are the manufacturing costs incurred in previous process centers and attached to units transferred into the current process center. In this example for assembly, the costs transferred in are $3.00 per unit, or $27,000 for the 9,000 units.

Assembly process center production data. The June 1 beginning work in process inventory (WIP) in assembly was 3,000 units with all assembly materials added and 30 percent complete in terms of assembly process center conversion. Of course the beginning work in process inventory of one period was the ending work in process inventory of the previous period. The $17,082 cost of the beginning work in process inventory includes $8,700 transferred in from the machining process center last month, plus $5,250 for materials costs, $1,404 for labor cost, and $1,728 for manufacturing overhead cost, incurred in the assembly department in the previous month.

During June, 9,000 units were transferred in from the machining process center at a cost of $3.00 per unit. The $27,000 of costs transferred in with these units appeared in the machining department cost of production report as costs transferred out. Costs added in the assembly department during June consist of materials, $16,200; labor, $17,808; and manufacturing overhead, $22,260. On June 30, 2,000 units were in ending work in process with all assembly department materials added and 75 percent of conversion completed.

Preparing the cost of production report. The cost of production report for the assembly process center is presented in Figure 17-4. It looks somewhat different from the machining cost of production report. The reason for the difference is that assembly had a beginning work in process inventory and machining did not. That may seem like a small difference, but it creates an accounting issue for inventory cost flows. In machining all costs were June production costs. In assembly there were June production costs, of course, but in addition there were costs in beginning inventory that have been carried over from the previous month's production. If the unit costs in beginning inventory are identical to unit costs in the current period, there is no difficulty. All units transferred out and units in ending inventory are accounted for using the same unit costs. However, identical unit costs are seldom the case. Even minor fluctuations in resource costs and production efficiencies create differing unit costs from one period to the next. All differences, major or minor, require the accountant to decide which costs should be transferred out of the process center and which costs should remain in ending work in process inventory. Accountants use the same inventory cost flow methods found in merchandising businesses. First in,

Fergus Valve Company
Cost of Production Report
R2 Gas Valve
June
Assembly Department

Units to account for:		**Units accounted for:**	
Beginning WIP	3,000	Transferred out	10,000
Transferred in, June	9,000	Ending WIP	2,000
Total units to account for	12,000	Total units accounted for	12,000

	Cost	Equivalent Units	Unit Cost
Costs to account for:			
Beginning work in process inventory:			
Prior departments	$ 8,700	3,000	$2.90
Materials	5,250	3,000	1.75
Labor	1,404	900	1.56
Manufacturing overhead	1,728	900	1.92
Total	17,082		$8.13
Current period production:			
Prior departments	27,000	9,000	$3.00
Materials	16,200	9,000	1.80
Labor	17,808	10,600	1.68
Manufacturing overhead	22,260	10,600	2.10
Total	83,268		$8.58
Total costs to account for	$100,350		

Costs accounted for:			
Transferred to next department:			
Prior departments	3,000 units @ $2.90	$ 8,700	
Prior departments	7,000 units @ 3.00	21,000	
Materials	3,000 units @ 1.75	5,250	
Materials	7,000 units @ 1.80	12,600	
Labor	900 units @ 1.56	1,404	
Labor	9,100 units @ 1.68	15,288	
Manufacturing overhead	900 units @ 1.92	1,728	
Manufacturing overhead	9,100 units @ 2.10	19,110	$ 85,080
Ending work in process inventory:			
Prior departments	2,000 units @ 3.00	6,000	
Materials	2,000 units @ 1.80	3,600	
Labor	1,500 units @ 1.68	2,520	
Manufacturing overhead	1,500 units @ 2.10	3,150	15,270
Total costs accounted for			$100,350

Schedule of Equivalent Units

	Materials	Conversion
Materials added this period to units in beginning inventory	0	
Conversion of 30% complete beginning inventory: 3,000 units, 70% conversion required to complete		2,100
Units started and completed during the period	7,000	7,000
Materials in ending work in process: 2,000 units with 100% of the material added	2,000	
Conversion of ending work in process: 2,000 units with 75% conversion		1,500
Equivalent units of output for the period	9,000	10,600

Figure 17-4
The June cost of production report for the assembly process center. Compare this report with the machining process center report in Figure 17-3 and notice the differences that arise because there is beginning inventory in assembly.

With beginning work in process, the accountant must use either FIFO or average costing to account for cost flows

first out (FIFO) and weighted average are the two most commonly used methods of costing production flows in process costing systems. We use FIFO to complete the Fergus Valve Company example, and we illustrate weighted average later in the chapter.

The units to account for section includes the 3,000 units in June 1 beginning WIP in the assembly process center plus the 9,000 units transferred in from machining during June. The 12,000 units are accounted for as follows: 10,000 units were completed during June and transferred to the finishing process center; 2,000 units were partially completed and remained in the finishing process center's ending work in process. The costs to account for section is larger than in the machining process center report because in assembly there is a section reporting the costs of beginning inventory in addition to the current period's production costs. Beginning inventory costs are computed separately so that FIFO can be used to account for the flow of product costs. Of course, the beginning inventory of one month is the ending inventory of the previous month, so the beginning inventory cost figures for June can be read directly from the May assembly process center's cost of production report.

Accounting for costs with beginning WIP. With FIFO costing accountants separate the costs of beginning inventory from current period production costs. Production quantity (equivalent units) must be computed for current period production and for units in beginning inventory in order to compute unit costs for each. In practice the total costs, equivalent units, and unit costs for beginning work in process inventory in June can be read from the ending work in process section of the May cost of production report. In the example, the May cost of production report is not presented, so unit costs are computed. Each cost in beginning inventory is divided by its equivalent units of production. For example, prior department costs and materials costs are divided by 3,000 equivalent units. Prior department costs are always 100 percent complete; otherwise, the units would not have been transferred to the current production center. All materials used in assembly are added early in the production process, so the 3,000 units in beginning inventory are 100 percent complete as to materials. Direct labor and manufacturing overhead are only 30 percent complete in beginning work in process. Therefore, the beginning inventory equivalent units are 900 for conversion (3,000 × .3). Total cost in beginning inventory in assembly is $17,082, and the average unit cost of a whole unit is $8.13.

Current period production consists of work done to complete the units in beginning work in process plus work done on the units transferred in during the month. First in, first out inventory assumes beginning inventory units are completed and transferred out first, followed by units transferred in during the period. The current period costs for each cost category are divided by the equivalent units of production for the period to determine unit costs. The $27,000 prior department cost in June in assembly is from the June cost of production report for units transferred out of machining at $3 per unit. Beginning inventory was already complete in terms of prior department costs on June 1. Similarly, the beginning inventory was complete in terms of materials added in the assembly department. Therefore, June materials costs in assembly pertain only to the 9,000 units transferred in during June.

Determining current period equivalent units with beginning inventory

Labor and overhead were used to complete beginning inventory and to process units transferred in during the month. Equivalent units for labor and overhead represent the amount of effort, measured in whole units of output, expended on completing the beginning work in process, starting and completing units during the month, and working on units in ending work in process. The computation of equivalent units in the assembly process center in June is shown in the schedule of equivalent units.

Schedule of Equivalent Units

	Materials	Conversion
Materials added this period to units in beginning inventory	0	
Conversion of 30% complete beginning inventory: 3,000 units, 70% conversion required to complete		2,100
Units started and completed during the period	7,000	7,000
Materials in ending work in process: 2,000 units with 100% of the material added	2,000	
Conversion of ending work in process: 2,000 units with 75% conversion		1,500
Equivalent units of output for the period	9,000	10,600

To measure **current period** equivalent units, we include the equivalent units required to **complete** the beginning work in process and **not** the amount of work that was already done on the units before the period started. In the previous period 30 percent of the conversion work was done on the units in beginning inventory. Therefore the amount of conversion done during the **current period** on the 3,000 units of beginning work in process inventory was 70 percent of 3,000 units, or 2,100 equivalent units.

The number of units started and completed during the period can be computed in two ways. One way is to deduct the units transferred into the period from the ending work in process inventory (9,000 units − 2,000 units = 7,000 units). This approach works if no units are lost or spoiled in the production process. A second approach is to subtract the number of units in beginning work in process inventory from the number of units transferred out of the department during the period (10,000 units − 3,000 units = 7,000 units). Both methods yield the correct answer.

The equivalent units for each cost element are divided into their corresponding cost to determine current period unit costs. In the assembly process center current period cost is $8.58 per unit, which is somewhat higher than unit cost in beginning inventory. The total costs to account for are $100,350, which includes beginning inventory costs and current period production costs.

Accounting for cost flows using FIFO. The costs accounted for section describes the disposition of the $100,350 of cost. Most of this cost is transferred out of the finishing process center with the 10,000 units completed in assembly, but some costs remain in the assembly process center with the units in ending work in process. Using FIFO, the beginning inventory costs are transferred out first, followed by current period production costs. If beginning inventory was composed of completed units, 3,000 units would be transferred at $8.13 a unit and 7,000 units would be transferred at the current period cost of $8.58. But by definition beginning inventory was only partially completed. It had all materials but only 30 percent (900 equivalent units) of conversion. Therefore, for prior department costs and materials costs the first 3,000 equivalent units are transferred out at beginning inventory costs, and the next 7,000 equivalent units are transferred out at current period costs. On the other hand, for labor and overhead costs the first 900 equivalent units are transferred out at beginning inventory costs and the next 9,100 equivalent units at current period costs. In total, **10,000** equivalent units of **each** cost element are transferred out using FIFO, for a total cost of $85,080.

The production costs remaining in assembly are for the partially completed units in ending work in process inventory. These units are all costed at the current period costs because all beginning inventory costs have been transferred out. There are 2,000 equivalent units of prior department costs and materials costs and 1,500 equivalent units of labor and overhead costs. The current period unit cost for each cost element is multiplied by its number of equivalent units in ending inventory. The total cost of ending work in process inventory in assembly is $15,270, which, when combined with the $85,080 of cost transferred out, accounts for all $100,350 of costs to account for.

An alternate method of reporting costs transferred out using the FIFO inventory method may be used. The total costs in beginning work in process are reported first, followed by the current period **costs incurred to complete beginning work in process.** The remaining costs transferred out are for units started and completed during the current period, which can be costed at the current period's total unit cost. The computation is shown below:

An alternate method of showing FIFO cost flows

Costs accounted for:			
Transferred to next process center:			
Beginning work in process		$17,082	
Required to complete beginning WIP:			
Direct labor	2,100 @ $1.68	3,528	
Manufacturing overhead	2,100 @ 2.10	4,410	
Current period production	7,000 @ 8.58	60,060	$ 85,080
Ending work in process:			
Prior department costs	2,000 @ 3.00	6,000	
Direct materials	2,000 @ 1.80	3,600	
Direct labor	1,500 @ 1.68	2,520	
Manufacturing overhead	1,500 @ 2.10	3,150	15,270
Total costs accounted for			$100,350

As you can see from this alternative computation, this reporting method reduces the list of costs transferred out for the period. Either method is acceptable and you should use the one you find easier.

Third process center: FIFO and weighted average costing. The last process center in the production of R2 gas valves is finishing, where the castings transferred in from assembly are completed by treating them with rust inhibitors, buffing, and packaging them. Completed units are transferred from finishing to finished goods inventory. We illustrate the cost of production report for this process center first using FIFO inventory for costing production cost flows. We then present the cost of production report for finishing using weighted average inventory flows.

Finishing process center production data. Beginning work in process in June is 5,000 units with all materials and 40 percent conversion. Ending WIP for June is 3,000 units with all materials and ⅓ conversion. Completed valves are transferred to finished goods. Finishing process center costs for beginning inventory were $41,670 of prior department costs, $1,400 for materials, $3,560 for labor, and $4,450 for manufacturing overhead. Current period costs in finishing were $85,080 of prior department costs, $3,100 for materials, $22,400 for labor, and $28,050 for manufacturing overhead. Figure 17-5 presents the cost of production report for finishing using FIFO inventory.

Preparing the cost of production report. The format and computation of the finishing process center cost of production report are similar to the format and computation of the assembly process center cost of production report. The costs in beginning inventory are divided by equivalent units in beginning inventory to find unit costs. Current period costs are divided by the current period equivalent units to find current period unit costs of production. Current period equivalent units are reported in the schedule at the bottom of Figure 17-5.

Using FIFO costing, $158,706 is transferred to the finished goods inventory for the 12,000 R2 gas valves completed in June. The first $51,080 came from beginning inventory and the remaining costs are the current period's costs required to finish the units in beginning inventory and the 7,000 units started and completed in finishing during June. The 3,000 units in ending work in process inventory have a cost of $31,044.

Notice that the current period's prior department unit cost is $8.508. The costs transferred out of assembly were composed of both beginning inventory costs and current period costs. The cost of the 10,000 units transferred into finishing from the assembly process center totaled $85,080. Dividing the **total costs** transferred into finishing by the **total number of units** transferred into finishing yields an **average unit cost** of $8.508. In other words, although FIFO is used to transfer costs out of a department, the transferred costs become averaged in the next process center.

Fergus Valve Company
Cost of Production Report
R2 Gas Valve
June
Finishing Department

Units to account for:		**Units accounted for:**	
Beginning WIP	5,000	Transferred out	12,000
Transferred in, June	10,000	Ending WIP	3,000
Total units to account for	15,000	Total units accounted for	15,000

	Cost	Equivalent Units	Unit Cost
Costs to account for:			
Beginning work in process inventory:			
Prior departments	$ 41,670	5,000	$ 8.334
Materials	1,400	5,000	.28
Labor	3,560	2,000	1.78
Manufacturing overhead	4,450	2,000	2.225
Total	51,080		$12.619
Current period production:			
Prior departments	85,080	10,000	$ 8.508
Materials	3,100	10,000	.31
Labor	22,440	11,000	2.04
Manufacturing overhead	28,050	11,000	2.55
Total	138,670		$13.408
Total costs to account for	$189,750		

Costs accounted for:				
Transferred to finished goods:				
Beginning work in process			$ 51,080	
To complete beginning WIP:				
Direct labor	3,000 units @	$ 2.04	6,120	
Manufacturing overhead	3,000 units @	2.55	7,650	
Current period production	7,000 units @	13.408	93,856	$158,706
Ending work in process inventory:				
Prior departments	3,000 units @	8.508	25,524	
Materials	3,000 units @	.31	930	
Labor	1,000 units @	2.04	2,040	
Manufacturing overhead	1,000 units @	2.55	2,550	31,044
Total costs accounted for				$189,750

Schedule of Equivalent Units

	Materials	Conversion
Materials added this period to units in beginning inventory	0	
Conversion of 40% complete beginning inventory: 5,000 units, 60% conversion required to complete		3,000
Units started and completed during the period	7,000	7,000
Materials in ending work in process: 3,000 units with 100% of the material added	3,000	
Conversion of ending work in process: 3,000 units with 33⅓% conversion		1,000
Equivalent units of output for the period	10,000	11,000

Figure 17-5
The June cost of production report for the finishing department is similar to the assembly process center report.

Weighted average inventory. The **weighted average inventory method,** sometimes called **average costing,** is a common alternative to FIFO costing and allows managers to average production costs of beginning inventory and the current period. Each cost is weighted by the quantity of beginning inventory and current period production. To illustrate weighted average costing we again prepare a cost of production report for June for the finishing process center, this time using weighted average costing in place of FIFO. The average costing June cost of production report for the finishing process center is shown in Figure 17-6.

Preparing the cost of production report. With average costing we do not have to report separately the beginning inventory costs and current period costs. Instead, for each of the cost elements we compute an average cost and use it to cost units transferred out and units in ending work in process inventory.

Computing the weighted average costs is a simple arithmetic process. For each cost element, we add the costs in beginning inventory to the current period costs. Then we divide this total by the sum of the equivalent units in beginning inventory and the equivalent units in current period production. The easiest method of computing the total equivalent units in weighted average process costing is as follows:

Schedule of Equivalent Units
Used to Compute Average Unit Costs
Finishing Process Center
June

	Materials	Conversion
Units transferred out during the period	12,000	12,000
Work done on ending work in process:		
Materials added in June: 3,000 units 100% complete	3,000	
Conversion: 3,000 with 33⅓% conversion		1,000
Total equivalent units represented by beginning work in process and current period production (sometimes referred to as weighted average equivalent units)	15,000	13,000

Equivalent units with average costing

It is important that you understand that FIFO and weighted average are two different methods of costing inventory flows in a process costing system. The actual production costs are not affected by the costing method used; what is affected is how the costs are distributed between units in ending inventory and units transferred out of the process center. One method is not correct or incorrect or even preferable to the other method. Instead, managers must decide which method offers the better information for internal and external reporting.

Fergus Valve Company
Cost of Production Report
R2 Gas Valve
June
Finishing Department

Units to account for:		**Units accounted for:**	
Beginning WIP	5,000	Transferred out	12,000
Transferred in, June	10,000	Ending WIP	3,000
Total units to account for	15,000	Total units accounted for	15,000

	Cost	Equivalent Units	Unit Cost
Costs to account for:			
Prior departments:			
Beginning WIP	$ 41,670		
Current period	85,080		
Total	126,750	15,000	$ 8.45
Materials:			
Beginning WIP	1,400		
Current period	3,100		
Total	4,500	15,000	.30
Labor:			
Beginning WIP	3,560		
Current period	22,440		
Total	26,000	13,000	2.00
Manufacturing overhead:			
Beginning WIP	4,450		
Current period	28,050		
Total	32,500	13,000	2.50
Total cost to account for	$189,750		$13.25

Costs accounted for:				
Transferred to finished goods	12,000 units @ $13.25			$159,000
Ending work in process inventory:				
Prior department	3,000 units @	8.45	$25,350	
Materials	3,000 units @	.30	900	
Labor	1,000 units @	2.00	2,000	
Manufacturing overhead	1,000 units @	2.50	2,500	30,750
Total costs accounted for				$189,750

Schedule of Equivalent Units

	Materials	Conversion
Units transferred out during the period	12,000	12,000
Materials in ending work in process:		
3,000 units with 100% of the material added	3,000	
Conversion of ending work in process:		
3,000 units with 33⅓% conversion		1,000
Weighted average equivalent units	15,000	13,000

Figure 17-6 The June cost of production report for the finishing department using a weighted average inventory cost flow rather than FIFO. The total cost is the same as in Figure 17-5, but the amounts transferred to finished goods and remaining in ending work in process are somewhat different from those obtained with FIFO.

The format of the unit cost computations in the cost of production report is somewhat different with weighted average costing. Instead of grouping all beginning inventory costs together and all current period costs together, as with FIFO, the costs are grouped by cost element. This is necessary to compute a weighted average cost for each cost element. The average cost is determined in the same way that any weighted average is found. For each cost element, the cost in beginning inventory is added to the current period cost and the total is divided by the sum of the beginning inventory and current period equivalent units. For example, materials cost in beginning inventory was $1,400. Current period materials cost is $3,100. The total of $4,500 is divided by the 15,000 total equivalent units for materials, yielding a weighted average cost of $.30 per unit.

Average unit costs in the finishing process center are $8.45 for prior department costs, $.30 for materials, $2.00 for labor, and $2.50 for overhead. The total is $13.25 per unit. The weighted average cost figure is used to cost the units transferred out of the department during the period and to cost ending work in process inventory.

Compare carefully the FIFO cost of production report in Figure 17-5 with the weighted average report in Figure 17-6. Observe the similarities and differences in the reports. The basic components of both reports are the same. The way unit costs are computed and reported are somewhat different, however.

Summary Product Cost Reports

Unit cost information from all process centers in a product's production cycle are reported in the summary product cost report

The cost of production reports illustrated in this chapter report the cost of making R2 gas valves during June. We can find the unit cost of producing the valves during June by looking at the finishing process center cost of production report in Figure 17-5. This report shows us the total cost transferred to finished goods and also the unit cost of materials, labor, and overhead in finishing. Materials, labor, and overhead costs per unit for the first two process centers, however, are buried in the figure for preceding department costs. If managers require more detailed manufacturing costs, accountants can prepare a **summary product cost report** as illustrated in Figure 17-7 on page 700. This report summarizes the unit cost of production in each process center for materials, labor, and overhead, as well as the cost per unit. If FIFO costing is used, the current period production costs are reported, as in our example. If average costing is used, the average unit cost is reported.

OTHER PRODUCT COSTING ISSUES

In addition to the basic concepts of process costing covered in this chapter, many other issues occur that complicate the measurement and reporting of costs. An in-depth study of process costing is beyond the scope of this book, but you should be aware of other issues in order to understand many actual process costing situations.

Fergus Valve Company
R2 Gas Valve Cost Report
June

	Units			
Physical Flow	**Machining**	**Assembly**	**Finishing**	**Total**
Beginning inventory	0	3,000	5,000	8,000
Started/transferred in	10,000	9,000	10,000	—
Ending inventory	1,000	2,000	3,000	6,000
Transferred out	9,000	10,000	12,000	—
	Unit Costs			
Cost Flow	**Machining**	**Assembly**	**Finishing**	**Total**
Materials	$1.20	$1.80	$ .31	$ 3.31
Labor	.80	1.68	2.04	4.52
Manufacturing overhead	1.00	2.10	2.55	5.65
Total	$3.00	$5.58	$4.90	$13.48

Figure 17-7 **This managerial accounting report summarizes the physical flow of units and the current period unit cost data found on the cost of production reports of the departments. The report provides information similar to that found on a departmental job cost sheet used in a job order cost system. The data in this report are based on FIFO costing.**

Change in Output Units

Sometimes the unit of measure changes as a product goes from one process center to the next

It is common for units of measure to change from one process center to another. For example, in a food processing plant output in the first process center may be measured in gallons, in the second process center the output measure may change to pounds, and in the final process center output may be in boxes of cereal. Accountants always measure and report costs in terms of the output units of each process center. When units change from one process center to the next, accountants merely express the output of the previous process center in terms of output in the current process center. As long as the accountant can translate the output from one process center's units to the next process center's output units, the measurement process is quite simple.

Spoilage and Lost Units

Some spoilage or lost units are common in manufacturing

Some spoilage or unit loss commonly occurs in manufacturing processes. The terms **lost units** and **spoiled units** often are used interchangeably, although in some production situations one seems more appropriate than in others. For example, *lost units* is more descriptive if gallons of a solution evaporate or disappear, whereas *spoiled units* is the better term if units are inspected and fail to meet quality control standards. Losses or spoilage often cannot be avoided. For example, a production employee may incorrectly set a machine to stamp out parts of the wrong size. Good parts may be discarded inadvertently with scrap material; some compound may be left too long in the curing process; or a machine may malfunction and perform unacceptable work on products. Regardless of the cause of the spoiled or lost units, the accountant must identify the loss, measure its cost, and account for it in the proper way.

The cost of normal spoilage is included as part of the necessary cost of production

Normal spoilage. The spoilage that occurs in manufacturing products often cannot be avoided. That is, given the quality of the materials and labor used to produce the product and the efficiency of the production machinery, some spoilage will occur in the normal course of operations. Such spoilage is called **normal spoilage** or **normal lost units.** The skill level of the employees, human errors, malfunctions of equipment, and random factors combine to cause some normal spoilage.

Managers try to avoid spoilage but they know that good units cannot be produced without production problems that cause some spoiled units. In effect, the cost of spoiled units is like any other manufacturing cost, such as machine maintenance or property taxes on the manufacturing facilities. Because spoiled units are an unavoidable part of many manufacturing processes, the cost of such spoilage is included as part of the manufacturing cost of good units. The accountant must measure the cost of the spoiled units and assign the cost to the good units.

For example, a firm manufactures control boards for microcomputers. The units are inspected and tested for quality at the end of the production process in the last process center. Units not passing inspection are scrapped because the cost of reworking them is too high to make rework economically feasible. During June the following production took place in the last process center:

Total units produced	10,000 units
Total units rejected at inspection and discarded	500
Total manufacturing costs	$522,500

If all the units were good, the cost of the control boards would be $52.25 per unit ($522,500/10,000 units). But we see that 500 units were faulty, leaving 9,500 good units. If the spoilage is normal, the lost units cannot be avoided. In other words, we need to produce 10,000 units in total to get the 9,500 good units. Therefore, the cost of the good units is $55 per unit ($522,500/9,500 units).

Measuring spoiled unit cost

Spoilage costs often are of particular interest to managers. Although some spoilage and lost units cannot be avoided, managers do not want spoilage to become excessive. Therefore, they monitor spoilage costs and attempt to spot trends toward unnecessary spoilage. Accountants may report spoilage costs separately to highlight them for management. For example, using the data above, we may report spoilage costs as follows:

Unit cost of production: $522,500/10,000 units		$52.25
Total cost of spoilage: 500 units × $52.25	$26,125	
Increase in cost of good units due to spoilage: $26,125/9,500		2.75
Total unit cost of good units		$55.00

Abnormal spoilage is not a product cost and is charged to a loss account in the period in which it occurs

Abnormal spoilage. When spoilage or lost units become excessive or result from unusual circumstances such as severe weather, managers realize such costs are not part of the **normal** and **necessary** costs of production. In that case, spoilage costs are removed from manufacturing costs and reported as an expense of the period. For example, if the spoilage above is considered unusual, the entry to record the **abnormal spoilage** is

	Abnormal loss due to spoilage	26,125	
	Work in process control		26,125
	To record the transfer of abnormal		
	spoiled units cost to a loss account.		

SUMMARY

Process costing is used to accumulate the costs of products manufactured in continuous-flow production processes. Manufacturing activities are separated into specific activities called **process centers,** for which cost data are accumulated. Periodically cost data are summarized and reported in **cost of production reports.** These reports describe the physical flow of units and the associated cost flows through the process center during the period. Cost data are accumulated for each cost element and unit costs are determined by dividing the production quantities, called **equivalent units,** into the product costs.

The cost of production report is divided into several sections. The first is the physical flow of production, which includes **units to account for** and **units accounted for.** The second section, **costs to account for,** reports the total and unit costs of production. Costs are identified for each cost element and for costs in total. The third section of the report is called **costs accounted for.** Here the costs are assigned to the units transferred out of the process center and to the units that remain in ending work in process. The quantity of production for the period is shown below in the **schedule of equivalent units.**

Since process costing is used to measure product costs for continuous-flow production processes, it is common to have beginning and ending work in process inventories. If the beginning inventory unit cost is different from the unit cost of the current period's production, some inventory cost-flow assumption must be used to transfer costs out of the process center and to cost ending inventory. The two common methods are first in, first out (FIFO) and weighted average.

With **first in, first out (FIFO)**, beginning inventory costs are grouped together and current period costs are grouped together. Costs are transferred out using FIFO. Costs and equivalent units are separated for beginning inventory and current production.

Weighted average requires grouping the costs together by cost element so that average costs may be computed easily. For each cost element, beginning inventory costs are totaled and divided by the total number of equivalent units for that cost. The average unit costs are used as the basis for costing inventory and transferring costs through process centers. Unit and total cost data for current period production and for beginning inventory sometimes are included in a weighted average cost of production report to provide managers with valuable cost data.

Unlike a job cost sheet, a cost of production report does not include the complete detailed cost data for a product. To obtain such data a manager must have cost of production reports for all of the process centers producing the product, or a **summary product cost report** must be prepared.

Spoiled or **lost units** are products that do not satisfy quality control requirements. **Normal spoiled units** are spoilage that cannot be avoided given the manufacturing environment. The cost of such units is part of the normal and necessary cost of manufacturing good units. Spoilage cost can be buried in the cost of the good units or reported separately in the cost of production report. Spoilage cost should be reported separately if the value of the information exceeds the cost of reporting it.

Occasionally, **abnormal spoilage** or **abnormal lost units** occur. The cost of such spoilage is **not** included in the manufacturing cost of the good products, but instead is treated as a loss of the period. The cost of abnormal spoilage is removed from the Work in Process Inventory and charged to a loss account.

KEY TERMS

abnormal spoiled unit cost *(702)*
conversion *(686)*
cost of production report *(684)*
costs to account for *(688)*
costs accounted for *(689)*
equivalent units *(683)*
equivalent whole units *(683)*
lost units *(700)*
normal lost units *(701)*
normal spoilage *(701)*
process center *(681)*
process costing *(680)*
schedule of equivalent units *(688)*
spoiled units *(700)*
summary product cost report *(699)*
transferred in costs *(690)*
units to account for *(688)*
units accounted for *(688)*

QUESTIONS

1. Describe the steps necessary to create and operate a process cost system.
2. Describe the purpose, format, and use of the cost of production report.
3. Explain what equivalent units are.
4. Why must we deal with inventory pricing methods, such as FIFO, with process costing, but not with job order costing?
5. Refer to the Fergus Valve Company example. What is the cost of ending work in process inventory on June 30, 1986, for the R2 gas valve production activity?

EXERCISES

Ex. 17-1 Equivalent units with no beginning WIP. Below are data on the quantity of production in five different process centers. Each situation described is completely **independent** of the other situations. None of the process centers has beginning work in process.

	Process Center				
	1	2	3	4	5
Units started or transferred in	10,000	50,000	40,000	30,000	60,000
Ending work in process	2,000	8,000	10,000	12,000	25,000
Percentage complete, conversion	50%	75%	20%	65%	25%

Required: Compute the equivalent units of conversion for the period for each process center.

Ex. 17-2 Equivalent units with beginning WIP. Below are inventory flow data for five **independent** situations.

	Situation				
	A	B	C	D	E
Beginning inventory	0	2,000	4,000	10,000	1,000
Percentage complete	—	25	50	60	80
Units transferred in	15,000	12,000	20,000	50,000	25,000
Ending inventory	5,000	0	6,000	8,000	5,000
Percentage complete	40%	—	30%	25%	80%

Required: For each situation above compute the equivalent units of production for the current period.

Ex. 17-3 Simple process costing. The Rainbow Industrial Products Company manufactures paints and rust inhibitors that it sells by the barrel. Below are September cost data for the first production process of white glossy paint.

transferred out = 16,000

Beginning work in process	0
Units started	20,000
Materials costs	$65,000
Direct labor costs	$85,500
Manufacturing overhead costs	$51,300
Ending work in process inventory	4,000 units, all materials, ¾ conversion

Required: Prepare a cost of production report for September.

Ex. 17-4 Cost of production report with no beginning WIP. Dapper Company uses process costing to account for the production of its basketballs, which are manufactured in a continuous-flow production process. Below are July production data for the product for the first process center in the production process.

Beginning work in process	0
Units started	20,000
Cost of materials added at the beginning	$75,000
Direct labor costs	$57,000
Manufacturing overhead costs	$85,500
Ending work in process	2,000 units, all materials, ½ conversion

Required: Prepare a cost of production report for July for the first process center.

Ex. 17-5 **Equivalent units for materials and conversion.** Below are inventory flow data for five **independent** situations.

	Situation				
	1	2	3	4	5
Beginning WIP:	0	6,000	10,000	2,000	7,000
Percentage complete materials	0	40	100	50	80
Percentage complete conversion	0	60	40	60	90
Units transferred in	12,000	34,000	80,000	8,000	42,000
Ending WIP:	3,000	4,000	5,000	1,200	9,000
Percentage complete materials	100	60	100	75	60
Percentage complete conversion	75	90	80	80	70

Required: For each situation compute the current period equivalent units for materials and conversion.

Ex. 17-6 **Cost of production report using FIFO.** Below are December production data for the first process center in the production of a chemical compound used in food processing. The company uses FIFO to cost production and transfer work in process.

a. Beginning work in process consists of 5,000 gallons, all materials, 60 percent conversion.
b. Beginning WIP costs include $5,050 materials, $1,860 labor, and $1,410 overhead.
c. Units started in May are 40,000 gallons.
d. Materials costs in May are $44,000.
e. Labor costs in May are $27,000.
f. Overhead costs in May are $21,600.
g. Ending work in process is 10,000 gallons, all materials, 40 percent conversion.

Required: Prepare the December cost of production report for the first process center using FIFO to cost production.

Ex. 17-7 **Cost of production report using average costing.** Refer to the data in Exercise 17-6 but assume the company uses weighted average inventory valuation to cost production and transfer units.

Required: Prepare the December cost of production report for the first process center using average costing to cost production.

Ex. 17-8 **Measuring production flows in process costing.** Summarized below are production activities in three process centers used in the production of a single product. The data for these three related process centers are for September manufacturing activities.

Process Center 1

Beginning work in process: 1,000 units with all materials and 70 percent conversion

Units started: 8,000

Ending work in process: 2,500 units with all materials and 60 percent conversion

Process Center 2

Beginning work in process: 1,200 units with all materials and ⅔ conversion

Ending work in process: 2,000 units with all materials and ⅖ conversion

Process Center 3

Beginning work in process: 3,000 units with all materials and 80 percent conversion

Ending work in process: 1,800 units with all materials and 75 percent conversion

Required: Compute the amount of output for each process center for each cost element for September.

Ex. 17-9 **FIFO cost of production report.** Whimawha Corporation uses FIFO inventory for its process costing system. The shearing process center is the first process center in the production of coat racks for commercial establishments. Following are production data for March.

Beginning work in process inventory is 8,000 units with all materials and 75 percent conversion.

Beginning inventory costs include $12,000 for materials, $6,000 for labor, and $3,000 for applied overhead.

There were 64,000 units started in March.

Materials costs for March were $102,400.

March labor costs were $63,825.

Applied manufacturing overhead was $36,075.

Ending work in process was 14,000 units with all materials and 25 percent conversion.

Required: Prepare a cost of production report in good form for the shearing process center for March.

Ex. 17-10 **Weighted average cost of production report.** Blossomwood Company manufactures plant food and other garden products. The first process center in the production of plant food is blending. During May the company transferred 4,000 units of product from blending to the next process center. Beginning work in process consisted of 2,000 units half complete in terms of conversion and with all materials. The ending work in process inventory had 4,000 units with all materials and ¼ converted.

Costs associated with beginning work in process include $7,700 for materials, $2,580 for direct labor, and $1,380 for manufacturing overhead. Current period costs in the blending process center are $24,300 for materials, $9,920 for labor, and $6,120 for overhead. The company uses the weighted average inventory method.

Required: Prepare the May cost of production report in good form for the blending process center.

Ex. 17-11 **Spoiled units.** The Haywood Company makes small electric motors for hobby projects. Completed units are inspected before transfer to finished goods inventory. Rejected units are discarded with no market value.

During July, 50,000 motors were completed. Of these, 4,000 units were rejected at inspection. Total production costs for the 50,000 units were $64,400.

Required:

- **a.** Compute the unit cost of the good units.
- **b.** Compute the total cost of spoiled units.
- **c.** Compute the increase in the unit cost of good units caused by the faulty units.

PROBLEMS

P. 17-1 **Process costing with no beginning WIP.** Memmerring Plastics Company makes bulk plastic which it sells to industrial manufacturing businesses. The K4A plastic is made in a series of four process centers. The final process center is curing. In February, 40,000 units of K4A were transferred into curing from the preceding department at a cost of $138,400. All but 6,000 units were completed in curing during the month and transferred to finished goods inventory. Ending work in process in curing had all materials and 70 percent conversion. February cost of materials in the process center was $18,800, and labor cost was $21,392. Manufacturing overhead is applied at the rate of 150 percent of direct labor cost. There was no beginning WIP inventory in February.

Required: Prepare a cost of production report in good form for the curing process center for February.

P. 17-2 **Cost of production report, no WIP.** The Standish Paper Products Company uses process costing to account for the production costs of all its products. Below are September production and cost data for the first process center in the production of one of its products.

Beginning work in process inventory	0
Units started in September	25,000
Materials costs	$46,250
Labor costs	$17,250
Overhead applied	$34,500
Ending work in process inventory	5,000 units, all materials, 60 percent conversion

Required: Prepare the September cost of production report in good form for the first process center.

P. 17-3 Cost of production report with beginning work in process. The Sodale Manufacturing Company uses process costing to account for production activities. Finishing is the last process center in the production process. During January, finishing had 4,000 units in beginning work in process inventory and 8,000 units were transferred in from the preceding process center. During the month, 10,000 units were transferred to finished goods. The beginning and ending work in process inventories were complete in terms of materials. The beginning inventory was 25 percent complete in terms of conversion and the ending inventory was 75 percent complete.

Beginning inventory costs were $13,600 for preceding department costs, $4,400 for materials, $1,600 for labor, and $1,000 for manufacturing overhead. During January, $28,800 of cost was transferred in from the preceding process center and materials cost of $10,400, labor cost of $15,750, and overhead of $9,975 were incurred. Sodale Manufacturing Company uses FIFO to account for production costs.

Required: Prepare the January cost of production report in good form for the finishing process center.

P. 17-4 Weighted average inventory method. Whitefish Bay Company makes paper products in continuous-flow production processes. The commercial division makes a variety of bond papers for businesses and other professional organizations. All production is accounted for using the weighted average inventory method.

In the last process center in the production of 20-pound bond paper, 10,000 units were transferred in during April from the preceding process center. Beginning work in process inventory in April consisted of 2,000 units with all materials and half conversion. The 4,000 units in ending work in process also had all materials and were half converted.

Costs in beginning work in process were $6,000 of preceding department cost, $2,100 of materials cost, $2,600 of labor cost, and $2,900 of applied manufacturing overhead. During April, $32,000 of preceding department costs were transferred into the process center. Materials costs for the month in the process center were $11,500, labor costs were $21,000, and overhead was $27,000.

Required: Prepare the April cost of production report for the process center.

P. 17-5 Understanding cost of production reports. The Kline Company is a small manufacturing business that started operations on January 2. The company produces a unique boat and automobile cleaning compound that it sells in gallon containers. The product is manufactured in two process centers—mixing and distilling. The cost of production reports for February for the two process centers are shown below and on the next page.

Kline Company
Cost of Production Report
Mixing Department
February

Units to account for:		**Units accounted for**	
Started during the period	10,000	Units transferred out	9,000
		Ending work in process	1,000
Total units to account for	10,000	Total units accounted for	10,000

		Costs	Equivalent Units	Unit Cost
Costs to account for:				
Direct material		$25,000	10,000	$2.50
Direct labor		19,600	9,800	2.00
Manufacturing overhead		14,700	9,800	1.50
Total costs to account for		$59,300		$6.00
Costs accounted for:				
Transferred out of the process center:	9,000 units @ $6.00			$54,000
Ending work in process inventory:				
Direct material	1,000 units @ 2.50		$2,500	
Direct labor	800 units @ 2.00		1,600	
Manufacturing overhead	800 units @ 1.50		1,200	5,300
Total costs accounted for				$59,300

Required: From the data presented in the cost of production reports and the problem description determine:

a. The ending work in process for the firm on February 28.
b. The number of equivalent units of conversion in ending work in process for the distilling process center.
c. The total manufacturing cost incurred during February.
d. The amount of direct materials used in February.
e. The cost of goods manufactured in February.
f. The unit cost in February for direct materials, direct labor, and manufacturing overhead.

Kline Company
Cost of Production Report
Distilling Department
February

Units to account for:		**Units accounted for:**	
Beginning work in process	2,000	Units transferred out	8,000
Transferred in this period	9,000	Ending work in process	3,000
Total units to account for	11,000	Total units accounted for	11,000

	Costs	Equivalent Units	Unit Cost
Costs to account for:			
Beginning work in process:			
Preceding department costs	$ 11,900	2,000	$ 5.95
Direct material	2,500	2,000	1.25
Direct labor	600	500	1.20
Manufacturing overhead	900	500	1.80
Total	15,900		$10.20
Current period production:			
Preceding department costs	54,000	9,000	$ 6.00
Direct material	11,700	9,000	1.30
Direct labor	11,875	9,500	1.25
Manufacturing overhead	18,050	9,500	1.90
Total	95,625		$10.45
Total costs to account for	$111,525		

Costs accounted for:			
Transferred out of the process center:			
Preceding department cost	2,000 units @ $5.95	$11,900	
Preceding department cost	6,000 units @ 6.00	36,000	
Direct material	2,000 units @ 1.25	2,500	
Direct material	6,000 units @ 1.30	7,800	
Direct labor	500 units @ 1.20	600	
Direct labor	7,500 units @ 1.25	9,375	
Manufacturing overhead	500 units @ 1.80	900	
Manufacturing overhead	7,500 units @ 1.90	14,250	$ 83,325
Ending work in process inventory:			
Preceding department cost	3,000 units @ 6.00	18,000	
Direct material	3,000 units @ 1.30	3,900	
Direct labor	2,000 units @ 1.25	2,500	
Manufacturing overhead	2,000 units @ 1.90	3,800	28,200
Total costs accounted for			$111,525

P. 17-6 Cost of production report with FIFO. Jamaica Foods produces various gourmet delights that are sold primarily to restaurants and institutions. One of them, a rum sauce for meats and poultry, is produced in a three-department production process, the last of which is the cooking department. January production data for the cooking department are presented below.

- **a.** Beginning inventory: 10,000 gallons, ⅖ materials, ⅗ conversion.
- **b.** Costs of beginning inventory: prior departments, \$9,000; materials, \$1,360; labor, \$2,400; MOH, \$1,200.
- **c.** Units transferred in during January: 60,000 gallons; cost, \$52,800.
- **d.** Cost of materials added in cooking department in January: \$16,500.
- **e.** Labor cost in January: \$27,280.
- **f.** MOH cost in January: \$13,640.
- **g.** Ending WIP inventory: 8,000 gallons, all materials, ¾ conversion.
- **h.** First in, first out inventory valuation is used in the cooking department.

Required: Prepare a January cost of production report for the cooking department.

P. 17-7 Two-department process costing without beginning WIP. Traverse Company makes a vinyl wall covering for commercial customers. The first process center is mixing, in which basic materials are combined and mixed to specifications. In the second process center, settling, additional materials are added to refine the product before it is sent to the last process center, sheeting.

Below are production and cost data for the month of February. Because of a recent strike there was no beginning work in process for the month in either process center.

In mixing, 1,200 units of product were started, and 800 units were completed and transferred to settling. The units in ending work in process had all materials and were ½ converted. During February, direct materials cost was \$12,000 and conversion cost was \$6,000 in mixing.

Settling incurred \$3,200 of direct materials costs and \$3,750 of conversion costs during February. Six hundred units of product were completed and transferred to the last process center and 200 units remained in ending inventory with all materials and ¾ conversion.

Required: Prepare the mixing and settling cost of production reports in good form for the month of February.

P. 17-8 Reporting product costs with FIFO costing. Below are March cost data for a finishing department of Redrocks Manufacturing Company. This department is the final production department in the manufacture of a certain type of bearing.

- **a.** Beginning work in process: 6,000 units, ⅔ materials, ¼ conversion.
- **b.** Costs of beginning work in process: prior departments, \$48,000; materials, \$10,000; labor, \$3,000; overhead, \$3,600.
- **c.** Transferred in 30,000 units; cost, \$243,000.
- **d.** Materials are added periodically; cost for March, \$81,200.
- **e.** Labor costs in March, \$65,600.
- **f.** Overhead costs in March, \$79,360.
- **g.** Ending work in process: 5,000 units, ⅖ materials, ½ conversion.
- **h.** FIFO inventory method is used.

Required: Prepare a March cost of production report in good form for the finishing department.

P. 17-9 Two-department process costing. Larry Lombard's Lasagna Factory produces high-quality lasagna noodles in a five-process production operation. The last two processes are cutting and packaging. Output in cutting is in pounds and output in packaging is in cases. There are 20 pounds of lasagna per case. Production data for March for these last two processes are presented below.

Cutting Department

a. Beginning WIP consists of 20,000 pounds, all materials, 30 percent conversion.
b. Costs of beginning WIP include materials, $800; direct labor, $300; MOH, $150; prior departments, $4,200.
c. Transferred in, 80,000 pounds at a cost of $17,600.
d. Materials, added at beginning at a cost of $4,000.
e. Direct labor, $4,600.
f. MOH, $2,300.
g. Ending WIP is 10,000 pounds, all materials, 80 percent conversion.
h. FIFO inventory valuation is used.

Packaging Department

a. Beginning WIP consists of 1,500 cases, all materials, ½ conversion.
b. Costs of beginning WIP include materials, $570; direct labor, $490; MOH, $620; prior departments, $10,570.
c. Transferred in ?
d. Materials added at a cost of $1,890.
e. Direct labor, $2,500.
f. MOH, $3,750.
g. Ending WIP is 1,000 cases, all materials, ¾ conversion.
h. Average cost inventory method is used.

Required: Prepare a cost of production report in good form for each department.

P. 17-10 Accounting for spoiled units. Eagle River Manufacturing Company makes printed circuit boards for hand calculators. The work is very demanding and some spoilage is expected due to employee fatigue, occasional faulty materials, and other random occurrences. In the week just ended, 5,000 circuit boards were completed and at final inspection 600 of the completed units were rejected and discarded. Manufacturing costs for the 5,000 units were $19,580.

Required: Respond to each **independent** situation:

a. Compute the unit cost of the good units.
b. Compute the total cost of spoiled units.
c. Compute the increase in unit cost of good units caused by the spoiled units.
d. Assuming the spoilage is normal, what journal entry is necessary for the spoiled units?
e. Assuming management expects no more than 10 percent of units to be faulty, what journal entry is necessary for the spoiled units?

CASE

Case 17-1 Two-period two-department process cost reporting. Blue Water Fishing Supply, Inc., makes a variety of fishing and boating products which it markets nationwide. A recent management analysis of product offerings indicated a need for a top-of-the-line double-tray tackle box. Company product engineers designed the new tackle box, which is manufactured in two process centers. In the fabricating process center, the top and bottom housings of the tackle box are cut and formed from rolled aluminum. The units are buffed and holes are drilled for the hinges and latches to be installed later. In the assembly process center, hinges, latches, and tackle box trays are installed. These parts are purchased from vendors.

Management believes the tackle box will sell quite favorably at a retail price of $35 each. The company sells its products to retailers at a discount of 30 percent of selling price and variable marketing costs typically average 8 percent of the company's sales revenue. The company's product policy is to earn a minimum 45 percent gross margin on product sales revenue.

Production of the tackle boxes began on October 1. The company uses the weighted average inventory method to account for production cost flows. Below are production quantity and cost data for the first 2 months of production.

October Production	**Fabricating**	**Assembly**
Beginning work in process	0	0
Units started during the month	15,000 units	—
Current period costs:		
Transferred in	—	?
Direct materials	$90,900	$24,600
Conversion	49,920	35,200
Units completed and transferred out	12,000 units	8,000 units
Ending work in process:	3,000 units	4,000 units
Percent complete materials	100%	100%
Percent complete conversion	33⅓%	75%

November Production	**Fabricating**	**Assembly**
Units started during the month	9,000 units	—
Current period costs:		
Transferred in	—	?
Direct materials	$53,820	$12,600
Conversion	36,160	15,600
Units completed and transferred out	6,000 units	7,000 units
Ending work in process:	6,000 units	3,000 units
Percent complete materials	100%	100%
Percent complete conversion	66⅔%	33⅓%

Required:

a. Prepare cost of production reports in goods form for both process centers for the first 2 months of production.

b. Prepare product cost summary reports for the first 2 months of production.

c. Compute the November percentage gross margin on product sales revenue for the new product, assuming all units produced are sold.

d. Compute the required retail sales price to satisfy the company's minimum gross margin requirement.

e. Assuming the maximum competitive retail price for the tackle box is $40, what is your evaluation of the potential for this product?

Cost Analysis Tools and Techniques 18

Accountants provide a wealth of cost data and other managerial accounting information that are reported to managers in many different internal accounting reports. Often, however, even more information can be obtained by a careful and systematic analysis of the available data. In this chapter we look at some of the more useful techniques for analyzing accounting data with the intention of providing managers with better or more complete information for decision making. When you have completed this chapter, you should understand:

1 The nature and use of quantitative managerial tools.

2 The meaning of central tendency measures.

3 The use of dispersion measures such as the standard deviation.

4 The use of regression-correlation analysis in analyzing cost behavior patterns and identifying trends.

5 The basic aspects of learning curves.

6 The concept of trend analysis using moving averages and exponential smoothing.

Cost behavior patterns have played an important role in the discussion of many different concepts in previous chapters. Cost-volume-profit, alternative choice decisions, flexible budgeting, variable costing, and manufacturing overhead variance analysis are some of the topics that require the use of cost behavior data.

Identifying cost behavior patterns is a difficult but important task, because of the frequent use of costs in managerial analysis. In Chapters 2 and 5, we discuss cost behavior and describe several simple techniques such as the high-low method and scatter diagram method for identifying behavior patterns. In this chapter we discuss and illustrate several more sophisticated methods for identifying and analyzing cost behavior patterns. The purpose and applicability of each method are described, followed by an illustration. For each method the computational process is carefully explained and finally more complex applications are discussed.

THE USE OF QUANTITATIVE METHODS

What role should quantitative analysis play in business?

Few business topics generate stronger opinions than the use of quantitative methods in business. Advocates argue the virtues of being able to describe and analyze business activities in quantitative terms. Dissenters maintain that there is no substitute for understanding the intricate interrelationships of a business and that quantitative models often miss the central issues of a problem. Part of the controversy arises from the fact that many quantitative tools have been introduced into business by people who found a technique and then went looking for a problem that it fit. The logical approach is to identify a problem and then look for an effective way to analyze and solve it.

Quantitative methods do not always yield correct or useful data. Our purpose in this chapter is to present some quantitative tools that are **potentially** useful in planning and control activities, as well as in managerial analysis and decision making. You should attempt to become proficient with these tools and use them when they prove fruitful, and you should have the courage and wisdom to ignore them when they are not useful. Wise managers fill their arsenal with a wide variety of tools that may be utilized when the situation requires. Quantitative tools should be part of that arsenal.

STATISTICS

A statistic is a numerical representation or description of something

The mere mention of the term *statistics* causes some people to envision complicated numerical analyses that are difficult to understand. Although some statistical analyses are complex, many statistical measures and analyses are not difficult and can provide managers with information useful in making decisions. In its simplest form, a **statistic** is merely a numerical representation or description of something. For instance, a person's age is a statistic that provides some information about the person. Additional statistics such as height, weight, and grade point average provide a more complete description of the person. Many statistics are used in business, both externally and internally. Earnings per share and dividend payments are two important statistics that investors, lenders, and others use to help evaluate the performance of businesses. Such statistics provide external users with descriptive measures of performance that may be compared among several firms or for a single firm over a period of time. Internally there are many different statistics that are used for planning, control, and decision making. Included are statistics on inventory turnover, daily cash receipts, average production costs, and average cost of spoilage.

In the course of developing the cost accounting data base, managers accumulate a wealth of data, much of which is assimilated and analyzed to provide relevant information for decision making. Much of the analysis involves statistical measures of central tendency and dispersion.

Measures of Central Tendency

Measures of central tendency are averages or middle values

One of the most commonly used business statistics is a measure of central tendency called an **average.** The average is a central number, a middle value representative of a set of data. For decision making an average is often the most important characteristic of a set of data. For example, daily cash receipts for a retail store during the past year ranged from $500 on the day of a blizzard to a high of $8,500 during peak sales, with an average of $5,200. The range of daily cash receipts may have some information value, but the average is more useful in predicting cash receipts for some future period. Average unit costs, average hourly wage rate, and average inventory size are all widely used in business.

There are several different ways of calculating averages. Each provides a different **measure of central tendency.** We use the data in Figure 18-1 to illustrate the calculation of several types of averages. The data consist of weekly cash receipts of the Streeter Company for a period of 9 weeks.

Figure 18-1
Nine weeks of cash receipts data for Streeter Company. The range of values is $2,700, but what is the expected amount of cash receipts each week?

Streeter Company
Weekly Cash Receipts

Week	Cash Collected
1	$5,800
2	4,300
3	6,500
4	7,000
5	6,800
6	5,500
7	5,400
8	6,500
9	6,200

The mean is used in many different statistical calculations

Mean. The most commonly used average is the **mean,** which is determined by adding the value of each element in a set of data and dividing the total by the number of data in the set. The mean is computed as follows:

$$\text{Mean} = \frac{x_1 + x_2 + x_3 + \cdots + x_n}{n}$$

$$= \frac{\Sigma x_i}{n}$$

where

x_i = individual values for the data elements with $i = 1, 2, \ldots, n$
n = number of data elements
Σ = summation sign indicating that the values of x_i are added together

$$\text{Mean} = \frac{\$5{,}800 + \$4{,}300 + \$6{,}500 + \$7{,}000 + \$6{,}800 + \$5{,}500 + \$5{,}400 + \$6{,}500 + \$6{,}200}{9}$$
$$= \frac{\$54{,}000}{9}$$
$$= \$6{,}000$$

The mean of the 9 weeks of cash flow data is $6,000. The mean, usually denoted as $\overline{X}$, is a very important value for many statistical calculations.

The median is the middle value of a set of data

Median. Another measure of central tendency is the **median,** which is the middle value of the data set. There is an equal number of values below and above the median value. The easiest way to determine the median value is to list all data in either descending or ascending order. For example, the cash receipts data in ascending order are

$4,300
5,400
5,500
5,800
6,200
6,500
6,500
6,800
7,000

Because there are nine values in the set, the middle value is the fifth value, or $6,200, with four values above the median and four values below.[1] The median is useful when the middle value is an important measure. For example, a few very low test scores can make the mean of a test much lower than the median. If students are more concerned with their relative class standing, the median may be more informative than the mean.

The mode is the most frequently occurring value

Mode. A third measure of central tendency is the **mode,** which is the most frequently occurring value in the data set. In the Streeter Company example in Figure 18-1 only the value $6,500 occurs more than once. Therefore, this amount is the mode. Like the median, the mode is determined by observing the data rather than by computing it mathematically. As the most frequently occurring value, the mode may suggest business patterns or other characteristics of a business. For example, the manager of a shoe store would be interested in knowing the most commonly purchased shoe size so as to order more shoes of the modal size for any given style. The mean or median shoe size is not as significant as the mode. Note that in any set of data there may be no mode, or several modes may exist. The mode is most useful as a qualitative measure and is seldom used in statistical analysis.

---

[1] If there is an even number of data elements, the median is the mean of the pair of middle values.

Measures of Dispersion

Dispersion measures the variation in values about the mean

Another important statistical measure is **dispersion,** which is the amount of variation in the values of data about the mean. The amount of variation can be important in planning. For example, look at the weekly sales volume data in Figure 18-2 for two fast-food restaurants.

Both restaurants have total sales for the 10-week period of $60,000 and mean weekly sales of $6,000. However, store B has significantly greater fluctuations in the amount of weekly sales. Such fluctuations affect planning for cash flows, employee staffing, inventory requirements, and other factors. A mere glance at the data in Figure 18-2 indicates the much greater dispersion of weekly sales for store B, but how much greater is the dispersion? Two measures of dispersion are the variance and the standard deviation.

Streeter Company
Weekly Sales Data

Week	Store A	Store B
1	$ 5,600	$ 7,400
2	6,100	4,900
3	5,700	8,600
4	5,900	4,200
5	6,300	9,100
6	6,200	8,300
7	6,400	3,700
8	5,900	4,800
9	5,800	5,600
10	6,100	3,400
Totals	$60,000	$60,000

Mean = $\overline{X}$ = $60,000/10 = $6,000

Figure 18-2
Two fast-food restaurants have identical mean weekly sales for a 10-week period, but one restaurant has significantly more fluctuation in weekly sales.

Variance. The **variance** is a measure of how much the items of data vary from the mean. It is computed as follows:

$$\text{Variance} = \frac{\Sigma\,(x_i - \overline{X})^2}{n - 1}$$

The difference between each value and the mean is found and squared, and the sum of the squared amounts is divided by the number of data elements minus one. The differences are squared to eliminate the problem of negative numbers. The value $n - 1$ is used because the calculation of variance is made using the mean $\overline{X}$, a value already computed from the same data, which causes a loss of a **degree of freedom**.

A discussion of the theory behind degrees of freedom is beyond the scope of this chapter, except to note that adjusting for degrees of freedom gives a less biased statistic. The variances, denoted S^2, for the weekly sales data of the two stores in Figure 18-2, are computed as follows:

$$S^2 = \frac{\Sigma (x_i - \bar{X})^2}{n - 1}$$

Store A		Store B	
$(\$5,600 - \$6,000)^2 =$	\$160,000	$(\$7,400 - \$6,000)^2 =$	\$ 1,960,000
$(6,100 - 6,000)^2 =$	10,000	$(4,900 - 6,000)^2 =$	1,210,000
$(5,700 - 6,000)^2 =$	90,000	$(8,600 - 6,000)^2 =$	6,760,000
$(5,900 - 6,000)^2 =$	10,000	$(4,200 - 6,000)^2 =$	3,240,000
$(6,300 - 6,000)^2 =$	90,000	$(9,100 - 6,000)^2 =$	9,610,000
$(6,200 - 6,000)^2 =$	40,000	$(8,300 - 6,000)^2 =$	5,290,000
$(6,400 - 6,000)^2 =$	160,000	$(3,700 - 6,000)^2 =$	5,290,000
$(5,900 - 6,000)^2 =$	10,000	$(4,800 - 6,000)^2 =$	1,440,000
$(5,800 - 6,000)^2 =$	40,000	$(5,600 - 6,000)^2 =$	160,000
$(6,100 - 6,000)^2 =$	10,000	$(3,400 - 6,000)^2 =$	6,760,000
	\$620,000		\$41,720,000
$S^2 = \$620,000/9 = \$68,889$		$S^2 = \$41,720,000/9 = \$4,635,556$	

Standard deviation. The variance for weekly sales data is much larger for store B, but the numbers are difficult to understand because the squaring of the differences made them so large. By taking the square root of the variance we find the **standard deviation,** S, which is a very useful statistic. For our example:

Store A

$$S^2 = \$68,889$$
$$S = \sqrt{\$68,889}$$
$$= \$262$$

Store B

$$S^2 = \$4,635,556$$
$$S = \sqrt{\$4,635,556}$$
$$= \$2,153$$

Formula for standard deviation

The calculation of the standard deviation using the square root of the variance formula can be quite cumbersome. It is easier to use the following formula for the standard deviation, which we present without explaining its derivation:

$$S = \sqrt{\frac{n\Sigma x_i^2 - (\Sigma x_i)^2}{n(n - 1)}}$$

This formula yields the same results and requires squaring each of the data elements, an easier task than squaring the differences between each data element and the mean.

The standard deviation has some useful statistical properties. As we explain shortly, under certain frequently occurring conditions, it is known that about 68 percent of the data can be found within one standard deviation on each side of the mean, and about 95 percent of the data can be found within two standard deviations of the mean. These characteristics enable managers to make estimates of the probability of certain events' occurring based on the mean and standard deviation calculated from the data. For example, the mean and standard deviation of the above data indicate that 68 percent of the time sales for store A will be between \$5,738 and \$6,262, calculated as:

$$\overline{X} \pm 1S$$

$$\$6{,}000 \pm \$262$$

Similarly, 95 percent of the time sales revenue for store A will be within two standard deviations of the mean, or between \$5,476 and \$6,524, calculated as \$6,000 ± 2(\$262). This kind of information is of obvious value to managers trying to project future sales revenue for the purpose of planning business operations. For example, in fast-food restaurants, sales revenue is usually the same as cash inflows, and knowledge of the range of future cash flows can help managers to plan when to borrow cash and when to invest idle funds or repay loans.

The estimate of weekly sales revenue for store B is much less precise. Store B has the same mean sales revenue of \$6,000, but revenue fluctuates much more. The standard deviation of store B's revenue is \$2,153. Therefore, 68 percent of the time sales revenue should be \$6,000 ± \$2,153, or between \$3,847 and \$8,153. Two standard deviations from the mean, or approximately 95 percent of the time, weekly sales should be in the range from \$1,694 to \$10,306, which is \$6,000 ± (2)(\$2,153). It is clear that even though the two fast-food restaurants have identical average weekly sales revenue, they face significantly different planning problems.

Sample Characteristics

The above estimates of sales, obtained from the mean and standard deviation, are based on two important assumptions:

1. The sample of data is representative of the population.
2. The population is normally distributed.

A sample should be representative of the population

Representative sample. The total set of data from which the sample data are collected is called the **population.** The **sample** of data taken from the population should be representative of the population in order for the mean and standard deviation calculated from the sample to be meaningful. We used 10 weeks of sales data as our sample of sales revenue. If the sample data are not representative of weekly sales revenue in general, the estimates of cash flows may be wrong. Most statistical analyses of accounting data are based on a sample of the total data. For example, quality-control programs frequently utilize sampling techniques to select every tenth or every twenty-fifth item to test for quality. Testing every item is too costly and sampling often provides very good quality control. Most business statistical analyses use sample data from which sample means, variances, and standard deviations are computed.

Normal distribution. The second assumption underlying estimates of the probability of various sales' occurring is the normal curve assumption. The **normal curve assumption** means that we assume the data in the population are normally distributed in a systematic and uniform pattern about the mean, and a **normal curve** is a diagram of normally distributed data. There is an equal probability that a value will fall on one side of the mean as on the other. The symmetrical nature of a normal distribution results in a bell-shaped curve illustrated at the top of Figure 18-3.

Not all data generate a bell-shaped curve, but a normal distribution is assumed for many business statistical analyses, because the data are often close enough to a normal distribution to provide useful statistics. The mathematical properties of the normal distribution have considerable practical value, such as enabling us to estimate easily the probabilities of the occurrence of many events.

The normal curve has very useful characteristics

Use of the normal curve. The area under the normal curve represents the probability of occurrence of an event that comes from a normally distributed population. The area under the curve on each side of the mean is 50 percent. You can now see where the 68 percent and 95 percent values mentioned earlier come from. The first normal curve shown in Figure 18-4 has a shaded area within one standard deviation of the mean. In the table in Figure 18-3, the area between the mean and one standard deviation is given as .3413. Since the shaded area in the first normal curve in Figure 18-4 is on each side of the mean, the value in the table must be doubled to obtain the total shaded area, and you see that $2 \times .3413 = .6826$, or slightly more than 68 percent. Similarly, the table gives the value .4772 for the area between the mean and two standard deviations away, or .9544 for the area on both sides of the mean, as illustrated by the second normal curve in Figure 18-4. This means that a data item or event occurs beyond two standard deviations away from the mean less than 5 percent of the time. The table can also be used to find the probability of an item's being at least as large as some value, or at least as small as some value.

For example, store B may want to know the probability that weekly sales revenue will fall between \$5,000 and \$7,000. These amounts are \$1,000 on either side of the mean value of \$6,000. One thousand dollars is only a portion of one standard deviation of \$2,153. In fact it is \$1,000/\$2,153, or .46 standard deviation from the mean. The .46 value is found in the normal curve table by finding .4 in the left column and going across that row to the .06 column, giving the value .1772 in the table. This value means that there is a 17.7 percent chance of being within .46 standard

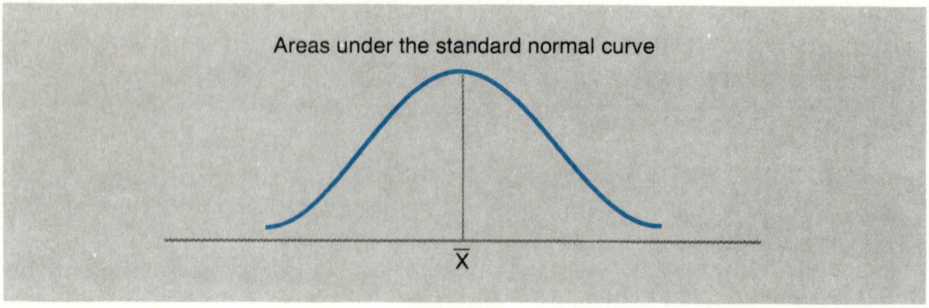

The following table provides percentage areas under the normal curve on one side of the mean.

Standard Deviation	.00	.01	.02	.03	.04	.05	.06	.07	.08	.09
0.0	.0000	.0040	.0080	.0120	.0160	.0199	.0239	.0279	.0319	.0359
0.1	.0398	.0438	.0478	.0517	.0557	.0596	.0636	.0675	.0714	.0753
0.2	.0793	.0832	.0871	.0910	.0948	.0987	.1026	.1064	.1103	.1141
0.3	.1179	.1217	.1255	.1293	.1331	.1368	.1406	.1443	.1480	.1517
0.4	.1554	.1591	.1628	.1664	.1700	.1736	.1772	.1808	.1844	.1879
0.5	.1915	.1950	.1985	.2019	.2054	.2088	.2123	.2157	.2190	.2224
0.6	.2257	.2291	.2324	.2357	.2389	.2422	.2454	.2486	.2518	.2549
0.7	.2580	.2612	.2642	.2673	.2704	.2734	.2764	.2794	.2823	.2852
0.8	.2881	.2910	.2939	.2967	.2995	.3023	.3051	.3078	.3106	.3133
0.9	.3159	.3186	.3212	.3238	.3264	.3289	.3315	.3340	.3365	.3389
1.0	.3413	.3438	.3461	.3485	.3508	.3531	.3554	.3577	.3599	.3621
1.1	.3643	.3665	.3686	.3708	.3729	.3749	.3770	.3790	.3810	.3830
1.2	.3849	.3869	.3888	.3907	.3925	.3944	.3962	.3980	.3997	.4015
1.3	.4032	.4049	.4066	.4082	.4099	.4115	.4131	.4147	.4162	.4177
1.4	.4192	.4207	.4222	.4236	.4251	.4265	.4279	.4292	.4306	.4319
1.5	.4332	.4345	.4357	.4370	.4382	.4394	.4406	.4418	.4429	.4441
1.6	.4452	.4463	.4474	.4484	.4495	.4505	.4515	.4525	.4535	.4545
1.7	.4554	.4564	.4573	.4582	.4591	.4599	.4608	.4616	.4625	.4633
1.8	.4641	.4649	.4656	.4664	.4671	.4678	.4686	.4693	.4699	.4706
1.9	.4713	.4719	.4726	.4732	.4738	.4744	.4750	.4756	.4761	.4767
2.0	.4772	.4778	.4783	.4788	.4793	.4798	.4803	.4808	.4812	.4817
2.1	.4821	.4826	.4830	.4834	.4838	.4842	.4846	.4850	.4854	.4857
2.2	.4861	.4864	.4868	.4871	.4875	.4878	.4881	.4884	.4887	.4890
2.3	.4893	.4896	.4898	.4901	.4904	.4906	.4909	.4911	.4913	.4916
2.4	.4918	.4920	.4922	.4925	.4927	.4929	.4931	.4932	.4934	.4936
2.5	.4938	.4940	.4941	.4943	.4945	.4946	.4948	.4949	.4951	.4952
2.6	.4953	.4955	.4956	.4957	.4959	.4960	.4961	.4962	.4963	.4964
2.7	.4965	.4966	.4967	.4968	.4969	.4970	.4971	.4972	.4973	.4974
2.8	.4974	.4975	.4976	.4977	.4977	.4978	.4979	.4979	.4980	.4981
2.9	.4981	.4982	.4982	.4983	.4984	.4984	.4985	.4985	.4986	.4986
3.0	.49865	.4987	.4987	.4988	.4988	.4989	.4989	.4989	.4990	.4990
4.0	.49997									

Figure 18-3 **The normal curve shows the symmetrical nature of a normal distribution. The table allows us to make probabilistic statements about a set of normally distributed data once the mean and the standard deviation have been computed.**

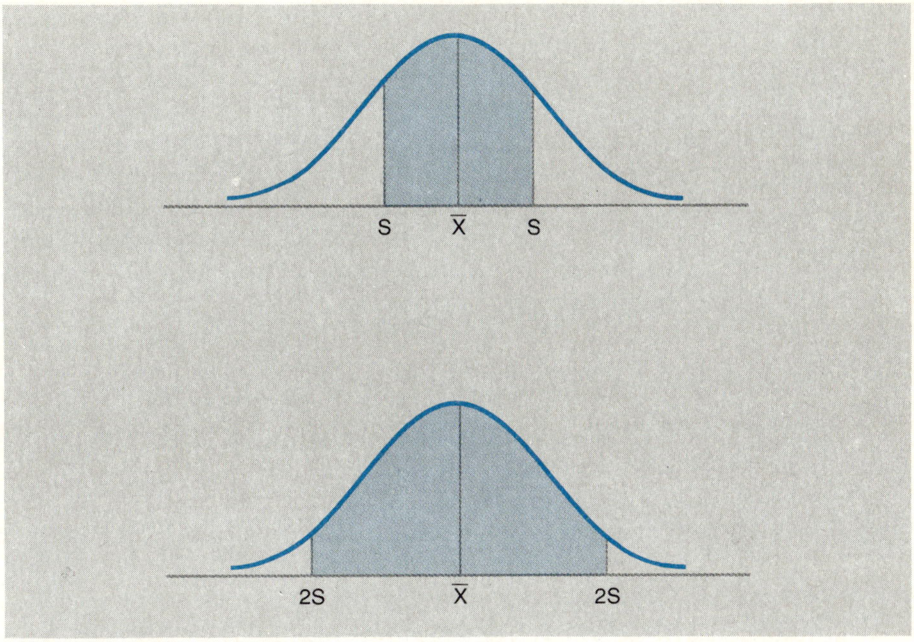

Figure 18-4
The normal curve with the shaded portions showing the areas under the curve for one and two standard deviations from the mean.

deviation of the mean. But this table only measures the probability of being away from the mean in one direction. The 17.7 percent is the probability of being between \$5,000 and \$6,000, or between \$6,000 and \$7,000. To find the probability of being between \$5,000 and \$7,000, the 17.7 percent is merely doubled to yield 35.4 percent.

Often managers are far more concerned about fluctuations in one direction than in another. For instance, the management of store B wants to know the probability of sales' being **at least** \$5,000. The probability of sales revenue's being between \$5,000 and the mean of \$6,000 is 17.7 percent. The probability of its being above the mean with a normal curve is 50 percent. Therefore, the probability of sales' being at least \$5,000 is 17.7 percent + 50 percent, or 67.7 percent.

REGRESSION-CORRELATION ANALYSIS

Another statistical tool important in business is regression-correlation analysis. It is used in cost planning and control to relate costs to activity levels for both actual costs and budgeted costs. Changes in costs as different activity levels occur have a significant impact on the planning and control functions. Some costs appear to be relatively fixed over a relevant range of activity and some vary with changes in activity level. Still others defy accurate description. Quantitative methods are especially useful for analyzing such varied cost behavior.

Regression-correlation is used to measure the nature and strength of the relationship between costs and activity

Regression-correlation analysis is used to determine the nature and strength of the relationship between costs and activity measures. Probably no other quantitative tool has as wide an applicability to accounting data as regression-correlation analysis. Its appeal stems from its ability to use one or more variables to predict the value of another variable. The prediction problem surfaces in many facets of budgeting, planning, and control. For example, in Chapters 2 and 5 we discussed separating mixed costs of production into fixed and variable components. This process is easily accomplished by regression analysis. Regression-correlation analysis is a two-step process, involving:

1. Determination of the nature of the association between two or more variables
2. Determination of the strength of the relationship between the variables

First we discuss simple linear regression and later we illustrate a more complex form of regression analysis.

Usually cost is the dependent variable in analyzing accounting data and activity level is the independent variable

Simple linear regression deals with two variables. The first is the **independent variable,** which typically is derived from historical data. The second is the **dependent variable,** whose value depends on the value of the independent variable and on the relationship between the two variables as described by a mathematical equation. For example, employee fringe benefits are related to the number of hours worked by employees. A company may use regression-correlation analysis to measure the relationship between the two variables. Here the independent variable is labor hours, and the dependent variable is employee fringe benefit cost. It is the dependent variable because its value depends on the number of labor hours and the relationship between labor hours and the amount of fringe benefit costs.

Computing the Regression Line

The first step is to compute the regression line

The **regression line** is a line whose equation best describes the linear relationship between the independent variable and the dependent variable. The linear regression line has the traditional form of the equation for a straight line, which is

$$Y_c = a + bX$$

where:

Y_c = the value of the dependent variable computed from a specific value of the independent variable.

a = the constant, which is the point where the regression line crosses the Y axis. It is the value of Y_c when $X = 0$.

b = the slope of the regression line. It describes the change in the value of Y_c for each unit change in the value of X. If Y_c increases when X increases, then the slope of the regression line is said to be positive. If Y_c decreases when X increases, the slope of the regression line is negative.

X = the value of the independent variable.

Figure 18-5 illustrates a regression line described by the equation $Y_c = 5 + 2X$. In this case $a = 5$, and $b = 2$. For any value of X, Y is equal to 5 + 2 times the value of X. The regression line is computed from the 10 data points shown on the graph. It is the straight line that minimizes the absolute vertical distance between the line and each datum. In other words, no other straight line can be drawn through the set of data that would reduce the total vertical distance between the data and the regression line, so the line is referred to as the **line of best fit.**

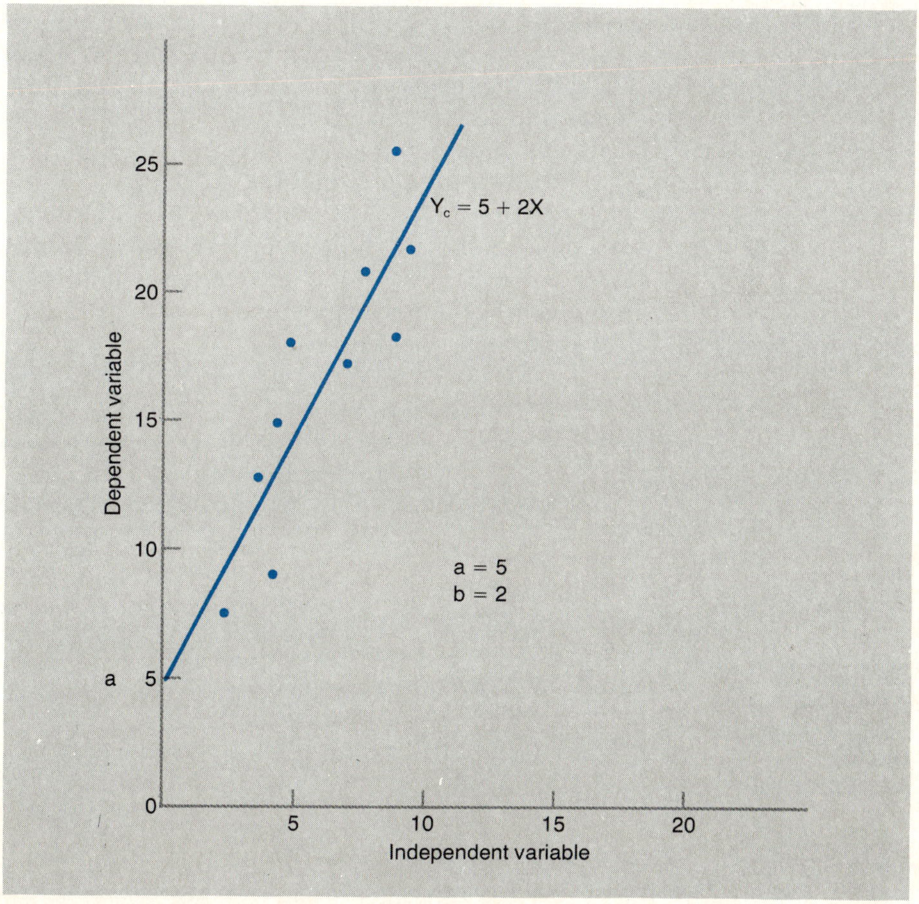

Figure 18-5 **Graph of a regression line showing the constant *a*, where the regression line crosses the *Y* axis, and the slope of the regression line *b*, which is the change in the value of *Y* for each unit change in the value of *X*.**

ILLUSTRATIVE EXAMPLE OF REGRESSION-CORRELATION ANALYSIS

To illustrate the computation and use of regression-correlation analysis, we present an example of the Wheat City Community Hospital. A schedule of weekly indirect costs and activity data is presented in Figure 18-6 for the hospital's emergency room.

These are historical data for 6 weeks of operating the emergency room. The indirect costs are given in column 1. Three different measures of activity are given in columns 2 through 4. In an effort to plan for and control the indirect costs of this patient care program, the hospital would like to be able to relate indirect costs to some measure of activity.

Regression Analysis

There are many ways to analyze these data, some more meaningful than others. For example, we could calculate the mean and standard deviation of the emergency room indirect costs. The mean is merely the sum of the weekly costs divided by the number of weeks, or $145,200/6 = $24,200, and the standard deviation is $2,361. As we discussed earlier, this information can be used to help plan activities and make decisions. However, even more useful information can be obtained if emergency room indirect costs are mathematically related to one of the activity variables presented in the schedule.

In simple linear regression only one independent variable can be related to the dependent variable. The hospital wants to predict indirect cost, which is the dependent variable. The independent variable can be any one of the three activity measures in Figure 18-6. For this illustration we choose patients served as the independent variable. Most regression lines are computed from some type of historical data such as monthly,

Wheat City Community Hospital
Weekly Emergency Room Cost and Activity Data

Week	1 Indirect Cost per Week	2 Patients Served	3 Direct Labor Hours Staff	4 Direct Labor Hours Medical
1	$ 22,500	110	600	150
2	25,800	132	620	180
3	28,000	184	760	190
4	23,400	115	570	170
5	21,500	91	550	140
6	24,000	148	610	135
Totals	$145,200	780	3,710	965

Figure 18-6
This schedule provides 6 weeks of data for indirect costs and three activity measures for a hospital emergency room.

weekly, or daily cost data, as in the hospital example. Here 6 weeks of emergency room data are used. This is a relatively small sample but it suffices for purposes of illustrating the computational process. Later we deal with significantly larger data bases, whose regression lines may be found easily with a computer.

Definition of variables. Several terms must be defined before we proceed:

- Y_i are the observed (actual) values of the dependent variable used in the computation of the regression line. In the example the Y_i values are the six weekly observations of the total indirect cost. For example, Y_1 is the \$22,500 indirect cost for week 1, and Y_2 is the \$25,800 cost for week 2.
- X_i are the observed (actual) values of the independent variable. Here X_i is the number of patients served each week. For example, X_1 is 110 patients in week 1 and X_2 is 132 patients in week 2.
- n is the number of observations used in computing the regression line. In our example there are 6 weeks of data, so $n = 6$.

A number of different approaches exist for computing the regression line. One approach is to solve the following set of simultaneous equations:

$$\Sigma Y_i = na + b\Sigma X_i \qquad (1)$$

$$\Sigma X_i Y_i = a\Sigma X_i + b\Sigma X_i^2 \qquad (2)$$

These two equations may look complex, but in fact they are easy to solve with basic algebra. First we explain the terms in the two equations.

- ΣY_i = the sum of all the observed values of the dependent variables Y_i, in this case the total of the weekly indirect costs
- ΣX_i = the sum of the observed values of the independent variables X_i, in this example the total number of patients served in the 6 weeks
- $\Sigma X_i Y_i$ = the sum of the products of each pair of X_i and Y_i
- ΣX_i^2 = the sum of the squared values of the independent variables X_i

Figure 18-7 provides all the necessary data to calculate the regression line equation. In addition, it contains values for Y_i^2, which are not needed to compute the regression line but are used later. Note that once these values are substituted into the two equations, the only variables without values are a and b, which are the two values necessary to describe the regression line.

Wheat City Community Hospital
Schedule of Data for Regression-Correlation Analysis

Week	Indirect Cost Y_i	Y_i^2	Patients Served X_i	X_i^2	X_iY_i
1	$ 22,500	$ 506,250,000	110	12,100	$ 2,475,000
2	25,800	665,640,000	132	17,424	3,405,600
3	28,000	784,000,000	184	33,856	5,152,000
4	23,400	547,560,000	115	13,225	2,691,000
5	21,500	462,250,000	91	8,281	1,956,500
6	24,000	576,000,000	148	21,904	3,552,000
Totals (Σ)	$145,200	$3,541,700,000	780	106,790	$19,232,100

Figure 18-7 Data necessary for computing the regression line relating indirect costs with number of patients served.

Solving for *a* and *b*. With two unknowns, *a* and *b*, and two equations, a solution is possible. The first step is to substitute the known values into the equations as follows:

$$\Sigma Y_i = na + b\Sigma X_i \qquad (1)$$
$$\$145{,}200 = 6a + 780b$$

$$\Sigma X_iY_i = a\Sigma X_i + b\Sigma X_i^2 \qquad (2)$$
$$\$19{,}232{,}100 = 780a + 106{,}790b$$

These two simultaneous equations may be solved either by substitution or by subtraction. We choose the latter method. The coefficient of *a* is smaller in each equation than the coefficient of *b*, so we eliminate *a* simply as a matter of convenience. When we multiply each term of equation (1) by 130, the coefficients of *a* in both equations become identical, and we can subtract one equation from the other. Multiplying by 130 we get

$$(130)\$145{,}200 = (130)6a + (130)780b \qquad (1)$$

Subtracting equation (1) from equation (2) we get

$$\begin{array}{lrcl r} \text{from} & \$19{,}232{,}100 & = & 780a + 106{,}790b & (2) \\ \text{subtract} & \$18{,}876{,}000 & = & 780a + 101{,}400b & (1) \\ \hline & \$\quad 356{,}100 & = & 0 + 5{,}390b & \end{array}$$

$$b = \frac{\$356{,}100}{5{,}390}$$

$$= \$66.06679$$

b is the variable cost per unit of activity

The value of b is the slope of the regression line. It means that for every unit increase in X, there is a \$66.06679 increase in Y. Since X is the number of patients served and Y is indirect costs, we can say that for each additional patient served indirect costs rise by \$66.07.

Once we have found b it is a simple matter to find a by substituting the value of b into equation (1) or (2). Again equation (1) is selected for computational ease, although either equation yields the same answer.

$$\$145{,}200 = 6a + 780(\$66.06679)$$

$$6a = \$145{,}200 - \$51{,}532.096$$

$$a = \frac{\$93{,}667.904}{6}$$

$$= \$15{,}611.317$$

The term a in the regression line equation is the Y intercept and represents the fixed component of indirect costs. The regression line equation is

$$Y_c = \$15{,}611.32 + \$66.07X$$

or total indirect cost is equal to the \$15,611.32 fixed cost plus \$66.07 for each patient served. Later you will see how the regression line is used for predicting, budgeting, or just helping managers understand costs and their relationships to other variables.

Correlation Analysis

Correlation measures the strength of the relationship between the two variables

The regression line describes the relationship that exists between the dependent and the independent variable, but it does not say how good the relationship is. Statistical techniques exist that measure the **strength of the relationship.** The regression line is the best-fitting straight line that can be fitted through the set of data, but it is possible that no regression line has a very good fit. We saw such a case in the scatter diagram in Chapter 5, Figure 5-2.

Interpreting positive and negative correlation

Coefficient of correlation. An important measure of how well the regression line fits the data is called the **coefficient of correlation,** denoted as r, which measures the degree of association between the dependent and the independent variables. It ranges in value from $+1$, representing perfect positive correlation, to -1, representing perfect negative correlation. **Positive correlation** means that as the independent variable increases or decreases so does the dependent variable. **Negative correlation** means that as the independent variable increases, the dependent variable decreases, and vice versa. Figure 18-8 illustrates the general relationship between r, the regression line, and the data.

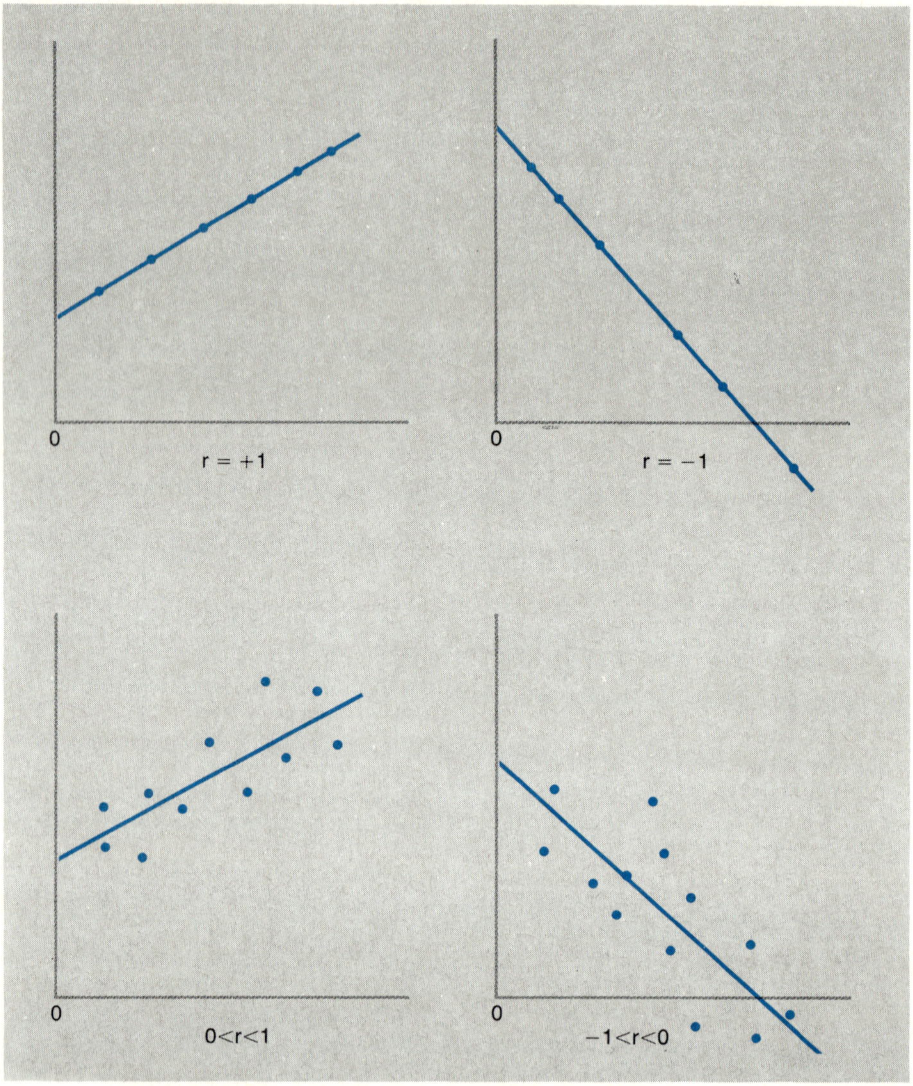

Figure 18-8
Graphs showing the general slopes and data distributions for correlations ranging from perfect positive correlation, +1, to perfect negative correlation, −1.

There are several computational approaches for finding r. One is to solve the following equation:

$$r = \frac{n\Sigma X_i Y_i - (\Sigma X_i)(\Sigma Y_i)}{\sqrt{n\Sigma X_i^2 - (\Sigma X_i)^2}\ \sqrt{n\Sigma Y_i^2 - (\Sigma Y_i)^2}} \tag{3}$$

All the data necessary for solving equation (3) are presented in Figure 18-7. Substituting the required data into equation (3), we get

$$r = \frac{(6)(\$19{,}232{,}100) - (780)(\$145{,}200)}{\sqrt{(6)(106{,}790) - (780)^2}\,\sqrt{(6)(\$3{,}541{,}700{,}000) - (\$145{,}200)^2}}$$

$$= \frac{\$115{,}392{,}600 - \$113{,}256{,}000}{\sqrt{32{,}340}\,\sqrt{\$167{,}160{,}000}}$$

$$= \frac{\$2{,}136{,}600}{\$2{,}325{,}070.7}$$

$$= .9189398$$

The closer r is to 1 or -1, the stronger the relationship between the dependent and the independent variables. The above calculation indicates a strong positive relationship. As r gets closer to zero it indicates a weaker relationship. The sign of r does not indicate the strength of the relationship, but only the direction. One must be careful in interpreting r; it measures the strength of the **linear** relationship between the dependent and independent variables. It is quite possible for r to be small, indicating a weak linear relationship, when the actual relationship between the variables is quite strong although it may not be linear. For example, Figure 18-9 shows two variables strongly related but having a weak linear relationship.

Different values of r must be interpreted carefully. An r of .8 does not indicate twice as good a linear relationship as an r of .4; the larger value actually indicates a relationship that is four times as strong as the smaller value. Similarly, an r of .75 is nine times as strong as an r of .25. You can see that as r doubles, the relationship increases by 2^2, and as r triples the relationship increases by 3^2. To make the interpretation of r more meaningful, therefore, the coefficient of correlation is often converted to the coefficient of determination, which is calculated as r^2, thereby eliminating the sign of r and enabling a more easily understood comparison to be made between the resulting values.

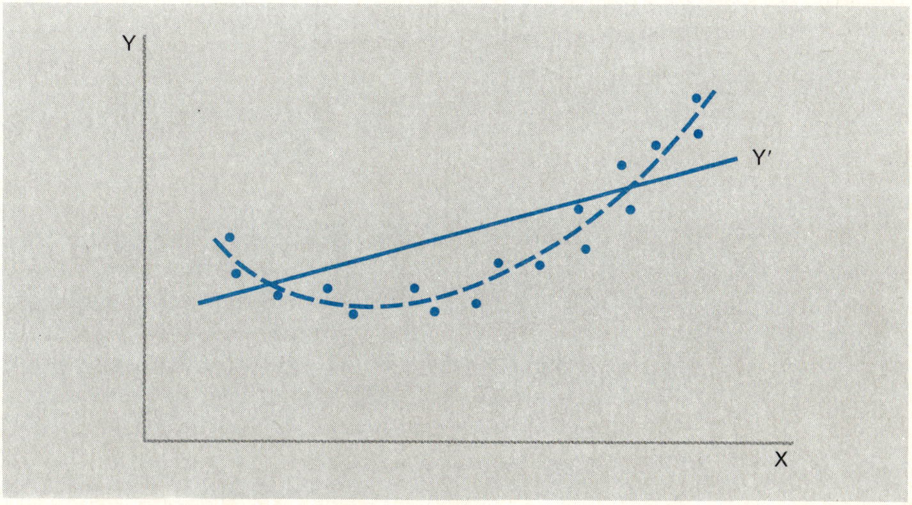

Figure 18-9
A correlation coefficient calculated for the linear regression line *Y* may indicate a poor correlation between the *X* and *Y* variables, but the broken line shows that the correlation is quite high, although it is not linear.

The **coefficient of determination** is another measure of the goodness of fit of the regression line to the data used in computing the regression line. It is a measure of the degree to which the two variables X and Y are related linearly. In the example above,

$$\begin{aligned} r^2 &= .9189398^2 \\ &= .84445036 \\ &= .84 \end{aligned}$$

To interpret this value of .84 it is first necessary to understand that r^2 is actually a ratio of two variances. Earlier we calculated the mean of emergency room costs of $24,200 and the standard deviation of $2,361. The standard deviation is the square root of the variance, and the variance is a measure of the fluctuation of costs about the mean, illustrated by diagram (a) in Figure 18-10. The costs also fluctuate about the regression line as illustrated by diagram (b) in Figure 18-10, and the coefficient of correlation tells us that the fluctuation of actual data about the regression line is relatively small. The mean and standard deviation give no indication why the costs fluctuate from week to week. The regression line relates the costs to the number of patients served in an attempt to explain some of the week-to-week fluctuations. The coefficient of determination of .84 indicates that of the total variance of indirect costs about the mean of $24,200, 84 percent of the fluctuation can be explained by knowing the number of patients served during the week.

What percentage of the total variation about the mean can be explained by the regression line?

Diagram (c) of Figure 18-10 shows the variation of the regression line Y_c about the mean $\overline{Y}$. You can see that where the vertical lines in diagram (b) are short, the vertical lines for the same data in diagrams (a) and (c) are similar in length. The coefficient of determination r^2 is actually the ratio of the variance of the regression line about the mean value of $24,200 to the total variance of the actual data about the mean. In other words, r^2 is the ratio of the variance in diagram (c) to the variance in diagram (a). Mathematically, it is expressed as:

$$r^2 = \frac{\Sigma(Y_c - \overline{Y})/(n - 1)}{\Sigma(Y_i - \overline{Y})/(n - 1)}$$

The numerator of the equation is the variance of the regression line about the mean [diagram (c)]; the denominator is the variance of the data about the mean [diagram (a)]. If the data all fell precisely on the regression line, that is, if $r = 1$, the variance of the regression line about the mean would be equal to the variance of the data about the mean, and the ratio r^2 would be equal to 1, which would mean that all the variance of indirect costs about the mean is explained by the number of patients visiting the emergency room. In our example, 84 percent of the variance is explained by the number of patients, and the remainder is due to other factors.

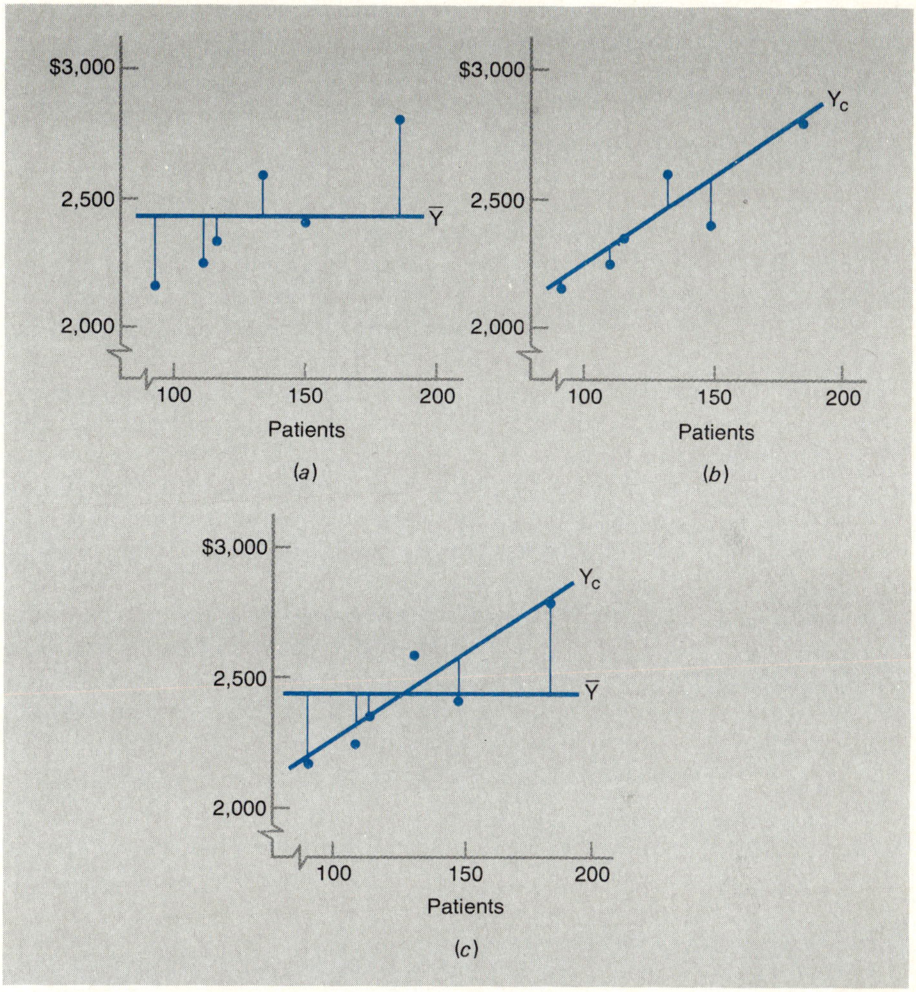

Figure 18-10
The indirect costs of Wheat City Community Hospital's emergency room are plotted against the number of patients served in each of 6 weeks. The same data are plotted in each diagram. The variance of the data about the mean are shown in (*a*), the variance about the regression line in (*b*), and the variance of the regression line about the mean in (*c*).

The portion of the variance that is not explained by the regression line relationship between the independent variable and dependent variable is $(1 - r^2)$ and is called the **coefficient of nondetermination,** whose value is .16 in our example. This portion of the variance must be explained by other independent variables or it results from random fluctuations.

Association Versus Causation

Many business decisions are influenced by managers' perceptions about the cause-and-effect relationships between activity variables and cost changes. Much of responsibility accounting rests on an ability to determine cause-and-effect relationships in business. Regression-correlation analysis measures the nature and association between two variables, usually based on historical data, but association—even strong association—does not prove cause-and-effect relationship. Many strong statistical associations exist that certainly suggest causal relationships but do not prove them.

Other Independent Variables

A coefficient of determination of .84 is very good. In practice an r^2 of .5 or even lower is often considered good enough to be useful to managers. It should be noted that a lack of strong correlation or even negative correlation does not mean a lack of information value for a manager. Frequently it is very useful to know that no relationship exists between two variables, particularly if managers have assumed a positive relationship in decision making. When the relationship is disproved, managers may look for better relationships. If an r^2 value is considered too low, a manager may choose to evaluate another independent variable to see whether it has a stronger relationship with the dependent variable. The Wheat City Community Hospital emergency room data in Figure 18-6 present three different measures of activity. We used patients served as the independent variable but either of the other two activity measures may be used as well.

One or both of the other two variables may have a stronger relationship to indirect emergency room cost, that is, a higher r^2, than number of patients served. To find out, we proceed as before. Each activity measure can be evaluated one at a time. Using direct labor hours for staff we compute a new regression line and r^2. Figure 18-11 presents the data necessary for the solution.

Wheat City Community Hospital
Schedule of Data for Regression-Correlation Analysis

Week	Indirect Costs Y_i	Y_i^2	Direct Labor Hours X_i	X_i^2	X_iY_i
1	$ 22,500	$ 506,250,000	600	360,000	$13,500,000
2	25,800	665,640,000	620	384,400	15,996,000
3	28,000	784,000,000	760	577,600	21,280,000
4	23,400	547,560,000	570	324,900	13,338,000
5	21,500	462,250,000	550	302,500	11,825,000
6	24,000	576,000,000	610	372,100	14,640,000
Totals (Σ)	$145,200	$3,541,700,000	3,710	2,321,500	$90,579,000

Figure 18-11 Data necessary for computing the regression line, as well as measures of correlation that describe how well the regression line fits the data.

Solving the two simultaneous equations to determine a and b for this regression line, we get

$$\Sigma Y_i = na + b\Sigma X_i \qquad (1)$$

$$\Sigma X_i Y_i = a\Sigma X_i + b\Sigma X_i^2 \qquad (2)$$

$$\$145{,}200 = 6a + 3{,}710b \qquad (1)$$

$$\$90{,}579{,}000 = 3{,}710a + 2{,}321{,}500b \qquad (2)$$

The multiplier for equation (1) is 3,710/6, or 618.3333. Multiplying equation (1) by 618.3333 and subtracting equation (1) from equation (2) we get

$$\$90{,}579{,}000 = 3{,}710\,a + 2{,}321{,}500b \qquad (2)$$

$$\underline{\$89{,}782{,}000 = 3{,}710a + 2{,}294{,}016.7b} \qquad (1)$$

$$\$797{,}000 = 27{,}483.3b$$

$$b = \$28.999429$$

To solve for a, we substitute the value of b into equation (1).

$$\$145{,}200 = 6a + (3{,}710)(\$28.999429) \qquad (1)$$

$$\$145{,}200 = 6a + \$107{,}587.88$$

$$6a = \$37{,}612.12$$

$$a = \$6{,}268.6867$$

The regression line using direct labor hours for staff is

$$Y_c = \$6{,}268.69 + \$29.00X$$

To find the value of r and r^2 we use equation (3):

$$r = \frac{(6)(\$90{,}579{,}000) - (3{,}710)(\$145{,}200)}{\sqrt{(6)(2{,}321{,}500) - (3{,}710)^2} \times \$12{,}929.037^*}$$

$$= \frac{\$543{,}474{,}000 - \$538{,}692{,}000}{\sqrt{164{,}900} \times \$12{,}929.037}$$

$$= \frac{\$4{,}782{,}000}{\$5{,}250{,}208}$$

$$= .91082106$$

* Note that this term, composed entirely of Y values, does not change when other independent variables are used and need not be computed again.

The coefficient of determination is

$$r^2 = .91082106^2$$
$$= .83$$

Medical direct labor hours may be use as an independent variable also. By substituting the necessary data into the analysis, we can compute the following regression line:

$$Y_c = \$10{,}546 + \$84.96X$$

The coefficients of correlation and determination are

$$r = .806226$$
$$r^2 = .65$$

You may want to compute both the regression line and r^2 to be certain you can arrive at the same answer using medical direct labor hours. Because r^2 for number of patients served is higher than for either medical or staff direct labor hours, we can state that the relationship between costs and number of patients is stronger than the relationship between costs and the other two variables. We now discuss how this information is used.

Using Linear Regression

A primary use of regression-correlation analysis is to aid in the planning process. Often accountants analyze historical cost data using various measures of activity in an attempt to determine the activity variable with the strongest relationship to cost. Then the variable is used as a basis for budgeting and other planning and analysis activities.

Because the number of patients served provides the highest coefficient of determination of the three activity variables analyzed, the hospital may use that variable as a basis for projecting emergency room indirect costs. With the regression equation available, management can project expected costs for any level of activity. It is only necessary to substitute the desired activity level into the equation for the value of X and calculate the value of Y. For example, to estimate indirect emergency room costs for a week when 150 patients are treated, we use this calculation:

$$\begin{aligned} Y_c &= \$15{,}611.32 + \$66.07X \\ &= \$15{,}611.32 + \$66.07(150) \\ &= \$15{,}611.32 + \$9{,}910.5 \\ &= \$25{,}522 \end{aligned}$$

The computations required in regression-correlation analysis can be made easily using inexpensive hand calculators many of which have internal programs that automatically compute a, b, and r^2. Regression-correlation software is readily available for computers.

The advantage of regression-correlation analysis is that it provides far more precision than the high-low or graphic methods discussed in Chapter 5. For instance, the high-low method gives the following results for the emergency room data:

		High-Low Method	Regression Line
Patients served			
$b = \dfrac{\$28,000 - \$21,500}{184 - 91}$	=	\$ 69.89	\$ 66.07
$a = \$28,000 - 184(\$69.892473)$	=	\$15,139.79	\$15,611.32
Staff labor hours			
$b = \dfrac{\$28,000 - \$21,500}{760 - 550}$	=	\$ 30.95	\$ 29.00
$a = \$28,000 - 760(\$30.952381)$	=	\$ 4,476.19	\$ 6,268.69
Medical labor hours			
$b = \dfrac{\$28,000 - \$21,500}{190 - 140}$	=	\$ 130.00	\$ 84.96
$a = \$28,000 - 190(\$130)$	=	\$ 3,300.00	\$10,546.00

In the first case the a and b values are reasonably close to those of the computed regression line; in the second case the b values are close but the a values are not; in the case of medical hours, the high-low estimate is poor. If high-low yields results similar to the regression line values, why not use the easier method? Because there is no way of knowing when high-low provides a good estimate and when it does not. There is no r^2, the goodness-of-fit measure. One of the real advantages of regression-correlation analysis is knowing how strong the relationship is between the two variables.

Two points of caution should be mentioned. One is that the regression line and r^2 are typically based on historical data. The resulting relationships may or may not hold in the future. Past data are often the best indicators of the future, but not always, and seldom is the past a perfect predictor of the future. Second, although there may be a strong cause-and-effect relationship between many linear regression variables, such as between utility bills and production output, regression-correlation analysis does not prove that there are causal relationships, only that a relationship may exist.

Multiple Linear Regression

An extension of simple linear regression is **multiple linear regression,** with two or more independent variables used simultaneously to predict the value of the dependent variable. In some instances using more than one independent variable can improve the forecast of the dependent variable by better explaining the past variations of the dependent variable. For example, if in the previous example the number of patient visits and number of medical staff hours could be related simultaneously to indirect labor costs, we might find that together they provide a stronger relationship than either of them alone.

Multiple regression includes more than one independent variable in the analysis

Multiple regression is the same two-step process as linear regression analysis: Compute the regression line and compute the strength of the relationship. The regression line takes the general form:

$$Y_c = a + b_1X_1 + b_2X_2 + b_3X_3 + \cdots + b_nX_n$$

where a is the Y intercept or the value of Y when all X terms have a zero value, and $b_1, \ldots b_n$ each represent the relationships between the dependent variable and one of the independent variables. Each independent variable has its own b coefficient and the number of terms in the regression line equation depends on the number of independent variables used in the analysis.

The strength of the relationships is measured by the **multiple coefficient of determination,** which is determined by

$$r^2 = \frac{\text{Explained variation}}{\text{Total variation}} = 1 - \frac{\Sigma(Y_i - Y_c)^2}{\Sigma(Y_i - \bar{Y})^2}$$

However, the computation of multiple r^2 is much more complex and tedious than that of r^2. Likewise, the complexity of computations for determining the regression line precludes solving multiple regression problems manually, but multiple regression programs are available on most computer systems.

LEARNING CURVES AND COST ANALYSIS

As learning takes place, labor efficiency improves

In financial planning and control and in managerial decision analysis, there is a tendency to view costs as fixed or directly variable. This view is convenient and often approximates cost behavior well enough for many purposes. However, there are situations in which cost behavior characteristics dictate a more precise analysis.

Some semivariable costs increase at a decreasing rate as the volume of activity increases. Such costs are called **learning curve costs** and the graphs of such costs are called **learning curves.** Many organizations have found and documented a learning effect in the production of goods or services. In other words, they have found that the amount of effort required to make a product or to provide a service declines over time, particularly with new products or processes. The improvement in labor efficiency produces reductions in labor costs per unit and other costs related to labor. Many products have relatively short life cycles, such as 6 months to 2 years. If learning curve effects occur for a year or more, product costs for a good portion of the product's life may be declining. In such cases learning curve cost analysis may be useful for estimating production costs and establishing product prices. Learning curves may be used to aid managers in predicting costs and in interpreting cause-and-effect relationships between activity measures and costs.

While learning is taking place, total labor time—and therefore total labor-related costs—continue to rise as units of output rise, but the labor time and costs rise at a decreasing rate. If this relationship is graphed with units of service or product on the horizontal axis and total cost on the vertical axis, it looks like Figure 18-12.

The broken line *OA* is a directly variable cost, with each unit change in activity level causing exactly the same change in total variable cost. The solid line *OB* is a learning curve cost. Although the total cost increases with activity, it is increasing at a decreasing rate. Depending on the degree of learning, called the **learning rate**, and the time period involved, the learning curve can have a different slope than the one in Figure 18-12.

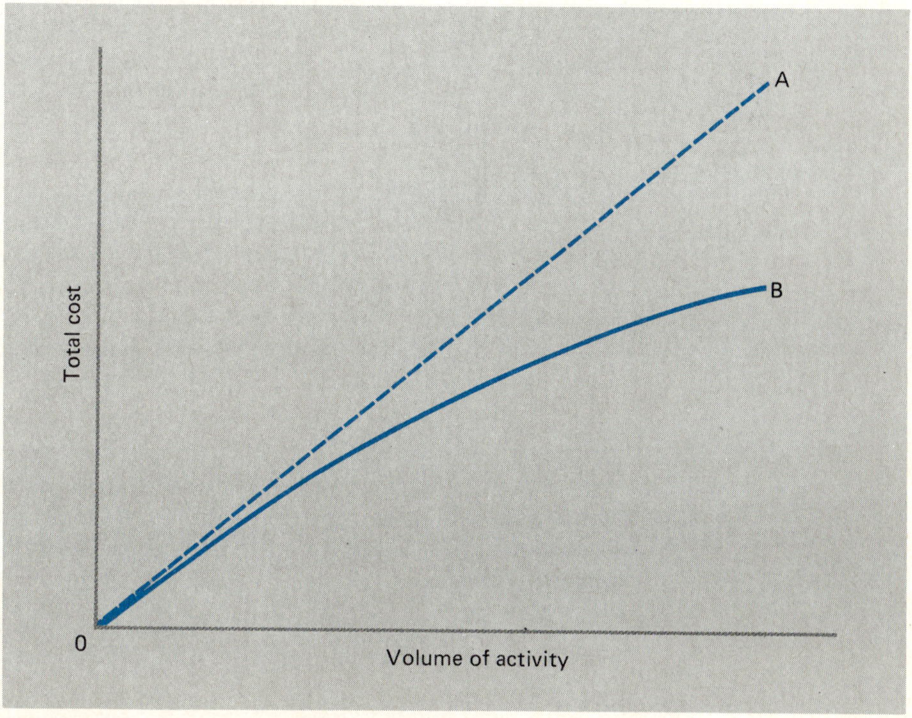

Figure 18-12
Learning curves are semivariable costs that increase at a decreasing rate. The dashed line *OA* is a directly variable cost, and the curved line *OB* is a learning curve that bends toward the *X* axis as learning takes place and labor cost per unit declines.

Computing Learning Curve Costs

The learning curve is an exponential function

In order to use learning curves for management planning and control, one must express the learning curve cost function in mathematical terms. The general form of the equation for a learning curve is

$$Y = aX^b$$

where:

Y = the average amount of time or cost per unit of output
a = the time or cost required to produce the first unit or batch of units
X = cumulative number of units or batches produced
b = the learning effect (index) = the logarithm of the learning rate divided by the logarithm of 2

Note that ***a*** and ***b*** have a different meaning in the notation for a learning curve than they do for the regression line. Be careful to use them correctly in each situation.

Substituting values into the equation makes it possible to determine specific values for labor time or cost for a particular situation. Some terminology is discussed before we work an example.

1. Learning is expressed as a percentage such as 70 percent, 90 percent, or 98 percent. Each time output doubles, the cumulative average labor cost of the output is equal to the learning curve percentage of the previous labor cost. In other words, when production doubles, the average labor cost of the product is a percentage of the cost at the last doubling. For example, it cost $100 to produce the first unit of a product and the learning curve is 95 percent. When the second unit is produced the cost of the **two** units produced so far is 95 percent of $100, or $95 per unit. When two more units are produced, output has again doubled and the average cost of each of the **four** units is 95 percent of $95, or 95 percent of 95 percent of the original $100 cost. The average cost of the four units is therefore $90.25.
2. The **higher** the learning curve percentage, the **lower** the learning effect. An 80 percent learning curve represents significantly more learning than a 95 percent learning curve. Also, note that a 100 percent learning curve represents no learning at all. In that case cost is directly variable and learning has reached what is known as a **steady state.**
3. The term ***a*** may represent a group of units rather than a single unit of service or product, such as the first 100 patients using a new service.
4. X is expressed in multiples of a for computational purposes. If

production has doubled once, X is 2; if it has doubled twice, X is 2^2, or 4; if it has doubled three times, X is 2^3, or 8; and so on. X can also be a figure like 3, or 4.7, representing a fraction of a doubling. If a is a single unit, and $X = 8$, then eight units have been produced in three doublings.

We now turn to a simple example using these learning curve concepts.

A Learning Curve Illustration

The Saverine Boat Company is a family-owned manufacturer of quality boats. It started as a producer of handmade canvas canoes and has branched into several specialized boat types. The most recent product line addition is a small bass boat that sells for $1,350. Like all Saverine's products, it is primarily manually produced except for basic fabricating processes. Consequently labor and labor-related costs comprise a large part of the product's total cost. The first quarter of 1986 was the first period of production for the new boat. Production data for the period are:

Boats produced	500
Direct materials	$200,000
Labor-related costs	120,000
Allocated fixed overhead	100,000

With the last three new boats added to the company's line, Saverine Boat Company has experienced a 90 percent learning effect for labor-related cost for the first several years of production. A similar learning curve effect is expected with the bass boat. The company would like to project product costs for this boat for the rest of 1986. The company estimates costs will remain stable for the 9-month period except for the learning curve effect, and production is expected to remain at 500 boats per quarter.

In order to prepare the budget for boat production for the last three quarters of the year, the company needs fixed and variable cost data. Fixed costs for the first quarter are $100,000, so for the last three quarters they are expected to total $300,000. Direct material is found easily by using unit variable costs from the data above:

$$\text{Direct material cost} = \$200{,}000 \text{ for } 500 \text{ boats}$$

$$\frac{\$200{,}000}{500 \text{ boats}} = \$400 \text{ per boat}$$

Direct labor cost poses a challenge because it changes as learning takes place. To complete the budget for the last three quarters of the year, the company must first calculate expected labor-related cost for production, using the learning curve.

Learning is computed in multiples of initial production

Finding labor costs with learning curves. The labor-related costs are expected to have a 90 percent learning curve effect, which means that each time the output **doubles,** the **cumulative average cost** of labor-related costs is 90 percent of what it was during the previous doubling. Therefore, for the first doubling of production from 500 boats to 1,000 boats, the cumulative average labor-related cost is 90 percent of the original cost. For the second doubling, from 1,000 boats to 2,000 boats, the cumulative average cost becomes 90 percent of 90 percent, or 81 percent of the original first batch cost. A schedule of labor-related costs for the production of the first 2,000 bass boats is presented in Figure 18-13.

The labor-related cost for the first 500 boats is $120,000, or an average of $240 per boat manufactured. The first doubling of output, from 500 to 1,000 boats, occurs during the second quarter. The **cumulative average cost** of production is 90 percent of $240, or $216. The total cumulative cost should be 1,000 units × $216, or $216,000. However, the cost of production for just the second quarter is $96,000, or an **incremental average cost** of $192 per boat ($96,000/500 boats). The next doubling, from 1,000 to 2,000 boats, will occur during the third and fourth quarters of the year. The cumulative average cost should be 90 percent of $216, or $194.40.

Another way of computing the same cost is to use the original cost and raise the learning effect to an exponential power equal to the number of doublings that have occurred. For instance, the cost for the second doubling is calculated as

$$\$240 \times (.9)^2 = \$240 \times .81 = \$194.40$$

Saverine Boat Company
Schedule of Labor-Related Costs for Bass Boats

Doubling	Cumulative Number of Units	Incremental Number of Units	Cumulative Cost	Incremental Cost	Total Average Unit Cost	Incremental Average Unit Cost
	500	500	$120,000	$120,000	$240.00	$240.00
1	1,000	500	216,000	96,000	216.00	192.00
2	2,000	1,000	388,800	172,800	194.40	172.80

Figure 18-13 **This schedule identifies the cumulative and incremental labor-related costs for producing the first two doublings of the original 500 units of production.**

If the cost of the third doubling were to be calculated it would be

$$\$240 \times (.9)^3 = \$174.96$$

Total cumulative labor-related cost for production of the first 2,000 boats is

$$\$194.40 \times 2{,}000 = \$388{,}800$$

As Figure 18-13 shows, the cost of production for the last two quarters only is $172,800, or an **incremental average cost** of $172.80. As you can see, the cost of producing the last boat is much less than the cost of producing the first boat. The learning curve formula, however, does not give the cost of producing the last unit. It gives the **average** unit cost of producing **all** units.

In Figure 18-13 the cumulative average cost is determined using the cost relationships described by the learning curve. The incremental cost is the cost of producing the additional increment of units. For example, the cumulative cost of producing the first 1,000 boats is $216,000. The cost of the first 500 boats is $120,000; therefore the remaining $96,000 is the labor-related cost of producing the second batch of 500 boats. Dividing the $96,000 by the 500-boat increment yields an incremental average unit cost of $192.00 for the 500-unit increment. The incremental average unit cost of the last 1,000 boats is similarly computed and is shown in Figure 18-13 as $172.80 per boat.

Saverine Boat Company has already produced the first 500 boats and the calculations in Figure 18-13 are made for the purpose of budgeting production for the last three quarters of the year. The cumulative labor-related cost is $388,800 for the first 2,000 boats, but that amount includes the $120,000 for the first 500 boats. Consequently the labor-related cost for the 1,500 boats to be produced during the last 9 months of 1986 is $268,800 ($388,800 − $120,000). Dividing $268,800 by 1,500 boats yields a labor-related cost of $179.20 per boat for the 1,500 boats. The budget for the last three quarters of 1986 for the 1,500 bass boats is as follows:

Direct materials	1,500 boats @ $400	=	$ 600,000
Labor-related costs	1,500 boats @ $179.20	=	268,800
Allocated fixed overhead		=	300,000
Total budgeted cost for last three quarters			$1,168,800

Using Logarithms to Compute Learning Curve Costs

In the boat company example, learning curve cost computations were quite simple, because the expected production precisely matched an exact dou-

Common or natural logarithms may be used in learning curve calculations

bling of the original production amount of 500 boats. The first doubling covered the second quarter and the second doubling matched expected production for the third and fourth quarters. But what if the expected production level is not an exact doubling? Suppose Saverine wants to budget costs for the first 6 months of 1987. At the current production level of 500 boats a quarter, it will produce 1,000 new boats in the first 6 months of 1987, which will be 3,000 in total since the first boat, but the next doubling of output occurs at 4,000 boats. A simple linear approximation can be made, but by definition learning curves are not straight lines, so some error will occur. To avoid the error, this and other learning curve problems can be solved using logarithms. The general form of the learning curve equation is

$$Y = aX^b$$

Using logarithms we can transform this to the linear form:

$$\ln Y = \ln a + b \ln X$$

If we know or can estimate a and b, it is possible to solve for any value of Y given any value of X whether or not X is a doubling multiple of the initial unit represented by a. Many inexpensive hand calculators have log function capabilities that make the computations very simple.

To illustrate, we again look at the boat company example. To solve the problem using logarithms, we use the logarithms of the variables.

> Y is the average amount of labor time or cost to produce X number of boats. It is the unknown value for which we want to solve.
>
> The number of units of service or product, in this case 3,000 boats, is expressed by X. However, X is not 3,000 boats; in our example the value of X is 6. This is because the first batch of boats produced consisted of 500 units and not just one. X in the learning curve formula is actually a multiple of the initial number of units. To solve for 3,000 boats when the initial number was 500, X is 3,000/500 boats, or 6.
>
> The value a is the average unit cost or labor time needed to produce a unit of service or product in the initial observation period. In this case it is \$240 per boat, as shown in Figure 18-13.
>
> The value b is the learning effect, which is equal to the log of the 90 percent learning rate divided by the log of 2[(ln .9)/(ln 2)].

Any learning curve problem with a 90 percent learning effect has a b value of $-.1520$, calculated as follows: the log of $.90 = -.1054$, and the log of $2 = .69315$, so $b = -.1054/.69315 = -.1520$. Values of b for any given learning effect are constant. Below are b values for some common learning rates:

Learning Rate	*b* Value
.70	−.5146
.75	−.4150
.80	−.3219
.85	−.2345
.90	−.1520
.95	−.0740
.98	−.0291

To summarize, the initial production run of 500 boats had average labor-related costs of $240 per unit, and the company experiences a 90 percent learning curve. We first repeat the previous calculation using logarithms to find the cost of production of 1,500 boats in the last three quarters of 1986. Then we calculate the cost for the first half of 1987, when 1,000 more boats are produced.

To compute the budgeted labor-related cost—Y in the learning curve equation—for the last three quarters of 1986, we merely substitute the necessary values into the learning curve equation.

$$Y = aX^b$$

$$\begin{aligned}\ln Y &= \ln a + b \ln X \\ &= \ln (\$240) + (-.1520) \ln 4\end{aligned}$$

where:

$\ln Y$ = the logarithm to the base e, or natural log, of the cost which is expressed as Y.
$\ln (\$240)$ = the natural log of the original unit cost of $240.
$-.1520$ = the value of b for a 90 percent learning curve.
$\ln 4$ = the natural log of the multiple of the initial quantity. Production for three quarters is 1,500 boats. Five hundred boats were already produced in the initial production run. Therefore, 2,000 boats will have been produced by year-end. Since 500 were in the initial production run, 2,000 is four times the initial amount, so the value of X is 4.

We can now substitute the appropriate values into the equation and solve for the log of Y and then for Y.

$$\begin{aligned}\ln Y &= 5.4806389 + (-.1520)\ 1.3862944 \\ &= 5.4806389 - .2107168 \\ &= 5.2699222\end{aligned}$$

$$Y = \$194.40$$

The value of Y is the antilogarithm of 5.2699222 and may be obtained from tables of natural logarithms or by means of a calculator.

Logarithms to the base e, or natural logs, are used here because they are most commonly found on hand calculators. However, logarithms to the base 10, or common logs, may be used just as easily.

The cumulative average cost for labor activities is $194.40, computed earlier and shown in Figure 18-13. The analysis is easily extended to compute the labor costs of boat production for the first 6 months of 1987. One thousand boats for the 6-month period means a total of 3,000 by the end of June 1987, which is six times the original production quantity of 500, so the value of X is 6. Substituting:

$$\begin{aligned} \ln Y &= \ln a + b \ln X \\ &= \ln (\$240) + (-.1520) \ln 6 \\ &= 5.4806389 + (-.1520)\ 1.7917595 \\ &= 5.4806389 - .2723474 \\ &= 5.2082915 \\ Y &= \$182.78 \end{aligned}$$

The cumulative average labor-related cost for 3,000 boats is $182.78 per unit. The total cumulative labor-related cost is $182.78 × 3,000 boats, or a total of $548,340. The cumulative labor-related cost for 2,000 boats completed in 1986 was computed earlier as $194.40 × 2,000 = $388,800. The difference between the total cost of $548,340 and the first-year cost of $388,800 is the incremental labor-related cost for the 1,000 boats to be produced in the first 6 months of 1987. The estimated amount the firm will have to spend for the labor-related costs of producing 1,000 boats in the first 6 months of 1987 is as follows:

Total labor cost for 3,000 boats	$548,340
Less labor cost for the first 2,000 boats	388,800
Labor cost for the last 1,000 boats	$159,540

Figure 18-14 shows the bass boat data presented in Figure 18-13 with cost estimates for 2,000 additional boats. As before, cumulative costs are presented together with the incremental cost of producing an additional amount.

The Steady State

The learning effect eventually stops for most new activities. Learning occurs for a period, and then the **steady state** is achieved when the costs

Saverine Boat Company
Schedule of Labor-Related Costs for Bass Boats

Doubling	Cumulative Number of Units	Incremental Number of Units	Cumulative Cost	Incremental Cost	Total Average Unit Cost	Incremental Average Unit Cost
	500	500	$120,000	$120,000	$240.00	$240.00
1	1,000	500	216,000	96,000	216.00	192.00
2	2,000	1,000	388,800	172,800	194.40	172.80
	3,000	1,000	548,340	159,540	182.78	159.54
3	4,000	1,000	699,840	151,500	174.96	151.50

Figure 18-14 The schedule of labor-related costs presented in Figure 18-13 is extended here in increments of 1,000 units to include production of the next 2,000 units.

When the steady state is reached the improvement in labor efficiency and cost stops

become directly variable, causing the curve to become a straight line at that point. Figure 18-15 shows a learning curve that reaches the steady state at production level X_1. When the steady state is reached the labor-related costs become directly variable and act in the manner of other variable costs. Once the steady state has been reached, the budgeting process becomes one of evaluating the directly variable costs.

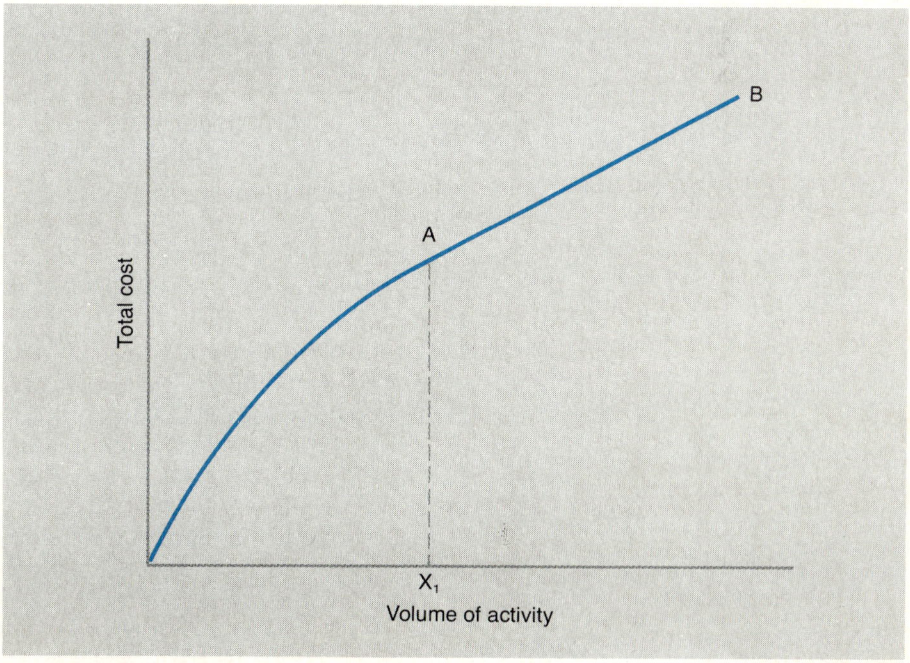

Figure 18-15 A plot of learning curve data. The learning curve is quite steep and does not decrease at a rapid rate because it represents a value of 90 percent, which is a relatively low rate of learning. Note the point where the steady state is reached, when the curve becomes a straight line, representing a directly variable cost.

TREND ANALYSIS

Trend analysis tracks cost over time

Many of the cost accounting data available to managers are generated at specific intervals of time or are in some way related to the passage of time. Inventory costs, sales, and prices vary over time and often in discernible patterns. Costs, sales, prices, and other variables recorded over successive time periods are called **time series,** and their systematic analysis is called **time series analysis** or **trend analysis.** The general purpose of time series analysis is to identify trends and to use the trends for planning and to improve decision making in general.

Methods used to analyze time series include regression analysis, moving averages, and exponential smoothing. With regression analysis, time is treated as the independent variable and each item of data has equal weight in the analysis. With exponential smoothing, more recent data may be given more or less weight than older data. Often, more recent data are better predictors of future events than older data because the more recent values result from current conditions that are more likely to approximate future conditions.

Trend analysis is used in forecasting

The primary use of trend analysis in business and economics is in forecasting. Managers may use moving average data or exponential smoothing data to predict sales, costs, cash receipts, activity levels, and other items. For example, a firm may use a moving average of monthly sales to predict the next month's sales, and a hospital may use exponential smoothing to predict weekly admittances. Trend analysis is useful because it allows managers to include new information in the analysis quite easily.

To illustrate trend analysis we use the following example of monthly payroll costs. The data for the past 6 months consist of the following:

Month	Payroll Costs
1	$83,000
2	80,000
3	88,000
4	91,000
5	90,000
6	96,000

The data and the following 4 months' payroll costs are used to analyze the trend in payroll costs using a moving average and then using exponential smoothing. We assume payroll costs for the following 4 months are as follows (though of course these values only become available as each month passes):

Month	Payroll Costs
7	$95,000
8	93,200
9	98,800
10	97,000

Moving Averages

The mean value of the first 6 months of payroll costs is $88,000, but if the costs are plotted for each month, as shown in Figure 18-16, you see that there is a general upward trend. Therefore the mean value may not be the best predictor of future costs, but it is a good start. If we observe the cost at the end of the seventh month, we can calculate the new mean of the seven available values, or we can calculate the **moving average** by dropping the first value of $83,000 and adding the latest value of $95,000 and computing the average of these six latest values. The new moving average after adding month 7 data and dropping month 1 data is $90,000. Each succeeding month, a new moving average is computed from the six latest values. For month 8 the moving average value is $92,200; for month 9 it is $94,000; and for month 10 it is $95,000.

The actual data and the moving average values can be plotted together to visualize the relationship of trend lines to actual data. The moving

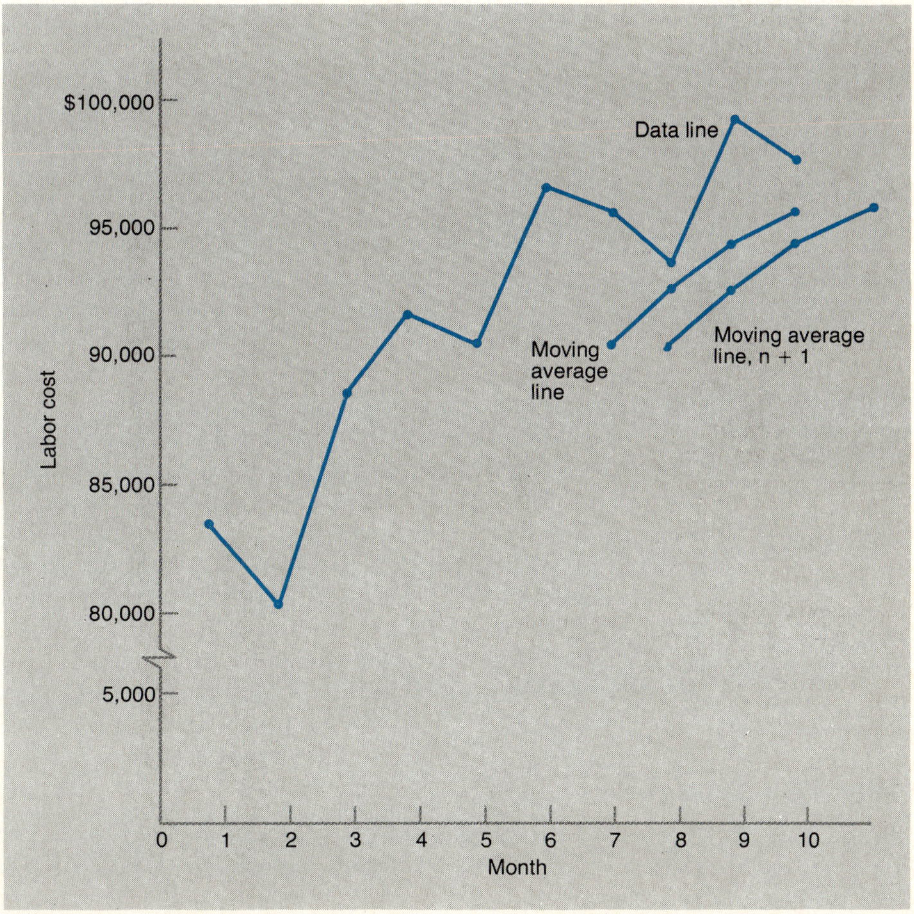

Figure 18-16
Actual data are plotted with the moving average line for the last 4 months. The moving average line is also plotted one time period ahead ($n + 1$) to compare with the next period's actual data.

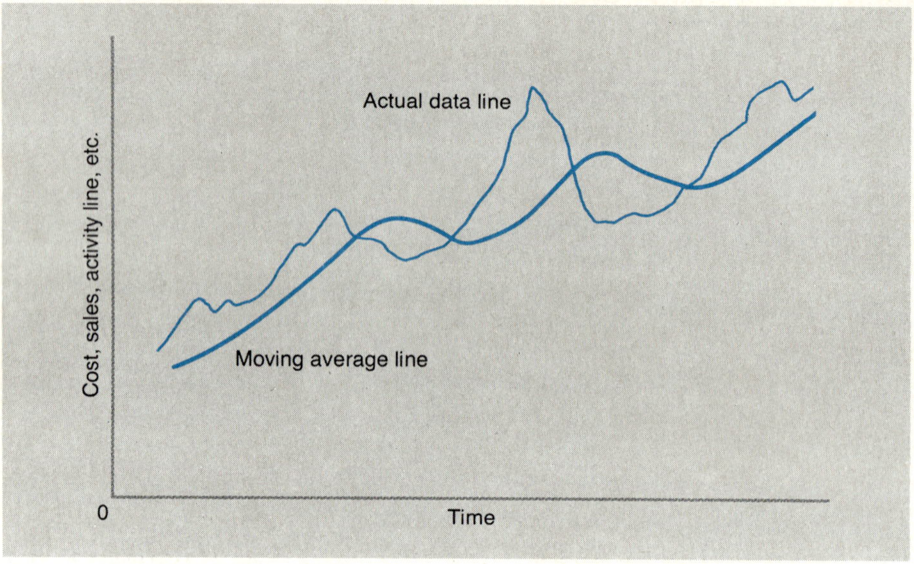

Figure 18-17
A moving average plotted over a long period of time together with actual data shows the general smoothing effect of the trend analysis. Note that the trend line lies below the data during rising trends and above the data during falling trends.

average may be plotted together with the most recent datum, as shown in Figure 18-16. For example, the moving average of $90,000 for month 7 is plotted with the $95,000 actual cost for month 7. However, the moving average computed with month 7 data will be used to forecast month 8 labor cost. Therefore, it is also logical to plot the moving average of one month with the actual datum of the next month to see how well the trend line predicted the actual results. This comparison is also graphed in Figure 18-16, and the trend line is identified as the $n + 1$ moving average curve.

The moving average lags behind the data from which it is computed

When plotted with the latest datum, the moving average is always below the data if the trend is up, and above the data if the trend is down. This means that the trend line always lags behind the actual data, and this fact must be kept in mind when the moving average is used in making predictions. The latest value of the moving average is not necessarily a good prediction of the next value of actual data, but it is usually a good prediction of the trend, or direction, in which future data can be expected to go. Figure 18-17 presents the moving average plotted over an extensive set of data, showing its smooth flow above or below the more erratic data. Sometimes the point where the moving average crosses above or below the data can be used to predict a change in trend direction.

Exponential Smoothing

A method of trend analysis that has some advantages over the moving average is called **exponential smoothing.** Exponential smoothing is easier to calculate than a moving average, especially if there is a large number of data. This method can assign more weight to the most recent value, so that the lag characteristic of the moving average can be minimized. A theoretical explanation of exponential smoothing is beyond the scope of this book, but it is not necessary to know the mathematical theory in order to understand and use this method of trend analysis.

To illustrate the use of exponential smoothing, we start with the first 6 months' data used in the moving average and the first mean of \$88,000 calculated on page 749.[2] When the next month's value of \$95,000 becomes available, it is made part of the next calculation. For this illustration we assume that the old data represent 70 percent of the available information, and the new item represents 30 percent. In practice, we can assume any percentage relationship we want, as we discuss later. Therefore the new information and the old are weighted and combined to yield a new point to add to the trend line:

$$\$88{,}000(.70) + \$95{,}000(.30) = \$90{,}100$$

When the value for the eighth month becomes available we again assign 70 percent to the old value and 30 percent to the new. The new exponentially smoothed trend line value for month 8 is

$$\$90{,}100(.70) + \$93{,}200(.30) = \$91{,}030$$

The next value of the trend line is calculated using the previous value and the month 9 datum as follows:

$$\$91{,}030(.70) + \$98{,}800(.30) = \$93{,}361$$

Finally, the value for month 10 is

$$\$93{,}361(.70) + \$97{,}000(.30) = \$94{,}453$$

With exponential smoothing managers can assign more or less weight to recent data

Both the moving average and exponential smoothing adjust to accommodate new data. With a moving average, the oldest data item is dropped and the most recent data item is added, so, in effect, this trend analysis method recognizes the impact of new information by dropping the oldest and adding the newest information. No data are dropped using exponential smoothing. Instead managers adjust for the importance of new information by assigning different weights, called an **alpha factor**, to the most recent data. Heavier weights make the most recent datum more important, which

[2] We use the \$88,000 for convenience. The exponentially smoothed value for month 7 could actually be different.

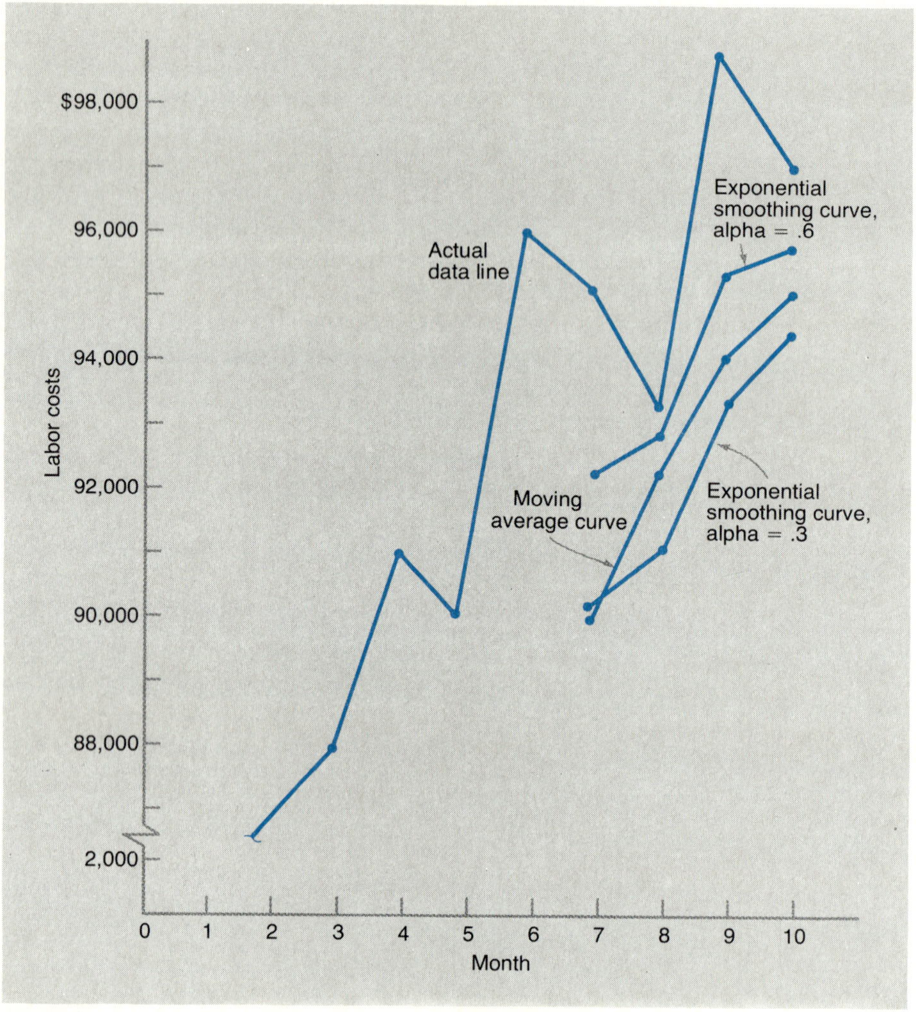

Figure 18-18
A data line is plotted for months 3 through 10 together with the moving average line and exponential smoothing lines with alphas of .3 and .6. The appropriate alpha factor must be determined for each situation.

means that a high alpha factor causes the exponential smoothing curve to react more quickly to changing trends. However, it also causes the curve to move away from the true trend when an unusual data point is encountered. For instance, a strike may cause payroll costs to drop to zero for a short period of time. Using experience, managers determine what alpha factor is most effective in analyzing and predicting costs, activity levels, or other variables.

The exponential smoothing curve looks quite different if we assign a different alpha factor to the most recent data. For example, an alpha of .6 for the payroll cost example means that the weight for the old data is (1 − alpha) or .4. Computing the values for the exponential smoothing curve we arrive at

Month 7: .4($88,000) + .6($95,000) = $92,200

For the other months the values are

Month	Value
8	.4($92,200) + .6($93,200) = $92,800
9	.4($92,800) + .6($98,800) = $96,400
10	.4($96,400) + .6($97,000) = $96,760

Both the .3 alpha and .6 alpha exponential smoothing curves are plotted in Figure 18-18 along with the moving average curve.

There is no generally accepted value for alpha. Managers should choose the value that appears to supply them with the most useful information over time.

Trend analysis is a useful management tool that can be complex. Here we provide only a very brief introduction to the topic. In other courses you may study trend analysis in more depth and apply it to accounting activities.

SUMMARY

Information about cost behavior patterns is important for many management accounting analyses and reporting activities. Simple techniques such as high-low and scatter diagram analysis are useful sometimes, but their information value is relatively limited. More sophisticated quantitative techniques may be used in planning and control. Quantitative methods do not provide useful information automatically. Managers must learn to use those techniques that are useful in each particular situation.

Among the more useful statistics are **measures of central tendency** and **measures of dispersion.** The **mean** is the arithmetic average of a data set. It is computed by summing the values in the data set and dividing by the number of data elements. The **median** is the middle value in a data set and the **mode** is the most commonly occurring value.

Measures of dispersion describe the fluctuation of the values in a data set about its mean. The **variance,** S^2, and the **standard deviation,** S, are two commonly used measures of dispersion. The standard deviation together with the mean may be used to make estimates about the probability of occurrence of certain values or events.

Use of the mean and standard deviation often assumes that the **population** from which the **sample** data are selected is normally distributed. A **normal distribution** of data means that the data are distributed symmetrically about the mean and satisfy certain statistical properties of the **normal curve.**

Among the more powerful quantitative tools for planning and controlling costs is **regression-correlation analysis. Simple linear regression** relates a single dependent variable to a single independent variable. The **independent variable** (X) is given or derived from historical data. The **dependent variable** (Y) is so called because its value depends on the value of the independent variable and the relationship between the two variables as described by an equation.

Regression-correlation analysis is a two-step process. The first step is to compute the **regression line,** which is a line whose equation best describes the linear relationship between the dependent and the independent variable. It is also called the **line of best fit.** The regression line can be computed by means of simultaneous equations and, once computed, can be used to predict any value of the dependent variable, given some value of the independent variable.

Correlation analysis measures the strength of the relationship between the two variables. The **coefficient of correlation** is denoted as r whose value ranges between -1 and $+1$. Positive correlation means that X and Y move in the same direction. Negative correlation means that X and Y move in opposite directions. The relationship between X and Y is strong if r is close to -1 or $+1$, and it is weaker as r approaches zero. To make interpretation of r easier, we usually convert it to r^2, which is called the **coefficient of determination.** Its value shows the percentage of fluctuation in the data that can be explained by the relationship between the dependent and the independent variable. The amount of fluctuation due to other factors is explained by the **coefficient of nondetermination.** If one independent variable does not yield a satisfactory r^2, another independent variable may be found to have a better fit.

With **multiple linear regression** more than one independent variable is used to predict the dependent variable. The purpose of using multiple independent variables is to improve the prediction process. The computation of the regression line and the coefficient of determination is significantly more complex than with simple linear regression.

Learning curves are a class of semivariable costs that increase with activity levels but at a decreasing rate. Such cost behavior is most commonly found in labor and labor-related costs as employees become more and more familiar with the production of a product or service. Learning curves are used to help managers predict the labor-related cost of producing new products or providing new services. Usually the learning effect lasts only for a period of time, after which the **steady state** is reached and the cost becomes directly variable.

Trend analysis is used to help managers identify trends in sales, costs, activities, or other items, and can be useful for budgeting and forecasting. Trend analysis allows new data to be incorporated easily into the analysis. With a **moving average trend analysis,** the most recent datum is added and the oldest datum is dropped each time a new average is calculated. Another form of trend analysis, called **exponential smoothing,** does not drop any data values but weights the relative importance of the old and the new data. The weight assigned to the new data may range from zero to 1 and is called the **alpha factor.** The weight assigned to the old data is always (1 − alpha). The more importance management assigns to recent data, the higher the alpha factor.

KEY TERMS

alpha factor *(751)*
average *(716)*
coefficient of correlation *(729)*
coefficient of determination *(732)*
coefficient of nondetermination *(733)*
cumulative average cost *(742)*
degrees of freedom *(718)*

dependent variable *(724)*
dispersion *(718)*
exponential smoothing *(750)*
independent variable *(724)*
learning curves *(738)*
learning rate *(739)*
line of best fit *(725)*
linear regression *(724)*
mean *(716)*
measures of central tendency *(716)*
measures of dispersion *(718)*
median *(717)*
mode *(717)*
moving average *(749)*
multiple coefficient of determination *(738)*
multiple linear regression *(737)*
negative correlation *(729)*
normal curve *(721)*
normal curve assumption *(721)*
normal distribution *(721)*
population *(720)*
positive correlation *(729)*
regression-correlation analysis *(724)*
regression line *(724)*
regression line equation *(724)*
sample *(720)*
simple linear regression *(724)*
standard deviation *(719)*
statistic *(715)*
steady state *(746)*
time series analysis *(748)*
trend analysis *(748)*
variance *(718)*

QUESTIONS

1. Define the mean, the median, and the mode. What are all three called?
2. Name the two common measures of dispersion and discuss why such measures are important.
3. In statistics, what is meant by a population and a sample? Give an illustration.
4. "These numbers just do not seem to make any sense, but they came out of our multiple regression model, so I guess they must be right." Comment.
5. What is the purpose of using regression-correlation analysis?
6. Explain the two steps in regression-correlation analysis?
7. Trymore Horticulture Laboratories, Inc., is attempting to develop new strains of carrots from seeds bought for that purpose from two different suppliers. The company wants to develop a strain that yields miniature carrots for use in preparing gourmet delicacies, and also a strain of giant carrots for making canned carrot juice. The process involves cultivating carrots from seeds that come from the largest or smallest carrots of subsequent plantings. In testing samples of seeds from the suppliers, the company finds that the mean length of carrots from supplier A is 5 inches with a standard deviation of 2.3 inches, while the mean length of carrots from supplier B is 5.2 inches with a standard deviation of 1.2 inches. Which supplier's seeds are more likely to produce the desired results?
8. In order to compare two brands of tires, a research organization tested five tires of each brand, measuring the mileage provided by each tire. The results of the test were as follows:

Mileage	
Brand A	**Brand B**
26,800	25,600
22,300	23,400
27,400	21,000
24,000	26,000
23,500	25,000

After the test, each tire manufacturer claimed that "on the average" its tires held up better than the other brand. Comment on these claims by discussing the meaning of the term "average" as used by the tire manufacturers.

9. A boat manufacturer builds boats of the following lengths, in feet: 10, 12, 14, 16, 18, 22, 23, 28, and 37. To plan next year's production, the company decided to hire a surveying firm to determine what size boat the public prefers. When the surveying firm quoted a price of $30,000 for the survey, the company decided to conduct the survey with its own staff. After some time, the surveying staff makes the following report: 22 percent of respondents preferred the mean size of the boats, which is 20 feet. Only 12 percent preferred the median size of 18 feet. Forty percent expressed a preference for 16-foot boats, 12 percent preferred boats smaller than 14 feet, and 13 percent preferred boats larger than 32 feet. Which measure of central tendency is most significant to the boat manufacturer? Why?
10. During a slack time in the personnel office, a clerk performed a regression-correlation analysis between shoe sizes of the company's employees and their salaries, with salaries as the dependent variable. She found that shoe sizes were negatively correlated with salaries, with an r^2 of .64, and she consequently recommended that in order to save money, the company should reject all employment applicants with small shoe sizes. Comment on the nature of the relationship between shoe sizes and salaries. What is the value of the coefficient of correlation? What do you think of the clerk's recommendation?
11. What is meant by a 90 percent learning curve? Does a 90 percent or a 70 percent learning curve show the greater learning effect?
12. "I've been looking over your 80 percent learning curve calculations on the cost of the new compressor. It says the steady state will be reached at a labor cost of $263 per unit. That is a bit too high. Why don't we switch to an 85 percent learning curve and a steady state of $250? Reducing the $263 by 5 percent yields about $250, giving us a lower labor cost for the compressor." Comment on the validity of the above statement and explain its fallacy by reference to learning curves and the steady state.
13. What is the purpose of using a moving average and exponential smoothing? How is exponential smoothing different from a moving average?

EXERCISES

Ex. 18-1 Measures of central tendency. Frothen Manufacturing Company wants to develop some statistics related to its employee's absenteeism. The cost accounting department has accumulated the following data on the total number of hours of labor time lost due to employee absenteeism during each of the last 25 work weeks.

Number of Hours Lost to Absenteeism in Each Pay Period

56	77	93	55	94
30	85	35	77	17
29	64	84	6	88
43	32	23	45	22
47	10	13	41	9

Required: Compute the mean, median, and mode for the number of hours of absenteeism.

Ex. 18-2 **Central tendency measures for a bank.** Rutherford Bank collected the following data on the number of deposits made by customers during a 3-week period:

	Week		
	1	2	3
Monday	337	593	430
Tuesday	413	798	566
Wednesday	586	936	721
Thursday	364	838	395
Friday	459	601	483

Required:

a. Compute the mean number of deposits per day.
b. Compute the mean number of weekly deposits.
c. Compute the median number of daily deposits for the 3-week period.
d. Find the modal deposit day and discuss briefly how the bank might use information about the mode.

Ex. 18-3 **Central tendency and dispersion.** A drugstore has the following daily cash sales for a 10-day period:

Day	Receipts
1	$350
2	260
3	410
4	385
5	440
6	325
7	370
8	310
9	290
10	360

Required:

a. Compute the mean.
b. Compute the standard deviation.

Ex. 18-4 **Use of mean and standard deviation.** The management of a company believes that its cash receipts are normally distributed. The mean daily cash receipts are $5,500 and the standard deviation is $500.

Required:

a. Compute the probability that cash receipts for a day will be between $5,000 and $6,000.
b. Compute the probability that cash receipts will be at least $4,500 for a day.
c. Find the probability of daily cash receipts' being greater than $6,000.
d. Determine the probability of cash receipts' being between $5,200 and $6,200.

Ex. 18-5 **Use of the normal curve table.** Biddle Keg Company uses white oak lumber to manufacture brandy barrels. Management believes that in the past it has had too much invested in its inventory of lumber and wants to develop some data that may help to manage the lumber inventory. From a random sample of weekly lumber use the company determines that mean weekly use is 900 board feet (bd ft) of white oak with a standard deviation of 100 bd ft. Management believes that lumber use is approximated by a normal distribution.

Required:

a. Compute the range of lumber use for 95 percent of the weeks.
b. Find the probability that lumber use will be between 800 and 1,000 bd ft.
c. Determine the probability that lumber use will be less than 800 bd ft per week.

Ex. 18-6 **Regression analysis.** The management of Crittenden Company wants to establish a flexible budget based on the following historical data on production and overhead costs, with all figures in thousands:

Production Quantity	Overhead Cost
3	$12
5	13
7	13
4	10
8	14

The flexible budget is to cover production of 6,000, 7,000, and 8,000 units of production.

Required:

a. Perform a regression analysis and develop a total cost formula for use with the flexible budget.
b. Use your total cost formula to estimate overhead cost for the three levels of production.

Ex. 18-7 **Calculation of regression line.** Below are machine hours and utility cost data for the Oolitic Chain Saw Company:

Month	Machine Hours	Utility Costs
January	1,200	$8,500
February	1,500	9,100
March	1,600	9,400
April	1,700	9,500
May	1,300	9,000
June	1,100	8,400

Required:

a. Compute a regression line from the above data using machine hours as the independent variable.
b. Use your solution to predict the expected cost of utilities when 1,800 machine hours are used.

Ex. 18-8 Spurious correlation. Mr. Nosebeek, an eccentric bird fancier, has made a hobby of counting the number of storks nesting each year on the chimneys of Eggley, the New England village where he lives. Recently the village elders published a history of Eggley which included data on the number of babies born in the village each year. Mr. Nosebeek wanted to compare the published birth data with his stork figures and prepared the following table:

Year	Storks X_i	X_i^2	Births Y_i	Y_i^2	X_iY_i
1986	40	1,600	59	3,481	2,360
1985	36	1,296	53	2,809	1,908
1984	42	1,764	75	5,625	3,150
1983	45	2,025	66	4,356	2,970
1982	37	1,369	48	2,304	1,776
1981	60	3,600	80	6,400	4,800
1980	46	2,116	74	5,476	3,404
	306	13,770	455	30,451	20,368

Mr. Nosebeek was aware that scientists had discarded the theory that storks bring babies. However, he never did trust scientists and in addition believed that he could use the stork data to decide when to buy or sell his investments in local companies that manufacture baby products.

Required:

a. Use the data to develop the regression line equation.
b. Compute r and r^2 for the data.
c. Discuss briefly the significance of the correlation.

Ex. 18-9 Regression and correlation. The manager of Flatone Brass Instruments Company believes that its utility costs are strongly correlated with production. He wants to develop a method of predicting utility costs with some reliability. Following are data collected over a 7-month period:

Utility Costs (× \$100)	Hundreds of Units Produced
\$11	7
9	8
14	5
23	9
13	8
8	3
12	9

Required:

a. Perform a regression analysis and develop the regression equation with production as the independent variable.
b. Calculate r and r^2.
c. Estimate utility cost for a production level of 600 units and comment briefly on the value of your estimate.

Ex. 18-10 Multiple regression. Towler Company has found that the cost of overhead on the production of its custom-designed simulated wood fireplace mantles is strongly related to the hourly wage of its production employees, kilowatt hours of electricity used, interest rate percentage, and molding machine time. The relationship is described by the following formula:

$$Y = 7.2X_1 + .28X_2 - 2.5X_3 + 3.6X_4$$

At the end of the current week of production the company has collected the following data:

X_1 = labor hours = 120
X_2 = kilowatt hours = 6
X_3 = interest rate = 15 percent
X_4 = molding machine hours = 100

Required: Estimate the cost of overhead for the current week using multiple regression.

Ex. 18-11 Use of learning curves. The Red Clay Pottery Company manufactures attractive handmade pottery items. New lines of pottery require some learning time and the management has noted a decline in labor time and cost as employees become used to the production of new products. The learning effect seems to approximate an 85 percent learning curve. Last summer the company produced 50 sets of a new line of pottery. The total labor cost was $3,000. This fall the company will produce an additional 150 sets for Christmas orders.

Required: Find the labor cost for the 150 sets of pottery using an 85 percent learning curve.

Ex. 18-12 Cost estimation with learning curves. Gedson, Inc., uses a learning curve of 90 percent for all new products it develops. A trial run of 1,000 units of a new product shows total labor-related costs of $150,000. Management plans to produce 3,000 units of the new product during the next year.

Required: Compute the expected labor-related cost for the year to produce the 3,000 units.

Ex. 18-13 Moving average. The Old Time Barbecue Restaurant experiences considerable fluctuations in sales, with lowest levels occurring in midweek and increasing to high levels on weekends. The company uses trend analysis to project sales for planning purchases and cash flows. Following are sales data for a 2-week period:

1	Monday	$1,260
2	Tuesday	1,120
3	Wednesday	970
4	Thursday	1,010
5	Friday	1,330
6	Saturday	1,580
7	Sunday	1,490
8	Monday	1,300
9	Tuesday	1,170
10	Wednesday	1,030
11	Thursday	990
12	Friday	1,480
13	Saturday	1,650
14	Sunday	1,590

Required: Calculate a 7-day moving average of sales revenue for the last 8 days of data.

Ex. 18-14 Exponential smoothing. Refer to the data in Exercise 18-13 on the sales revenue of the Old Time Barbecue Restaurant. The company uses exponential smoothing to predict average sales revenue for the purpose of planning cash flows and purchases. The average revenue projected on day 6 is $1,266. The weight assigned to the old value of the exponentially smoothed trend line is .70 and the weight assigned to the latest day's revenue is .30.

Required: Calculate the exponentially smoothed value of average daily revenue for days 7 through 14.

PROBLEMS

P. 18-1 Using the mean and standard deviation for business decisions. Curve-Ball Concessions operates the hot dog concession at a major league baseball park. The hot dogs sell for $.80 each and are a high-profit item, but sales fluctuate from game to game and it is hard to plan for adequate inventories without having some spoilage. Below are hot dog sales data for the first 11 games of the year.

Game	Hot Dogs Sold
1	24,000
2	18,000
3	16,000
4	28,000
5	25,000
6	14,000
7	9,000
8	12,000
9	19,000
10	18,000
11	15,000

Required:

a. Compute the mean, the mode, and the median for the hot dog sales.
b. Compute the standard deviation of hot dog sales.

c. If the concession wants to have enough hot dogs so it does not run out 85 percent of the time, determine how many hot dogs it should have available for each game.
d. Based on the data, determine what the range of hot dog sales is for 95.4 percent of the games.

P. 18-2 Use of mean and standard deviation. The Oyster Pearl Restaurant is popular with seafood fanciers who like its large variety of oyster dishes. The oyster sales fluctuate from day to day and planning inventories to minimize spoilage is difficult. The head chef proposes to have enough inventory on hand to satisfy customer demand 90 percent of the time. The general manager believes that the restaurant should limit its spoilage by having enough on hand to satisfy 80 percent of demand. The cost of oysters is $.40 each. Below are data on number of oysters sold during a 12-day period:

1	14,000	7	16,500
2	18,000	8	18,000
3	12,300	9	9,000
4	22,000	10	11,000
5	18,500	11	15,000
6	19,600	12	21,000

Required:

a. Compute the mean, mode, and median of oyster sales.
b. Compute the standard deviation of oyster sales.
c. Determine how many oysters the restaurant would have to buy daily in order to satisfy the general manager's proposal.
d. Compute the average cost of spoilage with the general manager's proposal. (Hint: Average spoilage is based on the difference between actual demand and average inventory.)
e. Determine how many oysters would have to be bought daily to satisfy the head chef's proposal.
f. Compute the average cost of spoilage with the chef's proposal and find how much greater the cost would be than if the general manager's proposal is adopted.

P. 18-3 Using the mean and standard deviation in business. Marge owns two neighborhood movie theaters, the North and the South. Frequently the North Theater has large weekly revenues and sometimes it experiences poor revenues. Marge engages you to analyze the data and suggest how they may be used to forecast future revenues.

Week	Admissions Revenue, North	Admissions Revenue, South
1	$1,200	$1,100
2	900	1,050
3	800	1,000
4	1,100	900
5	1,400	960
6	1,300	1,000
7	1,000	1,050
8	700	1,000
9	600	950
10	900	990

Required:

a. Compute the mean and standard deviation for weekly admission revenues for the two theaters.

b. Find the range of admission revenues for the two theaters 95.4 percent of the time, assuming a normal distribution.

c. Determine the probability that weekly admission revenue at the North Theater would be below $600.

P. 18-4 Using the mean and standard deviation. Willmar Company produces a variety of food products. Its 16-ounce bottles of concentrated black cherry juice cost $8.00 to produce and sell for $12 each. Sales are 10,000 bottles per month.

The company has received a number of letters from its customers, complaining that its 16-ounce bottles of black cherry concentrate contain less than 16 ounces of product. The bottles are filled by automatic equipment that can be set to fill any amount, but the amount actually placed into containers varies with a standard deviation of .5 ounce. The quantities dispensed by the equipment are normally distributed. Currently the equipment is set to dispense 16 ounces of product. Because of the complaints management decides that it must set the equipment to minimize the probability of underfilling the bottles. The manager of quality control wants the equipment adjusted so that there is a 98 percent probability that the bottles will contain at least 16 ounces of product. The marketing manager believes that 95 percent is a high enough probability.

Required:

a. Determine how to set the equipment in order to have a 98 percent probability of filling bottles with at least 16 ounces of product.

b. Calculate the additional cost of the product from the equipment adjustment to a 98 percent probability.

c. Determine how to set the equipment in order to have a 95 percent probability of filling bottles with at least 16 ounces of product.

d. Calculate the additional cost of the product from adjusting the equipment to a 95 percent probability.

e. What is the difference in monthly production cost between the marketing manager's and the quality control manager's proposals?

P. 18-5 Regression-correlation analysis for a utility. An electric utility is concerned about the number of customer complaints it has been receiving. Management is attempting to isolate the causes of rising customer complaints by investigating several suggested problem areas. One manager believes that most customer complaints are related to equipment failure or human errors made during periods of heavy demand for electricity. To support her idea, the manager submits the following data for the first 8 days of the month:

Day	Complaints	Electricity Generated (in thousands of kilowatt hours)
1	670	2,300
2	590	2,100
3	500	1,900
4	540	2,000
5	680	2,900
6	590	2,400
7	860	3,300
8	770	2,600

Required:

a. Complete a regression line equation for the data above using complaints as the dependent variable.
b. Compute the coefficient of determination.
c. Based on the results in parts *a* and *b*, agree or disagree with the manager's opinion of the relationship between the two variables. Tell management why you answered as you did, explaining carefully the meaning of the information you used in reaching your conclusion.
d. Based on the regression line you computed, find the expected number of complaints if the utility generates 3.8 million kilowatt hours in a day.

P. 18-6 Regression analysis for display space. Pamore & Byless Grocery wanted to determine if the amount of display space allocated to a specific brand of soft drink would have an effect on the amount of that product's sales. In alternate weeks it allocated 4, 8, and 12 square feet of space to display the soft drink and obtained the following data:

Sales	Space
$510	4
670	8
720	12
540	4
690	12
660	8

Required:

a. Perform a regression analysis with display space as the independent variable, and develop the regression equation.
b. Compute r and r^2 for the data.
c. Discuss your findings briefly and estimate the amount of revenue expected if 8 square feet are allotted to display the product.

P. 18-7 Use of regression line and r^2. The Fishing Shack is a general-purpose fishing tackle store that also rents fishing boats at a nearby lake. The heaviest rental times are on weekends, although the number of rentals varies from one weekend to another. The manager of the Fishing Shack thinks that boat rentals may be related to the number of campers staying at the campgrounds around the lake or to the number of visitors entering the state park located on the lake. To test his theory the manager gathered campground occupancy and state park visitation data for the last 6 weekends, which are presented below:

Week	Boat Rentals	Campers	Park Visitors
1	45	200	1,020
2	54	260	1,380
3	63	280	1,570
4	68	320	1,440
5	60	320	1,500
6	52	270	1,300

Required:

a. Compute the regression line using campers as the independent variable and boat rentals as the dependent variable.

b. Compute the regression line using park visitors as the independent variable and boat rentals as the dependent variable.
c. Compute r^2 for both regression lines.
d. State which of the two independent variables you would suggest using as a predictor of boat rentals. Explain why.

P. 18-8 Break-even point and profit with regression analysis. Pied Piper Company owns a unique process for exterminating rats from cities. Its fees are based on a city's population. The company charges a fee of $15,000 per city plus $1 per person. Below are revenue and operating data for the last six contracts.

City	Operating Cost	Rat Population	Total Revenue
Hummel	$ 70,000	400,000	$ 55,000
Hamilot	125,000	1,500,000	165,000
Himmel	80,000	500,000	85,000
Homily	90,000	1,000,000	130,000
Hamlet	110,000	1,350,000	140,000
Humer	115,000	1,200,000	120,000

The company is negotiating a contract with the city of Hamelin, which has a population of 110,000. The rat population is estimated at 1,100,000. (Hint: A break-even diagram should help you. You can save time by omitting the last three zeros from the data.)

Required:
a. Use the rat population and operating costs to perform a regression analysis and develop a total cost line.
b. Develop a total revenue line from the data provided.
c. Calculate the break-even point in units and dollars for the company's operations based on your estimates in parts *a* and *b*.
d. Use the city population and estimate of rat population for Hamelin to determine the expected profit or loss on the contract.

P. 18-9 Learning curve analysis. McGavren Manufacturing has recently started manufacturing a new industrial air compressor. During the first 6 months of the year 1,000 units are produced with average labor costs of $100 per unit. The firm expects to continue production of the air compressors for the next several years at the same level of output. The expected learning rates for labor costs are 70 percent for the rest of the current year, and for the next year.

Required:
a. Calculate expected labor cost for the first year.
b. Calculate expected labor cost for the second year.

P. 18-10 Learning curve analysis. Stahley Electronic Products Company finds that new product production has an 80 percent learning effect, and it takes at least 2 years to reach the steady state. A new digital CB radio had labor-related costs of $20 a unit for its initial production run of 2,000 units. During the first year of production the company expects to produce 6,000 new radios in addition to the initial run of 2,000. In the second year the company expects to produce 10,000 more radios.

Required:
a. Compute the labor-related costs of producing the radio for the first year.
b. Compute the labor-related production costs for the second year.
c. Find the average labor-related cost per unit for each year.

P. 18-11 Pricing with learning curve costs. Compaline Company is negotiating a contract for the manufacture of 3,000 staple guns, which require a large amount of manual assembly labor. Based on past experience company management believes that the first 400 units will be subject to an 80 percent learning curve. Management also estimates that 40 hours will be required to assemble the first 25 units.

The company has to establish a price for the contract and wants to earn a minimum rate of return of 20 percent on sales. However, if the staple gun is priced at $30 or more, management believes the company will not get the contract. The company's fixed cost to be allocated to this contract is $40,000. Direct labor cost is $8.20 per hour, direct materials cost is $2.18 per unit, and variable overhead is $4.60 per direct labor hour.

Required:

a. Prepare a labor time schedule similar to Figure 18-14 for the first 800 units of production. Round time estimates to two decimal places.
b. Compute the total time required to produce all 3,000 units in the contract.
c. Determine the selling price per unit.

P. 18-12 Trend analysis. The board of supervisors of Munrose County has authorized a study of deposits in savings and loan associations located in the county. Data collected for 20 years resulted in the following findings in millions of dollars:

1966	$46.0	1971	$ 90.3	1976	$130.8	1981	$226.0
1967	52.6	1972	98.2	1977	135.6	1982	241.3
1968	60.1	1973	109.8	1978	146.4	1983	288.1
1969	68.8	1974	114.6	1979	175.2	1984	291.0
1970	79.2	1975	122.5	1980	206.8	1985	305.6

The board wants to make some estimates of future savings and loans deposits in the county and asks you to perform some time series analysis for its use. The estimate of future deposits is based on the formula

$$\text{New deposits} = A + 1.2\,(D - A)$$

where A is the latest moving average or exponentially smoothed value and D is the latest item of deposit data.

Required:

a. Compute a 9-year moving average for the years 1975 through 1985. Carry your computations to two decimal places.
b. Compute the exponential smoothing trend line for the last 11 years of data, assuming that the value for 1974 is $72.00 and using an alpha of .2.
c. Use your computations and the formula provided to estimate the amount of deposits for 1986.

P. 18-13 Trend analysis of sales. The Sanfran Company wants to use trend analysis methods to help forecast monthly sales on a month-by-month basis. Below are January through December sales data. Starting with August, the company uses trend analysis in forecasting.

Month	Sales
January	$18,000
February	22,000
March	24,000
April	27,000
May	28,000
June	30,000
July	27,000
August	24,000
September	22,000
October	20,000
November	30,000
December	33,000

Required:

a. Calculate the moving average for each month from August through December, using 8 months in the average.

b. Using an alpha of .2, calculate the exponential smoothing values for August through December assuming the July estimate was $25,200.

c. State which method provides the better estimate of monthly sales for September through December. Explain.

d. Determine whether an alpha value of .4 provides a better exponential smoothing model for predicting monthly sales in this problem.

P. 18-14 Trend line analysis. Each quarter Belmor Company computes the average unit cost for manufacturing labor for each of its products. Below are data for the last 10 quarters for one product.

Quarter	Unit Labor Cost
1	$80
2	84
3	83
4	86
5	90
6	88
7	92
8	94
9	91
10	95

The company decides to use trend analysis to estimate labor cost for products for the next quarter. Five quarters of data that follow the ones above are as follows:

Quarter	Unit Labor Cost
11	$100
12	98
13	97
14	102
15	105

Required:

a. Using a 10-quarter moving average compute the moving average for quarters 10 through 15.

b. Compute the new average for quarters 10 through 15 using exponential smoothing and an alpha of .2, assuming that the exponentially smoothed value for the tenth quarter is $88.
c. Repeat part *b* using an alpha of .4.
d. Of the three trend lines computed in parts *a*, *b*, and *c*, determine which appears to be the best predictor of unit labor cost.

P. 18-15 Regression-correlation analysis (by computer). Warren Metal Products uses direct labor cost to apply overhead to production. The controller believes that other activity measures may be more closely related to the movement of overhead costs. The controller has decided to use regression-correlation analysis to test his belief. He has accumulated the following data:

Year	Direct Labor Cost	Direct Labor Hours	Machine Hours	Overhead Cost
1977	$100,000	30,000	19,000	$300,000
1978	110,000	31,000	18,500	340,000
1979	120,000	31,000	19,000	350,000
1980	125,000	31,500	20,000	380,000
1981	130,000	30,500	20,000	360,000
1982	160,000	32,000	20,500	410,000
1983	180,000	33,000	21,000	470,000
1984	200,000	32,500	20,800	460,000
1985	220,000	34,000	21,000	490,000
1986	240,000	34,500	21,500	520,000

Required:

a. Compute three regression lines using overhead cost as the dependent variable and each of the activity variables as independent variables.
b. Compute the coefficient of determination for each regression line.
c. Using the data determine which activity measure appears to be most closely related to overhead costs. Use regression-correlation information to support your answer.

CASE

Case 18-1 Regression-correlation analysis and cost prediction. The assembly department of the Walkoff Company makes engine housings requiring the use of materials, labor, and machinery in the production activity. Below are data on 8 weeks of production of engine housings.

Month	Units Produced	Total Production Cost	Machine Hours
December	132	$ 7,800	1,000
December	100	6,000	1,500
December	168	6,700	2,050
December	300	11,000	2,250
January	202	9,700	1,050
January	220	8,300	2,200
January	251	8,500	1,700
January	230	10,000	2,100

The company wants to use the above data to forecast the cost of production of engine housings in February, when 1,000 engine housings are expected to be produced.

Required:

a. Perform a complete regression-correlation analysis using total production costs as the dependent variable and units produced as the independent variable.

b. Perform a complete regression-correlation analysis using total production costs as the dependent variable and machine hours as the independent variable.

c. Recommend to management which variable should be used for predicting total production costs. Support your recommendations with a discussion of your findings.

d. Estimate the total production cost for February using the variable which you chose.

Financial Accounting Foundation for Managerial Accounting

part 5

A background in financial accounting is a prerequisite to the study of managerial accounting, and students using this book normally have such a background. In some cases however, a review of financial accounting concepts may be necessary. In addition, the financial accounting course taken by a class often cannot cover all necessary materials, and the topics not covered are completed in the following course. This part of the book contains the financial accounting material most likely still required of students prior to starting their study of managerial accounting. It includes two topics that integrate the students' financial accounting background and apply it in two areas. Chapter 19 covers financial statement analysis, providing an understanding of the information that can be obtained from accounting reports, and the ways such information is used by managers, investors, analysts, and others. Chapter 20 is a thorough presentation of the concepts and procedures underlying the preparation of the statement of changes in financial position, a report that normally cannot be understood well until a significant amount of accounting knowledge has been accumulated. In addition to these two chapters, a review of basic financial accounting concepts, including the accounting cycle and financial statements, is presented in an appendix.

Financial Statement Analysis

19

By drawing on a knowledge of accounting, finance, economics, and other related fields, you can use financial statements to evaluate the financial condition and performance of a business. This chapter is a synthesis of the many concepts, principles, and procedures you have studied. It will enable you to understand:

1. The meaning of financial analysis.
2. How to perform horizontal and vertical analyses of financial statements.
3. How to perform a ratio analysis of financial statements.
4. What tests you can perform to learn about the liquidity and solvency of a business organization.
5. Several measures of business profitability.
6. The purpose of market tests used by investors and analysts.
7. That a real appreciation and understanding of the value of accounting information requires a good knowledge of accounting and considerable experience with financial statement analysis.

By the time many corporations issue their annual report, thousands of transactions involving millions of dollars have taken place. The history of the transactions is recorded in voluminous journals and ledgers, but is reported in four brief, highly condensed, general-purpose statements. The balance sheet presents the financial condition of the entity. The income statement tells what was accomplished as a result of operations. A retained earnings statement explains the change in the earned portion of owners' equity. And a statement of changes in financial position describes the financing and investing activities of the business.

Each statement provides essential information, but the four statements **together** present a total picture which is complete only when the information in any one statement is **related** to the information in all the others.

Decision makers analyze financial statements in order to take future action. How can financial statements, which report on past history, help analysts to make decisions about the future? Often the best indicators of future conditions and events are data about the immediate past. Reading financial statements provides a considerable amount of information, but making good decisions requires a thorough analysis of the statements.

Financial analysis requires experience

A single chapter on **financial statement analysis** can only introduce the topic and discuss some of the information that emerges when financial statements are thoroughly analyzed. The integration of such information into a complete, coherent analysis can be accomplished only after much experience and more study of this and related topics.

Comparative figures enhance the analysis

The usefulness of most data in financial statements is enhanced significantly when statements of the current period can be compared with statements of previous accounting periods. Such comparisons may reveal trends and highlight important relationships that are not evident from the financial information of a single period. Therefore corporations provide annual reports with **comparative** financial statements—that is, reports that contain statements for at least two consecutive accounting periods. In addition, annual reports contain a great deal of information in the notes that accompany the financial statements.

The notes explain many aspects of business operations that cannot be shown clearly in the figures alone. These include several types of information required by the full disclosure principle. For example, the report discloses whether FIFO or LIFO is used for inventory valuation and whether depreciation is based on the straight-line or accelerated method. Items that may be shown as a single figure in the statements, such as contributed capital or funds provided by operations, are reported in detailed schedules. Various contingencies, such as pending lawsuits, are disclosed and any other data necessary to make the report complete are included.

Management is responsible for providing financial statements to users who need the information, but management cannot anticipate how the information will be used. Therefore the analysis of the information is left to the individual users, who must suit their investigation to their specific needs. Financial analysts develop a comprehensive picture of the financial status and future prospects of a firm by performing horizontal, vertical, and ratio analyses. To illustrate these three types of analysis, we use the financial statements of Megatrix Corporation for 1984 and 1985, shown in Figure 19-1.

HORIZONTAL ANALYSIS

Absolute and percentage changes are needed

Horizontal analysis is the comparison of figures reported in financial statements of two or more consecutive accounting periods. The analyst calculates the absolute changes—the difference between the figures of one year and the next—and also the percentage change from one year to the next, using the earlier year as the base period. Much additional information is obtained from financial statements in this manner. For example, in Figure 19-1, 1985 net income of $95,300 is a significant item of information. It becomes more significant, however, when it is seen as an increase of $7,700, or 8.8 percent, over the previous year, because it shows an upward trend. The information says even more about the performance of the company when we see that the 8.8 percent increase in earnings was achieved with a 3.3 percent decrease in total sales. This indicates that operations were more efficient in 1985 than in 1984, because cost of goods sold and operating expenses were a smaller percentage of sales than before.

The earlier year is usually the base period for calculating percentage changes. For example, Figure 19-1 shows that cash increased from 1984 to 1985 by $5,070. The percent increase is calculated as follows:

$$\frac{\text{Most recent value} - \text{Base period value}}{\text{Base period value}} = \text{Percentage change}$$

$$\frac{\$38{,}570 - \$33{,}500}{\$33{,}500} = \frac{\$5{,}070}{\$33{,}500} = .151\text{, or } 15.1\%$$

The absolute changes and the percentage changes between reported amounts must be interpreted carefully to prevent unusual circumstances from causing inappropriate conclusions. For example, if the base period amount is very small, the percentage change may appear extremely large although the absolute change is not especially significant. An example is the change in temporary investments in Megatrix Corporation's balance sheet, which shows an absolute change of $12,400. Although the change of 221.4 percent appears large, the amount of temporary investments in either year is not unusual for a corporation with assets of over $1 million. The percent change cannot be calculated if the base year amount is zero.

Trends are disclosed by analyses of several accounting periods

Horizontal analysis can provide an indication of significant **trends** in financial statement items. For this reason, corporations often provide comparative data for longer periods of time, such as 5 or 10 years, so that a number of year-to-year comparisons can be made. Note that horizontal analysis is not performed on the statement of changes because that statement already shows changes from one period to another.

Long-term comparisons are often more significant than comparisons for only two accounting periods, because more time periods can indicate the presence of trends in the figures. A change from one period to the next is not necessarily part of a longer trend, because it could be caused by unusual economic conditions or a few transactions that cannot be expected to recur. For example, a company experiences a sharp increase in earnings per share as a result of a profitable sale of investments which were acquired several years ago. The same surge in earnings cannot occur again once the investments are sold. Comparing only the past year's earnings with the current year's earnings might imply a sharp earnings uptrend. But comparing the past five years of earnings may indicate that the sharp upturn of earnings in the current year is not typical of the company's usual performance.

In addition to data for long-term comparisons, summaries of items such as total sales, total expenses, net income, earnings per share, and other important figures may be supplied in tables or graphs in the annual

Megatrix Corporation
Income Statements
For Years Ended December 31, 1985 and 1984

	1985	1984	Increase (decrease) Amount	%
Sales	$1,210,000	$1,251,400	$ (41,400)	(3.3)
Less cost of goods sold	666,500	713,800	(47,300)	(6.6)
Gross margin	543,500	537,600	5,900	1.1
Less expenses:				
Selling	142,800	158,100	(15,300)	(9.7)
Administrative	150,700	155,400	(4,700)	(3.0)
Other expenses	69,900	67,500	2,400	3.6
Interest expense	33,500	21,800	11,700	53.7
Total expenses	396,900	402,800	(5,900)	(1.5)
Income before tax	146,600	134,800	11,800	8.8
Income tax	51,300	47,200	4,100	8.7
Net income	$ 95,300	$ 87,600	$ 7,700	8.8
Earnings per common share	$9.53	$8.76	$.77	8.8

Megatrix Corporation
Statement of Retained Earnings
For Years Ended December 31, 1985 and 1984

	1985	1984	Increase (decrease) Amount	%
Retained earnings, Jan. 1	$ 139,600	$ 96,000	$ 43,600	45.4
Add net income	95,300	87,600	7,700	8.8
	234,900	183,600	51,300	27.9
Less dividends:				
Preferred	(3,000)	(3,000)	0	—
Common	(45,500)	(41,000)	(4,500)	11.0
Retained earnings, Dec. 31	$ 186,400	$ 139,600	$ 46,800	33.5

report to highlight the company's operations. Graphic presentations often illustrate financial relationships that are difficult to perceive by reading the statements alone. In addition, graphs can convey a large amount of

Megatrix Corporation
Balance Sheets
December 31, 1985 and 1984

	1985	1984	Increase (decrease) Amount	%
Assets				
Current assets:				
Cash	$ 38,570	$ 33,500	$ 5,070	15.1
Temporary investments	18,000	5,600	12,400	221.4
Accounts receivable (net)	91,280	79,700	11,580	14.5
Merchandise inventory	78,300	68,100	10,200	15.0
Prepaid expenses	9,350	18,200	(8,850)	(48.6)
Total current assets	235,500	205,100	30,400	14.8
Investments:				
Bond sinking fund	42,000	36,000	6,000	16.7
Investments in securities	182,000	181,300	700	.4
Total investments	224,000	217,300	6,700	3.1
Long-lived assets:				
Land	30,000	30,000	0	0
Buildings	330,000	280,000	50,000	17.9
Equipment	670,700	526,300	144,400	27.4
Less accumulated depreciation	(427,900)	(376,200)	(51,700)	13.7
Intangible assets	40,200	44,700	(4,500)	(10.1)
Total long-lived assets	643,000	504,800	138,200	27.4
Total assets	$1,102,500	$ 927,200	$175,300	18.9
Liabilities and Capital				
Current liabilities:				
Notes payable	$ 23,000	$ 30,000	$ (7,000)	(23.3)
Accounts payable	42,100	53,200	(11,100)	(20.9)
Taxes payable	12,600	10,700	1,900	17.8
Unearned revenues	38,400	43,700	(5,300)	(12.1)
Total current liabilities	116,100	137,600	(21,500)	(15.6)
Bonds payable, 9%, due 1997	350,000	200,000	150,000	75.0
Total liabilities	466,100	337,600	128,500	38.1
Capital:				
6% preferred stock, $100 par	50,000	50,000	0	0
Common stock, $10 par	100,000	100,000	0	0
Paid-in capital	300,000	300,000	0	0
Retained earnings	186,400	139,600	46,800	33.5
Total capital	636,400	589,600	46,800	7.9
Total liabilities and capital	$1,102,500	$ 927,200	$175,300	18.9

Figure 19-1 Horizontal analysis of financial statements. The difference between one year and the next for each item is computed both as an absolute and as a percentage change.

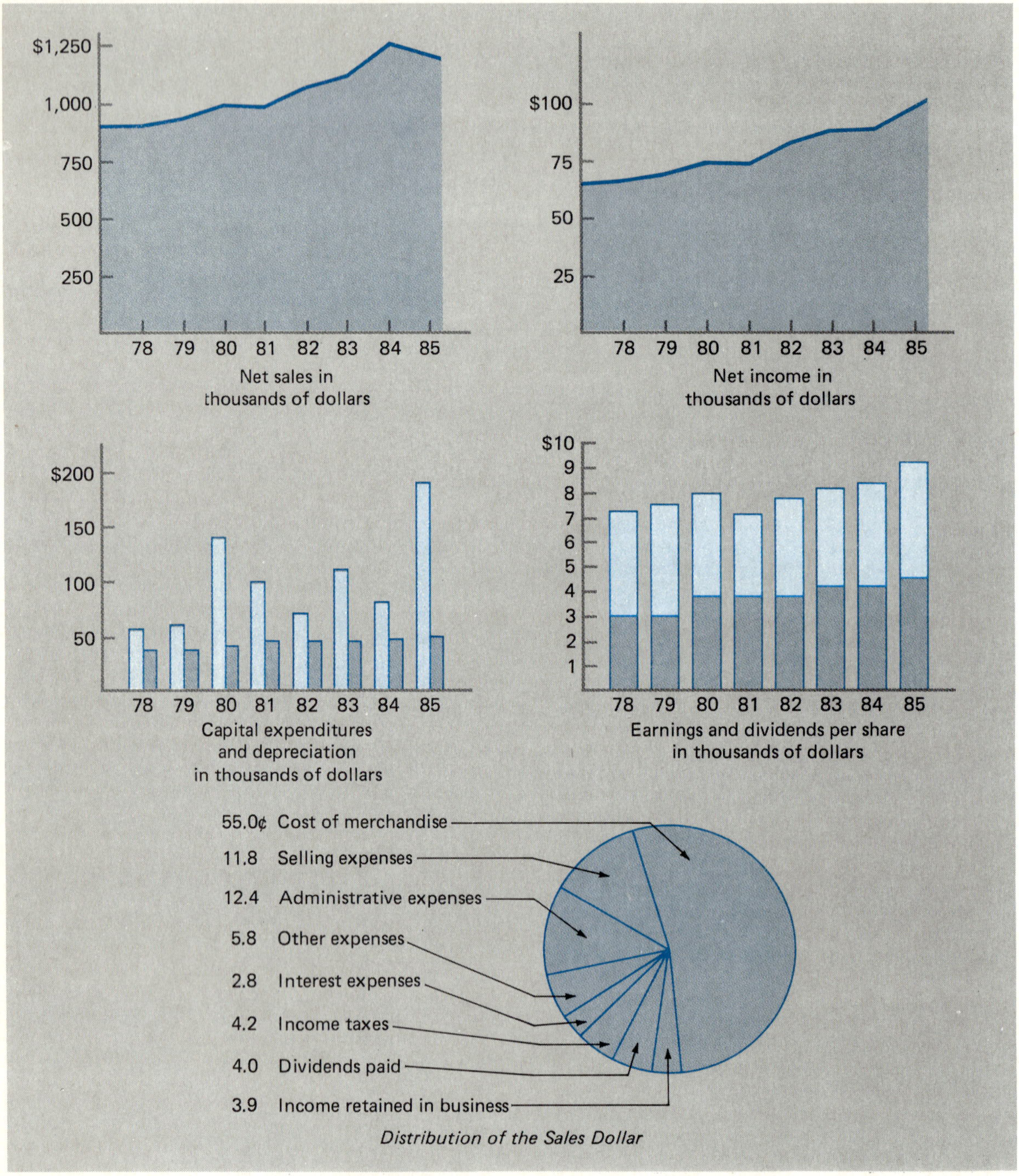

Figure 19-2 Many significant relationships and highlights of important financial data can be shown graphically in annual reports to supplement financial statements. The graphs shown here are only a small sample of the ways information can be presented.

information at a glance. Some examples of graphic illustrations are shown for Megatrix Corporation in Figure 19-2. Note the obvious presence of upwards trends in sales and income and the corresponding trend in earnings and dividends per share.

VERTICAL ANALYSIS

Statements can be converted to common units

Comparing figures in the financial statements of a single period is known as **vertical analysis**. All figures in a statement are converted to a common unit by expressing them as a percentage of a key figure in the statement, such as total sales in the income statement or total assets in a balance sheet. Figure 19-3 shows the income statement of Megatrix Corporation with each item expressed in dollars and as a percentage of sales. The statement of changes in financial position is expressed as a percentage of total sources or uses of funds, except for the schedule of working capital changes. Preparation of the statement of changes is covered in Chapter 20.

The individual percentages may reveal important proportional relationships among income statement items for each year or between the two years' figures. For instance, cost of goods sold as a percentage of sales decreased from 57 percent in 1984 to 55 percent in 1985. Total operating expenses increased from 32.2 to 32.8 percent. Net income as a percentage of sales was 7.9 percent in 1985 compared to 7.0 percent in 1984; thus despite a decrease in net sales, the company earned a higher net income primarily by reducing product expense. The implication is that management is controlling operating and product expenses carefully to counteract an adverse sales trend, which may be the result of temporary economic conditions.

Balance sheet items are usually expressed as percentages of total assets, as shown in Figure 19-4 for Megatrix Corporation. The component percentages show that current assets in 1985 are 21.4 percent of total assets, whereas current liabilities are only 10.5 percent of total equities. A comparison of the current asset components in the years 1984 and 1985 shows that the company reduced both receivables and inventories as a percentage of total assets. Although long-term investments increased in 1985, they are a smaller percentage of total assets than in 1984. The company is relying more heavily on creditors for its financing in 1985 than it did in 1984, with total liabilities increasing from 40.7 percent to 42.3 percent of total equities. But the company has shifted toward more long-term financing, as indicated by a decrease in the percentage of current liabilities. Reducing current assets as a percentage of total assets is consistent with the reduction in sales and shows careful management of working capital, which should lessen with declining sales. A shift to longer-term liabilities will preserve working capital and may improve financial leverage.

A change in a particular percentage may occur from a change in the individual item or a change in the total of several items. For example, if an asset increases from $100 to $120 while total assets increase from $1,000 to $1,500, the percentage change in the asset shows a decrease as follows:

	Current Year	%	Base Year	%	Actual Change
Supplies	$120	8	$100	10	$20 increase
	.	.	.	.	.
	.	.	.	.	.
Total assets	$1,500	100	$1,000	100	$500 increase

Percentage changes require careful analysis

The asset decreased from 10 percent of the total to 8 percent of the total although it increased in absolute terms. Often a change in an item or its percentage may indicate that further analysis is necessary to determine if there is a potential problem or potential improvement in future operations. Therefore, percentages should be used together with absolute values in any analysis.

RATIO ANALYSIS

A ratio is a number expressing the relationship between two other numbers. **Ratio analysis** is the examination of various ratios in order to learn something about the statements being analyzed. Both vertical and horizontal analyses produce ratios, because a percentage is a ratio obtained by dividing one figure into another. But ratio analysis typically includes measures that do not fall into either the vertical or horizontal category.

Different ratios are useful to different users

In earlier chapters we discussed measures such as the current ratio and the price-earnings ratio, and we indicated that they provide information useful for management and for financial analysis. Its degree of usefulness is a personal thing, however. Data useful to one decision maker may be of little interest to another who is making the same type of decision

Megatrix Corporation
Income Statement
For Years Ended December 31, 1985 and 1984

	1985	%	1984	%
Sales	$1,210,000	100.0	$1,251,400	100.0
Less cost of goods sold	666,500	55.1	713,800	57.0
Gross margin	543,500	44.9	537,600	43.0
Less operating expenses:				
Selling	142,800	11.8	158,100	12.6
Administrative	150,700	12.4	155,400	12.4
Other expenses	69,900	5.8	67,500	5.4
Interest expense	33,500	2.8	21,800	1.7
Total operating expenses	396,900	32.8	402,800	32.2
Income before tax	146,600	12.1	134,800	10.8
Income tax	51,300	4.2	47,200	3.8
Net income	$ 95,300	7.9	$ 87,600	7.0

but who places primary emphasis on other types of data. One analyst may view the current ratio as important in an analysis while another decides that it is of minor consequence. Therefore, the selection of the most meaningful ratios depends on the individual user of the information and on the type of decision or analysis being made.

For example, long-term creditors are interested in the solvency of the corporation, whereas short-term creditors are more interested in liquidity. In either case, they want to know something about the company's ability to repay its debts when they mature. Shareholders and potential investors are interested primarily in the company's profitability and in the way the company's stock behaves in the stock market. Managers want to know all

Megatrix Corporation
Statement of Changes in Financial Position
For Years Ended December 31, 1985 and 1984

	1985	%	1984	%
Sources of Working Capital				
From operations:				
Net income	$ 95,300	31.6	$ 87,600	42.3
Add Depreciation	51,700	17.1	49,800	24.1
Amortization	4,500	1.5	4,500	2.2
Working capital from operations	151,500	50.2	141,900	68.6
Other sources:				
Issuance of bonds payable	150,000	49.8	—	
Issuance of preferred stock	—		50,000	24.2
Sale of investments	—		15,000	7.2
Total sources of working capital	$ 301,500	100.0	$ 206,900	100.0
Uses of Working Capital				
Dividends	$ 48,500	16.1	$ 44,000	21.3
Purchase of equipment	144,400	47.9	125,500	60.7
Addition to buildings	50,000	16.6	—	
Purchase of investments	6,700	2.2	—	
Increase in working capital	51,900	17.2	37,400	18.1
Total uses of working capital	$ 301,500	100.0	$ 206,900	100.0
Increase (Decrease) in Working Capital				
Cash increased	$ 5,070	9.8	$ 8,680	23.2
Temporary investments	12,400	23.9	(5,800)	(15.5)
Accounts receivable	11,580	22.3	7,500	20.1
Merchandise inventory	10,200	19.7	9,600	25.7
Prepaid expenses	(8,850)	(17.1)	(1,250)	(3.3)
Notes payable	7,000	13.5	(5,000)	(13.4)
Accounts payable	11,100	21.4	12,650	33.8
Taxes payable	(1,900)	(3.7)	3,800	10.2
Unearned revenues	5,300	10.2	7,220	19.3
Increase in working capital	$ 51,900	100.0	$ 37,400	100.0

Figure 19-3 Vertical analysis of the income statement and statement of changes in financial position. The items in the income statement are reduced to a percentage of sales. In the statement of changes they are reduced to a percentage of total sources of working capital. The percentages are common units that facilitate comparisons within a statement and between statements.

Megatrix Corporation
Balance Sheets
December 31, 1985 and 1984

	1985	%	1984	%
Assets				
Current assets:				
Cash	$ 38,570	3.5	$ 33,500	3.6
Temporary investments	18,000	1.6	5,600	.6
Accounts receivable (net)	91,280	8.3	79,700	8.6
Merchandise inventory	78,300	7.1	68,100	7.3
Prepaid expenses	9,350	.8	18,200	2.0
Total current assets	235,500	21.4	205,100	22.1
Investments:				
Bond sinking fund	42,000	3.8	36,000	3.9
Investments in securities	182,000	16.5	181,300	19.6
Total investments	224,000	20.3	217,300	23.5
Long-lived assets:				
Land	30,000	2.7	30,000	3.2
Buildings	330,000	29.9	280,000	30.2
Equipment	670,700	60.8	526,300	56.8
Less accumulated depreciation	(427,900)	(38.8)	(376,200)	(40.6)
Intangible assets	40,200	3.6	44,700	4.8
Total long-lived assets	643,000	58.3	504,800	54.4
Total assets	$1,102,500	100.0	$ 927,200	100.0
Liabilities and Capital				
Current liabilities:				
Notes payable	$ 23,000	2.1	$ 30,000	3.2
Accounts payable	42,100	3.8	53,200	5.7
Taxes payable	12,600	1.1	10,700	1.2
Unearned revenues	38,400	3.5	43,700	4.7
Total current liabilities	116,100	10.5	137,600	14.8
Bonds payable, 9%, due 1997	350,000	31.7	200,000	21.6
Total liabilities	466,100	42.3	377,600	36.4
Capital:				
6% preferred stock, $100 par	50,000	4.5	50,000	5.4
Common stock, $10 par	100,000	9.1	100,000	10.8
Paid-in capital in excess of par	300,000	27.2	300,000	32.4
Retained earnings	186,400	16.9	139,600	15.1
Total capital	636,400	57.7	589,600	63.6
Total liabilities and capital	$1,102,500	100.0	$ 927,200	100.0

Figure 19-4
Vertical analysis of balance sheets. Each item is reduced to a percentage of total assets.

aspects of business operations to ensure that the financial statements reflect results that will be viewed favorably by creditors, shareholders, and potential investors. By maintaining adequate liquidity and an appropriate balance between assets, liabilities, and owners' equity, managers attempt to keep the company solvent and profitable over a long period of time. If a history of profitable operations develops, investors tend to view the company favorably, and their views are reflected in the market price of the company's stock. How do all these users of financial information measure solvency, liquidity, and profitability?

Ratio analysis can be useful to each class of decision makers for making such measurements. Ratios can be classified into four general categories, although there is some overlap. A specific ratio may fit into more than one category. The four categories are:

Tests of liquidity

1. Current ratio, also called the working capital ratio
2. Acid test ratio, also called the quick ratio
3. Receivables turnover, also called average collection period
4. Inventory turnover, also called average days' supply

Tests of solvency

5. Times interest earned
6. Debt-equity ratio
7. Debt ratio
8. Equity ratio
9. Funds flow to debt ratio

Tests of profitability

10. Return on sales, or profit margin
11. Return on total assets
12. Return on owners' equity
13. Financial leverage
14. Earnings per share (EPS)

Market tests

15. Book value per share
16. Price-earnings (P/E) ratio
17. Dividend yield
18. Dividend payout

Other ratios can be calculated as required for specific situations. Those listed above are discussed in connection with our analysis of Megatrix Corporation for the year 1985. A more complete analysis requires the calculation of comparative ratios so that trends can be examined as well as the ratios themselves. Our purpose, however, is not to perform an analysis but to show how each ratio is calculated and used. Our calculations are rounded to one decimal place as more precision is usually not warranted.

Tests of Liquidity

Liquidity is a measure of a company's ability to convert assets to cash to meet its current obligations. Current assets are used for current debt repayment, therefore measures of liquidity focus on the components of working capital.

1. Current ratio. The number of times that current assets could be used to repay current liabilities is called the **current ratio**. For Megatrix Corporation, the current ratio, or **working capital ratio**, is calculated as follows:

$$\text{Current ratio} = \frac{\text{Current assets}}{\text{Current liabilities}}$$

$$= \frac{\$235,500}{\$116,100} = 2.0 \text{ times}$$

Adequate values of ratios depend on the type of company and industry

The ratio shows that there are enough current assets to repay the current liabilities twice. For some businesses, this may be an adequate current ratio; for others it may be too high or too low. In evaluating the appropriateness of financial ratios, much depends on the nature of the business. If the current ratio is quite low, such as 1.2, sufficient cash may not be available to pay current liabilities. Not all current assets are readily convertible into cash to pay debts. For example, prepaid expenses are not converted to cash but instead are used in operations. Inventories are usually converted to receivables before the receivables can be converted to cash. Therefore, some of the current assets are considerably less liquid than others.

If the current ratio is high, such as 4.6, the company may have an excessive investment in current assets that do not produce a significant return. How does the current ratio in 1984 compare with the 1985 ratio calculated above?

2. Acid test ratio. To test the company's **immediate ability** to meet its current obligations, the **acid test ratio**, or **quick ratio**, is computed by omitting the less liquid current assets. The liquid, or quick, assets include cash and other assets that can be converted to cash quickly, such as temporary investments, notes receivable, and accounts receivable. In our example, merchandise inventory and prepaid expenses are excluded to obtain quick assets for 1985 ($235,500 of current assets − $78,300 of merchandise − $9,350 of prepaid expenses = $147,850 of quick assets).

$$\text{Acid test ratio} = \frac{\text{Liquid assets}}{\text{Current liabilities}}$$

$$= \frac{\$147,850}{\$116,100} = 1.3 \text{ times}$$

Many analysts believe that an acid test ratio of 1 indicates an adequate ability to satisfy current obligations, but you should beware of such general rules because they do not apply to all situations. A more significant evaluation is obtained by comparing the current and acid test ratios.

The adequacy of ratios depends on the industry in which the company operates

As an example, a company whose current and acid test ratios are 2.3 and 1.5, respectively, is much more liquid than one whose ratios are 2.3 and 1.1; but whether the former or the latter is in a more favorable situation depends on many other factors. The industry in which the business operates, or the type of credit terms it grants and receives, may require more or less liquid positions. A company that grants credit terms of 30 days but is allowed 60 days to pay its accounts payable does not need as high an acid test ratio as one that grants 60-day terms but must pay its own debts within 30 days. The former company collects its accounts faster and can get by with less cash on hand than the latter.

3. Receivables turnover. Another measure of liquidity is receivables turnover, which indicates how quickly accounts receivable are converted into cash. **Receivables turnover** is the time required for one complete cycle: from the time receivables are recorded through collection to the time new receivables are recorded. The faster the cycle is completed, the more quickly receivables are converted into cash. Receivables result directly from credit sales, and their turnover depends in part on the credit terms granted to customers. Ideally only credit sales should be used to calculate receivables turnover. However, this information often is not available in the financial statements, and net sales must be used instead. For Megatrix Corporation the calculation is as follows:

$$\text{Receivables turnover} = \frac{\text{Net sales}}{\text{Average receivables}}$$

$$= \frac{\$1{,}210{,}000}{(91{,}280 + \$79{,}700)/2}$$

$$= \frac{\$1{,}210{,}000}{\$85{,}490} = 14.2 \text{ times}$$

Average balance sheet figures are compared with income statement data

Notice the use of average receivables in the calculation rather than the ending balance of receivables. This is because the ratio relates income statement data to balance sheet data. Income statement information covers an entire accounting period, but balance sheet data are for a point in time. For the relationship to be meaningful, the balance sheet information should cover the same period as the income statement information. Therefore it is averaged in order to represent the entire accounting period as well. Calculating receivables turnover for 1984 would require use of the 1983 ending balance of accounts receivable, which is not available in Megatrix Corporation's statements.

The use of the beginning and ending balances to calculate averages may not provide the best average figure. Year-end balances may not be representative of account balances during most of the year due to seasonal variation in business volume. Therefore, when available, the current year's monthly or quarterly data should be used to calculate averages.

The liquidity of receivables is sometimes measured as the number of days' sales contained in the accounts receivable balance. The number of **days' sales in receivables**, also called the **average age of receivables** or the **average collection period**, is determined by calculating the average day's sales and then dividing the result into average receivables as follows:

$$\text{Average day's sales} = \frac{\text{Net sales}}{\text{Number of days in period}}$$

$$= \frac{\$1{,}210{,}000}{360 \text{ days}} = \$3{,}361 \text{ per day}$$

$$\text{Days' sales in receivables} = \frac{\text{Average receivables}}{\text{Average day's sales}}$$

$$= \frac{\$85{,}490}{\$3{,}361 \text{ per day}} = 25.4 \text{ days}$$

These calculations show that the receivables are held on the average for about 25 days before collection. If the company grants credit terms of n/30, this ratio indicates that customers are paying their accounts well within the credit period. In general, days' sales in receivables would indicate a collection problem if it exceeded the 30-day credit terms by a significant amount, such as 20 or 30 days. A collection problem caused by excessive delinquent accounts could in turn lead to a liquidity problem.

The same calculation can be made by dividing the receivables turnover into the number of days in the accounting period.

$$\text{Days' sales in receivables} = \frac{\text{Number of days in period}}{\text{Receivables turnover}}$$

$$= \frac{360 \text{ days}}{14.2} = 25.4 \text{ days}$$

We use 360 days in the calculation, but it is also possible to use 365 days or a 300-day business year, which excludes Sundays and holidays. The figure selected should be used consistently so that the resulting ratios are comparable.

4. Inventory turnover. The liquidity of inventories is measured by the number of times that average inventory is replaced during the period. **Inventory turnover** may be calculated by dividing average inventory into cost of goods sold. Average inventory is obtained by adding the beginning and ending inventory balance and dividing by 2. The inventory turnover for Megatrix Corporation is determined as follows:

$$\text{Inventory turnover} = \frac{\text{Cost of goods sold}}{\text{Average inventory}}$$

$$= \frac{\$666{,}500}{(\$78{,}300 + \$68{,}100)/2}$$

$$= \frac{\$666{,}500}{\$73{,}200} = 9.1 \text{ times}$$

A high turnover is generally more desirable than a low turnover, because each time merchandise is sold a profit is usually realized. However, too high a turnover may mean that sufficient goods are not on hand to satisfy customer needs; in that case the company may be losing some sales if merchandise is out of stock. Conversely, a low turnover may mean that merchandise is lying idle, and is an unproductive resource.

If inventory turns over slowly, gross margin must be higher than with rapid turnovers

Whether a particular turnover figure is too high or too low depends on the type of business. Inventory turnover rates vary tremendously by the types of merchandise that a business sells. Perishable merchandise requires a higher turnover than durable goods. To induce customers to buy perishable merchandise quickly, profit margins are kept to a minimum. Consequently, businesses that sell perishable merchandise usually have lower profit margins on each item. A high turnover compensates for a lower margin on each item, producing a normal profit for the business. On the other hand, a business that sells slow-moving goods must make up for the low turnover by a higher profit margin on each item sold. For example, a grocer may charge \$1 for an item that cost \$.90, but a jeweler may charge \$100 for an item that cost \$45. However, the jeweler may have to hold the \$100 item for a year before it is sold.

The liquidity of inventories may also be measured by the average number of days' supply of merchandise in the inventory balance. The **days' supply of inventory** is the number of days required to sell the average inventory on hand. The calculation for Megatrix Corporation is shown below.

$$\text{Average day's cost of goods sold} = \frac{\text{Cost of goods sold}}{\text{Number of days in period}}$$

$$= \frac{\$666{,}500}{360 \text{ days}} = \$1{,}851 \text{ per day}$$

$$\text{Days' supply of inventory} = \frac{\text{Average inventory}}{\text{Average day's CGS}}$$

$$= \frac{\$73{,}200}{\$1{,}851 \text{ per day}} = 39.5 \text{ days}$$

The company requires approximately 40 days to sell the inventory it normally keeps on hand. Whether this is good or bad depends on the type of inventory, industry standards, and management policy. The average days' supply of inventory can also be calculated by dividing the inventory turnover into the number of days in the period as follows:

$$\text{Days' supply of inventory} = \frac{\text{Number of days in period}}{\text{Inventory turnover}}$$

$$= \frac{360 \text{ days}}{9.1} = 39.6^{1} \text{ days}$$

Liquidity ratios are affected by the nature of the business, credit terms granted by the company, management policies, and the accounting method used. Analysts must be aware of each of these and allow for them when performing analyses or comparing the statements of several companies. A company using LIFO inventory valuation, for example, can be expected to have a lower current ratio than one using FIFO. The LIFO inventory may be undervalued, and may appear to have a higher turnover.

Tests of Solvency

An insolvent company cannot pay its bills

Liquidity is a measure of a company's ability to pay its current debts. **Solvency** refers to a company's ability to pay all of its debts as they come due, whether current or noncurrent. **Tests of solvency** focus on the company's ability to satisfy its long-term creditors. In order to service its bond indebtedness, a company must not only earn sufficient income to pay its interest expense in addition to paying all other expenses, it must also have a sufficient cash flow to service the debt. When the bonds payable mature, the company must have the ability to repay the debt from its own funds or from newly borrowed funds. The ability to obtain and to repay a long-term debt often depends on the firm's ability to obtain capital from shareholders. Therefore, the relationship between shareholders' equity and creditors' equity is evaluated.

5. Times interest earned. A company earns revenue from which it pays its expenses; any remainder is net income. If it earns only enough revenue to pay expenses, there is no income, but still the expenses are paid. A company that earns only enough to pay its interest and other expenses, with little or nothing left for net income, is less solvent than a company that can pay all its expenses and have a large net income. Analysts measure solvency by calculating how many times a company could pay its interest expense. The number of **times interest is earned** is calculated by dividing interest expense into earnings available for payment of interest expense.

---

[1] The difference between the first and second calculation of average days' supply of inventory is due to rounding of inventory turnover.

Interest is paid with before-tax dollars—therefore the cost of interest is less than the interest rate

Interest expense is first added back to income before tax, because the interest paid has also been earned in addition to the remaining income. Interest is a tax-deductible expense, so the before-tax figure is used because it is the maximum that could be paid as interest. For Megatrix Corporation, times interest earned for 1985 is calculated as follows:

$$\text{Times interest earned} = \frac{\text{Income before tax + Interest expense}}{\text{Interest expense}}$$

$$= \frac{\$146{,}600 + \$33{,}500}{\$33{,}500} = \frac{\$180{,}100}{\$33{,}500} = 5.4 \text{ times}$$

Income before tax plus interest expense is abbreviated as **EBIT**, derived from **E**arnings **B**efore **I**nterest and **T**axes. EBIT is used frequently in financial analysis.

6. Debt-equity ratio. Businesses obtain assets from owners and from creditors. The larger the portion provided by owners, the less risk is assumed by creditors. Liabilities expressed as a percentage of owners' equity is a ratio that indicates how much capital is provided by creditors compared to that provided by owners. If this ratio is 1, or 100%, each group provided an equal amount of capital. As the ratio increases, the amount of risk assumed by creditors increases, because the ratio indicates decreasing solvency. In our example, the ratio is as follows:

$$\text{Debt-equity ratio} = \frac{\text{Total liabilities}}{\text{Total owners' equity}}$$

$$= \frac{\$466{,}100}{\$636{,}400} = .732, \text{ or } 73.2\%$$

Owners provided more of the equities of Megatrix Corporation than creditors. Debt-equity ratios vary widely across industries. Financial institutions, such as banks or brokerage houses, typically have much higher debt-equity ratios than manufacturing companies or retail merchandisers. The relative amounts of debt and equity are also measured by the debt ratio or the equity ratio, as indicated below.

7. Debt ratio. Dividing total liabilities by total equities indicates the percentage of total assets provided by creditors. In our example the calculation is as follows:

$$\text{Debt ratio} = \frac{\text{Total liabilities}}{\text{Total equities}}$$

$$= \frac{\$466{,}100}{\$1{,}102{,}500} = .423, \text{ or } 42.3\%$$

8. Equity ratio. Subtracting the debt ratio of 42.3 percent from 100 percent yields 57.7 as the percent of assets provided by owners. The ratio can, of course, be calculated as follows:

$$\text{Equity ratio} = \frac{\text{Total owners' equity}}{\text{Total equities}}$$

$$= \frac{\$636{,}400}{\$1{,}102{,}500} = .577, \text{ or } 57.7\%$$

The relationship between owners' equity and liabilities is an indication of the company's use of financial leverage. The more debt, the more leverage the company has. Leverage is an indication of the use a company makes of borrowed funds to increase the return on owners' equity. If the borrowed money can be invested to return a yield higher than the interest rate paid on the borrowed money, the difference increases the profit for the owners. However, interest expense must be paid whether or not the company earns a profit, and with large amounts of debt, the company runs a greater risk of not having enough income to service the debt.

Debt is paid with cash, not with earnings

9. Funds flow to debt ratio. Liabilities are repaid with cash, and operations are the main source of cash for a business. The company's ability to generate cash from operations is reported in the statement of changes in financial position. External reports typically define funds as working capital, but for analytical purposes, it is assumed that working capital is a good surrogate for cash. After all, no one expects a company to repay all its debts at one time; the analyst only wants to assess its debt-paying ability. The ratio of **funds flow to debt** is calculated as follows:

$$\text{Funds flow to debt} = \frac{\text{Funds provided by operations}}{\text{Average total liabilities}}$$

$$= \frac{\$151{,}500}{(\$466{,}100 + \$337{,}600)/2}$$

$$= \frac{\$151{,}500}{\$401{,}850} = .377, \text{ or } 37.7\%$$

As with other calculations that involve both income statement and balance sheet figures, average balance sheet data are used. Megatrix Company generated enough funds from operations to repay about a third of its debt. Whether this is sufficient depends on the amount of debt that is ready to mature, and the company's ability to refinance the debt from sources other than operations. As with all other ratios, the analyst evaluates this one by reference to other information, such as the average funds flow to debt ratio for the industry. Some analysts like to include preferred stock in the denominator of the ratio, viewing preferred shares as debt rather than capital. Analysts sometimes use net income plus depreciation expense as the numerator of the ratio, on the assumption that other nonfund items in the income statement are usually not significant.

Tests of Profitability

In order to attract capital, businesses must earn enough profits to yield a satisfactory return to investors. If the profits do not materialize, a business will not be able to continue attracting capital from owners or creditors. The long-range survival of a business depends on its ability to earn enough revenue to satisfy all obligations and still provide a satisfactory return on the owners' investment. Several **tests of profitability** are available to measure the adequacy of income.

The basic calculation of return relates the amount of income earned to the amount of investment used to earn that income. Return is expressed as a percentage rate and is calculated as follows:

$$\text{Rate of return} = \frac{\text{Income earned on investment}}{\text{Amount of investment}}$$

Several different rates of return can be calculated, each using a different definition of income and investment.

10. Return on sales. The amount of net income earned on an average dollar of sales revenue is called the **return on sales**, or **profit margin**. Return on sales is calculated as a percentage of net sales as follows:

$$\text{Return on sales} = \frac{\text{Net income}}{\text{Net sales}}$$

$$= \frac{\$95{,}300}{\$1{,}210{,}000} = .079\text{, or } 7.9\%$$

High profit margins compensate for high risk

Each dollar of sales earned $.079, or about 8 cents of profit. Whether this profit margin is adequate depends on the type of business the company operates, and on the amount of assets invested in the business. If the assets turn over rapidly, the return on sales is usually lower than for businesses with slow turnovers. A business that holds slow-moving assets assumes more risk that those assets will become obsolete, more costly to replace, or less productive. In addition, assets tied up in one activity might earn a higher return if invested in another activity. The results obtained from assets with a high turnover are easier to predict, and holding such assets involves less risk. To compensate for high risk, businesses must earn higher returns.

Assets work the same whether they are acquired with debt or equity capital

11. Return on total assets. Income is earned by using assets productively. The more efficiently assets are used, the more profitable the business. Assets perform their function whether they are obtained from borrowed money or from owners; therefore, the return on assets should be calculated before deducting interest expense. If interest is not deducted, income taxes should not be deducted either because taxes are calculated on income after interest deductions. Consequently, EBIT is usually used to measure the return on assets.

$$\text{Return on total assets} = \frac{\text{Earnings before interest and taxes (EBIT)}}{\text{Average total assets}}$$

$$= \frac{\$146{,}600 + \$33{,}500}{(\$1{,}102{,}500 + \$927{,}200)/2}$$

$$= \frac{\$180{,}100}{\$1{,}014{,}850} = .177, \text{ or } 17.7\%$$

On the average, every dollar of assets earned 17.7 cents of income from which interest and taxes must be paid. When interest expense and tax data are not available because condensed statements are presented, the analyst has no choice but to calculate return on total assets by using net income instead of EBIT.

12. Return on owners' equity. The profit earned for the owners of a business is called **return on owners' equity** or **return on investment**. Return on owners' equity is an indication of the company's profitability because it shows how well the company is doing with the investment contributed by its owners. For Megatrix Corporation, return on total owners' equity is calculated as follows:

$$\text{Return on owners' equity} = \frac{\text{Net income}}{\text{Average owners' equity}}$$

$$= \frac{\$95{,}300}{(\$636{,}400 + \$589{,}600)/2}$$

$$= \frac{\$95{,}300}{\$613{,}000} = .155, \text{ or } 15.5\%$$

Net income is not shared equally by common and preferred shareholders. The return to preferred shareholders is limited to their preferred dividend—$3,000 per year for the Megatrix 6 percent preferred stock (6% of $50,000). All remaining income belongs to the common shareholders, whether or not it is paid to them in the form of dividends. For the common shareholders, therefore, return on investment should be calculated separately by excluding from total owners' equity the book value of preferred stock. Common equity therefore consists of total capital less $50,000 of preferred equity. Return on common equity for Megatrix is 16.4 percent, calculated as follows:

$$\text{Return on common equity} = \frac{\text{Net income} - \text{Preferred dividend requirement}}{\text{Average common equity}}$$

$$= \frac{\$95{,}300 - \$3{,}000}{(\$586{,}400 + \$539{,}600)/2}$$

$$= \frac{\$92{,}300}{\$563{,}000} = .164, \text{ or } 16.4\%$$

13. Financial leverage. If all of the assets of the business were contributed by shareholders, the entire return on these assets would belong to owners. If a business can borrow funds at an interest cost that is lower than the rate of return on assets, the owners can benefit from the borrowing. The benefit of borrowing money and investing at a rate higher than the cost of the funds is called **financial leverage**. For example, return on assets for a corporation is 12 percent, and the company issued 10 percent bonds. The bond proceeds can be invested at 12 percent, leaving 2 percent of the return for owners after paying the 10 percent interest. The same 12 percent return on assets now provides a greater return on owners' equity than without the use of borrowed money.

Leverage is the benefit obtained by using borrowed money

Precisely how much the return on common equity is increased by leverage depends on the proportion of assets borrowed, the interest rate, the rate of return on assets, and the income tax rate. For example, let us assume a company has \$20,000 of assets, no liabilities, income before tax of \$4,000, and a 40 percent income tax rate, leaving a net income of \$2,400. With no liabilities or interest expense, return on total assets is calculated on net income rather than on EBIT. We call this the **net return on assets**, and when there is no debt, net return on assets is the same as return on owners' equity, because total assets equal total owners' equity.

$$\text{Net return on assets} = \frac{\text{Net income}}{\text{Average total assets}} = \frac{\$2{,}400}{\$20{,}000} = .12, \text{ or } 12\%$$

$$\text{Return on common equity} = \frac{\text{Net income}}{\text{Common equity}} = \frac{\$2{,}400}{\$20{,}000} = .12, \text{ or } 12\%$$

Now we assume the company's equities consist of \$10,000 of common stock and \$10,000 of 10 percent bonds payable. The assets still earn \$4,000 before tax, but \$1,000 of this must be paid as interest, leaving \$3,000 of income subject to the 40 percent tax. This means that net income after tax is \$1,800 and return on common owners' equity is

$$\text{Return on common equity} = \frac{\text{Net income}}{\text{Common equity}} = \frac{\$1{,}800}{\$10{,}000} = .18, \text{ or } 18\%$$

By borrowing half of its assets, the company added 6 percent more return on owners' equity, although the assets earned the same amount of income. Notice, however, that net income is smaller because of the need to pay interest. But it is not \$1,000 smaller because less income also means less income tax. In fact, net income is smaller by the cost of interest less the tax saving created by the interest expense. The net-of-tax interest cost is only \$1,000 − .4(\$1,000), or \$600.

To measure financial leverage, we have to find the difference between return on common equity when all assets are contributed by owners and return on common equity when part of the assets are contributed by creditors. **Leverage** is the difference between the return on owners' equity and the net return on assets. But to find net return on assets when interest expense exists, we divide total assets into **net income plus the net-of-tax interest expense**. This way, net return on assets is precisely the same return the common stock would earn if all assets had been contributed by owners.

$$\text{Net return on assets} = \frac{\text{Net income} + \text{Net-of-tax interest expense}}{\text{Average total assets}}$$

$$= \frac{\$1{,}800 + \$600}{\$20{,}000} = \frac{\$2{,}400}{\$20{,}000} = .12, \text{ or } 12\%$$

$$\text{Financial leverage} = \text{Return on common equity} - \text{Net return on assets}$$

$$= .18 - .12 = .06, \text{ or } 6\%$$

Leverage can be positive or negative

In this example leverage is positive, providing 6 percent more return on common equity than would have been earned if the company had not made use of borrowed funds. However, if the net return on assets happens to be lower than the net-of-tax interest cost, leverage can be negative, often leaving shareholders with a smaller return or larger loss than would occur without borrowing. Once funds are borrowed, the company cannot simply stop paying interest if sales decline or costs increase. For this reason, managers must be careful not to increase owners' risk excessively by too much borrowing.

To illustrate negative leverage, suppose that EBIT of the company in our example decreases from \$4,000 to \$1,800. This 55 percent decrease in EBIT would be accompanied by a 73 percent decrease in return on common equity, from 18 percent to 4.8 percent, because the net return on assets would be less than the net-of-tax interest rate on debt. The calculations are shown below.

Net income before interest and tax (EBIT)	\$1,800
Less interest expense	1,000
Income before tax	800
Less income tax at 40 percent	320
Net income	\$ 480

$$\text{Return on assets} = \frac{\text{EBIT}}{\text{Average total assets}} = \frac{\$1{,}800}{\$20{,}000} = .090, \text{ or } 9.0\%$$

$$\text{Net return on assets} = \frac{\text{Net income} + \text{Net-of-tax interest expense}}{\text{Average total assets}}$$

$$= \frac{\$480 + \$600}{\$20{,}000} = \frac{\$1{,}080}{\$20{,}000} = .054, \text{ or } 5.4\%$$

$$\text{Return on common equity} = \frac{\text{Net income}}{\text{Common equity}}$$

$$= \frac{\$480}{\$10{,}000} = .048, \text{ or } 4.8\%$$

$$\text{Leverage} = \text{Return on common equity} - \text{Net return on assets}$$
$$= 4.8\% - 5.4\% = -.6\%$$

Now we return to our analysis of Megatrix Corporation for which we can calculate financial leverage. We already know the return on common equity is 16.4 percent. Net income and interest expense are available from the financial statements, and the income tax rate is calculated as 34.99 percent ($51,300/$146,600). This can be rounded to 35 percent for purposes of financial analysis. Below we calculate the net-of-tax interest expense and net return on assets:

Interest expense	$33,500
Less 35 percent tax	11,725
Net-of-tax interest expense	$21,775

The same calculation can be obtained as follows:

$$\text{Net of tax interest expense} = \text{Interest expense} \times (1 - \text{Tax rate})$$
$$= \$33{,}500\ (1 - .35)$$
$$= \$21{,}775$$

$$\text{Net return on assets} = \frac{\text{Net income} + \text{Net-of-tax interest expense}}{\text{Average total assets}}$$

$$= \frac{\$95{,}300 + \$21{,}775}{(\$1{,}102{,}500 + \$927{,}200)/2}$$

$$= \frac{\$117{,}075}{\$1{,}014{,}850} = .115, \text{ or } 11.5\%$$

$$\text{Leverage} = \text{Return on common equity} - \text{Net return on assets}$$
$$= 16.4\% - 11.5\% = 4.9\%$$

Megatrix Corporation's financial leverage is positive, providing 4.9 percent more return on owners' equity than would have been earned if the company had not made use of borrowed funds.

The existence of preferred stock can also provide leverage, because the preferred dividend is the same no matter how much or how little the company earns. When interest and tax data are not available, leverage is computed by using return on assets calculated on the basis of net income alone.

14. Earnings per share (EPS). The calculation of earnings per share can be complicated. EPS is one of the most important indicators of profitability because it can easily be compared to previous EPS figures and to the EPS figures of other companies. In addition, investors find it convenient to see the amount earned for a single share of stock. Interpreting this ratio properly requires a good understanding of how primary and fully diluted earnings per share are calculated. Since Megatrix Corporation does not have a complex capital structure, the calculation of earnings per share is simple.

$$\text{Earnings per share} = \frac{\text{Net income} - \text{Preferred dividend}}{\text{Weighted average no. of common shares}}$$

$$= \frac{\$95{,}300 - \$3{,}000}{10{,}000 \text{ shares}} = \frac{\$92{,}300}{10{,}000 \text{ shares}} = \$9.23$$

As with all ratios, the absolute value of EPS for the year is not as significant as the change from previous years. Therefore, financial analysis should include calculations of ratios for comparative statements.

The analyst should be aware of the effect on profitability ratios of alternative accounting methods and management policies. A company using accelerated depreciation, for instance, typically has a smaller asset base than it would have with straight-line depreciation, making the return on assets appear larger. A company that leases a large proportion of its assets may have a larger proportion of long-term liabilities than a company that buys its assets. A firm that uses operating leases extensively will seem to have a smaller amount of assets than it actually uses in its operations. Financial statements disclose a large amount of information in footnotes which the analyst must examine carefully in order to interpret the ratios computed from the figures in the main body of the statements.

Market Tests

Investors and shareholders are usually interested in the market price of a company's common stock, and in ratios that describe the stock's market performance. An investor has to pay the market price for a share of stock, therefore most market tests are based on the current price of the stock. Megatrix Corporation's common stock sells in the market at $70 per share.

15. Book value per share. The book value of a company often has little relationship to its market value. For companies with large amounts of financial assets, such as insurance companies, loan companies, and savings institutions, book value may be significant because a large portion of assets such as stock, bond, and mortgage investments and savings deposits usually has a book value that is close to market value. In that case, a comparison of book value and market value of the company's stock may reveal that a financial company's stock is trading in the market at bargain prices or at excessive prices.

Book value of stock is usually lower than market value

For most industrial companies with large amounts of fixed assets and inventories recorded at cost, book value of stock is often significantly below market value. Nevertheless, a comparison of book value and market value of stock sometimes gives an indication of how investors view the company. If market value is higher than book value, investors are attributing goodwill to the company or they are paying for undervalued assets, and their assessment of the company's asset value is reflected in the price of the stock. Book value may be calculated for preferred and common stock, but it is typically relevant only for common shares. Book value per common share is calculated by dividing total common equity (total capital − preferred equity) by the number of common shares. For Megatrix Corporation the calculation is:

$$\text{Book value per common share} = \frac{\text{Total common equity}}{\text{Number of common shares}}$$

$$= \frac{\$636{,}400 - \$50{,}000}{10{,}000 \text{ shares}} = \$58.64 \text{ per share}$$

With a market price of $70 per share, investors believe that the company's net assets are undervalued. The high returns on assets and on owners' equity provide justification for their assessment of the company's value.

16. Price-earnings (P/E) ratio. The price of a stock alone does not indicate whether or not the stock is expensive. A $60 stock may be a better buy than a $25 stock. To estimate value, the price should be related to the amount of income the company earns. The price-earnings (P/E) ratio reduces the stock to a common unit of measure for comparison with other stocks. It indicates how many dollars are required to buy $1 worth of earnings. In our example, the calculation is as follows:

The P/E ratio tells how expensive a stock is

$$\text{Price-earnings (P/E) ratio} = \frac{\text{Price per share}}{\text{Earnings per share}}$$

$$= \frac{\$70}{\$9.23} = 7.58 \text{ times}$$

This calculation shows that to buy $1 of Megatrix Corporation's annual earnings an investor must pay about 7.6 times that amount. Typically, companies whose earnings exhibit a rapid rate of growth have higher P/E ratios than those whose earnings are stable. Investors are willing to pay more for current earnings if they anticipate that future earnings will be higher. There is a very wide range of P/E ratios in the stock market. The average in the past few years has been between 6 and 12, but P/E ratios of over 100 occasionally occur.

Dividend yield is a rate of return

17. Dividend yield. Some investors buy common stock in order to earn dividend income. Others are more interested in the growth of their shares' market value. **Dividend yield** is one measure of rate of return on the investor's stock investment. It is calculated as follows:

$$\text{Dividend yield} = \frac{\text{Dividend per share}}{\text{Price per share}}$$

$$= \frac{\$4.55}{\$70} = .065, \text{ or } 6.5\%$$

If the company has a policy of paying regular dividends, the investor can expect a yield of 6.5 percent on an investment in the common stock of Megatrix Corporation. There is, of course, no guarantee that the company will continue to pay dividends. Many companies, however, try to maintain a stable dividend and to increase the dividend when possible, so that investors can depend on receiving a steady income from their shareholdings. Some companies, on the other hand, pay little or no dividend, because they attempt to grow by retaining and investing their earnings. Investors buy the stocks of such companies for their growth rather than for their dividend yield. Megatrix Corporation's dividend history, illustrated in Figure 19-2, indicates that current dividend rates will probably continue into the future.

18. Dividend payout. **Dividend payout** is the percentage of net income distributed by the company; it is an indication of the proportion of net income distributed to shareholders and the proportion retained by the business.

$$\text{Dividend payout} = \frac{\text{Total dividend}}{\text{Net income}}$$

$$= \frac{\$48{,}500}{\$95{,}300} = .51, \text{ or } 51\%$$

Slightly more than half of the income was distributed as dividends. The dividend payout can also be calculated from the point of view of common shareholders, by relating common dividends to net income less preferred dividends. The calculation may be made on the basis of total dividends and income, or on a per-share basis as follows:

$$\text{Dividend payout} = \frac{\text{Common dividend per share}}{\text{Earnings per share}}$$

$$= \frac{\$4.55}{\$9.23} = .49, \text{ or } 49\%$$

The portion of net income not paid to shareholders as dividends is retained by the company for the purpose of financing growth and expansion. Retained earnings do not provide a direct yield to the shareholder, but the shareholder can benefit from this portion of the company's income through growth in the market value of stock caused by the growth in retained earnings. With approximately half of its income retained, Megatrix Corporation is providing for its future growth and increased earnings.

All of the ratios discussed above are summarized in Figure 19-5, which shows how the ratios are calculated and their interpretation.

INTERPRETATION AND USE OF FINANCIAL RATIOS

The ratios presented in this chapter are some of the more common ones used by managers and financial analysts to assess the performance and future potential of a business. Other ratios can be calculated, and some of those presented may be calculated differently than shown here. Sometimes it is necessary to calculate only a small number of ratios in order to arrive at a decision about a business. More important than calculating the ratios is interpreting them. Evaluating ratios allows the analyst to determine whether specific areas of a business warrant further investigation.

An adequate financial analysis involves more than an understanding and interpretation of each of the individual ratios. An insight into the meaning of the interrelationships among the ratios and financial data in the statements is also needed. Gaining such an insight and understanding requires considerable experience in the analysis and interpretation of financial statements. Moreover, even experienced analysts cannot apply their skill equally well to all financial statements. Every industry has its own characteristics with which analysts must be familiar, and it is not possible for any one individual to understand all industries equally well.

Several financial services compile data and provide information on American industry and business corporations. Standard & Poor's *Corporation Records*, Moody's *Manual of Investments*, and Arnold Bernhard's *Value Line Investment Survey* are publications that provide large amounts of financial data, ratios, and financial analyses to help decision makers evaluate businesses. Dun & Bradstreet compiles lists of ratios that represent averages for many industries. Published industry averages, ratios, and financial analyses can be helpful, but the individual analyst must still rely on skill, insight, and even intuition in order to interpret the financial statements of a corporation and arrive at a decision. A comparison of historical ratios for a single company may indicate important trends, and may be more useful than published averages that obscure significant variations among companies.

In addition to the analysis of financial statements, analysts often use other available information about a company or an industry. The backlog of orders a company has, the new government contract it has just signed, or the successful test of a newly developed product, all can have a significant impact on future earnings. The analyst continuously seeks information to supplement the financial data available in accounting reports. What is the impact on a chemical company from legislation that prohibits use of certain pesticides because they pollute the environment? How will the auto industry be affected if Congress mandates that all cars must withstand a 5 mph crash without damage? What will happen to the earnings of domestic amateur movie camera makers when a foreign company introduces a low-priced color video camera for the amateur market? These and many other questions cannot be answered by reading the financial statements. But answers to such questions are of little value if they cannot be related to information in accounting reports.

Economic, social, and political factors enter into an analysis

In their search for information, financial analysts look to many sources. Information about new legislation, technological developments, foreign relations, and the state of the economy all can be relevant to an analysis of a single company. When necessary, an analyst will go directly to the company and ask questions. Financial analysts also have been instrumental in bringing about changes in the way accounting data are reported. For example, the statement of changes in financial position was not a part of the annual report of corporations until financial analysts began to demand that it be provided.

More recently financial analysts have been requesting that corporations publish forecasts and projections of future operations. Such **pro forma** financial statements are available only to management, and companies have been reluctant to provide them to external users. Managers prepare pro forma statements by adjusting the data in the current period's financial statements to reflect expected or planned changes. For example, if sales are $100,000 currently and management expects a 15 percent increase in sales, the pro forma income statement shows sales of $115,000. Other figures are similarly obtained from estimates, projections, budgets, and educated guesses. Pro forma statements can obviously prove to be quite different from actual results, but they are extremely useful to managers for planning operations and controlling business activities.

Financial forecasts may be included in future annual reports

Financial analysts would obviously find managements' projections useful in their assessment of future business performance. But the accounting profession is concerned about the way that pro forma statements should be verified and certified. There is a danger that forecasts could be viewed as actual expectations by external users, who may feel misled if the fore-

casted performance is not achieved. Nevertheless, in the futu
see annual reports containing pro forma financial statements in additi
historical data.

Name of Ratio	Method of Calculation	Interpretation
	Tests of Liquidity	
Current (working capital) ratio	$\frac{\text{Current assets}}{\text{Current liabilities}}$	Ability to pay current debts from current assets
Acid test (quick) ratio	$\frac{\text{Liquid assets}}{\text{Current liabilities}}$	Immediate ability to pay current debts from liquid assets
Receivables turnover	$\frac{\text{Net sales}}{\text{Average receivables}}$	Ability to convert receivables to cash measured by the number of collection cycles
Days' sales in receivables	$\frac{\text{Number of days in period}}{\text{Receivables turnover}}$	Effectiveness of credit terms measured by average age of receivables, or average collection period
Inventory turnover	$\frac{\text{Cost of goods sold}}{\text{Average inventory}}$	Ability to sell inventories measured by the number of purchase and sales cycles
Days' supply in inventory	$\frac{\text{Number of days in period}}{\text{Inventory turnover}}$	Time required to sell average inventory measured by average age of merchandise on hand
	Tests of Solvency	
Times interest earned	$\frac{\text{Earnings before interest and taxes (EBIT)}}{\text{Interest expense}}$	Ability to service long-term debt
Debt-equity ratio	$\frac{\text{Total liabilities}}{\text{Total owners' equity}}$	Proportion of assets provided by creditors compared with that provided by owners
Debt ratio	$\frac{\text{Total liabilities}}{\text{Total equities}}$	Proportion of total assets provided by creditors
Equity ratio	$\frac{\text{Total owners' equity}}{\text{Total equities}}$	Proportion of total assets provided by owners
Fund flows to debt ratio	$\frac{\text{Funds from operations}}{\text{Average total liabilities}}$	Ability to repay debts from funds generated by business operations
	Test of Profitability	
Return on sales	$\frac{\text{Net income}}{\text{Net sales}}$	Profit margin earned on each dollar of sales
Return on total assets	$\frac{\text{Earnings before interest and taxes (EBIT)}}{\text{Average total assets}}$	Efficiency with which managers use total assets to operate the business
Return on owners' equity	$\frac{\text{Net income}}{\text{Average owners' equity}}$	Rate of return earned by owners on their investment.
Net return on assets	$\frac{\text{Net income + Net-of-tax interest expense}}{\text{Average total assets}}$	Return on assets after tax and without interest, used for leverage calculations.
Leverage	Return on common equity − Net return on assets	Advantage to owners from using borrowed funds to earn a higher return on investment
Earnings per share (EPS)	$\frac{\text{Net income − Preferred dividend}}{\text{Weighted average no. of common shares}}$	Amount of net income earned by each common share
	Market Tests	
Book value per common share	$\frac{\text{Total common equity}}{\text{Number of common shares}}$	Amount of owners' equity in each share of stock
Price-earnings (P/E) ratio	$\frac{\text{Price per share}}{\text{Earnings per share}}$	Number of dollars required to buy $1 of earnings
Dividend yield	$\frac{\text{Dividend per share}}{\text{Price per share}}$	Return to owner on the investment required to buy one share of stock
Dividend payout	$\frac{\text{Common dividends}}{\text{Net income}}$ or $\frac{\text{Common dividend per share}}{\text{Earnings per share}}$	Proportion of earnings distributed as dividends

Figure 19-5 **Summary of financial ratios discussed in the chapter.**

SUMMARY

Analysis of financial statements requires a thorough understanding of the accounting principles and concepts used for measuring and reporting financial data, and of alternative accounting methods that may be selected by managers to present historical information. An adequate analysis requires the comparison of at least two accounting periods, and data on several consecutive periods are needed in order to perceive trends in the figures presented. A complete financial analysis may involve horizontal, vertical, and ratio analysis.

Horizontal analysis is the calculation of differences between account balances in the statements of two accounting periods. Such differences are computed in absolute and in percentage amounts and, if calculated for several accounting periods, may indicate significant trends in the figures. **Vertical analysis** is the comparison of figures within a financial statement of one period. The figures are expressed in common terms by converting them to a percentage of a significant value. In the income statement, all amounts are usually converted to a percentage of sales. In the balance sheet, amounts are usually converted to a percentage of total assets.

Ratio analysis is the calculation of the relationship between two figures which may come from the same statement or from two different statements. Ratios may be classified into tests of **liquidity, solvency, profitability,** and **market tests**. The most common of these ratios are summarized in Figure 19-5.

The interpretation of financial statements requires skills and insight which can be achieved only through experience. Published ratios and analyses may be helpful but they form only a part of the input that is needed to assess the past performance and future potential of a business.

KEY TERMS

acid test ratio *(784)*
average age of receivables *(786)*
average collection period *(786)*
book value per share *(796)*
current ratio *(784)*
days' sales in receivables *(786)*
day's supply of inventory *(787)*
debt-equity ratio *(789)*
debt ratio *(789)*
dividend payout *(798)*
dividend yield *(798)*
earnings per share (EPS) *(796)*
EBIT *(789)*
equity ratio *(790)*
financial leverage *(793)*
financial statement analysis *(774)*
funds flow to debt ratio *(790)*
horizontal analysis *(775)*
inventory turnover *(786)*
leverage *(794)*
liquidity *(783)*
market tests *(796)*
net return on assets *(793)*
price-earnings (P/E) ratio *(797)*
profit margin *(791)*
quick ratio *(784)*
ratio analysis *(780)*
receivables turnover *(785)*
return on owners' equity *(792)*
return on sales *(791)*
return on total assets *(792)*
solvency *(788)*
tests of liquidity *(783)*
tests of profitability *(791)*
tests of solvency *(788)*
times interest earned *(788)*
trends *(775)*
vertical analysis *(779)*
working capital ratio *(784)*

QUESTIONS

1. Discuss what is meant by external and internal decision makers, and the purposes for which they use financial statements.
2. What are the main purposes of analyzing financial statements?
3. What are some of the reasons for presenting comparative financial statements in annual reports?
4. Explain the main difference between horizontal and vertical analysis of financial statements.
5. Describe what is meant by ratio analysis of financial statements. What kind of tests can be performed with ratio analysis?
6. What advantage is offered by presenting financial statements of the past 5 to 10 years compared with presenting financial statements for only the current year and previous year?
7. Discuss the concept of financial leverage. What advantage can be derived by owners from financial leverage? What are the risks involved?
8. Stock A trades in the market at $60 per share. Stock B trades in the market at $20 per share. The price-earnings ratio of A is 9 and the price-earnings ratio of B is 12. While talking to his stock broker, Mr. Smith said, "I can't afford Stock A. It's too expensive. Buy 100 shares of Stock B." Discuss Mr. Smith's statement.
9. You are analyzing the financial statements of two companies which have virtually the same equity structure and net income. Company A uses FIFO inventory valuation and straight-line depreciation for its fixed assets. Company B uses LIFO inventory valuation and double-declining-balance depreciation. What are some of the differences you expect to find in the ratios of the two companies, and which ratios do you expect to differ?
10. Jack said to his friend Bill, "I just bought the stock of BDM Company at $50 per share. The dividend payout of 50 percent provides me with a yield of 10 percent on my investment and a chance for some growth." "That's nothing," replied Bill. "Six years ago I bought shares of UMS Company for $50 per share. The stock is now selling for $130 and the $10 dividend gives me a 20 percent return. I need a high return on my investments, because I depend on the dividends for half my income." "In that case you have better alternatives," suggested Jack. What are EPS and dividend per share on the BDM stock? Is Bill calculating return correctly? What does Jack mean by better alternatives?

EXERCISES

Ex. 19-1 **Using ratios to reconstruct financial data.** The annual report of Mattrix Company included the president's letter to shareholders, which stated: "Return on sales this year increased to 9 percent from 7.5 percent last year. The company's net income was $1,134,000 this year, up 8 percent over last year.

Required: Determine the percentage increase or decrease in sales from last year to the current year.

Ex. 19-2 **Using ratios to obtain financial data.** The current ratio of a company is 1.6, and working capital is $30,000. The company uses $8,000 of cash to repay a short-term note payable.

Required: Determine the amount of current assets, current liabilities, and the current ratio after the payment of the note.

Ex. 19-3 **Measures of liquidity.** Simian Company's current ratio is 2, and its quick ratio is 1.2. Listed below are several independent events or transactions, some of which affect the company's liquidity.

- **a.** Delivered merchandise costing $6,000 to a customer in exchange for $500 cash and a patent worth $5,500.
- **b.** Purchased merchandise on open account.
- **c.** Declared a cash dividend payable next month.
- **d.** Changed from terms of n/60 to 3/10, n/30 on accounts receivable.
- **e.** Purchased equipment on open account.
- **f.** Reduced selling price of merchandise and advertised special sale, thereby increasing volume of sales.
- **g.** Paid account payable.
- **h.** Sold merchandise for cash.
- **i.** Changed from FIFO to LIFO inventory method because prices are rising.
- **j.** Wrote off uncollectible account against allowance for bad debts.
- **k.** Collected account receivable.
- **l.** Paid dividend previously declared.
- **m.** Issued stock in exchange for land.
- **n.** Sold temporary investment at a profit.
- **o.** Added new line of durable goods to present line of perishable goods.

Required: Set up a table as shown below. For each item indicate what effect it will have on the company's current ratio, quick ratio, receivables turnover, and inventory turnover. Use a + to show an increase in the ratio, − to show a decrease, and 0 if the ratio is not affected or the effect cannot be determined. The first item is solved as an example.

Item	Current Ratio	Quick Ratio	Receivables Turnover	Inventory Turnover
a.	−	+	0	+

Ex. 19-4 **Measures of solvency and profitability.** Below is a list of independent transactions or events, each followed by some measures of solvency or profitability.

a. Issued capital stock for cash.
1. Debt-equity ratio
2. Return on sales
3. Debt ratio

b. Declared and paid cash dividend.
1. Equity ratio
2. Return on owners' equity
3. Debt-equity ratio

c. Notified by the city of a decrease in property taxes.
1. Return on sales
2. Fund flows to debt
3. Leverage

d. Bond holders converted bonds into common stock.
1. Leverage
2. Return on total assets
3. Fund flows to debt

e. Inventory turnover increased with no change in costs or selling prices.
1. Return on sales
2. Return on total assets
3. Times interest earned

f. Operating income increased 15 percent; interest expense increased 5 percent.
1. Return on owners' equity
2. Times interest earned
3. Leverage

Required: Indicate what effect each transaction would have on the ratios that follow it. Use a + or − to show an increase or decrease in the ratio, and a 0 to show that there is no change or the effect on the ratio cannot be determined.

Ex. 19-5 Profitability and leverage. Lancer Company has total assets of $3,000,000 and owners' equity of $1,200,000. Income after interest and before tax is $200,000, and interest expense is $80,000. The company is subject to a tax rate of 40 percent.

Required: Calculate the following ratios:

a. Times interest earned.
b. Return on total assets.
c. Return on equity.
d. Financial leverage.

Ex. 19-6 Effects on market measures. Below is a list of independent transactions or events, some of which affect market ratios of Bylo Company.

a. Issued 10 percent stock dividend followed by the regular quarterly cash dividend which had always been $1 per share.

b. Declared regular quarterly cash dividend.

c. Issued common stock for cash at market price, which is double the book value.

d. Effected a 2-for-1 stock split.

e. Won large court award in patent infringement suit.
f. Declared and issued 5 percent stock dividend.
g. Acquired profitable subsidiary in a pooling of interests. Prior to acquisition P/E ratio was 20 for Bylo stock and 6 for subsidiary stock.
h. The board of directors declared an increased dividend, payable next month.
i. Return on assets is 15 percent. Issued 12 percent bonds at par.
j. Net income increased, but the market price of the stock remained unchanged.
k. Earnings increased 20 percent, dividend payout remained unchanged.
l. Sales decreased, and return on sales is unchanged. Market price of stock remains the same.

Required: Set up a table as shown below. For each item indicate what effect it will have on the company's book value per share, earnings per share, price-earnings ratio, and dividend yield. Use a + or − to show an increase or decrease, and a 0 if there is no change or the change cannot be determined. The first item is solved as an example.

Book Value per Share	EPS	P/E	Dividend Yield
−	−	0	+

Ex. 19-7 **Turnover ratios.** Below are financial data taken from the records of Paemore Company.

Sales	$385,000
Cost of goods sold	170,000
Gross margin	215,000
Beginning inventory	19,950
Ending inventory	22,550
Beginning receivables	26,220
Ending receivables	28,780

Required: Calculate the following ratios:
a. Inventory turnover.
b. Receivables turnover.
c. Days' supply of inventory.
d. Days' sales in receivables.

Ex. 19-8 **Horizontal analysis.** Following are comparative financial statements of Kamasuto Corporation in condensed form.

Required: Perform a horizontal analysis of Kamasuto Corporation's financial statements by completing two additional columns, one for the amount of increase or decrease for 1985 over 1984, and the other for the percentage increase or decrease.

Kamasuto Corporation
Statements of Income and Retained Earnings
For the Years Ended December 31, 1985 and 1984

	1985	1984
Sales	$270,000	$252,000
Less cost of goods sold	156,000	153,600
Gross margin	114,000	98,400
Operating expenses	(60,960)	(56,160)
Depreciation expense	(10,800)	(9,600)
Interest expense	(6,240)	(6,240)
Income before taxes	36,000	26,400
Income taxes	10,800	7,680
Net income	25,200	18,720
Add beginning retained earnings	19,200	9,600
	44,400	28,320
Less dividends	20,400	9,120
Retained earnings ending balance	$ 24,000	$ 19,200

Kamasuto Corporation
Balance Sheets
December 31, 1985 and 1984

	1985	1984
Cash	$ 14,400	$ 19,200
Accounts receivable (net)	22,800	27,600
Inventories	55,200	51,600
Fixed assets (net)	96,000	84,000
Total assets	$188,400	$182,400
Current liabilities	$ 30,000	$ 28,800
Bonds payable, 10 percent	62,400	62,400
Common stock 6,000 shares	72,000	72,000
Retained earnings	24,000	19,200
Total equities	$188,400	$182,400
Year-end market price of stock	$37.75	$30.00

Ex. 19-9 Vertical analysis.

Required: Refer to the financial statements of Kamasuto Corporation in Exercise 19-8. Perform a vertical analysis of these statements by converting the statements to common units. Convert the income and retained earnings statement to percentages of sales. Convert the balance sheet to percentages of total assets.

Ex. 19-10 Ratio analysis.

Required: Refer to the financial statements of Kamasuto Corporation in Exercise 19-8. Perform a ratio analysis for the company for 1985, by calculating each of the ratios discussed in the text.

Ex. 19-11 Profitability and leverage. Lumpie Company had total assets of $900,000 at the beginning of the year and $1,100,000 at the end of the year. Net income before tax was $200,000, the tax rate is 40 percent, and the company paid $100,000 of interest expense. Average common equity for the year is $600,000 and return on sales was 8 percent.

Required: Calculate the return on total assets, return on common equity, leverage, and sales for the year.

Ex. 19-12 Understanding profitability and solvency. The rate of return on average total assets is 20 percent for Ypsilon Company. Its return on average common equity is 16 percent. The company is subject to an income tax rate of 40 percent, and its interest rate on average debt is 10 percent. There is no preferred stock outstanding. Average total assets are $3,200,000.

Required: Calculate average equity, debt, interest expense, times interest earned, and the debt ratio.

Ex. 19-13 Measuring liquidity. The current portions of the balance sheets of Blount Tool Corporation and Obtoose Cutlery Company are shown below.

	Blount	Obtoose
Current assets:		
Cash	$ 2,610	$ 2,370
Temporary investments	3,000	1,560
Notes receivable	1,470	1,170
Accounts receivable	4,140	3,450
Merchandise inventory	2,340	6,420
Prepaid expenses	750	2,850
Total current assets	$14,310	$17,820
Current liabilities:		
Notes payable	$ 1,740	$ 1,410
Taxes payable	900	960
Accounts payable	2,790	4,080
Salaries payable	2,520	2,910
Total current liabilities	$ 7,950	$ 9,360

Required:

a. Calculate the current ratio and working capital for each company.
b. Compare the current ratios and working capital for the two companies and discuss each company's ability to meet current obligations.
c. Calculate the acid test ratio for each company.
d. Explain each company's liquidity in terms of the acid test ratio.
e. What additional information did you gain by calculating the acid test ratio?

Ex. 19-14 Understanding market tests. Adrianne Company's stock trades in the market at $54 per share with a price-earnings ratio of 9. The company's dividend payout is 72 percent. It has 100,000 shares of common stock outstanding, and no preferred stock. Book value per share is $42.

Required: Calculate earnings per share, net income, dividends per share, dividend yield, and return on common equity.

Ex. 19-15 Understanding profitability and solvency ratios. Drubbing Company's return on total assets is 22 percent and its return on owners' equity is 16 percent. Average total assets for the year are $3,000,000 and beginning owners' equity is $2,070,000. The company is subject to a 40 percent income tax rate. There were no capital transactions during the year and no dividends were paid. Interest expense for the year was $60,000. There is no preferred stock outstanding and liabilities at the end of the year are the same as at the beginning.

Required: Calculate the debt-equity ratio for Drubbing Company at the end of the accounting period.

Ex. 19-16 Understanding liquidity ratios. Puzzel Company operates 360 days per year. Following are some data calculated from its financial statements.

a. There are 18 days' supply in ending inventory.
b. Cost of goods sold for the year was $1,296,000 which is 60 percent of sales.
c. There are 24 days' sales in ending accounts receivable.
d. Inventory and accounts receivable ending balances are the same as beginning balances.
e. The current ratio is 2.4 and the quick ratio is 1.86.
f. Current assets consist of cash, accounts receivable, and merchandise.

Required: Find the ending balance of each of the current assets.

PROBLEMS

P. 19-1 Horizontal analysis. The condensed financial statements of Gutierez Company, a sole proprietorship, are presented on the next page for the years ending December 31, 1984, 1985, and 1986.

	1986	1985	1984
Income statements:			
Sales	$60,000	$60,000	$63,000
Less cost of goods sold	22,500	25,500	27,000
Gross margin	37,500	34,500	36,000
Operating expenses	(19,950)	(19,050)	(20,550)
Depreciation expense	(7,800)	(7,650)	(7,500)
Interest expense	(2,250)	(1,800)	(1,950)
Net income	$ 7,500	$ 6,000	$ 6,000
Balance sheets:			
Current assets	$22,275	$18,900	$12,000
Investments	13,500	11,250	16,200
Fixed assets (net)	39,225	37,350	34,800
Total assets	$75,000	$67,500	$63,000
Current liabilities	$10,125	$10,500	$ 7,500
Long-term debt	18,000	15,000	16,500
Capital, Gutierez	46,875	42,000	39,000
Total equities	$75,000	$67,500	$63,000

Required:

a. Perform a horizontal analysis of the statements.
b. Explain any trends that appear to be significant.
c. Do you perceive any significant improvement in operations or financial position over the years presented? Explain.

P. 19-2 Vertical analysis. Refer to the financial statements of Gutierez Company in Problem 19-1.

Required:

a. Perform a vertical analysis for each of the three years.
b. Do you perceive any significant changes in the statements over the years presented? Explain.
c. What seems to be the primary reason for the increase in net income?

P. 19-3 Ratio analysis. Refer to the financial statements of Gutierez Company in Problem 19-1.

Required:

a. Calculate the following financial ratios for 1985 and 1984.
   1. Times interest earned
   2. Debt-equity ratio
   3. Debt ratio
   4. Equity ratio
   5. Funds flow to debt ratio
   6. Return on sales

7. Return on total assets
8. Return on owners' equity
9. Leverage

b. Do you perceive any significant trend in the rates of return? Explain.
c. Do the solvency measures indicate any significant trends? Explain.
d. Has the book value of the company increased faster or slower than net income over the past 2 years? Explain.

P. 19-4 Horizontal analysis. The condensed financial statements of Trendix Company are presented below for 3 years ending January 31.

	1986	1985	1984
Income statements:			
Sales	$ 80,000	$ 85,000	$ 83,000
Less cost of goods sold	38,000	40,000	37,000
Gross margin	42,000	45,000	46,000
Operating expenses	(6,900)	(8,325)	(7,350)
Depreciation	(3,000)	(2,700)	(2,800)
Interest	(4,600)	(4,600)	(4,600)
Income tax	(5,500)	(5,875)	(6,250)
Net income	$ 22,000	$ 23,500	$ 25,000
Balance sheets:			
Current assets	$103,500	$ 90,000	$ 72,000
Fixed assets (net)	126,000	112,500	108,000
Intangibles	40,500	42,750	45,000
Total	$270,000	$245,250	$225,000
Current liabilities	$ 63,000	$ 51,750	$ 38,250
Bonds payable, due 2001	90,000	90,000	90,000
Common stock $10 par	60,000	60,000	60,000
Retained earnings	57,000	43,500	36,750
Total	$270,000	$245,250	$225,000

Required:

a. Perform a horizontal analysis of the statements.
b. Discuss any trends that appear to be significant and any significant changes in operations or financial position over the years presented.

P. 19-5 Vertical analysis. Refer to the financial statements of Trendix Company in Problem 19-4.

Required:

a. Perform a vertical analysis for each of the 3 years.
b. Do you perceive any significant changes in the statements over the years presented? Explain.
c. What seems to be the primary reason for the decline in net income?

P. 19-6 Ratio analysis. Refer to the financial statements of Trendix Company in Problem 19-4.

Required:

a. Calculate the following financial ratios for each of the two latest years:
   1. Times interest earned
   2. Debt-equity ratio
   3. Debt ratio
   4. Equity ratio
   5. Fund flows to debt ratio
   6. Return on sales
   7. Return on total assets
   8. Return on owners' equity
   9. Financial leverage
   10. Current ratio

b. Explain any significant trends that you perceive in the ratios.

c. Is the book value increasing faster or slower than net income? Explain.

P. 19-7 Market tests. Refer to the financial statements of Trendix Company in Problem 19-4. The company paid cash dividends in 1985 and 1986 but not in 1984. The year-end market price per share of the company's stock was $36.75 in 1986, $35.25 in 1985, and $39.63 in 1984.

Required:

a. Calculate the amount of dividends paid by the company in 1985 and 1986.

b. Calculate the following ratios for each of the 3 years:
   1. Earnings per share
   2. Price-earnings ratio
   3. Dividend payout
   4. Dividend yield

c. Do you perceive any significant trends in the ratios you calculated? Explain.

P. 19-8 Complete financial analysis. Provided opposite are the comparative income statements and balance sheets of Niblix Company for 1985 and 1984.

Required:

a. Perform a vertical analysis on the 1985 statements and a horizontal analysis comparing the 1985 statements with those of 1984.

b. Calculate the following ratios for 1985:
   1. Current ratio
   2. Acid test ratio
   3. Inventory turnover
   4. Days' supply of inventory
   5. Receivables turnover
   6. Days' sales in receivables
   7. Return on sales

8. Return on total assets
9. Return on owners' equity
10. Financial leverage
11. Times interest earned
12. Debt-equity ratio
13. Gross margin percentage
14. Funds flow to debt ratio
15. Dividend payout ratio

Niblix Company
Income Statements
For the Years Ended December 31, 1985 and 1984

	1985	1984
Sales	$240,000	$210,000
Cost of goods sold	114,000	102,000
Gross margin	126,000	108,000
Operating expenses	(58,000)	(52,000)
Depreciation expense	(10,000)	(9,600)
Interest expense	(5,000)	(5,900)
Income tax expense	(21,200)	(16,200)
Net income	$ 31,800	$ 24,300

Niblix Company
Balance Sheet
December 31, 1985 and 1984

	1985	1984
Assets:		
Cash	$ 13,800	$ 17,000
Temporary investments	9,000	9,600
Accounts receivable	35,400	38,200
Merchandise	30,000	4,600
Prepaid expenses	1,800	2,400
Fixed assets	144,000	120,000
Accumulated depreciation	(48,000)	(42,000)
Total assets	$186,000	$170,600
Equities:		
Accounts payable	$ 34,200	$ 33,000
Accrued expenses	13,800	14,400
Long-term debt	36,000	48,000
Common stock	60,000	60,000
Retained earnings	42,000	15,200
Total equities	$186,000	$170,600

Johanson Company
Statement of Financial Position
December 31, 1985 and 1984
($000 omitted)

	1985	1984
Assets		
Current assets:		
Cash and temporary investments	$ 400	$ 380
Accounts receivable (net)	1,700	1,500
Inventories	2,200	2,120
Total current assets	4,300	4,000
Long-term assets:		
Land	500	500
Building and equipment (net)	4,700	4,000
Total long-term assets	5,200	4,500
Total assets	$9,500	$8,500
Liabilities and Capital		
Current liabilities:		
Accounts payable	$1,400	$ 700
Current portion of long-term debt	1,000	500
Total current liabilities	2,400	1,200
Long-term debt	3,000	4,000
Total liabilities	5,400	5,200
Stockholders' equity:		
Common stock	3,000	3,000
Retained earnings	1,100	300
Total stockholders' equity	4,100	3,300
Total liabilities and capital	$9,500	$8,500

Johanson Company
Statement of Income and Retained Earnings
For the Year Ended December 31, 1985
($000 omitted)

Net sales		$28,800
Less cost of goods sold	$15,120	
Selling expenses	7,180	
Administrative expenses	4,100	
Interest	400	
Income taxes	800	27,600
Net income		1,200
Retained earnings January 1		300
Subtotal		1,500
Cash dividends declared and paid		400
Retained earnings December 31		$ 1,100

P. 19-9 (CMA) Financial analysis. The 1985 financial statements for Johanson Company are reproduced on the opposite page.

Required: Select the best answer for each of the following questions:

1. The acid test ratio for 1985 is closest to
   a. 1.1 to 1 b. .9 to 1 c. 1.8 to 1 d. .2 to 1 e. .17 to 1
2. The average number of days' sales in receivables in 1985 is
   a. 18 days b. 360 days c. 20 days d. 4.4 days e. 80 days
3. Times interest earned ratio in 1985 is
   a. 3.0 times b. 1.0 times c. 72 times d. 2.0 times e. 6.0 times
4. The return on assets in 1985 is
   a. 26.7% b. 13.3% c. 25.3% d. 12.6% e. 23.1%
5. The inventory turnover in 1985 is
   a. 13.6 times b. 12.5 times c. .9 times d. 7.0 times e. 51.4 times
6. The return on sales in 1985 is
   a. 3.8% b. 47.5% c. 52.5% d. 95.8% e. 4.3%
7. The dividend payout ratio in 1985 is
   a. 33.3% b. 36% c. 20% d. 8.8% e. 100%
8. The return on owners' equity in 1985 is
   a. 12.6% b. 32.4% c. 29.3% d. 9.8% e. 10.8%

P. 19-10 Horizontal, vertical, and ratio analysis. The comparative balance sheets of Sylphia Company and its income statements for 1985 and 1984 are presented below and on the following page.

Sylphia Company
Balance Sheets
October 31, 1985 and 1984

	1985	1984
Cash	$ 4,000	$ 9,500
Accounts receivable	13,500	11,500
Merchandise	36,000	52,500
Prepaid expenses	2,500	2,500
Fixed assets	90,000	100,000
Accumulated depreciation	(32,000)	(35,000)
Total assets	$114,000	$141,000
Accounts payable	$ 20,000	$ 37,000
Accrued expenses	15,000	19,000
Notes payable, due 1989–1992	39,000	32,000
Capital, Sylvia	21,500	27,900
Capital, Sophia	18,500	25,100
Total equities	$114,000	$141,000

Sylphia Company
Income Statements
For the Years Ended October 31, 1985 and 1984

	1985	1984
Sales	$500,000	$505,000
Cost of goods sold	354,000	360,000
Operating expenses	112,380	106,500
Depreciation expense	8,120	9,200
Interest expense	5,500	5,300
Total expenses	480,000	481,000
Net income	$ 20,000	$ 24,000

Required:

a. Perform a vertical analysis of the 1985 statements and horizontal analysis comparing 1985 with 1984.

b. Calculate the following ratios for 1985:

1. Current ratio
2. Acid test ratio
3. Inventory turnover
4. Days' supply of inventory
5. Receivables turnover
6. Days' sales in receivables
7. Return on sales
8. Return on total assets
9. Return on owners' equity
10. Leverage
11. Times interest earned
12. Debt-equity ratio

P. 19-11 Reconstruction of balance sheet. The December 31, 1985, balance sheet of Erika Company, and its statement of changes in financial position for the year ending December 31, 1986, are presented below and on the following page.

Erika Company
Balance Sheet
December 31, 1985

Cash	$ 530	Accounts payable	$ 2,140
Accounts receivable	1,300	Bonds payable, due 1990	7,000
Merchandise inventory	2,370	Preferred stock	2,500
Land	9,800	Common stock	6,000
Equipment	12,200	Retained earnings	6,560
Accumulated depreciation	(2,000)		
Total assets	$24,200	Total equities	$24,200

Erika Company
Statement of Changes in Financial Position
For the Year Ended December 31, 1986

Sources		Uses	
From operations		Paid cash dividends	$ 360
Net income	$1,200	Retired preferred stock	2,500
Depreciation	600	Retired bonds payable	1,400
Gain on sale of land	(80)	Purchased equipment	3,000
Total from operations	1,720	Increase in working capital	340
Issued common stock	4,000		
Sold land	1,880		
Total sources	$7,600	Total uses	$7,600

Erika Company had the following financial ratios at the end of 1986:

Current ratio	2.20
Acid test ratio	.80
EBIT	$1,968
Return on average total assets	.08
Return on sales	.03
Turnover of average receivables	32.00
Dividend payout	.30

Required: Prepare the December 31, 1986, balance sheet for Erika Company without adding any new accounts.

P. 19-12 **Reconstruction of financial statements.** Following is the balance sheet of Detrex Company on December 31, 1985:

Detrex Company
Balance Sheet
December 31, 1985

Cash	$ 600	Accounts payable	$11,580
Accounts receivable	3,000	Bonds payable	30,000
Merchandise	11,000	Common stock, $10 par	10,000
Prepaid expenses	230	Additional paid-in capital	30,000
Fixed assets	110,000	Retained earnings	13,250
Accumulated depreciation	(30,000)		
Total assets	$ 94,830	Total equities	$94,830

The company did not buy or sell any fixed assets nor issue any stock during 1986. On December 31, 1986, the company's accountant obtained the following ratios and other data based on the 1986 operations:

Current ratio	2.0 times
Acid test ratio	.8 times
Inventory turnover	5.0 times
Receivables turnover	25.0 times
Equity ratio	58.8%
Debt ratio	41.2%
Times interest earned	6.0 times
Return on sales	7.0%
Gross margin percentage	52.0%
Book value per share	$58.80
Market price per share	$64.00
Earnings per share	$ 8.75
Dividend yield	5.0%
Federal income tax rate	30.0%
Depreciation rate	4.0%

Required: Use the above data to prepare the company's balance sheet on December 31,1986 and income statement for the year ending December 31, 1986. The following form is suggested for the income statement:

Detrex Company
Income Statement
For the Year Ended December 31, 1986

Sales
Less cost of goods sold
Gross margin
Less expenses
  Depreciation expense
  Interest expense
  Other expense
Total expenses
Income before tax
Federal income tax
Net income

CASE

Case 19-1 Analysis of pro forma statements

On the opposite page are the financial statements of Alexander Corporation. The company was established 6 years ago, and based on market studies and demand for the company's products, management has decided that it is time for a major expansion. To accomplish the expansion, the company needs a $100,000 infusion of capital. Two alternatives are considered by management. The company can issue additional common stock for $100,000 or it can obtain the same amount by issuing 12 percent bonds. The funds are to be used to buy new equipment for $70,000 and to increase working capital. The company pays no dividends and is subject to a 40 percent income tax rate. The stock or bonds are to be issued in early December 1986.

Alexander Corporation
Balance Sheet
November 30, 1986

Current assets	$ 25,000	Current liabilities	$ 14,000
Fixed assets	115,000	Note payable, 11%, 1998	30,000
Accumulated depreciation	(40,000)	Common stock, $10 par	40,000
		Retained earnings	16,000
Total assets	$100,000	Total equities	$100,000

Alexander Corporation
Income Statement
For the Year Ended November 30, 1986

Sales		$112,500
Selling and administrative expenses	$88,700	
Depreciation expense	5,500	
Interest expense	3,300	
Federal income tax	6,000	
Total expenses		97,500
Net income		$ 9,000

The following projections are made for the next year of operations:

a. The old equipment includes a fully depreciated machine that cost $10,000. This will be discarded as it has no salvage value. The remaining equipment is depreciated at an annual rate of 5 percent.

b. The new equipment will be depreciated at 10 percent per year with no salvage value. The equipment will be acquired in December 1986.

c. Sales are expected to increase by 40 percent and selling and administrative expenses by 30 percent over the current year.

d. Interest expense will remain the same if the stock is issued. If the bonds are issued, interest expense will increase.

e. Current liabilities are expected to increase by $30,000 by November 30, 1987.

Required:

a. Prepare pro forma financial statements for the year ending November 30, 1987 for each alternative method of financing the expanded operations.

b. Perform as complete a ratio analysis as possible on the 1986 statements and on the pro forma statements.

c. Recommend which alternative you prefer. Support your recommendation with the findings in your analysis.

Statement of Changes in Financial Position

20

The statement of changes in financial position is one of the basic financial statements found in the annual report of a company. It reports on the way funds flow into and out of the business. When you complete your study of this chapter, you should understand:

1. How financing and investing activities affect businesses, and the way the results of these activities are reported in the statement of changes.
2. Two definitions of funds that may be used in the preparation of the statement of changes.
3. The difference between net income earned and the amount of funds provided by operations.
4. What is meant by sources of funds and uses of funds and how they are reported.
5. The concept of nonfund items and the way they are used to convert net income to fund flows.
6. What is meant by the concept of all financial resources, and the way the concept affects the statement of changes.
7. How the statement of changes is used in decision making.
8. The use of working papers to prepare the statement of changes.

Your study of accounting up to this point has focused on the measurement of revenues and expenses and the valuation of assets, liabilities, and owners' equity. These measures provide the basis for determining net income from operations and for presenting financial position. However, the income statement and the balance sheet do not provide adequate information on the amount of cash flowing into and out of a business. Many internal and external decision makers require information on cash and working capital flows.

Financing and investing activities of a business

The **statement of changes in financial position,** often referred to as the **funds flow statement,** describes the financing and investing activities of a business enterprise. **Financing activities** are transactions that result in a flow of financial resources **into** the business. Examples are borrowing money or selling merchandise, both of which result in a business receiving cash. **Investing activities** are transactions that result in the flow of financial resources **out** of a business. Examples include the purchase of equipment or the repayment of debt, both of which result in cash outflows. The financial resources, or **funds,** obtained from financing activities are used to pay for investing activities.

The statement of changes reports the **sources** from which funds were obtained and the **uses** to which funds were put during an accounting period. In addition, it explains why the amount of funds on hand at the end of the accounting period is different from the amount of funds on hand at the beginning of the period. The purpose of this chapter is to discuss the nature of the statement of changes and the type of information it conveys.

THE NATURE OF CHANGES IN FINANCIAL POSITION

Funds are defined in one of two ways. Before the statement of changes in financial position can be prepared, it is necessary to understand which definition is being used.

Two definitions of funds

1. **Funds are defined as cash.**
2. **Funds are defined as working capital.**

The form of the statement of changes in financial position depends on the definition used. When **funds are defined as cash,** the statement of changes explains the amount of cash that various financing activities provided, the amount of cash used for various investing activities, and the resulting change in the cash balance from the beginning of the accounting period to the end as shown in the balance sheets. When **funds are defined as working capital,** the statement of changes explains how much working capital the financing and investing activities provided and used, and how working capital changed from the amount available at the beginning of the accounting period to the amount available at the end of the period.

The statement of changes with funds defined as cash is of interest primarily to internal managers. Managers need information on the day-to-day operations of the business, and must manage the flow of cash carefully. To monitor current operations and control the flow of current assets and liabilities, they must have detailed information on each component of working capital, including cash.

Funds are usually defined as working capital in statements prepared for external users. Investors, shareholders, financial analysts, and other external users are usually not interested in the detailed operations that are disclosed by cash flow information. They need a broad view of fund flows in order to determine the general well-being of the company and its ability to generate funds.

Sources and Uses of Funds

All financing and investing activities can be divided into a small number of categories. There are four types of financing activities that provide funds:

1. Operations that generate net income, the primary source of funds for most businesses
2. Capital contributions by owners during the accounting period
3. Borrowing from financial institutions or from the public
4. The sale of assets normally not held for sale

The funds made available by financing activities are used for making investments. There are four types of investing activities that require the use of funds. They are:

1. The acquisition of fixed assets in order to expand the business
2. Repayment of debt to creditors
3. Reacquisition of capital stock
4. The payment of dividends to shareholders

If a business obtains more funds from financing activities than it needs for investing activities, the unused funds increase the company's working capital or cash. This situation is described algebraically as follows, with hypothetical figures used to illustrate the equation:

$$\text{Sources} - \text{Uses} = \text{Increase in funds}$$

$$\$100{,}000 - \$90{,}000 = \$10{,}000 \text{ increase}$$

If the business obtains less funds from financing activities than it needs for investing, cash or working capital must be reduced to provide the balance of the funds used in investing activities. In that case, the situation is described algebraically as follows:

$$\text{Sources} - \text{Uses} = \text{Decrease in funds}$$

$$\$92{,}000 - \$100{,}000 = \$8{,}000 \text{ decrease}$$

The statement of changes in financial position reports all of the sources and uses of funds and is frequently prepared showing the change in funds as the difference between the sources and uses, as follows:

Sources	$ 92,000
Uses	100,000
Decrease in funds	$ 8,000

Some accountants prefer to prepare the statement in balanced form, with the change in funds viewed as if it were itself a source or use of funds, so that the algebraic representation is:

$$\text{Sources} = \text{Uses}$$

When the statement is viewed as a balanced equation, an increase in cash or working capital is reported together with the uses of funds, and a decrease is reported together with the sources. The first example, with an increase in funds, appears in the balanced form as follows:

$$\text{Sources} = \qquad \text{Uses}$$

$$\$100{,}000 = \$90{,}000 + \$10{,}000 \text{ increase in funds}$$

The second example, with a decrease in funds, appears in the balanced form as:

$$\text{Sources} \qquad = \text{Uses}$$

$$\$92{,}000 + \$8{,}000 \text{ decrease in funds} = \$100{,}000$$

The balanced form of the statement of changes in financial position is prepared as follows:

Sources	$ 92,000
Decrease in funds	8,000
Total	$100,000
Uses	$100,000

It does not matter which form is used, so long as you understand that the difference between total sources and total uses of funds is the change in funds for the period.

The statement of changes covers one accounting period

The information used to prepare the funds flow statement is obtained from the beginning and ending balance sheets and from the statements of income and retained earnings. In Figure 20-1 we illustrate how the statement of changes is related to the other three statements. As the name of

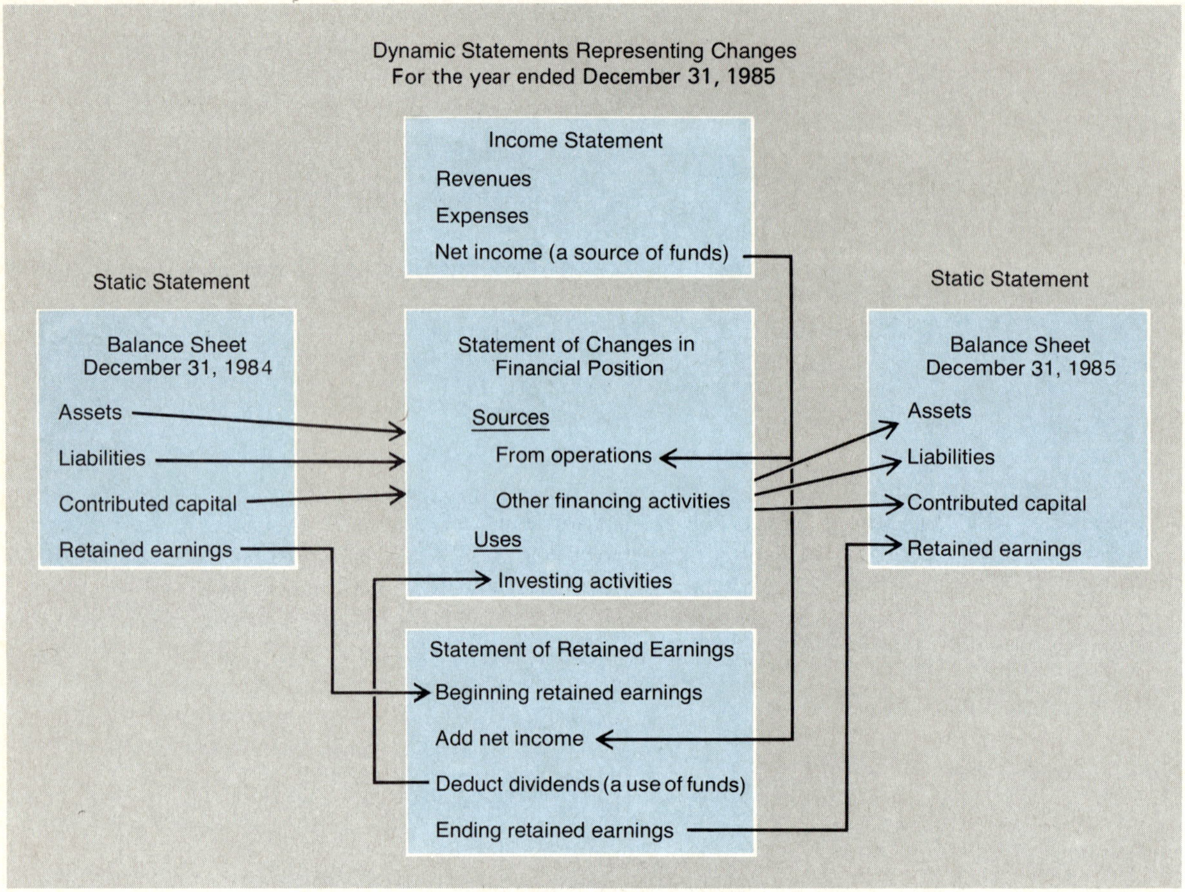

Figure 20-1 Relationship between static balance sheets and dynamic statements representing changes. The statement of changes in financial position describes the financing and investing activities of the business.

the statement implies, it reports the changes in financial position that took place between the beginning and ending balance sheets. The business employs its assets to operate in order to earn more assets. Operations are the primary source of funds that can be used to repay debts, acquire new assets, and pay dividends. In addition the company also obtains funds by selling old assets, issuing new stock, and incurring new debts. These financing and investing activities change the balance sheet accounts and the changes are explained in the statement of changes in financial position. In addition, the statement of changes shows the amount of funds provided by the operations reported in the income statement, and the amount of funds used to pay dividends, as reported in the retained earnings statement.

Of the four statements that make up the annual report, only the balance sheet is a static statement; it reports financial position at a specific point in time. The income statement, the statement of retained earnings, and the statement of changes in financial position are dynamic statements that report changes occurring during one accounting period.

Now that we have discussed the basic concepts and definitions of funds, we can proceed to an illustration that demonstrates how funds are reported in a statement of changes in financial position, and the differences between the definitions of funds. For this purpose we use the comparative balance sheets, income statement, and statement of retained earnings of Phoenix Corporation illustrated in Figure 20-2.

ANALYSIS OF BALANCE SHEET CHANGES

The cash balance of Phoenix Corporation changed from $67 on December 31, 1984, to $165 at the end of 1985. The statement of changes must explain this $98 increase if funds are defined as cash. Working capital is the difference between current assets and current liabilities. Phoenix Corporation's working capital on December 31, 1984, was $135 (current assets of $252 less current liabilities of $117), and at the end of 1985 working capital was $227 (current assets of $370 less current liabilities of $143). If funds are defined as working capital, the statement of changes must explain the $92 increase in working capital.

Because cash increased by $98 from the beginning of the period to the end, it is evident that the total financing activities provided $98 more cash than was needed to pay for total investing activities. Similarly, the $92 increase in working capital indicates that financing activities provided $92 more working capital than was needed to pay for total investing activities. The statement of changes in financial position must show the nature and amount of financing and investing activities and thereby explain the change in funds, however funds are defined.

Operations are a major source of funds

The most significant of the fund changes is the amount of funds provided by operations that result in net income. We first discuss the concept of funds provided by operations and explain why the fund inflow from operations is not the same as net income. Later we use the same example to illustrate preparation of the entire statement of changes with funds defined as working capital and also with funds defined as cash.

To explain the change in funds, we must analyze the change that took place in every balance sheet account from the end of 1984 to the end of 1985. These changes are analyzed in Figure 20-2 in the two columns next to the comparative balance sheet data, indicating the increases or decreases in asset and equity accounts from one year to the next. The increase in cash of $98 is denoted by a debit in Figure 20-2; the change in accounts receivable is an increase of $37, denoted by a debit; and the change in merchandise is a decrease of $17, denoted by a credit. All other changes are similarly calculated. Increases in liabilities are credits and decreases are debits. Obviously, since the balance sheets balance, the changes from one balance sheet to the next must also balance.

Phoenix Corporation
Comparative Balance Sheets
December 31, 1985 and 1984

			Changes	
	1985	**1984**	**dr Uses**	**cr Sources**
Assets				
Cash	$ 165	$ 67	98	
Accounts receivable (net)	127	90	37	
Merchandise	78	95		17
Total current assets	370	252		
Land	60	60		
Buildings	1,000	987	13	
Equipment	841	800	41	
Less accumulated depreciation	(706)	(660)		46
Total fixed assets	1,195	1,187		
Long-term investments	100	125		25
Patents	33	37		4
Total other assets	133	162		
Total assets	$1,698	$1,601		
Liabilities				
Accounts payable	$ 92	$ 74		18
Salaries payable	21	30	9	
Income taxes payable	20	13		7
Dividends payable	10			10
Total current liabilities	143	117		
Notes payable, due 1989	44			44
Bonds payable, due 1994	450	450		
Premium on bonds payable	16	18	2	
Total long-term liabilities	510	468		
Total liabilities	653	585		
Capital				
Preferred stock		48	48	
Common stock $1 par	510	500		10
Paid-in capital on common	260	220		40
Retained earnings	275	248		27
Total capital	1,045	1,016		
Total liabilities and capital	$1,698	$1,601	248	248

Net income is measured in accordance with the accrual concept rather than on the cash basis, so it must be converted to a fund inflow by appropriate adjustments. Transactions that affect the income statement also affect the balance sheet, so an examination of business operations should explain some of the balance sheet changes calculated in Figure 20-2. For example, net income changed the Retained Earnings account when the books were

Figure 20-2
The income statement, the statement of retained earnings, and the comparative balance sheets on page 826 are accompanied by a statement of changes in financial position to make a complete annual report. Note the two columns showing the balance sheet changes as debits and credits. These are not part of the balance sheet but are shown here because they are used in the text to explain preparation of the statement of changes. A statement of changes developed from the statements in this figure is presented in Figure 20-3 on page 836. Another is presented in Figure 20-4.

Phoenix Corporation
Income Statement
For the Year Ended December 31, 1985

Sales		$2,340
Less cost of goods sold:		
Beginning inventory	$ 95	
Add purchases	1,387	
Goods available for sale	1,482	
Less ending inventory	78	
Cost of goods sold		1,404
Gross margin		936
Less expenses:		
Administrative	317	
Salaries	306	
Depreciation	60	
Amortization of patent	4	
Interest	38	
Total expenses		725
Income from operations		211
Other income:		
Gain on sale of investments	5	
Loss on sale of equipment	(3)	2
Income before tax		213
Less income tax expense		96
Net income		$ 117

Phoenix Corporation
Statement of Retained Earnings
For the Year Ended December 31, 1985

Retained earnings, 12/31/84		$ 248
Add net income		117
		365
Deduct dividends:		
Cash dividends	$ 40	
2% stock dividend	50	90
Retained earnings, 12/31/85		$ 275

closed at the end of the year. Other balance sheet changes are the result of financing and investing activities that are not part of operations and are therefore not reported in the income statement.

Funds Provided by Operations with Funds Defined as Cash

The income statement in Figure 20-2 shows various revenues and expenses that resulted in a net income of $117. The change in retained earnings, however, is only a $27 increase because the company paid $90 of dividends during the year, as reported in the statement of retained earnings in Figure 20-2.

Now we look in detail at some of the transactions that occurred in 1985 as a result of operations. Note that these transactions were recorded during the year as they occurred. The journal entries are reproduced here to explain cash flows. Many similar transactions are aggregated into a single entry so that the overall effect on cash may be seen. From the income statement, we know that sales were $2,340, recorded as follows:

	Accounts receivable	2,340	
	Sales		2,340

Operations provided $2,340 of sales revenue, but only $2,303 of cash was collected from customers. This is evident from an examination of accounts receivable, which increased by $37. The beginning balance in Accounts Receivable was $90, and $2,340 was added as a result of the current year's sales. If the ending balance is $127, only $2,303 of accounts receivable was collected during the year. The collection of receivables is recorded as follows:

	Cash	2,303	
	Accounts receivable		2,303

These two entries are posted in the account below.

Accounts Receivable

Bal. 12/31/84	90	1985 collections	2,303
1985 sales	2,340		
Bal. 12/31/85	127		

Not all revenues are cash inflows

Given the beginning balance of $90, credit sales of $2,340, and the ending balance of $127, the credit to Accounts Receivable must have been $2,303. Therefore if accounts receivable increased during the period, cash collections are less than sales revenue. Conversely, if the balance of receivables decreased, the company must have collected more than its credit sales for the year. We can compute cash collections as follows:

Sales revenue	$2,340
Less increase in accounts receivable	37
Cash collected from customers[1]	$2,303

[1] The result is the same if all sales are not on credit.

By deducting the increase in accounts receivable from sales, we converted sales to a cash inflow. If accounts receivable had decreased, sales revenue would be converted to a cash inflow by adding the accounts receivable decrease. It is also possible to convert the net income figure to a cash flow in the same way, rather than the revenue figure.

The amounts recorded for expenses are not necessarily the same as the amounts of cash paid. For example, salaries required more cash than is reported on the income statement as salary expense; depreciation expense required no cash, and income taxes required less cash than reported as tax expense.

The journal entries to record expenses are given below. The payment of salaries includes not only the current year's salaries paid in cash, but also the payment of salaries payable accrued at the end of the previous year.

	Salaries payable	30	
	Salaries expense	285	
	Cash		315
	To pay current salaries and beginning		
	balance of salaries payable.		

The adjusting entry at the end of 1985 records salaries expenses which have not yet been paid but which are accrued at the end of the year.

	Salaries expense	21	
	Salaries payable		21
	To accrue salaries at end of 1985.		

Salaries Payable

1985 payments	30	Bal. 12/31/84	30
		12/31/85 accrual	21
		Bal. 12/31/85	21

Salaries Expense

Paid during the year	285		
Accrued at end of year	21		
Bal. 12/31/85	306		

All expenses are not cash outflows

The $315 of cash used to pay salaries during 1985 is clearly not the same as the $306 of salaries expense reported in the 1985 income statement. Cash paid for salaries is more than the reported expense because the company decreased its liability to its employees by $9 from $30 at the end of 1984 to $21 at the end of 1985.

Depreciation is neither a source nor a use of funds

Depreciation expense reported on the income statement does not require the use of either cash or working capital, because no current assets or liabilities are affected by the recording of depreciation. Depreciation is therefore known as a **nonfund** item on the income statement; it neither provides nor uses funds.

	Depreciation expense	60	
	Accumulated depreciation		60

The payment of taxes resulted in the use of $89 of cash, although tax expense is reported as $96. The difference is the result of the changes in the Income Taxes Payable account, which was $13 at the end of 1984 and $20 at the end of 1985. The tax expense is recorded as follows in 1985:

	Income tax expense	96	
	Income taxes payable		96

The beginning balance of Income Taxes Payable was $13. Therefore, this entry increases the Income Taxes Payable account to $109; to leave a $20 balance at the end of 1985, the following cash payment must have been made.

	Income taxes payable	89	
	Cash		89

To arrive at net income, the company deducted more income tax expense from revenues than was actually paid. By adding the increase in the tax liability to net income, we convert the net income figure to a cash inflow.

It is possible to analyze each change in current assets and current liabilities in a similar way, and to determine how it affected the amount of cash provided by operations. You have now seen that changes in some current accounts are used to convert revenue and expense items to cash flows. You also see that expenses such as depreciation do not result in a cash outflow. For the moment let us assume that sales revenue and the three expenses discussed above are the only items on the income statement. This assumption allows us to make the following summary analysis.

Income Statement Item		**Current Account Change**		**Cash Flow**
Sales	$2,340	Receivables increase	$(37)	$2,303
Salaries	(306)	Salaries payable decrease	(9)	(315)
Depreciation	(60)	Did not require cash payment		—
Income tax	(96)	Taxes payable increase	7	(89)
Income	$1,878	Cash provided by operations		$1,899

In this summary, each individual income statement item is converted to a cash flow. But we can accomplish the same thing by converting the single income figure to the same cash flow figure as follows:

Income	$1,878
Less receivables increase	(37)
Less salaries payable decrease	(9)
Add depreciation expense	60
Add taxes payable increase	7
Cash provided by operations	$1,899

Of course, this calculation is not complete because the income statement contains more than the above accounts. But the example serves to illustrate important cash flow concepts. As you can see from our analysis of sales and the change in accounts receivable, and also from the above calculation, an increase in current assets must be deducted from net income in order to convert the net income figure to a cash inflow. Conversely, a decrease in current assets must be added to net income to convert the figure to a cash inflow. With the salaries and tax examples, you see that a decrease in current liabilities increases the amount of cash used to pay expenses and should therefore be deducted to convert net income to a cash inflow, whereas an increase in current liabilities must be added to net income because less cash was used to pay the liability than was recorded as an expense. In addition, nonfund items such as depreciation that are deducted on the income statement are now added back to net income, and nonfund items such as gains that are added on the income statement are now deducted from net income. When all nonfund items and changes in current assets and current liabilities have been added to or deducted from net income, the net income figure has been converted to the amount of cash provided by operations.

The amount of cash used in operations and obtained from operations clearly depends on the changes in the current assets and current liabilities accounts that make up working capital. As you will see later in the chapter, the amount of cash provided by operations is $173, although net income is only $117. On the other hand, the amount of working capital provided by operations is $177. The difference is due to the fact that changes in working capital accounts affect the amount of cash provided by operations, but not the amount of working capital, as explained below.

Funds Provided by Operations with Funds Defined as Working Capital

Operations change the balances of working capital accounts

With funds defined as working capital, most of the revenues and expenses in the income statement are increases and decreases in working capital in the amount actually reported in the statement. For example, sales revenue was recorded as follows:

	Accounts receivable	2,340	
	Sales		2,340

Subsequently, $2,303 of accounts receivable was collected. But the collection of receivables does not change the amount of working capital. Consequently, sales provided $2,340 of working capital whether the goods were sold for cash or on open account, because both cash and accounts receivable are components of working capital.

Nonfund items on the income statement neither provide nor use funds

Similarly, salaries and taxes decreased working capital by the amount of salaries and tax expenses reported on the income statement. It does not matter whether the salaries and taxes are paid or accrued; the change in working capital is the same. On the other hand, depreciation expense had no effect on working capital, just as it had no effect on cash. Depreciation is a nonfund item and does not affect funds whichever definition of funds is used. Other nonfund items are discussed below.

You can see now that with funds defined as cash, the income statement must undergo considerable modification before the net income figure can be converted to a cash inflow figure. On the other hand, relatively little conversion is required if funds are defined as working capital. Only the nonfund items are used to convert the income figure to a fund flow.

Nonfund Items on the Income Statement

Net income measured under the accrual concept is not the same as the amount of funds obtained from operations. Some expenses and losses are deducted from revenues to arrive at net income, although they did not require the use of funds. Depreciation expense is an obvious example. Other nonfund deductions include amortization of intangibles, losses, deferred taxes, and amortization of bond discount. To convert the net income figure to a figure representing fund inflows from operations, such nonfund deductions must be added back to net income.

The income statement also contains items that are added in arriving at net income but that did not provide funds. Amortization of premium on bonds payable, gains, and income from stock investments accounted for by the equity method are examples. Because such nonfund items are not fund inflows, they must be deducted from net income to convert the net income figure to a fund inflow from operations. Some of these nonfund additions and deductions are explained below.

Depreciation and amortization. You already know that depreciation does not require the use of funds. No one writes a check to pay for depreciation expense. Amortization of intangible assets and depletion of natural resources do not require the use of funds. These items are added back to income in the funds flow statement because they are nonfund expenses that make revenue smaller than the fund inflow.

Premium on bonds payable. When bond discount or premium is amortized, the amount of interest expense reported in the income statement is not the same as the amount of cash paid for bond interest. Interest expense on bonds sold at a premium is smaller than the required interest payments. Phoenix Corporation's interest expense is $38, and on the balance sheet you see that premium on bonds payable changed from $18 to $16 because $2 of bond premium was amortized. Therefore, the entries to record interest expense must have been

	Interest expense	40	
	Cash		40

Cash paid to bond holders was $40, but the income statement reports only $38 of interest expense because at the end of the year, interest expense was adjusted and reduced to $38 when bond premium was amortized.

	Premium on bonds payable	2	
	Interest expense		2

Bond premium or discount amortization is a nonfund item

The $40 outflow of working capital for the payment of interest was greater than the $38 of interest expense deducted to arrive at net income. The difference, caused by $2 of bond premium amortization, is therefore a nonfund item that must be deducted from net income in order to convert the net income figure to funds obtained from operations.

If bond discount had been amortized instead of bond premium, the amortization of the discount would be added back to net income to arrive at funds provided by operations. A similar treatment is necessary for discount or premium amortization on long-term bond investments, because the amount of interest income recorded is not the same as the amount of cash received.

Gains and losses. When transactions result in gains or losses, the gain or loss reported in the income statement is only the net effect on owners' equity, and not the entire amount of funds obtained from the transaction. The fund flow effects of such transactions are quite different from the amount of gain or loss. Transactions that result in gains or losses may be either financing or investing activities. For example, the sale of fixed assets is a financing activity that may result in a gain or a loss. On the other hand, the early retirement of bonds payable is an investing activity that may result in a gain or loss.

A transaction resulting in a gain or a loss has an impact on fund flows that is usually greater than the gain or loss reported in the income statement. In addition, such transactions have nothing to do with the daily operations of a business, and therefore their effect on funds should not be part of funds provided by operations.

Gains and losses are nonfund items

If we examine the entry to record the sale of an asset, we see that the gain or loss is only a part of the entire transaction. It would be incorrect to show a part of the transaction as the fund flow. The entire amount of funds provided by the sale should be reported in the statement of changes, whereas only the gain or loss portion is shown in the income statement. Such gains or losses are nonfund items that must be added back to, or deducted from, net income to convert the net income figure to a number representing fund flows from operations.

For example, Phoenix Corporation sold equipment costing $25 and having a book value of $11. The sale of this fixed asset for $8 cash was recorded as follows:

	Cash	8	
	Accumulated depreciation	14	
	Loss on sale of fixed assets	3	
	Equipment		25

Deducting a loss in the income statement has the same effect on net income as deducting an expense for which a check was issued. The $3 loss is neither an inflow nor outflow of funds. The transaction actually provided $8 of cash because there was a transfer of $8 from fixed assets to current assets. Because equipment with a book value of $11 was exchanged for the cash, the difference is reported as a loss. But the company is not in the business of selling fixed assets, and this transaction does not belong in the category of sources of funds from operations, even though the loss is reported in the income statement. Therefore, the loss must be added back to net income in the funds flow statement, and the entire proceeds from the sale of the asset are reported among sources of funds from the sale of fixed assets.

If gains occur from sales of assets, they must be deducted from income to arrive at funds from operations. The gain itself is not an increase in funds, because the increase occurred from the entire proceeds of the sale.

Other Nonfund Transactions

Changes sometimes occur in capital accounts that appear to be sources or uses of funds when in fact they are not. The issuance of new stock provides a source of funds if assets are received when the stock is issued. However, if stock is issued as a result of a stock split, there is no effect on funds. Changes from stock splits do not appear on the statement of changes in financial position. Similarly, the issuance of a stock dividend neither provides nor uses funds. Therefore, the 2 percent stock dividend distributed by Phoenix Corporation is not disclosed in the funds flow statement although it appears in the statement of retained earnings.

The concepts discussed above are important for your understanding of the difference in the amount of funds provided by operations with different definitions of funds. In addition to funds provided by operations, other sources and uses of funds are reported on the statement of changes in financial position. Below we describe some of these and show how they are presented in the statement of changes, using the two definitions of funds.

Other Sources and Uses of Funds

The changes in balance sheet accounts shown in Figure 20-2 indicate that fixed assets were acquired, long-term investments were disposed of, long-term debt was increased, and capital stock was issued. Such changes result from financing and investing activities other than usual business operations and must be explained in the statement of changes. Before showing how these financing and investing activities are reported, we present a list of the transactions that will help to clarify the amounts reported in the statement of changes:

a. The company sold, for $8 cash, fixed assets that had a cost of $25 and a book value of $11 at the time of sale.

b. Preferred stock was redeemed at its book value and retired.

c. A 2 percent stock dividend was paid on the common stock, in addition to the cash dividends.

d. New equipment was acquired for $22 cash and a $44 long-term note payable.

Examine carefully the statement of changes to see how the fund flows from these and other transactions are reported. Figure 20-3 is the statement of changes with funds defined as working capital. Figure 20-4 is the statement with funds defined as cash. Funds provided by operations are shown as a single dollar amount in Figure 20-4. The detailed computation of the amount is reported in a separate schedule shown in Figure 20-5. Other than the amount of funds provided by operations, the sources and uses of funds are the same in both statements.

Phoenix Corporation
Statement of Changes in Financial Position
For the Year Ended December 31, 1985

Sources of Working Capital

Funds provided by operations:		
Net income		$117
Add items not requiring use of working capital:		
Depreciation expense	$ 60	
Amortization of patent	4	
Loss on sale of equipment	3	67
Less items not providing working capital:		
Amortization of bond premium		(2)
Gain on sale of investments		(5)
Working capital provided by operations		177
Other sources:		
Sale of equipment		8
Sale of long-term investments		30
Long-term borrowing used to finance purchase of new equipment		44
Total sources of working capital		$259

Uses of Working Capital

Payment of dividends	$ 40
Retirement of preferred stock	48
Addition to buildings	13
Purchase of new equipment, partly financed by new long-term borrowing	66
Increase in working capital	92
Total uses of working capital	$259

Schedule of Changes in Working Capital

	Working Capital Increase	Working Capital Decrease
Increase in cash	$ 98	
Increase in accounts receivable	37	
Decrease in merchandise		$ 17
Increase in accounts payable		18
Decrease in salaries payable	9	
Increase in income taxes payable		7
Increase in dividends payable		10
Total changes	144	52
Net increase in working capital		92
Totals	$144	$144

Figure 20-3
Statement of changes in financial position with funds defined as working capital. In addition to the sources and uses of working capital, the statement presents a schedule of changes in working capital, showing the change in each working capital component. This statement is in balanced form: Sources = Uses.

Note that the statement in Figure 20-3 is in the balanced form Sources = Uses, whereas the one in Figure 20-4 is in the form Sources − Uses = Change in funds. Both forms are commonly employed. The statement with funds defined as cash has a separate schedule detailing

Phoenix Corporation
Statement of Changes in Financial Position
For the Year Ended December 31, 1985

Sources of Cash

Cash provided by operations (see schedule, Figure 20-5)	$173	
Other sources of cash:		
Sales of equipment	8	
Sales of long-term investments	30	
Long-term borrowing used to finance purchase of new equipment	44	
Total sources of cash		$255

Uses of Cash

Payment of dividends	$ 30	
Retirement of preferred stock	48	
Additions to buildings	13	
Purchase of equipment, financed partly by new long-term borrowing	66	
Total uses of cash		157
Increase in cash balance		$ 98

Schedule of Changes in Working Capital

	Working Capital	
	Increase	**Decrease**
Increase in cash	$ 98	
Increase in accounts receivable	37	
Decrease in merchandise		$ 17
Increase in accounts payable		18
Decrease in salaries payable	9	
Increase in income taxes payable		7
Increase in dividends payable		10
Total changes	144	52
Net increase in working capital		92
Totals	$144	$144

Figure 20-4
Statement of changes in financial position with funds defined as cash. This statement is in the form: Sources − Uses = Change in cash. Note the reference to a separate schedule of funds provided by operations, which is shown in Figure 20-5. In Figure 20-3, this schedule is part of the main body of the statement.

the source of funds provided by operations. This schedule may be made a part of the statement as in Figure 20-3 and need not be presented separately. However funds are defined, the statement of changes has a section detailing changes in working capital for the period. The main difference between these two statements is the treatment of working capital. When funds are defined as cash, changes in working capital affect the amount of cash provided by operations, and such changes are therefore reported in the schedule showing how net income is converted to a cash inflow. In addition to working capital changes, this schedule shows the various nonfund items found in the income statement. When funds are defined as working capital, the conversion of net income to a fund inflow involves only the nonfund items.

Phoenix Corporation
Schedule of Cash Provided by Operations
For the Year Ended December 31, 1985

Net income		$117
Add depreciation expense	$ 60	
Amortization of patent	4	
Loss on sale of fixed assets	3	
Less gain on sale of investments	(5)	
Amortization of bond premium	(2)	60
Working capital provided by operations		177
Add decrease in merchandise	17	
Increase in accounts payable	18	
Increase in income taxes payable	7	
Less increase in accounts receivable	(37)	
Decrease in salaries payable	(9)	(4)
Total cash provided by operations		$173

Figure 20-5 **Schedule of cash provided by operations shows net income adjusted for nonfund items to isolate working capital provided by operations. This amount is further adjusted for changes in working capital accounts to arrive at cash provided by operations. Compare the form of this schedule with the same schedule in Figure 20-3.**

The Concept of All Financial Resources

Transactions that do not affect cash or working capital may take place during an accounting period. For example, common stock may be issued in exchange for land and buildings. Or a new 10-year bond payable may be issued in exchange for an old bond payable that is about to mature. Although such transactions do not affect funds, they nevertheless involve resource changes that must be disclosed in the statement of changes in financial position.

Exchanges represent both sources and uses of funds

The ability of a company to issue additional common stock is an important resource. The acquisition of new land and buildings in exchange for the stock is an important use of the company's resources although it does not affect funds. To ensure that all such resources are disclosed, the concept of **all financial resources** requires the reporting of the financing and investing aspects of exchanges.

An example of the way exchanges are treated is the acquisition of new equipment by Phoenix Corporation in exchange for cash and a long-term note payable. The cost of the equipment was $66 and Phoenix paid $22 cash. The transaction was recorded as follows:

	Equipment	66	
	Cash		22
	Notes payable		44

Only $22 of working capital was needed to acquire the new equipment. The company was able to obtain $44 of long-term financing for the acquisition of these assets. Although the note payable did not provide working capital, it does indicate the ability to borrow funds. Also, the purchase of assets represents $66 of investing activities, not just $22 represented by the use of cash.

If only the $22 of working capital effects of the above transaction were disclosed in the funds flow statement, the result would be to hide part of the company's investing and financing activities. Instead, as illustrated in Figure 20-3, such activities are reported and described in the statement to indicate that they do not involve working capital. Among sources of funds, the long-term borrowing is described as an exchange for equipment. Among the uses of funds, the acquisition of equipment is described as being financed partly by funds (the $22 cash payment) and partly by long-term borrowing.

Use of the Funds Flow Statement

Funds defined as working capital are useful to financial analysts

Phoenix Corporation's statements of changes in financial position provided in Figures 20-3 and 20-4 show that most of the company's funds were provided by business operations. A relatively small amount came from the sale of fixed assets, indicating that the business did not depend on such sales for its major source of funds. At the same time, the disposal of old assets and investment in new ones shows that the business is updating its plant and equipment and expanding its operations. The sale of long-term investments and the retirement of preferred stock may also indicate that management is revising its assets and equities structure to meet changing business conditions.

The increase in working capital seems to be rather large. A well-managed company normally does not maintain excessive working capital balances to avoid inefficient operations. The increases in working capital may be necessary if a larger volume of business is expected in the future. By examining the detailed changes in working capital, we see that funds have become much more liquid, with cash, temporary investments, and receivables increasing and liquid assets, such as merchandise and prepayments, decreasing. The company is therefore in a good position to improve its current ratio by repaying current liabilities, to finance expansion by new long-term investments, and to increase the volume of current operations, thereby possibly improving future profits.

Funds defined as cash are useful to managers

Managers are especially interested in the detailed analysis of the changes in current assets and current liabilities. They need information about cash flows in order to maintain good control over business operations and resources and to ensure adequate working capital. Managers undertake financing and investing activities that are eventually reflected in the financial statements that will be evaluated by external users of the company's annual report.

Financial analysts examine the statement of changes together with the other financial statements to assess the overall conditions and performance of a business. They may, for example, find a company to be an undesirable investment if it is paying cash dividends while it is obtaining more funds from the sale of fixed assets than from operations. The above discussions are only brief examples of the type of information that may be obtained from the statement of changes. At this point, however, you should try to understand the relationships among the numbers disclosed in the funds flow statement.

THE NATURE OF BALANCE SHEET CHANGES

Before we examine the techniques for preparing the statement of changes, it is important that you have a clear understanding of the nature of changes that are reported in the statement. We therefore start by illustrating why debits may be viewed as uses and credits as sources of funds, and by explaining the nature of nonfund items that are frequently found in the income statement.

The financial statements of Phoenix Corporation are used to illustrate the technical aspects of preparing the statement of changes in financial position. The resulting funds flow statements are shown in Figures 20-3 and 20-4, but now we show in detail specifically how they are derived. To review briefly the concept of sources and uses of funds, examine the comparative balance sheets and the income statement in Figure 20-2.

Debits and Credits as Uses and Sources of Funds

The changes in the balance sheet accounts are calculated and shown in Figure 20-2 in the two columns headed "Uses" and "Sources." The headings of these two columns also indicate that debits are uses of funds and credits are sources of funds. Why should this be the case? The reason is explained by reference to a change in a long-term liability or a fixed asset.

For example, Figure 20-2 shows that Phoenix Corporation did not have long-term notes payable outstanding in 1984 but does have them outstanding in 1985. It is therefore clear that the company borrowed money by issuing notes payable. When it did so the following entry was made:

	Cash	44	
	Notes payable		44

Credits are sources of funds

Issuing the note is a **financing activity** which **provides funds** and requires crediting a liability. The note payable is the **source** of the funds received, and it is recorded by a **credit.** If, instead, a liability had been reduced, it would have required the **use of funds,** and the decrease in the liability would be recorded as a **debit.** Therefore, credits represent sources of funds and debits represent uses of funds.

The same reasoning applies to a change in a fixed asset. Phoenix Corporation acquired buildings in 1985, resulting in the following entry:

	Buildings	13	
	Cash		13

Debits are uses of funds

Funds were **used** to acquire the buildings, whose increase is recorded with a **debit.** Therefore debits are uses of funds. Similarly, selling a fixed asset **provides funds.** The decrease in the asset account is a credit, so credits are sources of funds. This logic works with long-term liabilities and fixed assets. Do not make the mistake of using it on current accounts because those accounts **are** funds. The idea is to differentiate between funds and their sources and uses. Borrowing is the source which provides cash, or funds. The increase in the Building account is the use, which decreases cash.

The Concept of Nonfund Items

Operating a business is an important source of funds. **Revenues are sources and are recorded by credits; expenses are uses and are recorded by debits.** In the statement of changes in financial position we do not detail all sources and uses from operations. Instead we report the net source, which is the difference between revenue sources and expense uses.

Nonfund items are used to convert net income to fund flows

To convert net income to a **net source of funds,** the net income figure must be adjusted to eliminate the effects of the nonfund items and to **reflect only sources and uses of funds from operations.** The adjustments required to convert net income to net fund flows from operations is simple and logical. If a nonfund item, such as depreciation expense, was included in the income statement so that it reduced net income, that item is added back. If a nonfund item, such as a gain, was included in the income statement so that it increased net income, that item is deducted. Adjustments are needed for the following nonfund items commonly found in income statements:

- Nonfund items that reduced reported net income but do not actually use funds and therefore must be added back to net income include:

  Depreciation of fixed assets
  Depletion of natural resources
  Amortization of intangibles
  Discount amortization on bonds payable
  Premium amortization on bond investments
  Increases in deferred tax credits
  Decreases in deferred tax charges
  Losses

- Nonfund items that increase reported net income but do not actually provide funds and therefore must be deducted from net income include:

  Premium amortization on bonds payable
  Discount amortization on bond investments
  Decreases in deferred tax credits
  Increases in deferred tax charges
  Income from investment carried at equity
  Gains

DATA FOR STATEMENT PREPARATION

The comparative balance sheets, income statement, and retained earnings statement are the primary sources of information for preparing the statement of changes. Additional data from the accounting records may also be used to analyze the way specific transactions affect funds. Several relevant transactions are listed on page 835.

The statement of changes is prepared by means of a series of mechanical steps. They are designed to convert the information available above and in the company's financial statements into a statement of changes in financial positions. You cannot become entirely familiar with these procedures merely by reading about them; you must use them in order to comprehend them. The procedure consists of preparing working papers in a columnar worksheet. Entries are made in these working papers so that information is organized into a form from which the formal statement of changes in financial position may be prepared.

The entries used to prepare the statement of changes do not become part of the accounting records of the company. They are made in the working papers only, not in the books of account. The purpose of these entries is to enable the accountant to examine transactions that were recorded in the books previously. But now these transactions are examined to see their effect on funds rather than their effect on the accounting equation.

The changes in the balance sheet accounts, which the statement of changes explains, occurred as a result of transactions that were recorded in the books during the past accounting period. When the transactions were originally recorded, they were analyzed to determine their effect on the accounting equation. Now we need to analyze these same transactions to determine their effect on fund flows. The easiest way to analyze each transaction is to reproduce the journal entry that describes it and enter it into the working papers. As each entry is made it explains some of the changes in the account balances. When the change in each account in the working papers has been explained, sufficient information is accumulated to prepare the statement of changes.

First we illustrate the procedure with funds defined as working capital. Next we use the same method with funds defined as cash. The techniques employed for preparing the statement of changes depend on the definition of funds. With either definition, the concept of all financial resources is used.

PREPARING THE STATEMENT OF CHANGES WITH FUNDS DEFINED AS WORKING CAPITAL

The statement of changes reports the amount of working capital provided by operations and other sources of working capital. It also shows how working capital was used in investing activities, and the changes in working capital and its components.

Setting Up the Worksheet

The first two steps are procedures to calculate working capital, organize the working papers, and enter the available data in them. When these steps are completed, we are ready to start the analysis of income statement and balance sheet data. The completed worksheet is presented in Figure 20-6 and is discussed in the following pages.

Step 1. A four-column worksheet is established and the beginning and ending balances of all balance sheet accounts are entered in the extreme left and right columns respectively. Instead of entering all current assets and liabilities, however, only the working capital figures are entered. This simplifies the worksheet when funds are defined as working capital but of course it is not mandatory to condense the current items into a single number. Working capital is calculated at the beginning and end of the accounting period as shown below.

	1984	1985	Change
Current assets	$252	$370	$118 increase
Less current liabilities	117	143	26 increase
Working capital	$135	$227	$ 92 increase

Step 2. The two middle columns of the worksheet are left blank. They are used to explain the changes that occurred during the period. These two blank columns will be filled in with debit and credit entries that are needed to change the balance sheet accounts from their beginning balance to the ending balance. Space is also provided at the bottom of the worksheet to accumulate the fund flows. One section is labeled "Funds from Operations" and another is labeled "Funds Flow." The Funds Flow section accumulates all fund flows other than those from operations.

Phoenix Corporation
Worksheet for Statement of Changes in Financial Position
For the Year Ended December 31, 1985

	Beginning Balances 12/31/84	Balance Sheet Changes dr	Balance Sheet Changes cr	Ending Balances 12/31/85
Debits				
Working capital	135	l. 92		227
Land	60			60
Buildings	987	k. 13		1,000
Equipment	800	j. 66	f. 25	841
Long-term investments	125		e. 25	100
Patents	37		c. 4	33
Totals	2,144			2,261
Credits				
Accumulated depreciation	660	f. 14	b. 60	706
Notes payable, due 1989	—		j. 44	44
Bonds payable, due 1994	450			450
Premium on bonds payable	18	d. 2		16
Preferred stock	48	i. 48		—
Common stock $1 par	500		h. 10	510
Paid-in capital on common	220		h. 40	260
Retained earnings	248	g. 40 h. 50	a. 117	275
Totals	2,144	325	325	2,261
Funds from operations				
Sources of working capital from operations:				
Net income		a. 117		
Depreciation of equipment		b. 60		
Amortization of patent		c. 4		
Amortization of bond premium			d. 2	
Gain on sale of investments			e. 5	
Loss on sale of equipment		f. 3		
Funds flow				
Other sources of working capital				
Sale of long-term investments		e. 30		
Sale of equipment		f. 8		
Increase in long-term debt		j. 44		
Uses of working capital				
Payment of dividends			g. 40	
Retirement of preferred stock			i. 48	
Purchase of equipment			j. 66	
Addition to buildings			k. 13	
Increase in working capital			l. 92	
Totals		266	266	

Figure 20-6 **Worksheet used to prepare the statement in Figure 20-3. The bottom portion of the worksheet is divided into two parts, one for sources of funds from operations and the other, labeled "Funds Flow," for other sources and uses of funds.**

Examination of Income Statement

The purpose of the next two steps is to determine the amount of funds provided by operations. Operations generate net income, which changes retained earnings. But because net income is not the same as net fund inflows from operations, the net income figure must be converted to fund inflows by eliminating nonfund items that appear in the income statement.

Step 3. With this step, we use the net income figure to see how it changed the Retained Earnings account balance. The procedure results in entering net income in the bottom half of the worksheet where it is ready to be converted to funds provided by operations.

How does net income change the balance sheet? The change is in the Retained Earnings account, and it occurs when the books are closed and the balance in the Income Summary account is transferred to Retained Earnings. We now reproduce this entry here and enter it in the working papers in order to observe its effect on funds. From the net income reported in the income statement, we know that the entry to close the Income Summary account was as follows:

a.	Income summary	117	
	Retained earnings		117

The debit part of this entry shows where the funds came from—that is, the source of funds; the credit part shows which permanent account changed as a result of this source. The debit part of the entry is entered in the part of the worksheet in which we accumulate funds provided by operations. In this case the credit part explains part of the change in retained earnings and is, therefore, entered in the worksheet on the retained earnings line as entry *a*.

The $117 debit in the Funds from Operations section of the worksheet is the first component of funds provided by operations. The Retained Earnings account is credited, as it was when the books were originally closed, changing the balance in Retained Earnings. Because this credit to Retained Earnings does not change retained earnings from the beginning to the ending balance, other transactions must have affected this account. We know that these are dividend distributions and shall deal with them shortly.

As we examine transactions that caused changes in funds, it is necessary to accumulate the fund flows from these transactions in the appropriate parts of the worksheet. Therefore it helps to know how a transaction should be handled. You will always enter each transaction into the working papers correctly if you remember the following simple rules:

Rules for entering amounts in the worksheet

1. All temporary accounts are entered in the Funds from Operations section.

2. Permanent accounts are entered in the blank middle space in the top of the worksheet if the account title is listed.
3. Permanent accounts that represent funds, such as cash or other working capital accounts are entered in the working papers in the Funds Flow section.

You can see that these rules were followed with entry *a*. Income Summary is a temporary account and is therefore entered in Funds from Operations.

Step 4. Now we turn our attention to the rest of the income statement and examine each account reported in it to determine if there are any nonfund items that must be removed from income in order to convert net income to funds provided by operations.

The income statement is examined for nonfund items

Most revenues are inflows of working capital and most expenses are outflows of working capital. With funds defined as working capital, the net inflow from these revenues and expenses is already reflected in net income. Therefore we need only look for nonfund items. Starting at the top of the income statement, we note that sales are inflows of funds, and cost of goods sold is an outflow of funds. Neither contains any nonfund items. Similarly administrative expenses and salaries are outflows of funds which are already reflected in the net income figure.

An obvious nonfund item is depreciation expense. As soon as we find a nonfund item in the income statement, we can reproduce the journal entry that was originally used to record this item. The entry in our working papers to record depreciation is

b.	Depreciation expense (Operations)	60	
	Accumulated depreciation		60

Because Depreciation Expense is a temporary account, it is entered in Funds from Operations as a debit. Depreciation expense is a nonfund item that must be added back to net income to convert the net income figure to a cash inflow; therefore, both net income and depreciation expense appear as debits in the Funds from Operations section of the worksheet. The credit is entered on the accumulated depreciation line in our worksheet. It changes the beginning balance of Accumulated Depreciation by more than the $46 change in this account. This means that other transactions occurred that changed accumulated depreciation.

Returning to the income statement we find amortization of patents, another expense that does not require the use of funds, as can be seen when amortization expense is recorded. The entry to amortize the patent is

c.	Amortization expense (Operations)	4	
	Patents		4

This entry changes the Patents account and adds back the amortization expense to net income in the Funds from Operations section. The principle is the same as for depreciation expense.

The next item in the income statement is interest expense. When interest expense is paid, an outflow of funds occurs, but the amount of interest expense reported on the income statement is not necessarily the amount of cash used to pay the interest. A nonfund item may be hidden in the interest expense. This is because a year-end adjustment to amortize bond discount or premium may have affected the interest expense. In fact, there is a premium on bonds payable on the balance sheet, and $2 was amortized during the year. Therefore the amount of interest paid was not $38 as reported in the income statement, but $40, as explained on page 833.

The $40 cash paid for interest was an outflow of working capital, and interest expense appears on the income statement as a deduction, so we do not need to do anything with this entry, just as there is no need to make an adjustment for the payment of salaries or rent. However, at the end of the accounting period, the following adjusting entry was made to record the amortization of premium on bonds payable:

d.	Premium on bonds payable	2	
	Interest expense (Operations)		2

Entering entry *d* in the worksheet adds $2 to the credit side of Funds from Operations, reducing funds from operations by $2. The debit of $2 is entered on the premium on bonds payable line, causing that account to change from its beginning balance to the ending balance.

Proceeding further in our examination of the income statement, we find that a gain on sale of investments of $5 was recorded. Although this gain was added to arrive at net income, the inflow of cash from the sale of investments was not $5. Moreover, selling investments is not a part of usual business operations.

How do we know the amount of investments sold? The working papers provide a clue. The Long-Term Investments account in the working papers has a beginning balance of $125. It requires a credit of $25 in order to change it to its ending balance of $100. The sale of long-term investments, therefore, must have been recorded as follows:

e.	Cash (Funds flow)	30	
	Gain (Operations)		5
	Long-term investments		25

The sale of long-term investments is not part of operations. It is a different type of financing activity. Selling investments increased working capital by $30. Therefore, the $30 inflow will appear in the Funds Flow section of the worksheet as a debit. The $5 gain in the income statement is a nonfund item which did not provide any working capital; it is entered in the credit side of Funds from Operations. The $25 credit changes the Long-Term Investments account from its beginning balance to its ending balance.

The next item on the income statement is the loss on sale of equipment. Losses are nonfund items, and the sale of equipment does not provide funds from operations; it is one of the other categories of fund sources. The description of this equipment sale on page 835 says that the proceeds of the sale were $8 and the sold equipment had a cost of $25 and a book value of $11. If the sale resulted in a loss of $3, as reported in the income statement, it must have been recorded with the following journal entry:

f.	Cash (Funds flow)	8	
	Accumulated depreciation	14	
	Loss (Operations)	3	
	Equipment		25

The sale of equipment resulted in an $8 inflow of funds, but on the income statement there is a deduction of $3 for the loss. Clearly, the $3 loss did not result in an outflow of funds, yet this amount was deducted in arriving at net income. To convert the net income figure to the amount of funds flowing into the company as a result of operations, we must add this loss back to net income. The loss, a nonfund item, is automatically added to net income in the Funds from Operations section when the journal entry is entered in the worksheet.

The $14 debit to Accumulated Depreciation combined with the previous $60 credit entry is not enough to change the Accumulated Depreciation account from its beginning balance to its ending balance. Likewise, the $25 credit for equipment does not explain the entire change in the Equipment account. This means that there is yet another transaction to be analyzed to determine the overall change in equipment and accumulated depreciation.

The last expense reported in the income statement is federal income tax. We must decide whether the entire $96 expense was an outflow of funds, or whether more or less tax was actually paid. Tax expense and the tax payment are not the same if a deferred tax account was debited or credited. Deferred taxes are nonfund items that may be hidden in the tax expense, but in this case there is no deferred tax account whose balance changed in the balance sheet. Therefore nothing has to be done with tax expense.

We have now completed our examination of the income statement, and all nonfund items are entered in the Funds from Operations part of the worksheet in a way that converts the net income figure to funds provided by operations.

Examination of Retained Earnings Statement

The next step is the analysis of transactions that affected the retained earnings statement. The change caused by income from operations is already entered in the worksheet on the retained earnings line.

Step 5. The retained earnings statement in Figure 20-2 shows that net income was earned and dividends were paid in 1985. The $117 change caused by operations is already in the Funds from Operations section and on the retained earnings line in the worksheet. Therefore we can proceed directly to the dividends.

The cash dividend of $40 used working capital when it was declared. The entry is reproduced below. Entering it in the worksheet explains part of the change in the Retained Earnings account. The dividend declaration used $40 of working capital, which is entered in Funds Flow. When dividends are declared the Dividends Payable account is credited—$40 in this case. But the balance of dividends payable is $10, so cash must have been used to reduce the dividends payable liability from $40 to $10. Since both cash and dividends payable are components of working capital, the entire $40 is an outflow of funds.

g.	Retained earnings	40	
	Dividends payable or Cash (Funds flow)		40

The 2 percent stock dividend reported in the statement of retained earnings reduced retained earnings by $50. Originally 500 shares of $1 par common stock were outstanding, as shown in the 1984 balance sheet, and an additional 10 shares were issued as a stock dividend, as reported in the retained earnings statement and shown by the $510 ending common stock balance in the 1985 balance sheet. The entry to record the stock dividend is reproduced below.

h.	Retained earnings	50	
	Common stock		10
	Additional paid-in capital		40

The payment of a stock dividend has no effect on funds. When the entry is entered in the worksheet, it changes the Common Stock and Paid-in Capital accounts, as well as the Retained Earnings account, from their beginning to their ending balances.

Examination of Remaining Transactions

We have now completed the analysis of both the income statement and the retained earnings statement. This analysis enabled us to explain several of the balance sheet changes. We now examine the balance sheet accounts in the worksheet to determine if any changes have not yet been explained.

Step 6. In this step we complete the entries required to adjust all remaining balance sheet accounts in the worksheet to their ending balance. At this point we are left with two of the four transactions described on page 835: the retirement of preferred stock and the acquisition of equipment. Each of them must be analyzed to determine its effect on fund flows.

To find the amount of preferred stock that was retired, we look for a clue in the worksheet, where we see that the Preferred Stock account decreased by $48. To explain this change, we must debit the account. The acquisition and retirement of preferred stock at its book value is recorded as follows:

i.	Preferred stock	48	
	Cash (Funds flow)		48

The change in preferred stock explains why this account decreased. The $48 credit in entry *i* is a fund outflow and is entered in the Funds Flow section, representing funds used to retire the preferred stock.

The acquisition of equipment in exchange for cash and a note payable is an application of the **all financial resources** concept. Originally the transaction was recorded as follows, as described on page 838:

j.	Equipment	66	
	Cash		22
	Notes payable		44

The all financial resources concept applied

If this transaction were entered in the worksheet as journalized above, Equipment would be debited $66 and the Notes Payable account would be credited $44, but Funds Flow would be credited only $22. If the statement of changes is to report **all financial resources,** the company's ability to borrow funds for the purpose of acquiring assets must be fully disclosed. We therefore separate the above transaction into two components: one to record the source of funds from borrowing and the other to record the use of funds for buying equipment. The two component transactions are

j.	Cash (Funds flow)	44	
	Notes payable		44
	Equipment	66	
	Cash (Funds flow)		66

When these two entries are made in the worksheet, they have the same effect on the Equipment and Notes Payable accounts as the first version of entry *j*. But now the Funds Flow section shows all financial resources obtained and used in this transaction.

Only the changes in the Buildings account and in working capital have not yet been explained. We leave working capital for last. With access to the accounting records, the accountant can easily find out why the Buildings account changed. Even if we do not look at the underlying records, however, it is clear what occurred. To change the Buildings account beginning balance to its ending balance a debit of $13 is needed. This implies that buildings were acquired or additions were made to existing buildings, and such transactions use funds. The change in the Buildings account is explained with the following entry:

k.	Buildings	13	
	Funds flow		13

Any other accounts (except working capital) remaining with unexplained changes are treated similarly. For example, if a mortgage had been repaid, a Mortgage account would exist whose change would have to be shown in the worksheet as a debit. Debiting the Mortgage account would imply the use of funds to repay the debt. Any remaining changes in the worksheet can usually be made simply by debiting or crediting the account. The corresponding credit or debit part of the entry is typically a funds flow item.

Preparation of the Statement of Changes

To check the accuracy of our work, we need to find the balances of the two middle columns in the working papers. The lower part of the worksheet lists the sources and uses of working capital, and we can expect sources to exceed uses because working capital increased. Therefore if we transfer the change in working capital from the top part of the worksheet to the bottom part, the middle columns of the worksheet should balance. This transfer is accomplished with entry *l*.

l.	Working capital	92	
	Funds flow		92

The data in the lower part of the worksheet are used to prepare a formal statement of changes in financial position. The Funds from Operations section contains the details necessary to report the amount of working capital provided by operations, which may be shown in a separate schedule or included in the statement of changes as in Figure 20-3.

The total balance in the Funds from Operations section is found and entered in the worksheet so that this amount can be added to the items listed under Funds Flow. The Funds Flow section contains the remaining sources and uses of funds. Finding the totals of both columns in the lower part of the worksheet verifies that all entries balance and that total sources equal total uses. The sources and uses are organized in the statement as shown in Figure 20-3. In addition, to verify the change in working capital, the statement of changes must report all changes in working capital components in the schedule at the bottom of the statement.

PREPARING THE STATEMENT OF CHANGES WITH FUNDS DEFINED AS CASH

When funds are defined as cash, the statement of changes in financial position is somewhat more complex because reporting cash provided by operations requires more detail than reporting working capital provided by operations. The procedures, however, are not more difficult.

Every change in the balance sheet, including changes in current assets and current liabilities, must be explained to show the effect on cash. Changes in the current assets and current liabilities accounts affect cash primarily through operations. The change in accounts receivable affects the amount of cash provided by sales. Similarly, changes in accounts payable and merchandise affect the amount of cash used to pay for the goods sold.

Not all changes in current accounts are related to the operations of the company. For example, if equipment is purchased on open account, the increase in accounts payable is due to the purchase of fixed assets rather than the purchase of merchandise. A careful analysis of current accounts is necessary to determine if some of their changes result from nonoperating transactions. In general, however, you can assume that all changes in current accounts are due to operations. Therefore, current assets and liabilities are handled as follows in converting the net income from operations to a cash flow figure:

Item added to net income:
- Decreases in current assets
- Increases in current liabilities

Items deducted from net income:
- Increases in current assets
- Decreases in current liabilities

In addition, nonfund items such as depreciation expenses and gains are added or deducted as already illustrated.

The worksheet in Figure 20-7 is used for the preparation of the statement of changes with funds defined as cash. Steps 1 and 2 are now somewhat different.

Phoenix Corporation
Worksheet for Statement of Changes in Financial Position
For the Year Ended December 31, 1985

	Beginning Balances 12/31/84	Balance Sheet Changes dr	Balance Sheet Changes cr	Ending Balances 12/31/85
Debits				
Cash	67	1. 98		165
Accounts receivable (net)	90	2. 37		127
Merchandise	95		3. 17	78
Land	60			60
Buildings	987	k. 13		1,000
Equipment	800	j. 66	f. 25	841
Long-term investments	125		e. 25	100
Patents	37		c. 4	33
Totals	2,261			2,404
Credits				
Accounts payable	74		4. 18	92
Salaries payable	30	5. 9		21
Income taxes payable	13		6. 7	20
Dividends payable	—	g. 30	g. 40	10
Accumulated depreciation	660	f. 14	b. 60	706
Notes payable, due 1989	—		j. 44	44
Bonds payable, 1994	450			450
Premium on bonds payable	18	d. 2		16
Preferred stock	48	i. 48		—
Common stock $1 par	500		h. 10	510
Paid-in capital on common	220		h. 40	260
Retained earnings	248	g. 40 h. 50	a. 117	275
Totals	2,261	407	407	2,404
Funds from operations				
Sources of cash from operations:				
Net income		a. 117		
Increase in accounts receivable			2. 37	
Decrease in merchandise		3. 17		
Increase in accounts payable		4. 18		
Decrease in salaries payable			5. 9	
Increase in income taxes payable		6. 7		
Depreciation of equipment		b. 60		
Amortization of patent		c. 4		
Amortization of bond premium			d. 2	
Gain on sale of investments			e. 5	
Loss on sale of equipment		f. 3		
Funds flow				
Other sources of cash:				
Sale of long-term investments		e. 30		
Sale of equipment		f. 8		
Increase in long-term debt		j. 44		
Uses of cash:				
Payment of dividends			g. 30	
Retirement of preferred stock			i. 48	
Purchase of equipment			j. 66	
Addition to buildings			k. 13	
Increase in cash balance			1. 98	
Totals		308	308	

Figure 20-7 Worksheet used to prepare the statement in Figure 20-4. The changes in current assets and current liabilities are transferred to the portion of the worksheet used to accumulate funds from operation. Cash appears in the lower portion of the worksheet as a balancing item.

Setting Up the Worksheet

Step 1. Changes in current assets and current liabilities affect the amount of cash provided by operations. In Figure 20-6, the changes in these accounts were used to determine the net change in working capital. Now, instead of combining all current accounts into one working capital figure, we follow a somewhat different procedure and enter all beginning and ending balance sheet accounts in the worksheet.

With funds defined as cash, the change in cash is the difference between total sources and total uses of funds. The change in the Cash account will therefore be transferred to the Funds Flow section of the worksheet. This change in cash will appear on the statement of changes as the difference between total sources and total uses of cash. Another way of looking at this change in cash is to see it as the balancing item that makes sources of cash from all financing activities equal to uses of cash for all investing activities reported in the statement of changes. We can wait until all other entries have been made in the worksheet, as was done with the working capital approach, or we can transfer the change in cash to Funds Flow as the first step. Here we take the latter approach with the following entry:

1.	Cash	98	
	Funds flow		98

With funds defined as cash, current accounts are transferred to Operating Summary

We transfer the remaining current account changes, except the change in Dividends Payable, to the Funds from Operations section of the worksheet. We do this because these changes affect the amount of funds provided by operations when funds are defined as cash. Proceeding through the current accounts in the worksheet, the beginning balance of each operating current account is changed to its ending balance with the following entries in the worksheet:

2.	Accounts receivable	37	
	Operations		37
3.	Operations	17	
	Merchandise		17
4.	Operations	18	
	Accounts payable		18
5.	Salaries payable	9	
	Operations		9
6.	Operations	7	
	Income taxes payable		7

The only remaining current account is Dividends Payable. The change in this account is not transferred to Funds from Operations because dividends have nothing to do with operations.

Compare the worksheet in Figure 20-6 with the one in Figure 20-7 and observe the difference caused by the above entries. The Funds Flow section contains the change in cash, and the Funds from Operations section contains the changes of the current asset and current liability accounts that affect operations. Dividends Payable, a current account that does not affect operations, still remains unchanged. When funds are defined as cash, the Dividends Payable account is treated simply as if it is not part of working capital. The increase in this account means that the amount of cash used for the payment of dividends, which is an investing activity, was less than the total amount of dividends declared.

The main difference in the preparation of the statement of changes in financial position between the two definitions of funds is in the treatment of current accounts. When funds are defined as working capital, all of the current account changes are transferred to Funds Flow. When funds are defined as cash, only the change in cash is transferred to Funds Flow. Aside from these differences, the rest of the procedure is the same as described for funds defined as working capital.

We proceed through the entire example again with explanations only where they are necessary to illustrate the differences between the two approaches. Remember that the entries made at this time are not recorded in the books. They are simply reproduced in the working papers in order to analyze their effect on funds. The entries change the beginning balances of the accounts to their ending balances and accumulate all funds flows in the Funds from Operations and Funds Flow sections of the worksheet.

Examination of Income Statement

Step 3. The Income Summary account is closed in order to transfer net income to Retained Earnings.

a.	Income summary (Operations)	117	
	Retained earnings		117

Step 4. The income statement is examined for any nonfund items needed to convert the net income figure to a cash flow figure. Depreciation and amortization expense do not result in an outflow of cash and are added back to net income.

b.	Depreciation expense (Operations)	60	
	Accumulated depreciation		60
c.	Amortization expense (Operations)	4	
	Patents		4

Interest expense includes a nonfund item resulting from amortization of a bond premium. The change in the Bond Premium account is used to adjust Operations for premium amortization.

d.	Premium on bonds payable	2	
	Interest expense (Operations)		2

The sale of investments provided a $30 cash inflow. The gain originally added in the income statement must be deducted from net income because it is not an inflow of cash. The entry is reproduced and posted.

e.	Cash (Funds flow)	30	
	Gain (Operations)		5
	Long-term investments		25

The loss on sale of equipment is a nonfund item. The entry to record the transaction is entered in the working papers.

f.	Cash (Funds flow)	8	
	Accumulated depreciation	14	
	Loss (Operations)	3	
	Equipment		25

Examination of Retained Earnings Statement

Step 5. The payment of cash dividends is recorded with the following sequence of entries:

g.	Retained earnings	40	
	Dividends payable		40
	Dividends payable	30	
	Cash (Funds flow)		30

The effect of dividends payable on fund flows

These two entries change the Dividends Payable account. Now the Funds Flow section indicates that $30 of cash was used to pay dividends. Look closely at the treatment of dividends here as compared to the previous example. When funds are defined as working capital, nothing has to be done with the Dividends Payable account because it is one of the working capital components that determines the change in working capital.

When funds are defined as cash, however, we have to treat the Dividends Payable account separately. Not all dividend declarations result in cash outflows. Entry *g* ensures that only the amount of cash paid as dividends is reported in the statement of changes as a use of cash.

A 2 percent stock dividend is declared and paid, and there is no effect on cash.

h.	Retained earnings	50	
	Common stock		10
	Additional paid-in capital		40

Examination of Remaining Transactions

Step 6. Preferred stock is acquired and retired.

i.	Preferred stock	48	
	Cash (Funds flow)		48

The purchase of equipment for cash and a long-term note payable is recorded using the concept of all financial resources, which means the transaction is split into two components, one showing a source of funds and the other a use of funds.

j.	Cash (Funds flow)	44	
	Notes payable		44
	Equipment	66	
	Cash (Funds flow)		66

The Buildings account change has not been explained yet. The following entry changes the Buildings account from its beginning to its ending balance:

k.	Buildings	13	
	Funds flow		13

Preparation of the Statement of Changes

Step 7. All of the above entries are shown in Figure 20-7. Preparation of the cash flow statement is a matter of using the information in the lower part of the worksheet to organize the formal report shown in Figure 20-4 and the schedule in Figure 20-5. The Funds from Operations section of the worksheet contains the amount of cash provided by operations. The two middle columns can now be added to show that both the upper and lower portions balance. When cash provided by operations is a fairly complex computation as in this example, it is reported in a separate schedule with a reference in the statement of changes in financial position.

Look closely at the schedule of cash provided by operations shown in Figure 20-5, and compare it with the similar schedule in Figure 20-3. In Figure 20-5 net income is adjusted first for nonfund items, resulting in working capital provided by operations. Then this amount is adjusted for working capital items that affect cash from operations, yielding cash provided by operations. This approach illustrates the difference and the similarity between the two definitions of funds.

SUMMARY

The **statement of changes in financial position** describes the **financing** and **investing** activities of a business. Such activities are viewed as inflows and outflows of **funds,** which may be defined either as **cash** or as **net working capital.** Sources of funds are obtained from business operations and from such financing activities as the sale of fixed assets, the issuance of capital stock, and the borrowing of money. Funds obtained from financing activities are used for investment in new fixed assets, for the repayment of debts, and for the distribution of assets to shareholders in the form of dividends or by the reacquisition of capital stock. The difference between total sources of funds and total uses represents the change in cash or working capital.

The statement of changes in financial position is also known as a **funds flow statement.** It is a **cash flow statement** if funds are defined as cash. In either case the funds flow statement must be prepared in accordance with the concept of **all financial resources.**

One of the most important sources of funds is business operations. Net income is not the same as funds provided by operations, because the income statement includes some expenses, revenues, and other deductions and additions that do not use or provide funds. Such **nonfund items** include depreciation and amortization expense, gains and losses, amortization of bond premium and discount, and tax deferrals. The net income figure must be converted to a figure representing fund flows from operations.

When funds are defined as **working capital,** the net change in working capital is reported in a separate schedule of the funds flow statement to show how the working capital components changed during the period.

In most annual reports the funds flow statement is based on changes in working capital. External users of the statement analyze the relationships among the various sources and uses of funds to determine the effectiveness of management's investing and financing activities. For managerial purposes it is more useful to define funds as cash, because managers are interested in the more detailed day-to-day operations of the business. The components of working capital, and the way they affect cash, are of more interest to managers than is working capital as a whole.

Changes in balance sheet accounts represented by debits are uses of funds. Changes represented by credits are sources of funds. The source from operations is the net result of revenue credits and expense debits. Sources of **funds from operations** are important and should be reported in sufficient detail to explain how the net income figure is adjusted for nonfund items and converted to a figure representing net inflows of funds from operations.

To disclose fully a company's ability to obtain and use funds, exchanges must be accounted for using the concept of **all financial resources.** In the preparation of the funds flow statement, such transactions may be divided into two components. One component shows financial resources provided by the transaction and the other shows financial resources used. The source and use of financial resources is then reported in the funds flow statement as if the transaction had provided and used funds.

KEY TERMS

all financial resources *(838)*
cash flow statement *(858)*
financing activities *(821)*
funds *(821)*
funds flow statement *(821)*
funds provided by operations *(827)*
investing activities *(821)*
nonfund items *(830)*
statement of changes in financial position *(821)*
working capital *(821)*

QUESTIONS

1. What are the four major categories of financing activities? What are the four major categories of investing activities?
2. What is the effect on funds if the amount available from financing activities is greater than the amount needed for investing activities?
3. Why is depreciation added back to net income in order to arrive at cash generated by operations? Why not do the same with other expenses such as salaries expense?
4. Define working capital.
5. Explain why sales usually provide cash and working capital in different amounts. Under what circumstances do sales provide an equal amount of cash and working capital?
6. A company sold fixed assets at a loss. Describe the funds flow aspects of such a transaction, and explain why the loss is added back to net income in the funds flow statement.
7. What is meant by the concept of all financial resources? Describe a transaction that illustrates the concept.
8. Why does an increase in long-term notes payable affect working capital while an increase in short-term notes payable does not?
9. Explain why a purchase of merchandise on open account does not affect working capital, but a sale of merchandise on open account does.
10. A company issues 1,000 shares of common stock in exchange for land. What is the effect on funds, and how is this transaction reported on the statement of changes in financial position?

11. Equipment with a cost of $1,600 and a book value of $600 is sold for $250 cash and a $500 short-term note receivable. Describe the effect of this transaction on the accounting equation. Describe the effect on funds with funds defined as cash and also with funds defined as working capital.
12. During the year, a company declared dividends of $2,000. Of this amount, $500 remains unpaid at the end of the accounting period. What is the effect of the dividend on the accounting equation, on cash, and on working capital?
13. (AICPA) The statement of changes in financial position is normally a required basic financial statement for each period for which an earnings statement is presented. The reporting entity has the flexibility in form, content, and terminology of this statement to meet the objectives of differing circumstances. For example, the concept of "funds" may be interpreted to mean, among other things, cash or working capital. However, the statement should be prepared based on the all financial resources concept. What is the all financial resources concept? What are two types of financial transactions that would be disclosed under the all financial resources concept that would not be disclosed without this concept?

EXERCISES

Ex. 20-1 Change in working capital. The current asset and current liability account balances of Billco Corporation at the beginning and end of the accounting year were as follows:

	Beginning	Ending
Cash	$1,360	$2,110
Accounts receivable	3,050	3,490
Merchandise	7,510	6,790
Supplies	370	420
Accounts payable	2,300	2,490
Notes payable	1,980	1,710
Salaries payable	2,400	2,730
Taxes payable	1,530	1,500

Required: Calculate the change in working capital for the year.

Ex. 20-2 Effect of nonfund transactions on funds and income. Below is a list of independent transactions or events, each of which may have an effect on cash, working capital, or income.

a. Bought equipment for $1,000 cash and a $6,000, 12 percent 90-day note payable.
b. Sold equipment for $3,500 cash and a $5,000, 60-day note receivable. The equipment had a book value of $7,500.
c. Sold land with a book value of $2,500 for $8,500 cash.
d. Sold land with a book value of $9,000 for $4,000 cash and a $10,000 mortgage note.
e. Sold a patent with a book value of $5,000 for $3,200 cash.
f. Exchanged equipment with a book value of $3,200 for new equipment with a fair value of $3,000.
g. Retired long-term bonds payable with a book value of $10,300 for $9,800 cash.
h. Sold treasury stock that cost $5,000 for $4,750 cash.
i. Declared a cash dividend of $9,500 payable next month.

Required: On a sheet of paper list the letters *a* through *i* and headings as shown below. For each item indicate whether it caused cash, working capital, and income to increase or decrease, and by how much. Use a minus sign to show decreases. The first item is solved below as an example.

	Cash	Working Capital	Income
a.	−$1,000	−$7,000	0

Ex. 20-3 Effect of transactions on funds and income. Below is a list of transactions or events each of which may have an effect on cash, working capital, or income.

a. Sold merchandise from perpetual inventory for $1,000 on open account. The cost of the merchandise was $700.
b. Paid $3,000, 60-day 12 percent note payable on which $20 of interest was accrued at the end of the last period.
c. Used supplies costing $50 bought on open account last month.
d. Purchased merchandise for $2,000 on open account.
e. Wrote off $580 uncollectible account against allowance for bad debts.
f. Paid $1,000 of accounts payable recorded at net amount of $980 and recorded discount lost.
g. Received $500 cash and a $3,000, 30-day note from a customer in exchange for her $3,500 account receivable.
h. Sold temporary investment with a cost of $10,000 for $9,500 cash.
i. Paid $5,000 semiannual interest on bonds payable and amortized premium of $150. None of the interest had been recorded as an accrual.
j. Bought equipment for $2,500 cash and a $6,000, 4-year note payable.
k. Sold land with a book value of $9,000 for $4,000 cash and a $10,000 mortgage note.
l. Sold a patent with a book value of $5,000 for $1,200 cash and a $3,000, 90-day note receivable.
m. Exchanged land costing $4,000 and having a fair value of $6,000 for new equipment, and in addition paid $1,000 cash.
n. Paid $7,500 dividend payable declared earlier this year.
o. Recorded $800 of bad debt expense at end of year based on aging of accounts receivable.
p. Accrued $650 of interest receivable on bond investment at end of year.

Required: On a sheet of paper list the letters *a* through *p* and headings as shown below. For each item indicate whether it caused cash, working capital, and income to increase or decrease, and by how much. Use a minus sign to show decreases. The first item is solved below as an example.

	Cash	Working Capital	Income
a.	0	$300	$300

Ex. 20-4 Recognizing nonfund items. Certain nonfund items must be added to or deducted from net income to convert it to fund inflows from operations. Below is a list of items, some of which may have to be used to convert net income to fund flows.

a. Increase in bonds payable
b. Depreciation expense
c. Amortization of discount on bond investment

d. Gain on sale of land
e. Loss on redemption of bonds payable
f. Issuance of common stock
g. Amortization of intangibles
h. Retirement of preferred stock
i. Amortization of discount on bonds payable
j. Dividend income from temporary equity investments
k. Decrease in deferred tax credits
l. Loss on sale of equipment
m. Increase in deferred tax charges
n. Amortization of premium on bonds payable
o. Purchase of land
p. Income from investment carried on equity basis
q. Depletion of natural resources
r. Acquisition of treasury stock

Required: Code each item in the list to indicate whether it should be added to net income, deducted from net income, or does not affect funds from operations. Use the following codes:

0 No effect. Neither add to nor deduct from net income.
\+ Add to net income to arrive at fund flows.
− Deduct from net income to arrive at fund flows.

Ex. 20-5 Converting income to cash flows. Certain changes in current assets and liabilities must be added to or deducted from net income to convert it to cash inflows from operations. Below is a list of independent items, some of which may affect cash provided by operations.

a. Increase in accounts receivable
b. Decrease in supplies
c. Decrease in accounts payable
d. Increase in long-term debt
e. Increase in merchandise inventory
f. Increase in payroll taxes payable
g. Decrease in dividends payable
h. Decrease in land
i. Decrease in accounts receivable
j. Increase in cash
k. Increase in prepaid expenses
l. Decrease in salaries payable
m. Increase in interest payable
n. Decrease in interest receivable
o. Increase in retained earnings

Required: Code each item in the list to indicate whether it should be added to net income, deducted from net income, or does not affect the amount of cash provided by operations. Use the following codes:

0 No effect. Neither add to nor deduct from net income.
\+ Add to net income to arrive at cash flows.
− Deduct from net income to arrive at cash flows.

Ex. 20-6 **Calculating funds from operations.** Brooks Company reported net income of $40,000 for the year ending December 31, 1986. The income statement included depreciation expense of $3,500 and a gain on sale of land of $2,000. From the beginning to the end of the accounting period cash increased $1,500, accounts receivable increased $1,000, merchandise decreased $1,200, and current liabilities increased by $800.

Required:

a. Determine how much cash was provided by operations during 1986.

b. Determine how much working capital was provided by operations during 1986.

Ex. 20-7 **Calculation of net income from cash flows.** For the year ended December 31, 1986, Conn-Fuse Company, a maker of electrical connectors and fuses, had $75,000 of cash provided by operations. Depreciation expense for the year was $7,500 and the company incurred a loss of $1,000 on the sale of equipment. The cash flow statement prepared for management reported total uses of funds of $245,860. Following are data on the company's current asset and liability account balances:

	12/31/1986	12/31/1985
Cash	$36,800	$33,940
Accounts receivable	49,000	40,000
Merchandise	63,000	64,500
Prepaid expenses	19,460	19,460
Accounts payable	59,800	56,800
Accrued expenses	37,500	40,500
Taxes payable	29,750	29,750

Required: Calculate the company's net income for 1986, and the amount of cash provided from sources other than operations.

Ex. 20-8 **Cash collection and payments.** Slinger Company's fee revenue amounted to $28,000 in 1985. Salary expenses were $18,600, and supplies expenses were $1,700. Working capital balances were as follows:

	Beginning	Ending
Cash	$1,250	$1,760
Accounts receivable	2,150	2,830
Supplies	890	780
Accounts payable	1,180	1,050
Salaries	1,340	1,560

Required:

a. Calculate the amount of cash collected from clients in 1986.

b. Calculate the amount of cash paid for salaries and supplies in 1986, assuming that all accounts payable are owed for supplies.

Ex. 20-9 Interpretation of statement of changes. Examine carefully the following statement of changes:

Corion Company
Statement of Changes in Financial Position
For the Year Ended December 31, 1985

Sources of Funds		
From operations:		
Net loss	$(3,000)	
Add depreciation expense	12,000	
Add loss on sale of fixed assets	2,000	
Total		$ 11,000
Other sources:		
New 2-year note payable		15,000
Sale of land		30,000
Sale of equipment		10,000
Change in funds		9,000
Total sources		$ 75,000
Uses of Funds		
Repayment of mortgage		$ 40,000
Payment of dividends		8,000
Purchase of new equipment		27,000
Total uses		$ 75,000
Changes in Funds		
Cash decrease		$(23,000)
Accounts receivable increase		8,000
Merchandise increase		16,000
Accounts payable increase		(15,000)
Notes payable decrease		5,000
Change in funds		$ (9,000)

Required:

a. What is the definition of funds? Explain.
b. Did funds increase or decrease and by how much?
c. What was the company's main source of funds?
d. Explain how operations produced $11,000 of funds when the company operated at a loss.
e. What was the company's main use of funds?
f. What problems do you perceive with the composition of liabilities? The composition of working capital? The company's ability to generate funds in the future?
g. Discuss the soundness of the decision to pay a dividend.

Ex. 20-10 **Interpretation of funds from operations.** Examine the following schedule prepared by Knubble Corporation:

Knubble Corporation
Schedule of Funds Provided by Operations
For the Year Ended July 31, 1986

Sales		$32,760	
Add decrease in notes receivable		1,000	
Less increase in accounts receivable		(626)	
Inflows from operating revenues			$33,134
Cost of goods sold	$18,588		
Less decrease in merchandise	(212)		
Add decrease in trade payables	81	18,457	
Wages and salaries	5,284		
Less increase in wages payable	(12)	5,272	
Administrative expenses	3,066		
Add increase in prepaid expenses	11	3,077	
Property taxes		428	
Interest expense	532		
Add bond premium amortization	20	552	
Outflows for operating expenses			27,786
From operations			5,348
Rent income		207	
Add increase in unearned rent		3	210
Total			5,558
Federal income tax		1,330	
Less increase in deferred tax		50	1,280
Funds from operations			$ 4,278

Required:

a. What is the definition of funds?
b. What amount was reported as gross margin on the income statement?
c. How much rent was collected during the year?
d. How much rent was actually earned during the year?
e. How much cash was collected from customers?
f. As a result of changes in merchandise, did working capital increase or decrease and by what amount?
g. How much tax had to be paid to the federal government on the year's income?
h. What was the amount of tax expense reported on the income statement?

Ex. 20-11 **Working papers with funds defined as working capital.** Following are account balances of Simplitica Company, which reported $10,000 of net income for the year ended June 30, 1986:

	1986	1985
Cash	$ 7,200	$ 5,500
Accounts receivable	5,300	6,000
Equipment	59,000	54,000
Accumulated depreciation	(11,500)	(10,500)
Total assets	$60,000	$55,000
Accounts payable	$ 6,000	$ 7,800
Long-term debt	20,000	17,200
Capital	34,000	30,000
Total equities	$60,000	$55,000

During the fiscal year, the owner withdrew $6,000 from the business.

Required: Set up working papers for the preparation of a statement of changes in financial position with funds defined as working capital and complete the working papers.

Ex. 20-12 **Working papers with funds defined as cash.** Refer to the data for Simplitica Company in Exercise 20-11.

Required: Set up working papers for the preparation of a statement of changes in financial position with funds defined as cash and complete the working papers.

Ex. 20-13 **Interpretation of statement of changes.** Examine the following statement prepared by Faron Company's new treasurer.

Faron Company
Statement of Changes in Financial Position
December 31, 1986

Sources:	
Net income from income statement	$ 3,000
Accounts receivable decrease	6,000
Merchandise increase	(9,000)
Accounts payable increase	2,000
Depreciation	7,000
Total	9,000
Cost of land sold at loss of $4,000	24,000
New 3-year note payable	10,000
Change in funds	8,000
Total	$51,000
Uses:	
Debt	$30,000
Equipment	12,000
Dividends	9,000
Total	$51,000

Required:

a. Does the statement present information adequately? Explain.
b. What is the definition of funds? Explain.
c. Did funds increase or decrease and by how much?
d. What was the company's main source of funds?
e. What amount of funds was actually provided by the sale of land? Where should the loss on the sale appear?
f. What amount of funds was actually provided by operations? Explain how funds from operation can be so much greater than net income?
g. Does the statement indicate that current assets are becoming more or less liquid? Explain.
h. What was the main use of funds?
i. Does the decision to pay dividends appear to be sound?
j. Does the statement indicate the presence of potential problems for the company? Explain.

Ex. 20-14 **Recasting a statement of changes.** Examine the statement of changes in financial position presented in Exercise 20-13 and note any deficiencies in the presentation.

Required: Recast the statement in its proper form assuming it covers a 1-year period.

Ex. 20-15 **Interpreting a funds flow worksheet.** The controller of Elmer Corporation prepared the following worksheet on December 31, 1986:

	Beginning Balance	Changes		Ending Balance
		dr	cr	
Debits:				
Working capital	$ 200	g. 20		$ 220
Fixed assets	2,800	f. 581	b. 35	3,346
Long-term investments	1,500			1,500
Totals	$4,500			$5,066
Credits:				
Accumulated depreciation	400		c. 23	423
Long-term debt	1,000			1,000
Common stock	2,000		d. 400	2,400
Retained earnings	1,100	e. 17	a. 160	1,243
Totals	$4,500	618	618	$5,066
Sources and uses of funds:				
Net income		a. 160		
Gain on sale of fixed assets			b. 5	
Depreciation		c. 23		
Sales of fixed assets		b. 40		
Common stock issued		d. 400		
Dividends			e. 17	
Fixed assets acquired			f. 581	
Change in working capital			g. 20	
Totals		623	623	

Required:

a. What definition of funds is used in this worksheet? Explain.
b. Is it possible to determine the cost of the sold assets from the above data? Is it possible to determine the book value? Explain.
c. Did funds increase or decrease and by how much?
d. What was the amount of funds provided by operations?

Ex. 20-16 **Use of funds flow worksheet.** Refer to the worksheet of Elmer Corporation presented in Exercise 20-15.

Required: Use the data in the worksheet to prepare a statement of changes in financial position with funds defined as working capital. Omit the schedule of working capital changes.

Ex. 20-17 **Interpretation of funds flow worksheet.** Bleekey Company's internal auditor prepared the following worksheet on June 30, 1986:

	Beginning Balance	Changes		Ending Balance
		dr	cr	
Debits				
Cash	$ 1,200	m. 48		$ 1,248
Accounts receivable	1,900		a. 73	1,827
Merchandise	2,300	b. 105		2,405
Fixed assets	5,900	j. 332	c. 170	6,062
Patents	1,600		f. 10	1,590
Total debits	12,900			13,132
Credits				
Accumulated depreciation	1,800		d. 72	1,872
Accounts payable	1,600		e. 30	1,630
Long-term debt (net)	2,500	l. 150	g. 5	2,355
Preferred stock	2,300	i. 300		2,000
Common stock	3,000		h. 400	3,400
Retained earnings	1,700	k. 40	x. 215	1,875
Total credits	12,900	975	975	13,132
Sources of funds				
Net income		x. 215		
Accounts receivable		a. 73		
Merchandise			b. 105	
Gain on sale of land			c. 5	
Depreciation		d. 72		
Accounts payable		e. 30		
Amortization of patents		f. 10		
Bond discount		g. 5		
Land		c. 175		
Common stock		h. 400		
Uses of funds				
Preferred stock			i. 300	
Equipment			j. 332	
Dividends			k. 40	
Bonds			l. 150	
Cash			m. 48	
Totals		980	980	

Required:

a. What definition of funds is used in this worksheet? Explain.
b. What was the cost of the land that was sold? What was the selling price? Explain.
c. Which stock was retired, and which stock was issued during the period? Explain.
d. Was the amount of interest expense reported on the income statement greater or smaller than the amount actually paid to bond holders? Explain.
e. Calculate the change in working capital.

Ex. 20-18 **Use of funds flow worksheet.** Examine the worksheet presented for Bleekey Company in Exercise 20-17

Required: Use the data in the worksheet to prepare a statement of changes in financial position with funds defined as cash.

Ex. 20-19 **Change of funds definition.** Examine the worksheet presented for Bleekey Company in Exercise 20-17, which is prepared with funds defined as cash.

Required: Use the data in the worksheet to prepare a statement of changes in financial position but with funds defined as working capital.

PROBLEMS

P. 20-1 **Working capital basis statement of changes.** Comparative financial statements of Mars Company are provided below. Net income for the year was $3,980, and the company declared and paid $5,000 of dividends.

Mars Company
Comparative Balance Sheets
December 31, 1986 and 1985

	1986	1985
Assets:		
Cash	$ 680	$ 500
Accounts receivable	1,440	1,250
Merchandise	2,070	2,130
Land	7,700	5,600
Buildings	15,200	15,200
Accumulated depreciation	(5,300)	(4,100)
Total assets	$21,790	$20,580
Equities:		
Accounts payable	$ 1,160	$ 930
Bonds payable, due 1999	10,000	8,000
Common stock	5,000	5,000
Retained earnings	5,630	6,650
Total equities	$21,790	$20,580

Required: Prepare a statement of changes in financial position for the company with funds defined as working capital.

P. 20-2 Cash basis statement of changes. Use the data in Problem 20-1 to prepare a statement of changes in financial position for Mars Company with funds defined as cash.

P. 20-3 Interpreting a statement of changes. Examine the partial statement of changes shown below, as taken from the annual report of Jojoba Industries.

Jojoba Industries
Statement of Changes in Financial Position
For the Year Ended December 31, 1986

Sources of Funds		
From operations:		
Net income	$28,000	
Add depreciation	3,200	
Loss on sale of land	1,000	
Less increase in deferred tax	(500)	$31,700
Other sources:		
Issuance of bonds		10,000
Sale of land		19,000
Total sources		$60,700
Uses of Funds		
Payment of dividends		$15,000
Acquisition of plant		22,400
Retirement of preferred stock		18,500
Change in funds		4,800
Total uses		$60,700

Required:

a. What is the definition of funds?
b. Did funds increase or decrease and by how much?
c. What was the book value of the sold land?
d. What was the change in retained earnings?
e. Was the amount of tax expense more or less than the tax liability, and by how much?
f. Was the deferred tax account debited or credited, and by how much?
g. Was the preferred stock account debited or credited, and by how much?

P. 20-4 Recasting a statement of changes. The following statement was prepared by Burble Company on December 31, 1986:

Burble Company
Funds Flow Statement
For the Year 1986

Funds provided:		
Net income		$26,860
Depreciation		1,530
Amortization		600
Accounts receivable decrease		120
Accounts payable increase		150
Bond discount amortization		90
Sale of land		1,880
Sale of investments		1,090
Sale of stock		4,000
Total		$36,320
Funds applied:		
Dividends		$15,000
Merchandise increase		430
Notes payable, current, decrease		200
Gain on sale of land	$480	
Less loss on sale of investments	210	270
New buildings		16,100
New equipment		4,100
Change in cash		220
Total		$36,320

Required: Recast the above statement, using proper accounting terminology and form, with funds defined as working capital.

P. 20-5 Recasting a statement of changes. Refer to the statement provided by Burble Company in Problem 20-4.

Required: Recast the statement, using proper accounting terminology and form, with funds defined as cash.

P. 20-6 **Interpreting a statement of changes.** Examine the statement below from the annual report of Nikita Corporation.

Nikita Corporation
Statement of Changes in Financial Position
For the Year Ended December 31, 1986

Sources of funds		
From operations:		
Net income	$120,000	
Add depreciation	84,000	
Amortization of patents	36,000	
Increase in accounts payable	26,400	
Decrease in inventories	33,600	
Loss on sale of investments	28,800	
Less increase in accounts receivable	(10,800)	
Decrease in wages payable	(7,200)	
Gain on sale of equipment	(18,000)	$ 292,800
Other sources:		
Sale of equipment		696,000
Sale of investments		120,000
Issuance of stock		360,000
Total sources of funds		$1,468,800
Uses of funds		
Payment of dividends		$ 540,000
Retirement of bonds		780,000
Building improvements		132,000
Change in funds		16,800
Total uses of funds		$1,468,800

Required:

a. What definition of funds was used to prepare the statement?
b. What was the major source of funds?
c. Did funds increase or decrease and by how much?
d. What was the book value of the sold equipment?
e. What was the book value of the sold investment?
f. What was the book value of the retired bonds?
g. How much cash was required to retire bonds?
h. Discuss the source of funds provided by operations.
i. Assess the soundness of the dividend.
j. Do you perceive any problems with this company? Explain.
k. Prepare the schedule missing from the statement.

P. 20-7 **Funds defined as working capital.** The comparative financial statements of Venus Corporation are presented below. During 1986 the company issued new shares of its common stock in exchange for new equipment. The company declared and paid $16,140 in cash dividends in 1986.

Venus Corporation
Comparative Balance Sheets
December 31, 1986 and 1985

	1986	1985
Assets:		
Cash	$ 1,120	$ 900
Accounts receivable	2,710	2,830
Merchandise	5,180	4,750
Long-term investments	7,700	9,000
Land	6,000	7,400
Buildings	27,800	21,600
Equipment	21,340	17,340
Accumulated depreciation	(10,890)	(9,360)
Patents	5,000	5,600
Total	$65,960	$60,060
Equities:		
Notes payable	$ 1,800	$ 2,000
Accounts payable	2,310	2,160
Bonds payable	30,000	30,000
Discount on bonds payable	(660)	(750)
Common stock	14,000	10,000
Retained earnings	18,510	16,650
Total	$65,960	$60,060

Venus Corporation
Comparative Income Statements
For the Years Ended December 31, 1986 and 1985

	1986	1985
Sales	$82,520	$77,740
Gain on sale of land	480	
Total revenues	83,000	77,740
Expenses:		
Administrative	18,400	18,980
Salaries and wages	21,660	20,900
Depreciation of fixed assets	1,530	1,420
Amortization of patents	600	600
Loss on sale of investments	210	
Interest expense	4,000	3,840
Income taxes	18,600	15,400
Total expenses	65,000	61,140
Net income	$18,000	$16,600

Required: Prepare a statement of changes in financial position for the company with funds defined as working capital.

P. 20-8 Funds defined as cash. The comparative financial statements of Venus Corporation and other data on the company's operations are presented in Problem 20-7.

Required: Prepare a statement of changes in financial position for the company with funds defined as cash.

P. 20-9 Statement of changes. Below are the changes in account balances taken from the December 31, 1985 and 1986, balance sheets of Cusip Company.

	Changes dr (cr)
Cash	$ (560)
Accounts receivable	240
Merchandise	(860)
Land	(12,000)
Buildings	4,000
Equipment	7,550
Accumulated depreciation	(7,000)
Patents	900
Notes payable	(400)
Accounts payable	300
Mortgage payable	3,500
Bonds payable	(5,000)
Premium on bonds payable	180
Common stock	0
Retained earnings	9,150
	$ 0

The income statement reported $7,000 depreciation expense, $500 amortization of patent, a loss of $2,000 on the sale of land, and a net loss of $8,700 for the year ending December 31, 1986. Dividends in the amount of $450 were declared and paid in 1986.

Required: Prepare a statement of changes in financial position for Cusip Company with funds defined as working capital.

P. 20-10 Statement of changes. Use the data in Problem 20-9 to prepare a statement of changes in financial position for Cusip Company with funds defined as cash.

P. 20-11 Funds defined as working capital. The financial statements of Saturn Corporation are presented below. During the year, the company sold a parcel of land that had a cost of $2,000. It also sold equipment with a book value of $400 and a cost of $490 for $300 cash. In 1986 the company declared cash dividends of $358.

Saturn Corporation
Comparative Balance Sheets
December 31, 1986 and 1985

	1986	1985	Changes dr (cr)
Assets:			
Cash	$ 1,586	$ 2,064	(478)
Accounts receivable (net)	3,676	2,980	696
Merchandise inventory	1,688	1,960	(272)
Prepaid expenses	149	138	11
Property plant and equipment	29,582	26,670	2,912
Accumulated depreciation	(10,710)	(9,870)	(840)
Total assets	$25,971	$23,942	
Liabilities and capital:			
Notes payable	$ 990	$ 919	(71)
Accounts payable	2,147	2,190	43
Dividends payable	37	28	(9)
Bonds payable	5,000	3,000	(2,000)
Mortgage note payable	3,000	3,500	500
Common stock	8,000	8,000	
Retained earnings	7,797	6,305	(1,492)
Treasury stock	(1,000)		1,000
Total liabilities and capital	$25,971	$23,942	0

Saturn Corporation
Income Statement
For the Year Ended December 31, 1986

Sales		$39,290
Less expenses:		
Cost of goods sold	$25,347	
Selling and administrative	5,360	
Wages and salaries	4,025	
Depreciation	930	
Interest	520	36,182
Operating income		3,108
Gain on sale of land	72	
Loss on sale of equipment	(100)	(28)
Income before tax		3,080
Federal income tax		1,230
Net income		$ 1,850

Required: Prepare a statement of changes in financial position, working capital basis for Saturn Corporation for 1986.

P. 20-12 **Funds defined as cash.** The comparative balance sheets and the 1986 income statement of Saturn Corporation are presented in Problem 20-11, together with additional data on the company's operations.

Required: Prepare a statement of changes in financial position with funds defined as cash.

P. 20-13 **Statement of changes in financial position.** The 1986 financial statements of Pluto Corporation are provided below. The following information is also available:

a. The company declared and paid a cash dividend of $1,250 during 1986.
b. In June 1986, the company issued 100 shares of common stock at $37.50 per share.
c. During the year, the company sold land and building for $1,960. The land was carried at a cost of $630. The building was carried at a cost of $1,800 and a book value of $1,250.

Pluto Corporation
Income Statement
For the Year Ended December 31, 1986

Sales		$49,140
Less cost of goods sold:		
Beginning inventory	$ 2,250	
Purchases	29,150	
Goods available for sale	31,400	
Less ending inventory	1,930	
Cost of goods sold		29,470
Gross margin		19,670
Less expenses:		
Wages and salaries	7,920	
Selling and administrative	4,590	
Depreciation	1,260	
Property taxes	640	
Interest expense	790	15,200
Income from operations		4,470
Other income and expenses:		
Rent income	310	
Gain on sale of fixed assets	80	
Loss on sale of investments	(60)	330
Income before tax		4,800
Federal income tax		2,000
Net income		$ 2,800

Pluto Corporation
Comparative Balance Sheets
December 31, 1986 and 1985

	1986	1985	Changes dr (cr)
Assets			
Current assets:			
Cash	$ 2,070	$ 1,290	780
Notes receivable	300	1,800	(1,500)
Accounts receivable (net)	3,300	2,370	930
Merchandise	1,930	2,250	(320)
Prepaid expenses	70	50	20
Total current assets	7,670	7,760	
Fixed assets:			
Land	2,220	2,850	(630)
Plant and equipment	43,650	37,150	6,500
Accumulated depreciation	(15,510)	(14,800)	(710)
Total fixed assets	30,360	25,200	
Investments:			
Sinking fund	2,470	2,100	370
Common stock of subsidiaries	600	690	(90)
Total investments	3,070	2,790	
Total assets	$41,100	$35,750	
Liabilities and Capital			
Current liabilities:			
Notes payable	$ 750	$ 600	(150)
Accounts payable	1,790	1,920	130
Wages and salaries payable	460	440	(20)
Unearned rent income		30	30
Total current liabilities	3,000	2,990	
Long-term liabilities:			
Bond payable	9,750	9,750	
Premium on bonds payable	300	330	30
Deferred income taxes	1,420	1,350	(70)
Total long-term liabilities	11,470	11,430	
Total liabilities	14,470	14,420	
Capital:			
Common stock $15 par	13,500	12,000	(1,500)
Paid-in capital in excess of par	6,600	4,350	(2,250)
Retained earnings	6,530	4,980	(1,550)
Total capital	26,630	21,330	
Total liabilities and capital	$41,100	$35,750	

Required: Prepare a statement of changes in financial position for Pluto Corporation with funds defined as working capital.

P. 20-14 Statement of changes in financial position. The 1985 financial statements of Pluto Corporation and additional data on the company's operations are provided in Problem 20-13.

Required: Prepare a statement of changes in financial position with funds defined as cash.

CASES

Case 20-1 Reconstruction of lost records. Mr. Simkins has been waiting anxiously for the financial statements of Nebula Corporation, which he must present tomorrow to the board of directors of his company, Galaxie Enterprises. Galaxie has been negotiating for the acquisition of Nebula, and the statements are needed to support the company's offer to purchase the outstanding stock. Simkins is therefore relieved when he opens his mail and finds Nebula Corporation's materials. The enclosed letter states in part:

> You will be pleased to know that we completed the addition to our building for which the contractor agreed to accept 100 shares of our common stock as payment. In addition we were able to dispose of old equipment costing $3,000 permitting us to replace it with more modern equipment, putting us into a much better competitive position.

On close examination of the reports, Simkins notes with dismay that the balance sheet and retained earnings statements had been inadvertently omitted from the materials. He quickly reports the problem to his superior, Mrs. Brooks, and points out that it is not possible to obtain the missing reports in the time remaining before the board meeting.

"No problem," says Mrs. Brooks. "We have their annual report from last year." Going to a file, she retrieves the annual report which includes the 1985 balance sheet. "Here you are. You can use this balance sheet and the material you have to reconstruct the 1986 balance sheet. Any minor discrepancies will not matter for the purposes of this board meeting."

Simkins takes the annual report, returns to his office, and begins to review the following information in order to derive the missing report:

Nebula Corporation
Balance Sheet
December 31, 1985

Assets	
Cash	$10,280
Notes receivable	4,800
Accounts receivable (net)	2,370
Merchandise	2,050
Prepaid expenses	150
Land	12,000
Plant and equipment	42,150
Accumulated depreciation	(11,800)
Common stock of subsidiary	4,000
Total assets	$66,000
Liabilities and Capital	
Notes payable	$ 900
Accounts payable	6,050
Wages and salaries payable	240
Bond payable	18,000
Discount on bonds payable	(550)
Deferred income taxes	1,150
Common stock $30 par	10,000
Paid-in capital in excess of par	20,000
Retained earnings	10,210
Total liabilities and capital	$66,000

Nebula Corporation
Income Statement
For the Year Ended December 31, 1986

Sales		$90,380
Income from subsidiary carried at equity		800
Gain on sale of fixed assets		400
Total revenues		91,580
Less expenses:		
Cost of goods sold	$39,400	
Wages and salaries	19,550	
Selling and administrative	14,590	
Depreciation	4,720	
Interest expense	1,350	
Federal income tax	5,000	84,610
Net income		$ 6,970

Nebula Corporation
Statement of Changes in Financial Position
For the Year Ended December 31, 1986

Sources of working capital		
From operations:		
Net income		$ 6,970
Add depreciation	$ 4,720	
Bond discount amortization	50	
Increase in deferred tax	470	
Less gain on sale of fixed assets	(400)	
Income from subsidiary	(800)	4,040
Working capital provided by operations		11,010
Other sources:		
Stock issued in exchange for building addition		9,000
Sale of fixed assets		2,400
Total sources		$22,410
Uses of working capital		
Payment of dividends		2,800
Building construction financed by stock issuance		9,000
Purchase of fixed assets		5,500
Retirement of bonds payable		4,000
Increase in working capital		1,110
Total uses		$22,410
	Increase	**Decrease**
Changes in working capital		
Decrease in cash		$ 8,210
Increase in notes receivable	$ 1,200	
Increase in accounts receivable	2,930	
Increase in merchandise	3,880	
Increase in prepaid expenses	1,120	
Increase in notes payable		850
Decrease in accounts payable	1,260	
Increase in wages and salaries payable		220
	10,390	9,280
Increase in working capital		1,110
	$10,390	$10,390

After several attempts at reconstructing the 1986 balance sheet, Mr. Simkins realizes that he is hopelessly lost. He therefore comes to you and asks you to do the job.

Required: Use the available data to construct the December 31, 1986 balance sheet for Nebula Corporation.

Case 20-2 **(AICPA) Statement of changes.** Presented below are comparative statements of financial position of Kenwood Corporation as of December 31, 1986, and December 31, 1985, respectively and the company's income statement.

Kenwood Corporation
Statement of Financial Position

	December 31, 1986	December 31, 1985	Increase (Decrease)
Assets			
Current assets:			
Cash	$ 100,000	$ 90,000	$ 10,000
Accounts receivable (net)	210,000	140,000	70,000
Inventories	260,000	220,000	40,000
Total current assets	570,000	450,000	120,000
Land	325,000	200,000	125,000
Plant and equipment	580,000	633,000	(53,000)
Less accumulated depreciation	(90,000)	(100,000)	10,000
Patents	30,000	33,000	(3,000)
Total assets	$1,415,000	$1,216,000	$199,000
Liabilities and Shareholders' Equity			
Current liabilities:			
Accounts payable	$ 260,000	$ 200,000	$ 60,000
Accrued expenses	200,000	210,000	(10,000)
Total current liabilities	460,000	410,000	50,000
Deferred income taxes	140,000	100,000	40,000
Long-term bonds (due 1990)	130,000	168,000	(38,000)
Total liabilities	730,000	678,000	52,000
Shareholders' equity:			
Common stock, par value $5	250,000	210,000	40,000
Additional paid-in capital	233,000	170,000	63,000
Retained earnings	202,000	158,000	44,000
Total shareholders' equity	685,000	538,000	147,000
Total liabilities and shareholders' equity	$1,415,000	$1,216,000	$199,000

Kenwood Corporation
Income Statement
For the Year Ended December 31, 1986

Sales	$1,000,000
Expenses:	
Cost of sales	560,000
Salary and wages	190,000
Depreciation	20,000
Amortization	3,000
Loss on sale of equipment	4,000
Interest	16,000
Miscellaneous	8,000
Total expenses	801,000
Income before income taxes	199,000
Income taxes	
Current	50,000
Deferred	40,000
Provision for income taxes	90,000
Net income	$ 109,000
Earnings per share:	$2.21

Additional information:

- On February 2, 1986, Kenwood issued a 10 percent stock dividend to shareholders of record on January 15, 1986. The market price per share of the common stock on February 2 was $15.
- On March 1, Kenwood issued 3,800 shares of common stock for land. The common stock and land had current market values of approximately $40,000 on March 1.
- On April 15, Kenwood repurchased long-term bonds with a face value of $38,000 with no gain or loss.
- On June 30, Kenwood sold equipment costing $53,000, with a book value of $23,000, for $19,000 cash.
- On September 30, Kenwood declared and paid a $.04 per share cash dividend to shareholders of record August 1.
- On October 10, Kenwood purchased land for $85,000 cash.
- Deferred income taxes represent timing differences due to the use of ACRS depreciation for income tax reporting and straight-line depreciation for financial statement reporting.

Required: Using the working capital concept of funds, prepare a statement of changes in financial position of Kenwood Corporation for the year ended December 31, 1986. (Do not prepare a schedule of changes in working capital.)

Appendix A Basic Financial Accounting Concepts and the Accounting Cycle

Financial accounting is the process of identifying, collecting, classifying, recording, summarizing, and reporting information about events and transactions that affect a business organization. The information is reported in terms of dollars using **generally accepted accounting principles** (GAAP) that govern the measurement of income and financial position. Income and financial position are reported at the end of each **accounting period** in the form of an **income statement** and a **balance sheet.**

Accountants are able to provide relevant and accurate financial information by maintaining a concise and logical framework for identifying, recording, analyzing, and reporting an entity's financial activities. This framework is the **double-entry accounting system;** the processing of data in the system and the reporting of financial information summarized from the data are known as the **accounting cycle,** which is a series of logical, systematic procedures that include:

1. Identifying financial events and transactions and collecting data on them in **source documents**
2. Analyzing the transaction so that it can be recorded (journalized) in the accounting record known as the **journal**
3. Transferring the information in journal entries, by a process called **posting,** to individual **accounts** in the accounting record known as the **ledger**
4. **Adjusting** the account balances at the end of the accounting period to ensure that all events and transactions are reflected correctly
5. Using the correct account balances to prepare **financial statements,** such as the balance sheet and income statement
6. **Closing** the books at the end of the accounting period to prepare them for recording transactions in the next period

In this appendix we summarize briefly the accounting cycle concepts and procedures that result in financial reports of an **accounting entity** such as a corporation, a partnership, or an individual.

Events or transactions that can be measured in terms of money are recorded in the double-entry accounting system to reflect their effect on the accounting equation. The basic accounting equation is

$$\text{Assets} = \text{Liabilities} + \text{Owners' equity}$$

where liabilities and owners' equity together are known simply as **equities,** and **owners' equity** is also known as **capital.** When a transaction takes place, it has a dual effect on the accounting equation because the equation is always in balance and the equality of assets and equities cannot be violated. The dual aspect of transactions is recorded in the books of account consisting of a journal and a ledger. The **journal** is a chronological diary of transactions, and the **ledger** is a collection of individual accounts summarizing the effect of transactions on assets and equities.

THE DOUBLE-ENTRY ACCOUNTING SYSTEM

The double-entry accounting system consists of specific rules and procedures for recording financial events in the books of account. These rules and procedures enable the accounting records to accumulate information in a systematic manner so that it can be summarized periodically and reported in the financial statements. In order for the accounting system to represent the accounting equation, financial data are recorded in the accounts in a specific manner. Increases in assets are recorded on the left, or **debit,** side of an account and decreases are recorded on the right, or **credit,** side of the account. Conversely, increases in liabilities and capital are recorded as credits and decreases are recorded as debits. In this way, the accounting equation, Assets = Equities, remains in balance and also the debit balances of asset accounts equal the credit balances of equity accounts.

Assets = **Equities**

Asset Accounts		**Liability Accounts**		**Capital Accounts**	
Debit	Credit	Debit	Credit	Debit	Credit
+	−	−	+	−	+
Increase	Decrease	Decrease	Increase	Decrease	Increase

Total debits = **Total credits**

An account is maintained for each type of asset a company has, such as cash, land, and equipment, and for each type of equity, such as notes payable to banks, lease obligations, and common stock. Each time a financial transaction occurs, the balances in the accounts change, but the accounting equation remains in balance and the dollar amount of debits in the accounts equals the dollar amount of credits.

For example, if the owners of the business invest $5,000, the Cash account is debited because it increases, and the Capital account is credited because it increases. If $2,000 of the cash is used to buy equipment, the decrease in the Cash account is recorded with a credit, and the increase in the Equipment account is recorded with a debit.

Capital accounts change in two ways: One is by owners investing in the business, and the other is by business operations, which typically means selling goods or services for a profit. The major objective of most businesses is to increase capital by earning a satisfactory profit for their owners. Accountants measure the economic consequences of business transactions to determine their effect on owners' equity and on financial position. Many of the transactions that a business undertakes result in changes in capital. When a company performs a service or sells merchandise, it earns **revenue,** which increases capital. When a company purchases services or uses up assets, it incurs **expenses,** which decrease capital. The difference between revenues and expenses, called **income,** changes the balance of the capital accounts.

In order to obtain information about the operations that enable a company to earn income, a business needs detailed information on events that cause increases and decreases in capital. Therefore increases in capital that occur as a result of operations are recorded as revenues and decreases are recorded as expenses. Revenue and expense accounts are **temporary accounts,** which are subdivisions of the Capital account. Instead of various expenses being recorded as debits in the Capital account, they are recorded as debits in individual expense accounts. Similarly, revenues are recorded as credits in various revenue accounts rather than as credits in the Capital account. The temporary account balances are reported in the income statement at the end of the accounting period. In contrast, the asset, liability, and capital accounts are called **permanent accounts,** and their balances are reported in the balance sheet at the end of the accounting period.

If the business is a corporation, it must separate amounts contributed by shareholders in exchange for stock from amounts earned by operating the business. Contributions of shareholders are recorded in capital accounts such as **Common Stock** and **Preferred Stock**; income that is earned is recorded in a capital account called **Retained Earnings.** Revenues and expenses are therefore temporary subdivisions of the Retained Earnings account. At the end of the accounting period, the balances of temporary accounts are transferred to the Retained Earnings account prior to preparing the financial statements in order to be ready to start the next accounting cycle.

Recording Transactions

When a transaction takes place, it is analyzed to determine its effect on asset, liability, capital, revenue, and expense accounts. Then the transaction is recorded in the **journal,** identifying the date of the transaction, the accounts affected, and the amounts to be debited and credited. The journal thus accumulates a chronological record of all financial transactions, with each one fully described. Information in the journal is **posted** to individual accounts in the **general ledger.** Each ledger account accumulates information from the journal that affects that account only.

We illustrate the accounting process with the operations of Overton Company, which was formed on May 1 by issuing common stock to investors. Figure A-1 illustrates the journalizing and posting process for some of the company's transactions. The first transaction in the journal illustrates the receipt of cash and land in exchange for common stock. The Cash account and the Land account are debited, and the Common Stock account is credited. In the second transaction, the purchase of equipment is recorded by a debit, and the payment of cash for the equipment is recorded by a credit. In the third transaction a patent is obtained by incurring a liability, which is recorded as a note payable. You can see how the first entry has been posted in the three ledger accounts.

Similar transactions result in revenues and expenses that affect owners' equity. When the company provides services to customers, the following journal entry is recorded:

May 13	Accounts receivable	8,800	
	Cash	3,200	
	Service revenue		12,000
	Performed services for cash and		
	on open account.		

The revenue is recorded at the time it is earned although some of the cash will be collected later. In this way income is measured in the period in which services are performed. In order to operate the business and perform services, expenses must be incurred. The company pays salaries to employees, uses electric and utility services, uses supplies or materials, and pays rent.

May 14	Salary expense	2,400	
	Cash		2,400
	Paid biweekly salary.		
14	Prepaid rent	1,200	
	Cash		1,200
	Paid rent for 3 months in advance.		

Figure A-1 The general journal, showing entries posted to the general ledger.

General Journal

Page 1

Date		Ref	Debit	Credit
5/1	Cash	101	3,000	
	Land	131	5,000	
	Common stock	301		8,000
	Issued 4,000 shares capital			
	stock in exchange for cash			
	and 3 acres land.			
5/4	Equipment	134	360	
	Cash	101		360
	Purchased drill press			
	Check # 1219.			
5/12	Patents		2,000	
	Notes payable			2,000
	Purchased patent # 19427598			
	in exchange for 7%			
	6-month note.			

General Ledger

Acct # 101 Cash

Date		Ref	dr	Date		Ref	cr
5/1		1	3,000	5/4		1	350

Acct # 131 Land

Date		Ref	dr	Date		Ref	cr
5/1		1	5,000				

Acct # 301 Common Stock

Date		Ref	dr	Date		Ref	cr
				5/1		1	8,000

May 15	Office supplies expense	800	
	Accounts payable		800
	Acquired office supplies on open account.		
22	Utility expense	170	
	Cash		170
	Paid electric bill for May.		
25	Legal expenses	220	
	Accounts payable		220
	Received bill from attorney for drafting of contracts.		
26	Cash	250	
	Service revenue		250
	Received payment in advance for services to be performed later.		

Expenses are recorded in the period incurred, even if they are paid later. This way the expenses are matched with the revenues of the same period, resulting in a correct measure of income. The service revenue recorded on May 26 has not yet been earned. It will be earned later when the services are performed for the customer who made the advance payment. However, it is practical to record the receipt of cash as revenue if the company expects to perform the services in the current period.

Sometimes a business undertakes a transaction that increases or decreases owners' equity although the transaction is not part of the company's usual operations. Such changes in owners' equity are called **gains** or **losses.** In addition, a corporation may distribute some of its earnings to its shareholders in the form of dividends, thus reducing the balance in its Retained Earnings account. To illustrate such transactions, we show the sale of the company's patent and the distribution of a cash dividend to shareholders.

May 21	Cash	1,700	
	Notes receivable	1,200	
	Gain on sale of assets		900
	Patent		2,000
	Sold patent which was found unsuitable.		
26	Dividends	600	
	Cash		600
	Distributed cash dividend to shareholders.		

Many other transactions occur in the course of business that change the balances of asset, liability, and owners' equity accounts. Some examples are:

May 27	Cash	6,600	
	Accounts receivable		6,600
	Collected accounts from customers.		
28	Salary expense	2,600	
	Cash		2,600
	To record payroll for 2 weeks.		
30	Notes payable	2,000	
	Interest expense	7	
	Cash		2,007
	Early repayment of a 7% 6-month note		
	given in exchange for patent 18 days ago.		
	$\$2,000 \times .07 \times 18/360 = \$7$		

All of these transactions are posted in the ledger accounts. At the end of the accounting period, the ending balances of the accounts are used to prepare the income statement and the balance sheet. Before this can be done, however, a number of end-of-period procedures must be performed.

Trial Balance

To ensure that the dollar amounts of debits and credits are equal in the ledger, we prepare a **trial balance** by listing all the accounts, placing their balances in either the debit or credit column, and finding the totals of debits and credits.

The trial balance taken from the ledger of Overton Company on May 31 is shown in Figure A-2. Note that the balance of Retained Earnings is zero because all changes in this account were recorded in temporary revenue, expense, gains, and dividends accounts.

Before the account balances in the trial balance can be used to prepare financial statements, it is necessary to ensure that these balances are correct and that all transactions and events that occurred have been recorded. During the accounting period, most transactions are recorded from source documents. In some cases source documents are not available until after earnings or expenses occur. In a few cases, source documents are not prepared at all. Consequently, some events are not recorded by the end of the accounting period, and incorrect balances exist in some accounts. The incorrect balances occur because the passage of time causes changes in account balances that are not yet reflected in the records. At the end of each accounting period the accountant must examine the accounts and determine which ones need adjusting.

Overton Company
Trial Balance
May 31

	Debit	Credit
Cash	$ 5,413	
Notes receivable	1,200	
Accounts receivable	2,200	
Prepaid rent	1,200	
Land	5,000	
Equipment	360	
Accounts payable		$ 1,020
Common stock		8,000
Retained earnings		0
Dividends	600	
Service revenue		12,250
Gain on sale of assets		900
Salary expense	5,000	
Office supplies expense	800	
Utility expense	170	
Legal expense	220	
Interest expense	7	
Totals	$22,170	$22,170

Figure A-2
Trial balance prior to adjusting and closing the books.

ADJUSTING ENTRIES

Journal entries used to bring incorrect account balances to their correct amounts are called **adjusting entries.** Financial statements can be prepared only after all accounts have correct balances. The adjusting process is a crucial part of end-of-period procedures. It enables accountants to arrive at proper measures of income and financial position.

Basically there are five types of adjustments. Two are called accruals, two are called deferrals; and the remaining one consists of allocations.

ACCRUALS AND DEFERRALS

Accruals are adjustments that must be made for events that will require a future cash payment or receipt, but the payment or receipt has not yet occurred. **Deferrals** are adjustments that must be made for events that were recorded when a cash payment or receipt took place but at the end of the accounting period the resource was not used up or the revenue was not earned. Accruals and deferrals are timing concepts.

To **accrue** means to accumulate, or build up, as a result of the passage of time. For example, a note receivable accumulates, or accrues, interest even though the receipt of the interest may take place only when the note is collected. The earning of interest expense is continuous. To **defer** means to postpone, or leave until a later time. For example, a company may buy fuel oil to heat its plant. Heating the plant uses up the oil and is an expense. However, the company may buy the fuel in the summer and postpone, or defer, burning the oil until winter.

Accrual adjustments are required when:

1. Revenue is earned but not recorded because payment has not been received.
2. Expense is incurred but not recorded because payment has not been made.

Deferral adjustments depend on the way a payment or receipt is initially recorded. Such adjustments are required when:

3a. Payment is made and recorded as an asset, but some or all of the asset has expired, or

3b. Payment is made and recorded as an expense, but some or all of the resource acquired is not yet used.

4a. Payment is received and recorded as revenue, but all the revenue is not yet earned, or

4b. Payment is received and recorded as unearned revenue (a liability), but some or all of the revenue is earned.

Accrued Revenues (Receivables)

Earning is a flow process that occurs when effort is expended. If no payment takes place during the effort, revenue still accrues (accumulates). For example, a company performs a service. Until the bill is prepared and sent to the client, the revenue is not recorded because the source document does not exist. The company has nevertheless earned revenue and should recognize the existence of assets in the form of receivables by recording the asset and accruing the revenue.

Some revenues are earned merely with the passage of time. A company may invest some of its money in government bonds that pay interest every 6 months. The interest is earned continuously as long as the money is invested, although interest is received only every 6 months. The receipt of the interest does not always coincide with the end of the accounting period. If interest on bond investments has been earned but not received, it must be recorded and reported in the financial statements.

For example, on May 21, Overton Company sold its patent in exchange for \$1,700 cash and a \$1,200, 9 percent note receivable due in 60 days. By May 31, when the company's accounting period ends, the company has earned 10 days' interest income of \$3. Because the cash has not yet been received, however, the income is not yet recorded. To report income accurately, the company should record the interest income in the current period, even though the money will be received later. The following entry adjusts the accounts:

May 31	Interest receivable	3	
	Interest income		3
	To accrue interest on note receivable.		
	$1,200 × .09 × 10/360 = $3		

The interest receivable, often recorded as accrued interest receivable, is an asset that appears on the balance sheet. The credit to Interest Income increases the balance in the revenue account. After the adjusting entry is posted, the two accounts appear as follows:

Interest Receivable			
May 31	3		

Interest Income			
		May 31	3

Accrued Expenses (Payables)

There are many situations in which a company has received goods or services but has not yet paid for them. The firm therefore has a liability that is not yet recorded. For example, the firm's employees provide services to the company. Periodically the company pays for the services and records salary expense. If the end of the accounting period does not coincide with a payday, the company accrues (accumulates) the salary expenses since the last payday and recognizes the existence of its payroll obligation in the form of payables. The accrued employee salaries are an expense in the period in which the work is performed even though payment will not be made until the next accounting period.

For example, Overton Company has a policy of paying its employees every other Friday. It paid salaries on May 14 and May 28 as shown earlier. The next payment of salaries will normally take place on Friday, June 11, but the accounting period ends on May 31. The company receives the services of its employees from May 28 to May 31, and it should record these services as expenses even though it will pay for them in June. Otherwise, salary expense for the period will be incorrect. Assuming that salaries of $500 have been earned by employees since their last payday, the following adjusting entry is made:

May 31	Salary expense	500	
	Salaries payable		500
	To accrue payroll from May 28 to end		
	of month.		

The debit to Salary Expense increases the expense account so that the proper balance will appear on the income statement. The credit to Salaries

Payable, also commonly called accrued salaries, creates the liability account that will appear on the balance sheet. The fact that the cash outflow for these wages will occur later does not change the amount of services obtained during the current accounting period. After the adjustment is posted, the two accounts appear as follows:

Salaries Payable

Debit		Credit	
		May 31	500

Salary Expense

Debit		Credit
May 14	2,400	
28	2,600	
May 31	500	
Bal.	5,500	

Prepaid (Deferred) Expenses

An expenditure of money does not necessarily result in an expense. Often it results in the exchange of cash for another asset. The expense occurs when the asset is used. For example, when coal is burned, the using up of the coal stockpile is an expense; the company no longer has the coal available as a resource. But if the coal is not used in the current period, the company has an asset whose use is deferred to the next period; when the coal is used later, it will become an expense. The recognition of the expense is deferred (postponed) until a future period.

It is possible to record some transactions in more than one way; the method chosen depends on what is most suitable for a particular business. For example, Overton Company uses office supplies continuously in its operations. If most supplies are used shortly after they are acquired, it may be convenient to record the acquisition of supplies as an expense. Another business may record the purchase of office supplies as the acquisition of an asset called Supplies, a prepaid expense.

Whichever method is adopted, accounts must be adjusted at year-end if some of the supplies are used and some still remain on hand at the end of the year. To illustrate, office supplies costing $800 were purchased during the accounting period, and a physical count of the inventory disclosed that supplies costing $275 were on hand at the end of the period. This means that $525 of supplies have been used.

Purchase recorded as an expense. Overton Company recorded the purchase of office supplies as an expense. The entry, as shown earlier, was as follows:

May 15	Office supplies expense	800	
	Accounts payable		800
	Purchased office supplies on open		
	account.		

At the end of the period, the Office Supplies Expense account has a debit balance of $800. The correct balance at year-end in this account is $525. The remaining $275 of supplies on hand are an asset, not an expense of this period. The use of this asset is deferred until the next period. The following adjusting entry is needed:

May 31	Office supplies	275	
	Office supplies expense		275
	To adjust expense account based on		
	physical count of supplies on hand.		

The debit of $275 to Office Supplies creates a prepaid expense account, which appears in the May 31 balance sheet as an asset. The credit to the Office Supplies Expense account reduces the $800 balance of this account to the correct balance of $525. After the adjusting entry is posted, the two accounts appear as follows:

Office Supplies

May 31	275		

Office Supplies Expense

May 15	800	May 31	275
Bal.	525		

The asset account, Office Supplies, did not exist previously and is created with the adjusting entry so that this asset may appear in the balance sheet. The Office Supplies Expense account balance will be reported in the income statement. If the adjusting entry had not been made, assets would have been understated and expenses would have been overstated.

Purchase recorded as asset. Purchases of goods and services such as supplies and rent can also be recorded as prepaid expenses. Overton Company could have recorded the purchase of office supplies as the acquisition of an asset. In that case, the entry would have been:

May 15	Office supplies	800	
	Accounts payable		800
	Purchased office supplies on open		
	account.		

At the end of the accounting period, the physical count of office supplies shows that the Office Supplies account should have a debit balance of $275, the cost of the supplies still on hand. The necessary entry to adjust the account and record the supplies used as an expense is

May 31	Office supplies expense	525	
	Office supplies		525
	To adjust expense account based on		
	physical count of supplies on hand.		

Regardless of how the transaction was initially recorded, the ending balances of the Office Supplies account and the Office Supplies Expense account must report the amount of supplies on hand and the amount used. A similar adjustment must be made in the Prepaid Rent account. On May 14 Overton Company recorded the payment of 3 months' rent as an asset. The entry resulted in debiting the asset, Prepaid Rent, $1,200 for May, June, and July rent as follows:

May 14	Prepaid rent	1,200	
	Cash		1,200
	Paid rent for 3 months in advance.		

By the end of May, 1 month's rent had been used up and 2 months' rent is deferred and will provide future benefits. To adjust the Prepaid Rent account, it is necessary to remove from the account the rent expense that has been incurred. The entry is

May 31	Rent expense	400	
	Prepaid rent		400
	To reduce Prepaid Rent account and		
	record rent expense for May.		

The debit records the expense, and the credit reduces the asset account so that its proper balance will appear in the balance sheet. When the adjusting entry is posted, the two accounts appear as follows:

Prepaid Rent

May 14	1,200	May 31	400
Bal.	800		

Rent Expense

May 31	400		

Unearned (Deferred) Revenue

A company may collect money before it performs services, as happened with Overton Company on May 26. If a customer pays in advance for a service to be performed later, there is a resulting obligation to provide the service. The obligation may be recorded as a liability that will be discharged as time passes. The revenue will be earned in the future when the service is performed. However, the service may be performed very soon after the collection of advance payments. Therefore it may be more convenient to record the revenue when the cash is received, as Overton Company did, on the assumption that it will be earned before the end of the accounting period.

Receipt recorded as revenue. If the cash receipt is recorded as revenue, the Service Revenue account may contain some unearned revenue at the end of the accounting period. For example, Overton Company made the following two entries earlier:

May 13	Accounts receivable	8,800	
	Cash	3,200	
	Service revenue		12,000
	Performed services on open account.		
May 26	Cash	250	
	Service revenue		250
	Received payment in advance for		
	services to be performed later for		
	customer.		

As a result of these entries, the credit balance in the Service Revenue account is $12,250. On May 31 it is necessary to remove from the account any revenue that has been collected but not yet earned. If by the end of the month only $150 of services were performed for the customer who paid $250 in advance for services, the unearned portion must be removed from the revenue account with the following adjusting entry:

May 31	Service revenue	100	
	Unearned revenue		100
	To remove unearned receipt from		
	service revenue.		

The debit reduces the balance in the Service Revenue account to $12,150, which is the amount of revenue actually earned during the accounting period. The Unearned Revenue account represents an obligation that the company owes to its customer. This obligation is properly shown in the balance sheet as a liability. The two accounts appear as follows:

Unearned Revenue

		May 31	100

Service Revenue

May 31	100	May 14	12,000
		May 26	250
		Bal.	12,150

Receipt recorded as liability. In some cases it may be more appropriate to credit a liability account when advance payments are received and to record the revenue earned only at the end of the accounting period. For example, Overton Company could have made the following entry to record receipt of money in advance of performing a service:

May 26	Cash	250	
	Unearned revenue		250
	Received advance payment from		
	customer.		

By May 31, $150 of services have been performed for this customer, and part of the obligation has been discharged. However, the revenue has not been recorded, and the Unearned Revenue account is now overstated. The amount earned must be removed from the liability account and recorded as revenue. The entry is as follows:

May 31	Unearned revenue	150	
	Service revenue		150
	To record earned revenue		
	from services.		

The Service Revenue and Unearned Revenue accounts now have correct balances as shown below.

Unearned Revenue

May 31	150	May 26	250
		Bal.	100

Service Revenue

		May 14	12,000
		May 31	150
		Bal.	12,150

Note that the ending balances in the two accounts after adjustment are the same regardless of how the receipt of unearned revenue is originally recorded. This occurs because the accounting system reports economic facts no matter how the records are maintained. The economic facts are that the company has earned $12,150 of revenue by performing services, and it owes $100 of services to be performed in the next accounting period. If the financial statements are to be accurate, they must report these amounts. The liability account is a deferred revenue; that is, the earning of the revenue is postponed until the next accounting period although the receipt of cash for the future service has already occurred.

ALLOCATIONS

Allocation is the process of assigning costs and expenses to specific accounting periods. Two common examples are depreciation and uncollectible accounts. Adjustments requiring allocations are not specifically related to cash flows. Moreover, the amounts of such adjustments must be estimated and are not as precise as accruals and deferrals.

Depreciation

When a firm buys fixed assets such as buildings or machinery, it expects to use them for a number of accounting periods. The assets are expected to provide the firm with benefits, such as facilitating the earning process or generating revenues. Because the useful life of a fixed asset is longer than one accounting period, the entire cost of the asset should not be recorded as an expense of the period in which it is purchased. The entire cost is recorded as an asset at the time of purchase, whether or not all of it was paid in cash. To satisfy the matching principle, the company must spread the cost of the asset over its useful life and must allocate an appropriate portion of the cost to each period of the asset's life.

For example, Overton Company acquired equipment on May 4 for $360. The equipment is expected to last 5 years and will have no salvage value. Each month that the equipment is used, $1/60$ of its cost, or $6, may be recorded as an expense for that month. On May 31 the following adjusting entry is made:

May 31	Depreciation expense	6	
	Accumulated depreciation		6
	To record straight-line depreciation on		
	equipment for 1 month.		

The original cost of the equipment remains in the asset account. The depreciation is credited to Accumulated Depreciation, a contra-asset account, and the two accounts together indicate the book value of the asset. The depreciation expense reported in the income statement is the portion of the equipment's original cost that is allocated to the current month. After the adjusting entry is posted, these accounts appear as follows:

Equipment

May 4	360		

Accumulated Depreciation

		May 31	6

Depreciation Expense

May 31	6		

The depreciation expense of $6 will appear in the income statement. The Equipment account and its related Accumulated Depreciation account are both permanent accounts and are reported together in the balance sheet. The Accumulated Depreciation account accumulates the amount of cost assigned to each period in which the asset was used. Therefore, the balance of the Accumulated Depreciation account increases over time. On the other hand, Depreciation Expense is a temporary account, and it starts each period with a zero balance.

At the end of the second month of use, the same adjusting entry will be made. The balance of the Accumulated Depreciation account will then be $12, indicating that this much of the original cost of the asset has been expensed. The depreciation expense of $6 will again appear in the income statement, showing the amount of expense allocated to the second month.

Summary of Accruals, Deferrals, and Allocations

Note that every adjusting entry involves both temporary and permanent accounts and therefore affects both the income statement and the balance sheet. Accruals and deferrals that require recording expenses reduce assets or increase liabilities; if they require recording revenues, they increase assets or reduce liabilities.

Allocations differ from accruals and deferrals because they necessitate estimating the amount of the adjustment. Depreciation expense is based on an estimate of expected useful life of the asset. Bad debts expense is based on an estimate of uncollectible amounts of receivables. In addition, allocations are not related to the timing of cash flows. On the other hand, accruals and deferrals can be calculated precisely and are directly related to cash flows.

Figure A-3 summarizes and explains these adjustments, gives examples, and shows the balance sheet and income statement treatment of deferrals, accruals, and allocations.

CLOSING THE BOOKS

After all the accounts have been adjusted, an adjusted trial balance may be prepared. The adjusted trial balance of Overton Company is shown in Figure A-4. From the account balances in this trial balance, the company can prepare the income statement, the balance sheet and the statement of retained earnings. Prior to preparing statements, however, it is necessary to transfer all temporary account balances to the Retained Earnings account. This process is known as **closing the books** and it creates zero balances in all temporary accounts.

If all the expenses and revenues had been recorded directly in the Retained Earnings account, the balance in the account would have increased by the net income earned. Revenues and gains would have increased Retained Earnings, whereas expenses and losses would have

	Balance Sheet Treatment	Explanation	Examples	Income Statement Treatment
DEFERRALS	**Assets** are recorded as prepaid expenses.	Cash outflow has occurred. Goods or services have been received but not yet used.	Prepaid insurance, office supplies, or prepaid rent.	An **expense** is recorded for the portion of the asset used during the period. The unused portion is an asset and will become an expense in future periods.
	Liabilities are recorded as unearned revenues.	Cash inflow has occurred. Payment has been received for goods and services that have not yet been delivered.	Rent received in advance or subscriptions collected in advance.	**Revenue** is recorded for the portion of goods and services delivered. The portion not delivered is a liability which will become revenue in future periods.
ACCRUALS	**Assets** are recorded as receivables.	Cash inflow has not occurred. The earning process is complete, but no assets have been received.	Interest on bond investments or unbilled services.	**Revenues** are recognized and recorded in the period in which the earning process is complete.
	Liabilities are recorded as payables.	Cash outflow has not occurred. Benefits have been used or received, but no cash has been paid.	Interest on bonds payable, salaries payable, or taxes payable.	**Expenses** are recognized and recorded in the period in which benefits are consumed.
ALLOCATIONS	Recorded as reduction in asset or increase in contra asset.	Cash outflow occurred when the asset was bought, or it continues to occur if periodic payments are made on installment purchase. The cost of the asset is allocated to each period of its expected useful life.	Depreciation of equipment, amortization of intangibles, or depletion of natural resources.	**Expense** is recognized in each period in which the asset is used. Timing of cash flows does not affect the income statement. The expense does not result in any payments. The amount must be estimated.
		Services or goods have been provided, but payment has not been received. Payment is expected in future period but may not take place.	Bad debts on credit sales.	**Expense** is recorded in the period in which sales takes place for amounts which are expected to be uncollectible. The amount must be estimated.

Figure A-3 Accruals, deferrals, and allocations are end of period adjustments that affect the balance sheet and the income statement.

decreased it. But with revenues, gains, and expenses recorded in temporary accounts, the balance in the Retained Earnings account is still zero. Closing the temporary accounts brings the Retained Earnings balance to its correct amount.

Overton Company
Trial Balance
May 31

	Debit	Credit
Cash	$ 5,413	
Notes receivable	1,200	
Accounts receivable	2,200	
Interest receivable	3	
Prepaid rent	800	
Office supplies	275	
Land	5,000	
Equipment	360	
Accumulated depreciation		$ 6
Accounts payable		1,020
Salaries payable		500
Unearned revenue		100
Common stock		8,000
Retained earnings		0
Dividends	600	
Service revenue		12,150
Gain on sale of assets		900
Interest income		3
Salary expense	5,500	
Rent expense	400	
Office supplies expense	525	
Utility expense	170	
Legal expense	220	
Depreciation expense	6	
Interest expense	7	
Totals	$22,679	$22,679

Figure A-4
Adjusted trial balance prior to closing the books and preparing financial statements.

The balances of the temporary revenue and expense accounts are used to calculate net income, which is the **net** change in retained earnings resulting from the period's operations. Retained earnings also changed as a result of dividend payments, but dividends are capital transactions and have nothing to do with the determination of income. The Dividend account, however, is also a temporary account and it must also be closed.

Use of the Income Summary Account

Closing the books is a two-step process. First, all the revenue and expense account balances are transferred to a new temporary account called **Income Summary.** The balance in this account is, of course, net income. The second step is to close the Income Summary account by transferring its balance to retained earnings.

Closing entries. A closing entry transfers the balance of a temporary account to Income Summary or Retained Earnings, leaving revenue and expense accounts with zero balances. To illustrate, the Service Revenue account has a credit balance of $12,150, which is to be transferred to the Income Summary account. The following entry creates, or opens, the Income Summary account and transfers the Service Revenue balance to it, leaving Service Revenue with a zero balance:

May 31	Service revenue	12,150	
	Income summary		12,150
	To close Service Revenue account.		

When this entry is posted, the Service Revenue account is closed, and the two accounts appear as follows:

Service Revenue

5/31	100	5/14	12,000
		5/27	250
To close	12,150	Bal.	12,150

Income Summary

		5/31	12,150

The Gain on Sale of Assets and the Interest Income accounts are closed in the same way.

31	Gain on sale of assets	900	
	Interest income	3	
	Income summary		903
	To close gain and interest accounts.		

Next, we close the expense accounts. They can be closed individually, or all at once as follows:

31	Income summary	6,828	
	Salary expense		5,500
	Rent expense		400
	Office supplies expense		525
	Utility expense		170
	Legal expense		220
	Depreciation expense		6
	Interest expense		7
	To close expense accounts.		

Closing Income Summary and Dividends. After these entries are posted, the only temporary accounts that still have balances are the Income Summary account and the Dividends account. These are closed directly to Retained Earnings. The journal entries are as follows:

May 31	Income summary	6,225	
	Retained earnings		6,225
	To close Income Summary account and		
	transfer net income to retained earnings.		
31	Retained earnings	600	
	Dividends		600
	To close Dividends account.		

The posting of these two entries is illustrated in Figure A-5, which shows how the Retained Earnings account is increased by the amount of net income and decreased by the amount of dividends, leaving a balance of $5,625 to be reported in the balance sheet.

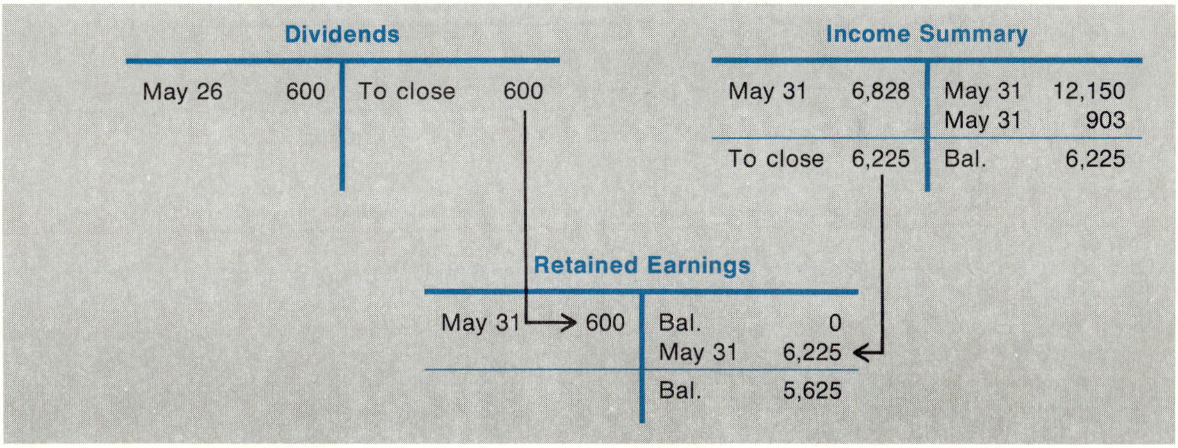

Figure A-5 Income Summary and Dividends accounts closed to Retained Earnings. The results of the period's operations are now reflected in the new Retained Earnings balance.

FINANCIAL STATEMENTS

The financial statements prepared for Overton Company on May 31 are shown in Figure A-6. They consist of the Income Statement, the Statement of Retained Earnings, and the Balance Sheet. The Statement of Changes in Financial Position, which is also reported at the end of the accounting period, is discussed in Chapter 20 and is not shown here.

Overton Company
Income Statement
For the Month Ended May 31

Service revenue		$12,150
Gain on sale of assets		900
Interest income		3
Total revenues		13,053
Less expenses:		
Salary expense	$5,500	
Rent expense	400	
Office supplies expense	525	
Utility expense	170	
Legal expense	220	
Depreciation expense	6	
Interest expense	7	6,828
Net income		$ 6,225

Overton Company
Statement of Retained Earnings
For the Month Ended May 31

Retained earnings, May 1	$ 0
Add net income	6,225
	6,225
Less dividends	600
Retained earnings, May 31	$5,625

Overton Company
Balance Sheet
May 31

Current Assets			**Current Liabilities**		
Cash		$ 5,413	Accounts payable		$ 1,020
Notes receivable		1,200	Salaries payable		500
Accounts receivable		2,200	Unearned revenue		100
Interest receivable		3	Total liabilities		1,620
Prepaid rent		800			
Office supplies		275			
Total current assets		9,891			
Fixed Assets			**Capital**		
Land		5,000	Common stock	$8,000	
Equipment	$360		Retained earnings	5,625	
Accumulated depreciation	(6)	354	Total capital		13,625
Total assets		$15,245	Total liabilities and capital		$15,245

Figure A-6 **Financial statements of Overton Company.**

The Income Statement

The ending balances of temporary accounts (except Dividends) are used to prepare the income statement. These accounts may be organized in various classifications, or the statement may be prepared in **single-step** form as shown in Figure A-6, with all revenues and gains shown together and all expenses deducted together. In a **multiple-step** income statement, revenues are classified as operating and nonoperating, and expenses are classified as operating or nonoperating, with operating expenses sometimes further organized into selling and administrative categories.

The Retained Earnings Statement

The change in retained earnings from the beginning of the period to the end is reported in the statement of retained earnings. Net income from the income statement is added to the beginning balance of retained earnings, any dividends declared during the period are deducted from the total, and the resulting ending balance is reported in the year-end balance sheet.

The Balance Sheet

The balance sheet reports the company's financial position at a point in time, typically the end of the accounting period, which may be a calendar year or a fiscal year. The balance sheet in Figure A-6 shows assets classified into current and long-term. Liabilities are also classified in a similar manner, and owners' equity is reported in several capital accounts showing contributed capital separately from retained earnings.

YEAR-END PROCEDURES FOR MERCHANDISING COMPANIES

Businesses that sell goods rather than services must account for the cost of their merchandise in addition to other expenses. The inventory of merchandise may be maintained in a perpetual inventory system or in a periodic inventory system. With a perpetual inventory system, all purchases of merchandise are recorded in the Merchandise Inventory account. When a sale takes place, the sales revenue is recorded and the sold merchandise is removed from the inventory account and its cost is recorded as an expense called Cost of Goods Sold. Below are hypothetical entries to record a sale of goods.

June 4	Accounts receivable	4,000	
	Sales revenue		4,000
	Sold goods on open account.		
	Cost of goods sold	2,800	
	Merchandise inventory		2,800
	To remove cost of sold goods from		
	merchandise account.		

With a periodic inventory system, purchases of goods are recorded in a Purchases account rather than in the Merchandise Inventory account. The Inventory account does not change during the accounting period but simply contains the balance of inventory that was on hand at the end of the previous period. When a sale takes place, only the sales revenue is recorded. Cost of goods sold is not recorded because it is not readily determinable or known at the time of sale. At the end of the accounting period a physical count of goods on hand is taken and is used to determine cost of goods sold for the entire period.

The beginning inventory balance plus the balance in the Purchases account together make up the total cost of goods available for sale. The inventory of goods on hand at the end of the period is the portion of total goods available that has not been sold. By deducting ending inventory from goods available for sale, the business determines the cost of the goods that were sold. The calculation is made by means of a special journal entry at the end of the accounting period. This entry eliminates the balance of the Inventory account and that of the Purchases account, opens the Cost of Goods Sold account, and adjusts the Inventory account by putting in the ending balance as determined by the physical count. A hypothetical example is as follows:

June 30	Merchandise inventory	3,500	
	Cost of goods sold	46,600	
	Purchases		46,800
	Merchandise inventory		3,300
	To adjust Merchandise, close Purchases,		
	and open Cost of Goods Sold account.		

The two credits together total the cost of goods available for sale. The debit to the inventory account is the amount of goods on hand at the end of the period and establishes the correct balance in that account. The remaining goods have been sold and are recorded as cost of goods sold, which will appear in the income statement as a deduction from sales revenue to arrive at gross margin from sales. The Cost of Goods Sold account is closed to Income Summary together with all other expense accounts when the books are closed.

Appendix B Time Value of Money

Money available today is more valuable than money available in the future. The compensation for waiting is the time value of money, called **interest.**

COMPOUND INTEREST

Compound interest occurs when interest earned during the previous period itself earns interest in the next and subsequent periods. If $1,000 is placed into a savings account paying 6 percent interest per year, interest accumulates as follows:

Principal invested in first year	$1,000.00
Interest for first year ($1,000 × .06 × 1)	60.00
Amount available at end of first year	1,060.00
Interest for second year ($1,060 × .06 × 1)	63.60
Amount available at end of second year	$1,123.60

The interest earned in the second year is greater than $60 because it is earned on the principal **plus** the first year's interest. If the savings account pays 6 percent interest compounded quarterly, 1.5 percent interest is added to the account each quarter, as follows:

Principal invested in first year	$1,000.00
Interest for first quarter ($1,000 × .06 × 1 × ¼)	15.00
Amount available at end of first quarter	1,015.00
Interest for second quarter ($1,015 × .06 × 1 × ¼)	15.23
Amount available at end of second quarter	1,030.23
Interest for third quarter ($1,030.23 × .06 × 1 × ¼)	15.45
Amount available at end of third quarter	1,045.68
Interest for fourth quarter ($1,045.68 × .06 × 1 × ¼)	15.69
Amount available at end of first year	$1,061.37

With quarterly compounding, the initial investment of $1,000 earned $1.37 more interest in the first year than with annual compounding. To deal with compound interest, we define the following terms:

P = the principal sum that earns interest
i = the interest rate per period
n = the number of periods during which compounding takes place. A period can be any length of time

Future Value of $1

A sum of money invested today at compound interest accumulates to a larger sum called the **amount** or **future value.** The future value of $1,000 invested at 6 percent compounded annually for 2 years is $1,123.60, as shown above. The future value includes the original principal and the accumulated interest.

The future value varies with the interest rate, the compounding frequency, and the number of periods. If we know the future value of a $1 principal investment, we can use it to calculate the future value of any amount invested. For example, at 8 percent interest per period, $1 accumulates as follows:

Future value of $1 at 8% for 1 period	= $1.00000 × 1.08	= $1.08000
Future value of $1 at 8% for 2 periods	= $1.08000 × 1.08	= $1.16640
Future value of $1 at 8% for 3 periods	= $1.16640 × 1.08	= $1.25971

The above table can be diagramed as follows:

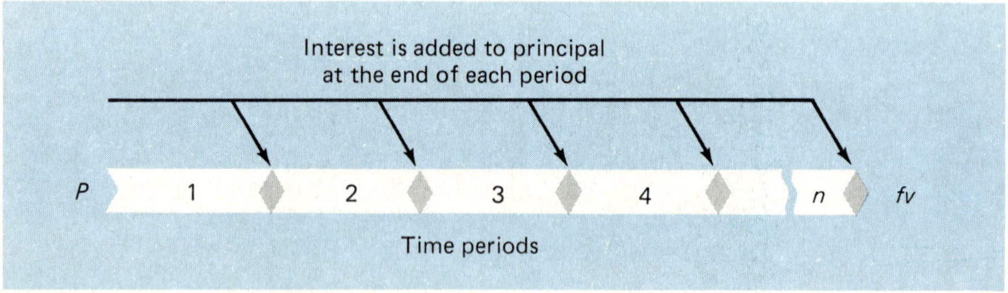

The end of each period is designated by a small diamond. The arrows pointing to the end of each period indicate that payments are made into the investment. The general formula for the future value of $1, with n representing the number of compounding periods is

$$fv = (1 + i)^n$$

Using this formula, future values can be calculated for any interest rate and any number of time periods. Table I on page 000 shows future values of $1 for many interest rates and time periods. To obtain the future value of any principal other than $1, it is only necessary to multiply the principal by the factor found in the table for the future value of $1.

$$fv = P(1 + i)^n$$

or

$$fv = Pf$$

where f is the factor in the future value of $1 table, with interest rate i and number of periods n.

Problem 1. Bonzer Company invests $4,000,000 in certificates of deposit that earn 16 percent interest per year, compounded semiannually. What will be the future value of this investment at the end of 5 years when the company plans to use it to build a new plant?

Solution 1. Compounding is semiannual and there are 5 years, so the number of half-year periods is 10. The semiannual interest rate is half the 16 percent annual rate, or 8 percent. Using Table I, with $i = 8$ percent and $n = 10$, the factor in the table is 2.15892. Multiplying this factor by the principal investment, we get

$$\begin{aligned} fv &= P \times f(n = 10, i = 8\%) \\ &= \$4{,}000{,}000 \times 2.15892 \\ &= \$8{,}635{,}680 \end{aligned}$$

COMPOUND DISCOUNT

If $1 can be invested at 8 percent today to become $1.08 in the future, then $1 is the **present value** of the future amount of $1.08. The present value of future receipts of money is important in business decision making. Frequently it is necessary to decide how much future receipts are worth today in order to determine whether an investment should be made or how much should be invested. Finding the present value of future receipts involves discounting the future value to the present. **Discounting** is the opposite of compounding. It involves finding the present value of some future amount of money that is assumed to include interest accumulations.

Present Value of $1

Knowing the present value of $1 is useful because it enables you to find the present value of any future payment. Assuming 8 percent interest per period, a table of present values of $1 can be constructed as follows:

$$\text{Present value of \$1 discounted for 1 period at 8\%} = \frac{\$1.00000}{1.08} = \$.92593$$

$$\text{Present value of \$1 discounted for 2 periods at 8\%} = \frac{\$.92593}{1.08} = .85734$$

$$\text{Present value of \$1 discounted for 3 periods at 8\%} = \frac{\$.85734}{1.08} = .79383$$

The general formula for the present value of $1 is

$$pv = \frac{1}{(1 + i)^n}$$

Table II on pages 918 and 919 is constructed from this formula. To find the present value of any future amount, the appropriate factor from the table is multiplied by the amount.

Problem 2. Alpha Company can invest at 16 percent compounded annually. Beta Company can invest at 16 percent compounded semiannually. Each company will need $200,000 four years from now. How much must each invest today?

Solution 2. With annual compounding $n = 4$ and $i = 16$ percent. With semiannual compounding $n = 8$ and $i = 8$ percent. Using Table II we find the present value factors and multiply by the future value to obtain the present value. For Alpha Company,

$$\begin{aligned} pv &= fv \times f(n = 4, i = 16\%) \\ &= \$200{,}000 \times .55229 \\ &= \$110{,}458 \end{aligned}$$

For Beta Company,

$$\begin{aligned} pv &= fv \times f(n = 8, i = 8\%) \\ &= \$200{,}000 \times .54027 \\ &= \$108{,}054 \end{aligned}$$

The more frequent the compounding, the smaller the present value. Beta Company needs to invest less than Alpha Company because its investment grows faster due to more frequent compounding.

ANNUITIES

An **annuity** is a series of equal payments made at equal time intervals, with compounding or discounting taking place at the time of each payment.

Each annuity payment is called a **rent.** There are several different types of annuities, but we discuss only ordinary annuities. In an **ordinary annuity,** each rent is paid or received at the **end** of each period. There are as many rents as there are periods. Installment purchases, long-term bonds, pension plans, and capital budgeting all involve annuities.

Future Value of Annuity of $1

If you open a savings account that compounds interest each month, and at the end of each month you deposit $100 in the savings account, your deposits are the rents of an annuity. After 1 year, you will have made 12 deposits of $100 each, or a total of $1,200, but the account will have more than $1,200 in it because each deposit earns interest. If the interest rate is 6 percent a year compounded monthly, your balance is $1,233.56. The **future value of an annuity** or **amount of annuity** is the sum accumulated in the future from all the rents paid and the interest earned by the rents. The abbreviation ***FV*** is used for the future value of an annuity to differentiate it from the lowercase ***fv*** used for the future value of $1.

To obtain a table of future values of annuities, we assume payments of $1 each period made into a fund that earns 8 percent interest compounded each period. The following diagram illustrates an annuity of four payments of $1, each paid at the end of each period, with interest of 8 percent compounded each period.

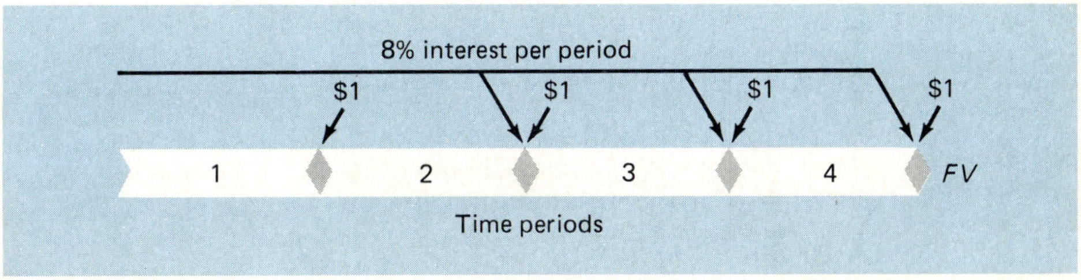

Notice that there are four rents and four periods, each rent is paid at the **end** of each period. At the end of the first period, $1 is deposited and earns interest for three periods. The next rent earns interest for two periods, and so on. We want the amount at the end of the fourth period. It can be determined by calculating the future value of each individual $1 deposit as follows:

Future value of $1 at 8% for 3 periods	=	$1.25971
Future value of $1 at 8% for 2 periods	=	1.16640
Future value of $1 at 8% for 1 period	=	1.08000
The fourth rent of $1 earns no interest	=	1.00000
Total for 4 rents		$4.50611

The formula for the future value of an annuity of $1 can be used to produce tables for a variety of periods and interest rates.

$$FV = \frac{(1 + i)^n - 1}{i}$$

Table III on page 000 is derived from this formula. You should know how to use the table to solve annuity problems.

Problem 3. In the beginning of 1986, the directors of Malloy Corporation decided that plant facilities will have to be expanded in a few years. The company plans to invest $50,000 every year, starting on June 30, 1986, into a trust fund that earns 11 percent interest compounded annually. How much money will be in the fund on June 30, 1990, after the last deposit has been made?

Solution 3. The first deposit is made at the end of the first 1-year period, and there is a total of 5 periods. The last deposit, made on June 30, 1990, earns no interest. The investment is an ordinary annuity, with $n = 5$ and $i = 11$ percent. From Table III we find that the amount of an ordinary annuity of $1 is 6.22780.

$$\begin{aligned} FV &= \text{Rent} \times f(n = 5, i = 11\%) \\ &= \$50{,}000 \times 6.22780 \\ &= \$311{,}390 \end{aligned}$$

If the company needs a total of $300,000 on June 30, 1990, how much would it have to deposit every year? Here we have to solve for the rent, given the future value, as follows:

$$\begin{aligned} FV &= \text{Rent} \times f(n = 5, i = 11\%) \\ \$300{,}000 &= \text{Rent} \times 6.22780 \\ \text{Rent} &= \frac{\$300{,}000}{6.22780} \\ &= \$48{,}171.10 \end{aligned}$$

The company has to deposit $48,171 each time in order to accumulate the necessary $300,000 by June 30, 1990.

Present Value of Annuity of $1

The present value of an annuity is the sum that must be invested today at compound interest in order to obtain periodic rents over some future time.

Notice that we use the abbreviation ***PV*** for the present value of an annuity, as differentiated from the lowercase ***pv*** for the present value of $1. By using the present value of $1, we can obtain a table for the present value of an ordinary annuity of $1. The present value of an annuity of $1 can be illustrated as follows:

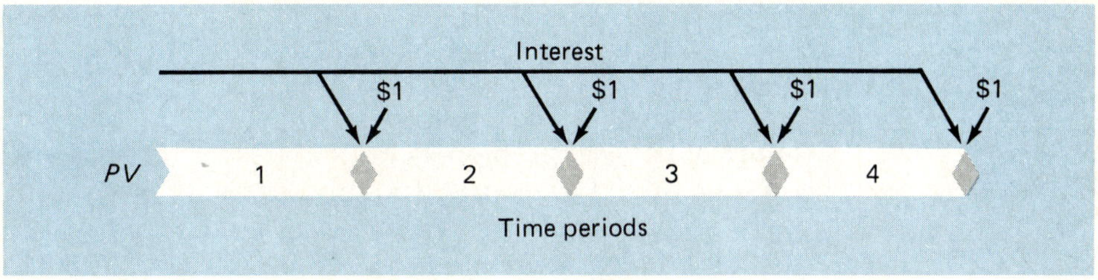

With each rent available at the **end** of each period, when compounding takes place, the number of rents is the same as the number of periods. By discounting each future rent to the present, we find the present value of the entire annuity.

Present value of first $1 discounted for 1 period at 8%	= $ .92593
Present value of second $1 discounted for 2 periods at 8%	= .85734
Present value of third $1 discounted for 3 periods at 8%	= .79383
Present value of fourth $1 discounted for 4 periods at 8%	= .73503
Present value of annuity of 4 rents at 8%	$3.31213

The first rent is worth more than the others because it is received earlier. Table IV on page 000 may be used to solve problems involving the present value of annuities. The formula used to construct Table IV is:

$$PV = \frac{1 - \dfrac{1}{(1 + i)^n}}{i}$$

Problem 4. Mr. Floryn, the owner of Floryn Corporation, is retiring and wants to use the money from the sale of his company to establish a retirement plan for himself. The plan is to provide an income of $50,000 per year for the rest of his life. An insurance company calculates that his life expectancy is 32 more years and offers an annuity that yields 9 percent compounded annually. How much will the insurance company want now in exchange for the future annuity payments?

Solution 4. The investment today is the present value of an annuity of $50,000 per year, with $n = 32$ and $i = 9$ percent. In Table IV, we find the factor 10.40624, which is the present value if the rents were $1.

$$\begin{aligned} PV &= \text{Rent} \times f(n = 32, i = 9\%) \\ &= \$50{,}000 \times 10.40624 \\ &= \$520{,}312 \end{aligned}$$

To assure an income of $50,000 per year, the insurance company must be paid $520,312 today. The first rent will be paid at the end of the first period. What happens if Mr. Floryn lives longer than 32 years?[1]

Solution of Managerial Problems

Many business problems are solved by use of compound interest and present value tables. For example, Barrett Corporation is investigating two possible investments. Project A is the purchase of a mine for $200,000. Net income from the sale of ore is expected to be $48,000 per year for 10 years, at which time the mine will be depleted. The property will then be sold at an estimated price of $60,000. Project B is the purchase of an office building that is leased for 15 years. The lease provides annual receipts of $40,000 at the end of each of the next 4 years, and annual receipts of $45,000 for the remaining life of the lease. The purchase price is $200,000. Barrett Corporation requires a 20 percent return on its investments. Which investment is preferable?

Solution. Project A can be diagramed as follows:

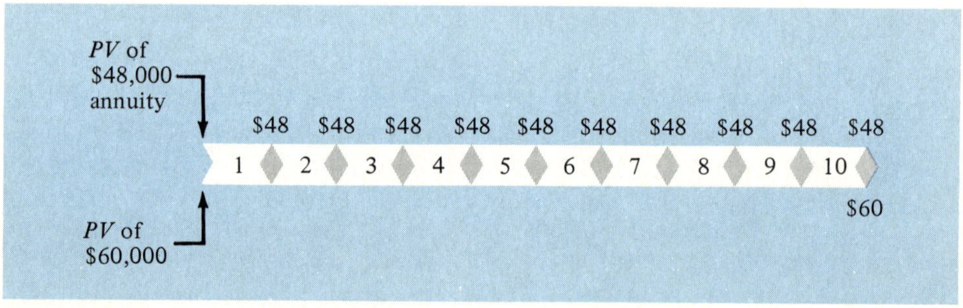

To evaluate the project, we need to find the present value of the future income stream of $48,000 per year plus the present value of the future sales price of $60,000, both discounted to the present at the company's required rate of return of 20 percent.

PV of annuity of $48,000 ($n$ = 10, i = 20%) = $48,000 × 4.19247	$201,238.56
pv of $60,000 ($n$ = 10, i = 20%) = $60,000 × .16151	9,690.60
Total present value of Project A cash inflows	$210,929.16

[1] The insurance company keeps making the payments. Its calculations are based on probabilities. What it pays to those living longer than expected, it makes up from those who die earlier than expected.

Project B can be diagramed as follows:

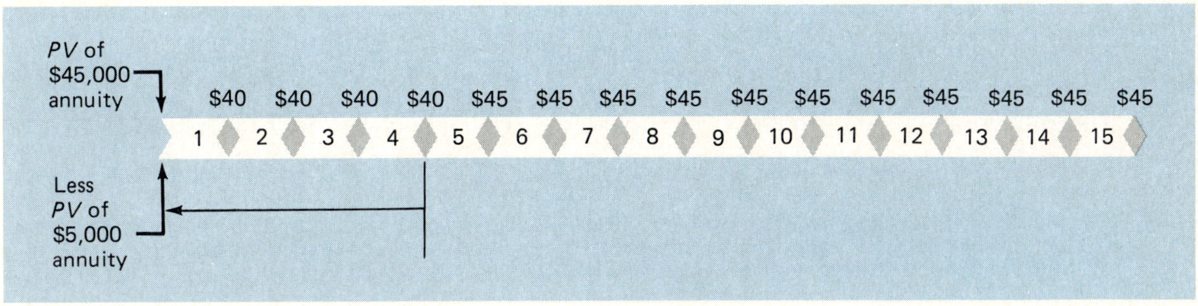

The problem can be broken down into two separate annuities, one with receipts of $45,000 per year for 15 years and the other with payments of $5,000 for 4 years. The present value of the two annuities can be found by computing the present value of an annuity of $45,000 for 15 years at 20 percent minus an annuity of $5,000 for 4 years at 20 percent.

PV of annuity of $45,000 ($n$ = 15, i = 20%) = $45,000 × 4.67547	$210,396.15
PV of annuity of $ 5,000 (n = 4, i = 20%) = $ 5,000 × 2.58873	(12,943.65)
Total present value of Project B cash inflows	$197,452.50

By discounting each project at the company's required rate of return, we find that Project A cash inflows have a present value of $210,929.16 and Project B cash inflows have a present value of $197,452.50. Since the asking price of each project is $200,000, Project B should not be accepted. The value of Project A is greater than the asking price, therefore the company should acquire Project A. By paying less than the present value of the project, the company will obtain a rate of return greater than 20 percent.

Table I
Future Value of $1

n	8%	9%	10%	11%	12%	13%	14%	15%	16%	17%	18%	n
1	1.08000	1.09000	1.10000	1.11000	1.12000	1.13000	1.14000	1.15000	1.16000	1.17000	1.18000	1
2	1.16640	1.18810	1.21000	1.23210	1.25440	1.27690	1.29960	1.32250	1.34560	1.36890	1.39240	2
3	1.25971	1.29503	1.33100	1.36763	1.40493	1.44290	1.48154	1.52087	1.56090	1.60161	1.64303	3
4	1.36049	1.41158	1.46410	1.51807	1.57352	1.63047	1.68896	1.74901	1.81064	1.87389	1.93878	4
5	1.46933	1.53862	1.61051	1.68506	1.76234	1.84244	1.92541	2.01136	2.10034	2.19245	2.28776	5
6	1.58687	1.67710	1.77156	1.87041	1.97382	2.08195	2.19497	2.31306	2.43640	2.56516	2.69955	6
7	1.71382	1.82804	1.94872	2.07616	2.21068	2.35261	2.50227	2.66002	2.82622	3.00124	3.18547	7
8	1.85093	1.99256	2.14359	2.30454	2.47596	2.65844	2.85259	3.05902	3.27841	3.51145	3.75886	8
9	1.99900	2.17189	2.35795	2.55804	2.77308	3.00404	3.25195	3.51788	3.80296	4.10840	4.43545	9
10	2.15892	2.36736	2.59374	2.83942	3.10585	3.39457	3.70722	4.04556	4.41144	4.80683	5.23384	10
11	2.33164	2.58043	2.85312	3.15176	3.47855	3.83586	4.22623	4.65239	5.11726	5.62399	6.17593	11
12	2.51817	2.81266	3.13843	3.49845	3.89598	4.33452	4.81790	5.35025	5.93603	6.58007	7.28759	12
13	2.71962	3.06580	3.45227	3.88328	4.36349	4.89801	5.49241	6.15279	6.88579	7.69868	8.59936	13
14	2.93719	3.34173	3.79750	4.31044	4.88711	5.53475	6.26135	7.07571	7.98752	9.00745	10.14724	14
15	3.17217	3.64248	4.17725	4.78459	5.47357	6.25427	7.13794	8.13706	9.26552	10.53872	11.97375	15
16	3.42594	3.97031	4.59497	5.31089	6.13039	7.06733	8.13725	9.35762	10.74800	12.33030	14.12902	16
17	3.70002	4.32763	5.05447	5.89509	6.86604	7.98608	9.27646	10.76126	12.46768	14.42646	16.67225	17
18	3.99602	4.71712	5.55992	6.54355	7.68997	9.02427	10.57517	12.37545	14.46251	16.87895	19.67325	18
19	4.31570	5.14166	6.11591	7.26334	8.61276	10.19742	12.05569	14.23177	16.77652	19.74838	23.21444	19
20	4.66096	5.60441	6.72750	8.06231	9.64629	11.52309	13.74349	16.36654	19.46076	23.10560	27.39303	20
21	5.03383	6.10881	7.40025	8.94917	10.80385	13.02109	15.66758	18.82152	22.57448	27.03355	32.32378	21
22	5.43654	6.65860	8.14027	9.93357	12.10031	14.71383	17.86104	21.64475	26.18640	31.62925	38.14206	22
23	5.87146	7.25787	8.95430	11.02627	13.55235	16.62663	20.36158	24.89146	30.37622	37.00623	45.00763	23
24	6.34118	7.91108	9.84973	12.23916	15.17863	18.78809	23.21221	28.62518	35.23642	43.29729	53.10901	24
25	6.84848	8.62308	10.83471	13.58546	17.00006	21.23054	26.46192	32.91895	40.87424	50.65783	62.66863	25
26	7.39635	9.39916	11.91818	15.07986	19.04007	23.99051	30.16658	37.85680	47.41412	59.26966	73.94898	26
27	7.98806	10.24508	13.10999	16.73865	21.32488	27.10928	34.38991	43.53531	55.00038	69.34550	87.25980	27
28	8.62711	11.16714	14.42099	18.57990	23.88387	30.63349	39.20449	50.06561	63.80044	81.13423	102.9666	28
29	9.31727	12.17218	15.86309	20.62369	26.74993	34.61584	44.69312	57.57545	74.00851	94.92705	121.5005	29
30	10.06266	13.26768	17.44940	22.89230	29.95992	39.11590	50.95016	66.21177	85.84988	111.0647	143.3706	30
31	10.86767	14.46177	19.19434	25.41045	33.55511	44.20096	58.08318	76.14354	99.58586	129.9456	169.1774	31
32	11.73708	15.76333	21.11378	28.20560	37.58173	49.94709	66.21483	87.56507	115.5196	152.0364	199.6293	32
33	12.67605	17.18203	23.22515	31.30821	42.09153	56.44021	75.48490	100.6998	134.0027	177.8826	235.5626	33
34	13.69013	18.72841	25.54767	34.75212	47.14252	63.77744	86.05279	115.8048	155.4432	208.1226	277.9638	34
35	14.78534	20.41397	28.10244	38.57485	52.79962	72.06851	98.10018	133.1755	180.3141	243.5035	327.9973	35
36	15.96817	22.25123	30.91268	42.81808	59.13557	81.43741	111.8342	153.1519	209.1643	284.8991	387.0368	36
37	17.24563	24.25384	34.00395	47.52807	66.23184	92.02428	127.4910	176.1246	242.6306	333.3319	456.7034	37
38	18.62528	26.43668	37.40434	52.75616	74.17966	103.9874	145.3397	202.5433	281.4515	389.9983	538.9100	38
39	20.11530	28.81598	41.14478	58.55934	83.08122	117.5058	165.6873	232.9248	326.4838	456.2981	635.9139	39
40	21.72452	31.40942	45.25926	65.00087	93.05097	132.7816	188.8835	267.8636	378.7212	533.8687	750.3783	40
41	23.46248	34.23627	49.78518	72.15096	104.2171	150.0432	215.3272	308.0431	439.3165	624.6264	885.4465	41
42	25.33948	37.31753	54.76370	80.08757	116.7231	169.5488	245.4730	354.2495	509.6072	730.8129	1044.827	42
43	27.36664	40.67611	60.24007	88.89720	130.7299	191.5901	279.8392	407.3870	591.1443	855.0511	1232.896	43
44	29.55597	44.33696	66.26408	98.67589	146.4175	216.4968	319.0167	468.4950	685.7274	1000.410	1454.817	44
45	31.92045	48.32729	72.89048	109.5302	163.9876	244.6414	363.6791	538.7693	795.4438	1170.479	1716.684	45
46	34.47409	52.67674	80.17953	121.5786	183.6661	276.4448	414.5941	619.5847	922.7148	1369.461	2025.687	46
47	37.23201	57.41765	88.19749	134.9522	205.7061	312.3826	472.6373	712.5224	1070.349	1602.269	2390.311	47
48	40.21057	62.58524	97.01723	149.7970	230.3908	352.9923	538.8066	819.4007	1241.605	1874.655	2820.567	48
49	43.42742	68.21791	106.7190	166.2746	258.0377	398.8814	614.2395	942.3108	1440.262	2193.346	3328.269	49
50	46.90161	74.35752	117.3909	184.5648	289.0022	450.7359	700.2330	1083.657	1670.704	2566.215	3927.357	50

Table I
Future Value of $1 (continued)

n	19%	20%	21%	22%	23%	24%	25%	26%	28%	30%	32%	*n*
1	1.19000	1.20000	1.21000	1.22000	1.23000	1.24000	1.25000	1.26000	1.28000	1.30000	1.32000	1
2	1.41610	1.44000	1.46410	1.48840	1.51290	1.53760	1.56250	1.58760	1.63840	1.69000	1.74240	2
3	1.68516	1.72800	1.77156	1.81585	1.86087	1.90662	1.95312	2.00038	2.09715	2.19700	2.29997	3
4	2.00534	2.07360	2.14359	2.21533	2.28887	2.36421	2.44141	2.52047	2.68435	2.85610	3.03596	4
5	2.38635	2.48832	2.59374	2.70271	2.81531	2.93163	3.05176	3.17580	3.43597	3.71293	4.00746	5
6	2.83976	2.98598	3.13843	3.29730	3.46283	3.63522	3.81470	4.00150	4.39805	4.82681	5.28985	6
7	3.37932	3.58318	3.79750	4.02271	4.25928	4.50767	4.76837	5.04190	5.62950	6.27485	6.98261	7
8	4.02139	4.29982	4.59497	4.90771	5.23891	5.58951	5.96046	6.35279	7.20576	8.15731	9.21704	8
9	4.78545	5.15978	5.55992	5.98740	6.44386	6.93099	7.45058	8.00451	9.22337	10.60450	12.16649	9
10	5.69468	6.19174	6.72750	7.30463	7.92595	8.59443	9.31323	10.08569	11.80592	13.78585	16.05977	10
11	6.77667	7.43008	8.14027	8.91165	9.74891	10.65709	11.64153	12.70796	15.11157	17.92160	21.19890	11
12	8.06424	8.91610	9.84973	10.87221	11.99116	13.21479	14.55192	16.01204	19.34281	23.29809	27.98254	12
13	9.59645	10.69932	11.91818	13.26410	14.74913	16.38634	18.18989	20.17516	24.75880	30.28751	36.93696	13
14	11.41977	12.83918	14.42099	16.18220	18.14143	20.31906	22.73737	25.42071	31.69127	39.37376	48.75678	14
15	13.58953	15.40702	17.44940	19.74229	22.31396	25.19563	28.42171	32.03009	40.56482	51.18589	64.35895	15
16	16.17154	18.48843	21.11378	24.08559	27.44617	31.24259	35.52714	40.35792	51.92297	66.54166	84.95382	16
17	19.24413	22.18611	25.54767	29.38442	33.75879	38.74081	44.40892	50.85097	66.46140	86.50416	112.1390	17
18	22.90052	26.62333	30.91268	35.84899	41.52331	48.03860	55.51115	64.07223	85.07059	112.4554	148.0235	18
19	27.25162	31.94800	37.40434	43.73577	51.07368	59.56786	69.38894	80.73100	108.8904	146.1920	195.3911	19
20	32.42942	38.33760	45.25926	53.35764	62.82062	73.86415	86.73617	101.7211	139.3797	190.0496	257.9162	20
21	38.59101	46.00512	54.76370	65.09632	77.26936	91.59155	108.4202	128.1685	178.4060	247.0645	340.4494	21
22	45.92331	55.20614	66.26408	79.41751	95.04132	113.5735	135.5253	161.4924	228.3596	321.1839	449.3932	22
23	54.64873	66.24737	80.17953	96.88936	116.9008	140.8312	169.4066	203.4804	292.3003	417.5391	593.1990	23
24	65.03199	79.49685	97.01723	118.2050	143.7880	174.6306	211.7582	256.3853	374.1444	542.8008	783.0227	24
25	77.38807	95.39622	117.3909	144.2101	176.8593	216.5420	264.6978	323.0455	478.9049	705.6410	1033.590	25
26	92.09181	114.4755	142.0429	175.9364	217.5369	268.5121	330.8723	407.0373	612.9982	917.3333	1364.339	26
27	109.5893	137.3706	171.8719	214.6424	267.5704	332.9550	413.5903	512.8670	784.6377	1192.533	1800.927	27
28	130.4112	164.8447	207.9651	261.8637	329.1116	412.8642	516.9879	646.2124	1004.336	1550.293	2377.224	28
29	155.1893	197.8136	251.6377	319.4737	404.8072	511.9516	646.2349	814.2276	1285.550	2015.381	3137.935	29
30	184.6753	237.3763	304.4816	389.7579	497.9129	634.8199	807.7936	1025.927	1645.505	2619.996	4142.075	30
31	219.7636	284.8516	368.4228	475.5046	612.4328	787.1767	1009.742	1292.668	2106.246	3405.994	5467.539	31
32	261.5187	341.8219	445.7916	580.1157	753.2924	976.0991	1262.177	1628.761	2695.995	4427.793	7217.151	32
33	311.2073	410.1863	539.4078	707.7411	926.5496	1210.363	1577.722	2052.239	3450.873	5756.130	9526.639	33
34	370.3366	492.2235	652.6834	863.4441	1139.656	1500.850	1972.152	2585.821	4417.118	7482.970	12575.16	34
35	440.7006	590.6682	789.7470	1053.402	1401.777	1861.054	2465.190	3258.135	5653.911	9727.860	16599.22	35
36	524.4337	708.8019	955.5938	1285.150	1724.186	2307.707	3081.488	4105.250	7237.006	12646.22	21910.97	36
37	624.0761	850.5623	1156.269	1567.883	2120.748	2861.557	3851.860	5172.615	9263.367	16440.08	28922.48	37
38	742.6506	1020.675	1399.085	1912.818	2608.520	3548.330	4814.825	6517.495	11857.11	21372.11	38177.67	38
39	883.7542	1224.810	1692.893	2333.638	3208.480	4399.930	6018.531	8212.044	15177.10	27783.74	50394.52	39
40	1051.668	1469.772	2048.400	2847.038	3946.430	5455.913	7523.164	10347.18	19426.69	36118.86	66520.77	40
41	1251.484	1763.726	2478.564	3473.386	4854.110	6765.336	9403.955	13037.44	24866.16	46954.52	87807.41	41
42	1489.266	2116.471	2999.063	4237.531	5970.555	8389.011	11754.94	16427.18	31828.69	61040.88	115905.8	42
43	1772.227	2539.765	3628.866	5169.788	7343.782	10402.37	14693.68	20698.24	40740.72	79353.15	152995.6	43
44	2108.950	3047.718	4390.928	6307.141	9032.852	12898.94	18367.10	26079.78	52148.12	103159.1	201954.2	44
45	2509.651	3657.262	5313.023	7694.712	11110.41	15994.69	22958.87	32860.53	66749.59	134106.8	266579.6	45
46	2986.484	4388.714	6428.757	9387.549	13665.80	19833.42	28698.59	41404.26	85439.48	174338.9	351885.1	46
47	3553.916	5266.457	7778.796	11452.81	16808.94	24593.44	35873.24	52169.37	109362.5	226640.5	464488.3	47
48	4229.160	6319.749	9412.344	13972.43	20674.99	30495.86	44841.55	65733.41	139984.0	294632.7	613124.5	48
49	5032.701	7583.698	11388.94	17046.36	25430.24	37814.87	56051.94	82824.10	179179.6	383022.5	809324.4	49
50	5988.914	9100.438	13780.61	20796.56	31279.20	46890.43	70064.92	104358.4	229349.9	497929.2	1068308.2	50

Table II
Present Value of $1

n	8%	9%	10%	11%	12%	13%	14%	15%	16%	17%	18%	n
1	.92593	.91743	.90909	.90090	.89286	.88496	.87719	.86957	.86207	.85470	.84746	1
2	.85734	.84168	.82645	.81162	.79719	.78315	.76947	.75614	.74316	.73051	.71818	2
3	.79383	.77218	.75131	.73119	.71178	.69305	.67497	.65752	.64066	.62437	.60863	3
4	.73503	.70843	.68301	.65873	.63552	.61332	.59208	.57175	.55229	.53365	.51579	4
5	.68058	.64993	.62092	.59345	.56743	.54276	.51937	.49718	.47611	.45611	.43711	5
6	.63017	.59627	.56447	.53464	.50663	.48032	.45559	.43233	.41044	.38984	.37043	6
7	.58349	.54703	.51316	.48166	.45235	.42506	.39964	.37594	.35383	.33320	.31393	7
8	.54027	.50187	.46651	.43393	.40388	.37616	.35056	.32690	.30503	.28478	.26604	8
9	.50025	.46043	.42410	.39092	.36061	.33288	.30751	.28426	.26295	.24340	.22546	9
10	.46319	.42241	.38554	.35218	.32197	.29459	.26974	.24718	.22668	.20804	.19106	10
11	.42888	.38753	.35049	.31728	.28748	.26070	.23662	.21494	.19542	.17781	.16192	11
12	.39711	.35553	.31863	.28584	.25668	.23071	.20756	.18691	.16846	.15197	.13722	12
13	.36770	.32618	.28966	.25751	.22917	.20416	.18207	.16253	.14523	.12989	.11629	13
14	.34046	.29925	.26333	.23199	.20462	.18068	.15971	.14133	.12520	.11102	.09855	14
15	.31524	.27454	.23939	.20900	.18270	.15989	.14010	.12289	.10793	.09489	.08352	15
16	.29189	.25187	.21763	.18829	.16312	.14150	.12289	.10686	.09304	.08110	.07078	16
17	.27027	.23107	.19784	.16963	.14564	.12522	.10780	.09293	.08021	.06932	.05998	17
18	.25025	.21199	.17986	.15282	.13004	.11081	.09456	.08081	.06914	.05925	.05083	18
19	.23171	.19449	.16351	.13768	.11611	.09806	.08295	.07027	.05961	.05064	.04308	19
20	.21455	.17843	.14864	.12403	.10367	.08678	.07276	.06110	.05139	.04328	.03651	20
21	.19866	.16370	.13513	.11174	.09256	.07680	.06383	.05313	.04430	.03699	.03094	21
22	.18394	.15018	.12285	.10067	.08264	.06796	.05599	.04620	.03819	.03162	.02622	22
23	.17032	.13778	.11168	.09069	.07379	.06014	.04911	.04017	.03292	.02702	.02222	23
24	.15770	.12640	.10153	.08170	.06588	.05323	.04308	.03493	.02838	.02310	.01883	24
25	.14602	.11597	.09230	.07361	.05882	.04710	.03779	.03038	.02447	.01974	.01596	25
26	.13520	.10639	.08391	.06631	.05252	.04168	.03315	.02642	.02109	.01687	.01352	26
27	.12519	.09761	.07628	.05974	.04689	.03689	.02908	.02297	.01818	.01442	.01146	27
28	.11591	.08955	.06934	.05382	.04187	.03264	.02551	.01997	.01567	.01233	.00971	28
29	.10733	.08215	.06304	.04849	.03738	.02889	.02237	.01737	.01351	.01053	.00823	29
30	.09938	.07537	.05731	.04368	.03338	.02557	.01963	.01510	.01165	.00900	.00697	30
31	.09202	.06915	.05210	.03935	.02980	.02262	.01722	.01313	.01004	.00770	.00591	31
32	.08520	.06344	.04736	.03545	.02661	.02002	.01510	.01142	.00866	.00658	.00501	32
33	.07889	.05820	.04306	.03194	.02376	.01772	.01325	.00993	.00746	.00562	.00425	33
34	.07305	.05339	.03914	.02878	.02121	.01568	.01162	.00864	.00643	.00480	.00360	34
35	.06763	.04899	.03558	.02592	.01894	.01388	.01019	.00751	.00555	.00411	.00305	35
36	.06262	.04494	.03235	.02335	.01691	.01228	.00894	.00653	.00478	.00351	.00258	36
37	.05799	.04123	.02941	.02104	.01510	.01087	.00784	.00568	.00412	.00300	.00219	37
38	.05369	.03783	.02673	.01896	.01348	.00962	.00688	.00494	.00355	.00256	.00186	38
39	.04971	.03470	.02430	.01708	.01204	.00851	.00604	.00429	.00306	.00219	.00157	39
40	.04603	.03184	.02209	.01538	.01075	.00753	.00529	.00373	.00264	.00187	.00133	40
41	.04262	.02921	.02009	.01386	.00960	.00666	.00464	.00325	.00228	.00160	.00113	41
42	.03946	.02680	.01826	.01249	.00857	.00590	.00407	.00282	.00196	.00137	.00096	42
43	.03654	.02458	.01660	.01125	.00765	.00522	.00357	.00245	.00169	.00117	.00081	43
44	.03383	.02255	.01509	.01013	.00683	.00462	.00313	.00213	.00146	.00100	.00069	44
45	.03133	.02069	.01372	.00913	.00610	.00409	.00275	.00186	.00126	.00085	.00058	45
46	.02901	.01898	.01247	.00823	.00544	.00362	.00241	.00161	.00108	.00073	.00049	46
47	.02686	.01742	.01134	.00741	.00486	.00320	.00212	.00140	.00093	.00062	.00042	47
48	.02487	.01598	.01031	.00668	.00434	.00283	.00186	.00122	.00081	.00053	.00035	48
49	.02303	.01466	.00937	.00601	.00388	.00251	.00163	.00106	.00069	.00046	.00030	49
50	.02132	.01345	.00852	.00542	.00346	.00222	.00143	.00092	.00060	.00039	.00025	50

Table II
Present Value of $1 (continued)

n	19%	20%	21%	22%	23%	24%	25%	26%	28%	30%	32%	*n*
1	.84034	.83333	.82645	.81967	.81301	.80645	.80000	.79365	.78125	.76923	.75758	1
2	.70616	.69444	.68301	.67186	.66098	.65036	.64000	.62988	.61035	.59172	.57392	2
3	.59342	.57870	.56447	.55071	.53738	.52449	.51200	.49991	.47684	.45517	.43479	3
4	.49867	.48225	.46651	.45140	.43690	.42297	.40960	.39675	.37253	.35013	.32939	4
5	.41905	.40188	.38554	.37000	.35520	.34111	.32768	.31488	.29104	.26933	.24953	5
6	.35214	.33490	.31863	.30328	.28878	.27509	.26214	.24991	.22737	.20718	.18904	6
7	.29592	.27908	.26333	.24859	.23478	.22184	.20972	.19834	.17764	.15937	.14321	7
8	.24867	.23257	.21763	.20376	.19088	.17891	.16777	.15741	.13878	.12259	.10849	8
9	.20897	.19381	.17986	.16702	.15519	.14428	.13422	.12493	.10842	.09430	.08219	9
10	.17560	.16151	.14864	.13690	.12617	.11635	.10737	.09915	.08470	.07254	.06227	10
11	.14757	.13459	.12285	.11221	.10258	.09383	.08590	.07869	.06617	.05580	.04717	11
12	.12400	.11216	.10153	.09198	.08339	.07567	.06872	.06245	.05170	.04292	.03574	12
13	.10421	.09346	.08391	.07539	.06780	.06103	.05498	.04957	.04039	.03302	.02707	13
14	.08757	.07789	.06934	.06180	.05512	.04921	.04398	.03934	.03155	.02540	.02051	14
15	.07359	.06491	.05731	.05065	.04481	.03969	.03518	.03122	.02465	.01954	.01554	15
16	.06184	.05409	.04736	.04152	.03643	.03201	.02815	.02478	.01926	.01503	.01177	16
17	.05196	.04507	.03914	.03403	.02962	.02581	.02252	.01967	.01505	.01156	.00892	17
18	.04367	.03756	.03235	.02789	.02408	.02082	.01801	.01561	.01175	.00889	.00676	18
19	.03670	.03130	.02673	.02286	.01958	.01679	.01441	.01239	.00918	.00684	.00512	19
20	.03084	.02608	.02209	.01874	.01592	.01354	.01153	.00983	.00717	.00526	.00388	20
21	.02591	.02174	.01826	.01536	.01294	.01092	.00922	.00780	.00561	.00405	.00294	21
22	.02178	.01811	.01509	.01259	.01052	.00880	.00738	.00619	.00438	.00311	.00223	22
23	.01830	.01509	.01247	.01032	.00855	.00710	.00590	.00491	.00342	.00239	.00169	23
24	.01538	.01258	.01031	.00846	.00695	.00573	.00472	.00390	.00267	.00184	.00128	24
25	.01292	.01048	.00852	.00693	.00565	.00462	.00378	.00310	.00209	.00142	.00097	25
26	.01086	.00874	.00704	.00568	.00460	.00372	.00302	.00246	.00163	.00109	.00073	26
27	.00912	.00728	.00582	.00466	.00374	.00300	.00242	.00195	.00127	.00084	.00056	27
28	.00767	.00607	.00481	.00382	.00304	.00242	.00193	.00155	.00100	.00065	.00042	28
29	.00644	.00506	.00397	.00313	.00247	.00195	.00155	.00123	.00078	.00050	.00032	29
30	.00541	.00421	.00328	.00257	.00201	.00158	.00124	.00097	.00061	.00038	.00024	30
31	.00455	.00351	.00271	.00210	.00163	.00127	.00099	.00077	.00047	.00029	.00018	31
32	.00382	.00293	.00224	.00172	.00133	.00102	.00079	.00061	.00037	.00023	.00014	32
33	.00321	.00244	.00185	.00141	.00108	.00083	.00063	.00049	.00029	.00017	.00010	33
34	.00270	.00203	.00153	.00116	.00088	.00067	.00051	.00039	.00023	.00013	.00008	34
35	.00227	.00169	.00127	.00095	.00071	.00054	.00041	.00031	.00018	.00010	.00006	35
36	.00191	.00141	.00105	.00078	.00058	.00043	.00032	.00024	.00014	.00008	.00005	36
37	.00160	.00118	.00086	.00064	.00047	.00035	.00026	.00019	.00011	.00006	.00003	37
38	.00135	.00098	.00071	.00052	.00038	.00028	.00021	.00015	.00008	.00005	.00003	38
39	.00113	.00082	.00059	.00043	.00031	.00023	.00017	.00012	.00007	.00004	.00002	39
40	.00095	.00068	.00049	.00035	.00025	.00018	.00013	.00010	.00005	.00003	.00002	40
41	.00080	.00057	.00040	.00029	.00021	.00015	.00011	.00008	.00004	.00002	.00001	41
42	.00067	.00047	.00033	.00024	.00017	.00012	.00009	.00006	.00003	.00002	.00001	42
43	.00056	.00039	.00028	.00019	.00014	.00010	.00007	.00005	.00002	.00001	.00001	43
44	.00047	.00033	.00023	.00016	.00011	.00008	.00005	.00004	.00002	.00001	.00000	44
45	.00040	.00027	.00019	.00013	.00009	.00006	.00004	.00003	.00001	.00001	.00000	45
46	.00033	.00023	.00016	.00011	.00007	.00005	.00003	.00002	.00001	.00001	.00000	46
47	.00028	.00019	.00013	.00009	.00006	.00004	.00003	.00002	.00001	.00000	.00000	47
48	.00024	.00016	.00011	.00007	.00005	.00003	.00002	.00002	.00001	.00000	.00000	48
49	.00020	.00013	.00009	.00006	.00004	.00003	.00002	.00001	.00001	.00000	.00000	49
50	.00017	.00011	.00007	.00005	.00003	.00002	.00001	.00001	.00000	.00000	.00000	50

Table III
Future Value of Annuity of $1

n	8%	9%	10%	11%	12%	13%	14%	15%	16%	17%	18%	n
1	1.00000	1.00000	1.00000	1.00000	1.00000	1.00000	1.00000	1.00000	1.00000	1.00000	1.00000	1
2	2.08000	2.09000	2.10000	2.11000	2.12000	2.13000	2.14000	2.15000	2.16000	2.17000	2.18000	2
3	3.24640	3.27810	3.31000	3.34210	3.37440	3.40690	3.43960	3.47250	3.50560	3.53890	3.57240	3
4	4.50611	4.57313	4.64100	4.70973	4.77933	4.84980	4.92114	4.99337	5.06650	5.14051	5.21543	4
5	5.86660	5.98471	6.10510	6.22780	6.35285	6.48027	6.61010	6.74238	6.87714	7.01440	7.15421	5
6	7.33593	7.52333	7.71561	7.91286	8.11519	8.32271	8.53552	8.75374	8.97748	9.20685	9.44197	6
7	8.92280	9.20043	9.48717	9.78327	10.08901	10.40466	10.73049	11.06680	11.41387	11.77201	12.14152	7
8	10.63663	11.02847	11.43589	11.85943	12.29969	12.75726	13.23276	13.72682	14.24009	14.77325	15.32700	8
9	12.48756	13.02104	13.57948	14.16397	14.77566	15.41571	16.08535	16.78584	17.51851	18.28471	19.08585	9
10	14.48656	15.19293	15.93742	16.72201	17.54874	18.41975	19.33730	20.30372	21.32147	22.39311	23.52131	10
11	16.64549	17.56029	18.53117	19.56143	20.65458	21.81432	23.04452	24.34928	25.73290	27.19994	28.75514	11
12	18.97713	20.14072	21.38428	22.71319	24.13313	25.65018	27.27075	29.00167	30.85017	32.82393	34.93107	12
13	21.49530	22.95338	24.52271	26.21164	28.02911	29.98470	32.08865	34.35192	36.78620	39.40399	42.21866	13
14	24.21492	26.01919	27.97498	30.09492	32.39260	34.88271	37.58107	40.50471	43.67199	47.10267	50.81802	14
15	27.15211	29.36092	31.77248	34.40536	37.27971	40.41746	43.84241	47.58041	51.65951	56.11013	60.96527	15
16	30.32428	33.00340	35.94973	39.18995	42.75328	46.67173	50.98035	55.71747	60.92503	66.64885	72.93901	16
17	33.75023	36.97370	40.54470	44.50084	48.88367	53.73906	59.11760	65.07509	71.67303	78.97915	87.06804	17
18	37.45024	41.30134	45.59917	50.39594	55.74971	61.72514	68.39407	75.83636	84.14072	93.40561	103.7403	18
19	41.44626	46.01846	51.15909	56.93949	63.43968	70.74941	78.96923	88.21181	98.60323	110.2846	123.4135	19
20	45.76196	51.16012	57.27500	64.20283	72.05244	80.94683	91.02493	102.4436	115.3798	130.0329	146.6280	20
21	50.42292	56.76453	64.00250	72.26514	81.69874	92.46992	104.7684	118.8101	134.8405	153.1385	174.0210	21
22	55.45676	62.87334	71.40275	81.21431	92.50258	105.4910	120.4360	137.6316	157.4150	180.1721	206.3448	22
23	60.89330	69.53194	79.54302	91.14788	104.6029	120.2048	138.2970	159.2764	183.6014	211.8013	244.4869	23
24	66.76476	76.78981	88.49733	102.1742	118.1552	136.8315	158.6586	184.1678	213.9776	248.8076	289.4945	24
25	73.10594	84.70090	98.34706	114.4133	133.3339	155.6196	181.8708	212.7930	249.2140	292.1049	342.6035	25
26	79.95442	93.32398	109.1818	127.9988	150.3339	176.8501	208.3327	245.7120	290.0883	342.7627	405.2721	26
27	87.35077	102.7231	121.0999	143.0786	169.3740	200.8406	238.4993	283.5688	337.5024	402.0323	479.2211	27
28	95.33883	112.9682	134.2099	159.8173	190.6989	227.9499	272.8892	327.1041	392.5028	471.3778	566.4809	28
29	103.9659	124.1354	148.6309	178.3972	214.5828	258.5834	312.0937	377.1697	456.3032	552.5121	669.4475	29
30	113.2832	136.3075	164.4940	199.0209	241.3327	293.1992	356.7869	434.7452	530.3117	647.4391	790.9480	30
31	123.3459	149.5752	181.9434	221.9132	271.2926	332.3151	407.7370	500.9569	616.1616	758.5038	934.3186	31
32	134.2135	164.0370	201.1378	247.3236	304.8477	376.5161	465.8202	577.1005	715.7475	888.4494	1103.496	32
33	145.9506	179.8003	222.2515	275.5292	342.4295	426.4632	532.0350	664.6655	831.2671	1040.486	1303.125	33
34	158.6267	196.9823	245.4767	306.8374	384.5210	482.9034	607.5199	765.3654	965.2698	1218.368	1538.688	34
35	172.3168	215.7108	271.0244	341.5896	431.6635	546.6808	693.5727	881.1702	1120.713	1426.491	1816.652	35
36	187.1022	236.1247	299.1268	380.1644	484.4631	618.7493	791.6729	1014.346	1301.027	1669.995	2144.649	36
37	203.0703	258.3760	330.0395	422.9825	543.5987	700.1867	903.5071	1167.498	1510.191	1954.894	2531.686	37
38	220.3160	282.6298	364.0434	470.5106	609.8305	792.2110	1030.998	1343.622	1752.822	2288.225	2988.389	38
39	238.9412	309.0665	401.4478	523.2667	684.0102	896.1985	1176.338	1546.166	2034.274	2678.224	3527.299	39
40	259.0565	337.8825	442.5926	581.8261	767.0914	1013.704	1342.025	1779.090	2360.757	3134.522	4163.213	40
41	280.7810	369.2919	487.8518	646.8269	860.1424	1146.486	1530.909	2046.954	2739.478	3668.391	4913.591	41
42	304.2435	403.5281	537.6370	718.9779	964.3595	1296.529	1746.236	2354.997	3178.795	4293.017	5799.038	42
43	329.5830	440.8457	592.4007	799.0655	1081.083	1466.078	1991.709	2709.247	3688.402	5023.830	6843.865	43
44	356.9497	481.5218	652.6408	887.9627	1211.813	1657.668	2271.548	3116.633	4279.547	5878.881	8076.760	44
45	386.5056	525.8587	718.9048	986.6386	1358.230	1874.165	2590.565	3585.129	4965.274	6879.291	9531.577	45
46	418.4261	574.1860	791.7953	1096.169	1522.218	2118.806	2954.244	4123.898	5760.718	8049.770	11248.26	46
47	452.9002	626.8628	871.9749	1217.747	1705.884	2395.251	3368.838	4743.482	6683.433	9419.231	13273.95	47
48	490.1322	684.2804	960.1723	1352.700	1911.590	2707.633	3841.475	5456.005	7753.782	11021.50	15664.26	48
49	530.3427	746.8657	1057.190	1502.497	2141.981	3060.626	4380.282	6275.406	8995.387	12896.16	18484.83	49
50	573.7702	815.0836	1163.909	1668.771	2400.018	3459.507	4994.521	7217.716	10435.65	15089.50	21813.09	50

Table III
Future Value of Annuity of $1 (continued)

n	19%	20%	21%	22%	23%	24%	25%	26%	28%	30%	32%	n
1	1.00000	1.00000	1.00000	1.00000	1.00000	1.00000	1.00000	1.00000	1.00000	1.00000	1.00000	1
2	2.19000	2.20000	2.21000	2.22000	2.23000	2.24000	2.25000	2.26000	2.28000	2.30000	2.32000	2
3	3.60610	3.64000	3.67410	3.70840	3.74290	3.77760	3.81250	3.84760	3.91840	3.99000	4.06240	3
4	5.29126	5.36800	5.44566	5.52425	5.60377	5.68422	5.76562	5.84798	6.01555	6.18700	6.36237	4
5	7.29660	7.44160	7.58925	7.73958	7.89263	8.04844	8.20703	8.36845	8.69991	9.04310	9.39833	5
6	9.68295	9.92992	10.18299	10.44229	10.70794	10.98006	11.25879	11.54425	12.13588	12.75603	13.40579	6
7	12.52271	12.91590	13.32142	13.73959	14.17077	14.61528	15.07349	15.54575	16.53393	17.58284	18.69564	7
8	15.90203	16.49908	17.11892	17.76231	18.43004	19.12294	19.84186	20.58765	22.16343	23.85769	25.67825	8
9	19.92341	20.79890	21.71389	22.67001	23.66895	24.71245	25.80232	26.94043	29.36919	32.01500	34.89529	9
10	24.70886	25.95868	27.27381	28.65742	30.11281	31.64344	33.25290	34.94495	38.59256	42.61950	47.06178	10
11	30.40355	32.15042	34.00131	35.96205	38.03876	40.23787	42.56613	45.03063	50.39847	56.40535	63.12155	11
12	37.18022	39.58050	42.14158	44.87370	47.78767	50.89495	54.20766	57.73860	65.51005	74.32695	84.32045	12
13	45.24446	48.49660	51.99132	55.74591	59.77883	64.10974	68.75958	73.75063	84.85286	97.62504	112.3030	13
14	54.84091	59.19592	63.90949	69.01001	74.52796	80.49608	86.94947	93.92580	109.6117	127.9126	149.2399	14
15	66.26068	72.03511	78.33049	85.19221	92.66940	100.8151	109.6868	119.3465	141.3029	167.2863	197.9967	15
16	79.85021	87.44213	95.77989	104.9345	114.9834	126.0108	138.1086	151.3766	181.8677	218.4722	262.3557	16
17	96.02175	105.9306	116.8937	129.0201	142.4295	157.2534	173.6357	191.7345	233.7907	285.0139	347.3095	17
18	115.2659	128.1167	142.4413	158.4045	176.1883	195.9942	218.0446	242.5855	300.2521	371.5180	459.4485	18
19	138.1664	154.7400	173.3540	194.2535	217.7116	244.0328	273.5558	306.6577	385.3227	483.9734	607.4721	19
20	165.4180	186.6880	210.7584	237.9893	268.7853	303.6006	342.9447	387.3887	494.2131	630.1655	802.8631	20
21	197.8474	225.0256	256.0176	291.3469	331.6059	377.4648	429.6809	489.1098	633.5927	820.2151	1060.779	21
22	236.4385	271.0307	310.7813	356.4432	408.8753	469.0563	538.1011	617.2783	811.9987	1067.280	1401.229	22
23	282.3618	326.2369	377.0454	435.8608	503.9166	582.6298	673.6264	778.7707	1040.358	1388.464	1850.622	23
24	337.0105	392.4842	457.2249	532.7501	620.8174	723.4610	843.0330	982.2511	1332.659	1806.003	2443.821	24
25	402.0425	471.9811	554.2422	650.9551	764.6055	898.0916	1054.791	1238.636	1706.803	2348.803	3226.844	25
26	479.4306	567.3773	671.6330	795.1653	941.4647	1114.634	1319.489	1561.682	2185.708	3054.444	4260.434	26
27	571.5224	681.8528	813.6759	971.1016	1159.002	1383.146	1650.361	1968.719	2798.706	3971.778	5624.772	27
28	681.1116	819.2233	985.5479	1185.744	1426.572	1716.101	2063.952	2481.586	3583.344	5164.311	7425.699	28
29	811.5228	984.0680	1193.513	1447.608	1755.683	2128.965	2580.939	3127.798	4587.680	6714.604	9802.923	29
30	966.7122	1181.882	1445.151	1767.081	2160.491	2640.916	3227.174	3942.026	5873.231	8729.985	12940.86	30
31	1151.387	1419.258	1749.632	2156.839	2658.404	3275.736	4034.968	4967.953	7518.735	11349.98	17082.93	31
32	1371.151	1704.109	2118.055	2632.344	3270.836	4062.913	5044.710	6260.620	9624.981	14755.98	22550.47	32
33	1632.670	2045.931	2563.847	3212.460	4024.129	5039.012	6306.887	7889.382	12320.98	19183.77	29767.62	33
34	1943.877	2456.118	3103.254	3920.201	4950.678	6249.375	7884.609	9941.621	15771.85	24939.90	39294.26	34
35	2314.214	2948.341	3755.938	4783.645	6090.334	7750.225	9856.761	12527.44	20188.97	32422.87	51869.43	35
36	2754.914	3539.009	4545.685	5837.047	7492.111	9611.279	12321.95	15785.58	25842.88	42150.73	68468.64	36
37	3279.348	4247.811	5501.279	7122.197	9216.297	11918.99	15403.44	19890.83	33079.88	54796.95	90379.61	37
38	3903.424	5098.374	6657.547	8690.080	11337.05	14780.54	19255.30	25063.44	42343.25	71237.03	119302.1	38
39	4646.075	6119.048	8056.632	10602.90	13945.57	18328.87	24070.12	31580.94	54200.36	92609.14	157479.8	39
40	5529.829	7343.858	9749.525	12936.54	17154.05	22728.80	30088.66	39792.98	69377.46	120392.9	207874.3	40
41	6581.496	8813.629	11797.93	15783.57	21100.48	28184.72	37611.82	50140.16	88804.15	156511.7	274395.0	41
42	7832.981	10577.36	14276.49	19256.96	25954.59	34950.05	47015.77	63177.60	113670.3	203466.3	362202.5	42
43	9322.247	12693.83	17275.55	23494.49	31925.14	43339.06	58770.72	79604.77	145499.0	264507.2	478108.2	43
44	11094.47	15233.59	20904.42	28664.28	39268.92	53741.43	73464.40	100303.0	186239.7	343860.3	631103.9	44
45	13203.42	18281.31	25295.35	34971.42	48301.77	66640.38	91831.50	126382.8	238387.8	447019.4	833058.1	45
46	15713.07	21938.57	30608.37	42666.13	59412.18	82635.07	114790.4	159243.3	305137.4	581126.2	1099637.7	46
47	18699.56	26327.29	37037.13	52053.68	73077.98	102468.5	143489.0	200647.6	390576.9	755465.1	1451522.8	47
48	22253.48	31593.74	44815.92	63506.49	89886.92	127061.9	179362.2	252817.0	499939.5	982105.6	1916011.1	48
49	26482.64	37913.49	54228.27	77478.92	110561.9	157557.8	224203.8	318550.4	639923.5	1276738.3	2529135.6	49
50	31515.34	45497.19	65617.20	94525.28	135992.2	195372.6	280255.7	401374.5	819103.1	1659760.7	3338460.0	50

Table IV
Present Value of Annuity of $1

n	8%	9%	10%	11%	12%	13%	14%	15%	16%	17%	18%	n
1	0.92593	0.91743	0.90909	0.90090	0.89286	0.88496	0.87719	0.86957	0.86207	0.85470	0.84746	1
2	1.78326	1.75911	1.73554	1.71252	1.69005	1.66810	1.64666	1.62571	1.60523	1.58521	1.56564	2
3	2.57710	2.53129	2.48685	2.44371	2.40183	2.36115	2.32163	2.28323	2.24589	2.20958	2.17427	3
4	3.31213	3.23972	3.16987	3.10245	3.03735	2.97447	2.91371	2.85498	2.79818	2.74324	2.69006	4
5	3.99271	3.88965	3.79079	3.69590	3.60478	3.51723	3.43308	3.35216	3.27429	3.19935	3.12717	5
6	4.62288	4.48592	4.35526	4.23054	4.11141	3.99755	3.88867	3.78448	3.68474	3.58918	3.49760	6
7	5.20637	5.03295	4.86842	4.71220	4.56376	4.42261	4.28830	4.16042	4.03857	3.92238	3.81153	7
8	5.74664	5.53482	5.33493	5.14612	4.96764	4.79877	4.63886	4.48732	4.34359	4.20716	4.07757	8
9	6.24689	5.99525	5.75902	5.53705	5.32825	5.13166	4.94637	4.77158	4.60654	4.45057	4.30302	9
10	6.71008	6.41766	6.14457	5.88923	5.65022	5.42624	5.21612	5.01877	4.83323	4.65860	4.49409	10
11	7.13896	6.80519	6.49506	6.20652	5.93770	5.68694	5.45273	5.23371	5.02864	4.83641	4.65601	11
12	7.53608	7.16073	6.81369	6.49236	6.19437	5.91765	5.66029	5.42062	5.19711	4.98839	4.79322	12
13	7.90378	7.48690	7.10336	6.74987	6.42355	6.12181	5.84236	5.58315	5.34233	5.11828	4.90951	13
14	8.24424	7.78615	7.36669	6.98187	6.62817	6.30249	6.00207	5.72448	5.46753	5.22930	5.00806	14
15	8.55948	8.06069	7.60608	7.19087	6.81086	6.46238	6.14217	5.84737	5.57546	5.32419	5.09158	15
16	8.85137	8.31256	7.82371	7.37916	6.97399	6.60388	6.26506	5.95423	5.66850	5.40529	5.16235	16
17	9.12164	8.54363	8.02155	7.54879	7.11963	6.72909	6.37286	6.04716	5.74870	5.47461	5.22233	17
18	9.37189	8.75563	8.20141	7.70162	7.24967	6.83991	6.46742	6.12797	5.81785	5.53385	5.27316	18
19	9.60360	8.95011	8.36492	7.83929	7.36578	6.93797	6.55037	6.19823	5.87746	5.58449	5.31624	19
20	9.81815	9.12855	8.51356	7.96333	7.46944	7.02475	6.62313	6.25933	5.92884	5.62777	5.35275	20
21	10.01680	9.29224	8.64869	8.07507	7.56200	7.10155	6.68696	6.31246	5.97314	5.66476	5.38368	21
22	10.20074	9.44243	8.77154	8.17574	7.64465	7.16951	6.74294	6.35866	6.01133	5.69637	5.40990	22
23	10.37106	9.58021	8.88322	8.26643	7.71843	7.22966	6.79206	6.39884	6.04425	5.72340	5.43212	23
24	10.52876	9.70661	8.98474	8.34814	7.78432	7.28288	6.83514	6.43377	6.07263	5.74649	5.45095	24
25	10.67478	9.82258	9.07704	8.42174	7.84314	7.32998	6.87293	6.46415	6.09709	5.76623	5.46691	25
26	10.80998	9.92897	9.16095	8.48806	7.89566	7.37167	6.90608	6.49056	6.11818	5.78311	5.48043	26
27	10.93516	10.02658	9.23722	8.54780	7.94255	7.40856	6.93515	6.51353	6.13636	5.79753	5.49189	27
28	11.05108	10.11613	9.30657	8.60162	7.98442	7.44120	6.96066	6.53351	6.15204	5.80985	5.50160	28
29	11.15841	10.19828	9.36961	8.65011	8.02181	7.47009	6.98304	6.55088	6.16555	5.82039	5.50983	29
30	11.25778	10.27365	9.42691	8.69379	8.05518	7.49565	7.00266	6.56598	6.17720	5.82939	5.51681	30
31	11.34980	10.34280	9.47901	8.73315	8.08499	7.51828	7.01988	6.57911	6.18724	5.83709	5.52272	31
32	11.43500	10.40624	9.52638	8.76860	8.11159	7.53830	7.03498	6.59053	6.19590	5.84366	5.52773	32
33	11.51389	10.46444	9.56943	8.80054	8.13535	7.55602	7.04823	6.60046	6.20336	5.84928	5.53197	33
34	11.58693	10.51784	9.60857	8.82932	8.15656	7.57170	7.05985	6.60910	6.20979	5.85409	5.53557	34
35	11.65457	10.56682	9.64416	8.85524	8.17550	7.58557	7.07005	6.61661	6.21534	5.85820	5.53862	35
36	11.71719	10.61176	9.67651	8.87859	8.19241	7.59785	7.07899	6.62314	6.22012	5.86171	5.54120	36
37	11.77518	10.65299	9.70592	8.89963	8.20751	7.60872	7.08683	6.62881	6.22424	5.86471	5.54339	37
38	11.82887	10.69082	9.73265	8.91859	8.22099	7.61833	7.09371	6.63375	6.22779	5.86727	5.54525	38
39	11.87858	10.72552	9.75696	8.93567	8.23303	7.62684	7.09975	6.63805	6.23086	5.86946	5.54682	39
40	11.92461	10.75736	9.77905	8.95105	8.24378	7.63438	7.10504	6.64178	6.23350	5.87133	5.54815	40
41	11.96723	10.78657	9.79914	8.96491	8.25337	7.64104	7.10969	6.64502	6.23577	5.87294	5.54928	41
42	12.00670	10.81337	9.81740	8.97740	8.26194	7.64694	7.11376	6.64785	6.23774	5.87430	5.55024	42
43	12.04324	10.83795	9.83400	8.98865	8.26959	7.65216	7.11733	6.65030	6.23943	5.87547	5.55105	43
44	12.07707	10.86051	9.84909	8.99878	8.27642	7.65678	7.12047	6.65244	6.24089	5.87647	5.55174	44
45	12.10840	10.88120	9.86281	9.00791	8.28252	7.66086	7.12322	6.65429	6.24214	5.87733	5.55232	45
46	12.13741	10.90018	9.87528	9.01614	8.28796	7.66448	7.12563	6.65591	6.24323	5.87806	5.55281	46
47	12.16427	10.91760	9.88662	9.02355	8.29282	7.66768	7.12774	6.65731	6.24416	5.87868	5.55323	47
48	12.18914	10.93358	9.89693	9.03022	8.29716	7.67052	7.12960	6.65853	6.24497	5.87922	5.55359	48
49	12.21216	10.94823	9.90630	9.03624	8.30104	7.67302	7.13123	6.65959	6.24566	5.87967	5.55389	49
50	12.23348	10.96168	9.91481	9.04165	8.30450	7.67524	7.13266	6.66051	6.24626	5.88006	5.55414	50

Table IV
Present Value of Annuity of $1 (continued)

n	19%	20%	21%	22%	23%	24%	25%	26%	28%	30%	32%	n
1	0.84034	0.83333	0.82645	0.81967	0.81301	0.80645	0.80000	0.79365	0.78125	0.76923	0.75758	1
2	1.54650	1.52778	1.50946	1.49153	1.47399	1.45682	1.44000	1.42353	1.39160	1.36095	1.33150	2
3	2.13992	2.10648	2.07393	2.04224	2.01137	1.98130	1.95200	1.92344	1.86844	1.81611	1.76629	3
4	2.63859	2.58873	2.54044	2.49364	2.44827	2.40428	2.36160	2.32019	2.24097	2.16624	2.09567	4
5	3.05763	2.99061	2.92598	2.86364	2.80347	2.74538	2.68928	2.63507	2.53201	2.43557	2.34521	5
6	3.40978	3.32551	3.24462	3.16692	3.09225	3.02047	2.95142	2.88498	2.75938	2.64275	2.53425	6
7	3.70570	3.60459	3.50795	3.41551	3.32704	3.24232	3.16114	3.08331	2.93702	2.80211	2.67746	7
8	3.95437	3.83716	3.72558	3.61927	3.51792	3.42122	3.32891	3.24073	3.07579	2.92470	2.78595	8
9	4.16333	4.03097	3.90543	3.78628	3.67310	3.56550	3.46313	3.36566	3.18421	3.01900	2.86815	9
10	4.33893	4.19247	4.05408	3.92318	3.79927	3.68186	3.57050	3.46481	3.26892	3.09154	2.93041	10
11	4.48650	4.32706	4.17692	4.03540	3.90185	3.77569	3.65640	3.54350	3.33509	3.14734	2.97759	11
12	4.61050	4.43922	4.27845	4.12737	3.98524	3.85136	3.72512	3.60595	3.38679	3.19026	3.01332	12
13	4.71471	4.53268	4.36235	4.20277	4.05304	3.91239	3.78010	3.65552	3.42718	3.22328	3.04040	13
14	4.80228	4.61057	4.43170	4.26456	4.10816	3.96160	3.82408	3.69485	3.45873	3.24867	3.06091	14
15	4.87586	4.67547	4.48901	4.31522	4.15298	4.00129	3.85926	3.72607	3.48339	3.26821	3.07644	15
16	4.93770	4.72956	4.53637	4.35673	4.18941	4.03330	3.88741	3.75085	3.50265	3.28324	3.08822	16
17	4.98966	4.77463	4.57551	4.39077	4.21904	4.05911	3.90993	3.77052	3.51769	3.29480	3.09713	17
18	5.03333	4.81219	4.60786	4.41866	4.24312	4.07993	3.92794	3.78613	3.52945	3.30369	3.10389	18
19	5.07003	4.84350	4.63460	4.44152	4.26270	4.09672	3.94235	3.79851	3.53863	3.31053	3.10901	19
20	5.10086	4.86958	4.65669	4.46027	4.27862	4.11026	3.95388	3.80834	3.54580	3.31579	3.11288	20
21	5.12677	4.89132	4.67495	4.47563	4.29156	4.12117	3.96311	3.81615	3.55141	3.31984	3.11582	21
22	5.14855	4.90943	4.69004	4.48822	4.30208	4.12998	3.97049	3.82234	3.55579	3.32296	3.11805	22
23	5.16685	4.92453	4.70251	4.49854	4.31063	4.13708	3.97639	3.82725	3.55921	3.32535	3.11973	23
24	5.18223	4.93710	4.71282	4.50700	4.31759	4.14281	3.98111	3.83115	3.56188	3.32719	3.12101	24
25	5.19515	4.94759	4.72134	4.51393	4.32324	4.14742	3.98489	3.83425	3.56397	3.32861	3.12198	25
26	5.20601	4.95632	4.72838	4.51962	4.32784	4.15115	3.98791	3.83670	3.56560	3.32970	3.12271	26
27	5.21513	4.96360	4.73420	4.52428	4.33158	4.15415	3.99033	3.83865	3.56688	3.33054	3.12326	27
28	5.22280	4.96967	4.73901	4.52810	4.33462	4.15657	3.99226	3.84020	3.56787	3.33118	3.12369	28
29	5.22924	4.97472	4.74298	4.53123	4.33709	4.15853	3.99381	3.84143	3.56865	3.33168	3.12400	29
30	5.23466	4.97894	4.74627	4.53379	4.33909	4.16010	3.99505	3.84240	3.56926	3.33206	3.12425	30
31	5.23921	4.98245	4.74898	4.53590	4.34073	4.16137	3.99604	3.84318	3.56973	3.33235	3.12443	31
32	5.24303	4.98537	4.75122	4.53762	4.34205	4.16240	3.99683	3.84379	3.57010	3.33258	3.12457	32
33	5.24625	4.98781	4.75308	4.53903	4.34313	4.16322	3.99746	3.84428	3.57039	3.33275	3.12467	33
34	5.24895	4.98984	4.75461	4.54019	4.34401	4.16389	3.99797	3.84467	3.57062	3.33289	3.12475	34
35	5.25122	4.99154	4.75588	4.54114	4.34472	4.16443	3.99838	3.84497	3.57080	3.33299	3.12481	35
36	5.25312	4.99295	4.75692	4.54192	4.34530	4.16486	3.99870	3.84522	3.57094	3.33307	3.12486	36
37	5.25472	4.99412	4.75779	4.54256	4.34578	4.16521	3.99896	3.84541	3.57104	3.33313	3.12489	37
38	5.25607	4.99510	4.75850	4.54308	4.34616	4.16549	3.99917	3.84556	3.57113	3.33318	3.12492	38
39	5.25720	4.99592	4.75909	4.54351	4.34647	4.16572	3.99934	3.84569	3.57119	3.33321	3.12494	39
40	5.25815	4.99660	4.75958	4.54386	4.34672	4.16590	3.99947	3.84578	3.57124	3.33324	3.12495	40
41	5.25895	4.99717	4.75998	4.54415	4.34693	4.16605	3.99957	3.84586	3.57128	3.33326	3.12496	41
42	5.25962	4.99764	4.76032	4.54438	4.34710	4.16617	3.99966	3.84592	3.57132	3.33328	3.12497	42
43	5.26019	4.99803	4.76059	4.54458	4.34723	4.16627	3.99973	3.84597	3.57134	3.33329	3.12498	43
44	5.26066	4.99836	4.76082	4.54473	4.34734	4.16634	3.99978	3.84601	3.57136	3.33330	3.12498	44
45	5.26106	4.99863	4.76101	4.54486	4.34743	4.16641	3.99983	3.84604	3.57138	3.33331	3.12499	45
46	5.26140	4.99886	4.76116	4.54497	4.34751	4.16646	3.99986	3.84606	3.57139	3.33331	3.12499	46
47	5.26168	4.99905	4.76129	4.54506	4.34757	4.16650	3.99989	3.84608	3.57140	3.33332	3.12499	47
48	5.26191	4.99921	4.76140	4.54513	4.34762	4.16653	3.99991	3.84610	3.57140	3.33332	3.12499	48
49	5.26211	4.99934	4.76149	4.54519	4.34766	4.16656	3.99993	3.84611	3.57141	3.33332	3.12500	49
50	5.26228	4.99945	4.76156	4.54524	4.34769	4.16658	3.99994	3.84612	3.57141	3.33333	3.12500	50

Table V
Areas Under the Normal Curve

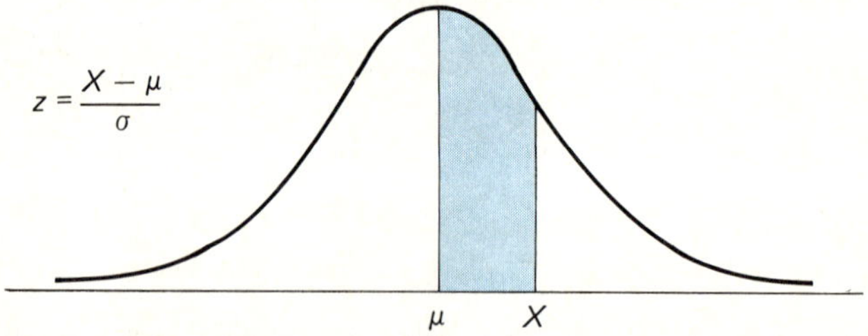

z	.00	.01	.02	.03	.04	.05	.06	.07	.08	.09
.00	.00000	.00399	.00798	.01197	.01595	.01994	.02392	.02790	.03188	.03586
.10	.03983	.04379	.04776	.05172	.05567	.05962	.06356	.06749	.07142	.07534
.20	.07926	.08317	.08706	.09095	.09483	.09871	.10257	.10642	.11026	.11409
.30	.11791	.12172	.12551	.12930	.13307	.13683	.14058	.14431	.14803	.15173
.40	.15542	.15910	.16276	.16640	.17003	.17364	.17724	.18082	.18438	.18793
.50	.19146	.19497	.19847	.20194	.20540	.20884	.21226	.21566	.21904	.22240
.60	.22575	.22907	.23237	.23565	.23891	.24215	.24537	.24857	.25175	.25490
.70	.25803	.26115	.26424	.26730	.27035	.27337	.27637	.27935	.28230	.28523
.80	.28814	.29103	.29389	.29673	.29954	.30234	.30510	.30785	.31057	.31327
.90	.31594	.31859	.32121	.32381	.32639	.32894	.33147	.33397	.33645	.33891
1.00	.34134	.34375	.34613	.34849	.35083	.35314	.35543	.35769	.35993	.36214
1.10	.36433	.36650	.36864	.37076	.37285	.37493	.37697	.37900	.38100	.38297
1.20	.38493	.38686	.38877	.39065	.39251	.39435	.39616	.39796	.39973	.40147
1.30	.40320	.40490	.40658	.40824	.40988	.41149	.41308	.41465	.41620	.41773
1.40	.41924	.42073	.42219	.42364	.42506	.42647	.42785	.42922	.43056	.43189
1.50	.43319	.43448	.43574	.43699	.43822	.43943	.44062	.44179	.44295	.44408
1.60	.44520	.44630	.44738	.44845	.44950	.45053	.45154	.45254	.45352	.45448
1.70	.45543	.45637	.45728	.45818	.45907	.45994	.46079	.46164	.46246	.46327
1.80	.46407	.46485	.46562	.46637	.46711	.46784	.46856	.46926	.46994	.47062
1.90	.47128	.47193	.47257	.47320	.47381	.47441	.47500	.47558	.47615	.47670
2.00	.47725	.47778	.47831	.47882	.47932	.47982	.48030	.48077	.48124	.48169
2.10	.48213	.48257	.48300	.48341	.48382	.48422	.48461	.48500	.48537	.48574
2.20	.48610	.48645	.48679	.48713	.48745	.48777	.48809	.48840	.48870	.48899
2.30	.48928	.48956	.48983	.49010	.49036	.49061	.49086	.49111	.49134	.49158
2.40	.49180	.49202	.49224	.49245	.49266	.49286	.49305	.49324	.49343	.49361
2.50	.49379	.49396	.49413	.49430	.49446	.49461	.49477	.49491	.49506	.49520
2.60	.49534	.49547	.49560	.49573	.49585	.49598	.49609	.49621	.49632	.49643
2.70	.49653	.49664	.49674	.49683	.49693	.49702	.49711	.49720	.49728	.49736
2.80	.49744	.49752	.49760	.49767	.49774	.49781	.49788	.49795	.49801	.49807
2.90	.49813	.49819	.49825	.49831	.49836	.49841	.49846	.49851	.49856	.49860
3.00	.49865	.49869	.49874	.49878	.49882	.49886	.49889	.49893	.49896	.49900
3.10	.49903	.49906	.49910	.49913	.49916	.49918	.49921	.49924	.49926	.49929
3.20	.49931	.49934	.49936	.49938	.49940	.49942	.49944	.49946	.49948	.49950
3.30	.49952	.49953	.49955	.49957	.49958	.49960	.49961	.49962	.49964	.49965
3.40	.49966	.49968	.49969	.49970	.49971	.49972	.49973	.49974	.49975	.49976

Glossary

The number in parentheses after each term refers to the chapter in which the term is first described.

abnormal spoiled unit cost (17) The manufacturing costs incurred in making products that are lost or spoiled in the production process.

absorption costing (10) A product costing method in which all costs of production, direct and indirect, fixed and variable, are included in the costs of products. Also called full costing.

Accelerated Cost Recovery System (ACRS) (13) A system of asset depreciation required for tax reporting purposes for assets acquired after December 31, 1980.

accounting information (1) Financial information that is relevant, timely, and accurate and is produced by an entity's accounting system

accounting rate of return (ARR) (13) A method of capital expenditure investment analysis that uses accounting measures of income and investment as the basis for evaluating investment projects.

accuracy (1) A characteristic of accounting information referring to accounting information that is free from error.

acid test ratio (19) The ratio of liquid assets to current liabilities, used as a measure of liquidity. Also called the quick ratio.

activity costing (2) The process of determining costs for activities of a business other than manufacturing.

actual cost (2) The cost actually incurred in producing a product or providing a service. Also called historical cost.

actual cost transfer price (11) A price assigned to products or services transferred between segments of an organization. The price is based on the actual cost of making the product or providing the service.

actual hours (9) The number of direct labor hours actually worked during some reporting period. Usually reported in a labor summary report.

administrative expense budget (7) Estimated administrative expenses for a specified time period, such as a month or a year.

all financial resources (20) The concept of reporting all financing and investing activities in the statement of changes in financial position, including those that do not affect cash or working capital, such as exchanges of stock or long-term debt for fixed assets.

allocation (4) The process of assigning common costs to cost objectives in some systematic manner in accordance with the matching principle. **(14)** One of the three basic objectives of public finance, intended to provide socially desirable goods and services in the right amount.

allocation base (4) An activity or use measure used to assign common costs to cost objectives.

alternative choice decision (6) A decision involving the choice between two or more decision alternatives or courses of action.

application base (4) A measure of some activity, such as direct labor hours, units of production, sales revenue, or machine hours, used to compute an overhead application rate.

assets employed (11) An asset base used to measure performance of a segment of an organization. The base includes all assets except those not employed in the normal course of business activities.

average age of receivables (19) *See* days' sales in receivables.

average collection period (19) *See* days' sales in receivables.

average cost (15) Inventory valuation method that weights the cost of beginning and current period inventory. The method is used for perpetual and periodic inventory systems. **(17)** In process costing, used to cost the production of units produced during the period.

average cost inventory method (15) A method of inventory valuation in which the total cost of inventory is divided by the number of units to determine the weighted average cost. This cost is used for valuing ending inventory and for charging product costs to cost of goods sold.

average cumulative cost (18) The average unit cost of all units produced at some specific volume of production in a production environment in which a learning effect occurs.

average days' supply in inventory (19) A ratio used to measure liquidity, calculated by dividing inventory turnover into the number of days in the accounting period.

average incremental cost (18) In a learning curve environment, the average unit cost of the incremental units that are produced.

average standard contribution margin (16) The average contribution margin provided by the expected product sales mix.

average standard cost of inputs (16) The average unit cost of production inputs at the standard mix of inputs.

bail-out (13) A capital budgeting project evaluation method that measures how quickly the project's investment can be recovered from the combination of cash savings and the salvage value of the investment at any point in time.

basic standards (8) Long-term standards created for a period of 2 to 5 years or more. Used as a benchmark for long-term comparison.

benefit-cost analysis (2) The comparison of costs and benefits in evaluating alternative courses of action. (14) The formal project evaluation phase of budgeting using the federal government Planning, Programming, Budgeting System (PPBS).

break-even point (5) The activity level that yields zero profit, where total revenue equals total costs.

budget (7) A comprehensive quantitative plan for utilizing the resources of an entity for some specified period of time.

budget variance (7) The difference between budgeted data and actual results.

budget variance report (7) An internal report that shows the difference between budget data and actual results

budgeted activity level (4) The estimated amount of activity for the coming accounting period expressed in terms of the application base, e.g., 10,000 direct labor hours. The budgeted activity level is estimated before the accounting period begins.

budgeted hours (9) The number of direct labor hours budgeted before the accounting period begins. Usually used in creating the manufacturing overhead rate and in computing manufacturing overhead volume variances in a standard cost system.

budgeted income statement (7) Estimated revenues and expenses for an entity for some specified time period in the form of a pro forma income statement.

budgeted overhead cost (4) The estimated amount of overhead costs determined before the accounting period begins. Used in the computation of a predetermined overhead rate.

budgeted overhead rate (4) A rate for applying overhead to production during the accounting period, e.g., $5 per machine hour; the rate is determined before the accounting period begins. Also called a predetermined overhead rate.

budgeted statement of financial position (7) An estimated statement of financial position for some specific future point in time. Also called a budgeted balance sheet.

by-product (4) A product of relatively small economic value that results from the production of a main product or group of products, e.g., particle board made from sawdust in the production of lumber.

capacity costs (2) Cost required to provide and operate a production facility, sometimes called occupancy costs.

capital budgeting (13) The systematic process of identifying and evaluating capital investment projects to arrive at a capital expenditure budget.

capital expenditure budget (7) The report identifying an organization's plans for investing in capital projects with lives typically exceeding one accounting year and representing relatively large expenditures.

capital rationing (13) The process of selecting the more desirable projects from a series of profitable investments.

carrying costs (15) Costs such as inventory storage and handling costs that are essential in maintaining an inventory of goods ready for sale or for use in the production process.

cash budget (7) Estimated cash receipts and disbursements of an entity for some specified time period, starting with the expected beginning cash balance and ending with the expected ending cash balance.

cash flow statement (20) The statements of changes in financial position with funds defined as cash; primarily used for internal decision making.

Certificate in Management Accounting (CMA) (1) A certificate granted by the Institute of Management Accounting to candidates who have successfully completed a rigorous professional examination administered by the institute and have met certain work experience requirements.

certified public accountant (CPA) (1) A professional accountant who has passed a professional examination, obtained practical experience, satisfied other requirements, and is certified to practice public accounting and to audit financial statements in his state of residence.

clearing account (3) An account used to accumulate costs until they can be distributed to various cost objectives or expense accounts. The Payroll account is an example. Also called a holding account.

coefficient of correlation (18) A statistic known as r whose value ranges from -1 to $+1$ and that explains the strength of the relationship between the movement of two sets of data. If r has a value close to -1 or $+1$ it represents a strong relationship; a value close to zero represents a weak relationship.

coefficient of determination (18) A statistic known as r^2 that is obtained by squaring the coefficient of correlation. Its value ranges from zero to 1 and it measures the strength of the relationship between two sets of data, with the stronger relationship designated by values closer to 1 and the weaker relationship designated by values closer to zero.

coefficient of nondetermination (18) A statistic calculated as $1 - r^2$ where r^2 is the coefficient of determination. The coefficient of nondetermination explains random fluctuation in a set of data and fluctuations caused by variables other than the independent variable.

committed fixed costs (2) The fixed costs of providing production facilities and other relatively long-term commitments of resources. Fixed costs that cannot be easily or quickly eliminated.

common cost (2) A cost that is not identifiable with a single cost objective but instead is shared by, or common to, more than one cost objective, e.g., the salary of a production plant manager shared by all producing departments in the manufacturing plant.

contribution approach (10) A cost reporting approach that highlights cost behavior characteristics rather than functional cost characteristics. Variable costs are deducted from sales to determine the amount contributed toward covering fixed costs and providing profit.

contribution approach pricing (12) A form of cost-plus pricing using variable costs plus an amount or percentage as the basis for setting the price.

contribution margin (5) The difference between the selling price and the variable cost of a product or service. Both the manufacturing and nonmanufacturing variable costs per unit are deducted from the selling price to determine the contribution margin. In aggregate, contribution margin is the difference between total sales and total variable costs.

contribution margin variance (16) A measure of the difference between the standard contribution margin and the actual contribution margin generated by a product for some time period.

control (7) The concept of monitoring activities and taking action to correct undesirable performance, often using budgets as a basis for measuring performance.

control account (2) An account whose balance represents the total of all balances in accounts of a related subsidiary ledger. Accounts Receivable is the control account for the individual accounts of amounts owed by customers.

controllable cost (2) A cost over which a manager has direct control or significant influence.

controllable variance (9) The difference between actual manufacturing overhead and a flexible overhead budget based on actual output in the two-variance method of overhead variance analysis. Equal to the sum of the spending and efficiency variances in a three-way overhead variance analysis.

conversion cost (2) Direct labor cost and manufacturing overhead cost combined.

cost (2) The amount of resource given up for some product or service.

cost accounting (1) The process of determining the cost of some product or activity.

cost accounting data base (1) The set of cost accounting data used for both internal and external accounting reports.

Cost Accounting Standards Board (CASB) (1) A five-member board that was created by Congress to establish cost accounting standards and procedures for costing goods and services provided under contracts negotiated with the federal government. The board is no longer in existence but its pronouncements still are in effect.

cost after split-off (4) The joint product production cost that occurs after the split-off point and therefore is identifiable with a specific product.

cost allocation (2) The process of assigning common costs to cost objectives in accordance with the matching principle.

cost analyzing (1) A basic activity in cost accounting dealing with the systematic evaluation of cost data to solve problems and to provide relevant information.

cost behavior (2) The way a cost changes with respect to changes in the level of activity. Usually classified as fixed, variable, semifixed, semivariable, or mixed.

cost-benefit analysis (1) The process of analyzing the benefits derived from some project or activity with the cost necessary to do it. To be acceptable the benefits must be greater than the costs.

cost of capital (13) The amount that an organization pays for the capital that it uses.

cost center (11) A responsibility center in which managers are held responsible for the costs under their control.

cost determination (1) A basic activity of cost accounting dealing with the measurement of costs for some specific product or activity.

cost elements (2) The three basic components of product cost—direct materials, direct labor, and manufacturing overhead.

cost of estimation error (15) The cost that arises from incorrectly estimating the value of variables used in management decision making.

cost of goods manufactured (2) The cost of the products transferred from work in process inventory to finished goods inventory during a period. Usually reported in a cost of goods manufactured schedule showing beginning work in process, current period production costs, and ending work in process.

cost indifference point (6) The activity level at which the total costs of two alternatives are identical. At this level of activity managers are indifferent between the two alternatives in terms of cost.

cost objective (2) The product or activity whose cost is being determined.

cost-plus pricing (12) A type of pricing model using costs plus an amount or percentage as the basis for determining the price.

cost of production report (17) A report used to summarize production costs in a process center of a process costing system.

cost recording (1) The process of recording cost data in the formal accounting records of an organization.

cost reporting (1) Communicating cost information in the form of internal and external reports.

cost-volume-profit analysis (5) Analyses that deal with how costs and profits change in relation to changes in the volume of activity.

cost-volume-profit chart (5) A graphic presentation of cost-volume-profit relationships. Often called a CVP chart. Frequently useful for presenting complex cost relationships graphically.

costs to account for (17) The section of the cost of production report that reports the production costs incurred in the process center during the period.

costs accounted for (17) The section of a cost of production report that shows the disposition of costs that occurred in the process center during the reporting period. Typically costs are transferred to the next process center or remain in the process center's ending work in process inventory.

currently attainable standards (8) Standards that describe desired levels of performance but that reflect the realities of the operating environment, such as machine breakdowns.

daily time ticket (3) A document used by employees to record how they spent their workday. A source document used to identify labor cost with cost objectives.

data (1) The basic facts and figures that constitute a data base; the building blocks of an information system.

data base (1) The foundation of data supporting an information system or a portion of an information system; the data drawn on by users to meet information needs.

days' sales in receivables (19) A ratio used to measure liquidity, calculated by dividing the receivables turnover into the number of days in the accounting period.

debt/equity ratio (19) A measure of solvency calculated by dividing total liabilities by total owners' equity.

debt ratio (19) A measure of solvency calculated by dividing total liabilities by total equities, indicating the percentage of equities provided by creditors.

decentralization (11) The process of delegating decision authority to various levels in the organization.

decision model (1) A description of how a particular decision is made.

decision theory (1) The body of knowledge concerning the process of decision making.

delegation (11) The process of assigning decision authority and responsibility to managers of various segments of an organization.

demand (12) The total amount of product or service all purchasers are willing to buy at all possible prices.

demand curve (12) A graphic presentation showing the amount buyers in aggregate are willing to buy at all possible prices.

demand elasticity (12) A measure of the way demand for goods or services changes with changing prices. If demand is elastic, a decrease in price results in higher revenue because demand increases more than enough to offset the lower price. The opposite is true of inelastic demand.

departmental job cost sheet (3) A job cost sheet that identifies manufacturing costs by department or production function as well as by cost elements.

departmental overhead rates (4) Manufacturing overhead rates created for individual departments or groups of departments rather than one overhead rate for an entire production plant. The purpose of departmental rates is to do a better job of matching overhead costs with the revenues generated by the sale of products.

dependent variable (18) The variable whose value is to be predicted by means of a linear regression line and that depends on the values of the independent variable.

differential cost (6) A cost that differs between decision alternatives.

direct allocation (4) A method of allocating service department overhead costs directly to producing departments without any allocation to other service departments.

direct costing (10) *See* variable costing.

direct labor (2) Labor that is directly identifiable with a specific product or activity.

direct labor budget (7) Estimated direct labor costs and quantities of an entity for some time period.

direct materials (2) Raw materials used in the production process that can be identified with specific products.

direct materials budget (7) A formal plan describing the use of direct materials for some specific time period. Part of the master budget.

discounted cash flows (DCF) (13) Capital budgeting and other types of analyses that rely on the time value of money. All cash flows are discounted at some interest rate to their present value.

discretionary fixed costs (2) Fixed costs that can be eliminated at managements' discretion in a relatively short period of time, e.g., some administrative salaries, research and development costs, and new systems development costs.

dispersion (18) A measure of the amount by which data fluctuate about some measure of central tendency.

distribution (14) A basic objective of public finance concerned with who should receive the economic benefits of society and in what amount.

dividend payout (19) A ratio indicating what percentage of net income is paid by a corporation in the form of dividends, calculated by dividing dividends per share by earnings per share.

dividend yield (19) The rate of return on common stock, calculated as the dividend per share divided by the price per share of stock.

division contribution statement (10) A contribution report identifying the amount of contribution margin provided by each division of a company.

division income statement (10) An income statement identifying net income by division.

dynamic budget (9) *See* flexible budget.

EBIT (19) Earnings before interest and taxes.

economic order quantity (EOQ) (15) The optimum order size that results in the lowest total inventory cost for some specific inventory item.

efficiency variance (9) The difference in variable manufacturing overhead caused by using more or fewer hours than standard. Also used to describe labor variances caused by using more or fewer hours than standard.

engineering standards (8) Very tight standards assuming no production problems, sometimes called ideal standards.

equity ratio (19) A measure of solvency calculated by dividing total owners' equity by total equities, indicating the percentage of equities contributed by shareholders.

equivalent units (17) A measure of the amount of production in a process center. The amount of equivalent whole units that would have been produced if all efforts had been devoted to starting and completing units rather than completing units in beginning inventory and starting but not completing units in ending inventory.

estimated activity level (4) *See* budgeted activity level.

estimated overhead cost (4) *See* budgeted overhead cost.

expected contribution margin (16) The contribution margin expected from sales based on the expected mix of product sales. The same as the weighted average contribution margin except the expected contribution margin is based on expected data rather than historical data.

exponential smoothing (18) A statistical technique of trend analysis using an alpha factor to assign weights to new data for the purpose of calculating a trend line.

external reporting (1) *See* financial accounting.

factory burden (3) *See* manufacturing overhead.

factory overhead rate (3) *See* manufacturing overhead rate.

favorable variance (8) The amount by which standard costs exceed actual costs. Any variance in which actual cost is less than standard cost.

Federal Trade Commission (FTC) (1) An agency of the federal government primarily involved in ensuring the use of fair practices in business and trade activities. The Robinson-Patman Act and lines of business reporting are administered by the FTC.

FICA tax (3) Social security tax required to be withheld from employees with an equal amount matched and paid by employers.

financial accounting (1) Accounting for the financial affairs of entities for the purpose of reporting such affairs to those outside the entity. Also called external reporting.

Financial Accounting Standards Board (FASB) (1) An independent rule-making body charged with issuing financial accounting rules known as Standards.

financial analysis (19) The interpretation of financial statements for the purpose of assessing past business performance, evaluating present business conditions, and predicting future potential for business success.

financial budget (7) The set of budgets including the capital expenditures budget, cash budget, budgeted balance sheet, and budgeted statement of changes in financial position.

financial leverage (19) The benefit obtained by borrowing money at one rate of interest and investing it at a higher rate of interest so that the return on the investor's equity is greater than it would be without borrowing.

financing activities (20) Business activities that provide funds, reported in the statement of changes in financial position. Examples include operations that generate net income, investment by owners, borrowing, and sale of noncurrent assets.

finished goods (2) Products in a manufacturing firm that have been completed and are ready for sale.

first in, first out (FIFO) (15) The inventory valuation method that assumes that the inventory acquired earliest is the first to be used or sold. The method refers to the flow of costs rather than to the physical flow of goods.

fiscal policy (14) One of the two instruments of economic stabilization policy dealing with the taxing and spending actions of government.

fixed budget (7) A budget prepared for a single expected level of activity. Also called a static budget.

fixed cost (2) A cost that does not change with the level of activity. Described by the general formula $Y = a$.

fixed overhead (7) The portion of manufacturing overhead that does not change with changing levels of activity.

flexible budget (9) A budget prepared for more than one level of activity, covering several levels within the relevant range of activity. Also called a dynamic budget.

full costing (10) *See* absorption costing.

functional budget (14) *See* line budget.

funds (20) Cash or working capital whose change is reported in the statement of changes in financial position.

funds flow statement (20) *See* statement of changes in financial position.

funds provided by operations (20) The amount of cash or working capital provided by operating the business rather than from other sources, generally consisting of net income adjusted for nonfund items and reported in the statement of changes in financial position.

gross payroll (3) The payroll cost for a period, computed as the wage rate multiplied by the time worked. The amount of pay from which employee withholdings are deducted to arrive at net pay.

gross profit allocation method (4) A method of assigning joint product costs to products so that each product contributes an equal percentage of gross margin on sales.

high-cost input (16) An input used in a multiple-resource production process that costs more than the average standard cost of inputs.

high-low method (5) A method of estimating the fixed and variable cost components of a mixed cost. Based on the difference between the highest and lowest costs experienced in a specific time period and the difference in activity level.

high-profit product (16) A product that provides a profit or contribution margin that is higher than the average profit or contribution margin provided by all products.

historical costs (2) Costs that have already occurred. Also called actual costs.

horizontal analysis (19) Financial analysis involving the comparison of figures in financial statements of two or more consecutive accounting periods.

ideal standards (8) Very tight, hard-to-achieve standards assuming ideal production conditions.

independent variable (17) The variable whose value is used in linear regression analysis to predict the value of the dependent variable.

indirect costs (2) Costs that cannot be identified directly with a cost objective.

indirect labor (2) Manufacturing labor that cannot be identified directly with products.

indirect materials (2) Materials necessary for the production process, but not identifiable with a specific product.

inferior goods (12) Products whose demand is the inverse of normal products. Price increases cause an increase in demand, and price decreases cause a decrease in demand.

information (1) Data assembled in usable form. Information increases a person's knowledge or decreases the risk of making an incorrect decision.

internal rate of return (IRR) (13) The interest rate that discounts the cash inflows from a project to the present value, which is identical to the present value of the cash outflows of that project.

internal reporting (1) *See* managerial accounting.

Internal Revenue Service (IRS) (1) The tax-collecting arm of the federal government. The IRS issues some accounting rules.

inventoriable cost (2) Necessary cost of production that increases the value of a product and becomes part of the cost of the product.

inventory acquisition (3) All activities necessary to purchase and receive inventory and move it into the inventory storage area.

inventory control (15) The process of planning and monitoring inventory.

inventory distribution (3) All activities associated with transferring raw materials into production.

inventory profits (15) Profits higher than normal caused by matching current revenues with older inventory costs.

inventory turnover (19) A measure of liquidity calculated by dividing cost of goods sold for a period by average inventory of the same period.

investing activities (20) Business activities that require the use of funds, such as acquisition of assets, repayment of debt, payment of dividends, and reacquisition of stock.

investment center (11) A form of responsibility center in which managers are held responsible for the return on assets invested in that segment of the organization.

job cost sheet (3) A report used to summarize the production costs for a specific production job in a job order costing system.

job number (3) An identification number assigned to each job cost sheet. The number may be designed to allow accountants to analyze costs easily in a variety of ways.

job order costing (3) A cost accounting system used to accumulate costs for products produced in batches or intermittent production runs. Job order production is characterized by an identifiable starting and completion time for the batch of production. Production costs are summarized on a job cost sheet.

job time ticket (3) A source document used to identify labor costs with cost objectives. Employees prepare this document for each job on which they work.

joint cost (4) Production costs associated with joint products before the split-off point and allocated to products by means such as the gross margin method or the physical units method.

joint cost allocation (4) The process of assigning joint costs to joint products.

joint product (4) A product that is produced as part of a group of products and not distinguishable as a separate product until the split-off point.

joint production process (4) A production process that yields two or more different products.

kinked demand curve (12) A demand curve occurring in oligopolistic markets in which the action of one supplier causes a kink or sharp break in the demand curve for products of other suppliers.

labor distribution report (3) A report summarizing the use of labor for some time period, such as a week or month.

labor efficiency variance (8) A variance caused by using more or fewer labor hours than standard.

labor mix variance (16) The amount of labor variance that results from changing the mix of labor inputs from the standard mix.

labor rate variance (8) The amount of labor variance that results from paying labor more or less than the standard rate.

last in, first out (LIFO) (15) Inventory valuation method that assumes the goods purchased most recently are the first ones sold or used. The method refers to the flow of inventory costs and not to the physical flow of the goods.

lead time (15) The time between placing and receiving an order.

lead time demand (15) The amount of inventory required during lead time.

learning curve cost (2) A semivariable cost that increases at a decreasing rate. It indicates the cost effect of labor becoming more efficient as new tasks and processes are learned.

learning curves (2) A class of semivariable costs that

increase at a decreasing rate, such as labor costs resulting during a period when a new task is being learned.

learning rate (18) The rate at which learning takes place, expressed as a percentage that determines the shape of the learning curve.

least squares regression line (18) *See* regression line.

leverage (19) *See* financial leverage.

line budget (14) A budget prepared along organizational or functional lines, such as marketing, administrative, and manufacturing.

liquidity (19) The speed with which assets can be converted to cash. The ability of an entity to pay its current debts as they mature.

loss leader (12) A product priced very low, perhaps below cost, intended to attract customers to the business to buy products at normal prices as well as the loss leader items.

lost unit cost (17) The cost of manufacturing units that are identified as spoiled or lost units.

low-cost input (16) In a multiple-resource production process, an input that costs less than the average cost of all inputs at the standard mix.

low-profit item (16) A product whose profit or contribution margin is less than the average profit or contribution margin at the standard sales mix.

make-buy decision (6) A decision involving the choice between buying a product or service or producing it.

management by objective (8) A management method whereby managers establish specific performance criteria and investigate situations only when actual performance varies significantly from the performance criteria. Also called management by exception.

managerial accounting (1) The accounting and reporting of information to managers within the organization. Also called internal reporting.

manufacturing contribution margin (10) The difference between sales and the variable manufacturing expenses.

manufacturing overhead (2) All necessary costs of manufacturing other than direct labor and direct materials. The indirect costs of manufacturing.

manufacturing overhead applied (3) The account used to accumulate the amount of overhead applied to production. The account normally has a credit balance. The term also refers to the amount of overhead charged to a particular cost objective.

manufacturing overhead budget (4) The estimated amount of manufacturing overhead costs for an entity for a specific time period. Estimated indirect manufacturing costs, both fixed and variable.

manufacturing overhead control (3) The account used to accumulate actual manufacturing overhead costs as they are incurred. The account normally has a debit balance.

manufacturing overhead rate (3) A predetermined rate used for applying manufacturing overhead costs to products, e.g., $6 per direct labor hour.

manufacturing overhead variance analysis (9) The systematic process of analyzing the difference between actual manufacturing overhead and applied manufacturing overhead. The two-variance and three-variance methods are common ways of analyzing overhead variances.

margin of safety ratio (5) A measure of the relative amount that actual activity differs from break-even activity. The difference is expressed as a ratio of actual activity, with a range of possible values from $-\infty$ to $+1$. Values above zero indicate the firm is operating above the break-even point.

marginal cost (12) The amount of increase in total cost caused by a one-unit increase in output.

marginal revenue (12) The amount of increase in total revenue caused by a one-unit increase in sales.

market equilibrium (12) The intersection of the supply and demand curves; it occurs when the amount buyers are willing to buy at a particular price coincides with the amount sellers are willing to supply at that price.

market price (11) The price for some product or service determined by the market mechanisms external to the business.

market tests (19) That part of financial analysis that involves the calculation of financial ratios, such as dividend yield, price-earnings ratio, and others derived from stock market data.

marketing expense budget (7) Estimated marketing costs of an entity for a specific time period.

master budget (7) The total budget package of an organization, including both the operating and financial budgets. Sometimes referred to as the profit plan.

material mix variance (16) The amount of the materials variance caused by using a different proportion of material inputs than the standard mix.

material price variance (8) A variance caused by paying more or less than the standard price for a raw material.

material quantity variance (8) A variance caused by using more or less material than the standard quantity.

materials budget (7) Estimated materials use for an entity for some specified period.

materials requisition (3) A document sent to the inventory storeroom area to start raw materials into production.

mean (18) A measure of central tendency calculated by adding all items in a set of data and dividing by the number of items.

measures of central tendency (18) Statistics that describe average characteristics of a set of data, such as the mean, the median, or the mode.

measures of dispersion (18) Statistics that describe how data fluctuate around some measure of central tendency.

median (18) A measure of central tendency calculated as the middle value of an ordered set of data.

mixed cost (2) A cost composed of both fixed and variable cost components. Described by the general equation $Y = a + bX$. Y is the total cost, a is the fixed component, and b is the variable cost per unit of activity.

mode (18) A measure of central tendency representing the value of a set of data that occurs most frequently.

modified cost (11) A form of transfer price based on cost and modified to reflect special conditions or management's attitudes.

modified market price (11) A transfer price based on market price and adjusted to reflect such factors as the absence of marketing costs in interdivision sales.

monetary policy (14) One of the two instruments of economic stabilization policy dealing with the quantity of money and the cost of money in the economy.

monopolistic competition (12) A market in which there are many suppliers of similar, but not identical, products.

monopoly (12) A market with only one supplier.

moving average (18) A mean calculated for a set of data by deleting the oldest data element and adding the newest data element as it becomes available.

multiple-alternative choice decision (6) A decision involving more than two alternative courses of action.

multiple linear regression (18) A statistical technique using two or more independent variables to predict the value of one dependent variable.

multiyear costing (14) The process of identifying costs with a project for the life of the project rather than just for the next budget year. An element of PPBS.

negative correlation (18) The relationship described by the coefficient of correlation when increases in the values of the independent variable are accompanied by decreases in the values of the dependent variable.

negotiated price (11) A form of transfer price in which the buying and selling parties negotiate the transfer price.

net pay (3) Gross pay less withholding items. The amount actually paid to employees.

net present value (NPV) (13) A capital budgeting analysis method that is used to discount all cash inflows and outflows from a project to their present value. The firm's cost of capital or target rate of return is used as the interest rate.

nonfund items (20) Those expenses, revenues, gains, and losses reported in the income statement that do not provide or use cash or working capital. Items that are added to or deducted from net income to arrive at funds from operations.

nonmanufacturing activities (10) All activities other than manufacturing, e.g., marketing, accounting, and administration.

normal capacity (9) The expected activity level for the accounting period assuming normal operating conditions. The activity level is expressed in units of output, direct labor hours, machine hours, or some other measure of activity.

normal curve (18) *See* normal distribution.

normal distribution (18) A symmetrical bell-shaped curve describing the normal probability distribution found in many types of statistical data.

normal lost units (17) Spoiled or lost units that occur in the normal production process and therefore are included as part of the cost of producing good units.

normal spoilage (17) *See* normal lost units.

normal spoiled unit cost (17) The cost associated with normal spoilage.

not-for-profit sector (14) The sector of the economy comprising governments, universities, charities, and other organizations that provide services to the public without attempting to generate a profit.

occupancy costs (2) *See* capacity costs.

oligopoly (12) A market in which there are several large sellers that dominate the market and compete with one another.

operating budget (7) The set of budgets for the normal operations of a business, including all activities involved in generating operating income.

opportunity cost (2) The benefit foregone by rejecting one alternative so that another can be accepted.

ordering costs (15) The total cost associated with ordering a particular inventory item, typically including the costs of obtaining current prices, securing order approval, preparing purchase documents, and receiving the order.

overapplied overhead (3) The amount by which applied overhead exceeds actual overhead.

overhead (2) *See* manufacturing overhead.

payback (13) A capital budgeting analysis method used to determine how long it will take to recover the initial investment of a proposed project.

payback reciprocal (13) A capital budgeting evaluation method that is an estimate of the internal rate of return. The payback reciprocal is computed by dividing the payback period into 1.

payout ratio (19) *See* dividend payout.

payroll taxes (3) Taxes on the wages of employees that must be paid by the employer. Included are the employer's share of FICA taxes, federal and state unemployment taxes, and workmens' compensation taxes.

perfectly competitive market (12) A market in which there are many buyers and sellers, none of whom can affect the market price by their individual actions. The product or service sold in the market is homogeneous, resources can flow freely into and out of the market, and all market participants have perfect knowledge of prices and costs.

performance reporting (7) The comparison of actual results with the expected results embodied in the budget, often resulting in the reporting of variances.

period costs (2) The cost of goods and services that are recorded as expenses in the period in which they are consumed.

periodic inventory system (2) A method of accounting for inventories in which the inventory account is adjusted only at year-end after a physical count of the inventory. Inventory purchases are recorded in a Purchases account and the cost of goods sold is determined at the end of the accounting period by summing beginning inventory and purchases and subtracting ending inventory.

perpetual inventory system (2) A method of accounting for inventories in which all inventory increases and decreases are recorded directly in the Inventory account. Cost of goods sold is determined at the time of sale.

physical units allocation method (4) A method of joint cost allocation in which each unit of product in the joint product group receives the same amount of joint cost.

planning (7) The process of developing the set of budgets used in achieving organizational goals. A design or scheme for achieving specific goals or objectives.

Planning, Programming, Budgeting System (PPBS) (14) A comprehensive budget review, evaluation, and preparation process first initiated in the federal government in 1965 and subsequently used in similar forms in various state and local governments.

positive correlation (18) The relationship described by the coefficient of correlation when increases in the values of the independent variable are accompanied by increases in the values of the dependent variable.

predetermined overhead rate (3) *See* budgeted overhead rate.

present value (13) The current value of an amount to be received in the future.

price-earnings ratio (19) The ratio calculated by dividing the market price of a stock by its earnings per share.

price indifference point (6) The activity level at which the new price produces a profit identical to the profit generated by the old price and activity level.

pricing (12) The process of assigning a selling price to products or services sold by the organization.

prime cost (2) Direct materials cost and direct labor cost combined.

private sector (14) The sector of the economy consisting of privately owned organizations primarily engaged in providing services and selling products to earn profits.

pro forma statements (19) Financial statements of future accounting periods, consisting of expected future account balances prepared on the basis of projections and expectations of future events.

problem definition (1) The process of determining precisely what problem is being addressed.

process center (17) A separate identifiable production activity characterized by homogeneous output and by work that is identical for each unit.

process costing (17) A cost accounting system used to accumulate costs of products manufactured in continuous-flow production processes. There is no identifiable starting and completion time for production activity, so production costs must be summarized periodically in cost of production reports.

producing department (4) A department that is directly involved in furthering the production of products by performing some production process, such as drilling, assembly, or finishing.

product contribution statement (10) A contribution report that identifies the amount of contribution margin provided by each product.

product cost (2) All costs, both direct and indirect, of producing a product in a manufacturing firm or the cost of acquiring a product in a merchandising business and making it ready for sale.

product profitability report (10) A report identifying profit by product.

production budget (7) Estimated production quantities and costs for an entity for some specified period of time.

production mix variance (16) A measure of the dollar amount of variance caused by changing from the standard mix of production inputs to some other mix.

profit center (11) A form of responsibility center in which managers are held responsible for both expenses and revenues.

profit margin (19) *See* return on sales.

profit plan (7) A company's total budget used in achieving a desired profit goal. Sometimes the term refers only to the operating budget, and sometimes it is used synonymously with the term master budget.

profit-volume chart (5) A special form of cost-volume-profit chart that highlights the break-even point and profit. The horizontal center line of the chart is the zero profit line.

profitability index (PI) (13) The ratio of the present value of cash inflows to the present value of cash outflows. A capital budgeting evaluation method that adjusts for the difference in the size of project costs.

profitability ratios (19) *See* tests of profitability.

program accounting (14) An accounting system with an ability to attach accounting data to specific programs to show the resources used or budgeted for each objective.

program budget (14) A budget prepared for programs or outputs of an organization.

public finance (14) The entire area of government economic activity including resource allocation, income distribution to people, and the financing function of government.

public sector (14) The portion of the not-for-profit sector consisting of publicly owned organizations and institutions, such as city governments, state universities, federal parks, and others whose purpose is to provide services to the public without earning a profit.

purchase order (3) A business document prepared by the purchasing department to order some resource or service.

purchase price (12) The amount paid for some resource acquired by a firm.

purchase requisition (3) A business document indicating that some item or service needs to be ordered.

purchasing agent (3) The individual who has responsibility for all purchasing activities.

quantity variance (8) *See* material quantity variance.

quick ratio (19) *See* acid test ratio.

ratio analysis (19) A method of analyzing financial statements by calculating ratios between specific items of data presented in the statements for the purpose of obtaining measures of liquidity, solvency, and profitability.

raw materials (2) The basic materials used in production by a manufacturing firm. Most raw materials are direct materials, but some are indirect materials.

receivables turnover (19) A measure of liquidity calculated by dividing net sales by average accounts receivable, indicating the speed with which receivables are collected and converted to cash.

receiving report (3) A business document indicating the receipt of some inventory item or items and the amount received.

reciprocal allocation (4) A method of allocating service department costs to producing departments and service departments in proportion to costs of services used. All service department costs are then assigned to producing departments. This allocation method requires the use of linear algebra.

regression-correlation analysis (18) The analysis of statistical data performed by calculating a regression line, the coefficient of correlation, and the coefficient of determination and then interpreting the results of the calculations.

regression line (18) A straight line that best fits through a set of data by minimizing the absolute distances between the data points and the line. Also called the line of best fit and the least squares regression line.

regression line equation (18) The equation that describes mathematically the intercept and slope of the regression line.

reinvestment rate (13) The rate at which cash inflows from capital projects can be invested.

relevance (1) The characteristic of accounting information requiring that information meets the needs of users.

relevant cost (6) A cost useful in the decision-making process and having two characteristics: it is an expected future cost and a differential cost.

relevant range assumption (2) The assumption that the identified behavior pattern of a cost may exist only for a certain range of activity. At an activity level above or below the relevant range the cost may have a different behavior pattern.

reorder point (15) The inventory level at which a new order is placed for some specific inventory item.

residual income (11) The difference between actual net income and a specified target net income.

responsibility accounting (11) The process of reporting on how well managers meet their responsibilities.

responsibility centers (11) Clearly identified segments of an organization in which managers are held responsible for the performance of the organization segment. Cost centers, profit centers, and investment centers are the three common forms of responsibility centers.

return on investment (11) A measure of the amount earned on an investment project.

return on owners' equity (19) A measure of profitability calculated by dividing net income by average owners' equity.

return on sales (19) A measure of profitability calculated by dividing net income by net sales.

return on total assets (19) A measure of profitability calculated by dividing net income before interest and taxes by total average assets.

returned materials report (3) An internal report that shows the cost and quantity of unused materials returned to inventory from production activities.

Robinson-Patman Act (1) A federal law that prohibits discriminatory pricing of products or services except in certain special situations.

safety stock (15) An additional amount of inventory in excess of lead time demand intended to minimize or eliminate the possibility of a stockout.

sales budget (7) Estimate of sales volume of an entity for some specified period of time. Prepared first because most other budgets are derived, at least in part, from the sales budget.

sales mix variance (16) A measure of the profit consequences of selling products in different amounts from the standard sales mix.

sales quantity variance (16) A measure of the amount of variance in profits caused by selling more or less units than standard.

sample (18) A set of data collected from a population so that it is representative of the population.

scatter diagram (5) A chart or graph used to plot cost data that may provide managers with a visual representation of cost trends or patterns.

schedule of equivalent units (17) A schedule in a cost of production report that shows the physical quantity of output for the process center for the reporting period.

Securities and Exchange Commission (SEC) (1) A regulatory body of the United States government charged with overseeing the operation of stock markets and regulation of public corporations.

segment reports (10) Reports that identify costs, revenues, profits, contribution margin, or other variables for parts or segments of an organization.

selling the budget (7) The process of convincing the budget review committee of the merits of some budget proposal.

selling price (12) The amount charged by an organization for some product or resource that it sells to others.

semifixed cost (2) A cost that increases with activity in jumps or steps. It remains constant for a range of activity and then jumps to a higher amount. Also called a step function cost.

semivariable cost (2) A cost that increases continuously, but not proportionately, with activity. Learning curve costs increase at a decreasing rate. Other semivariable costs increase at an increasing rate.

sensitivity analysis (15) The process of determining how sensitive the output of a model is to changes in the inputs or changes in the model parameters.

service department (4) A department, such as maintenance or inventory storeroom, that facilitates or supports production activities, but is not directly involved in producing products.

shortage costs (15) The cost in lost sales or inefficient production of running out of an inventory item.

simple linear regression (18) Regression analysis involving one dependent variable and one independent variable.

single-product decision (6) A joint product production or sales decision that affects only one of the joint products.

solvency (19) The ability to repay all debts and obligations as they come due.

special order (6) An order that has characteristics different from regular orders. Typically a one-time order that provides the opportunity to utilize unused capacity.

spending variance (9) The difference between actual manufacturing overhead cost and a flexible budget based on actual inputs. One of the variances isolated by using the three-variance method.

split-off point (4) The point in the production process when a by-product separates from the main product or when joint products become identifiable as separate products.

spoiled unit cost (17) The cost of spoiled or lost units.

stabilization (14) An objective of public finance aimed at keeping the economy running smoothly with acceptable growth and few economic fluctuations. Fiscal and monetary policy are the two instruments of stabilization.

standard cost (8) A carefully predetermined cost. A measure of what a cost should be.

standard cost transfer price (11) A transfer price based on the standard cost of the good or service transferred between business segments.

standard deviation (18) A measure of dispersion describing the variation of data from their mean.

standard hours (9) The number of hours that should have been worked given the standard number of hours per unit and the quantity of output manufactured during the period.

standard setting (8) The process of establishing standard costs.

standards committee (8) A group of people within an organization whose function is to establish standards and reevaluate them periodically.

statement of changes in financial position (20) One of the basic financial statements presented in annual reports, describing the financing and investing activities of a business enterprise. Also called funds flow statement or cash flow statement.

static budget (9) *See* fixed budget.

statistic (18) Any item of information that describes some characteristic of a subject under investigation.

steady state (18) The point on a learning curve when no more learning takes place and each subsequent repetition of the learned task requires as much time or cost as the previous repetition.

step function cost (2) A cost that remains fixed for a given range of activity but makes incremental jumps as some activity level is reached, whereupon it again remains fixed for a new range of activity.

stockout (15) The zero inventory level for some specific inventory when there is demand for the item.

stockout cost (15) The cost associated with running out of inventory; includes lost sales, customer ill will, and production inefficiencies.

subsidiary ledger (2) The set of individual accounts that are summarized by a control account in the general ledger, e.g., individual accounts receivable for each customer that sum to the balance in the Accounts Receivable Control account.

summary product cost report (17) A product cost report used in a process costing system that summarizes the manufacturing costs for all process centers used in the production of a particular product.

sunk cost (6) A cost that has already been incurred and cannot be changed and therefore is not relevant to the decision process.

supply (12) The total amount all suppliers are willing to sell at each possible selling price.

supply curve (12) A graphic presentation of the amount suppliers in aggregate are willing to sell at each possible selling price.

target income (5) A desired level of income expressed as an amount or a percentage of investment or sales.

target profit pricing (12) The process of establishing prices based on desired profit levels.

target profit transfer price (11) A transfer price based on covering all costs and providing a desired level of income.

tests of liquidity (19) That portion of financial analysis that involves the calculation of ratios, such as the current ratio, quick ratio, and various turnovers, that provide an indication of a company's liquidity.

tests of profitability (19) That portion of financial analysis that involves the calculation of ratios, such as rates of return, that provide information on the profitability of a business.

tests of solvency (19) That portion of financial analysis that involves the calculation of ratios, such as the debt/equity ratio, and other tests that provide an indication of a company's ability to pay its debts as they mature.

three-variance method (9) A method of overhead variance analysis that isolates three variances—spending, efficiency, and volume.

time assumption (2) The assumption that cost behavior patterns may change over time and an identified pattern may be valid only for a specific period of time.

time value of money (13) The notion that money in the present is worth more than money in the future, and the cost of waiting for future money requires payment in the form of interest.

timeliness (1) An information characteristic requiring that accounting information be very current.

times interest earned (19) A measure of solvency calculated as net income before interest and taxes divided by the required interest expense.

total cost of spoiled units (17) The total cost associated with the production of units that are identified as spoiled or lost.

total cumulative cost (18) The total cost of manufacturing a particular number of units in a production environment with a learning curve effect.

total net assets (11) Total assets less any contra-asset accounts, such as Accumulated Depreciation.

total net assets employed (11) Total assets less contra-asset accounts less any assets not currently employed in generating net income.

transfer pricing (11) The process of pricing the transfer of goods and services between segments of an organization.

trend analysis (18) A statistical technique using moving averages or exponential smoothing to determine the trend in a set of data, usually for the purpose of predicting future values of the data. **(19)** Analysis of financial statements for the purpose of measuring trends in sales, earnings, or other aspects of business performance.

two-alternative decisions (6) A decision that involves selecting one of two alternatives being evaluated.

two-variance method (9) A method of overhead variance analysis that isolates two variances—controllable and volume.

underapplied overhead (3) The amount by which actual overhead exceeds applied overhead.

unfavorable variance (8) The amount by which actual costs exceed standard costs. Any variance in which actual cost is greater than standard cost.

unit cost (2) The cost of one unit of product. Typically an average unit cost of producing the product during some time period, such as a month.

units to account for (17) The portion of a cost of production report that identifies the number of units that must be accounted for in the process center during the period.

units accounted for (17) The portion of a cost of production report that identifies the disposition of units in production in the process center during the period.

variable cost (2) A cost that increases proportionately with the level of activity. Described by the equation $Y = bX$ where Y is total cost and b is the variable cost per unit of activity.

variable costing (10) A product costing method that includes all variable costs of manufacturing in the cost of the product and excludes any fixed costs. Also called direct costing.

variable overhead (7) The portion of manufacturing overhead costs that vary directly with the level of activity.

variance (18) A measure of dispersion describing the fluctuation of data about their mean.

variance analysis (8) The systematic process of identifying, reporting, and explaining variances.

vertical analysis (19) Financial analysis that involves the comparison of figures within a financial statement or between financial statements of a single period.

volume variance (9) The amount of overhead variance caused by operating at an activity level different from budgeted. The difference between applied overhead and a budget based on actual output.

withholdings (3) Amounts deducted from gross payroll and paid to various recipients such as governments, unions, and insurance companies.

work in process (2) Inventory that is in the process of being manufactured. Partially completed inventory.

working capital (19) The net current assets of a business not required for the payment of current liabilities, calculated as current assets minus current liabilities. **(20)** One of the definitions of funds, used in the preparation of the statement of changes in financial position.

yield variance (16) The difference between the standard and actual output obtained from a given amount of inputs.

zero-base budgeting (14) A method of budget review and evaluation that requires all projects and programs, new and old, to justify all resources. Each project starts the budget evaluation process without a resource commitment even if it is an ongoing project.

Key Figures

CHAPTER 1

P. 1-1 Income from repair business, $965 per month
P. 1-3 Expected monthly income during the first 6 months, $2,200
P. 1-4 Total cost of delivery per pound, $.23

CHAPTER 2

Ex. 2-2 1986 net income, $139,000
Ex. 2-3 Total direct cost, $68,103
Ex. 2-4 a. Monthly distribution cost, $65,000 + $.12*Y*
Ex. 2-6 Cost of goods manufactured, $600,000
Ex. 2-7 B. Beginning Work in Process, $11,000
Ex. 2-9 c. Expense for the period, $7,500
Ex. 2-10 f. Change in per-unit profit, $.75, or 45%, increase
Ex. 2-11 a. Average unit cost of goods made in 1986, $57.50
Ex. 2-12 D. Cost of goods sold, $62,000
P. 2-1 b. Cost of goods sold, $41,360
P. 2-2 Cost of goods manufactured, $1,247,625
P. 2-3 Net income, $16,600
P. 2-4 d. Total overhead cost, $300,000 + $8.00(*X*)
P. 2-5 b. Net income, $5,900
P. 2-6 Net income, $78,000
P. 2-7 b. Net income, $(1,000)
P. 2-8 d. Total manufacturing costs incurred during the year, $539,640
P. 2-9 a. Raw materials 6/30, $13,000
P. 2-10 g. Unit cost of production, $4.00
P. 2-11 a. Cost of goods sold, $433,000
P. 2-12 d. Difference in amount paid, $276,000
Case 2-1 c. Cost of goods manufactured, $1,963,200

CHAPTER 3

Ex. 3-1 b. Cost of materials used in production, $138,920
Ex. 3-2 Total vacation pay for period, $608.70
Ex. 3-3 c. Total labor cost for the week, $559.60
Ex. 3-4 a. Overhead charged in January, $128,160
Ex. 3-5 c. Direct labor cost charged to production, $2,990
Ex. 3-6 c. Actual overhead per direct labor hour, $28.15
Ex. 3-7 Unit cost of product, $71.00
Ex. 3-8 b. Total overhead, $(9,000) overapplied
Ex. 3-9 b. Gross profit as a percentage of sales, 37.2%
Ex. 3-11 Total per-unit manufacturing cost, $85.195
Ex. 3-12 b. Required selling price, $2,840
P. 3-1 c. Total cost of 1 direct labor hour, $14.18
P. 3-2 a. Direct labor cost for the week, $1,152
P. 3-3 a. Cost per hour worked, proposed contract, $8.50
P. 3-4 b. Cost per unit of job number 2001, $102.33
P. 3-5 d. New hourly rate, $18.50
P. 3-6 e. Single rate for repairs, $20.84 per hour
P. 3-7 b. Underapplied overhead, $191,000
P. 3-9 f. Overhead of $6,600 is applied to production
P. 3-10 a. Average unit cost of producing all mowers, $119.49
P. 3-11 1, c; 4, b
P. 3-12 a. Target price based on average cost for the year, $119.31
P. 3-13 b. Production costs charged to Work in Process, $780,800
P. 3-14 Cost of ending Work in Process, $13,037
P. 3-15 f. Ending balance in Raw Materials, $16,000
P. 3-16 d. Net income, $66,250
Case 3-1 e. Balance in ending Work in Process, $17,590

CHAPTER 4

Ex. 4-1 a. Manufacturing overhead rate, 160% of DLC
Ex. 4-2 f. Manufacturing overhead rate, 61% of prime cost
Ex. 4-4 Budgeted assembly department overhead cost, $114,577
Ex. 4-5 Production department overhead rate, $4.68 per direct labor hour
Ex. 4-6 Total manufacturing overhead, underapplied by $46,000, or 3.4%
Ex. 4-7 b. Total allocated joint cost to PH-444, $10,667
Ex. 4-8 b. Total allocated joint cost to PH-222, $72,800

Ex. 4-9 Total unit cost of SA-3, $9.40
Ex. 4-10 a. Total joint cost allocated to CLAY-A, $58,800
Ex. 4-11 Total unit product cost of Buzie-Whamo, $1.85
Ex. 4-12 Product cost as a percentage of sales, 86%
Ex. 4-13 Applied overhead for Patton, $43,600
P. 4-1 b. Total production cost, $885,000
P. 4-2 d. Overapplied overhead using direct labor hours, $(28,000)
P. 4-3 a. Finishing division MOH rate using DLH, $4 per DLH
P. 4-4 a. Applied manufacturing overhead in Assembly, $893,750
P. 4-5 c. Total applied overhead, $83,660
P. 4-6 a. Total budgeted overhead in Finishing, $105,000
P. 4-7 a. Manufacturing overhead rate for Packaging, 92% of shipping cost
P. 4-8 c. Total gross margin for September, $119,800
P. 4-9 b. Per-unit joint cost of Reslin, $4.444
P. 4-10 e. Total cost of ending inventory, $210,375
P. 4-11 c. Per-unit joint cost of GFC-3, $9.60
P. 4-12 b. Average cost per pound of output, $3.26
Case 4-1 c. Gross margin percentage, 22%

CHAPTER 5

Ex. 5-2 a. Cost equation, $Y = \$2{,}212 + \$93X$
Ex. 5-3 b. Estimated utility cost, $1,181
Ex. 5-4 b. Estimated costs using patients served, $1,376,000
Ex. 5-5 Break-even sales revenue, $360,000
Ex. 5-6 c. Required sales with proposed target profit, 75,294 units
Ex. 5-7 a. Break-even point, $60,000
Ex. 5-8 b. July net income, $5,400
Ex. 5-9 d. Margin of safety ratio, .349, or 34.9%
Ex. 5-10 2, a; 5, e
Ex. 5-11 Profit, $5,040
Ex. 5-12 b. Net income with proposed changes, $17,250
Ex. 5-13 a. Break-even point in total units, 940,000 units
P. 5-1 c. Manufacturing overhead rate, $8.90 per machine hour
P. 5-2 d. Expected sales using newspaper advertising, $95,000
P. 5-3 d. Break-even point with cost increases: 60,000 units
P. 5-4 a. Estimated building permits with 16% interest, 570.88 permits
P. 5-5 e. Break-even point with marketing program, 380,000 units
P. 5-6 B. Sales price per unit, $31
P. 5-7 c. Required sales level with target profit, $130,000
P. 5-8 c. Expected profit from the city of Hamelin, $17,184
P. 5-9 1, b; 4, a
P. 5-10 b. Break-even in sales dollars, $630,000
P. 5-11 a. Break-even volume, 5,000 kg
P. 5-12 b. Required sales volume, 4,050,000 units
Case 5-1 b. Third-quarter break-even point, 3,750 total units
Case 5-2 c. Break-even point in sale dollars, $172,812.50

CHAPTER 6

Ex. 6-1 a. Cost indifference point, 8,000 units
Ex. 6-2 a. Cost indifference point, 175,000,000 gallons
Ex. 6-3 a. Cost indifference point, 43,750 wheel assemblies
Ex. 6-4 a. Break-even point for automated system, 13,125 units
Ex. 6-5 b. Cost indifference point, 80,000 tons
Ex. 6-6 c. Monthly cost of Bill-Fast with 50,000 customers, $33,000
Ex. 6-7 b. Cost of incorrect decision, $18,000
Ex. 6-8 a. Selling at split-off would cost the company $1.20 per unit
Ex. 6-9 a. Price indifference point, 15,000 units
Ex. 6-10 c. Expected net income with the new selling price, $130,000
Ex. 6-11 b. Change in profit if order is accepted, $11,100 increase
Ex. 6-12 a. A-10–A-50 cost indifference point, 6,000 units
P. 6-1 b. Cost indifference point, 18,000 units
P. 6-2 d. Cost savings from using the manual system, $6,000
P. 6-3 c. New cost indifference point, 28,909 units
P. 6-4 c. Cost of selecting Data-Trex with 108,000 requests, $3,600
P. 6-5 c. Expected net income, $760,000
P. 6-6 a. Break-even point with proposed system, 12,000 ft of fence
P. 6-7 d. Minimum price for Morning Flower cologne, $8.33 per unit
P. 6-8 b. Expected net income for the coming season, $8,000
P. 6-9 Effect on net income of accepting the order, $44,000 increase
P. 6-11 d. Cost savings from the automated system, $7,080
P. 6-12 a. Copy-A–Copy-B cost indifference point, 140,000 copies

Case 6-1	a. Enrollments could drop by as much as 3,789 students

CHAPTER 7

Ex. 7-1	Total budgeted sales, 371,280 units, or $1,215,480
Ex. 7-2	First-quarter budgeted purchases of 25-horsepower motors, 280 units
Ex. 7-3	Total budgeted direct labor, 105,000 hours, or $630,000
Ex. 7-4	Total budgeted manufacturing overhead costs, $128,000
Ex. 7-5	Nylon-cord tires budgeted February purchases, 240 tires
Ex. 7-6	April direct labor budget, 12,650 hours, or $99,500
Ex. 7-7	Budgeted April cash receipts, $131,921
Ex. 7-8	Nitrate budgeted first-quarter purchases, 13,600 pounds, or $8,160
Ex. 7-9	Total budgeted manufacturing overhead costs, $3,540
Ex. 7-10	Total variance, $2,750 U
Ex. 7-11	Total budgeted manufacturing overhead costs, $107,625
Ex. 7-12	Total overhead budget variance, $125 F
P. 7-1	Total budgeted sales revenue for the year, $1,475,000
P. 7-2	Required first-quarter ending inventory for plywood, 15,825 sq ft
P. 7-3	Sales manager's second-quarter production budget, 1,100 units
P. 7-4	Total budgeted second-quarter sales, $579,200
P. 7-5	a. March production quantity budget, 320 tables
P. 7-6	Budgeted first-quarter ending cash balance, $85,400
P. 7-7	1, d; 3, b
P. 7-8	g. Budgeted cost of goods sold, $6,298
P. 7-9	a. Total budgeted production quantity, 22,000 units
P. 7-10	a. Total budgeted sales revenue, $600,000
P. 7-11	e. Budgeted cost of goods sold, $279,610
Case 7-1	i. Budgeted net income, $48,423

CHAPTER 8

Ex. 8-1	Material quantity variance, $210 F
Ex. 8-2	Labor rate variance, $2,850 U
Ex. 8-3	Total labor variance, $7,600 U
Ex. 8-4	Total materials variance, $400 F
Ex. 8-5	Total materials price variance, $96 F
Ex. 8-6	Standard cost of direct materials put into production, $51,400
Ex. 8-7	Total labor variance, $451 F
Ex. 8-8	Standard labor cost per 5,000 sq ft of lawn, $10.80
Ex. 8-9	Expected production costs of electric motors, $119
Ex. 8-11	b. Standard quantity of materials, 11,100 units
Ex. 8-12	Total labor rate variance, $65 U
Ex. 8-13	Labor efficiency variance, $600 U
P. 8-1	Total labor variance for April, $1,460 F
P. 8-2	c. Total actual prime cost, $22.85 per can
P. 8-3	c. Net income based on standard costs, $80,000
P. 8-4	a. Total direct labor variance, $920 U
P. 8-5	a. Number of standard direct labor hours, 11,250 hours
P. 8-6	a. Material quantity variance, $756 U
P. 8-7	a. Material purchase price variance for B, $2,000 U
P. 8-8	b. Actual prime cost per unit, $1.07
P. 8-9	a. Standard cost of 1 sport coat, $60.00 per unit
P. 8-10	d. Total product cost variance, $39,205 U
Case 8-1	a. Total materials quantity variance, $256,600 U

CHAPTER 9

Ex. 9-1	Budgeted net income at sales of $400,000, $38,000
Ex. 9-2	Total budget variance, $2,900 F
Ex. 9-3	b. Manufacturing overhead rate, $4,675 per unit
Ex. 9-4	b. Break-even point for cafeteria, 170,769 meals
Ex. 9-5	b. Total flexible budget variance, $7,000 U
Ex. 9-6	Volume variance, $13,440 F
Ex. 9-7	Efficiency variance, $10,560 U
Ex. 9-8	Volume variance: A, F; B, F; C, U
Ex. 9-9	c. Actual machine hours, 10,700 hours
Ex. 9-10	c. Price of government contract, $196,000
Ex. 9-11	1, c; 3, a
Ex. 9-12	b. Overhead volume variance, $500 U
Ex. 9-13	2, b; 4, d
P. 9-1	Total budget variance, $18,000 F
P. 9-2	a. Budgeted profit at 51,000 DLH, $281,800
P. 9-3	a. Total budget variance, $3,400 F
P. 9-4	Total budget variance, $72,000 U
P. 9-5	Budgeted total expenses at 136,000 DLH, $5,576,800
P. 9-6	b. Standard cost of conversion, $27 per unit
P. 9-7	Volume variance, $1,200 F
P. 9-8	b. Spending variance, $8,520 F

P. 9-9 d. Actual overhead, $158,000
P. 9-10 b. Fixed amount, $18,000
P. 9-11 e. Actual direct labor hours, 21,000 hours
P. 9-12 Total standard cost of October production, $41,600
P. 9-13 e. Total actual unit cost of a pound of candy, $1.439
P. 9-14 Efficiency variance, $18,000 U
P. 9-15 a. Total direct materials variance, $1,540 U
Case 9-1 g. Expected profit at 240 units, $1,231,600

CHAPTER 10

Ex. 10-1 Selling cost as a percentage of revenue, 1.3%
Ex. 10-2 Total unit cost of data entry, $.74 per unit
Ex. 10-3 Total labor variance for June, $8,330 U
Ex. 10-4 Contribution of 18-inch fan product, $22,000
Ex. 10-5 Northern sales region contribution, $71,900
Ex. 10-6 Model 300 product contribution, $21,000
Ex. 10-7 Net income, $20,000
Ex. 10-8 Net income, $20,000
Ex. 10-9 d. Difference in net income, full costing income $46,000 higher
Ex. 10-10 Variable costing net income, $543,000
Ex. 10-11 Year 2 absorption costing net income, $720,000
Ex. 10-12 Income before taxes, $380
Ex. 10-13 a. Absorption costing net income, $268,000
P. 10-1 b. July net income, $765
P. 10-2 a. Unit cost of cutting lawns, $12.42
P. 10-3 Fishing boat division income, $210,000
P. 10-4 Product profit for 20-foot canoes, $33,350
P. 10-5 Guitar division contribution, $38,000
P. 10-6 Standard guitar product contribution, $40,100
P. 10-7 Western sales region contribution, 27,800
P. 10-8 b. Difference in net income, full costing income $16,000 lower
P. 10-9 c. Variable costing ending inventory cost, $168,000
P. 10-10 Absorption costing year 2 net income, $340,000
P. 10-11 b. Break-even point, $500,667 of sales
P. 10-12 1987 variable costing net income, $111,000
Case 10-1 Labor hours required in excess of effective capacity, 10,000 hours

CHAPTER 11

Ex. 11-1 b. ROI on net assets, 25%
Ex. 11-2 c. Residual income on 12% of gross assets employed, $88,000
Ex. 11-3 a. ROI on beginning owners' equity, 25%
Ex. 11-4 d. ROI on ending owners' equity, 16.7%
Ex. 11-5 b. ROI of Division Z, 25%
Ex. 11-6 b. ROI on total net assets, 19%
Ex. 11-7 b. ROI of western region, 4.5%
Ex. 11-8 b. ROI on gross assets, 7.8%
Ex. 11-9 b. Transfer price based on actual cost, $53 per unit
Ex. 11-10 e. Transfer price based on product cost plus 30%, $37.27 per dozen
Ex. 11-11 b. Target profit transfer price, $44.47 per dozen
Ex. 11-13 b. Computer charges to police using core hours, $250,000
P. 11-1 e. Residual income, $(85,000)
P. 11-2 b. 1986 ROI on total gross assets, 9.77%
P. 11-3 e. Division B residual income, $(20,250)
P. 11-4 d. Amount of assets not employed in operations, $375,000
P. 11-5 b. Ending balance in owners' equity, $2,390,000
P. 11-6 d. Net income with a market transfer price, $140,000
P. 11-7 a1. Transfer price to cover all costs, $.60 per pound
P. 11-8 a. Transfer price of standard product cost plus 28%, $1,004.80
P. 11-10 b. Patrol hours purchased at full cost, 1,800 hours
P. 11-11 d. Return on sales, 14.7%
P. 11-12 a3. Modified market price, $95 per ton
P. 11-13 a. Full product cost transfer price, $53 per windshield
P. 11-14 a. Advantage to company of producing product, $1.00 per unit
Case 11-1 h. Net income with target profit transfer price, $28,865

CHAPTER 12

Ex. 12-1 b. Net income, $520
Ex. 12-2 Equilibrium point for both chemicals, 50 million pounds at $10 per pound
Ex. 12-3 Equilibrium point, 220,000 tons at $8 per ton
Ex. 12-4 b. Net income at optimum strategy, $9,200

Ex. 12-5 b. Net income at optimum strategy, $1,600
Ex. 12-6 b. Price should be set at $85 per unit, yielding demand of 24 units.
Ex. 12-7 a. Full product cost plus 50% for Extralite, $142.50
Ex. 12-8 Moist dinners selling price, $.99 per package
Ex. 12-9 a. Total profit added by special order, $6,000
Ex. 12-10 Required selling price, $38 per unit
Ex. 12-11 b. Number of students per lesson, 8
Ex. 12-12 c. Prime cost plus 115%, $288 per unit
Ex. 12-13 a. Profit from special order, $6,000
Ex. 12-14 c. Total cost plus 25%, $14.00 per unit
P. 12-1 Equilibrium, 400 tons at $12 per ton
P. 12-2 b. Supply curve at equilibrium, $Y = \$1.84 + \$.16X$
P. 12-3 a. Supply curve at equilibrium, $Y = \$5.70 + \$.04X$
P. 12-4 b. Price including labor cost, $97 per unit
P. 12-5 a. Maximum per-unit variable manufacturing cost, $270 per unit
P. 12-6 b. Minimum required price, $9.50 per unit
P. 12-7 d. Effect on net income, $1,000 decrease in profits
P. 12-8 Year 3 net income with $60 camera price, $480,000
P. 12-9 d. Required sales volume for a discount store, $350,000
P. 12-10 Price rocket kits at $74 each.
P. 12-11 Expected loss for 1986, $(58,000)
Case 12-1 d. Required price per day, $81.4286
Case 12-2 b. Required admission price, $.85 per visitor

CHAPTER 13

Ex. 13-1 IRR, a little higher than 15%
Ex. 13-2 IRR, 15.6%
Ex. 13-3 a. Net present value of machine Y, $34,577
Ex. 13-4 Net present value of project, $7,959.32
Ex. 13-5 Payback, 4 years
Ex. 13-6 Accounting rate of return, 12.5%
Ex. 13-7 Maximum amount the company should invest, $111,565
Ex. 13-8 Net present value, $8,251
Ex. 13-9 Net present value, $5,228; IRR, 19.3%
Ex. 13-10 Cost of capital, 16.3%
Ex. 13-11 b. Payback reciprocal, 29.9%
Ex. 13-12 b. Accounting rate of return, 30.3%
Ex. 13-13 Weighted average cost of capital, 8.62%
P. 13-1 d. Net present value, $7,294
P. 13-2 c. Required annual cost savings, $2,155.66
P. 13-3 b. Profitability index, 1.04
P. 13-4 c. IRR, slightly less than 17%
P. 13-5 a. Project C payback period, 5.11 years
P. 13-6 a. Maximum bid, $66,905
P. 13-7 b. Profitability index project A, .99
P. 13-8 a2. IRR for project A, 12%
P. 13-9 b. Net present value of project C, $430
P. 13-10 b. NPV of project, $240,466.60
P. 13-12 c. NPV of project Black, $(3,381)
P. 13-13 b. NPV of project, $643,334
P. 13-14 b. NPV of project, $15,638
P. 13-15 a. NPV of purchase proposal, $18,371
Case 13-1 a. NPV of project, $(2,805,821.52)

CHAPTER 14

Ex. 14-5 b. Percentage change in budget, 7.8%
Ex. 14-8 Percentage change in budget, 10.6%
Ex. 14-9 Total budget for year, $350,000
Ex, 14-10 Total budgeted expenditures for 1987, $257,430
Ex. 14-11 Salary cost for community education, $52,500
P. 14-1 Total variance, $12,300 U
P. 14-2 Total budgeted revenue, $10,943,500
P. 14-3 Total budgeted expenditures, $11,279,530
P. 14-4 Budgeted student tuition, $6,048,000
P. 14-5 Total budgeted revenues, $13,975,390
P. 14-6 Total budgeted expenditures, $967,448
P. 14-7 Budgeted gasoline cost, $225,351
P. 14-8 Total budget variance, $37,000
P. 14-9 Budgeted drivers' salaries, $312,000
P. 14-10 Total budget, $115,140
P. 14-11 Total budgeted cost for business minor program, $287,320
P. 14-12 Estimated total funds to be raised by local taxes, $1,355,600
Case 14-1 Total budget variance in correct report, $289,500 U

CHAPTER 15

Ex. 15-1 EOQ, 2,500 units
Ex. 15-2 b. Cost of inventory, $3,750
Ex. 15-3 b. Number of orders, 20 per year
Ex. 15-4 c. Annual inventory ordering cost for the 3 products, $5,100
Ex. 15-5 Optimum safety stock, 72 units
Ex. 15-6 a. EOQ, 1,500 packs of paper
Ex. 15-7 Cost of incorrectly estimating demand, $100
Ex. 15-8 c. Weighted average cost of goods sold, $3,012.48

Ex. 15-9 b. Perpetual inventory LIFO cost of goods sold, $1,780
Ex. 15-10 b. LIFO ending inventory, $2,048
Ex. 15-11 a. FIFO ending inventory, $51,550
Ex. 15-12 c. Inventory costs added to WIP with moving average, $31,226.923
P. 15-1 d. Reorder point with safety stock, 3,168 cans
P. 15-2 a. EOQ, 3,366.50 units
P. 15-3 b. Lead time demand, 20 life jackets
P. 15-4 b. Total inventory cost, $1,200
P. 15-5 c. Reorder point, 16,000 gallons
P. 15-6 e. Cost of incorrectly estimating carrying cost, $350.16
P. 15-7 a. EOQ, 2,400 gallons
P. 15-8 b. LIFO cost of inventory used, $58,520
P. 15-9 c. Moving average cost of ending inventory, $27,675.35
P. 15-10 c. Operating income with LIFO inventory, $104,200
P. 15-11 c. Ending inventory with moving average valuation, $48,694
P. 15-12 b. Materials issued to production using LIFO perpetual, $62,420
P. 15-13 Cost of goods sold using weighted average, $116,900
Case 15-1 a. Ordering cost, $20 per order

CHAPTER 16

Ex. 16-1 b. Material quantity variance, $1,110 U
Ex. 16-2 b. Labor efficiency variance, $3,880 U
Ex. 16-3 a. Total material variance, $680 U
Ex. 16-4 Material mix variance for Zoline-4, $1,620 F
Ex. 16-5 Material yield variance, $400 U
Ex. 16-6 b. Total material mix variance, $468 U
Ex. 16-7 f. Actual cost per unit, $2.80
Ex. 16-8 a. Total labor efficiency variance, $50 U
Ex. 16-9 Sales mix variance, $14.00 F
Ex. 16-10 b. Sales mix variance for 14-foot boats, $11,800 U
Ex. 16-11 Total sales mix variance, $5,800 F
Ex. 16-12 Standard material cost per 10-liter container, $53.10
P. 16-1 Total material variance, $9 F
P. 16-2 Total labor efficiency variance, $6,100 F
P. 16-3 a. Total material price variance, $420 U
P. 16-4 d. Material yield variance, $1,000 U
P. 16-5 c. Actual cost of instructor, $30.13 per student
P. 16-6 Average standard cost of inputs, $6.85 per labor hour
P. 16-7 b. Total labor variance for the program, $1,455 U
P. 16-8 Total material quantity variance, $396 F
P. 16-9 c. Total material mix variance, $129.32 F
P. 16-10 c. Actual product contribution, $2,180
P. 16-11 Total marketing variance, $11,000 U
P. 16-12 Total contribution margin variance, $3,000 U
P. 16-13 a. Total variance, $290 F
P. 16-14 d. Total standard per-unit cost of candy, $1.391 per pound
Case 16-1 c. Total variable manufacturing cost variance, $49,600

CHAPTER 17

Ex. 17-1 Equivalent units for process center 2, 48,000 units
Ex. 17-2 Equivalent units for process center E, 24,200 units
Ex. 17-3 Unit cost transferred out of process center, $10.45 per unit
Ex. 17-4 Cost of ending work in process inventory, $15,000
Ex. 17-5 Equivalent units of conversion process center 4, 8,560 units
Ex. 17-6 Total costs transferred to finished goods, $84,520
Ex. 17-7 Average unit cost of production during period, $2.42 per unit
Ex. 17-8 Process center 3 equivalent units of conversion, 5,850 units
Ex. 17-9 Total costs transferred out during the period, $194,600
Ex. 17-10 Cost of ending work in process inventory, $20,000
Ex. 17-11 c. Increase in unit costs of good units, $.112 per unit
P. 17-1 Labor cost in ending work in process inventory, $2,352
P. 17-2 Cost of ending work in process inventory, $16,000
P. 17-3 Total cost transferred out during the period, $72,050
P. 17-4 Average unit cost of production for the period, $9.65
P. 17-5 d. Amount of material cost used in February, $36,700
P. 17-6 Total cost transferred out of center during period, $111,180
P. 17-7 Settling department total unit cost for the period, $25.00
P. 17-8 Current period total unit cost of production, $15.43

P. 17-9 Cost of ending work in process in packaging, $8,240
P. 17-10 b. Total cost of spoiled units, $2,349.60
Case 17-1 Assembly department, November costs transferred out, $106,330

CHAPTER 18

Ex. 18-1 Mean, 47 hours
Ex. 18-2 a. Mean number of daily deposits, 568 deposits
Ex. 18-3 Standard deviation, 55.13
Ex. 18-4 c. Probability of cash receipts greater than $6,000, 15.9%
Ex. 18-5 a. Range of lumber use 95% of time, 704 to 1,096 bd ft
Ex. 18-6 a. Regression line equation, $Y = \$9,540 + \$530X$
Ex. 18-7 b. Estimated utility cost, $9,725.93
Ex. 18-8 a. Regression line equation, $Y = 11.89 + 1.215X$
Ex. 18-9 b. Coefficient of determination, .232425
Ex. 18-10 Estimated cost of overhead, $1,225.305
Ex. 18-11 Labor cost of 150 sets, $5,670
Ex. 18-12 Production labor cost for the year, $336,000
Ex. 18-13 Period 14 moving average, $1,316
Ex. 18-14 Period 14 exponential smoothing value, $1,432
P. 18-1 b. Standard deviation, 5,762
P. 18-2 a. Mean, 16,241.67
P. 18-3 a. South mean, $1,000; South standard deviation, $56.96
P. 18-4 b. Cost after adjustment, $8.5125 per bottle
P. 18-5 a. Regression line equation, $Y = 97 + .227X$
P. 18-6 b. Coefficient of determination, .883235
P. 18-7 a. Regression line equation, $Y = 11.95 + .16382X$
P. 18-8 c. Break-even point in units, 756,320 units
P. 18-9 a. Total labor-related cost of first year, $140,000
P. 18-10 b. Total labor-related cost for year 2, $75,080
P. 18-11 c. Selling price, $27.59
P. 18-12 c. Predicted 1986 deposits using moving average, $391.92
P. 18-13 d. Exponential smoothing value for October, $22,179
P. 18-14 a. Moving average period 11 value, $90.30
P. 18-15 a. Regression line equation for DLH, $Y = -\$1,128 + \$48X$
Case 18-1 Regression line, $Y = -75.83 + .03X$

CHAPTER 19

Ex. 19-1 Increase in sales, 10%
Ex. 19-2 Current ratio, 1.7
Ex. 19-5 a. Times interest earned, 3.5
Ex. 19-7 d. Days sales in receivables, 25.7 days
Ex. 19-10 l. Return on sales, 9.3%
Ex. 19-11 Leverage, 2%
Ex. 19-12 Return on common equity, 16%
Ex. 19-13 a. Current ratio of Blount, 1.80
Ex. 19-14 Price-earnings ratio, 9 times
Ex. 19-15 Ending assets, $3,180,000
Ex. 19-16 Quick ratio, 1.86
P. 19-3 a2. Debt-equity ratio, .607
P. 19-6 a4. Equity ratio, .42
P. 19-7 b. 1985 EPS, $3.67
P. 19-8 b8. Return on total assets, 32.5%
P. 19-10 b2. Acid test ratio, .5 times
P. 19-11 Net income, $8,750
Case 19-1 Total interest expense if bonds are issued, $10,500

CHAPTER 20

Ex. 20-1 Total change in working capital, $300 increase
Ex. 20-6 a. Cash provided by operations, $40,900
Ex. 20-7 Net income, $71,000
Ex. 20-8 Total cash paid for salaries and supplies, $20,100
Ex. 20-10 e. Cash collected from customers, $33,134
Ex. 20-11 Changes, $13,800
Ex. 20-12 Changes, $14,500
Ex. 20-14 Total sources of cash, $51,000
Ex. 20-15 d. Working capital provided by operations, $178
Ex. 20-16 Working capital provided from operations, $178
Ex. 20-17 e. Cash increased by $50
Ex. 20-18 Total sources of cash, $870
Ex. 20-19 Total sources of working capital, $872
P. 20-1 Increase in working capital, $80
P. 20-2 Sources of cash from operations, $7,280
P. 20-3 c. Book value of sold land, $20,000
P. 20-4 Total working capital provided by operations, $28,810
P. 20-5 Total cash provided by operations, $28,450
P. 20-6 Book value of sold investments, $148,800
P. 20-7 Total sources of working capital other than operations, $6,970
P. 20-8 Total changes in working capital, increased by $580
P. 20-9 Total sources of working capital, $16,900

P. 20-10 Cash provided by operations, $1,340
P. 20-11 Total other sources of working capital, $4,372
P. 20-12 Total cash provided by operations, $2,311
P. 20-13 Total decrease in working capital, $100
P. 20-14 Total sources of cash, $10,700
P. 20-15 December 31, 1986, retained earnings balance, $7,400
Case 20-1 Total assets on December 31, 1986, $75,500
Case 20-2 Total working capital provided by operations, $176,000

Index